The Foundations of Modern Macroeconomics

The Foundations of Modern Macroeconomics

Ben J. Heijdra

Frederick van der Ploeg

OXFORD
UNIVERSITY PRESS

OXFORD

UNIVERSITY PRESS

Great Clarendon Street, Oxford OX2 6DP

Oxford University Press is a department of the University of Oxford.
It furthers the University's objective of excellence in research, scholarship,
and education by publishing worldwide in

Oxford New York

Auckland Bangkok Buenos Aires Cape Town Chennai
Dar es Salaam Delhi Hong Kong Istanbul Karachi Kolkata
Kuala Lumpur Madrid Melbourne Mexico City Mumbai Nairobi
São Paulo Shanghai Singapore Taipei Tokyo Toronto

with an associated company in Berlin

Oxford is a registered trade mark of Oxford University Press
in the UK and in certain other countries

Published in the United States
by Oxford University Press Inc., New York

British Library Cataloguing in Publication Data

Data available

Library of Congress Cataloging in Publication Data

Heijdra, Ben J.
    Foundations of modern macroeconomics / Ben J. Heijdra, Frederick van der Ploeg.
        p. cm.
    Includes bibliographical references.
        1. Macroeconomics.   I. Ploeg, Frederick van der, 1956–   II. Title.
    HB172.5 .H437 2002   339—dc21   2001055718

ISBN 0-19-877618-7
ISBN 0-19-877617-9 (pbk.)

10 9 8 7 6 5 4 3 2 1

Typeset by Newgen Imaging Systems (P) Ltd, Chennai, India
Printed in Great Britain
on acid-free paper by T.J. International Ltd., Padstow, Cornwall

Preface

In this book we try to present a balanced overview of modern macroeconomic theory. We have adhered to two guiding principles in writing this book. First, we have adopted a rather eclectic approach by paying attention not just to the most recent insights in the field but also to developments that are currently less fashionable. In doing so we hope to provide the students with a better overview of current and past debates in macroeconomic theory. We have thus chosen to include discussions of the IS–LM model, the adaptive expectations hypothesis, and the quantity rationing models of the early 1970s. Though these theories are currently less fashionable (and, as some economists argue, may even be "outdated") it is our firm conviction that they nevertheless provide important insights. For example, to fully appreciate the importance of the rational expectations hypothesis, a good understanding of the adaptive expectations hypothesis (its immediate predecessor) is indispensable. Similarly, to really understand the contributions made in recent years by Real Business Cycle economists it is useful to have a firm understanding of the IS-LM model, whilst a familiarity with the quantity rationing literature helps in appreciating the New Keynesian insights. Finally, "old habits die slowly" and the IS-LM model is still used extensively even though, as Blanchard has pointed out recently, many people may not even know they are using it (2000b, p. 1405).

Our second guiding principle concerns the adopted style of the book. In addition to introducing the different theories by verbal and graphical means, we have also aimed to successively develop "the tools of the trade" of modern macroeconomics. In this aspect our book is related to Allen's (1967) marvellous macroeconomic toolbook. So instead of only providing students with a verbal/intuitive understanding of the material (valuable as it is), we also want to teach them the basic modelling tricks of modern macroeconomics. Where needed we present the full details of both the models and their solutions. We expect that students who have worked through our book should have little or no problems with more advanced graduate textbooks like Blanchard and Fischer (1989), Farmer (1993), Obstfeld and Rogoff (1996), Romer (2001), Turnovsky (1997, 2000), Sargent (1987a), and Ljungqvist and Sargent (2000). Similarly, the student should be well prepared to read (and appreciate) the magnificent survey articles in the recent macroeconomics handbook by Taylor and Woodford (1999).

How did this book get written? We started to think about writing this book in 1993 when we were both employed at the University of Amsterdam. The second author benefited much from his experience teaching courses in macroeconomic theory and policy at the London School of Economics together with Charles Bean and John Hardman Moore. Handwritten notes on the first ten chapters were developed by the second author and expanded into a set of typed lecture notes by the first author in early 1995. These notes carried the provisional title of *Macroeconomics in Sixteen Frames*, even though only ten "frames" existed at that time. (Recall that projection at a rate of at least sixteen frames per second underlies the principle of motion pictures. The working title was thus intended to signal that the book presents a smooth overview of modern macroeconomics.) We determined the contents of the remaining frames and the Mathematical Appendix together and the first author completed the work on the book on a part-time basis during the period 1995–2001.

Our book can be used both in the undergraduate and the graduate curriculum. In the undergraduate curriculum, Chapters 1–11 can be used in a second (intermediate) macroeconomics course whilst Chapters 12–17 are aimed at final-year advanced undergraduates. For example, we have ourselves used Chapters 1–10 in our second-year macroeconomics courses at the Universities of Amsterdam and Groningen. Students in these institutions typically study a book like Mankiw (2000a) in their first-year course. In the graduate curriculum, the book can be used as the main text in a first-semester macro course or as a supplementary text for an advanced graduate macro course. The book is well suited for beginning graduate students with no or insufficient previous training in macroeconomic theory. Parts of Chapters 13–17 were used in the various graduate courses we have taught over the years for the Netherlands Network of Economics (NAKE) and the Tinbergen Institute. Graduate courses based on the material in this book were also given in the European University Institute (Florence), the Institute for Advanced Studies (Vienna), and SERGE (Prague).

Despite considerable effort on our part (and that of the editorial team of Oxford University Press), we are almost sure that some typos and errors are still "out there" to be discovered. We pledge to publish all such errors and typos as we become aware of them. We will make the errata documents available through the home page of the first-mentioned author. At the time of writing, the link is: http://www.eco.rug.nl/medewerk/heijdra. On this home page we will also place the problem sets for the book as they become available.

We have received comments from many students and colleagues over the years. Particularly detailed comments were received from two anonymous referees, Jaap Abbring, Leon Bettendorf, Lans Bovenberg, Erik Canton, Robert Dur, Switgard Feuerstein, Christian Groth, Albert van der Horst, Jan-Peter Kooiman, Jenny Ligthart, and Partha Sen. Peter Broer provided technical assistance on Chapters 15–17 and Thijs Knaap helped with the impulse-response graphs in Chapter 15. The first drafts of Chapters 16–17 were written during a visit of the first-mentioned author to the Economic Policy Research Unit (EPRU) of the University of Copenhagen in January 2000. We are grateful to EPRU for its hospitality and excellent research facilities.

We were very fortunate to work with Andrew Schuller of Oxford University Press. Despite the fact that we missed many deadlines over the years, and ultimately handed in a typescript almost twice the size we originally promised, Andrew has maintained a cheerful disposition and a steady interest in the project. During the fine tuning of the book we benefited tremendously from the efforts of Rebecca Bryant, also of Oxford University Press.

Ben J. Heijdra
Rick van der Ploeg

Contents

Contents

Detailed Contents

List of Figures

List of Figures

List of Figures

List of Tables

List of Tables

Who is Who in Macroeconomics?

The purpose of this chapter is to achieve three goals:

1. To investigate the effectiveness of monetary and fiscal policy on output, employment, the interest rate, and the price level,

2. To introduce the most important past and current schools of thought in macroeconomics, and

3. To (partially) refresh and extend the macroeconomic knowledge from first-year courses.

In order to achieve these goals, we first have to discuss some elementary concepts relating to the *aggregate labour market* and the *demand for money*. It turns out that the most important differences of opinion between (most varieties of) Classical and Keynesian economists can be traced back to their respective assumptions regarding the labour market, expectation formation, and money demand.

1.1 The Aggregate Labour Market

Our discussion of the labour market in this chapter is very basic. In Chapters 7–9 we return to this important topic in more detail. The stylized account of the labour market uses the devices of the aggregate demand for and supply of labour.

1.1.1 The demand for labour

The central element in the basic theory of labour demand is the production function. Perfectly competitive profit-maximizing entrepreneurs utilize this production function under the restriction that the capital stock is given in the short run. The production function is thus given by:

$$Y = F(N, \bar{K}), \tag{1.1}$$

where Y is real output, $\bar{K}$ is the given capital stock (machines, PCs, cars), N is the amount of labour employed, and $F(.,.)$ is the production function. The marginal products of labour and capital are denoted by F_N and F_K, respectively. Furthermore, we assume that the marginal product of labour (capital) declines as employment (capital) is increased, i.e. $F_{NN} < 0$ ($F_{KK} < 0$). Too many cooks in the kitchen spoil the broth. We also assume that the factors are cooperative in the sense that increasing one factor raises the marginal productivity of the other factor ($F_{KN} = F_{NK} > 0$). The use of robot mixers in the kitchen thus enhances the productivity of the cooks. Finally, we assume constant returns to scale so that doubling all factors of production induces a doubling of output. More precisely, $F(\lambda N, \lambda \bar{K}) = \lambda F(N, \bar{K})$ with λ any positive constant.

Short-run profits are defined as revenues minus the wage bill:

$$\Pi \equiv PY - WN, \tag{1.2}$$

where Π is nominal profit, P is the price charged by the firm, and W is the nominal wage rate. In words, all revenue (PY) that is not paid to the variable production factor labour in terms of wages (WN) is considered profit, which is the reward that accrues to the owners of the capital stock (note that we ignore taxes for the moment).

We assume perfect competition on the aggregate goods market, so that the individual firm cannot exert any influence on its price. Hence, the only choice that is open to the firm (in the short run) is to determine the amount of production (Y) and employment (N) such that profit is maximized. By substituting the production function in the profit definition, we see that once employment is chosen, output is also automatically chosen. The problem for the firm is thus to choose N to maximize Π:

$$\max_{\{N\}} \Pi \equiv PF(N, \bar{K}) - WN. \tag{1.3}$$

The firm can do no better than to follow the following decision rule:

$$\frac{d\Pi}{dN} = 0 : \quad PF_N(N, \bar{K}) - W = 0, \tag{1.4}$$

where the second-order condition implies that (1.4) describes a maximum: $d^2\Pi/dN^2 = PF_{NN} < 0$. The interpretation of (1.4) is clear; the firm should keep expanding its employment up to the point where the marginal unit of labour exactly breaks even (in the sense that the additional output produced by the marginal worker yields a revenue that exactly covers the wage that is paid to the worker). In terms of Figure 1.1, the profit maximum occurs at point A. (At points B and C the firm makes no profits.)

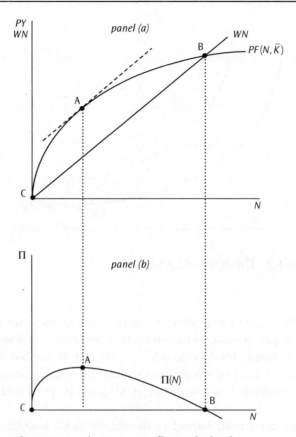

Figure 1.1. Short-run profit maximization

The decision rule (1.4) is a vitally important element in the macroeconomic labour market story. It is also relatively uncontroversial: virtually all macroeconomists believe in some version of equation (1.4). We can easily transform (1.4) into the demand for labour, a schedule which shows how much labour a firm wants to hire for a given real wage rate. Formally, we can view equation (1.4) as an implicit relationship between N^D (the superscript "D" stands for **d**emand) on the one hand and the real wage (W/P) and the given capital stock $\bar{K}$ on the other. The partial derivatives of this implicit relationship can be obtained by using the trick of implicit functions. First, we totally differentiate equation (1.4):

$$dF_N(N^D, \bar{K}) = d(W/P) \quad \Rightarrow \quad F_{NN}dN^D + F_{NK}d\bar{K} = d(W/P), \tag{1.5}$$

or, after rearranging terms:

$$dN^D = -(F_{NK}/F_{NN})\, d\bar{K} + (1/F_{NN})\, d(W/P). \tag{1.6}$$

3

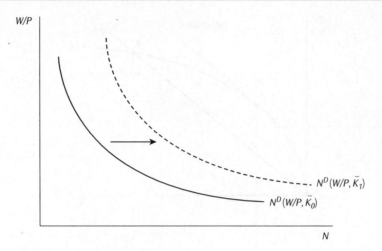

Figure 1.2. The demand for labour

Since $F_{NN} < 0$, the marginal product of labour falls as more units of labour are employed. As a result, equation (1.6) states that a higher real wage ($d(W/P) > 0$) diminishes the demand for labour ($dN^D < 0$) ceteris paribus (i.e. holding $\bar{K}$ constant). Hence, $(1/F_{NN})$ in equation (1.6) has the interpretation of the partial derivative of the implicit function between N^D and $(W/P, \bar{K})$ with respect to the real wage (W/P).

The partial derivative with respect to the capital stock is obtained in a similar fashion (and is equal to $-F_{NK}/F_{NN} > 0$). Since labour and capital are cooperative factors of production, increasing the capital stock raises the marginal product of labour. For a given real wage rate, the profit-maximizing firm thus hires more labour.

In summary, we can write:

$$N^D = N^D(W/P, \bar{K}), \quad N^D_{W/P} \equiv 1/F_{NN} < 0, \quad N^D_{\bar{K}} \equiv -F_{NK}/F_{NN} > 0. \tag{1.7}$$

In terms of Figure 1.2, varying the real wage rate implies a movement along a given demand for labour curve, whilst increasing the capital stock shifts the demand curve to the right. A higher cost of labour or a lower capital stock necessitates a higher marginal productivity of labour and thus a lower demand for labour.

1.1.2 The supply of labour

In the previous section we implicitly assumed that firms can freely observe the actual values of the price level and the wage rate (P and W). This is realistic enough, because all the individual firm must do is to observe its *own* price and the wage paid to its *own* workers.

Matters are somewhat more complicated for the households, who are the suppliers of labour in our stylized account of the labour market. Indeed, in the decision about goods consumption and labour supply, the households may know their own nominal wage (W) with certainty, but they may not know how much they can actually consume with that wage. The household has to estimate the price of a whole basket of goods, a task inherently more difficult than the one facing the individual firm. The simplest way to introduce this asymmetry in information is to assume that the household forms a guess about the aggregate price level, denoted by P^e (where the superscript "e" stands for expected).

The household derives utility from goods consumption (denoted by C) and leisure ($1 - N^S$). The household "owns" one unit of time, of which N^S units are spent working, so that time available for leisure is equal to $1 - N^S$. We write the utility function in general terms as $U(C, 1 - N^S)$ and assume positive but diminishing marginal utilities: $U_C > 0$, $U_{1-N} > 0$, $U_{CC} < 0$, $U_{1-N,1-N} < 0$. Some extra consumption of goods and leisure is fun, but less so if you already consume a lot or have plenty of spare time to enjoy.

The household chooses that combination of C and $1 - N^S$ for which the highest possible satisfaction is attained (as measured by $U(.,.)$), *given* the expected price level (P^e) and the (expected) budget restriction $P^e C = W N^S$. We assume that the household has no sources of income other than wages. Formally, we can thus write the problem for the household as follows:

$$\max_{\{C,N^S\}} U \equiv U(C, 1 - N^S) \quad \text{subject to} \quad P^e C = W N^S. \tag{1.8}$$

This problem looks rather prohibitive, but we can make it easier by substituting the level of consumption implied by the budget restriction ($C = (W/P^e)N^S$) into the utility function. The household then only has to choose the level of labour supply:

$$\max_{\{N^S\}} U \equiv U[(W/P^e)N^S, 1 - N^S]. \tag{1.9}$$

This yields a straightforward decision rule for the household:

$$\frac{dU}{dN^S} = 0: \quad (W/P^e)U_C - U_{1-N} = 0. \tag{1.10}$$

The first term on the left-hand side (i.e. $(W/P^e)U_C$) measures the marginal benefit of supplying one extra unit of labour to the labour market. By working more, the household obtains more income, especially if the real wage is high, and hence more consumption. The second term (i.e. U_{1-N}) measures the marginal cost of that extra unit. By supplying more labour, the household misses out on valuable leisure time. In an optimum the household sets the marginal benefit equal to the marginal cost of supplying an additional unit of labour.

In principle we could now proceed by investigating what happens to labour supply and consumption if the expected real wage rate is varied. Mathematically

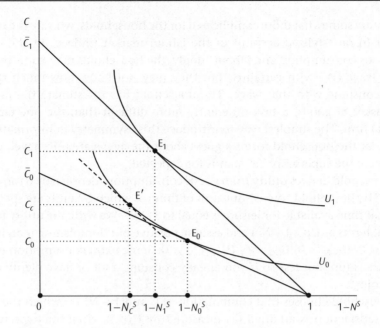

Figure 1.3. The consumption-leisure choice

this is slightly more involved than for the labour demand equation, so that we first derive the basic intuition concerning labour supply by graphical means. (The mathematical derivation of labour supply is given in an intermezzo in Chapter 7).

In Figure 1.3 we plot consumption on the vertical axis and leisure on the horizontal axis. The initial expected real wage is $(W/P^e)_0$, and the budget line goes through $\bar{C}_0$ ($\equiv (W/P^e)_0$) on the C-axis, and 1 on the $(1 - N^S)$-axis. The optimal consumption-leisure choice occurs at the point where an indifference curve has a tangency with the budget line. This occurs at point E_0, where consumption is C_0, leisure is $1 - N_0^S$, and the level of utility is U_0. By plotting the implied value of labour supply (N_0^S) against the real wage rate in Figure 1.4, we obtain the first point on the labour supply curve.

Suppose now that the expected real wage is a bit higher, say $(W/P^e)_1$. In terms of Figure 1.3 this implies that the budget line rotates in a clockwise fashion around the intersection point on the leisure axis. The new intersection on the consumption axis is at $\bar{C}_1$ ($\equiv (W/P^e)_1$). For the case drawn, the new optimum choice occurs at point E_1, which lies above and to the left of the initial point E_0. Consumption is C_1, leisure is $1 - N_1^S$, and the level of utility is U_1. By plotting the implied value of labour supply (N_1^S) against the real wage rate in Figure 1.4, we obtain the second point on the labour supply curve. By connecting the two points we obtain the labour supply schedule N^S, which for the case drawn slopes upward.

Unlike the labour demand curve, which always slopes downwards, the slope of the labour supply curve is not necessarily positive. The reason is that there are two,

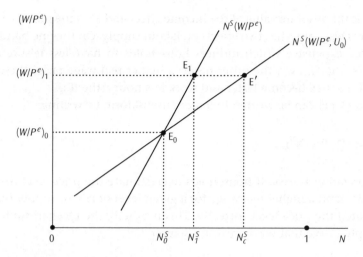

Figure 1.4. The supply of labour

potentially offsetting, effects that confront the household when the expected real wage rises. The first effect is called the *pure substitution effect*. To determine this effect, we ask ourselves the question what combination of consumption and leisure the household would choose at the higher expected real wage if it were somehow restricted to remain at the initial level of utility U_0. In Figure 1.3, we see that the household would choose point E′, where consumption is C_C, leisure is $1 - N_C^S$, and labour supply is N_C^S (the subscript "C" stands for compensated). The move from the initial point E_0 to the (hypothetical) compensated point E′ constitutes the pure substitution effect (i.e. *SE*). Intuitively, the pure substitution effect says that a household will buy less of anything for which the price has risen. A rise in the expected real wage rate means that the price of leisure has gone up. Consequently, the household buys less of it. This gives us an interesting result: *the compensated labour supply curve is always upward sloping* (see $N^S(W/P^e, U_0)$ in Figure 1.4).

The second effect is called the *income effect*. It says that, for a given initial level of labour supply N_0^S, a higher expected real wage implies a higher expected real income, or, $(W/P^e)_1 N_0^S > (W/P^e)_0 N_0^S$. Provided leisure is a normal good the household would react to this higher income by purchasing *more* leisure not less. Hence, the income effect, which is represented by the move from point E′ to E_1 (i.e. *IE*), works in the opposite direction to the pure substitution effect. As it happens, Figure 1.3 has been drawn for the case where the substitution effect dominates the income effect, so that labour supply slopes up. The other cases cannot be excluded on a priori grounds, however, and the issue can only be fully resolved by empirical means (see Chapter 7).

Mathematically, we can represent the labour supply curve in general form by:

$$W/P^e = g(N^S), \qquad g_N \gtreqless 0 \quad \Leftrightarrow \quad SE \gtreqless |IE|, \tag{1.11}$$

7

where $|IE|$ is the absolute value of the income effect and SE is the substitution effect. A higher real wage thus has two effects on labour supply. On the one hand, it makes leisure more expensive which induces households to have less leisure and work more hours (the SE). On the other hand, a higher real wage raises the income of households so they become lazier and work less hours (the IE).

Equation (1.11) can be written in a more useful form by writing:

$$W/P = (P^e/P)g(N^S). \tag{1.12}$$

The interpretation is easy. If households overestimate the price level (i.e. $P^e > P$), they will demand a higher real wage for a given level of labour supply than if they had estimated the price level correctly. This is exactly the mechanism behind the Lucas Supply Curve that we discuss in Chapter 3.

1.1.3 Aggregate supply in the goods market: Adaptive expectations

We have now developed a logically consistent description of the aggregate labour market consisting of equations (1.7) and (1.12). We must now assume something about the way in which households form their expectations. Since we shall return to this issue in Chapters 3 and 4 in more detail, we simply postulate two alternative assumptions regarding the expected price level: (i) the *adaptive expectations hypothesis* (AEH) and (ii) the *perfect foresight hypothesis* (PFH).

Under the AEH the expected price level is given in the short run, but moves slowly to correct for past expectational errors. Using t as an index for time (e.g. years), the AEH mechanism is:

$$P^e_{t+1} = P_t + (1 - \lambda)\left[P^e_t - P_t\right] \quad 0 < \lambda < 1. \tag{1.13}$$

This equation says that households expect the price in the future period $t + 1$ to be equal to the actual price in the current period t if their expectations proved correct in the current period. If, instead, they have mis-estimated the price level in the current period ($P^e_t \neq P_t$), they incorporate part of the expectational error in the revision of their expectation in the current period, where λ represents the speed with which households update their price expectations. We find it convenient to use the short-hand notation for the AEH:

$$\Delta P^e = \lambda[P - P^e] \quad 0 < \lambda < 1 \quad \text{(AEH)}, \tag{1.14}$$

where the Δ-operator stands for the change in a variable from one period to the next. Equation (1.14) captures sluggish adjustment of expectations regarding the price level.

The second, diametrically opposed, assumption regarding expectations is the PFH. It simply states that households expect the price level that actually holds:

$$P^e = P \quad \text{(PFH)}. \tag{1.15}$$

The PFH can be seen as the deterministic counterpart to the rational expectations hypothesis (REH) discussed in Chapter 3.

The labour market description can be used, in combination with either AEH or PFH, to describe the supply curve (AS) on the aggregate goods market. Obviously, the form of this AS curve depends on the particular expectations hypothesis used. We first consider the AS curve under the AEH. This is illustrated in Figure 1.5. Suppose that the initial price level is P_0 and that the expected price level is equal to this, i.e. $P_0^e = P_0$. In that case, households make no expectational error, supply the "correct" amount of labour, labour market equilibrium determines the right amount of employment and the correct real wage, and output is (via the short-run production function) equal to potential output Y^*. In terms of Figure 1.5, north-west panel, the labour supply function (1.11) is given as $W = P_0^e g(N^S)$ and the labour demand function (1.7) is given implicitly by $W = P_0 F_N(N^D, \bar{K})$ (note that we have put the **nominal** wage on the vertical axis). The nominal wage is W_0 and employment is N^*, so that $Y^* = F(N^*, \bar{K})$. Now consider a higher actual price level, say P_1. The expected price level is still equal to P_0^e and the labour supply curve is unchanged.

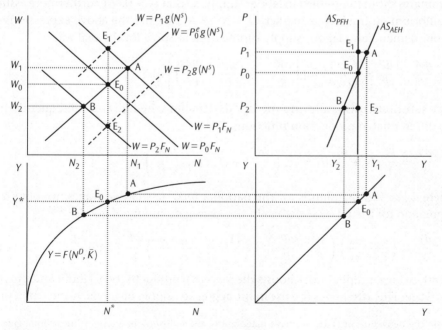

Figure 1.5. Aggregate supply and expectations

The demand for labour shifts up, to $W = P_1 F_N(N^D, \bar{K})$, so that labour market equilibrium is at point A, the nominal wage rate is W_1, employment is N_1 (greater than N^*), and output is Y_1 (greater than Y^*). This yields the second point on the AS curve. Employment and output are larger because the **actual** real wage is lower. This is due to the fact that households have underestimated the price level and consequently overestimated their real wage. Point B corresponds to a lower actual price level and a lower level of aggregate supply of goods; it can be derived in a similar fashion as point A.

The AS curve under the PFH is even easier to derive. Expected and actual prices always coincide, so labour supply is always based on the correct information (as is labour demand), employment is always equal to N^*, output is equal to Y^*, and the AS curve is vertical. This is also illustrated in Figure 1.5.

Before we move on, we find it instructive to give an analytical derivation of the AS curve. The labour demand and labour supply curves (1.7) and (1.11) may be written in terms of elasticities:

$$\frac{dN^D}{N^D} = \frac{d\bar{K}}{\bar{K}} - \epsilon_D \left[\frac{dW}{W} - \frac{dP}{P} \right], \tag{1.16}$$

$$\frac{dN^S}{N^S} = \epsilon_S \left[\frac{dW}{W} - \frac{dP^e}{P^e} \right], \tag{1.17}$$

where $\epsilon_D \equiv -F_N/(NF_{NN})$ and $\epsilon_S \equiv g(N)/(Ng_N)$ denote the wage elasticities of labour demand and labour supply, respectively.[1] We assume that the substitution effect dominates the income effect in labour supply, so that $\epsilon_S > 0$. We furthermore assume equilibrium on the labour market, $N = N^D = N^S$, so that the above expressions for labour demand and labour supply can be used to solve for the real wage:

$$\frac{dW}{W} - \frac{dP}{P} = \left(\frac{1}{\epsilon_D + \epsilon_S} \right) \left[\frac{d\bar{K}}{\bar{K}} - \epsilon_S \left(\frac{dP}{P} - \frac{dP^e}{P^e} \right) \right]. \tag{1.18}$$

If we substitute this result into the labour demand schedule and subsequently into the differentiated production function,

$$\frac{dY}{Y} = \frac{F_N}{Y} dN + \frac{F_K}{Y} d\bar{K} = \omega_N \left(\frac{dN}{N} \right) + (1 - \omega_N) \left(\frac{d\bar{K}}{\bar{K}} \right), \tag{1.19}$$

where $\omega_N \equiv WN/PY$ stands for the national income share of wages, we obtain an expression for the relative change in the aggregate supply of goods:

$$\frac{dY}{Y} = \left(\frac{\omega_N \epsilon_D \epsilon_S}{\epsilon_D + \epsilon_S} \right) \left(\frac{dP}{P} - \frac{dP^e}{P^e} \right) + \left(\frac{(1 - \omega_N)\epsilon_D + \epsilon_S}{\epsilon_D + \epsilon_S} \right) \frac{d\bar{K}}{\bar{K}} \quad \text{(AS).} \tag{1.20}$$

Clearly, a bigger capital stock boosts the marginal productivity of labour and thus the real wage. This attenuates the rise in the aggregate supply of goods. Anticipated price

---

[1] In the derivation of (1.16) we have made use of the following property of linear homogeneous production functions: $KF_{NK} = -NF_{NN}$. See the Intermezzo in Chapter 4 on production theory for further properties.

changes ($dP^e/P^e = dP/P$) do not affect real wages, employment, or the aggregate supply of goods. Unanticipated price changes, however, do affect these variables. For example, if the actual price level turns out to be bigger than the expected price level, the real wage falls and thus employment and the aggregate supply of output rise.

Expression (1.20) corresponds to the AS curve derived graphically in Figure 1.5. Under the PFH we clearly have a vertical AS curve which shifts to the right if the capital stock expands. Under the AEH, the expected price level is fixed in the short run so that the AS curve slopes upwards. In this case, the AS curve also shifts to the right if the capital stock rises. Over time expectations regarding the price level may be adjusted which leads to shifts in the AS curve. For example, if in any period the actual price level rises above the expected price level, in subsequent periods the expected price level will be revised upwards. This lowers the purchasing power households expect from their wage income, so households decide to work fewer hours. This induces a rise in the real wage and thus a fall in labour demand and employment. Consequently, aggregate supply of output falls. This argument shows why a rise in the expected price level shifts the AS curve to the left.

1.1.4 Nominal wage rigidities

In order to have an effect of the price level on aggregate supply, we can assume the AEH. We now consider an alternative assumption. Modigliani (1944) demonstrated that there is a way in which an upward-sloping (segment of the) aggregate supply curve can be generated even if we adopt the PFH. Modigliani assumes that *nominal* wages are inflexible downwards, but perfectly flexible in the upward direction. Workers hate wage cuts, but love a rise. In Figure 1.6, we assume that the rigid nominal wage is equal to W_0 and that P_0 is the price level at which full employment holds. We assume the PFH (1.15). The situation for price levels exceeding P_0 is straightforward. The nominal wage rises to keep the real wage constant and maintain full employment. The situation is different for a lower price level than P_0, however. For example, if $P = P_2$, the demand for labour is given by $W = P_2 F_N(N^D, \bar{K})$, but the effective supply of labour is the horizontal line segment $W_0 C$. Since we assume that the nominal wage rate is not allowed to fall, employment equals N_2 ($< N^*$) and there are $N_2^S - N_2$ units of labour unemployed. By not allowing their wages to fall in nominal terms, the households end up partially pricing themselves out of the labour market.

1.2 Aggregate Demand: Review of the IS-LM Model

From our first-year course in macroeconomics, we recall that the demand side of the economy can be described by means of the IS–LM model. For the closed economy

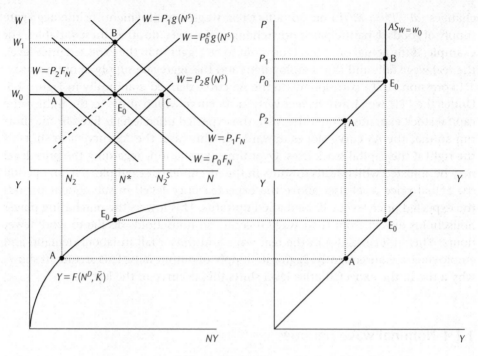

Figure 1.6. Aggregate supply with downward nominal wage rigidity

this model can be written as:

$$Y = C + I + G, \tag{1.21}$$

$$C = C(Y - T), \quad 0 < C_{Y-T} < 1, \tag{1.22}$$

$$I = I(R), \quad I_R < 0, \tag{1.23}$$

$$T = T(Y), \quad 0 < T_Y < 1, \tag{1.24}$$

$$M/P = l(Y, R), \quad l_Y > 0, l_R \leq 0, \tag{1.25}$$

where I is investment, G is government spending, T represents taxes, and R is the rate of interest. Equation (1.21) is the usual national income accounting identity, (1.22) is the consumption function expressing C as a function of disposable income $(Y - T)$, where C_{Y-T} denotes the marginal propensity to consume out of disposable income. The investment equation is given in (1.23). A higher rate of interest means that the cost of capital is high, leading entrepreneurs to lower the level of investment. Equation (1.24) shows that tax receipts depend on the level of income generated in the economy; T_Y stands for the marginal tax rate. Equations (1.21)–(1.24) implicitly define the IS curve, that is the combinations of R and Y for which there exists spending equilibrium. Finally, equation (1.25) is the money market equilibrium condition, equating the real money supply (M/P) to the real demand for money. This last schedule has proved a real bone of contention between the different schools of thought in macroeconomics, and consequently it warrants some further discussion.

1.2.1 The demand for money

Why do people hold money, even though it does not pay any interest? This is one of the unresolved questions in macroeconomic theory. Over the centuries, some of the finest minds in economics have broken their heads over this issue, and some (partial) answers are indeed available. Keynes claimed that the money theory proposed in his *General Theory* represented a radical break with the traditional wisdom of his days. In this section we show in what sense Keynes may have meant this statement.

There are two main motives for holding money balances, the *transactions motive* and the *speculative motive*. The transactions motive runs as follows. People like to consume goods steadily over the course of the month (say), but usually only get their income paid once a month or once a week. Since cash is used as payment in many transactions, people need a certain amount of cash during the period in between pay cheques. They could, of course, put their income in the bank in an interest-earning savings account and get the necessary amount needed for transactions each day (hour, minute, second?) but that would involve a lot of trips to the bank and involve substantial transaction costs and a loss of valuable leisure time. A more reasonable approach would be for the households to decide on an optimal cash management problem: choose the number of trips to the bank such that the marginal costs and benefits of the savings account are equated. Out of this cash management problem we would certainly obtain an interest sensitivity of money demand, since interest represents the income foregone when wealth is held in the form of money. We would also expect that the transactions demand for money would depend positively on the real stream of transactions that the household wishes to conduct. Economy-wide we can proxy this effect on real money demand with the specification (1.25).

Intermezzo

Baumol's transactions theory of the demand for money. Let k be the number of transactions per period (month or week), so that average money holdings are given by $M/P = \frac{1}{2}(Y/k)$. Households choose the number of transactions and thus average money holdings by minimizing the sum of foregone interest on money holdings (the opportunity cost) and transactions costs: $RY/(2k) + ck$, where c denotes the cost per transaction (bank costs plus leisure time). Minimization yields the first-order condition:

$$-\frac{RY}{2k^2} + c = 0.$$

The second-order condition is $RY/k^3 > 0$, confirming that the optimum is indeed a minimum. The first-order condition implies the following optimum number of transactions and demand for money:

$$k = \sqrt{\frac{RY}{2c}}, \quad \frac{M}{P} = \frac{Y}{2k} = \sqrt{\frac{cY}{2R}}.$$

Hence, the higher the cost per transaction (c) and the lower the opportunity cost of holding money (R), the higher the demand for real money balances. Money demand rises with the square root of income and is proportional to the price level.

Another motive for holding money that was stressed by Keynes is the so-called speculative motive (called "the demand for money to hold as an asset" by Modigliani (1944)). Money has two important properties: it is very liquid, and it is risk free in the absence of inflation (a guilder is still a guilder tomorrow). Other assets such as shares and bonds fluctuate in value (even in real terms, once corrected for inflation) and are hence both more risky and less liquid. Keynes (and Modigliani, 1944) suggests regressive expectations as a rationale behind the liquidity preference. The story runs as follows. If the rate of interest is very low then prices of bonds are very high (the price of a consol that pays 1 guilder indefinitely is $P_B = (1+R)^{-1}+(1+R)^{-2}+\cdots = 1/R$. Hence, bond prices and interest rates move in opposite directions). Investors expect that high prices of bonds cannot persist forever, and thus anticipate that bond prices will fall (P_B falls, or R rises). In other words, they expect a capital loss on bonds, which prompts them to hold most of their wealth in the form of money (we take into account the differences in riskiness of money and bonds to avoid the conclusion that the agents choose a corner solution: either all money or all bonds). The speculative demand for money thus motivated depends negatively on the interest rate, i.e. $l_R \leq 0$.

Keynes suggested that the liquidity preference function $l(Y, R)$ may have the form as drawn in Figure 1.7. If the rate of interest is very high ($R \geq R^{MAX}$), households will not hold any cash for speculative purposes. Bond prices are very low and capital gains on bonds are expected. So why hold money? On the other hand, Keynes argued, if the rate of interest is very low ($R \leq R^{MIN}$) then people would become indifferent between holding their wealth in terms of money or bonds. The liquidity preference function would become perfectly elastic at that minimum rate of interest, R^{MIN}. This is called the liquidity trap.

1.2.2 The IS-LM model

The money market is represented by equation (1.25). The LM curve represents all combinations of output Y and the rate of interest R for which the money market is

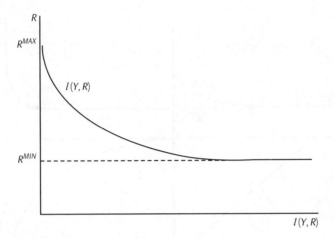

Figure 1.7. The liquidity preference function

in equilibrium. Formally, the properties of the LM curve can be found by using the implicit function trick once again:

$$d(M/P) = l_Y \, dY + l_R \, dR \quad \Rightarrow \quad dR = \frac{d(M/P) - l_Y \, dY}{l_R}. \tag{1.26}$$

The slope of the LM curve is thus $-l_Y/l_R \geq 0$, while the effect of the real money supply on the rate of interest is equal to $(1/l_R) \leq 0$. Graphically, the LM curve is derived as in Figure 1.8.[2] We have shown with equation (1.26) that the LM curve, typically, slopes upwards and shifts to the right if real money balances expand. A higher interest rate lowers money demand, so national income must be higher to boost money demand back to the unchanged level of money supply. A higher money supply or a lower price level pushes up bond prices and thus lowers the interest rate. We note that the LM curve is vertical for high rates of interest, and horizontal for low rates of interest (provided we accept Keynes' liquidity preference function as drawn in Figure 1.7).

The IS curve represents combinations of output Y and the rate of interest R for which there exists aggregate spending balance. Formally, by using equations (1.21)–(1.24) we derive the IS curve as follows:

$$Y = C(Y - T(Y)) + I(R) + G \quad \Rightarrow$$
$$dY = C_{Y-T}(1 - T_Y)dY + I_R dR + dG, \tag{1.27}$$

or, after rearranging:

$$dY = \frac{dG + I_R \, dR}{1 - C_{Y-T}(1 - T_Y)}. \tag{1.28}$$

---

[2] For the special case where the demand for money is additively separable and can be written as $k(Y) + l(R)$.

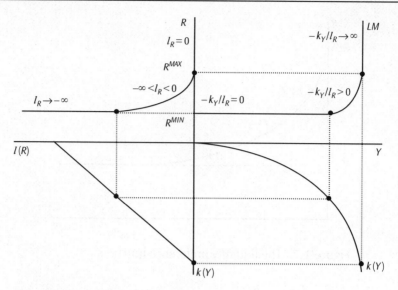

Figure 1.8. Derivation of the LM curve

Increasing government spending stimulates output for a given level of the interest rate. Students are invited to derive the IS curve graphically as well.

1.2.3 The AD curve

As we know from first-year courses in macroeconomics, the demand side of the economy is in equilibrium if there is simultaneous spending and money market equilibrium. This demand-side equilibrium corresponds to the intersection of the IS and LM curves and is summarized by the AD curve, that is those combinations of output Y and the price level P for which there is money market equilibrium and spending equilibrium. By using (1.26) and (1.28), the expression for the AD curve can be obtained:

$$dY = \frac{dG + (I_R/l_R)(M/P)\,[dM/M - dP/P]}{1 - C_{Y-T}(1 - T_Y) + l_Y I_R/l_R} \qquad \text{(AD)}. \qquad (1.29)$$

The AD curve can also be derived graphically. This is left as an exercise for the students. The intuition is as follows. A higher price level erodes the real value of money balances and thus exerts an upward pressure on the interest rate. This depresses aggregate investment and thus lowers the aggregate demand for goods. Consequently, the AD curve generally slopes downwards. A higher level of public spending or a boost to the nominal money supply boosts aggregate demand and thus shifts out the AD curve. The former case induces a rise while the latter case a fall in the interest rate.

1.2.4 Effectiveness of fiscal and monetary policy

The output multiplier for public spending given in equation (1.28) equals the inverse of the marginal propensity to save out of income plus the marginal tax rate, i.e. $1/[1 - C_{Y-T}(1 - T_Y)]$, and thus exceeds unity.[3] This multiplier is relevant when the interest rate is exogenous or investment does not depend on the interest rate and was first derived by a colleague of John Maynard Keynes, namely Richard Kahn (1931). An instructive way to write this multiplier is as follows:

$$\frac{d\dot{Y}}{dG} = 1 + C_{Y-T}(1 - T_Y) + C_{Y-T}^2(1 - T_Y)^2 + C_{Y-T}^3(1 - T_Y)^3 + \cdots$$

$$= \frac{1}{1 - C_{Y-T}(1 - T_Y)}. \tag{1.30}$$

Let us assume for the sake of argument a marginal propensity to consume of 75 per cent ($C_{Y-T} = 0.75$) and a marginal tax rate of one third ($T_Y = 1/3$). The impact effect of a one million guilder bond-financed increase in public spending yields a one million guilder increase in aggregate demand and national income. Of that increase in national income one sixth of a million is saved and another one third of a million is taken by the tax men. The remainder, i.e. half a million guilders, is consumed and is the second-round boost to national income. Of that second-round boost one twelfth of a million is saved and one sixth of a million is brought to the tax men. A quarter of a million is left for consumption and induces the third-round boost to national income. This multiplier process is continued *ad infinitum* leading to a total increase in national income of two million guilders (namely $1 + 0.5 + 0.25 + 0.125 + \cdots$) and corresponding to a Kahn multiplier of two. Hence, for every guilder pumped by the government into the economy, national income expands by two guilders.

The magnitude of the Kahn multiplier is smaller if saving leakage and tax leakage are substantial, that is if the marginal propensity to consume is small and the marginal tax rate is large. For example, if the marginal tax rate is zero, the multiplier is four instead of two. For a small open economy, this multiplier is smaller again if there is a lot of import leakage (see Chapter 11).

Expression (1.29) shows the Keynesian multiplier for a bond-financed rise in public spending, which is relevant when the interest rate is endogenous and the price level is rigid (at least in the short run). This multiplier is thus only relevant under the assumption of sticky prices. The Keynesian multiplier is smaller in magnitude than the Kahn multiplier given by expression (1.30) on account of crowding out of private investment. This is captured by the additional positive term $l_Y I_R/l_R$ in the denominator of the Keynesian multiplier. The intuition is as follows. A bond-financed rise in public spending leads to a greater supply of government bonds and

---

[3] Aggregate saving is defined as $S(Y) \equiv Y - C(Y - T(Y)) - T(Y)$ so that the marginal propensity to save out of income equals $S_Y \equiv (1 - T_Y)(1 - C_{Y-T})$, which clearly satisfies $0 < S_Y < 1$. The savings identity furthermore implies that $C_Y \equiv 1 - (S_Y + T_Y)$, from which it follows that $0 < S_Y + T_Y < 1$ since $0 < C_Y < 1$. Hence, the multiplier exceeds unity.

thus exerts a downward pressure on bond prices and an upward pressure on interest rates. This leads to a fall in private investment and a fall in aggregate demand and employment, so that the Keynesian multiplier is smaller in magnitude than the Kahn multiplier. The extent of crowding out is more significant if private investment is very sensitive to changes in the interest rate ($|I_R|$ large) while money demand is not very sensitive ($|l_R|$ small) to changes in the interest rate and sensitive to changes in national income (l_Y large).

1.3 Schools in Macroeconomics

We now have all the ingredients that are needed to characterize the different schools of thought in macroeconomics. We briefly distinguish: (1) the classical economists, (2) the Keynesians, (3) proponents of the neo-Keynesian synthesis, (4) the monetarists, (5) the new classical economists, (6) the supply siders, and last but not least (7) the new Keynesians.

1.3.1 Classical economists

Names that spring to mind are Adam Smith, David Hume, David Ricardo, John Stuart Mill, Knut Wicksell, Irving Fisher, and Keynes of the *Treatise on Money* of 1930. We can roughly characterize the classical view on money by the crude quantity theory of money. In terms of our model, the LM curve (1.25) is replaced by a special case in which money demand does not depend on the interest rate:

$$M = kPY. \tag{1.31}$$

Hence, there is no reason to hold money for speculative purposes ($l_R \equiv 0$) and the velocity of circulation ($1/k$) is constant. The classical view regarding the supply side of the economy is characterized by a strong belief in markets and the efficacy of the price mechanism. In terms of our model, this implies flexible wages and prices, perfect foresight, labour market clearing, and a vertical AS curve. See Figure 1.9. Hence, fiscal and monetary policy cannot affect the levels of employment and output.

The classical model can be seen as a special case of the IS-LM-AS model developed above, with $l_Y = k = $ constant and $l_R = 0$. This means that the LM curve is vertical, so that fiscal policy is useless in affecting employment and output. Increasing government spending leads to a higher rate of interest and full crowding out of private investment, but not to changes in the price level. Monetary policy, on the other hand, has no effects on the real sphere of the economy, and only leads to a higher price level. This property is called the neutrality of monetary policy. The classical economists thus believed in a dichotomy: the real and monetary sectors could essentially be studied separately. Demand-side policies merely affect the

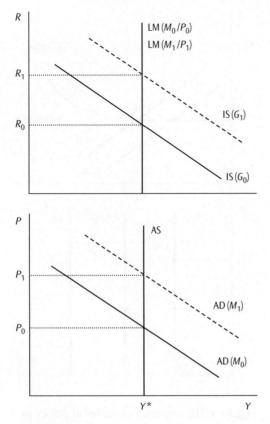

Figure 1.9. Monetary and fiscal policy in the classical model

interest rate and/or the price level, while supply-side policies affect the real wage, employment, and output.

1.3.2 Keynesians

Will we ever know what Keynes really meant when he wrote the *General Theory*? Probably not, but a number of insights into what Keynes may have meant can be obtained by following Modigliani's (1944) suggestion that the main Keynesian innovations consist of the liquidity preference schedule and the assumption of nominal wage rigidity.

With respect to his liquidity preference theory of money, Keynes himself used the classical economists as scapegoats. In doing so, he used the gimmick of the liquidity trap. Suppose, Keynes argued, that the rate of interest is so low that the economy is on the horizontal part of the LM curve. Suppose furthermore, that the level of

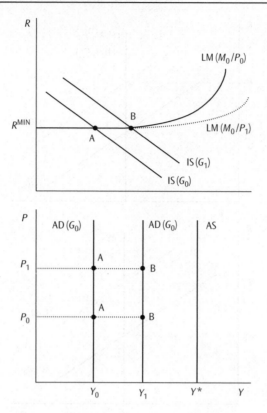

Figure 1.10. Monetary and fiscal policy in the Keynesian model

spending at that interest rate is too low to support full employment of the factors of production, and that prices and wages are flexible. In terms of Figure 1.10, the rate of interest is R^{MIN}, and output is $Y_0 < Y^*$. Keynes came to the startling conclusion that the classical model is inconsistent in that case. Aggregate supply is vertical at $Y = Y^*$, but demand falls short of Y^*, and no amount of price/wage reductions will restore equilibrium. The self-correcting feature of the market, which is of course the hallmark of classical theory, simply does not work.

Monetary policy will not help, according to Keynes, because the additional money will simply be absorbed by investors with no noticeable effect on the interest rate. Fiscal policy, on the other hand, will work really well. In terms of Figure 1.10, the additional government spending will stimulate aggregate demand (corresponding to a shift in the IS curve) and hence employment and output.

Nowadays, the liquidity trap is seen as a nice way to get people to take notice of the Keynesian ideas. In fact, Keynes' classical colleague and contemporary, A. C. Pigou, quickly pointed out that Keynes' result disappears once a wealth effect is introduced in the consumption function. In that case, the position of the IS curve will depend on real money balances M/P, the AD curve will slope downwards (and not be vertical, as Keynes suggested), and full employment will be restored provided prices and wages are flexible.

1.3.3 The neo-Keynesian synthesis

The neo-Keynesian synthesis was developed by neoclassical economists who allowed for a short run with Keynesian properties and a long run with classical properties. Since it contains classical and Keynesian elements, the approach is often referred to as the neoclassical synthesis. Names of neo-Keynesian synthesizers: Franco Modigliani, Paul Samuelson, James Tobin, Robert Solow, and in the 1950s and 1960s virtually all macroeconomists *except* Milton Friedman. There are actually different versions of the neo-Keynesian synthesis, depending on the assumption made about the labour market. The first version maintains (as does Modigliani, 1944) that nominal wages are rigid downwards. This opens up the possibility of unemployment and an upward sloping section of the AS curve (see section 1.1.4 and Figure 1.6). To get some adjustment over time, we add a Phillips curve relationship to the model, i.e. $\dot{W} = \alpha U$ ($\alpha < 0$). Introduction of a Phillips curve thus makes the change in nominal wages dependent on the amount of unemployment, where unemployment (U) is defined as $U \equiv (N^S - N)/N^S$. As a result, full employment will be restored after some time.

The second version of the neoclassical synthesis allows nominal wages to be fully flexible, but uses the AEH (1.14) to make the expected price level a slowly moving variable. The model corresponding to the neo-Keynesian synthesis corresponds to the AS curve (1.20), the AD curve (1.29), and the AEH (1.14). Again, full employment will eventually be restored, depending on the speed at which agents adapt to expectational errors. The effects of fiscal and monetary policy are illustrated in Figure 1.11. A bond-financed rise in public spending from G_0 to G_1 induces an outward shift of the IS curve and thus the AD curve. On impact, output rises above Y^* even though there is some crowding out of private investment on account of the rise in the rate of interest. The impact multiplier is, in fact, smaller than the Keynesian multiplier contained in expression (1.29). The reason is that the rise in aggregate demand caused by the increase in public spending causes on impact the price level to rise from P_0 to P_1 (through an upward move along the AS curve). The higher price level induces a contraction in the supply of real money balances and thus causes a rise in the interest rate and a fall in aggregate demand (associated with the backward shift in the LM curve). Consequently, the short-run multiplier is smaller than the Keynesian multiplier. We thus conclude that the short-run employment and output multipliers for a bond-financed rise in public spending are lower if saving, tax, and import leakages are substantial, crowding out of private investment is substantial, and the price level rises a lot. The short-run effects on employment and output are small and on the price level are large if the AD curve is relatively steep and the AS curve is relatively flat. In subsequent periods households revise their expectations regarding the price level upwards. This lowers the expected real wage and the supply of labour. Hence, the AS curve shifts backwards over time until output and employment are cut back to their equilibrium levels. The long-run effect of the fiscal expansion is thus merely a rise in the price level with no effect on employment or output.

Figure 1.11 may also be used to investigate the effects of an expansion of the nominal money supply from M_0 to M_1 under the AEH. The outward shift of the LM curve lowers the interest rate and pushes up aggregate demand. Consequently, the AD curve shifts out. On impact the price level also rises, which attenuates the rise in national income. Over time the expected price level is revised upwards and the AS curve shifts back until the original equilibrium of employment and output are reached again. In the short run a monetary expansion thus induces a boom in employment and output and a fall in the interest rate, but in the long run employment and output are unaffected and the price level rises in proportion with the rise in the nominal money supply. Although money is not neutral in the short run, it is neutral in the long run.

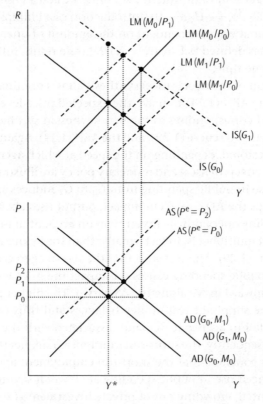

Figure 1.11. Monetary and fiscal policy in the neo-Keynesian synthesis model

1.3.4 The monetarists

Names: Milton Friedman and his friends. They assumed that the interest sensitivity of investment is very high (i.e. I_R large in absolute value) so that the IS curve is very flat. Consequently, fiscal policy leads to strong crowding out of private investment. Furthermore, the monetarists, like the classical economists, had strong sympathy for the quantity theory of money which implies a steep or vertical LM curve. In contrasts to the classical economists, Friedman does **not** accept the REH. Instead, he adopted the AEH. Fiscal policy is under monetarist assumptions unable to influence employment and output. This is why the monetarists were so vehemently against the Keynesians who believed in pump priming the economy in recessions.

Undoubtedly, the monetarists' assumptions imply that monetary policy has real effects. Indeed, from the quantity theory we have $M = kPY$, so that $dM > 0$ implies that $dPY = (1/k) dM > 0$. The distribution of the total effect (dPY) over real effects (dY) and nominal effects (dP) depends on the assumptions made about the labour market and the formation of expectations. Under AEH there are temporary effects on real output. The policy maker may therefore be tempted to use a monetary expansion to combat unemployment. The policy maker is, however, according to the monetarists, not very good at timing monetary policy. There are long and variable lags before a macroeconomic problem is recognized, before an appropriate macroeconomic policy is implemented, and before a policy has the required effect. As a result, monetary policy can actually accentuate business cycle fluctuations in the economy (if the policy is set too late, for example). This is why Friedman (1968) suggests that the central bank should follow a constant growth rule for some monetary aggregate and not tinker with monetary policy in order to try to influence aggregate demand and employment.

1.3.5 New classical economists

Names: Robert Lucas, Thomas Sargent, Robert Barro. Natural successors of the classical economists. These modern day classical economists stress mathematical techniques and are called "fresh water" economists, because they work (or used to) at universities near the big lakes in the Mid West (Chicago, Carnegie-Mellon, Minneapolis) and should be contrasted with the more Keynesian, "salt water" economists who work at US universities on the East coast (Harvard, MIT, Yale, Princeton).

These new classical economists have shed themselves more thoroughly of the neo-Keynesian synthesis than the monetarists, and firmly back classical ideas such as flexible prices and wages, rational expectations or perfect foresight, the efficiency of the market, and full employment. All fluctuations that we observe in the economy are due not to nominal rigidities but to rational agents responding to the incentives as they observe them. Strong endorsement of rational expectations and microeconomic underpinning of macroeconomic relations, such as the consumption function, the investment function, and the labour market. An early gimmick that was used to get the profession's attention was the so-called policy ineffectiveness proposition (PIP), according to which the policy maker either cannot (strong PIP) or should not (weak PIP) use countercyclical policy—see also the discussion of the classical proposition that monetary policy is neutral at the end of section 1.3.1. This school of thought will be discussed in more detail in Chapter 3.

1.3.6 Supply siders

Names: Arthur Laffer, Robert Mundell. Radical conservatives who despise government intervention in markets and emphasize the distorting effects of taxation. Beautifully chastised by Krugman (1994). Their policy advice was quite simple: cut tax rates and thus stimulate the economy. They argued that there was no need to cut government spending because the tax cut would pay for itself. Reagan loved the story, especially as it suggested that you could have your cake and eat it: no need to restrain public spending on defence while having an excuse to substantially cut the tax rate.

Central element was the so-called Laffer curve, first derived on the back of an envelope. This Laffer curve can be derived from a small modification of our model of the labour market, namely equations (1.7) and (1.12). Assume that there is only one tax, levied on labour income and paid by households, denoted by t_L, and that there is perfect foresight (so that $P^e = P$). The labour market model is then given by:

$$(1 - t_L)W/P = g(N^S), \quad W/P = F_N(N^D, \bar{K}), \quad N^D = N^S = N, \tag{1.32}$$

It is easy to see (from (1.12)) that $1 - t_L$ plays the same role as P/P^e in the expression for the AS curve (1.20), hence we can write the relative change in national income as:

$$\frac{dY}{Y} = -\left(\frac{\omega_N \epsilon_D \epsilon_S}{\epsilon_D + \epsilon_S}\right)\left(\frac{dt_L}{1 - t_L}\right) + \left(\frac{(1 - \omega_N)\epsilon_D + \epsilon_S}{\epsilon_D + \epsilon_S}\right)\frac{d\bar{K}}{\bar{K}}. \tag{1.33}$$

This expression can be used to find the relative change in revenue from the tax on labour in real terms (i.e. $T \equiv t_L(W/P)N = t_L\omega_N Y$):

$$\frac{dT}{T} \equiv \left[1 - \left(\frac{t_L}{1 - t_L}\right)\left(\frac{\omega_N \epsilon_D \epsilon_S}{\epsilon_D + \epsilon_S}\right)\right]\frac{dt_L}{t_L} + \left(\frac{(1 - \omega_N)\epsilon_D + \epsilon_S}{\epsilon_D + \epsilon_D}\right)\frac{d\bar{K}}{\bar{K}}, \tag{1.34}$$

where we assume that the share of labour in value added (ω_N) is constant as will be the case for a Cobb-Douglas production function. The first term in square brackets on the right-hand side shows the direct revenue (also called the tax rate) effect of the labour tax for a given level of wage income. The second term in square brackets on the right-hand side shows the tax base effect. If the labour tax rate is increased and labour supply slopes upwards ($\epsilon_S > 0$), labour supply and employment decrease. Hence, labour tax revenue will fall as well. We note that, for small labour tax rates

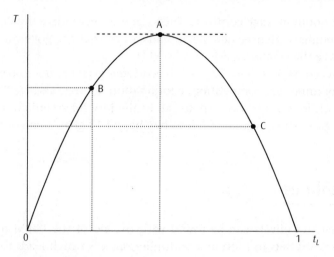

Figure 1.12. The Laffer curve

($t_L \approx 0$), the (negative) tax base effect is dominated by the (positive) tax rate effect on public revenue so that public revenue increases with the tax rate.

For large labour tax rates, however, the (positive) tax rate effect can be dominated by the (negative) tax base effect, especially if labour demand and labour supply are very elastic. In that case, labour tax revenue declines as the tax rate increases. Conversely, cutting the labour tax rate may actually boost revenue. Similar reasoning led Laffer to suggest that the revenue function would look like a parabola: for high tax rates the disincentive effect of the tax would be so strong that revenue would actually decline as the tax rate is increased further. This occurs beyond point A in Figure 1.12 at which tax revenue is maximized. If the tax rate is small, e.g. at point B, a rise in the tax rate boosts public revenue. Beyond point A, say at point C, a **reduction** in the tax rate would lead to an **increase** in tax revenue. Clearly, when the tax rate is zero or unity, tax revenue is zero.

Although Laffer's advice itself is logically correct and appeals to wishful thinkers, it was empirically irrelevant: the US economy was at a point like B in Figure 1.12. As a result, huge deficits and a massive build-up of government debt occurred despite substantial tax cuts in the US during the Reagan years.

1.3.7 New Keynesians

Names: (1970s) Edmund Phelps, John B. Taylor, Stanley Fischer, (1980s) Olivier-Jean Blanchard, Greg Mankiw. These are "salt water" economists who derive their main inspiration from the insights of John Maynard Keynes. Markets may not be as perfect as the classical economists suggest. Early new Keynesians accepted the REH but stressed the existence of nominal rigidities, arising from, for example, multi-period nominal wage contracts. Such rigidities invalidate the PIP of the new classical economists. Hence, new Keynesians argue that the government can and should stabilize the economy, even under REH.

The most recent wave of new Keynesian economics is more micro-based. The predominance of imperfect competition, coordination failures, and credit restrictions are stressed. Although it is too early to call in the jury for a verdict, it is clear that this is a very promising avenue of research. Chapter 13 gives some of the details.

1.4 Punchlines

Aggregate demand effects can be found with the aid of the IS-LM model. A rise in public spending sets in motion a multiplier process which leads to a larger rise in national income. However, the multiplier process is dampened by saving, tax, and import leakages. In addition, there is crowding out of private investment on account of the higher interest rate. In an open economy with capital mobility there may also be crowding out of net exports as the real exchange rate appreciates. An expansion of the nominal money supply or a fall in the aggregate price level also boosts aggregate demand and employment. In this case the interest rate falls so that private investment is boosted. In a small open economy the real exchange rate depreciates which gives a boost to net exports. Aggregate demand thus falls as the price level rises.

Aggregate supply is essentially determined by equilibrium in the labour market. Labour demand rises if there is a cut in the real wage or a boost to the capital stock. The wage elasticity of labour supply is positive if the substitution effect dominates the income effect in labour supply, that is if the elasticity of substitution between consumption and leisure in utility exceeds unity. If the income effect dominates the substitution effect, the wage elasticity of labour supply is negative. Labour supply declines as the tax system becomes more progressive, but is a positive function of the average income tax rate. Due to asymmetry in information, firms observe the wages to be paid to workers while households have to form expectations regarding the aggregate price level when deciding on their labour supply. Hence, equilibrium employment and the aggregate supply of goods thus rises if the capital stock expands, the average tax wedge falls, the tax system becomes less progressive, and if there is an unanticipated rise in the price level.

Macroeconomic equilibrium occurs when aggregate demand and aggregate supply of goods match up. The easiest case is the one assumed by classical economists: a quick clearing of all markets and perfect foresight. In that case, monetary policy is neutral in the sense that it cannot affect the real wage, employment, or output, neither in the short nor in the long run. A doubling of the money supply simply leads to a doubling of the aggregate price level. A fiscal expansion is fully crowded out by a fall in private investment (and net exports) on account of a rise in the interest rate (and an appreciation of the currency), so that neither employment nor output is affected. Hence, only supply-side policies, such as changes in the capital stock or in the various tax rates, can affect employment and output. Modern day versions of the classical economists are the new classicals, also called the "fresh water" economists, who stress rational expectations in stochastic environments and microeconomic foundations of macroeconomic relationships. A related breed of macroeconomists are the supply siders who believe in cutting taxes as this would boost tax revenue and alleviate the need to cut public spending. The supply siders were very influential in the 1980s, but have largely been discredited.

The older variety of Keynesian economists assumed sticky prices in the short run, so that employment and output were mainly determined by aggregate demand in the short run. A recent school of new Keynesians give the microeconomic underpinnings by stressing imperfect competition, coordination failures, and credit restrictions. The neo-Keynesian synthesis allows for a Keynesian short run and classical long run by introducing the assumption of adaptive expectations regarding the price level. In the short run the multiplier associated with a fiscal expansion is further reduced due to the rise in the price level. This leads to a contraction in real money balances, a further rise in the interest rate, and thus a dampening of the expansion in aggregate demand. Over time households revise their expectations upwards. As a result, aggregate supply and employment fall until the original equilibrium is restored again. The long-run output and employment multipliers for a rise in government spending are thus zero because any expansion of aggregate demand is fully offset by reductions in private investment (and net exports) caused by a higher interest rate (and appreciation of the currency).

Monetarists are somewhere in between the classical and Keynesian economists. They allow for adaptive expectations, but believe in the ineffectiveness of fiscal policy and the potential harmfulness of using monetary policy to manage aggregate demand. Monetarists believe in long and variable lags in monetary policy and therefore advocate a constant and modest rate of monetary growth. Clearly, monetarists are also deeply suspicious of using fiscal policy to fight unemployment.

Further Reading

The classic statement of the IS-LM model is presented by Hicks (1937). Most intermediate textbooks contain a thorough discussion of the IS-LM model. The ones we are familiar with are: Burda and Wyplosz (1997), Mankiw (2000a), Blanchard (2000a), and Abel and Bernanke (2001). The expectations-augmented Phillips curve was proposed independently by Friedman (1968) and Phelps (1967). Phelps et al. (1970) is a classic collection of the first wave of articles aiming to improve the microeconomic foundations of macroeconomics. Gordon (1974) presents a nice overview of the discussion between the monetarist Friedman and his various critics. Students interested in the historical aspects of the quantity theory of money should consult Laidler (1991). Feldstein (1986) presents an interesting discussion of supply side economics. Mankiw and Romer (1991) present a number of key articles in the new Keynesian school. To celebrate the arrival of a new millennium a number of very nice articles have appeared giving an overview of twentieth century developments in macro—see Blanchard (2000b) and Woodford (forthcoming). Snowdon, Vane, and Wynarczyk (1994) also present a nice overview of the various schools of thought. Klamer (1984) contains interviews with some of the principal new classical economists and some critics of this approach. Students interested in a through treatment of labour demand should refer to Hamermesh (1993).

2

Dynamics in Aggregate Supply and Demand

The purpose of this chapter is to achieve four goals, which are all related to the intrinsic dynamics that exist in the IS-LM model (or can be added to it quite easily). In particular, we study the following four issues:

1. The AEH and stability of the IS-LM-AS model under the neo-Keynesian synthesis,
2. The concept of hysteresis or path dependence arising in a model where the equilibrium rate of unemployment is determined by the past rate of unemployment and temporary shocks have permanent effect,
3. A theory of investment and the implied stock-flow interaction between investment and the capital stock, and,
4. A first view of the government budget restriction and the implied stock-flow interaction between the government deficit and debt or money, which allows a comparison of stability and effectiveness of money-financed and bond-financed increases in government spending.

In all cases the notion of stability will play a fundamental role. A *stable system* may be defined as one in which the unique equilibrium (also called stationary state) is eventually restored following a shock to one or more of the exogenous variables. Obviously, to operationalize this definition we must in each case indicate exactly what we mean by an equilibrium, and which variables we classify as exogenous. When the system has multiple equilibria (or stationary points), there may be stable or unstable equilibria. If there is a unique stable equilibrium, we shall choose that equilibrium as the relevant one and can still speak of a stable system.

The reason that economists like to focus attention on stable systems is that the alternative is unpalatable: unstable systems are not very useful for understanding the economy. An unstable system has no stable equilibria. Such an unstable system may very well have one or more unstable equilibria, but it is not likely to be at any of those equilibria at any point in time. Indeed, even if such a system starts in an equilibrium, a very small shock will permanently displace the system from that equilibrium. Only by pure coincidence would the system be in an equilibrium. Since economists know a lot more about equilibria than they do about disequilibrium situations, they like to study models that predict that the system converges along an equilibrium adjustment path to a stable equilibrium (see also Chapter 4). Note that this notion of equilibrium can also be extended to uncertain environments, in which case one would talk, for example, of stochastic steady states (see Chapter 3).

A very useful piece of methodological advice is contained in the so-called *correspondence principle*, which was transplanted from physics to economics by Paul Samuelson in his *Foundations of Economic Analysis* of 1947. In words, the correspondence principle states that we should believe and use only stable systems. As it will turn out, adherence to this principle often yields important information on the comparative static (or even comparative dynamic) predictions that can be derived from a theory. More precisely, the mathematical conditions that are necessary to have a stable system often enable macroeconomists to sign the steady-state multipliers for changes in government policy or other exogenous variables. We will give a number of applications of the correspondence principle during the course of this chapter.

In this chapter we restrict attention to models exhibiting a particular form of stability, the one that is most familiar to students of physical systems. All models discussed in this chapter display stability of a *backward-looking* kind. At a particular instant in time, the model determines the endogenous variables as a function of the exogenous variables and the predetermined state variables. Loosely put, history (as summarized by the state variables) determines the present situation. These backward-looking models are fairly mechanical, very much as switching on a machine will cause effects now and in the future but a machine will not switch itself on in anticipation of a future operation. In Chapter 4 we shall look at models exhibiting a completely different kind of stability, namely *forward-looking stability*. There history and the future jointly determine the current situation. Such forward-looking models are not considered in this chapter. These models arise in cases where economic psychology is relevant; for example, firms investing in anticipation of an investment subsidy being abolished in the future or a little boy who starts salivating at the promise of a Chelsea bun.

We also look in section 2 of this chapter at a macroeconomic model for which the steady state is not uniquely defined. Instead, the equilibrium at which the economy finally settles down depends on the course of history. Although this property seems eminently reasonable to historians and other social scientists, the steady-state equilibrium of most economic models does not depend on the course of history. Mathematically, such systems are characterized by a zero eigenvalue of the Jacobian matrix in the continuous-time case or a unit root in the discrete-time case. An interesting feature of models with the hysteresis property is that temporary shocks can have permanent effects. For example, a temporary adverse shock to the labour market can lead to lasting increases in the rate of unemployment.

2.1 The Adaptive Expectations Hypothesis and Stability

In Chapter 1 we saw that one variant of the neo-Keynesian synthesis model can be obtained under flexible wages and prices by assuming that price expectations are formed according to the adaptive expectations hypothesis (AEH). The model can be written in a very compact form as:

$$Y = AD(G, M/P), \tag{2.1}$$

$$Y = Y^* + \phi [P - P^e], \quad \phi > 0, \tag{2.2}$$

$$\dot{P}^e = \lambda [P - P^e], \quad \lambda > 0. \tag{2.3}$$

Equation (2.1) is the AD curve, which summarizes the simultaneous occurrence of money market equilibrium and spending equilibrium. The partial derivatives of the AD curve with respect to its arguments have been interpreted in Chapter 1 and follow immediately from equation (1.29):

$$AD_G \equiv \frac{1}{1 - C_{Y-T}(1 - T_Y) + l_Y I_R/l_R} > 0, \tag{2.4}$$

$$AD_{M/P} \equiv \frac{(I_R/l_R)}{1 - C_{Y-T}(1 - T_Y) + l_Y I_R/l_R} > 0. \tag{2.5}$$

Clearly, aggregate demand rises if government spending or real money balances are increased.

Equation (2.2) is the specification for aggregate supply in the goods market. Potential output, also called the full-employment level of output (Y^*), depends on supply-side variables. For example, potential output is an increasing function of the capital stock—see expression (1.20). Due to the fact that the expected and the actual price levels do not always coincide under the assumption of adaptive expectations, labour supply and consequently output can differ (in the short run) from their respective full-employment levels. The parameter ϕ follows from the AS curve (1.20):

$$\phi \equiv AS_P = \left(\frac{\omega_N \epsilon_D \epsilon_S}{\epsilon_D + \epsilon_S} \right) \frac{Y}{P} > 0. \tag{2.6}$$

Hence, the parameter ϕ determines the slope of the short-run AS curve—the higher a value of ϕ, the flatter the short-run AS curve, and the larger the output fluctuations that occur as a result of a given shift in aggregate demand:

$$P = P^e + (1/\phi) [Y - Y^*], \quad \left(\frac{dP}{dY} \right)_{P^e = P_0^e} = 1/\phi. \tag{2.7}$$

The gap between the full-employment level of output and the actual level of output, $Y^* - Y$, is sometimes called Okun's gap. It is also a measure of (involuntary) unemployment.

Finally, equation (2.3) is the continuous time version of the AEH expressed in equation (1.14). Agents revise their expectations regarding the price level if there is a discrepancy between the actual and the expected price level. The parameter λ is an indicator for the speed at which agents adapt their expectations (i.e. the speed at which they correct their mistakes). A crucial aspect of the AEH is that the expected price level is a *state variable*, which means that its value is given at a particular instant in time. Hence, under the AEH the expected price level, P^e, is treated just like the capital stock, namely as something that is determined in the past. To illustrate the point, we solve the differential equation (2.3) to obtain the following expression for the expected price level:

$$\dot{P}^e(\tau) + \lambda P^e(\tau) = \lambda P(\tau) \quad \Rightarrow \quad P^e(t) = \int_{-\infty}^{t} \lambda P(\tau) e^{-\lambda(t-\tau)} d\tau. \tag{2.8}$$

The expected price level in period t, denoted by $P^e(t)$, depends on the entire path of (exponentially weighted) price levels in the past. Due to the discounting, distant prices have relatively little influence on the expectation of the current price level.

The neo-Keynesian model of aggregate demand and supply summarized by equations (2.1)–(2.3) can be solved quite easily for the short run, the transition period, and the long run. Graphically, the solution has already been discussed in Chapter 1 and is illustrated again in Figure 2.1. The initial situation is point E_0, where output is equal to its potential level ($Y = Y^*$), the rate of interest is equal to R_0, and the price level is equal to P_0. Now consider the following experiment in order to determine the stability of our model: does the economy automatically return to an equilibrium after a shock, say an increase in government spending? The (affirmative) answer is easily illustrated with the aid of the diagram. Following the increase in government spending ($dG > 0$), the IS curve and hence the AD curve both shift to the right. Expectations are given in the short run, so that the economy operates along the short-run aggregate supply curve through E_0. At point A the price level has increased from P_0 to P' and output has also increased (to Y'). Is there an equilibrium at point A or, more precisely from a mathematical point of view, is A a stationary point? Clearly, there is equilibrium in the sense that the AD curve and short-run AS curve intersect. Given their price expectations, households are happy to supply the amount of labour they do, and all markets clear. There is, however, a disequilibrium regarding expectations: at point A households base their plans on the expectation that the price is P_0 but the actual price level is higher (P'). The AEH suggests that this discrepancy will be eliminated over time. Hence, A is not a stationary point. As the expected price level is increased, the short-run AS curve will start to shift up and to the left and the economy will move along the new AD curve towards point E_1. Point E_1 is a point of full equilibrium, because all markets clear and there is an expectational equilibrium. Hence, point E_1 is both an equilibrium from an economic point of view and a stationary point. Consequently, the IS-LM-AS model is stable.

It is not always so easy to use graphical devices to demonstrate stability. For that reason the following, slightly more formal method, may be used. Recall that in the

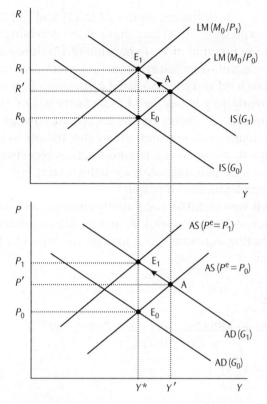

Figure 2.1. Fiscal policy under adaptive expectations

short run, the expected price level P^e is a predetermined- or state variable. Consequently, we can use expressions (2.1)–(2.2) to solve for the short-run equilibrium values of output, Y, and the price level, P, conditional on the exogenous variables $(G, Y^*,$ and $M)$ and the predetermined state variable (P^e). By totally differentiating equations (2.1)–(2.2) we obtain:

$$dY = AD_G dG + (M/P)AD_{M/P}\left(\frac{dM}{M} - \frac{dP}{P}\right), \tag{2.9}$$

$$dY = \phi[dP - dP^e] + dY^*. \tag{2.10}$$

These two expressions can be solved for the change in the price level, dP, and in output, dY:

$$dP = \frac{\phi dP^e + AD_G dG + (1/P)AD_{M/P}dM - dY^*}{\phi + (M/P^2)AD_{M/P}}, \tag{2.11}$$

$$dY = \frac{\phi[AD_G dG + (1/P)AD_{M/P}[dM - (M/P)dP^e]] + (M/P^2)AD_{M/P}dY^*}{\phi + (M/P^2)AD_{M/P}}. \tag{2.12}$$

33

Since $\phi > 0$ and $AD_{M/P} > 0$, the numerator of (2.11) and (2.12) is guaranteed to be positive. Hence, expression (2.11) says that P is an increasing function of P^e, G, and M but a decreasing function of Y^*. Expression (2.12) shows that the Keynesian multiplier which is relevant when prices are sticky, i.e. AD_G, is weakened on account of the rise in the price level and the associated contraction in real money balances. The extent of this weakening is captured by the factor $\phi/[\phi + (M/P^2)AD_{M/P}] < 1$. We see that the flatter the AS curve, i.e. the smaller the change in the price level caused by a change in aggregate demand, the smaller the rise in the price level and the dampening of the short-run Keynesian multiplier. A very steep AS curve implies that a rise in government spending yields a relatively large boost to the price level and a small rise in employment and output.

Expression (2.11) is very useful for our stability analysis, because it summarizes all the effects that influence the price level, P, at a particular instant in time. Indeed, by totally differentiating equation (2.3), and substituting (2.11), we obtain the differential equation:

$$d\dot{P}^e = \lambda \left[dP - dP^e \right]$$

$$= \lambda \left[\frac{AD_G dG + (1/P)AD_{M/P} [dM - (M/P)dP^e] - dY^*}{\phi + (M/P^2)AD_{M/P}} \right]$$

$$\Leftrightarrow \dot{P}^e = \Omega \left(P^e, G, M, Y^* \right). \tag{2.13}$$

The interpretation of (2.13) is as follows. The model given in (2.1)-(2.3) implies an implicit dynamic relationship, $\dot{P}^e = \Omega(P^e, G, M, Y^*)$. The partial derivatives of this implicit function are given by the coefficients on the right-hand side of (2.6) and imply $\Omega_G, \Omega_M > 0$ and $\Omega_{P^e}, \Omega_{Y^*} < 0$.

Let us now return to the stability experiment mentioned above. We leave exogenous variables other than government spending unchanged (i.e. $dM = dY^* = 0$ and $dG > 0$) and determine the "laws of motion" of the expected price level. The resulting *phase diagram* is found in Figure 2.2. From the expressions in (2.13) it is clear that $\dot{P}^e = \Omega[.]$ is a negative function of P^e (since $\Omega_{P^e} < 0$). The initial equilibrium or steady state is given by point E_0. If government spending is increased, the $\dot{P}^e$ line shifts up and to the right (since $\Omega_G > 0$). Even though P^e is fixed in the short run, $\dot{P}^e$ jumps to a positive value (point A). The expected price level starts to rise, which is represented by the arrows along the new $\dot{P}^e$ line. Eventually, the economy reaches point E_1, which is the new equilibrium and steady state. This experiment shows that the crucial property that is needed for stability is that changes in the expected price level should taper off. More formally, stability implies (and is implied by) $\partial \dot{P}^e / \partial P^e \equiv \Omega_{P^e} < 0$. If this stability condition holds, the model is, of course, stable in the face of shocks to other kinds of exogenous variables as well.

In order to test one's understanding of the material it is useful to examine the stability of an alternative neo-Keynesian synthesis model, namely one where the

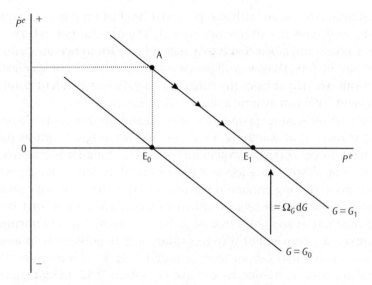

Figure 2.2. Stability and adaptive expectations

nominal wage adjusts sluggishly in response to conditions in the labour market. This is left as an exercise.

2.2 Hysteresis: Temporary Shocks can have Permanent Effects

We now consider a special class of models that have the *hysteresis* property. With hysteresis we mean a system whose steady state is not given, but can wander about and depends on the past path of the economy. Mathematically, we will see that this property implies that the Jacobian matrix of a continuous-time system has, apart from some "stable" eigenvalues (i.e. with a negative real part), a zero eigenvalue. For a discrete-time system there will be a unit root next to the other eigenvalues that are supposed to be smaller than one in absolute value. Systems with hysteresis can thus be viewed as being in the twilight zone between stable and unstable systems. Such systems are important in macroeconomics, because they allow us to depart from the rigid framework of equilibrium, a-historical economics. The best economic example of hysteresis is due to people becoming alienated from the labour market if they remain unemployed for a long enough period of time.

2.2.1 Alienation of the unemployed

So far, we have assumed that the equilibrium, steady-state, or potential level of output (Y^*) depends on the (exogenous) capital stock and supply-side policies (e.g. tax rates on labour). Associated with the potential level of output is an equilibrium, steady-state, or *natural* rate of unemployment. The implied natural rate of unemployment is a constant, albeit that it may depend on various tax rates, and does not depend on past history. Here we will develop a different model of aggregate supply. In order to this, we depart from the concept of a path-independent natural rate of unemployment.[1] We will assume a discrete-time system.

The idea is rather simple: people that stay unemployed become alienated from the labour market, stop searching for a job, and no longer count as part of the potential work force. Potential explanations are that long-term unemployed lose skills if they remain without a job or are stigmatized by firms. Hence, people that stay unemployed for long enough no longer add to downward wage pressure and become part of the natural rate of unemployment. We assume that the natural unemployment rate at any point in time is determined by the past unemployment rate. A simple, but convenient way to capture this hypothesis is to assume that the potential (or natural) output level at time $t + 1$, Y_{t+1}^*, is given by the actual output level at time t, Y_t. Hence, we can use expression (2.12) to write next period's potential level of output as a function of the current levels of potential output, the expected price, government spending and the money supply:

$$dY_{t+1}^* = dY_t - d\sigma_t = \frac{\phi d\delta_t - \alpha\phi dP_t^e + \alpha dY_t^* - (\phi + \alpha)d\sigma_t}{\phi + \alpha}, \tag{2.14}$$

where $\alpha \equiv (M/P^2)AD_{M/P} > 0$, $d\delta_t \equiv AD_G dG_t + (1/P)AD_{M/P}dM_t$ is an aggregate demand shock in period t, and where $d\sigma_t$ stands for an adverse aggregate supply shock in period t. Hence, a recession caused by tight monetary or fiscal policy or other falls in aggregate demand can lead to a future fall in potential output and thus a future rise in the corresponding natural unemployment rate.

2.2.2 History matters

The discrete-time equivalent for the expression of next period's expected price level as a function of the current levels of the expected price, potential output, government spending, and the money supply becomes:

$$dP_{t+1}^e = (1 - \lambda)dP_t^e + \lambda dP_t = \frac{\lambda d\delta_t - \lambda dY_t^* + [(1 - \lambda)\alpha + \phi]dP_t^e}{\phi + \alpha}, \tag{2.15}$$

where the expectational adjustment coefficient satisfies $0 < \lambda < 1$.

The dynamic system defined by the difference equations (2.14) and (2.15) generates the dynamics in the potential level of output, Y_t^*, and the expected price level,

---

[1] Indeed, this hysteresis effect is already present in the analysis of Phelps (1972, pp. 76–78).

P_t^e. The Jacobian matrix, say A, corresponding to this system is given by:

$$A = (\phi + \alpha)^{-1} \begin{bmatrix} \alpha & -\phi\alpha \\ -\lambda & (1-\lambda)\alpha + \phi \end{bmatrix}. \tag{2.16}$$

Since the product of the two eigenvalues of this Jacobian matrix is given by the determinant, $|A| = \alpha(1-\lambda)/(\alpha + \phi)$, and the sum of the two eigenvalues is given by the trace, $\mathrm{tr}(A) = [(2-\lambda)\alpha + \phi]/(\alpha + \phi)$, the two eigenvalues of the Jacobian matrix of this system are, respectively, unity and $0 < \alpha(1-\lambda)/(\alpha + \phi) < 1$.

In order to analyse the dynamic properties of this system in more detail, we use a trick and write the Jacobian matrix as follows:

$$AS = S\Lambda, \quad \text{where } \Lambda \equiv \begin{bmatrix} 1 & 0 \\ 0 & \dfrac{\alpha(1-\lambda)}{\alpha + \phi} \end{bmatrix} \tag{2.17}$$

denotes the diagonal matrix of eigenvalues and S is the matrix whose columns correspond to the eigenvectors of the Jacobian matrix A.[2] It is easy to show that the matrix S and its inverse S^{-1} are given by:

$$S = \begin{bmatrix} -\alpha & \phi \\ 1 & \lambda \end{bmatrix} \quad \text{and} \quad S^{-1} = (\alpha\lambda + \phi)^{-1} \begin{bmatrix} -\lambda & \phi \\ 1 & \alpha \end{bmatrix}. \tag{2.18}$$

The system (2.14)–(2.15) can be written in compact matrix form as:

$$x_{t+1} = Ax_t + a_t, \quad x_t \equiv \begin{bmatrix} dY_t^* \\ dP_t^e \end{bmatrix}, \quad a_t \equiv (\alpha + \phi)^{-1} \begin{bmatrix} \phi d\delta_t - (\alpha + \phi)d\sigma_t \\ \lambda d\delta_t \end{bmatrix}. \tag{2.19}$$

By defining auxiliary variables $z_t \equiv S^{-1}x_t$ and $b_t \equiv S^{-1}a_t$, the transformed system can be written as:

$$z_{t+1} = \Lambda z_t + b_t, \quad b_t \equiv (\alpha + \phi)^{-1} \begin{bmatrix} 0 \\ 1 \end{bmatrix} d\delta_t + (\alpha\lambda + \phi)^{-1} \begin{bmatrix} \lambda \\ -1 \end{bmatrix} d\sigma_t. \tag{2.20}$$

This transformed system is much easier to analyse than the original system because Λ is diagonal, so that there are no simultaneity effects anymore. The transformed system in fact consists of two first-order difference equations stacked on top of each other. For shocks to aggregate demand, we can easily find the solution to this system

---

[2] In formal terms, since A has distinct eigenvalues, its eigenvectors are linearly independent so that A can be diagonalized as $S^{-1}AS = \Lambda$ (Strang, 1988, pp. 254–260). By pre-multiplying both sides of this expression by S, the result in the text is found. See also Azariadis (1993, pp. 34–38) and the Mathematical Appendix.

of difference equations by recursive substitution:

$$z_t \equiv \begin{bmatrix} z_{1,t} \\ z_{2,t} \end{bmatrix} = \begin{bmatrix} 0 \\ z_{2,t} \end{bmatrix} \quad \text{with } z_{2,t} = (\alpha + \phi)^{-1} \sum_{i=0}^{\infty} \left[\frac{\alpha(1-\lambda)}{\alpha+\phi} \right]^i d\delta_{t-1-i}, \quad (2.21)$$

where

$$dY_t^* = \phi z_{2,t} \quad \text{and} \quad dP_t^e = \lambda z_{2,t}. \quad (2.22)$$

Hence, in contrast to economies in which hysteresis is not present, demand-side policies have real effects in the long run as well as in the short run. For example, the long-run effects of a sustained increase in government spending (i.e. $dM_t = 0$ and $d\delta_t \equiv AD_G dG$) on the actual and potential levels of output are easily seen to be equal to:

$$\left(\frac{dY^*}{dG} \right)^{LR} = \left(\frac{\phi}{\alpha+\phi} \right) \sum_{i=0}^{\infty} \left[\frac{\alpha(1-\lambda)}{\alpha+\phi} \right]^i AD_G = \left(\frac{\phi}{\alpha\lambda+\phi} \right) AD_G. \quad (2.23)$$

Clearly, temporary shocks to the aggregate demand for goods do not induce permanent effects on the levels of output.

To demonstrate that temporary shocks to aggregate supply may in the presence of hysteresis indeed lead to permanent changes in output and the natural rate of unemployment, we solve the system of difference equations when there are adverse shocks to aggregate supply $d\sigma_t$:

$$z_t = \left(\frac{1}{\alpha\lambda+\phi} \right) \begin{bmatrix} \lambda \sum_{i=0}^{\infty} d\sigma_{t-1-i} \\ -\sum_{i=0}^{\infty} \left[\frac{\alpha(1-\lambda)}{\alpha+\phi} \right]^i d\sigma_{t-1-i} \end{bmatrix}. \quad (2.24)$$

We immediately observe an essential difference between shocks to aggregate supply and shocks to aggregate demand. Although the effects of temporary shocks to aggregate demand fade out with time, the effects of temporary shocks to aggregate supply are long-lasting. Hence, temporary shocks in aggregate supply have permanent effects:

$$\frac{dY_t^*}{d\sigma_{t-j}} = -(\alpha\lambda+\phi)^{-1} \left[\alpha\lambda + \phi \left(\frac{\alpha(1-\lambda)}{\alpha+\phi} \right)^{j-1} \right]. \quad (2.25)$$

The second term in the square brackets fades out as j increases, but the first term does not fade out and is the reason why temporary shocks have permanent effects.

2.3 Investment, the Capital Stock, and Stability

In section 1 of this chapter we saw an example of stability analysis involving expectations. In this section and the next, we look at stability in a class of dynamic systems that stresses the interaction between stocks and flows. A very prominent example of interaction between stocks and flows is the one between the level of the capital stock and the rate of investment. This interaction is typically ignored in the IS-LM model, which renders the IS-LM model less useful for understanding transient and long-run issues. Notable exception to this ad hoc approach are Tobin and Buiter (1976) and Sargent (1987b). Before turning to the stability issue in the context of investment-capital dynamics, we first briefly introduce a theory of investment (by the typical firm) that is based on microeconomic foundations. This theory will be further developed in Chapter 4, but is used here to motivate the form of the investment function that is appropriate if dynamic issues are taken into account.

2.3.1 Adjustment costs and the theory of investment

Firms invest in order to add units of capital to the stock they already have and to replace the worn out capital stock. They do this because they want to conduct their operations in the most profitable way. In Chapter 1 we have already described a very basic *static* model of producer behaviour. The objective of this section is to expand our basic model of producer behaviour to a *dynamic* setting. By doing so, the issue of optimal investment plans can be studied.

We make the following assumptions regarding the typical firm. First, the firm has static expectations regarding all prices and the interest rate. Second, technology is constant. Third, the firm is a perfect competitor in the markets for its inputs and its output. Fourth, the investment process is subject to *adjustment costs*. Adding new machines is disruptive to the production process and leads to lost revenue. For low levels of investment these adjustment costs are low, but these costs rise more than proportionally with the level of investment. The adjustment cost function is (for simplicity) assumed to be quadratic: $bP^I I^2$, where b is a positive constant, P^I is the price of new machines, and I is the level of gross investment by the firm. The adjustment cost function is illustrated in Figure 2.3. The production function is still given by $Y = F(N, K)$ and has the properties stated in Chapter 1.

Finally, we assume that the typical firm maximizes the present value of the net payments it can make to the owners of its capital stock (i.e. the shareholders), subject to the restrictions of the production function and the capital accumulation identity. The market rate of interest on bonds R is used as the discount factor. In an intermezzo to this chapter we demonstrate that this assumption is justified in a decentralized market setting with a well-functioning stock market.

Since the problem of the firm is essentially dynamic, all variables must be given a time index. In order to obtain the simplest possible expressions, the derivation proceeds in discrete time. Nominal cash flow at the beginning of period t, Π_t, is defined as:

$$\Pi_t = PF(N_t, K_t) - WN_t - P^I I_t - bP^I I_t^2, \tag{2.26}$$

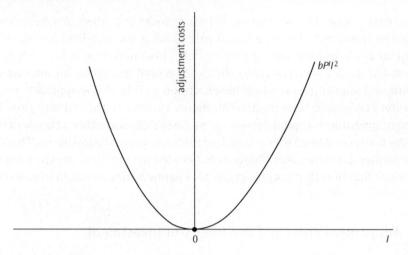

Figure 2.3. Adjustment costs of investment

where N_t is employment in period t, K_t is the capital stock at the beginning of period t, and I_t is the level of investment in period t. Note that the prices of goods and labour (P, P^I, W) have no time index, because we assume that firms expect these to be constant over time. The first two terms on the right-hand side of (2.26) represent sales revenue minus the wage bill; they are familiar from Chapter 1. The third term represents the current outlays on new investment goods, and the fourth term represents the adjustment costs. The identity linking rates of investment and the capital stock is given in discrete time as:

$$K_{t+1} - K_t = I_t - \delta K_t, \tag{2.27}$$

where δ represents the constant rate of physical deterioration of the capital stock due to wear and tear.

In period 0 ("today") the objective function of the firm, i.e. the present value of present and future cash flow streams, can be written as:

$$\bar{V}_0 \equiv \sum_{t=0}^{\infty} \left(\frac{1}{1+R}\right)^t \Pi_t$$

$$= \sum_{t=0}^{\infty} \left(\frac{1}{1+R}\right)^t \left[PF(N_t, K_t) - WN_t - P^I I_t - bP^I I_t^2\right]. \tag{2.28}$$

Due to the dynamic nature of the problem, the firm must formulate plans regarding production now and in the indefinite future (Y_t, for $t = 0, 1, 2, \ldots, \infty$). It does so by choosing paths (for time periods $t = 0, 1, 2, \ldots, \infty$), for employment ($N_t$), investment ($I_t$), and the capital stock (K_{t+1}) such that (2.28) is maximized subject to (2.27).

Intermezzo

The cost of capital. Which rate should the firm use to discount its present and future profits? Does the firm's dividend policy matter to the valuation of its shares on the stock market? These and related questions were first analysed in a number of highly influential papers by Modigliani and Miller (1958), Miller and Modigliani (1961), and Miller (1977). Miller and Modigliani (1961, p. 413) consider the following scenario: suppose a firm wants to invest by buying a $100 machine. How should it finance this investment—by reducing dividends (and thus relying on retained earnings) or by issuing new shares? Their surprising answer is that, in an ideal economy characterized by perfect capital markets, rational behaviour, and perfect certainty, the firm's dividend policy does not matter. This is the famous *Modigliani-Miller Theorem* (MMT hereafter). As it turns out this theorem also gives an answer to our first question concerning the appropriate discount rate for the firm.

Before giving a simple demonstration of the MMT it is important to emphasize the assumptions upon which its validity is based (Miller and Modigliani, 1961, p. 412). By *perfect capital markets* it is meant that no buyer or seller of securities has market power. There are no brokerage fees, transaction costs, and tax distortions. By *rational behaviour* it is meant that investors prefer more wealth to less and do not care about the form in which their wealth accrues (e.g. by cash payments or by valuation changes). Finally, by *perfect certainty* it is meant that all investors are fully aware of all future investment programmes and the future profits of every corporation. Presumably because these assumptions are rather stringent, Modigliani himself reputedly always adds the proviso "to a first approximation" when talking about the validity of the MMT (see Blanchard and Fischer, 1989, p. 314 fn. 35).

Suppose that there are many firms (indexed with i), facing identical technology and adjustments costs, and that the shares of all firms are traded in the stock market. Assume furthermore that, apart from holding shares in the various companies, investors can also hold a one-period government bond which pays $(1 + R)$ dollars per dollar invested each period. We assume that the firms issue no (corporate) debt and that the interest rate, wages, and prices are constant, both at present and in the future. Under the assumption made, the *fundamental principle of valuation* says that the yield per dollar invested must be the same for all financial assets:

$$\frac{d_t^i + p_{t+1}^i - p_t^i}{p_t^i} = R, \tag{a}$$

where d_t^i is the dividend per share paid by firm i at the end of period t, p_t^i is the price of a share in firm i (exclusive of period $t - 1$ dividend) at the start of period t. The left-hand side of (a) shows that the yield on one dollar invested in shares of firm i consists of dividend plus capital gains expressed in terms of the price of a share in that firm. The right-hand side of (b) shows that this common yield on shares must be equal to the yield on one-period government bonds.

Note that (a) can be rewritten as:

$$p_t^i = \left(\frac{1}{1+R}\right)\left[d_t^i + p_{t+1}^i\right].$$ (b)

This expression can be rewritten in terms of the value of the firm as a whole by defining $V_t^i \equiv p_t^i n_t^i$, where n_t^i is the number of shares of firm i at the beginning of period t:

$$
\begin{aligned}
V_t^i &= \left(\frac{1}{1+R}\right)\left[n_t^i d_t^i + n_t^i p_{t+1}^i\right] \\
&= \left(\frac{1}{1+R}\right)\left[n_t^i d_t^i + \left(n_t^i + n_{t+1}^i - n_{t+1}^i\right)p_{t+1}^i\right] \\
&= \left(\frac{1}{1+R}\right)\left[D_t^i + V_{t+1}^i - m_{t+1}^i p_{t+1}^i\right],
\end{aligned}
$$ (c)

where $D_t^i \equiv n_t^i d_t^i$ is total dividends paid at the end of period t to owners of the n_t^i "old" stockholders and $m_{t+1}^i \equiv n_{t+1}^i - n_t^i$ is the number of new shares sold during period t at the ex-dividend closing price p_{t+1}^i. Suppose that $P^I I_t^i (1 + b I_t^i)$ is the given firm's investment level (inclusive of adjustment costs) and that $X_t^i \equiv PF(K_t^i, N_t^i) - WN_t^i$ is the firm's gross profit, both measured at the beginning of period t. Then the amount of outside capital that the firm needs to finance its investment plans at the beginning of period $t + 1$ is:

$$m_{t+1}^i p_{t+1}^i = P^I I_{t+1}^i (1 + b I_{t+1}^i) + D_t^i - X_{t+1}^i.$$ (d)

By substituting (d) into (c) we obtain the following expression for the value of the firm at the start of period t:

$$V_t^i = \left(\frac{1}{1+R}\right)\left[X_{t+1}^i - P^I I_{t+1}^i (1 + b I_{t+1}^i) + V_{t+1}^i\right].$$ (e)

The crucial thing to note is that the level of dividends does not affect anything in (e)! Hence, the current value of the firm is independent of its current dividend policy. Solving (e) by repeated substitution of terms like V_{t+1}^i, V_{t+2}^i etc., we find the following expression for V_t^i after T substitutions:

$$V_t^i = \sum_{s=t+1}^{t+T} \left(\frac{1}{1+R} \right)^{s-t} \Pi_s^i + \left(\frac{1}{1+R} \right)^T V_{t+T}^i, \tag{f}$$

where we have used the definition of cash flow, Π_s^i (cf. the one given in (2.26)). By letting $T \to \infty$ in (f) we obtain:

$$V_t^i = \sum_{s=t+1}^{\infty} \left(\frac{1}{1+R} \right)^{s-t} \Pi_s^i. \tag{g}$$

As is pointed out by Auerbach (1979b, p. 437), the expression in (g) holds provided the value of the firm grows at a slower rate than R so that $\lim_{T \to \infty} (1+R)^{-T} V_{t+T}^i = 0$ in (f). This is a so-called *No Ponzi Game* (NPG) condition which prohibits the firm from running a "chain letter scheme" by supporting dividend payments solely from new share issues. (We shall encounter NPG conditions in various setting throughout the book).

By dropping the now superfluous firm index i and noting that the firm also has some cash flow at the beginning of the period t, we find that the objective function of the firm can be written as:

$$\bar{V}_t \equiv V_t + \Pi_t = \sum_{s=t}^{\infty} \left(\frac{1}{1+R} \right)^{s-t} \Pi_s. \tag{h}$$

By normalizing the planning period $t = 0$ we obtain the expression (2.28) in the text. Cash flows should be discounted by the cost of capital which, in the present setting, equals the rate of return on government bonds.

The Modigliani-Miller Theorem has been extended and generalized over the last four decades. Useful extensions in a macroeconomic setting are Auerbach (1979b), Sinn (1987), and Turnovsky (1995, ch. 10). All these authors focus on the effect of real world taxes on the validity of the MMT.

Two things are noteworthy. First, the choices regarding investment and the capital stock are not independent because the capital accumulation identity (2.27) implies a path of the capital stock once a path for investment is chosen. Second, the firm has an installed capital stock already, so that K_0 is not a choice variable to the firm. Formally, the maximization problem can be solved by means of the Lagrange multiplier method. The Lagrangian is:

$$\mathcal{L}_0 \equiv \sum_{t=0}^{\infty} \left(\frac{1}{1+R} \right)^t \left[PF(N_t, K_t) - WN_t - P^I I_t - bP^I I_t^2 \right]$$

$$- \sum_{t=0}^{\infty} \frac{\lambda_t}{(1+R)^t} \left[K_{t+1} - (1-\delta)K_t - I_t \right], \tag{2.29}$$

where λ_t is the Lagrange multiplier for the capital accumulation constraint that is relevant in period t (in order to simplify the notation these multipliers are weighted by the discount factor). The first-order conditions are (for $t = 0, \ldots, \infty$):

$$\frac{\partial \mathcal{L}_0}{\partial N_t} = \left(\frac{1}{1+R}\right)^t [PF_N(N_t, K_t) - W] = 0, \tag{2.30}$$

$$\frac{\partial \mathcal{L}_0}{\partial K_{t+1}} = \left(\frac{1}{1+R}\right)^t \left[\frac{PF_K(N_{t+1}, K_{t+1}) + \lambda_{t+1}(1 - \delta)}{1+R} - \lambda_t\right] = 0, \tag{2.31}$$

$$\frac{\partial \mathcal{L}_0}{\partial I_t} = \left(\frac{1}{1+R}\right)^t [-P^I - 2bP^I I_t + \lambda_t] = 0. \tag{2.32}$$

(Note the timing of the Lagrange multiplier in the first-order condition for capital!)

Although (2.30)–(2.32) look monstrously difficult, they can nevertheless be readily interpreted. First, equation (2.30) amounts to the marginal productivity condition for the labour input that was already derived for the static case (see equation (1.04)). It is intuitively obvious that these two first-order conditions coincide: labour is a fully flexible factor of production, and the choice of how much labour to use is not a dynamic one.

Equations (2.31) and (2.32) can be combined to yield an expression for the optimal path of investment. First, (2.32) is used to get expressions for λ_t and λ_{t+1}:

$$\lambda_t = P^I[1 + 2bI_t], \quad \lambda_{t+1} = P^I[1 + 2bI_{t+1}]. \tag{2.33}$$

By substituting these expressions into (2.31), we obtain the first-order condition for investment:

$$PF_K(N_{t+1}, K_{t+1}) + \lambda_{t+1}(1 - \delta) - \lambda_t(1 + R) = 0 \Rightarrow$$

$$PF_K(N_{t+1}, K_{t+1}) + (1 - \delta)P^I[1 + 2bI_{t+1}] - (1 + R)P^I[1 + 2bI_t] = 0 \Rightarrow$$

$$I_{t+1} - \left(\frac{1+R}{1-\delta}\right)I_t + \frac{PF_K(N_{t+1}, K_{t+1}) - P^I(R + \delta)}{2bP^I(1-\delta)} = 0. \tag{2.34}$$

This equation is an unstable difference equation for investment, since the coefficient for I_t is greater than unity. The steady-state solution for investment is found by setting $I_{t+1} = I_t = I$:

$$I = \frac{1}{2b}\left[\frac{PF_K(N, K)}{P^I(R + \delta)} - 1\right]. \tag{2.35}$$

The intuition behind expression (2.35) is very simple. If the value of the marginal product of capital (PF_K) is greater than the rental price of capital (i.e. the opportunity cost of capital plus the depreciation charge, $(R + \delta)P^I$), the firm should invest. Note furthermore that in the absence of adjustment costs ($b = 0$), the firm has no well-defined optimal *investment* policy. In that case (2.35) reduces to $PF_K = P^I(R + \delta)$, which is a static condition determining the optimal *capital stock* for the firm. Hence,

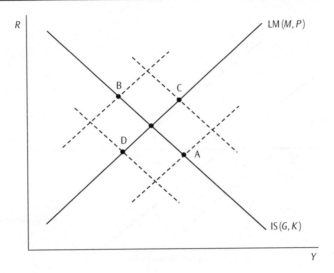

Figure 2.4. Comparative static effects in the IS-LM model

Recall that the stability requirement is that changes in the capital stock must taper off, i.e. stability requires that $\partial \dot{K}/\partial K \equiv I_R H_K + I_K + I_Y AD_K - \delta < 0$ holds. Stabilizing influences exist because $I_K < 0$, $I_Y AD_K < 0$, and $-\delta < 0$. A high capital stock (and thus a low level of output) imply a low level of gross investment. In addition, a high capital stock implies a high level of depreciation. Hence, net investment is at a low level and the capital stock will fall in future periods back to its equilibrium value. However, a destabilizing influence is clearly the term $I_R H_K > 0$. Intuitively, the destabilizing effect is due to the fact that a higher capital stock induces a lower interest rate (as $H_K < 0$) and stimulates investment (as $I_R < 0$).

What would the typical economist do in such a situation where stability is not guaranteed? Typically, one would appeal to Samuelson's correspondence principle and simply assume stability, i.e. postulate that the destabilizing effect of $I_R H_K > 0$ is dominated by the sum of the stabilizing effects $(I_K + I_Y AD_K - \delta) < 0$. This is the approach taken here also.

Given that stability has been assumed, what happens if the government increases its expenditure on goods and services $(dG > 0)$? Equation (2.47) says that the $\dot{K}$ line may shift up or down depending on the sign of $\partial \dot{K}/\partial G \equiv I_R H_G + I_Y AD_G$. A typical monetarist (see Chapter 1) would suggest a strong interest rate effect on investment ($|I_R|$ large), and a large effect on the interest rate but a small effect on output of a rise in government spending (H_G large and AD_G small). Consequently, a monetarist might suggest that $\partial \dot{K}/\partial G$ is negative. This is illustrated in Figure 2.5. According to the monetarist view, the $\dot{K}$ line shifts down, and in the long run the capital stock is crowded out by government spending.

A typical Keynesian might argue the reverse: $|I_R|$ small, H_G small, and AD_G large, so that $\partial \dot{K}/\partial G > 0$. This implies that the $\dot{K}$ line shifts up and to the right, so that the

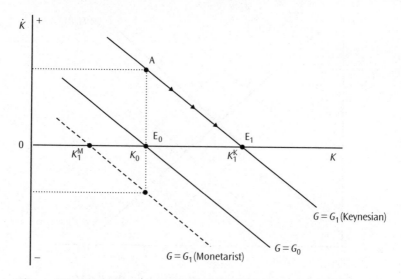

Figure 2.5. The effect on capital of a rise in public spending

capital stock is stimulated in the long run by a rise in government spending. The Keynesian predictions regarding the effects on the rate of interest and output have been illustrated in Figure 2.6. In the short run the capital stock is fixed (at K_0) and the IS curve shifts to the right. The economy moves from E_0 to A, and output and employment increase. Despite the higher interest rate, firms wish to add to their capital stock ($\dot{K} > 0$ in A) and the IS curve starts to shift back towards the ultimate equilibrium point E_1.

The long-run effect on output is guaranteed to be positive (though more so under the Keynesian assumptions). This can be shown as follows. In the long run it must be the case that $\dot{K} = 0$, so that $I^{LR} = \delta K^{LR}$ and $dI^{LR} = \delta dK^{LR} > 0$ (where the superscript LR denotes long-run values). Gross investment equals replacement investment in the steady state and is increased by a rise in public spending. By using (2.47) we obtain the long-run effect on investment and the capital stock:

$$\left(\frac{dI}{dG}\right)^{LR} = \delta\left(\frac{dK}{dG}\right)^{LR} = \frac{\delta[I_R H_G + I_Y AD_G]}{-[I_R H_K + I_K + I_Y AD_K - \delta]}, \tag{2.48}$$

where stability ensures that the denominator is positive. To a Keynesian, the additional government spending "crowds in" the capital stock and the numerator is positive, and the reverse holds for a monetarist. By using the long-run investment effect (2.38) and the IS-LM multipliers, we obtain the following long-run output multiplier for a rise in public spending:

$$\left(\frac{dY}{dG}\right)^{LR} = \frac{I_R(I_K - \delta)}{I_R(I_K - \delta)[1 - C_{Y-T}(1 - T_Y)] - \delta[I_Y I_R - I_R I_Y]} > 0, \tag{2.49}$$

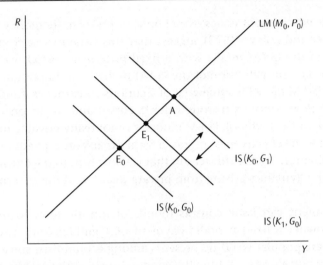

Figure 2.6. Capital accumulation and the Keynesian effects of fiscal policy

where the denominator of this expression is proportional to $-\partial \dot{K}/\partial K$ and is thus (by stability) guaranteed to be positive. Samuelson's correspondence principle thus yields useful information on the sign of the denominator. Since the numerator of expression (2.49) is negative as well, output must rise in the long run. The Keynesian assumptions imply that investment is not very sensitive to the rate of interest while money demand is very sensitive to changes in the interest rate (a steep IS curve and a flat LM curve) and that investment reacts strongly to changes in output. In that case, crowding out of private investment is small relative to the output effect on investment. It thus follows that output and capital both rise after an increase in public spending. The monetarist assumptions are the opposite (a steep LM curve, a flat IS curve, and a small output effect on investment). Hence, a rise in public spending depresses capital and output rises by less in the long run.

This example must not be taken too seriously, of course, in view of the fact that it is highly implausible that the actual AS curve is horizontal (as was assumed in this section). It merely serves to illustrate the stability issues surrounding the stock-flow interaction between the capital stock and investment.

2.4 Wealth Effects and the Government Budget Constraint

Another example of stock-flow interaction are the intrinsic dynamics in the IS-LM models that arise once we allow for the wealth effects in consumption and money demand if the government issues extra bonds or prints more money to finance its deficit. Blinder and Solow (1973) suggest that this issue can be fruitfully studied with the aid of the IS-LM model with a fixed price level, which we normalize at unity (i.e. $P = 1$). This extension of the IS-LM model is an important one, because the textbook IS-LM model is somewhat of a curious construct as it measures in one diagram both flow concepts (through the IS curve) and stock concepts (through the LM curve). In the textbook IS-LM model it is not really possible to even ask the question of how the effectiveness of, say, a fiscal expansion depends on the mode of government finance. It is for this reason that we now turn to the crucial question of allowing for the dynamics arising from private wealth and the government budget restriction.

The government can issue consols (bonds of infinite term to maturity) that promise the owner a fixed periodic payment of 1 guilder from now to infinity. Such consols are popular wedding presents among economists, since they remind the partners to buy a rose each time the coupon is paid at the wedding anniversary. If the rate of interest is R, how much would an investor be willing to pay for such a bond? Obviously, the price of the bond P_B would be exactly equal to the present value of the stream of income derived from the bond, or, in continuous time:

$$P_B = \int_0^\infty 1 e^{-R\tau} d\tau = -(1/R)\left[e^{-R\tau}\right]_0^\infty = 1/R. \tag{2.50}$$

If the government has issued B of such bonds in the past, then the payments it must make each period are equal to B times 1 guilder. Hence, B represents both the number of consols with the public and the interest payments of the government to the public. If the government issues new consols ($\dot{B} > 0$), it receives $P_B\dot{B}$ in revenue from this bond sale. Furthermore, the government can meet its obligations by simply printing money ($\dot{M} > 0$). With goods prices fixed at unity, the government budget restriction can be written as:

$$G + B = T + \dot{M} + (1/R)\dot{B}. \tag{2.51}$$

The left-hand side represents the nominal spending level of the government inclusive of interest payments to private agents. The right-hand side of the government budget restriction shows the three financing methods open to the government: taxation, money finance, and bond finance.

The level of taxation (T) depends on all income received by the households, i.e. inclusive of real interest receipts B:

$$T = T(Y + B), \quad 0 < T_{Y+B} < 1. \tag{2.52}$$

The total amount of real financial wealth in the economy (A) is the sum of the fixed capital stock ($\bar{K}$), the real money supply, and the real value of bond holdings by the public:

$$A \equiv \bar{K} + M/P + B/R. \tag{2.53}$$

As a final modification, Blinder and Solow (1973) suggest that both consumption and money demand depend positively on the level of wealth:

$$C = C(Y + B - T, A), \quad 0 < C_{Y+B-T} < 1, \; C_A > 0, \tag{2.54}$$

$$M/P = l(Y, R, A), \quad l_Y > 0, \; l_R < 0, \; 0 < l_A < 1. \tag{2.55}$$

Equation (2.54) is a mixture of two theoretical notions. As we shall see in Chapter 6, the forward-looking theory of consumption requires households to have unlimited access to a perfect capital market. This suggests that private consumption should depend on total wealth (i.e. financial wealth plus human wealth, the present value of lifetime earnings) and, possibly, the rate of interest as well. Furthermore, bonds should not be counted as part of private wealth. In contrast, the Keynesian theory of consumption suggests a central role for current income. As we shall see in Chapter 6, however, there is an empirically plausible rationale for the specification adopted in (2.54). For now we simply use (2.54) without further comment and leave some of these issues as an exercise and for Chapter 6.

Money demand, given by the right-hand side of (2.55), is also different from the one used in equation (1.25). The rationale for this money demand function is a portfolio allocation model. The household chooses to allocate its total financial wealth (A) over the three different financial assets that exist in the model: bonds, claims to physical capital, and money. Under the assumption that claims to physical capital and bonds are perfectly substitutable, the rate of return on these assets must be the same (and equal to R). This explains why only R (or the consol price) appears in (2.55). Obviously, if wealth rises, one would expect all components of the wealth portfolio to rise, including the demand for money. This explains the wealth effect in money demand.

2.4.1 Short-run macroeconomic equilibrium

In the short run, the money supply and the level of government debt are predetermined variables. The IS curve is obtained by combining (2.52)–(2.23) with the investment function (1.23) and the national income identity (1.21):

$$Y = C\left[Y + B - T(Y + B), \bar{K} + M/P + B/R\right] + I(R) + G, \tag{2.56}$$

and the LM curve is given by equation (2.55). The short-run equilibrium values of output Y and the rate of interest R can once again be expressed in terms of the predetermined and exogenous variables:

$$Y = AD(P, G, \bar{K}, B, M), \qquad R = H(P, G, \bar{K}, B, M) \tag{2.57}$$

where the relevant partial derivatives are obtained in the usual manner

$$AD_B = \frac{C_{Y+B-T}(1 - T_{Y+B}) + C_A/R - \phi l_A/R}{1 - C_{Y+B-T}(1 - T_{Y+B}) + \phi l_Y}, \tag{2.58}$$

$$H_B = \frac{-(l_A/R)\left[1 - C_{Y+B-T}(1 - T_{Y+B})\right]}{(l_R - l_A B/R^2)\left[1 - C_{Y+B-T}(1 - T_{Y+B}) + \phi l_Y\right]}$$
$$- \frac{l_Y(C_{l+B-T}(1 - T_{Y+B}) + (C_A/R))}{(l_R - l_A B/R^2)\left[1 - C_{Y+B-T}(1 - T_{Y+B}) + \phi l_Y\right]} > 0, \tag{2.59}$$

$$AD_G = \frac{1}{1 - C_{Y+B-T}(1 - T_{Y+B}) + \phi l_Y} > 0, \tag{2.60}$$

$$H_G = \frac{-l_Y}{(l_R - l_A B/R^2)\left[1 - C_{Y+B-T}(1 - T_{Y+B}) + \phi l_Y\right]} > 0 \tag{2.61}$$

$$AD_M = -(P/M)AD_P > 0, \quad H_M = -(P/M)H_P, \quad \phi \equiv \frac{l_R - C_A B/R^2}{l_R - l_A B/R^2} > 0. \tag{2.62}$$

The interpretation of these partial derivatives is facilitated with the aid of Figure 2.7. For example, an increase in government spending shifts the IS curve from IS(G_0,M_0) to IS(G_1,M_0). In point A income is higher than before and there is an excess demand for money (an excess supply of bonds). This causes a fall in bond prices, i.e. a rise in the interest rate, which moves the economy to point B. In terms of Figure 2.7, both output and the rate of interest are higher, hence $AD_G > 0$ and $H_G > 0$. The partial derivatives for changes in M and B are discussed below.

In Figure 2.7 we have shown that an increase in government spending causes a short-run increase in output Y and the rate of interest R. This is not the end of the story, of course, since we have not yet taken the government budget restriction into account. Blinder and Solow (1973) consider two extreme cases. In the first case, the government prints new money to finance the additional government spending. Consequently, the money stock changes over time to balance the government's books, i.e. $\dot{M} \neq 0$ and $\dot{B} = 0$. In the second case considered by Blinder and Solow (1973), the government balances its books by issuing additional bonds, i.e. $\dot{M} = 0$ and $\dot{B} \neq 0$. The questions that can be analysed now are: (i) is the model stable under both financing methods, and (ii) what is the relationship between the different output multipliers for government spending with respect to different modes of government finance. At first blush one would ignore wealth effects and suggest that a money-financed increase in government spending boosts output by more than a bond-financed rise in government spending, because it is associated with a fall in the interest rate and thus an additional boost to aggregate money demand as the LM curve shifts out. At second blush this may not turn out to be correct as the wealth effects in consumption and money demand affect the multipliers as well. We now investigate this in more detail.

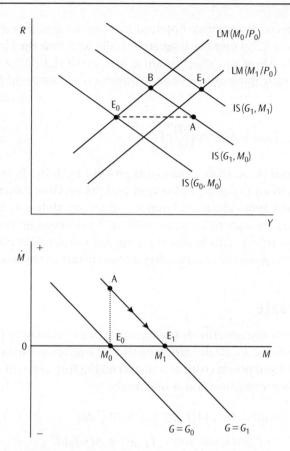

Figure 2.7. The effects of fiscal policy under money finance

2.4.2 Money finance

Under money finance the government budget restriction reduces to $\dot{M} = G + B - T(Y+B)$, where B is fixed. This government budget restriction thus represents a function relating $\dot{M}$ to government spending G and output Y. By totally differentiating this function and taking into account equation (2.57), the following differential equation is obtained:

$$d\dot{M} = dG - T_{Y+B}[AD_G dG + AD_M dM]$$

$$= (1 - T_{Y+B}AD_G)dG - T_{Y+B}AD_M dM. \qquad (2.63)$$

Hence, it is immediately obvious that the model is stable under money finance. Indeed, we have $\partial\dot{M}/\partial M \equiv -T_{Y+B}AD_M < 0$ so that changes in the money stock dampen out over time. Furthermore, the initial effect of the fiscal impulse is to cause a budget deficit, i.e. $\partial\dot{M}/\partial G \equiv (1 - T_{Y+B}AD_G) > 0$. The impact, transition, and long-run effects of a money-financed increase in government spending are illustrated in Figure 2.7. From the diagram it is obvious that the long-run effect on output exceeds the short-run effect (point E_1 lies to the right of point B). With the aid of the steady-state government budget restriction we derive the long-run output multiplier:

$$\left(\frac{dY}{dG}\right)_{MF}^{LR} \equiv 1/T_{Y+B} > AD_G \equiv \left(\frac{dY}{dG}\right)_{MF}^{SR}. \tag{2.64}$$

Money finance leads to a stable adjustment process. Both the IS and the LM curve shift out leading to an expansion of output and tax revenue thereby reducing the government deficit until balanced budget and steady state are reached. Output has to rise by just enough to generate sufficient tax revenue to pay for the rise in government spending. This is why the long-run output multiplier for a money-financed increase in government spending is equal to one over the marginal tax rate.

2.4.3 Bond finance

Under bond finance the government budget restriction reduces to $(1/R)\dot{B} = G + B - T(Y + B)$ and M is fixed. By totally differentiating the government budget restriction around an initial equilibrium (with $\dot{B} = 0$) and taking into account equation (2.57), the following differential equation is obtained:

$$(1/R)d\dot{B} = dG + dB - T_{Y+B}[AD_G dG + AD_B dB + dB]$$
$$= (1 - T_{Y+B}AD_G)dG + [1 - T_{Y+B}(1 + AD_B)]dB. \tag{2.65}$$

Hence, it is not at all obvious that the model is stable under bond finance. Recall that the model is stable if (and only if) changes in debt eventually dampen over time, i.e. $\partial \dot{B}/\partial B < 0$. Hence, the stability condition is:

$$\frac{\partial \dot{B}}{\partial B} < 0 \quad \Leftrightarrow \quad 1 - T_{Y+B}(1 + AD_B) < 0 \quad \Leftrightarrow \quad AD_B > \frac{1 - T_{Y+B}}{T_{Y+B}} > 0. \tag{2.66}$$

The stability condition says that the wealth effect on aggregate demand, AD_B, must be positive and sufficiently large. In (2.57) we showed, however, that AD_B cannot be signed a priori. This is because a rise in the level of debt boosts private wealth, private consumption, and thus aggregate demand and output (the outward shift of the IS curve), but it also increases money demand and thus depresses aggregate demand and output (inward shift of the LM curve). Hence, a necessary condition for stability is that the wealth effect on consumption dominates the wealth effect on money demand.

But this is not sufficient for stability, because the additional debt also gives rise to additional government outlays on interest payments and the potential danger of a self-fuelling explosion of government debt. The interest payments must ultimately be financed by means of higher tax revenues for otherwise the government books will not be balanced (i.e. it must be the case that eventually $\dot{B} = 0$). This is why the marginal tax rate plays a role in the stability condition. More precisely, with a high marginal tax rate, more tax revenues are generated for a given expansion of output and thus it is more likely that the deficit is eliminated and the build-up of government debt is arrested (i.e. stability is ensured).

The impact, transition, and long-run effects of a bond-financed rise in government spending are illustrated in Figure 2.8 for the stable case. From the diagram it is obvious that the long-run effect on output exceeds the short-run effect. Indeed, from the steady-state government budget restriction we can derive the long-run output multiplier:

$$\left(\frac{dY}{dG}\right)^{LR}_{BF} \equiv AD_G - AD_B \left(\frac{1 - T_{Y+B}AD_G}{1 - T_{Y+B}(1 + AD_B)}\right) > AD_G \equiv \left(\frac{dY}{dG}\right)^{SR}_{BF}. \tag{2.67}$$

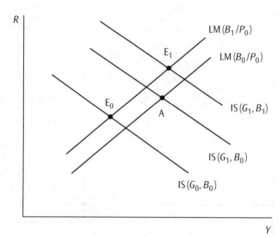

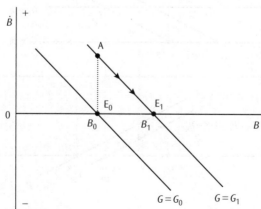

Figure 2.8. Fiscal policy under (stable) bond financing

As a final remark, consider the long-run multipliers under the two financing methods. It is obvious from (2.64) and (2.67) that, provided the stability condition (2.66) holds, the bond-financed output multiplier exceeds the money-financed multiplier:

$$\left(\frac{dY}{dG}\right)_{BF}^{LR} \equiv AD_G - AD_B \left(\frac{1 - T_{Y+B}AD_G}{1 - T_{Y+B}(1 + AD_B)}\right) > \frac{1}{T_{Y+B}} \equiv \left(\frac{dY}{dG}\right)_{MF}^{LR}. \tag{2.68}$$

The intuition is straightforward. The long-run increase in output under bond finance must exceed the one under money finance, because the additional interest payments must also be financed by means of higher tax receipts and this requires a higher national income. This has been illustrated in Figure 2.9, where point E_0

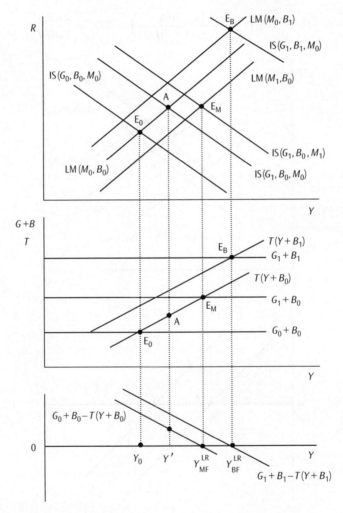

Figure 2.9. Long-run effect of fiscal policy under different financing modes

indicates the initial equilibrium, point A stands for the short-run outcome, and points E_M and E_B represent the long-run outcome under money finance and bond finance, respectively. Figure 2.9 clearly shows that bond finance (if it is stable) yields a bigger long-run multiplier than money finance even though the interest rate rises by more. Providing the intuition behind the shifts in the IS, LM, and tax schedules is left as an exercise.

2.5 Punchlines

We have extended the static IS-LM-AS model by adding some essential dynamic features to do with adaptive expectations, capital accumulation, and the build-up of government debt. Allowing for adaptive expectations in aggregate supply ensures that anticipated fiscal and monetary policy can have transient real effects. This is why this extension corresponds to a neo-Keynesian synthesis with a Keynesian short run and a classical long run. Hence, an expansion of aggregate demand leads in the short and medium run to a rise in output but as expectations catch up with the rise in prices the initial gains in output are wiped out. Money is thus neutral in the long run. Stability of the expectational adjustment process is guaranteed, because the price level rises in the short run less than proportionally with the expected price level as a consequence of the short-run contraction in the aggregate supply.

We also provided an example of hysteresis, or path dependence of the steady state, by suggesting that the natural level of output depends on the past level of output. Alternatively, the natural unemployment rate is supposed to be determined by the past unemployment rate. This captures the phenomenon that the long-term unemployed become alienated from the labour market, stop searching for a job, and no longer exert downward wage pressure. Two lessons can be drawn from this analysis. First, permanent changes in fiscal and monetary policy have lasting effects on employment and output. Second, as far as supply-side policy and shocks are concerned, even temporary changes have permanent effects on employment and output. Temporary adverse supply shocks can thus lead to permanently higher levels of unemployment. The mathematical condition for hysteresis to occur is the presence of a zero eigenvalue in the Jacobian matrix of continuous-time or a unit eigenvalue in discrete-time systems.

Another popular method to allow for dynamics in aggregate demand and supply is to have an augmented Phillips curve relating nominal wage inflation to expected price inflation and the gap between actual and potential output. If expected inflation equals last year's actual inflation, we obtain the acceleration hypothesis: the change in the rate of inflation (i.e. the acceleration of the price level) rises with the gap between actual and potential output. Clearly, it is then only possible to sustain an unemployment rate lower than the natural rate, if inflation rises steadily over time.

Monetary disinflation, i.e. a cut in the monetary growth rate, eventually leads to a corresponding cut in the inflation rate, but causes in the interim period transitory unemployment losses.

To allow for finite speeds of investment and sluggish adjustment in the capital stock, it is useful to introduce adjustment costs when investment takes place. In that case, employment still follows from the condition that the marginal productivity of labour must equal the real wage but the marginal productivity of capital no longer equals the user cost of capital (i.e. the rental charge plus the depreciation charge). Instead, investment is high if the gap between the marginal productivity of capital and the user cost of capital is large. This amounts to an investment function which states that investment increases if output rises and the capital stock or the interest rate declines. Such a specification also arises if one adopts an accelerator view of investment. Introducing this specification of investment and the capital accumulation identity into the basic model of aggregate demand, typically, does not lead to instability. Under the Keynesian assumptions, i.e. investment not very sensitive, but money demand very sensitive to changes in the interest rate, a rise in public spending leads to higher levels of capital and output. However, under the monetarist assumptions, i.e. investment very sensitive, but money demand insensitive to changes in the interest rate, an increase in public spending crowds out capital and thus depresses output in the long run. It is straightforward to extend these multiplier-accelerator models to allow for investment lags and other lags. One finds stable adjustment processes as long as the investment lag is long enough and the propensity to consume small enough.

A final extension to allow for dynamics in the basic IS-LM-AS model is to incorporate wealth effects in consumption and money demand. This extension is essential, because the basic IS-LM framework compares apples with pears as the IS curve refers to flow concepts while the LM curve relates to stock concepts. There is something fundamentally wrong with seeking equilibrium in both stock and flow concepts without allowing for a time dimension. To allow for this time dimension, we assume that consumption and money demand rise if wealth (consisting of claims to physical capital, real money balances and government bonds) increases. Consumption also depends on disposable income, where taxes are levied on both production and interest income. The government budget constraint states that the public sector financial deficit, i.e. primary public spending plus interest payments minus tax revenue, must be financed by printing money or issuing bonds. Since a money-financed increase in public spending induces downward pressure on the interest rate while a bond-financed increase in public spending induces upward pressure on the interest rate, one might think at first sight that money finance is more expansionary than bond finance. Although this may be so in the short run, this turns out to be not the case in the long run. In fact, the long-run bond-financed multiplier is larger than the money-financed multiplier because national income has to rise to generate sufficient tax revenue not only to cover the rise in public spending but also the interest on the accumulated government debt. The money-financed multiplier simply equals one over the marginal tax rate, whereas the bond-financed multiplier is larger than this. Money finance leads to a stable process, since the initial government deficit is gradually eliminated as money supply expands, the interest rate falls, and national income and tax revenue rise. Bond finance may lead to a never-ending explosion of government debt if over time the build-up of government debt raises money demand and pushes up the interest rate so much that national income and tax revenue fall. The result is an ever-increasing government deficit. This instability can only be stopped if the wealth effect in consumption is strong enough, that is if the rise in private wealth and consumption boosts aggregate demand, national income and tax revenue sufficiently to ensure that the government deficit becomes smaller over time. Hence, to ensure stability under bond finance the wealth effect in consumption must be relatively strong compared to the wealth effect in money demand.

Further Reading

Key readings in the adjustment cost approach to investment are Eisner and Strotz (1963), Lucas (1967), Gould (1968), and Treadway (1969). Abel (1990) gives an overview of this literature. The classic articles on the government budget constraint are Blinder and Solow (1973, 1976). See also Tobin and Buiter (1976), Turnovsky (1977), and Scarth (1988). For early applications of dynamic methods to the study of the macroeconomy readers are referred to Samuelson (1947), Baumol (1959), and Allen (1967). See Cross (1988) for a collection of papers dealing with hysteresis.

Rational Expectations and Economic Policy

The purpose of this chapter is to discuss the following issues:

1. What do we mean by rational expectations (also called model-consistent expectations)?

2. What are the implications of the rational expectations hypothesis (REH) for the conduct of economic policy? What is the meaning of the so-called policy-ineffectiveness proposition (PIP)?

3. What are the implications of the REH for the way in which we specify and use macroeconometric models, and what is the Lucas critique?

4. What is the lasting contribution of the rational expectations revolution?

3.1 What is Rational Expectations?

3.1.1 The basic idea

More than three decades ago, John Muth published an article in which he argued forcefully that economists should be more careful about their informational assumptions, in particular about the way in which they model expectations. Muth's (1961) point can be illustrated with the aid of the neoclassical synthesis model under the AEH that was discussed in Chapter 2. Consider Figure 3.1, which illustrates the effects of monetary policy over time. The initial equilibrium is at point E_0, with output equal to Y^* and the price level equal to P_0. There is an expectational equilibrium, because $P = P^e$ at point E_0. If the monetary authority increases the money supply (in a bid to stimulate the economy), aggregate demand is boosted (the AD curve shifts to AD_1), the economy moves to point A, output increases to Y^*, and the price level rises to P'. In A there is a discrepancy between the expected price level and the

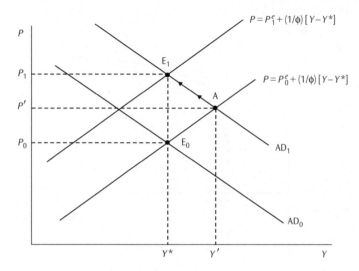

Figure 3.1. Monetary policy under adaptive expectations

actual price level. This discrepancy is slowly removed by an upward revision of the expected price level, via the adaptive expectations mechanism (e.g. equation (1.14)). In the diagram this is represented by a gradual movement along the new AD curve towards point E_1, which is the new full equilibrium.

The adjustment path of expectations is very odd, however, because agents (e.g. households supplying labour) make *systematic mistakes* along this path. The time paths for the actual and expected price levels are illustrated in Figure 3.2, as is the expectational error ($P^e - P$). The initial shock causes an expectational error that is slowly eliminated. All along the adjustment path, the error is negative and stays negative, and agents keep guessing wrongly.

This is very unsatisfactory, Muth (1961) argued, because it is diametrically opposed to the way economists model human behaviour in other branches of economics. There, the notion of rational decision making (subject to constraints) occupies centre stage, and this does not appear to be the case under the AEH. As a result, Muth proposed that: "expectations, since they are informed predictions of future events, are essentially the same as the predictions of the relevant economic theory" (1961, p. 316).

With respect to the model illustrated in Figure 3.1, this would mean that agents hear at time t_0 that the money supply has been increased from M_0 to M_1, use the relevant economic theory (equations (2.1)–(2.2)), calculate that the correct price level for the new money supply is P_1, adjust their expectations to that new money supply ($P_1^e = P_1$), and supply the correct amount of labour. As a result, the economy jumps from E_0 to E_1, output is equal to Y^* and the price level is P_1. Of course, this adjustment story amounts to the PFH version of the policy-ineffectiveness proposition. Since there is no uncertainty in the model, forecasting is not difficult for

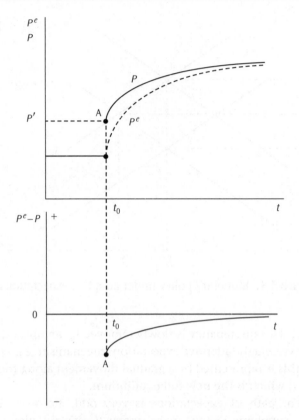

Figure 3.2. Expectational errors under adaptive expectations

the agents. They realize that a higher money supply induces a higher price level and thus adjust their wages upwards. As a result, the real wage, employment, and output are unaffected.

In reality all kinds of chance occurrences play an important role. In a macroeconomic context one could think of stochastic events such as fluctuation in the climate, natural disasters, shocks to world trade (German reunification, OPEC shocks, the Gulf War), etc. In such a setting, forecasting is a lot more difficult. Muth (1961) formulated the hypothesis of rational expectations (REH) to deal with situations in which stochastic elements play a role. The basic postulates of the REH are: (i) information is scarce and the economic system does not waste it, and (ii) the way in which expectations are formed depends in a well-specified way on the structure of the system describing the economy.

In order to clarify these postulates, consider the following example of an isolated market for a non-storable good (so that inventory speculation is not possible). This market is described by the following linear model:

$$Q_t^D = a_0 - a_1 P_t, \quad a_1 > 0, \tag{3.1}$$

$$Q_t^S = b_0 + b_1 P_t^e + U_t, \quad b_1 > 0, \tag{3.2}$$

$$Q_t^D = Q_t^S \quad [\equiv Q_t], \tag{3.3}$$

where P_t is the price of the good in period t, Q_t^D is the quantity demanded, Q_t^S is the quantity supplied, and P_t^e is the price level that suppliers expect in period $t-1$ to hold in period t. The random variable U_t represents all stochastic elements that impinge on the supply curve. If the good in question is an agricultural commodity, U_t could summarize all the random elements introduced in the supply decision by the weather, crop failures, insect plagues, etc.

Equation (3.1) shows that demand only depends on the actual price of the good. In other words, the agents know the price of the good, and there are no stochastic events occurring on the demand side of the market, such as random taste changes, income fluctuations, etc. Equation (3.2) implies that there is a production lag: suppliers must decide on the production capacity before knowing exactly what will be the price at which they can sell their goods. They make this decision on the basis of all information that is available to them. In the context of this model, the information they possess in period $t-1$ is summarized by the so-called *information set*, Ω_{t-1}:

$$\Omega_{t-1} \equiv \{P_{t-1}, P_{t-2}, ...; Q_{t-1}, Q_{t-2}, ...; a_0, a_1, b_0, b_1; U_t \sim N(0, \sigma^2)\} \tag{3.4}$$

What does this mean? First, the agents know all prices and quantities up to and including period $t-1$ (they do not forget relevant past information). Obviously, the information set Ω_{t-1} does not include P_t, Q_t, and U_t. Second, the agents know the structure of the market they are in (recall: "the relevant economic theory" is used by agents). Hence, the model parameters a_0, a_1, b_0, and b_1 are known to the agents as is the structure of the model given in (3.1)–(3.3). Third, although the actual realization of the stochastic error term U_t is not known for period t, the probability distribution of this stochastic variable is known. For simplicity, we assume that U_t is distributed as a normal variable with an expected value of zero ($EU_t = 0$), no autocorrelation ($EU_t U_s = 0$ for $t \neq s$), and a constant variance of σ^2 [$\equiv E(U_t - EU_t)^2$], where $E(.)$ is the unconditional expectations operator. This distributional assumption is written in short-hand notation as $N(0, \sigma^2)$. Recall from first-year statistics that the normal distribution looks like the symmetric bell-shaped curve drawn in Figure 3.3. Fourth, past realizations of the error terms are, of course, known. Agents know past observations on Q_{t-i} and P_{t-i}, and can use the model (3.1)–(3.3) to find out what the corresponding realizations of the shocks must have been (i.e. U_{t-i}).

The REH can now be stated very succinctly as:

$$P_t^e = E[P_t \mid \Omega_{t-1}] \equiv E_{t-1} P_t, \tag{3.5}$$

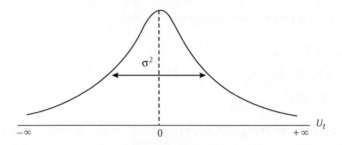

Figure 3.3. The normal distribution

where E_{t-1} is short-hand notation for $E(. \mid \Omega_{t-1})$, which is the *conditional expectation* operator. In words, equation (3.5) says that the *subjective* expectation of the price level in period t formed by agents in period $t-1$ (P_t^e) coincides with the conditional *objective* expectation of P_t, given the information set Ω_{t-1}.

How does the REH work in our simple model? First, equilibrium outcomes are calculated. Hence, (3.3) is substituted into (3.1) and (3.2), which can then be solved for P_t and Q_t in terms of the parameters and the expected price P_t^e:

$$P_t = \frac{a_0 - b_0 - b_1 P_t^e - U_t}{a_1}, \tag{3.6}$$

$$Q_t = b_0 + b_1 P_t^e + U_t. \tag{3.7}$$

Equation (3.6) is crucial. It says that the actual price in period t depends on the price expected to hold in that period, and the realization of the stochastic shock U_t. More precisely, a higher expected price level or a positive supply shock (bigger P_t^e or U_t) boosts the supply of goods and thus the equilibrium price level must fall in order to clear the market. The REH postulates that individual agents can also calculate (3.6) and can take the conditional expectation of P_t:

$$E_{t-1} P_t = E_{t-1} \left[\frac{a_0 - b_0 - b_1 P_t^e - U_t}{a_1} \right]$$

$$= \left(\frac{a_0 - b_0}{a_1} \right) - \left(\frac{b_1}{a_1} \right) E_{t-1} P_t^e - \left(\frac{1}{a_1} \right) E_{t-1} U_t. \tag{3.8}$$

Consider the three terms on the right-hand side of (3.8) in turn. The first term is obvious: the conditional expectation of a known constant is that constant itself. The second term can similarly be simplified: P_t^e is a known constant, so that $E_{t-1} P_t^e = P_t^e$. The third term can be simplified by making use of our knowledge concerning the distribution of U_t. Since U_t is not autocorrelated, the conditional expectation of it is equal to its unconditional expected value, i.e. $E_{t-1} U_t = 0$. As a result of all these simplifications, $E_{t-1} P_t$ can be written as:

$$E_{t-1} P_t = \left(\frac{a_0 - b_0}{a_1} \right) - \left(\frac{b_1}{a_1} \right) P_t^e. \tag{3.9}$$

But the REH states in (3.5) that the objective expectation, $E_{t-1}P_t$, and the subjective expectation, P_t^e, coincide. Hence, by substituting $E_{t-1}P_t = P_t^e$ into (3.9) we obtain the solution for P_t^e:

$$P_t^e = \frac{a_0 - b_0}{a_1} - \left(\frac{b_1}{a_1}\right) P_t^e \quad \Rightarrow \quad P_t^e = E_{t-1}P_t = \left(\frac{a_0 - b_0}{a_1 + b_1}\right). \tag{3.10}$$

The final expression is the rational expectations solution for the *expected* price level. The actual price level P_t is stochastic (of course, since it depends on the stochastic supply shock U_t). By substituting (3.10) into (3.6), the expression for P_t is obtained:

$$P_t = \left(\frac{a_0 - b_0}{a_1 + b_1}\right) - \left(\frac{1}{a_1}\right) U_t = \bar{P} - \left(\frac{1}{a_1}\right) U_t, \tag{3.11}$$

where $\bar{P} \equiv (a_0 - b_0)/(a_1 + b_1)$ is the equilibrium price that would obtain if there were no stochastic elements in the market. Equation (3.11) says that the actual price P_t fluctuates randomly around $\bar{P}$. The expectational error is equal to $P_t - E_{t-1}P_t = -(1/a_1)U_t$, and exhibits no predictable pattern. Also, the average of this error is zero, so that agents do not make systematic mistakes. If there is an expected negative supply shock, for example due to an agricultural disaster, the price level rises.

What would have been the case under the AEH? Obviously, under AEH, the expectational errors do display a predictable pattern. Recall (from (1.14)) that the AEH says that the expected price level can be written as a weighted average of last period's actual price level and last period's expected price level:

$$P_t^e = \lambda P_{t-1} + (1 - \lambda)P_{t-1}^e, \quad 0 < \lambda < 1. \tag{3.12}$$

By using (3.6) and (3.12), the model can be solved under the AEH:

$$P_t - (1 - \lambda)P_{t-1}$$
$$= \left(\frac{\lambda(a_0 - b_0)}{a_1}\right) - \left(\frac{b_1}{a_1}\right)(P_t^e - (1 - \lambda)P_{t-1}^e) - \left(\frac{1}{a_1}\right)(U_t - (1 - \lambda)U_{t-1}),$$
$$= \left(\frac{\lambda(a_0 - b_0)}{a_1}\right) - \left(\frac{\lambda b_1}{a_1}\right)P_{t-1} - \left(\frac{1}{a_1}\right)(U_t - (1 - \lambda)U_{t-1}) \quad \Rightarrow$$
$$P_t = \left(\frac{\lambda(a_0 - b_0)}{a_1}\right) + \left[1 - \lambda\left(\frac{a_1 + b_1}{a_1}\right)\right]P_{t-1} - \left(\frac{1}{a_1}\right)(U_t - (1 - \lambda)U_{t-1}). \tag{3.13}$$

Equation (3.13) shows that the equilibrium price P_t under the AEH displays a clearly recognizable pattern, because P_t depends on its own lagged value P_{t-1} and the error term displays autocorrelation.

The issue can be illustrated with the aid of Figures 3.4 and 3.5, which show the paths of the price level and the expectational errors that are made under, respectively, the REH and the AEH. The diagrams were produced as follows. First, the computer was instructed to draw 100 (quasi-) random numbers from a normal distribution with mean zero and variance $\sigma^2 = 0.01$. These random numbers are the

U_t of the model. The parameters of demand and supply were set at $a_0 = 3$, $a_1 = 1$, $b_0 = 1$, and $b_1 = 1$, which implies that the deterministic equilibrium price is $\bar{P} = 1$. Obviously, from (3.10) it is clear that under the REH, $P_t^e = \bar{P} = 1$. This is the dashed line in Figure 3.4. The actual price level under the REH is given by (3.11), and is drawn as a solid line fluctuating randomly around the dashed line. In Figure 3.5 the

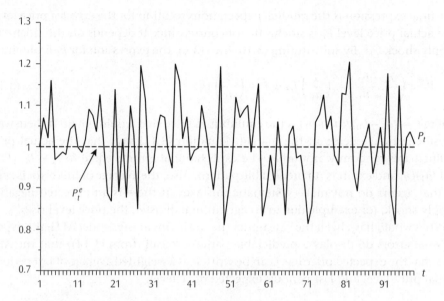

Figure 3.4. Actual and expected price under REH

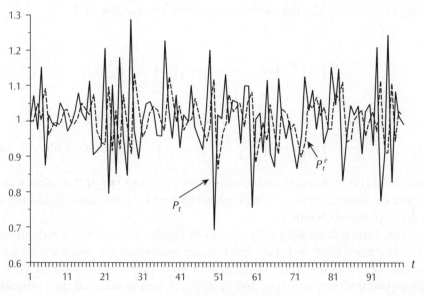

Figure 3.5. Actual and expected price under AEH

expected and actual price levels have been drawn for the same stochastic U_t terms as before. Not surprisingly, there is a clear pattern in the way expectations continually lag behind actual price movements (as (3.12) of course suggests theoretically).

3.1.2 Do we really believe the idea?

In the previous section we have postulated the REH in the form of a statement like (3.5). Muth (1961) offers an intuitive defence for the equality of conditional and subjective expectations. First, if the conditional expectation of the price level based on the model ($E_{t-1}P_t$) were considerably better at forecasting P_t than the subjective expectation of suppliers (P_t^e), there would be an opportunity for making larger than normal profits for an alert "insider", i.e. someone who does use the information contained in the model. This insider could, for example, start his/her own business, engage in inventory speculation (in the case of storable goods), or operate a consulting firm specialized in selling forecasting services to the existing suppliers.

It has unfortunately proved very difficult indeed to come up with a formal model of this "market for information". One of the reasons is that (i) information is costly to get, and (ii) is at least partially a public good. Agents that possess information can, by their actions in the market place, unwittingly reveal the content of this information to agents who have not acquired it. As a result, there may be a strong "free-rider" problem in the market for information. Using this type of argument, Grossman and Stiglitz (1980) conclude that it is impossible for the market for information to be efficient. Other authors investigate the question whether agents can learn to converge to rational expectations—see, for example, Friedman (1979), DeCanio (1979), and Pesaran (1987). The conclusion of this literature suggests that is not always the case. To quote DeCanio, "the economical use of information will not necessarily generate rational expectations" (1979, p. 55).

So there are good reasons to believe that the use of the REH cannot be justified as an outcome of an informational cost-benefit analysis. Yet, many economists today accept the REH as the standard assumption to make in macro-models involving uncertainty. The reason for this almost universal acceptance is again the correspondence principle. Since we know little about actual learning processes, and the REH describes an equilibrium situation, it is the most practical hypothesis to use. Of course, the equilibrium described by models involving the REH is inherently stochastic. For that reason, REH solutions for models can be referred to as *stochastic steady-state solutions*.

3.2 Applications of REH in Macroeconomics

The idea behind rational expectations remained unused for a decade, before new classicals like Robert Lucas, Thomas Sargent, Neil Wallace, and Robert Barro applied it to macroeconomic issues. They took most of their motivation from Friedman's (1968) presidential address to the American Economic Association, and consequently focused on the role of monetary policy under the REH.

Their basic idea can be illustrated with a simple loglinear model, that is based on Sargent and Wallace (1975).

$$y_t = \alpha_0 + \alpha_1(p_t - E_{t-1}p_t) + u_t, \quad \alpha_1 > 0, \tag{3.14}$$

$$y_t = \beta_0 + \beta_1(m_t - p_t) + \beta_2 E_{t-1}(p_{t+1} - p_t) + v_t, \quad \beta_1, \beta_2 > 0, \tag{3.15}$$

$$m_t = \mu_0 + \mu_1 m_{t-1} + \mu_2 y_{t-1} + e_t, \tag{3.16}$$

where $y_t \equiv \log Y_t$, $m_t \equiv \log M_t$, and $p_t \equiv \log P_t$ are, respectively, output, the money supply, and the price level, all measured in logarithms. The random terms are given by u_t, v_t, and e_t, and are assumed to be independent from themselves in time, and from each other, i.e. $Ev_t = 0$, $Ev_t^2 = \sigma_V^2$, $Eu_t = 0$, $Eu_t^2 = \sigma_U^2$, $Ee_t = 0$, and $Ee_t^2 = \sigma_E^2$.

Equation (3.14) is the expectations based short-run aggregate supply curve (e.g. (2.2)). If agents underestimate the price level, they supply too much labour and output expands. Note that the coefficient α_0 plays the role of potential output, $\alpha_0 = y_t^* \equiv \log Y_t^*$. Equation (3.15) is the AD curve. The real balance term, $m_t - p_t$, reflects the influence of the LM curve, i.e. the Keynes effect, and the expected inflation rate, $E_{t-1}(p_{t+1} - p_t)$, represents a Tobin effect. Investment depends on the real interest rate, so that, ceteris paribus the nominal interest rate, a higher rate of expected inflation implies a lower real rate of interest, and a higher rate of investment and hence aggregate demand. Finally, equation (3.16) is the policy rule followed by the government. This specification nests several special cases: (i) Friedman would advocate a constant money supply (since there is no real growth in the model) and would set $\mu_1 = \mu_2 = 0$, so that $m_t = \mu_0$; (ii) a Keynesian like Tobin would believe in a countercyclical policy rule, i.e. $\mu_1 = 0$ but $\mu_2 < 0$. If output in the previous period is low (relative to potential, for example), then the monetary authority should stimulate the economy by raising the money supply in this period. The interpretation of the error term in the money supply rule is not that the monetary authority deliberately wishes to make the money supply stochastic, but rather that she has imperfect control over this aggregate. We could also allow money supply to depend on other elements of the information set, i.e. $p_{t-1}, p_{t-2}, \ldots,$ $m_{t-2}, m_{t-3}, \ldots, y_{t-2}, y_{t-3}, \ldots$, but that does not affect the qualitative nature of our conclusions regarding the effectiveness of monetary policy whatsoever.

How do we solve the model given in (3.14)–(3.16)? It turns out that the solution method explained above can be used in this model also. First, we equate aggregate supply (3.14) and demand (3.15) and solve for the price level:

$$p_t = \frac{\beta_0 - \alpha_0 + \beta_1 m_t + \alpha_1 E_{t-1}p_t + \beta_2 E_{t-1}[p_{t+1} - p_t] + v_t - u_t}{\alpha_1 + \beta_1}. \tag{3.17}$$

Second, we take expectations of p_t, conditional on the information set Ω_{t-1}:

$$E_{t-1}p_t = \frac{\beta_0 - \alpha_0 + \beta_1 E_{t-1}m_t + \alpha_1 E_{t-1}E_{t-1}p_t}{\alpha_1 + \beta_1}$$
$$+ \frac{\beta_2 E_{t-1}E_{t-1}[p_{t+1} - p_t] + E_{t-1}(v_t - u_t)}{\alpha_1 + \beta_1}. \quad (3.18)$$

But the conditional expectation of a conditional expectation is just the conditional expectation itself, i.e. we only need to write E_{t-1} once on the right-hand side of (3.18). The shock terms v_t and u_t are not autocorrelated, so the conditional expectation of these shocks is zero, i.e. $E_{t-1}v_t = 0$ and $E_{t-1}u_t = 0$. In other words, knowing the actual realization of these shocks in the previous period (v_{t-1} and u_{t-1}), as the agents do, does not convey any information about the likely outcome of these shocks in period t. After substituting all these results into (3.18), one obtains a much simplified expression for $E_{t-1}p_t$:

$$E_{t-1}p_t = \frac{\beta_0 - \alpha_0 + \beta_1 E_{t-1}m_t + \alpha_1 E_{t-1}p_t + \beta_2 E_{t-1}[p_{t+1} - p_t]}{\alpha_1 + \beta_1}. \quad (3.19)$$

By deducting (3.19) from (3.17), a very simple expression for the price surprise is obtained:

$$p_t - E_{t-1}p_t = \left(\frac{\beta_1}{\alpha_1 + \beta_1}\right)[m_t - E_{t-1}m_t] + \left(\frac{1}{\alpha_1 + \beta_1}\right)[v_t - u_t]. \quad (3.20)$$

Only unanticipated shocks to AD and AS, and unanticipated changes in the money supply can cause agents to be surprised. Indeed, (3.16) implies that $m_t - E_{t-1}m_t = e_t$, so that (3.20) and (3.14) imply the following expression for output:

$$y_t = \alpha_0 + \frac{\alpha_1 \beta_1 e_t + \alpha_1 v_t + \beta_1 u_t}{\alpha_1 + \beta_1}, \quad (3.21)$$

where the parallel with equation (3.11) should be obvious. Equation (3.21) represents the stochastic steady-state solution for output. Given the model and the REH, output fluctuates according to (3.21).

Equation (3.21) has an implication that proved very disturbing to many economists in the early 1970s. It says that monetary policy is completely ineffective at influencing output (and hence employment): regardless of the policy rule adopted by the government (passive monetarist or activist Keynesian), output evolves according to (3.21) *which contains no parameters of the policy rule!* This is, in a nutshell, the basic message of the policy-ineffectiveness proposition (PIP). In the words of Sargent and Wallace:

In this system, there is no sense in which the authority has the option to conduct counter-cyclical policy. To exploit the Phillips curve, it must somehow trick the public. By virtue of the assumption that expectations are rational, there is no feedback rule that the authority can employ and expect to be able systematically to fool the public. This means that the authority cannot exploit the Phillips curve even for one period. (1976, p. 177)

Of course, the PIP caused an enormous stir in the ranks of the professional economists. Indeed, it seemed to have supplied proof that macroeconomists are useless. If macroeconomic demand management is ineffective, then why should society fund economists engaging themselves in writing lengthy scholarly treatises on the subject of stabilization policy?

On top of this came the second strike of the new classicals against the then predominantly Keynesian army of policy-oriented macroeconomists. Lucas argued that the then popular large macroeconometric models (with a strong Keynesian flavour) are useless for the exact task for which they are being used, namely the evaluation of the effects of different types of economic policy. This so-called *Lucas critique* can be illustrated with the aid of our model. Suppose that the economy has operated under the policy rule (3.16) for some time, that agents know and understand it, and that the economy is in a stochastic steady state, so that output follows the stochastic process given by (3.21).

By solving (3.16) for e_t and substituting the result into (3.21), it is clear that output can be written as follows:

$$y_t = \phi_0 + \phi_1 y_{t-1} + \phi_2 m_t + \phi_3 m_{t-1} + \xi_t, \tag{3.22}$$

where

$$\phi_0 \equiv \frac{\alpha_0(\alpha_1 + \beta_1) - \mu_0\alpha_1\beta_1}{\alpha_1 + \beta_1}, \quad \phi_1 \equiv -\frac{\mu_2\alpha_1\beta_1}{\alpha_1 + \beta_1}, \quad \phi_2 \equiv \frac{\alpha_1\beta_1}{\alpha_1 + \beta_1} \tag{3.23}$$

$$\phi_3 \equiv -\frac{\mu_1\alpha_1\beta_1}{\alpha_1 + \beta_1}, \quad \xi_t \equiv \frac{\alpha_1 v_t + \beta_1 u_t}{\alpha_1 + \beta_1}. \tag{3.24}$$

An econometrician running regressions like (3.22) would find a well-fitting model. An innocent but popular interpretation might suggest that a monetary expansion would yield an expansion of employment and output. Indeed, many use simulations of econometric models to give policy recommendations. Lucas pointed out, however, that the model would be useless for policy simulations because its coefficients are not invariant to the policy rule under the REH. Indeed, suppose that the government would switch to a strong countercyclical viewpoint, reflected in a more negative value for the parameter μ_2. Predictions with the model based on the existing estimates of the ϕ_i-parameters would seriously misrepresent the real effects of this policy switch, due to the fact that the actual ϕ_i-parameters would change. For example, an increase in $|\mu_2|$ would increase the actual value of $|\phi_1|$.

Of course, Lucas is right *in principle*. Provided one compares only stochastic steady states, the effects mentioned by him will indeed obtain. But in practice the Lucas critique may be less relevant, especially in the short run. As we have argued above, very little is known about the learning processes that may prompt agents to converge to a rational expectations equilibrium. To the extent that it may take agents some time to adapt to the new policy rule, it may well be that both (3.22) and (3.16) give the wrong answers. This may explain why full-scale models embodying the REH are still relatively scarce.

3.3 Should We Take the PIP Seriously?

Shortly after the publication of Sargent and Wallace's (1976) seemingly devastating blow to advocates of (Keynesian) countercyclical policy, it was argued that PIP is not the inevitable outcome of the REH (that, of course, made a lot of Keynesians happy again, and may have promoted the broad acceptance of the REH). The crucial counter-example to PIP was provided by Stanley Fischer (1977), a new Keynesian economist. His argument is predictable, in view of Modigliani's (1944) interpretation of Keynes' contribution. What happens with PIP if money wages are rigid, for example due to nominal wage contracts?

3.3.1 One-period nominal wage contracts

Fischer's (1977) model is very simple. The AD curve is monetarist in nature:

$$y_t = m_t - p_t + v_t,\qquad(3.25)$$

which can be seen as a special case of (3.15) with $\beta_0 = \beta_2 = 0$ and $\beta_1 = 1$. The supply side of the economy consists of workers signing one-period or two-period nominal wage contracts, after which the demand for labour curve determines the actual amount of employment. We first consider the case of one-period wage contracts. We assume that workers aim (and settle) for a nominal wage contract for which they expect full employment in the next period, when the wage contract is in operation. This is illustrated in Figure 3.6. Workers know the supply and demand schedules for

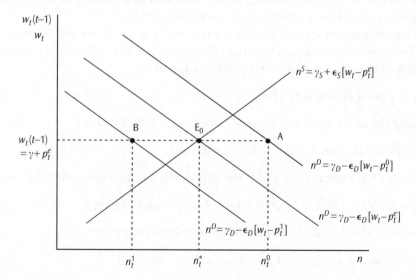

Figure 3.6. Wage setting with single-period contracts

labour, and estimate the market clearing real wage. Since the contract is specified before the price in period t is known, the workers use the expected price level to determine the market clearing real wage. If their price expectation is p_t^e, then expected full employment occurs at point E_0. If the actual price level in period t is higher (lower) then employment occurs at point A (B). Let $w_t(t-1)$ denote the (logarithm of the) nominal wage that is specified at the end of period $t-1$, to hold in period t. Assume furthermore that the real wage that clears the labour market is equal to γ. Then $w_t(t-1)$ is set as:

$$w_t(t-1) = \gamma + E_{t-1}p_t, \tag{3.26}$$

where we can simplify notation further by normalizing $\gamma = 0$. The supply of output depends on the actual real wage:

$$y_t = [p_t - w_t(t-1)] + u_t, \tag{3.27}$$

so that (3.26) and (3.27) imply a Lucas-type supply curve:

$$y_t = [p_t - E_{t-1}p_t] + u_t. \tag{3.28}$$

Note that (3.28) is a special case of (3.14) with $\alpha_0 = 0$ and $\alpha_1 = 1$.

We assume that the policy rule adopted by the policy maker has the following form:

$$m_t = \sum_{i=1}^{\infty} \mu_{1i} u_{t-i} + \sum_{i=1}^{\infty} \mu_{2i} v_{t-i}. \tag{3.29}$$

Hence, the policy maker is assumed to react to past shocks in aggregate demand and supply (below we shall see that it is in fact sufficient to react to shocks only lagged once and lagged twice, so that $\mu_{1i} = \mu_{2i} = 0$ for $i = 3, 4, \ldots, \infty$).

Not surprisingly, in view of the similarities with our earlier model, Fischer's one-period contract model implies that the PIP is valid. The REH solution is constructed as follows. First, solving (3.25) and (3.28) for p_t yields:

$$p_t = \tfrac{1}{2}\left[m_t + v_t - u_t + E_{t-1}p_t\right]. \tag{3.30}$$

By taking conditional expectations of both sides, (3.30) becomes:

$$E_{t-1}p_t = \tfrac{1}{2}\left[E_{t-1}m_t + E_{t-1}v_t - E_{t-1}u_t + E_{t-1}p_t\right]. \tag{3.31}$$

Deducting (3.31) from (3.30) yields the expression for the expectational error:

$$p_t - E_{t-1}p_t = \tfrac{1}{2}\left[(m_t - E_{t-1}m_t) + (v_t - E_{t-1}v_t) - (u_t - E_{t-1}u_t)\right]. \tag{3.32}$$

Now assume that the shock terms display autocorrelation, i.e.:

$$u_t = \rho_U u_{t-1} + \epsilon_t, \quad |\rho_U| < 1, \quad v_t = \rho_V v_{t-1} + \eta_t, \quad |\rho_V| < 1, \tag{3.33}$$

where ϵ_t and η_t are uncorrelated white noise terms (often referred to as *innovations*): $E\epsilon_t = 0$, $E\epsilon_t^2 = \sigma_\epsilon^2$, $E\eta_t = 0$, and $E\eta_t^2 = \sigma_\eta^2$.

What does the surprise term (3.32) look like? First, (3.29) implies that agents know the money supply in period t once they have lagged information (there is no stochastic element in the policy rule). Hence, $m_t - E_{t-1}m_t = 0$. The fact that the shocks are autocorrelated implies that agents can use information on the shocks in the previous period (i.e. v_{t-1} and u_{t-1}) to forecast the shocks in period t:

$$E_{t-1}u_t = \rho_U u_{t-1}, \quad E_{t-1}v_t = \rho_V v_{t-1}. \tag{3.34}$$

By using these forecasts in equation (3.32), and substituting the price surprise into (3.28), the REH solution for output is obtained:

$$y_t = \tfrac{1}{2}\left[\eta_t - \epsilon_t\right] + u_t. \tag{3.35}$$

The coefficients of the policy rule (i.e. μ_{1i} and μ_{2i}) do not influence the path of output, so that PIP holds. In other words, anticipated monetary policy is unable to cause deviations of output from its natural level.

3.3.2 Overlapping wage contracts

Now consider the case where nominal contracts are decided on for two periods. We continue to assume that nominal wages are set such that the expected real wage is consistent with full employment. Hence, in period t there are two nominal wage contracts in existence. Half of the workforce is on the wage contract agreed upon in period $t - 1$ (to run in periods t and $t + 1$), and the other half has a contract formulated in period $t - 2$ (to run in periods $t - 1$ and t). In symbols:

$$w_t(t - 1) \equiv E_{t-1}p_t, \quad w_t(t - 2) \equiv E_{t-2}p_t. \tag{3.36}$$

Notice the difference in the information set used for the two contracts. The economy is perfectly competitive, so that there is only one output price, and aggregate supply is equal to:

$$y_t = \tfrac{1}{2}\left[p_t - w_t(t - 1) + u_t\right] + \tfrac{1}{2}\left[p_t - w_t(t - 2) + u_t\right], \tag{3.37}$$

where the first term in brackets on the right-hand side is the output of firms with workers on one-year old contracts, and the second term is the output of firms with workers on two-year old (expiring) contracts. By substituting (3.36) into (3.37), we obtain the aggregate supply curve for the two-period contract case:

$$y_t = \tfrac{1}{2}\left[p_t - E_{t-1}p_t\right] + \tfrac{1}{2}\left[p_t - E_{t-2}p_t\right] + u_t. \tag{3.38}$$

Hence, this supply curve has two different surprise terms, differing in the information set. The rest of the model consists of the aggregate demand curve (3.25) and the money supply rule (3.29).

The model can be solved by repeated substitution. First, (3.25) and (3.38) can be solved for p_t:

$$p_t = \frac{1}{2} \left[m_t + v_t - u_t + \frac{1}{2} \left(E_{t-1} p_t + E_{t-2} p_t \right) \right]. \tag{3.39}$$

By taking expectations conditional upon period $t - 2$ information of both sides of (3.39), we obtain:

$$E_{t-2} p_t = \frac{1}{2} \left[E_{t-2} m_t + E_{t-2} v_t - E_{t-2} u_t + \frac{1}{2} \left(E_{t-2} E_{t-1} p_t + E_{t-2} E_{t-2} p_t \right) \right]. \tag{3.40}$$

We already know that $E_{t-2} E_{t-2} p_t = E_{t-2} p_t$, but what does $E_{t-2} E_{t-1} p_t$ mean? In words, it represents what agents expect (using period $t - 2$ information) to expect in period $t - 1$ about the price level in period t. But a moment's contemplation reveals that this cannot be different from what the agents expect about p_t using $t - 2$ information, i.e. $E_{t-2} E_{t-1} p_t \equiv E_{t-2} p_t$. This is an application of the so-called Law of Iterated Expectations. In words this law says that you do not know ahead of time how you are going to change your mind. Only genuinely new information makes you change your expectation. Hence, (3.40) can be solved for $E_{t-2} p_t$:

$$E_{t-2} p_t = E_{t-2} m_t + E_{t-2} v_t - E_{t-2} u_t. \tag{3.41}$$

Similarly, by taking expectations conditional upon period $t - 1$ information of both sides of (3.39), we obtain:

$$E_{t-1} p_t = \frac{1}{2} \left[E_{t-1} m_t + E_{t-1} v_t - E_{t-1} u_t + \frac{1}{2} \left(E_{t-1} E_{t-1} p_t + E_{t-1} E_{t-2} p_t \right) \right]. \tag{3.42}$$

Obviously, $E_{t-1} E_{t-1} p_t = E_{t-1} p_t$, but what does $E_{t-1} E_{t-2} p_t$ mean? In words, it represents what agents expect (using period $t - 1$ information) to expect in period $t - 2$ about the price level in period t. But $E_{t-2} p_t$ is known in period $t - 1$, so that $E_{t-1} E_{t-2} p_t \equiv E_{t-2} p_t$ (the expectation of a constant is the constant itself). By substituting (3.41) into (3.42), the solution for $E_{t-1} p_t$ is obtained:

$$E_{t-1} p_t = \frac{2}{3} E_{t-1} m_t + \frac{1}{3} E_{t-2} m_t + \frac{2}{3} \left[E_{t-1} v_t - E_{t-1} u_t \right] + \frac{1}{3} \left[E_{t-2} v_t - E_{t-2} u_t \right]. \tag{3.43}$$

If we now substitute (3.41) and (3.43) into (3.39), the REH solution for the price level is obtained:

$$p_t = \frac{2}{3} E_{t-1} m_t + \frac{1}{3} E_{t-2} m_t + \frac{1}{2} (v_t - u_t) + \frac{1}{6} E_{t-1} (v_t - u_t) + \frac{1}{3} E_{t-2} (v_t - u_t). \tag{3.44}$$

This can be substituted into the AD equation (3.25) to obtain the expression for y_t:

$$\begin{aligned}
y_t &= m_t - \left[\frac{2}{3} E_{t-1} m_t + \frac{1}{3} E_{t-2} m_t + \frac{1}{2} (v_t - u_t) + \frac{1}{6} E_{t-1} (v_t - u_t) + \frac{1}{3} E_{t-2} (v_t - u_t) \right] + v_t \\
&= \frac{1}{3} \left[m_t - E_{t-2} m_t \right] - \frac{1}{2} (v_t - u_t) - \frac{1}{6} E_{t-1} (v_t - u_t) - \frac{1}{3} E_{t-2} (v_t - u_t) + v_t, \tag{3.45}
\end{aligned}$$

where we have used the fact that $E_{t-1} m_t = m_t$.

The monetary surprise $(m_t - E_{t-2}m_t)$ must now be calculated. Using (3.29), we find that:

$$m_t = \mu_{11}u_{t-1} + \mu_{21}v_{t-1} + \sum_{i=2}^{\infty} \mu_{1i}u_{t-i} + \sum_{i=2}^{\infty} \mu_{2i}v_{t-i}, \tag{3.46}$$

and:

$$E_{t-2}m_t = \mu_{11}E_{t-2}u_{t-1} + \mu_{21}E_{t-2}v_{t-1} + \sum_{i=2}^{\infty} \mu_{1i}u_{t-i} + \sum_{i=2}^{\infty} \mu_{2i}v_{t-i}$$

$$= \rho_U\mu_{11}u_{t-2} + \rho_V\mu_{21}v_{t-2} + \sum_{i=2}^{\infty} \mu_{1i}u_{t-i} + \sum_{i=2}^{\infty} \mu_{2i}v_{t-i}, \tag{3.47}$$

where we have used the fact that (3.33) implies $E_{t-2}U_{t-1} = \rho_U u_{t-2}$ and $E_{t-2}v_{t-1} = \rho_V v_{t-2}$. Using (3.46) and (3.47) we find:

$$m_t - E_{t-2}m_t = \mu_{11}[u_{t-1} - \rho_U u_{t-2}] + \mu_{21}[v_{t-1} - \rho_V v_{t-2}]$$

$$= \mu_{11}\epsilon_{t-1} + \mu_{21}\eta_{t-1}. \tag{3.48}$$

Equation (3.48) is intuitive. Agents can perfectly forecast the money supply *one* period ahead (i.e. $E_{t-1}m_t = m_t$) but not *two* periods ahead. That is because in period $t - 1$ an innovation in the demand and supply shock occurs (equal to ϵ_{t-1} and η_{t-1}, respectively) that the monetary policy maker will react to. In other words, the innovation that occurs in period $t - 1$ is not forecastable by agents who have signed their contract in period $t - 2$.

If we substitute (3.48) into (3.45), the final expression for output is obtained:

$$y_t = \tfrac{1}{3}[\mu_{11}\epsilon_{t-1} + \mu_{21}\eta_{t-1}] + \tfrac{1}{2}(v_t + u_t) - \tfrac{1}{6}E_{t-1}(v_t - u_t) - \tfrac{1}{3}E_{t-2}(v_t - u_t)$$

$$= \tfrac{1}{2}[\eta_t + \epsilon_t] + \tfrac{1}{3}[\mu_{11} + 2\rho_U]\epsilon_{t-1} + \tfrac{1}{3}[\mu_{21} + \rho_V]\eta_{t-1} + \rho_U^2 u_{t-2}. \tag{3.49}$$

This is the crucial counter-example to the PIP. Equation (3.49) contains the policy parameters μ_{11} and μ_{21}, so that output can be affected by monetary policy even under rational expectations. As Fischer puts it, the intuitive reason for his result is that "...between the time the two-year contract is drawn up and the last year of operation of that contract, there is time for the monetary authority to react to new information about recent economic disturbances" (1977, p. 269). Because of the two-period contracts, half of the workers have implicitly based their contract wage on "stale" information.

But Fischer's blow to the new classicals was made even more devastating by the following. Clearly, output *can* be affected by monetary policy. But *should* it be affected, and if so, how? Clearly, (3.49) implies that output fluctuates stochastically, so some measure of the degree of fluctuations over time is warranted. The appropriate measure is the *asymptotic variance* of y_t, designated by σ_Y^2 (see the Intermezzo below). Intuitively, the asymptotic variance measures the severity of the fluctuations in output. Using standard (but tedious) techniques, the asymptotic variance of the output path described by (3.49) can be written as:

$$\sigma_Y^2 \equiv \sigma_\epsilon^2 \left[\frac{1}{4} + \frac{\rho_U^4}{1 - \rho_U^2} + \frac{1}{9}(\mu_{11} + 2\rho_U)^2 \right] + \sigma_\eta^2 \left[\frac{1}{4} + \frac{1}{9}(\mu_{21} + \rho_V)^2 \right]. \tag{3.50}$$

So, to the extent that fluctuations in output are a good proxy for loss of economic welfare, the policy maker could attempt to minimize the asymptotic variance of output by choosing its reaction coefficients μ_{11} and μ_{21} appropriately. It turns out that the optimal values for these parameters are equal to:

$$\mu_{11} = -2\rho_U, \quad \mu_{21} = -\rho_V. \tag{3.51}$$

Intuitively, the policy parameters should be set at values that neutralize the effects of the shocks that occur in period $t - 1$. In view of (3.49), the coefficients given in (3.51) do exactly that. Of course, not all output fluctuations can be eliminated by the policy maker. This is because the first and the last terms on the right-hand side of (3.49) cannot be affected by the policy maker. The first, because the policy maker has no better information about the innovations in the present period than the public possesses. The last, because u_{t-2} was known when the oldest contracts were signed in period $t - 2$, and is hence incorporated in the oldest contract.

In a recent paper, Chadha (1989) has extended Fischer's (1977) analysis to the multi-period overlapping contract setting using the insights of Calvo (1982) that are discussed in detail below in Chapter 13. In his model, he is able to analyse contracts of any particular duration (not just one-period and two-period contracts as in Fischer's model). He is furthermore able to express the asymptotic variance in output as a function of the contract length. This diagram is given in Figure 3.7. The

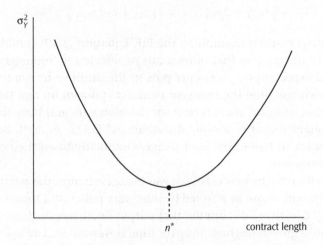

Figure 3.7. The optimal contract length

conclusion is very surprising indeed: there is an optimal contract length of $n^* > 0$, which Chadha estimates to be around 3.73 quarters for the US economy (1989, p. 492). Hence, intuitively, contracts act as "shock absorbers" of the economy.

There are a number of other reasons why PIP fails–see Buiter (1980) for an interesting discussion. For example, private agents may not have rational expectations, or there may be nominal price stickiness. Furthermore, even though anticipated monetary policy may not be able to cause deviations of output from its natural level, anticipated monetary policy may affect the natural rate itself. A theoretic (albeit empirically not so relevant) example is the Mundell-Tobin effect: a higher monetary growth rate depresses the real interest rate, and this boosts capital accumulation and the natural level of output.

Intermezzo

Asymptotic variance Rational expectations models often use the asymptotic variance of output as a welfare measure. Intuitively, the asymptotic variance measures the degree of fluctuations over time in output. An economy with violent (mild) fluctuations has a high (low) asymptotic variance. Suppose that the path for output is described by the following equation:

$$y_t = \lambda y_{t-1} + x_t + \epsilon_t, \quad |\lambda| < 1, \tag{a}$$

where y_t is output, x_t is some (vector of) deterministic exogenous variable(s), and ϵ_t is a white noise stochastic error term with mean zero and variance σ_ϵ^2. How would a Martian judge the degree of fluctuations in output, not knowing any realizations of output and the error term, but in full knowledge of equation (a) and the stochastic process of the error terms. The answer is that he would calculate the asymptotic variance:

$$\sigma_Y^2 \equiv E_{t-\infty} [y_t - E_{t-\infty} y_t]^2, \tag{b}$$

where the notation $E_{t-\infty}$ formalizes the idea of no information about the actual realizations mentioned above. It is as if the Martian makes his calculations at the beginning of time.

The asymptotic variance of output implied by the process in (a) is calculated as follows. First, we write $E_{t-\infty} y_t = \lambda E_{t-\infty} y_{t-1} + x_t$ and work out the square:

$$
\begin{aligned}
[y_t - E_{t-\infty} y_t]^2 &= [\lambda y_{t-1} + x_t + \epsilon_t - \lambda E_{t-\infty} y_{t-1} - x_t]^2 \\
&= [\lambda (y_{t-1} - E_{t-\infty} y_{t-1}) + \epsilon_t]^2 \\
&= \lambda^2 [y_{t-1} - E_{t-\infty} y_{t-1}]^2 + \epsilon_t^2 + 2\lambda \epsilon_t [y_{t-1} - E_{t-\infty} y_{t-1}].
\end{aligned} \tag{c}
$$

Taking expectations of both sides of (c) yields:

$$E_{t-\infty}\,[y_t - E_{t-\infty}y_t]^2 = \lambda^2 E_{t-\infty}\,[y_{t-1} - E_{t-\infty}y_{t-1}]^2$$
$$+ E_{t-\infty}\epsilon_t^2 + 2\lambda E_{t-\infty}\epsilon_t\,[y_{t-1} - E_{t-\infty}y_{t-1}]. \tag{d}$$

The second term on the right-hand side is the variance of the error term (σ_ϵ^2), and the third term is zero because the error term is independent of lagged output. The term on the left-hand side is the asymptotic variance of y_t, and the first term on the right-hand side is λ^2 times the asymptotic variance of y_{t-1}. Because the process in (a) is stationary ($|\lambda| < 1$), these two asymptotic variances are identical. Using all this information, the final expression for the asymptotic variance becomes:

$$\sigma_Y^2 = \lambda^2 \sigma_Y^2 + \sigma_\epsilon^2 \quad \Rightarrow \quad \sigma_Y^2 = \frac{\sigma_\epsilon^2}{1 - \lambda^2}. \tag{e}$$

Intuitively, the asymptotic variance of output is a multiple of the variance of the error term due to the persistence effect via lagged output. If λ is close to unity, there is a lot of persistence and the variance multiplier is very large.

3.4 Punchlines

To most economists, one of the unsatisfactory aspects of the adaptive expectations hypothesis (AEH) is that it implies that agents make systematic mistakes along the entire adjustment path from the initial to the ultimate equilibrium. In the early 1960s, John Muth argued that such an outcome is difficult to square with the predominant notion adopted throughout economics, namely that agents use scarce resources (like information) wisely. He formulated the rational expectations hypothesis (REH) which, in essence, requires the subjective expectation of households regarding a particular variable to be equal to the objective expectation for that variable conditional upon the information set available to the agent.

Muth's idea was introduced into the macroeconomic literature in the early 1970s by a number of prominent new classical economists. They argued that under the REH, monetary policy is ineffective (at influencing aggregate output and employment) because agents cannot be systematically fooled into supplying too much or too little labour. This is the so-called policy irrelevance proposition (PIP) which caused a big stir in the ranks of professional macroeconomists in the mid-1970s. Another implication of the REH is that, according to the Lucas critique, the then predominant macroeconometric models are useless for the task of evaluating the effects of different macroeconomic policies.

As was quickly pointed out by proponents of the new Keynesian school, the REH does not necessarily imply the validity of the PIP. Stanley Fischer pointed out that if nominal wage contracts are set for more than one period in advance (and are not indexed) then even under rational expectations monetary policy can (and indeed should) be used to stabilize the economy. Hence, the validity of PIP hinges not so much of the REH but rather on the type of model that is used. If REH is introduced in a classical model then the implications are classical whereas a Keynesian model with REH yields Keynesian implications.

It is almost universally agreed that the PIP cannot be taken seriously, except perhaps as an extreme position taken to promote a discussion. Furthermore, due to the fact that Fischer and others demonstrated that the REH does not necessarily imply PIP, acceptance of the REH as a modelling device is also almost universal. The Lucas critique is valid, but its empirical short-run relevance is seriously doubted by both theoretical econometricians (Favero and Hendry, 1992) and applied policy modellers. A reason for this luke-warm reception may be the absence of a credible theory of how agents learn new policy rules.

Further Reading

The classic articles setting out rational expectations are Lucas (1972, 1973), Sargent (1973), Sargent and Wallace (1975, 1976), and Barro (1976). Papers stressing the stickiness of wages or prices include Fischer (1977), Phelps and Taylor (1977), Barro (1977), Gray (1976, 1978), and Taylor (1979, 1980). For good surveys of this literature, see McCallum (1980), Maddock and Carter (1982), and Attfield, Demery, and Duck (1985). Several key articles on the rational expectations approach are collected in Lucas and Sargent (1981), Miller (1994), and Hoover (1992). The interested reader should also consult the collections of essays by Lucas (1981) and Sargent (1993). See Frydman and Phelps (1983) for a collection of essays on learning under rational expectations.

As was acknowledged by Lucas himself, an early statement of the Lucas critique is found in Marschak (1953). For an early application of the rational expectations hypothesis to finance, see Samuelson (1965). McCallum (1983b) presents a model of the liquidity trap and finds the rational expectations solution. The pre-REH literature on optimal stabilization policy is well surveyed by Turnovsky (1977, chs. 13–14). See also the classic analysis by Poole (1970) on the optimal choice of policy instruments within the stochastic IS-LM model. For an early analysis of economic policy under rational expectations, see Fischer (1980b).

4

Anticipation Effects and Economic Policy

The purpose of this chapter is to discuss the following issues:

1. To complete our discussion of the dynamic theory of investment by firms that was commenced in Chapter 2,

2. Use the investment theory to determine how the government can use tax incentives (such as an investment subsidy) to stimulate capital accumulation. This is an example of fiscal policy where the government changes a relative price in order to prompt a substitution response,

3. Embed the investment theory in an IS-LM framework. How do anticipation effects influence the outcome of traditional budgetary policies?

4.1 Dynamic Investment Theory

In Chapter 2 we sketched a theory of investment by firms that is based on forward-looking behaviour and adjustment costs of investment. For reasons of intuitive clarity, the model was developed in discrete time. It turns out, however, that working in continuous time is much more convenient from a mathematical point of view. The first task that must be performed therefore is to redevelop and generalize the model in continuous time.

4.1.1 The basic model

Assume that the real profit of the representative firm is given by what is left of revenue after the production factor labour and investment outlays have been paid:

$$\pi(t) \equiv F(N(t), K(t)) - w(t)N(t) - p^I(t) [1 - s_I(t)] \Phi(I(t)), \tag{4.1}$$

where $\pi(t)$ is real profit in period t, $F(.,.)$ is the constant returns to scale production function, $w(t)$ is the real wage rate ($\equiv W(t)/P(t)$), $p^I(t)$ is the relative price of investment goods ($\equiv P^I(t)/P(t)$), $s_I(t)$ is the investment subsidy, and $\Phi(.)$ is the adjustment cost function, with $\Phi_I > 0$ and $\Phi_{II} > 0$. By assuming that the good produced by the firm is the same as the investment good (the so-called single good assumption), we obtain the simplification $p^I(t) = 1$. In some cases it is convenient to assume that the adjustment cost function is quadratic:

$$\Phi(I(t)) = I(t) + b\,[I(t)]^2, \quad b > 0. \tag{4.2}$$

The capital accumulation identity is given by:

$$\dot{K}(t) = I(t) - \delta K(t), \quad \delta > 0. \tag{4.3}$$

The firm must choose a path for its output such that the present value of its profits is maximized. Since *real* profits are defined in (4.1), the appropriate discount rate is the *real* rate of interest on alternative financial assets. This real interest rate is denoted by r and is assumed to be constant over time throughout this chapter. Under these assumptions, the net present value of the stream of profits now and in the future is given by:

$$V(0) \equiv \int_0^\infty \pi(t)e^{-rt}dt$$

$$= \int_0^\infty \left[F(N(t), K(t)) - w(t)N(t) - [1 - s_I(t)]\,\Phi(I(t))\right]e^{-rt}dt. \tag{4.4}$$

To the extent that shares of this company are traded in the stock exchange, and share prices are based on fundamentals and not on the speculative whims and fancies of irrational money sharks, its value on the stock market should equal $V(0)$ in real terms, or $P(0)V(0)$ in nominal terms.

The firm maximizes (4.4) under the restriction (4.3). With the aid of the Maximum Principle the solution to this problem can be found quite easily.[1] The current-value Hamiltonian can be written as:

$$\mathcal{H}(t) \equiv e^{-rt}\big[F(N(t), K(t)) - w(t)N(t) - [1 - s_I(t)]\,\Phi(I(t))$$

$$+ q(t)\,[I(t) - \delta K(t)]\big]. \tag{4.5}$$

Formally, $q(t)$ plays the role of the Lagrange multiplier for the capital accumulation restriction. The economic interpretation of $q(t)$ is straightforward. It can be shown that $q(0)$ represents the shadow price of installed capital $K(0)$. In words, $q(0)$ measures by how much the value of the firm would rise ($dV(0)$) if the initial capital

---

[1] Note that the method sketched here is a generalization of the Lagrange multiplier method used in Chapter 2. An explanation of the Maximum Principle based mainly on pure economic intuition can be found in Dorfman (1969). Other excellent sources are Dixit (1990) and Intriligator (1971). See also the Mathematical Appendix.

stock were increased slightly ($dK(0)$), i.e. $q(0) \equiv dV(0)/dK(0)$ (see the Intermezzo on Tobin's q below).

The firm can freely choose employment and the rate of investment at each instant, so that the following first-order conditions (for $t \in [0, \infty]$) should be intuitive:

$$\frac{\partial \mathcal{H}(t)}{\partial N(t)} = e^{-rt} [F_N(N(t), K(t)) - w(t)] = 0, \tag{4.6}$$

$$\frac{\partial \mathcal{H}(t)}{\partial I(t)} = e^{-rt} [q(t) - (1 - s_I(t))\Phi_I(I(t))] = 0. \tag{4.7}$$

The interpretation of (4.6) is the usual one: the firm must choose the amount of labour such that the marginal product of labour equals the real wage rate. Note that (4.7) implies a very simple investment function:

$$(1 - s_I(t))\Phi_I(I(t)) = q(t) \quad \Rightarrow \quad I(t) \equiv I(q(t), s_I(t)), \tag{4.8}$$

where $I_q \equiv 1/[(1 - s_I)\Phi_{II}] > 0$ and $I_s \equiv \Phi_I/[(1 - s_I)\Phi_{II}] > 0$. In words, higher values for q and s_I both imply a higher rate of investment. Indeed, for the quadratic adjustment cost function (4.2), the investment function has a very simple form:

$$\Phi_I(I(t)) = 1 + 2bI(t) = \frac{q(t)}{1 - s_I(t)} \quad \Rightarrow \quad I(t) = \frac{1}{2b}\left[\frac{q(t)}{1 - s_I(t)} - 1\right]. \tag{4.9}$$

The parallel with the expression derived in Chapter 2 (i.e. equation (2.36)) should be noted. Note that we have not used the symbol q for nothing: The investment theory developed here is formally known as Tobin's q-theory, after its inventor James Tobin (1969).

The first expression in equation (4.8) allows a very simple interpretation of the optimality condition for investment. It instructs the firm to equate the marginal cost of investment (equal to $(1 - s_I)\Phi_I$) to the shadow price of capital, which is the marginal benefit of investment. In other words, by spending money today on investment you add value to your company. This added value is measured by the shadow price.

Equations (4.6)–(4.7) are in essence static conditions of the form "marginal cost equals marginal benefit". The truly *intertemporal* part of the problem is solved by choosing an optimal path for the shadow price of capital. The first-order condition for this choice is:

$$\frac{d\left[q(t)e^{-rt}\right]}{dt} = -\frac{\partial \mathcal{H}(t)}{\partial K(t)} \quad \Rightarrow$$

$$e^{-rt}[\dot{q}(t) - rq(t)] = -e^{-rt}[F_K(N(t), K(t)) - \delta q(t)]. \tag{4.10}$$

This condition can be written in several ways, two of which are:

$$\dot{q}(t) = (r + \delta)q(t) - F_K(N(t), K(t)), \tag{4.11}$$

and:

$$\frac{\dot{q}(t) + F_K(N(t), K(t))}{q(t)} = r + \delta. \tag{4.12}$$

Equation (4.12) allows for a very intuitive interpretation. The shadow return on the possession and use of physical capital is the sum of the shadow capital gain ($\dot{q}(t)$) and the marginal product of capital [$F_K(N(t), K(t))$], expressed in terms of the shadow price (to make it a *rate* of return). This shadow rate of return must equal the market rate of return on other financial assets (that are perfect substitutes for shares) *plus* the rate of physical deterioration of the capital stock. The depreciation costs must be counted as a cost item because capital evaporates over time, regardless of whether the firm uses the capital for production or not. Hence, in determining the optimal path for $q(t)$ the firm is guided by the implicit arbitrage equation (4.12).

We have developed Tobin's *marginal* q-theory of investment in this section. It is shown in an intermezzo to this chapter that, provided some more specific assumptions are made about the adjustment cost function, Tobin's *average* q-theory coincides with his marginal q-theory. Average q for the firm is defined as $\bar{q}(0) \equiv V(0)/K(0)$. In words, $\bar{q}$ represents the value that the stock market ascribes to each unit of installed capital of the firm (at replacement cost, see the Intermezzo).

And this is exactly where the great beauty of the theory lies. In principle one can look up the stock market value of a firm from the financial pages in the newspapers, and divide this by the replacement value of its capital stock (slightly more work), and calculate the firm's q. The value of q that is obtained in this manner reflects all information that is (according to the stock market participants) of relevance to the particular firm (see Hayashi (1982) for further remarks).

Intermezzo

Tobin's q-theory of investment. In this intermezzo we show that Tobin's average and marginal q coincide under certain conditions. The proof is adapted from Hayashi (1982). Suppose that the profit function in equation (4.1) is adjusted by including the existing capital stock in the adjustment cost function:

$$\pi(t) \equiv F(N(t), K(t)) - w(t)N(t) - p^I(t)\left[1 - s_I(t)\right]\Phi\left[I(t), K(t)\right],$$

where $\pi(t)$ is real profit, $w(t)$ is the real wage rate [$\equiv W(t)/P(t)$], $p^I(t)$ is the relative price of investment goods [$\equiv P^I(t)/P(t)$], and $s_I(t)$ is the investment subsidy. The adjustment cost function is homogeneous of degree one in $I(t)$ and $K(t)$, with $\Phi_I > 0$, $\Phi_K < 0$, $\Phi_{II} > 0$, $\Phi_{IK} < 0$, and $\Phi_{KK} > 0$. Hence, adjustment costs are decreasing in the capital stock. Large firms experience less disruption for a given level of investment than small firms.

The firm is assumed to maximize the present value of profits, using the (time-varying) real interest rate $r(t)$ as the discount factor. Equation (4.4) is altered to:

$$V(0) \equiv \int_0^\infty \big[F(N(t), K(t)) - w(t)N(t)$$
$$- p^I(t)(1 - s_I(t))\Phi\,[I(t), K(t)] \big]e^{-R(t)}dt,$$

where $V(0)$ is the real stockmarket value of the firm, and $R(t)$ is a discounting factor that depends on the entire path of short interest rates up to t:

$$R(t) \equiv \int_0^t r(\tau)\,d\tau \;\Rightarrow\; \frac{dR(t)}{dt} = r(t).$$

The counterpart to (4.5) is:

$$\mathcal{H}(t) \equiv e^{-R(t)}\big[F(N(t), K(t)) - w(t)N(t) - p^I(t)(1 - s_I(t))\Phi\,[I(t), K(t)] \big]$$
$$+ e^{-R(t)}\lambda(t)\,[I(t) - \delta K(t)],$$

where $\lambda(t)$ is the Lagrange multiplier. The first-order conditions for this problem are:

$$\frac{\partial \mathcal{H}(t)}{\partial N(t)} = 0: \quad F_N(N(t), K(t)) - w(t) = 0, \tag{a}$$

$$\frac{\partial \mathcal{H}(t)}{\partial I(t)} = 0: \quad \lambda(t) - p^I(t)(1 - s_I(t))\Phi_I(I(t), K(t)) = 0, \tag{b}$$

$$\frac{d\big[\lambda(t)e^{-R(t)}\big]}{dt} = -\frac{\partial \mathcal{H}(t)}{\partial K(t)}:$$

$$\dot{\lambda}(t) - [r(t) + \delta]\lambda(t) = -F_K\,[N(t), K(t)]$$
$$+ p^I(t)(1 - s_I(t))\Phi_K\,[I(t), K(t)], \tag{c}$$

where we have already deleted the (non-zero) exponential term $e^{-R(t)}$ from the expressions. These expressions generalize (4.6), (4.7), and (4.10) to the case of a linear homogeneous adjustment cost function and a time-varying rate of interest.

In order to establish the relationship between the Lagrange multiplier ($\lambda(0)$), the capital stock ($K(0)$), and the real stockmarket value of the firm ($V(0)$), we first derive the definition:

$$\frac{d}{dt}\Big[\lambda(t)K(t)e^{-R(t)}\Big] \equiv \big[K(t)\dot{\lambda}(t) + \lambda(t)\dot{K}(t) - r(t)\lambda(t)K(t)\big]e^{-R(t)}. \tag{d}$$

The term in square brackets on the right-hand side of (d) can be expanded by substituting the capital accumulation identity, and equation (c). Ignoring time indexes for now, we obtain:

$$[\ldots] = K\left[(r+\delta)\lambda - F_K + p^I(1-s_I)\Phi_K\right] + \lambda\left[I - \delta K\right] + r\lambda K$$

$$= -F_K K + p^I(1-s_I)\Phi_K K + \lambda I$$

$$= -F_K K + p^I(1-s_I)\left[\Phi - \phi_I I\right] + \lambda I = -\pi. \qquad (e)$$

In the final step we have used the linear homogeneity of Φ (i.e. $\Phi = \Phi_I I + \Phi_K K$), equation (b), and the following result:

$$\pi = F_N N + F_K K - wN - p^I(1-s_I)\Phi$$

$$= F_K K + N\left[F_N - w\right] - p^I(1-s_I)\Phi$$

$$= F_K K - p^I(1-s_I)\Phi,$$

where we have used the linear homogeneity of F (i.e. $F = F_N N + F_K K$), and equation (a). By substituting (e) into (d) and integrating we obtain:

$$\int_0^\infty d\left[\lambda(t)K(t)e^{-R(t)}\right] = -\int_0^\infty \pi(t)e^{-R(t)}dt \equiv -V(0) \quad \Rightarrow$$

$$\left[\lim_{t\to\infty} \lambda(t)K(t)e^{-R(t)}\right] - \lambda(0)K(0) = -V(0) \quad \Rightarrow$$

$$V(0) = \lambda(0)K(0), \qquad (f)$$

where the term in square brackets on the left-hand side vanishes due to the transversality condition. The final expression of (f) shows that Tobin's *average* q (designated by $\bar{q}$) equals *marginal* q:

$$\bar{q}(0) \equiv \frac{V(0)}{p^I(0)K(0)}, \quad q(0) = \frac{\lambda(0)}{p^I(0)} \quad \Rightarrow \quad \bar{q}(0) = q(0).$$

The nominal stockmarket value of the firm is $P(0)V(0)$ and the nominal replacement value of its capital stock is $P^I(0)K(0)$. As a result, Tobin's average q is $P(0)V(0)/(P^I(0)K(0))$, which equals $V(0)/(p^I(0)K(0))$.

4.1.2 Fiscal policy: Investment stimulation

The model can now be used to investigate the immediate, transitional, and long-run effects of governmental efforts to stimulate investment. Omitting the (now almost superfluous) time index, the model consists of equations (4.3), (4.6), (4.8),

85

and (4.11):

$$\dot{K} = I(q, s_I) - \delta K,$$ (4.13)

$$\dot{q} = (r + \delta)q - F_K(N, K),$$ (4.14)

$$w = F_N(N, K).$$ (4.15)

Despite its simplicity, the model allows several economically interesting variations to be considered within the same framework. Clearly, in view of (4.15), some assumption must be made about the real wage rate w. At least three types of labour market assumptions can be distinguished: (i) the model is interpreted at firm level and the real wage is assumed to be exogenously given (and constant); the model is interpreted at the level of the aggregate economy and (ii) full employment of labour is postulated or (iii) a macroeconomic labour supply equation is added to it (e.g. equation (1.11) with $P^e = P$). We consider these three cases in turn.

The effects of the investment subsidy under constant real wages

If the real wage rate is constant, the assumption of perfect competition in the goods market (and the implied homogeneity of the production function) renders the model very simple indeed. Of course, aside from the microeconomic interpretation given above, this case is also relevant for an entire economy with rigid real wages. Since the production function is homogeneous of degree one (constant returns to scale), the marginal products of labour and capital are homogeneous of degree zero (see the Intermezzo). This implies that $F_N(N, K)$ can be written as $F_N(1, K/N)$, which depends on the capital-labour ratio only. Equation (4.15) says that $w = F_N(1, K/N)$, which uniquely determines the K/N ratio for the firm, which is constant over time because w is constant over time. This also implies that the marginal product of capital is constant, since $F_K(N, K) = F_K(1, K/N) = F_K$, a constant.

By assuming a constant real wage, the labour demand equation can be ignored, and the model consists of equations (4.13)–(4.14). The qualitative content of the model can be summarized graphically by means of Figure 4.1. The $\dot{K} = 0$ line represents all combinations of K and q such that the capital stock is in equilibrium. In view of (4.13), this implies that gross investment is exactly equal to replacement investment along the $\dot{K} = 0$ line. Formally, we obtain from (4.13):

$$d\dot{K} = I_q \, dq + I_s \, ds_I - \delta \, dK,$$ (4.16)

which implies that the slope of the $\dot{K} = 0$ line is:

$$\left(\frac{\partial q}{\partial K} \right)_{\dot{K}=0} = \frac{\delta}{I_q} > 0.$$ (4.17)

In words, a higher capital stock necessitates a higher level of steady-state gross investment. This is only forthcoming if q is also higher.

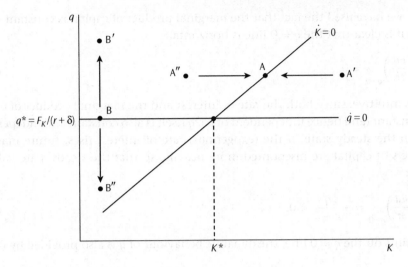

Figure 4.1. Investment with constant real wages

Equation (4.16) also implies that an increase in the investment subsidy shifts the $\dot{K} = 0$ line down and to the right:

$$\left(\frac{\partial q}{\partial s_I}\right)_{\dot{K}=0} = -\frac{I_s}{I_q} < 0. \tag{4.18}$$

The after-subsidy cost of investing falls and as a result firms are willing to invest the same amount for a lower value of q.

For points off the $\dot{K} = 0$ line, the dynamics of the capital stock is also provided by equation (4.16):

$$\frac{\partial \dot{K}}{\partial K} = -\delta < 0. \tag{4.19}$$

The graphical interpretation is as follows. In point A the capital stock is in equilibrium. If K is slightly higher (say at A' to the right of point A), (4.19) predicts that depreciation exceeds gross investment so that the capital stock falls over time, i.e. $\dot{K} < 0$. This dynamic effect is indicated by a horizontal arrow towards the $\dot{K} = 0$ line. Obviously, for points to the left of the $\dot{K} = 0$ line, the arrows point the other way (see point A''). The basic insight is, of course, that the capital accumulation process is self-correcting, i.e. for a given value of q, K has an automatic tendency to return to the $\dot{K} = 0$ line.

The $\dot{q} = 0$ line represents all points for which the firm's investment plans are in equilibrium. By differentiating (4.14) we obtain:

$$d\dot{q} = (r + \delta)\, dq + q\, dr, \tag{4.20}$$

where we have used the fact that the marginal product of capital is constant. From (4.20) it is clear that the $\dot{q} = 0$ line is horizontal:

$$\left(\frac{\partial q}{\partial K}\right)_{\dot{q}=0} = 0. \tag{4.21}$$

This is intuitive: since both the rate of interest and the marginal product of capital are constant (and hence independent of K), q itself is also constant and independent of K in the steady state. If the (exogenous) rate of interest rises, future marginal products of capital are discounted more heavily, so that the steady-state value of q falls:

$$\left(\frac{\partial q}{\partial r}\right)_{\dot{q}=0} = -\frac{q}{r+\delta} < 0. \tag{4.22}$$

For points off the $\dot{q} = 0$ line, the dynamic behaviour of q is also provided by (4.20):

$$\frac{\partial \dot{q}}{\partial q} = r + \delta > 0. \tag{4.23}$$

The graphical interpretation is as follows. At point B the value of q is consistent with an equilibrium investment plan. Now take a slightly higher value of q, say the one associated with point B', directly above point B. Clearly, in view of the fact that both r and F_K are constant, this higher value of q can only satisfy the arbitrage equation (4.12) if a (shadow) capital gain is expected, i.e. if $\dot{q} > 0$. The opposite holds at points below the $\dot{q} = 0$ line (say point B', as is indicated with the arrows in Figure 4.1). Intuitively, therefore, the q-dynamics is inherently unstable. Slight moves away from the $\dot{q} = 0$ line are not self-correcting but reinforcing.

By combining the information regarding the K-dynamics and q-dynamics, the forces operating on points in different regions of Figure 4.1 are obtained and summarized by the arrows. For example, at point B' there are automatic forces shifting the (q, K) combination in a north-easterly direction. In Figure 4.2, a number of representative *trajectories* have been drawn. Note especially what happens if a trajectory crosses through the $\dot{K} = 0$ line. Take point A, for example. As it moves in a south-easterly direction, it gets closer and closer to the $\dot{K} = 0$ line. As it reaches this line (at point A'), however, the value of q keeps falling and the level of gross investment becomes too low to sustain the given capital stock. As a result, the trajectory veers off in a south-westerly direction towards point A'' (never to be heard of again).

From the different trajectories that have been drawn in Figure 4.2, it can be judged that the model appears to be very unstable: all trajectories seem to lead away from the steady-state equilibrium point at E_0. There is, however, one path that does give rise to stable adjustment, namely the $\dot{q} = 0$ line itself. Consider, for example, point C. It lies on the $\dot{q} = 0$ line (so there are no forces operating to change the value of q over time), but it lies to the left of the $\dot{K} = 0$ line. But, the K-dynamics is stable, so the capital stock will automatically rise towards its level at point E_0. A similar conclusion holds for point C'.

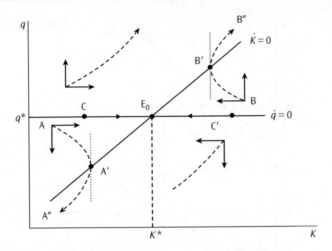

Figure 4.2. Derivation of the saddle path

In conclusion, for each given initial level of the capital stock, *there is exactly one path towards the steady-state equilibrium*. And this is very fortunate indeed, because one would have an embarrassment of riches if this were not the case. Indeed, suppose that the model were globally stable, so that "all roads lead to Rome", i.e. all (q, K) combinations would eventually return to point E_0. That would lead to a very troublesome conclusion, namely that the shadow price of capital (q) is not determined at any point in time!

The particular type of stability that is exemplified by the model is called *saddle-point stability*: there is exactly one stable adjustment path (called the saddle path) that re-establishes equilibrium after a shock. Technically speaking, the requirement that the economy be on the saddle path has more justification than just convenience: ultimately, an exploding solution is seen by agents not to be in their own best interests, so that they have good reason to restrict attention to the saddle-path solution. The remainder of this chapter will be used to demonstrate the remarkable predictive content of models incorporating saddle-point stability.

Consider the case of an *unanticipated and permanent increase in the investment subsidy*. This means that at some time t_A the government announces that s_I will be increased "as of today". In other words, the policy change is implemented immediately. For future reference, the implementation date is denoted by t_I. Hence, an unanticipated shock is a shock for which announcement and implementation dates coincide, i.e. $t_A = t_I$. The effects of the policy measure can be derived graphically with the aid of Figure 4.3. We have already derived that an increase in s_I shifts the $\dot{K} = 0$ line to the right, so that the ultimate equilibrium will be at point E_1. How does the adjustment occur? Very simple. Since E_0 is on the $\dot{q} = 0$ line (which is also the saddle path for this model), the higher subsidy gives rise to higher gross investment and the adjustment path is along the saddle path from E_0 to E_1. Note that the capital stock adjusts *smoothly*, due to the fact that adjustment costs make

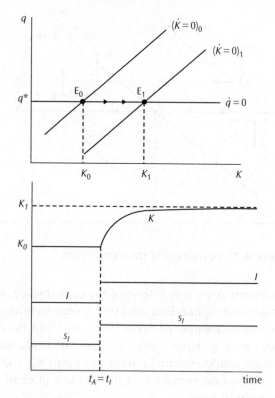

Figure 4.3. An unanticipated permanent
increase in the investment subsidy

very uneven investment plans very expensive. The adjustment over time has also
been illustrated in Figure 4.3.

As a second "finger exercise" with the model, consider an unanticipated permanent increase in the exogenous rate of interest r as illustrated in Figure 4.4. Equation
(4.22) shows that this shifts the $\dot{q} = 0$ line down due to the heavier discounting of
future marginal products of capital. What does the adjustment path look like now?
Clearly, the new equilibrium is at point E_1 and the only path to this point is the
saddle path going through it. Since K is fixed in the short run, the only stable adjustment path is the one with a "financial correction" at the time of the occurrence of
the shock (in t_A): q jumps down from point E_0 to point A directly below it. The intuition behind this financial correction is aided by solving the differential equation
for q given in (4.14):

$$q(t) \equiv \int_t^\infty F_K(\tau) \exp\left[-\int_t^\tau [r(s) + \delta]\, ds \right] d\tau. \tag{4.24}$$

Hence, as was already hinted at above, q represents the discounted value of present
and future marginal products of capital, so that an increase in r (either now or in

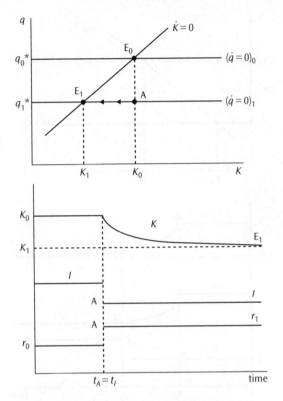

Figure 4.4. An unanticipated permanent
increase in the rate of interest

the future) immediately leads to a revaluation of this stream of returns. After the
immediate financial correction, the adjustment proceeds smoothly along the saddle
path towards the ultimate steady-state equilibrium point E_1.

As a final example of how the model works, consider the case where the firm hears
at time t_A that interest rates will rise permanently at some future date t_I. This is an
example of a so-called *anticipated shock*. Formally, an unanticipated shock is one that
is known to occur at some later date. Obviously, the only real news reaches the agent
at time t_A. Everything that happens after that time is known to the agent. What
happens to the value of q can already be gleaned from (4.24). Discounting of future
marginal products becomes heavier (than before the shock) after the rate of interest
has actually risen, i.e. for $t \geq t_I$. Hence, q must fall at the time the news becomes
available. But by how much? This is best illustrated with the aid of Figure 4.5.
Consider the following intuitive solution principle: a discrete adjustment in q must
occur at the time the news becomes available (i.e. at t_A), and there cannot be a
further discrete adjustment in q after t_A. Intuitively, an *anticipated* jump in q would
imply an infinite (shadow) capital gain or loss (since there would be a finite change
in q in an infinitesimal amount of time). Hence, the solution principle amounts to

91

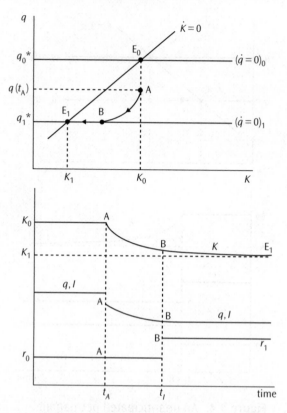

Figure 4.5. An anticipated permanent increase
in the rate of interest

requiring that all jumps occur when something truly unexpected occurs (which is at time t_A). Obviously, at t_A there is an infinite capital loss, but it is unanticipated.

With the aid of this solution principle, the adjustment path can be deduced. We work backwards. At the time of the interest rate increase the (q, K) combination must be on the new saddle path, i.e. at point B. If it were to reach B too soon ($t < t_I$) or too late ($t > t_I$), equilibrium would never be re-established without further jumps in q that are prohibited. Between t_A and t_I the dynamic forces determining q and K are those associated with the old equilibrium E_0 (see the arrows). Working backwards, there is exactly one trajectory starting at point A at t_A that arrives at point B at the right time t_I. Hence, the unique path that re-establishes equilibrium after the shock is the one comprised of a discrete adjustment at t_A from E_0 to A, followed by gradual adjustment from A to B in the period before the interest rate has risen, arrival at point B at t_I, followed by further gradual adjustment in the capital stock from B to E_1.

In comparison with the case of an unanticipated rise in the interest rate, the paths of q and investment are more smooth in the anticipated case (compare Figures 4.4

and 4.5, lower panel). The reason is, of course, that the firm in the case of an anticipated shock has an opportunity to react to the worsened investment climate in the future.

The effects of the investment subsidy with full employment in the labour market

Up to now we have interpreted the model given in (4.13)-(4.14) as applying to a single firm facing a constant real wage. Suppose that we re-interpret the model at a macroeconomic level, i.e. I and K now represent economy-wide gross investment and the capital stock, respectively, and the interpretation of q is likewise altered. Assume furthermore that the economy is characterized by full employment in the labour market. By normalizing employment to unity ($N = 1$), the model consists of:

$$\dot{K} = I(q, s_I) - \delta K, \tag{4.25}$$

$$\dot{q} = (r + \delta)q - F_K(1, K), \tag{4.26}$$

where it is clear that the major change caused by our re-interpretation is that the marginal product of capital is no longer constant. Intuitively, since the labour input is fully employed, the economy experiences diminishing returns to capital, since $F_{KK} < 0$. This also causes the $\dot{q} = 0$ line to be affected:

$$\left(\frac{\partial q}{\partial K}\right)_{\dot{q}=0} = \frac{F_{KK}}{r + \delta} < 0, \quad \left(\frac{\partial q}{\partial r}\right)_{\dot{q}=0} = -\frac{F_K}{(r + \delta)^2} < 0, \quad \frac{\partial \dot{q}}{\partial q} = r + \delta > 0. \tag{4.27}$$

Intuitively, steady-state q is downward sloping in K because the more capital is used, the lower is its marginal product. As a result, the discounted stream of marginal products (which is q) falls.

In Figure 4.6, the saddle path is derived graphically. The dynamic forces are much more complicated in this case. This is because the steady-state level of q and the q-dynamics itself are now both dependent on K. In addition to trajectories from points like A and C, there are now also trajectories from points like B and D that pass through the $\dot{q} = 0$ line. The major alteration compared to our earlier case is that the saddle path no longer coincides with the $\dot{q} = 0$ line.

As a first policy measure, consider an *anticipated abolition* of the investment subsidy, as was for example the case in the Netherlands in the late 1980s. Using the solution principle introduced above, the effects of this announced policy measure can be derived with the aid of Figure 4.7. The ultimate effect of the abolition of the subsidy is to increase the relative price of investment goods and to shift the $\dot{K} = 0$ line up and to the left. In the long run the economy ends up at point E_1, with a lower capital stock and a higher value of q (due to the higher steady-state marginal product of capital). Since the discrete adjustment in q must occur at the time of the announcement t_A, and the economy must be on the new saddle path at the time of implementation t_I, the adjustment path must look like the one sketched in the diagram. At t_A there is a financial correction that pushes the economy from

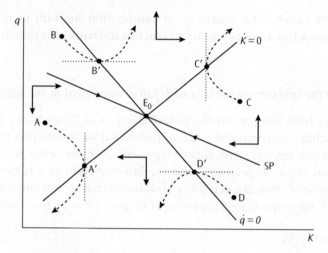

Figure 4.6. Investment with full employment in the labour market

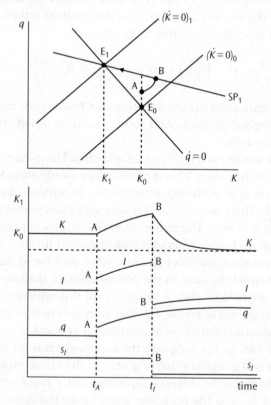

Figure 4.7. An anticipated abolition of the investment subsidy

E_0 to A directly above it (recall that K is fixed in the short run). Between t_A and t_I the economy moves in a north-easterly direction towards point B, where it arrives at t_I. After that, there is gradual adjustment from B to the new steady state at E_1.

The striking (though intuitive) conclusion is that investment goes up initially! Firms in this economy rush to put in their investment orders in order to be able to get the subsidy while it still exists. This is of course exactly what happened in the Dutch case. The adjustment paths for all variables have been drawn in the lower panel of Figure 4.7. The conclusion of this experiment must be that anticipation effects are very important and can give rise to (at first glance) unconventional dynamic adjustment.

Temporary or permanent investment subsidy?

Suppose that the policy maker wishes to stimulate the economy and has decided to do so by creating investment incentives in the form of an investment subsidy. If the policy maker desires the maximum stimulus to emerge for a given subsidy, should she introduce a permanent or a temporary investment subsidy? Intuition would suggest that a temporary subsidy would have a larger impact on current investment because firms would squeeze in their investments while the subsidy exists. This is an intertemporal substitution argument: firms are tempted to bring forward their intertemporal investment plans to "make hay while the sun shines". It turns out that our simple model in fact predicts this kind of response.

The temporary subsidy is announced and introduced in $t_A = t_I$ and simultaneously announced to be abolished again at some fixed time in the future t_E ($> t_A$ of course). Our heuristic solution principle can again be used to graphically derive the adjustment path with the aid of Figure 4.8. Working backwards in time, the following must hold: (i) at t_E the economy must be on the saddle path towards the eventual steady-state equilibrium E_0; (ii) between t_A and t_E the dynamic forces operating on q and K are those associated with the equilibrium E_1 (that is relevant if the subsidy were permanent). The arrows are drawn in Figure 4.8. At t_A the capital stock is given (at K_0) and the discrete financial adjustment must take place.

Using all this information, the adjustment path is easily seen to consist of a jump from E_0 to A at time t_A, gradual adjustment from A to B between t_A and t_E, followed by gradual adjustment from B to E_0 after t_E. The time paths for all variables are drawn in the lower panel of Figure 4.8.

Of course, the path associated with a *permanent* subsidy is an immediate jump at t_A from E_0 to A′ followed by gradual adjustment from A′ to E_1. This shows that the effect on current investment (i.e. $I(t_A)$) is highest for a temporary investment subsidy (compare points A and A′). This is because, for a given investment subsidy, the value of q falls by less in the case of a temporary subsidy. Hence, if the policy maker is concerned about stimulating current investment, a temporary investment subsidy is one way to achieve it.

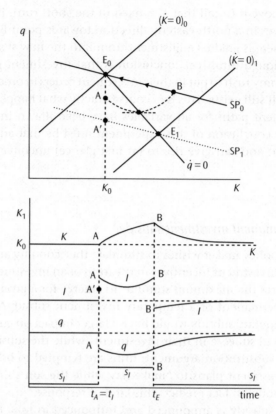

Figure 4.8. A temporary increase in the investment subsidy

Interaction with the labour supply decision

As a final application of the model, we now consider the general case where the model is interpreted at a macroeconomic level, and equations (4.13)–(4.15) are appended with a labour supply equation of the form familiar from Chapter 1:

$$w(1 - t_L) = g(N), \tag{4.28}$$

where t_L is the tax rate on labour income.

What happens to investment and employment if the tax on labour is reduced? And how do these effects occur over time? Obviously, in order to examine the effect on investment, the effect on the steady-state value of q must be determined. Since the economy is operating under perfect competition, the production function is linear homogeneous (constant returns to scale), and F_N and F_K depend only on K/N. The expressions for F_N and F_K can be linearized as follows (see the

Intermezzo below):

$$\tilde{F}_N = [(1 - \omega_L)/\sigma_{KN}]\left[\tilde{K} - \tilde{N}\right] = \tilde{w}, \tag{4.29}$$

$$\tilde{F}_K = -(\omega_L/\sigma_{KN})\left[\tilde{K} - \tilde{N}\right], \tag{4.30}$$

$$\tilde{N} = \epsilon_S\left[\tilde{w} - \tilde{t}_L\right], \tag{4.31}$$

where $\tilde{F}_K \equiv dF_K/F_K$, $\tilde{F}_N \equiv dF_N/F_N$, $\tilde{N} \equiv dN/N$, $\tilde{K} \equiv dK/K$, $\tilde{w} \equiv dw/w$, $\tilde{t}_L \equiv dt_L/(1-t_L)$, $\omega_L \equiv NF_N/Y$, $\epsilon_S \equiv g(N)/(Ng_N)$, and $\sigma_{KN} \equiv F_N F_K/(YF_{NK})$. In words, a variable with a tilde represents the proportional rate of change in that variable, ω_L is the share of income paid out to the factor labour, ϵ_S is the labour supply elasticity (see Chapter 1) that is assumed to be positive, and σ_{KN} (≥ 0) is the substitution elasticity between capital and labour. Intuitively, it measures how easy it is to substitute one factor of production for the other. The easier the substitution, the higher the value for σ_{KN}. Note that we have already imposed that the labour market is in equilibrium.

Intermezzo

Some production theory. If $Y = F(N, K)$ is a linear homogeneous production function, it possesses several very useful properties (see e.g. Ferguson, 1969, pp. 94–96):

(P1) $F_N N + F_K K = Y$ (Euler's Theorem);

(P2) F_N and F_K are homogeneous of degree zero in N and K, hence;

(P3) $NF_{NN} = -KF_{NK}$ and $KF_{KK} = -NF_{KN}$;

(P4) $\sigma_{KN} \equiv F_N F_K/(YF_{KN})$.

Also, Young's Theorem ensures that $F_{NK} = F_{KN}$. Armed with these useful properties equations (4.29) and (4.30) can be derived. First, totally differentiate $F_N(N, K)$:

$$dF_N = F_{NN}\, dN + F_{NK}\, dK. \tag{a}$$

But (P3) ensures that $F_{NN} = -(K/N)F_{NK}$, so that (a) can be written as:

$$dF_N = -(K/N)F_{NK}\, dN + F_{NK}\, dK = -F_{NK}K\left[\frac{dN}{N} - \frac{dK}{K}\right] \Rightarrow$$

$$\frac{dF_N}{F_N} = \left(\frac{F_{NK}K}{F_N}\right)\left[\frac{dK}{K} - \frac{dN}{N}\right]. \tag{b}$$

It remains to be shown that $F_{NK}K/N$ can be written in terms of an income share and the substitution elasticity defined in (P4):

$$\frac{F_{NK}K}{F_N} = \left(\frac{F_K K}{Y}\right)\left(\frac{F_{NK}Y}{F_N F_K}\right) = \frac{1 - \omega_L}{\sigma_{KN}}. \tag{c}$$

Combining (c) and (b) yields (4.29). Note that we have used (P1) and (c) to derive that $F_K K/Y = 1 - F_N N/Y = 1 - wN/Y = 1 - \omega_L$. The derivation of (4.30) is left as an exercise.

By using (4.29) and (4.31), the equilibrium employment level and the wage rate can be written as a function of $\tilde{K}$ and $\tilde{t}_L$:

$$\tilde{w} = \frac{(1 - \omega_L)\left[\tilde{K} + \epsilon_S \tilde{t}_L\right]}{\sigma_{KN} + (1 - \omega_L)\epsilon_S}, \tag{4.32}$$

$$\tilde{N} = \frac{\epsilon_S(1 - \omega_L)\tilde{K} - \epsilon_S \sigma_{KN} \tilde{t}_L}{\sigma_{KN} + (1 - \omega_L)\epsilon_S}. \tag{4.33}$$

By substituting (4.33) into (4.30), the expression for $\tilde{F}_K$ is obtained:

$$\tilde{F}_K = -\frac{\omega_L\left[\tilde{K} + \epsilon_S \tilde{t}_L\right]}{\sigma_{KN} + (1 - \omega_L)\epsilon_S}. \tag{4.34}$$

This expression is particularly important. It says that the marginal product of capital increases if the tax on labour is reduced. The reason is that a decrease in the labour tax stimulates employment (since $\epsilon_S > 0$), which means that capital becomes more productive (since $F_{KN} > 0$).

The immediate, transitional, and long-run effects of a permanent unanticipated reduction in the labour income tax have been illustrated in Figure 4.9. As the labour tax falls, the marginal product of capital rises (for all levels of the capital stock) and the $\dot{q} = 0$ line shifts up and to the right. The economy jumps from E_0 to A, and the value of q jumps from q_0 to q'. Entrepreneurs observe a very good business climate and feel a strong incentive to expand business by investing. The economy moves smoothly along the saddle path from A to E_1. The situation in the labour market is depicted in Figure 4.10. The immediate effect of the tax reduction is an expansion of labour supply from N_0^S to N_1^S. Employment is immediately stimulated and rises from N_0 to N'. This is not the end of the story, however. Due to the fact that more capital is put in place (factories are expanded) labour becomes more productive as well. In terms of Figure 4.10, the labour demand schedule starts to gradually shift up and to the right, and employment expands further. The ultimate steady-state equilibrium is at E_1. The time paths for all variables have been sketched in the bottom panel of Figure 4.9.

4.2 A Dynamic IS-LM Model

Tobin's q-theory has become very popular among macroeconomists. The reason is that it allows for a very simple description of the dynamics of the investment

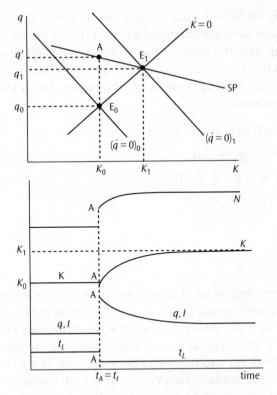

Figure 4.9. A fall in the tax on labour
income: investment and employment effects

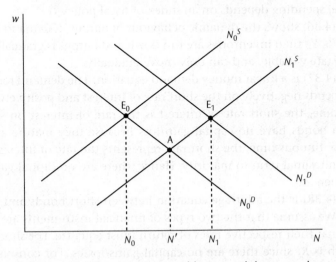

Figure 4.10. The short-run and long-run labour market
effects

process, and gives predictions that are not grossly contradicted by empirical evidence. In this section we discuss Blanchard's (1981) IS-LM model which incorporates the q-theory along with the assumptions of fixed prices and slow quantity adjustment. This allows us to study the macroeconomic effects of traditional fiscal policy in an explicit forward-looking framework. The model that is used is described by the following equations:

$$Y^D = aq + \beta Y + G, \quad a > 0, \ 0 < \beta < 1, \tag{4.35}$$

$$\dot{Y} = \sigma \left[Y^D - Y \right], \quad \sigma > 0, \tag{4.36}$$

$$M/P = kY - lR_S, \quad k > 0, \ l > 0, \tag{4.37}$$

$$R_S = R_L - (1/R_L)\dot{R}_L, \tag{4.38}$$

$$\frac{\dot{q} + \pi}{q} = R_S, \tag{4.39}$$

$$\pi = \alpha_0 + \alpha_1 Y, \tag{4.40}$$

where Y^D is real spending on goods and services, q is Tobin's average q, Y is the level of real production (and income), G is an index of fiscal policy, $\dot{Y}$ [$\equiv dY/dt$] is the change in output, R_S is the short rate of interest, R_L is the rate of interest on consols (the long rate), M is the nominal money supply, and P is the fixed price level.

Equations (4.35)–(4.36) together describe a dynamic IS curve. Equation (4.35) shows that spending depends on Tobin's average q, both because of its positive effect on investment and (potentially) because of positive wealth effects in consumption (recall that qK is the value of the nation's capital stock. To the extent that domestic households own the firms, qK is part of wealth which may affect consumption). Furthermore, spending depends on an index of fiscal policy G.

Equation (4.36) shows the dynamic behaviour of output. If demand exceeds production ($Y^D > Y$) then inventories are run down and output is gradually increased. Output is a state variable, and can only move gradually.

Equation (4.37) is a linear money demand equation. The demand for real money balances depends negatively on the short rate of interest and positively on income. In discrete time, the short rate of interest is the rate of interest on single-period bonds. Such bonds have no capital gain/loss because they mature after a single period. In continuous time, the short rate represents the rate of interest on a bond with an infinitesimal term to maturity. Hence, there are no capital gains/losses in this case either.

Equation (4.38) is the arbitrage equation between short bonds and consols (see Chapter 2). We assume that the two types of financial instruments are perfect substitutes, so that their respective rates of return must equalize. For short bonds this rate of return is R_S since there are no capital gains/losses. For consols there may, however, be capital gains/losses. Recall that the price of consols is the inverse of the rate of interest on consols, i.e. $P_B \equiv 1/R_L$. The rate of return on a consol is equal to the sum of the coupon payment (1 guilder each period) plus the expected capital gain ($\dot{P}_B$) expressed in terms of the price of the consol (P_B):

$$\text{return on consol} \equiv \frac{1 + \dot{P}_B}{P_B} = \frac{1 - (1/R_L^2)\dot{R}_L}{1/R_L} = R_L - (1/R_L)\dot{R}_L, \tag{4.41}$$

where we have used $P_B \equiv 1/R_L$ and $\dot{P}_B = (-1/R_L^2)\dot{R}_L$ to arrive at the final expression. This rate of return on consols must be the same as the short rate of interest:

$$\dot{R}_L/R_L = R_L - R_S. \tag{4.42}$$

Equation (4.42) is known as the *term structure of interest rates*.

Equation (4.39) is another arbitrage equation. Since q measures the value of shares, the rate of return on shares is the sum of the periodic dividend payment (π) plus the expected capital gain ($\dot{q}$) on shares, expressed in terms of the share price (q) itself:

$$\text{return on share} \equiv \frac{\pi + \dot{q}}{q}, \tag{4.43}$$

Since shares and the other financial instruments are perfect substitutes, the rate of return on shares must be the same as the short rate of interest. This is what (4.39) says. Finally, equation (4.40) is an ad hoc relationship between profit (or dividends) and output. If output is high, the marginal product of capital is also high (for a given capital stock) and so are profits.

The model can be condensed to three equations by means of simple substitutions:

$$\dot{Y} = \sigma[aq - bY + G], \quad b \equiv 1 - \beta, \quad 0 < b < 1, \tag{4.44}$$

$$R_S = (k/l)Y - (1/l)(M/P), \tag{4.45}$$

$$R_S = \frac{\dot{q} + \alpha_0 + \alpha_1 Y}{q}. \tag{4.46}$$

The $\dot{Y} = 0$ line is linear and upward sloping. Increasing government spending shifts the $\dot{Y} = 0$ line down and to the right, and the dynamic forces operating on points off the $\dot{Y} = 0$ line are stabilizing, i.e. for a given level of q, output automatically returns to the equilibrium line over time.

$$\left(\frac{\partial q}{\partial Y}\right)_{\dot{Y}=0} = \frac{b}{a} > 0, \quad \left(\frac{\partial q}{\partial G}\right)_{\dot{Y}=0} = -\frac{1}{a} < 0, \quad \frac{\partial \dot{Y}}{\partial Y} = -\sigma b < 0. \tag{4.47}$$

The $\dot{q} = 0$ line is slightly more complicated due to its non-linearity. Its slope depends on the relative strength of two effects: if Y increases, both profits and the short rate of interest rise. As a result, the net effect on the steady-state value for q [$\equiv (\alpha_0 + \alpha_1 Y)/R_S$] is not a priori clear. In this section we assume that the profit effect of output is dominated by the interest rate effect. This case is labelled the "bad news case" by Blanchard (1981). To calculate the properties of the $\dot{q} = 0$ line, we totally differentiate (4.46):

$$\dot{q} = R_S q - \alpha_0 - \alpha_1 Y \quad \Rightarrow$$

$$d\dot{q} = [qk/l - \alpha_1] \, dY + R_S \, dq - q \, d(M/Pl). \tag{4.48}$$

From (4.48) we can derive that the slope of $\dot{q} = 0$ is:

$$\left(\frac{\partial q}{\partial Y} \right)_{\dot{q}=0} = \frac{\alpha_1 - qk/l}{R_S}. \tag{4.49}$$

Hence, the "bad news" case holds if $\alpha_1 < qk/l$, which is likely if the LM curve is relatively steep (as the monetarists would have it). Equation (4.48) also implies that an increase in the money supply shifts the $\dot{q} = 0$ line up and to the right. Also, the dynamics of q for points off the $\dot{q} = 0$ line is destabilizing:

$$\left(\frac{\partial q}{\partial M} \right)_{\dot{q}=0} = \frac{q}{lPR_S} > 0, \quad \frac{\partial \dot{q}}{\partial q} = R_S > 0. \tag{4.50}$$

The dynamic behaviour of the model can once again be determined graphically with the aid of Figure 4.11 (the $\dot{q} = 0$ line is drawn as a linear line for convenience). The model is saddle-point stable, and the initial equilibrium is at E_0, with output equal to Y_0 and Tobin's q equal to q_0.

Now consider what happens if the policy maker announces a permanent fiscal expansion to be implemented some time in the future (hence $t_I > t_A$). Using the heuristic solution principle used extensively in this chapter, the adjustment path is easily derived. At t_A there is a stockmarket correction and q jumps from q_0 to q'. Agents know that output will expand in the future and as a result short interest rates will rise. Even though profits will rise also, the interest rate effect dominates in this case, so that the discounted value of profits (i.e. q) must fall. Between t_A and t_I output actually falls. This is because aggregate spending (Y^D) has collapsed due to the fall in q (recall that the additional government spending has not yet materialized). At t_I the fiscal impulse happens and demand exceeds production ($Y^D > Y$), which leads to a gradual increase in production along the saddle path from B to E_1. Ultimately, the economy ends up with a higher level of output and a lower value of q.

What happens to the other variables over time has been illustrated in the lower panel of Figure 4.11. The path of the short rate of interest is implied by the path for income Y and the LM curve (4.37). The long rate of interest must satisfy (4.38). We know that in the long run both the short- and the long rate must rise ($dR_L = dR_S > 0$). In view of the solution principle, R_L can only jump at time t_A since no anticipated infinitely large capital gains/losses are allowed. If R_L were to jump down to a level below R_L, equilibrium would never be restored since $\dot{R}_L = R_L(R_L - R_S) < 0$, and R_L would continue to fall over time (whereas its steady-state level is higher than before the shock). Hence, R_L must jump up at time t_A to a level above R_S (but below its new steady-state level). Thereafter, $\dot{R}_L = R_L(R_L - R_S) > 0$, and R_L gradually starts to rise further over time towards its new steady-state level.

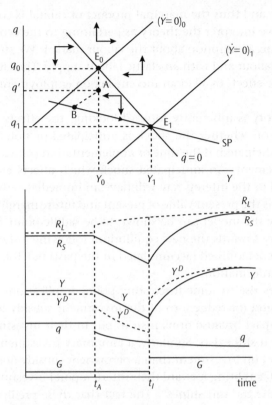

Figure 4.11. Anticipated fiscal policy

4.3 Punchlines

The key concept that is developed in this chapter is that of saddle-point stability. To illustrate this concept we develop Tobin's q theory of investment in continuous time. This theory, which was also discussed briefly in discrete time in Chapter 2, is quite attractive because it is very simple but nevertheless yields predictions which accord with intuition and (some of the) empirical evidence. In the q-theory, investment by firms depends on the shadow price of installed capital goods, which is called Tobin's marginal q. This shadow price is a forward-looking concept and it incorporates all the information that is of relevance to the firm. Under some conditions Tobin's marginal q coincides with average q, which can be measured in a relatively straightforward fashion by looking at the stockmarket value of the firm.

In order to understand the capital dynamics implied by Tobin's q theory, we study the effect of an investment subsidy in a number of different settings. In the simplest possible setting we interpret the theory at the level of an individual firm for which the real wage rate and thus the marginal product of capital is constant. In a more complex setting we interpret the theory as pertaining to the economy as a whole. This necessitates an assumption about the labour market. We study the cases with a fixed supply of labour and with an elastic labour supply. The latter case allows for a discussion of the effects of a labour income tax on employment, investment, and the capital stock.

Since the q-theory is inherently forward looking, the effects of a policy shock depend critically on whether the shock is anticipated or not. A policy shock is unanticipated (anticipated) if the time of implementation coincides (postdates) the time of announcement. An anticipated shock which affects either the marginal product of capital or the interest rate will have an immediate effect on investment because Tobin's q is the present value of present and future marginal capital productivity. Graphically the model can be shown to be saddle-point stable, i.e. there is a unique trajectory towards the new equilibrium following a shock. At impact the capital stock is predetermined (accumulated in the past) but Tobin's q can jump to incorporate new information.

The model gives rise to some interesting policy implications. For example, an anticipated abolition (or reduction) of the investment subsidy leads to an investment boom at impact because firms rush to put in their investment orders to get the subsidy while it still exists. Similarly, a temporary investment subsidy causes a larger impact effect on investment than a permanent subsidy does. Intuitively this happens because firms bring forward their intertemporal investment plans in order to "make hay while the sun shines". The fact that these predictions accord with intuition lends the theory some credibility.

Another attractive feature of Tobin's q theory is that it is easily incorporated in the IS-LM model. In doing so one of the objections raised against that model, namely that it contains only rudimentary dynamics, is substantially weakened. By also introducing a simple (forward-looking) term structure of interest rates into the model, the dynamic IS-LM model gives rise to a rich array of intertemporal effects. For example, with an anticipated increase in government consumption it is possible that output falls during the early phase of the transition. This is because the downward jump in Tobin's q causes a fall in investment and aggregate demand which is not counteracted because the additional government consumption has not yet materialized. In the long run, of course, output rises beyond its initial level.

Further Reading

The material on the investment subsidy is motivated in part by the analyses of Abel (1982) and Summers (1981). Abel (1981) shows how the investment model can be generalized by allowing for a variable utilization rate of capital. The recent investment literature stresses the irreversibility of investment and/or non-convex adjustment costs. Key articles are: Abel and Eberly (1994), Abel et al. (1996), Dixit and Pindyck (1994), and Caballero and Leahy (1996). A good survey is Caballero (1999).

Sargent (1987b) and Nickell (1986) develop a dynamic theory of labour demand based on adjustment costs on the stock of labour. Hamermesh and Pfann (1996) present a recent survey of this literature. In Chapter 11 we show how saddle-point equilibria naturally arise in the open economy context. Key papers are Dornbusch (1976) and Buiter and Miller (1981, 1982), and a good survey is Scarth (1988, ch. 9).

and Mankiw (1996), Davis (1990), Davis and Haltiwanger (1996), and Caballero and others (1996), and ... (1990).

Second (1982) and Sneddon (1996) discuss ... and ... Lindbeck and Snower, ... a great ... Finally, in Chapter 12 we discuss how ... (not directly ...) and ... Finley 1996, and Sneddon and ... Sneddon (1990, 1993).

5

The Macroeconomics of Quantity Rationing

The purpose of this chapter is to discuss the following issues:

1. To introduce the first attempt by (neo-) Keynesians to provide microeconomic foundations of Keynesian macroeconomics,
2. To analyse the effects of fiscal and monetary policy in the different disequilibrium configurations,
3. To ascertain the lasting contributions made by the quantity rationing approach.

5.1 (Neo-) Keynesians go Micro

Without any doubt, the Keynesian camp was in great disarray during the middle and late 1970s. First of all, the neoclassical synthesis was under great stress from the attacks by the monetarists at first and the new classicals later on. Furthermore, the Lucas critique had caused serious doubts as to the validity of macroeconomic models that are not based on a firm microeconomic underpinning (which describes a great many Keynesian models of those days).

Not surprisingly, a new research programme was launched by predominantly Keynesian macroeconomists such as Robert Barro (!) and Herschel Grossman (1971, 1976), and Edmond Malinvaud (1977), building on earlier work by Robert Clower (1965) and Don Patinkin (1965), that was specifically aimed at providing Keynesian macroeconomics with firm micro-foundations. (Note, however, that Barro "jumped ship" in the late 1970s and became one of the leaders of the new classical school. See Barro (1979b) for his reasons.) In this chapter we wish to provide a selective survey of what these neo-Keynesian theories amount to.

5.1.1 The basic ideas

Not surprisingly, in view of Modigliani's interpretation of the Keynesian innovation, the crucial assumption that the neo-Keynesians use is the notion of comprehensive price and wage fixity (in the short run). As we have already seen in the previous chapters, the non-functioning of a price signal implies the automatic emergence of a quantity signal. For example, a large part of the Amsterdam market for rental accommodation is price regulated. As a result the price signal is not allowed to do its job (of clearing the market) and large waiting periods of up to ten years or more are the consequence (that is the quantity signal). Similarly, the long queues one used to routinely observe in the Eastern Bloc countries are a tell-tale sign of quantity signals taking over where price signals are not allowed to work.

Hence, given the assumption that prices and wages are fixed, it should come as no surprise that macroeconomic quantities such as output and employment will be influenced. More precisely: we should expect *rationing* to emerge in one or more markets. For example, if the real wage W/P is "too high", one would expect the demand for labour to be "too low" *vis-à-vis* labour supply and unemployment to exist. (As it turns out, however, this basic intuition in some cases provides an incorrect causal link between the level of real wages and unemployment.) But if agents are unemployed, they are likely to change their consumption plans also. In other words, the problem that exists in one market (e.g. an excessive real wage) also has an effect in the other market (e.g. lower demand for goods because the unemployed consume less). This is an example of so-called *spillover effects* that may exist between markets.

It is clear that we have to be very specific about the kind of restrictions that agents face when making their decisions. Clower (1965) formulated the *dual decision hypothesis* for this purpose. Loosely speaking, the dual decision hypothesis suggests that agents, when formulating their optimal plans in one market, take into account the possible quantity restrictions that they may face in one or more different markets. The plans that are made according to the dual decision hypothesis are called *effective* plans. Plans that are based only on the usual budget restriction are called *notional* plans.

A final element in the theories to be discussed is the *minimum transaction rule*, according to which the short side of the market determines the quantity that is actually traded. The idea can be illustrated with the aid of Figure 5.1, which depicts a market for some particular good in isolation. The demand and supply schedules are Q^D and Q^S, respectively, and the fixed price is equal to P_0. This price is too low for the market to clear, and there exists an excess demand for the good, i.e. $Q^D(P_0) > Q^S(P_0)$. If we postulate that exchange in this market is voluntary, nobody is forced to trade more than he/she wishes, and the actual amount traded is the minimum of demand and supply:

$$Q = \min\left[Q^S(P_0), Q^D(P_0)\right], \tag{5.1}$$

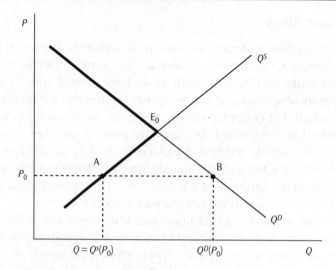

Figure 5.1. The minimum transaction rule

which equals $Q^S(P_0)$ in the case depicted. Equation (5.1) is a formal representation of the minimum transaction rule. By trying several different price levels, the minimum transaction rule is obtained graphically as the thick line in Figure 5.1.

5.1.2 Notional behaviour of households

We assume that there is a representative household that consumes goods (C), leisure ($1 - N$), and real money balances ($m \equiv M/P$, where M is the nominal money supply and P is the price level). There are no interest-bearing assets so the household can only save by holding money. The household's utility function is given by:

$$U_H = U(C, 1 - N, m), \tag{5.2}$$

where $U_C > 0$, $U_{1-N} > 0$, and $U_m > 0$. Real money balances appear in the utility function as a proxy for future consumption possibilities (see Muellbauer and Portes (1978) for an explicit two-period approach). The budget restriction of the representative household is:

$$m - m_0 = \pi_0 + wN - C, \tag{5.3}$$

where π_0 [$\equiv \Pi_0/P$] is real profit income received at the beginning of the period, m_0 [$\equiv M_0/P$] is initial real money balances, and w [$\equiv W/P$] is the real wage rate. Equation (5.3) says that the excess of income over consumption spending is to be saved in the form of additional money balances. The budget restriction can also be written in a more intuitive form:

$$C + w(1 - N) + m = m_0 + \pi_0 + w, \tag{5.4}$$

where the right-hand side of (5.4) is the definition of full income, i.e. the maximum amount of income the household can generate by working the maximum amount of hours at its disposal (and not consuming any leisure). The left-hand side of (5.4) says that this full income can be spent on three spending categories: consumption of goods, consumption of leisure, and real money balances.

The *notional* plans for the household are obtained by maximizing (5.2) subject to (5.4). The first-order conditions characterizing the notional plans are easily derived by using the Lagrange multiplier method (see Chapter 2 and the Mathematical Appendix). The Lagrangean is:

$$\mathcal{L} \equiv U(C, 1 - N, m) + \lambda \left[m_0 + \pi_0 + w - C - w(1 - N) - m \right], \tag{5.5}$$

where λ is the Lagrange multiplier associated with the budget restriction (5.4). The first-order conditions for C, $1 - N$, and m are:

$$\frac{\partial \mathcal{L}}{\partial C} = U_C - \lambda = 0, \tag{5.6}$$

$$\frac{\partial \mathcal{L}}{\partial (1 - N)} = U_{1-N} - \lambda w = 0, \tag{5.7}$$

$$\frac{\partial \mathcal{L}}{\partial m} = U_m - \lambda = 0, \tag{5.8}$$

where, of course, the final first-order condition, $\partial \mathcal{L}/\partial \lambda = 0$, implies the household budget restriction (5.4). By substituting the Lagrange multiplier λ, equations (5.6)–(5.8) can be summarized by two first-order conditions: $U_C = U_m$ and $U_{1-N}/U_C = w$. In words, the first condition states that the marginal rate of substitution between consumption and money should equal unity, and the second condition states that the marginal rate of substitution between consumption and leisure should equal the opportunity cost of leisure (i.e. the real wage rate). Of course, the second condition has already been discussed extensively in Chapter 1. In order to get the simplest possible expressions, we use a Cobb–Douglas utility function to represent the household's preferences:

$$U = C^\alpha (1 - N)^\beta m^\gamma, \tag{5.9}$$

with $0 < \alpha, \beta, \gamma < 1$ and $\alpha + \beta + \gamma = 1$. The advantage of using this specific form is that the solutions for C, N, and m that satisfy the first-order conditions plus the household budget restriction are very straightforward:[1]

$$C^D = C^D(w, P, M_0 + \Pi_0) = \alpha \left[\left(\frac{M_0 + \Pi_0}{P} \right) + w \right], \tag{5.10}$$

$$N^S = N^S(w, P, M_0 + \Pi_0) = 1 - \left(\frac{\beta}{w} \right) \left[\left(\frac{M_0 + \Pi_0}{P} \right) + w \right], \tag{5.11}$$

$$m^D = m^D(w, P, M_0 + \Pi_0) = \gamma \left[\left(\frac{M_0 + \Pi_0}{P} \right) + w \right], \tag{5.12}$$

where C^D is the notional demand for goods, N^S is the notional supply of labour, and m^D is the notional demand for real money balances. Equations (5.10)–(5.12) imply that consumption, leisure, and real money balances are all normal goods: as full income increases more of each is purchased. The following partial derivatives will be useful below.

$$C_w^D \equiv \frac{\partial C^D}{\partial w} = \alpha > 0, \quad C_P^D \equiv \frac{\partial C^D}{\partial P} = -\frac{\alpha(M_0 + \Pi_0)}{P^2} < 0, \tag{5.13}$$

$$C_M^D \equiv \frac{\partial C^D}{\partial M_0} = \frac{\alpha}{P} > 0, \quad N_w^S \equiv \frac{\partial N^S}{\partial w} = \frac{\beta(M_0 + \Pi_0)}{Pw^2} > 0, \tag{5.14}$$

$$N_P^S \equiv \frac{\partial N^S}{\partial P} = \frac{\beta(M_0 + \Pi_0)}{wP^2} > 0, \quad N_M^S \equiv \frac{\partial N^S}{\partial M_0} = -\frac{\beta}{wP} < 0. \tag{5.15}$$

These effects are intuitive. Note that, due to the Cobb–Douglas assumption, the notional labour supply equation is guaranteed to be upward sloping in the wage rate, i.e. the income effect is dominated by the substitution effect. Note finally, that the effects of the absolute price level operate via a wealth effect: a rise in the price erodes the real value of the initial profit income and money balances (since $\pi_0 \equiv \Pi_0/P$ and $m_0 \equiv M_0/P$).

5.1.3 Notional behaviour of firms

We model firms in the simplest possible way. Unlike Muellbauer and Portes (1978), we do not allow for the possibility of simultaneous rationing of firms in both the goods market and the labour market.[2] Firms are assumed to be unable to hold

---

[1] Notation is a perennial problem in rationing models. After some soul-searching we settled on the following conventions. Superscripts "D" and "S" stand for *notional* demands and supplies, respectively. Superscripts "DE" and "SE" stand for *effective* demands and supplies, respectively. Quantity variables with a bar refer to *actually traded* quantities (and perceived quantity constraints). For example, N^D is the notional demand for labour, N^{SE} is the effective supply of labour, and $\bar{N}$ is the actual amount of labour traded.

[2] If the firms can also make a non-trivial inventory decision, it is possible for them to be simultaneously rationed in both the labour market and the goods market. The resulting *underconsumption* regime is rarely observed in practice, and including it does not seem worth the effort.

inventories, nor to be able to invest. As a consequence, the firm maximizes its profit:

$$\pi = Y - wN = F(N) - wN, \tag{5.16}$$

where π is current period real profit (to be handed over to households in the future), $Y = F(N)$ is production in the current period (there is no physical capital). Below we will occasionally make use of the following Cobb–Douglas specification to get simple expressions:

$$Y = F(N) \equiv N^\epsilon, \quad 0 < \epsilon < 1. \tag{5.17}$$

In the absence of rationing, the firm chooses its production level Y and its demand for labour N such that (5.16) is maximized. The first-order condition is obtained in the usual fashion:

$$\frac{d\pi}{dN} = 0: \quad F_N(N) = w. \tag{5.18}$$

Equation (5.18) says that the marginal product of labour should be equated to the real wage rate. Obviously (5.18) and the production function imply two implicit functions relating the notional demand for labour (N^D) and the notional supply of goods (Y^S) to the real wage rate.

$$N^D = N^D(w), \quad N^D_w = 1/F_{NN} < 0, \tag{5.19}$$

$$Y^S = F\left(N^D(w)\right) = Y^S(w), \quad Y^S_w = F_N/F_{NN} < 0. \tag{5.20}$$

5.1.4 Walrasian equilibrium

The government levies no taxes and pays no transfers, but it does consume goods (denoted by G), and pays for these goods by issuing new money. The government budget restriction can be written as:[3]

$$(m - m_0) + (\pi - \pi_0) = G, \tag{5.21}$$

which says that the net acquisition of financial assets by the private sector (households plus firms) equals government consumption.

Before we discuss disequilibrium in product and labour markets, it is useful first to consider the Walrasian equilibrium (WE) in which prices and wages are flexible and all markets clear. Since households and firms face no constraints due to quantity

---

[3] The national income identity is $Y = C + G$. By substituting this identity, as well as the profit definition (5.16), into the household budget constraint (5.3) we obtain (5.21).

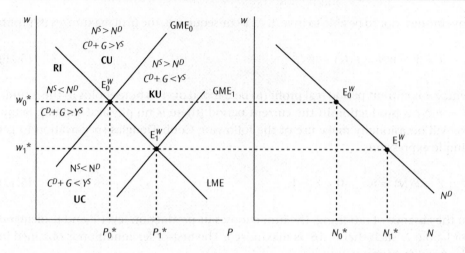

Figure 5.2. The Walrasian equilibrium and the effects of fiscal policy

rationing, the model is closed by the following two equilibrium conditions:

$$Y^S(w) = C^D(w, P, M_0 + \Pi_0) + G, \tag{GME}$$

$$N^D(w) = N^S(w, P, M_0 + \Pi_0), \tag{LME}$$

where GME and LME stand for, respectively, the **goods market equilibrium** and **labour market equilibrium**.

The Walrasian equilibrium can be illustrated with the aid of Figure 5.2. By differentiating the GME we obtain:

$$Y_w^S \, dw = C_w^D \, dw + C_P^D \, dP + C_M^D \, dM_0 + dG \quad \Rightarrow$$

$$dw = \frac{-C_P^D \, dP - C_M^D \, dM_0 - dG}{C_w^D - Y_w^S}. \tag{5.22}$$

From this we conclude that GME is upward sloping in (w, P) space, and shifts down and to the right if government spending or the money supply are increased:

$$\left(\frac{\partial w}{\partial P}\right)_{GME} \equiv -\frac{C_P^D}{C_w^D - Y_w^S} > 0, \quad \left(\frac{\partial w}{\partial G}\right)_{GME} \equiv -\frac{1}{C_w^D - Y_w^S} < 0, \tag{5.23}$$

$$\left(\frac{\partial w}{\partial M_0}\right)_{GME} \equiv -\frac{C_M^D}{C_w^D - Y_w^S} < 0. \tag{5.24}$$

In words, if w rises, the demand for goods is increased but the supply of goods is reduced. As a result, there is an excess demand for goods that can only be eliminated if the price of these goods rises. Similarly, an increase in government consumption (or the money supply) creates an excess demand for goods (for a given real wage rate), which can only be eliminated if the price level rises and household demand for goods is sufficiently cut back.

By differentiating the LME, we obtain the following:

$$N_w^S \, dw + N_P^S \, dP + N_M^S \, dM_0 = N_w^D \, dw \quad \Rightarrow \quad dw = \frac{-N_P^S \, dP - N_M^S \, dM_0}{N_w^S - N_w^D}. \tag{5.25}$$

Hence, the LME is downward sloping in (w, P) space, and shifts up and to the right if the money supply is increased:

$$\left(\frac{\partial w}{\partial P} \right)_{LME} \equiv -\frac{N_P^S}{N_w^S - N_w^D} < 0, \quad \left(\frac{\partial w}{\partial M_0} \right)_{LME} \equiv -\frac{N_M^S}{N_w^S - N_w^D} > 0. \tag{5.26}$$

In words, for a given level of the real wage rate w, an increase in the price level increases labour supply and induces an excess supply of labour that only disappears if the real wage rate falls. Similarly, for a given price level, an increase in the money supply reduces labour supply (as households are wealthier) and creates an excess demand for labour that vanishes if the real wage rate rises.

The effects of fiscal policy have been illustrated in Figure 5.2. The initial Walrasian equilibrium is at E_0^W. An increase in G shifts GME down and to the right. This leads to a fall in the real wage rate and a rise in the price level. Employment rises: households work harder despite the fall in real wages because of the negative effect on wealth of the higher price level.

Monetary policy, consisting of a helicopter drop of money balances at the beginning of the period (i.e. $dM_0 > 0$) has an ambiguous effect on employment and the real wage rate. This is because both GME and LME curves shift to the right: the wealth effect causes households to consume more and work less.

5.1.5 Effective demands and supplies of households

The household can face quantity restrictions in the labour market, the goods market, or both. Starting with the first case, suppose that the household faces a binding restriction on the number of hours of work equal to $\bar{N}$ ($< N^S$). In the face of this restriction, the household formulates effective demands for goods and real money balances (C^{DE} and m^{DE}, respectively). These are obtained by maximizing (5.5) by choice of C and m, with the restriction $N = \bar{N}$ substituted in. The first-order conditions consist of (5.6) and (5.8) and the budget restriction:

$$C + m = m_0 + \pi_0 + w\bar{N}. \tag{5.27}$$

For the Cobb–Douglas preferences given in (5.9), the solutions are:

$$C^{DE} = C^{DE}(w\bar{N}, P, M_0 + \Pi_0) = \left(\frac{\alpha}{\alpha + \gamma} \right) \left[\left(\frac{M_0 + \Pi_0}{P} \right) + w\bar{N} \right], \tag{5.28}$$

$$m^{DE} = m^{DE}(w\bar{N}, P, M_0 + \Pi_0) = \left(\frac{\gamma}{\alpha + \gamma} \right) \left[\left(\frac{M_0 + \Pi_0}{P} \right) + w\bar{N} \right]. \tag{5.29}$$

Obviously, since $\bar{N} < N^S$ (the constraint is binding) equation (5.28) implies that $C^{DE} < C^D$. Due to the rationing in the labour market, households cut back consumption. For the Cobb–Douglas case we can use (5.10) and (5.28) to obtain an alternative expression for C^{DE} which clearly shows the spillover effect from the labour market to the goods market:

$$C^{DE} = C^D - \left(\frac{\alpha}{\alpha + \gamma}\right) w [N^S - \bar{N}]. \tag{5.30}$$

If the employment ration ($\bar{N}$) happens to coincide with the notional supply of labour (N^S) then effective and notional demands for goods will coincide, i.e. $C^{DE} = C^D$ (students should verify that $m^{DE} = m^D$ also in that case). From equation (5.28) we obtain the following partial derivatives which will prove useful below:

$$C_w^{DE} \equiv \frac{\partial C^{DE}}{\partial w} = \frac{\alpha \bar{N}}{\alpha + \gamma} > 0, \quad C_N^{DE} \equiv \frac{\partial C^{DE}}{\partial \bar{N}} = \frac{\alpha w}{\alpha + \gamma} > 0, \tag{5.31}$$

$$C_P^{DE} \equiv \frac{\partial C^{DE}}{\partial P} = -\frac{\alpha (M_0 + \Pi_0)}{(\alpha + \gamma) P^2} < 0, \quad C_M^{DE} \equiv \frac{\partial C^{DE}}{\partial M_0} = \frac{\alpha}{(\alpha + \gamma) P} > 0. \tag{5.32}$$

Now suppose that the household is restricted in the amount of consumption goods it can purchase at the given price level, i.e. $C \leq \bar{C}$. The *effective* supply of labour and demand for money are in this case obtained by maximizing (5.5) with respect to N and m, subject to the restriction $C = \bar{C}$, and the budget restriction:

$$w(1 - N) + m = m_0 + \pi_0 + w - \bar{C}. \tag{5.33}$$

The solutions are, for the Cobb–Douglas case:

$$N^{SE} = N^{SE}(w, P, \bar{C}, M_0 + \Pi_0) = 1 - \left(\frac{\beta}{(\beta + \gamma)w}\right) \left[\left(\frac{M_0 + \Pi_0}{P}\right) + w - \bar{C}\right], \tag{5.34}$$

$$m^{DE} = m^{DE}(w, P, \bar{C}, M_0 + \Pi_0) = \left(\frac{\gamma}{\beta + \gamma}\right) \left[\left(\frac{M_0 + \Pi_0}{P}\right) + w - \bar{C}\right]. \tag{5.35}$$

Obviously, since $\bar{C} < C^D$ (the constraint is binding) equation (5.28) implies that $N^{SE} < N^S$. Due to the rationing in the goods market, households cut back their labour supply. This is intuitive: if you cannot buy goods with your labour earnings, then why bother working so hard? By using (5.11) and (5.34) we obtain an alternative expression for effective labour supply which shows the spillover from the goods market to the labour market:

$$N^{SE} = N^S - \left(\frac{\beta}{\beta + \gamma}\right) \left(\frac{1}{w}\right) [C^D - \bar{C}]. \tag{5.36}$$

If the consumption ration ($\bar{C}$) happens to coincide with the notional demand for goods (C^D) then the effective and notional labour supplies coincide, i.e. $N^{SE} = N^S$ (and thus also $m^{DE} = m^D$).

Once again, the following partial derivatives will prove useful below:

$$0 < N_w^{SE} \equiv \frac{\partial N^{SE}}{\partial w} = \frac{\beta}{(\beta + \gamma)w^2} \left[\left(\frac{M_0 + \Pi_0}{P} \right) - \bar{C} \right] < N_w^S, \tag{5.37}$$

$$0 < N_P^{SE} \equiv \frac{\partial N^{SE}}{\partial P} = \frac{\beta(M_0 + \Pi_0)}{(\beta + \gamma)wP^2} < N_P^S, \tag{5.38}$$

$$0 > N_M^{SE} \equiv \frac{\partial N^{SE}}{\partial M_0} = -\frac{\beta}{(\beta + \gamma)wP} > N_M^S, \tag{5.39}$$

$$N_C^{SE} \equiv \frac{\partial N^{SE}}{\partial \bar{C}} = \frac{\beta}{(\beta + \gamma)w} > 0. \tag{5.40}$$

Hence, the effective labour supply is less elastic than notional labour supply.

Finally, if households are simultaneously rationed in both markets, i.e. $\bar{C} < C^D$ and $\bar{N} < N^S$, their choice problem is trivial: they simply accumulate money balances as implied by the budget restriction:

$$m = m_0 + \pi_0 + w\bar{N} - \bar{C}. \tag{5.41}$$

The money balances yield utility to the household in the form of future consumption possibilities.

5.1.6 Effective demands and supplies of firms

When firms cannot get all the labour they wish to purchase according to their notional plans, $\bar{N} < N^D$, and the effective supply of goods is obtained by substituting $\bar{N}$ into the production function:

$$Y^{SE} = F(\bar{N}) \quad \Rightarrow \quad Y^{SE} = Y^{SE}(\bar{N}), \quad Y_N^{SE} = F_N > 0. \tag{5.42}$$

Obviously, since $\bar{N} < N^D$ the effective supply is less than the notional supply of goods, i.e. $Y^{SE} < Y^S$. For the Cobb–Douglas production function we can use (5.20) and (5.42) to obtain an alternative expression for the effective supply of goods:

$$\log Y^{SE} = \log Y^S - \epsilon \left[\log N^D - \log \bar{N} \right]. \tag{5.43}$$

If the firm is restricted in the amount of goods it can sell at the given price level, $Y = \bar{Y} < Y^S$, and the firm expresses an effective demand for labour. This is equal to the amount of labour needed to produce $\bar{Y}$:

$$F(N^{DE}) = \bar{Y} \quad \Rightarrow \quad N^{DE} = N^{DE}(\bar{Y}), \quad N_Y^{DE} = 1/F_N > 0. \tag{5.44}$$

For the Cobb–Douglas case we can combine (5.19) and (5.44) to obtain:

$$\log N^{DE} = \log N^D - \left(\frac{1}{\epsilon} \right) \left[\log Y^S - \log \bar{Y} \right]. \tag{5.45}$$

Obviously, the firm cannot be rationed in both markets simultaneously. Either the labour constraint is binding, or the output constraint is. This is because the firm has no real choice left if either output or employment is determined.

5.1.7 The full model

Depending on the particular combination of the real wage rate w and the price level P, there are three possible regimes that the economy can find itself in. These regimes are summarized in Table 5.1. The different regimes can be depicted graphically by means of Figure 5.3. The dashed lines are the notional GME and LME schedules discussed in section 1.4 above. In order to determine the effective goods- and labour market clearing loci, we must be very precise about the different regimes.

Table 5.1. Effective regime classification

		Labour market	
		(Effective) Excess Supply (ESL)	(Effective) Excess Demand (EDL)
Goods market	(Effective) Excess Supply (ESG)	Keynesian Unemployment $\bar{C} = C^{DE} < Y^S - G$ $\bar{N} = N^{DE} < N^S$	Impossible
	(Effective) Excess Demand (EDG)	Classical Unemployment $C^{DE} + G > Y^S = \bar{Y}$ $\bar{N} = N^D < N^{SE}$	Repressed Inflation $C^D + G > Y^{SE} = \bar{Y}$ $N^D > N^{SE} = \bar{N}$

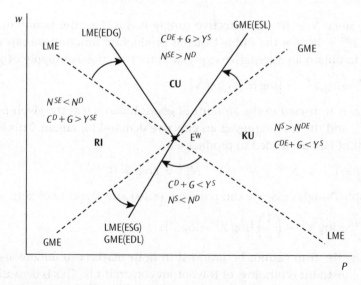

Figure 5.3. Effective equilibrium loci and the three regimes

Consider first the goods market equilibrium locus if there is excess supply of labour. This locus is labelled GME(ESL) and is defined by:

$$Y^S(w) = C^{DE}(w\bar{N}, P, M_0 + \Pi_0) + G, \quad \bar{N} = N^D(w). \tag{GME(ESL)}$$

GME(ESL) is upward sloping and lies to the left of GME. For a given real wage, w_0, the left-hand sides of GME and GME(ESL) are the same and thus $C^D(w_0, P_0, M_0 + \Pi_0) = C^{DE}(w_0\bar{N}, P_1, M_0 + \Pi_0)$. We know, however, that when evaluated at the same wage-price combination the effective demand falls short of the notional demand because unemployed workers spend less on consumption, i.e. $C^{DE}(w_0\bar{N}, P_0, M_0 + \Pi_0) < C^D(w_0, P_0, M_0 + \Pi_0)$. It follows that P_1 must be lower than P_0, i.e. GME(ESL) lies to the left of GME in Figure 5.3. (Obviously, at the Walrasian equilibrium point GME and GME(ESL) coincide because there $C^{DE} = C^D$.)

Goods market equilibrium when there is excess demand for labour is denoted by GME(EDL) and is defined by:

$$Y^{SE}(\bar{N}) = C^D(w, P, M_0 + \Pi_0) + G, \quad \bar{N} = N^S(w, P, M_0 + \Pi_0). \tag{GME(EDL)}$$

Since firms are rationed in their demand for labour, they supply fewer goods ($Y^{SE} < Y^S$) and, for a given real wage rate, the price level has to rise (thus eroding wealth) in order to reduce consumption demand and increase the supply of labour. Alternatively, for a given price level, the real wage rate has to fall in order to restore goods market equilibrium. It follows that GME(EDL) must be steeper than the relevant section of the GME schedule.

Labour market equilibrium with an excess demand for goods is denoted by LME(EDG) and is defined by:

$$N^D(w) = N^{SE}(w, P, \bar{C}, M_0 + \Pi_0), \quad \bar{C} = Y^S(w) - G. \tag{LME(EDG)}$$

LME(EDG) is downward sloping and lies to the right of LME. For a given real wage rate, w_0, the left-hand sides of LME and LME(EDG) are the same so that $N^{SE}(w_0, P_1, Y^S(w_0) - G, M_0 + \Pi_0) = N^S(w_0, P_0, M_0 + \Pi_0)$. For the wage-price combination (w_0, P_0) households cannot buy as many goods as they wish and effective labour supply falls short of the notional supply, i.e. $N^{SE}(w_0, P_0, Y^S(w_0) - G, M_0 + \Pi_0) < N^S(w_0, P_0, M_0 + \Pi_0)$. It follows that P_1 is higher than P_0, i.e. LME(EDG) lies to the right of the LME schedule.

Finally, labour market equilibrium with an excess supply of goods is denoted by LME(ESG) and is defined by:

$$N^S(w, P, M_0 + \Pi_0) = N^{DE}(\bar{Y}), \quad \bar{Y} = C^D(w, P, M_0 + \Pi_0) + G. \tag{LME(ESG)}$$

It is straightforward to show that LME(ESG) coincides with GME(EDL).

5.1.8 The effectiveness of fiscal and monetary policy

In the regime of *Classical Unemployment* (CU), households are rationed in both markets, so that the rationing equilibrium is described by:

$$\bar{N} = N^D(w), \tag{LME(CU)}$$

$$\bar{Y} = Y^S(w). \tag{GME(CU)}$$

These expressions contain neither G nor M_0, so it is obvious that both fiscal and monetary policy are ineffective. All that happens if the government increases its consumption is that private consumption is crowded out one-for-one.

In the regime of *Keynesian Unemployment* (KU) there is excess supply in both markets, and rationing equilibrium is described by:

$$\bar{N} = N^{DE}(\bar{Y}), \tag{LME(KU)}$$

$$\bar{Y} = C^{DE}(w\bar{N}, P, M_0 + \Pi_0) + G. \tag{GME(KU)}$$

The comparative static effects of changes in G and M_0 are obtained in the usual fashion:

$$d\bar{Y} = C_N^{DE} d\bar{N} + C_M^{DE} dM_0 + dG = C_N^{DE} N_Y^{DE} d\bar{Y} + C_M^{DE} dM_0 + dG \quad \Rightarrow$$

$$d\bar{Y} = \frac{dG + C_M^{DE} dM_0}{1 - C_N^{DE} N_Y^{DE}}, \tag{5.46}$$

where the numerator is guaranteed to be positive.

These effects can be illustrated with the aid of Figure 5.4. An increase in G (or M_0) boosts effective demand for goods and shifts the GME(KU) schedule up and to the

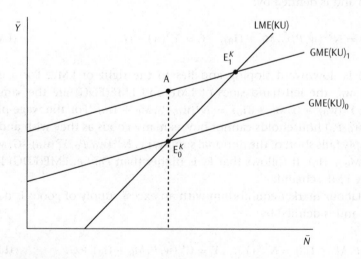

Figure 5.4. The Keynesian unemployment equilibrium and fiscal policy

left. For a given level of employment (at point A), firms experience a greater demand for their products and a relaxation of their sales constraint. As a result, output rises as does the effective demand for labour and hence employment. This gives rise to a multiplier effect due to the additional labour income received by households. The new equilibrium is at E_1^K, with higher employment and output.

In the regime of *Repressed Inflation* (RI), there is generalized excess demand, so that the rationing equilibrium is given by:

$$\bar{N} = N^{SE}(w, P, \bar{Y} - G, M_0 + \Pi_0), \qquad \text{(LME(RI))}$$

$$\bar{Y} = Y^{SE}(\bar{N}), \qquad \text{(GME(RI))}$$

where we have substituted the consumption ration, i.e. $\bar{C} = \bar{Y} - G$, in the effective supply of labour equation (LME(EDG)) to obtain LME(RI). Fiscal and monetary policy are now counterproductive. Fiscal policy worsens the rationing that households face in the goods markets ($d\bar{C} < 0$) and reduces the effective labour supply and hence employment even further. In terms of Figure 5.5, LME(RI) shifts up and to the left. Firms experience a worsening of the labour constraint and are forced to cut back production even further. This causes a "supply multiplier" effect due to the additional reduction of the effective supply of labour. Eventually, the economy ends up at point E_1^R, with lower output and employment. The output supply multiplier is easily obtained:

$$d\bar{Y} = Y_N^{SE}\left[N_C^{SE}\left(d\bar{Y} - dG\right) + N_M^{SE} dM_0\right] \quad \Rightarrow$$

$$d\bar{Y} = \frac{-Y_N^{SE} N_C^{SE} dG + Y_N^{SE} N_M^{SE} dM_0}{1 - Y_N^{SE} N_C^{SE}}. \qquad (5.47)$$

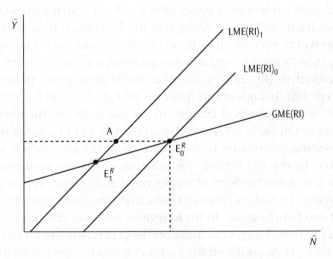

Figure 5.5. The repressed inflation equilibrium and fiscal policy

Table 5.2. Effects on output and employment of changes in government spending and the money supply

	Government spending	Money supply
Keynesian unemployment	$\dfrac{\partial \bar{N}}{\partial G} = \dfrac{N_Y^{DE}}{1 - C_N^{DE} N_Y^{DE}} > 0$	$\dfrac{\partial \bar{N}}{\partial M_0} = \dfrac{C_M^{DE} N_Y^{DE}}{1 - C_N^{DE} N_Y^{DE}} > 0$
	$\dfrac{\partial \bar{Y}}{\partial G} = \dfrac{1}{1 - C_N^{DE} N_Y^{DE}} > 0$	$\dfrac{\partial \bar{Y}}{\partial M_0} = \dfrac{C_M^{DE}}{1 - C_N^{DE} N_Y^{DE}} > 0$
Classical unemployment	$\dfrac{\partial \bar{N}}{\partial G} = 0$	$\dfrac{\partial \bar{N}}{\partial M_0} = 0$
	$\dfrac{\partial \bar{Y}}{\partial G} = 0$	$\dfrac{\partial \bar{Y}}{\partial M_0} = 0$
Repressed inflation	$\dfrac{\partial \bar{N}}{\partial G} = \dfrac{-N_C^{SE}}{1 - N_C^{SE} Y_N^{SE}} < 0$	$\dfrac{\partial \bar{N}}{\partial M_0} = \dfrac{N_M^{SE}}{1 - N_C^{SE} Y_N^{SE}} < 0$
	$\dfrac{\partial \bar{Y}}{\partial G} = \dfrac{-Y_N^{SE} N_C^{SE}}{1 - N_C^{SE} Y_N^{SE}} < 0$	$\dfrac{\partial \bar{Y}}{\partial M_0} = \dfrac{Y_N^{SE} N_M^{SE}}{1 - N_C^{SE} Y_N^{SE}} < 0$

Hence, it is clear that the effect of a monetary impulse is also to reduce output due to the adverse effect on labour supply.

The effects of fiscal and monetary policy have been summarized in Table 5.2. The crucial policy conclusion that must be drawn from this table is that the choice of the correct policy response depends very much on which particular regime the economy finds itself in. If the economy is in the KU regime, then clearly Keynesian fiscal impulses will be very effective. If, on the other hand, the economy is in the CU or RI regime, then Keynesian demand management is either impotent (CU regime) or counterproductive (RI regime). So what is the appropriate policy measure in these latter regimes? To answer this question we turn to Table 5.3, which contains the comparative static effects of changes in the real wage and the price level.

The information in Table 5.3 shows that in the CU and RI regimes there is ample scope for economic policy that is aimed directly at the level of real wages and/or the price level. In the CU regime, for example, real wage moderation is a very effective way to increase the level of employment and output. This is intuitive: real wages are too high for full employment, and anything that lowers them is good for employment and hence output. In the RI regime, however, the appropriate policy is to allow for a rise in real wages (to choke off the excess demand for labour) and/or a rise in the price level (to choke off the excess demand for goods). All this presumes, of course, that the policy maker has the instruments to interfere directly with real wages and/or the price level.

Table 5.3. Effects on output and employment of changes in the real wage rate and the price level

	Real wage	Price level
Keynesian unemployment	$\dfrac{\partial \bar{N}}{\partial w} = \dfrac{C_w^{DE} N_Y^{DE}}{1 - C_N^{DE} N_Y^{DE}} > 0$	$\dfrac{\partial \bar{N}}{\partial P} = \dfrac{C_P^{DE} N_Y^{DE}}{1 - C_N^{DE} N_Y^{DE}} < 0$
	$\dfrac{\partial \bar{Y}}{\partial w} = \dfrac{C_w^{DE}}{1 - C_N^{DE} N_Y^{DE}} > 0$	$\dfrac{\partial \bar{Y}}{\partial P} = \dfrac{C_P^{DE}}{1 - C_N^{DE} N_Y^{DE}} < 0$
Classical unemployment	$\dfrac{\partial \bar{N}}{\partial w} = N_w^D < 0$	$\dfrac{\partial \bar{N}}{\partial P} = 0$
	$\dfrac{\partial \bar{Y}}{\partial w} = Y_w^S < 0$	$\dfrac{\partial \bar{Y}}{\partial P} = 0$
Repressed inflation	$\dfrac{\partial \bar{N}}{\partial w} = \dfrac{N_w^{SE}}{1 - N_C^{SE} Y_N^{SE}} > 0$	$\dfrac{\partial \bar{N}}{\partial P} = \dfrac{N_P^{SE}}{1 - N_C^{SE} Y_N^{SE}} > 0$
	$\dfrac{\partial \bar{Y}}{\partial w} = \dfrac{Y_N^{SE} N_w^{SE}}{1 - N_C^{SE} Y_N^{SE}} > 0$	$\dfrac{\partial \bar{Y}}{\partial P} = \dfrac{Y_N^{SE} N_P^{SE}}{1 - N_C^{SE} Y_N^{SE}} > 0$

5.1.9 Wage and price dynamics

So far, we have assumed that wages and prices are fixed altogether. What would happen if prices and wages respond over time to disequilibrium situations? One possibility is to assume that real wages react to the (effective) excess demand for labour and the price level reacts to the (effective) excess demand for goods:

$$\dot{w} = \lambda_N \left[N^{D(E)} - N^{S(E)} \right], \quad \lambda_N > 0, \tag{5.48}$$

$$\dot{P} = \lambda_G \left[C^{D(E)} + G - Y^{S(E)} \right], \quad \lambda_G > 0, \tag{5.49}$$

where the notation indicates that effective and notional quantities appear in an alternating fashion, i.e. in the KU regime the relevant labour market disequilibrium measure is $(N^{DE} - N^S)$ but in the CU and RI regimes it is $(N^D - N^{SE})$. The dynamic adjustment over time has been indicated with arrows in Figure 5.6. Suppose that the economy starts in a Keynesian unemployment equilibrium at point E_0^K. There is an effective excess supply of labour, so that the real wage rate falls over time, and effective excess supply of goods, which leads to price reductions. Eventually the economy moves into the regime of Repressed Inflation, where the real wage and price dynamics are sharply reversed (point A). The cyclical adjustment is stable and eventually restores the Walrasian equilibrium E^W.

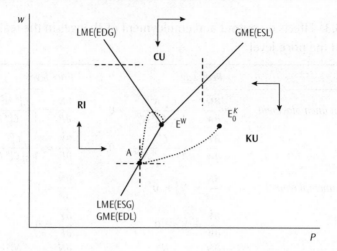

Figure 5.6. Wage and price dynamics and stability

5.2 Rationing in Small Open Economies

For policy purposes it is important to consider the implications of rationing for a small open economy. Dixit (1978) discusses the effects of rationing in a one-sector model of a small open economy with no inventories, immobile labour, tradeable goods, prices determined on the world market (so that purchasing power parity (PPP) holds, $P = EP^*$, where P^* is the world price level and E is the nominal exchange rate), and fixed exchange rates. In fact, rationing in such an open economy is much simpler than in a closed economy. Any effective excess demand for (supply of) goods is met by importing (exporting) goods from (to) the rest of the world. Hence, there can never be any spillover effects from the goods market onto the labour market, and thus whether unemployment or overemployment prevails depends entirely on whether the real wage is too high or too low.

The balance of trade (net exports, X) follows from the absorption approach, that is, the excess of production over absorption. When there is excess supply of labour, it is given by:

$$X = F(N^D(w)) - C^{DE}(wN^D(w), EP^*, M_0 + \Pi_0) - G, \tag{5.50}$$

where we have substituted the constraint on the labour market ($\bar{N} = N^D(w)$) and PPP ($P = EP^*$). When there is excess demand for labour and firms are rationed in the labour market, the expression for the trade balance is:

$$X = F(N^S(w, EP^*, M_0 + \Pi_0)) - C^D(w, EP^*, M_0 + \Pi_0) - G, \tag{5.51}$$

where we have again substituted the labour market constraint ($\bar{N} = N^S(.)$) and PPP. We assume that there is real wage rigidity, so that w is fixed in the short run,

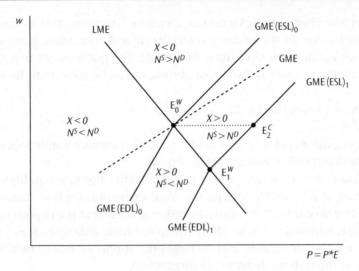

Figure 5.7. Rationing in a simple model of the small open economy

irrespective of whether exchange rates are fixed or floating. Figure 5.7 presents the four possible outcomes and has some similarity with the familiar Mundell-Swan diagram.

We first consider the case of *fixed exchange rates*. In the short run, the economy may experience a trade surplus (deficit), but in the long run this leads (in the absence of sterilization) to an increase (decrease) in foreign reserves, the money supply, and wealth, and hence to a downward shift of the effective GME locus and an upward (downward) shift of the LME locus. A trade surplus leads to more wealth, which in the presence of unemployment increases the household's effective demand for goods and thus chokes off some of the trade surplus. When firms are rationed, the increase in wealth reduces the supply of labour and thus the supply of goods, increases the demand for goods, and thus chokes off the trade surplus in two ways. However, in the latter case the initial excess demand for labour is worsened. These adjustment processes are of course related to David Hume's specie-flow mechanism and the monetary approach to the balance of payments.

The adjustment process under *floating exchange rates* is quite different. When there is an incipient trade surplus, the nominal exchange rate appreciates (i.e. E falls), the home price level falls, and thus real wealth is boosted. This chokes off the excess supply of goods, so that the economy never diverges from the effective GME locus and balanced trade.

A fiscal expansion in an economy with fixed exchange rates shifts the Walrasian equilibrium from E_0^W to E_1^W, so that on impact the trade deficit rises by exactly the same amount as the increase in government spending. As the budget deficit must be financed by money creation, next period's stock of real money balances increases by the change in government spending. However, this is exactly offset by the decrease due to the ensuing trade deficit and thus there is no change in the short-run equilibrium over time. Effectively, the government uses its foreign reserves to purchase commodities from abroad, as can be seen from the identity:

$$(m - m_0) + (\pi - \pi_0) = G + X, \tag{5.52}$$

i.e. the net acquisition of financial assets by the private sector must equal the sum of the government deficit and the trade surplus.[4]

With floating exchange rates and real wage rigidity the new equilibrium lies to the north-east of E_1^W, say E_2^C, so that the fiscal expansion leads to classical unemployment. The reason for this counterintuitive result is that the depreciation of the exchange rate, required to choke off the incipient trade deficit, increases the home price level, erodes real wealth, and increases the supply of labour (whilst the real wage rate and thus labour demand are unaffected).

Note that a devaluation in a situation of unemployment erodes the real value of wealth and therefore reduces the effective demand for goods and causes a trade surplus. (If there were nominal rather than real wage rigidity, labour demand and output increase.) A devaluation in a situation of excess demand for labour increases labour supply and output, decreases demand, and improves the trade balance.

5.3 Intertemporal Spillovers

As a final example of the macroeconomic quantity rationing literature we now discuss a simplified version of the closed-economy model developed by Neary and Stiglitz (1983). They extend the static disequilibrium analysis of Barro and Grossman (1971) and Malinvaud (1977) by allowing for intertemporal considerations. In doing so they are able to demonstrate the critical role of constraint expectations and intertemporal spillovers. Indeed, it is possible to show that when agents expect unemployment tomorrow, it will be more likely that there is unemployment today. Hence there exists a so-called "bootstrap" effect in the sense that pessimistic expectations can lead to bad outcomes today (see also Persson and Svensson, 1983).

We start with a brief description of the model. Households have an inelastic supply of labour (normalized to equal unity) and decide on their lifetime consumption plans on the basis of subjective point expectations about future wages, prices, and constraint levels. To keep things as simple as possible, only the first two periods are studied ("today" and "tomorrow") and the rest of the future is summarized by the inclusion of money balances in the utility function. The representative household

---

[4] The national income identity for the open economy is $Y = C + G + X$. By using this identity plus the profit definition (5.3) in (5.16) we obtain (5.52).

has a simple Cobb–Douglas utility function:

$$U_H = C_1^{\alpha_1} C_2^{\alpha_2} m_2^{\gamma}, \tag{5.53}$$

with $\alpha_1, \alpha_2, \gamma > 0$ and $\alpha_1 + \alpha_2 + \gamma = 1$. In (5.53), C_i represents consumption of goods in period i and $m_2 \equiv M_2/P_2$ denotes real money holdings at the end of the second period, where M_2 is nominal money balances and P_i is the price level in period i. The intertemporal budget constraint facing the household is given by:

$$P_1 C_1 + P_2 C_2 + M_2 = Y \equiv M_0 + P_1 Y_1 + P_2 Y_2, \tag{5.54}$$

where M_0 denotes the household's initial endowment of nominal money balances, Y denotes total income, and Y_i is production in period i. The first equality in (5.54) says that total household income can either be spent on goods consumption in the two periods or can be carried over into the future. The second equality in (5.54) says that, in contrast to what we assumed in section 1, profits and wages are distributed instantaneously to the household sectors. The notional demand functions of the household are obtained by maximizing (5.53) subject to (5.54):

$$C_1^D = \alpha_1 \left(\frac{Y}{P_1} \right), \tag{5.55}$$

$$C_2^D = \alpha_2 \left(\frac{Y}{P_2} \right), \tag{5.56}$$

$$m_2^D = \gamma \left(\frac{Y}{P_2} \right). \tag{5.57}$$

The objective function of the representative firm is the sum of current and future profits:

$$\Pi \equiv \pi_1 + \pi_2$$
$$= P_1 F(N_1) - W_1 N_1 + P_2 F(N_2) - W_2 N_2, \tag{5.58}$$

where W_i and N_i are, respectively, the nominal wage and demand for labour in period i, and $F()$ is the production function featuring positive but diminishing marginal productivity of labour ($F_N > 0 > F_{NN}$). The notional demands for labour and output supplies are obtained by maximizing (5.58) with respect to N_1 and N_2. The resulting expressions are:

$$N_i^D = N^D(w_i), \quad N_w^D = 1/F_{NN} < 0,$$
$$Y_i^S = F\left(N^D(w_i) \right) = Y^S(w_i), \quad Y_w^S = F_N/F_{NN} < 0,$$

where $w_i \equiv W_i/P_i$ is the real wage in period i. Note that, unlike Neary and Stiglitz (1983), we ignore the possibility of firm investment.

The final agent in the model is the government which can purchase goods in each period (denoted by G_i) and can make transfer payments to households thereby increasing their initial endowment M_0. The government finances its policy actions by printing money.

125

5.3.1 Walrasian expectations

We first consider the case where agents do not expect to be constrained either today or tomorrow. This leads to the following goods market equilibrium (GME$_i$) and labour market equilibrium (LME$_i$) loci:

$$Y^S(w_i) = \alpha_i \left(\frac{M_0 + P_1 F(1) + P_2 F(1)}{P_i} \right) + G_i, \tag{GME$_i$}$$

$$1 = N^D(w_i). \tag{LME$_i$}$$

The equilibrium condition (GME$_i$) equates notional goods supply in period i (the left-hand side) to total notional goods demand in period i (right-hand side) given that household income is consistent with full employment of labour in both periods (i.e. $Y_i = F(N_i) = F(1)$ in the two periods). Similarly, the equilibrium condition (LME$_i$) equates labour supply (left-hand side) to notional labour demand (right-hand side) in the two periods. If prices and wages are perfectly flexible, then (LME$_i$) determines the equilibrium real wage in both periods and (GME$_i$) determines the nominal prices (and thus the nominal wage) in both periods. The Walrasian price-wage vector is denoted by (W_i^*, P_i^*).

To reduce the dimensionality of the model somewhat we assume that P_1 and W_2 remain always at their Walrasian level, i.e. we assume that $P_1 = P_1^*$ and $W_2 = W_2^*$ and concentrate on variations in W_1 and P_2. The notional equilibria can be illustrated with the aid of Figure 5.8. In this figure, the LME$_1$ locus is horizontal at $W_1 = W_1^*$, which implies that $w_1 = w_1^*$ also since $P_1 = P_1^*$. For points above (below) the LME$_1$ line the real wage is too high (low) and there is excess supply of (demand for) labour. The GME$_1$ locus is downward sloping because an increase in today's real wage (w_1)

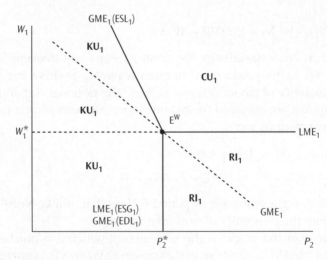

Figure 5.8. Notional and effective equilibria with Walrasian expectations

reduces aggregate supply and a reduction in tomorrow's price level reduces total income and therefore reduces aggregate demand. For points above (below) the GME_1 line today's real wage is too high (low), supply is too low (high) and there is excess demand for (supply of) goods.

Now consider the case where agents expect the Walrasian equilibrium to prevail tomorrow yet allow for the possibility of quantity constraints today. This leads to the same type of spillover effects that were discussed above. When there is unemployment today ($N^D(W_1/P_1^*) < 1$) then households' effective demand for goods will be less than their notional demand and therefore, to maintain goods market equilibrium, today's real wage rate has to rise. The effective goods market equilibrium locus is given by:

$$Y^S\left(\frac{W_1}{P_1^*}\right) = \alpha_1\left(\frac{M_0}{P_1^*} + F\left(N^D\left(\frac{W_1}{P_1^*}\right)\right)\right) + \left(\frac{P_2}{P_1^*}\right)F(1)\right) + G_1, \qquad (\text{GME}_1(\text{ESL}_1))$$

where the first term on the right-hand side of ($\text{GME}_1(\text{ESL}_1)$) represents the effective demand for goods in period 1 by households (Y_1^{DE}). It follows in a straightforward fashion that $\text{GME}_1(\text{ESL}_1)$ is steeper than the GME_1 line.

When there is excess demand for labour today ($N^D(W_1/P_1^*) > 1$) firms are constrained in their hiring of labour and their effective supply of goods is less than their notional supply ($Y^{SE}(1) = F(1) < Y^S(W_1/P_1^*)$). The $\text{GME}_1(\text{EDL}_1)$ is given by:

$$F(1) = \alpha_1\left(\frac{M_0}{P_1^*} + F(1) + \left(\frac{P_2}{P_1^*}\right)F(1)\right) + G_1. \qquad (\text{GME}_1(\text{EDL}_1))$$

Since W_2 does not feature in ($\text{GME}_1(\text{EDL}_1)$) it follows that $\text{GME}_1(\text{EDL}_1)$ is vertical.

If there is an excess supply of goods today, firms' demand for labour is constrained by the demand for goods and therefore the $\text{LME}_1(\text{ESG}_1)$ locus coincides with the $\text{GME}_1(\text{EDL}_1)$ line. This obviously rules out the regime of underconsumption due to the fact that there are no inventories. For obvious reasons, the $\text{LME}_1(\text{EDG}_1)$ locus coincides with the LME_1 locus because the supply of labour is exogenous by assumption.

The resulting effective goods market and labour market equilibrium loci divide up the space into three regimes, i.e. Keynesian unemployment (KU), classical unemployment (CU), and repressed inflation (RI). This is indicated in Figure 5.8.

5.3.2 Bootstrap effects

We now consider intertemporal spillover effects, that is, the effects of expectations of future quantity constraints on the current behaviour of households and firms. One of the objectives of Neary and Stiglitz (1983) was to demonstrate the existence of "bootstrap" phenomena. By this we mean that when households expect to be unemployed today, and when firms expect they cannot sell all their goods tomorrow, it is also more likely that firms will be unable to sell all their goods today. Such

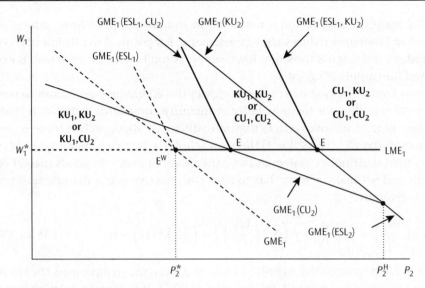

Figure 5.9. Effective equilibria with expectations of future Keynesian or classical unemployment

phenomena lead to the possibility of multiple equilibria for a given level of current and expected future wages and prices. For ease of exposition, we concentrate on the effects of expected Keynesian unemployment or classical unemployment.[5]

Since the supply of labour is inelastic, the effective LME_1 locus coincides with the notional LME_1 locus as long as firms face no quantity constraints in the current period. When households expect to be constrained in their sale of labour tomorrow, their human wealth declines and therefore current consumption falls. The $GME_1(ESL_2)$ locus is defined as follows:

$$Y^S\left(\frac{W_1}{P_1^*}\right) = \alpha_1\left[\frac{M_0}{P_1^*} + F(1) + \left(\frac{P_2}{P_1^*}\right)F\left(N^D\left(\frac{W_2^*}{P_2}\right)\right)\right] + G_1. \qquad \text{(GME}_1\text{(ESL}_2\text{))}$$

The comparison of (GME$_i$) (for period 1) and (GME$_1$(ESL$_2$)) reveals that $GME_1(ESL_2)$ lies to the right of the GME_1 locus. In Figure 5.9, GME_1, $GME_1(ESL_1)$, and LME_1 have all been reproduced from Figure 5.8 for convenience. The $GME_1(ESL_2)$ line has also been drawn and cuts the LME_1 line at point E''. When firms expect to be unable to sell all their goods tomorrow, this does not affect the current effective supply of goods as we abstract from the intertemporal spillover effects arising from (reduced) inventories. This means that the $GME_1(KU_2)$ coincides with the $GME_1(ESL_2)$ locus, where the notation KU_2 stands for Keynesian unemployment in the second period, i.e. the combination of ESL_2 and ESG_2. This has also been illustrated in Figure 5.9.

If households expect that tomorrow there will be classical unemployment (CU_2, consisting of excess demand for goods (EDG_2) and excess supply of labour (ESL_2)),

---

[5] We have simplified the Neary–Stiglitz model by ruling out inventory holdings of firms. As a result, the behaviour of firms is entirely static and intertemporal spillovers only occur via household behaviour.

then they will have less incentive to save as they cannot buy all the goods they want tomorrow anyway. Therefore current consumption increases. Indeed, the effective demand for goods in period 1 given that the household faces a constraint in the goods market ($C_2 \leq \bar{C}_2$) in period 2 is obtained by maximizing (5.53) subject to (5.54) and the constraint. If the second-period constraint is binding (so that $C_2 = \bar{C}_2$), we obtain:

$$C_1^{DE} = \left(\frac{\alpha_1}{\alpha_1 + \gamma}\right)\left[\frac{Y}{P_1} - \left(\frac{P_2}{P_1}\right)\bar{C}_2\right]. \tag{5.59}$$

The $\text{GME}_1(\text{CU}_2)$ locus is then defined as:

$$Y^S\left(\frac{W_1}{P_1^*}\right) = \left(\frac{\alpha_1}{\alpha_1 + \gamma}\right)\left[\frac{M_0}{P_1^*} + F(1) + \left(\frac{P_2}{P_1^*}\right)\left(F\left(N^D\left(\frac{W_2^*}{P_2}\right)\right) - \bar{C}_2\right)\right] + G_1.$$

$$(\text{GME}_1(\text{CU}_2))$$

Of course, the $\text{GME}_1(\text{CU}_2)$ locus is only relevant for those values of P_2 for which the household actually faces a constraint in the goods market tomorrow. This implies the following constraint:

$$[C_2^D \equiv]\alpha_2\left[\frac{M_0}{P_2} + \left(\frac{P_1^*}{P_2}\right)F(1) + F\left(N^D\left(\frac{W_2^*}{P_2}\right)\right)\right] > \bar{C}_2. \tag{5.60}$$

The right-hand side of this inequality is the notional demand for period-2 consumption. Let $P_2^H(\bar{C}_2)$ denote that value for P_2 for which the constraint in (5.60) holds with equality. Then it follows that the $\text{GME}_1(\text{CU}_2)$ locus coincides with the $\text{GME}_1(\text{ESL}_2)$ line for P_2 in excess of $P_2^H(\bar{C}_2)$. Since future consumption is constrained, $P_2^H(\bar{C}_2)$ lies to the right of the Walrasian level P_2^*—see Figure 5.9.

So far, we have looked at the notional first-period loci when there are expectations of future quantity constraints. Now consider the effective loci when there are expectations of either Keynesian or classical unemployment. The effective $\text{GME}_1(\text{ESL}_1,\text{KU}_2)$ line is given by:

$$Y^S\left(\frac{W_1}{P_1^*}\right) = \alpha_1\left[\frac{M_0}{P_1^*} + F\left(N^D\left(\frac{W_1}{P_1^*}\right)\right) + \left(\frac{P_2}{P_1^*}\right)F\left(N^D\left(\frac{W_2^*}{P_2}\right)\right)\right] + G_1,$$

$$(\text{GME}_1(\text{ESL}_1,\text{KU}_2))$$

whilst the effective $\text{GME}_1(\text{ESL}_1,\text{CU}_2)$ line is given by:

$$Y^S\left(\frac{W_1}{P_1^*}\right) = \left(\frac{\alpha_1}{\alpha_1 + \gamma}\right)\left[\frac{M_0}{P_1^*} + F\left(N^D\left(\frac{W_1}{P_1^*}\right)\right)\right.$$
$$\left. + \left(\frac{P_2}{P_1^*}\right)\left(F\left(N^D\left(\frac{W_2^*}{P_2}\right)\right) - \bar{C}_2\right)\right] + G_1. \quad (\text{GME}_1(\text{ESL}_1,\text{CU}_2))$$

These two loci are only relevant above the LME_1 locus, that is, when there is unemployment today. Obviously, they pivot to the right because the existence of current unemployment means that today's demand for goods will be less and therefore the supply of goods needs to be choked off with a higher real wage in order to maintain goods market equilibrium in the first period. Clearly, the $GME_1(ESL_1,KU_2)$ line lies completely to the right of the $GME_1(ESL_1,CU_2)$ line. It is now possible to divide the (W_1,P_2) space bordered by the loci LME_1, $GME_1(ESL_1,CU_2)$, and $GME_1(ESL_1,KU_2)$ into combinations of current and expected regimes–see Figure 5.9. The regime that lies above the LME_1 line and between $GME_1(ESL_1,CU_2)$, and $GME_1(ESL_1,KU_2)$ is the most interesting one and it consists of either Keynesian unemployment in both periods (KU_1,KU_2) or classical unemployment in both periods (CU_1,CU_2).

The first thing to note is that the vector of current and future wages and prices consistent with Walrasian equilibrium is not unique since it depends on the nature of expectations about future quantity constraints. If W_1 and P_2 are flexible, all points between E^W and E'' on LME_1 are possible Walrasian equilibria, each associated with a different configuration of constraint expectations. The second point to notice is the non-uniqueness of effective equilibria for particular constellations of current and future wages and prices. The region above the LME_1 line and between $GME_1(ESL_1,CU_2)$, and $GME_1(ESL_1,KU_2)$ in Figure 5.9 is compatible with either KU_1 or CU_1, depending on what agents expect tomorrow. The final point to notice is the "bootstrap" effect, that is, Keynesian (classical) unemployment is more likely to occur today when it is expected to prevail tomorrow. In terms of Figure 5.9, the region for which there is KU_1 is larger if KU_2 is expected than if CU_2 is expected. Conversely, the region for which there is CU_1 is larger if CU_2 is expected than if KU_2 is expected.

5.3.3 Rational constraint expectations

The previous subsection employed arbitrary expectations about future quantity constraints, which is undoubtedly the main reason for the non-uniqueness of the Walrasian and effective equilibria. In order to avoid this problem, one might borrow the assumption of rational expectations from the new classical school of macroeconomics (see Chapter 3). Although the assumption of rational expectations may be within the spirit of market clearing and other assumptions of the new classical school, it is a rather far-fetched assumption within a macroeconomic model with rationing. The assumption of rational constraint expectations presumes that agents have an enormous amount of information in order to be able to calculate the *aggregate* future quantity constraints in a rational fashion. However, it does not require knowledge of *individual* demands and supplies. This is just as well, since if this were the case firms and households could engage in bilateral bargaining which contradicts the fundamental assumption of fixed wages and prices. Due to the difficulties in the coordination of the behaviour of individual households and firms when information (at a disaggregated level) is imperfect, the assumption of rational constraint expectations may be a first step in removing the arbitrariness of expectations.

To understand rational constraint expectations, let us focus on the case where there is unemployment today and Keynesian unemployment is expected tomorrow. It is important at this stage to distinguish between real and nominal wage rigidity. If there is real wage rigidity (w_2 constant), then the $GME_1(ESL_1, KU_2)$ locus is also the locus that pertains under rational constraint expectations. However, if there is nominal wage rigidity (W_2 constant), one has to take account of the fact that second-period income, $Y_2 = F(N^D(W_2/P_2))$, is an increasing function of the second-period price, since a higher price erodes the real wage and thus boosts labour demand, employment, and income. This means that the locus under rational constraint expectations, say the RCE locus, lies to the right of the $GME_1(ESL_1)$ locus.[6]

The main implication of the above argument is that the set of (W_1, P_2) combinations consistent with Keynesian rather than classical unemployment today is greater when Keynesian unemployment rather than when Walrasian equilibrium is expected to prevail tomorrow, so that rational constraint expectations increase the likelihood of Keynesian unemployment today. Hence, the "bootstrap" property still holds when constraint expectations are rational. The assumption of rational constraint expectations does reduce non-uniqueness of the set of equilibria.

Neary and Stiglitz (1983) also show that, under the assumption of rational constraint expectations, the effects of an increase in government spending on employment and output during a Keynesian regime is greater than under static expectations of Keynesian unemployment tomorrow and greater still than under Walrasian expectations about the future. The main reason for this interesting result is that an increase in government spending is more effective when firms are pessimistic about their future sales prospects. Also, the increase in government spending relaxes the constraint on current sales and therefore firms might plan to hire more labour and produce more output tomorrow. Under the assumption of rational constraint expectations, households realize that this increases their life-cycle income and they therefore increase consumption both today and tomorrow which in turn increases the effective demand for labour today.

Note the sharp contrast with the policy neutrality results of the new classical school. Their neutrality results depend on price flexibility (market clearing) and rational expectations. Rational expectations actually enhance the effectiveness of fiscal policy in the rationing approach. Hence, it follows that the essential ingredient of the policy neutrality propositions of the new classical school is market clearing rather than rational expectations. This, of course, was the message of Fischer (1977) which we discussed in detail in Chapter 3 above.

---

[6] Neary and Stiglitz (1983, pp. 216–219) discuss an iterative procedure to obtain consistency of expectations and of actual outcomes, which demonstrates that this remains the case even when there are intertemporal spillover effects arising from inventories.

5.4 Punchlines

We study the macroeconomic implications of two key insights in this chapter. First, if the price system does not work then quantity signals take over as a coordination device in the economy. Second, if there is quantity rationing in one market this may spill over into one or more other markets and affect conditions in these markets in a meaningful way. In the presence of quantity rationing so-called effective demands and supplies are relevant. These differ from the conventionally defined (or notional) demands and supplies in that they take the quantity restrictions into account. For example, for a household the notional demand for consumption goods is obtained by maximizing utility subject to the household budget constraint. In contrast, if the household is unable to sell all the labour it wants to sell, it faces a quantity restriction in the labour market. The effective demand for consumption goods is then obtained by maximizing utility subject to the budget restriction and the quantity constraint in the labour market.

In the early to mid-1970s a number of Keynes-inspired economists built general (dis-) equilibrium models of the macroeconomy, in which the price level and real wage are fixed and quantity rationing exists in the markets for good and labour. The aim of these economists was to weaken the challenge of the new classicals by providing Keynesian economics with firm microeconomic foundations.

In the standard models there are three macroeconomic regimes depending on the configuration of the real wage and the price level. In the Keynesian unemployment (KU) regime, there is excess supply of goods and labour, in the classical unemployment regime (CU) there is excess supply of labour and excess demand for goods, and in the Repressed Inflation regime there is simultaneous excess demand for goods and labour.

A rather interesting prediction of the standard model is that the effects of fiscal and monetary policy depend critically on the regime that the economy happens to be in. An increase in government consumption, for example, has a positive effect on output and employment in the KU regime, has no effect in the CU regime, and decreases output and employment in the RI regime. Whilst the first two cases are familiar from our discussion of Keynesians and classicals in Chapter 1, the third case is novel and somewhat surprising. The intuition behind the so-called supply multiplier is that the increase in government consumption worsens the quantity restriction experienced by households in the goods market. As a result, these households supply even less labour and thus aggregate employment and output fall.

In a similar vein, the effects of policy measures directly impacting on the real wage or the price level also depend critically on the regime the economy is in. To alleviate unemployment and boost output the real wage should fall in the classical regime (as expected from our earlier discussion). In sharp contrast, the real wage should rise if the economy is in the KU or the RI regime. The reasons for this result are different for the two regimes. In the KU regime an increase in the real wage boosts aggregate demand for goods because the household experiences a higher (labour) income. This in turn reduces the severity of the constraint experienced by firms and prompts them to hire more workers and thus to boost output. In contrast, in the RI regime the increase in the real wage boosts employment and output because the supply of labour expands.

The standard model has been extended in a number of directions, the most interesting of which are the setting of a small open economy and the intertemporal setting. In the intertemporal disequilibrium model there is the possibility of intertemporal spillovers. It is possible, for example, to show that there may be an intertemporal bootstrap effect in the sense that pessimistic expectations about constraints in the future may increase the likelihood of such constraints in the present.

What is the lasting contribution of the rationing approach? Perhaps the single most important contribution of this approach to macroeconomics has been to clarify the nature of disequilibrium situations in an explicit general equilibrium framework. Due to disequilibria, notional plans lose their relevance and must be replaced by effective plans. The additional insights that flow from the approach are plentiful. Real wages may have nothing to do with unemployment in some cases, whereas they are of vital importance in others.

The quantity rationing approach suffers from one major defect, however, in the sense that the rigidity of prices and wages is simply *postulated* and not derived from maximizing principles. Indeed, it is straightforward to show that the rationing equilibria are in fact Pareto-inefficient. This begs the question why prices and wages are not changed by the economic agents. In that sense, the rationing approach resembles "Hamlet without the Prince" or "A pub without beer". The main character of neoclassical economics (i.e. the price mechanism) has been omitted from the play without any justification.

On the other hand, however, the slow adjustment of prices and wages seems to be a fact of life. See, for example, Blinder (1994) for empirical evidence on price adjustment by firms. In that sense, the rationing models may present a relevant description of the world as it actually is.

One strand of literature has instead chosen to remedy the lack of a "theory of pricing" by adopting explicit price- and wage-setting agents in the form of monopolistically competitive firms and labour unions. This literature will be discussed in detail in Chapter 13 which deals with new Keynesian economics.

Further Reading

An influential and highly readable reinterpretation of Keynes is found in Leijonhufvud (1968). Surveys of the quantity rationing literature are given by Drazen (1980), van der Ploeg (1987a), Bénassy (1982, 1993b), and Silvestre (1993). Neary (1980) extends the Dixit model by including a non-traded goods sector. For excellent surveys of the open economy quantity rationing models the reader is referred to Neary (1990) and Cuddington, Johansson, and Löfgren (1984).

6

The Government Budget Deficit

The purpose of this chapter is to discuss the following issues:

1. To explain and assess the validity of the Ricardian equivalence theorem, and to show how it operates in a simple two-period optimizing model of consumption behaviour;

2. To explain the notion of tax smoothing and the golden financing rule, and

3. To show how the fiscal stance of the government should be measured.

6.1 Ricardian Equivalence

The Ricardian equivalence theorem was formulated, as the name suggests, by the British classical economist David Ricardo (1817, p. 245), who immediately dismissed it as being irrelevant in practice. In an influential paper, however, the new classical economist Robert Barro (1974) forcefully argued that the Ricardian equivalence theorem is worthy of professional attention and yields important policy prescriptions.

Loosely speaking, the Ricardian equivalence theorem amounts to the following: for a given path of government spending the particular method used to finance these expenditures does not matter, in the sense that real consumption, investment, and output are unaffected. Specifically, whether the expenditures are financed by means of taxation or debt, the real consumption and investment plans of the private sector are not influenced. In that sense government debt and taxes are equivalent.

In other words, government debt is simply viewed as delayed taxation: if the government decides to finance its deficit by issuing debt today, private agents will save more in order to be able to redeem this debt in the future through higher taxation levels. Consequently, if the Ricardian equivalence theorem is valid, the Blinder and Solow (1973) model (discussed extensively in Chapter 2) is seriously flawed. In that model real private consumption depends on net wealth, *which includes government debt*! Under Ricardian equivalence, government debt in the hands of the public should not be counted as net wealth since it is exactly matched by the offsetting liability in the form of future taxation.

6.1.1 A simple model

Suppose that historical time from now into the indefinite future is split into two segments. The first segment (called period 1) is the present, and the second segment (called period 2) is the future (obviously, by construction, there is no period 3). There is perfect foresight on the part of both households and the government. We look at the behaviour of the representative household first. It lives as long as the government does, and achieves utility by consuming goods in both periods. Labour supply is exogenous and household income consists of exogenous "manna from heaven". Lifetime utility V is given by:

$$V = U(C_1) + \left(\frac{1}{1+\rho}\right) U(C_2), \quad \rho > 0, \tag{6.1}$$

where C_t is consumption in period $t\ (= 1, 2)$, $U(.)$ is the instantaneous utility function, ρ is the pure rate of time preference, representing the effects of "impatience". The higher ρ, the heavier future utility is discounted, and the more impatient is the household. At the end of period 0 (i.e. the "past"), the household has financial assets amounting in real terms to A_0 over which it also receives interest payments at the beginning of period 1 equal to rA_0, where r is the real rate of interest, which is assumed fixed for convenience. The exogenous non-interest income payments are denoted by Y_1 and Y_2, respectively, so that the budget restrictions in the two periods are:

$$A_1 = (1+r)A_0 + (1-t_1)Y_1 - C_1, \tag{6.2}$$

$$A_2 = (1+r)A_1 + (1-t_2)Y_2 - C_2 = 0, \tag{6.3}$$

where t_1 and t_2 are the proportional tax rates on income in the two periods, and $A_2 = 0$ because it makes no sense for the household to die with a positive amount of financial assets ($A_2 \leq 0$), and it is also assumed that it is impossible for the household to die in debt ($A_2 \geq 0$). (Below, we modify the model and show that households with children may wish to leave an inheritance.) Note that (6.2)–(6.3) incorporate the assumption that interest income is untaxed.

If the household can freely borrow or lend at the going interest rate r, A_1 can have either sign and equations (6.2)–(6.3) can be consolidated into a single lifetime budget restriction. Technically, this is done by substituting out A_1 from (6.2)–(6.3):

$$A_1 = \frac{C_2 - (1-t_2)Y_2}{1+r} = (1+r)A_0 + (1-t_1)Y_1 - C_1 \Rightarrow$$

$$C_1 + \frac{C_2}{1+r} = (1+r)A_0 + H, \tag{6.4}$$

where the right-hand side of (6.4) represents total wealth, which is the sum of initial financial wealth inclusive of interest received, $(1 + r)A_0$, and human wealth, H:

$$H \equiv (1 - t_1)Y_1 + \frac{(1 - t_2)Y_2}{1 + r}. \tag{6.5}$$

Equation (6.4) says that the *present value* of consumption expenditure during life must equal total wealth.

In order to demonstrate the Ricardian equivalence theorem, we need to introduce the government and its budget restriction. We start as simple as possible by assuming that the government buys goods for its own consumption (G_1 and G_2), and finances its expenditure by taxes and/or debt. There is no money in the model, so money financing is impossible. The government, like the household, exists for two periods, and can borrow or lend at the interest rate r. In parallel with (6.1)–(6.3), the government's budget identities are:

$$(D_1 \equiv) \quad rB_0 + G_1 - t_1Y_1 = B_1 - B_0, \tag{6.6}$$

$$(D_2 \equiv) \quad rB_1 + G_2 - t_2Y_2 = B_2 - B_1 = -B_1, \tag{6.7}$$

where D_i and B_i denote, respectively, the deficit and government debt in period i ($i = 1, 2$), respectively, and $B_2 = 0$ because the government, like the household, cannot default on its debt and is assumed to remain solvent (no banana republic!). Using the same trick as before, equations (6.6)–(6.7) can be consolidated into a single government budget restriction:

$$(1 + r)B_0 + G_1 - t_1Y_1 = \frac{t_2Y_2 - G_2}{1 + r} \quad \Rightarrow$$

$$(1 + r)B_0 + G_1 + \frac{G_2}{1 + r} = t_1Y_1 + \frac{t_2Y_2}{1 + r}, \tag{6.8}$$

where the left-hand side of (6.8) represents the present value of the net liabilities of the government, and the right-hand side is the present value of net income of the government (i.e. the tax revenue).

Since government bonds are the only financial asset in the toy economy, household borrowing (lending) can only take the form of negative (positive) holdings of government bonds. Hence, equilibrium in the financial capital market implies that:

$$A_i = B_i, \tag{6.9}$$

for $i = 0, 1, 2$.

The first demonstration of the Ricardian equivalence theorem is obtained by solving the government budget restriction for $(1 + r)B_0$, and substituting the result into the household budget restriction (6.4) taking (6.9) into account:

$$C_1 + \frac{C_2}{1+r} = (1+r)B_0 + \left[(1-t_1)Y_1 + \frac{(1-t_2)Y_2}{1+r}\right]$$

$$= t_1 Y_1 + \frac{t_2 Y_2}{1+r} - G_1 - \frac{G_2}{1+r} + (1-t_1)Y_1 + \frac{(1-t_2)Y_2}{1+r}$$

$$= Y_1 - G_1 + \frac{Y_2 - G_2}{1+r} \equiv \Omega. \tag{6.10}$$

The final expression shows that the tax parameters drop out of the household's budget restriction altogether. Only the present value of (exogenously given) government spending affects the level of net wealth of the household. Consequently, the choice of C_1 and C_2 do not depend on the tax parameters t_1 and t_2 either. The way in which the government finances its expenditure has no real effects on consumption.

So if consumption plans are unaffected by the timing of taxation, then what is? The answer is, of course, household saving. In order to demonstrate this, and to facilitate the subsequent discussion, we use a specific form for the utility function $U(.)$; one that yields very simple expressions for the optimal consumption and saving plans:

$$U(C_t) = \log C_t. \tag{6.11}$$

The household chooses C_1 and C_2 such that (6.1) is maximized subject to (6.10) and given the utility function (6.11). Again the optimality conditions can be obtained by using the Lagrange multiplier method. The Lagrangean is:

$$\mathcal{L} \equiv \log C_1 + \left(\frac{1}{1+\rho}\right) \log C_2 + \lambda \left[\Omega - C_1 - \frac{C_2}{1+r}\right], \tag{6.12}$$

so that the first-order conditions are:

$$\frac{\partial \mathcal{L}}{\partial C_1} = \frac{1}{C_1} - \lambda = 0, \tag{6.13}$$

$$\frac{\partial \mathcal{L}}{\partial C_2} = \frac{1}{(1+\rho)C_2} - \frac{\lambda}{1+r} = 0, \tag{6.14}$$

and the third condition, $\partial \mathcal{L}/\partial \lambda = 0$, yields the budget restriction (6.10). By combining (6.13)–(6.14), the so-called consumption Euler equation is obtained:

$$\lambda = \frac{1}{C_1} = \frac{1+r}{(1+\rho)C_2} \quad \Rightarrow \quad \frac{C_2}{C_1} = \frac{1+r}{1+\rho}. \tag{6.15}$$

In words, (6.15) says that, for example, if $r > \rho$, $C_2/C_1 > 1$ or $C_2 > C_1$. The household wishes to enjoy relatively high consumption in the second period. This is understandable in view of the fact that a low value of ρ (relative to r) implies that the household has a lot of patience, and hence a strong willingness to postpone consumption.

Equation (6.15) determines the *optimal time profile* of consumption, i.e. it shows consumption in the future relative to consumption now. The *level* of consumption is obtained by substituting (6.15) into the household budget restriction (6.10):

$$C_1 = \left(\frac{1+\rho}{2+\rho}\right)\Omega, \quad C_2 = \left(\frac{1+r}{2+\rho}\right)\Omega. \tag{6.16}$$

The expression for household saving (S_1) is determined by the identity $S_1 \equiv A_1 - A_0 = B_1 - B_0$, or:

$$S_1 = rB_0 + (1-t_1)Y_1 - \left(\frac{1+\rho}{2+\rho}\right)\Omega, \tag{6.17}$$

from which we see immediately that the tax rate t_1 does not vanish from the expression for household saving in the first period.

Now consider the following Ricardian experiment. The government reduces the tax rate in the first period ($dt_1 < 0$) but keeps its goods consumption (G_1 and G_2) constant. Then equation (6.17) implies that

$$dS_1 = -Y_1 \, dt_1 > 0, \tag{6.18}$$

(as $d\Omega = drB_0 = 0$) but the government budget restriction (6.8) implies that taxes in the second period must satisfy:

$$Y_1 dt_1 + \left(\frac{Y_2}{1+r}\right) dt_2 = 0 \quad \Rightarrow \quad dt_2 = -\left(\frac{(1+r)Y_1}{Y_2}\right) dt_1 > 0, \tag{6.19}$$

as the present value of government liabilities are unchanged by assumption. Hence, the reaction of the household to this Ricardian experiment is to increase its saving in the first period ($dS_1 > 0$) in order to be able to use the extra amount saved plus interest in the second period to pay the additional taxes. In Figure 6.1, the experiment has been illustrated graphically.

The initial *income endowment* point is E_0^Y. It represents the point at which the household makes no use of debt in the first period (i.e. $B_1 = 0$) and simply consumes according to (6.2)–(6.3). Since the household can freely lend/borrow at the going rate of interest r, however, it can choose any (C_1, C_2) combination along the budget line AB. Suppose that the optimal consumption point is at E^C, where there is a tangency between an indifference curve ($dV = 0$) and the budget line. The optimal consumption levels are given by C_1^* and C_2^*, respectively. As a result of the Ricardian experiment, income rises in the first period and falls in the second period, but the net wealth of the household (Ω) is unchanged. Hence, the income endowment point shifts *along* the given budget line in a south-easterly direction to E_1^Y. The optimal consumption point does not change, however, since nothing of importance has changed for the household. Hence, the only thing that happens is that the household increases its saving in the first period and it does so by purchasing more bonds from the government.

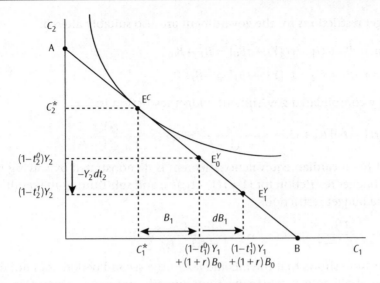

Figure 6.1. Ricardian equivalence experiment

There are many theoretical objections that can be levelled at the Ricardian equivalence theorem. In the next subsections we discuss the most important theoretical reasons causing Ricardian equivalence to fail. The interested reader is referred to the recent symposium on the budget deficit for further details (see Barro (1989) and other papers in the same issue of the *Journal of Economic Perspectives*).

6.1.2 Distorting taxes

Up to this point we have assumed that income in the two periods is exogenous. It is easy to imagine that, for example due to an endogenous labour supply decision, income depends on the tax rate on labour income (see Chapter 1). If that is the case, we should write $Y_1(t_1, t_2)$ and $Y_2(t_1, t_2)$, and the path of taxes may directly influence the income endowment point, and potentially also the level of net household wealth. Consequently, Ricardian equivalence should be expected to fail.

An even simpler example of a distorting tax can be provided with the aid of the model introduced above. Assume that non-interest income is exogenous but that there is a comprehensive income tax, and that interest income is also taxable. Equations (6.2)–(6.3) are modified to:

$$B_1 = B_0 + (1 - t_1)[Y_1 + rB_0] - C_1, \tag{6.20}$$

$$B_2 = B_1 + (1 - t_2)[Y_2 + rB_1] - C_2 = 0, \tag{6.21}$$

where we have already incorporated (6.9). The consolidated budget restriction for the household becomes:

$$C_1 + \frac{C_2}{1 + r(1 - t_2)} = [1 + r(1 - t_1)]B_0 + \left[(1 - t_1)Y_1 + \frac{(1 - t_2)Y_2}{1 + r(1 - t_2)}\right]. \tag{6.22}$$

The budget restrictions for the government are also suitably altered:

$$(D_1 \equiv) \quad rB_0 + G_1 - t_1 [Y_1 + rB_0] = B_1 - B_0, \tag{6.23}$$

$$(D_2 \equiv) \quad rB_1 + G_2 - t_2 [Y_2 + rB_1] = -B_1, \tag{6.24}$$

so that the consolidated government budget restriction is:

$$[1 + r(1 - t_1)] B_0 + G_1 + \frac{G_2}{1 + r(1 - t_2)} = t_1 Y_1 + \frac{t_2 Y_2}{1 + r(1 - t_2)}. \tag{6.25}$$

Failure of the Ricardian equivalence theorem is demonstrated by solving the government budget restriction for $(1 + r(1 - t_1))B_0$, and substituting the result into the household budget restriction:

$$C_1 + \frac{C_2}{1 + r(1 - t_2)} = Y_1 - G_1 + \frac{Y_2 - G_2}{1 + r(1 - t_2)} \equiv \Omega(t_2). \tag{6.26}$$

This expression shows that the income tax in the second period does not drop out of the household budget constraint. Consequently, optimal consumption plans are affected by the timing of taxation. Obviously, t_1 does not appear in (6.26) because it operates like a lump-sum tax. Households are taxed on their interest income in the first period and can do nothing to avoid having to pay that tax (since B_0 is predetermined and is hence a "sitting duck" for the tax man). The tax in the second period changes the intertemporal price of consumption now versus later, and as a result distorts the saving decision.[1]

Intermezzo

The two-period consumption model. Because the two-period consumption model has played such an important role in the macroeconomic literature it pays to understand its basic properties well. Assume that the representative household's lifetime utility function is given in general terms by:

$$V = V(C_1, C_2), \tag{a}$$

where C_i is consumption in period i, and we assume positive but diminishing marginal utility of consumption in both periods, i.e. $V_i \equiv \partial V / \partial C_i$ and $V_{ii} \equiv \partial^2 V / \partial C_i^2 < 0$. Note that (6.1) is a special case of (a) incorporating a zero cross

---

[1] Indeed, optimal C_1 and C_2 are modified from (6.16) to:

$$C_1 = \left(\frac{1 + \rho}{2 + \rho}\right) \Omega(t_2), \quad C_2 = \left(\frac{1 + r(1 - t_2)}{2 + \rho}\right) \Omega(t_2)$$

from which we conclude that $\partial C_1 / \partial t_2 > 0$ and $\partial C_2 / \partial t_2 = -(r/(2 + \rho))(Y_1 - G_1) < 0$. So the tax leads to a shift of consumption from the future to the present.

derivative $V_{12} \equiv \partial^2 V / \partial C_1 \partial C_2$. In the general case considered here, no such restriction is placed on V_{12}.

Abstracting from taxes, the household's periodic budget identities are given by $A_1 + C_1 = (1+r_0)A_0 + Y_1$ and $C_2 = (1+r_1)A_1 + Y_2$ which can be consolidated to yield the lifetime budget constraint:

$$C_1 + \frac{C_2}{1+r_1} = (1+r_0)A_0 + \left[Y_1 + \frac{Y_2}{1+r_1} \right] \equiv \Omega, \tag{b}$$

where Y_i is exogenous non-interest income in period i, A_0 is initial financial wealth, Ω is initial total wealth (i.e. the sum of financial and human wealth), and r_i is the interest rate in period i. The household chooses C_1 and C_2 in order to maximize lifetime utility (a) subject to the lifetime budget constraint (b). The first-order conditions are given by (b) and the Euler equation:

$$\frac{V_1(C_1, C_2)}{V_2(C_1, C_2)} = 1 + r_1, \tag{c}$$

where we indicate explicitly that V_i in general depends on both C_1 and C_2 (because $V_{12} \neq 0$ is not excluded a priori).

Equations (b)–(c) define implicit functions relating consumption in the two periods to the interest rate and total wealth which can be written in general terms as $C_i = C_i(\Omega, r_1)$ for $i = 1, 2$. To find the partial derivatives of these implicit functions we employ our usual trick and totally differentiate (b)–(c) to obtain the following matrix expression:

$$\Delta \begin{bmatrix} dC_1 \\ dC_2 \end{bmatrix} = \begin{bmatrix} 1 \\ 0 \end{bmatrix} d\Omega + \begin{bmatrix} \dfrac{C_2}{(1+r_1)^2} \\ V_2 \end{bmatrix} dr_1, \tag{d}$$

where the matrix Δ on the left-hand side of (d) is defined as:

$$\Delta \equiv \begin{bmatrix} 1 & \dfrac{1}{1+r_1} \\ V_{11} - (1+r_1)V_{12} & V_{12} - (1+r_1)V_{22} \end{bmatrix}, \tag{e}$$

where we have already incorporated Young's theorem according to which $V_{12} = V_{21}$ (Chiang, 1984, p. 313). The second-order conditions for utility maximization ensure that the determinant of Δ is strictly positive (see Chiang (1984, pp. 400-408) for details), i.e. $|\Delta| > 0$. This means that the implicit function theorem can be used (Chiang, 1984, p. 210).

Let us first consider the effects of a marginal change in wealth. We obtain from (d):

$$\frac{\partial C_1}{\partial \Omega} = \frac{V_{12} - (1+r_1)V_{22}}{|\Delta|} \gtrless 0, \tag{f}$$

$$\frac{\partial C_2}{\partial \Omega} = \frac{(1+r_1)V_{12} - V_{11}}{|\Delta|} \gtrless 0. \tag{g}$$

Several observations can be made reading these expressions. First, the effect of wealth changes on consumption in both periods is ambiguous in general. Second, if lifetime utility satisfies $V_{12} \geq 0$ then $\partial C_i/\partial \Omega > 0$ for $i = 1, 2$, and present and future consumption are both normal goods. Third, if $V_{12} < 0$ then either present consumption or future consumption may be an inferior good ($\partial C_i/\partial \Omega < 0$). It follows from (b), however, that at most one good can be inferior, i.e.:

$$\frac{\partial C_1}{\partial \Omega} + \left(\frac{1}{1+r_1}\right)\frac{\partial C_2}{\partial \Omega} = 1. \tag{h}$$

Next we consider the effects of a marginal change in the interest rate r_1. It follows from the budget restriction (b) that a change in r_1 not only changes the relative price of future consumption (on the left-hand side of (b)) but also affects the value of human wealth (and thus total wealth) given in square brackets on the right-hand side of (b). Indeed, in view of the definition of Ω, we find $\partial\Omega/\partial r_1 = -Y_2/(1+r_1)^2 < 0$, i.e. an increase in the interest rate reduces the value of human capital because future wage income is discounted more heavily. By taking this (human) wealth effect into account we obtain the following partial derivatives from (d):

$$\frac{\partial C_1}{\partial r} = \left(\frac{V_{12} - (1+r_1)V_{22}}{|\Delta|}\right)\left(\frac{A_1}{1+r_1}\right) - \left(\frac{1}{|\Delta|}\right)\left(\frac{V_2}{1+r_1}\right) \gtrless 0, \tag{i}$$

$$\frac{\partial C_2}{\partial r} = \left(\frac{(1+r_1)V_{12} - V_{11}}{|\Delta|}\right)\left(\frac{A_1}{1+r_1}\right) + \left(\frac{1}{|\Delta|}\right)V_1 \gtrless 0, \tag{j}$$

where we have used the second period budget identity, $(1 + r_1)A_1 = C_2 - Y_2$ to simplify these expressions. Again several observations can be made regarding the expressions in (i)–(j). First, without further restrictions on V_{12} and A_1 the effects are ambiguous. By differentiating the lifetime budget equation (b) we find:

$$\frac{\partial C_1}{\partial r_1} + \left(\frac{1}{1+r_1}\right)\frac{\partial C_2}{\partial r_1} = \frac{A_1}{1+r_1}, \tag{k}$$

from which we deduce that for an agent who chooses to save ($A_1 > 0$) either present or future consumption (or both) rise if the interest rate rises. Second, if

$A_1 > 0$ and $V_{12} \geq 0$ then $\partial C_1/\partial r \gtrless 0$ and $\partial C_1/\partial r > 0$. Third, if the agent's utility maximum happens to coincide with its endowment point (so that $A_1 = 0$) then it neither saves nor dissaves and it follows that $\partial C_1/\partial r < 0$ and $\partial C_1/\partial r > 0$.

In the literature it is often assumed that the utility function is *homothetic*. A homothetic utility function can be written as $V(C_1, C_2) = G[H(C_1, C_2)]$, where $G[.]$ is a strictly increasing function and $H(C_1, C_2)$ is homogeneous of degree one in C_1 and C_2 (see e.g. Sydsæter and Hammond, 1995, p. 573). We recall the following properties of such functions from the intermezzo in Chapter 4: (P1) $H_1 C_1 + H_2 C_2 = H$, (P2) H_1 and H_2 are homogeneous of degree zero in C_1 and C_2, (P3) $H_{12} = -(C_1/C_2)H_{11} = -(C_2/C_1)H_{22}$ and thus $H_{11} = (C_2/C_1)^2 H_{22}$, and (P4) $\sigma_{12} \equiv -d\log(C_1/C_2)/d\log(H_1/H_2) = H_1 H_2/(HH_{12}) \geq 0$. Since $H_{ii} < 0$ it follows from (P3) that $H_{12} > 0$ and from (f) to (g) that present and future consumption are both normal goods. To study the effect of a change in the interest rate we note that the first-order condition (c) becomes $H_1/H_2 = 1 + r_1$. Since the H_i are homogeneous of degree zero, this Euler equation pins down a unique C_1/C_2 ratio as a function of $1 + r_1$. By loglinearizing the Euler equation and the budget restriction (b) (holding $(1+r_0)A_0$, Y_1, and Y_2 constant) we obtain the following expression:

$$\begin{bmatrix} \omega_1 & 1-\omega_1 \\ -1 & 1 \end{bmatrix} \begin{bmatrix} \frac{dC_1}{C_1} \\ \frac{dC_2}{C_2} \end{bmatrix} = \begin{bmatrix} (A_1/\Omega) \\ \sigma_{12} \end{bmatrix} \left(\frac{dr_1}{1+r_1} \right), \tag{l}$$

where $\omega_1 \equiv C_1/\Omega$ and $1 - \omega_1 \equiv C_2/((1 + r_1)\Omega)$ are the budget shares of, respectively, first- and second-period consumption. Solving (l) we obtain the comparative static effects:

$$\frac{\partial C_1}{\partial r_1} = \frac{C_1}{1+r_1} \left[(1-\omega_1) - \frac{Y_2}{(1+r_1)\Omega} - (1-\omega_1)\sigma_{12} \right], \tag{m}$$

$$\frac{\partial C_2}{\partial r_1} = \frac{C_2}{1+r_1} \left[(1-\omega_1) - \frac{Y_2}{(1+r_1)\Omega} + \omega_1\sigma_{12} \right], \tag{n}$$

where we have also used $(1 + r_1)A_1 = C_2 - Y_2$. The three terms appearing in square brackets on the right-hand sides of (m) and (n) represent, respectively, the *income effect*, the *human wealth effect*, and the *substitution effect* (see also Obstfeld and Rogoff (1996, p. 30) for this terminology). We illustrate these effects in Figure 6.2.

The ultimate effect of an increase in the interest rate r_1 is given by the move from E_0 to E_1. This total effect can be decomposed into the usual Hicksian fashion. In doing so we exploit the fact that for homothetic utility functions the slope of the indifference curves is the same along a straight ray from the origin. Two such rays are drawn in Figure 6.2, one for the old and one for the new interest rate. The move from E_0 to E' is the substitution effect (SE) and the move from E' to E'' is the income effect (IE). If the household were to have

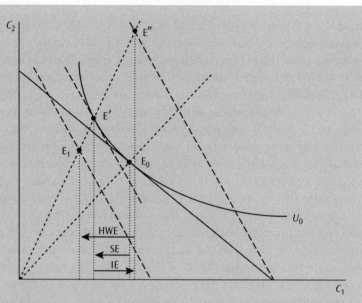

Figure 6.2. Income, substitution, and human wealth effects

no non-interest income in the second period ($Y_2 = 0$) this would be all as the human wealth effect would be absent. If Y_2 is positive, however, the increase in the interest rate reduces the value of human capital and shifts the budget restriction inward. Hence, the human wealth effect (HWE) is represented by the move from E'' to E_1. Students should check their understanding of homothetic utility functions by drawing the case for which the substitution effect is zero. Further results on the two-period model are presented by Obstfeld and Rogoff (1996, ch. 1).

6.1.3 Borrowing restrictions

In the basic case we have assumed that households can borrow/lend at the same rate of interest as the government. In practice this is unlikely to be the case, as is evidenced by the prevalence of credit rationing of young agents with high earning potential but no tangible appropriable collateral (slavery is not allowed, so future labour income typically cannot serve as collateral). Furthermore, households are more risky to lend to than (stable) governments, suggesting that the former may pay a larger risk premium than the latter. It turns out that borrowing restrictions can invalidate the Ricardian equivalence proposition.

For simplicity we assume that a household is unable to borrow altogether but can lend money at the going interest rate r. In the case discussed so far, this would be no problem because the household chose to be a net *lender* in the first period. Let us now augment the scenario by assuming that income is low in the first period and high in

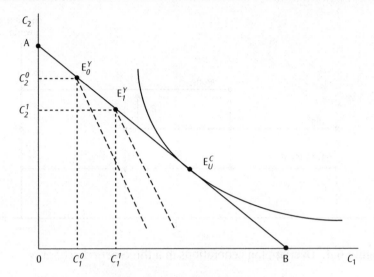

Figure 6.3. Liquidity restrictions and the Ricardian experiment

the second period. This case has been drawn in Figure 6.3. The income endowment point is E_0^Y, and the optimal consumption point *in the absence of borrowing restrictions* is E_U^C. This point is not attainable, however, since it involves borrowing in the first period, which is by assumption not possible for the household. The effective choice set is consequently only $AE_0^Y C_1^0 0$ and the optimal consumption point (C_1^0, C_2^0) is at the kink in the budget line (in point E_0^Y).

If we now conduct the Ricardian experiment of a tax cut in the first period matched by a tax increase in the second, the income endowment point shifts along the unrestricted budget line AB, say to point E_1^Y. As a result, the severity of the borrowing constraint is relaxed and the consumption point (C_1^1, C_2^1) moves to point E_1^Y. The effective choice set has expanded to $AE_1^Y C_1^1 0$ and real consumption plans (and household utility) have changed for the better.

Obviously, a similar story holds in the less extreme case where the borrowing rate is not infinite (as in the case discussed here) but higher than the rate the government faces. In that case the budget line to the right of the income endowment point is not vertical but downward sloping, and steeper than the unrestricted budget line AB (see the dashed line segments). As a result, the Ricardian experiment still leads to an expansion of the household's choice set and real effects on the optimal consumption plans.

6.1.4 Finite lives

Everybody knows that there are only two certainties in life: death and taxes. Hence, one should feel ill at ease if Ricardian equivalence only holds if households live

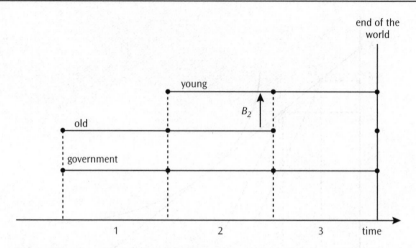

Figure 6.4. Overlapping generations in a three-period economy

forever. In the example discussed so far, households, the government, and the entire economy last for two periods, which effectively amounts to saying that the household has an infinite life. Suppose that we change the model slightly by introducing two households, that each live for only two periods, and that the government and the economy last for three periods. The old household lives in periods 1 and 2, whilst its offspring, the young household, lives in periods 2 and 3. The structure of the overlapping generations is drawn in Figure 6.4.

We describe the *old generation* first. They are assumed to possess the following lifetime utility function:

$$V^O = \log C_1^O + \left(\frac{1}{1+\rho}\right) \log C_2^O + \alpha V^Y, \quad \alpha \geq 0, \tag{6.27}$$

where the superscript "O" designates the old generation, and "Y" the young generation. Equation (6.27) says that if $\alpha > 0$, the old generation loves its offspring, in the sense that a higher level of welfare of the young also gives rise to a higher welfare of the old. The old can influence the welfare of the young by leaving an inheritance. Assume that this inheritance, if it exists, is given to the young just before the end of period 2 (see Figure 6.4). The inheritance is the amount of bonds left over at the end of the old generation's life, i.e. B_2^O. Clearly, it is impossible to leave a negative inheritance, so that the only restriction is that $B_2^O \geq 0$.

The consolidated budget restriction of the old generation is derived in the usual fashion. The periodic budget restrictions are:

$$B_1^O = (1+r)B_0 + (1-t_1)Y_1^O - C_1^O, \tag{6.28}$$

$$B_2^O = (1+r)B_1^O + (1-t_2)Y_2^O - C_2^O, \tag{6.29}$$

from which B_1^O can be eliminated to yield:

$$C_1^O + \frac{C_2^O + B_2^O}{1+r} = (1+r)B_0 + \left[(1-t_1)Y_1^O + \frac{(1-t_2)Y_2^O}{1+r} \right] \equiv \Omega^O, \tag{6.30}$$

where Ω^O is total wealth of the old generation, and the term in square brackets is human wealth of the old generation denoted by H^O. Equation (6.30) says that the present value of consumption expenditure (including the bequest to the young) during life must equal total wealth. In order to determine the appropriate size of the bequest, the link between the size of the inheritance and lifetime utility of the young generation must be determined, i.e. we must find $V^Y = \Phi(B_2^O)$.

By assumption the *young generation* has no offspring (presumably because "the end of the world is nigh"), does not love the old generation, and hence has the standard utility function which only depends on own consumption levels:

$$V^Y = \log C_2^Y + \left(\frac{1}{1+\rho} \right) \log C_3^Y. \tag{6.31}$$

Its consolidated budget restriction is derived in the usual fashion. The periodic budget restrictions are:

$$B_2^Y = (1-t_2)Y_2^Y - C_2^Y, \tag{6.32}$$
$$B_3^Y = (1+r)\left[B_2^O + B_2^Y \right] + (1-t_3)Y_3^Y - C_3^Y = 0, \tag{6.33}$$

from which B_2^Y can be eliminated to yield:

$$C_2^Y + \frac{C_3^Y}{1+r} = B_2^O + \left[(1-t_2)Y_2^Y + \frac{(1-t_3)Y_3^Y}{1+r} \right] \equiv \Omega^Y, \tag{6.34}$$

where Ω^Y is total wealth of the young generation, and the term in square brackets is the human wealth of this generation denoted by H^Y.

The optimal plan for the young generation is to choose C_2^Y and C_3^Y such that (6.31) is maximized subject to (6.34). The solutions are similar to those given in (6.16):

$$C_2^Y = \left(\frac{1+\rho}{2+\rho} \right) \Omega^Y, \quad C_3^Y = \left(\frac{1+r}{2+\rho} \right) \Omega^Y. \tag{6.35}$$

By substituting these optimal plans into the utility function (6.31), we obtain the expression relating optimal welfare of the young generation as a function of the exogenous variables, including the inheritance B_2^O:

$$V^Y \equiv \Phi(B_2^O) = \log \left(\frac{1+\rho}{2+\rho} \right) + \left(\frac{1}{1+\rho} \right) \log \left(\frac{1+r}{2+\rho} \right) + \left(\frac{2+\rho}{1+\rho} \right) \log \Omega^Y$$

$$= \Phi_0 + \left(\frac{2+\rho}{1+\rho} \right) \log \left[B_2^O + H^Y \right]. \tag{6.36}$$

The *old generation* is aware of the relationship given in (6.36), and uses it in the decision regarding its own optimal plan. Hence, the old generation chooses C_1^O,

C_2^O, and B_2^O such that (6.27) is maximized subject to (6.30), (6.36), and the inequality restriction $B_2^O \geq 0$. The first-order conditions are obtained by postulating the Lagrangian:

$$\mathcal{L} \equiv \log C_1^O + \left(\frac{1}{1+\rho}\right) \log C_2^O + \alpha \Phi(B_2^O) + \lambda \left[\Omega^O - C_1^O - \frac{C_2^O + B_2^O}{1+r}\right], \tag{6.37}$$

so that the first-order conditions are:

$$\frac{\partial \mathcal{L}}{\partial C_1^O} = \frac{1}{C_1^O} - \lambda = 0, \tag{6.38}$$

$$\frac{\partial \mathcal{L}}{\partial C_2^O} = \frac{1}{(1+\rho)C_2^O} - \frac{\lambda}{1+r} = 0, \tag{6.39}$$

$$\frac{\partial \mathcal{L}}{\partial B_2^O} = \left[\alpha\left(\frac{dV^Y}{dB_2^O}\right) - \frac{\lambda}{1+r}\right] \leq 0, \quad B_2^O \geq 0, \quad B_2^O\left(\frac{\partial \mathcal{L}}{\partial B_2^O}\right) = 0. \tag{6.40}$$

(The fourth condition, $\partial \mathcal{L}/\partial \lambda = 0$, yields the budget restriction (6.30).) Equation (6.40) is the Kuhn-Tucker condition for the optimal inheritance B_2^O that must be used because of the inequality restriction (see e.g. Chiang (1984, ch. 21) and the Mathematical Appendix). The mathematical details need not worry us at this point because the economic interpretation is straightforward. If $\alpha = 0$ (unloved offspring), then equation (6.40) implies that $\partial \mathcal{L}/\partial B_2^O = -\lambda/(1+r) < 0$ (a strict inequality, because (6.38) shows that $\lambda = 1/C_1^O > 0$) so that $B_2^O(\partial \mathcal{L}/\partial B_2^O) = 0$ implies also $B_2^O = 0$. In words, no inheritance is given to offspring that is unloved. More generally, if α is so low that $\partial \mathcal{L}/\partial B_2^O < 0$, giving an inheritance would detract from the old generation's lifetime utility, which means that the inheritance is set at the lowest possible value of $B_2^O = 0$.

Hence, a positive inheritance implies that the first expression in (6.40) holds with equality. Using (6.36) it can then be written as:

$$B_2^O > 0 \Rightarrow \frac{\partial \mathcal{L}}{\partial B_2^O} = 0 \Leftrightarrow \frac{\alpha(2+\rho)}{(1+\rho)\left[B_2^O + H^Y\right]} = \frac{\lambda}{1+r} = \frac{1}{(1+\rho)C_2^O}, \tag{6.41}$$

where we have also used (6.39) in the final step. Furthermore, (6.38)–(6.39) can be combined to yield the familiar Euler equation for consumption.

$$C_2^O = \left(\frac{1+r}{1+\rho}\right) C_1^O. \tag{6.42}$$

By using (6.30), and (6.41)–(6.42), the solutions for optimal consumption and the (positive) inheritance can be solved:

$$C_1^O = \frac{(1+\rho)\left[\Omega^O + H^Y/(1+r)\right]}{(2+\rho)(1+\alpha)}, \tag{6.43}$$

$$C_2^O = \frac{(1+r)\Omega^O + H^Y}{(2+\rho)(1+\alpha)}, \tag{6.44}$$

$$B_2^O = \frac{\alpha(1+r)\Omega^O - H^Y}{(1+\alpha)}. \tag{6.45}$$

These results are intuitive. First, if α is very large (unbounded love for the offspring) the old generation consumes next to nothing, and the inheritance approaches its maximum value of $(1+r)\Omega^O$. Second, if there is a lot of growth in the economy, H^Y is high and the young have high human wealth. This means that the marginal utility of bequests falls, so that the inheritance is reduced ($\partial B_2^O/\partial H^Y < 0$). Since the offspring is wealthier, the old generation consumes more in both periods of life ($\partial C_1^O/\partial H^Y > 0$ and $\partial C_2^O/\partial H^Y > 0$).

It can now be demonstrated that, provided the optimal bequest stays positive, Ricardian equivalence holds in this economy despite the fact that households have shorter lives than the government. The government budget restriction is now:

$$(1+r)B_0 + G_1 + \frac{G_2}{1+r} + \frac{G_3}{(1+r)^2} = t_1 Y_1^O + \frac{t_2(Y_2^O + Y_2^Y)}{1+r} + \frac{t_3 Y_3^Y}{(1+r)^2}. \tag{6.46}$$

Consider the following Ricardian experiment: the government reduces the tax rate in period 1 ($dt_1 < 0$) and raises it in period 3 ($dt_3 > 0$), such that (6.46) holds for an unchanged path of government consumption, i.e.:

$$0 = Y_1^O dt_1 + \frac{Y_3^Y}{(1+r)^2} dt_3 \quad \text{(balanced-budget)}. \tag{6.47}$$

What do (6.43)–(6.45) predict will be the result of this Ricardian experiment? Clearly, from (6.43) we have that:

$$dC_1^O = \frac{(1+\rho)\left[d\Omega^O + (1/(1+r))dH^Y\right]}{(2+\rho)(1+\alpha)}. \tag{6.48}$$

But (6.30) predicts that

$$d\Omega^O = -Y_1^O dt_1 > 0, \tag{6.49}$$

and (6.34) says that

$$dH^Y = -\left(\frac{Y_3^Y}{1+r}\right) dt_3 = (1+r)Y_1^O dt_1, \tag{6.50}$$

(where we have used (6.47) to relate dt_3 to dt_1) so that $d\Omega^O + (1/(1+r))dH^Y = 0$, and (6.48) is reduced to

$$\frac{dC_1^O}{dt_1} = 0, \tag{6.51}$$

and, of course, also (by (6.44))

$$\frac{dC_2^O}{dt_1} = 0. \tag{6.52}$$

The Ricardian experiment does not affect the consumption plans of the old generation at all. What is the intuition behind this result? The answer is found in (6.45).

$$dB_2^O = \left(\frac{\alpha(1+r)dA^O - dH^Y}{1+\alpha} \right) dt_1$$

$$= \left(\frac{-\alpha(1+r)Y_1^O - (1+r)Y_1^O}{1+\alpha} \right) dt_1 = -(1+r)Y_1^O dt_1 > 0. \tag{6.53}$$

The entire tax cut is simply added to the inheritance. In period 1 the old generation buys government bonds (that have just been emitted by the government to finance its deficit, hence no upward pressure on the bond price!) on which it receives interest. The additional bonds plus interest are added to the inheritance so that the young generation is able to meet its higher tax bill. Equations (6.34)–(6.35) and (6.53) therefore predict that the consumption of the young generation is unchanged as well.

$$d\Omega^Y = dB_2^O - \left(\frac{Y_3^Y}{1+r} \right) dt_3$$

$$= -(1+r)Y_1^O dt_1 - \left(\frac{Y_3^Y}{1+r} \right) \left(-\frac{Y_1^O(1+r)^2}{Y_3^Y} \right) = 0, \tag{6.54}$$

which implies that

$$dC_2^Y = dC_3^Y = 0. \tag{6.55}$$

In conclusion, the fact that individual lives are finite does not mean that Ricardian equivalence automatically fails. Provided future generations are linked to the current generation through a whole chain of operative bequests, the unbroken chain of connected generations ensures that Ricardian equivalence holds. Of course, once a single link of the chain snaps (zero bequests, childless couples), generations are no longer linked and Ricardian equivalence does not hold in general. Leaving no inheritance is the optimal strategy if the degree of "altruism" α is low, or if future income growth is high.[2] Students should test their understanding of this material by showing that Ricardian equivalence also fails, even if there are positive inheritances, if there is an inheritance tax that is varied in the experiment.

6.1.5 Some further reasons for Ricardian non-equivalence

A further reason why Ricardian equivalence may fail is the occurrence of *net population growth*. Intuitively, the burden of future taxation is borne by more shoulders, so that the burden per capita is lower for future generations than for current generations. Hence, one expects real effects from a Ricardian experiment that shifts taxation to the future. (We demonstrate this with a formal model in Chapter 14 below.)

A fifth reason why Ricardian equivalence may fail has to do with issues such as irrationality, myopic behaviour, and lack of information. Households may not be as farsighted and rational as we have assumed so far, and may fail to fully understand the implications of the government budget restriction. Furthermore, they may simply not have the cognitive power to calculate an optimal dynamic consumption plan, and simply stick to static "rule of thumb" behaviour like "spend a constant fraction of current income on consumption goods".

A sixth reason why Ricardian equivalence may fail has to do with the "bird in the hand" issue. A temporary tax cut, accompanied by a rise in government debt, acts as an insurance policy and thus leads to less precautionary saving and a rise in private consumption (Barsky et al., 1986). The main idea is that the future rise in the tax rate reduces the variance of future after-tax income, so that risk-averse households have to engage in less precautionary saving. A temporary tax cut thus has real effects, because it is better to have one bird in the hand than ten in the air. This critique of Ricardian debt equivalence relies on the absence of complete private insurance markets. A related reason for failure of debt equivalence is that people are uncertain of what their future income and thus also what their future bequests will be (Feldstein, 1988). People may thus value differently, on the one hand, spending a sum now, and, on the other hand, saving the sum of money and then bequeathing.

Finally, a frequently stated but incorrect "reason". A popular argument is that government debt matters in as far as it has been sold to foreigners. The idea is that in the future our children face a burden, because they have to pay higher taxes in order for the government to be able to pay interest on and redeem government debt to the children of foreigners. A rise in government debt is thus thought to constitute a transfer of wealth abroad. However, the original sale of government debt to foreigners leads to an inflow of foreign assets whose value equals the present value of the future amount of taxes levied on home households which is then

---

[2] Barring transfers in the opposite direction, i.e. from child to parent.

paid as interest and principal to foreigners. Hence, this critique of Ricardian debt equivalence turns out to be a red herring.

6.1.6 Empirical evidence

The Ricardian equivalence theorem has been the subject of many tests ever since its inception by Barro (1974). The existing literature is ably surveyed in a recent paper by Seater (1993). There is a substantial part of the empirical literature that finds it hard to reject the Ricardian equivalence theorem. Nevertheless, the jury is still out as solid tests with microeconomic data still have to be performed. Even though Seater (1993) concludes that debt equivalence is a good approximation, Bernheim (1987) in his survey comes to the conclusion that debt equivalence is at variance with the facts. Even though debt equivalence is from a theoretical point of view invalid and according to most macroeconomists empirically invalid as well, one might give the supporters of Ricardian debt equivalence, for the time being, the benefit of the doubt when they argue that the Ricardian proposition is from an empirical point of view not too bad. Hence, in the following section we see what role there is for government debt if Ricardian equivalence is assumed to hold.

6.2 The Theory of Government Debt Creation

Is there any role for government debt if it barely affects real economic outcomes such as investment and consumption? According to the neoclassical view of public finance, there is still a role for government debt in smoothing intratemporal distortions arising from government policy. In particular, government debt may be used to smooth tax and inflation rates and therefore private consumption over time. Such neoclassical views on public finance give prescriptions for government budget deficits and government debt that are more or less observationally equivalent to more Keynesian views on the desirability of countercyclical policy. After a simple discussion of the intertemporal aspects of the public sector accounts, we review the principle of tax smoothing. In the light of this discussion we are able to comment on the golden rule of public finance.

6.2.1 A simple model of tax smoothing

Assume that the policy maker can only raise revenue by means of a distorting tax system (e.g. labour taxes). Assume furthermore, that there are costs associated with enforcing the tax system, so-called "collection costs", and suppose that we can measure the welfare loss of taxation (L_G) as a quadratic function of the tax rates

$(t_1$ and $t_2)$, and a linear function of income levels in the two periods $(Y_1$ and $Y_2)$.

$$L_G \equiv \tfrac{1}{2}t_1^2 Y_1 + \tfrac{1}{2}\frac{t_2^2 Y_2}{1+\rho_G}, \tag{6.56}$$

where ρ_G is the (policy maker's) political pure rate of time preference. We continue to assume that household income is exogenous. The government budget restriction is augmented somewhat by distinguishing between consumption and investment expenditure by the government, denoted by G_t^C and G_t^I, respectively $(t = 1, 2)$. Instead of equations (6.6)–(6.7) we have:

$$(D_1 \equiv) \; rB_0 + G_1^C + G_1^I - t_1 Y_1 = B_1 - B_0, \tag{6.57}$$

$$(D_2 \equiv) \; rB_1 + G_2^C - R_2^I - t_2 Y_2 = B_2 - B_1 = -B_1, \tag{6.58}$$

where R_2^I is the gross return on public investment obtained in period 2, so that the *rate* of return r_G can be written as:

$$R_2^I = (1 + r_G)G_1^I. \tag{6.59}$$

Obviously it makes no sense for the government to invest in period 2 since the world ends at the end of that period (hence $G_2^I = 0$). Note furthermore that (6.57)–(6.58) also imply the following relationship between the deficits in the two periods and the initial debt level:

$$D_1 + D_2 + B_0 = 0. \tag{6.60}$$

To the extent that there is an initial debt $(B_0 > 0)$, the sum of the deficits in the two periods must be negative (i.e. amount to a surplus). The consolidated government budget restriction can be obtained in the usual fashion:

$$(1+r)B_0 + G_1^C + G_1^I - t_1 Y_1 = \frac{t_2 Y_2 + (1+r_G)G_1^I - G_2^C}{1+r} \; [\equiv B_1] \quad \Rightarrow$$

$$[\Xi_1 \equiv] \; (1+r)B_0 + G_1^C + \frac{G_2^C}{1+r} + \frac{(r - r_G)G_1^I}{1+r} = t_1 Y_1 + \frac{t_2 Y_2}{1+r}, \tag{6.61}$$

where Ξ_1 is the present value of the net liabilities of the government. We immediately see the *golden rule of government finance*: as long as $r_G = r$, government investment expenditure can be debudgeted from the government budget constraint. In words, public investments that attain the market rate of return give rise to no net liability of the government and hence do not lead to present or future taxation. They can be financed by means of debt without any problem.

The growth rate of income in this economy is defined as $\gamma \equiv Y_2/Y_1 - 1$, so that we can write $Y_2 = (1+\gamma)Y_1$, and everything can be written in terms of Y_1. Specifically, the right-hand side of (6.61) can be rewritten as:

$$\xi_1 \equiv \frac{\Xi_1}{Y_1} = t_1 + \left(\frac{1+\gamma}{1+r}\right)t_2, \tag{6.62}$$

where ξ_1 is net government liabilities expressed as a share of income in the first period.

The policy maker is assumed to minimize the welfare loss due to distortionary taxation, subject to the revenue requirement restriction (6.62). The Lagrangean is:

$$\mathcal{L} \equiv \tfrac{1}{2} t_1^2 Y_1 + \tfrac{1}{2} t_2^2 \left(\frac{1+\gamma}{1+\rho_G} \right) Y_1 + \lambda \left[\xi_1 - t_1 - \left(\frac{1+\gamma}{1+r} \right) t_2 \right], \tag{6.63}$$

so that the first-order conditions are:

$$\frac{\partial \mathcal{L}}{\partial t_1} = t_1 Y_1 - \lambda = 0, \tag{6.64}$$

$$\frac{\partial \mathcal{L}}{\partial t_2} = t_2 \left(\frac{1+\gamma}{1+\rho_G} \right) Y_1 - \lambda \left(\frac{1+\gamma}{1+r} \right) = 0, \tag{6.65}$$

and the third condition, $\partial \mathcal{L}/\partial \lambda = 0$, yields the revenue requirement restriction (6.62). By combining (6.64)–(6.65), the *"Euler equation"* for the government's optimal taxation problem is obtained:

$$\lambda = t_1 Y_1 = \left(\frac{1+r}{1+\rho_G} \right) t_2 Y_1 \quad \Rightarrow \quad t_1 = \left(\frac{1+r}{1+\rho_G} \right) t_2. \tag{6.66}$$

This expression is intuitive: a *short-sighted government* (ρ_G greater than r) would choose a low tax rate in the current period and a high one in the future. In doing so, the "pain" of taxation is postponed to the future. The opposite holds for a very patient policy maker.

Equations (6.62) and (6.66) can be combined to solve for the levels of the two tax rates:

$$t_1 = \frac{(1+r)^2 \xi_1}{(1+r)^2 + (1+\gamma)(1+\rho_G)}, \tag{6.67}$$

$$t_2 = \frac{(1+\rho_G)(1+r)\xi_1}{(1+r)^2 + (1+\gamma)(1+\rho_G)}, \tag{6.68}$$

where the optimal path for government debt is also implicitly determined by equations (6.67)–(6.68). We observe that the existing debt exerts an influence on the optimal tax rates only via ξ_1. In that sense it is only of historical significance. The debt was created in the past and hence leads to taxation now and in the future. The optimal taxation problem is illustrated in Figure 6.5. The straight line through the origin is the Euler equation (6.66), and the downward sloping line is the revenue requirement line (6.62). The concave curves are iso-welfare loss curves (i.e. combinations of t_1 and t_2 for which L_G is constant, or $dL_G = 0$). The closer to the origin, the smaller the welfare costs of taxation. The given revenue is raised with the smallest welfare loss in a point of tangency between the revenue requirement line and an iso-welfare loss curve. This happens at point E.

A special case of the tax-smoothing theory is obtained by assuming that $r = \rho_G$. In that case, (6.67)–(6.68) predict that the two tax rates are equal in the two periods:

$$t_1 = t_2 = \left(\frac{1+r}{2+r+\gamma} \right) \xi_1. \tag{6.69}$$

Debt is used to keep the tax rates constant, hence the name "tax smoothing".

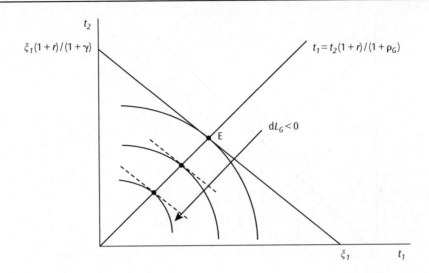

Figure 6.5. Optimal taxation

The left-hand side of (6.61) can also be expressed in terms of shares of current national income. After some manipulation we obtain:

$$
\xi_1 \equiv \frac{G_1^C}{Y_1} + \left(\frac{1}{1+r}\right)\frac{G_2^C}{Y_1} + \left(\frac{r - r_G}{1+r}\right)\frac{G_1^I}{Y_1} + (1+r)\frac{B_0}{Y_1}
$$

$$
= g_1^C + \left(\frac{1+\gamma}{1+r}\right)g_2^C + \left(\frac{r - r_G}{1+r}\right)g_1^I + (1+r)b_0, \tag{6.70}
$$

where $g_t^C \equiv G_t^C/Y_t$, $g_1^I \equiv G_1^I/Y_1$, and $b_0 \equiv B_0/Y_1$. Furthermore, using (6.57), the deficit in period 1 can also be written in terms of national income in period 1:

$$
d_1 \equiv \frac{D_1}{Y_1} = \frac{rB_0 + G_1^C + G_1^I - t_1 Y_1}{Y_1} = rb_0 + g_1^C + g_1^I - t_1. \tag{6.71}
$$

The *spending point* is defined as the point where $D_1 = 0$, and is drawn as point E_0^S in Figure 6.6. The *optimal taxation point* is given by point E_0^T.

With the aid of this simple model a number of "rules of thumb" can be derived for the government's finances. First, as was mentioned above, government investment projects earning a market rate of return can be financed by means of debt. Second, consumption spending and losses on public investment projects should be financed by means of taxation. Third, tax rates should be smoothed as much as possible to minimize the welfare loss due to taxation. Fourth, a *temporary* rise in government consumption may be financed by means of debt. Formally, a temporary increase does not raise the revenue requirement of the government (ξ_1 is constant since $dG_2^C = -(1+r)dG_1^C$ implies that $d\Xi_1 = 0$), so that the revenue requirement line stays put. In terms of Figure 6.6, the spending point moves from E_0^S to E_1^S, the optimal taxes remain unchanged, and the temporary increase in government spending

155

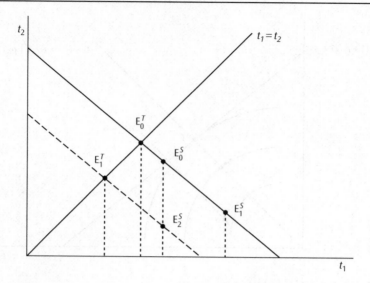

Figure 6.6. Optimal taxation and tax smoothing

is accommodated by an increase in the deficit (and hence debt) in the first period. This is a neoclassical policy prescription that looks a lot like old-fashioned Keynesian countercyclical policy. During (temporary) recessions there is no harm in letting the debt increase a little bit. Fifth, if it appears that the government's spending level has *permanently* increased ($d\xi_1 > 0$), tax rates should be increased immediately. For example, if we know that unemployment has permanently increased (and not due to a recession), taxes should be increased in order to finance the additional unemployment benefits. Sixth, if the government credibly announces that it is permanently lowering government spending, tax rates should be lowered immediately. This is a so-called "balanced decline" of the public sector. Seventh, if the government credibly announces that it will lower its consumption spending in the future ($dg_2^C < 0$), then the tax rates should be lowered immediately. In terms of Figure 6.6, the revenue requirement line shifts down and to the left, and the spending point moves from E_0^S to E_2^S directly below it. The deficit in the first period (and hence debt) increases as a result. Indeed, (6.69) and (6.70)–(6.71) predict that $dd_1/dg_1^C = (1+\gamma)/(2+r+\gamma) > 0$.

In Chapter 10 we shall return to the issue of debt management and the nation's finances. We do this in the context of models in which the political process is made endogenous, the so-called "endogenous politicians" or New Political Economy approach to macroeconomics. In that context it is much more natural to discuss the otherwise "hard to swallow" debt and deficit norms agreed upon by members of the European Community in the Maastricht Treaty. For those who cannot wait, the article by Buiter, Corsetti, and Roubini (1993) makes excellent reading.

6.3 Punchlines

In this chapter two concepts, both relating to the government budget constraint, are introduced and analysed, namely the so-called Ricardian equivalence theorem (RET) and the theory of tax smoothing.

Starting with the first of these, the RET can be defined as follows. *For a given path of government spending*, the particular financing method used by the government (bonds or taxes) does not matter. More precisely, when the RET is valid, the financing method of the government does not affect real consumption, investment, output, and welfare and government debt is seen as a form of delayed taxation. It must be stressed that the RET is not a statement about the effects of government consumption but rather deals with the way these expenditures are paid for by the government.

The intuition behind the RET is quite simple. If the government cuts taxes today and finances the resulting deficit by means of debt, then households will realize that, since total resources claimed by the government have not changed in present value terms, eventually the tax will have to be raised again sometime in the future. To ensure that it will be able to meet its future tax bills, the household reacts to the tax cut by saving it. The tax cut does not affect the lifetime resources available to the households and thus does not affect their consumption plans either.

Although the RET was not taken seriously by David Ricardo himself, it was (and still is) taken seriously by most new classical economists. A lot of objections have, however, been raised against the strict validity of the RET. First, if the Ricardian experiment involves changing one or more taxes which distort economic decisions (like a comprehensive income tax) then RET will fail. Intuitively, the lifetime resources available to the households will in that case depend on the particular time path of taxes and not just on the present value of taxes.

Second, if the household is unable to borrow freely, for example because future labour income cannot be used as collateral, then RET fails. Again, the reason for this failure is that the household choice set (and the severity of the household's borrowing constraints) is affected by the time path of taxes chosen by the government.

Third, if households have finite lives whilst the government (and the economy as a whole) is infinitely lived, RET may or may not be valid. It turns out that it matters whether the overlapping generations which populate the economy are altruistically linked with each other or not. Generations are altruistically linked if they care about each other's welfare (like children caring for their parents or vice versa). In the absence of intergenerational altruism, the RET fails. Intuitively, a tax cut now matched (in present value terms) by a tax hike later on will make present generations wealthier and future generations poorer. With intergenerational altruism it is possible that the RET holds because transfers between generations will take place. Intuitively, a tax cut today will be passed on to future generations in the form of an (additional) inheritance.

Other objections to the RET relate to net population growth, informational problems (irrationality, myopia, and lack of information), and the so-called "bird in the hand" fallacy. The upshot of the discussion is that there are ample theoretical reasons to suspect that the RET is not strictly valid. Unfortunately, as is often the case, the empirical evidence regarding the approximate validity of the RET is inconclusive.

Even if one is willing to assume that the RET is valid, this does not mean that public debt has no role to play in the economy. Indeed, according to the theory of tax smoothing the government can use public debt to smooth its tax rates over time. To the extent that these tax rates are distorting the behaviour of private agents, tax smoothing is socially beneficial because it minimizes the distortions of the tax system as a whole. A number of intuitive "rules of thumb" follow from the theory. First, government investment projects earning the market rate of return do not represent a net claim by the government on private sector resources and thus can be financed with government debt. Second, government consumptive spending (including losses on public investment programmes) should be financed by means of taxes. Third, tax rates should be smoothed and not display large fluctuations over time. Fourth, temporary spending shocks can be financed with debt but permanent shocks should be financed with taxes.

Further Reading

The theory of tax smoothing is due to Barro (1979a). Readers interested in the various issues surrounding the government budget constraint and the deficit are referred to Buiter (1985, 1990). The intertemporal consumption model used in this chapter is due to Fisher (1930). See Deaton (1992) and Attanasio (1999) for recent surveys of intertemporal consumption theory.

7

A Closer Look at the Labour Market

The purpose of this chapter is to discuss the following issues:

1. What are some of the most important stylized facts about the labour market in advanced capitalist economies?

2. How can we explain some of these stylized facts in the standard model of the labour market used so far? How do these theories fall short of providing a full explanation?

3. How can we explain real wage rigidity as the outcome of an implicit contractual arrangement between risk-neutral firms and risk-averse workers?

4. What do we mean by efficiency wages and how do they lead to equilibrium unemployment?

7.1 Some Stylized Facts

The stylized facts about the labour market in advanced capitalist countries can be subdivided into the two categories of *time series* evidence and *cross-section* information. The main indicator of labour market performance is the unemployment rate. Ever since the Great Depression of the 1930s this has been at the forefront of macroeconomic research. The following stylized facts about unemployment can be established for most countries in the Western world (see, e.g. Layard et al., 1991, ch. 1).

Fact 1: The unemployment rates fluctuates over time   In Figures 7.1–7.3, we plot the unemployment rate for a number of regions and countries since 1967.[1] As is evident from Figure 7.1, unemployment was relatively low and stable in the EC

---

[1] The data are taken from various issues of the *OECD Economic Outlook*. Where possible we make use of standardized unemployment data.

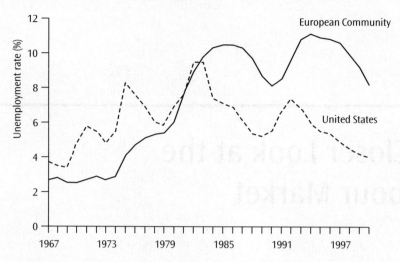

Figure 7.1. Unemployment in the European Community and the United States

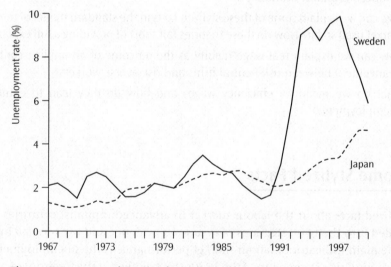

Figure 7.2. Unemployment in Japan and Sweden

up until the time of the first oil shock in 1973. After that, for about a decade, the employment rate followed a steady trend upward, peaking in 1985–1986 and again in 1995. Unemployment in 1997 is estimated to be 10.6% in the EC (this amounts to 17.8 million people out of work!). Unemployment in the US seems to be hovering around 6% during that same period, and in 1997 it stands at 4.9%.

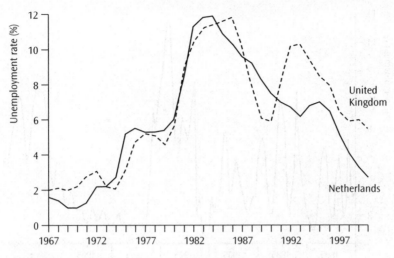

Figure 7.3. Unemployment in the United Kingdom and the Netherlands

The unemployment experience in the US and the EC differs markedly from that in Japan and Sweden.[2] As is shown in Figure 7.2, until the early 1990s, the latter countries have had a stable and low unemployment rate of around 2%. The unemployment experience in the UK looks very much like the EU pattern whereas Dutch unemployment has dropped off rather dramatically during the last few years—see Figure 7.3.

Fact 2: Unemployment fluctuates more between business cycles than within business cycles In Figures 7.4 and 7.5, we plot the unemployment rate for the US and the United Kingdom for extended periods of time.[3] The Great Depression truly deserves its name, especially in the US. Unemployment was very high for a prolonged period of time and peaked at close to 25%! Another thing to note is that, if unemployment were purely a business-cycle phenomenon, one would expect a much more regular pattern than the one observed in these figures. To put the same argument slightly differently, the time series of unemployment displays a lot of *persistence*, much more than is consistent with the business cycle. For example, by regressing unemployment on its own lagged variable, Layard, Nickell, and Jackman

---

[2] We focus on the figures for Sweden because it is a representative member of the European Free Trade Area (EFTA). Other member countries are Norway, Sweden, Finland, Austria, and Switzerland. Lack of data have precluded us from constructing a consistent unemployment index for the EFTA countries.

[3] The data for the period until 1993 have been taken from Mitchell (1998a, pp. 163, 165, 168–169) for the United Kingdom and from Mitchell (1998b, pp. 112, 114) for the United States. The data for the period 1994–2000 have been taken from OECD (2001, Table 21).

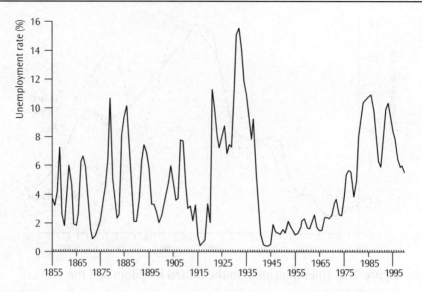

Figure 7.4. Unemployment in the United Kingdom, 1855–2000

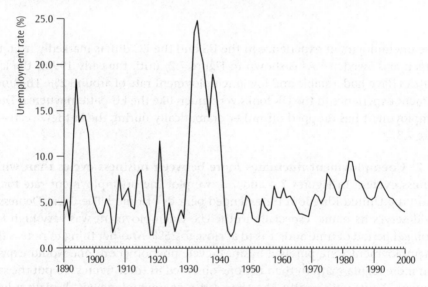

Figure 7.5. Unemployment in the United States, 1890–2000

(1991, p. 77) obtain the following fit for the UK during the period 1900–1989:

$$\hat{U}_t = 0.0041 + \underset{(0.039)}{0.934}\ U_{t-1}, \tag{7.1}$$

and for the US:

$$\hat{U}_t = 0.0080 + \underset{(0.051)}{0.877}U_{t-1}, \tag{7.2}$$

where U_t is the actual unemployment rate at time t and $\hat{U}_t$ is the unemployment rate predicted by the regression equation. The numbers in parentheses are the estimated standard error of the coefficient estimates. In both countries the coefficient for lagged unemployment is high (and close to unity) and significant. This suggests a lot of persistence in the unemployment time series. High persistence implies that it takes a long time before the effects of a particular shock die out (see below).

Fact 3: The rise in European unemployment coincides with an enormous increase in long-term unemployment Almost half of Europe's unemployed have been unemployed for more than one year. In Table 7.1, which is taken from Bean (1994, p. 575), we show the unemployment composition for a number of regions of the developed world for 1979 and 1988. The column "Annual Inflows" measures the percentage inflow into unemployment, i.e. the number of people who lose their job expressed as a percentage of the number of employed people. The column "Annual Outflows" measures the flow out of unemployment, i.e. the number of people that find a job expressed as a percentage of the number of unemployed people.

The striking pattern that can be observed in Table 7.1 is that the inflow rates are relatively similar in the two years, but that the outflow rate in the EC has halved between 1979 and 1988! In words, the high unemployment level in the EC is caused not so much by an increased probability of losing one's job, but rather by a reduction in the probability of finding a job when one is unemployed (Bean, 1994, p. 576).

The same pattern is observed in Table 7.2 which has been taken from Layard, Nickell, and Jackman (1991, ch. 1). Between 1979 and 1990, the total level of unemployment has risen in most countries, but in the ten EC countries the

Table 7.1. The nature of unemployment

		Annual Inflows[a]	Annual Outflows[a]	Long-term Unemployment[b]
European Community	1979	0.27	9.8	29.3
	1988	0.33	5.0	54.8
United States	1979	2.07	43.5	4.2
	1988	1.98	45.7	7.4
Japan	1979	0.31	19.1	16.5
	1988	0.37	17.2	20.6
Non-EC Europe[c]	1979	0.70	38.1	5.3
	1988	0.80	30.4	7.3

Notes:
[a] Percentage of source population
[b] Percentage of total unemployment
[c] Nordic countries only

Source: Bean (1994)

Table 7.2. Unemployment duration by country

	1990			1979		
	All	Under 1 year	Over 1 year	All	Under 1 year	Over 1 year
Belgium	8.7	1.9	6.8	8.2	3.4	4.8
Denmark	9.6	6.8	2.8	6.2	–	–
France	8.9	5.4	3.5	5.9	4.1	1.8
Germany	5.0	2.6	2.4	3.2	2.6	0.6
Ireland	14.0	4.8	9.2	7.1	4.8	2.3
Italy	7.9	2.4	5.5	5.2	3.3	1.9
Netherlands	7.6	3.8	3.8	5.4	3.9	1.5
Portugal	5.1	2.5	2.6	4.8	–	–
Spain	16.2	6.7	9.5	8.5	6.1	2.4
United Kingdom	6.5	3.6	2.9	5.0	3.8	1.3
Australia	6.8	5.2	1.6	6.2	5.1	1.1
New Zealand	7.6	–	–	1.9	–	–
Canada	8.1	7.6	0.5	7.4	7.1	0.3
United States	5.5	5.2	0.3	5.8	5.6	0.2
Japan	2.1	1.7	0.4	2.1	1.7	0.4
Austria	3.3	2.9	0.4	1.7	1.5	0.2
Finland	3.4	2.8	0.6	5.9	4.8	1.1
Norway	5.3	4.7	0.6	2.0	1.9	0.1
Sweden	1.6	1.5	0.1	1.7	1.6	0.1
Switzerland	1.8	–	–	0.9	–	–

Source: Layard, Nickell, and Jackman (1991, p. 6)

rise in long-term unemployment has been much larger than that in short-term unemployment. We shall return to this issue below.

Fact 4: In the very long run unemployment shows no trend   This fact has been graphically illustrated in Figures 7.4 and 7.5. Although there are sharp peaks and deep troughs, there does not seem to be any noticeable trend in the unemployment rate for the US and the UK. This is all the more remarkable in view of the enormous productivity gains that have been made in the last century and a half. Apparently, the nineteenth century luddite fear of physical capital permanently pushing workers into unemployment has proved unfounded.

More formally, and in terms of equations (7.1)–(7.2), the coefficient of the lagged unemployment rate is high but less than unity. Ultimately, there are mechanisms at work whereby unemployment returns to some average level. The convergence to this average level is very slow, however, as can be demonstrated as follows. From equations like (7.1)–(7.2) we can determine the long-term steady-state unemployment rate $\bar{U}$:

$$U_t = \alpha_0 + \alpha_1 U_{t-1} \;\Rightarrow\; \bar{U} = \frac{\alpha_0}{1 - \alpha_1}, \tag{7.3}$$

which would equal 6.21% for the UK, for example.[4] From (7.3) we can compute the adjustment speed by solving the difference equation for U_t. Suppose that the unemployment rate at time $t = 0$ (the reference period) is equal to U_0. Then (7.3) can be solved by repeated substitutions of the kind:

$$U_1 = \alpha_0 + \alpha_1 U_0,$$

$$U_2 = \alpha_0 + \alpha_1 U_1 = \alpha_0 + \alpha_1 [\alpha_0 + \alpha_1 U_0]$$

$$\vdots \quad \vdots$$

$$U_t = \alpha_0 \left[1 + \alpha_1 + \alpha_1^2 + \dots + \alpha_1^{t-1} \right] + \alpha_1^t U_0. \tag{7.4}$$

This expression can be rewritten in the following (more elegant) form:[5]

$$U_t - \bar{U} = [U_0 - \bar{U}] \alpha_1^t. \tag{7.5}$$

Equation (7.5) can be used to determine how long it takes for any discrepancy between U_0 and $\bar{U}$ to be eliminated. Suppose that the unemployment rate is currently U_0 and the long-run unemployment rate is $\bar{U}$. How many periods (t_H) does it take, for example, before half of the difference $(U_0 - \bar{U})$ is eliminated? We can use t_H as the indicator for the adjustment speed in the system. It is calculated as follows:

$$\left[U_{t_H} - \bar{U} \right] \equiv \left[U_0 - \bar{U} \right] \alpha_1^{t_H} = \tfrac{1}{2} \left[U_0 - \bar{U} \right] \;\Rightarrow\;$$

$$\alpha_1^{t_H} = \tfrac{1}{2} \;\Rightarrow\;$$

$$t_H \log \alpha_1 = -\log 2 \;\Rightarrow\; t_H = -\frac{\log 2}{\log \alpha_1}. \tag{7.6}$$

For the UK this amounts to $t_H = 10.15$ years (see (7.1)). Hence, it takes slightly more than a decade before even half of the difference between the actual and the long-run unemployment rate is eliminated.

---

[4] We ignore the fact that we are using estimates for α_0 and α_1, and should really be constructing confidence intervals for $\bar{U}$.

[5] The trick is to write the term in square brackets as:

$$1 + \alpha_1 + \alpha_1^2 + \cdots + \alpha_1^{t-1} = \frac{1 - \alpha_1^t}{1 - \alpha_1}$$

By using this result plus the definition of $\bar{U}$ (given in (7.3), equation (7.5) is obtained.

Fact 5: Unemployment differs a lot between countries As we can see from Table 7.2, the level of unemployment differs a lot even between the countries of Europe. It is very high for countries of the (original) EC, whilst it is very low (and unchanged over time) for other European countries like Norway, Sweden, Finland, Austria, and Switzerland. As we shall see in Chapter 8, a reason for this different unemployment experience may be the different labour market institutions that exist in this second group of countries.

Fact 6: Few unemployed have themselves chosen to become unemployed Only a very small minority of the unemployed have quit a job in order to become unemployed (for example, to search for a new job). The vast majority of unemployment occurs because the workers are laid off by their employer. This fact will prove important in Chapter 9, where we discuss search behaviour.

Fact 7: Unemployment differs a lot between age groups, occupations, regions, races, and sexes Examples are easy to come by. Table 7.3 shows the unemployment rates of workers, by age and by sex, for different countries. Women experience much higher unemployment rates than men, and the young have higher unemployment rates than older workers. The statistics on Italy and Spain are particularly dramatic in this respect! Furthermore, unemployment differs a lot for occupations as well. In Table 7.4 the unemployment rates for blue collar workers and white collar workers are shown for a number of countries. Blue collar workers experience about double the unemployment rate of their (more fortunate) white collar colleagues.

As these stylized facts show, there is quite a lot to be explained about the labour market. The next section is aimed at showing how the standard labour market story used so far can explain some of the stylized facts. We also show in which important aspects it fails to provide an adequate explanation. One of these failures concerns the observed (relative) inflexibility of the real wage rate with respect to demand and productivity shocks. For that reason we also discuss two theories that can explain real wage inflexibility in the final section of this chapter.

7.2 The Standard Macroeconomic Labour Market Theory

7.2.1 Flexible wages and clearing markets

Up to this point we have modelled the labour market in the same way we would model the market for peanuts, i.e. by looking at the aggregate demand and supply schedules (for labour in this case; see Chapter 1). Although a high level of aggregation is the hallmark of macroeconomics, this approach flies in the face of the evidence unearthed in the previous section. For example, suppose that one wishes to use the standard approach to explain why blue collar workers experience a higher

Table 7.3. Sex composition of unemployment

	All	Over 25		Under 25	
		Men	Women	Men	Women
Belgium	11.0	5.6	15.3	16.0	27.1
Denmark	7.8	5.2	9.4	9.3	11.9
France	10.5	6.4	10.1	19.6	27.9
Germany	6.2	5.1	7.5	6.1	8.5
Greece	7.4	3.8	6.7	15.5	35.1
Ireland	17.5	13.5	18.5	27.2	22.6
Italy	7.9	2.3	6.5	21.0	30.1
Netherlands	9.6	6.8	11.7	14.2	14.3
Portugal	7.0	3.3	5.6	13.1	21.5
Spain	20.1	11.9	16.8	39.9	50.1
United Kingdom	10.2	8.8	8.0	16.9	14.6
Australia	8.0	5.6	6.1	15.0	14.5
New Zealand	4.1	1.9	2.4	6.1	5.5
Canada	8.8	7.0	8.4	14.9	12.5
United States	6.1	4.8	4.8	12.6	11.7
Japan	2.8	2.6	2.4	5.4	5.0
Austria	3.8	3.4	3.7	4.4	4.7
Finland	5.0	5.0	3.8	9.7	8.1
Norway	2.1	1.8	1.5	3.8	3.9
Sweden	1.9	1.4	1.5	4.4	4.0
Switzerland	2.4	–	–	–	–

Source: Layard, Nickell, and Jackman (1991, p. 7)

unemployment rate than white collar workers (see Fact 7). Obviously, this can be done by distinguishing two types of labour. Call the blue collar workers "unskilled" labour (denoted by N_U) and the white collar workers "skilled" labour (N_S). The production function of the representative firm is given by:

$$Y = G(N_U, N_S, \bar{K}) = G(N_U, N_S, 1) \equiv F(N_U, N_S), \tag{7.7}$$

where Y is output, and the capital stock is fixed in the short run at $\bar{K} = 1$. Hence, $F(N_U, N_S)$ is the short-run production function that satisfies $F_U \equiv \partial F/\partial N_U > 0$, $F_S \equiv \partial F/\partial N_S > 0$, $F_{UU} \equiv \partial^2 F/\partial N_U^2 < 0$, and $F_{SS} \equiv \partial^2 F/\partial N_S^2 < 0$.

The representative firm maximizes profit by choosing the optimal production level. With perfect competition in the output market and both input markets, the output price P and the wage rates W_U and W_S are taken as given by the firm and

Table 7.4. The skill composition of unemployment

		Blue Collar	White Collar
Australia	1986	6.6	3.2
	1987	6.5	3.3
	1992	9.9	4.2
	1993	8.9	4.0
Canada	1983	15.9	8.9
	1984	14.4	8.7
	1991	15.0	7.7
	1992	15.6	8.6
	1993	15.2	8.6
United Kingdom	1985	9.7	5.3
	1986	9.6	5.2
	1992	13.2	5.8
	1993	13.9	6.3
United States	1983	13.5	6.3
	1984	9.8	5.0
	1991	9.4	4.7
	1992	10.1	5.3
	1993	9.0	4.9

Source: OECD (1994, p. 15)

the choice problem is:

$$\max_{\{N_U, N_S\}} \Pi \equiv PF(N_U, N_S) - W_U N_U - W_S N_S, \tag{7.8}$$

which yields the usual marginal productivity conditions:

$$PF_U(N_U, N_S) = W_U, \quad PF_S(N_U, N_S) = W_S. \tag{7.9}$$

In words, the value of the marginal product of each type of labour must be equated to its wage rate. Obviously, the expressions in equation (7.9) can be used to derive the demand functions for the two types of labour. By total differentiation of the two equations, we obtain the following matrix expression:

$$\begin{bmatrix} dN_S \\ dN_U \end{bmatrix} = \left(\frac{1}{F_{SS}F_{UU} - F_{SU}^2} \right) \begin{bmatrix} F_{UU} & -F_{SU} \\ -F_{SU} & F_{SS} \end{bmatrix} \begin{bmatrix} dw_S \\ dw_U \end{bmatrix}, \tag{7.10}$$

where $w_S \equiv W_S/P$, $w_U \equiv W_U/P$, and $F_{SU} \equiv \partial^2 F/\partial N_S N_U$. The term in round brackets on the right-hand side of (7.10) is positive for any well-behaved production function. Equation (7.10) can be used to find all the comparative static results of the demand functions for the two types of labour:

$$N_S^D = N_S^D(w_S, w_U), \quad N_U^D = N_U^D(w_S, w_U), \tag{7.11}$$

where the "own" real wage effects are guaranteed to be negative:

$$N_{SS}^D \equiv \frac{\partial N_S^D}{\partial w_S} < 0, \quad N_{UU}^D \equiv \frac{\partial N_U^D}{\partial w_U} < 0. \tag{7.12}$$

The "cross" real wage effects cannot be signed without making further assumptions. Assume that skilled and unskilled labour are *gross substitutes*. This implies that F_{SU} is negative, and the cross partial derivatives are both positive:

$$N_{SU}^D \equiv \frac{\partial N_S^D}{\partial w_U} > 0, \quad N_{US}^D \equiv \frac{\partial N_U^D}{\partial w_S} > 0. \tag{7.13}$$

In words, if unskilled labour becomes dearer, the demand for skilled labour increases, and similarly if skilled labour becomes more expensive, the demand for unskilled labour increases. This is because the two factors can be used as substitutes in the production process.

In order to close the model as simply as possible, we assume that the supply curves of the two types of labour are perfectly inelastic.

$$N_S^S = \bar{N}_S, \quad N_U^S = \bar{N}_U. \tag{7.14}$$

The equilibrium in the two labour markets can be drawn as in Figure 7.6.

If wages are perfectly flexible, full employment is attained in both markets. This is the case at points E_0^S and E_0^U, respectively. How can we nevertheless provide an explanation for the high unemployment rate among unskilled workers? A simple explanation runs as follows. Suppose that there is a minimum wage law, which states

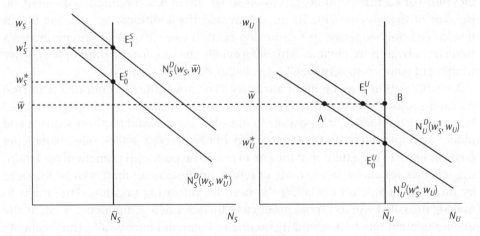

Figure 7.6. The markets for skilled and unskilled labour

that the *real* wage of *any* worker (irrespective of that worker's skill level) must not fall below $\bar{w}$. This minimum wage is at a level below the market clearing real wage in the market for skilled labour, but above the equilibrium real wage in the unskilled labour market. As a result, the minimum wage is binding in the market for unskilled labour, and unemployment emerges in that market equal to the segment AB in the right-hand panel of Figure 7.6. This is not the end of the story, however, since the high real wage of unskilled workers prompts the representative firm to substitute skilled for unskilled labour. The demand for skilled labour shifts to the right, and the skilled real wage rate rises. This partially offsets the initial unemployment effect by stimulating the demand for unskilled labour a little. Ultimately, the unemployment equilibrium with minimum wages occurs at points E_1^S and E_1^U, respectively.

We have developed a very simple representation of the bottom end of the labour market. There is unemployment in the market for unskilled labour because this type of labour is too expensive: the marginal product of this type of labour is simply too low, given the existence of a binding minimum wage, to be consistent with full employment. We recognize (from Chapter 5) that the minimum wage causes *Classical Unemployment* in the market for unskilled labour.

A number of policy options exist to solve this type of unemployment. First, the minimum wage could be abolished. This will obviously work, but may cause politically undesirable income distribution effects, social unrest, etc. Hence, some package of transfers to unskilled workers may be unavoidable. Second, unskilled labour could be subsidized. In terms of Figure 7.6, this amounts to shifting the demand for unskilled labour up and to the right. The demand for unskilled labour is artificially stimulated to make the minimum wage less of a disequilibrium wage. Third, the government can directly employ some unskilled workers at the going minimum wage. Again, the demand for unskilled labour shifts to the right, and unemployment is reduced. The problem with this option is that the jobs that are created tend to be "dead-end" jobs (like having three men guarding the Town Clerk's bicycle). For all three options discussed so far, there is a revenue requirement on the part of the government. To the extent that the additional tax revenue that is needed can only be raised in a distorting fashion (see Chapter 6), the net benefits to society are far from obvious. This is especially the case for the third option, since nothing of value to society may be created in dead-end jobs.

A fourth option may be more attractive. The government could invest in (re-) training projects specifically targeted at unskilled workers. By making unskilled labour more productive, it is possible to stimulate the demand for those workers and reduce unemployment. In the terminology of Chapter 6, a golden rule of financing could be used: to the extent that the rate of return on public investment in (re-) training schemes equals the market rate of return, such schemes may even be financed by means of debt, thus obviating the need for distorting taxation. The return to making unskilled workers more productive includes two components. First, as the unemployment rate falls, spending on unemployment benefits falls, thus reducing the government's revenue requirement. Second, as the previously unemployed find work, they also start to pay taxes, thus further reducing the government's revenue requirement.

In conclusion, even our very simple standard model can be used to derive sensible conclusions about the labour market. If we look at the Dutch situation, for example, the relative wage of unskilled versus skilled labour (i.e. W_U/W_S) has risen during the last decade! Hence, this is a possible explanation for stylized Fact 7: unemployment among unskilled workers is high because this type of labour is too dear. Most economists agree that this is partially true, but that other elements also play a role.

7.2.2 The effects of taxation

Before leaving the standard model of the aggregate labour market, we turn to an analysis of the effects of taxation on employment and the real wage rate. This analysis was commenced in Chapter 1 (see section 3.6 on the supply siders) and is completed here. Attention is restricted to the short run, i.e. the capital stock is assumed to be constant (and equal to $\bar{K}$). There is only one type of labour, and the representative firm maximizes short-run profit which is defined as:

$$\Pi \equiv PF(N, \bar{K}) - W(1 + t_E)N, \tag{7.15}$$

where t_E is an *ad valorem* tax levied on the firm's use of labour (e.g. the employer's contribution to social security). The usual argument leads to the marginal productivity condition for labour, $F_N(N, \bar{K}) = W(1 + t_E)/P$. This expression can be loglinearized:

$$\tilde{N}^D = -\epsilon_D \left[\tilde{w} + \tilde{t}_E \right], \tag{7.16}$$

where $w \equiv W/P$ is the gross real wage, $\epsilon_D \equiv -F_N/(NF_{NN})$ is the absolute value of the labour demand elasticity, $\tilde{N}^D \equiv dN^D/N^D$, $\tilde{t}_E \equiv dt_E/(1 + t_E)$, and $\tilde{w} \equiv dw/w$.

Most income tax systems in use in the developed countries are *progressive*, in the sense that the tax rate rises with the tax base (labour income in this case). Since we wish to investigate the effects of progressivity on the labour supply decision by households, we specify the general tax function $T(WN^S)$. The marginal tax rate t_M facing households coincides with the derivative of this function with respect to income, i.e. $t_M \equiv dT(WN^S)/d(WN^S)$. In the absence of taxable income from other sources, the average tax rate is simply $t_A \equiv T(WN^S)/(WN^S)$. The household's utility function is assumed to be of the usual kind:

$$U = U(C, 1 - N^S), \tag{7.17}$$

with $U_C > 0$, $U_{1-N} > 0$, $U_{CC} < 0$, $U_{1-N,1-N} < 0$. In addition to facing (progressive) income taxes, the household also has to pay an *ad valorem* tax on consumption goods (e.g. a value-added tax, t_C), so that the household budget restriction is:

$$P(1 + t_C)C = WN^S - T(WN^S) \equiv (1 - t_A)WN^S. \tag{7.18}$$

The household maximizes utility by choosing the optimal level of consumption and labour supply. The Lagrangean is:

$$\mathcal{L} \equiv U(C, 1 - N^S) + \lambda \left[(1 - t_A)WN^S - P(1 + t_C)C \right], \tag{7.19}$$

yielding the first-order conditions:

$$\frac{\partial \mathcal{L}}{\partial C} = U_C - \lambda P(1 + t_C) = 0, \tag{7.20}$$

$$\frac{\partial \mathcal{L}}{\partial N^S} = -U_{1-N} + \lambda W \left[(1 - t_A) - N^S \left(\frac{dt_A}{dN^S} \right) \right] = 0. \tag{7.21}$$

In view of the definition of the tax function, however, it is straightforward to derive that $N^S(dt_A/dN^S) = t_M - t_A$, so that (7.20)–(7.21) can be combined to yield the expansion path:[6]

$$\lambda = \frac{U_C}{P(1 + t_C)} = \frac{U_{1-N}}{W(1 - t_M)} \quad \Rightarrow$$

$$\frac{U_{1-N}}{U_C} = w \left(\frac{1 - t_M}{1 + t_C} \right), \tag{7.22}$$

where we have used the definition of the gross real wage w. Equation (7.22) drives home a very important point: the marginal rate of substitution between leisure and consumption depends on the marginal (and not on the average) tax rate facing households!

In order to facilitate the discussion to come, we assume that the utility function (7.17) is homothetic and define the substitution elasticity between consumption and leisure as follows:

$$\sigma_{CM} = \frac{\%\text{ge change in } C/(1 - N^S)}{\%\text{ge change in } U_{1-N}/U_C} \equiv \frac{d \log(C/(1 - N^S))}{d \log(U_{1-N}/U_C)} \geq 0. \tag{7.23}$$

Intuitively, σ_{CM} measures how "easy" it is (in utility terms) for the household to substitute consumption for leisure. A household with a very low value of σ_{CM}, finds substitution very difficult, whereas a household with a high σ_{CM} is quite

---

[6] The average tax rate is defined as $t_A \equiv T(WN^S)/(WN^S)$. By differentiating with respect to N^S we obtain:

$$\frac{dt_A}{dN^S} = \frac{1}{W} \left(\frac{N^S WT'(WN^S) - T(WN^S)}{(N^S)^2} \right).$$

By rearranging this expression we obtain the result mentioned in the text.

happy to substitute consumption for leisure. In graphical terms, the former house-hold has sharp kinks in its indifference curves,[7] whereas the latter has relatively flat indifference curves. The substitution elasticity can be used in the linearization of (7.22):

$$d \log (U_{1-N}/U_C) = \tilde{w} - \tilde{t}_M - \tilde{t}_C = (1/\sigma_{CM})\left[\tilde{C} - \widetilde{(1 - N^S)}\right] \quad \Rightarrow$$

$$\tilde{C} + (1/\omega_L)\tilde{N}^S = \sigma_{CM}\left[\tilde{w} - \tilde{t}_M - \tilde{t}_C\right], \tag{7.24}$$

where $\tilde{t}_M \equiv dt_M/(1 - t_M)$, $\tilde{t}_C \equiv dt_C/(1 + t_C)$, and $\omega_L \equiv (1 - N^S)/N^S$ is the initial ratio of leisure to labour supply. The budget restriction (7.18) can also be linearized:

$$\tilde{C} + \tilde{t}_C = \tilde{w} - \tilde{t}_A + \tilde{N}^S, \tag{7.25}$$

where $\tilde{t}_A \equiv dt_A/(1 - t_A)$. Hence, the average income tax rate influences the budget restriction of the household.

By solving (7.24)–(7.25) for the change in labour supply, the following expression is obtained:

$$\tilde{N}^S = (1 - N^S)\left[(\sigma_{CM} - 1)\tilde{w} - \sigma_{CM}(\tilde{t}_M + \tilde{t}_C) + \tilde{t}_A + \tilde{t}_C\right]$$

$$= \bar{\epsilon}_{SW}\left[\tilde{w} - \tilde{t}_M - \tilde{t}_C\right] + \epsilon_{SI}\left[\tilde{t}_A + \tilde{t}_C - \tilde{w}\right]$$

$$= \epsilon_{SW}\left[\tilde{w} - \tilde{t}_C\right] - \bar{\epsilon}_{SW}\tilde{t}_M + \epsilon_{SI}\tilde{t}_A, \tag{7.26}$$

where $\bar{\epsilon}_{SW} \equiv \sigma_{CM}(1 - N^S)$ is the *compensated* wage elasticity, and $\epsilon_{SI} \equiv (1 - N^S)$ is the income elasticity. The compensated wage elasticity corresponds to the substitution effect and is always non-negative. The income elasticity of labour supply corresponds to the income effect and is always negative. The total effect of a change in the gross wage is measured by the *uncompensated* wage elasticity, $\epsilon_{SW} \equiv \bar{\epsilon}_{SW} - \epsilon_{SI} = (\sigma_{CM} - 1)(1 - N^S)$, which may be positive, zero, or even negative, depending on the magnitude of σ_{CM}. If the elasticity of substitution between leisure time and consumption (σ_{CM}) exceeds unity, the substitution effect dominates the income effect and thus labour supply is an increasing function of the real wage. Otherwise, the income effect dominates the substitution effect and labour supply slopes back-wards. Empirical studies report that the wage elasticity of labour supply (ϵ_S) is fairly small for males, but bigger for females (see Pencavel, 1986 and Killingsworth and Heckman, 1986).

The demand and supply equations of the standard model of the labour mar-ket (expanded with various tax rates) are given in linearized form by, respectively, equations (7.16) and (7.26). There are several ways to close the model. For example,

---

[7] This does not imply that this household is kinky. It just means that the household is very reluctant to deviate from a fixed proportion between consumption and leisure. In case $\sigma_{CM} = 0$, the indifference curves are at right angles, and nothing will make the household deviate from a fixed proportion between consumption and leisure.

Table 7.5. Taxes and the competitive labour market

	(a) Flexible wage			(b) Fixed consumer wage		
	$\tilde{w}$	$\tilde{N}$	dU	$\tilde{w}$	$\tilde{N}$	dU
$\tilde{t}_M$	$\dfrac{\bar{\epsilon}_{SW}}{\epsilon_{SW}+\epsilon_D}$	$-\dfrac{\epsilon_D\bar{\epsilon}_{SW}}{\epsilon_{SW}+\epsilon_D}$	0	0	0	$-\bar{\epsilon}_{SW}$
$\tilde{t}_A$	$-\dfrac{\epsilon_{SI}}{\epsilon_{SW}+\epsilon_D}$	$\dfrac{\epsilon_D\epsilon_{SI}}{\epsilon_{SW}+\epsilon_D}$	0	1	$-\epsilon_D$	$\bar{\epsilon}_{SW}+\epsilon_D$
$\tilde{t}_M=\tilde{t}_A$	$\dfrac{\epsilon_{SW}}{\epsilon_{SW}+\epsilon_D}$	$-\dfrac{\epsilon_D\epsilon_{SW}}{\epsilon_{SW}+\epsilon_D}$	0	1	$-\epsilon_D$	ϵ_D
$\tilde{t}_E$	$-\dfrac{\epsilon_D}{\epsilon_{SW}+\epsilon_D}$	$-\dfrac{\epsilon_D\epsilon_{SW}}{\epsilon_{SW}+\epsilon_D}$	0	0	$-\epsilon_D$	ϵ_D
$\tilde{t}_C$	$-\dfrac{\epsilon_{SW}}{\epsilon_{SW}+\epsilon_D}$	$-\dfrac{\epsilon_D\epsilon_{SW}}{\epsilon_{SW}+\epsilon_D}$	0	1	$-\epsilon_D$	ϵ_D
$\tilde{w}_C$	$-$	$-$	$-$	1	$-\epsilon_D$	$\epsilon_{SW}+\epsilon_D$

the equilibrium interpretation postulates flexible wages and assumes continuous market clearing ($\tilde{N} = \tilde{N}^D = \tilde{N}^S$). Since we also wish to discuss the effect of different tax rates on unemployment, the *disequilibrium* interpretation requires the real wage to be fixed at a level that is too high for market clearing. In Table 7.5 we calculate the effects of the different taxes on employment, the gross real wage rate, and unemployment for both the equilibrium and disequilibrium interpretations of the model.

Tax effects with flexible wages and a clearing labour market

Suppose that the policy maker wishes to make the tax system more progressive, without however, changing the average tax rate. In terms of Table 7.5(a), this means that $\tilde{t}_M > 0$ and all other tax rates remain constant ($\tilde{t}_A = \tilde{t}_E = \tilde{t}_C = 0$). Due to the higher marginal tax rate, households supply less labour at the same gross real wage rate, and labour supply shifts to the left. In terms of Figure 7.7, the equilibrium moves from E_0 to E_1, and the gross wage rate increases.[8] Part of the tax is shifted from households to the firms (segment E_1B) because they have to pay higher wages to the households. The degree of tax shifting depends on the elasticities of the demand and supply curves.

If, on the other hand, the policy maker increases the average income tax, keeping the marginal tax and all other taxes unchanged, the effects on the labour market are completely different. The situation (for $\epsilon_{SW} > 0$) is also depicted in Figure 7.7. As

---

[8] This holds regardless of the sign of ϵ_{SW}, provided the stability condition $\epsilon_{SW} + \epsilon_D > 0$ is satisfied. In terms of Figure 7.5, the labour supply curve can be downward sloping but it must be steeper than the labour demand curve. Otherwise, high wages would be associated with excess demand for labour. There is no plausible real wage adjustment mechanism that would lead to stability in that case.

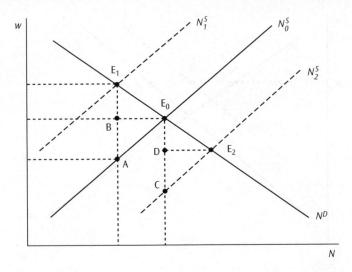

Figure 7.7. The effects of taxation when wages are flexible

a result of the higher average tax, households feel poorer and start to supply more labour. This shifts the labour supply curve to the right, the equilibrium moves from E_0 to E_2 so that the real wage falls and employment rises.

Tax effects with rigid consumer wages and unemployment

Assume now that (for whatever reason) the real consumer wage is exogenously fixed above the level consistent with full employment. The real consumer wage is defined as the real wage after income taxes and the tax on goods have been taken into account, i.e. $w_C \equiv w(1 - t_A)/(1 + t_C)$. In loglinearized form we have that:

$$\tilde{w}_C \equiv \tilde{w} - \tilde{t}_A - \tilde{t}_C. \tag{7.27}$$

In view of this definition, equations (7.16) and (7.26) can be rewritten in terms of the exogenous real consumer wage:

$$\tilde{N}^D = -\epsilon_D \left[\tilde{w}_C + \tilde{t}_A + \tilde{t}_E + \tilde{t}_C \right], \tag{7.28}$$

$$\tilde{N}^S = \epsilon_{SW} \tilde{w}_C + \bar{\epsilon}_{SW} \left[\tilde{t}_A - \tilde{t}_M \right]. \tag{7.29}$$

By assumption the real consumer wage is too high for full employment, so that the minimum transaction rule says that employment is determined by the demand for labour (see Chapter 5), i.e. $N = N^D$ which implies in loglinearized form that $\tilde{N} = \tilde{N}^D$. Unemployment is defined as $U \equiv (N^S - N^D)/N^D \approx \log N^S - \log N^D$, so that

175

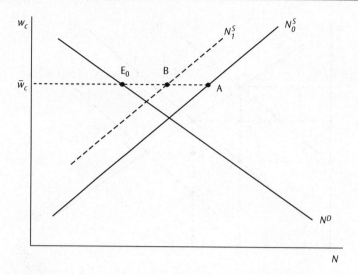

Figure 7.8. The effects of taxation with a fixed consumer wage

we have for the change in unemployment:

$$dU = \tilde{N}^S - \tilde{N}^D. \tag{7.30}$$

Equations (7.28)–(7.30) determine employment, labour supply, and the unemployment rate as a function of the tax rates and the exogenous real consumer wage. Equation (7.27) can be used to determine what happens to the gross real wage.

Consider what happens if the marginal tax rate on labour is increased, leaving all other taxes unchanged. For the given real consumer wage, labour supply is decreased and labour demand is unchanged. Consequently, unemployment is reduced. Some of the unemployed hours of labour are no longer supplied due to the disincentive effect of the higher marginal tax rate. This policy experiment has been illustrated in Figure 7.8. The economy is initially at E_0 and stays there. The reduction in unemployment is represented by the horizontal segment BA. The students are advised to work through the entries of Table 7.5(b), and verify their understanding by drawing pictures.

7.3 Real Wage Rigidity

There exists a fundamental tension in the labour market theories that are based on perfectly competitive behaviour and flexible wages. From microeconometric research we know that the labour supply curve of (especially male) workers is highly inelastic (almost vertical). Macroeconometric research, on the other hand, shows

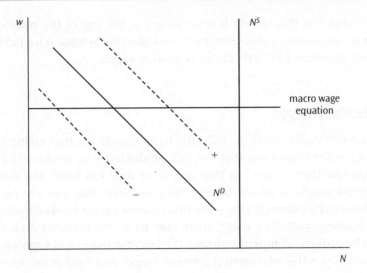

Figure 7.9. Labour demand and supply and the macroeconomic wage equation

that employment does fluctuate, for example due to productivity or demand shocks. In terms of Figure 7.9, this implies that the macroeconomic supply equation is not vertical but almost horizontal. What could be the microeconomic rationale behind such a horizontal real wage equation? In other words, why are real wages inflexible? A number of theories have been proposed to answer this question.

7.3.1 Implicit contracts

The theory of implicit contracts was formulated in the mid-1970s by Azariadis (1975) in the hope (and expectation) that it could ultimately provide the microeconomic foundation for the quantity rationing models that are characterized by real wage rigidity (see Chapter 5). Although implicit contract models are relatively complex, the basic idea is quite simple. There is uncertainty about the state of the world, for example due to random productivity shocks. Households dislike uncertainty and are *risk averse*. Firms, on the other hand, do not care much about uncertainty, and are *risk neutral*.

Under these circumstances, a Pareto-efficient trade is possible between the firm and its workers (the households). In exchange for a stable real wage, employees pay an *insurance premium* to the employer by agreeing to work at a lower real wage. This means that wages are, in equilibrium, "too low" (compared to the Walrasian outcome without implicit contracts) so that employment is "too high" (compared to the Walrasian outcome without implicit contracts). Hence, implicit contract theory does provide a rationale for real wage rigidity but not for (involuntary) unemployment. For that reason it is no longer at the top of the research agenda of most macroeconomists studying the labour market. Instead, a lot of them have turned their attention to the theory of efficiency wages.

7.3.2 Efficiency wages

As is argued by Stiglitz (1986, p. 182), the basic hypothesis underlying the family of efficiency wage theories is that the net productivity of workers is a function of the wage rate they receive. In that case firms may not lower the wage even if there is excess supply of labour because they may fear that the adverse effect on worker productivity outweighs the reduction in the wage per worker, thus increasing actual total labour cost. As a result, there may be unemployment even in a world populated by perfectly competitive firms. The law of demand and supply is repealed. Furthermore, since the relationship between wages and worker productivity may differ between industries, wages (for otherwise identical workers) may also differ across industries, thus repealing the law of one price.

As Stiglitz (1986) shows, there are at least five different explanations for the link between wages and workers' productivity. First, it has been argued in the development literature that there is a direct link between productivity and the level of nutrition, especially at low levels of nutrition. This link gives rise to an S-shaped wage–productivity curve as is drawn, for example, in Figure 7.10. The second theory leading to efficiency wage effects is based on labour turnover. The lower the wage, the higher the rate of labour turnover. To the extent that the firm must incur training costs for new workers, this mechanism gives rise to a link between the wage and the worker's productivity. The third theory is based on imperfect information

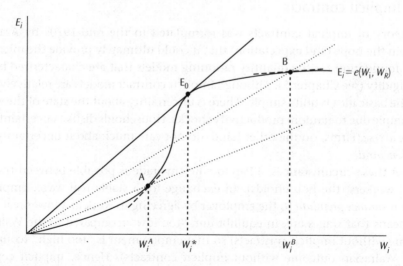

Figure 7.10. Efficiency wages

on the part of the firm about the characteristics of the worker. By paying a high wage the firm obtains a high quality labour force. The fourth theory is based on the imperfect information that the firm has about the workers' actions and the cost of monitoring them. Unemployment works as a disciplining device (Shapiro and Stiglitz, 1984): if workers are caught shirking on the job, they are fired and become unemployed (for some time). Note that there are other (potentially more efficient) means by which the firm can induce the good behaviour of its work force. An example is the use of bonding. Upon entering employment in the firm, the worker pays a bond up front, to be forfeited to the firm if he/she is caught shirking. Apart from the moral hazard problem that the firm may have (wrongfully accusing the worker of shirking, leading to the forfeit of her/his bond), poor workers may have no way to borrow the money for the performance bond. Hence, to the extent that poor/unskilled workers have restricted access to the capital market, this theory may explain why these groups experience a higher unemployment rate (Stiglitz, 1986, p. 186). The fifth theory suggests that workers' performance depends on whether they believe they are being treated fairly. In this sociological theory the workers are particularly interested in their wage relative to that of other workers.

A simple model of efficiency wages

Suppose that the effort level of a worker in firm i is denoted by E_i, and depends positively on the wage paid in firm i (W_i) and negatively on the wage that can be obtained elsewhere (W_R):

$$E_i \equiv e(W_i, W_R), \quad e_W > 0, \quad e_{W_R} < 0. \tag{7.31}$$

The idea is simple: if you pay your workers well (as did Henry Ford), they are likely to display a lot of effort. Conversely, "if you pay peanuts, you get (lazy) monkeys". Let N_i denote the number of workers that are employed in firm i, so that $L_i \equiv E_i N_i$ is the total number of efficiency units of labour employed by the firm. In the absence of capital, these efficiency units of labour lead to output via the production function $F(L_i)$. The firm maximizes profits, that are defined as follows:

$$\Pi_i \equiv P_i A F(E_i N_i) - W_i N_i, \tag{7.32}$$

where A is an index for general productivity, and P_i is the price charged by firm i for its product. The firm chooses its level of employment (N_i) and wage rate (W_i) in order to maximize profit. The first-order conditions are:

$$\frac{\partial \Pi_i}{\partial N_i} = P_i A E_i F_L(E_i N_i) - W_i = 0, \tag{7.33}$$

$$\frac{\partial \Pi_i}{\partial W_i} = P_i A N_i F_L(E_i N_i) e_W(W_i, W_R) - N_i = 0, \tag{7.34}$$

where F_L is the marginal product of labour measured in efficiency units. By substituting these two conditions, the expression determining the *efficiency wage* for firm

i is obtained:

$$\frac{W_i e_W(W_i, W_R)}{e(W_i, W_R)} = 1. \tag{7.35}$$

This expression says that the firm should find the wage for which the elasticity of the effort function equals unity. The firm should keep increasing its wage rate as long as the effort rises faster than the wage rate (and the wage per unit of effort keeps falling). In terms of Figure 7.10, the optimum is at point E_0. This is the only point where the tangent of the effort curve goes through the origin, thus ensuring that the unit-elasticity condition (7.35) is satisfied.[9]

Once the efficiency wage and hence the optimal effort level have been determined, the number of workers that are employed by the firm is determined by equation (7.33). By aggregating over all firms the aggregate demand for labour (measured in terms of workers) is obtained. From the structure of the model, there is no reason at all to expect that full employment will prevail. Productivity shocks have no effect on the efficiency wage chosen by the firms, and hence only affect employment. Hence, this model provides a partial equilibrium reason for the horizontal real wage equation drawn in Figure 7.9.

Up to this point we have not yet determined W_R. The model developed by Summers (1988) provides a particularly simple illustration of how W_R may depend on the unemployment rate and the level of unemployment benefits. The effort function is specialized to:

$$E_i = (W_i - W_R)^\epsilon, \quad 0 < \epsilon < 1, \tag{7.36}$$

where ϵ measures the strength of the productivity-enhancing effects of high wages, which we call the *leap-frogging effect*. Assume that W_R represents the value of the outside option for the workers, i.e. it represents what workers get if they are not employed by firm i. We assume that W_R is a weighted average of the average wage paid by other firms in the economy ($\bar{W}$) and the unemployment benefit (B):

$$W_R = (1 - U)\bar{W} + UB = \bar{W}[1 - U + \beta U], \tag{7.37}$$

where U is the unemployment rate, and $\beta \equiv B/\bar{W}$ is the unemployment benefit expressed as a proportion of the average wage paid in the economy (the so-called replacement rate). We assume that β is constant, i.e. the government indexes the unemployment benefit to the average wage rate.

---

[9] The ray from the origin has slope E_i/W_i. At point E_0 this ray is tangent to the effort curve, i.e. $E_i/W_i = e_W$ or $W_i e_W/E_i = 1$ at that point. At point A (B) the effort curve is steeper (flatter) than the ray from the origin and $W_i e_W/E_i > 1$ (< 1). Hence, W_i^A is too low, and W_i^B is too high.

In view of (7.35) and (7.36), the efficiency wage is easily calculated:

$$\frac{W_i}{E_i}\frac{\partial E_i}{\partial W_i} = 1 \quad \Rightarrow \quad \left(\frac{W_i - W_R}{W_i}\right) = \epsilon \quad \Leftrightarrow \quad W_i = \frac{W_R}{1-\epsilon}. \tag{7.38}$$

The firm pays a constant markup $(1/(1-\epsilon))$ times the value of the outside option. But equation (7.38) is not the end of the story. If all firms are treated symmetrically in equilibrium, we have that the average wage that is paid coincides with the optimal wage paid by firm i (determined in (7.38)), i.e. $W_i = \bar{W}$. By substituting this into (7.37), and using (7.38) we obtain the expression for the equilibrium unemployment rate U^*:

$$W_i = \bar{W} = \frac{W_R}{1-\epsilon} = \frac{\bar{W}(1 - U + \beta U)}{1-\epsilon} \quad \Rightarrow \quad U^* = \frac{\epsilon}{1-\beta}. \tag{7.39}$$

Obviously, a meaningful solution is only obtained if the unemployment benefit is strictly less than the average wage, or $0 < \beta < 1$. Even though the model underlying (7.39) is extremely simple, it provides some very clear and intuitive conclusions. First, the higher the leapfrogging coefficient, the higher is the equilibrium unemployment rate. Second, the lower the indexing coefficient β, the lower is equilibrium unemployment.

The mechanism behind these results can be illustrated with the aid of Figure 7.11. On the vertical axis we plot the optimal wage of firm i relative to the average wage paid by other firms in the economy $(W_i/\bar{W})$. By using (7.37)–(7.38), the relative wage paid by firm i can be written as:

$$\frac{W_i}{\bar{W}} = \frac{1 - (1-\beta)U}{1-\epsilon}, \quad \text{RW curve.} \tag{7.40}$$

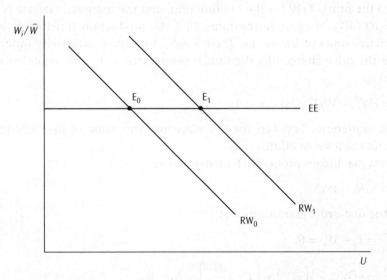

Figure 7.11. The relative wage and unemployment

The relative wage curve (RW) is a downward-sloping function of the unemployment rate U. The labour market is in symmetric (unemployment) equilibrium if firm i pays the same wage as all other firms (which therefore also equals the market average wage). Hence, the horizontal line EE gives the equilibrium condition, $W_i/\bar{W} = 1$. The equilibrium is at E_0. Suppose that the government increases the indexing coefficient β. This shifts the RW locus up and to the right. For a given level of unemployment, the pain associated with being unemployed is reduced and firm i must pay a higher relative wage than before in order to attract workers. This cannot be an equilibrium, however, since every firm wishes to pay a higher relative wage (thus driving $W_i/\bar{W}$ back to unity), thereby leading the economy to the new equilibrium at E_1, with a higher level of unemployment.

As is pointed out by Summers (1988, p. 385), the model can explain why unemployment is high in particular segments of the population. For example, young people may value leisure more highly than older people, and consequently have a higher rate of turnover and hence a higher value of ϵ. As equation (7.39) shows, the unemployment rate for young people is also higher in that case. Similarly, mobility for (blue collar) construction workers is higher than for other occupations, again suggesting a higher value for ϵ and a higher unemployment rate for this group of workers.

Progressive taxation and efficiency wages

As a final application of the efficiency wage model, we now consider the effects of progressive taxation on the unemployment rate. We assume that the wage rate received after tax is equal to $W_i^N = (1 - t_A)W_i$, where t_A is the average tax rate paid by the worker, and $t_A \equiv T(W_i)/W_i$ (recall that each worker supplies one unit of labour to the firm). $T(W_i)$ is the tax function, and the marginal tax rate is defined as $t_M \equiv dT/dW_i$. Assume furthermore that the production function is linear in the efficiency units of labour, i.e. $F(L_i) = E_i N_i$, that the productivity index $A = 1$, and that the price charged by the firm is normalized at $P_i = 1$. Equation (7.36) is modified to:

$$E_i = \left(W_i^N - W_R\right)^\epsilon, \quad 0 < \epsilon < 1, \tag{7.41}$$

where the difference between the net wage and the value of the outside option determines the level of effort.

The firm maximizes profits that are defined as:

$$\Pi_i \equiv E_i N_i - W_i N_i, \tag{7.42}$$

so that the first-order conditions are:

$$\frac{\partial \Pi_i}{\partial N_i} = E_i - W_i = 0, \tag{7.43}$$

$$\frac{\partial \Pi_i}{\partial W_i} = \epsilon(W_i^N - W_R)^{\epsilon-1} N_i \left[1 - \frac{dT}{dW_i}\right] - N_i = 0. \tag{7.44}$$

By combining (7.43)–(7.44) and noting the definitions of t_A and t_M, we obtain the expression for the efficiency wage:

$$\left(W_i^N - W_R\right)^{\epsilon-1} (1 - t_M) = \frac{1}{\epsilon} \quad \Rightarrow$$

$$\frac{\left(W_i^N - W_R\right)^{\epsilon}}{W_i^N - W_R} = \frac{1}{\epsilon(1 - t_M)} = \frac{W_i}{W_i^N - W_R} \quad \Rightarrow$$

$$\left(\frac{W_i^N - W_R}{W_i^N}\right) = \epsilon s \quad \Rightarrow \quad W_i^N = \frac{W_R}{1 - \epsilon s}, \tag{7.45}$$

where s is an index of progressivity of the tax system, that is defined as:

$$s \equiv \left(\frac{1 - t_M}{1 - t_A}\right). \tag{7.46}$$

For a progressive tax system, the marginal tax rate is higher than the average tax rate ($t_M > t_A$) and $s < 1$. An increase in the progressivity of the tax system is represented by a decrease in s. Equation (7.45) shows that the firm, as before, pays a constant markup times the value of the outside option but this markup now also depends on the degree of progressivity of the tax system s.

The value of the outside option is determined as before:

$$W_R = (1 - t_A)\bar{W}\left[1 - U + \beta U\right], \tag{7.47}$$

where we have assumed that the unemployment benefit is indexed to the net average wage paid in the economy, i.e. $B \equiv \beta(1 - t_A)\bar{W}$. In the symmetric equilibrium, all firms pay the same wage ($W_i = \bar{W}$), and equations (7.45) and (7.47) can be used to solve for the equilibrium unemployment rate U^*:

$$W_i(1 - t_A) = (1 - t_A)\bar{W} = \frac{W_R}{1 - \epsilon s} = \frac{(1 - t_A)\bar{W}(1 - U + \beta U)}{1 - \epsilon s} \quad \Rightarrow$$

$$U^* = \frac{\epsilon s}{1 - \beta}. \tag{7.48}$$

Equation (7.48) shows that the *average* tax rate has no effect on the equilibrium unemployment level, provided the degree of progressivity of the tax system s is constant. Increasing the unemployment benefit index parameter β increases equilibrium unemployment. Perhaps the most surprising conclusion is that increasing the degree of progressivity (decreasing s) *reduces* unemployment! The intuition behind this result is, however, straightforward. A move to a more progressive tax system reduces the scope for leapfrogging by firms, and punishes firms for paying excessive wages. As a result, wages are lowered and unemployment falls.

The comparative static effects on gross and net wages with respect to the different tax parameters can be obtained as follows. After some manipulation we obtain a simple expression for W_i:[10]

$$W_i = [\epsilon(1 - t_M)]^{\epsilon/(1-\epsilon)}. \tag{7.49}$$

By loglinearizing (7.49) we obtain:

$$\tilde{W}_i = -\left(\frac{\epsilon}{1-\epsilon}\right)\tilde{t}_M = \left(\frac{\epsilon}{1-\epsilon}\right)\left(\tilde{s} - \tilde{t}_A\right), \tag{7.50}$$

where $\tilde{W}_i \equiv dW_i/W_i$, $\tilde{t}_M \equiv dt_M/(1 - t_M)$, $\tilde{t}_A \equiv dt_A/(1 - t_A)$, and $\tilde{s} \equiv ds/s \equiv \tilde{t}_A - \tilde{t}_M$. Furthermore, in view of the fact that $W_i^N \equiv W_i(1 - t_A)$ we also have that:

$$\tilde{W}_i^N = \tilde{W}_i - \tilde{t}_A = -\left(\frac{\epsilon}{1-\epsilon}\right)\tilde{t}_M - \tilde{t}_A, \tag{7.51}$$

A higher average tax rate has no effect on the gross wage, so that workers bear the full brunt of the tax. If the marginal and average tax rates are both increased, the degree of progressivity of the tax system is unchanged and the net wage rate falls by more than 100%, because the gross wage also falls. Workers bear more than 100% of the burden of the tax.

7.4 Punchlines

We started this chapter by establishing some stylized facts about the labour market in advanced capitalistic economies. In such economies, unemployment shows a lot of fluctuations over time which are quite persistent (more so than the business cycle). In Europe the recent rise in unemployment is due to a rise in long-term unemployment. Once unemployed, European workers find it hard to exit the pool of the jobless by finding a new job. Looking at very long data sets reveals that there is no long-run trend in the unemployment rate. The unemployment rate differs between apparently similar countries suggesting an explanatory role for dissimilar labour market institutions. The majority of job loss (inflow into unemployment) is due to layoffs by firms not voluntary quits by workers. Finally, the unemployment rate differs between age groups, occupation, regions, races, and sexes.

The standard labour market model employed in the early chapters of this book can easily be augmented to explain some of these stylized facts. For example, the higher unemployment rate among blue collar workers *vis-à-vis* white collar workers can be modelled by distinguishing two types of workers, skilled and unskilled, and by assuming that there is a minimum (real) wage which is binding for the latter type of workers. In that case there is unemployment in the market for unskilled workers. The unemployment is classical as it is directly caused by the binding minimum wage.

---

[10] By substituting (7.48) into (7.47) we find that $W_R = (1-t_A)\bar{W}(1-\epsilon s)$ so that $W_i^N - W_R = (1-t_M)\epsilon\bar{W}$. By using this result in (7.41) and noting (7.43) we obtain (7.49).

Abolishing the minimum wage would solve the unemployment problem because the unskilled wage rate would fall to clear the market.

The standard model is also quite useful to study the impact of a variety of taxes on the aggregate labour market. We consider a wide array of taxes, namely a progressive system of (labour) income taxes, a payroll tax, as well as a tax on consumption. In the standard model with flexible wages, taxes affect equilibrium wages and employment but do not give rise to unemployment. Ceteris paribus the average income tax rate, an increase in the marginal income tax chokes off labour supply and leads to lower employment, a higher producer wage, and a lower consumer wage. On the other hand, if the marginal tax is kept unchanged and the average tax is increased then labour supply increases (because leisure is a normal good), both producer and consumer wages fall, and employment rises. Simple expressions can be derived which show which side of the labour market ends up paying the tax (so-called tax incidence).

If the consumer wage is assumed to be fixed above the market clearing level then employment is demand determined and unemployment emerges. Now, the effects of the tax system on employment and the unemployment rate can be traced. Raising the marginal income tax or lowering the average tax both lead to a reduction in the unemployment rate. In the former case labour demand (and hence employment) is unchanged but labour supply drops off. In the latter case labour demand (and employment) is boosted and labour supply falls.

Although the standard labour demand model is thus quite flexible there is one stylized fact for which it cannot easily furnish a credible explanation, namely the fact that the real wage appears to be rather rigid in the face of productivity and demand shocks. The standard model can be made consistent with this rigidity by assuming a highly elastic labour supply curve but that assumption is grossly at odds with microeconometric evidence. For that reason, a number of economists have started to look for alternative reasons for real wage rigidity.

A highly influential answer is provided by the theory of efficiency wages. The basic hypothesis underlying this theory is that the net productivity of workers is a function of the wage rate they are paid. A famous example of efficiency wages is provided by the case of Henry Ford, who paid very high wages and achieved a very high level of productivity as a result. The implications of the efficiency–wage hypothesis are quite far-reaching. First, the law of demand and supply is no longer relevant. Even if there is excess supply of labour, the firm may not lower its wage rate because the adverse effect on its workers' productivity may outweigh the beneficial reduction in the wage bill. Furthermore, the law of one price is also repealed. Since the effort–wage relationship may differ across industries, wages may also differ for otherwise identical workers.

In the final part of this chapter we develop a simple model in which efficiency wages lead to real wage rigidity and a positive equilibrium unemployment rate. Crucial determinants of the equilibrium unemployment rate are the replacement rate (the ratio of unemployment benefits and the after-tax wage rate), the so-called leap-frogging coefficient (summarizing the productivity-enhancing effect of high wages), and the degree of progressivity of the income tax system.

Further Reading

All serious students of the macroeconomic labour market should take notice of Layard, Nickell, and Jackman (1991) and Bean (1994). Key readings on the efficiency wage theory are collected in Akerlof and Yellen (1986). Katz (1986), Stiglitz (1986), and Weiss (1991) present very good surveys. Hoel (1990) studies the impact of progressive income taxes in an efficiency wage model. On dual labour markets, see Saint-Paul (1992) and Bulow and Summers (1986). Good surveys on the implicit contract literature are Azariadis (1981), Azariadis and Stiglitz (1983), and Rosen (1985). For a good survey article on tax incidence in macro models, see Kotlikoff and Summers (1987).

8

Trade Unions and the Labour Market

The purpose of this chapter is to discuss the following issues:

1. What models of trade union behaviour exist, and what do they predict about unemployment?
2. What do we mean by corporatism and how can it explain some of the stylized facts about the labour market?
3. How can so-called insider-outsider models be used to explain hysteresis?
4. How does taxation affect unemployment in trade union models?
5. How do trade unions affect investment by firms?

8.1 Some Models of Trade Union Behaviour

The typical layman's sentiment about trade unions probably runs as follows. Powerful trade unions are just like monopolists. They sell labour dearly, cause high real wages, and hence are really to blame for low employment and high unemployment. In this section we evaluate this sentiment within the context of several partial equilibrium models of trade union behaviour. The typical setting is one where a single representative union interacts with a single representative firm.

Suppose that the representative trade union has a utility function $V(w, L)$ with the following form:

$$V(w, L) \equiv \left(\frac{L}{N}\right) u(w) + \left[1 - \left(\frac{L}{N}\right)\right] u(B), \tag{8.1}$$

where N is the (fixed) number of union members, L is the number of employed members of the union ($L \leq N$), w is the real wage rate, B is the pecuniary value of being unemployed (referred to as the unemployment benefit), and $u(.)$ is the indirect utility function of the representative union member.[1] Equation (8.1) can be interpreted in two ways. First, L/N can be interpreted as the probability that a union member will be employed, in which case the union cares about the expected utility of its representative member. This is the probabilistic interpretation. The second, utilitarian, interpretation runs as follows. The union calculates the average utility attained by its employed and unemployed members, and takes that as its index of performance.

The representative firm is modelled in the standard fashion. The production function is $Y = AF(L, \bar{K})$, where Y is output, $\bar{K}$ is the fixed capital stock, A is a productivity index, and $F(.,.)$ features constant returns to scale and positive but diminishing marginal labour productivity ($F_L > 0 > F_{LL}$). The (short-run) real profit function is defined as:

$$\pi(w, L) \equiv AF(L, \bar{K}) - wL. \tag{8.2}$$

All models discussed in this section can be solved graphically. In order to do so, however, a number of graphical schedules must be derived. First, the labour demand schedule is obtained by finding all (w, L) combinations for which profit is maximized by choice of L. Formally, we have $\pi_L \equiv \partial\pi/\partial L = 0$, which yields:

$$\pi_L = AF_L(L, \bar{K}) - w = 0 \quad \Leftrightarrow \quad L^D = L^D(w, A, \bar{K}), \tag{8.3}$$

where $L_w^D < 0$, $L_A^D > 0$, and $L_{\bar{K}}^D > 0$. The labour demand curve is downward sloping in (w, L) space.

The second graphical device that is needed is the *iso-profit curve*. It represents the combinations of w and L for which profits attain a given level. It can be interpreted as the firm's indifference curve. The slope of an iso-profit curve can be determined in the usual fashion:

$$d\pi = 0: \quad \Rightarrow \quad \pi_w dw + \pi_L dL = 0 \quad \Rightarrow \quad \left(\frac{dw}{dL}\right)_{d\pi=0} = -\frac{\pi_L}{\pi_w}. \tag{8.4}$$

We know from equation (8.2) that $\pi_w = -L < 0$, so that the slope of an iso-profit line is determined by the sign of π_L. But $\pi_L \equiv AF_L - w$, and $F_{LL} < 0$, so that π_L is positive for a low employment level, becomes zero (at the profit-maximizing point), and then turns negative as employment increases further. Hence, in terms of Figure 8.1, the iso-profit curves are upward sloping to the left of the labour demand schedule, downward sloping to the right of labour demand, and attain a maximum for points on the labour demand schedule. In Figure 8.1 a number of iso-profit curves have been drawn, each associated with a different level of profit. Obviously, for a given

---

[1] An indirect utility function differs from the usual, direct, utility function in that it depends on prices and income rather than on quantities. The two are intricately linked, however. Indeed, the indirect utility function is obtained by substituting the optimal quantity choices of the household back into the direct utility function.

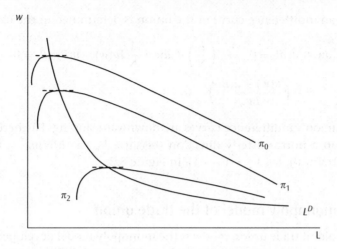

Figure 8.1. The iso-profit locus and labour demand

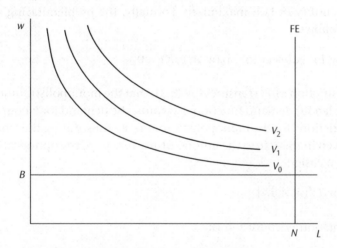

Figure 8.2. Indifference curves of the union

level of employment L, the level of profit is increased if the wage rate falls, i.e. $d\pi/dw = \pi_w < 0$. Hence, the level of profit increases the further down the demand for labour curve the firm operates, i.e. $\pi_0 < \pi_1 < \pi_2$.

Trade union behaviour can also be represented graphically. The third schedule to be derived concerns the union's indifference curve. Obviously, the union will not supply any workers to the firm at a wage rate below the unemployment benefit. Hence, in terms of Figure 8.2, the restriction $w \geq B$, translates into the horizontal line BB. Furthermore, the union is unable to supply any more workers than its current membership. Hence, there is an additional restriction $L \leq N$, which is the full employment line FE in Figure 8.2. Within the feasible region ($w \geq B$ and $L \leq N$),

189

the slope of an indifference curve of the union is determined in the usual way:

$$dV = V_w dw + V_L dL = 0 \quad \Rightarrow \quad \left(\frac{L}{N}\right) u_w dw + \frac{1}{N} \left[u(w) - u(B)\right] dL = 0 \quad \Rightarrow$$

$$\left(\frac{dw}{dL}\right)_{dV=0} = -\left(\frac{u(w) - u(B)}{L u_w}\right) < 0. \tag{8.5}$$

Hence, the union's indifference curves are downward sloping. Furthermore, union utility rises in a north-easterly direction (because $V_w \equiv (L/N)u_w > 0$ and $V_L \equiv (u(w) - u(B))/N > 0$), i.e. $V_2 > V_1 > V_0$ in Figure 8.2.

8.1.1 The monopoly model of the trade union

Perhaps the oldest trade union model is the monopoly model developed by Dunlop (1944). The trade union is assumed to behave like a monopolistic seller of labour. It faces the firm's demand for labour (defined implicitly in (8.3)) and sets the real wage such that its utility (8.1) is maximized. Formally, the problem facing a monopoly union is as follows:

$$\max_{\{w\}} V(w, L) \quad \text{subject to} \quad \pi_L(w, A, L, \bar{K}) = 0, \tag{8.6}$$

where the restriction $\pi_L = 0$ ensures (by (8.3)) that the monopolistic union chooses a point on the labour demand function. In words, the demand for labour acts like the "budget restriction" for the monopolistic union. By substituting the labour demand function (given in (8.3)) into the union's utility function, the optimization problem becomes even easier:

$$\max_{\{w\}} V\left[w, L^D(w, A, \bar{K})\right], \tag{8.7}$$

so that the first-order condition is:

$$\frac{dV}{dw} = 0: \quad V_w + V_L L_w^D = 0, \tag{8.8}$$

which implies that $V_w/V_L = -L_w^D$. The slope of the union's indifference curve should be equated to the slope of the demand for labour.[2]

The monopoly union solution is illustrated in Figure 8.3. The wage rate is set at w^M, the union attains a utility level V^M, and employment is L^M. The union has $(N - L^M)$ of its members unemployed. How does this unemployment level compare to the competitive solution? If there were no unions, the forces of the free market would force the wage rate down to $w = B$, so that point C in Figure 8.3 represents the competitive point. Employment is equal to L^C which is greater than employment

---

[2] It is possible that the union cannot choose this interior solution because the firm would make too little profit there. In such a case a corner solution is attained, and (8.8) does not hold with equality. We ignore this case here.

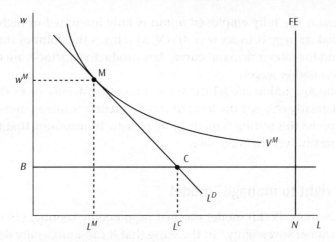

Figure 8.3. Wage setting by the monopoly union

with monopoly unions, i.e. $L^C > L^M$. Hence, the monopoly union causes more unemployment than would be the case under perfect competition, and the layman's sentiments mentioned in the introduction are confirmed.

Recall that one of the reasons for being interested in models of union behaviour is to investigate their potential in explaining the (near) horizontal real wage equation (see Figure 7.9). What happens if there is a productivity shock in the monopoly model? In the competitive solution (point C in Figure 8.3) there is only an effect on real wages if the productivity shock (dA) is very large, i.e. if the new labour demand equation intersects with the FE line at a wage rate above B. Something similar happens in the monopoly union model. In order to derive the real wage effects of a productivity shock, we first rewrite (8.8) in a more intuitive form:

$$V_w + V_L L_w^D = \left(\frac{L}{N}\right) u_w + \frac{1}{N}[u(w) - u(B)] L_w^D = 0$$

$$= \left(\frac{L}{wN}\right)\left[w u_w + [u(w) - u(B)] w L_w^D / L\right] = 0$$

$$\Rightarrow \frac{u(w) - u(B)}{w u_w} = \frac{1}{\epsilon_D}, \tag{8.9}$$

where $\epsilon_D \equiv -w L_w^D / L$ is the absolute value of the labour demand elasticity. If this demand elasticity is constant (as is the case for a Cobb–Douglas production function), then a productivity shock has no effect on the real wage rate chosen by the monopoly union. Only employment reacts to a productivity shock, and the model indeed predicts a rigid real wage.

Obviously, as for the competitive case, this conclusion must be qualified if the union is fully employed ($L = N$). In that case the union's effective utility function is (via (8.1)) equal to $V(w, L) = U(w)$, which no longer depends on the employment

191

level. As a result, the fully employed union is only interested in high real wages, and its optimal strategy is to set $w = AF_L(N, \bar{K})$. This is the point of intersection of the FE line and the labour demand curve. Any productivity shocks are immediately translated into higher wages.

In the monopoly union model the trade union unilaterally picks the wage and the firm unilaterally chooses the level of employment it wants at that wage. In the next union model this setting is made more realistic by assuming that the firm and the union bargain over the wage rate.

8.1.2 The "right to manage" model

The right to manage (RTM) model was first proposed by Leontief (1946). The firm still has "consumer sovereignty" in the sense that it can unilaterally determine the employment level (hence the name "right to manage"), but there is bargaining between the firm and the union over the real wage. The outcome of the bargaining process is modelled as a so-called generalized Nash bargaining solution (see e.g. Binmore and Dasgupta, 1987, and Booth, 1995, pp. 150–151). According to this solution concept, the real wage that is chosen after bargaining maximizes the geometrically weighted average of the gains to the two parties. In logarithmic terms we have:

$$\max_{\{w\}} \Omega \equiv \lambda \log \left[V(w, L) - \bar{V} \right] + (1 - \lambda) \log \left[\pi(w, L) - \bar{\pi} \right]$$

$$\text{subject to } \pi_L(w, A, L, \bar{K}) = 0, \tag{8.10}$$

where $\bar{V} \equiv U(B)$ is the fall-back position of the union, $\bar{\pi}$ is the fall-back position of the firm, and λ represents the relative bargaining strength of the union ($0 \leq \lambda \leq 1$). Obviously, the monopoly union model is obtained as a special case of the RTM model by setting $\lambda = 1$. We have already argued that the union has no incentive to accept wages lower than the unemployment benefit B, where utility of the union is at its lowest value of $V(w, L) = V(B, L) = U(B)$. This rationalizes the fall-back position of the union. For the firm a similar fall-back position will generally exist. To the extent that the firm has fixed costs, minimum profit must be positive, i.e. $\bar{\pi} > 0$.

By substituting the labour demand function (8.3) into (8.10), the problem is simplified substantially:

$$\max_{\{w\}} \Omega \equiv \lambda \log \left[V(w, L^D(w, A, \bar{K})) - \bar{V} \right] + (1-\lambda) \log \left[\pi(w, L^D(w, A, \bar{K})) - \bar{\pi} \right], \tag{8.11}$$

for which the first-order condition is:

$$\frac{d\Omega}{dw} = \lambda \left(\frac{V_w + V_L L_w^D}{V - \bar{V}} \right) + (1 - \lambda) \left(\frac{\pi_w + \pi_L L_w^D}{\pi - \bar{\pi}} \right) = 0. \tag{8.12}$$

The numerator of the first term on the right-hand side of (8.12) can be simplified to:

$$V_w + V_L L_w^D = \left(\frac{L}{wN} \right) [w u_w - \epsilon_D [u(w) - u(B)]]. \tag{8.13}$$

Furthermore, the second term on the right-hand side of (8.12) becomes:

$$\pi_w + \pi_L L_w^D = \pi_w = -L, \tag{8.14}$$

since the solution lies on the labour demand curve, so that $\pi_L = 0$. By substituting (8.13)–(8.14) into (8.12), and simplifying, we obtain the real wage expression for the RTM model (the counterpart to (8.9)):

$$\lambda \left(V - \bar{V} \right)^{-1} \left[V_w + V_L L_w^D \right] = -(1 - \lambda) \left(\pi - \bar{\pi} \right)^{-1} \pi_w \quad \Rightarrow$$

$$\frac{L}{wN} \left[w u_w - \epsilon_D \left[u(w) - u(B) \right] \right] = \left(\frac{(1 - \lambda)(V - \bar{V})}{\lambda(\pi - \bar{\pi})} \right) L \quad \Rightarrow$$

$$w u_w - \epsilon_D \left[u(w) - u(B) \right] = \left(\frac{(1 - \lambda)wL}{\lambda(Y - wL - \bar{\pi})} \right) \left[u(w) - u(B) \right], \tag{8.15}$$

where we have used the definition of π (in (8.2)) and the fact that $V - \bar{V} = (L/N)(u(w) - u(B))$ in the final step. Continuing the derivation, we obtain:

$$\frac{u(w) - u(B)}{w u_w} = \frac{1}{\epsilon_D + \phi}, \quad \phi \equiv \frac{(1 - \lambda)\omega_L}{\lambda(1 - \omega_L - \omega_\pi)} \geq 0, \tag{8.16}$$

where $\omega_L \equiv wL/Y$ is the share of labour income in total income, and $\omega_\pi \equiv \bar{\pi}/Y$ is the share of the minimum profit level in total income.

Equation (8.16) shows that the real wage markup that rolls out of the bargaining process is lower than under the monopoly union model (unless the union has all the bargaining power, in which case $\lambda = 1$, $\phi = 0$, and (8.9) and (8.16) coincide). The RTM solution can be illustrated with the aid of Figure 8.4. For ease of reference, the monopoly solution M and associated iso-profit curve π^M have also been drawn. The RTM solution lies on the labour demand curve, but at a wage level below that for the monopoly solution. It is indicated by point R where the profit level of the firm is $\pi^R > \pi^M$. Compared to the competitive solution (at point C), there is still too little employment, and too much unemployment. Compared to the monopoly solution, however, unemployment is lower.

The exact location of point R depends on the bargaining strength of the union, as represented by the parameter λ. The higher is λ, the closer point R lies to point M. On the other hand, if λ is very low, then ϕ is very large (see (8.16)) and the wage is close to the competitive solution, i.e. $w \approx B$. Hence, depending on the magnitude of λ, R can be anywhere on the labour demand curve between points M and C.

A major problem with the RTM solution is that the chosen wage-employment outcome is Pareto-inefficient, i.e. it is possible to make one of the parties involved in the bargain better off without harming the other party. This can be demonstrated with the aid of Figure 8.4. At point R, the union attains a utility level of V^R and the firm has a profit level of π^R. The firm is indifferent for all (w, L) combinations along the iso-profit curve π^R, but the union's utility strictly increases if a point off the labour demand curve is chosen. Indeed, the efficient solution occurs at the

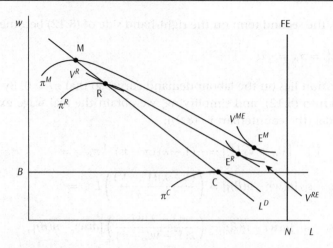

Figure 8.4. Wage setting in the right-to-manage model

point where there is a tangency between the iso-profit curve π^R and an indifference curve for the union. This occurs at point E^R, where the union attains a utility level $V^{RE} > V^R$. (For the same reason, point M is also inefficient, but point C is efficient. Verify these claims.)

Economists are not particularly fond of inefficient solutions, especially in the "small numbers" case—that we are considering here—with only two parties bargaining. One would expect that the two parties would be sufficiently smart to eliminate the type of inefficiency that exists in the RTM and monopoly model. For that reason, the efficient bargaining model was developed by McDonald and Solow (1981).

8.1.3 The efficient bargaining model

McDonald and Solow (1981) analyse the case where the union and the firm bargain simultaneously over wages and employment. Again the bargaining problem can be analysed within a generalized Nash bargaining setup. Now the negotiations lead to the maximization of Ω by choice of the appropriate wage-employment combination:

$$\max_{\{w,L\}} \Omega \equiv \lambda \log \left[V(w,L) - \bar{V} \right] + (1 - \lambda) \log \left[\pi(w,L) - \bar{\pi} \right]. \tag{8.17}$$

The first-order conditions for this problem are:

$$\frac{\partial \Omega}{\partial w} = \left(\frac{\lambda}{V - \bar{V}} \right) V_w + \left(\frac{1 - \lambda}{\pi - \bar{\pi}} \right) \pi_w = 0, \tag{8.18}$$

$$\frac{\partial \Omega}{\partial L} = \left(\frac{\lambda}{V - \bar{V}} \right) V_L + \left(\frac{1 - \lambda}{\pi - \bar{\pi}} \right) \pi_L = 0. \tag{8.19}$$

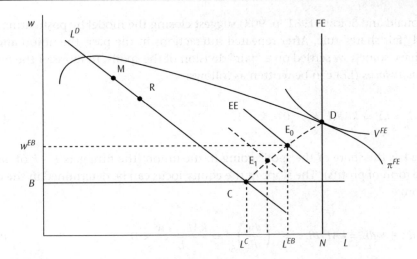

Figure 8.5. Wages and employment under efficient bargaining

By combining (8.18)-(8.19), the so-called *contract curve* is obtained:

$$-\left(\frac{1-\lambda}{\pi-\bar{\pi}}\right) = \left(\frac{\lambda}{V-\bar{V}}\right)\frac{V_w}{\pi_w} = \left(\frac{\lambda}{V-\bar{V}}\right)\frac{V_L}{\pi_L} \Rightarrow \frac{V_L}{V_w} = \frac{\pi_L}{\pi_w}. \tag{8.20}$$

In words, the contract curve (CD in Figure 8.5) represents the locus of (w, L) combinations for which efficient bargaining solutions are obtained. For any point on the contract curve, there is no (w, L) combination that makes one party better off without simultaneously harming the other party. In graphical terms, the contract curve represents all tangency points between iso-profit curves and union indifference curves.

One immediate implication of the efficient bargaining model is that the real wage exceeds the marginal product of labour. Indeed, (8.20) says that $\pi_L = V_L\pi_w/V_w < 0$ (since $V_L > 0$, $V_w > 0$, and $\pi_w < 0$). Hence:

$$\pi_L \equiv AF_L(L, \bar{K}) - w < 0 \quad \Leftrightarrow \quad w > AF_L(L, \bar{K}). \tag{8.21}$$

Hence, with the exception of the competitive solution, efficient contracts are not on the labour demand curve. Of course, we have already discussed three points on the contract curve, namely points C, E^R and E^M in Figure 8.4.

In Figure 8.5, the entire contract curve is drawn as the dashed line connecting points C and D. We assume that full employment is possible in principle. This means that the profit level associated with the full employment level on the contract curve (point D) exceeds the fall-back profit level of the firm (i.e. $\pi^{FE} > \bar{\pi}$). In that case, the entire line segment CD constitutes the contract curve. As it stands, the model is not yet fully specified because it does not yield a prediction about any *particular* wage-employment outcome—all (w, L) combinations along the line CD are efficient.

McDonald and Solow (1981, p. 903) suggest closing the model by postulating a so-called "fair share" rule. After repeated interactions in the past, the union and the firm have somehow settled on a "fair" division of the spoils. In terms of the model, the *equity locus* (EE) can be written as follows:

$$wL = kY = kAF(L, \bar{K}), \quad 0 < k < 1, \tag{8.22}$$

where k is the share of the spoils going to the union (the firm gets $1 - k$ of output in the form of profits). The slope of the equity locus can be determined in the usual fashion:

$$Ldw + wdL = kAF_L dL \quad \Rightarrow \quad \left(\frac{dw}{dL}\right)_{EE} = \frac{kAF_L - w}{L} < 0, \tag{8.23}$$

where the sign follows from the fact that $\pi_L \equiv AF_L - w < 0$ (solution lies to the right of the labour demand function) so that *a fortiori* $w > kAF_L$. The equity locus is downward sloping and shifts up and to the right if labour's share of the pie (k) is increased.

By combining the equity locus EE and the contract curve CD, the equilibrium wage-employment combination is obtained at E_0. A very surprising conclusion is reached. Compared to the competitive solution (point C), employment is higher (and unemployment is lower) under the efficient bargaining model ($L^{EB} > L^C$). The layman's sentiment, mentioned in the introduction to this chapter, is only partially correct. Wages are higher than in the competitive solution ($w^{EB} > B$) but employment is also higher than in the competitive solution. The intuition behind this result is that the union prevents the firm from grabbing the maximum profit level (at point C), and instead turns some of this profit into jobs for union members.

In that sense the next conclusion that can be drawn on the basis of the efficient bargaining model is perhaps less paradoxical than it may appear at first sight. Wage moderation, as modelled by a smaller share of the pie for labour ($dk < 0$), turns out to be bad for employment! Graphically, a lower k shifts the EE locus down and to the left, shifting the equilibrium from E_0 to E_1. The power of the firm is *de facto* increased, and the wage-employment combination is forced closer to the competitive solution.

Hence, the efficient wage bargaining model yields some surprising conclusions. The problem with the model appears to be its tenuous empirical relevance. Although simultaneous bargaining over wages and employment is efficient, it is hardly ever observed in practice. It therefore appears that the RTM model (which includes the monopoly model as a special case) has a closer affinity to reality than the efficient bargaining model. In other words, in the real world the relevant case appears to be that firms and unions negotiate over the wage rate, but that the firm can unilaterally determine the employment level.

8.1.4 Trade unions in a two-sector model

Before turning to the next issue, it is instructive to study the effects of trade union behaviour in a two-sector setting. This allows us to study the spillover effects that unions may have on the non-unionized sector of the economy. Suppose that labour is homogeneous, but that there are two sectors in the economy. The first sector, called the *primary sector*, is unionized, and the second, called the *secondary sector*, has a competitive system of wage determination. The labour force is fixed, and equal to N. Employment in sector i is denoted by L_i, and U is the number of unemployed workers, so that $N = L_1 + L_2 + U$. We assume that a monopoly union sets the wage in the primary sector. The demand for labour in the two sectors is given by $L_1^D(w_1)$ and $L_2^D(w_2)$, respectively, where w_i is the wage in sector i. These schedules are drawn in Figure 8.6. In the primary sector, the monopoly union selects the tangency point for a union indifference curve and the demand for labour (point M). The wage rate is w_1^M and employment is L_1^M. In the absence of a union, and with perfect mobility of labour between the two sectors, the common wage rate would be at the market clearing competitive level w^C, and employment in the two sectors would be L_1^C and L_2^C, respectively. If the union sets the wage in the primary sector at w_1^M, however, all workers that cannot find a job in that sector supply their labour inelastically to the secondary sector, so that the wage rate in that sector is w_2^M and employment is $L_2^M = N - L_1^M$. Hence, with a monopoly union in the primary sector, there is *full employment* of labour at the aggregate level, but wage disparity between the primary and secondary sectors. Workers in the secondary sector would rather work in the

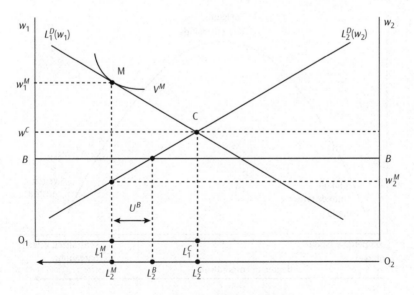

Figure 8.6. Unemployment in a two-sector model

197

primary sector (because wages are higher there), but are prevented from getting work there because of the union's wage-setting power.

Suppose now, however, that unemployment benefits equal B, and that B exceeds the wage for which full employment would prevail in the economy, i.e. $B > w_2^M$. In such a case, employment in the two sectors would equal L_1^M and L_2^B, respectively, and unemployment would be equal to U^B.

8.2 Corporatism

Our fifth stylized fact in Chapter 7 suggests that there are large differences in the unemployment rates of countries of the developed world. We saw that (at least up until the early 1990s) countries such as the US, Japan, Austria, Sweden, Norway, and Finland are characterized by low unemployment, whilst countries such as Belgium and the Netherlands have high unemployment. Calmfors and Driffill (1988) suggest that the unemployment rate may have something to do with the degree of *corporatism* that exists in the economy, and that the relationship is parabolic, as is drawn in Figure 8.7. Although the concept of corporatism is hard to define precisely, Calmfors and Driffill intend it to mean the degree of centralization of the wage-setting process. In terms of Figure 8.7, a low degree of corporatism is found in countries such as Japan, Switzerland, Canada, and the US, since these countries are characterized by relatively competitive labour markets. A very high degree

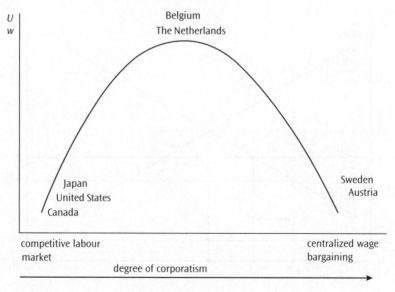

Figure 8.7. Unemployment, real wages, and corporatism

of corporatism is found in countries such as Austria, Norway, Sweden, Denmark, and Finland. An intermediate degree of corporatism is found in the Netherlands, Belgium, and Australia.

The reason why highly corporatist countries have a good unemployment record may be that highly centralized unions tend to internalize external effects that smaller unions would cause. First, higher wages at the microeconomic level translate to a higher price level at the macroeconomic level. Small unions do not take this wage-price spiral into account, but large national unions may. Second, higher wages mean both higher unemployment, and in most countries, higher civil servants' wages (via the indexing clauses), thus raising the government's revenue requirement. To the extent that the additional revenue must be raised by means of higher tax rates, union members may not experience an increase in their after-tax wages. Again, large unions are more likely to internalize this external effect than small unions. Third, it is possible that leapfrogging effects (see Chapter 7) are important when there are small unions. With a high degree of centralization, however, these effects will be absent. A national union cannot overbid its own wage claim (Layard et al., 1991, p. 30).

The reason why countries with a low degree of centralization fare well on the unemployment front is that unions, if they exist at all, are very small, have very little power and are hence rather harmless. As a result, the fact that these small unions do not internalize externalities does not matter much, because the externalities themselves are small in that case.

Unemployment is at its worst for intermediate cases. There, unions are large enough to cause some damage (in the form of higher wage claims and lower employment levels), but too small to feel inclined to internalize the external effects mentioned above. By being neither one nor the other, the countries characterized by an intermediate degree of centralization inherit the bad features of both extreme cases.

8.3 Fiscal Increasing Returns

In a recent article, Blanchard and Summers (1987a) argue that the countries in the EC are characterized by so-called *fiscal increasing returns* due to the existence of a large public sector. Their idea is very simple: an increase in employment can be associated with a rise in the after-tax real wage rate. Put in more colloquial terms, a tax cut can pay for itself. Their argument is not based on the assumption that the economy is located on the downward-sloping part of the Laffer curve (see Chapter 1), but rather on the fact that high employment means low expenditure on unemployment benefits. The basic mechanism can be demonstrated with the aid of a very simple model. There is perfect competition on the goods market and output Y is produced with the following constant returns to scale production function:

$$Y = F(L, \bar{K}), \quad F_L > 0 > F_{LL}, \tag{8.24}$$

where L is employment and $\bar{K}$ is the fixed capital stock. Assume that the government keeps its budget deficit constant if unemployment is diminished. The government budget restriction is:

$$G + \beta w(1 - t)[N - L] = tY, \tag{8.25}$$

where G is exogenous government spending on goods and services, t is the tax rate (so that tY is tax revenue), N is the given labour force (so that $N - L$ is the number of unemployed members of the labour force), $w_N \equiv w(1 - t)$ is the after-tax real wage rate, and β is the constant *replacement ratio* ($0 < \beta < 1$). It is assumed that the unemployment benefit is linked to the after-tax real wage. The tax rate t ensures that the government budget is balanced.

With perfect competition in the goods market, the demand for labour is implicitly defined by the marginal productivity condition:

$$F_L(L, \bar{K}) = w. \tag{8.26}$$

Equations (8.24)–(8.26) contain four endogenous variables (Y, L, w, and t), so that a macroeconomic relationship between after-tax real wages w_N and employment L can be deduced:

$$w_N \equiv w(1 - t) = F_L(L, \bar{K}) \left[\frac{F(L, \bar{K}) - G - \beta w(1 - t)(N - L)}{F(L, \bar{K})} \right]. \tag{8.27}$$

Equation (8.27) has a hump-shaped form, as has been illustrated in Figure 8.8. If employment is very low, the effect of diminishing returns to labour is dominated by the decrease in the tax rate which is made possible by the larger tax base. As a result, net wages can rise. When employment is high, on the other hand, the reverse happens: the tax rate effect is dominated by the decreasing returns to labour, and the net wage falls as employment expands.

More formally, the slope of (8.25) can be calculated as follows (see the Intermezzo below):

$$\frac{dw_N}{dL} = \left(\frac{(1 - t)w_N}{(1 - \omega_G)L} \right) \left[-\frac{1 - \omega_L}{\sigma} + \left(\beta + \frac{t}{1 - t} \right) \omega_L \right], \tag{8.28}$$

where ω_G is the share of government spending in output, ω_L is the share of labour income in output, t is the initial tax rate, and σ is the substitution elasticity between capital and labour in the production function (see Chapter 4).

Blanchard and Summers (1987a, p. 548) close the model by assuming that the after-tax real wage rate is fixed at some exogenous level, say $\bar{w}_N$ in Figure 8.8. This could be either because of extensive indexing or due to the influence of trade unions.

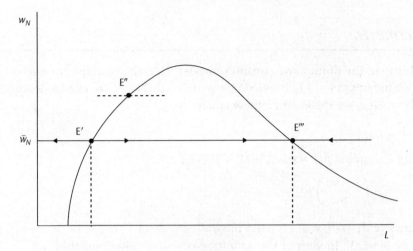

Figure 8.8. Fiscal increasing returns

At that level of net wages, there are two equilibria; a "bad" equilibrium at E′ characterized by low employment, and a "good" equilibrium at E‴, where employment is high. It is likely that (some of) the EC countries may find themselves in the bad equilibrium. If this is indeed the case, a rather perverse policy conclusion is reached. A rise in the union's wage claim turns out to be good for employment! The bad equilibrium shifts from E′ to E‴. Conversely, wage moderation is bad for employment. Furthermore, there is scope for a wage-tax deal between the government and the unions. By keeping the after-tax real wage rate unchanged (at $\bar{w}_N$), a simultaneous reduction in the tax rate and gross real wages can shift the economy from the bad to the good equilibrium.

Blanchard and Summers (1987a) suggest, however, that the bad equilibrium is unstable. To demonstrate this instability, we postulate the following ad hoc adjustment rule for the tax rate:

$$\dot{t} = \gamma \left[G + \beta w(1-t) \left[N - L \right] - tF(L, \bar{K}) \right], \quad \gamma > 0, \tag{8.29}$$

where the gross real wage is given by (8.26) and we retain the assumption of a fixed after-tax real wage $\bar{w}_N$. As is shown in the Intermezzo, around point E′, we have that $\partial \dot{t}/\partial t > 0$: unless the economy is exactly at point E′, a small deviation away from this equilibrium is self-perpetuating, so that the equilibrium is unstable. For point E‴, on the other hand, we have that $\partial \dot{t}/\partial t < 0$, which implies stability. Hence, to the extent that $\bar{w}_N$ is truly fixed, there are two possibilities if a country finds itself in a bad equilibrium. Either there is automatic adjustment from the bad to the good equilibrium, or there is a gradual deterioration of the employment performance accompanied by ever increasing tax rates. Of course, a wage-tax deal would help in getting the EC countries from the bad to the good equilibrium.

Intermezzo

Stability in the Blanchard-Summers model. The relationship between w_N and the employment level L, implied by equations (8.24)–(8.26) can be deduced as follows. First, we loglinearize these equations:

$$\tilde{Y} = \omega_L \tilde{L}, \tag{a}$$

$$(t - \omega_G)\tilde{w}_N - \beta(1 - t)\omega_L \tilde{L} = t\tilde{Y} + (1 - t)\tilde{t}, \tag{b}$$

$$\tilde{w} = -\left(\frac{1 - \omega_L}{\sigma}\right)\tilde{L}, \tag{c}$$

where $\tilde{Y} \equiv dY/Y$, $\tilde{L} \equiv dL/L$, $\tilde{w}_N \equiv dw_N/w_N$, $\tilde{t} \equiv dt/(1-t)$, $\tilde{w} \equiv dw/w$, $\omega_G \equiv G/Y$, and $\omega_L \equiv wL/Y$. In view of the definition of w_N, we also have that:

$$\tilde{w}_N = \tilde{w} - \tilde{t}. \tag{d}$$

By substituting (a)–(c) into (d) and simplifying, the following expression is obtained.

$$\tilde{w}_N = \left(\frac{1 - t}{1 - \omega_G}\right)\left[-\left(\frac{1 - \omega_L}{\sigma}\right) + \omega_L\left(\beta + \frac{t}{1 - t}\right)\right]\tilde{L}. \tag{e}$$

Since $\tilde{L} \equiv dL/L$ and $\tilde{w}_N \equiv dw_N/w_N$ we can rewrite (e) to obtain (8.28).

Stability of the equilibria E′ and E‴ can be investigated as follows. The adjustment mechanism (8.29) is linearized as follows:

$$d\dot{t} = -\gamma Y\left[\beta(1 - t)\omega_L \tilde{L} + t\tilde{Y} + (1 - t)\tilde{t}\right]. \tag{f}$$

By using (a) and (c), and recognizing that $\tilde{w}_N = 0$, so that $\tilde{w} = \tilde{t}$, we obtain from (a):

$$d\dot{t} = \left(\frac{\gamma\sigma Y}{1 - \omega_L}\right)\left[-\left(\frac{1 - \omega_L}{\sigma}\right) + \omega_L\left(\beta + \frac{t}{1 - t}\right)\right]dt. \tag{g}$$

Hence, by (e), $d\dot{t}/dt < 0$ if w_N depends negatively on L and $d\dot{t}/dt > 0$ in the opposite case. Hence, point E′ is unstable and point E‴ is stable.

8.4 Hysteresis and the Persistence of Unemployment

The second and fourth stylized facts from Chapter 7 demonstrate that there is a high degree of persistence in the European unemployment rate. How can models based on trade unions explain this phenomenon? The key to the solution is found in the membership rule of the union. Up to this point we have assumed that the typical union has a fixed number of members (say N members, as in section 2). It is possible, however, that unemployed union members either quit the union, or worse, are kicked out. What may happen in such a case is illustrated with the aid of the simple model by Blanchard and Summers (1986, 1987b).

Suppose that the demand for each firm's product depends on the real money supply (an index of aggregate demand) and the relative price of the product *vis-à-vis* the general price index:

$$y_i = (m - p) - a(p_i - p), \quad a > 1, \tag{8.30}$$

where all variables are measured in logarithms, y_i is output, m is the money supply, p_i is the price charged by firm i, and p is the aggregate price index. There are constant returns to scale, and only labour is used in the production process. The production function is $y_i = l_i$, where l_i is employment in firm i. Perfect competition in the goods market implies that price is set equal to marginal cost, so that $p_i = w_i$. Hence, the demand for labour is given by:

$$l_i = (m - w) - a(w_i - w), \tag{8.31}$$

where w is an aggregate index of nominal wages.

Each firm has a given number n_i^* of attached workers. Only the interests of these workers are taken into account in the wage bargaining process, for which reason these workers are referred to as the *insiders*. Only if all insiders are employed by the firm, is the firm allowed to hire any *outsiders*. We assume that the group of insiders has sufficient bargaining power to set the wage unilaterally. Furthermore, it is assumed that the wage is set such that the expected employment is equal to the number of insiders:

$$El_i = n_i^*, \tag{8.32}$$

where E is the expectations operator. By using (8.31)–(8.32), we derive that $El_i = Em - Ew - a(w_i - Ew) = n_i^*$. All firms are identical and all insider groups have the same size, so that the equilibrium is symmetric. Consequently, all insider groups choose the same nominal wage, so that:

$$w_i = w = Ew. \tag{8.33}$$

It follows that $n_i^* = Em - w$. By substituting this expression into (8.31) we obtain the final expression for employment (per firm):

$$l_i = m - w - a(w_i - w) = m - Em + n_i^* \quad \Rightarrow$$

$$l = (m - Em) + n^*, \tag{8.34}$$

where the firm index i can be dropped in the final step due to symmetry. Equation (8.34) shows that only the unexpected shock in aggregate demand has any effect on employment (per firm). Suppose that the membership rule of the group of insiders is as follows: $n_i^* = l_i(-1)$, i.e. only insiders that were employed in the previous period will belong to the group of insiders in the current period. By substituting this membership rule into (8.34), the *hysteresis effect* is obtained:

$$l = (m - Em) + l(-1), \tag{8.35}$$

which, for a given labour force $\bar{n}$, can be rewritten in terms of the unemployment rate U as:[3]

$$U = -(m - Em) + U(-1). \tag{8.36}$$

Equation (8.36) yields the very strong conclusion that the unemployment rate follows a random walk. To the extent that aggregate demand surprises are random, the change in unemployment, ΔU is random also. There is no tendency for the unemployment rate to converge to any particular level. The intuition behind this result is straightforward. After a bad shock, employment falls (by (8.35)). The unemployed become outsiders, and the remaining insiders are not inclined to lower wages to get their former comrades back into a job. The opposite holds after a positive aggregate demand shock.

Of course, the hysteresis result is far too strong, both for empirical and theoretical reasons. Empirically, as we saw in Chapter 7, the unemployment rates in the UK and US display a lot of persistence but no hysteresis. The autoregressive coefficient in the unemployment process (see (7.3)) is high but not equal to unity. Theoretically, an unsatisfying assumption made so far is that the insiders have all the bargaining power and can set the wage unilaterally. Firms, in other words, are unable to appoint the unemployed who may be willing to work at a lower wage.

It turns out, however, that the model can be salvaged quite easily. Following Blanchard (1991), the bargaining process between the firm and the group of insiders is made more interesting by recognizing an explicit role for the unemployment rate. Unemployment has two distinct effects in the bargaining process. First, there is the *fear effect* that we also encountered in the efficiency wage models (see Chapter 7). If unemployment is high, a typical insider is a bit more modest in his/her wage claims. If unemployed, it may not be so easy to find another job. Second, the *threat effect* exists. If unemployment is high, employers can threaten current employees (the insiders) that they will be replaced by (hungry) unemployed workers.

A simple model that includes both aspects is the following. Labour demand is very simple:

$$l = -w + \epsilon, \tag{8.37}$$

where ϵ is a stochastic shock (with $E\epsilon = 0$), l is employment, and w is the wage rate (all in logarithms). Just as in the previous model, it is assumed that wages are set such

---

[3] In levels, the unemployment rate is given by $U \equiv (\bar{N} - L)/\bar{N} = 1 - (L/\bar{N}) \approx -\log(L/\bar{N}) = \bar{n} - l$, where the approximation is valid for small unemployment rates.

that the insiders (of which there are $l(-1)$) expect to have a job in the current period, i.e. $w^* = -l(-1)$. An unemployed person receives the unemployment benefit plus the utility value of leisure, the sum of which can be expressed in pecuniary terms by the *reservation* or *unemployment wage*, w_R (if all workers were to receive w_R, expected employment would be equal to $l_R = -w_R$). Assuming that unemployment is the correct indicator for labour market conditions for both the firm and the insiders, the actual wage w is assumed to be set as follows:

$$w = aw^* + (1 - a)w_R - b(\bar{n} - l), \quad 0 \le a \le 1, b \ge 0. \tag{8.38}$$

Equation (8.38) says that the actual wage (w) is a weighted average of the wage insiders would choose (w^*) and the reservation wage (w_R) (with weight a, representing the bargaining strength of the insiders), with a correction for the unemployment situation in the labour market. If unemployment $U \equiv \bar{n} - l$ is very high, insiders are more modest in their wage claims, and the wage is lower. By simple substitutions the following expression for the unemployment process is obtained:

$$U = \left(\frac{a}{1+b}\right)U(-1) + \left(\frac{1-a}{1+b}\right)w_R + \left(\frac{1-a}{1+b}\right)\bar{n} - \left(\frac{1}{1+b}\right)\epsilon. \tag{8.39}$$

Since $0 \le a \le 1$ and $b \ge 0$, (8.39) shows that the unemployment rate displays persistence but no hysteresis. If b is high (strong influence of unemployment on the bargained wage rate) then there is little persistence. Furthermore, if insider power is high (a close to unity), persistence is high. Hence, this version of the insider-outsider model does indeed deliver more sensible predictions.

8.5 Applications of Trade Union Models

In this section some of the union models discussed in this chapter are used to study two issues. First, we continue our study of the effects of taxation on employment, wages, and unemployment. Second, we study the effects of unions on the rate of investment by the firm.

8.5.1 The effects of taxation

In order not to unduly test the reader's patience, only one tax experiment is conducted. Suppose that the system of income taxes is progressive, that unemployment benefits are untaxed, and that the tax function is given by $T(w)$, so that the marginal tax rate is $t_M \equiv dT/dw$ and the average tax rate is $t_A \equiv T/w$. It is assumed that the monopoly union model applies, and that the union's utility function is augmented (from (8.1)) to include income taxes:

$$V(w, L) \equiv \left(\frac{L}{N}\right) u(w(1 - t_A)) + \left[1 - \left(\frac{L}{N}\right)\right] u(B), \tag{8.40}$$

so that the first-order condition for the optimal wage is:

$$\frac{dV}{dw} = [u(w(1 - t_A)) - u(B)] L_w^D + L^D u_{w(1-t_A)} \left[(1 - t_A) - w\frac{dt_A}{dw}\right] = 0. \tag{8.41}$$

This expression can be simplified by using the result that $wdt_A/dw = t_M - t_A$ and using the labour demand elasticity ϵ_D (defined below (8.9)):

$$\frac{u(w(1 - t_A)) - u(B)}{w(1 - t_A)u_{w(1-t_A)}} = \frac{s}{\epsilon_D}, \tag{8.42}$$

where $s \equiv (1 - t_M)/(1 - t_A)$ is the index of progressivity of the tax system. For a progressive tax system, $t_M > t_A$, so that $s < 1$. Recall from Chapter 7 that an increase in progressivity of the tax system is represented by a decrease in s.

For example, assume that the representative union member's indirect utility function is given by $U(.) \equiv \log(.)$. Then the markup equation (8.42) is simplified to:

$$\log w(1 - t_A) = \log B + s/\epsilon_D \quad \Rightarrow \quad w = \left(\frac{B}{1 - t_A}\right) e^{s/\epsilon_D}. \tag{8.43}$$

From (8.43) we can see that the gross wage w (and thus unemployment U) rises if the unemployment benefit (B) rises, the degree of progressivity falls (s rises), and the average tax rate (t_A) rises. These conclusions are very similar to those that were obtained for the efficiency wage model in Chapter 7.

8.5.2 Unions and investment

Are unions good or bad for investment? Intuitively one would think the latter. The argument might go as follows. When capital is a variable production factor, the demand for labour becomes more elastic. This creates a conflict between what is optimal for the union in the short run and in the long run. Take, for example, the case of the monopoly union discussed in section 1.1. There it was shown that the wage markup bears an inverse relationship with the labour demand elasticity. A short-sighted union will push for high wages and suffer the consequences in the future as firms accumulate capital and labour demand becomes more elastic. Far-sighted unions, on the other hand, will demand a lower wage, in the hope that the firm will not invest too much, so that the wage in the future will be comparable. A kind of *wage smoothing* behaviour may emerge.

This is not the end of the story, however, since there is a *credibility problem* associated with the wage smoothing union, due to the fact that investment is largely irreversible. The union can announce to the firm that it will follow a smooth (and moderate) wage policy, after which the firm will invest. Once the firm has invested, however, the firm is a "sitting duck" for the union. The capital stock cannot be shifted easily so the union can renege on its promise of moderate wages and skim off a large part of the firm's profits. But the firm knows beforehand that the union has this incentive to cheat, and consequently will not believe the union's announcement of smooth and moderate wages. As a result, it invests less, in order to minimize the risk and impact of being cheated in the future. This is the famous *underinvestment* result, discussed for example in van der Ploeg (1987b). We shall return to credibility issues in Chapter 10, where we shall also illustrate how reputational forces can overcome (some of) the problems associated with dynamically inconsistent behaviour.

The remainder of this section serves to demonstrate the underinvestment result in a simple two-period model of the interaction between a monopoly trade union and a firm. This example is a simplification of the model presented in van der Ploeg (1987b). The firm exists for two periods (now and in the future) and has a given capital stock K_1 at the beginning of period 1. Real profits in the two periods are equal to:

$$\pi_1 \equiv F(L_1, K_1) - w_1 L_1 - \Phi(I_1), \tag{8.44}$$

$$\pi_2 \equiv F(L_2, K_1 + I_1) - w_2 L_2, \tag{8.45}$$

where π_t is real profit in period t $(= 1, 2)$, L_t is employment, I_t is investment, w_t is the real wage rate, $F(., .)$ is a constant returns to scale production function, and $\Phi(.)$ is the installation function for investment. As we have shown in Chapter 4, this function captures the existence of internal adjustment costs that are rising (at an increasing rate) in the rate of investment, i.e. $\Phi_I > 0$ and $\Phi_{II} > 0$. Obviously the firm does not invest in the second period because our stylized world comes to a close at the end of that period. Furthermore, we have assumed for convenience that the capital stock does not depreciate. The firm chooses its employment and investment levels in order to maximize the present value of its stream of profits, which is defined as:

$$\Pi = \pi_1 + \frac{\pi_2}{1+r}$$

$$\equiv F(L_1, K_1) - w_1 L_1 - \Phi(I_1) + \left(\frac{F(L_2, K_1 + I_1) - w_2 L_2}{1+r} \right), \tag{8.46}$$

where r is the real interest rate. The first-order conditions for the optimization problem are:

$$\frac{\partial \Pi}{\partial L_1} = F_L(L_1, K_1) - w_1 = 0, \tag{8.47}$$

$$\frac{\partial \Pi}{\partial I_1} = -\Phi_I(I_1) + \left(\frac{1}{1+r} \right) F_K(L_2, K_1 + I_1) = 0, \tag{8.48}$$

$$\frac{\partial \Pi}{\partial L_2} = \left(\frac{1}{1+r} \right) [F_L(L_2, K_1 + I_1) - w_2] = 0. \tag{8.49}$$

In order to keep the model as simple as possible, we work with specific functional forms for the firm's production and adjustment cost functions, and the utility function of the representative union member. The adjustment cost function is quadratic (see (4.2)), i.e. $\Phi(.) = I_1(1 + bI_1)$, and the production function is assumed to be Cobb-Douglas, i.e. $Y_t = L_t^\alpha K_t^{1-\alpha}$, with $0 < \alpha < 1$ and Y_t representing output. By using these specific functions, (8.47)–(8.49) can be written as:

$$L_1^D = \left(\frac{\alpha}{w_1}\right)^{\epsilon_D} K_1, \tag{8.50}$$

$$L_2^D = \left(\frac{\alpha}{w_2}\right)^{\epsilon_D} [K_1 + I_1], \tag{8.51}$$

$$I_1 = \frac{q-1}{2b}, \tag{8.52}$$

$$q \equiv \frac{F_K(L_2, K_1 + I_1)}{1+r} = \left(\frac{1-\alpha}{1+r}\right)\left(\frac{\alpha}{w_2}\right)^{\alpha\epsilon_D}, \tag{8.53}$$

where $\epsilon_D \equiv 1/(1-\alpha)$, L_t^D is the firm's demand for labour in period t, and q is Tobin's q-ratio discussed extensively in Chapter 4. Equations (8.50)–(8.51) show that the elasticity of labour demand is constant. Equation (8.52) shows that investment is increasing in Tobin's q, which itself depends negatively on the exogenously given real rate of interest r and the real wage rate in the second period w_2.

The monopoly trade union has the following lifetime utility function:

$$\Omega \equiv V(w_1, L_1) + \left(\frac{1}{1+\rho}\right) V(w_2, L_2), \tag{8.54}$$

where ρ is the pure rate of time preference (see Chapter 6), and $V(w_t, L_t)$ is the instantaneous utility of the union, that is defined as follows:

$$V(w_t, L_t) \equiv \left(\frac{L_t}{N}\right) u(w_t) + \left[1 - \left(\frac{L_t}{N}\right)\right] u(B), \tag{8.55}$$

which indicates that membership of the union is fixed at N, and the unemployment benefit is constant over time. The optimal plan for the union consists of choosing w_1 and w_2 such that (8.54) is maximized given (8.55) and the labour demand functions (8.50)–(8.51). The necessary conditions for this optimization problem are:

$$\frac{\partial \Omega}{\partial w_1} = \frac{\partial V}{\partial w_1} + \frac{\partial V}{\partial L_1}\frac{\partial L_1^D}{\partial w_1} = 0, \tag{8.56}$$

$$\frac{\partial \Omega}{\partial w_2} = \frac{\partial V}{\partial w_2} + \frac{\partial V}{\partial L_2}\left(\frac{\partial L_2^D}{\partial w_2} + \frac{\partial L_2^D}{\partial I_1}\frac{\partial I_1}{\partial q}\frac{\partial q}{\partial w_2}\right) = 0. \tag{8.57}$$

Equation (8.56) has a form identical to the one obtained for the static case (see e.g. (8.8)). A point of tangency is found between a union's indifference curve and the labour demand curve. Assuming that the utility function of the representative union member is logarithmic ($u(.) = \log(.)$) equation (8.56) can be rewritten by using (8.50) to yield:

$$\frac{1}{\epsilon_D} = \frac{u(w_1) - u(B)}{w_1 u_w(w_1)} = \log w_1 - \log B \quad \Rightarrow$$

$$\log w_1^* = \log B + \frac{1}{\epsilon_D}. \tag{8.58}$$

Equation (8.57) is slightly more involved. The union realizes that the wage that it chooses for the second period influences the firm's investment decision: the higher the wage in the second period, the lower the rate of investment by the firm. Compared to the static case with no investment, therefore, the demand for labour in the second period is more elastic, and the wage rate chosen by the union is lower. Specifically, we can easily derive that:

$$\frac{1}{\epsilon_D + \phi} = \frac{U(w_2) - U(B)}{w_2 U_w(w_2)} = \log w_2 - \log B \quad \Rightarrow$$

$$\log w_2^* = \log B + \frac{1}{\epsilon_D + \phi}, \tag{8.59}$$

where ϕ is defined as:

$$\phi \equiv -\frac{\partial L_2^D}{\partial I_1} \frac{\partial I_1}{\partial w_2} \frac{w_2}{L_2^D} = \left(\frac{\alpha \epsilon_D}{L_2^D}\right) \left(\frac{1 - \alpha}{1 + r}\right) \left(\frac{\alpha}{w_2}\right)^{\epsilon_D(1+\alpha)} > 0. \tag{8.60}$$

Comparing the optimal wage rates in the two periods (as given in (8.58) and (8.59)), it is clear that the wage is lower in the second period, i.e. $w_1^* > w_2^*$. By offering low wages in the second period, the firm is encouraged to invest a lot.

The problem with the optimal union wage profile (w_1^*, w_2^*) is that the firm will not believe that the union will stick to it! Indeed, if a legally binding agreement is impossible, the union will not stick to the wage rate w_2^* it has announced to the firm when period 2 comes along. The reason is not that it has changed its mind in the light of new information, but rather that it faces a different incentive structure when period 2 comes along. In technical terms, the optimal policy for the union is *dynamically inconsistent*. The reason why the firm does not believe that the union will set the wage at w_2^* in period 2 is easy to demonstrate. Suppose that the firm did believe the union, and decided its investment plans according to (8.52)–(8.53) with w_2^* substituted (call this investment level I_1^*). At the beginning of period 2, the firm has invested a lot and has a total capital stock of $K_1 + I_1^*$, and demands labour according to (8.51) with $K_1 + I_1^*$ substituted. The union, however, observes this demand for labour, knows that the capital stock cannot be shifted any more, and makes its decision on the optimal wage in the second period on the basis of the demand curve:

$$L_2^D = \left(\frac{\alpha}{w_2}\right)^{\epsilon_D} [K_1 + I_1^*],$$

(8.61)

which is iso-elastic with wage elasticity ϵ_D (in absolute terms), so that the union sets the wage in the second period at the same level as in the first period, i.e. $\hat{w}_2 = w_1 > w_2^*$. The firms knows this, and hence is not going to believe the union if it announces w_2^*.

So what is the solution to this conundrum? Although a more complete treatment will have to wait until Chapter 10, common sense suggests a solution for our present problem. The firm knows that it is going to get ripped off in the second period "come hell or high water". Hence, it expects to be charged the wage rate $w_t^C = w_1^*$ in both periods ($t = 1, 2$), and bases its investment decision on this knowledge. Indeed, this assumption on the part of the firm is consistent with the actual behaviour of the union. For that reason, the wage profile (w_1^C, w_2^C) is called the *time-consistent* policy of the union. But, since $w_1^* > w_2^*$ (and thus $w_2^C > w_2^*$), and investment depends negatively on the wage rate in the second period, the firm will also invest less under the consistent wage profile (w_1^C, w_2^C) than under the inconsistent wage profile (w_1^*, w_2^*). Hence, the effect of a union that is unable to stick to its promises is to stifle investment.

8.6 Punchlines

In this chapter the three most important models of trade union behaviour have been studied, namely the monopoly union model, the right-to-manage model, and the efficient bargaining model. The objective function of the union is the expected (or average) utility of the union's members. In most of the discussion we assume that the number of union members is fixed.

In the monopoly union model, the union unilaterally picks a wage rate such that union utility is maximized subject to the proviso that the solution lies on the labour demand curve. The union thus acts as the monopolistic seller of labour exploiting the downward-sloping labour demand curve of the firm. The optimal wage choice of the union can be represented as a simple markup expression involving unemployment benefit and the elasticity of the labour demand function. The union's choice implies that both the wage and the unemployment rate are above their respective competitive levels. Productivity shocks typically lead only to employment changes so that the model is consistent with real wage rigidity. (The proviso must be made because a union which is fully employed is only interested in higher wages so that positive productivity shocks do not translate into employment expansions.)

In the right-to-manage model, the firm is still allowed to decide on employment but the wage is the outcome of a bargaining process between the union and the firm.

Using the concept of generalized Nash bargaining, the resulting wage can again be written in a markup format. In addition to unemployment benefit and demand elasticity an additional component entering the markup solution is the relative bargaining strength of the union. An attractive feature of the right-to-manage model is that it contains the monopoly union solution and the competitive solution as special (extreme) cases. An unattractive feature of the right-to-manage solution is that it is Pareto inefficient, i.e. it is possible to make one of the parties involved in the bargaining strictly better off without making the other party worse off.

The efficient bargaining model solves this problem by assuming that the firm and the union bargain over both the wage and the employment level. The outcome of this bargaining process is a range of efficient wage-employment combinations. When combined with a "fair share" rule, dividing output over the two parties, the model predicts a unique wage-employment solution. Interestingly, wage and employment are higher than under the competitive solution as the union turns profits into jobs. Wage moderation, consisting of a smaller share of the output going to labour, is bad for employment because the wage-employment solution moves closer to the competitive solution.

In the remainder of this chapter we show a number of applications of the various union models. In Chapter 7 we saw that one of the stylized facts about the labour market is that institutions may be an important determinant of the unemployment rate. We briefly discuss the hypothesis that corporatism, loosely defined as the degree of centralization of the wage-setting process, may be such an important institution. Some authors have claimed that unemployment is low if there are either many very small or few very large unions but that unemployment is high in the intermediate case. Hence, high or low corporatism both lead to a low unemployment rate but intermediate corporatism does not. Intuitively, small unions do little harm, large nation-wide unions practise wage moderation because they internalize the outcomes of excessive wage claims, but middle-sized unions are both strong yet do not take into account all the adverse consequences of their wage claims on the macroeconomy.

Another stylized fact that can be explained with the aid of a union model is the high degree of persistence in the unemployment rate (the near-hysteresis effect). The membership rule of the union turns out to form a key model ingredient explaining hysteresis. If the unemployed union insiders become outsiders the next period, then strict hysteresis applies. If the outsiders are allotted a role in the wage bargaining process, via the reservation wage, then the model becomes more realistic and predicts a high degree of persistence.

As a final application of the union model, we study the effects of a monopoly union on the investment plans of firms. It turns out that unions may be bad for firm investment because of the hold-up problem. The optimal choice of the union is to offer low wages in the future in order to induce the firm to invest a lot. This offer is not credible to the firm, however, because once the firm has invested the union will renege on its promise and demand higher wages. Intuitively, the union "holds up" (as in a Western movie) the firm's capital stock. The firm will formulate its optimal investment and production plans in the full knowledge that it will be held up in the future and will therefore invest less than it would otherwise have done. This is the famous underinvestment result. The scenario sketched is an example of the dynamic inconsistency which arises is many different settings in macroeconomics. In Chapter 10 we return to this important issue.

Further Reading

On the interaction between union wage setting and firm investment, see Grout (1984), van der Ploeg (1987b), Anderson and Devereux (1988), and Devereux and Lockwood (1991). Gottfries and Horn (1987) present a union-based model of unemployment persistence. Lindbeck and Snower (1988) is a good reference to the insider-outsider literature. Manning (1987) embeds the union model in a sequential bargaining framework. Koskela and Vilmunen (1996) study the effects of income taxes in a union model. For good surveys of the union literature, see Oswald (1982, 1985), Farber (1986), Pencavel (1991), and Booth (1995). See Cross (1988) for an interesting collection of articles on hysteresis.

9

Search in the Labour Market

The purpose of this chapter is to discuss the following issues:

1. How can we explain the duration of unemployment? We introduce a simple model of search in the labour market.

2. How does taxation affect the equilibrium unemployment rate? How can we reduce the equilibrium unemployment rate?

3. How can the search-theoretic approach explain observed persistence in the unemployment rate?

9.1 Search in the Labour Market

The labour market in many countries is characterized by huge gross flows of workers leaving a job and entering unemployment and vice versa. For example, for the US the flow of workers entering or leaving a job amounts to 7 million per month (Blanchard and Diamond, 1989, p. 1)! It would be tempting to argue that these enormous flows, due to the simultaneous occurrence of job creation and job destruction, are bound to cause problems. There are a lot of workers looking for jobs, and vice versa. At a macroeconomic level, however, it appears that (at least in the US) the labour market is relatively efficient at matching jobs and workers. As we saw in Chapter 7, US unemployment seems to be relatively low and stable. The modern theory of search behaviour in the labour market is specifically aimed at describing this matching process that takes place in the labour market. This theory is radically different from the previous labour market theories discussed so far in that the notion of an aggregate labour market is abandoned. As Diamond (1982, p. 217) explains, rather than assuming that the market is the mechanism by which workers and jobs are brought together, the modern approach assumes that there is a search process which stochastically brings together unemployed workers and vacant jobs in a pair-wise fashion. This search process takes time and consequently causes loss of output. When a worker and a job meet each other, negotiations take place to determine the wage.

9.1.1 A simple model[1]

The modern theory of search makes use of the so-called *matching function*. This is a hypothetical concept, not unlike the production function, which turns out to be very convenient analytically. A matching function determines the number of jobs that are created ("matches") each instant, as a function of the number of unemployed job-seeking workers and the number of vacancies that exist (plus exogenous variables). Firms have jobs that are either *filled* or *vacant*. It is assumed that only vacant jobs are on offer. The firm is not searching for workers to replace existing (but unsatisfactory) workers. Workers either have a job or are unemployed, and only the unemployed engage in search. There is no on-the-job search in the model discussed in this section. By making these assumptions, the two activities of production of goods and trade in labour are strictly separate activities.

Firms and workers know the job-matching technology, and know that there is an exogenously given *job separation process*.[2] At each moment in time, a proportion of the existing filled jobs are destroyed, say because of firm-specific shocks making previously lucrative jobs unprofitable. In equilibrium, there is thus a constant inflow into unemployment, and the model predicts an *equilibrium unemployment rate* that is strictly greater than zero.

It is assumed that there are many firms and many workers, and that every agent behaves as a perfect competitor. The fixed labour force consists of N workers, and each worker who has a job supplies one unit of labour. (There is no decision on hours of work by the worker, and effort of each worker is constant.) The unemployment rate is defined as the fraction of the labour force without a job, and is denoted by U. The vacancy rate is the number of vacancies expressed as a proportion of the labour force, and is denoted by V. Hence, at each moment in time, there are UN unemployed workers and VN vacant jobs "trying to find each other".

The number of successful matches each instant in time depends on UN and VN according to the matching function:

$$XN = G(UN, VN), \tag{9.1}$$

where XN is the total number of matches, so that X is the matching *rate*, and $G(.,.)$ is a linearly homogeneous function, with $G_U > 0$, $G_V > 0$, $G_{UU} < 0$, $G_{VV} < 0$, and $G_{UU}G_{VV} - G_{UV}^2 > 0$. The intuitive idea behind (9.1) is that at each instant XN

---

[1] The exposition given in this section closely follows Pissarides (1990, ch. 1).
[2] Mortensen and Pissarides (1994) and Pissarides (2000, ch. 2) develop a matching model with an endogenous job destruction rate.

meetings occur between an unemployed worker and a firm with a job vacancy. Which particular worker meets which particular job vacancy is selected randomly.

Consider a small time interval dt. During that time interval, there are $XN\,dt$ matches and VN vacant jobs, so that the probability of a vacancy being filled during dt equals $(XN/VN)dt$. By defining $q \equiv XN/VN = X/V$, we can use equation (9.1) to write q as:

$$q \equiv \frac{G(UN, VN)}{VN} = \frac{VNG(UN/VN, 1)}{VN} = G(U/V, 1) \equiv q(\theta), \tag{9.2}$$

where $\theta \equiv V/U$ is the vacancy–unemployment ratio that plays a crucial role in the analysis. Obviously, since $q(\theta)dt$ measures the probability that a vacancy will be filled in the time interval dt, $q(\theta)$ can be interpreted as the *instantaneous* probability of a vacancy being filled, and the expected duration of a job vacancy is $1/q(\theta)$. All these results are derived more formally in the Intermezzo below.

In view of the assumptions about $G(.,.)$, the following properties of the $q(\theta)$ function can be demonstrated:

$$\frac{dq}{d\theta} = -\frac{G_U}{\theta^2} < 0, \tag{9.3}$$

and

$$\eta(\theta) \equiv -\frac{\theta}{q}\frac{dq}{d\theta} = \frac{G_U}{\theta q} \quad \Rightarrow \quad 0 < \eta(\theta) < 1, \tag{9.4}$$

where $\eta(\theta)$ is the absolute value of the elasticity of the $q(\theta)$ function.[3]

Unemployed workers also find a match in a stochastic manner. For workers, the instantaneous probability of finding a firm with a vacancy is given by XN/UN, the number of vacancies expressed as a fraction of the number of unemployed workers. This instantaneous probability can be written in terms of θ also:

$$\frac{G(UN, VN)}{UN} = \frac{VNG(UN/VN, 1)}{UN} = (V/U)G(U/V, 1) = \theta q(\theta) \equiv f(\theta). \tag{9.5}$$

The $f(\theta)$ function has the following elasticity:

$$\frac{\theta}{f(\theta)}\frac{df}{d\theta} = \left[q(\theta) + \theta\frac{dq}{d\theta}\right]\frac{\theta}{\theta q(\theta)} = 1 + \frac{\theta}{q}\frac{dq}{d\theta} = 1 - \eta(\theta) > 0. \tag{9.6}$$

Since $f(\theta)$ represents the instantaneous probability of an unemployed worker finding a job, the expected duration of unemployment equals $1/f(\theta) = 1/(\theta q(\theta))$. This is intuitive, since unemployed workers find it easier to locate a job (and hence expect a shorter duration of unemployment) if θ is high, i.e. if there are relatively many vacancies. The definitions of $q(\theta)$ and $f(\theta)$ in (9.2) and (9.5) show that there is

---

[3] The trick is to write (9.1) as $XN = G_U UN + G_V VN$, which implies $q = G_U/\theta + G_V$. Hence, $\eta(\theta) = G_U/(q\theta) = 1 - G_V/q$, which is between 0 and 1 because $0 < G_V < q$.

an intricate connection between the process linking workers to jobs, and the one linking jobs to workers. This is obvious, since workers and vacancies meet in pairs.

The variable θ is the relevant parameter measuring labour market pressure to both parties involved in the labour market. This parameter plays a crucial role because the dependence of the search probabilities on θ implies the existence of a *trading external-ity*. There is stochastic rationing occurring in the labour market (firms with unfilled vacancies, workers without a job) which cannot be solved by the price mechanism, since worker and vacancy must first get together before the price mechanism can play any role. The degree of rationing is, however, dependent on the situation in the labour market, which is summarized by θ. If θ rises, the probability of rationing is higher for the average firm and lower for the average worker. The particular exter-nal effect that is present in the model is called the *congestion* or *search externality* by Pissarides (1990, p. 6).

For simplicity it is assumed that there is an exogenously given *job destruction pro-cess* that ensures that a proportion s of all filled jobs disappears at each instant. These jobs could be destroyed, for example, because of firm-specific shocks making previously profitable jobs unprofitable. Hence, in a small time interval dt, the prob-ability that an employed worker loses his/her job and becomes unemployed is given by sdt (with the same holding for filled jobs, of course). Hence, the average number of workers that become unemployed in a time interval dt equals $s(1 - U)N\,dt$ and the average number of unemployed who find a job is given by $\theta q(\theta)UN\,dt$. In the steady-state the unemployment rate is constant, so that the expected inflow and outflow must be equal to each other:

$$s(1 - U)N\,dt = \theta q(\theta)UN\,dt. \tag{9.7}$$

By assuming that the labour force N is large, expected and actual inflows and out-flows can be assumed the same, so that (9.7) can be solved for the actual equilibrium unemployment rate:

$$U = \frac{s}{s + \theta q(\theta)}, \tag{9.8}$$

which implies that $\partial U/\partial s > 0$ and $\partial U/\partial \theta < 0$.

Intermezzo

Some statistical theory. The search-theoretic approach makes use of some statistical techniques that may not be immediately obvious. In this intermezzo some important notions are reviewed. Further details can be found in Ross (1993, ch. 5).

A very convenient probability distribution is the exponential distribution. A continuous random variable X is exponentially distributed if its probability density function has the form:

$$f(x) = \begin{cases} \lambda e^{-\lambda x} & x \geq 0 \\ 0 & x < 0 \end{cases} \tag{a}$$

which implies that the cumulative distribution function is given by:

$$F(x) \equiv \int_{-\infty}^{x} f(y)\, dy = \begin{cases} 1 - e^{-\lambda x} & x \geq 0 \\ 0 & x < 0 \end{cases} \tag{b}$$

The cumulative distribution function $F(x)$ measures the probability that the random variable X attains a value less than or equal to x, or in symbols:

$$F(x) \equiv P\{X \leq x\}. \tag{c}$$

The exponential distribution has the following properties. First, $E(X) = 1/\lambda$, the expected value of X is $1/\lambda$. Second, the variance of X is $V(X) \equiv E(X^2) - [E(X)]^2 = 1/\lambda^2$. Third, the random variable X is *memoryless*. Suppose that X is the lifetime of some light bulb. Then, if the light bulb is still working at some time t, the distribution of the remaining amount of time that it will continue to shine light is the same as the original distribution. Colloquially speaking, the light bulb does not "remember" that it has already shone for t periods. Formally, a random variable is memoryless if the following holds:

$$P\{X > s + t \mid X > t\} = P\{X > s\}. \tag{d}$$

The memoryless property implies a very simple expression for the *failure rate* function (often called the *hazard rate* function). The failure rate function $r(t)$ represents the conditional probability density that a t-year old item (such as a light bulb or a human being) fails. It is defined as:

$$r(t) \equiv \frac{f(t)}{1 - F(t)}. \tag{e}$$

For the exponential distribution, the memoryless property implies that the distribution of remaining life for a t-year old item is the same as for a new item. As a result, the failure rate function should be constant. Using (a)–(c), we find that this is indeed the case:

$$r(t) \equiv \frac{f(t)}{1 - F(t)} = \frac{\lambda e^{-\lambda t}}{e^{-\lambda t}} = \lambda. \tag{f}$$

We shall have the opportunity to use this property in economically very interesting applications in the present chapter and in Chapter 16.

The search-theoretic approach also makes extensive use of the notion of a *Poisson process*. A Poisson process is a *counting process* with a number of properties. A stochastic process $\{M(t), t \geq 0\}$ is called a counting process if $M(t)$ represents the number of "events" that have occurred up to time t. For example, if $M(t)$ represents the number of goals scored by one's favourite soccer star by time t, an "event" consists of your star hitting the back of the net once more. In the context of matching, $M(t)$ represents the number of all matches that have occurred by time t. The counting process $M(t)$ must satisfy: (i) $M(t) \geq 0$; (ii) $M(t)$ is integer valued; (iii) if $s < t$, then $M(t) - M(s) \geq 0$; and (iv) for $s < t$, $M(t) - M(s)$ equals the number of events that have occurred in the interval (s, t) (Ross, 1993, p. 208).

A Poisson process is a specific kind of counting process. Formally, the counting process $\{M(t), t \geq 0\}$ is called a Poisson process with rate $\lambda (> 0)$ if: (i) $M(0) = 0$; (ii) the process has independent increments; (iii) the number of events in any interval length t is Poisson distributed with mean λt. Hence,

$$P\{M(t + s) - M(s) = m\} \equiv e^{-\lambda t} \frac{(\lambda t)^m}{m!}, \tag{g}$$

for $m = 0, 1, 2, 3, \ldots$ For our purposes it is important to know something about interarrival times. Suppose that we have a Poisson process $M(t)$, and that the first event has occurred at time T_1. We define T_n as the elapsed time between the $(n - 1)$st and the nth event (for $n > 1$), and refer to T_n as the interarrival time. Of course, T_n is stochastic. A very useful property of the Poisson process is that T_n $(n = 1, 2, 3, \ldots)$ are independent identically distributed exponential random variables with parameter λ and hence have a mean of $1/\lambda$ (Ross, 1993, p. 214).

Within the context of the matching model this is a very handy property. Since interarrival times are distributed exponentially, the hazard rate $r(t) = \lambda$ is constant and $\lambda \, dt$ represents the probability that a failure will take place in the time interval dt. Note that a "failure" implies that a match has occurred in this context. Hence, λ can be interpreted as the instantaneous probability of a match occurring.

Firms

Each firm is extremely small, has a risk-neutral owner, and has only one job, which is either filled or vacant. If the job is filled, the firm hires physical capital K at a given interest rate r, and produces output $F(K, 1)$. The production function is constant returns to scale and satisfies $F_K > 0 > F_{KK}$ and $F_L > 0 > F_{LL}$. If the job is vacant, on the other hand, the firm is actively searching for a worker and incurs a constant search cost of γ_0 per time unit. As was pointed out above, the probability that the firm finds a worker in time interval dt is given by $q(\theta) \, dt$. Since each firm only has one job, the number of jobs and firms in the economy coincide, and the free entry/exit condition determines the number of jobs/firms.

Let J_O denote the present value of the profit stream originating from a firm with an occupied job, and let J_V designate the same for a firm with a vacancy. With a perfect capital market the firm can borrow freely at the given interest rate, and the following steady-state *arbitrage equation* holds for a firm with a vacancy:

$$rJ_V = -\gamma_0 + q(\theta)[J_O - J_V]. \tag{9.9}$$

In words, equation (9.9) says that a vacant job is an asset of the firm. In equilibrium, the value of this asset must be such that the capital cost rJ_V is exactly equal to the return from the asset. The return consists of two parts, i.e. the constant search cost that must be incurred each time unit $(-\gamma_0)$ plus the expected capital gain due to the fact that the vacant job can be filled in the future (with instantaneous probability $q(\theta)$). The capital gain is the difference in value of a filled and a vacant job, i.e. $J_O - J_V$.

Since anyone who is prepared to incur the constant search cost each time unit can set up a firm (with a vacancy) and start looking for a worker, free entry of firms will occur until the value of a vacant job is exactly equal to zero. Conversely, if a vacant job is worth a negative amount, exit of firms takes place and vacancies disappear. This implies the following expression:

$$J_V = 0 \quad \Rightarrow \quad 0 = -\gamma_0 + q(\theta)J_O \quad \Rightarrow \quad J_O = \gamma_0/q(\theta). \tag{9.10}$$

The final expression is intuitive. The expected duration of a vacancy is $1/q(\theta)$ during which the search cost γ_0 must be incurred. In equilibrium the number of jobs/firms must be such that the expected profit of a filled job is exactly equal to the expected cost of the vacancy.

For a firm with a filled job, the following steady-state arbitrage equation can be derived:

$$rJ_O = F(K, 1) - (r + \delta)K - w - sJ_O, \tag{9.11}$$

where $(r + \delta)$ is the rental charge on capital goods, and w is the real wage rate. Equation (9.11) says that the asset value of a filled job is J_O and its capital cost equals rJ_O. This must equal the return from the filled job, which consists of two parts. The first part is the surplus created in production, i.e. (the value of) output that remains after the production factors capital and labour have been paid (this equals $F(K, 1) - (r + \delta)K - w$). The second part is the expected capital loss due to job destruction (sJ_O).

The size of each firm with a filled job is determined in the usual manner. The firm chooses the amount of capital it wants to rent such that the value of the firm is maximized. In terms of (9.11) we can write this problem as:

$$\max_{\{K\}} (r + s) J_O \equiv F(K, 1) - (r + \delta)K - w \;\Rightarrow\; F_K(K, 1) = r + \delta. \tag{9.12}$$

This is the usual condition equating the marginal product of capital to the rental charge on capital. By substituting (9.10) and (9.12) into (9.11), we obtain:[4]

$$\frac{(r + s)\gamma_0}{q(\theta)} = F(K, 1) - F_K(K, 1)K - w \;\Rightarrow$$

$$\frac{F_L(K, 1) - w}{r + s} = \frac{\gamma_0}{q(\theta)}. \tag{9.13}$$

The left-hand side of (9.13) represents the value of an occupied job, equalling the present value of rents (accruing to the firm during the job's existence) using the risk-of-job-destruction-adjusted discount rate, $r + s$, to discount future rents. The right-hand side of (9.13) is the expected search costs. With free exit/entry of firms, the value of an occupied job exactly equals the expected search costs (see above).[5]

Workers

The worker is risk neutral and lives forever, and consequently only cares about the expected discounted value of income (Diamond, 1982, p. 219). A worker with a job earns the wage w, whilst an unemployed worker obtains the exogenously given "unemployment benefit" z. This may consist of a real transfer payment from the government but may also include the pecuniary value of leisure. Let Y_E denote the present value of the expected stream of income of a worker with a job, and let Y_U denote the same for an unemployed worker. Then the following steady-state arbitrage equation can be derived for a worker without a job:

$$rY_U = z + \theta q(\theta) [Y_E - Y_U]. \tag{9.14}$$

In words, equation (9.14) says that the asset Y_U is the human capital of the unemployed worker. The capital cost of the asset must be equal to the return, which consists of the unemployment benefit, z, plus the expected capital gain due to finding a job, i.e. $Y_E - Y_U$. As Pissarides (1990, p. 10) points out, rY_U can be interpreted in two ways. First, it is the yield on human capital of an unemployed worker during search. It measures the minimum amount for which the worker would be willing to stop searching for a job, and hence has the interpretation of a *reservation wage*. The second

---

[4] We have used the linear homogeneity of the production function, which implies that $F = F_K K + 1 \times F_L$, so that $F - F_K K = F_L$.

[5] If there were no search costs for the firm ($\gamma_0 = 0$), the model would yield the standard productivity condition for labour ($F_L = w$). With positive search costs, however, the factor labour receives less than its marginal product. This is because the marginal product of labour must be sufficiently large to cover the capital cost of the expected search costs.

interpretation is that of "normal" or "permanent" income: the amount that the unemployed worker can consume whilst still leaving his/her human capital intact.

For a worker with a job the steady-state arbitrage equation reads as follows.

$$rY_E = w - s[Y_E - Y_U]. \tag{9.15}$$

The permanent income of an employed worker differs from the wage rate because there is a non-zero probability of job destruction causing a capital loss of $Y_E - Y_U$.

By solving (9.14)-(9.15) for rY_U and rY_E, the following expressions are obtained:

$$rY_U = \frac{(r+s)z + \theta q(\theta)w}{r+s+\theta q(\theta)}, \tag{9.16}$$

$$rY_E = \frac{sz + [r+\theta q(\theta)]w}{r+s+\theta q(\theta)} = \frac{r(w-z)}{r+s+\theta q(\theta)} + rY_U, \tag{9.17}$$

where the second expression in (9.17) shows that $w \geq z$ must hold for anybody to be willing to search for a job.

Wages

What happens when a job seeker encounters a firm with a vacancy? Clearly there is a *pure economic rent* created by the encounter, existing of the sum of the foregone expected search costs by the firm and the worker. But how is this surplus shared between the two parties? In this search context, it is clearly not possible to refer to some going market wage rate, because the concept of an aggregate labour market with impersonal exchange has been abandoned. The exchange that takes place between the two parties is one-on-one, and the division of the rent is a matter of bargaining. Fortunately, as we saw in Chapter 8, there is a useful solution concept in two-person bargaining situations, called the *generalized Nash bargaining* solution.

We assume that all firm-worker pairings are equally productive, so that the wage rate is the same everywhere. This allows us to focus on the *symmetric* equilibrium solution of the model, which is reasonable because the aim of this chapter is to discuss the macroeconomic implications of search theory, not to develop an empirically adequate description of the labour market. We furthermore assume that each firm-worker pair that is involved in wage negotiations takes the behaviour of other such pairings as given.

Consider a particular firm-worker pairing i. What does the firm get out of a deal? Obviously the firm changes status from a firm with a vacancy (with value $J_V^i = 0$, due to free exit/entry) to a firm with an occupied job (with value J_O^i). Hence, the expected gain to the firm is:

$$rJ_O^i = F(K_i, 1) - (r+\delta)K_i - w_i - sJ_O^i \implies$$

$$J_O^i = \frac{F_L(K_i, 1) - w_i}{r+s}, \tag{9.18}$$

where K_i denotes the capital stock of firm i, and we have used (9.12) and linear homogeneity of the firm's production function to obtain the final expression involving the marginal product of labour. (Upon reaching agreement with the worker, the firm rents capital such that $F_K(K_i, 1) = r + \delta$.) Equation (9.18) shows what the firm is after: it wants to squeeze as much surplus as possible out of the worker by bargaining for a wage far below the marginal product of the worker.

What does the worker get out of the deal? If a deal is struck, the worker changes status from unemployed to employed worker, which means that the net gain to the worker is:

$$r\left(Y_E^i - Y_U\right) = w_i - s\left[Y_E^i - Y_U\right] - rY_U,$$
(9.19)

where Y_U does not depend on w_i, but rather on the expectation regarding the wage rate in the economy as a whole (see (9.16)). If the worker does not accept this job offer (and the wage on offer w_i) then he/she must continue searching as one of many in the "pool of the unemployed". The relevant wage rate that the unemployed worker takes into account to calculate the value of being unemployed is not w_i but rather the *expected* wage rate elsewhere in the economy.

Using the generalized Nash bargaining solution, the wage w_i is set such that Ω is maximized:

$$\max_{\{w_i\}} \Omega \equiv \beta \log\left[Y_E^i - Y_U\right] + (1 - \beta) \log\left[J_O^i - J_V\right], \quad 0 < \beta < 1,$$
(9.20)

where J_V ($= 0$) and Y_U can be interpreted as the "threat" points of the firm and the worker, respectively. The relative bargaining strengths of the worker and the firm are given by, respectively, β and $1 - \beta$. The usual rent-sharing rule rolls out of the bargaining problem defined in (9.20):

$$\frac{d\Omega}{dw_i} = \beta \left(\frac{\Omega}{Y_E^i - Y_U}\right) \frac{dY_E^i}{dw_i} + (1 - \beta) \left(\frac{\Omega}{J_O^i - J_V}\right) \frac{dJ_O^i}{dw_i} = 0 \quad \Rightarrow$$

$$\frac{\beta}{r + s} \left(\frac{1}{Y_E^i - Y_U}\right) - \frac{1 - \beta}{r + s} \left(\frac{1}{J_O^i - J_V}\right) = 0 \quad \Rightarrow$$

$$Y_E^i - Y_U = \left(\frac{\beta}{1 - \beta}\right) \left[J_O^i - J_V\right].$$
(9.21)

This rent-sharing rule can be turned into a more convenient *wage equation* in two ways.

First, by substituting (9.18)–(9.19) into (9.21) and imposing $J_V = 0$ (due to free exit/entry) we obtain:

$$(1 - \beta)Y_E^i = \beta J_O^i + (1 - \beta)Y_U \Rightarrow$$

$$(1 - \beta)\left[\frac{w_i + sY_U}{r + s}\right] = \beta\left[\frac{F_L(K_i, 1) - w_i}{r + s}\right] + (1 - \beta)Y_U \Rightarrow$$

$$(1 - \beta)[w_i + sY_U] = \beta[F_L(K_i, 1) - w_i] + (1 - \beta)(r + s)Y_U \Rightarrow$$

$$w_i = (1 - \beta)rY_U + \beta F_L(K_i, 1). \tag{9.22}$$

The worker gets a weighted average of his/her reservation wage (rY_U) and marginal product (F_L). The stronger is the bargaining position of the worker, the larger is β and the closer is the wage to the marginal product of labour.

The second expression for the wage equation is obtained as follows. From (9.12) we know that each firm with an occupied job chooses the same capital stock, so that $K_i = K$. Hence, the wage rate chosen by firm i is also the same for all firms, $w_i = w$. This implies that rY_U can be written as follows:

$$rY_U = z + \theta q(\theta)[Y_E - Y_U] = z + \theta q(\theta)\left(\frac{\beta}{1 - \beta}\right)J_O$$

$$= z + \theta q(\theta)\left(\frac{\beta}{1 - \beta}\right)\frac{\gamma_0}{q(\theta)} = z + \frac{\beta\theta\gamma_0}{1 - \beta}. \tag{9.23}$$

This result is intuitive. The reservation wage is increasing in the unemployment benefit, the relative bargaining strength of the worker, the employers' search cost, and the tightness in the labour market. By substituting (9.23) into (9.22) we obtain the alternative wage equation:

$$w = (1 - \beta)z + \beta[F_L(K, 1) + \theta\gamma_0]. \tag{9.24}$$

Workers get a weighted average of the unemployment benefit and the surplus, which consists of the marginal product of labour plus the expected search costs that are saved if the deal is struck (recall that $\gamma_0\theta \equiv \gamma_0 V/U$ represents the average hiring costs per unemployed worker).

9.1.2 Market equilibrium

We now have all the necessary ingredients of the model. For convenience, the full model is summarized by the following four equations which together determine the equilibrium values for the endogenous variables, K, w, θ, and U.

$$F_K(K, 1) = r + \delta, \tag{9.25}$$

$$\frac{F_L\left[K(r + \delta), 1\right] - w}{r + s} = \frac{\gamma_0}{q(\theta)}, \tag{9.26}$$

$$w = (1 - \beta)z + \beta\left[F_L\left[K(r + \delta), 1\right] + \theta\gamma_0\right], \tag{9.27}$$

$$U = \frac{s}{s + \theta q(\theta)}. \tag{9.28}$$

Equation (9.25) is the marginal productivity condition for capital, determining the optimal capital stock (and thus the optimal size of production) of each firm with a filled job. Since the marginal productivity of capital diminishes as more capital is added ($F_{KK} < 0$), (9.25) relates the optimal capital stock (K^*) to the (exogenous) rental rate on capital, i.e. $K^* = K(r + \delta)$ with $K' < 0$. By plugging this function into, respectively, (9.13) and (9.24) we obtain (9.26) and (9.27). Equation (9.26) is a form of the zero profit condition implied by the assumption of free exit/entry of firms, and (9.27) is the wage-setting equation that rolls out of the Nash bargaining between a firm with a vacancy and an unemployed job seeker. Finally, (9.28) is the expression for the equilibrium unemployment rate. This equation is also known as the *Beveridge curve* (Blanchard and Diamond, 1989).

The model is recursive under the assumption of a fixed real rate of interest. First, (9.25) determines the optimal size of each producing firm as a function of the interest rate. Then (9.26)–(9.27) determine equilibrium values for w and θ as a function of that optimal capital stock. Finally, (9.28) determines the unemployment rate, U, as a function of θ. Once θ and U are known, the number of jobs is given by $(1 - U)N + \theta UN$ and employment equals $L = (1 - U)N$.

The graphical representation of the model is given in Figure 9.1. In panel (a) the ZP curve is the zero-profit condition (9.26). It is downward sloping in (w, θ) space:

$$\left(\frac{dw}{d\theta}\right)_{ZP} = \frac{(r + s)\gamma_0}{q(\theta)^2} q'(\theta) < 0. \tag{9.29}$$

Intuitively, a reduction in the wage increases the value of an occupied job and thus raises the left-hand side of (9.26). To restore the zero-profit equilibrium the expected search cost for firms (the right-hand side of (9.26)) must also increase, i.e. $q(\theta)$ must fall and θ must rise.

Also in panel (a), the WS curve is the wage-setting curve (9.27). This curve is upward sloping in (w, θ) space:

$$\left(\frac{dw}{d\theta}\right)_{WS} = \beta\gamma_0 > 0. \tag{9.30}$$

Intuitively, the wage rises with θ because the worker receives part of the search costs that are foregone when he strikes a deal with a firm with a vacancy (see above).

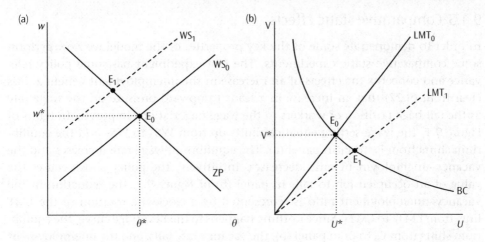

Figure 9.1. Search equilibrium in the labour market

By combining ZP and WS_0 in panel (a), the equilibrium wage, w^*, and vacancy–unemployment ratio, θ^*, are determined—see point E_0 in panel (a).

In panel (b) of Figure 9.1 the equilibrium vacancy–unemployment ratio (the indicator for labour market tightness) is represented by the line LMT_0 from the origin and BC is the Beveridge curve (9.28) rewritten in (V, U) space. By using $V \equiv \theta U$ in (9.28), the Beveridge curve can be loglinearized:

$$\tilde{V} = \left(\frac{1}{1-\eta} \right) \tilde{s} - \left(\frac{s+f\eta}{f(1-\eta)} \right) \tilde{U}, \tag{9.31}$$

where $\tilde{U} \equiv dU/U$, $\tilde{V} \equiv dV/V$, and $\tilde{s} \equiv ds/s$, and where η and f are given, respectively, in (9.4) and (9.5).[6] The Beveridge curve is downward sloping (since $0 < \eta < 1$). Intuitively, for a given unemployment rate, a reduction in vacancy rate leads to a fall in the instantaneous probability of finding a job (f), i.e. for points below the BC curve the unemployment rate is less than the rate required for flow equilibrium in the labour market ($U < s/(s+f)$). To restore flow equilibrium the unemployment rate must rise. Equation (9.31) also shows that an increase in the job destruction rate s shifts the Beveridge curve up and to the right, a result which will be used below.

---

[6] This expression is obtained as follows. Starting with (9.28) and noting that $f(\theta) \equiv \theta q(\theta)$ we find:

$$[s + f(\theta)] \, dU + U \, df(\theta) = 0 \quad \Rightarrow$$

$$\frac{s}{U} dU + U \, df(\theta) = (1 - U) ds \quad \Rightarrow$$

$$s\tilde{U} + Uf(\theta) [1 - \eta(\theta)] \tilde{\theta} = s(1 - U)\tilde{s} \quad \Rightarrow$$

$$[s - f(\theta)U(1 - \eta(\theta))] \tilde{U} + Uf(\theta)(1 - \eta(\theta))\tilde{V} = s(1 - U)\tilde{s}.$$

By using $U = s/(s + f)$ in the final expression and rewriting we obtain (9.31).

225

9.1.3 Comparative static effects

In order to demonstrate some of the key properties of the model we now perform some comparative static experiments. The first experiment has some policy relevance and concerns the effects of an increase in the unemployment benefit z. It is clear from (9.27) that an increase in z leads to upward pressure on the wage rate as the fall-back position of workers in the wage negotiations improves. In terms of Figure 9.1, the wage setting equation shifts up from WS_0 to WS_1 and the equilibrium shifts from E_0 to E_1 in panel (a). The equilibrium wage rate increases and the vacancy–unemployment ratio decreases. Intuitively, the policy shock causes the value of an occupied job to fall. In panel (b) of Figure 9.1, the reduction in the vacancy–unemployment ratio is represented by a clockwise rotation of the LMT line, from LMT_0 to LMT_1. Since nothing happens to the Beveridge curve, the equilibrium shifts from E_0 to E_1 in panel (b), the vacancy rate falls, and the unemployment rate rises.

As a second comparative static experiment we consider what happens when the exogenous rate of job destruction s rises. This shock is more complicated than the first one because it affects both the incentive for firms to create vacancies and the Beveridge curve itself. It is clear from (9.26) that, ceteris paribus the wage, the increase in the job destruction rate reduces the value of an occupied job as the rents accruing to the firm are discounted more heavily. Hence, in terms of panel (a) of Figure 9.2, the ZP curve shifts to the left from ZP_0 to ZP_1. Since nothing happens to the wage-setting curve, the equilibrium in panel (a) shifts from E_0 to E_1 and both the wage and the vacancy–unemployment ratio fall. In panel (b) of Figure 9.2, the LMT curve rotates in a clockwise fashion from LMT_0 to LMT_1. As was noted above, the direct effect of an increase in the job destruction rate is to shift the Beveridge curve outward, say from BC_0 to BC_1 in panel (b). We show in the appendix that

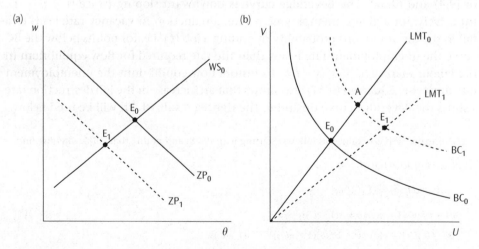

Figure 9.2. The effects of a higher job destruction rate

the outward shift in the Beveridge curve dominates the clockwise rotation in the LMT curve (provided a very mild sufficient condition is satisfied) so that the new equilibrium E_1 lies in a north-easterly direction from the initial equilibrium E_0 so that both the unemployment and vacancy rates increase.

9.2 Applications of Search Models

In this section we use the search-theoretic approach to study three issues. First, we continue our study of the effects of taxation on the labour market. Second, we study the idea of treating workers like empty beer bottles. Specifically, we look at what happens if employers must pay (receive) a deposit if they lay off (hire) a worker. Finally, we briefly investigate how the search-theoretic approach can be used to explain the observed persistence in the unemployment rate.

9.2.1 The effects of taxation

We assume that there are two separate taxes levied on labour. First, the employer must pay an *ad valorem* tax on the use of labour (a payroll tax), which is denoted by t_E. Second, the household faces a proportional tax on labour income, denoted by t_L.

The effects of the employers' tax on labour are as follows. First, equation (9.11) is modified to:

$$rJ_O = F(K, 1) - (r + \delta)K - w(1 + t_E) - sJ_O, \tag{9.32}$$

so that the marginal productivity condition for capital (equation (9.12)) is unaffected, but the free entry/exit condition (9.13) is modified to:

$$\frac{F_L\left[K(r + \delta), 1\right] - w(1 + t_E)}{r + s} = \frac{\gamma_0}{q(\theta)}, \tag{9.33}$$

where we have also substituted the implicit expression determining the optimal capital stock (i.e. $K^* = K(r + \delta)$).

The effects of the labour income tax are as follows. First, since the unemployment benefit is untaxed and exogenous, equation (9.14) is unchanged, but the after-tax real wage rate $w(1 - t_L)$ appears in (9.15), so that (9.16)-(9.17) are modified to:

$$rY_U = \frac{(r + s)z + \theta q(\theta)w(1 - t_L)}{r + s + \theta q(\theta)}, \tag{9.34}$$

$$rY_E = \frac{sz + [r + \theta q(\theta)]\,w(1 - t_L)}{r + s + \theta q(\theta)} = \frac{r\,[w(1 - t_L) - z]}{r + s + \theta q(\theta)} + rY_U, \tag{9.35}$$

where the second expression in (9.35) shows that $w(1 - t_L) \geq z$ must hold for anybody to be willing to search, i.e. the labour income tax must not be too high.

227

The second effect of the income tax operates via the wage bargaining process. By following the derivation in section 1.1, the rent-sharing rule (9.21) is modified to:

$$Y_E^i - Y_U = \left(\frac{\beta}{1-\beta}\right) \left(\frac{1-t_L}{1+t_E}\right) \left[J_O^i - J_V\right],\tag{9.36}$$

so that the wage equation (9.22) becomes:

$$w_i = (1-\beta)\left(\frac{rY_U}{1-t_L}\right) + \beta\left(\frac{F_L(K_i, 1)}{1+t_E}\right),\tag{9.37}$$

and (9.24) can be written as:

$$w = (1-\beta)\left(\frac{z}{1-t_L}\right) + \beta\left(\frac{F_L[K(r+\delta), 1] + \theta\gamma_0}{1+t_E}\right),\tag{9.38}$$

where we have once again substituted $K^* = K(r+\delta)$.

The core part of the model consists of the Beveridge curve (9.28), the zero-profit curve (9.33), and the wage-setting curve (9.38). It is possible to explain the intuition behind the comparative static effects of the various tax rates by graphical means. (The formal derivations are found in the appendix.)

First we consider in Figure 9.3 the effects of an increase in the payroll tax, t_E. It follows from (9.33) that the zero profit curve shifts to the left (from ZP_0 to ZP_1 in panel (a)) as a result of the shock. Ceteris paribus the gross wage rate, the tax increase reduces the value of an occupied job so that the zero profit equilibrium is consistent with a lower vacancy–unemployment ratio. The payroll tax also features in the wage-setting equation. Indeed, it follows from (9.38) that the increase in the payroll tax puts downward pressure on the wage rate. Intuitively this is because the firm is interested in the net surplus of the match (equal to $(F_L + \theta\gamma_0)/(1+t_E)$), i.e. it takes the payroll tax into account. Part of this surplus features in the wage which

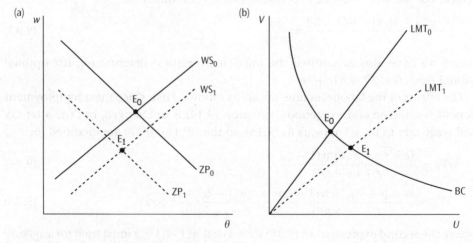

(a)

(b)

Figure 9.3. The effects of a payroll tax

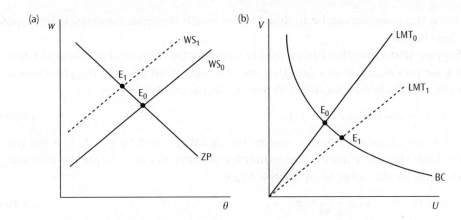

Figure 9.4. The effects of a labour income tax

thus falls on that account. In terms of Figure 9.3, the wage-setting curve shifts down from WS_0 to WS_1 in panel (a). The equilibrium shifts from E_0 to E_1, and both the wage rate and the vacancy–unemployment ratio fall (see Appendix). In panel (b) the LMT curve rotates in a clockwise fashion from LMT_0 to LMT_1 and the equilibrium shifts from E_0 to E_1. The equilibrium vacancy rate falls and the unemployment rate increases.

As a second comparative statics exercise we now consider the effects of an increase in the labour income tax, t_L. The effects of this shock are illustrated in Figure 9.4. The increase in the labour income tax has no effect on the zero-profit curve but the wage-setting equation shifts up from WS_0 to WS_1 in panel (a). Intuitively, it follows from (9.38) that the tax increase raises the outside option for the household in the wage bargaining process because the unemployment benefit is untaxed. This leads, ceteris paribus, to upward pressure on the wage rate. In panel (a) the equilibrium shifts from E_0 to E_1, the gross wage rate increases, and the vacancy–unemployment ratio falls. In panel (b) the LMT curve rotates in a clockwise fashion from LMT_0 to LMT_1, the equilibrium shifts from E_0 to E_1, and equilibrium vacancies fall whilst the unemployment rate rises. The tax shock works in exactly the same way as an increase in the unemployment benefit.

9.2.2 Deposits on workers?

Some people return empty bottles to the store because they find it unacceptable from an environmental point of view to litter them. Most people, however, are less interested in this noble pursuit of a responsible attitude towards the natural environment, and only return the bottles because there is money to be made in the form of a deposit that will be refunded. One could argue that a similar system should be tried in the labour market. Why not have the firm pay a deposit when it fires a worker, to be refunded when it (re-) hires that (or another) worker? It turns out that this question can be analysed in the search-theoretic framework developed in this chapter.

Suppose that a firm that hires a worker receives a fixed once-off payment of b from the government, but that a firm that fires a worker must pay b to the government. Clearly, (9.9) would be modified to reflect this payment:

$$rJ_V = -\gamma_0 + q(\theta)\left[J_O + b - J_V\right].\tag{9.39}$$

If a firm with a vacancy finds a worker, its capital gain will be $J_O - J_V$ *plus* the payment from the government. Free exit/entry of firms will then imply the following expression for the value of an occupied job:

$$J_V = 0 \quad \Rightarrow \quad J_O = \frac{\gamma_0}{q(\theta)} - b.\tag{9.40}$$

Equation (9.40) shows that the deposit acts like a lump-sum subsidy to firms with a vacancy. The expected search costs $\gamma_0/q(\theta)$ are reduced by the lump-sum payment received from the government.

For a firm with a filled job, the steady-state arbitrage equation reads as follows:

$$rJ_O = F(K, 1) - (r + \delta)K - w - s\left[J_O + b\right].\tag{9.41}$$

If the job is destroyed, the firm not only loses the value of the occupied job, but must also pay back the deposit on its worker to the government. As a result, the expected capital loss is $s(J_O + b)$. (Since the job destruction rate s is exogenous, the firm can do nothing to reduce the probability of an adverse job-destroying shock.) The marginal productivity condition for capital (9.12) still holds. By combining (9.12) with (9.40)–(9.41), the zero profit condition (given in (9.13)) is changed to:

$$(r + s)\left[\frac{\gamma_0}{q(\theta)} - b\right] = F(K, 1) - F_K(K, 1)K - w - sb \quad \Rightarrow$$

$$\frac{\gamma_0}{q(\theta)} = \frac{F_L(K, 1) - w + rb}{r + s}.\tag{9.42}$$

The capital value of the deposit acts like a subsidy on the use of labour.

The rent-sharing rule (equation (9.21)) is modified to reflect the payment the firm receives if it employs the worker:

$$Y_E^i - Y_U = \left(\frac{\beta}{1 - \beta}\right)\left[J_O^i + b - J_V\right],\tag{9.43}$$

so that the wage equation (9.22) becomes:

$$w_i = (1 - \beta)rY_U + \beta\left[F_L(K_i, 1) + rb\right].\tag{9.44}$$

Since the reservation wage is still given by (9.23), the wage equation (9.44) can be rewritten for the symmetric case (with $w_i = w$) as:

$$w = (1 - \beta)z + \beta\left[F_L(K, 1) + rb + \theta\gamma_0\right].\tag{9.45}$$

The model consists of equations (9.25), (9.28), (9.42), and (9.45).

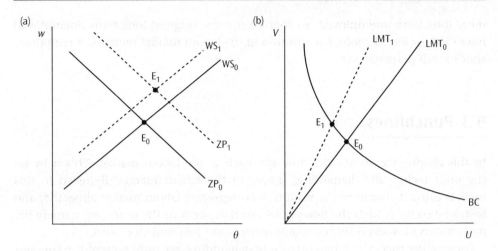

Figure 9.5. The effects of a deposit on labour

In Figure 9.5 we illustrate the effects of an increase in the deposit, b. It follows from (9.42) that the zero profit curve shifts up (from ZP_0 to ZP_1 in panel (a)) because the interest payments the firm earns on the deposit increase the value of an occupied job. These interest payments, however, also influence the wage rate via the wage-setting equation (9.45). Hence, the wage-setting equation shifts up from WS_0 to WS_1 in panel (a). It is shown in the appendix that both the wage and the vacancy–unemployment ratio rise as a result of the shock, i.e. point E_1 lies to the north-east of the initial equilibrium E_0. In panel (b) the LMT curve rotates in a counterclockwise fashion from LMT_0 to LMT_1 and the equilibrium shifts from E_0 to E_1. The equilibrium vacancy rate rises and the unemployment rate falls.

9.2.3 Search unemployment, loss of skills, and persistence

As we saw in Chapter 7, one of the stylized facts about the labour markets of advanced economies is the persistence of the unemployment rate. How can this persistence be explained in the search-theoretic framework? In a recent contribution, Pissarides (1992) has shown that one of the mechanisms by which temporary shocks can persist for a long time has to do with loss of skills. If the unemployed lose some of their skills, they become less productive, and hence less attractive to the firms. By sitting at home without a job, they lose some of their human capital. As a result, there are less vacancies in the next period, and the expected duration of unemployment increases. Furthermore, because of the fact that average human capital has decreased (due to the loss of skills by the long-term unemployed), the market becomes "thin", in the sense that average labour productivity has decreased. There are less profitable matches in the economy than would have been the case if the unemployed had not lost some of their skills. There will, on average, be more long-term unemployed, so that even if the original long-term unemployed have died (or found a job), the thinness of the labour market remains. A temporary shock is self-perpetuating.

9.3 Punchlines

In this chapter we discuss the flow approach to the labour market. This is by far the most technically demanding theory of the labour market discussed in this book because it abandons the notion of an aggregate labour market altogether and instead directly models the flows of labour that occur in the economy, namely the movements of workers from unemployment into jobs and vice versa.

Because the theory is inherently quite demanding, we only present the simplest possible search model. The central elements in the model are the following. First, there are frictions in the process by which job-seeking unemployed workers come into contact with firms that are looking for a worker to fill a vacancy. These frictions are costly and time consuming. Second, the crucial analytical device that makes the model tractable is the so-called matching function. (This function plays a similar role in the flow approach to the labour market that the neoclassical production function plays in the theory of factor productivity and growth.) The matching function relates the probabilities of workers meeting firms (and firms meeting workers) as a function of an aggregate labour market tightness variable. This tightness indicator is the ratio of vacancies and unemployed workers.

If the vacancy–unemployment ratio is high (low) then the probability that an unemployed job seeker finds a firm with a vacancy is high (low) and expected duration of the search for a job is low (high). The matching function also explains the conditions facing the other party on the market. Indeed, if the vacancy–unemployment ratio is high (low), then there are many (few) firms trying to locate an unemployed worker so that the probability that an individual firm is successful is low (high) and the expected duration of the firm's search process is high (low).

The third key ingredient of the search model concerns the wage formation process. Once a firm with a vacancy meets an unemployed worker a pure economic rent is created consisting of the sum of foregone expected search costs by the firm and the worker. This surplus must be divided somehow between the firm and the worker. The typical assumption in this literature is that the two parties bargain over the wage.

The fourth ingredient of the model is the so-called Beveridge curve which relates the equilibrium unemployment rate to the (exogenous) job destruction rate (regulating the flow into unemployment) and the workers' job finding rate (regulating the flow out of unemployment). The job destruction rate is strictly positive because previously profitable firm-worker matches are destroyed due to idiosyncratic shocks.

The model yields a general equilibrium solution for, inter alia, the unemployment rate and the vacancy rate as a function of the exogenous variables. We perform various comparative static experiments. For example, an increase in the job destruction rate leads to an increase in both the unemployment and vacancy rates and to a decrease in the vacancy–unemployment ratio.

We complete this chapter by applying the search model in a number of different settings. First, we show how the search equilibrium is affected by the tax system. Second, we show that a worker-deposit scheme can be used to affect the equilibrium unemployment rate. (Under the scheme the firm receives a grant from the government when it hires a worker but must repay the grant when the job is destroyed again.) Finally, we briefly argue that a modified search model can account for one of the stylized facts of the labour market, namely that there is strong persistence in the unemployment rate. The key notion here is that the unemployed may lose their skills while unemployed and become less attractive employees to firms (and thus face a longer search process) as a result.

Further Reading

Key references to the modern search-theoretic literature are Mortensen (1978, 1982a, 1982b, 1986, 1989), Diamond (1984a, 1984b), Mortensen and Pissarides (1994), Pissarides (1994), and Blanchard and Diamond (1994). Mortensen and Pissarides (1999a, 1999b) present good (but advanced) surveys of the literature. Hosios (1990) studies the welfare-theoretic properties of the search model. Microeconomic evidence on the job destruction /creation process is presented by Davis, Haltiwanger, and Schuh (1996). For a recent and very extensive survey of the matching function, see Petrongolo and Pissarides (2001).

Appendix

In section 1.3 we graphically derive some results regarding shocks to the unemployment benefit, z, and the job destruction rate, s. In this appendix we derive these results analytically. First we loglinearize equations (9.26)–(9.27) holding constant r and δ (and thus also F_K, F_L, and K). After some manipulation we obtain:

$$
\begin{bmatrix} \eta(w - F_L) & -1 \\ -\beta\gamma_0\theta & 1 \end{bmatrix} \begin{bmatrix} \tilde{\theta} \\ dw \end{bmatrix} = \begin{bmatrix} (F_L - w)\left[\tilde{\gamma}_0 + (s/(r+s))\tilde{s}\right] \\ (1 - \beta)dz + \beta\gamma_0\theta\tilde{\gamma}_0 \end{bmatrix},
\tag{A9.1}
$$

where η is defined in (9.4), $\tilde{\theta} \equiv d\theta/\theta$, $\tilde{\gamma}_0 \equiv d\gamma_0/\gamma_0$, and $\tilde{s} \equiv ds/s$. Solving (A9.1) yields the solutions for $\tilde{\theta}$ and dw:

$$
\tilde{\theta} \equiv \tilde{V} - \tilde{U} = \frac{-(F_L - w + \beta\theta\gamma_0)\tilde{\gamma}_0 - (F_L - w)(s/(r+s))\tilde{s} - (1-\beta)dz}{\eta(F_L - w) + \beta\theta\gamma_0},
\tag{A9.2}
$$

$$
dw = (F_L - w)\left[\frac{-\beta\theta\gamma_0\left[(1-\eta)\tilde{\gamma}_0 + (s/(r+s))\tilde{s}\right] + \eta(1-\beta)dz}{\eta(F_L - w) + \beta\theta\gamma_0}\right].
\tag{A9.3}
$$

It follows that an increase in the unemployment benefit ($dz > 0$) raises the wage ($dw > 0$) and reduces the vacancy–unemployment ratio ($\tilde{\theta} > 0$) as is illustrated in Figure 9.1. An increase in the job separation rate ($\tilde{s} > 0$) leads to a reduction in both the wage and the vacancy–unemployment ratio ($dw < 0$ and $\tilde{\theta} < 0$) as is illustrated in Figure 9.2. Finally, an increase in the search costs ($\tilde{\gamma}_0 > 0$) reduces both the wage and the vacancy–unemployment ratio ($dw < 0$ and $\tilde{\theta} < 0$). Students are invited to draw the corresponding graph and to provide the economic intuition.

It remains to show that an increase in the job destruction rate raises both the unemployment and vacancy rates, as is asserted in the discussion surrounding Figure 9.2. By using (9.31) and (A9.2) (and setting $\tilde{\gamma}_0 = dz = 0$) we obtain a system in $\tilde{V}$ and $\tilde{U}$:

$$
\begin{bmatrix} 1 & \dfrac{s+f\eta}{f(1-\eta)} \\ 1 & -1 \end{bmatrix} \begin{bmatrix} \tilde{V} \\ \tilde{U} \end{bmatrix} = \begin{bmatrix} 1 \\ -\left(\dfrac{s}{r+s}\right) \dfrac{(1-\eta)(F_L - w)}{\eta(F_L - w) + \beta\gamma_0\theta} \end{bmatrix} \dfrac{\tilde{s}}{1-\eta}.
\tag{A9.4}
$$

Solving (A9.4) yields the following expressions:

$$
\tilde{V} = \left(\dfrac{f}{s+f}\right) \left[1 - \left(\dfrac{s+f\eta}{f}\right) \left(\dfrac{s}{r+s}\right) \dfrac{F_L - w}{\eta(F_L - w) + \beta\gamma_0\theta}\right] \tilde{s} \gtrless 0,
\tag{A9.5}
$$

$$
\tilde{U} = \left(\dfrac{f}{s+f}\right) \left[1 + \left(\dfrac{s}{r+s}\right) \dfrac{(1-\eta)(F_L - w)}{\eta(F_L - w) + \beta\gamma_0\theta}\right] \tilde{s} > 0.
\tag{A9.6}
$$

Unemployment unambiguously rises but the effect on the vacancy rate is ambiguous in general. It is not difficult to show, however, that the term in square brackets on the right-hand side of (A9.5) is positive if a rather weak sufficient condition is satisfied. First we note that (9.26) gives rise to the following result:

$$
\dfrac{F_L - w}{\eta(F_L - w) + \beta\gamma_0\theta} = \dfrac{r+s}{\eta(r+s) + \beta f}.
\tag{A9.7}
$$

By using (A9.7) the term in square brackets on the right-hand side of (A9.5) can be simplified to:

$$
\begin{aligned}
[.] &= 1 - \left(\dfrac{s+f\eta}{f}\right) \left(\dfrac{s}{r+s}\right) \dfrac{r+s}{\eta(r+s) + \beta f} \\
&= \dfrac{f[r\eta + \beta f] - s^2}{f[\eta(r+s) + \beta f]} \\
&= \dfrac{fr\eta + f^2[\beta - (s/f)^2]}{f[\eta(r+s) + \beta f]}.
\end{aligned}
\tag{A9.8}
$$

The denominator in (A9.8) is positive and, since $fr\eta > 0$, a *sufficient* condition for the numerator to be positive also is $\beta > (s/f)^2$ or:

$$
\beta > \left(\dfrac{U}{1-U}\right)^2,
\tag{A9.9}
$$

where we have used the fact that $U = s/(s+f)$. Provided the relative bargaining power of the worker (β) is not very small, the inequality in (A9.9) is satisfied and the term in square brackets on the right-hand side of (A9.5) is positive. In fact, the sufficient condition is quite weak. Even for the relatively high unemployment rate of 25% ($U = 0.25$) the condition is satisfied if $\beta > 1/9$. See, also Pissarides (1990, p. 16) who derives a more stringent sufficient condition.

In section 2.1 we modify the model to take into account the effects of taxation on the labour market. An increase in the labour income tax rate operates just like an increase in the unemployment benefit so the results follow immediately. Keeping all exogenous variables other than the payroll tax constant we find by differentiating (9.33) and (9.38):

$$
\begin{bmatrix} \eta \left(\dfrac{w(1+t_E) - F_L}{1+t_E} \right) & -1 \\ -\dfrac{\beta \gamma_0 \theta}{1+t_E} & 1 \end{bmatrix} \begin{bmatrix} \tilde{\theta} \\ dw \end{bmatrix} = \begin{bmatrix} w \\ -\dfrac{\beta \gamma_0 \theta}{1+t_E} \end{bmatrix} \tilde{t}_E,
\tag{A9.10}
$$

where $\tilde{t}_E \equiv dt_E/(1+t_M)$. Solving (A9.10) yields the solutions for $\tilde{\theta}$ and dw:

$$
\tilde{\theta} = - \left(\frac{w(1+t_E) - \beta \theta \gamma_0}{\eta \left[F_L - w(1+t_E) \right] + \beta \theta \gamma_0} \right) \tilde{t}_E < 0,
\tag{A9.11}
$$

$$
dw = - \left(\frac{\beta \theta \gamma_0 \left[(1-\eta)w + \frac{F_L}{1+t_E} \right]}{\eta \left[F_L - w(1+t_E) \right] + \beta \theta \gamma_0} \right) \tilde{t}_E < 0,
\tag{A9.12}
$$

where it follows from (9.38) that the numerator of (A9.11) is positive.

In section 2.2 we study the effects of an increase in the deposit on labour, b. Keeping all exogenous variables other than the deposit constant we find by differentiating (9.42) and (9.45):

$$
\begin{bmatrix} \eta \left(w - F_L - rb \right) & -1 \\ -\beta \gamma_0 \theta & 1 \end{bmatrix} \begin{bmatrix} \tilde{\theta} \\ dw \end{bmatrix} = \begin{bmatrix} -1 \\ \beta \end{bmatrix} r \, db.
\tag{A9.13}
$$

Solving for $\tilde{\theta}$ and dw yields:

$$
\tilde{\theta} = \left(\frac{1-\beta}{\eta \left(F_L + rb - w \right) + \beta \theta \gamma_0} \right) r \, db > 0,
\tag{A9.14}
$$

$$
dw = \left(\frac{\beta \left[\theta \gamma_0 + \eta \left(F_L + rb - w \right) \right]}{\eta \left(F_L + rb - w \right) + \beta \theta \gamma_0} \right) r \, db > 0.
\tag{A9.15}
$$

10

Macroeconomic Policy, Credibility, and Politics

The purpose of this chapter is to discuss the following issues:

1. What do we mean by dynamic inconsistency. When is economic policy dynamically inconsistent and hence not credible?
2. How can reputation effects come to the rescue if the optimal policy is inconsistent?
3. Why does it sometimes pay to appoint a conservative to head the central bank?
4. How can the taxation of capital give rise to dynamic inconsistency?

10.1 Dynamic Inconsistency

10.1.1 A classic tale

As anyone with more than a fleeting interest in literature knows, Ulysses had a hard time getting back to his island of Ithaca after helping the Greeks win the war against the Trojans. Apparently the Greeks had forgotten to suitably thank the gods upon winning the war, and this had irritated them to such an extent that they decided to make the Greeks suffer. To cut a long story short, it took Ulysses ten years plus a lot of trouble to get home. During this journey he and his men have to pass the island of the Sirens. These Sirens were twin sisters and excellent singers but had a dangerous streak to them. As the witch Circe warns Ulysses:

Your next encounter will be with the Sirens, who bewitch everybody that approaches them. There is no home-coming for the man who draws near them unawares and hears the Sirens' voices; no welcome from his wife, no little children brightening at their father's return. For with the music of their song the Sirens cast their spell upon him, as they sit there in a meadow piled high with the mouldering skeletons of men, whose withered skin still hangs upon their bones. (Homer, 1946, p. 190)

Ulysses is facing a difficult choice. He would like to listen to the Sirens (who would not?) but he does not want to end up as a skeleton just yet. Fortunately Circe also suggests a solution to the decision problem Ulysses faces. As Ulysses later tells his men, their ears should be plugged with beeswax so that they cannot hear the Sirens, and:

I alone ... might listen to their voices; but you must bind me hard and fast, so that I cannot stir from the spot where you will stand me, by the step of the mast, with the rope's end lashed round the mast itself. *And if I beg you to release me, you must tighten and add to my bonds.* (Homer, 1946, p. 193; emphasis added)

The plan is executed, they sail past the Sirens' island, and Ulysses instructs his men to release him. He wants to go to the island. His men, suitably instructed, ignore his pleas and add to his bonds. They escape the perilous Sirens with no additional problems.

Ulysses' decision problem is a classic example of dynamic inconsistency, and Circe's suggestion constitutes a smart solution to the problem. The *optimal* policy for Ulysses and his men is to listen to the Sirens and continue the journey to Ithaca. After all, they are good singers. Unfortunately, this policy is *inconsistent*, since it leads to death and decay, and Ithaca will not be reached. Circe's solution is to make Ulysses *commit* himself to his long-term goal of reaching Ithaca by plugging the ears of his crew, and tying himself to the mast. By giving up his authority for a brief spell, he and his men are better off as a result. The commitment solution is consistent but *suboptimal*, as his men don't get to hear the music.[1]

10.1.2 A neoclassical tale

Dynamic inconsistency also features prominently in the economics literature. One of the simplest examples of dynamic inconsistency concerns the conduct of monetary policy with an expectations-augmented Phillips curve (Kydland and Prescott, 1977). Our version of their example makes use of the Lucas supply curve. Aggregate supply of goods y depends on the full employment level of output $\bar{y}$, the inflation surprise $\pi - \pi^e$, and a stochastic error term ϵ (with properties $E\epsilon = 0$ and $E\epsilon^2 = \sigma^2$):

$$y = \bar{y} + \alpha \left[\pi - \pi^e\right] + \epsilon, \quad \alpha > 0, \tag{10.1}$$

where y and $\bar{y}$ are both measured in logarithms. If the actual inflation rate, π, exceeds the expected inflation rate, π^e, workers have overestimated the real wage, labour supply is too high, and output is higher than its full-employment level.

We assume that agents hold rational expectations (REH, see Chapter 3), so that the expected inflation rate coincides with the mathematical expectations of the actual

---

[1] One wonders why Ulysses did not tie all his men but one to the mast, and plug that one man's ears with beeswax. That way a higher level of welfare would have been attained and consistency would have been ensured. Homer does not explain. Perhaps the mast only held one person.

inflation rate predicted by the model, i.e. $\pi^e \equiv E\pi$. The policy maker is assumed to have an objective function (often referred to as a *social welfare function*) which depends on inflation and an output target y^* that is higher than the full employment level of output ($\bar{y} > y^*$). Although this may appear odd, the policy maker deems the full-employment level of output to be too low from a societal point of view. This is for example, due to the existence of distorting taxes or unemployment benefits.[2] The cost function of the policy maker is given by:

$$\Omega \equiv \frac{1}{2} [y - y^*]^2 + \frac{\beta}{2}\pi^2, \quad \beta > 0, \tag{10.2}$$

where β measures the degree of inflation aversion of the policy maker. The higher β, the higher the welfare costs associated with inflation, and the stronger is the inflation aversion. The policy maker cannot directly influence the expectations held by the private agents and consequently takes π^e as given in its optimization problem. There is *information asymmetry* in the sense that the policy maker can observe the realization of the supply shock, ϵ, but the public cannot. As a result, the policy-ineffectiveness proposition (PIP) fails and economic policy has real effects (see Chapter 3). The policy maker chooses the inflation rate and output level such that social costs (10.2) are minimized subject to the Lucas supply curve (10.1). The Lagrangean for this problem is:

$$\min_{\{\pi, y\}} \mathcal{L} \equiv \frac{1}{2} [y - y^*]^2 + \frac{\beta}{2}\pi^2 + \lambda \left[y - \bar{y} - \alpha(\pi - \pi^e) - \epsilon\right], \tag{10.3}$$

so that the first-order conditions are:

$$\frac{\partial \mathcal{L}}{\partial y} = (y - y^*) + \lambda = 0, \tag{10.4}$$

$$\frac{\partial \mathcal{L}}{\partial \pi} = \beta\pi - \alpha\lambda = 0. \tag{10.5}$$

By combining (10.4)–(10.5) we obtain the "social expansion path", giving all combinations of inflation and output for which social costs are minimized:

$$y - y^* = -(\beta/\alpha)\pi \quad \Leftrightarrow \quad \pi = -(\alpha/\beta) [y - y^*]. \tag{10.6}$$

This downward-sloping line has been drawn in Figure 10.1. Graphically the line represents all points of tangency between an iso-cost curve of the policy maker and a Lucas supply curve. In view of the definition of the social welfare function (10.2), the iso-cost curves are concentric ovals around the bliss point E, where $\pi = 0$ and

---

[2] Obviously, the first-best policy would be to remove these pre-existing distortions directly. It is assumed that this is impossible, however, so that monetary policy is used as a second-best instrument to boost output. See Persson and Tabellini (1989, p. 9).

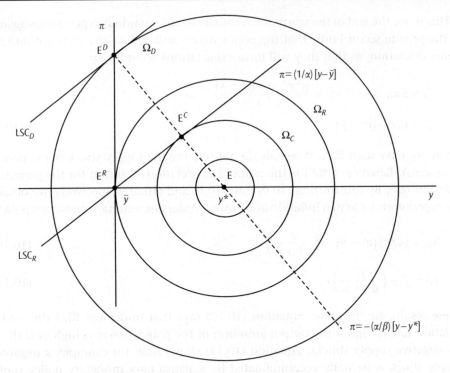

Figure 10.1. Consistent and optimal monetary policy

$y = y^*$. The slope of the iso-cost curves is obtained in the usual fashion:

$$d\Omega = 0: \quad \frac{d\pi}{dy} = -\frac{(y - y^*)}{\beta\pi}. \tag{10.7}$$

It follows that the iso-cost curve is horizontal ($d\pi/dy = 0$) for $y = y^*$ and is vertical ($d\pi/dy \to \infty$) for $\pi = 0$.

By combining (10.1) and (10.6), we obtain the expression for inflation under *discretion*, denoted by π_D:

$$\pi = \pi^e + (1/\alpha)[y - \bar{y} - \epsilon] = \pi^e + (1/\alpha)[-(\beta/\alpha)\pi + y^* - \bar{y} - \epsilon] \quad \Rightarrow$$

$$(1 + \beta/\alpha^2)\pi = \pi^e + (1/\alpha)[y^* - \bar{y} - \epsilon] \quad \Rightarrow$$

$$\pi_D = \frac{\alpha^2\pi^e + \alpha[y^* - \bar{y} - \epsilon]}{\alpha^2 + \beta}. \tag{10.8}$$

We use the term "discretion" because the policy maker chooses the optimal inflation rate in each period as it pleases, i.e. after it has observed the supply shock ϵ. Equation (10.8) says that inflation under discretion is high if expected inflation is high, if the ambition of the policy maker (i.e. $y^* - \bar{y}$) is large, and if there is a negative aggregate supply shock ($\epsilon < 0$, which is the case, for example, with an OPEC shock).

This is not the end of the story, of course, since under rational expectations agents in the private sector know that the policy maker will choose the inflation rate π_D under discretion, so that they will form expectations accordingly:

$$\pi_D^e \equiv E\pi_D \quad \Rightarrow \quad \pi_D^e = \frac{\alpha^2 \pi_D^e + \alpha\,[y^* - \bar{y}]}{\alpha^2 + \beta} \quad \Rightarrow$$

$$\pi_D^e \equiv (\alpha/\beta)\,[y^* - \bar{y}], \tag{10.9}$$

where we have used $E\epsilon = 0$ (agents do not observe the supply shock but expect it to be zero). Equation (10.9) is the rational expectations solution for the expected inflation rate. By substituting (10.9) into (10.8) and (10.6), respectively, we obtain the expressions for actual inflation and output under discretionary monetary policy:

$$\pi_D = (\alpha/\beta)\,[y^* - \bar{y}] - \left(\frac{\alpha}{\alpha^2 + \beta}\right)\epsilon, \tag{10.10}$$

$$y_D = \bar{y} + \left(\frac{\beta}{\alpha^2 + \beta}\right)\epsilon. \tag{10.11}$$

These results are intuitive. Equation (10.10) says that under the REH the actual inflation rate is high if the output ambition of the policy maker is high or if there are negative supply shocks. Equation (10.11) shows that, for example, a negative supply shock is partially accommodated by expansionary monetary policy (only partially as $\beta/(\alpha^2 + \beta) < 1$). This is especially the case if the policy maker has "leftist" preferences, i.e. has a low aversion towards inflation, represented by a low value of β. A left-wing policy maker attaches a greater importance to the stabilization of output (and hence, employment) fluctuations. A similar conclusion is obtained if the Lucas supply curve is very flat. In that case, α is very large and a large degree of accommodation takes place.

The problem with the discrete solution is that it is *suboptimal*! This can be demonstrated graphically with the aid of Figure 10.1. The discrete solution is represented by point E^D, where we have drawn the Lucas supply curve, LSC_D, for a realization of the supply shock equal to $\epsilon = 0$. Suppose, however, that the policy maker could announce to the public that it would choose a zero inflation rate, i.e. $\pi = 0$. If the public believes this announcement, the REH implies that expected inflation will also be zero, i.e. $\pi^e = 0$, so that the relevant Lucas supply curve would be the one through the origin (i.e. LSC_R which passes through point E^R). Through this point, there is an iso-cost curve Ω^R that is closer to the bliss point E, and consequently involves strictly lower social costs, i.e. $\Omega^R < \Omega^D$. Hence, for this case the solution is:

$$\pi_R = \pi_R^e = 0, \tag{10.12}$$

$$y_R = \bar{y} + \epsilon, \tag{10.13}$$

where we have used the subscript "R" to designate that this is policy under a *rule*. Instead of choosing the optimal inflation and output combination each period, the policy maker follows a simple money growth rule that ensures that the inflation rate is zero, as promised. Equation (10.13) shows that no accommodation of supply shocks is possible under this rule (obviously, since accommodation would lead to inflation, which violates the promise). The advantage is that there is no inflation under the rule, as (10.12) shows.

The problem with this optimal policy is that it is *inconsistent*! This can also be illustrated with the aid of Figure 10.1. The solution under the inflation rule $\pi_R = 0$ is given at point E^R, and the relevant Lucas supply curve goes through that point (LSC$_R$). But the policy maker has an even more attractive option than E^R if it faces LSC$_R$, namely the "cheating" point E^C, where there is a tangency between LSC$_R$ and the iso-cost curve Ω^C. In the cheating solution, the policy maker creates an inflation surprise $\pi > \pi_R = \pi_R^e = 0$ in order to boost output $y > \bar{y}$.

Formally, the cheating solution for inflation, denoted by π_C, is obtained by substituting $\pi^e = \pi_R = 0$ into (10.8):

$$\pi_C = \frac{\alpha \left[y^* - \bar{y} - \epsilon \right]}{\alpha^2 + \beta}, \tag{10.14}$$

so that output is:

$$y_C = \left(\frac{\beta}{\alpha^2 + \beta} \right) \bar{y} + \left(\frac{\alpha^2}{\alpha^2 + \beta} \right) y^* + \left(\frac{\beta}{\alpha^2 + \beta} \right) \epsilon. \tag{10.15}$$

The upshot of this is, of course, that the solution under the zero-inflation rule is not *credible*. Only if the policy maker is able to commit himself by being tied to the "mast" of zero inflation (just like Ulysses), does the rules solution have credibility.

Before turning to one possible commitment mechanism, we summarize the argument up to this point. There are three possible options that the policy maker has in the current setup. It can pursue discretionary policy (equations (10.10)–(10.11)), follow a zero-inflation rule (equations (10.12)–(10.13)), or cheat (equations (10.14)–(10.15)). By substituting the different solutions for output and inflation into the welfare cost function (10.2) (assuming $\epsilon = 0$ for simplicity), we obtain the following expressions:

$$\Omega_C = \frac{1}{2} \left(\frac{\beta}{\alpha^2 + \beta} \right) [\bar{y} - y^*]^2, \tag{10.16}$$

$$\Omega_R = \frac{1}{2} [\bar{y} - y^*]^2, \tag{10.17}$$

$$\Omega_D = \frac{1}{2} \left(\frac{\alpha^2 + \beta}{\beta} \right) [\bar{y} - y^*]^2, \tag{10.18}$$

from which we infer that $\Omega_D > \Omega_R > \Omega_C > 0$. The cheating solution is closest to the bliss point, is credible but it violates the REH. The rules solution is optimal and satisfies REH, but is open to temptation and is hence not credible. Finally, the solution under discretion is suboptimal, satisfies REH, and is credible.

10.1.3 Reputation as an enforcement mechanism

In the previous subsection we have shown that the only policy which is both credible and consistent with rational expectations is the suboptimal discretionary policy. Given the structure of the problem, it appears that the economy is likely to end up in the worst possible equilibrium. In an influential article, however, Barro and Gordon (1983b) have demonstrated that *reputation effects* can come to the rescue, and prevent this worst-case scenario from materializing. Their argument can be made with the aid of the model developed in section 1.2. In order to develop the simplest possible model, we assume that there are no stochastic shocks ($\epsilon \equiv 0$). There is repeated interaction between the policy maker and the public (represented, for example, by the unions who set the nominal wage rate).

The cost function of the policy maker consists of the present value of the costs incurred each period, and is defined as:

$$V \equiv \Omega_0 + \frac{\Omega_1}{1+r} + \frac{\Omega_2}{(1+r)^2} + \cdots = \sum_{t=0}^{\infty} \frac{\Omega_t}{(1+r)^t}, \tag{10.19}$$

where r is the real discount factor (e.g. the real rate of interest), and Ω_t is the cost incurred in period t:

$$\Omega_t \equiv \tfrac{1}{2} [y_t - y^*]^2 + \frac{\beta}{2} \pi_t^2, \tag{10.20}$$

and the Lucas supply curve is given by:

$$y_t = \bar{y} + \alpha [\pi_t - \pi_t^e], \quad \alpha > 0. \tag{10.21}$$

It is assumed for simplicity that both y^* and $\bar{y}$ are constant over time and thus do not feature a time subscript.

As in section 1.2, there are again a number of choices that the policy maker can make. A discretionary policy involves setting inflation according to (10.10) in each period (with $\epsilon = 0$ imposed). This yields a cost level of Ω_D in each period (see (10.18)), so that the present value of social costs equals V^D:

$$V^D \equiv \left(\frac{1+r}{r} \right) \Omega_D. \tag{10.22}$$

Now consider what happens if the policy maker chooses to follow a *constant-inflation* rule, $\pi_t = \pi_R$, where we generalize the previous discussion by allowing the constant inflation rate π_R to be non-zero. If this inflation rate is believed by the public, it will come to expect it, so that the expected inflation rate will also be equal to π_R in each period, so that output will equal $\bar{y}$ in each period. By substituting these solutions into (10.20) the periodic cost level under the rule is obtained:

$$\Omega_R(\pi_R) = \Omega_R + \frac{\beta}{2} \pi_R^2, \tag{10.23}$$

where Ω_R is the welfare cost under the zero-inflation rule as defined in (10.17), and we have indicated that under the more general inflation rule, the cost level depends positively on the chosen inflation level. By substituting (10.23) into (10.19), the present value of costs incurred under the rule $V^R(\pi_R)$ is obtained:

$$V^R(\pi_R) \equiv \left(\frac{1+r}{r}\right)\left[\Omega_R + \frac{\beta}{2}\pi_R^2\right]. \tag{10.24}$$

Finally, as before, the cheating solution is derived by determining the optimal choice for the policy maker given that the public expects it to stick to the announced inflation rate π_R. By substituting $\pi^e = \pi_R$ into equation (10.8), and setting $\epsilon = 0$, the expression for the cheating inflation rate π_C is obtained:

$$\pi_C = \frac{\alpha^2 \pi_R + \alpha\,[y^* - \bar{y}]}{\alpha^2 + \beta}, \tag{10.25}$$

which implies that output under cheating is given by:

$$y_C = \left(\frac{\beta}{\alpha^2 + \beta}\right)\bar{y} + \left(\frac{\alpha^2}{\alpha^2 + \beta}\right)y^* - \left(\frac{\alpha\beta}{\alpha^2 + \beta}\right)\pi_R. \tag{10.26}$$

By substituting (10.25)–(10.26) into (10.20), the periodic cost level associated with cheating is obtained:

$$\Omega_C(\pi_R) = \frac{1}{2}\left[\left(\frac{\beta}{\alpha^2 + \beta}\right)[\bar{y} - y^*] - \left(\frac{\alpha\beta}{\alpha^2 + \beta}\right)\pi_R\right]^2$$

$$+ \frac{\beta}{2}\left[\left(\frac{\alpha^2}{\alpha^2 + \beta}\right)\pi_R + \left(\frac{\alpha}{\alpha^2 + \beta}\right)[y^* - \bar{y}]\right]^2, \tag{10.27}$$

where Ω_C depends on the chosen inflation level under the rule. Obviously, (10.27) and (10.16) coincide for $\pi_R = 0$, and $\Omega_C(\pi_R)$ is greater than Ω_C for any non-zero value of π_R.

We are now in a position to introduce the policy maker's *reputation* into the analysis. Suppose that the public trusts the policy maker in period t, if it has kept its promise in the previous period $t - 1$ (in the sense that it did as it was expected to do). If that is the case, the public expects that the rule will be followed in period t so that inflation will be set at π_R. On the other hand, if the policy maker did not keep its promise in period $t - 1$, the public loses trust in the policy maker, and instead expects the discrete solution to obtain in period t. In formal terms, the postulated mechanism adopted by the public can be written as follows.

$$\pi_t^e = \begin{cases} \pi_R & \text{if } \pi_{t-1} = \pi_{t-1}^e \\ \pi_{D,t} & \text{if } \pi_{t-1} \neq \pi_{t-1}^e \end{cases} \tag{10.28}$$

Equation (10.28) implies that the public adopts the tit-for-tat strategy in the repeated prisoner's dilemma game that it plays with the policy maker. If the policy maker "misbehaves" it gets punished by the public for one period. To see that this is indeed the case, consider the following possible sequences of events. We start in period 0

243

and assume that the policy maker has credibility in that period (i.e. in period -1 it has kept its promise) and so expected inflation in period 0 equals the level specified by the rule, i.e. $\pi_0^e = \pi_R$.

The first scenario that the policy maker can follow in period 0 is to keep its promise, and to produce inflation equal to π_R. The public observes this inflation rate, concludes that the policy maker is trustworthy, and continues to expect that inflation will be set according to the rule. By sticking to its promise, the policy maker has maintained its reputation, and no punishment takes place.

The second scenario that the policy maker can follow is to cheat in period 0. It has an incentive to do so since the periodic cost level attained in period 0 is then given by (10.27) which is lower than periodic cost under the rule as given in (10.23). In fact, the *temptation* that the policy maker is subjected to in period 0 can be calculated:

$$T(\pi_R) \equiv \Omega_R(\pi_R) - \Omega_C(\pi_R)$$

$$= \frac{1}{2}[\bar{y} - y^*]^2 + \frac{\beta}{2}\pi_R^2 - \frac{1}{2}\left[\left(\frac{\beta}{\alpha^2 + \beta}\right)[\bar{y} - y^*] - \left(\frac{\alpha\beta}{\alpha^2 + \beta}\right)\pi_R\right]^2$$

$$- \frac{\beta}{2}\left[\left(\frac{\alpha^2}{\alpha^2 + \beta}\right)\pi_R + \left(\frac{\alpha}{\alpha^2 + \beta}\right)[y^* - \bar{y}]\right]^2, \tag{10.29}$$

where we have used (10.27) and (10.23), and $T(\pi_R)$ is the temptation to cheat if the policy rule stipulates an inflation rate π_R. In Figure 10.2 we have plotted this quadratic temptation function. Several points of this function are easy to find. If the

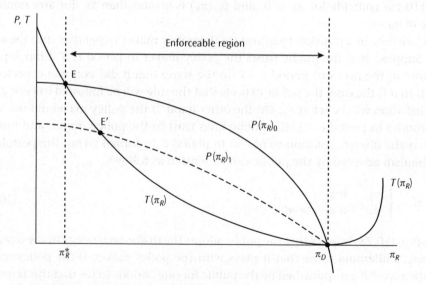

Figure 10.2. Temptation and enforcement

rule inflation rate $\pi_R = 0$, $T(0)$ is equal to:

$$T(0) \equiv \Omega_R - \Omega_C = \frac{1}{2} \left(\frac{\alpha^2}{\alpha^2 + \beta} \right) [y^* - \bar{y}]^2 , \qquad (10.30)$$

and $T(\pi_R) = 0$ if the rule inflation equals the discrete inflation rate π_D given in (10.10) (with $\epsilon = 0$ imposed):

$$T(\pi_D) = 0. \qquad (10.31)$$

The inflation rate under discretion is also the point where temptation is minimized. For higher inflation rates, the $T(\pi_R)$ curve starts to rise again.

But under the second scenario, the policy maker is punished in period 1, because it did not keep its promise in period 0. The public has lost confidence in the policy maker, and expects the discrete solution for period 1. This causes costs in period 1 to be higher than they would have been, since $\Omega_D > \Omega_R(\pi_R)$, and these additional costs must be taken into account in the decision about whether or not to stick to the rule in period 0. From the point of view of the policy maker, the punishment it receives consists of the discounted value of the additional costs it incurs in period 1:

$$P(\pi_R) \equiv \frac{\Omega_D - \Omega_R(\pi_R)}{1 + r}$$

$$= \left[\frac{1}{2} \left(\frac{\alpha^2 + \beta}{\beta} \right) [\bar{y} - y^*]^2 - \frac{1}{2} [\bar{y} - y^*]^2 - \frac{\beta}{2} \pi_R^2 \right] \left(\frac{1}{1 + r} \right)$$

$$= \left[\frac{1}{2} \frac{\alpha^2}{\beta} [\bar{y} - y^*]^2 - \frac{\beta}{2} \pi_R^2 \right] \left(\frac{1}{1 + r} \right) , \qquad (10.32)$$

where we have used (10.18) and (10.23). Again, a number of points on the punishment curve can be found easily. First, if the rule inflation $\pi_R = 0$, $P(0)$ is equal to:

$$P(0) = \frac{1}{2} \left(\frac{1}{1 + r} \right) \frac{\alpha^2}{\beta} [\bar{y} - y^*]^2 . \qquad (10.33)$$

By comparing (10.33) and (10.30) it is clear that $P(0) < T(0)$. Furthermore, $P(\pi_R) = 0$ for the discrete inflation rate π_D:

$$P(\pi_D) = 0. \qquad (10.34)$$

Finally, for rule inflation rates larger than π_D, $P(\pi_R) < 0$. The quadratic punishment function $P(\pi_R)$ has been drawn in Figure 10.2.

In period 1 the public expects the policy maker to produce the discretionary inflation rate π_D, and given this expectation it is also optimal for the policy maker to do so. Hence, in period 1 expected and actual inflation coincide, and confidence in the policy maker is restored (see (10.28)). As a result, the public expects the rule inflation rate to be produced in period 2. And by assumption the policy maker does indeed produce the rule inflation because we have investigated the effects of a single act of cheating by the policy maker. No further costs are associated with the cheating that takes place in period 0, and $P(\pi_R)$ and $T(\pi_R)$ fully summarize the relevant costs and benefits of a single act of cheating in period 0.[3]

Clearly, if the temptation of cheating exceeds the punishment, the policy maker will submit to temptation and cheat. The public knows this and does not believe the rule at all in such a case. In technical terms, the rule inflation is then *not enforceable*. This immediately explains that the zero inflation rule is not enforceable. The temptation to cheat is simply too large for $\pi_R = 0$ to be enforceable. In terms of Figure 10.2, only rule inflation rates in the interval $[\pi_R^*, \pi_D]$ are enforceable. The *optimal enforceable* rule inflation rate is of course the lowest possible enforceable inflation rate π_R^* (point E). This is because for all rule inflation rates there are no inflation surprises (otherwise a punishment would occur) so that there are only costs associated with inflation and no benefits (through higher than full-employment output). Consequently, the lowest enforceable inflation rate minimizes these costs. Just as in the repeated prisoner's dilemma game analysed inter alia by Axelrod (1984), the enforcement mechanism in the form of loss of reputation ensures that the economy does not get stuck in the worst equilibrium with discretionary monetary policy.

The optimal enforceable rule inflation rate π_R^* can be calculated by equating $P(\pi_R)$ and $T(\pi_R)$ given in (10.29) and (10.32), respectively. After some manipulation we obtain:

$$\pi_R^* \equiv \left(\frac{\alpha \, [y^* - \bar{y}]}{\beta} \right) \left[\frac{1 - \zeta}{1 + \zeta} \right], \quad \zeta \equiv \frac{\alpha^2 + \beta}{\beta(1 + r)}. \tag{10.35}$$

Hence, the optimal enforceable rule inflation rate is a weighted average of the unenforceable zero-inflation rule and the enforceable but suboptimal discretionary inflation rate π_D, which equals the term in round brackets (Barro and Gordon, 1983b, p. 113).[4]

As a final application of this model, consider what happens if the real interest rate r rises. In terms of Figure 10.2, nothing happens to the temptation line $T(\pi_R)$, but the punishment line $P(\pi_R)$ rotates in a counter-clockwise fashion around the discretionary point. As a result, the enforceable region shrinks, and the optimal enforceable rule inflation rate rises. This is intuitive. Due to the fact that punishment occurs one period after the offence, higher discounting of the future implies a smaller punishment ceteris paribus. This result is confirmed by the expression in (10.35).

---

[3] At the beginning of period 2 the policy maker faces exactly the same problem as at the beginning of period 0. Hence, if it pays to cheat in period 0 it also does in period 2. Vice versa, if it does not pay to cheat in period 0 then it also does not pay in period 2. For that reason we only need to check whether cheating pays for one deviation.

[4] We assume that the interest rate is not too low (i.e. $r > \alpha^2/\beta$) so that $0 < \zeta < 1$ and the optimal enforceable inflation rate is strictly positive. See also Figure 10.2.

10.2 The Voting Approach to Optimal Inflation

In a seminal paper, Rogoff (1985) asks himself the question why it is the case that central bankers are often selected from the conservative ranks of society. It turns out, once again, that the answer relies on the benefits of a commitment mechanism (like Ulysses' mast). In order to make the point as simply as possible, we utilize the model of section 1.2 with some minor modifications. Following Alesina and Grilli (1992), we use a median voter model to determine which person is elected to head the central bank and conduct monetary policy. Assume that person i has the following cost function:

$$\Omega_i \equiv \tfrac{1}{2}[y - y^*]^2 + \tfrac{\beta_i}{2}\pi^2, \tag{10.36}$$

where the only difference with (10.2) is that the degree of inflation aversion differs from person to person. The Lucas supply curve is still given by (10.1), so that if person i were elected to head the central bank, he would choose the discretionary inflation rate and associated output level (denoted by π_D^i and y_D^i, respectively). In view of (10.10)–(10.11), these would amount to:

$$\pi_D^i = \left(\frac{\alpha}{\beta_i}\right)[y^* - \bar{y}] - \left(\frac{\alpha}{\alpha^2 + \beta_i}\right)\epsilon, \tag{10.37}$$

$$y_D^i = \bar{y} + \left(\frac{\beta_i}{\alpha^2 + \beta_i}\right)\epsilon. \tag{10.38}$$

The preferences regarding inflation are diverse, and are summarized by the frequency distribution of β_i's as given in Figure 10.3. Agents with a very low value of

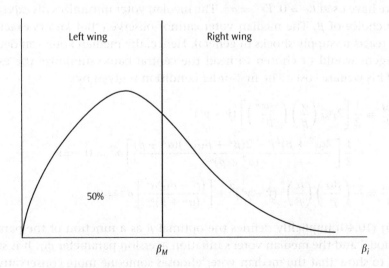

Figure 10.3. The frequency distribution of the inflation aversion parameter

β_i are called "left wing" in that they do not worry much about inflation but a great deal about output and employment stabilization. At the other end of the political spectrum, "right-wing" agents with a very high β_i have a strong aversion against inflation and worry very little about output stabilization.

We assume that the agents choose from among themselves the agent who is going to head the central bank. Voting is on a pairwise basis and by majority rule. The agent that is chosen has an inflation aversion parameter β. For this agent there exists no other agent β_i such that β_i is preferred by a majority of the people over β. Since there is a single issue (namely the choice of β) and preferences of the agents are single-peaked in β, the *median voter theorem* holds (see Mueller, 1989, pp. 65–66). In words this theorem says that the median voter determines the choice of β. The median voter has an inflation aversion parameter β_M that is illustrated in Figure 10.3. Exactly 50% of the population is more left wing than this voter and 50% is more right wing than the median voter.

But the median voter knows exactly what an agent with inflation aversion parameter β would choose, since that is given by (10.37)–(10.38) by setting $\beta_i = \beta$. By substituting (10.37)–(10.38) into the *median voter's cost function*, we obtain:

$$
\Omega_M \equiv \frac{1}{2} E\left[\left(y_D^i - y^*\right)^2 + \beta_M \left(\pi_D^i\right)^2\right]
$$

$$
= \frac{1}{2} E\left[\left(\bar{y} - y^* + \left(\frac{\beta}{\alpha^2 + \beta}\right)\epsilon\right)^2 + \beta_M \left(\frac{\alpha}{\beta}(y^* - \bar{y}) - \left(\frac{\alpha}{\alpha^2 + \beta}\right)\epsilon\right)^2\right]
$$

$$
= \frac{1}{2}\left[1 + \beta_M \left(\frac{\alpha}{\beta}\right)^2\right](\bar{y} - y^*)^2 + \frac{1}{2}\left[\frac{\beta^2 + \beta_M \alpha^2}{(\alpha^2 + \beta)^2}\right]\sigma^2, \tag{10.39}
$$

where we have used $E\epsilon = 0$, $E\epsilon^2 = \sigma^2$. The median voter minimizes his *expected* cost level by choice of β. The median voter cannot observe ϵ but knows exactly how agent β reacts to supply shocks in general. Hence, the median voter can determine which agent would (if chosen to head the central bank) minimize the expected value of his welfare costs. The first-order condition is given by:

$$
\frac{d\Omega_M}{d\beta} = \frac{1}{2}\left[2\beta_M \left(\frac{\alpha}{\beta}\right)\left(\frac{-\alpha^2}{\beta}\right)\right](\bar{y} - y^*)^2
$$

$$
+ \frac{1}{2}\left[\frac{2(\alpha^2 + \beta)^2\beta - 2(\beta^2 + \beta_M\alpha^2)(\alpha^2 + \beta)}{(\alpha^2 + \beta)^4}\right]\sigma^2 = 0 \quad \Rightarrow
$$

$$
\frac{d\Omega_M}{d\beta} = -\left(\frac{\beta_M}{\beta}\right)\left(\frac{\alpha}{\beta}\right)^2 (\bar{y} - y^*)^2 + \left[\frac{(\beta - \beta_M)\alpha^2}{(\alpha^2 + \beta)^3}\right]\sigma^2 = 0. \tag{10.40}
$$

Equation (10.40) implicitly defines the optimal β as a function of the parameters of the model and the median voter's inflation aversion parameter β_M. It is straightforward to show that the median voter chooses someone more conservative than himself, i.e. $\beta > \beta_M$. The proof runs as follows. If we evaluate $d\Omega_M/d\beta$ for $\beta = \beta_M$, equation (10.40) shows that $d\Omega_M/d\beta < 0$. Since the second-order condition for cost minimization requires that $d^2\Omega_M/d\beta^2 > 0$, $d\Omega_M/d\beta$ rises as β rises, so that $d\Omega_M/d\beta = 0$ for a value of β larger than β_M. Hence, the median voter delegates the conduct of monetary policy to someone more inflation averse than himself, and in this manner commits himself to a lower inflation rate.[5]

Furthermore, it is also possible to derive the following comparative static results with respect to the variance of the shocks (σ^2), the degree of inflation aversion of the median voter (β_M), and the ambitiousness of monetary policy ($y^* - \bar{y}$):

$$\frac{\partial \beta}{\partial \sigma^2} \equiv -\frac{\beta^3(\beta - \beta_M)}{3\beta_M(y^* - \bar{y})^2(\alpha^2 + \beta)^2(\alpha^2/\beta) + \sigma^2\beta^3} < 0, \tag{10.41}$$

$$\frac{\partial \beta}{\partial \beta_M} \equiv \frac{(\alpha^2 + \beta)^3(y^* - \bar{y})^2 + \sigma^2\beta^3}{3\beta_M(y^* - \bar{y})^2(\alpha^2 + \beta)^2(\alpha^2/\beta) + \sigma^2\beta^3} > 0, \tag{10.42}$$

$$\frac{\partial \beta}{\partial (y^* - \bar{y})} \equiv \frac{2\beta_M(\alpha^2 + \beta)^3(y^* - \bar{y})}{3\beta_M(y^* - \bar{y})^2(\alpha^2 + \beta)^2(\alpha^2/\beta) + \sigma^2\beta^3} > 0. \tag{10.43}$$

In words, more uncertainty (a higher σ^2) and a more left-wing population (a lower β_M) both lead to the appointment of a more left-wing central banker (a lower β). Higher output ambition, however, leads to the appointment of a more conservative central banker.

10.3 Dynamic Consistency and Capital Taxation

Up to this point the economic policy applications of the notion of dynamic inconsistency have all been in the area of monetary policy. This is not to say that this is the only area where this phenomenon is encountered.[6] Indeed, the purpose of this section is to demonstrate that exactly the same issues are relevant for fiscal policy as well. We demonstrate this with the aid of a simple model of optimal taxation and public goods adapted from Fischer (1980). As in Chapter 6, time is split into two periods, with period 1 representing the present and period 2 the future. The representative household has the following utility function:

$$U \equiv \frac{C_1^{1-1/\epsilon_1}}{1 - 1/\epsilon_1} + \left(\frac{1}{1+\rho}\right)\left[C_2 + \alpha\left(\frac{(1-N_2)^{1-1/\epsilon_2}}{1 - 1/\epsilon_2}\right) + \beta\left(\frac{G_2^{1-1/\epsilon_3}}{1 - 1/\epsilon_3}\right)\right], \tag{10.44}$$

---

[5] An even easier way to demonstrate that $\beta_M > \beta$ is to write (10.40) as:

$$\frac{(\beta - \beta_M)\sigma^2}{(\alpha^2 + \beta)^3} = \frac{\beta_M(y^* - \bar{y})^2}{\beta^3} > 0,$$

from which the result follows immediately.

[6] Indeed, we came across dynamic inconsistency in Chapter 8 where we analysed the interaction between wage setting by the union and capital investment by the firm. There we showed that the future wage offer of the union is dynamically inconsistent and thus not credible.

where C_t is goods consumption in period t ($= 1, 2$), N_2 is labour supply in the future, and G_2 is the level of public goods provision in the future. Notice that for simplicity labour supply and public goods provision are zero in the present period. Nothing of substance is affected by these simplifications. At the beginning of period 1, there is an existing capital stock built up in the past, equal to K_1. Capital does not depreciate and the constant marginal product of capital is equal to b (see below). The resource constraint in the current period is:

$$C_1 + [K_2 - K_1] = bK_1. \tag{10.45}$$

In words, (10.45) says that consumption plus investment in the present period must equal production (and capital income). In the second period, total demand for goods equals $C_2 + G_2$, which must equal production $F(N_2, K_2)$ plus the capital stock (which can be consumed during period 2. Think of capital as "corn"). Assuming a linear production function, the resource constraint in the second period is given by:

$$C_2 + G_2 = F(N_2, K_2) + K_2 = aN_2 + (1 + b)K_2, \tag{10.46}$$

where a is the constant marginal product of labour.[7]

10.3.1 The first-best optimum

Let us first study the so-called *command optimum*. Suppose that there is a benevolent social planner who must decide on the optimal allocation by maximizing the utility of the representative household subject to the restrictions (10.45)–(10.46). The Lagrangean for this optimal social plan is:

$$\mathcal{L} \equiv \frac{C_1^{1-1/\epsilon_1}}{1 - 1/\epsilon_1} + \left(\frac{1}{1 + \rho}\right) \left[C_2 + \alpha \left(\frac{(1 - N_2)^{1-1/\epsilon_2}}{1 - 1/\epsilon_2}\right) + \beta \left(\frac{G_2^{1-1/\epsilon_3}}{1 - 1/\epsilon_3}\right) \right]$$
$$- \lambda \left[C_1 + \frac{C_2 + G_2 - aN_2}{1 + b} - (1 + b)K_1 \right], \tag{10.47}$$

---

[7] Assuming a linear production function simplifies the exposition substantially. Technically, a linear production function is obtained by imposing an infinite elasticity of substitution between capital and labour, i.e. $\sigma_{KN} \to \infty$ (see Chapter 4). It also means that the demands for labour and capital are infinitely elastic, and that both factors are *inessential*, in the sense that output can be produced with only one of the two production factors.

which yields the first-order conditions:

$$\frac{\partial \mathcal{L}}{\partial C_1} = C_1^{-1/\epsilon_1} - \lambda = 0, \tag{10.48}$$

$$\frac{\partial \mathcal{L}}{\partial C_2} = \frac{1}{1+\rho} - \frac{\lambda}{1+b} = 0, \tag{10.49}$$

$$\frac{\partial \mathcal{L}}{\partial G_2} = \frac{\beta G_2^{-1/\epsilon_3}}{1+\rho} - \frac{\lambda}{1+b} = 0, \tag{10.50}$$

$$\frac{\partial \mathcal{L}}{\partial N_2} = -\frac{\alpha(1-N_2)^{-1/\epsilon_2}}{1+\rho} + \frac{a\lambda}{1+b} = 0. \tag{10.51}$$

Equation (10.49) implies that the marginal utility of income (given by λ) is constant: $\lambda = (1+b)/(1+\rho)$. By substituting this value of λ into (10.48) and (10.50)–(10.51), the optimal values for C_1, N_2, and G_2 are obtained.

$$C_1 = \left(\frac{1+b}{1+\rho}\right)^{-\epsilon_1}. \tag{10.52}$$

$$1 - N_2 = (a/\alpha)^{-\epsilon_2}, \tag{10.53}$$

$$G_2 = \beta^{-\epsilon_3}. \tag{10.54}$$

Finally, by using (10.52)–(10.54) in the consolidated resource constraint, the level of consumption in the second period can be calculated:

$$C_2 = (1+b)^2 K_1 + a - (1+b)C_1 - G_2 - a(1-N_2)$$
$$= a + (1+b)^2 K_1 - (1+\rho)^{\epsilon_1}(1+b)^{1-\epsilon_1} - \alpha^{\epsilon_2} a^{1-\epsilon_2} - \beta^{\epsilon_3}, \tag{10.55}$$

where we assume that the non-negativity restriction on consumption in the second period is non-binding (i.e. $C_2 \geq 0$). The command optimum is the best possible outcome for the representative household, given the availability of resources and the state of technology.

In practice, the policy maker may have direct control over the level of public goods provision G_2, but it is not likely to have direct control over the variables chosen by the representative household such as C_1, C_2, and N_2 (even in the former centrally planned Eastern bloc countries this proved to be difficult). This does not in and of itself imply that the first-best optimum cannot be attained in a decentralized economy. Indeed, if the government chooses G_2 optimally and has lump-sum taxes at its disposal, the first-best plan as given in (10.52)–(10.55) can be *decentralized*.

In the decentralized economy, households own the capital stock which they rent out to firms at an interest rate r. Households furthermore sell their labour to these firms, for which they receive a real wage W_2 (recall that they do not work in period 1). The budget restriction of the representative household in the first period is:

$$C_1 + [K_2 - K_1] = r_1 K_1, \tag{10.56}$$

where r_1 is the interest rate in period 1, so that $r_1 K_1$ is the interest income received by the household. This income is spent either on consumption goods or by purchasing additional investment goods. In the second period, the budget restriction is:

$$C_2 = W_2 N_2 + (1 + r_2)K_2 - Z_2, \tag{10.57}$$

where Z_2 is lump-sum taxes and r_2 is the real interest rate, both in period 2. The household does not invest in period 2 since the model world ends at the end of that period.

The representative firm produces output by hiring capital and/or labour from the representative household. Profit in period t is equal to:

$$\pi_t \equiv F(K_t, N_t) - W_t N_t - r_t K_t, \tag{10.58}$$

so that profit-maximizing behaviour implies that $r_t = F_K = b$ and $W_t = F_N = a$. In period 1 there is no labour supply and only capital is used, and in period 2 both labour and capital are used in production. Hence, for the linear production function we have:

$$r_1 = r_2 = b, \quad W_2 = a. \tag{10.59}$$

The real interest rate is constant and equal to b and the real wage in the second period is also constant and equal to a. Since both factors of production are paid exactly their respective marginal product, and the production function is constant returns to scale, the representative firm makes no profit.

The government purchases goods in period 2 and pays for these goods by lump-sum taxes levied on the representative household. Hence, the government budget restriction is:

$$G_2 = Z_2. \tag{10.60}$$

By substituting (10.59)–(10.60) into (10.56)–(10.57) and consolidating, we obtain:

$$C_1 + \frac{C_2 + G_2}{1 + b} = \frac{a N_2}{1 + b} + (1 + b)K_1. \tag{10.61}$$

The representative household maximizes its utility (10.44) by choice of C_1, C_2, and N_2, taking G_2 and its consolidated budget restriction (10.61) as given. Provided the government sets G_2 appropriately (i.e. at the level given in (10.54)) the thus chosen values of C_1, C_2, and N_2 coincide with the first-best optimum values given in (10.52)–(10.53) and (10.55). Hence, the social optimum can be decentralized if the government has access to lump-sum taxes.

10.3.2 The second-best problem

In practice the policy maker does not have (non-distorting) lump-sum taxes at its disposal. Instead, it must finance its spending by means of taxes on the different income categories. Suppose that t_L is the tax on labour income and t_K is the tax on capital income in the second period.[8] The household's budget restrictions become:

$$C_1 + [K_2 - K_1] = bK_1, \tag{10.62}$$

$$C_2 = a(1 - t_L)N_2 + [1 + b(1 - t_K)]K_2, \tag{10.63}$$

where we have already imposed the expressions in (10.59). By consolidating (10.62)–(10.63) we obtain:

$$C_1 + \frac{C_2}{1 + b(1 - t_K)} = \frac{a(1 - t_L)N_2}{1 + b(1 - t_K)} + (1 + b)K_1, \tag{10.64}$$

which is the counterpart to (10.61). The representative household maximizes its utility (10.44) by choice of C_1, C_2, and N_2, taking G_2 and its budget restriction (10.64) as given. The Lagrangean for this problem is:

$$\mathcal{L} \equiv \frac{C_1^{1-1/\epsilon_1}}{1 - 1/\epsilon_1} + \left(\frac{1}{1 + \rho}\right)\left[C_2 + \alpha\left(\frac{(1 - N_2)^{1-1/\epsilon_2}}{1 - 1/\epsilon_2}\right) + \beta\left(\frac{G_2^{1-1/\epsilon_3}}{1 - 1/\epsilon_3}\right)\right]$$
$$- \lambda\left[C_1 + \frac{C_2 - a(1 - t_L)N_2}{1 + b(1 - t_K)} - (1 + b)K_1\right], \tag{10.65}$$

which yields the first-order conditions:

$$\frac{\partial \mathcal{L}}{\partial C_1} = C_1^{-1/\epsilon_1} - \lambda = 0, \tag{10.66}$$

$$\frac{\partial \mathcal{L}}{\partial C_2} = \frac{1}{1 + \rho} - \frac{\lambda}{1 + b(1 - t_K)} = 0, \tag{10.67}$$

$$\frac{\partial \mathcal{L}}{\partial N_2} = -\frac{\alpha(1 - N_2)^{-1/\epsilon_2}}{1 + \rho} + \frac{a(1 - t_L)\lambda}{1 + b(1 - t_K)} = 0, \tag{10.68}$$

which can be solved for C_1, C_2, and N_2:

$$C_1 = \left(\frac{1 + b(1 - t_K)}{1 + \rho}\right)^{-\epsilon_1}, \tag{10.69}$$

$$C_2 = a(1 - t_L) + (1 + b)[1 + b(1 - t_K)]K_1 \tag{10.70}$$
$$- (1 + \rho)^{\epsilon_1}[1 + b(1 - t_K)]^{1-\epsilon_1} - \alpha^{\epsilon_2}[a(1 - t_L)]^{1-\epsilon_2},$$

$$1 - N_2 = \left(\frac{a(1 - t_L)}{\alpha}\right)^{-\epsilon_2}. \tag{10.71}$$

---

[8] A tax on capital income in the first period is abstracted from as it would amount to a lump-sum tax.

Finally, by substituting these optimal solutions back into the utility function, the *indirect utility function* is obtained:

$$V \equiv \left(\frac{1}{\epsilon_1 - 1}\right)\left(\frac{1 + b(1 - t_K)}{1 + \rho}\right)^{1 - \epsilon_1} + \left(\frac{I_F}{1 + \rho}\right)$$
$$+ \left(\frac{\alpha}{1 + \rho}\right)\left(\frac{1}{\epsilon_2 - 1}\right)\left(\frac{a(1 - t_L)}{\alpha}\right)^{1 - \epsilon_2} + \left(\frac{\beta}{1 + \rho}\right)\left(\frac{G_2^{1 - 1/\epsilon_3}}{1 - 1/\epsilon_3}\right), \tag{10.72}$$

where I_F is *full income* of the representative household, which is defined as:

$$I_F \equiv a(1 - t_L) + [1 + b(1 - t_K)](1 + b)K_1. \tag{10.73}$$

Full income represents the maximum amount of income the household could have in period 2, i.e. by not consuming anything in period 1 and by supplying the maximum amount of labour in period 2.

The government budget restriction in the absence of lump-sum taxes is:

$$G_2 = t_K b K_2 + t_L a N_2. \tag{10.74}$$

Government spending on public goods must be financed by the revenue from the capital and labour taxes. The policy maker maximizes indirect utility of the representative household (given in (10.72)) subject to the government budget restriction (10.74). The Lagrangean for the policy maker's problem is:

$$\mathcal{P} \equiv V(G_2, t_L, t_K) - \mu\left[G_2 - t_K b\left[(1 + b)K_1 - C_1\right] - t_L a N_2\right], \tag{10.75}$$

where we have substituted the expression for gross saving by the household, $K_2 \equiv (1 + b)K_1 - C_1$, and μ is the Lagrange multiplier associated with the government budget restriction (10.74). The first-order conditions for the policy maker's problem are the constraint (10.74) and:

$$\frac{\partial \mathcal{P}}{\partial G_2} = \frac{\partial V}{\partial G_2} - \mu = 0, \tag{10.76}$$

$$\frac{\partial \mathcal{P}}{\partial t_L} = \frac{\partial V}{\partial t_L} + \mu a\left[N_2 + t_L\frac{\partial N_2}{\partial t_L}\right] = 0, \tag{10.77}$$

$$\frac{\partial \mathcal{P}}{\partial t_K} = \frac{\partial V}{\partial t_K} + \mu b\left[K_2 + t_K\frac{\partial K_2}{\partial t_K}\right] = 0. \tag{10.78}$$

In the appendix it is shown that the first-order conditions can be rewritten in the following, more intuitive, form:

$$\beta G_2^{-1/\epsilon_3} = \eta, \tag{10.79}$$

$$\eta = \frac{1}{1 - \left(\frac{t_L}{1 - t_L}\right)\epsilon_L}, \tag{10.80}$$

$$\eta = \frac{1}{1 - \left(\frac{t_K}{1 - t_K}\right)\epsilon_K}, \tag{10.81}$$

where ϵ_L is the uncompensated wage elasticity of labour supply ($\epsilon_L > 0$), ϵ_K is the uncompensated interest elasticity of gross saving ($\epsilon_K > 0$), and $\eta \equiv \mu/(\partial V/\partial I_F)$ is the *marginal cost of public funds* (MCPF). Intuitively, the MCPF measures how much it "costs" to raise a guilder of public revenue. If there are non-distorting taxes it costs exactly one guilder to raise a guilder, and the MCPF is unity. On the other hand, if taxes distort real decisions by the private sector, it costs more than one guilder to raise one guilder of public revenue and the MCPF exceeds unity.

Equation (10.79) is the modified Samuelson rule for the optimal provision of public goods (see Atkinson and Stern, 1974). In words, (10.79) says that the marginal benefits of public goods (the left-hand side of (10.79)) should be equated to the marginal cost of financing these public goods, i.e. the MCPF. If there are non-distorting taxes, $\eta = 1$, and society can afford the first-best optimum level of public consumption. With distorting taxes, $\eta > 1$, and fewer public goods are provided. Equations (10.80)–(10.81) determine the optimal mix of taxes. Indeed, by rewriting (10.80)–(10.81) we obtain:

$$\frac{t_L}{1 - t_L} = \left(1 - \frac{1}{\eta}\right)\frac{1}{\epsilon_L}, \tag{10.82}$$

$$\frac{t_K}{1 - t_K} = \left(1 - \frac{1}{\eta}\right)\frac{1}{\epsilon_K}. \tag{10.83}$$

Equations (10.82)–(10.83) are expressions for the so-called *Ramsey taxes* on capital and labour (named after the British economist Frank Ramsey). Intuitively, these taxes raise a given amount of government revenue in the least distorting fashion. In order to facilitate the interpretation of (10.82)–(10.83), suppose that labour supply is perfectly inelastic (i.e. $\epsilon_L = 0$). Then we know that a tax on labour income works exactly like a (non-distorting) lump-sum tax. Equation (10.80) says that in that case the MCPF is unity, so that (10.83) says that capital should not be taxed at all, and the entire revenue should be raised by means of the labour tax. The reverse case holds if the savings function is very interest inelastic and the labour supply is very wage elastic. In that case capital should be taxed heavily and labour should be taxed lightly. In the general case, however, (10.82)–(10.83) say that both tax rates should be set at some positive level.

10.3.3 Dynamic inconsistency of the optimal tax plan

The problem with the optimal tax plan calculated in the previous section is that it is dynamically inconsistent. In the first period the policy maker announces that it will tax both labour income and capital income in the second period. But it turns out that once the second period has commenced it is no longer optimal for the policy maker to stick to its plan. This can easily be demonstrated with the aid of the model. At the beginning of the second period, the representative household has a capital stock of K_2 and chooses C_2 and N_2 to maximize remaining lifetime utility,

$$U_2 \equiv C_2 + \alpha \left(\frac{(1 - N_2)^{1-1/\epsilon_2}}{1 - 1/\epsilon_2} \right) + \beta \left(\frac{G_2^{1-1/\epsilon_3}}{1 - 1/\epsilon_3} \right), \tag{10.84}$$

subject to the budget restriction:

$$C_2 = a(1 - t_L)N_2 + [1 + b(1 - t_K)] K_2. \tag{10.85}$$

Following the usual steps, the solutions for C_2 and N_2 are obtained:

$$C_2 = a(1 - t_L) + [1 + b(1 - t_K)] K_2 - \alpha^{\epsilon_2} [a(1 - t_L)]^{1-\epsilon_2}, \tag{10.86}$$

$$1 - N_2 = \left(\frac{a(1 - t_L)}{\alpha} \right)^{-\epsilon_2}. \tag{10.87}$$

By substituting (10.86)–(10.87) into (10.84) the indirect utility function for period 2 is obtained:

$$V_2 \equiv [a(1 - t_L) + [1 + b(1 - t_K)] K_2]$$
$$+ \left(\frac{\alpha}{\epsilon_2 - 1} \right) \left(\frac{a(1 - t_L)}{\alpha} \right)^{1-\epsilon_2} + \beta \left(\frac{G_2^{1-1/\epsilon_3}}{1 - 1/\epsilon_3} \right). \tag{10.88}$$

Obviously, (10.86)–(10.87) coincide with the expressions given in (10.70)–(10.71), respectively, if the policy maker keeps his word and produces the tax rates as given in (10.82)–(10.83).

The problem is that, from the perspective of period 2, the policy maker will set different tax rates. Intuitively, the reason is that once the capital stock K_2 is in place, taxing capital income is non-distorting (since the capital income is like a "sitting duck") and the optimal Ramsey tax solution is to set $t_L = 0$ (since the labour tax is distorting) and $t_K > 0$.[9] As a result of this, the optimal tax rates as given in (10.82)–(10.83) are not believed by the public.

Of course, there is a consistent solution to the problem. This solution is obtained by working backwards in time, starting in period 2. The public knows that the government will set $t_L = 0$ in period 2 and raise its revenue by means of the tax on capital income only. The public also knows that G_2 will be set according to the level given in (10.54) because the policy maker has a non-distorting tax at its disposal in period 2. As a result of the higher level of public spending and the higher capital tax, the public will save less in period 1.

---

[9] Formally, the policy maker chooses G_2, t_L, and t_K in order to maximize (10.88) subject to the government budget restriction (10.74). By following the same steps as before it can be shown that these results follow. Notice also that the government's plan regarding public goods provision is also dynamically inconsistent. Provided enough revenue can be raised from the capital income tax, the policy maker will set G_2 at the first-best optimum level as given in (10.54). This is a higher level than was announced in the first period.

10.4 Punchlines

The discussion in this chapter focuses on the phenomenon of dynamic inconsistency. The classic example of dynamic inconsistency and its potential resolution can be traced to the ancient Greek author Homer. In this chapter, however, we study examples of dynamic inconsistency in governmental economic policy. We study three examples, two of which deal with monetary policy and one with fiscal policy.

To prepare for the first two examples of dynamic inconsistency we develop a simple model in which the policy maker faces a (stochastic) Lucas supply curve and attempts to steer output towards a higher than full employment level by setting the inflation rate (using monetary policy instruments to do so). The cost function of the policy maker depends positively on the deviation of output from its target level and on the inflation rate. A simple parameter measures the relative aversion of the policy maker against inflation. The higher this parameter the more "right wing" we shall call the policy maker. There is informational asymmetry in the model because the policy maker can observe the realization of the stochastic supply shock in the Lucas supply curve but the public cannot. As a result of this asymmetry, monetary policy is effective at influencing output despite the fact that private agents formulate rational expectations.

We can distinguish three different solutions to the policy maker's optimization problem. Under the discretionary solution, the policy maker chooses inflation (and thus output) in each period. Since private agents know the structure of the model they can compute the rational expectations solution under discretion which then feeds back into the Lucas supply curve. The rational expectations solution for the discretionary policy has two features. First, the chosen inflation rate depends positively on the output ambition of the policy maker (the gap between target and full employment output) and negatively on the supply shock. Second, the degree of accommodation of supply shocks by monetary policy depends in an intuitive fashion on the political orientation of the policy maker. Indeed, a left-wing (right-wing) policy maker cares little (strongly) about inflation and cares strongly (little) about deviations in output from full employment.

The discretionary solution is suboptimal, however, in that the policy maker can steer closer to its bliss point under an alternative rule-based solution. The rule-based solution is as follows. The policy maker announces to the public that it will follow a monetary policy rule which produces zero inflation in every period. If the public believed that the policy maker would stick to its promise the expected inflation rate would also be zero and no output stabilization would take place.

The problem with the rule-based solution is, however, that it is dynamically inconsistent. A policy maker has a strong incentive to exploit the Lucas supply curve based on zero expected inflation and to accommodate supply shocks by accommodating surprise inflation. This is the so-called cheating solution which derives its name from the fact that the policy maker does not stick to its promises of no inflation. The cheating solution is closest to the policy maker's bliss point but it violates the rational expectations assumption.

The upshot of the discussion so far is that the only policy which is both believed by private agents (and is said to be credible) and is consistent with rational expectations is the discretionary policy. Of all policies considered however, the discretionary policy yields the policy maker the lowest level of welfare (i.e. the highest level of social cost). It would seem that the economy gets stuck with the worst possible outcome.

In an ingenious paper, Barro and Gordon have shown that the reputation of the policy maker can act as an enforcement device, making it possible that the superior rule-based equilibrium is credibly selected in equilibrium. These authors proxy the policy maker's reputation as follows. If the policy maker has kept its promise (whatever it was) in the previous period then the public will believe the policy maker's announcement that it will follow the monetary rule in the present period. In contrast, if the policy maker did not keep its promise in the previous period, the public discounts the policy maker's reputation and expects that the discretionary solution will be selected in the present period. This is an example of a "tit-for-tat" strategy adopted by the private agents in their repeated prisoner's dilemma game with the policy maker. The approach implies that a rule-based solution may be enforceable which features a positive inflation rate.

In the remainder of this chapter we give two more examples of dynamic inconsistency (and its possible resolution). In the first of these we show that in a voting model, the median voter will elect somebody to act as the central banker who is more conservative (and has a higher aversion against inflation) than he is himself. In doing so, the median voter commits himself to a lower inflation rate than he would have chosen had he himself been the monetary policy maker.

In the final example we develop a simple toy model of optimal taxation of labour and capital income when lump-sum taxes are not available. Two key results are derived. First, abstracting from issues of dynamic inconsistency, the optimal tax rates on both labour and capital are non-zero and these rates depend on the elasticities of the respective tax bases. Second, the optimal taxes are dynamically inconsistent. Once the future capital stock is in place, the tax base for capital income tax is inelastic and the policy maker can raise public revenue in a non-distorting fashion by not taxing labour income and taxing capital income as much as possible.

Further Reading

The key references to the reputational model of inflation are Barro and Gordon (1983a, 1983b), and Backus and Driffill (1985). See also Cukierman and Meltzer (1986) and Cukierman (1992). Persson and Tabellini (1994b) present a collection of the most important articles. Recently a number of monographs have appeared on the political economy approach to economic policy–see Persson and Tabellini (1989), Dixit (1996), Persson and Tabellini (2000), and Drazen (2000). For a review of the last two books, see Saint-Paul (2000). Readers interested in the optimal taxation literature are referred to Atkinson and Stiglitz (1980). Persson and Tabellini (1994a) study capital taxation in a model of a representative democracy. Van der Ploeg (1995) studies the political economy of monetary and fiscal policy in a dynamic macroeconomic model.

Appendix

Derivation of equations (10.80)–(10.81)

Equation (10.80) is derived as follows. First, we calculate $\partial V/\partial t_L$ from the indirect utility function given in (10.72).

$$\frac{\partial V}{\partial t_L} = -\frac{a}{1+\rho} + \frac{a}{1+\rho}\left(\frac{a(1-t_L)}{\alpha}\right)^{-\epsilon_2} = -\left(\frac{a}{1+\rho}\right)N_2, \tag{A10.1}$$

where we have used (10.71) in the final step. By substituting (A10.1) into (10.77) we obtain:

$$-\left(\frac{a}{1+\rho}\right)N_2 + \mu a N_2\left[1 + \frac{t_L}{N_2}\frac{\partial N_2}{\partial t_L}\right] = 0 \quad \Rightarrow$$

$$\mu(1+\rho)\left[1 - \left(\frac{t_L}{1-t_L}\right)\epsilon_L\right] = 1, \tag{A10.2}$$

where $\eta \equiv \mu(1+\rho)$ is the marginal cost of public funds, and ϵ_L is the uncompensated wage elasticity of labour supply:

$$\epsilon_L \equiv \frac{\partial N_2}{\partial a(1-t_L)}\frac{a(1-t_L)}{N_2} = -\left(\frac{1-t_L}{t_L}\right)\frac{\partial N_2}{\partial t_L}\frac{t_L}{N_2} = \omega_H\epsilon_2 > 0, \tag{A10.3}$$

where $\omega_H \equiv (1-N_2)/N_2$ is the leisure/work ratio. By rewriting (A10.2), equation (10.80) is obtained.

Equation (10.81) is obtained in a similar fashion. First, we calculate $\partial V/\partial t_K$ from the indirect utility function given in (10.72).

$$\frac{\partial V}{\partial t_K} = -\frac{b}{1+\rho}(1+b)K_1 + \frac{b}{1+\rho}\left(\frac{1+b(1-t_K)}{1+\rho}\right)^{-\epsilon_1}$$

$$= \left(\frac{b}{1+\rho}\right)[C_1 - (1+b)K_1] = -\left(\frac{b}{1+\rho}\right)K_2, \tag{A10.4}$$

where we have used (10.69) and the definition of K_2 in the two final steps. By substituting (A10.4) into (10.78) we obtain:

$$-\left(\frac{b}{1+\rho}\right)K_2 + \mu b K_2\left[1 + \frac{t_K}{K_2}\frac{\partial K_2}{\partial t_K}\right] = 0 \quad \Rightarrow$$

$$\mu(1+\rho)\left[1 - \left(\frac{t_K}{1-t_K}\right)\epsilon_K\right] = 1, \tag{A10.5}$$

where ϵ_K is the uncompensated interest elasticity of gross saving:

$$\epsilon_K \equiv \frac{\partial K_2}{\partial b(1 - t_K)} \frac{b(1 - t_K)}{K_2} = -\left(\frac{1 - t_K}{t_K}\right) \frac{\partial K_2}{\partial t_K} \frac{t_K}{K_2} = \omega_C \epsilon_1 > 0, \tag{A10.6}$$

where ω_C is defined as:

$$\omega_C \equiv \frac{b(1 - t_K)C_1}{[1 + b(1 - t_K)]K_2}. \tag{A10.7}$$

By rewriting (A10.5), equation (10.81) is obtained.

11

The Open Economy

The purpose of this chapter is to discuss the following issues:

1. How do we add the international sector to the IS-LM model? The Mundell-Fleming contribution.
2. What are the implications of openness on the effects of fiscal and monetary policy? How do the degree of capital mobility and the exchange rate system affect the conclusions?
3. How are shocks transmitted across countries and how does international policy coordination work?
4. How can we introduce forward-looking behaviour into the model?

11.1 The International Sector in the IS-LM Model

11.1.1 Some bookkeeping

From national income accounting principles we know that for the open economy aggregate output can be written as:

$$Y \equiv C + I + G + (EX - IM), \tag{11.1}$$

where Y is aggregate output, C is private consumption, G is government consumption, EX is exports, and IM are imports. Aggregate spending by domestic residents is called *absorption* and is defined as $A \equiv C + I + G$. Exports are added to domestic absorption in the calculation of aggregate output because foreigners also spend on our goods, but imports must be deducted because what we import (i.e. parts of C, I, and G) does not lead to domestic production.

In view of the definition of absorption A, (11.1) can also be written as:

$$Y \equiv A + (EX - IM), \tag{11.2}$$

which says that income equals aggregate spending by domestic residents plus *net* exports.

We also recall that aggregate output in an economy can be measured in different manners. Particularly, total output produced within the country is measured by gross domestic product (GDP), whereas total output produced by residents of the country (anywhere in the world) is measured by gross national product (GNP). For the first definition the relevant criterion is "where is it produced" and for the second definition "who produces it". The difference between GNP and GDP therefore depends on net factor payments received from abroad (such as income from capital in the form of interest and dividends, and labour income received by domestic residents from abroad). In practice we shall ignore the difference between the two concepts regarding aggregate output.

Yet another definition is obtained from (11.1) by adding international transfer receipts TR and deducting net taxes T (total taxes minus domestic transfers) on both sides:

$$Y + TR - T \equiv C + I + (G - T) + (EX + TR - IM), \tag{11.3}$$

where the left-hand side of (11.3) gives the definition of disposable income of residents. By noting that aggregate saving by the private sector S is defined as $S \equiv Y + TR - T - C$, equation (11.3) can be written as:

$$(S - I) + (T - G) \equiv (EX + TR - IM) \equiv CA. \tag{11.4}$$

The current account surplus CA is identically equal to the private sector savings surplus $S - I$ plus the government budget surplus $T - G$. The current account surplus measures the rate at which the aggregate economy is adding to its net external assets: by spending less than your income (as a nation) you build up claims on the rest of the world. Hence, ignoring valuation changes of the existing stock of net foreign assets (NFA) we have:

$$\Delta NFA \equiv CA, \tag{11.5}$$

or, equivalently,

$$\Delta NFA \equiv (S - I) + (T - G). \tag{11.6}$$

Hence, a country for which $S = I$ and $G > T$ is of necessity running down its stock of net foreign assets (it is "borrowing from the rest of the world").

As a final step we must link the situation of the balance of payments to what happens in the financial sector by means of some elementary money accounting. In

Balance sheet of the central bank

Assets		Liabilities	
Net foreign assets	NFA^{cb}		
Domestic credit	DC	High powered money	H

equation (11.6) the *aggregate* change in net foreign assets is determined (i.e. lumping together all sectors of the economy such as the central bank, commercial banks, treasury, and the non-bank private sector). We denote what happens to the central bank's net foreign asset position by ΔNFA^{cb}. The monetary authority's balance sheet can be written (in stylized form) as above.

Here NFA^{cb} includes foreign exchange reserves less liabilities to foreign official holders, and DC includes securities held by the central bank (such as T-bills), loans, and other credit. High powered money consists of currency C^P (cash in vaults and currency in the hands of the public) plus commercial bank deposits at the central bank RE (so that $H \equiv C^P + RE$). High powered money is often referred to as "base money".

By taking first differences we can derive from the central bank's balance sheet that the change in the net foreign asset position of the central bank is equal to the difference between the rate of high powered money creation minus the rate of domestic credit creation:

$$\Delta NFA^{cb} \equiv \Delta H - \Delta DC. \tag{11.7}$$

Equation (11.7) demonstrates an important mechanism due to the eighteenth-century Scottish philosopher and economist David Hume. If the monetary authority intervenes in the foreign exchange market (by buying or selling foreign exchange) the stock of net foreign assets changes and, by (11.7), the stock of high powered money changes as well, i.e. $\Delta H = \Delta NFA^{cb}$. Hence, foreign exchange sales (purchases) automatically reduce (increase) the stock of high powered money (and, by the money multiplier, the money stock as well; see below).

The monetary authority can (temporarily) break this automatic link between H and NFA^{cb} by engaging in so-called *sterilization* operations. In terms of (11.7) the central bank can sterilize the effect of changes in its net foreign asset position by manipulating domestic credit, i.e. $\Delta H = 0$ if $\Delta DC = -\Delta NFA^{cb}$. For example, if the central bank sells foreign exchange reserves (so that $\Delta NFA^{cb} < 0$) and simultaneously uses an expansionary open market operation (a purchase of domestic bonds on the open market) of appropriate magnitude, so that $\Delta DC = -\Delta NFA^{cb} > 0$, then $\Delta H = 0$.

In a fractional reserve banking system commercial banks are required to hold a fraction of their deposits in the form of reserves with the central bank. The money stock, M^S, as measured by the sum of deposits, D, at the commercial banks plus currency, C^P, is then a multiple of the stock of high powered money:

$$M^S \equiv D + C^P = \mu H \quad \Leftrightarrow \quad \Delta M^S = \mu \Delta H, \tag{11.8}$$

where $\mu > 1$ is the money multiplier.[1]

11.1.2 The modified IS-LM model for a small open economy

Up to this point all we have done is manipulate some unexciting (but rather essential) identities. We can give the story some theoretical content by specifying the behavioural equations of the model. First, we write (11.2) in the form of a condition for spending equilibrium in the aggregate goods market as:

$$Y = A(r, Y) + G + X(Y, Q), \tag{11.9}$$

where $A(r, Y)$ is the part of domestic absorption that depends on the rate of interest r and the level of aggregate output Y, G is the exogenous level of government spending, and $X(Y, Q)$ is net exports ($\equiv EX - IM$) as a function of output and the relative price of foreign goods $Q \equiv EP^*/P$, where E is the nominal exchange rate (domestic currency per unit of foreign currency), P^* is the foreign price level, and P is the domestic price level. In view of the definition of the exchange rate, a depreciation (or devaluation) of the domestic currency is represented by an increase in E.

Since investment depends negatively on the interest rate and the marginal propensity to consume out of current income is between zero and unity, we have that $A_r < 0$ and $0 < A_Y < 1$. Furthermore, the net export function satisfies $X_Y < 0$ (since imports depend positively on income) and $X_Q > 0$ (as it is assumed that the *Marshall–Lerner condition* holds). Equation (11.9) is the open economy IS curve. Like its closed economy counterpart, it is downward sloping in (r, Y) space, but the import leakage makes it steeper than for the closed economy.

The money market can be modelled in the standard fashion.

$$M^D/P = L(r, Y), \tag{11.10}$$

$$M^S = \mu \left[NFA^{cb} + DC \right], \tag{11.11}$$

$$M^D = M^S = M, \tag{11.12}$$

with $L_r < 0$ and $L_Y > 0$ (see Chapter 1). Equations (11.10)–(11.11) define the open economy LM curve, which is upward sloping in (r, Y) space. The modification brought about by the recognition of the openness of the economy consists of

---

[1] Assume that the commercial banks are required by law to hold a fraction c_1 of their deposits as reserves with the central bank, $RE = c_1 D$, where $0 < c_1 < 1$. Suppose furthermore that the public desires a constant ratio between currency holdings and deposits, say $C^P/D = c_2$. Then, since $M^S \equiv D + C^P = (1 + c_2)D$ and $H = (c_1 + c_2)D$, we can derive that $M^S = \mu H$, where $\mu \equiv (1 + c_2)/(c_1 + c_2) > 1$. A higher legal reserve requirement or a lower desired currency-deposits ratio both decrease the money multiplier.

the potential endogeneity of the money supply through changes in the stock of net foreign assets of the central bank. The model is closed by assuming that both domestic and foreign prices are fixed (and normalized to unity, i.e. $P^* = P = 1$), and by making an assumption regarding the degree of international capital mobility.

11.1.3 Capital mobility and economic policy

We can distinguish several degrees of "financial openness" of an economy. First, it can be assumed that the small open economy (SOE) has no trade in financial assets with the rest of the world (ROW). This extreme case is referred to as one of *capital immobility*. This case was relevant during the 1940s and early 1950s when many countries had capital controls. A second case is that of *perfect capital mobility*. Financial capital is perfectly mobile and flows to that location where it earns the highest yield. Domestic and foreign bonds are perfect substitutes and portfolio adjustment is instantaneous so that yields are equated across the world. This case is often deemed to be relevant to the situation in the 1980s and 1990s. Finally, the intermediate case is referred to as one of *imperfect capital mobility*.

The balance of payments B can be written as the sum of the current account and the capital account. Ignoring net international transfers the former coincides with the trade account:

$$B \equiv X(Y, Q) + KI(r - r^*) \equiv \Delta NFA^{cb}, \tag{11.13}$$

where B is the balance of payments, KI is net capital inflows, and r^* is the interest rate in the ROW. If KI is positive this means that domestic residents are selling more financial assets (such as bonds) to the ROW than they are buying from the ROW. In that case the country as a whole is a net borrower from the ROW. The three assumptions regarding capital mobility that were mentioned above can now be made more precise. Capital immobility (case (i)) means that $KI(r - r^*) \equiv 0$ so that balance of payments equilibrium coincides with equilibrium on the current account, i.e. $B = \Delta NFA^{cb} = X(Y, Q) = 0$. With perfect capital mobility (case (ii)), arbitrage in the capital markets and the resulting capital flows ensure that $r = r^*$ always, which can be represented mathematically by $KI_r \to \infty$. Finally, for the case of imperfect capital mobility (case (iii)) differences between r and r^* can exist in equilibrium and $0 < KI_r \ll \infty$. Figure 11.1 shows the balance of payments (BP) curves in (r, Y) space for the different cases. The slope of the BP curve can be obtained by differentiating (11.13):

$$\left(\frac{dr}{dY} \right)_{B=0} = -\frac{X_Y}{KI_r} \geq 0. \tag{11.14}$$

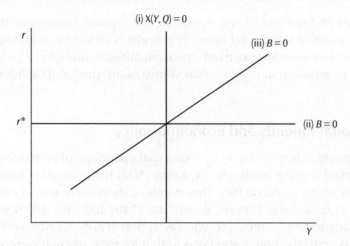

Figure 11.1. The degree of capital mobility and the balance of payment

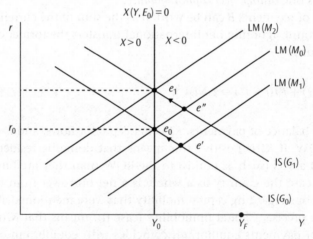

Figure 11.2. Monetary and fiscal policy with immobile capital and fixed exchange rates

Monetary and fiscal policy with immobile capital and fixed exchange rates

The IS curve is given by (11.9), the LM curve in (11.10)–(11.12), and the BP curve in (11.13) (with $B = 0$ and $KI \equiv 0$ imposed). Graphically the situation in the economy can be drawn as in Figure 11.2. The initial IS-LM-BP equilibrium is at point e_0 where output is Y_0 and the interest rate is r_0. Note that for points to the right of the BP curve output and imports are too high and the current account is in deficit ($X < 0$), with the reverse holding for points to the left of the BP curve. It is assumed that output is below full employment output Y_F and that the policy maker wishes to conduct economic policy aimed at restoring full employment.

Since the money supply is generally endogenous in the open economy operating under fixed exchange rates, we must be precise about what is meant by *monetary policy*. An open market operation in the form of a purchase of bonds by the central bank leads to an increase in domestic credit $\Delta DC > 0$, and, by (11.11), to an increase in the money supply $\Delta M^S = \mu \Delta DC > 0$. In terms of Figure 11.2, the LM curve shifts from $LM(M_0)$ to $LM(M_1)$ in the short run. At point e′, output is higher and the interest rate is lower than before the shock, but the current account is in deficit ($B = X < 0$). Since the country is spending more than it is earning, the demand for foreign exchange exceeds the supply of foreign exchange. Since the monetary authority is committed to maintaining a fixed exchange rate, however, it must satisfy the excess demand for foreign exchange by running down its international reserves, i.e. $\Delta NFA^{cb} < 0$. In the absence of sterilization, this means, by equation (11.11), that the money stock starts to decrease again. This causes the LM curve to *gradually* shift to the left, and the economy moves along the IS curve back to point e_0. Ultimately, the initial increase in domestic credit is exactly offset by the loss in foreign exchange reserves and only the composition (but not the size) of the central bank's portfolio has been changed as a result of the monetary policy.

Now consider what happens if the policy maker wishes to stimulate the economy by means of fiscal policy, consisting of a bond-financed increase in government spending.[2] Assume furthermore that government spending is entirely on domestically produced goods (a simplification that is relaxed below in section 2). In terms of Figure 11.2, the IS curve shifts from $IS(G_0)$ to $IS(G_1)$ and the new short-run equilibrium is at point e″. In view of the increase in output, imports are higher, the current account is in deficit ($X < 0$), and the money supply gradually declines (from M_0 to M_1) as the central bank foreign exchange reserves dwindle. The ultimate equilibrium is at point e_1, at which output is unchanged and the interest rate is higher.

In conclusion, neither monetary nor fiscal policy can (permanently) raise the level of income in the absence of capital mobility. The balance of payments is only in equilibrium if the current account is, but the latter does not itself depend on the rate of interest. This very strong conclusion is modified once the extreme assumption of capital immobility is relaxed.

Monetary and fiscal policy with perfect capital mobility under fixed exchange rates

With perfect capital mobility, the BP curve is horizontal. In terms of Figure 11.3, the initial equilibrium is at e_0. Monetary policy, consisting of an increase in domestic

---

[2] The Treasury issues *new* bonds to pay for the additional government spending. This ensures that the money supply stays constant as the level of domestic credit is unchanged. The money raised by the bond sale is spent again on the additional government goods.

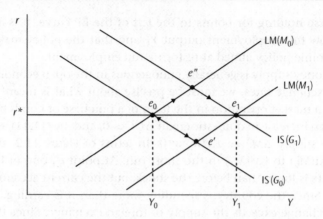

Figure 11.3. Monetary and fiscal policy with perfect capital mobility and fixed exchange rates

credit, shifts the LM curve from LM(M_0) to LM(M_1). At point e' the domestic interest rate is below the world interest rate and a massive capital outflow would occur, which worsens the capital account. Since output (and hence imports) is higher, the current account is also worse than at point e_0. The money supply will decrease (instantaneously) as investors purchase foreign exchange in order to buy profitable foreign financial assets. Since the exchange rate is fixed, the monetary authority sells them the required foreign exchange, which means that its stock of net foreign assets decreases, i.e. $\Delta NFA^{cb} < 0$. The adjustment occurs instantaneously, since all that happens is a portfolio reshuffling by investors. Hence, the economy stays at point e_0. The shift in LM due to the increase in domestic credit is immediately reversed by the loss of foreign exchange reserves, or, in terms of (11.7), $\Delta NFA^{cb} + \Delta DC \equiv \Delta H = 0$. Monetary policy is totally ineffective even in the short run.

Fiscal policy, on the other hand, is very effective in this case. Consider again a bond-financed increase in government spending. In terms of Figure 11.3, the IS curve shifts to the right from IS(G_0) to IS(G_1). This puts upward pressure on the domestic interest rate (at point e'') which causes massive net capital inflows. As investors from the ROW wish (in net terms) to buy domestic securities, the supply of foreign exchange outstrips the demand for foreign exchange. In order to maintain the fixed exchange rate, the central bank purchases the excess supply of foreign exchange and its stock of net foreign assets and hence the money supply increases (instantaneously), i.e. $\Delta M^S = \mu \Delta NFA^{cb} > 0$. This causes the LM curve to shift from LM(M_0) to LM(M_1). Only at point e_1 are the domestic and foreign interest rates equated and the money supply stabilized. Since capital is perfectly mobile, the shift from e_0 to e_1 occurs instantaneously. Hence, fiscal policy is highly effective in a small open economy under perfect capital mobility.

Monetary and fiscal policy with perfect capital mobility under flexible exchange rates

Under flexible exchange rates variations in the value of the domestic currency (E) ensure that the balance of payments is always in equilibrium. Indeed, the exchange rate is determined by balance of payments equilibrium, since it implies that the demand for and supply of foreign exchange are equated:

$$B \equiv \Delta NFA^{cb} = 0 \quad \Leftrightarrow \quad X(Y,E) + KI(r - r^*) = 0, \tag{11.15}$$

where we have substituted $P^* = P = 1$ so that $Q = E$ in the expression for net exports. Suppose that there is a current account deficit, so that exports are smaller than imports. Since exports give rise to a supply of foreign exchange and imports cause a demand for foreign exchange, this means that $X < 0$ represents an excess demand for foreign exchange. This excess demand for foreign exchange is met by capital inflows, consisting of investors from the ROW buying domestic bonds. Since they have to pay for these bonds, the capital inflow gives rise to a supply of foreign exchange. In equilibrium, therefore, E adjusts until $X(Y,E) = -KI(r - r^*)$ since only then does demand equal supply in the foreign exchange market.

This has an important consequence for economic policy, since the monetary authority has control over the domestic money supply under flexible exchange rates. The reason is that the central bank, by allowing the exchange rate to float freely, does not need to intervene in the foreign exchange market. This means that its stock of net foreign assets is fixed, so that changes in domestic credit translate directly into changes in the money supply.

The equilibrium exchange rate follows from the IS-LM equilibrium with $r = r^*$ imposed. By using (11.9)–(11.12) and imposing $r = r^*$, equilibrium in the money market and the (demand side of the) goods market implies:

$$M = L(r^*, Y), \tag{11.16}$$

$$Y = A(r^*, Y) + G + X(Y,E), \tag{11.17}$$

where we have also substituted $P = 1$ in (11.16). Equation (11.16) represents money market equilibrium at the given world interest rate r^*. Since the money supply is constant (11.16) determines a unique level of output that is independent of the exchange rate. In terms of Figure 11.4, this curve is drawn as $LL(M_0)$. Equation (11.17) represents domestic spending equilibrium at the world rate of interest. Since a high value for E (a weak domestic currency) stimulates net exports, (11.17) implies a positive relationship between output and the exchange rate that has been drawn as the schedule YY in Figure 11.4. Indeed, the slope of the YY schedule can be obtained from (11.17) as:

$$\left(\frac{dE}{dY} \right)_{YY} = \frac{1 - A_Y - X_Y}{X_Q} > 0. \tag{11.18}$$

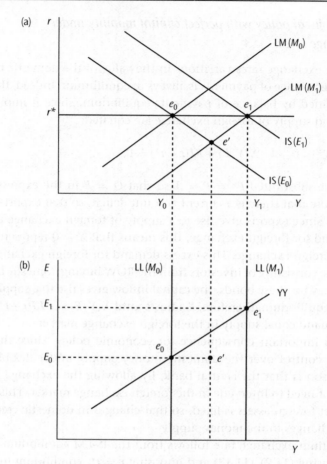

Figure 11.4. Monetary policy with perfect capital mobility and flexible exchange rates

Monetary policy is highly effective in this case. In terms of Figure 11.4, an increase in domestic credit shifts the LM curve in panel (a) from $LM(M_0)$ to $LM(M_1)$ and the LL curve from $LL(M_0)$ to $LL(M_1)$. At point e' the domestic interest rate is below the world interest rate, and a massive capital outflow occurs. There is excess demand for foreign exchange which leads to an instantaneous depreciation of the domestic currency (from E_0 to E_1 in panel (b)). This stimulates net exports as domestic goods are now cheaper to foreigners and shifts the IS curve from $IS(E_0)$ to $IS(E_1)$. The new equilibrium, which is attained instantaneously, is at point e_1 where output is increased.

Fiscal policy, in the form of a bond-financed increase in government spending, turns out to be entirely ineffective (as was to be expected from the discussion surrounding the LL and YY curves). In terms of Figure 11.5, the fiscal impulse shifts the IS curve in panel (a) from $IS(G_0, E_0)$ to $IS(G_1, E_0)$, and the YY curve in panel (b) from

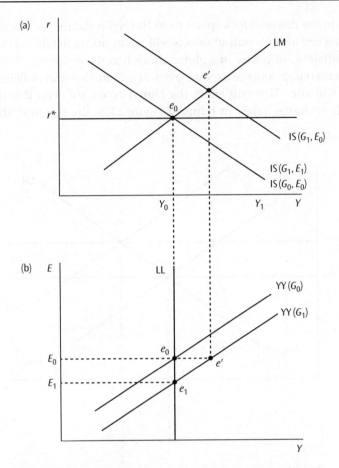

Figure 11.5. Fiscal policy with perfect capital mobility and flexible exchange rates

$YY(G_0)$ to $YY(G_1)$. This puts upward pressure on domestic interest rates and at point e' massive capital inflows occur leading to an excess supply for foreign exchange. In response, the domestic currency appreciates (E falls from E_0 to E_1), which leads to a deterioration of the current account and shifts IS back from $IS(G_1, E_0)$ to $IS(G_1, E_1)$, which coincides with $IS(G_0, E_0)$. In the new equilibrium, which is again attained instantaneously, output and the rate of interest are unchanged and the exchange rate has appreciated. Fiscal policy is completely ineffective under flexible exchange rates.

An immediate policy consequence of this ineffectiveness result is that the small open economy operating under flexible exchange rates is, in a sense, insulated from foreign spending disturbances (such as shocks to the demand for its exports), *provided* these shocks are uncoordinated and consequently have no effect on the world rate of interest. For example, if a spending bust occurs in Germany leading to a decrease in the demand for exports from the Netherlands, the Dutch exchange rate will depreciate and no output effects will occur under flexible exchange rates. Matters are different, of course, if a global shock hits the economy. If all countries, except the Netherlands, pursue expansionary aggregate demand policies, the world interest rate will rise. This will affect the Dutch economy even if it is operating under flexible exchange rates. In terms of Figure 11.6, the rise in r^* shifts the YY

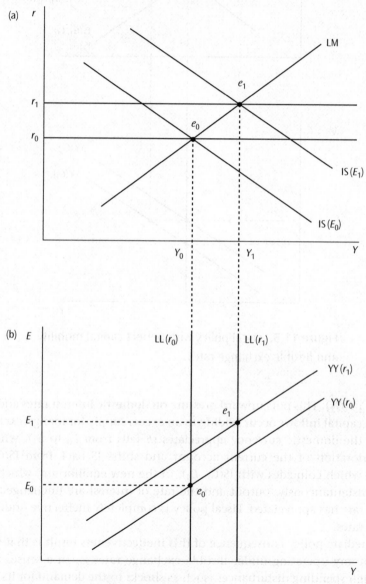

Figure 11.6. Foreign interest rate shocks with perfect capital mobility and flexible exchange rates

curve to the left and the LL curve to the right. The domestic currency depreciates, due to the capital outflows, and output increases. A global shock is transmitted to the small open economy through its effect on the world rate of interest. We return to the issue of shock transmission below.

Imperfect capital mobility

If financial capital is imperfectly mobile, we have a weighted average of the two previous extreme cases. The balance of payments curve is upward sloping (see (11.14)) and points to the left (right) of the BP curve are consistent with a balance of payments surplus (deficit). The IS, LM, and BP curves have been drawn in Figure 11.7, where the BP curve has been drawn flatter than the LM curve. Instead of discussing fiscal and monetary policy under fixed and flexible exchange rates by graphical means, we present the different comparative static effects in mathematical form in Table 11.1. The results in Table 11.1 are obtained as follows. First we totally differentiate the IS, LM, and BP curves. After some manipulations we obtain:

$$
\begin{bmatrix}
L_Y & L_r & 0 & -1 \\
1 - A_Y - X_Y & -A_r & -X_Q & 0 \\
(X_Y/KI_r) & 1 & (X_Q/KI_r) & 0
\end{bmatrix}
\begin{bmatrix}
dY \\
dr \\
dE \\
dM
\end{bmatrix}
=
\begin{bmatrix}
0 \\
dG \\
dr^*
\end{bmatrix}.
\qquad (11.19)
$$

Of course, equation (11.19) cannot be used to solve for all four variables appearing on the left-hand side since we only have three equations. This "problem" is solved however, by specifying the exchange rate regime. Under flexible exchange rates the

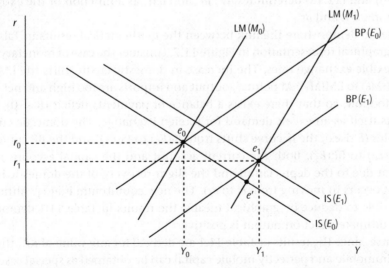

Figure 11.7. Monetary policy with imperfect capital mobility and flexible exchange rates

Table 11.1. Capital mobility and comparative static effects

	dG	dM	dr^*
Flexible exchange rates			
dY	$-\dfrac{L_r X_Q/KI_r}{|\Delta|} \gtreqless 0$	$\dfrac{X_Q(1 - A_r/KI_r)}{|\Delta|} > 0$	$-\dfrac{L_r X_Q}{|\Delta|} > 0$
dr	$\dfrac{L_Y X_Q/KI_r}{|\Delta|} \gtreqless 0$	$-\dfrac{X_Q(1 - A_Y)/KI_r}{|\Delta|} \lesseqgtr 0$	$0 < \dfrac{L_Y X_Q}{|\Delta|} \leq 1$
dE	$\dfrac{L_r X_Y/KI_r - L_Y}{|\Delta|} \lesseqgtr 0$	$\dfrac{1 - A_Y - X_Y + A_r X_Y/KI_r}{|\Delta|} > 0$	$\dfrac{-A_r L_Y - L_r(1 - A_Y - X_Y)}{|\Delta|} > 0$
Fixed exchange rates			
dY	$\dfrac{1}{|\Gamma|} > 0$	$\dfrac{X_Q(1 - A_r/KI_r)}{|\Gamma|} > 0$	$\dfrac{A_r}{|\Gamma|} < 0$
dr	$-\dfrac{X_Y/KI_r}{|\Gamma|} \gtreqless 0$	$-\dfrac{(1 - A_Y)X_Q/KI_r}{|\Gamma|} < 0$	$0 < \dfrac{1 - A_Y - X_Y}{|\Gamma|} \leq 1$
dM	$\dfrac{L_Y - L_r X_Y/KI_r}{|\Gamma|} \gtreqless 0$	$\dfrac{|\Delta|}{|\Gamma|} > 0$	$\dfrac{A_r L_Y + L_r(1 - A_Y - X_Y)}{|\Gamma|} < 0$

Notes: $|\Delta| \equiv X_Q\left[L_Y(1 - A_r/KI_r) - L_r(1 - A_Y)/KI_r\right] > 0$
$|\Gamma| \equiv 1 - A_Y - X_Y + A_r X_Y/KI_r > 0$

money supply is exogenous (and the column for dM is moved to the right-hand side of (11.19)) and (11.19) determines dY, dr, and dE, as a function of the exogenous variables dM, dG, and dr^*. Under fixed exchange rates, on the other hand, the exchange rate is exogenous (and the column for dE is moved to the right-hand side of (11.19)) and (11.19) determines dY, dr, and dM, as a function of the exogenous variables dE, dG, and dr^*.

In order to demonstrate the link between the mathematical results in Table 11.1 and the graphical representation in Figure 11.7, consider the case of monetary policy under flexible exchange rates. The increase in domestic credit shifts the LM curve from LM(M_0) to LM(M_1). At point e', output and imports are too high and net capital inflows too low, so that there exists a balance of payments deficit ($B < 0$), which manifests itself as an excess demand for foreign exchange. The domestic currency depreciates (E rises), the IS curve shifts from IS(E_0) to IS(E_1), and the BP curve shifts from BP(E_0) to BP(E_1). Both the current account and the capital account recover somewhat due to the depreciation and the slight recovery of the domestic interest rate (that occurs in moving from e' to e_1). The new equilibrium is at e_1. Although it is impossible to deduce by graphical means, the results in Table 11.1 demonstrate that the ultimate effect on output is positive.

Of course, since the results of Table 11.1 are derived for any value of KI_r, the polar cases of immobile and perfectly mobile capital can be obtained as special cases from the table by setting $KI_r = 0$ and $KI_r \to \infty$, respectively. The students are advised to verify that this is indeed the case.

11.1.4 Aggregate supply considerations

Up to this point we have assumed that domestic and foreign price levels are constant ($P = P^* = 1$). Whilst this may be appropriate under some conditions (e.g. in the very short run), it is nevertheless important to add a *supply side* to the Mundell–Fleming model of the small open economy. We use a model inspired by Argy and Salop (1979), Armington (1969), and Branson and Rotemberg (1980) to demonstrate the importance of supply-side effects. This model will also be used (in simplified form) in section 2 on the transmission of shocks and the coordination of economic policy in a two-country model of the world. We restrict attention to the case of perfect capital mobility and flexible exchange rates.

The Armington approach

Now that we wish to model the production side of the economy, we have to be more precise about the various price indexes. There are two goods, a *domestic good* with price P, and a *foreign good* with price P^* in foreign currency (EP^* is the price of the foreign good in domestic currency). These goods are *imperfect substitutes* for each other (otherwise one would expect purchasing power parity (PPP) to hold, so that the real exchange rate, EP^*/P, would be identically equal to unity at all times). Real household consumption C and investment I are assumed to be determined by the usual macro-relations:

$$C = C(Y), \quad I = I(r), \tag{11.20}$$

with $0 < C_Y < 1$ and $I_r < 0$, and real government spending G is exogenously given.

We now need to confront the issue of *sourcing* of the goods. For example, once the households know how much they wish to consume in the aggregate and in real terms, the next issue for them is to decide on where to purchase the goods (and the same holds for investment by firms and government consumption). The trick that was devised by Armington (1969) is to assume that, for example, C is in fact "constructed" out of domestically produced goods (labelled by C_d) and foreign produced goods (labelled by C_f). Since the two goods are assumed to be imperfect substitutes, we cannot simply add C_d and C_f to find C (a German apple is not quite the same as a Dutch apple, even though they are both round and taste good). A particularly simple way to capture the imperfect substitution idea is to assume that:

$$C = C_d^\alpha C_f^{1-\alpha}, \tag{11.21}$$

with $0 < \alpha < 1$ denoting the relative weight given to domestically produced goods used in consumption.

In the decision about sourcing, the households wish to attain the composite consumption level C (that is determined by (11.20) once Y is known) as cheaply as possible. Since the (domestic currency) prices of domestic and foreign goods are P

and EP^*, respectively, the households decide on C_d and C_f such that total nominal consumption spending, $P_C C \equiv P C_d + EP^* C_f$, is minimized given the restriction imposed by (11.21). (Here, P_C is a consumer price index (CPI) for which an expression is deduced below.) The household chooses the optimal ratio between C_d and C_f on the basis of the relative (domestic currency) price of the two goods:

$$\frac{C_d}{C_f} = \left(\frac{\alpha}{1-\alpha}\right)\left(\frac{EP^*}{P}\right), \tag{11.22}$$

which is intuitive: if the relative price of foreign goods rises, households choose a larger proportion of consumption goods from domestic sources. By substituting (11.22) into the budget restriction, we obtain:

$$P C_d = \alpha P_C C, \quad EP^* C_f = (1-\alpha) P_C C, \tag{11.23}$$

which says that spending shares on domestic and foreign goods are constant.[3] Also, by substituting (11.23) into (11.21), we obtain the expression for the CPI:

$$C = \left[\frac{\alpha P_C C}{P}\right]^\alpha \left[\frac{(1-\alpha)P_C C}{EP^*}\right]^{1-\alpha} = \alpha^\alpha (1-\alpha)^{1-\alpha} P_C C P^{-\alpha} \left(EP^*\right)^{-(1-\alpha)} \Rightarrow$$

$$P_C \equiv \Omega_0 P^\alpha \left(EP^*\right)^{1-\alpha}, \tag{11.24}$$

where $\Omega_0 \equiv [\alpha^\alpha (1-\alpha)^{1-\alpha}]^{-1} > 0$ is some constant. The weights that define the consumption bundle C (α and $1-\alpha$) also appear in the CPI.

By substituting (11.20) and (11.24) into (11.23), we obtain intuitive expressions for C_d and C_f in terms of aggregate income Y and the real exchange rate ($Q \equiv$) EP^*/P:

$$C_d = \alpha \Omega_0 \left(\frac{EP^*}{P}\right)^{1-\alpha} C(Y), \quad C_f = (1-\alpha)\Omega_0 \left(\frac{EP^*}{P}\right)^{-\alpha} C(Y). \tag{11.25}$$

For a given real exchange rate, a rise in real income raises the demand for both domestic and foreign consumption goods. For a given level of aggregate income, the real exchange rate determines where the goods to be used for consumption are bought.

---

[3] Constant spending shares are a feature of the Cobb-Douglas specification for composite consumption C, given in (11.21). This sharp prediction is altered if (11.21) is changed to, for example, a CES specification.

By using the same approach for investment and government spending, we obtain expressions for I_d, I_f, G_d, and G_f:[4]

$$I_d = \alpha\Omega_0 \left(\frac{EP^*}{P}\right)^{1-\alpha} I(r), \quad I_f = (1-\alpha)\Omega_0 \left(\frac{EP^*}{P}\right)^{-\alpha} I(r), \tag{11.26}$$

$$G_d = \alpha\Omega_0 \left(\frac{EP^*}{P}\right)^{1-\alpha} G, \quad G_f = (1-\alpha)\Omega_0 \left(\frac{EP^*}{P}\right)^{-\alpha} G. \tag{11.27}$$

Real exports are denoted by EX and are sold to the ROW at the same price that domestic customers pay for these goods (P), and spending on imported goods (in terms of domestic currency) equals $EP^*(C_f + I_f + G_f)$, so that the national income identity (11.1) can be written as:

$$PY \equiv P_C C + P_C I + P_C G + PEX - EP^* \left[C_f + I_f + G_f\right]$$

$$= PC_d + PI_d + PG_d + PEX \quad \Rightarrow$$

$$Y \equiv C_d + I_d + G_d + EX, \tag{11.28}$$

which shows (more clearly than (11.1)) that only domestically produced goods enter into the aggregate production measure for the domestic economy. In summary, by looking in more detail at the sourcing issue we now have an IS equation (similar in form to (11.9)) in which the real exchange rate affects domestic spending equilibrium.

By defining net exports (in real terms) by $X \equiv EX - -(EP^*/P)[C_f + I_f + G_f]$, noting (11.25)–(11.27) and assuming that the demand for exports depends on the real exchange rate,

$$EX = EX_0 \left(\frac{EP^*}{P}\right)^{\beta} = EX_0 Q^{\beta}, \quad \beta \geq 0, \tag{11.29}$$

(where EX_0 represents all exogenous influences on the country's exports) we obtain the net export function defined by the model:

$$X[r, Y, Q, G, EX_0] \equiv EX_0 Q^{\beta} - Q(1-\alpha)\Omega_0 Q^{-\alpha} [A(r, Y) + G], \tag{11.30}$$

where $A(r, Y) \equiv C(Y) + I(r)$. Several features are worth noting in the comparison between (11.30) and the net export function used throughout section 1 (i.e. $X(Y, Q)$). First, domestic absorption, and not just aggregate domestic income, appears in (11.30). Since domestic absorption depends on the rate of interest and some investment goods are purchased from the ROW, the BP curve has a positive slope even under perfectly immobile capital (compare section 1.3). A higher rate of interest chokes off aggregate investment, decreases imports of investment goods,

---

[4] We assume for the sake of convenience that I and G are similar composites as C, i.e. $I = I_d^{\alpha} I_f^{1-\alpha}$ and $G = G_d^{\alpha} G_f^{1-\alpha}$. This assumption ensures that the price indices for investment and government spending are the same as the CPI, so that the real exchange rate does not affect relative prices within a country.

and causes a trade account surplus. To restore equilibrium on the trade account, income (and hence imports) must rise.

A second feature of (11.30) is that we can now be more precise about the *Marshall-Lerner condition*. Indeed, by differentiating (11.30) with respect to the real exchange rate Q (holding $A + G$) fixed, we obtain:

$$\frac{X_Q}{Y} = \frac{\beta E X_0 Q^{\beta-1}}{Y} - \frac{(1-\alpha)^2 \Omega_0 Q^{-\alpha} [A(r, Y) + G]}{Y} = \frac{\beta \omega_X - (1-\alpha)\omega_M}{Q}, \tag{11.31}$$

where $X_Q \equiv \partial X/\partial Q$, $\omega_X \equiv EX/Y$, and $\omega_M \equiv Q(C_f + I_f + G_f)/Y$ are, respectively, the domestic output shares of exports and imports. This expression shows that net exports improve as a result of a real exchange rate depreciation if the following condition holds:

$$\frac{Q X_Q}{Y} = \beta \omega_X - (1-\alpha)\omega_M > 0, \tag{11.32}$$

or, if the trade balance is initially in equilibrium (so that imports and exports are of equal magnitude and $\omega_M = \omega_X$), the condition is:

$$\beta + \alpha - 1 > 0. \tag{11.33}$$

This is the famous Marshall-Lerner condition: if the sum of the elasticities of export and import demand exceeds unity, a depreciation of the currency improves the trade account, so that $X_Q > 0$. The intuition behind the Marshall-Lerner condition is as follows. A depreciation of the currency (a rise in Q) makes domestic goods cheaper for the ROW and increases export earnings. This improves net exports. The rise in Q also makes foreign goods more expensive to domestic residents. If real imports were unchanged, *spending* on imports would rise because of the depreciation, which would worsen net exports. Domestic residents, however, substitute domestic goods for foreign goods, as a result of the depreciation, and this effect mitigates the rise in import spending and its adverse effect on net exports. The strength of the export effect is regulated by the export elasticity β and that of the import spending effect is regulated by $1 - \alpha$. The Marshall-Lerner condition ensures that the export effect dominates the import spending effect, which translates as $\beta > 1 - \alpha$ or, equivalently, $\beta + \alpha > 1$.

The extended Mundell-Fleming model

By using (11.25)–(11.29) the IS curve for the model is obtained:

$$Y = \alpha \Omega_0 Q^{1-\alpha} [A(r, Y) + G] + EX_0 Q^\beta, \tag{11.34}$$

which can be written in loglinearized form as:

$$\tilde{Y} = (1 - \omega_X)\left[\omega_C \tilde{C} + \omega_I \tilde{I} + (1 - \omega_C - \omega_I)\tilde{G} + (1 - \alpha)\tilde{Q}\right]$$

$$+ \omega_X \left[\widetilde{EX}_0 + \beta \tilde{Q}\right], \tag{11.35}$$

where $\tilde{Y} \equiv dY/Y$, $\tilde{C} \equiv dC/C$, $\tilde{I} \equiv dI/I$, $\tilde{G} \equiv dG/G$, $\tilde{Q} \equiv dQ/Q$, $\widetilde{EX}_0 \equiv dEX_0/EX_0$, and $\omega_C \equiv C/[A+G]$ and $\omega_I \equiv I/[A+G]$ denote, respectively, the share of consumption and investment in total domestic absorption. Aggregate consumption and investment (see (11.20)) can be loglinearized to:

$$\tilde{C} = \epsilon_{CY}\tilde{Y}, \quad \tilde{I} = -\epsilon_{IR}dr, \tag{11.36}$$

where $0 < \epsilon_{CY} \equiv YC_Y/C \equiv \text{MPC/APC} < 1$ and $\epsilon_{IR} \equiv -I_r/I > 0$ are, respectively, the income elasticity of the aggregate consumption function and (the absolute value of) the interest semi-elasticity of the investment function.[5] Note that ϵ_{CY} equals the marginal propensity over the average propensity to consume, which is less than unity for the usual Keynesian consumption function.

The money market of the model is summarized by the LM curve $M/P = L(r, Y)$, which can be loglinearized to:

$$\tilde{M} - \tilde{P} = -\epsilon_{MR}\,dr + \epsilon_{MY}\tilde{Y}, \tag{11.37}$$

where $\epsilon_{MY} \equiv YL_Y/L > 0$ and $\epsilon_{MR} \equiv -L_r/L > 0$ are, respectively, the income elasticity and (the absolute value of) the interest semi-elasticity of the money demand function.

Since we assume perfect capital mobility, the world interest rate determines the domestic rate ($r = r^*$), so that:

$$dr = dr^*. \tag{11.38}$$

The supply side of the model also contains some new elements. Domestic firms are perfectly competitive (and do not attempt to exploit the export demand function (11.29)) and maximize short-run profit $\Pi \equiv PF(N, \bar{K}) - WN$, where N is employment, W is the nominal wage, and $\bar{K}$ is the given capital stock. The labour demand function is implicitly defined by the marginal productivity condition $PF_N(N, \bar{K}) = W$, which can be loglinearized to:

$$\tilde{P} + \tilde{F}_N = \tilde{W} \quad \Rightarrow \quad \tilde{N} = -\epsilon_{NW}\left[\tilde{W} - \tilde{P}\right], \tag{11.39}$$

where $\epsilon_{NW} \equiv -F_N/(NF_{NN}) > 0$ is the (absolute value of the) real wage elasticity of labour demand. It is assumed, following Branson and Rotemberg (1980), that the labour market is characterized by unemployment because the wage is too high. We model this by assuming that the nominal wage is set according to the wage-setting rule $W = W_0 P_C^\lambda$, where W_0 is exogenous and $0 \leq \lambda \leq 1$. This rule can be loglinearized to:

$$\tilde{W} = \tilde{W}_0 + \lambda\tilde{P}_C. \tag{11.40}$$

---

[5] We use the term semi-elasticity to indicate that ϵ_{IR} relates the *percentage* rate of change of investment to the *absolute* change in the interest rate. In the case of interest rates, the use of semi-elasticities is natural. For example, if $\epsilon_{IR} = 2$, a one percentage *point* increase in the rate of interest (say a rise in r from 5 to 6% per annum) causes a fall in investment of 2%.

Workers care about their wage in terms of the CPI but may suffer from money illusion (if $0 < \lambda < 1$). In case $\lambda = 0$, workers have a *nominal wage target*, and if $\lambda = 1$ they have a *real wage target*. Branson and Rotemberg (1980) suggest on the basis of empirical evidence that $\lambda = 0$ is relevant for the US economy in which there is little or no indexing of nominal wages, and $\lambda = 1$ is more relevant to the situation in the UK, Germany, Italy, and Japan, where wage indexing is much more common.

Once the wage rate is set, domestic producers determine employment (by (11.39)), after which output is determined by the production function which can be loglinearized to:

$$\tilde{Y} = \omega_N \tilde{N}, \tag{11.41}$$

where $0 < \omega_N \equiv WN/Y < 1$ is the share of labour income in aggregate output.

The full model consists of the IS curve (11.35)–(11.36), the LM curve (11.37), the BP curve (11.38), and the AS curve (11.39)–(11.41). For convenience, the equations are gathered in Table 11.2, where we have substituted the BP curve into the IS and LM curves. The endogenous variables are aggregate output, the domestic price level, and the real exchange rate. Once the latter two are determined, the nominal exchange rate is also determined since $\tilde{E} \equiv \tilde{P} + \tilde{Q} - \tilde{P}^*$, where $\tilde{P}^*$ is exogenous due to the small open economy assumption. The other exogenous variables are $\tilde{M} \equiv dM/M$, $\tilde{G} \equiv dG/G$, dr^*, $\widetilde{EX}_0 \equiv dEX_0/EX_0$, and $\tilde{W}_0 \equiv dW_0/W_0$. The comparative static effects can be obtained in the standard fashion and have been collected in Table 11.3.

Graphically these effects can be illustrated as follows. Consider the case of a positive demand shock (say $\tilde{G} > 0$). In the standard Mundell-Fleming model with fixed prices and flexible exchange rates, such a shock does not affect aggregate output (and hence employment). This is the well-known insulation property of flexible exchange rates. The results in Table 11.3 suggest that this insulation property no

Table 11.2. The Extended Mundell–Fleming Model

$$\tilde{Y} = \frac{(1 - \omega_X)\left[-\omega_I \epsilon_{IR} dr^* + (1 - \omega_C - \omega_I)\tilde{G}\right] + \omega_X \widetilde{EX}_0}{1 - (1 - \omega_X)\omega_C \epsilon_{CY}}, \tag{T2.1}$$
$$+ \frac{[(1 - \alpha)(1 - \omega_X) + \beta \omega_X]\tilde{Q}}{1 - (1 - \omega_X)\omega_C \epsilon_{CY}}$$

$$\tilde{M} - \tilde{P} = -\epsilon_{MR} dr^* + \epsilon_{MY} \tilde{Y}, \tag{T2.2}$$

$$\tilde{Y} = -\omega_N \epsilon_{NW}\left[\tilde{W}_0 + \lambda(1 - \alpha)\tilde{Q} - (1 - \lambda)\tilde{P}\right] \tag{T2.3}$$

Notes: Endogenous variables are $\tilde{Y} \equiv dY/Y$, $\tilde{Q} \equiv dQ/Q$, $\tilde{P} \equiv dP/P$, exogenous variables are dr^*, $\tilde{M} \equiv dM/M$, $\tilde{G} \equiv dG/G$, $\tilde{W}_0 \equiv dW_0/W_0$, $\widetilde{EX}_0 \equiv dEX_0/EX_0$. Absorption share of consumption is ω_C, absorption share of investment is ω_I, export share in GDP is ω_X, labour income share of output is ω_N. Income elasticity of aggregate consumption is ϵ_{CY}, interest semi-elasticity of aggregate investment is ϵ_{IR}, income elasticity of money demand is ϵ_{MY}, interest semi-elasticity of money demand is ϵ_{MR}, wage elasticity of labour demand is ϵ_{NW}, real exchange rate export elasticity is β, real exchange rate import spending elasticity is $1 - \alpha$. Money illusion exists if $0 < \lambda < 1$, real wage rigidity if $\lambda = 1$, nominal wage rigidity if $\lambda = 0$.

Table 11.3. Wage rigidity and demand and supply shocks

	$\omega_G(1-\omega_X)\tilde{G}$ $\omega_X\tilde{EX}_0$	$\tilde{M}$	$\omega_N\epsilon_{NW}\tilde{W}_0$
$\tilde{Y}$	$\dfrac{\lambda(1-\alpha)\omega_N\epsilon_{NW}}{|\Delta|} \geq 0$	$\dfrac{(1-\lambda)\delta_1\omega_N\epsilon_{NW}}{|\Delta|} \geq 0$	$-\dfrac{\delta_1}{|\Delta|} < 0$
$\tilde{Q}$	$-\dfrac{1+(1-\lambda)\epsilon_{MY}\omega_N\epsilon_{NW}}{|\Delta|} < 0$	$\dfrac{(1-\lambda)\delta_2\omega_N\epsilon_{NW}}{|\Delta|} \geq 0$	$-\dfrac{\delta_2}{|\Delta|} < 0$
$\tilde{P}$	$-\dfrac{\lambda(1-\alpha)\epsilon_{MY}\omega_N\epsilon_{NW}}{|\Delta|} \leq 0$	$\dfrac{\lambda(1-\alpha)\delta_2\omega_N\epsilon_{NW}+\delta_1}{|\Delta|} > 0$	$\dfrac{\delta_1\epsilon_{MY}}{|\Delta|} > 0$
$\tilde{E}$	$-\dfrac{1+(1-\alpha\lambda)\epsilon_{MY}\omega_N\epsilon_{NW}}{|\Delta|} < 0$	$\dfrac{(1-\alpha\lambda)\delta_2\omega_N\epsilon_{NW}+\delta_1}{|\Delta|} > 0$	$\dfrac{\delta_1\epsilon_{MY}-\delta_2}{|\Delta|} \gtrless 0$
$\tilde{P}_C$	$-\dfrac{(1-\alpha)(1+\epsilon_{MY}\omega_N\epsilon_{NW})}{|\Delta|} < 0$	$\dfrac{(1-\alpha)\delta_2\omega_N\epsilon_{NW}+\delta_1}{|\Delta|} > 0$	$\dfrac{\delta_1\epsilon_{MY}-(1-\alpha)\delta_2}{|\Delta|} \gtrless 0$

Notes: $\delta_1 \equiv (1-\alpha)(1-\omega_X) + \beta\omega_X > 0$
$\delta_2 \equiv 1 - (1-\omega_X)\omega_C\epsilon_{CY}, \quad 0 < \delta_2 < 1$
$|\Delta| \equiv \lambda(1-\alpha)\omega_N\epsilon_{NW}\delta_2 + [1+(1-\lambda)\epsilon_{MY}\omega_N\epsilon_{NW}]\delta_1 > 0$

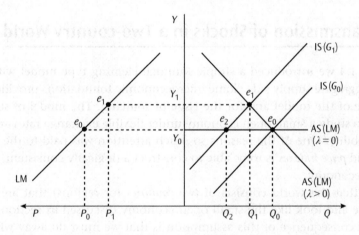

Figure 11.8. Aggregate demand shocks under wage rigidity

longer holds for the augmented Mundell-Fleming model developed in this section (as $dY/dG > 0$), unless there exists nominal wage rigidity ($\lambda = 0$). The basic intuition behind this result can be explained with the aid of Figure 11.8. In the left-hand side of Figure 11.8, the LM curve is drawn, expressing the negative relationship between the domestic price level and output. The IS curve is an upward sloping relationship between output and the real exchange rate. The AS(LM) curve is obtained by substituting the LM curve into the AS curve:

$$\tilde{Y} = \frac{-\omega_N\epsilon_{NW}\left[\tilde{W}_0 + \lambda(1-\alpha)\tilde{Q} - (1-\lambda)\left(\tilde{M} + \epsilon_{MR}\,dr^*\right)\right]}{1+(1-\lambda)\epsilon_M\omega_N\epsilon_{NW}}. \qquad \text{(AS(LM))}$$

281

If there is real wage rigidity ($\lambda = 1$), the AS(LM) curve is downward sloping and independent of the price level (see (T2.3) in Table 11.2) so that the money supply and the world interest rate have no effect on its position. If there is nominal wage rigidity ($\lambda = 0$), on the other hand, the AS(LM) curve is independent of the real exchange rate (horizontal). An increase in government spending shifts the IS curve up from IS(G_0) to IS(G_1). In the absence of nominal wage rigidity ($\lambda > 0$), the real exchange rate appreciates (from Q_0 to Q_1), but not by enough to undo the expansionary effect of increased government spending on output. The domestic price level falls as does the nominal exchange rate ($\tilde{E} < \tilde{P} < 0$). If there is nominal wage rigidity ($\lambda = 0$), on the other hand, output and the domestic price level are unchanged, and the real exchange rate appreciation exactly reverses the stimulative effect of the additional government spending. Since real output depends on what happens to real wages (as producers do not have money illusion), nominal wages must be free to fall (along with the domestic price level) if there are to be any positive output effects. This explains why output effects are zero under nominal wage rigidity.

11.2 Transmission of Shocks in a Two-country World

In section 1.4 we introduced a simple Mundell-Fleming type model with a rudimentary aggregate supply side. Some microeconomic foundations provided for the supply side of the model and for the issue of sourcing. The model of section 1.4 was used to study a small open economy under flexible exchange rates and perfect capital mobility. One of the reasons so much attention was paid to the details of *sourcing* and *price indexes* is to be able to construct a (logically consistent) model of the world economy.

Assume that the world consists of *two countries* (or regions) that are identical in structure and look like the small open economy discussed in section 1.4. One immediate consequence of this assumption is that we must do away with the ad hoc export demand function (11.29), since we know from (11.25)–(11.27) that the domestic economy's demand for imports is given by:

$$C_f + I_f + G_f = (1 - \alpha)\Omega_0 \left(\frac{EP^*}{P} \right)^{-\alpha} [C(Y) + I(r) + G]$$

$$= (1 - \alpha)\Omega_0 \left(\frac{EP^*}{P} \right)^{-\alpha} [A(r, Y) + G]. \tag{11.42}$$

But the domestic economy's exports are (in a two-country world) just the foreign country's demand for imports which, in view of the symmetry assumption, take a form similar to (11.42):

$$EX \equiv C_f^* + I_f^* + G_f^* = (1 - \alpha)\Omega_0 \left(\frac{EP^*}{P} \right)^{\alpha} [A(r^*, Y^*) + G^*], \tag{11.43}$$

where stars denote foreign variables, e.g. C_f^* is the demand for domestically produced consumption goods by foreign residents.[6] By loglinearizing (11.43) we obtain:

$$\widetilde{EX} = \alpha \tilde{Q} + \omega_C \epsilon_{CY} \tilde{Y}^* - \omega_I \epsilon_{IR} \, dr^* + (1 - \omega_C - \omega_I) \tilde{G}^*. \tag{11.44}$$

By substituting this export demand function in the domestic economy's IS curve (equation (T2.1) in Table 11.2) we obtain the IS curve for the domestic economy in a two-country setting:

$$
\begin{aligned}
\tilde{Y} = {} & \frac{-\omega_I \epsilon_{IR} \, dr^* + \omega_G \left[(1 - \omega_X) \tilde{G} + \omega_X \tilde{G}^* \right] + \omega_X \omega_C \epsilon_{CY} \tilde{Y}^*}{1 - (1 - \omega_X) \omega_C \epsilon_{CY}} \\
& + \frac{\left[(1 - \omega_X)(1 - \alpha) + \omega_X \alpha \right] \tilde{Q}}{1 - (1 - \omega_X) \omega_C \epsilon_{CY}},
\end{aligned}
\tag{11.45}
$$

where we have used the fact that $dr = dr^*$ due to perfect capital mobility. By comparing (T2.1) and (11.45), it is clear that the IS curve is augmented in a number of ways. First, the interest rate exerts a stronger effect on domestic production than before. The reason is that changes in the interest rate decrease investment in *both* countries, and since some investment goods are imported, spillover effects exist. Second, foreign government spending spills over into the domestic economy, both directly (via the term involving $\tilde{G}^*$) and indirectly (via the term with $\tilde{Y}^*$).

Of course, the foreign country also has an IS curve (labelled IS*) which is similar in form to (11.45). By making the appropriate substitutions, the IS* curve can be written as:

$$
\begin{aligned}
\tilde{Y}^* = {} & \frac{-\omega_I \epsilon_{IR} \, dr^* + \omega_G \left[(1 - \omega_X) \tilde{G}^* + \omega_X \tilde{G} \right] + \omega_X \omega_C \epsilon_{CY} \tilde{Y}}{1 - (1 - \omega_X) \omega_C \epsilon_{CY}} \\
& - \frac{\left[(1 - \omega_X)(1 - \alpha) + \omega_X \alpha \right] \tilde{Q}}{1 - (1 - \omega_X) \omega_C \epsilon_{CY}},
\end{aligned}
\tag{11.46}
$$

where we have once again used $dr = dr^*$. The real exchange rate affects foreign spending negatively because it is measured from the point of view of the domestic country (i.e. $Q \equiv EP^*/P$). By using (11.45)–(11.46) to solve for Y and Y^*, the

---

[6] Note that the real exchange rate from the perspective of the foreign country is $P/(EP^*) \equiv 1/Q$. This explains the positive sign of the exponent on the real exchange rate in (11.43). Comparing (11.43) and (11.29) shows that the two coincide if $\alpha = \beta$ and $EX_0 \equiv (1 - \alpha)\Omega_0[A(r^*, Y^*) + G^*]$. This shows that EX_0 is no longer exogenous in a two-country model.

following simplified expressions for IS and IS* are obtained:

$$\tilde{Y} = \frac{-(1+\gamma)\omega_I \epsilon_{IR} dr^* + \omega_G \left([1 - \omega_X(1-\gamma)]\,\tilde{G} + [\gamma + \omega_X(1-\gamma)]\,\tilde{G}^*\right)}{(1+\gamma)(1-\gamma)[1 - (1-\omega_X)\omega_C \epsilon_{CY}]}$$

$$+ \frac{(1-\gamma)\left[(1-\omega_X)(1-\alpha) + \omega_X\alpha\right]\tilde{Q}}{(1+\gamma)(1-\gamma)[1 - (1-\omega_X)\omega_C \epsilon_{CY}]}, \tag{11.47}$$

$$\tilde{Y}^* = \frac{-(1+\gamma)\omega_I \epsilon_{IR} dr^* + \omega_G \left([1 - \omega_X(1-\gamma)]\,\tilde{G}^* + [\gamma + \omega_X(1-\gamma)]\,\tilde{G}\right)}{(1+\gamma)(1-\gamma)[1 - (1-\omega_X)\omega_C \epsilon_{CY}]}$$

$$- \frac{(1-\gamma)\left[(1-\omega_X)(1-\alpha) + \omega_X\alpha\right]\tilde{Q}}{(1+\gamma)(1-\gamma)[1 - (1-\omega_X)\omega_C \epsilon_{CY}]}, \tag{11.48}$$

where $0 < \gamma \equiv \omega_X \omega_C \epsilon_{CY}/[1 - (1-\omega_X)\omega_C \epsilon_{CY}] < 1$.

Domestic output depends on both domestic and foreign government spending in this symmetric model of the world economy. It is, however, not a priori clear which effect dominates, the "own" effect (via $\tilde{G}$) or the spillover effect (via $\tilde{G}^*$). By comparing the coefficients for $\tilde{G}$ and $\tilde{G}^*$ in (11.47)–(11.48), it can be seen that the own effect is larger than the spillover effect provided the economies are not "too open", i.e. provided the share of exports in GDP is less than one-half ($\omega_X < \frac{1}{2}$). This requirement is intuitive, since a high value of ω_X implies that the two economies are more sensitive to foreign than to domestic influences (in colloquial terms, if the foreign country sneezes, the domestic country catches a cold if ω_X is high).

Since it is more convenient to work with the logarithmic version of the model (and in order to cut down on notation), equations (11.47)–(11.48) are rewritten in logarithmic form as equations (T3.1) and (T3.2) in Table 11.4.

In order to discover how the model works, we look at some prototypical cases before studying the empirically relevant application of the model.

11.2.1 Nominal wage rigidity in both countries

If there exists nominal wage rigidity in both countries, the relevant model is obtained from Table 11.4 by setting $\lambda = \lambda^* = 0$. The resulting model can then be studied graphically with the aid of Figure 11.9. The LM(AS$_N$) curve is obtained by substituting the AS curve (i.e. equations (T3.5) and (T3.7) combined and with $\lambda = 0$ imposed, hence the subscript "N" for **n**ominal) into the LM curve (LM*(AS$_N^*$) is obtained in an analogous fashion). The resulting expressions for price and output levels are:

$$p = \frac{m + \epsilon_{MR} r^* + \omega_N \epsilon_{NW} \epsilon_{MY} w_0}{1 + \omega_N \epsilon_{NW} \epsilon_{MY}}, \quad p^* = \frac{m^* + \epsilon_{MR} r^* + \omega_N \epsilon_{NW} \epsilon_{MW} w_0^*}{1 + \omega_N \epsilon_{NW} \epsilon_{MW}}, \tag{11.49}$$

Table 11.4. A two-country extended Mundell–Fleming model

$$y = -\epsilon_{YR} r^* + \epsilon_{YQ} q + \epsilon_{YG} [g + \eta g^*], \tag{T3.1}$$

$$y^* = -\epsilon_{YR} r^* - \epsilon_{YQ} q + \epsilon_{YG} [g^* + \eta g], \tag{T3.2}$$

$$m - p = \epsilon_{MY} y - \epsilon_{MR} r^*, \tag{T3.3}$$

$$m^* - p^* = \epsilon_{MY} y^* - \epsilon_{MR} r^*, \tag{T3.4}$$

$$y = -\omega_N \epsilon_{NW} [w - p], \tag{T3.5}$$

$$y^* = -\omega_N \epsilon_{NW} [w^* - p^*], \tag{T3.6}$$

$$w = w_0 + \lambda p_C, \tag{T3.7}$$

$$w^* = w_0^* + \lambda^* p_C^*, \tag{T3.8}$$

$$p_C = \omega_0 + p + (1 - \alpha) q, \tag{T3.9}$$

$$p_C^* = \omega_0 + p^* - (1 - \alpha) q, \tag{T3.10}$$

Notes: All variables except the interest rate are in logarithms and starred variables refer to the foreign country. Endogenous variables are the outputs (y, y^*), the real exchange rate (q), the rate of interest (r^*), price levels (p, p^*), nominal wages (w, w^*), and consumer price indexes (p_C, p_C^*). Exogenous are government spending (g, g^*), the money stocks (m, m^*), and the wage targets (w_0, w_0^*). Elasticities of (T3.1)–(T3.2) can be recovered from (11.47)–(11.48), and $\omega_0 \equiv \log \Omega_0$.

and

$$y = \frac{\omega_N \epsilon_{NW} [m + \epsilon_{MR} r^* - w_0]}{1 + \omega_N \epsilon_{NW} \epsilon_{MY}}, \tag{LM(AS$_N$)}$$

$$y^* = \frac{\omega_N \epsilon_{NW} [m^* + \epsilon_{MR} r^* - w_0^*]}{1 + \omega_N \epsilon_{NW} \epsilon_{MY}}. \tag{LM*(AS$_N^*$)}$$

The curves $\text{LM(AS}_N)$ and $\text{LM}^*(\text{AS}_N^*)$ are drawn in the left-hand panel of Figure 11.9, and coincide in the initial equilibrium due to the symmetry assumption. The goods market equilibrium schedule under nominal wage rigidity, GME_N, is obtained by substituting $\text{LM(AS}_N)$ into the IS curve and solving for r^* in terms of the real exchange rate and the exogenous variables (and similarly for GME_N^*):

$$r^* = \frac{(1 + \omega_N \epsilon_{NW} \epsilon_{MY}) [\epsilon_{YQ} q + \epsilon_{YG} (g + \eta g^*)] + \omega_N \epsilon_{NW} [w_0 - m]}{\epsilon_{YR} (1 + \omega_N \epsilon_{NW} \epsilon_{MY}) + \omega_N \epsilon_{NW} \epsilon_{MR}}, \tag{GME$_N$}$$

$$r^* = \frac{(1 + \omega_N \epsilon_{NW} \epsilon_{MY}) [-\epsilon_{YQ} q + \epsilon_{YG} (g^* + \eta g)] + \omega_N \epsilon_{NW} [w_0^* - m^*]}{\epsilon_{YR} (1 + \omega_N \epsilon_{NW} \epsilon_{MY}) + \omega_N \epsilon_{NW} \epsilon_{MR}}. \tag{GME$_N^*$}$$

GME_N is upward sloping in (r^*, q) space because a real depreciation (a rise in q) stimulates domestic output and, consequently, the demand for real money balances. Money market equilibrium can only be restored if the interest rate is higher (the slope of GME_N^* is reversed since $-q$ measures the real exchange rate from the foreign country's perspective).

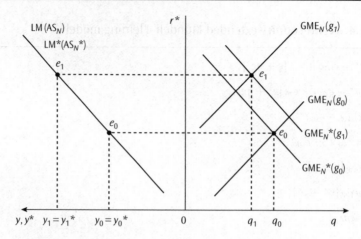

Figure 11.9. Fiscal policy with nominal wage rigidity in both countries

Fiscal policy in the domestic country (represented by a rise in g) shifts up both GME_N and GME_N^* but, provided the own effect of government spending dominates (so that $\eta < 1$), the former shifts by more than the latter (i.e. $\partial r^*/\partial g$ is largest for GME_N). The new equilibrium is at e_1, the domestic economy experiences a real appreciation, and output in *both countries* rises. Hence, the fiscal stimulus in the domestic economy also stimulates the foreign economy. This is why this phenomenon is called a *locomotive policy*: the one country is able to pull itself and the other country out of a recession by means of fiscal policy. Why does it work? The increased government spending in the domestic economy leads to upward pressure on domestic interest rates. The resulting capital inflows cause the domestic currency to appreciate, so that the demand for foreign goods is increased. This stimulates output in the foreign country. The resulting increase in the interest rate causes the price levels of both countries to rise by the same amount. Since nominal wages are fixed, the real producer wage falls in both countries, which explains the increase in output and employment.

For future reference we derive the expressions for the output multipliers. First, we use (GME_N) and (GME_N^*) to derive the effect of domestic and foreign fiscal policy on the world interest rate:

$$\frac{dr^*}{dg} = \frac{dr^*}{dg^*} = \frac{(1+\eta)\epsilon_{YG}(1+\omega_N\epsilon_{NW}\epsilon_{MY})}{2\left[\epsilon_{YR}(1+\omega_N\epsilon_{NW}\epsilon_{MY}) + \omega_N\epsilon_{NW}\epsilon_{MR}\right]} > 0. \tag{11.50}$$

Next, we use ($LM(AS_N)$), ($LM(AS_N^*)$), and (11.50) to derive the output effects:

$$\frac{dy}{dg} = \frac{dy}{dg^*} = \frac{dy^*}{dg} = \frac{dy^*}{dg^*} = \frac{(1+\eta)\omega_N\epsilon_{YG}\epsilon_{NW}\epsilon_{MR}}{2\left[\epsilon_{YR}(1+\omega_N\epsilon_{NW}\epsilon_{MY}) + \omega_N\epsilon_{NW}\epsilon_{MR}\right]} > 0. \tag{11.51}$$

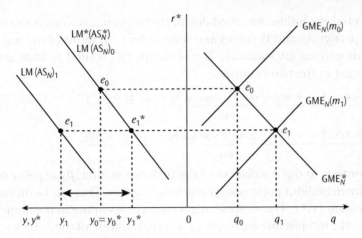

Figure 11.10. Monetary policy with nominal wage rigidity in both countries

The key thing to note is that own and foreign fiscal policy affect have the same output effects in both countries.

Monetary policy in the domestic country, on the other hand, does not benefit but harm the foreign country. This is illustrated with the aid of Figure 11.10. The increase in the domestic money stock shifts the domestic goods market equilibrium locus from $GME_N(m_0)$ to $GME_N(m_1)$ and the LM(AS) curve from $LM(AS_N)_0$ to $LM(AS_N)_1$. There is downward pressure on domestic interest rates, and the capital outflows lead to a depreciation of the currency. This shifts domestic demand towards domestically produced goods and away from foreign goods. Also, foreigners shift towards goods produced in the domestic economy. In view of (11.49), the foreign price level falls and consequently the real producer wage rises. This explains the fall in output and employment in the foreign country. For obvious reasons monetary policy is referred to as a *beggar-thy-neighbour policy*: the domestic economy is stimulated at the expense of the foreign economy.

11.2.2 Real wage rigidity in both countries

If both countries experience real wage rigidity, the relevant model is obtained from Table 11.4 by setting $\lambda = \lambda^* = 1$. Again the resulting model is amenable to graphical analysis. Under real wage rigidity, the aggregate supply curves in the two countries are equal to:

$$y = -\omega_N \epsilon_{NW} \left[\omega_0 + w_0 + (1 - \alpha)q \right], \tag{AS_R}$$

$$y^* = -\omega_N \epsilon_{NW} \left[\omega_0 + w_0^* - (1 - \alpha)q \right]. \tag{AS_R^*}$$

The goods market equilibrium schedules for the two countries are obtained by equating the respective AS and IS curves and solving for r^* in terms of the real exchange rate and the exogenous variables. The subscript "R" is used to indicate that real wages are rigid in the two countries.

$$r^* = \frac{\omega_N \epsilon_{NW} [\omega_0 + w_0] + (\epsilon_{YQ} + \omega_N \epsilon_{NW})q + \epsilon_{YG} [g + \eta g^*]}{\epsilon_{YR}}, \qquad (\text{GME}_R)$$

$$r^* = \frac{\omega_N \epsilon_{NW} [\omega_0 + w_0^*] - (\epsilon_{YQ} + \omega_N \epsilon_{NW})q + \epsilon_{YG} [g^* + \eta g]}{\epsilon_{YR}}. \qquad (\text{GME}_R^*)$$

In sharp contrast to our conclusion in the previous section, *fiscal policy* constitutes a beggar-thy-neighbour policy under real wage rigidity. This can be illustrated with the aid of Figure 11.11. The increase in government spending in the domestic country (g) raises the interest rate and causes a real appreciation of the domestic economy (provided $\eta < 1$, which we assume). Since consumer wages are fixed, the producer wage falls in the domestic economy and output and employment are stimulated. The opposite holds in the foreign country, where the producer wage rises. By raising g, the domestic policy maker causes the foreign producer wage to rise, as foreign workers demand higher nominal wages in order to keep their consumption wage constant after the real depreciation of the foreign currency. For future reference we derive the expressions for the various output multipliers. First we use (GME_R) and (GME_R^*) to derive the effect of domestic and foreign fiscal policy on the real exchange rate:

$$\frac{dq}{dg} = -\frac{dq}{dg^*} = -\frac{(1 - \eta)\epsilon_{YR}\epsilon_{YG}}{2[\epsilon_{YQ} + \omega_N \epsilon_{NW}]} < 0. \qquad (11.52)$$

Next, we use (AS_R), (AS_R^*), and (11.52) to derive the output effects:

$$\frac{dy}{dg} = -\frac{dy}{dg^*} = \frac{dy^*}{dg^*} = -\frac{dy^*}{dg} = \frac{(1 - \eta)(1 - \alpha)\omega_N \epsilon_{NW} \epsilon_{YR}\epsilon_{YG}}{2[\epsilon_{YQ} + \omega_N \epsilon_{NW}]} > 0. \qquad (11.53)$$

Equation (11.53) provides a clear statement of the beggar-thy-neighbour property of fiscal policy when both countries experience real wage rigidity.

Not surprisingly, monetary policy has no real effects under real wage rigidity. As none of the equilibrium conditions is affected, the interest rate, output levels, and the real exchange rate are also unaffected and the increase in m causes an (equal) increase in the domestic price level and the nominal wage rate ($dp = dw$). Since the real exchange rate is unaffected, the nominal exchange rate depreciates by the full amount of the change in the domestic price ($de = dp$).

11.2.3 Real wage rigidity in Europe and nominal wage rigidity in the United States

In an influential paper, Branson and Rotemberg (1980) argue on the basis of empirical evidence, that nominal wage rigidity characterizes the US economy whilst real

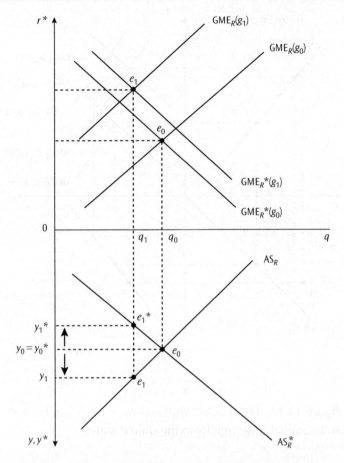

Figure 11.11. Fiscal policy with real wage rigidity in both countries

wage rigidity well describes the European countries. Letting Europe denote the home country and the US the foreign country (and ignoring the rest of the world for the time being), the model describing this configuration is obtained from Table 11.4 by setting $\lambda = 1$ and $\lambda^* = 0$. The analysis of the effects of fiscal and monetary policy can once again proceed by graphical means. Since Europe experiences real wage rigidity, it is fully described by GME_R and AS_R (given in (GME_R) and (AS_R), respectively). The US economy, on the other hand, experiences nominal wage rigidity, and is described by $LM^*(AS_N^*)$ and GME_N^* (given in $(LM^*(AS_N^*))$ and (GME_N^*), respectively). The different schedules have been drawn in Figure 11.12. The initial equilibrium is at e_0.

A *European fiscal expansion* (a rise in g) leads to an upward shift of both GME_R and GME_N^*, with the former experiencing the larger shift (as $\eta < 1$). The real

289

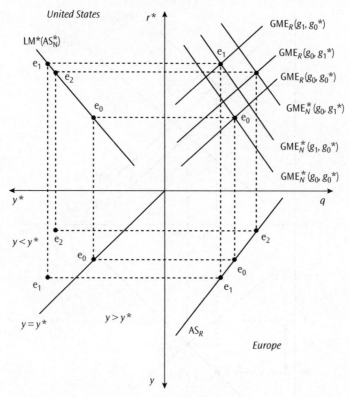

Figure 11.12. Fiscal policy with real wage rigidity in Europe and nominal wage rigidity in the United States

exchange rate of Europe appreciates and the new equilibrium is at e_1. Both y and y^* increase, though the latter increases by more than the former (see the third quadrant). The European fiscal impulse constitutes a locomotive policy since it ends up simultaneously stimulating US output and employment.

A *US fiscal expansion* (a rise in g^*) shifts both GME_R and GME_N^*. In terms of Figure 11.12, the new equilibrium is at e_2. The rate of interest is higher, there is a real depreciation in Europe, but output falls because real producer wages in Europe rise. Output and employment in the US rise, so that the US fiscal expansion constitutes a beggar-thy-neighbour policy. It leads to lower output and higher unemployment in Europe.

A *monetary expansion in Europe* has no real effects (see above), but *expansionary US monetary policy* (a rise in m^*) constitutes a locomotive policy for Europe. This has been illustrated in Figure 11.13. The increase in the US money stock shifts GME_N^* down and $LM^*(AS_N^*)$ to the left. The European real exchange rate appreciates and the interest rate falls. Both y and y^* rise, and the US impulse thus stimulates both economies. By inflating the foreign price level, the real producer wage abroad falls.

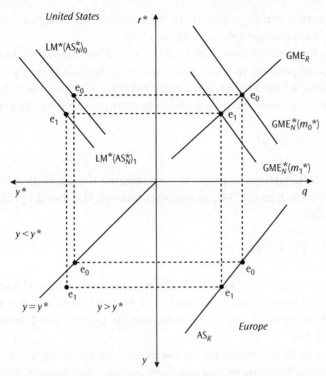

Figure 11.13. Monetary policy with real wage rigidity in
Europe and nominal wage rigidity in the United States

This explains why foreign output rises. Similarly, the real exchange rate appreciation causes European producer wages to fall, thus also enabling an increase in output there.

11.2.4 International policy coordination

The symmetric two-country model of the world economy that was developed in the previous subsections can be used to study the issue of international policy coordination. Since we do not wish to carry on with the rather extensive notational burden introduced in the development of this model, the insights of the two-country model are summarized by means of the following reduced form expressions for domestic and foreign output:

$$y = g + \zeta g^*, \quad y^* = g^* + \zeta^* g, \tag{11.54}$$

where g and g^* are indexes of fiscal policy, $\zeta = \zeta^* = 1$ if there is nominal wage rigidity in both countries (which is the case studied in section 2.1), $\zeta = \zeta^* < 0$ if there is real wage rigidity in both countries (see section 2.2), and, finally, $\zeta < 0$ and

291

$0 < \zeta^* < 1$ if there is real wage rigidity in the domestic economy and nominal wage rigidity in the foreign economy (see section 2.3).

Assume that the *domestic* government is interested in stimulating domestic output (to get as close as possible to some given full employment target, $\bar{y} > 0$) without, however, creating a large government sector (which could give rise to large deficits). We assume that the domestic policy maker minimizes some cost function, L_G:

$$L_G \equiv \tfrac{1}{2}\left(y - \bar{y}\right)^2 + \frac{\theta}{2}g^2, \tag{11.55}$$

subject to the reduced form expression summarizing the domestic economy, given by the first expression in (11.54). In a similar fashion, the foreign policy maker has the loss function:

$$L_G^* \equiv \tfrac{1}{2}\left(y^* - \bar{y}\right)^2 + \frac{\theta}{2}\left(g^*\right)^2, \tag{11.56}$$

that it minimizes subject to the constraint imposed by the reduced form expression for foreign output (the second equation in (11.54)). It is assumed that the domestic and foreign policy makers have the same output targets, i.e. $\bar{y}$ features in both (11.55) and (11.56).

Suppose that both governments choose their own spending level *independently*, i.e. without taking the possible repercussions for the other country into account. In this case, fiscal policy is *uncoordinated* and each country chooses its spending level conditional upon the other country's spending level. For example, the policy maker in the domestic economy solves:

$$\min_{\{g\}} L_G \equiv \tfrac{1}{2}\left(g + \zeta g^* - \bar{y}\right)^2 + \frac{\theta}{2}g^2, \tag{11.57}$$

which yields the domestic country's *reaction function*, RR:

$$\frac{\partial L_G}{\partial g} = \left(g + \zeta g^* - \bar{y}\right) + \theta g = 0 \quad \Rightarrow \quad g = \frac{\bar{y} - \zeta g^*}{1 + \theta}, \quad \text{RR.} \tag{11.58}$$

Similarly, the foreign country has a reaction function (RR*) which relates its optimal (non-coordinated) level of government spending to its full employment target and the spending level of the domestic country:

$$\frac{\partial L_G^*}{\partial g^*} = \left(g^* + \zeta^* g - \bar{y}\right) + \theta g^* = 0 \quad \Rightarrow \quad g^* = \frac{\bar{y} - \zeta^* g}{1 + \theta}, \quad \text{RR*.} \tag{11.59}$$

The *non-cooperative Nash equilibrium* is defined as that equilibrium in which each country's spending plan is optimal given the other country's spending plan. Since the reaction functions designate such conditionally optimal spending plans, the non-cooperative Nash equilibrium is obtained by finding the intersection of RR

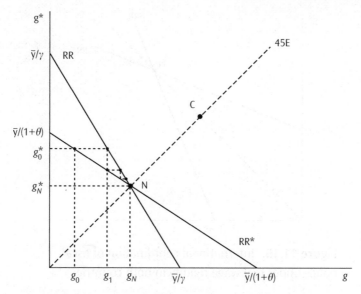

Figure 11.14. International coordination of fiscal policy under nominal wage rigidity in both countries

and RR*, i.e. by solving (11.58)–(11.59) for g and g^*. For the special case of $\zeta = \zeta^*$, we obtain:

$$g_N = g_N^* = \frac{\bar{y}}{1 + \zeta + \theta}, \quad \text{for } \zeta = \zeta^*, \tag{11.60}$$

where the subscript "N" indicates that these solutions are non-cooperative. In terms of Figures 11.14 and 11.15, the two reaction functions can be drawn as RR and RR*, respectively. In both diagrams we impose that $\zeta = \zeta^*$, which means that the two countries have the same wage-setting regime. In Figure 11.14 both countries have nominal wage rigidity ($\zeta = \zeta^* = 1$), and in Figure 11.15 both countries experience real wage rigidity ($\zeta = \zeta^* < 0$). In both cases the stable[7] non-cooperative solution is at point N, where the two reaction functions intersect.

What would a *coordinated policy* look like? In the coordinated solution, the policy maker in one country takes into account the (positive or negative) effect that its own spending has on the other country. One way to analyse the coordinated policy is to assume that both policy makers relinquish control over spending to some international agency which is instructed to minimize the total welfare loss, $L_G + L_G^*$, by choosing spending levels in the two countries. Formally, the problem solved

---

[7] It is easy to show that the non-cooperative Nash equilibrium is stable. In terms of Figure 11.14, suppose that $g = g_0$ initially. It is then optimal for the foreign policy maker to choose $g^* = g_0^*$. But for this value of g^*, it is optimal for the domestic policy maker to set $g = g_1$. Repeating the argument shows that the only stable Nash equilibrium is at point N.

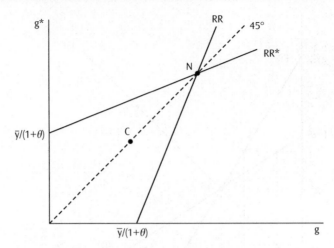

Figure 11.15. International coordination of fiscal policy under real wage rigidity in both countries

under a coordinated fiscal policy is:

$$\min_{\{g^*,g\}} L_G + L_G^* \equiv \tfrac{1}{2}\left(g + \zeta g^* - \bar{y}\right)^2 + \tfrac{1}{2}\left(g^* + \zeta^* g - \bar{y}\right)^2$$

$$+ \frac{\theta}{2}g^2 + \frac{\theta}{2}\left(g^*\right)^2, \tag{11.61}$$

which yields the first-order conditions:

$$\frac{\partial(L_G + L_G^*)}{\partial g} = \left(g + \zeta g^* - \bar{y}\right) + \zeta^*\left(g^* + \zeta^* g - \bar{y}\right) + \theta g = 0, \tag{11.62}$$

$$\frac{\partial(L_G + L_G^*)}{\partial g^*} = \zeta\left(g + \zeta g^* - \bar{y}\right) + \left(g^* + \zeta^* g - \bar{y}\right) + \theta g^* = 0. \tag{11.63}$$

By comparing these first-order conditions under cooperative behaviour to the ones relevant under non-cooperative behaviour (given in equations (11.58)–(11.59)), it is clear that in the cooperative solution the policy maker explicitly takes into account the international spill-over effects that exist (represented by the terms premultiplied by ζ and ζ^* in (11.62) and (11.63), respectively). By solving (11.62)–(11.63) for g and g^* (again for the special case $\zeta = \zeta^*$), the spending levels under coordination are obtained:

$$g_C = g_C^* = \frac{\bar{y}}{1 + \zeta + \frac{\theta}{1+\zeta}}, \quad \text{for } \zeta = \zeta^*, \tag{11.64}$$

where the subscript "C" is used to designate cooperation.

The relative size of government spending in the cooperative and non-cooperative scenario's can be judged by comparing (11.60) and (11.64). If there is nominal wage rigidity in both countries ($\zeta = \zeta^* = 1$), the cooperative solution involves the higher spending levels in the two countries. This is illustrated in Figure 11.14, where point C designates the cooperative solution. The intuition behind this result is obvious. With nominal wage rigidity in both countries, fiscal policy constitutes a locomotive policy. In the absence of coordination, however, individual countries do not take into account that their own fiscal spending also aids the other country. They therefore both underestimate the benefit of their own spending and consequently choose spending levels that are too low. In the cooperative solution, on the other hand, this external effect is internalized, and spending levels are raised to make full use of the locomotive feature of fiscal policy.

The opposite holds if there is real wage rigidity in both countries ($\zeta = \zeta^* < 0$), as is illustrated in Figure 11.15. Fiscal policy constitutes a beggar-thy-neighbour policy and uncoordinated actions by national governments lead to spending levels that are too high. The coordinated policy solution internalizes this "pollution-like" aspect of government spending and consequently leads to lower spending levels.

Up to this point we have only analysed the symmetric cases of either nominal or real wage rigidity in both countries. As a final case, consider the mixed case where there is real wage rigidity in the domestic country (Europe) and nominal wage rigidity in the foreign country (the US). This configuration implies that $\zeta < 0$ and $0 < \zeta^* < 1$. Following the same reasoning as before, but noting that now $\zeta \neq \zeta^*$, it is possible to derive the uncoordinated and coordinated solutions for government spending:

$$g_N = \frac{(1+\theta-\zeta)\bar{y}}{(1+\theta)^2 - \zeta\zeta^*} = \frac{\bar{y}}{1+\zeta+\theta+\left[\frac{\zeta(\zeta-\zeta^*)}{1+\theta-\zeta}\right]}, \tag{11.65}$$

$$g_N^* = \frac{(1+\theta-\zeta^*)\bar{y}}{(1+\theta)^2 - \zeta\zeta^*} = \frac{\bar{y}}{1+\zeta+\theta-\left[\frac{(1+\theta)(\zeta-\zeta^*)}{1+\theta-\zeta}\right]}, \tag{11.66}$$

so that:

$$g_C - g_N = \frac{(1+\theta+\zeta^2)\zeta^*\theta g_N^* - (\zeta+\zeta^*)\zeta\theta g_N}{\left[1+\theta+(\zeta^*)^2\right](1+\theta+\zeta^2) - (\zeta+\zeta^*)^2} > 0, \tag{11.67}$$

$$g_C^* - g_N^* = \frac{\left[1+\theta+(\zeta^*)^2\right]\zeta\theta g_N - (\zeta+\zeta^*)\zeta^*\theta g_N^*}{\left[1+\theta+(\zeta^*)^2\right](1+\theta+\zeta^2) - (\zeta+\zeta^*)^2} < 0. \tag{11.68}$$

From (11.65) we can conclude that g_N is larger, and g_N^* is smaller, in the asymmetric than under the symmetric case (for which $\zeta = \zeta^* > 0$)—compare (11.65)–(11.66) and (11.60). Furthermore, in view of (11.65)–(11.66) and (11.67)–(11.68) we observe that $g_N < g_C$ and $g_N^* > g_C^*$. This means that, in the absence of cooperation, the world interest rate is too high, the dollar is too strong, and there is high unemployment in Europe due to the economic policy pursued by the US. This result is intuitive since fiscal policy is a beggar-thy-neighbour policy for the US, which consequently spends too much in the absence of coordination. Under cooperation this external effect is internalized. Similarly, European fiscal policy is a locomotive policy, which consequently spends too little.

11.3 Forward-looking Behaviour in International Financial Markets

Up to this point we have been somewhat inconsistent in our discussion of the economy operating under flexible exchange rates. The nature of this inconsistency can be gleaned by looking at the *uncovered interest parity* condition. Consider a domestic investor who has $f\,100$ to invest either at home, where the interest rate on bonds is r, or in the US, where the interest rate on bonds is r^*. If the investor chooses to purchase a domestic bond, he will get $f\,100 \times (1 + r)$ at the end of the period, so that the gross yield on his investment is equal to $1 + r$. If, on the other hand, the investor purchases the US bond, he must first change currency (from guilders to dollars), and purchase US bonds to the amount of $(f\,100 \times (1/E_0) = \$100$, where E_0 is the nominal exchange rate at the beginning of the period (the dimension of E is, of course, f per $\$$). At the end of the period he receives $(\$100E_0) \times (1 + r^*)$, which he converts back into guilders by taking his dollars to the foreign exchange market, thus obtaining $(1 + r^*) \times (\$100E_0)/E_1 = f\,100 \times (1 + r^*) \times (E_1/E_0)$. Of course, the investor must decide at the beginning of the period on his investment, and he does not know the actual exchange rate that will hold at the end of the period. The *estimated* gross yield on his foreign investment therefore equals $(1 + r^*) \times (E_1^e/E_0)$, where E_1^e is the exchange rate the investor expects at the beginning of the period to hold at the end of the period. If the investor is risk-neutral, he chooses the domestic (foreign) bond if $1 + r > (<)(1 + r^*) \times (E_1^e/E_0)$, and is indifferent between the two investment possibilities if the expected yields are equal.

The point of all this is that the expected yield differential between domestic and foreign investments depends not only on the interest rates in the two countries (r and r^*) but also on what is expected to happen to the exchange rate in the period of the investment:

$$\text{yield gap} \equiv (1+r) - (1+r^*)\frac{E_1^e}{E_0} = (1+r) - (1+r^*)\left(1 + \frac{\Delta E^e}{E_0}\right)$$

$$= (1+r) - \left(1 + r^* + \frac{\Delta E^e}{E_0} + r^*\frac{\Delta E^e}{E_0}\right) \approx r - \left(r^* + \frac{\Delta E^e}{E_0}\right), \tag{11.69}$$

where the cross-term $r^*\Delta E^e/E_0$ can be ignored because it is of second-order magnitude. Equation (11.69) can be written in continuous time as:

$$\text{yield gap} = r - (r^* + \dot{e}^e), \tag{11.70}$$

where $e \equiv \log E$, so that $\dot{e}^e \equiv de^e/dt \equiv \dot{E}^e/E$. Expressions (11.69) and (11.70) are intuitive. If the domestic currency is expected to appreciate during the period ($\dot{e}^e < 0$), then the domestic currency yield on the US bond is reduced because the dollar earnings on the bond are expected to represent fewer guilders than if no appreciation is expected. In the case of perfect capital mobility, arbitrage will ensure that the yield differential is eliminated, in which case (11.70) reduces to the famous uncovered interest parity condition:

$$r = r^* + \dot{e}^e. \tag{11.71}$$

11.3.1 The Dornbusch model

Up to this point we have always assumed that $r = r^*$ under perfect capital mobility, which would be correct if investors never expect the exchange rate to change. Whilst this may be reasonable under a (tenable) fixed exchange rate regime, it is a somewhat inconsistent assumption to make about investors' expectations in a regime of freely flexible exchange rates. Investors know that the exchange rate can (and generally will) fluctuate, and consequently will form expectations about the change in the exchange rate. The seminal contribution by Dornbusch (1976) was to introduce the assumption of perfect foresight (the deterministic counterpart to rational expectations; see Chapters 1 and 3) into a model of a small open economy facing perfect capital mobility and sticky prices. The model is summarized in Table 11.5. Equations (T5.1) and (T5.2) are, respectively, the IS curve and the LM curve for a small open economy. Uncovered interest parity is given in equation (T5.3) and equation (T5.4) is the Phillips curve. If output is higher than its full employment level $\bar{y}$, prices *gradually* adjust to eliminate Okun's gap. The adjustment speed of the price level is finite, due to the assumption of sticky prices. This means in formal terms that $0 < \phi < \infty$. Finally, equation (T5.5) represents the assumption of perfect foresight. Agents' expectations regarding the path of the exchange rate coincide with the actual path of the exchange rate.

The model exhibits long-run monetary neutrality, as $\dot{p} = 0$ implies that $y = \bar{y}$ and $\dot{e} = 0$ implies that $r = r^*$, so that (T5.2) shows that $m - p$ is constant. In the long run, the domestic price level and the nominal money supply move together. Furthermore, there is also a unique equilibrium real exchange rate, defined by (T5.1) with $y = \bar{y}$ and $r = r^*$ substituted. This equilibrium exchange rate is not affected

Table 11.5. The Dornbusch Model

$y = -\epsilon_{YR}r + \epsilon_{YQ}\left[p^* + e - p\right] + \epsilon_{YG}g,$	(T5.1)
$m - p = -\epsilon_{MR}r + \epsilon_{MY}y,$	(T5.2)
$r = r^* + \dot{e}^e,$	(T5.3)
$\dot{p} = \phi\left[y - \bar{y}\right],$	(T5.4)
$\dot{e}^e = \dot{e}.$	(T5.5)

by monetary policy, but can be affected by fiscal policy. But we are really interested in the short-run dynamics implied by the model. To study this, we first reduce the model to two differential equations in e and p. For given values of the nominal exchange rate and the domestic price level, the domestic interest rate and output can be written as:

$$y = \frac{\epsilon_{MR}\epsilon_{YQ}[p^* + e - p] + \epsilon_{MR}\epsilon_{YG}g + \epsilon_{YR}(m - p)}{\epsilon_{MR} + \epsilon_{MY}\epsilon_{YR}},$$ (11.72)

$$r = \frac{\epsilon_M\epsilon_{YQ}[p^* + e - p] + \epsilon_{MY}\epsilon_{YG}g - (m - p)}{\epsilon_{MR} + \epsilon_{MY}\epsilon_{YR}}.$$ (11.73)

By substituting (11.72)–(11.73) and (T5.5) into (T5.3) and (T5.4), we obtain the dynamic representation of the model:

$$\begin{bmatrix} \dot{e} \\ \dot{p} \end{bmatrix} = \begin{bmatrix} \dfrac{\epsilon_M\epsilon_{YQ}}{\epsilon_{MR} + \epsilon_M\epsilon_{YR}} & \dfrac{1 - \epsilon_M\epsilon_{YQ}}{\epsilon_{MR} + \epsilon_M\epsilon_{YR}} \\ \dfrac{\phi\epsilon_{MR}\epsilon_{YQ}}{\epsilon_{MR} + \epsilon_M\epsilon_{YR}} & -\dfrac{\phi(\epsilon_{YR} + \epsilon_{MR}\epsilon_{YQ})}{\epsilon_{MR} + \epsilon_M\epsilon_{YR}} \end{bmatrix} \begin{bmatrix} e \\ p \end{bmatrix}$$
$$+ \begin{bmatrix} \dfrac{\epsilon_M\epsilon_{YQ}p^* + \epsilon_M\epsilon_{YG}g - m}{\epsilon_{MR} + \epsilon_M\epsilon_{YR}} - r^* \\ \dfrac{\phi[\epsilon_{MR}\epsilon_{YQ}p^* + \epsilon_{MR}\epsilon_{YG}g + \epsilon_{YR}m]}{\epsilon_{MR} + \epsilon_M\epsilon_{YR}} - \phi\bar{y} \end{bmatrix}.$$ (11.74)

The only sign that is ambiguous in the Jacobian matrix on the right-hand side of (11.74) is the one for $\partial\dot{e}/\partial p$. This is because an increase in the domestic price level has an ambiguous effect on the domestic interest rate. On the one hand, real money balances decrease, which leads to upward pressure on the interest rate, but on the other hand the domestic price increase also leads to a real appreciation of the exchange rate which decreases output and hence the (transactions) demand for money. This money demand effect causes downward pressure on the interest rate. We assume for simplicity that the money supply effect dominates the money demand effect, so that $\epsilon_{MY}\epsilon_{YQ} < 1$ and $\partial\dot{e}/\partial p > 0$.

The model can be analysed with the aid of Figure 11.16. The $\dot{e} = 0$ line is obtained by taking the first equation in (11.74) and solving it for e as a function of p and the exogenous variables:

$$e + p^* = \frac{-(1 - \epsilon_{MY}\epsilon_{YQ})p - \epsilon_{MY}\epsilon_{YG}g + m + (\epsilon_{MR} + \epsilon_{MY}\epsilon_{YR})r^*}{\epsilon_{MY}\epsilon_{YQ}}.$$ (11.75)

Along the $\dot{e} = 0$ line the domestic interest rate equals the foreign interest rate ($r = r^*$). It is downward sloping in view of our assumption (made above) that $\epsilon_{MY}\epsilon_{YQ} < 1$. For points above the $\dot{e} = 0$ line the nominal (and the real) exchange rate is too high, output is too high, and the domestic rate of interest is higher than the world rate ($r > r^*$). Uncovered interest parity predicts that an exchange rate depreciation is expected and occurs ($\dot{e}^e = \dot{e} > 0$). The opposite holds for points below the $\dot{e} = 0$ line. These dynamic forces on the nominal exchange rate are indicated by vertical

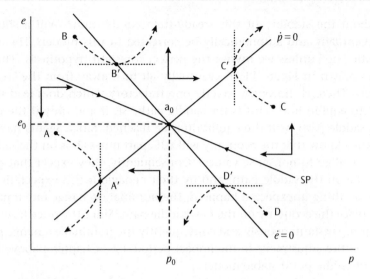

Figure 11.16. Phase diagram for the Dornbusch model

arrows in Figure 11.16. More formally we can derive the same result by noting that (11.74) implies:

$$\left(\frac{\partial \dot{e}}{\partial e}\right) = \frac{\epsilon_{MY}\epsilon_{YQ}}{\epsilon_{MR} + \epsilon_{MY}\epsilon_{YR}} > 0, \tag{11.76}$$

which shows that the interest parity condition introduces an unstable element into the economy in the sense that exchange rate movements are magnified, rather than dampened, according to (11.76).

The $\dot{p} = 0$ line is obtained by taking the second equation in (11.74) and solving it for e as a function of p and the exogenous variables:

$$e + p^* = \frac{(\epsilon_{YR} + \epsilon_{MR}\epsilon_{YQ})p - \epsilon_{MR}\epsilon_{YG}g - \epsilon_{YR}m + (\epsilon_{MR} + \epsilon_{MY}\epsilon_{YR})\bar{y}}{\epsilon_{MR}\epsilon_{YQ}}. \tag{11.77}$$

Along the $\dot{p} = 0$ line there is full employment ($y = \bar{y}$). It is upward sloping because an increase in the domestic price level reduces output via the real balance effect. To restore full employment, the nominal exchange rate must depreciate. For points to the right of the $\dot{p} = 0$ line, output is below its full employment level ($y < \bar{y}$) and the domestic price level is falling. The opposite holds for points to the left of the $\dot{p} = 0$ line. The dynamic forces operating on the price level are indicated by horizontal arrows in Figure 11.16. In formal terms, the second equation of (11.74) shows that the real side of the model exerts a stabilizing influence on the economy:

$$\left(\frac{\partial \dot{p}}{\partial p}\right) = -\frac{\phi(\epsilon_{YR} + \epsilon_{MR}\epsilon_{YR})}{\epsilon_{MR} + \epsilon_{MY}\epsilon_{YQ}} < 0. \tag{11.78}$$

The long-run steady-state equilibrium is at point a_0 in Figure 11.16, where $\dot{p} = \dot{e} = 0$ so that both $r = r^*$ and $y = \bar{y}$ hold.

What about the stability of this steady-state equilibrium? Will a shock away from a_0 eventually and automatically be corrected in this model? The answer is an emphatic "no" unless we invoke the perfect foresight hypothesis. The dashed trajectories drawn in Figure 11.16 eventually all turn away from the steady-state equilibrium. There is, however, exactly one trajectory which does lead the economy back to equilibrium. This is the saddle path, SP. If and only if the economy is on this saddle path, will the equilibrium be reached. Since agents have perfect foresight they know that the economy will fall apart unless it is on the saddle path (p and/or e will go to nonsense values). Consequently, they expect that the economy must be on the saddle path, and by their behaviour this expectation is also correct. If anything unexpected happens, the nominal exchange rate immediately adjusts to place the economy on the new saddle path. Since the price level is sticky, it cannot jump instantaneously and consequently the nominal exchange rate takes care of the entire adjustment in the impact period. (See Chapter 4 above for other examples of saddle-point stable models.)

As an example of adjustment, consider the case of an *unanticipated expansionary fiscal policy*. In terms of Figure 11.17, the increase in g shifts the $\dot{p} = 0$ line to the right and the $\dot{e} = 0$ line to the left, leaving the long-run price level unchanged. At impact the exchange rate adjusts downward from point a_0 to a_1. There is no transitional dynamics, and the Dornbusch model predicts exactly the same adjustment pattern as the traditional Mundell–Fleming approach does in this case. Since there is no need for a long-run price adjustment the assumption of price stickiness plays no role in the adjustment process, and because the fiscal impulse is unanticipated, the interest parity condition does not introduce transitional dynamics into the

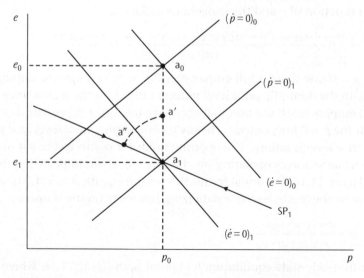

Figure 11.17. Fiscal policy in the Dornbusch model

exchange rate in this case. Students are advised to verify that the announcement of a future permanent increase in government spending leads to an immediate appreciation of the currency, followed by falling prices and a further appreciation of the exchange rate, in the period between announcement and implementation of the policy. Once government spending has gone up, the price level starts to rise again and the exchange rate appreciates further. In the long run, the equilibrium is at a_1, with a permanently lower exchange rate and the same price level, and the adjustment path is a_0 to a' at impact, gradual movement from a' to a'' between announcement and implementation, followed by gradual movement from a'' to a_1 after implementation.

An *unanticipated and permanent expansionary monetary policy* produces the famous overshooting result in this case. In terms of Figure 11.18, an increase in the money supply shifts both the $\dot{e} = 0$ line and the $\dot{p} = 0$ line to the right, leaving the long-run equilibrium real exchange rate unchanged (recall that money is neutral in the long run). In the short run, however, prices are sticky and the exchange rate makes a discrete adjustment from e_0 to e'. The depreciation of the currency leads to an increase in the demand for aggregate output ($y > \bar{y}$) and the domestic price level starts to rise. A gradual adjustment along the saddle path SP_1, with an appreciating real exchange rate, leads the economy back to the long-run equilibrium. The nominal exchange rate actually overshoots its long-run target in the impact period. The intuition behind this result is that agents expect a long-run depreciation of the nominal exchange rate, and hence domestic assets are less attractive. There is a net capital outflow and the spot rate depreciates. The exchange rate overshoots in order for domestic residents to be compensated (for the fact that $r < r^*$) during adjustment by an exchange rate appreciation. Hence, point a_1 must be approached from a north-westerly direction.

Price stickiness and overshooting

The finite speed of adjustment in the goods market (a distinctly Keynesian feature) plays a crucial role in the exchange rate overshooting result. Suppose, for example, that $\phi \to \infty$, so that (T5.4) predicts that $y = \bar{y}$ always, as prices adjust infinitely fast. This means that we can solve (T5.1)–(T5.2) for the domestic rate of interest and price level as a function of the nominal exchange rate e and the exogenous variables. For the domestic interest rate we obtain:

$$r = \frac{(\epsilon_{YQ}\epsilon_{MY} - 1)\bar{y} + \epsilon_{YQ}(p^* + e) + \epsilon_{YG}g - \epsilon_{YQ}m}{\epsilon_{MR} + \epsilon_{YQ}\epsilon_{MR}}, \tag{11.79}$$

which, together with (T5.5), can be substituted into (T5.3) to get the expression for the rate of depreciation of the exchange rate under perfectly flexible prices:

$$\dot{e} = \frac{(\epsilon_{YQ}\epsilon_M - 1)\bar{y} + \epsilon_{YQ}(p^* + e) + \epsilon_{YG}g - \epsilon_{YQ}m}{\epsilon_{MR} + \epsilon_{YQ}\epsilon_{MR}} - r^*. \tag{11.80}$$

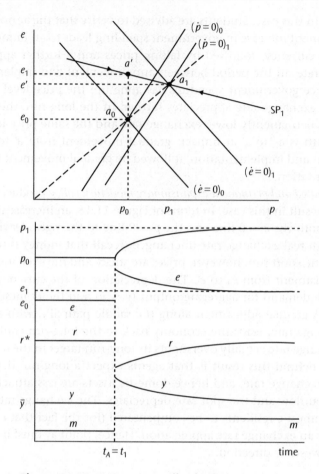

Figure 11.18. Monetary policy in the Dornbusch model

This is an unstable differential equation in e only (it does not feature the price level, p). In terms of Figure 11.19, the only stable solution, following an unanticipated increase in the money supply, is an immediate discrete adjustment of the exchange rate from e_0 to e_1. Consequently, both immediately before and immediately after the shock, the exchange rate is constant ($\dot{e} = 0$) so that the domestic rate of interest stays equal to the world rate at all times ($r = r^*$). Unanticipated monetary policy does not lead to overshooting if prices are perfectly flexible.

This does not mean, of course, that overshooting is impossible when the price level is fully flexible. In some cases, anticipation effects can also cause overshooting of the exchange rate. Assume that the monetary impulse is announced at time t_A to be implemented at some later time t_I ($>t_A$). If agents have perfect foresight, the adjustment path will be an immediate depreciation at time t_A from e_0 to e', followed

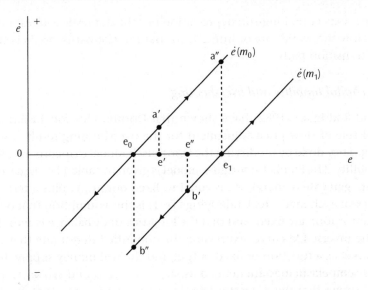

Figure 11.19. Exchange rate dynamics with perfectly flexible prices

by gradual further depreciation between t_A and t_I, represented by the movement from point a' to a" along the $\dot{e}(m_0)$ line. Exactly at time t_I the money supply is increased (as was announced), the $\dot{e} = 0$ line shifts to the right to $\dot{e}(m_1)$, and the exchange rate settles at its new equilibrium level e_1. Agents anticipate a depreciation of the currency in the long run since the money supply increases. There can be no anticipated jumps in the exchange rate, since these would imply infinitely large expected capital gains/losses, so that one side of the market would disappear. Consequently, interest parity dictates adjustment, and the exchange rate starts to depreciate immediately.[8] There is still no overshooting in this case.

Matters are different if the monetary impulse is implemented immediately ($t_A = t_I$) but is of a temporary nature. Specifically, it is announced (and believed by the agents) that the money supply will be decreased to its old level at some time t_E in the future. In that case, the adjustment path is given by an immediate depreciation at $t_A = t_I$ from e_0 to e'', followed by gradual appreciation between t_A and t_E (described by the movement from point b' to b"). At the time the money supply is decreased again, the exchange rate has fallen back to its initial level, the $\dot{e} = 0$ line shifts from $\dot{e}(m_1) = 0$ to $\dot{e}(m_0) = 0$, and equilibrium is restored. A temporary monetary expansion causes the exchange rate to overshoot its long-run (unchanged)

---

[8] The smaller the difference between implementation and announcement dates ($t_I - t_A$), the larger is the jump in the exchange rate at impact. This can be seen intuitively, by noting that if ($t_I - t_A$) → 0, the jump is instantaneous from e_0 to e_1, and if ($t_I - t_A$) → ∞, the policy measure is postponed indefinitely, and nothing happens to the exchange rate.

level. Agents expect no long-run depreciation but the domestic interest rate is temporarily below the world rate of interest, so that interest parity predicts that $\dot{e} < 0$ along the transition path.

Imperfect capital mobility and overshooting

Frenkel and Rodriguez (1982) have shown that Dornbusch's conclusion regarding the crucial role of slow price adjustment for the overshooting result is somewhat misleading. They do so by modifying the Dornbusch model to incorporate imperfect capital mobility. The Frenkel-Rodriguez model is given in Table 11.6. Equation (T6.1) shows that aggregate demand, y^d, is equal to fixed output, $\bar{y}$, plus a term depending on the real exchange rate. Underlying (T6.1) is the assumption that output and domestic absorption are fixed, and that the long-run trade balance is zero. Equation (T6.2) is the inverse LM curve, expressing the domestic interest rate that clears the money market as a function of fixed output and the real money supply. In view of (T5.2), the semi-elasticities are defined as: $\epsilon_{RY} \equiv \epsilon_{MY}/\epsilon_{MR}$ and $\epsilon_{RM} \equiv 1/\epsilon_{MR}$. Equation (T6.3) shows that the domestic price level changes as a result of goods market disequilibrium, and (T6.4) shows that the trade balance, X, depends positively on the real exchange rate. In (T6.5), net capital inflows, KI, depend on the yield gap between domestic and foreign assets (see (11.70)). Depending on the value of ξ, (T6.5) can be used to describe different assumptions regarding capital mobility. If capital is immobile, $\xi = 0$, if it is perfectly mobile, $\xi \to \infty$, and the intermediate case of imperfect capital mobility is obtained if $0 < \xi \ll \infty$. Under perfect capital mobility, yield gaps are closed instantaneously, uncovered interest parity holds ($r = r^* + \dot{e}$), and the balance of payments restriction (T6.6) is redundant (since it holds as an identity in that case).

By using (T6.1) and (T6.3), the price adjustment equation is obtained:

$$\dot{p} = \phi \epsilon_{DQ} \left[p^* + e - p \right], \tag{11.81}$$

which shows that the price exerts a stable influence, i.e. $\partial \dot{p}/\partial p = -\phi \epsilon_{DQ} < 0$. Similarly, by substituting (T6.2), (T6.4), and (T6.5) into (T6.6), the dynamic

Table 11.6. The Frenkel–Rodriguez Model

$y^d = \bar{y} + \epsilon_{DQ} \left[p^* + e - p \right],$	(T6.1)
$r = \epsilon_{RY} \bar{y} - \epsilon_{RM} \left[m - p \right],$	(T6.2)
$\dot{p} = \phi \left[y^d - \bar{y} \right],$	(T6.3)
$X = \epsilon_{XQ} \left[p^* + e - p \right],$	(T6.4)
$KI = \xi \left[r - (r^* + \dot{e}) \right],$	(T6.5)
$KI + X = 0.$	(T6.6)

equation for the exchange rate is obtained:

$$\dot{e} = (\epsilon_{XQ}/\xi)\,[p^* + e - p] + \epsilon_{RY}\bar{y} - \epsilon_{RM}\,[m - p] - r^*, \tag{11.82}$$

which shows that, just as in the Dornbusch model, the instability originates from the exchange rate, i.e. $\partial\dot{e}/\partial e = \epsilon_{XQ}/\xi \geq 0$. Following the same procedures as above, the $\dot{p} = 0$ and $\dot{e} = 0$ lines can be derived:

$$e = p - p^*, \tag{11.83}$$

$$e = [1 - \xi\epsilon_{RM}/\epsilon_{XQ}]\,p + (\xi/\epsilon_{XQ})\,[\epsilon_{RM}m - \epsilon_{RY}\bar{y} + r^*]. \tag{11.84}$$

The $\dot{p} = 0$ line (11.83) is upward sloping, but the slope of the $\dot{e} = 0$ line (11.84) is ambiguous. If capital mobility is low (ξ low), it is likely to be upward sloping, but if capital mobility is high it will be downward sloping. The two cases are drawn in Figures 11.20 and 11.21, respectively.

Figure 11.20 illustrates that there is no overshooting of the exchange rate after a monetary impulse under low capital mobility. At impact, the higher money supply causes the domestic interest rate to fall. This causes net capital outflows ($KI < 0$). At the same time, the exchange rate depreciates and the trade account improves. If capital mobility is low, the former effect is dominated by the latter, and balance of payments equilibrium requires a slight appreciation of the currency (to ensure that $X + KI = 0$ at time $t = 0$). After that, the domestic price level and the exchange rate rise along the saddle path towards their new equilibrium levels. The opposite case with high mobility of capital is illustrated in Figure 11.21. Here, both the $\dot{e} = 0$ line and the associated saddle path are downward sloping. The exchange rate overshoots its long-run level at impact, as the capital inflow effect dominates the effect on the trade account at impact.

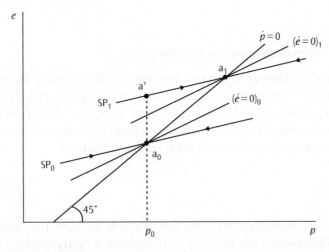

Figure 11.20. Exchange rate dynamics with low capital mobility

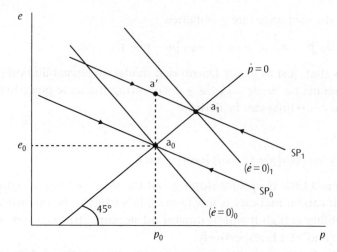

Figure 11.21. Exchange rate dynamics with high capital mobility

So what is the lesson that is learnt from this model? The role of asset market adjustment speed is vital in the discussion about overshooting. As long as the speed of price adjustment is finite, the sign of the parameter ($\epsilon_{XQ} - \xi\epsilon_{RM}$) determines whether or not there is overshooting. In other words, the assumption of sticky prices is *necessary but not sufficient* for the exchange rate overshooting result. By only considering the extreme case of perfect capital mobility, one is unable to disentangle the effects of adjustment speeds in goods- and assets markets, and one is tempted to infer (incorrectly) that price stickiness alone automatically implies exchange rate overshooting.

Monetary accommodation and overshooting

Up to this point we have assumed that the policy maker pursues discrete monetary policy, consisting of once-off changes in the money supply. Suppose now, however, that the policy maker wishes to accommodate any price shocks that may occur. Specifically, we continue to use the Dornbusch model of Table 11.5, but we postulate that the money supply reacts to the price level according to:

$$m = \bar{m} + \delta p, \tag{11.85}$$

where δ is the accommodation coefficient. If $\delta = 0$, we have the "pure float" case analysed by Dornbusch, but if $0 < \delta < 1$, we have a "dirty float". There is some degree of exchange rate management in the form of adjustments in the money supply.

Since the money supply is no longer exogenous, equations (11.72)–(11.73) are replaced by:

$$y = \frac{\epsilon_{MR}\epsilon_{YQ}\left[p^* + e - p\right] + \epsilon_{MR}\epsilon_{YG}g + \epsilon_{YR}\left[\bar{m} - (1-\delta)p\right]}{\epsilon_{MR} + \epsilon_{MY}\epsilon_{YR}}, \tag{11.86}$$

$$r = \frac{\epsilon_{MY}\epsilon_{YQ}\left[p^* + e - p\right] + \epsilon_{MY}\epsilon_{YG}g - \bar{m} + (1-\delta)p}{\epsilon_{MR} + \epsilon_{MY}\epsilon_{YR}}. \tag{11.87}$$

so that the $\dot{p} = 0$ and $\dot{e} = 0$ lines are changed to:

$$e = \frac{\left[(1-\delta)\epsilon_{YR} + \epsilon_{MR}\epsilon_{YQ}\right]p + (\epsilon_{MR} + \epsilon_{MY}\epsilon_{YR})\bar{y}}{\epsilon_{MR}\epsilon_{YQ}}$$

$$- \frac{\epsilon_{MR}\epsilon_{YQ}p^* + \epsilon_{MR}\epsilon_{YG}g + \epsilon_{YR}\bar{m}}{\epsilon_{MR}\epsilon_{YQ}} \tag{11.88}$$

$$e = \frac{\left[1 - \delta - \epsilon_M\epsilon_{YQ}\right]p - \epsilon_M\epsilon_{YQ}p^* - \epsilon_M\epsilon_{YG}g + \bar{m} + (\epsilon_{MR} + \epsilon_M\epsilon_{YR})r^*}{\epsilon_M\epsilon_{YQ}}. \tag{11.89}$$

The $\dot{p} = 0$ line (11.88) is still unambiguously upward sloping, but the slope of the $\dot{e} = 0$ line (11.89) is ambiguous:

$$\left(\frac{de}{dp}\right)_{y=\bar{y}} = \frac{\epsilon_{MR}\epsilon_{YQ} + (1-\delta)\epsilon_{YR}}{\epsilon_{MR}\epsilon_{YQ}} \geq 1, \tag{11.90}$$

$$\left(\frac{de}{dp}\right)_{r=r^*} = -\frac{1 - \delta - \epsilon_{MY}\epsilon_{YQ}}{\epsilon_{MY}\epsilon_{YQ}}. \tag{11.91}$$

If there is *little accommodation* ($0 < \delta < 1 - \epsilon_{MY}\epsilon_{YQ}$), expansionary monetary policy (a rise in $\bar{m}$) leads to overshooting (as was the case in the Dornbusch model for which $\delta = 0$ and $1 - \epsilon_{MY}\epsilon_{YQ} > 0$). If there is a lot of accommodation ($\delta > 1 - \epsilon_{MY}\epsilon_{YQ} > 0$), however, the overshooting result disappears and undershooting of the exchange rate is the result. This can be illustrated with the aid of Figure 11.22. An increase in $\bar{m}$ shifts both the $\dot{p} = 0$ and $\dot{e} = 0$ lines but leaves the long-run equilibrium real exchange rate unaffected. If the initial equilibrium is at a_0 (initial schedules have not been drawn to avoid cluttering the diagram), an increase in $\bar{m}$ shifts the long-run equilibrium to a_1. Adjustment is instantaneous from a_0 to a', followed by gradual adjustment from a' to a_1. The time paths of the different variables are given in the lower panel of Figure 11.22. Note that, since the money supply rises along with the price level, it is possible to approach the new equilibrium with a falling interest rate. The change in the money supply has a more than 100% effect on the price level in the long run. Recall that in the steady state, $y = \bar{y}$ and $r = r^*$, so that the real exchange rate is constant. In view of (11.87) we observe that $dp(\infty) = d\bar{m}/(1-\delta) > d\bar{m}$ (since $0 < \delta < 1$). The reason for this result is, of course, that m increases by more than $\bar{m}$ if there is accommodation.

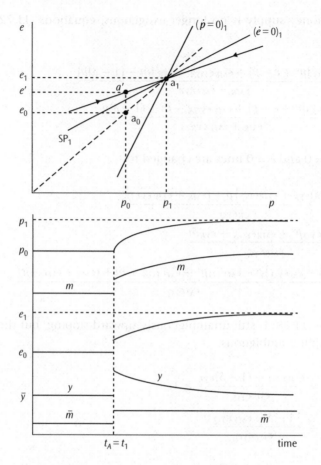

Figure 11.22. Monetary accommodation and undershooting

11.4 Punchlines

In this chapter we conclude our discussion of the IS-LM model that was commenced in Chapter 1, by discussing the contributions made by Mundell and Fleming (MF) and subsequent work in the area. In the MF framework it is explicitly recognized that most countries are open economies, i.e. they trade goods and financial assets with each other. There are two crucial aspects characterizing the open economy, namely its "financial openness" and the exchange rate system it maintains.

By financial openness we mean the ease with which domestic residents substitute domestic and foreign assets in their portfolios as yields between assets differ. If substitution is very easy then yields will equalize. This situation is often referred to as one of perfect capital mobility. At the other extreme, if domestic residents are not willing to hold foreign assets at all (or if there are strictures against it) then the economy is "financially closed" and there is said to be no capital mobility at all. The intermediate case, with imperfectly mobile capital, can also be distinguished.

There are two prototypical exchange rate systems. Under a system of fixed exchange rates, the monetary authority keeps the exchange rate for the domestic currency fixed by means of interventions on the foreign exchange market. Unless the policy maker engages in sterilization operations, the money supply will be endogenous under this regime. With a system of flexible exchange rates, the monetary authority does not intervene in the foreign exchange market. As a result the equilibrium exchange rate is endogenously determined by the forces of demand and supply in the foreign exchange market.

The results of monetary and fiscal policy depend both on the degree of capital mobility and on the exchange rate system. With immobile capital and under fixed exchange rates neither monetary nor fiscal policy can permanently affect aggregate output. With perfectly mobile capital and fixed (flexible) exchange rates, monetary policy is ineffective (effective) and fiscal policy is effective (ineffective) at influencing output. All these results are based on the assumption of a fixed price level.

In order to endogenize the price level we add a simple model of aggregate supply to the MF framework. The key features of this model are as follows. First, perfectly competitive firms set prices of the domestic good. Second, domestic and foreign goods are distinct and are imperfect substitutes for each other. Third, to give the model some Keynesian features it is assumed that the (real or nominal) consumer wage is fixed and that the demand for labour determines employment and output. Finally, because domestic consumers use both domestic and foreign goods, the consumer price index, upon which the wage claims are potentially based, depends on both the domestic and the foreign price (and thus on the nominal exchange rate).

Armed with this extended MF model we investigate the effects of monetary and fiscal policy under perfect capital mobility. Not surprisingly, the wage setting regime plays a crucial role. Under real (nominal) wage rigidity, monetary policy is ineffective (effective). With real wage rigidity fiscal policy boosts output, reduces the domestic price, and leads to an appreciation of both the nominal and the real exchange rate. In contrast, with nominal wage rigidity fiscal policy does not affect output and the domestic price and merely leads to an appreciation of the real and nominal exchange rate. All these results hold for a small open economy which faces an exogenously given world interest rate.

In order to endogenize the world interest rate we assume that the world consists of two identical countries which can each be described by the extended MF model. The two-country MF model shows how shocks are transmitted internationally. Depending on the configuration of wage-setting regimes in the two countries' policy initiatives may spill over across countries. As an application of the two-country model we show the effects of policy coordination.

In the last part of this chapter we introduce forward-looking elements in a sticky-price model of a small open economy facing perfect capital mobility. A striking feature of this model is that an unanticipated and permanent monetary expansion may produce overshooting of the exchange rate. Intuitively, agents expect a long-run depreciation of the nominal exchange rate which, ceteris paribus, makes domestic assets less attractive than foreign assets. There is a net capital outflow and the spot exchange rate depreciates. During transition the domestic interest rate falls short of the world interest rate. As a result the exchange rate overshoots its long-run equilibrium value because part of the yield on domestic assets consists of a gradual appreciation of the exchange rate.

The overshooting result caused a big stir in the late 1970s because it provided an economically intuitive rationale for the large swings that are often observed in the exchange rate. Large changes in the exchange rate need not be due to the behaviour of irrational currency speculators after all! In the final part of the chapter we demonstrate that price stickiness is a necessary but not a sufficient condition for the overshooting result to hold. Both a high degree of capital mobility and price stickiness are needed to produce overshooting.

Further Reading

Obstfeld and Rogoff (1996) is a recent graduate text focusing on the open economy. The classic references on the open economy IS-LM model are Mundell (1968) and Fleming (1962). See Frenkel and Razin (1987) for a review article. Open economy models incorporating the rational expectations (or perfect foresight) hypothesis were developed by Dornbusch (1976, 1980, 1983), Kouri (1976), Niehans (1977), Buiter and Miller (1981, 1982), and Obstfeld and Rogoff (1984). See Gärtner (1993) for a recent survey. Obstfeld and Rogoff (1995a) present a micro-founded model of the small open economy with sticky prices.

Students interested in multi-country models and the issue of policy coordination are referred to Cooper (1968), Mussa (1979), Aoki (1986), McKibbin (1988), Canzoneri and Henderson (1991), and McKibbin and Sachs (1991). Key references to the intertemporal approach to the current account are Sachs (1981), Buiter (1981), Obstfeld (1982), and Svensson and Razin (1983). A good survey of this literature is presented by Obstfeld and Rogoff (1995b). For empirical evidence, see Feldstein and Horioka (1980) and Feldstein (1994).

Calvo and Rodriguez (1977) study a perfect foresight model with currency substitution. For good surveys of the literature on balance of payments crises, see Agénor, Bhandari, and Flood (1992) and Blackburn and Sola (1993).

12

Money

The purpose of this chapter is to discuss the following issues:

1. What are the principal functions of money in advanced economies?
2. How can the role of money be captured in simple models?
3. What is the socially optimal quantity of money?
4. How does money affect the government budget constraint (nominal money growth as an inflation tax)?

12.1 Functions of Money

The question "What is money?" will be answered with full confidence when asked of any man or woman in the street. Indeed, the typical response one may expect from such a question would probably consist of the person in question taking out his/her wallet and showing a colourful piece of paper with some numbers printed on it and possibly the portrait of some past or present monarch or president. If the question had been asked a few centuries ago, the object produced from the wallet would probably have been made of some precious metal rather than (hard to counterfeit) paper but the intended answer would have been the same: money is the stuff which sits in one's wallet and can be used to purchase goods and services.[1]

Economists will show considerably less confidence if confronted with the same question and instead of formulating a straight answer will propose a number of functions performed by this elusive thing called "money". In other words, instead of designating what money "is" economists describe what money "does," or more precisely what something must do in order for it to be called money. In broad terms

[1] An exhaustive and highly readable historical treatment of the emergence of money in different societies is found in Einzig (1949). See also Davies (1994), Jevons (1875), Menger (1892), Fisher (1913), Wicksell (1935), and Jones (1976).

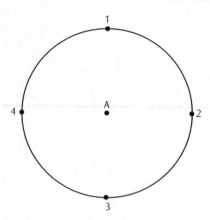

Figure 12.1. The barter economy

three major functions of money can be distinguished: (1) money as a medium of exchange, (2) money as a medium of account, and (3) money as a store of value (McCallum, 1989a, pp. 16–18).

The various aspects of money can be illustrated with the aid of Figure 12.1. Suppose there are four agents (labelled 1 through 4) in the economy who each produce a unique commodity but like to consume not just their own product but also all other products in the economy. In a *barter* economy all agents formulate their supply of the own good and demands for the other goods, meet at a central market place (which is located, say, at point A in Figure 12.1) in which the equilibrium *relative* prices are determined. Since there are four goods in our example, there are in total six relative prices which are determined.[2] Exchange takes place without the use of money, namely good 1 is directly exchanged ("bartered") for good 2, etc. Aside from obvious complications relating to indivisibilities of goods etc., a centralized market place would function perfectly well without money. Intuitively, without some kind of "friction" money is not likely to be a very useful thing to have.

In reality, of course, not all transactions take place in a centralized full-information setting and the process of trading becomes more complicated. Assume that the central market place in Figure 12.1 exists, but that the agent does not know beforehand which other trader he is going to meet there at any particular time. Suppose that at most two traders meet randomly at this market in each period. Then agents are confronted with a major problem due to the need for a double coincidence of wants. For example, agent 1 may find himself paired with agent 2 who may or may not want to trade with him. In fact, in the absence of money, an exchange of goods will only take place if agent 1 meets an agent who wants to have his good

---

[2] These are the rates at which the goods are exchanged pair-wise. Denoting p_{ij} as the relative price of good i in terms of good j, we have the following relative prices: p_{12}, p_{13}, p_{14}, p_{23}, p_{24}, and p_{34}. Obviously, we have that $p_{ij} \equiv 1/p_{ji}$.

and who himself has a good which agent 1 is looking for. Hence, in such a setting it may take a lot of effort and a long time before agent 1 can actually trade.

Even if agents are perfectly informed about the location of trading partners, the problem may still persist. Cass and Yaari (1966) present a case in which the double coincidence of wants always fails. Assume that agents only wish to consume their own good and the good produced by the agent located closest (in a clockwise direction), i.e. agent 1 would like to consume the bundle (1,2), agent 2 (2,3), agent 3 (3,4), and agent 4 (4,1). Assume that the goods are non-storable and that each agent can at most travel halfway towards his adjacent neighbours. This means that agent 1, for example, can attempt to trade with agents 4 and 2, agent 2 with 1 and 3, etc. It is easy to see, however, that no trading will actually take place. Agent 1, for example, cannot trade with 2 because the latter is not interested in good 1 at any price. Similarly, agent 1 will not trade with agent 4 for the same reason. The double coincidence of wants fails, all agents consume only their own good, and a situation of autarky persists.

Now assume there is a durable "thing" which is storable and can be transferred across agents at zero cost, and call this thing money. Then agents will actually be able to trade with each other by using this money rather than bartering. Agent 1, for example, sells his good to agent 4, and receives money for it with which he purchases good 2 from agent 2. Since the other agents do the same with their neighbours, an equilibrium can be attained in which all agents are better off (in welfare terms) as a result of the existence of a medium of exchange called money.

Of course, the circle model is a highly stylized account of the trading process but it is nevertheless useful because it motivates the following medium-of-exchange "test". Something serves the role of medium of exchange if its existence ensures that agents can attain a higher level of welfare.[3] In the "random-encounters" model and in the "circle" model money serves as a medium of exchange in the sense of this proposed definition. Indeed, in the former model the trading friction is reduced (but not totally eliminated)[4] by the existence of a medium of exchange, whereas in the latter the friction is completely eliminated.

There is nothing in the theory which suggests that the medium of exchange must be an intrinsically valuable commodity such as gold or silver (or rare shells) which enhance people's utility or can be put to productive uses. Indeed, an intrinsically low-valued good (such as paper) can also serve as a medium of exchange provided it is generally accepted in exchange. To the extent that gold and silver are better

---

[3] This test is similar to (but more general than) the one suggested by McCallum (1983b). His requirement is more strict in that it requires the medium of exchange to expand production possibilities. Indeed, he call this the "traditional presumption" (1983, p. 24).

[4] Agent 1 may meet an agent from whom he does not want to buy anything but who does want to buy good 1. The transaction takes place against money, which agent 1 can use at some later encounter. If agent 1 instead meets an agent who does not want good 1 and whose good agent 1 does not want, then no trade takes place. Hence, some frictions remain in the random-encounters model.

used for productive purposes, it is actually preferable for society to use intrinsically low-valued material as a medium of exchange (McCallum, 1989a, p. 17).

The second major function of money is that of *medium of account*. As was explained above, an economy with four distinct goods exhibits six distinct relative prices. For an economy with N different goods the number of distinct relative prices amounts to $N(N-1)/2$, which is a rather large number even for a modestly large N. If all goods are expressed in terms of money, and money is thus the medium of account, then only N different (absolute) prices for the different goods need be recorded. Denoting these absolute prices by p_i $(i = 1, \ldots, N)$ the relative prices are then implied, e.g. $p_{ij} \equiv p_i/p_j$.

The third function of money is that of *store of value*. In a monetary economy money can be used to buy goods and vice versa, not only today but (more than likely) also tomorrow. Hence, a stock of money represents "future purchasing power". In the future the money can be exchanged for goods which can be consumed or used in the production process. Money is thus capable of being used as a store of value, but there are other assets (bonds, company shares, real estate, etc.) which typically outperform it in this role because they yield a positive rate of return whereas money (typically) does not.

Of the three major roles played by money, only the medium-of-exchange role is the distinguishing feature of money. Any commodity can serve as a medium of account (without at the same time serving as a medium of exchange) and there are various non-money assets which can serve as a store of value.

12.2 Modelling Money as a Medium of Exchange

In Chapter 1 we discussed the Baumol (1952)–Tobin (1956) inventory-theoretic model of money demand in an intermezzo. The basic idea behind that model is that money is held through the period between income receipts, despite the fact that it does not yield any interest, because it is needed to make purchases. The baker will sell you a loaf of bread in exchange for money but not for bonds. At a more general level the model suggests that money facilitates transactions. Of course, the Baumol–Tobin model is rather restrictive in its scope and partial equilibrium in nature, and the task of this section is to study how money as a medium of exchange can be cast in a general equilibrium framework. In what follows the Baumol–Tobin model is shown to be a special case of a more general framework in which money helps to "grease the wheels" of the economy by minimizing liquidity costs.

12.2.1 Setting the stage

Suppose an individual agent lives for two periods, "now" (period 1) and "in the future" (period 2), and possesses stocks of bonds (B_0) and money (M_0) that were accumulated in the past. The agent has fixed real endowment income in the two periods (Y_1 and Y_2, respectively) and consumes in the two periods (C_1 and C_2, respectively). The price of the good in the two periods is denoted by P_1 and P_2, respectively. The periodic budget identities are then given by:

$$P_1 Y_1 + M_0 + (1 + R_0)B_0 = P_1 C_1 + M_1 + B_1, \tag{12.1}$$

$$P_2 Y_2 + M_1 + (1 + R_1)B_1 = P_2 C_2 + M_2 + B_2, \tag{12.2}$$

where R_i is the nominal interest rate on bonds in period i. The left-hand side in these expressions represents the total resources available to the household whereas the right-hand side represents what these resources can be spent on.

Since the agent will not be around in period 3 and there is no bequest motive (see Chapter 6), he will not wish to die with positive stocks of money and/or bonds (i.e. $M_2 \leq 0$ and $B_2 \leq 0$). The financial sector will not allow him to die indebted ($B_2 \geq 0$) and the agent cannot create money ($M_2 \geq 0$). Hence, combining all these requirements yields $M_2 = B_2 = 0$, so that (12.1)–(12.2) can be combined into the following consolidated budget constraint:

$$[A \equiv] \ Y_1 + \frac{Y_2}{1 + r_1} + \left(\frac{P_0}{P_1}\right) m_0 + (1 + r_0)b_0 = C_1 + \frac{C_2}{1 + r_1} + \frac{R_1 m_1}{1 + R_1}, \tag{12.3}$$

where $m_t \equiv M_t/P_t$ is real money balances, $b_t \equiv B_t/P_t$ is real bonds (or real debt if b_t is negative), and r_t is the real rate of interest which is defined as:

$$r_t = \frac{P_t(1 + R_t)}{P_{t+1}} - 1. \tag{12.4}$$

If the price level is stable (rising, falling), the real interest rate equals (falls short of, exceeds) the nominal interest rate.

The agent has the usual lifetime utility function which depends on consumption in the two periods in a time-separable manner:

$$V = U(C_1) + \left(\frac{1}{1 + \rho}\right) U(C_2), \tag{12.5}$$

where $\rho > 0$ is the pure rate of time preference and $U(.)$ has the usual properties (see Chapter 6). The household chooses consumption in the two periods (C_1 and C_2) and its desired money holding (m_1) in order to maximize (12.5) subject to (12.3) and the non-negativity condition on money holdings ($m_1 \geq 0$), and given the predetermined stocks of money and bonds (m_0 and b_0). The Lagrangean associated with this problem is:

$$\mathcal{L} \equiv U(C_1) + \left(\frac{1}{1 + \rho}\right) U(C_2) + \lambda \left[A - C_1 - \frac{C_2}{1 + r_1} - \frac{R_1 m_1}{1 + R_1}\right], \tag{12.6}$$

where λ is the Lagrangean multiplier. The first-order conditions are:

$$\frac{\partial \mathcal{L}}{\partial C_1} = U'(C_1) - \lambda = 0, \tag{12.7}$$

$$\frac{\partial \mathcal{L}}{\partial C_2} = \left(\frac{1}{1+\rho}\right) U'(C_2) - \frac{\lambda}{1+r_1} = 0, \tag{12.8}$$

$$\frac{\partial \mathcal{L}}{\partial m_1} \equiv \lambda \left(\frac{-R_t}{1+R_1}\right) \leq 0, \quad m_1 \geq 0, \quad m_1 \frac{\partial \mathcal{L}}{\partial m_1} = 0. \tag{12.9}$$

Equations (12.7)–(12.8) are exactly the same as in a model without money and in combination yield the usual Euler equation relating the optimal time profile of consumption to the divergence between the real interest rate and the rate of time preference. The existence of money does not affect this aspect of the intertemporal model. Equation (12.9) is new and warrants some further discussion. First consider the normal case with a strictly positive rate of interest ($R_1 > 0$) so that the term in round brackets in (12.9) is strictly negative and the complementary slackness condition suggests that no money is held by the agent:

$$m_1 = 0 \quad \text{if } R_1 > 0. \tag{12.10}$$

The intuition behind this result is that the opportunity cost of holding money consists of foregone interest, which is positive. Since money is not "doing" anything useful in the model developed thus far, the rational agent refrains from using money altogether.

The second, at first view rather *pathological*, case describes the situation in which the nominal interest rate is negative ($R_1 < 0$), so that the term in round brackets in (12.9) is positive. Now the agent wishes to hold as many money balances as possible. By simply holding these money balances they appreciate in value (relative to goods). To put it differently, money has a positive yield if the interest rate is negative.

$$m_1 \to \infty \quad \text{if } R_1 < 0. \tag{12.11}$$

Of course, negative nominal interest rates do not represent a particularly realistic phenomenon. We shall nevertheless have a need to return to this case in section 4.2 below where we discuss the optimal quantity of money argument. In the remainder of this section, however, we restrict attention to the normal case, i.e. we assume that the nominal interest rate is strictly positive. The challenge is then to modify the basic model in such a way that money will play a non-trivial role for the agent (and thus for the economy as a whole).

12.2.2 Shopping costs

In section 1 it was argued that money as a medium of exchange reduces the transactions costs associated with the trading process between agents. A particularly simple and elegant way to capture this aspect of money was suggested by McCallum (1983b, 1989a). He assumes that households value leisure time and that part of their time endowment is spent on "shopping around" for goods. Money is useful in the sense that it makes shopping easier, i.e. by using money the agent can save leisure time otherwise spent on shopping. We now modify our basic model to incorporate shopping costs.

Suppose that the household has a time endowment of unity, works a fixed amount of time units, $\bar{N}$, and spends S_t units of time on shopping. Then the agent enjoys $(1 - \bar{N} - S_t)$ units of leisure in period t. The utility function is modified to take into account that the agent likes leisure time:

$$V = U(C_1, 1 - \bar{N} - S_1) + \left(\frac{1}{1+\rho}\right) U(C_2, 1 - \bar{N} - S_2), \quad \rho > 0. \tag{12.12}$$

The intertemporal budget constraint is still given by (12.3), with endowment income now representing real labour income, $Y_t \equiv (W_t/P_t)\bar{N}$, where W_t is the nominal wage rate in period t. The shopping technology is assumed to take the following form:

$$1 - \bar{N} - S_t = \psi(m_{t-1}, C_t), \tag{12.13}$$

where the $\psi(.)$ function is assumed to have the following properties. First, for a given level of goods consumption, raising the level of real money balances results in a finite reduction of time spent shopping and thus an increase in available leisure, i.e. $\psi_m(.) > 0$. Second, the reduction in shopping cost due to a given increase in money balances decreases as more money balances are used, i.e. $\psi_{mm}(.) < 0$ or, in words, the shopping technology features diminishing marginal productivity of money balances. Third, increasing consumption requires more shopping costs but at a diminishing rate, i.e. $\psi_C(.) < 0$ and $\psi_{CC}(.) > 0$. Finally, the shopping costs are bounded, i.e. $0 < \psi(\infty) < \psi(0) < 1 - \bar{N}$.

The household chooses C_t, S_t (for $t = 1, 2$), and m_1 (m_0 being predetermined) in order to maximize (12.12) subject to (12.3), (12.13), and the non-negativity constraint on money balances ($m_1 \geq 0$). The Lagrangean expression is:

$$\mathcal{L} \equiv U(C_1, 1 - \bar{N} - S_1) + \left(\frac{1}{1+\rho}\right) U(C_2, 1 - \bar{N} - S_2)$$

$$+ \lambda \left[A - C_1 - \frac{C_2}{1+r_1} - \frac{R_1 m_1}{1+R_1}\right] - \sum_{t=1}^{2} \lambda_t \left[1 - \bar{N} - S_t - \psi(m_{t-1}, C_t)\right], \tag{12.14}$$

where λ_t are the Lagrangean multipliers associated with the shopping technology in the two periods. The first-order conditions are:

$$\frac{\partial \mathcal{L}}{\partial C_1} = U_C(C_1, 1 - \bar{N} - S_1) - \lambda + \lambda_1 \psi_C(m_0, C_1) = 0, \tag{12.15}$$

$$\frac{\partial \mathcal{L}}{\partial C_2} = \left(\frac{1}{1+\rho}\right) U_C(C_2, 1 - \bar{N} - S_2) - \frac{\lambda}{1+r_1} + \lambda_2 \psi_C(m_1, C_2) = 0, \tag{12.16}$$

$$\frac{\partial \mathcal{L}}{\partial S_1} = -U_L(C_1, 1 - \bar{N} - S_1) + \lambda_1 = 0, \tag{12.17}$$

$$\frac{\partial \mathcal{L}}{\partial S_2} = -\left(\frac{1}{1+\rho}\right) U_L(C_2, 1 - \bar{N} - S_2) + \lambda_2 = 0, \tag{12.18}$$

$$\frac{\partial \mathcal{L}}{\partial m_1} \equiv \lambda \left(\frac{-R_1}{1+R_1}\right) + \lambda_2 \psi_m(m_1, C_2) \leq 0, \quad m_1 \geq 0, \quad m_1 \frac{\partial \mathcal{L}}{\partial m_1} = 0, \tag{12.19}$$

where $U_C(.)$ and $U_L(.)$ denote the marginal utility of consumption and leisure, respectively.

The first thing to note about these expressions concerns equation (12.19), which is the first-order condition for optimal money balances. Comparing this expression to its counterpart in the basic model (i.e. equation (12.9)) reveals that the existence of shopping costs indeed gives rise to an additional positive term in the first expression of (12.19), $U_L(C_2, 1 - \bar{N} - S_2)\psi_m(m_1, C_2)/(1 + \rho)$ (we have used (12.18) to eliminate λ_2). This term represents the marginal utility of money balances. It must be stressed, however, that this does not in-and-of-itself ensure that the agent will choose to hold positive money balances. Indeed, given the assumptions made so far, it is quite possible that $m_1 = 0$ is the best available option for the household. Specifically if the marginal utility of leisure and/or the marginal productivity of money balances are low, the first expression in (12.19) will be strictly negative so that the complementary slackness condition ensures that $m_1 = 0$ is optimal, as in the basic model. Intuitively, no money is held in that case because the agent does not really mind shopping (U_L low) and/or because money does not reduce shopping costs by much (ψ_m low).

In the remainder of this section we assume that ψ_m and/or U_L are high enough to ensure that a strictly positive amount of money is held by the agent. The first expression in (12.19) holds with equality and the Lagrange multipliers (λ_1 and λ_2) can be eliminated by combining (12.15)–(12.18) after which the following optimality conditions are obtained:

$$\lambda = U_C(C_1, 1 - \bar{N} - S_1) + U_L(C_1, 1 - \bar{N} - S_1)\psi_C(m_0, C_1)$$

$$= \left(\frac{1+r_1}{1+\rho}\right) \left[U_C(C_2, 1 - \bar{N} - S_2) + U_L(C_2, 1 - \bar{N} - S_2)\psi_C(m_1, C_2)\right]$$

$$= \frac{U_L(C_2, 1 - \bar{N} - S_2)\psi_m(m_1, C_2)(1 + R_1)}{(1 + \rho)R_1}, \tag{12.20}$$

where λ represents the marginal utility of wealth (see Chapter 6). In planning his optimal consumption levels, the agent equates the marginal utility of wealth to the *net* marginal utility of consumption, which consists of the direct marginal utility of consumption ($U_C(.)$ in the first and second lines of (12.20)) minus the disutility caused by the additional shopping costs which must be incurred (the $U_L(.)\psi_C(.)$ terms). For consumption taking place in the future the expression is augmented by a net discounting factor (see the second line of (12.20)). The third line in (12.20) shows that the marginal utility of money balances ($U_L(.)\psi_m(.)$) must be equated to the opportunity costs associated with holding these balances expressed in utility terms.

12.2.3 Money in the utility function

Inspection of equations (12.12)–(12.13) of the shopping-cost model reveals that this approach in effect amounts to putting money directly into the utility function, i.e. by substituting (12.13) into the felicity function $U(C_t, 1 - \bar{N} - S_t)$ we obtain an *indirect* felicity function, $\tilde{U}(C_t, m_{t-1}) \equiv U(C_t, \psi(m_{t-1}, C_t))$, which only depends on consumption and money balances. Hence, the shopping cost approach can be used to rationalize the conventional practice in macroeconomic modelling of putting money directly into the utility function.

In a recent paper, Feenstra (1986) has provided further justifications for this practice by demonstrating that there exists a functional equivalence between, on the one hand, models with money entered as an argument into the utility function and, on the other hand, models in which money does not enter utility but instead affects "liquidity costs" which in turn show up in the budget restriction. Since the Baumol–Tobin model gives rise to such liquidity costs, Feenstra (1986) has demonstrated that, in a general equilibrium setting, it too is equivalent to a model with money in the utility function.

In a classic paper on the micro-foundations of monetary theory, Clower (1967) complained that (at least in models such as developed up to this point) money is not allowed to play a distinctive role in the economy. Indeed, by looking at the budget identities (12.1)–(12.2), it is clear that money enters these expressions in exactly the same way that goods and bonds do. Implicitly, this suggests that any item (be it goods, money, or bonds) can be directly exchanged for any other item, i.e. goods for bonds, bonds for money, etc. This makes Clower complain that: "... an economy that admits of this possibility clearly constitutes what any Classical economist would regard as a barter rather than a money economy. The fact that fiat money is included among the set of tradeable commodities is utterly irrelevant; the role of money in economic activity is analytically indistinguishable from that of any other commodity" (Clower, 1967, p. 83). In a pure monetary economy, Clower argues, there is a single good, "money", which is used in all transactions, and "money buys goods and goods buy money; but goods do not buy goods" (1967, p. 86).

In the context of our basic model of section 2.1, Clower's idea can be formalized by requiring that spending on consumption goods cannot exceed cash balances carried over from the previous period.[5] The so-called *Clower* or *cash-in-advance constraint* thus amounts to:

$$P_t C_t \leq M_{t-1} \quad \Leftrightarrow \quad C_t \leq (P_{t-1}/P_t)m_{t-1}. \tag{12.21}$$

The basic model, augmented with the Clower constraint (12.21), can be solved as follows. To keep things simple, we assume that the Clower constraint holds with equality in the first period. Since m_0 is predetermined, the same then holds for consumption in the first period, i.e. $C_1 = P_0 m_0 / P_1$. The household chooses C_2 and m_1 in order to maximize (12.5), subject to (12.3) and (12.21). The Lagrangean is:

$$\mathcal{L} \equiv U((P_0/P_1)m_0) + \left(\frac{1}{1+\rho}\right) U(C_2) + \lambda_2 \left[(P_1/P_2)m_1 - C_2\right]$$
$$+ \lambda \left[A - (P_0/P_1)m_0 - \frac{C_2}{1+r_1} - \frac{R_1 m_1}{1+R_1}\right], \tag{12.22}$$

where λ_2 is the Lagrangean multiplier associated with the Clower constraint. The first-order conditions consist of the budget constraint (12.3) and:

$$\frac{\partial \mathcal{L}}{\partial C_2} \equiv \left(\frac{1}{1+\rho}\right) U'(C_2) - \frac{\lambda}{1+r_1} - \lambda_2 \leq 0, \quad C_2 \geq 0, \quad C_2 \frac{\partial \mathcal{L}}{\partial C_2} = 0, \tag{12.23}$$

$$\frac{\partial \mathcal{L}}{\partial m_1} \equiv -\lambda \left(\frac{R_1}{1+R_1}\right) + \lambda_2 (P_1/P_2) \leq 0, \quad m_1 \geq 0, \quad m_1 \frac{\partial \mathcal{L}}{\partial m_1} = 0, \tag{12.24}$$

$$\frac{\partial \mathcal{L}}{\partial \lambda_2} \equiv (P_1/P_2)m_1 - C_2 \geq 0, \quad \lambda_2 \geq 0, \quad \lambda_2 \frac{\partial \mathcal{L}}{\partial \lambda_2} = 0. \tag{12.25}$$

The marginal utility of wealth is strictly positive, i.e. $\lambda > 0$, so that (by (12.23)) the marginal utility of consumption is bounded. Since $\lim_{C_t \to \infty} U'(C_t) = 0$ by assumption, this implies that the consumer chooses a strictly positive consumption level in period 2, i.e. $C_2 > 0$ and (by the first inequality in (12.25)) $m_1 > 0$. Hence, the cash-in-advance constraint does indeed deliver the "goods" desired by Clower. Money is essential, not because it is valued intrinsically, but rather because households wish to consume in the second period. It can also be shown that the household will not hold excess cash balances. Since $m_1 > 0$, the first expression in (12.24) holds with equality, which ensures that the shadow price of cash balances is strictly positive:

$$\lambda_2 = \lambda (P_2/P_1) \left(\frac{R_1}{1+R_1}\right) > 0. \tag{12.26}$$

This implies that the first expression in (12.25) holds with an equality, i.e. the household will hold just enough cash to be able to finance their optimal consumption plan in the future. This result is not specific to our simple two-period model and easily generalizes to a multi-period setting.

[5] For simplicity we assume that the cash-in-advance constraint does not affect purchases of bonds.

As is the case for the shopping model and the Baumol–Tobin model, the cash-in-advance approach can also be shown to be equivalent to a utility-of-money approach. Indeed, as the Clower constraint always holds with equality $(C_t = (P_{t-1}/P_t)m_{t-1})$, the same results are obtained if the indirect felicity function $\tilde{U}(C_t, m_{t-1}) \equiv \min[C_t, m_{t-1}]$ is maximized subject to the budget constraint only (see Feenstra, 1986, p. 285). An important aspect of this indirect felicity function is that the substitution elasticity between consumption and money balances is zero. In this aspect the cash-in-advance formulation differentiates itself from both the shopping model and the Baumol–Tobin model.

12.3 Money as a Store of Value

In the basic model of section 2.1 above, both bonds and money can be used by the individual agent to transfer resources across time and both assets are thus capable of serving as a store of value, although the former does so in a superior fashion to the latter as it yields a higher rate of return. For that reason, money is not generally held in the basic model. It thus does not actually serve as a store of value even though it is technically capable of doing so.

Bewley (1980) presents a model in which money is used as a store of value. His approach can be illustrated with the aid of our basic model. The key assumption he makes is that money is the only asset available to the agent, i.e. $B_0 = B_1 = B_2 = 0$ in the budget equations (12.1)–(12.2). These can then be expressed in real terms as:

$$Y_1 + \frac{m_0}{1 + \pi_0} = C_1 + m_1, \quad Y_2 + \frac{m_1}{1 + \pi_1} = C_2, \quad m_1 \geq 0, \tag{12.27}$$

where $\pi_t \equiv P_{t+1}/P_t - 1$ is the inflation rate.[6] The agent chooses consumption in the two periods and money holdings (C_1, C_2, m_1) in order to maximize lifetime utility (12.5) subject to (12.27). The Lagrangean for this problem is given by:

$$\mathcal{L} \equiv U(C_1) + \left(\frac{1}{1+\rho}\right) U(C_2) + \lambda_1 \left[Y_1 + \frac{m_0}{1 + \pi_0} - C_1 - m_1\right]$$
$$+ \lambda_2 \left[Y_2 + \frac{m_1}{1 + \pi_1} - C_2\right], \tag{12.28}$$

---

[6] If m_1 is strictly positive, the first two expressions in (12.27) can be consolidated:

$$A \equiv Y_1 + (1 + \pi_1)Y_2 + \frac{m_0}{1 + \pi_0} = C_1 + (1 + \pi_1)C_2,$$

which shows that the "implicit interest rate" on money satisfies $1 + r_t^M \equiv 1/(1 + \pi_t)$, i.e. $r_t^M \equiv -\pi_t/(1 + \pi_t) \approx -\pi_t$.

where λ_1 and λ_2 are the Lagrangean multipliers associated with the two budget restrictions. The first-order conditions are the two budget constraints and:

$$\frac{\partial \mathcal{L}}{\partial C_1} = U'(C_1) - \lambda_1 = 0, \tag{12.29}$$

$$\frac{\partial \mathcal{L}}{\partial C_2} = \left(\frac{1}{1+\rho}\right) U'(C_2) - \lambda_2 = 0, \tag{12.30}$$

$$\frac{\partial \mathcal{L}}{\partial m_1} \equiv -\lambda_1 + \frac{\lambda_2}{1+\pi_1} \leq 0, \quad m_1 \geq 0, \quad m_1 \frac{\partial \mathcal{L}}{\partial m_1} = 0. \tag{12.31}$$

Equations (12.29)–(12.31) can be combined to yield the following expression:

$$\frac{\partial \mathcal{L}}{\partial m_1} \equiv \frac{U'(C_2)}{1+\rho}\left[\frac{1}{1+\pi_1} - \frac{(1+\rho)U'(C_1)}{U'(C_2)}\right] \leq 0, \tag{12.32}$$

$$m_1 \geq 0, \quad m_1 \frac{\partial \mathcal{L}}{\partial m_1} = 0.$$

The intuition behind (12.32) can be illustrated with the aid of Figure 12.2. The consolidated budget equation is drawn as the straight line segment AB with slope $dC_2/dC_1 = -1/(1+\pi_1)$. The indifference curve, V_0, has a slope of $dC_2/dC_1 = -(1+\rho)U'(C_1)/U'(C_2)$ and has a tangency with the budget line at point E^C. This is the privately optimal consumption point ignoring the non-negativity constraint on money holdings. If the income endowment point lies north-west of point E^C, say at E_0^Y, money is of no use as a store of value to the agent. In economic terms, the agent would like to be a net supplier of money in order to attain the consumption point E^C but this is impossible. Graphically, the indifference curve through E_0^Y (the dashed curve) is steeper than the budget line, the choice set is only $AE_0^Y C$, and the best the agent can do is to consume his endowments in the two periods.

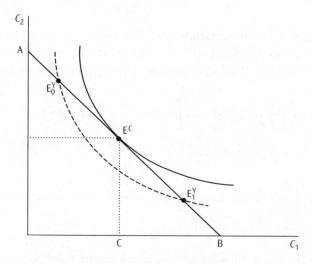

Figure 12.2. Money as a store of value

In mathematical terms, the slope configuration implies that $\partial \mathcal{L}/\partial m_1 < 0$ (lifetime utility rises by supplying money) and complementary slackness results in $m_1 = 0$.

In the alternative case, for which the income endowment point lies south-east of the consumption point (say at E_1^Y) the agent saves in the first period by holding money and the first expression in (12.32) holds with equality so that the Euler equation becomes:

$$\frac{U'(C_2)}{U'(C_1)} = (1 + \rho)(1 + \pi_1). \tag{12.33}$$

The upshot of the discussion so far is that money will be held under certain circumstances because it provides a means by which intertemporal consumption smoothing can be achieved.

Of course, the Bewley approach is rather specific and somewhat unrealistic in that interest-bearing financial instrument are widely available in modern market economies. This fact does not, in-and-of-itself invalidate the argument, however, as the following example, inspired by Sargent and Wallace (1982) reveals. Suppose that there are poor agents (with low income endowments) and rich agents (with high income endowments) in the economy, and assume that both types of agents wish to save in the first period. Suppose furthermore that interest-bearing bonds exist but that they come in minimum denominations, say due to legal restrictions or otherwise, and assume there are no savings banks. In this setting the poor agents save too small an amount to be able to purchase even a single bond and they are thus forced to save by holding money. On the other hand, the rich agents will hold all (or part) of their saving in higher-yielding bonds. Aggregating over all agents in the economy, the indivisibility of bonds results in a positive demand for money to be held as a store of value.

12.3.1 Overlapping-generations model of money

In the model of the previous section, money is used as a store of value by an individual agent provided there is some friction which prevents him from using higher-yielding assets for this task. The argument is based on a partial equilibrium investigation, and the first task of this section is to embed the notion of money as a store of value in a general equilibrium economy-wide model. Instead of using the legal restrictions argument of Sargent and Wallace (1982), we introduce an *inter-generational friction*, of the type first emphasized by Samuelson (1958), in order to motivate a meaningful role for money. This allows us to introduce and discuss the so-called *overlapping-generations* model of money, which has been extremely influential in modern monetary theory.

At time t the population consists of $N/2$ young agents and $N/2$ old agents and we normalize N to unity to simplify the notation. All agents live for two periods, so the young have two periods to live and the old only one. Agents receive an endowment, Y, when young, but do not have any endowment income when they are old. The output Y is potentially storable and for each unit stored in period t, $1/(1 + \delta)$ units of output will be left over in period $t + 1$, where $\delta > -1$. This storage technology nests several special cases. Particularly, if $\delta \to \infty$, goods spoil immediately and are thus non-storable. If $\delta = 0$, goods keep indefinitely, and if $-1 < \delta < 0$ goods reproduce without supervision by the storage process.[7]

The (representative) young agent can either consume his output in youth (C_t^Y, where the superscript denotes "young"), store it (K_t of which $K_t/(1 + \delta)$ is available in period $t + 1$), or trade it for fiat money. Since the money price of output is P_t, the last option yields the agent real money balances at the end of period t ($m_t \equiv M_t/P_t$). The budget identity facing a young agent in his youth is thus:

$$Y = C_t^Y + K_t + M_t/P_t. \tag{12.34}$$

Now consider the budget identity of an old agent in period t. This agent stored output in youth (K_{t-1}) as well as nominal money balances (M_{t-1}) with which he can purchase goods, facing the period-t price level (P_t). In addition, the agent receives a transfer from the government (T_t), the amount of which he takes as given. The budget identity of an old agent is thus:

$$C_t^O = K_{t-1}/(1 + \delta) + T_t + (P_{t-1}/P_t)m_{t-1}, \tag{12.35}$$

where the superscript denotes "old". But the agent who is young in period t will himself be old in period $t + 1$, and will thus face a constraint similar to (12.35) but dated one period later in the last period of his life:

$$C_{t+1}^O = K_t/(1 + \delta) + T_{t+1} + (P_t/P_{t+1})m_t. \tag{12.36}$$

The lifetime utility function of the young agent in period t is given by:

$$V_t^Y = U(C_t^Y) + \left(\frac{1}{1 + \rho}\right) U(C_{t+1}^O), \quad \rho > 0, \tag{12.37}$$

and the agent chooses C_t^Y, C_{t+1}^O, K_t, and m_t in order to maximize (12.37) subject to (12.34) and (12.36) as well as non-negativity conditions on money holdings and stored output ($M_t \geq 0$ and $K_t \geq 0$, respectively). The Lagrangean is:

$$\mathcal{L} \equiv U(C_t^Y) + \left(\frac{1}{1 + \rho}\right) U(C_{t+1}^O) + \lambda_{1,t} \left[Y - C_t^Y - K_t - m_t\right]$$
$$+ \lambda_{2,t} \left[K_t/(1 + \delta) + T_{t+1} + (P_t/P_{t+1})m_t - C_{t+1}^O\right], \tag{12.38}$$

where $\lambda_{1,t}$ and $\lambda_{2,t}$ are the Lagrangean multipliers of the budget identities in youth and old age respectively. The first-order conditions consist of the budget identities

[7] Samuelson gives the examples of rabbits and yeast for this case. In a more serious vein, a negative value for δ captures the notion of net productivity in the economy (1958, p. 468).

(12.34) and (12.36) and:

$$\frac{\partial \mathcal{L}}{\partial C_t^Y} = U'(C_t^Y) - \lambda_{1,t} = 0, \tag{12.39}$$

$$\frac{\partial \mathcal{L}}{\partial C_{t+1}^O} = \left(\frac{1}{1+\rho}\right) U'(C_{t+1}^O) - \lambda_{2,t} = 0, \tag{12.40}$$

$$\frac{\partial \mathcal{L}}{\partial m_t} \equiv -\lambda_{1,t} + \lambda_{2,t}/(1+\pi_t) \le 0, \quad m_t \ge 0, \quad m_t \frac{\partial \mathcal{L}}{\partial m_t} = 0, \tag{12.41}$$

$$\frac{\partial \mathcal{L}}{\partial K_t} \equiv -\lambda_{1,t} + \lambda_{2,t}/(1+\delta) \le 0, \quad K_t \ge 0, \quad K_t \frac{\partial \mathcal{L}}{\partial K_t} = 0, \tag{12.42}$$

where $\pi_t \equiv P_{t+1}/P_t - 1$ is the inflation rate. In view of our assumptions regarding the utility function, agents wish to consume in both periods of their lives so that $\lambda_{1,t} > 0$ and $\lambda_{2,t} > 0$. Equations (12.41)–(12.42) imply that, provided $\pi_t \neq \delta$, the young agent will choose a single type of asset to serve as a store of value, depending on which one has the highest yield. Particularly, if inflation is relatively low ($\pi_t < \delta$) then only money will be held ($K_t = 0$ and $m_t > 0$), and if it is relatively high ($\pi_t > \delta$) then only goods will be stored ($K_t > 0$ and $m_t = 0$). In terms of Figure 12.3, in the first case the storage technology is not productive enough and yields a budget line AB which lies below the budget line associated with holding money as a store of value (the line AC). The line configuration is switched in the second case with high inflation ($\pi_t > \delta$).

The behaviour of the old in period t is quite straightforward. Although they entered life (in period $t-1$) possessing a utility function analogous to (12.37) (and designated by V_{t-1}^Y), their behaviour in period $t-1$ (their youth) constitutes "water

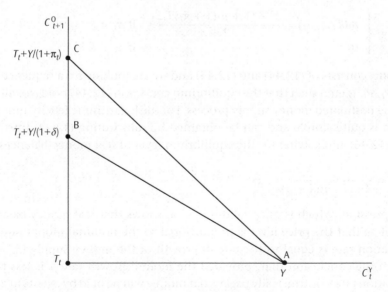

Figure 12.3. Choice set with storage and money

under the bridge" in the sense that it cannot be undone in period t (it is irreversible or "sunk" in economic terms). All that remains for them is to maximize remaining lifetime utility, $U(C_t^O)$ subject to the budget identity (12.35). They simply consume their entire budget.

Following Wallace (1980) we assume that the government pursues a simple money supply rule:

$$M_t = (1 + \mu)M_{t-1}, \tag{12.43}$$

with $\mu > -1$ representing the constant rate of nominal money growth. The additional money is used to finance the transfer to the old, i.e. the government budget restriction is $M_t - M_{t-1} = P_t T_t$ which implies that the transfer in period $t + 1$ is:

$$T_{t+1} = \frac{M_{t+1} - M_t}{P_{t+1}} = \frac{\mu M_t}{P_t} \frac{P_t}{P_{t+1}} = \frac{\mu m_t}{1 + \pi_t}. \tag{12.44}$$

Equilibrium in the model requires both money and goods markets to be in equilibrium in all periods. By Walras' Law, however, the goods market is in equilibrium provided the money market is, i.e. provided demand and supply are equated in the money market:

$$m(T_{t+1}, \pi_t) = M_t/P_t, \tag{12.45}$$

where $m(.)$ is a function, representing the demand for money by the young in period t, which is implied by the first-order conditions (12.39)–(12.42). For example, if the felicity function in (12.37) is logarithmic, $U(x) \equiv \log x$, then this money demand function has the following form:

$$m_t = \begin{cases} m(T_{t+1}, \pi_t) = \dfrac{Y - (1 + \rho)(1 + \pi_t)T_{t+1}}{2 + \rho} & \text{if } \pi_t < \delta \\ 0 & \text{if } \pi_t > \delta. \end{cases} \tag{12.46}$$

The model consists of (12.44) and (12.45) and we are looking for a sequence of price levels $(P_t, P_{t+1}, \text{etc.})$ such that the equilibrium condition (12.44) holds for all periods given the postulated money supply process. For the logarithmic felicity function the solution is quite simple and can be obtained by substituting (12.44) into the first line of (12.46) and solving for the equilibrium level of real money balances:

$$m_t = \frac{Y}{2 + \rho + \mu(1 + \rho)} \quad \Leftrightarrow \quad P_t = \left(\frac{2 + \rho + \mu(1 + \rho)}{Y}\right) M_t. \tag{12.47}$$

This expression, which is only valid if $\pi_t < \delta$, shows that real money balances are constant so that the price level is proportional to the nominal money supply and the inflation rate is equal to the rate of growth of the money supply ($\pi_t = \mu$). So we reach the conclusion that, provided the money growth rate μ is less than the depreciation rate δ, intrinsically useless fiat money will be held by agents in a general equilibrium setting. Intuitively, money is the best available financial instrument to serve as a store of value as it outperforms the storage technology in that case. Of course, if the storage technology yields net productivity ($\delta < 0$) then the monetary equilibrium will only obtain if the money growth rate is negative ($\mu < \delta < 0$), i.e. if there is a constant rate of deflation of the price level. In contrast, if goods are perishable ($\delta \rightarrow \infty$) then the monetary equilibrium will always hold since money represents the only store of value in that case.

The existence of a monetary equilibrium is quite tenuous in the overlapping-generations model. Indeed, if $\mu > \delta$ then the storage technology outperforms money as a store of value and consequently the demand for real money balances will be zero (see the second line in (12.46)). Despite the fact that fiat money exists ($M_t > 0$) and is distributed to agents in the economy, it is not used by these agents as a store of value. This implies that money is valueless and the nominal price level is infinite, i.e. $1/P_t = 0$ for all t.

12.3.2 Uncertainty and the demand for money

In the basic model discussed in section 2.1 above, the respective yields on money and bonds are known by the agent who consequently only has to compare these yields in order to decide upon the optimal instrument to use as a store of value. In the basic model the yield on bonds is higher than that on money so that only the former are used as a store of value. In this section we introduce a friction into the basic model by assuming that the yield on bonds (though higher on average than that on money) is not known with certainty by the agent when making his decisions regarding consumption and saving in the first period. Sandmo (1970, p. 353) refers to this situation as one in which there exists *capital risk*; the investor is uncertain as to the yield on his investment. We assume that endowment income in both periods is known with certainty (there is no *income risk*). Furthermore, the yield on money is known with certainty so that money constitutes a "safe" asset from the point of view of the investor. To simplify the notation somewhat we define the yield on money as $1 + r_t^M \equiv 1/(1 + \pi_t)$. The periodic budget identities (12.1)–(12.2) can then be expressed in real terms as:

$$Y_1^* + \left(1 + r_0^M\right) m_0 + (1 + r_0)b_0 = C_1 + m_1 + b_1, \tag{12.48}$$

$$(1 + r_1^M)m_1 + (1 + \tilde{r}_1)b_1 = \tilde{C}_2, \tag{12.49}$$

where we have already incorporated the fact that $m_2 = b_2 = 0$. Note that Y_1^* represents the present value of present and future endowment income, capitalized at the risk-free rate, i.e. $Y_1^* \equiv Y_1 + Y_2/(1 + r_1^M)$. The tilde above r_1 denotes that the yield on bonds is a stochastic variable, the realization of which (r_1) will only be known to the agent at the end of the first period, i.e. after consumption and savings plans have been made (C_1, m_1, b_1).[8] This means (by (12.49)) that consumption in the second

[8] Of course, r_0 is not stochastic as it is a realization of $\tilde{r}_0$ which is known at the beginning of the first period.

period is also a stochastic variable, i.e. $\tilde{C}_2$ appears in (12.49). In the terminology of Drèze and Modigliani (1972, p. 309) the model implies that investing in bonds represents a *temporal uncertain prospect*, i.e. time must elapse before the uncertainty is removed.

Below it will turn out to be useful to write the budget identities (12.48)–(12.49) in a slightly different manner:

$$Y_1^* + A_1 = C_1 + \frac{\tilde{A}_2}{(1 + r_1^M)\omega_1 + (1 + \tilde{r}_1)(1 - \omega_1)}, \tag{12.50}$$

$$\tilde{A}_2 = \tilde{C}_2, \tag{12.51}$$

where $A_t \equiv (1 + r_{t-1}^M)m_{t-1} + (1 + r_{t-1})b_{t-1}$ represents total assets inclusive of interest receipts available at the beginning of period t and where $\omega_1 \equiv m_1/(m_1 + b_1)$ represents the portfolio share of money. In the first period the agent chooses consumption C_1 and the portfolio share ω_1, not knowing how high will be the value of his assets at the beginning of the second period because the yield on the risky investment is uncertain.

Since $\tilde{r}_1$ (and thus $\tilde{C}_2$ and $\tilde{A}_2$) is stochastic, the agent must somehow evaluate the utility value of the uncertain prospect $\tilde{C}_2$. The theory of *expected utility*, which was developed by Von Neumann and Morgenstern (1944) postulates (as indeed its name suggests) that the agent will evaluate the expected utility in order to make his optimal decision, i.e. instead of using V in (12.5) as the welfare indicator the agent uses the expected value of V, denoted by $E(V)$.[9] We assume that the agent bases his decisions on a subjective assessment of the probability distribution of the yield on his investment, the density function of which is given by $f(\tilde{r}_1)$. We furthermore assume that $\tilde{r}_1$ is restricted to lie in the interval $[-1, \infty)$, with the lower bound representing "losing your entire investment principal and all" and the upper bound denoting "striking it lucky by hitting the jackpot". Finally, we assume that the parameters of the model and the stochastic process for $\tilde{r}_1$ are such that we can ignore the non-negativity constraint for money holdings. Since there is no sign restriction on bond holdings, this means that we only need to study an internal optimum.

The expected utility of the agent can now be written as follows:

$$E(V) \equiv \int_{-1}^{\infty} \left[U(C_1) + \left(\frac{1}{1 + \rho} \right) U(\tilde{C}_2) \right] f(\tilde{r}_1) \, d\tilde{r}_1$$

$$= U(C_1) + \left(\frac{1}{1 + \rho} \right) \int_{-1}^{\infty} U[S_1 \left[(1 + r_1^M)\omega_1 + (1 + \tilde{r}_1)(1 - \omega_1) \right]] f(\tilde{r}_1) \, d\tilde{r}_1, \tag{12.52}$$

where $S_1 \equiv A_1 + Y_1^* - C_1$. The agent chooses C_1 (and thus S_1) and ω_1 in order to maximize his expected utility, $E(V)$. Straightforward computation yields the following

---

[9] The expected utility theory is discussed in more detail by Hirshleifer and Riley (1992).

first-order conditions (for ω_1 and C_1, respectively):

$$0 = (1 + \rho)^{-1} \int_{-1}^{\infty} U'(\tilde{C}_2)(A_1 + Y_1^* - C_1)(r_1^M - \tilde{r}_1)f(\tilde{r}_1)d\tilde{r}_1 \quad \Leftrightarrow$$

$$0 = E\left(U'(\tilde{C}_2)(A_1 + Y_1^* - C_1)(r_1^M - \tilde{r}_1)\right). \tag{12.53}$$

$$U'(C_1) = (1 + \rho)^{-1} \int_{-1}^{\infty} U'(\tilde{C}_2)\left[(1 + r_1^M)\omega_1 + (1 + \tilde{r}_1)(1 - \omega_1)\right]f(\tilde{r}_1)d\tilde{r}_1 \quad \Leftrightarrow$$

$$U'(C_1) = (1 + \rho)^{-1}EU'(\tilde{C}_2)\left[(1 + r_1^M) + (1 + \tilde{r}_1)(1 - \omega_1)\right], \tag{12.54}$$

Technically, (12.53) is the expression determining the optimal composition of the investment portfolio in terms of money (which has a certain yield r_1^M) and bonds (carrying a stochastic yield $\tilde{r}_1$). Intuitively (12.53) says that the expected marginal utility per dollar invested should be equated for the two assets (see Sandmo, 1969, pp. 588, 590). Equation (12.54) is the Euler equation, determining the optimal time profile of consumption, generalized for the existence of capital uncertainty.

In order to simplify the discussion, we now assume that the agent has a felicity function, $U(C_t)$, which takes the following, iso-elastic form:

$$U(C_t) = \begin{cases} (1/\gamma)\left[C_t^{\gamma} - 1\right] & \text{if } \gamma \neq 0 \\ \log C_t & \text{if } \gamma = 0, \end{cases} \tag{12.55}$$

where $\gamma < 1$ represents the *degree of risk aversion* exhibited by the agent (see below). The first-order condition for ω_1 (given in (12.53)) collapses to:

$$0 = E\left[\tilde{C}_2^{\gamma-1}(A_1 + Y_1^* - C_1)(r_1^M - \tilde{r}_1)\right]$$

$$= E\left[(A_1 + Y_1^* - C_1)^{\gamma}\left[(1 + r_1^M)\omega_1 + (1 + \tilde{r}_1)(1 - \omega_1)\right]^{\gamma-1}(r_1^M - \tilde{r}_1)\right]$$

$$= E\left[\left[(1 + r_1^M)\omega_1 + (1 + \tilde{r}_1)(1 - \omega_1)\right]^{\gamma-1}(r_1^M - \tilde{r}_1)\right]. \tag{12.56}$$

In going from the first to the second line we have substituted the expression for $\tilde{C}_2$ from (12.51), and in the final step we have made use of the fact that A_1, C_1, and Y_1^* are non-stochastic variables. Equation (12.56) implicitly determines the optimal portfolio share, ω_1^*, as a function of r_1^M, γ, and parameters characterizing the probability distribution of $\tilde{r}_1$. The important thing to note is that ω_1^* maximizes the subjective mean return on the portfolio, r^*, which is defined as:

$$(1 + r^*)^{\gamma} \equiv \max_{\omega_1} E\left[(1 + r_1^M)\omega_1 + (1 + \tilde{r}_1)(1 - \omega_1)\right]^{\gamma}$$

$$= E\left[(1 + r_1^M)\omega_1^* + (1 + \tilde{r}_1)(1 - \omega_1^*)\right]^{\gamma}. \tag{12.57}$$

For the iso-elastic felicity function (12.55), the first-order condition for C_1 (given in (12.54)) collapses to:

$$C_1^{\gamma-1} = (1+\rho)^{-1}E\left[\tilde{C}_2^{\gamma-1}\left[(1+r_1^M)\omega_1 + (1+\tilde{r}_1)(1-\omega_1)\right]\right]$$

$$= (1+\rho)^{-1}(A_1 + Y_1^* - C_1)^{\gamma-1}E\left[(1+r_1^M)\omega_1 + (1+\tilde{r}_1)(1-\omega_1)\right]^{\gamma}$$

$$= (1+\rho)^{-1}(A_1 + Y_1^* - C_1)^{\gamma-1}(1+r^*)^{\gamma} \quad \Rightarrow$$

$$C_1 = c\left[A_1 + Y_1^*\right], \tag{12.58}$$

where c is the marginal propensity to consume out of total wealth:

$$c \equiv \frac{(1+r^*)^{\gamma/(\gamma-1)}}{(1+\rho)^{1/(\gamma-1)} + (1+r^*)^{\gamma/(\gamma-1)}}. \tag{12.59}$$

In going from the second to the third line in (12.58) we have made use of the expression for r^* in (12.57). The striking thing to note about (12.58)–(12.59) is that the optimal consumption plan for the first period looks very much like the solution that would be obtained under certainty. Indeed, in the absence of uncertainty about the bond yield, maximization of lifetime utility would give rise to the expression in (12.58)–(12.59) but with r^* replaced by $\max[\bar{r}_1, r_1^M]$, where $\bar{r}_1$ is the certain return on bonds. Furthermore, in the case of a logarithmic felicity function ($\gamma = 0$), r^* drops out of (12.58)–(12.59) altogether and the capital risk does not affect present consumption at all (see Blanchard and Fischer (1989, p. 285) on this point).

With iso-elastic felicity functions, there thus exists a "separability property" between the savings problem (choosing when to consume) and the portfolio problem (choosing what to use as a savings instrument).[10] Since (as we shall see in subsequent chapters) modern macroeconomics makes almost exclusive use of such felicity functions, it is instructive to turn to a more detailed discussion of the pure portfolio problem. In doing so, we are not only able to characterize more precisely the factors influencing the choice of money versus bonds but it also allows us to introduce the liquidity preference theory of money that was developed by Tobin (1958). This so-called portfolio approach to money played a major role in macroeconomics in the 1960s and 1970s.

The portfolio decision

An important implication of the theory discussed above is that for a certain class of felicity functions, the expected-utility-maximizing household wishes to consume a fraction c of total wealth whilst saving the remaining fraction $1 - c$. Designating the amount to be invested by $S_1 = (1 - c)[A_1 + Y_1^*]$, the budget equation for the

[10] This was first demonstrated by Samuelson (1969b, pp. 243–245) in a multi-period discrete-time setting and generalized to continuous time for a more general class of felicity functions by Merton (1971). See also the discussion by Drèze and Modigliani (1972, pp. 317–323) on the separability property in the context of a two-period model with both capital and income risk.

portfolio problem is $S_1 = m_1 + b_1$ and the household wishes to choose m_1 and b_1 such as to maximize expected utility of end-of-period wealth, $E(U(\tilde{A}_2))$, where $\tilde{A}_2 \equiv S_1[(1 + r_1^M)\omega_1 + (1 + \tilde{r}_1)(1 - \omega_1)]$.

Stepping back somewhat from the specifics of our two-period model, the general form of the portfolio problem as analysed by Tobin (1958) and Arrow (1965) takes exactly this form. The investor chooses the portfolio share of money ω in order to maximize expected utility:

$$EU(\tilde{Z}), \quad \tilde{Z} \equiv S\big[(1 + r^M)\omega + (1 + \tilde{r})(1 - \omega)\big], \tag{12.60}$$

where $\tilde{Z}$ is end-of-period wealth, S is the amount to be invested, and r^M is the risk-free rate (S and r^M are both exogenously given parameters). The first-order condition for this problem is:

$$EU'(\tilde{Z})(r^M - \tilde{r}) = 0. \tag{12.61}$$

Apart from a slight change of notation, (12.61) coincides with the first-order condition for ω_1 in the two-period model (see (12.53) above).

In order to further develop intuition behind the first-order condition (12.61) we now turn to the *mean-variance model*, which can be seen as an approximation/special case of the model discussed so far.[11] The first step in the argument is to expand the utility function, $U(\tilde{Z})$, by means of a Taylor approximation around the expected value (or mean) of $\tilde{Z}$, denoted by $E(\tilde{Z})$:

$$U(\tilde{Z}) \approx U(E(\tilde{Z})) + U'(E(\tilde{Z}))\big[\tilde{Z} - E(\tilde{Z})\big] + \tfrac{1}{2}U''(E(\tilde{Z}))\big[\tilde{Z} - E(\tilde{Z})\big]^2$$
$$+ \tfrac{1}{6}U'''(E(\tilde{Z}))\big[\tilde{Z} - E(\tilde{Z})\big]^3 + \cdots \tag{12.62}$$

Taking expectations on both sides of (12.62) yields the (approximate) expression for expected utility:

$$EU(\tilde{Z}) \approx EU(E(\tilde{Z})) + EU'(E(\tilde{Z}))\big[\tilde{Z} - E(\tilde{Z})\big] + \tfrac{1}{2}EU''(E(\tilde{Z}))\big[\tilde{Z} - E(\tilde{Z})\big]^2 + \cdots$$
$$= U(E(\tilde{Z})) + \tfrac{1}{2}U''(E(\tilde{Z}))E\big[\tilde{Z} - E(\tilde{Z})\big]^2 + \cdots \tag{12.63}$$

In going from the first to the second line in (12.63) we use the fact that the expected value of a constant is that constant itself. The expected utility associated with end-of-period wealth can thus be approximated by the utility of expected wealth (first term on the right-hand side in the second line), a term involving the variance of end-of-period wealth (second term), plus higher-order terms subsumed in the dots.

The second step in the argument amounts to ignoring all higher-order terms in (12.63) so that preferences of the investor are (assumed to be) fully described by

---

[11] See Hirshleifer and Riley (1992, pp. 69–73) for a further discussion.

only the mean and the variance of end-of-period wealth; hence the name of the mean-variance approach. In summary, we write expected utility as:

$$EU(\tilde{Z}) = U(E(\tilde{Z})) - \eta E \left[\tilde{Z} - E(\tilde{Z}) \right]^2, \tag{12.64}$$

where $\eta \equiv -\frac{1}{2}U''(E(\tilde{Z}))$. The sign of η fully characterizes the investor's attitude towards risk. Indeed, if $\eta = 0$, the variance term drops out of (12.64) altogether and the investor is only interested in the expected value of end-of-period wealth. Such an investor, who totally disregards the variance of end-of-period wealth, is called *risk neutral*. In terms of Figure 12.4, the underlying utility function, $U(\tilde{Z})$, is simply a straight line from the origin ($U'(\tilde{Z}) > 0$ and $U''(\tilde{Z}) = 0$ in this case).

In real life, most people do care whether the return they receive is certain (has a zero variance) or is subject to fluctuations and can be much higher or lower than expected (has a positive variance). *Risk-averse* investors are therefore characterized by a positive value of η. In terms of Figure 12.4, a risk-averse investor has an underlying utility function which is concave ($U'(\tilde{Z}) > 0$ and $U''(\tilde{Z}) < 0$). In order to take on additional risk (a "bad" rather than a good) a risk-averse agent must be compensated in the form of a higher expected return, i.e. he must receive a *risk premium*. In formal terms the risk-premium, π_R, is such that the agent is indifferent between the risky prospect $\tilde{Z}$ and the certain prospect $E(\tilde{Z})$ (see Pratt, 1964):

$$U(E(\tilde{Z}) - \pi_R) = EU(\tilde{Z}). \tag{12.65}$$

In general π_R depends on the distribution of $\tilde{Z}$ but a simple example can be used to illustrate what is going on. Suppose that the distribution of $\tilde{Z}$ is such that $\tilde{Z} = Z_0 - h$

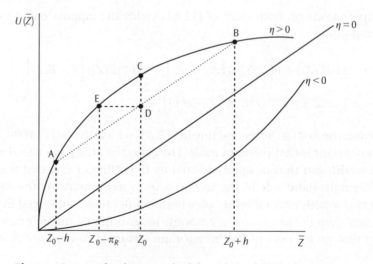

Figure 12.4. Attitude towards risk and the felicity function

or $\tilde{Z} = Z_0 + h$ with equal probability $\frac{1}{2}$ so that $E(\tilde{Z}) = Z_0$. The risk premium associated with this distribution is found by applying (12.65). In terms of Figure 12.4, the right-hand side of (12.65) is represented by point D which lies halfway along the straight line connecting points A and B. Concavity of the utility function ensures that the utility of the expected outcome, $U(E(\tilde{Z})) = U(Z_0)$, is higher than expected utility, $E(U(\tilde{Z}))$, i.e. point C lies above point D. To find the risk premium we must determine the certain prospect $(Z_0 - \pi_R)$ such that (12.65) holds. In Figure 12.4 this is done by going to point E, which lies directly to the left of point D. The horizontal distance between points D and E represents the risk premium π_R. In order to feel indifferent between, on the one hand, receiving $Z_0 - \pi_R$ for sure and, on the other hand, receiving $Z_0 - h$ or $Z_0 + h$ with equal probability, the risk-averse investor must receive a risk premium equal to π_R.

The third type of agent is described by (12.64) with a negative value for η inserted. Such an agent is called a *risk-lover* because he prefers an uncertain over a certain outcome when both have equal expected value. He thus enjoys the thrill of a gamble and is willing to pay (rather than receive) a risk premium. In terms of Figure 12.4, a risk-lover has a convex underlying utility function ($U'(\tilde{Z}) > 0$ and $U''(\tilde{Z}) > 0$). In the remainder of this section we focus attention on the portfolio behaviour of risk-averse investors.

Up to this point, we have described the agent's expected utility in terms of the variable $\tilde{Z}$ which is stochastic only because the return on the risky asset, $\tilde{r}$, is. Hence, the next step in our exposition of the mean-variance approach consists of postulating a particular probability distribution for $\tilde{r}$. A particularly simple and convenient distribution to choose in this context is the normal distribution:

$$\tilde{r} \sim N(\bar{r}, \sigma_R^2), \tag{12.66}$$

where "$\sim$" means "is distributed as," "N" stands for "normal or Gaussian distribution", $\bar{r}$ is the mean of the distribution, and σ_R^2 its variance. The advantage of working with the normal distribution lies in the fact that it is fully characterized by only two parameters, $\bar{r}$ and σ_R^2. All higher-order uneven terms, such as $E(\tilde{r} - \bar{r})^i$ (for $i = 3, 5, 7, \cdots$) are equal to zero as the distribution is symmetric around its mean. Furthermore, the higher-order even terms, such as $E(\tilde{r} - \bar{r})^i$ (for $i = 4, 6, 8, \cdots$) can be expressed in terms of $\bar{r}$ and σ_R^2 (Hirshleifer and Riley, 1992, p. 72). This implies that (12.63) can always be written as in (12.64) even without ignoring the higher-order terms, i.e. preferences are fully described by only two parameters. Another advantage of using the normal distribution is that it enables us to conduct simple comparative static experiments pertaining to $\bar{r}$ and σ_R^2 and the optimal portfolio choice below.

Armed with the distributional assumption in (12.66), the probability distribution of end-of-period wealth can be determined by noting the definition of $\tilde{Z}$ in (12.60). After some manipulation we derive that $\tilde{Z}$ is distributed normally (i.e. $\tilde{Z} \sim N(\bar{Z}, \sigma_Z^2)$)

with parameters depending on the portfolio fraction of money ω:

$$\bar{Z} \equiv E(\tilde{Z}) = S\left[(1 + r^M)\omega + (1 - \omega)(1 + \bar{r})\right],$$
$$\sigma_Z^2 \equiv E\left[\tilde{Z} - E(\tilde{Z})\right]^2 = S^2(1 - \omega)^2\sigma_R^2. \tag{12.67}$$

By manipulating the portfolio share of money, the investor can influence both the expected value of, and the risk associated with, end-of-period wealth. For example, if only money is held in the portfolio ($\omega = 1$), end-of-period wealth equals $S(1 + r^M)$ for sure ($\sigma_Z = 0$). This determines point A in Figure 12.5. The top panel of that figure plots combinations of expected return (vertical axis) and risk (horizontal axis), whilst the lower panel plots the relationship between risk and the portfolio share of money.[12] At the other extreme, if no money is held at all ($\omega = 0$), expected end-of-period wealth equals $S(1 + \bar{r})$ and the standard deviation is $\sigma_Z = S\sigma_R$. In order to have any non-trivial solution at all, the mean return on the risk asset must exceed that on money, otherwise a risk-averse agent would never hold any risky assets. Hence, $\bar{r} > r^M$ must be assumed to hold. This in turn ensures that point B lies north-east of point A in the top panel of Figure 12.5. By connecting points A and B in the top panel we obtain the upward-sloping constraint representing feasible trade-off opportunities between average return and risk. In the lower panel, σ_Z and ω are related by the second definition in (12.67) which can be rewritten as $1 - \omega = \sigma_Z/(\sigma_R S)$.

The final step in our exposition of the mean-variance model consists of introducing the appropriate indifference curve. According to (12.64), expected utility depends on both $\bar{r}$ and σ_R^2 and the indifference curve satisfies $dEU(\tilde{Z}) = U'(\bar{Z})d\bar{Z} - 2\eta\sigma_Z d\sigma_Z = 0$ from which we derive:

$$\frac{d\bar{Z}}{d\sigma_Z} = \frac{2\eta\sigma_Z}{U'(\bar{Z})} > 0, \quad \frac{d^2\bar{Z}}{d\sigma_Z^2} = 2\eta\left[\frac{U'(\bar{Z}) - \sigma_Z U''(\bar{Z})\left(d\bar{Z}/d\sigma_Z\right)}{\left[U'(\bar{Z})\right]^2}\right] > 0. \tag{12.68}$$

Hence, the typical indifference curve of a risk-averse agent is upward sloping and convex; see for example EU_0 in the top panel in Figure 12.5. Since expected return is a "good" and risk is a "bad" for such an agent, expected utility increases if the indifference curve shifts in a north-westerly direction.

It is clear from the slope configuration in Figure 12.5 that a risk-averse investor will typically choose a *diversified portfolio*.[13] Rather than choosing the safe haven of only money (point A) it is optimal for him to "trade risk for return", i.e. to accept some risk by holding a proportion of his portfolio in the form of the risky asset. In exchange the investor receives a higher expected yield on his portfolio. In Figure 12.5 the optimum occurs at point E_0 where the indifference curve is

---

[12] It is convenient to work with the standard deviation of $\tilde{Z}$ (rather than its variance) because it is in the same units as the mean of $\tilde{Z}$ which facilitates the economic interpretation to follow.

[13] For a discussion of possible corner solutions, see Tobin (1958, pp. 77–78).

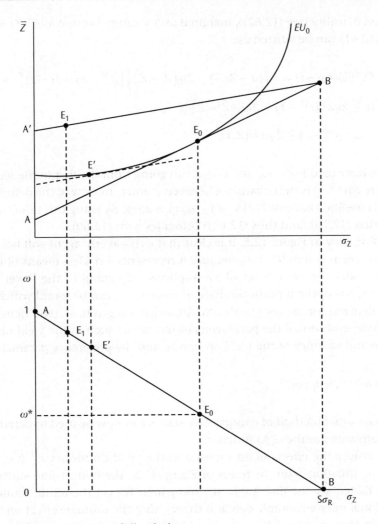

Figure 12.5. Portfolio choice

tangential to the budget line.[14] In technical terms we have:

$$\left(\frac{d\bar{Z}}{d\sigma_Z}\right)_{IC} \equiv \frac{2\eta\sigma_Z}{U'(\bar{Z})} = \frac{\bar{r} - r^M}{\sigma_R} \equiv \left(\frac{d\bar{Z}}{d\sigma_Z}\right)_{BL}. \tag{12.69}$$

The left-hand side of (12.69) represents the slope of the indifference curve (subscript "IC") whereas the right-hand side is the slope of the budget line (subscript "BL").

Although (12.69) looks different from (12.61), it is not difficult to show that the former is merely a special case of the latter. Since we work with a second-order

---

[14] The budget line is given by $\bar{Z} = S/[1 + \bar{r} + \omega(r^M - \bar{r})]$ which can be written in terms of σ_Z by noting that $1 - \omega = \sigma_Z/(\sigma_R S)$.

expansion of utility (see (12.62)), marginal utility can be written as $U'(\tilde{Z}) = a - 2\eta\tilde{Z}$, so that (12.61) can be written as:

$$
\begin{aligned}
0 = EU'(\tilde{Z})(r_M - \tilde{r}) &= E\left[(a - 2\eta\bar{Z}) - 2\eta\left(\tilde{Z} - \bar{Z}\right)\right]\left[(r^M - \bar{r}) - (\tilde{r} - \bar{r})\right] \\
&= (a - 2\eta\bar{Z})\left(r^M - \bar{r}\right) + 2\eta E\left(\tilde{Z} - \bar{Z}\right)(\tilde{r} - \bar{r}) \\
&= U'(\bar{Z})\left(r^M - \bar{r}\right) + 2\eta\text{cov}(\tilde{Z}, \tilde{r}),
\end{aligned}
\tag{12.70}
$$

where we have used $E(\tilde{Z}) = \bar{Z}$ and $E(\tilde{r}) = \bar{r}$ in going from the first to the second line and where $\text{cov}(\tilde{Z}, \tilde{r})$ is the covariance between $\tilde{Z}$ and $\tilde{r}$. In view of the definition of $\tilde{Z}$ in (12.61) we find that $\text{cov}(\tilde{Z}, \tilde{r}) = S(1 - \omega)\sigma_R^2 = \sigma_Z\sigma_R$. By using this result in (12.70) we find that (12.70) (and thus (12.61)) coincides with (12.69).

Returning now to Figure 12.5, it is clear that a risk-averse agent will hold money even if its return is zero ($r^M = 0$) because it represents a riskless means of investing (at least, under the present set of assumptions). By going to the lower panel of Figure 12.5, the optimal portfolio share of money, ω^*, can be found which implies that the demand for money equals $\omega^* S$. Although S is given, ω^* (and hence money demand) depends on all the parameters of the model such as the yield on money, the mean and variance of the yield on bonds, and the preference parameter(s):

$$
\omega^* = \omega^*(r^M, \bar{r}, \sigma_R^2, \eta).
\tag{12.71}
$$

The conventional method of comparative statics can now be used to determine the partial derivatives of the $\omega^*(.)$ function.

First consider the effects of an increase in the yield on money r^M (i.e. a reduction in the inflation rate). In terms of Figure 12.5, the budget line shifts up and becomes flatter; see the line A'B in the top panel. We get the result, familiar from conventional microeconomic demand theory, that the ultimate effect on the portfolio share of money (and thus money demand) can be decomposed into income and pure substitution effects. On the one hand, an increase in r^M narrows the yield gap between money and the risky asset which induces the investor to substitute towards the safe asset and to hold a higher portfolio share of money. This is the pure substitution effect represented in Figure 12.5 by the move from E_0 to E'. On the other hand, an increase in r^M also increases expected wealth and the resulting income (or wealth) effect also leads to an upward shift in ω. Hence, both income and substitution effects work in the same direction and the new optimum lies at point E_1, where the move from E' to E_1 represents the income effect.

In formal terms, the total effect on ω of an increase in r^M can be expressed in the form of a conventional Slutsky equation:

$$
\frac{\partial\omega}{\partial r^M} = \left(\frac{\partial\omega}{\partial r^M}\right)_{dEU=0} + \omega S\left(\frac{\partial\omega}{\partial\bar{Z}}\right) > 0,
\tag{12.72}
$$

where the first term on the right-hand side represents the pure substitution or "compensated" effect and the second term is the income effect:

$$\left(\frac{\partial \omega}{\partial r^M}\right)_{dEU=0} \equiv \frac{(1-\omega)\sigma_R^2}{(\bar{r}-r^M)\left[\sigma_R^2+(r^M-\bar{r})^2\right]} > 0, \qquad (12.73)$$

$$\left(\frac{\partial \omega}{\partial \bar{Z}}\right) \equiv \frac{\bar{r}-r^M}{S\left[\sigma_R^2+(r^M-\bar{r})^2\right]} > 0. \qquad (12.74)$$

The second, much more interesting, comparative static experiment concerns the effect on the money portfolio share of an increase in the expected yield on the risky asset. Throughout this book we have made use of money demand functions which are downward sloping in "the" interest rate, i.e. in terms of our model we have implicitly assumed that $\partial \omega/\partial \bar{r}$ is negative. The question is now whether this result is actually necessarily true in our model. In terms of Figure 12.6, an increase in $\bar{r}$ causes the budget line to rotate in a counter-clockwise fashion around point A. In contrast to the previous case, income and substitution effects now operate in opposite directions and the Slutsky equation becomes:

$$\frac{\partial \omega}{\partial \bar{r}} = \left(\frac{\partial \omega}{\partial \bar{r}}\right)_{dEU=0} + (1-\omega)S\left(\frac{\partial \omega}{\partial \bar{Z}}\right) > 0, \qquad (12.75)$$

where $(\partial \omega/\partial \bar{r})_{dEU=0} = -(\partial \omega/\partial r^M)_{dEU=0} < 0$ and where $(\partial \omega/\partial \bar{Z}) > 0$ (see (12.74)). In terms of Figure 12.6, the pure substitution effect is the move from E_0 to E' and the income effect is the move from E' to E_1^1 if the substitution effect dominates or E_1^2 if the income effect dominates. It is thus quite possible that money demand depends positively on the expected yield on the risky asset in the portfolio model of Tobin (1958). Under the usual assumption of a dominant substitution effect (which we have employed time and again throughout this book), however, the portfolio approach does indeed deliver a downward-sloping money demand function as postulated by Keynes and his followers.

The third and final comparative static experiment concerns the effect on money demand of the degree of risk associated with the risky asset as measured by the standard deviation of the yield, σ_R. In terms of Figure 12.7, a number of things happen if σ_R rises. First, in the top panel the budget line becomes flatter and rotates in a clockwise fashion around point A. In order to get the same expected return, the investor must be willing to hold a riskier portfolio, i.e. to accept a higher value of σ_Z. In the bottom panel, the line relating the standard deviation of the portfolio to the portfolio share of money becomes flatter and rotates in a counter-clockwise fashion around point A. The Slutsky equation associated with the change in σ_R is:

$$\frac{\partial \omega}{\partial \sigma_R} = \left(\frac{\partial \omega}{\partial \sigma_R}\right)_{dEU=0} - (1-\omega)S\left[(\bar{r}-r^M)/\sigma_R\right]\left(\frac{\partial \omega}{\partial \bar{Z}}\right) > 0, \qquad (12.76)$$

where $\partial \omega/\partial \bar{Z}$ is given in (12.74) and the pure substitution effect is given by:

$$\left(\frac{\partial \omega}{\partial \sigma_R}\right)_{dEU=0} \equiv \frac{(1-\omega)\left[2\sigma_R^2+(r^M-\bar{r})^2\right]}{\sigma_R\left[\sigma_R^2+(r^M-\bar{r})^2\right]} > 0. \qquad (12.77)$$

337

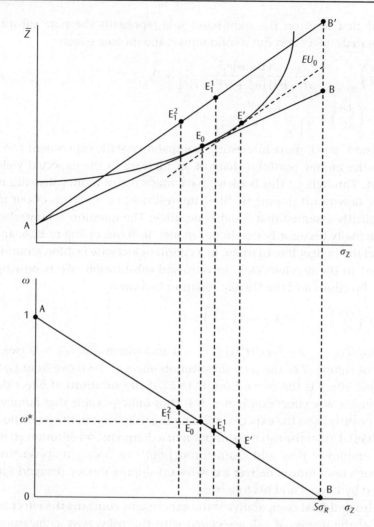

Figure 12.6. Portfolio choice and a change in the expected yield on the risky asset

The substitution effect dominates the income effect and money demand rises if the return on the risky asset becomes more volatile.

12.4 The Optimal Quantity of Money

In the previous two sections we have reviewed the main models of money which have been proposed in the postwar literature. We now change course somewhat by

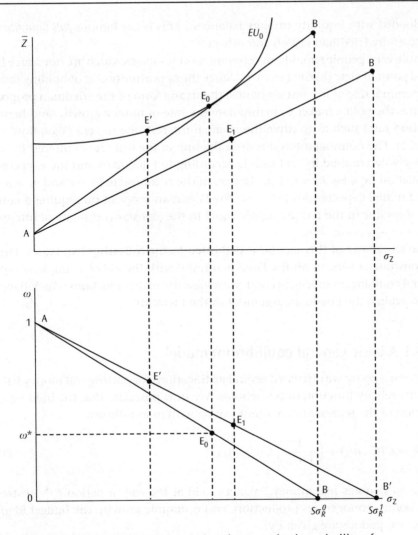

Figure 12.7. Portfolio choice and an increase in the volatility of the risky asset

taking for granted that money exists and plays a significant role in the economic process and by posing the question concerning the socially optimal quantity of money. If fiat money is useful to economic agents then how much of it should the policy maker bring into circulation? This question received an unambiguous answer from Friedman (1969). Social optimality requires marginal social benefits and costs of money to be equated. Since the production of fiat money (intrinsically useless tokens) imposes little or no costs on society, the money supply should be expanded up to the point where the marginal benefit of money is (close to) zero and agents are flooded with liquidity (money balances). This is the famous *full liquidity* result proposed by Friedman (1969) and others.[15]

Intuitively, people should not economize on resources which are not scarce from a social point of view (like fiat money). Since the opportunity cost of holding money is the nominal rate of interest on bonds, the strong form of the Friedman proposition requires the policy maker to manipulate the rate of money growth (and hence the inflation rate) such as to drive the *nominal* interest rate to zero (Woodford, 1990, p. 1071). The nominal interest is itself the sum of the real rate of interest (r_t, which is largely determined by real factors according to Friedman) and the expected rate of inflation (π_t^e), i.e. $R_t = r_t + \pi_t^e$. Hence, in the steady state ($r_t = r$ and $\pi_t = \mu_t$) and with fulfilled expectations ($\pi_t^e = \pi_t$) the Friedman proposition requires a constant rate of decline in the money supply equal to the (constant) real rate of interest, i.e. $R_t = 0 \Leftrightarrow -\mu_t = -\pi_t = r$.

The remainder of this section is dedicated to the following two issues. First, we demonstrate (a version of) the Friedman result with the aid of a simple two-period general equilibrium model. Second, we review the main objections which have been raised against the Friedman argument in the literature.

12.4.1 A basic general equilibrium model

In section 2 above we discussed several justifications for putting real money balances into the felicity function of households. We now postulate that the lifetime utility function of the representative agent can be written as follows:

$$V = U(C_1, m_1) + \left(\frac{1}{1+\rho}\right) U(C_2, m_2), \tag{12.78}$$

where m_t denotes real money balances held at the *end* of period t.[16] Abstracting from bonds, endogenous production, and economic growth, the budget identities in the two periods are given by:

$$P_1 Y + M_0 + P_1 T_1 = P_1 C_1 + M_1, \tag{12.79}$$

$$P_2 Y + M_1 + P_2 T_2 = P_2 C_2 + M_2, \tag{12.80}$$

where M_0 is given and $P_t T_t$ represents lump-sum cash transfers received from the government. The representative agent takes these transfers as parametrically given in making his optimal plans, but in general equilibrium they are endogenously determined.

---

[15] Other important contributors to the debate are Bailey (1956) and Samuelson (1968b, 1969a). An excellent survey of this vast literature is Woodford (1990).

[16] We thus change the timing of the utility-yielding effect of money in comparison to the arguments in section 2. We do so in order to simplify the argument and to retain consistency with Brock's (1975) model of which our model is a special case.

We postulate a simple money supply process according to which the rate of nominal money growth is constant:

$$\frac{\Delta M_t}{M_{t-1}} = \mu,$$ (12.81)

where μ is a policy instrument of the government. The increase in the nominal money supply is disbursed to the representative agent in the form of lump-sum transfers:

$$P_t T_t = \Delta M_t.$$ (12.82)

The household chooses C_t and M_t (for $t = 1, 2$) in order to maximize (12.78) subject to (12.79)–(12.80). Assuming an interior solution, the first-order conditions for this problem are:

$$\frac{U_C(C_1, m_1)}{P_1} = \frac{U_m(C_1, m_1)}{P_1} + \left(\frac{1}{1+\rho}\right)\frac{U_C(C_2, m_2)}{P_2},$$ (12.83)

$$U_C(C_2, m_2) = U_m(C_2, m_2),$$ (12.84)

where $U_C(.) \equiv \partial U(.)/\partial C_t$ and $U_m(.) \equiv \partial U(.)/\partial m_t$. Equation (12.83) says that the marginal utility of spending one dollar on consumption (the left-hand side) must be equated to the marginal utility obtained by holding one dollar in the form of money balances (the right-hand side). The latter is itself equal to the marginal utility due to reduced transaction costs (first term) plus that due to the store-of-value function of money (second term). In the final (second) period, money is not used as a store of value so only the transactions demand for money motive is operative. This is what the expression in (12.84) says.

In the absence of goods consumption by the government, and public and private investment, the product market clearing condition says that endowment income equals private consumption in both periods:

$$Y = C_1 = C_2.$$ (12.85)

By multiplying the expression in (12.83) by M_1 and using (12.81), (12.84), and (12.85), the perfect foresight equilibrium for the economy can be written as:

$$[U_C(Y, m_1) - U_m(Y, m_1)]\, m_1 = \frac{m_2 U_C(Y, m_2)}{(1+\rho)(1+\mu)},$$ (12.86)

$$U_C(Y, m_2) = U_m(Y, m_2).$$ (12.87)

These two equations recursively determine the equilibrium values for the real money supply. The trick is to work backwards in time. First, equation (12.87) is solved for m_2. Second, by using this optimal value, say m_2^*, in the right-hand side of (12.86), an equation determining m_1^* is obtained. Since the path of the nominal money supply is determined by the policy maker, the nominal price level associated with the solution is given by $P_t^* \equiv M_t/m_t^*$.

In our simple two-period model the solution method is quite simple, but the bulk of the literature on the optimal money supply is based on the notion of an infinitely lived representative agent for which a general solution is much harder to obtain. Indeed, in that literature the discussion is often based on simple special cases. In order to facilitate comparison with that literature and to simplify the exposition of our model, we now assume that the felicity function is *additively separable*:

$$U(C_t, m_t) \equiv u(C_t) + v(m_t), \tag{12.88}$$

with $u'(C_t) > 0$, $u''(C_t) < 0$, $v'(m_t) > 0$ for $0 < m_t < m^*$, $v'(m_t) = 0$ for $m_t = m^*$, $v'(m_t) < 0$ for $m_t > m^*$ and $v''(m_t) < 0$. Marginal utility of consumption is positive throughout but satiation with money balances is possible provided the real money supply is sufficiently high.

By using (12.88) in (12.86)–(12.87) we obtain:

$$\left[u'(Y) - v'(m_1)\right] m_1 = \frac{m_2 u'(Y)}{(1 + \rho)(1 + \mu)} \tag{12.89}$$

$$u'(Y) = v'(m_2). \tag{12.90}$$

In Figure 12.8 these two equilibrium conditions have been drawn. Equation (12.90) is represented by the horizontal line TC, where "TC" stands for "terminal condition". Equation (12.89) is an Euler-like equation and is drawn in the figure as the upward-sloping EE line.[17] The equilibrium is at point E_0. Before going on to the issue of social optimality of the perfect foresight equilibrium at E_0, it is instructive to conduct some comparative dynamic experiments. An increase in the money growth rate, for example, leads to an upward shift in the EE line, say to EE_1 in Figure 12.8. The equilibrium shifts to E_1 and real money balances in the first period fall, i.e. $dm_1^*/d\mu < 0$. Hence, even though only the level of future nominal money balances is affected (M_1 stays the same and M_2 rises), the rational representative agent endowed with perfect foresight foresees the consequences of higher money growth and as a result ends up bidding up the nominal price level not only in the future but also in the present. A similar effect is obtained if the rate of pure time preference is increased.

12.4.2 The satiation result

We have seen that, in our simple two-period model, the optimal real money balances in the two periods are determined recursively by the expressions in (12.86)–(12.87)

---

[17] The slope of the EE line is:
$$\frac{dm_2}{dm_1} = \frac{(1 + \rho)(1 + \mu)\left[u'(Y) - v'(m_1) - m_1 v''(m_1)\right]}{u'(Y)} > 0.$$

and can thus be expressed as implicit functions of taste and endowment parameters and the money growth rate, i.e. we can write $m_1^* = m_1^*(\rho, Y, \mu)$ and $m_2^* = m_2^*(\rho, Y, \mu)$. For the separable case of (12.88) these implicit functions feature the following partial derivatives with respect to the money growth rate: $\partial m_1^*/\partial \mu < 0$ and $\partial m_2^*/\partial \mu = 0$. Since the rate of money growth is a policy variable it follows that the policy maker has the instrument needed to influence the equilibrium of money balances, at least in the first period. By substituting $m_t^*(.)$ and (12.85) into the utility function of the representative agent (12.88) we obtain:

$$V = u(Y) + v\left(m_1^*(\rho, Y, \mu)\right) + \left(\frac{1}{1+\rho}\right)\left[u(Y) + v\left(m_2^*(\rho, Y)\right)\right]. \tag{12.91}$$

A utilitarian policy maker can pursue an optimal monetary policy by choosing the money growth rate for which the welfare of the representative agent is at its highest level. By maximizing (12.91) by choice of μ we obtain (a variant of) the Friedman satiation result:

$$\frac{dV}{d\mu} = v'\left(m_1^*(\rho, Y, \mu^*)\right)\left(\frac{dm_1^*}{d\mu}\right) = 0 \quad \Rightarrow \quad v'\left(m_1^*(\rho, Y, \mu^*)\right) = 0, \tag{12.92}$$

where μ^* is the optimal money growth rate. This optimal growth rate of the money supply is such that the corresponding demand for current real money balances chosen by the representative household is such that the marginal utility of these balances is zero (and thus equal to the social cost of producing these balances). In terms of Figure 12.8, the social optimum is at point E^{SO} and corresponds to a higher level of real money balances and a lower money growth rate than at point E_0.

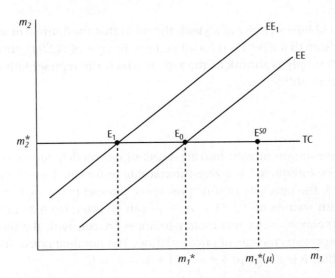

Figure 12.8. Monetary equilibrium in a perfect foresight model

The satiation result does not hold in the final period, of course, as the terminal condition pins down a positive marginal utility of money balances needed for transaction purposes (see (12.87)). It is straightforward to generalize the Friedman result to a setting with an infinitely lived representative agent.[18] In that case terms like $(1+\rho)^{t-1}U(C_t, m_t)$ are added to the utility function in (12.78) and budget equations like $P_t Y + M_{t-1} + P_t T_t = P_t C_t + M_t$ are added to (12.79) (both for $t = 3, 4, 5, \ldots, \infty$). Equation (12.86) is then generalized to:

$$\left[u'(Y) - v'(m_t)\right] m_t = \frac{m_{t+1} u'(Y)}{(1+\rho)(1+\mu)} \quad (t = 1, 2, 3, \ldots, \infty). \tag{12.93}$$

The thing to note about (12.93) as compared to (12.89)–(12.90) is that the terminal condition is no longer relevant. Brock (1975, pp. 138–141) shows that the equilibrium solution to (12.93) will in fact be the steady-state solution for which $m_t = m_{t+1} = m^*$:

$$v'(m^*) = \left[1 - \frac{1}{(1+\rho)(1+\mu)}\right] u'(Y) \quad \Rightarrow \tag{12.94}$$

$$\frac{dm^*}{d\mu} = \frac{u'(Y)}{(1+\rho)(1+\mu)^2 v''(m^*)} < 0. \tag{12.95}$$

Since both the endowment and real money balances are constant over time, lifetime utility of the infinite lived representative agent is equal to:

$$V = \left(\frac{1+\rho}{\rho}\right) \left[u(Y) + v\left(m^*(\mu)\right)\right]. \tag{12.96}$$

Maximizing (12.96) by choice of μ yields the result that the optimal money supply is such as to ensure that $v'(m^*) = 0$ for all periods. In view of (12.94), this is achieved if the money supply is shrunk at the rate at which the representative household discounts future utility:

$$\mu^* = -\frac{\rho}{1+\rho}. \tag{12.97}$$

Although there are no interest-bearing assets in our model, equation (12.97) can nevertheless be interpreted as a zero-interest rate result (see Turnovsky and Brock, 1980). Indeed, the pure rate of time preference represents the psychological costs associated with waiting and $\rho/(1+\rho)$ ($\approx \rho$) can be interpreted as the real rate of interest. Furthermore, since real money balances are constant, the money growth rate μ^* also represents the rate of price inflation. The nominal rate of interest in the optimum is thus $R \equiv \rho/(1+\rho) + \pi = \rho/(1+\rho) + \mu^* = 0$.

---

[18] Much of modern macroeconomic theory makes use of such a fictional agent. See e.g. section 4.4 below and Chapters 14–17.

12.4.3 Critiques of the full liquidity rule

The Friedman satiation rule, according to which the policy maker should use its money growth instrument in order to drive the marginal utility of real money balances to zero, has come under severe criticism in the literature. We now wish to demonstrate the two most important mechanisms by which the full liquidity result is invalidated. In order to do so we return to the two-period setting but we enrich the basic model of section 4.1 above by moving from an endowment to a production economy and by introducing (potentially) distorting taxes.

Introducing endogenous production

We assume that the representative household derives utility not only from consumption of goods and real money balances but also from leisure. Hence, equation (12.78) is replaced by:

$$V = U(C_1, 1 - L_1, m_1) + \left(\frac{1}{1 + \rho}\right) U(C_2, 1 - L_2, m_2), \qquad (12.98)$$

where the time endowment is unity, L_t is labour supply, and $1 - L_t$ is leisure in period t $(= 1, 2)$. The household budget identities in the two periods are:

$$W_1^N(1 - \tau_1)L_1 + M_0 + P_1 T_1 = P_1 C_1 + M_1, \qquad (12.99)$$

$$W_2^N(1 - \tau_2)L_2 + M_1 + P_2 T_2 = P_2 C_2 + M_2, \qquad (12.100)$$

where M_0 is given, $P_t T_t$ represents lump-sum cash transfers received from the government, W_t^N is the nominal wage rate, and τ_t is the tax rate on labour. To keep things simple we assume that production is subject to constant returns to scale and that the production function is given by $Y_t = L_t$. Perfectly competitive producers set price equal to marginal cost which implies that $P_t = W_t^N$. As before, the government does not consume any goods so that the goods market clearing condition requires consumption by households to equal production in both periods. In summary, we have that:

$$C_t = Y_t = L_t, \quad W_t^N = P_t. \qquad (12.101)$$

Rather than analysing the behaviour of the representative household and firm separately, it is legitimate to incorporate (12.101) into (12.99)–(12.100) and to have the household-producer choose consumption (and thus production) and real money balances directly. Assuming an interior solution, the first-order conditions characterizing the optimum are given by:

$$U_{1-L}(x_t) = (1 - \tau_1)U_C(x_t), \quad t = 1, 2, \qquad (12.102)$$

$$[U_C(x_1) - U_m(x_1)] m_1 = \frac{m_2 U_C(x_2)}{(1 + \rho)(1 + \mu)}, \qquad (12.103)$$

$$U_C(x_2) = U_m(x_2), \qquad (12.104)$$

where $x_t \equiv [C_t, 1 - C_t, m_t]$ and we have used the definition of the money growth rate (given in (12.81)) to simplify (12.103). Equation (12.102) shows that the household equates the marginal rate of substitution between leisure and consumption to the after-tax wage in both periods. Equations (12.103)–(12.104) generalize (12.86)–(12.87) by accounting for an endogenous labour supply (and thus production) choice. Armed with this minor modification to our original model, the robustness of the full liquidity result can be examined.

Non-separability

The model is solved recursively by working backwards in time, just as in section 4.1 above. We assume that both tax rates are constant. Equations (12.102) (for $t = 2$) and (12.104) then pin down optimal levels of consumption (and labour supply) and money balances for the final period (C_2^* and m_2^*, respectively) which are constant and independent of the rate of money growth μ. Given these values for C_2^* and m_2^*, equations (12.102) (for period $t = 1$) and (12.103) together constitute a system of implicit equations expressing C_1^* and m_1^* in terms of the rate of money growth μ (as well as ρ, τ_1, and τ_2, but these are held constant). Denoting these implicit functions by $C_1^*(\mu)$ and $m_1^*(\mu)$, we obtain the following derivatives by means of standard techniques:

$$\frac{dC_1^*}{d\mu} = \frac{m_2^* \left[U_{1-L,m} - (1 - \tau_1)U_{Cm} \right]}{(1 + \rho)(1 + \mu)^2 |\Delta|}, \tag{12.105}$$

$$\frac{dm_1^*}{d\mu} = -\frac{m_2^* \left[U_{1-L,C} - U_{1-L,1-L} - (1 - \tau_1)\left(U_{CC} - U_{C,1-L} \right) \right]}{(1 + \rho)(1 + \mu)^2 |\Delta|}, \tag{12.106}$$

where $|\Delta|$ is the (negative) Jacobian of the system and where the partial derivatives U_{CC}, U_{Cm}, $U_{C,1-L}$, $U_{1-L,1-L}$, and $U_{1-L,m}$ are all evaluated in the optimum point (C_1^*, $1 - C_1^*, m_1^*$).

The expression in (12.106) shows that the sign of $dm_1^*/d\mu$ is ambiguous in the generalized model. The existence of diminishing marginal utility of leisure and consumption ensures that $U_{1-L,1-L}$ and U_{CC} are both negative, but the cross-term, $U_{1-L,C} \equiv U_{C,1-L}$, can have either sign. Turnovsky and Brock (1980, p. 197) argue that it is reasonable to assume on economic grounds that $U_{C,1-L}$ is positive, i.e. the marginal utility of consumption rises with leisure. With that additional assumption it is clear that optimal money holdings in the current period fall as the money growth rate is increased, i.e. $dm_1^*/d\mu < 0$. This conclusion generalizes our earlier result obtained for the basic model of section 4.1 above (see (12.95)).

As the expression in (12.105) shows, the sign of $dC_1^*/d\mu$ is also ambiguous in general as it depends on the cross-partial derivatives $U_{1-L,m}$ and U_{Cm} which can have either sign and about which economic theory does not suggest strong priors. In economic terms the ambiguity arises because it is not a priori clear how (or even whether) the rate of money growth affects the marginal rate of substitution between consumption and leisure, i.e. how μ influences the consumption-leisure trade-off.

The issue can be investigated more formally by writing the marginal rate of substitution between leisure and consumption (for period $t = 1$) in a general functional form as $g(C_1, m_1)$:

$$g(C_1, m_1) \equiv \frac{U_{1-L}(C_1, 1 - C_1, m_1)}{U_C(C_1, 1 - C_1, m_1)}. \tag{12.107}$$

By partially differentiating $g(.)$ with respect to m_1 we obtain the following result:

$$\begin{aligned} g_m(C_1, m_1) &= \frac{U_C U_{1-L,m} - U_{1-L} U_{Cm}}{[U_C]^2} \\ &= \frac{U_{1-L,m} - g(C_1, m_1) U_{Cm}}{U_C} \\ &= \frac{U_{1-L,m} - (1 - \tau_1) U_{Cm}}{U_C}, \end{aligned} \tag{12.108}$$

where we have used (12.102) in the final step). The expression in (12.108) shows the intimate link which exists between $g_m(C_1, m_1)$ and the sign of $dC_1^*/d\mu$ in (12.105): if the marginal rate of substitution between leisure and consumption rises (falls) with real money balances, $g_m(C_1, m_1) > 0 \ (< 0)$, then an increase in the money growth rate leads to an increase (decrease) in goods consumption, i.e. $dC_1^*/d\mu > 0 \ (< 0)$.

The upshot of the discussion so far is that C_2^* and m_2^* do not depend on the rate of money growth and that C_1^* and m_1^* do so but in an ambiguous fashion. By plugging $C_1^*(\mu)$ and $m_1^*(\mu)$ into the utility function (12.98) we obtain an expression for household utility in terms of the policy variable μ:

$$V \equiv U\left(C_1^*(\mu), 1 - C_1^*(\mu), m_1^*(\mu)\right) + \left(\frac{1}{1+\rho}\right) U(C_2^*, 1 - C_2^*, m_2^*). \tag{12.109}$$

The policy maker selects the optimal money growth rate μ^* in order to maximize V, a problem which yields the following first-order condition:

$$\frac{dV}{d\mu} = \tau_1 U_C \left(\frac{dC_1^*}{d\mu}\right) + U_m \left(\frac{dm_1^*}{d\mu}\right) = 0, \tag{12.110}$$

where we have used equation (12.102) to simplify (12.110). Armed with this expression we can re-examine the validity of the Friedman full-liquidity result according to which μ^* should be set such as to drive the marginal utility of money balances to zero. Equation (12.110) shows the various cases under which this result continues to hold in our extended model. First, if there is no initial tax on labour in the first period ($\tau_1 = 0$) then the leisure-consumption choice is undistorted so that a change in the money growth rate does not create a first-order welfare effect even if it does affect consumption in the first period. In terms of (12.110), $U_C = U_{1-L}$ in that case and the sign (or magnitude) of $dC_1^*/d\mu$ does not matter. The first term on the right-hand side of (12.110) drops out and, provided $dm_1^*/d\mu \neq 0$, the optimal money growth rate entails driving U_m to zero.

The second case for which the satiation result obtains is one for which the tax is strictly positive ($\tau_1 > 0$) but consumption is independent of the money growth rate ($dC_1^*/d\mu = 0$). This case was emphasized by Turnovsky and Brock (1980). In terms of (12.110) and (12.108) this holds if the marginal rate of substitution between leisure and consumption does not depend on μ. If that result obtains, the felicity function $U(.)$ is said to be *weakly separable* in ($C_t, 1 - L_t$) on the one hand and m_t on the other. It can then be written as:

$$U(C_t, 1 - L_t, m_t) = U[Z(C_t, 1 - L_t), m_t], \tag{12.111}$$

where $Z(.)$ is some sub-felicity function. Note that (12.111) implies that the marginal rate of substitution between leisure and consumption only depends on the properties of $Z(.)$, as $U_{1-L}/U_C = U_Z Z_{1-L}/(U_Z Z_C) = Z_{1-L}/Z_C$ and thus does not depend on m_t.

In summary, the Friedman satiation result holds in our model if (i) there is no initial tax on labour income ($\tau_1 = 0$), and (ii) if τ_1 is positive but preferences display the weak separability property. In general, however, (12.109) implicitly defines the optimal money growth rate and U_m will not be driven to zero. Turnovsky and Brock refer to (12.110) as a "distorted" Friedman liquidity rule (1980, p. 197).

The government budget restriction

The second major argument against the validity of the Friedman result is based on the notion that steady-state inflation (caused by nominal money growth) can be seen as a tax on money balances and thus has repercussions for the government budget constraint especially in a "second-best" world in which lump-sum taxes are not available to the policy maker. In such a world, Phelps (1973) argues, government revenue must be raised by means of various distorting taxes, of which the "inflation tax" is only one. The literature initiated by Phelps is often called the "public finance" approach to inflation and optimal money growth. Briefly put, the Phelps approach is an application to monetary economics of the optimal taxation literature in the tradition of Ramsey (1927).[19] We return to the insights of Phelps (1973) below.

12.4.4 An infinite horizon model

Up to this point we have employed simple two-period models in order to demonstrate (some of) the key issues in monetary macroeconomics. Although such two-period models are convenient for some purposes, they also have some undesirable features. For example, as the model only distinguishes two periods ("today" and the "future"), there is no third period and the model economy "closes down" at the end of period 2. The aim of this subsection is to get rid of this rather unattractive feature of the model. To that effect, we develop a general equilibrium model of a

---

[19] We briefly discussed Ramsey taxation in the context of Chapter 10 above.

monetary economy in which the economy does not come to a full stop at some time in the future but instead runs on indefinitely through time. We subsequently use this multi-period model to demonstrate the validity of the Friedman rule under different assumptions regarding government financing.

Households

We assume that the behaviour of households in the economy can be captured with the fictional representative agent who is infinitely lived and has the following lifetime utility function:

$$V = \sum_{t=1}^{\infty} \left(\frac{1}{1+\rho}\right)^{t-1} U(C_t, 1 - L_t, m_t), \tag{12.112}$$

where the felicity function, $U(.)$, has the usual properties: (i) there is positive but diminishing marginal felicity for both consumption and leisure, (ii) there exists a satiation level for real money balances, $\bar{m}$, and (iii) marginal felicity of real money is diminishing. Since timing issues will prove extremely important below, we simplify the notation by defining $x_t \equiv [C_t, 1 - L_t, m_t]$ and by writing the properties of the felicity function as follows:

$$
\begin{aligned}
U_C(x_t) &\equiv \frac{\partial U(x_t)}{\partial C_t} > 0, & U_{CC}(x_t) &\equiv \frac{\partial^2 U(x_t)}{\partial C_t^2} < 0, \\
U_{1-L}(x_t) &\equiv \frac{\partial U(x_t)}{\partial [1 - L_t]} > 0, & U_{1-L,1-L}(x_t) &\equiv \frac{\partial^2 U(x_t)}{\partial [1 - L_t]^2} < 0, \\
U_m(x_t) &\equiv \frac{\partial U(x_t)}{\partial m_t} \gtreqless 0 \quad \text{for } m_t \lesseqgtr \bar{m}, & U_{mm}(x_t) &\equiv \frac{\partial^2 U(x_t)}{\partial m_t^2} < 0.
\end{aligned}
$$

$$\tag{12.113}$$

To keep the model as simple as possible we continue to abstract from physical capital, and assume that the representative household can shift resources through time by means of government bonds and/or money. The periodic budget constraint in period t $(= 1, 2, ...)$ is given in nominal terms by:

$$(1 + R_{t-1})B_{t-1} + W_t^N(1 - \tau_t)L_t + M_{t-1} + P_t T_t = P_t C_t + M_t + B_t, \tag{12.114}$$

where B_{t-1} is the stock of government bonds held at the end of period $t - 1$, R_{t-1} is the nominal interest on government bonds paid at the end of period $t - 1$, M_t is the stock of money balances at the beginning of period t, W_t^N is the nominal wage rate, τ_t is the proportional tax on labour income, and $P_t T_t$ is transfers received from the government. Equation (12.114) generalizes (12.1)–(12.2) by adding taxes and transfers, recognizing endogenous labour income (rather than exogenous endowment income), and by distinguishing multiple periods.

By dividing both sides of (12.114) by the current price level, P_t, we obtain the household's budget identity in real terms:

$$(1 + r_{t-1})b_{t-1} + W_t(1 - \tau_t)L_t + \frac{m_{t-1}}{1 + \pi_{t-1}} + T_t = C_t + m_t + b_t, \tag{12.115}$$

where $b_t \equiv B_t/P_t$ is the stock of real bonds, $W_t \equiv W_t^N/P_t$ is the real wage rate, $\pi_t \equiv P_{t+1}/P_t - 1$ is the inflation rate, and $r_t \equiv P_t(1+R_t)/P_{t+1} - 1$ is the real interest rate.

The household's budget identity is a difference equation in bond holdings, b_t, which can be solved forwards in time by repeated substitutions. After some tedious but straightforward manipulations we find the following general expression (see the appendix to this chapter):

$$A_0 = \sum_{t=1}^{1+k} q_t^0 \left[C_t + \left(\frac{R_t}{1 + R_t} \right) m_t - W_t(1 - \tau_t)L_t - T_t \right]$$

$$+ q_{k+1}^0 b_{k+1} + q_{k+1}^0 \left(\frac{m_{k+1}}{1 + R_{k+1}} \right), \tag{12.116}$$

where $A_0 \equiv (1 + r_0)b_0 + m_0/(1 + \pi_0)$ and q_t^0 is a rather complicated discount factor involving the real interest rates in future periods:

$$q_t^0 \equiv \begin{cases} 1 & \text{for } t = 1 \\ \prod_{i=1}^{t-1} \left(\frac{1}{1+r_i} \right) & \text{for } t = 2, 3, \ldots \end{cases} \tag{12.117}$$

By letting $k \to \infty$, we find that (12.116) simplifies to:

$$A_0 = \sum_{t=1}^{\infty} q_t^0 \left[C_t + \left(\frac{R_t}{1 + R_t} \right) m_t - W_t(1 - \tau_t)L_t - T_t \right], \tag{12.118}$$

provided the following so-called *transversality conditions* hold:

$$\lim_{k \to \infty} q_{k+1}^0 b_{k+1} = 0, \tag{12.119}$$

$$\lim_{k \to \infty} \frac{q_{k+1}^0 m_{k+1}}{1 + R_{t+k}} = 0. \tag{12.120}$$

We postpone a more extended discussion of transversality conditions to Chapter 14. *Intuitively*, equation (12.119) means that the household's assets (b_t positive) cannot grow faster than the rate of interest. In the case of household debt (b_t negative) the household would, of course, be perfectly happy to let the expression in (12.119) be negative but there will be no lenders in the market allowing this to happen. *Technically*, (12.119) is a terminal condition on the household's debt as time goes to infinity. It does the same thing in the infinite-horizon model as the assumption of $B_2 = 0$ does in the two-period model of section 12.2.1, namely to ensure that the household is *solvent*. The intuition behind (12.120) is similar.

Equation (12.118) is the present-value budget constraint of the household. It shows that the excess of spending on consumption and money balances over the after-tax wage income plus government transfers (right-hand side) must be equal in present-value terms to the pre-existing wealth of the household (left-hand side). Equation (12.118) is the infinite-horizon counterpart to (12.3).

The household chooses sequences for its consumption, labour supply, and real money balances (i.e. $\{C_t\}_{t=1}^{\infty}$, $\{L_t\}_{t=1}^{\infty}$, and $\{m_t\}_{t=1}^{\infty}$) in order to maximize lifetime utility (12.112) subject to the lifetime budget constraint (12.118). The Lagrangian expression associated with this optimization programme is:

$$\mathcal{L} \equiv \sum_{t=1}^{\infty} \left(\frac{1}{1+\rho}\right)^{t-1} U(C_t, 1 - L_t, m_t) \tag{12.121}$$

$$+ \lambda \left[A_0 - \sum_{t=1}^{\infty} q_t^0 \left[C_t + \left(\frac{R_t}{1+R_t}\right) m_t - W_t(1-\tau_t)L_t - T_t \right] \right],$$

where λ is the Lagrangian multiplier. The first-order conditions for an interior optimum are the constraint (12.118) and:

$$\frac{\partial \mathcal{L}}{\partial C_t} = 0: \quad \left(\frac{1}{1+\rho}\right)^{t-1} U_C(x_t) = \lambda q_t^0, \tag{12.122}$$

$$\frac{\partial \mathcal{L}}{\partial L_t} = 0: \quad \left(\frac{1}{1+\rho}\right)^{t-1} U_{1-L}(x_t) = \lambda q_t^0 W_t(1-\tau_t), \tag{12.123}$$

$$\frac{\partial \mathcal{L}}{\partial m_1} \equiv 0: \quad \left(\frac{1}{1+\rho}\right)^{t-1} U_m(x_t) = \lambda q_t^0 \left(\frac{R_t}{1+R_t}\right). \tag{12.124}$$

By eliminating the Lagrange multiplier from these expressions we obtain the usual conditions equating marginal rates of substitution to relative prices:

$$\frac{U_{1-L}(x_t)}{U_C(x_t)} = W_t(1-\tau_t), \tag{12.125}$$

$$\frac{U_m(x_t)}{U_C(x_t)} = \frac{R_t}{1+R_t}. \tag{12.126}$$

In each period, the marginal rate of substitution between leisure and consumption should be equated to the after-tax wage rate, whilst the marginal rate of substitution between real money balances and consumption should be equated to the opportunity cost of holding real money balances.

Firms, government, and Walras' Law

The firm sector is very simple. There is no capital in the economy and goods are produced with labour only. The production function is given by $Y_t = L_t$ and the representative firm maximizes profits, $\Pi_t \equiv P_t Y_t - W_t^N L_t$, given this linear technology. The perfectly competitive solution implies marginal cost pricing, $P_t = W_t^N$, i.e. the real wage rate is equal to unity:

$$W_t = 1, \tag{12.127}$$

and profits are zero ($\Pi_t = 0$).

The government budget identity is given in nominal terms by:

$$R_{t-1}B_{t-1} + P_t G_t + P_t T_t = \tau_t W_t^N L_t + (M_t - M_{t-1}) + (B_t - B_{t-1}), \tag{12.128}$$

where G_t is the consumption of goods by the government. The sum of spending on interest payments on outstanding debt plus government consumption and transfers to households (left-hand side) must be equal to the sum of the labour income tax revenue, newly issued money balances, and newly issued government debt (right-hand side). By dividing both sides of (12.128) by the current price level, and noting (12.4) and the definition of the real interest rate, we obtain the government budget identity in real terms:

$$(1 + r_{t-1})b_{t-1} + G_t + T_t = \tau_t W_t L_t + m_t - \left(\frac{m_{t-1}}{1 + \pi_{t-1}}\right) + b_t. \tag{12.129}$$

Before discussing the key features of the model we check Walras' Law. By combining the household budget identity (12.115) with the government budget identity (12.129) we obtain $W_t L_t = C_t + G_t$ (which is the resource constraint). But $W_t = 1$ (by (12.127)) and the production function implies $Y_t = L_t$ so it follows that $Y_t = C_t + G_t$. So, provided the household and government budget identities are satisfied, so is the economy-wide resource constraint.

The adjusted household budget constraint

In order to prepare for our discussion of the optimal rate of money growth it is useful to derive the so-called "adjusted household budget constraint" (Ljungqvist and Sargent, 2000, pp. 319–325). This adjusted budget constraint is obtained by substituting the household's first-order conditions (12.122)–(12.124) into the regular, unadjusted, household budget constraint (12.118). After some manipulation we obtain the following expression:

$$A_0 = \sum_{t=1}^{\infty} q_t^0 [C_t - T_t] + \sum_{t=1}^{\infty} q_t^0 \left(\frac{R_t}{1 + R_t}\right) m_t - \sum_{t=1}^{\infty} q_t^0 W_t (1 - \tau_t) L_t$$

$$= \frac{1}{\lambda} \sum_{t=1}^{\infty} \left(\frac{1}{1 + \rho}\right)^{t-1} [U_C(x_t) [C_t - T_t] + U_m(x_t) m_t - U_{1-L}(x_t) L_t], \tag{12.130}$$

where we have used (12.122)–(12.124) to get from the first to the second line. By applying (12.122) for $t = 1$ and noting that $q_1^0 = 1$ (from (12.117)) we derive that λ equals the marginal utility of consumption in the first period, i.e. $\lambda = U_C(x_1)$.

By substituting this result in (12.130) we obtain the final expression for the adjusted household budget constraint:

$$A_0 U_C(x_1) = \sum_{t=1}^{\infty} \left(\frac{1}{1+\rho} \right)^{t-1} [U_C(x_t)[C_t - T_t] + U_m(x_t)m_t - U_{1-L}(x_t)L_t]. \quad (12.131)$$

The advantage of working with (12.131) instead of with (12.118) is that the former expression no longer contains the distorting tax instruments of the government (namely τ_t and μ_t). This facilitates the characterization of the optimal taxation problem because the social planning problem can be conducted directly in quantities (rather than in terms of tax rates).[20]

Optimal money growth revisited

We now have all the ingredients needed to study the optimal tax problem of the government. The social planner chooses sequences for consumption, employment, and real money balances (i.e. $\{C_t\}_{t=1}^{\infty}$, $\{L_t\}_{t=1}^{\infty}$, and $\{m_t\}_{t=1}^{\infty}$) in order to maximize lifetime utility of the representative household (12.112) subject to the adjusted household budget constraint (12.131) and the economy-wide resource constraint $L_t = C_t + G_t$. We assume that the sequence of government consumption, $\{G_t\}_{t=1}^{\infty}$, is exogenously given. The Lagrangian associated with this optimization programme is:

$$\mathcal{L}_G \equiv \sum_{t=1}^{\infty} \left(\frac{1}{1+\rho} \right)^{t-1} \Big[U(C_t, 1 - L_t, m_t) + \lambda_t^G [L_t - C_t - G_t]$$

$$+ \theta^G \Big(U_C(x_t)[C_t - T_t] + U_m(x_t)m_t - U_{1-L}(x_t)L_t \Big) \Big]$$

$$- \theta^G A_0 U_C(x_1), \quad (12.132)$$

where θ^G is the Lagrange multiplier for the adjusted household budget constraint and $\{\lambda_t^G\}_{t=1}^{\infty}$ is the sequence of Lagrange multipliers for the resource constraint.

Let us first assume that the policy maker can freely adjust the level of transfers, T_t, in each period. It is clear that this scenario includes the case of lump-sum financing because negative transfers are allowed. What is the optimal rate of money growth in this economy? The first-order conditions for the sequence of transfers, $\{T_t\}_{t=1}^{\infty}$, take the following form:

$$\frac{\partial \mathcal{L}_G}{\partial T_t} = -\theta^G \left(\frac{1}{1+\rho} \right)^{t-1} U_C(x_t) = 0. \quad (12.133)$$

But, since the discounting factor on the right-hand side of (12.133) is strictly positive, and we have ruled out satiation of consumption ($U_C(x_t) > 0$—see (12.113)),

---

[20] The approach followed here is called the "primal" approach to the Ramsey problem because it uses outputs and the direct utility function. See Atkinson and Stiglitz (1980, pp. 376–382) for a discussion of the primal approach to Ramsey taxation in static models. Jones et al. (1997) and Ljungqvist and Sargent (2000, pp. 319–325) follow Lucas and Stokey (1983) by applying the primal methods in a dynamic context.

it follows from (12.133) that $\theta^G = 0$. Intuitively, the availability of the lump-sum instruments means that the adjusted household budget constraint does not represent a constraint on the social optimization programme. The remaining first-order conditions of the social plan are obtained by setting $\partial \mathcal{L}_G / \partial C_t = \partial \mathcal{L}_G / \partial L_t = \partial \mathcal{L}_G / \partial m_t = 0$ (for $t = 1, 2, \ldots$) and noting that $\theta^G = 0$. After some straightforward manipulation we find:

$$\frac{U_{1-L}(x_t)}{U_C(x_t)} = 1, \tag{12.134}$$

$$U_m(x_t) = 0. \tag{12.135}$$

Equation (12.134) shows that the marginal rate of substitution between leisure and consumption should be equated to the marginal rate of transformation between labour and goods (which is unity since the production function is linear). Equation (12.135) is the Friedman rule requiring the policy maker to satiate the representative household with money balances. Equations (12.134)–(12.135) characterize the socially optimal allocation in terms of quantities. In the final step we must find out what tax instruments the planner can use to ensure that these conditions hold in the decentralized economy. By comparing (12.134)–(12.135) to the first-order conditions for the household, given in (12.125)–(12.126), we find that they coincide if there is no tax on labour income and the nominal interest rate is zero, i.e. $\tau_t = R_t = 0$. With a constant level of government consumption ($G_t = G$ for all t) the optimal allocation is constant, i.e. $C_t = C$, $L_t = L$, $b_t = b$, $m_t = m$, $W_t = W$, and $T_t = T$ for all t. The real interest rate is equal to the rate of pure time preference, $r_t = \rho$, and, since the nominal rate is zero, it follows that the rate of inflation is constant and equal to $\pi_t = -\rho/(1 + \rho)$. Since m is constant, the rate of money growth equals the rate of inflation, i.e. $\mu_t = -\rho/(1 + \rho)$.

Ramsey taxation

Matters are not as simple if the policy maker does not have access to a freely adjustable lump-sum instrument like T_t. In the absence of such an instrument the policy maker is forced to raise the required revenue, needed to finance the government's consumption path, in a distortionary fashion, i.e. by means of a tax on labour income and/or by means of money growth (the inflation tax). In the remainder of this subsection we briefly sketch the complications which arise in this setting. As before, the social planner chooses sequences $\{C_t\}_{t=1}^{\infty}$, $\{L_t\}_{t=1}^{\infty}$, and $\{m_t\}_{t=1}^{\infty}$ which maximize (12.112) subject to (12.131) and the resource constraint $L_t = C_t + G_t$. We now assume, however, that $T_t = 0$ for all t.

The first-order conditions for an interior solution for real money balances is given by $\partial \mathcal{L}_G / \partial m_t = 0$ for all t. By using (12.132) we derive the following conditions for, respectively, m_1 and m_t $(t = 2, 3, \ldots)$:

$$U_m(x_1) + \theta^G \left[U_m(x_1) + m_1 U_{mm}(x_1)\right] + \theta^G (1 + r_0) U_{Cm}(x_1) = 0, \tag{12.136}$$

$$U_m(x_t) + \theta^G \left[U_m(x_t) + m_t U_{mm}(x_t)\right] = 0, \tag{12.137}$$

where the term involving $U_{Cm}(x_1)$ appearing in (12.136) is due to the fact that the marginal utility of consumption in the first period in general depends on real money balances. In contrast to the lump-sum case, the Lagrange multiplier θ^G is now strictly positive. Intuitively, θ^G measures the utility cost of raising government revenue through distortionary taxes (Ljungqvist and Sargent, 2000, p. 323). An immediate consequence which follows from the first-order conditions (12.136)–(12.137) is that the full liquidity rule is no longer optimal even if the felicity function is separable in consumption and real money balances (so that $U_{Cm}(x_t) = 0$). Indeed, in the separable case (12.136) and (12.137) coincide and can be simplified to:

$$U_m(x_t) = -m_t U_{mm}(x_t) \left(\frac{\theta^G}{1 + \theta^G}\right) > 0. \tag{12.138}$$

The optimal level of real money balances falls short of its satiation level and the Friedman result no longer obtains in this setting.

12.5 Punchlines

Money performs three major functions in the economy: it is a medium of exchange, serves as a store of value, and performs the role of a medium of account. Of these three functions, the first is the most distinguishing function of money. Despite the fact that every layman knows what money is (and what it can do) it has turned out to be difficult to come up with a convincing model of money. In the first part of this chapter we discuss some of the more influential models that have been proposed in the literature.

The medium of exchange role of money has been modelled by assuming that money reduces the transactions costs associated with the trading process between agents. In this view, the existence of money reduces the time needed for shopping. Since leisure is valued by the agents, the same holds for money. This so-called shopping cost approach is one way to rationalize the conventional practice in macroeconomic modelling of putting money balances directly into the household's utility function. The cash-in-advance approach is another possible rationalization for this practice.

The role of money as a store of value has been modelled in two major ways. In the first model, intrinsically useless money may be held if it allows agents to engage in intertemporal consumption smoothing *and* either (i) there are no other financial assets available for this purpose at all, or (ii) such assets exist but carry an inferior rate of return. The second model of money as a store of value is based on the notion that assets carrying a higher yield than money may also be more risky. In the simplest possible application of this idea, the yield on money is assumed to be certain and equal to zero (no price inflation) whilst the yield on a risky financial asset is stochastic. The risky asset carries a positive *expected* yield. The actual (realized) rate of return on such an asset is, however, uncertain and may well be negative. In such a setting the risk-averse household typically chooses a diversified portfolio, consisting of both money and the risky asset, which represents the optimal trade-off between risk and return.

In the second part of this chapter we take for granted that money exists and plays a useful role in the economic process and study the socially optimal quantity of money. If fiat money is useful to economic agents then how large should the money supply be? Friedman proposes a simple answer to this question: since fiat money is very cheap to produce, the money supply should be expanded up to the point where the marginal social benefit of money is (close to) zero. This is the famous *full liquidity* or *satiation* result. We first demonstrate the validity of the satiation result in a very simple two-period model of an endowment economy with money entering the utility function of the households. Next we extend the model by endogenizing the labour supply decision of households and demonstrate the various reasons why full liquidity may not be socially optimal.

Further Reading

Good textbooks on monetary economics are Niehans (1978), McCallum (1989a), and Walsh (1998). Diamond (1984), Kiyotaki and Wright (1993), and Trejos and Wright (1995) use the search-theoretic approach to model money. The demand for money by firms is studied by Miller and Orr (1966) and Fischer (1974). Romer (1986, 1987) embeds the Baumol–Tobin model in a general equilibrium model. Saving (1971) presents a model of money based on transactions costs. McCallum and Goodfriend (1987) give an overview of money demand theories. Fischer (1979) studies monetary neutrality in a monetary growth model.

On the public finance approach to inflation, see Chamley (1985), Turnovsky and Brock (1980), Mankiw (1987), Gahvari (1988), Chari et al. (1996), Correia and Teles (1996), Batina and Ihori (2000, ch.10), and Ljungqvist and Sargent (2000, ch. 17). On the unpleasant monetarist arithmetic argument, see Drazen and Helpman (1990), Sargent and Wallace (1993), and Liviatan (1984).

Appendix

In this appendix we derive equation (12.116) in the text. As a preparatory step we write (12.115) in short-hand format as follows:

$$b_{t-1} = \frac{b_t + z_t}{1 + r_{t-1}},$$
(A12.1)

where z_t is the forcing term of the difference equation:

$$z_t \equiv C_t + m_t - \frac{m_{t-1}}{1 + \pi_{t-1}} - W_t(1 - \tau_t)L_t - T_t. \tag{A12.2}$$

We wish to solve (A12.1) forwards in time, taking account of the fact that in period $t = 1$, b_0 is given. By using (A12.1) we find the following expression after two substitutions:

$$b_0 = \left(\frac{1}{1 + r_0}\right)[b_1 + z_1]$$

$$= \left(\frac{1}{1 + r_0}\right)\left[\left(\frac{1}{1 + r_1}\right)[b_2 + z_2] + z_1\right]$$

$$= \left(\frac{1}{1 + r_0}\right)\left[\left(\frac{1}{1 + r_1}\right)\left[\left(\frac{1}{1 + r_2}\right)[b_3 + z_3] + z_2\right] + z_1\right] \Leftrightarrow$$

$$(1 + r_0)b_0 = \left(\frac{1}{1 + r_1}\right)\left(\frac{1}{1 + r_2}\right)b_3 + z_1 + \left(\frac{1}{1 + r_1}\right)z_2 + \left(\frac{1}{1 + r_1}\right)\left(\frac{1}{1 + r_2}\right)z_3.$$

From the ultimate expression it is easy to recognize the pattern and to conclude that after k substitutions we get:

$$(1 + r_0)b_0 = \left(\frac{1}{1 + r_1}\right)\left(\frac{1}{1 + r_2}\right)\cdots\left(\frac{1}{1 + r_k}\right)b_{k+1}$$

$$+ z_1 + \left(\frac{1}{1 + r_1}\right)z_2 + \ldots + \left(\frac{1}{1 + r_1}\right)\left(\frac{1}{1 + r_2}\right)\cdots\left(\frac{1}{1 + r_k}\right)z_{k+1}$$

$$= \prod_{i=1}^{k}\left(\frac{1}{1 + r_i}\right)b_{k+1} + z_1 + \sum_{t=2}^{1+k}\prod_{i=1}^{t-1}\left(\frac{1}{1 + r_i}\right)z_t. \tag{A12.3}$$

By using the definition for q_t^0 given in equation (12.117) in the text, we find that (A12.3) can be written in a compact form as:

$$(1 + r_0)b_0 = q_{k+1}^0 b_{k+1} + \sum_{t=1}^{1+k} q_t^0 z_t. \tag{A12.4}$$

Next we must simplify the second term on the right-hand side of (A12.4). By using (A12.2) we can write this term as:

$$\sum_{t=1}^{1+k} q_t^0 z_t = \sum_{t=1}^{1+k} q_t^0 [C_t - W_t(1 - \tau_t)L_t - T_t] + \sum_{t=1}^{1+k} q_t^0 \left[m_t - \frac{m_{t-1}}{1 + \pi_{t-1}}\right]. \tag{A12.5}$$

The first term on the right-hand side of (A12.5) is already in the required format but the second term can be further simplified. We note that it follows by definition that

$q_t^0 = q_{t-1}^0 / (1 + r_{t-1})$ for $t \geq 2$. By using this result we obtain:

$$\sum_{t=1}^{1+k} q_t^0 \left[m_t - \frac{m_{t-1}}{1 + \pi_{t-1}} \right] = \sum_{t=1}^{1+k} q_t^0 m_t - \frac{m_0}{1 + \pi_0} - \sum_{t=2}^{1+k} \frac{q_{t-1}^0 m_{t-1}}{(1 + r_{t-1})(1 + \pi_{t-1})}$$

$$= \sum_{t=1}^{1+k} q_t^0 m_t - \sum_{s=1}^{k} \frac{q_s^0 m_s}{1 + R_s} - \frac{m_0}{1 + \pi_0}$$

$$= \sum_{t=1}^{1+k} q_t^0 m_t \left[1 - \frac{1}{1 + R_t} \right] + \frac{q_{k+1}^0 m_{k+1}}{1 + R_{k+1}} - \frac{m_0}{1 + \pi_0}, \qquad (A12.6)$$

where we have used the fact that the nominal interest rate, R_t, satisfies $1 + R_t = (1 + r_t)(1 + \pi_t)$ in going from the first to the second line. By using (A12.5) and (A12.6) in (A12.4) and rearranging we obtain equation (12.116) in the text.

13

New Keynesian Economics

The purpose of this chapter is to discuss the following issues:

1. Can we provide microeconomic foundations behind the "Keynesian" multiplier?

2. What are the welfare-theoretic aspects of the monopolistic competition model? What is the link between the output multiplier of government consumption and the marginal cost of public funds (MCPF)?

3. Does monetary neutrality still hold when there exist costs of adjusting prices?

4. What do we mean by nominal and real rigidity and how do the two types of rigidity interact?

13.1 Reconstructing the "Keynesian" Multiplier

The challenge posed by a number of authors in the 1980s is to provide microeconomic foundations for Keynesian multipliers by assuming that the goods market is characterized by monopolistic competition. This is, of course, not the first time such micro-foundations are proposed, a prominent predecessor being the fixed-price disequilibrium approach of the early 1970s (see Chapter 5). The problem with that older literature is that prices are simply assumed to be fixed, which makes these models resemble Shakespeare's *Hamlet* without the Prince, in that the essential market coordination mechanism is left out. Specifically, fixed (disequilibrium) prices imply the existence of unexploited gains from trade between restricted and unrestricted market parties. There are $f100$ bills lying on the footpath, and this begs the question why this would ever be an equilibrium situation.

Of course some reasons exist for price stickiness, and these will be reviewed here, but a particularly simple way out of the fixity of prices is to assume price-setting behaviour by monopolistically competitive agents.[1] This incidentally also solves Arrow's (1959) famous critical remarks about the absence of an auctioneer in the perfectly competitive framework.

13.1.1 A static model with monopolistic competition

In this subsection we construct a simple model with monopolistic competition in the goods market. There are three types of agents in the economy: households, firms, and the government. The representative household derives utility from consuming goods and leisure and has a Cobb-Douglas utility function:

$$U \equiv C^\alpha (1 - L)^{1-\alpha}, \quad 0 < \alpha < 1, \tag{13.1}$$

where U is utility, L is labour supply, and C is (composite) consumption. The household has an endowment of one unit of time and all time not spent working is consumed in the form of leisure, $1 - L$. The composite consumption good consists of a bundle of closely related product "varieties" which are close but imperfect substitutes for each other (e.g. red, blue, green, and yellow ties). Following the crucial insights of Spence (1976) and Dixit and Stiglitz (1977), a convenient formulation is as follows:

$$C \equiv N^\eta \left[N^{-1} \sum_{j=1}^{N} C_j^{(\theta-1)/\theta} \right]^{\theta/(\theta-1)}, \quad \theta > 1, \ \eta \geq 1, \tag{13.2}$$

where N is the number of different varieties that exist, C_j is a consumption good of variety j, and θ and η are parameters. This specification, though simple, incorporates two economically meaningful and separate aspects of product differentiation. First, the parameter θ regulates the ease with which any two varieties (C_i and C_j) can be substituted for each other. In formal terms, θ represents the *Allen-Uzawa cross-partial elasticity of substitution* (see Chung, 1994, ch. 5). Intuitively, the higher is θ, the better substitutes the varieties are for each other. In the limiting case (as $\theta \to \infty$), the varieties are perfect substitutes, i.e. they are identical goods from the perspective of the representative household.

The second parameter appearing in (13.2), η, regulates "preference for diversity" (PFD, or "taste for variety" as it is often called alternatively). Intuitively, diversity preference represents the utility gain that is obtained from spreading a certain amount of production over N varieties rather than concentrating it on a single variety (Bénassy, 1996b, p. 42). In formal terms *average* PFD can be computed by comparing the value of composite consumption (C) obtained if N varieties and X/N units per variety are chosen with the value of C if X units of a single variety

---

[1] See the recent surveys by Bénassy (1993a), Silvestre (1993), Matsuyama (1995), and the collection of papers in Dixon and Rankin (1995).

are chosen ($N = 1$):

$$\text{average PFD} \equiv \frac{C(X/N, X/N, ..., X/N)}{C(X, 0, ..., 0)} = N^{\eta-1}. \tag{13.3}$$

The elasticity of this function with respect to the number of varieties represents the *marginal* taste for additional variety[2] which plays an important role in the monopolistic competition model. By using (13.3) we obtain the expression for the marginal preference for diversity (MPFD):

$$\text{MPFD} = \eta - 1. \tag{13.4}$$

It is now clear how and to what extent η regulates MPFD: if η exceeds unity MPFD is strictly positive and the representative agent exhibits a love of variety. The agent does not enjoy diversity if $\eta = 1$ and MPFD $= 0$ in that case.

The household faces the following budget constraint:

$$\sum_{j=1}^{N} P_j C_j = W^N L + \Pi - T, \tag{13.5}$$

where P_j is the price of variety j, W^N is the nominal wage rate (labour is used as the numeraire later on in this section), Π is the total profit income that the household receives from the monopolistically competitive firms, and T is a lump-sum tax paid to the government. The household chooses its labour supply and consumption levels for each available product variety (L and $C_j, j = 1, \ldots, N$) in order to maximize utility (13.1), given the definition of composite consumption in (13.2), the budget constraint (13.5), and taking as given all prices ($P_j, j = 1, \ldots, N$), the nominal wage rate, profit income, and the lump-sum tax.

By using the convenient trick of *two-stage budgeting*, the solutions for composite consumption, consumption of variety j, and labour supply are obtained:

$$PC = \alpha \left[W^N + \Pi - T \right], \tag{13.6}$$

$$\left(\frac{C_j}{C} \right) = N^{-(\theta+\eta)+\eta\theta} \left(\frac{P_j}{P} \right)^{-\theta}, \quad j = 1, \ldots, N, \tag{13.7}$$

$$W^N \left[1 - L \right] = (1 - \alpha) \left[W^N + \Pi - T \right], \tag{13.8}$$

where P is the so-called *true price index* of the composite consumption good C. Intuitively, P represents the price of one unit of C given that the quantities of all varieties are chosen in an optimal (utility-maximizing) fashion by the household. It is defined as follows:

$$P \equiv N^{-\eta} \left[N^{-\theta} \sum_{j=1}^{N} P_j^{1-\theta} \right]^{1/(1-\theta)}. \tag{13.9}$$

---

[2] As is often the case in economics, the marginal rather than the average concept is most relevant. Bénassy presents a clear discussion of average and marginal preference for diversity (1996, p. 42).

Intermezzo

Two-stage budgeting. As indeed its name strongly suggests, the technique of two-stage budgeting (or more generally, multi-stage budgeting) solves a relatively complex maximization problem by breaking it up into two (or more) much less complex sub-problems (or "stages"). An exhaustive treatment of two-stage budgeting is far beyond the scope of this book. Interested readers are referred to Deaton and Muellbauer (1980, pp. 123–137) which contains a more advanced discussion plus references to key publications in the area.

We illustrate the technique of two-stage budgeting with the aid of the maximization problem discussed in the text. Since C and $1 - L$ appear in the utility function (13.1) and only C_j ($j = 1, \ldots, N$) appear in the definition of C in (13.2) it is natural to subdivide the problem into two stages. In stage 1 the choice is made (at the "top level" of the problem) between composite consumption and leisure, and in stage 2 (at the "bottom" level) the different varieties are chosen optimally, conditional upon the level of C chosen in the first stage.

Stage 1. We postulate the existence of a price index for composite consumption and denote it by P. By definition total spending on differentiated goods is then equal to $\sum_j P_j C_j = PC$ so that (13.5) can be re-written as:

$$PC + W^N(1 - L) = W^N + \Pi - T \equiv I_F, \tag{a}$$

which says that spending on consumption goods plus leisure (the left-hand side) must equal full income (I_F on the right-hand side). The top-level maximization problem is now to maximize (13.1) subject to (a) by choice of C and $1 - L$. The first-order conditions for this problem are the budget constraint (a) and:

$$\frac{U_{1-L}}{U_C} = \frac{W^N}{P} \Rightarrow \frac{W^N}{P} = \frac{1 - \alpha}{\alpha} \frac{C}{1 - L}. \tag{b}$$

The marginal rate of substitution between leisure and composite consumption must be equated to the real wage rate which is computed by deflating the nominal wage rate with the price index of composite consumption (and not just the price of an individual product variety!). By substituting the right-hand expression of (b) into the budget identity (a), we obtain the optimal choices of C and $1 - L$ in terms of full income:

$$PC = \alpha I_F, \quad W^N(1 - L) = (1 - \alpha)I_F. \tag{c}$$

Finally, by substituting these expressions into the (*direct*) utility function (13.1) we obtain the *indirect* utility function expressing utility in terms of full income and a cost-of-living index:

$$V \equiv \frac{I_F}{P_V},$$ (d)

where P_V is the true price index for utility, i.e. it is the cost of purchasing one unit of utility (a "util"):

$$P_V \equiv \left(\frac{P}{\alpha}\right)^{\alpha} \left(\frac{W^N}{1-\alpha}\right)^{1-\alpha}.$$ (e)

Stage 2. In the second stage the agent chooses varieties, C_j ($j = 1, 2, ..., N$), in order to "construct" composite consumption in an optimal, cost-minimizing, fashion. The formal problem is:

$$\underset{\{C_j\}}{\text{Max}} \; N^{\eta} \left[N^{-1} \sum_{j=1}^{N} C_j^{(\theta-1)/\theta} \right]^{\theta/(\theta-1)} \qquad \text{subject to} \qquad \sum_{j=1}^{N} P_j C_j = PC,$$ (f)

for which the first-order conditions are the constraint in (f) and:

$$\frac{\partial C/\partial C_j}{\partial C/\partial C_k} = \frac{P_j}{P_k} \;\; \Rightarrow \;\; \left(\frac{C_k}{C_j}\right)^{1/\theta} = \frac{P_j}{P_k}, \quad \text{for } j, k = 1, 2, ..., N.$$ (g)

The marginal rate of substitution between any two product varieties must be equated to the relative price of these two varieties. By repeatedly substituting the first-order condition (g) into the definition of C (given in (13.2)), we obtain the following expression for C_j:

$$C_j = \frac{N^{-\eta} C P_j^{-\theta}}{\left[\sum_{k=1}^{N} N^{-1} P_k^{1-\theta} \right]^{-\theta/(1-\theta)}}.$$ (h)

By substituting (h) into the constraint given in (f) the expression for the price index P is obtained:

$$\sum_{j=1}^{N} P_j C_j = \frac{N^{\theta/(\theta-1)-\eta} C \left[\sum_{j=1}^{N} P_j^{1-\theta} \right]}{\left[\sum_{j=1}^{N} P_j^{1-\theta} \right]^{-\theta/(1-\theta)}} = PC \;\; \Rightarrow$$

$$P \equiv N^{\eta} \left[N^{-\theta} \sum_{j=1}^{N} P_j^{1-\theta} \right]^{1/(1-\theta)}.$$ (i)

By using this price index we can re-express the demand for variety j of the consumption good (given in (h)) in a more compact form as:

$$\left(\frac{C_j}{C}\right) = N^{-(\theta+\eta)+\eta\theta} \left(\frac{P_j}{P}\right)^{-\theta}, \quad j = 1, ..., N,$$ (j)

which is the expression used in the text (namely equation (13.7)).

It must be pointed out that we could have solved the choice problem facing the consumer in one single (and rather large) maximization problem, instead of by means of two-stage budgeting, and we would, of course, have obtained the same solutions. The advantages of two-stage budgeting are twofold: (i) it makes the computations more straightforward and mistakes easier to avoid, and (ii) it automatically yields useful definitions for true price indexes as by-products.

Finally, although we did not explicitly use the terminology, the observant reader will have noted that we have already used the method of two-stage budgeting before in Chapter 10. There we discussed the Armington approach to modelling international trade flows and assumed that a domestic composite good consists of a domestically produced good and a good produced abroad.

The firm sector is characterized by monopolistic competition, i.e. there are very many small firms each producing a variety of the differentiated good and each enjoying market power in its own output market. The individual firm j uses labour to produce variety j and faces the following production function:

$$
Y_j = \begin{cases} 0 & \text{if } L_j \leq F \\ (1/k)\left[L_j - F\right] & \text{if } L_j \geq F \end{cases},
\tag{13.10}
$$

where Y_j is the marketable output of firm j, L_j is labour used by the firm, F is fixed cost in terms of units of labour, and k is the (constant) marginal labour requirement. The formulation captures the notion that the firm must expend a minimum amount of labour ("overhead labour") before it can produce any output at all (see Mankiw, 1988, p. 9). As a result, there are *increasing returns to scale* at firm level as average cost declines with output.

The profit of firm j is denoted by Π_j and equals revenue minus total costs:

$$
\Pi_j \equiv P_j Y_j - W^N\left[k Y_j + F\right],
\tag{13.11}
$$

which incorporates the assumption that labour is perfectly mobile across firms, so that all firms are forced to pay a common wage (W^N does not feature an index j). The firm chooses output in order to maximize its profits (13.11) subject to its price-elastic demand curve. We assume that it acts as a *Cournot* competitor in that firm j takes other firms' output levels as given, i.e. there is no strategic interaction between producers of different product varieties.

In formal terms, the choice problem takes the following form:

$$
\underset{\{Y_j\}}{\text{Max}} \ \Pi_j = P_j(Y_j)Y_j - W^N\left[k Y_j + F\right],
\tag{13.12}
$$

where the notation $P_j(Y_j)$ is used to indicate that the choice of output affects the price which firm j will fetch (downward-sloping demand implies $\partial P_j / \partial Y_j < 0$).

The first-order condition yields the *pricing rule* familiar from first-year microeconomic texts:

$$\frac{d\Pi_j}{dY_j} = P_j + Y_j \left(\frac{\partial P_j}{\partial Y_j} \right) - W^N k = 0 \quad \Rightarrow$$

$$P_j = \mu_j W^N k, \tag{13.13}$$

where μ_j is the markup of price over marginal cost (i.e. variable labour cost) and ϵ_j is the (absolute value of the) price elasticity of demand facing firm j:

$$\mu_j \equiv \frac{\epsilon_j}{\epsilon_j - 1}, \quad \epsilon_j \equiv -\frac{\partial Y_j}{\partial P_j} \frac{P_j}{Y_j}. \tag{13.14}$$

The higher is the elasticity of demand, the smaller is the markup and the closer is the solution to the perfectly competitive one. Clearly, the pricing rule in (13.13) is only sensible if μ_j is positive, i.e. demand must be elastic and ϵ_j must exceed unity.

The government does three things in this model: it consumes a composite good (G, given below), it levies lump-sum taxes on the representative household (T), and it employs civil servants (L_G). To keep things simple we assume that G is defined analogously to C in (13.2):

$$G \equiv N^\eta \left[N^{-1} \sum_{j=1}^{N} G_j^{(\theta-1)/\theta} \right]^{\theta/(\theta-1)}, \tag{13.15}$$

where G_j is the government's demand for variety j. It is assumed that the government is efficient in the sense that it chooses varieties G_j ($j = 1, \ldots, N$) in an optimal, cost-minimizing, fashion, taking a certain level of composite public consumption (G) as given. This implies that the government's demand for variety j is:

$$\frac{G_j}{G} = N^{-(\theta+\eta)+\eta\theta} \left(\frac{P_j}{P} \right)^{-\theta}, \quad j = 1, \ldots, N, \tag{13.16}$$

where the similarity to (13.7) should be apparent to all and sundry. Since C and G feature the same functional form, the price index for the public good is given by P in (13.9).

Total demand facing each firm j equals $Y_j \equiv C_j + G_j$, which in view of (13.7) and (13.16) shows that the demand elasticity facing firm j equals $\epsilon_j = \theta$ so that the markup is constant and equal to $\mu_j = \mu = \theta/(\theta - 1)$. In this simplest case, the composition of demand does not matter. The model is completely symmetric: all firms face the same production costs and use the same pricing rule and thus set the same price, i.e. $P_j = \bar{P} = \mu W^N k$. As a result they all produce the same amount, i.e. $Y_j = \bar{Y}$, for $j = 1, \ldots, N$. A useful quantity index for real aggregate output can then

Table 13.1. A simple macro model with monopolistic competition

---

$$Y = C + G \tag{T1.1}$$

$$PC = \alpha I_F, \ I_F \equiv \left[W^N + \Pi - T \right] \tag{T1.2}$$

$$\Pi \equiv \sum_{j=1}^{N} \Pi_j = \theta^{-1} PY - W^N NF \tag{T1.3}$$

$$T = PG + W^N L_G \tag{T1.4}$$

$$P = N^{1-\eta} \bar{P} = N^{1-\eta} \mu W^N k \tag{T1.5}$$

$$W^N (1 - L) = (1 - \alpha) I_F \tag{T1.6}$$

$$P_V = \left(\frac{P}{\alpha} \right)^\alpha \left(\frac{W^N}{1 - \alpha} \right)^{1-\alpha}, \ V = \frac{I_F}{P_V} \tag{T1.7}$$

---

be defined as:

$$Y \equiv \frac{\sum_{j=1}^{N} P_j Y_j}{P}, \tag{13.17}$$

so that the aggregate goods market equilibrium condition can be written as in (T1.1) in Table 13.1.

For convenience, we summarize the model in aggregate terms in Table 13.1. Equation (T1.1) is the aggregate goods market clearing condition and (T1.2) is household demand for the composite consumption good (see (13.6)). Equation (T1.3) relates aggregate profit income (Π) to aggregate spending (PY) and firms' outlays on overhead labour ($W^N NF$). This expression is obtained by using the symmetric pricing rule, $P_j = \bar{P} = \mu W^N k$, in the definition of firm profit in (13.11) and aggregating over all active firms. The government budget restriction (T1.4) says that government spending on goods (PG) plus wage payments to civil servants ($W^N L_G$) must equal the lump-sum tax (T). By using the symmetric pricing rule in the definition of the price index (13.9) expression (T1.5) is obtained. Labour supply is given by (T1.6). Finally, (T1.7) contains some welfare indicators to be used and explained below in section 1.4.

Equilibrium in the labour market implies that the supply of labour (L) must equal the number of civil servants employed by the government (L^G) plus the number of workers employed in the monopolistically competitive sector:

$$L = L_G + \sum_{j=1}^{N} L_j. \tag{13.18}$$

Walras' Law ensures that the labour market is in equilibrium, i.e. (T1.1)–(T1.6) together imply that (13.18) holds.

There is no money in the model so *nominal* prices and wages are indeterminate. It is convenient to use leisure as the numeraire, i.e. W^N is fixed and everything is measured in wage units. The model can be analysed for two polar cases. In the first case, the number of firms is constant and fluctuations in profits emerge. This version of the model is deemed to be relevant for the short run and gives rise to short-run multipliers (Mankiw, 1988). In the second case, the number of firms is variable and exit/entry of firms ensures that profits return to zero following a shock. Following Startz (1989) this can be seen as the long-run version of the model.

13.1.2 The short-run balanced-budget multiplier

In the (very) short run, Mankiw (1988) argued, the number of firms is fixed (say $N = N_0$) and the model in Table 13.1 exhibits a positive balanced-budget multiplier. This can be demonstrated as follows. By substituting (T1.3) and (T1.4) into (T1.2), the aggregate consumption function can be written in terms of aggregate output and constants:

$$C = c_0 + (\alpha/\theta)Y - \alpha G, \tag{13.19}$$

where $c_0 \equiv \alpha [1 - N_0 F - L_G] W$ and $W \equiv W^N/P$ is the real wage. It follows from (T1.5) that the real wage rate is constant in the short run.[3] The consumption function looks rather Keynesian and has a slope between zero and unity since $0 < \alpha < 1$ and $\theta > 1$. Additional output boosts real profit income to the household which spends a fraction of the extra income on consumption goods (and the rest on leisure). The consumption function has been drawn in Figure 13.1 for an initial level of government spending, G_0. By vertically adding G_0 to C, aggregate demand is obtained. The initial equilibrium is at point E_0 where aggregate demand equals production and equilibrium consumption and output are, respectively, C_0 and Y_0.

Now consider what happens if the government boosts its consumption, say from G_0 to G_1, and finances this additional spending by an increase in the lump-sum tax. Such a balanced-budget policy has two effects in the short run. First, it exerts a negative effect on the aggregate consumption function (see (13.19)) because households have to pay higher taxes, i.e. the consumption function shifts down by $\alpha \, dG$ in Figure 13.1. Second, the spending shock also boosts aggregate demand one-for-one because the government purchases additional goods. Since the marginal propensity to consume out of full income, α, is less than unity, this direct spending effect dominates the private consumption decline and aggregate demand increases (by $(1 - \alpha) \, dG$), as is illustrated in Figure 13.1. The equilibrium shifts from E_0 to E_1,

---

[3] The number of product varieties (N) is fixed as are (by assumption) the markup (μ) and the marginal labour requirement (k).

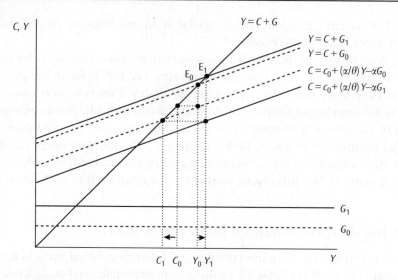

Figure 13.1. Government spending multipliers

output increases from (Y_0 to Y_1), but consumption falls (C_0 to C_1). Formally, the short-run income and profit multipliers are:

$$\left(\frac{dY}{dG}\right)^{SR}_{T} = \left(\frac{\theta d\Pi}{PdG}\right)^{SR}_{T} = (1-\alpha)\left[1 + \sum_{i=1}^{\infty}(\alpha/\theta)^i\right] = \frac{1-\alpha}{1-\alpha/\theta} > 1-\alpha. \qquad (13.20)$$

An increase in government spending increases aggregate demand on impact by $(1-\alpha)dG$ and causes additional real profits to the tune of $\theta^{-1}(1-\alpha)dG$. Although aggregate household consumption declines at impact by αdG, the rise in profit income mitigates this reduction somewhat. This furnishes a second round in the multiplier process, which ultimately converges to the expression given in (13.20). Under perfect competition, there is no profit effect and hence the ultimate effect of a change in government consumption coincides with the impact effect, $1-\alpha$.

Although (13.20) looks like a Keynesian multiplier (and certainly was sold as one by the initial authors),[4] some features are distinctly un-Keynesian. For one, household consumption falls as a result of the increase in government consumption:

$$-\alpha < \left(\frac{dC}{dG}\right)^{SR}_{T} = -\left(\frac{\theta-1}{\theta-\alpha}\right)\alpha < 0, \qquad (13.21)$$

which is at odds with the usual Haavelmo balanced-budget multiplier (see Chapter 1). Furthermore, it turns out that the same reason that makes households cut back consumption (i.e. the higher tax burden, which lowers full income) also

---

[4] With the notable exception of Dixon (1987) who argued that the multiplier was more Walrasian than Keynesian.

makes them cut back on leisure consumption (since leisure is a normal good, see (13.8)) and increase labour supply. In aggregate terms we have:

$$0 < W \left(\frac{dL}{dG} \right)^{SR}_T = \left(\frac{\theta - 1}{\theta - \alpha} \right) (1 - \alpha) < (1 - \alpha). \tag{13.22}$$

Hence, the Keynesian multiplier is really explained by the fact that households supply more labour because they feel poorer. This is a mechanism more usually associated with the new classical school to be discussed below in Chapter 15.

13.1.3 The short-run multiplier in isolation

Mankiw (1988) uses an ingenious argument to mimic the effect of bond financing in a static model (like the one in Table 13.1). Suppose that the additional government consumption is not financed by additional taxes (as in the previous subsection) but instead is paid for by firing civil servants. As in the case of bond financing,[5] the representative household's budget constraint is unaffected by the spending shock and the consumption function (13.19) is replaced by:

$$C = \alpha [1 - NF] W + (\alpha/\theta)Y - \alpha(T/P), \tag{13.23}$$

where the real tax bill (T/P) is constant. The various multipliers are now:

$$\left(\frac{dY}{dG} \right)^{SR}_{LG} = \left(\frac{\theta d\Pi}{PdG} \right)^{SR}_{LG} = \left[1 + \sum_{i=1}^{\infty} (\alpha/\theta)^i \right] = \frac{1}{1 - \alpha/\theta} > 1, \tag{13.24}$$

$$\left(\frac{dC}{dG} \right)^{SR}_{LG} = \frac{\alpha}{\theta - \alpha} > 0, \quad W \left(\frac{dL}{dG} \right)^{SR}_{LG} = -\left(\frac{1 - \alpha}{\theta - \alpha} \right) < 0. \tag{13.25}$$

The output multiplier exceeds unity (as in the traditional Keynesian cross-model). As the representative household is wealthier because of the additional profit income, consumption rises and labour supply (and hence employment) falls. The additional units of labour that are needed to produce the additional output are released from the public sector. The intersectoral re-allocation of labour (from the public to the private sector) dominates the reduction in labour supply so that aggregate output can expand.

13.1.4 The "long-run" multiplier

Startz (1989) suggested that the multiplier stories that were told in the previous two subsections are incomplete because they implicitly assume that there are f 100 bills lying around on the footpath. Just as in the fixed-price approach discussed

---

[5] And with disconnected generations so that Ricardian equivalence does not hold; see section 1.4 in Chapter 6.

in Chapter 5, not all trading opportunities are exhausted in the short-run equilibrium that emerges following a public spending shock. Indeed, as both (13.20) and (13.24) demonstrate, additional profits emerge as a result of the increase in government spending. In the absence of barriers to entry, one would expect new firms to commence operations as long as super-normal profits persist. Following Heijdra and van der Ploeg (1996, p. 1291) we capture this idea with the following simple specification:

$$\dot{N} = \gamma_N(\Pi/P) = \gamma_N\left[\theta^{-1}Y - WNF\right], \quad \gamma_N > 0, \tag{13.26}$$

where $\dot{N} \equiv dN/dt$ is the rate of change in the number of firms over time and γ_N is finite so that exit/entry occurs gradually over time.

To keep the discussion as simple as possible, it is assumed in the remainder of this section that the government employs no civil servants (i.e. $L_G = 0$). The goods market equilibrium (GME) condition is obtained by substituting (T1.2)–(T1.4) into (T1.1):

$$Y = \alpha\left[1 - NF\right]W + (\alpha/\theta)Y + (1 - \alpha)G$$

$$= \left[\frac{\alpha(1 - NF)}{\mu k(1 - \alpha/\theta)}\right]N^{\eta-1} + \left[\frac{1 - \alpha}{1 - \alpha/\theta}\right]G \quad \text{(GME)}, \tag{13.27}$$

where we have solved for output and used the pricing rule (given in (T1.5) above) to relate the real wage to the number of firms in the second line of (13.27). For future reference we rewrite this pricing rule as follows:

$$W = \frac{N^{\eta-1}}{\mu k}. \tag{13.28}$$

Finally, the zero-profit condition, ZP, which is obtained by setting $\Pi = 0$ in (T1.3), collapses to $Y = \theta WNF$ which can be re-expressed with the aid of the pricing rule (13.28) in terms of the number of firms:

$$Y = \frac{\theta FN^{\eta}}{\mu k} \quad \text{(ZP)}. \tag{13.29}$$

The intuition behind the short-run, transitional, and long-run effects of a tax-financed increase in public consumption can now be explained with the aid of Figure 13.2. In the top panel ZP represents combinations of output and the number of firms for which profits are zero. In view of (13.29) the ZP line goes through the origin and is upward sloping:

$$\left(\frac{dY}{dN}\right)_{ZP} = \eta\left(\frac{Y}{N}\right) > 0. \tag{13.30}$$

Furthermore, (13.26) shows that profits are positive (negative) for points to the left (right) of the ZP line so that the entry dynamics is as indicated by horizontal arrows. Still in the top panel, GME$_0$ represents the initial goods market equilibrium locus

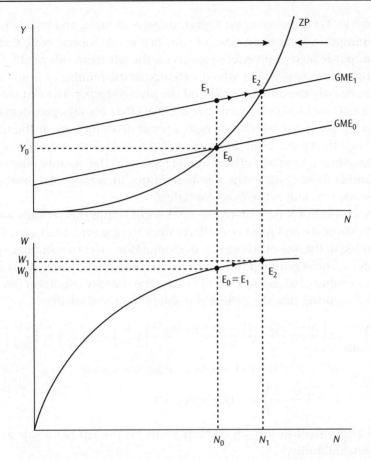

Figure 13.2. Multipliers and firm entry

as defined in equation (13.27). In order to study the properties of the GME-locus we differentiate (13.27) around an initial zero-profit equilibrium:

$$[1 - \alpha/\theta] \frac{dY}{Y} = \frac{\alpha W}{Y} [1 - NF] \frac{dW}{W} - \frac{\alpha WNF}{Y} \frac{dN}{N} + (1 - \alpha) \frac{dG}{Y}$$

$$= [1 - (1 - \alpha)\omega_G] \frac{dW}{W} - \frac{\alpha}{\theta} \left[\frac{dW}{W} + \frac{dN}{N} \right] + (1 - \alpha) \frac{dG}{Y}$$

$$= (\eta - 1) [\alpha + (1 - \alpha)\omega_C] \frac{dN}{N} - \frac{\alpha\eta}{\theta} \frac{dN}{N} + (1 - \alpha) \frac{dG}{Y}, \qquad (13.31)$$

where we have used the zero-profit condition (in levels) in going from the first to the second line and the pricing rule in going from the second to the third line. The initial output shares of private and public consumption are given, respectively, by $\omega_C \equiv C/Y$ and $\omega_G \equiv 1 - \omega_C = G/Y$.

Equation (13.31) shows that, for a given number of firms, an increase in government consumption leads to an upward shift of the GME-locus. Note furthermore that the output-related profit effect appears on the left-hand side of (13.31). There are two distinct mechanisms by which a change in the number of firms affects the GME-locus, namely the *diversity effect* and the *fixed-cost effect*. The first term on the right-hand side of (13.31) represents the positive effect on aggregate demand of an increase in the real wage which occurs as a result of an increase in the number of firms provided the agents exhibit love of variety ($\eta > 1$). This is the diversity effect. The second term is potentially offsetting and represents the negative effect on aggregate demand of fixed costs: as the number of firms increases, total overhead costs rise and profits fall. This is the fixed-cost effect.

The overall effect of N on Y along the GME-locus is thus theoretically ambiguous because the diversity and fixed-cost effects work in opposite directions. Our usual ploy to be used in the face of ambiguity, the Samuelsonian correspondence principle (see Chapter 2), does not help to resolve this issue because the model is stable for all parameter values. Indeed, in view of (13.26) the stability condition ($\partial \dot{N}/\partial N < 0$) amounts to requiring that the ZP line is steeper than the GME line.

$$\left(\frac{\partial Y}{\partial N}\right)_{GME} \equiv \left[\frac{(\eta - 1)\left[\alpha + (1 - \alpha)\omega_C\right] - \alpha\eta/\theta}{1 - \alpha/\theta}\right]\left(\frac{Y}{N}\right) < \eta\left(\frac{Y}{N}\right) \equiv \left(\frac{\partial Y}{\partial N}\right)_{ZP}$$

$$\Leftrightarrow \quad (\eta - 1)\left[\alpha + (1 - \alpha)\omega_C\right] - \alpha\eta/\theta < \eta - \alpha\eta/\theta$$

$$\Leftrightarrow \quad \left(\frac{\eta - 1}{\eta}\right)\left[\alpha + (1 - \alpha)\omega_C\right] < 1, \tag{13.32}$$

where the latter inequality holds as both terms on the left-hand side are strictly between zero and unity.[6]

Two often-used approaches lead to a resolution of the ambiguity regarding the slope of the GME-locus. In the first approach the ambiguity is resolved by ignoring the conceptual distinction between the price elasticity of demand (θ) and the preference for diversity (η) and imposing a single utility parameter to regulate these two effects. Technically, the standard Dixit and Stiglitz (1977, p. 298) formulation is used for composite consumption by setting $\eta = \mu \equiv \theta/(\theta - 1)$ in (13.2). Since $\theta > 1$ is required to guarantee a meaningful monopolistically competitive equilibrium (i.e. to ensure that $\mu > 1$), diversity preference is operative ($\eta > 1$) **and** strong enough to render the slope of the GME-locus positive:

$$\left(\frac{\partial Y}{\partial N}\right)_{GME}^{\eta = \mu} \equiv \frac{(1 - \alpha)\omega_C}{(\theta - 1)\left[1 - \alpha/\theta\right]} > 0. \tag{13.33}$$

This is the case drawn in Figure 13.2. An increase in government consumption shifts the GME locus from GME_0 to GME_1. At impact the number of firms is predetermined

---

[6] For a more general utility function than (13.1), the stability condition does furnish additional information that is useful for comparative static purposes. See Heijdra and van der Ploeg (1996, p. 1291), Heijdra and Ligthart (1997, p. 817), and Heijdra et al. (1998, p. 86) for different examples.

(at $N = N_0$) and output rises as the economy jumps from E_0 to E_1. This is the short-run multiplier given in (13.20). At point E_1 there are super-normal profits to be had and entry of new firms occurs. Gradually, the economy moves along GME_1 from E_1 to E_2 and both output and the number of firms increase towards their new equilibrium values. Furthermore, as the lower panel of Figure 13.2 shows, the real wage rate also increases during transition. So, even though the model may not be vintage Keynesian in its basic mechanism, it does have some Keynesian features since the real wage and aggregate output move pro-cyclically.

Whereas in the first approach the long-run output multiplier exceeds the short-run multiplier, this conclusion is reversed in the second approach. Startz (1989, p. 741) implicitly resolves the ambiguity concerning the slope of the GME locus by eliminating preference for diversity altogether, i.e. by setting $\eta = 1$ in (13.2). The GME locus is downward sloping in that case as entry of firms only does bad things to the economy (such as using up additional resources in the form of overhead labour):

$$\left(\frac{\partial Y}{\partial N} \right)_{GME}^{\eta=1} \equiv -\frac{\alpha/\theta}{1 - \alpha/\theta} < 0. \tag{13.34}$$

Furthermore, the pricing rule (13.28) implies a constant real wage in that case. In a diagram like Figure 13.2, the GME curve is downward sloping in the top panel and the wage curve is horizontal in the bottom panel. At impact the multiplier is as in (13.20) but during transition the increase in the number of firms leads to a reduction in aggregate output. The long-run effect on output is equal merely to the first round of the multiplier process in (13.20) (i.e. the impact effect of the shock):

$$0 < \left(\frac{dY}{dG} \right)_T^{LR,\eta=1} = (1 - \alpha) < \frac{1 - \alpha}{1 - \alpha/\theta} \equiv \left(\frac{dY}{dG} \right)_T^{SR}. \tag{13.35}$$

This prompts Startz (1989, p. 747) to conclude that "... in the long run the short-run multiplier is eliminated by free entry".

In the most general version of the model, with η unrestricted, the long-run multiplier can be solved by combining (13.29) and (13.31):

$$\left(\frac{dY}{dG} \right)_T^{LR} = \eta W \left(\frac{dL}{dG} \right)_T^{LR} = \frac{1 - \alpha}{1 - ((\eta - 1)/\eta)\left[\alpha + (1 - \alpha)\omega_C\right]} > 1 - \alpha, \tag{13.36}$$

where the inequality follows from the fact that the denominator is strictly between zero and unity if $\eta > 1$ (see (13.32)). Hence, whereas fluctuations in profit income explain the multiplication of the impact effect in the short run, it is the preference for diversity effect which plays this role in the long run.

Although Startz (1989, p. 751 n. 13) justifies the elimination of diversity preference by appealing to computational advantages, it is not an innocuous assumption at all as the discussion above reveals. In essence, if the diversity parameter (η) is greater than unity there are economy-wide increasing returns to scale that help explain the "long-run" multiplier under free exit/entry of firms. Indeed, in the long run profits are zero and $Y = \theta WNF = WL$ which implies (by (13.29)) that the macroeconomic "production function" can be written as:

$$Y = \left(\frac{(\theta F)^{1-\eta}}{\mu k} \right) L^{\eta}. \tag{13.37}$$

Changes in the aggregate supply of the production factor(s) (labour in this case) are magnified more than proportionally. The importance of increasing returns to scale for Keynesian economics has been stressed time and again by seasoned warriors like Weitzman (1982, 1984, 1994) and Solow (1986, 1998) and allowing for preference for diversity is one particularly simple way to introduce scale economies.[7]

13.1.5 Welfare effects

In a famous passage in the *General Theory*, Keynes argued that seemingly useless government consumption could actually improve welfare for the agents in the economy:

If the Treasury were to fill old bottles with bank-notes, bury them at suitable depths in disused coal-mines which are then filled up to the surface with town rubbish, and leave it to private enterprise on well-tried principles of *laissez-faire* to dig the notes up again (...), there need be no more unemployment and, with the help of the repercussions, the real income of the community, and its capital wealth also, would probably become a good deal greater than it actually is. (1936, p. 129)

In the jargon of modern economics, Keynes suggests in this quotation that the marginal cost of public funds (MCPF, see Chapter 10) is zero or even negative: useless spending turns out to be useful after all! To conclude this section we now investigate the link between fiscal policy multipliers and the welfare of the representative agent. It turns out that the monopolistic competition model has some Keynesian aspects in this regard although they are not quite as extreme as the quotation suggests.

One of the major advantages of macroeconomic models based on explicit microeconomic foundations is that they provide an explicit link between macroeconomic concepts (such as aggregate output, employment, etc.) and the level of welfare experienced by the representative household. To conduct the welfare analysis for the monopolistic competition model it is convenient to use the so-called *indirect utility function*, rather than the direct utility function given in (13.1). The indirect utility function is obtained by substituting the optimal plans of the representative

---

[7] In the model developed here (and in most models in the literature) all scale economies are external to the firm in the long run. With a constant markup the zero profit condition in combination with markup pricing implies a unique (constant) optimal long-run firm size: $\bar{Y} \equiv F/[(\mu - 1)k]$. Hence, aggregate output expansion is solely due to increases in the number of firms in the long run.

household (namely (13.6) and (13.8)) into the direct utility function (13.1) (see the Intermezzo above for details):

$$V \equiv \frac{I_F}{P_V} \equiv \frac{W + \Pi/P - T/P}{P_V/P}, \quad \frac{P_V}{P} \equiv \frac{W^{1-\alpha}}{\alpha^\alpha(1-\alpha)^{1-\alpha}}. \tag{13.38}$$

Armed with this expression we can evaluate the welfare effects of expansionary fiscal policy. In the interests of brevity, we only analyse the short-run multipliers discussed above in subsections 1.2. and 1.3.

First consider the case in which the increase in government consumption is financed by means of a lump-sum tax increase. By substituting the expression for real aggregate profit income (T1.3) and the government budget constraint (T1.4) in (13.38) we obtain the following expression:

$$V \equiv \frac{[1 - NF - L_G]W + (1/\theta)Y - G}{P_V/P}. \tag{13.39}$$

Since N and thus also W, P, P_V are constant in the short run, the welfare effect of a tax-financed fiscal expansion is simply the derivative of V with respect to G:

$$\left(\frac{dV}{dG}\right)_T^{SR} = \left(\frac{P}{P_V}\right)\left[\frac{1}{\theta}\left(\frac{dY}{dG}\right)_T^{SR} - 1\right] = -\left(\frac{P}{P_V}\right)\left(\frac{\theta - 1}{\theta - \alpha}\right) < 0, \tag{13.40}$$

where we have substituted the output multiplier (given in (13.20)) to simplify the expression. Under monopolistic competition, there is an intimate link between the multiplier and the welfare effect of public spending which is absent under perfect competition. The intuition is that under monopolistic competition there is a distortion in the goods market and the economy is "too small" from a societal point of view. By raising government spending output rises and that in itself constitutes a move in the right, welfare-enhancing, direction. Of course government consumption must also be financed somehow (here by means of lump-sum taxes) so that the expansion is not costless. Indeed, (13.40) shows that the overall effect of a lump-sum financed fiscal expansion is negative.

So unless there are other reasons (such as public goods aspects due to government spending discussed by Heijdra and van der Ploeg, 1996) the government does not increase welfare as a result of its increased spending and Keynes' insight does not hold. This un-Keynesian element of the monopolistic competition model is explained by two of its key properties: (1) the real wage is flexible and clears the labour market, and (2) every unit of labour contributes to production in the economy.

The importance of the second property of the model can be demonstrated by studying the case (discussed in detail in subsection 1.3) in which the spending shock is financed by reducing the number of (unproductive) civil servants (i.e. $dG = -WdL_G$). In that case the lump-sum tax is constant and the relevant expression for indirect utility is:

$$V \equiv \frac{[1 - NF]\, W + (1/\theta)Y - T/P}{P_V/P},\tag{13.41}$$

from which we obtain the welfare effect:

$$\left(\frac{dV}{dG}\right)^{SR}_{LG} = \left(\frac{P}{P_V}\right)\frac{1}{\theta}\left(\frac{dY}{dG}\right)^{SR}_{LG} = \left(\frac{P}{P_V}\right)\left(\frac{1}{\theta - \alpha}\right) > 0.\tag{13.42}$$

In this case only the beneficial effect of government-induced output expansion is operative and welfare rises. The intuition is the same as in Keynes' story: units of labour are shifted from socially unproductive to productive activities. The monopolistically competitive sector absorbs the former civil servants without prompting a change in the real wage.

Intermezzo

Multipliers and the marginal cost of public funds. There exists a simple relationship between the macroeconomic concept of the output multiplier and the public finance concept of marginal cost of public funds (MCPF). This link is particularly useful to study issues of optimal public spending and taxation. As was pointed out in Chapter 10, MCPF measures how much it costs to raise a guilder of public revenue. In the context of the monopolistic competition model MCPF is defined as follows:

$$MCPF \equiv -\frac{1}{U_C}\frac{dV}{dG},\tag{a}$$

where U_C is the marginal utility of composite consumption. Intuitively, the minus sign appears on the right-hand side to convert benefits into costs (a negative benefit is equivalent to a positive cost!) and the division by U_C occurs in order to compare "likes with likes" and to render MCPF dimensionless.

It is not difficult to show that U_C equals P/P_V. Recall that the representative household maximizes utility, $U(C, 1 - L)$, subject to the budget constraint, $I_F = PC + W^N(1 - L)$. The first-order conditions for this problem are $U_C = \lambda P$ and $U_{1-L} = \lambda W^N$, where λ is the Lagrange multiplier of the budget constraint representing the marginal utility of (full) income, i.e. $\lambda = dU/dI_F$ (see Intriligator, 1971, ch. 3). The indirect utility function (13.38) shows that $dV/dI_F = 1/P_V = dU/dI_F$. By combining these results we derive that $U_C = P/P_V$ so that (13.40) and (13.42) can be re-expressed in terms of MCPF:

$$0 < MCPF^{SR}_T \equiv -\frac{1}{U_C}\left(\frac{dV}{dG}\right)^{SR}_T = \frac{\theta - 1}{\theta - \alpha} < 1,\tag{b}$$

$$MCPF^{SR}_{LG} \equiv -\frac{1}{U_C}\left(\frac{dV}{dG}\right)^{SR}_{LG} = -\frac{1}{\theta - \alpha} < 0.\tag{c}$$

Hence, it costs (more than zero but) less than one guilder to raise a guilder of revenue if lump-sum taxes are used (expression (b)) and the MCPF is even negative if useless civil servants can be made socially productive (expression (c)). Heijdra and van der Ploeg (1996) develop a more general monopolistic competition model and use the concept of MCPF to derive the conditions under which optimal public spending is countercyclical.

13.2 Monopolistic Competition and Money

In the monopolistic competition model used throughout the previous section (and summarized in Table 13.1) money is abstracted from and as a result **nominal** prices and the nominal wage are indeterminate although, of course, **relative** prices are determined within the model. The objective of this section is to introduce money into the model and study its properties. Although there are several ways to ensure that money plays a role in the model (see Chapter 12), we focus attention on the simplest of these and postulate that real money balances yield utility to the representative household. The utility function (13.1) is changed to:

$$U \equiv \left[C^{\alpha}(1-L)^{1-\alpha} \right]^{\beta} (M/P)^{1-\beta}, \quad 0 < \alpha, \ \beta < 1, \tag{13.43}$$

where M is nominal money balances. The household has an initial endowment of money, M_0, and the budget constraint (13.5) is changed to:

$$PC + W^N(1-L) + M = M_0 + W^N + \Pi - T, \tag{13.44}$$

which says that the sum of spending on consumption, leisure, and money balances (the left-hand side) must equal total wealth (the right-hand side of (13.44)).

The household chooses composite consumption (C), labour supply (L), and money balances (M) in order to maximize (13.43) subject to (13.44). The solutions are:[8]

$$PC = \alpha\beta I_F, \quad I_F \equiv M_0 + W^N + \Pi - T, \tag{13.45}$$

$$W^N(1-L) = \beta(1-\alpha)I_F, \tag{13.46}$$

$$M = (1-\beta)I_F. \tag{13.47}$$

The first two expressions are qualitatively the same as before (see (13.6) and (13.8)), although I_F now includes initial money balances. Furthermore, equation (13.47) shows that money demand is proportional to full income. For future reference we

---

[8] The demand for variety j of the composite consumption good is still given by (13.7).

Table 13.2. A simple monetary monopolistic competition model

$$Y = C + G \tag{T2.1}$$

$$C = \alpha\beta(I_F/P), \quad I_F/P \equiv M_0/P + W^N/P + \Pi/P - T/P \tag{T2.2}$$

$$\Pi/P \equiv \theta^{-1}Y - (W^N/P)NF \tag{T2.3}$$

$$T/P = G + (W^N/P)L_G \tag{T2.4}$$

$$P/W^N = \mu k N^{1-\eta} \tag{T2.5}$$

$$(W^N/P)(1 - L) = \beta(1 - \alpha)(I_F/P) \tag{T2.6}$$

$$M_0/P = (1 - \beta)(I_F/P) \tag{T2.7}$$

$$V = \frac{I_F}{P_V}, \quad P_V = \left(\frac{P}{\alpha\beta}\right)^{\alpha\beta} \left(\frac{W^N}{\beta(1-\alpha)}\right)^{\beta(1-\alpha)} \left(\frac{P}{1-\beta}\right)^{1-\beta} \tag{T2.8}$$

substitute the solutions (13.45)–(13.47) back into the direct utility function (13.43) to obtain the indirect utility function–see equation (T2.8) in Table 13.2 above.

Assuming a constant money supply (M_0), the money market equilibrium condition is:

$$M = M_0. \tag{13.48}$$

The rest of the model is unchanged and we summarize the main equations of the monetary monopolistic competition model in Table 13.2.

It is tempting (though wrong) to conclude from the form of the indirect utility function (T2.8) that the government could increase the welfare of the representative household by simply bringing more money into circulation (and boosting full income, I_F, in the process), for example by engineering a helicopter drop of money ($dM_0 > 0$). The reason why such a ploy would not work is that money is neutral in this model and the classical dichotomy holds (see Chapter 1). This can be demonstrated formally by noting that the equilibrium conditions (in Table 13.2) are homogeneous of degree zero in W^N, P, T, Π, I_F, and M_0 (see Dixon, 1987, p. 141). By substituting ζW^N, ζP, ζT, $\zeta\Pi$, ζI_F, and ζM_0 ($\zeta > 0$) into Table 13.2 the real equilibrium is unaffected. All that happens if the money supply is multiplied by ζ is that all nominal variables are increased equiproportionally and all real variables are unchanged. Hence, a helicopter drop of money does not succeed in raising household welfare because both I_F **and** P_V go up by the same proportional amount thus keeping V in (T2.8) unchanged. The upshot of this discussion is that monopolistic competition *in and of itself* does not introduce monetary non-neutrality. Put differently, if money is neutral in a model-economy without monopolistic competition then it is also neutral if monopolistic competition is introduced into the model (Silvestre, 1993, p. 122).

The model can be summarized with two equations. The goods market equilibrium (GME) locus is obtained by using (T2.2)–(T2.4) and (T2.6) in (T2.1). The money market equilibrium (MME) locus is obtained by using the second expression of (T2.2) as well as (T2.3)–(T2.4) in (T2.7):

$$Y = \frac{\alpha \left[1 - NF - L_G \right] W + (1 - \alpha)G}{1 - \alpha/\theta} \quad \text{(GME)}, \tag{13.49}$$

$$\frac{M_0}{P} = \left(\frac{1 - \beta}{\beta} \right) \left[\left[1 - NF - L_G \right] W + (1/\theta)Y - G \right] \quad \text{(MME)}. \tag{13.50}$$

The two loci provide a clear demonstration of the classical dichotomy. In the short run, N and thus W are fixed and GME determines equilibrium output. Since the money supply does not appear in (13.49), monetary policy cannot affect equilibrium output. According to (13.50), an increase in the money supply leads to an equiproportional increase in the price level.

The GME and MME loci can also be used to compute the short-run effects of a tax-financed increase in public consumption. An increase in G leads to a boost in output Y but a reduction in the demand for real money balances (as real full income falls). Since nominal money balances M_0 are constant, the price P rises to bring demand and supply of real money balances back into equilibrium. The nominal wage and prices of different varieties also rise equi-proportionally. In summary:

$$0 < \left(\frac{dY}{dG} \right)_T^{SR} = \frac{1 - \alpha}{1 - \alpha/\theta} < 1, \quad \left(\frac{dW^N}{W^N} \right)_T^{SR} = \left(\frac{dP}{P} \right)_T^{SR} = \left(\frac{d\bar{P}}{\bar{P}} \right)_T^{SR}, \tag{13.51}$$

$$\left(\frac{dM_0/P}{dG} \right)_T^{SR} = - \left(\frac{M_0}{P^2} \right) \left(\frac{dP}{dG} \right)_T^{SR} = - \frac{(1 - \beta)(\theta - 1)}{\beta(\theta - \alpha)} < 0.$$

From the monetary side of things the model is more classical than Keynesian if prices and wages are flexible.

13.3 Sticky Prices and the Non-neutrality of Money

In the previous section it was demonstrated that the presence of monopolistically competitive agents in the economy does not in and of itself render money non-neutral. This is not to say that the introduction of price-setting agents in a macroeconomic model is merely a theoretical nicety yielding no novel insights or additional predictions. Indeed, in the first section of this chapter it was shown how the monopolistic competition model with flexible prices and wages generates results that are quite different from the standard competitive model. An additional advantage of assuming monopolistic, rather than perfect, competition is that one can do away with the fictional notion of the Walrasian auctioneer.

By modelling price-setting agents explicitly, it is also possible to study quite precisely the conditions under which such an agent would change his price (or keep it unchanged) following a shock in some nominal variable such as the money supply or the money wage rate (Rotemberg, 1987, p. 71). The key ingredient of the New Keynesian approach is to postulate that it costs the firm real resources in order to change its price. As a result, prices may not be adjusted after some nominal shock and money may be non-neutral. In the remainder of this section a number of the main macroeconomic price-adjustment models will be discussed. The key feature distinguishing these models lies in the nature of the price adjustment cost that are postulated.

As is pointed out by Rotemberg (1982, p. 522) there are two main reasons why prices may be costly to change. First, there may be administrative costs having to do with informing dealers, reprinting price lists, etc. Such costs tend to have the nature of a fixed cost per price change, independent of the magnitude of the change: it costs the same to reprint your restaurant menu card when you double or triple your prices. Such price adjustment costs are often referred to as *menu costs* in the new Keynesian literature. The second reason why prices may be costly to change is that there may be an implicit cost due to an adverse reaction of customers to large price changes. According to this view customers may prefer **frequent small** price changes over **infrequent but large** price adjustments. It is conventional to assume that such costs are increasing and convex in the price change.[9]

We now turn to a discussion of some of the most popular models of price setting. In the first model only menu costs play a role (subsection 3.1) whilst in the second we assume that price adjustment costs are quadratic (subsection 3.2). In subsection 3.3 we discuss an alternative setting in which price adjustment costs are random and are either infinite or zero in any particular period. The models in subsections 3.2–3.3 both give rise to a new Keynesian Phillips curve which is similar in form (though not in interpretation) to the expectations-augmented Phillips curve of Friedman and Phelps (see Roberts, 1995, pp. 979–980).

13.3.1 Menu costs, real rigidity, and monetary neutrality

In this subsection we develop a simple monetary monopolistic competition model in which price-setting firms face small menu costs if they wish to change their prices. The model is a simplified version of Blanchard and Kiyotaki (1987) in that the labour market is assumed to be competitive and populated by wage-taking agents (firms and the representative household). Hence, the nominal wage is flexible and

---

[9] Such costs are reminiscent of the adjustment costs often postulated in the theory of firm investment. See the discussion of Tobin's q theory of investment in Chapters 2 and 4.

labour demand and supply are equated. The main advantage of assuming a competitive labour market is that it facilitates the exposition of the main results and identifies in a straightforward fashion some of the empirical problems the menu-cost argument runs into.

As in Blanchard and Kiyotaki (1987, p. 649) the representative household has a utility function which is additively separable in composite consumption and real money on the one hand and labour hours on the other.

$$U(C, M/P, L) \equiv U^1(C, M/P) - U^2(L)$$

$$= C^\alpha (M/P)^{1-\alpha} - \gamma_L \left[\frac{L^{1+1/\sigma}}{1+1/\sigma} \right], \quad 0 < \alpha < 1, \ \sigma > 0, \quad (13.52)$$

where $\gamma_L > 0$ is a simple scaling factor (to be used in the computer simulations below) and σ regulates the slope of the labour supply function (see below). The budget restriction is given by:

$$PC + M = W^N L + M_0 + \Pi - T \ (\equiv I), \quad (13.53)$$

where I represents total wealth of the household (including labour income). Composite consumption is defined by (13.2) and it is assumed that the diversity effect is absent (i.e. we set $\eta = 1$). This is a useful and innocuous simplification as it is assumed that the number of firms is constant. The household chooses consumption, money balances, and labour supply in order to maximize (13.52) subject to (13.53). Again a simple two-stage procedure can be used to find the solutions. In the first stage the household chooses C and M/P to maximize the sub-utility function $U^1(C, M/P)$ subject to the budget restriction $PC + M = I$. This yields the following expressions:

$$PC = \alpha I, \quad (13.54)$$

$$M = (1 - \alpha)I, \quad (13.55)$$

$$V^1(I/P) = \alpha^\alpha (1 - \alpha)^{1-\alpha}(I/P), \quad (13.56)$$

where $V^1(I/P)$ is the indirect sub-utility function associated with $U^1(C, M/P)$.[10] In the second stage, the household chooses L and thus I in order to maximize $V^1(I/P) - U^2(L)$ subject to the definition of I (given on the right-hand side of (13.53)). This yields the expressions for labour supply and real household wealth including labour income:

$$L = \left(\frac{\alpha^\alpha (1 - \alpha)^{1-\alpha}}{\gamma_L} \right)^\sigma \left(\frac{W^N}{P} \right)^\sigma, \quad (13.57)$$

$$\frac{I}{P} = \left(\frac{\alpha^\alpha (1 - \alpha)^{1-\alpha}}{\gamma_L} \right)^\sigma \left(\frac{W^N}{P} \right)^{1+\sigma} + \frac{M_0 + \Pi - T}{P}. \quad (13.58)$$

---

[10] It is obtained by substituting the optimal values for C and M/P into the direct sub-utility function $U^1(.)$.

By using the utility specification (13.52), there is no income effect in labour supply and only the substitution effect survives. The advantage of this specification is that it enables us to demonstrate the crucial role played by the elasticity of labour supply with respect to the real wage. If σ is very high, labour supply is highly elastic and large labour supply changes result from only a small increase in the real wage. Conversely, if σ is low labour supply is relatively inelastic and a large change in the real wage is needed to produce a given increase of labour supply.

Each firm in the monopolistically competitive sector faces a demand for its product from the private sector (see (13.7)) and from the government (see (13.16)). Since we abstract from diversity effects ($\eta = 1$), total demand facing firm j can be written as:

$$Y_j(P_j, P, Y) = \left(\frac{P_j}{P}\right)^{-\theta} \left(\frac{Y}{N}\right), \tag{13.59}$$

where Y is aggregate demand:

$$Y = C + G = \left(\frac{1-\alpha}{\alpha}\right)\left(\frac{M}{P}\right) + G, \tag{13.60}$$

and where we have used (13.54)–(13.55) to relate private consumption to real money balances.

For reasons that will become clear below, we use a slightly more general description of technology than before. Instead of (13.10) we use the following production function:

$$Y_j = \begin{cases} 0 & \text{if } L_j \leq F \\ \left[\frac{L_j - F}{k}\right]^{\gamma} & \text{if } L_j \geq F \end{cases}, \tag{13.61}$$

with $0 < \gamma \leq 1$. If γ is strictly less than unity, the marginal physical product of labour declines with output and the average cost curve of the firm is U-shaped (see Dixon and Lawler, 1996, p. 223). Of course, if $\gamma = 1$ (13.61) and (13.10) coincide.

Firm j chooses its price, P_j, in order to maximize its profit:[11]

$$\Pi_j(P_j, P, Y) \equiv P_j Y_j(P_j, P, Y) - W^N \left[k\left(Y_j(P_j, P, Y)\right)^{1/\gamma} + F\right]. \tag{13.62}$$

The optimal price of firm j must satisfy the following first-order condition:

$$\begin{aligned}
\frac{d\Pi_j(P_j, P, Y)}{dP_j} &= [P_j - MC_j]\left(\frac{\partial Y_j(P_j, P, Y)}{\partial P_j}\right) + Y_j(P_j, P, Y) \\
&= Y_j(P_j, P, Y)\left[1 + \left(\frac{P_j - MC_j}{P_j}\right)\left(\frac{P_j}{Y_j(.)}\frac{\partial Y_j(.)}{\partial P_j}\right)\right] \\
&= Y_j(P_j, P, Y)\left[1 - \theta\left(\frac{P_j - MC_j}{P_j}\right)\right] = 0,
\end{aligned} \tag{13.63}$$

---

[11] The reason why we introduce the rather elaborate notation for demand $Y_j(P_j, P, Y)$ and profit $\Pi_j(P_j, P, Y)$ will be made apparent below.

where MC_j is marginal costs of firm j and where we have substituted the price elasticity of demand (θ) in going from the second to the third line. An active firm is one which produces a positive amount of goods ($Y_j(.) > 0$) and sets price according to:

$$P_j = \mu MC_j \Rightarrow P_j = \left(\frac{\mu k}{\gamma}\right) W^N Y_j^{(1-\gamma)/\gamma}, \quad \mu = \frac{\theta}{\theta - 1} > 1. \qquad (13.64)$$

This pricing rule generalizes the one derived in section 1 of this chapter (i.e. equation (13.13)) by allowing for an upward-sloping marginal cost curve (if $\gamma < 1$). Apart from this generalization, another important thing to note is that in section 1 it was assumed that the firm sets its output level in a profit-maximizing fashion taking other producers' output levels as given (the Cournot assumption). In contrast, in this section the firm sets its price in an optimal (profit-maximizing) fashion, taking other producers' prices as given (the Bertrand assumption). In the absence of menu costs the two assumptions yield the same pricing rule. As is shown below, however, this equivalence does not necessarily hold in the presence of menu costs.

We now have all the ingredients of the model, though still abstracting from menu costs. The main equations have been collected in Table 13.3. Equation (T3.2) expresses consumption (and equilibrium real money balances) as a function of factors influencing real wealth. It is obtained by using (13.54)–(13.55), (13.58), imposing money market equilibrium (13.48), and substituting the government budget constraint $G = T/P$ (we again abstract from civil servants and set $L_G = 0$ in (T2.4)). Equation (T3.3) is the expression for aggregate profit income. It is obtained by substituting the optimal price (13.64) into the definition of profit income (13.62) and simplifying by using the definition of Y in (13.17). Finally,

Table 13.3. A simplified Blanchard-Kiyotaki model (no menu costs)

$$Y = C + G \qquad (T3.1)$$

$$C = \left(\frac{\alpha}{1-\alpha}\right)\left(\frac{M_0}{P}\right) = \begin{cases} \alpha\left[\omega^{-\sigma}\left(\frac{W^N}{P}\right)^{1+\sigma} + \frac{M_0}{P} + \frac{\Pi}{P} - G\right] (\text{if } \sigma < \infty) \\ \alpha\left[\left(\frac{W^N}{P}\right)L + \frac{M_0}{P} + \frac{\Pi}{P} - G\right] (\text{if } \sigma \to \infty) \end{cases} \qquad (T3.2)$$

$$\Pi/P \equiv \left(\frac{\mu - \gamma}{\mu}\right)Y - (W^N/P)NF \qquad (T3.3)$$

$$P/W^N = (\mu k/\gamma)\left(\frac{Y}{N}\right)^{(1-\gamma)/\gamma} \qquad (T3.4)$$

$$\frac{W^N}{P} = \begin{cases} \omega L^{1/\sigma} (\text{if } \sigma < \infty) \\ \omega (\text{if } \sigma \to \infty) \end{cases} \qquad (T3.5)$$

Notes: $\omega \equiv \gamma_L[\alpha^\alpha(1-\alpha)^{1-\alpha}]^{-1} > 0$ and $\mu \equiv \theta/(\theta - 1)$.

(T3.4) is the price-setting rule in the symmetric equilibrium, and (T3.5) is the labour supply function.

Before turning to the implications of menu costs, we first study the properties of the model under perfect price flexibility. By studying the flex-price version of the models first, it is easier to understand the implications of menu costs later on. It is clear that money is neutral: multiplying W^N, P, and M_0 by $\zeta > 0$ does not change anything real and just changes all nominal variables (such as nominal wealth, I, and nominal profit, Π) equi-proportionally. On the monetary side of things the models of Tables 13.2 and 13.3 are thus similar in that they both exhibit monetary neutrality when prices and wages are flexible. There is an important difference between the two models, however, in the area of fiscal policy. Indeed, because there is no income effect in labour supply (see (T3.5)), fiscal policy is completely ineffective in the model of this section. Using the expressions in Table 13.3 it is easy to show that a tax-financed increase in public consumption leads to one-for-one crowding out of private consumption, no effect on output, real profits, employment, and real wages, and an increase in the price level. In that sense the model used here is even more classical than the one used in the previous section. In the next subsection we study if and to what extent the notion of menu costs can give this hyper-classical model a more Keynesian flavour.

The basic menu-cost insight

Sometimes the answer to an apparently simple question can be quite surprising. A beautiful example of this phenomenon is provided by Akerlof and Yellen's (1985a) question whether "small deviations from rationality make significant differences to equilibria". Alternatively, the question could be rephrased in terms of transactions costs: can small costs of changing one's actions have large effects on the economic equilibrium and social welfare? Nine out of ten people would probably answer this question with an unequivocal "no". The thought experiment would probably lead them to reject the notion that a small "impulse" can produce a "large effect". In terms of Matsuyama's (1995) terminology, most people are unfamiliar with the notion of macroeconomic complementarities and cumulative processes. It turns out, however, that the answer to Akerlof and Yellen's question can be quite a bit more complex.

In the context of our model, the task at hand is to investigate whether, following a shock in aggregate demand, price stickiness can (a) be privately efficient and (b) exist in general equilibrium, whilst (c) the effect on social welfare can be large. If both parts (a) and (b) are demonstrated, Akerlof and Yellen's question is answered in the affirmative. Part (a) can be easily demonstrated to hold in our model and relies on a simple application of the *envelope theorem*. The proof of part (b) is more complex as it relies on the general equilibrium implications of price stickiness. Once (a) and (b) have been demonstrated, part (c) follows readily.

Intermezzo

The envelope theorem The envelope theorem is extremely useful in economic theory. Broadly speaking the theorem says that the change in the objective function due to a change in an exogenous parameter is the same whether or not the decision variable is adjusted as a result of the change in the parameter. In more colloquial terms, the theorem says that objective functions are flat at the top (Rotemberg, 1987, p. 76).

Consider the formal demonstration by Varian (1992, pp. 490–491). Suppose that $f(x, z)$ is the objective function, x is the decision variable, and z is the (vector of) exogenous variables and parameters. The first-order condition for an optimum of $f(x, z)$ by choice of x is:

$$\frac{\partial f(x, z)}{\partial x} = 0. \tag{a}$$

But (a) can itself be interpreted as an implicit function relating the optimal choice for the decision variable (x^*) to the particular values of z, say $x^* = x^*(z)$. By plugging x^* back into the objective function we obtain the so-called optimal value function:

$$V(z) \equiv \underset{\{x\}}{\text{Max}}\, f(x, z) = f(x^*(z), z). \tag{b}$$

It is useful to note that we have in fact encountered many such optimal value functions throughout the book. For example, in this chapter the indirect utility function (13.38) is an example of a maximum value function: it expresses maximum attainable utility (the objective) in terms of full income and a true price index (the parameters that are exogenous to the household). Similarly, the true price index for the composite differentiated good (13.9) is an example of a minimum value function.

Using the optimal value function (b) we can determine by how much the objective function changes if (an element of) z changes by a small amount. By totally differentiating (b) we obtain:

$$\frac{dV(z)}{dz} = \left[\frac{\partial f(x, z)}{\partial x} \right]_{x=x^*(z)} \left(\frac{dx^*(z)}{dz} \right) + \frac{\partial f(x^*(z), z)}{\partial z}. \tag{c}$$

The second term on the right-hand side of (c) is the direct effect on the objective function of the change in z keeping the decision variable unchanged. The first term on the right-hand side is the indirect effect on the objective function that is induced by the change in x^* itself. The point to note, however, is that in the optimum the objective function is flat (i.e. (a) shows that $\partial f(.)/\partial x = 0$ for

$x = x^*$) so that the indirect effect is zero. Hence, equation (c) reduced to:

$$\frac{dV(z)}{dz} = \frac{\partial f(x^*(z), z)}{\partial z} \equiv \frac{\partial V(z)}{\partial z}. \tag{d}$$

This is the simplest statement of the envelope theorem. The total and partial derivatives are the same, i.e. at the margin the change in the objective function is the same whether or not the decision variable is changed.

We close with an anecdote from times past. As is argued by Silberberg (1987), the discovery of the envelope theorem is due in part to a dispute between the famous economist Jacob Viner and his draftsman Dr Y. K. Wong. Viner was working on his famous paper about the relationship between short-run (AC_{SR}) and long-run average cost (AC_{LR}) curves (see Viner, 1931). He instructed Dr Wong to draw AC_{LR} in such a way that it was never above any portion of any AC_{SR} curve and that it would pass through the minimum points of all AC_{SR} curves. Dr Wong, being a mathematician, refused to do so and pointed out to Viner that his instructions were actually inconsistent. Unfortunately, Viner, not being a mathematician, could not understand Dr Wong's point and ended up drawing AC_{LR} through all the minima of the AC_{SR} curves (see his chart IV and footnote 16). Samuelson (1947), being both an economist and mathematician, ultimately solved the puzzle by pointing out that AC_{LR} is the envelope of all AC_{SR} curves. Wong was right after all! If this anecdote has any lesson at all, it must be that economists should also be reasonably good mathematicians to avoid falling into puzzles that cannot be solved by graphical means alone.

What happens to the optimal price of firm j if aggregate demand changes by a small amount? The answer is provided by the envelope theorem (see the Intermezzo). In particular, (13.59) and (13.64) together yield an expression for the optimal price in terms of the parameters that are exogenous to firm j, i.e. $P_j^* = P_j(P, Y, W^N)$:

$$\frac{P_j^*}{P} = \left[\left(\frac{\mu k}{\gamma} \right) \left(\frac{W^N}{P} \right) \left(\frac{Y}{N} \right)^{(1-\gamma)/\gamma} \right]^{\gamma/[\gamma + \theta(1-\gamma)]}. \tag{13.65}$$

By substituting $P_j^*(.)$ into (13.62) we obtain the maximum profit function, $\Pi_j^*(P, Y, W^N)$, of firm j:

$$\Pi_j^*(P, Y, W^N) \equiv P_j^*(.)Y_j(P_j^*(.), P, Y) - W^N \left[k \left(Y_j(P_j^*(.), P, Y) \right)^{1/\gamma} + F \right]. \tag{13.66}$$

By differentiating this expression with respect to aggregate demand we obtain the result that it doesn't really matter to the profit of firm j whether or not it changes its price following a shock in aggregate demand:

$$
\begin{aligned}
\frac{d\Pi_j^*(.)}{dY} &= \left[\left[P_j^*(.) - MC_j^*(.) \right] \left(\frac{\partial Y_j(P_j, P, Y)}{\partial P_j} \right)_{P_j = P_j^*} + Y_j(P_j^*(.), P, Y) \right] \left(\frac{dP_j^*(.)}{dY} \right) \\
&\quad + \left[P_j^*(.) - MC_j^*(.) \right] \left(\frac{\partial Y_j(P_j^*(.), P, Y)}{\partial Y} \right) \\
&= \left[\frac{\partial \Pi_j(.)}{\partial P_j} \right]_{P_j = P_j^*} \left(\frac{dP_j^*(.)}{dY} \right) + \left[P_j^*(.) - MC_j^*(.) \right] \left(\frac{\partial Y_j(P_j^*(.), P, Y)}{\partial Y} \right) \\
&= \left[P_j^*(.) - MC_j^*(.) \right] \left(\frac{\partial Y_j(P_j^*(.), P, Y)}{\partial Y} \right) \equiv \frac{\partial \Pi_j(.)}{\partial Y},
\end{aligned}
\tag{13.67}
$$

where $MC_j^*(.)$ is short-hand notation for the marginal cost of firm j evaluated in the optimum. Hence, to a first-order of magnitude, the effect on the profit of firm j of a change in aggregate demand is the same whether or not firm j changes its price optimally following the aggregate demand shock.

The envelope result can be illustrated with the aid of a diagram originally suggested by Akerlof and Yellen (1985a, p. 710). In Figure 13.3 firm j's price and profit level are put on the horizontal and vertical axes respectively. Initially aggregate demand is Y_0 and the optimal price is at the top of the "profit hill" at point A. The optimal price-profit combination is denoted by $(P_j^*(P, Y_0, W_0^N), \Pi_j^*(P, Y_0, W_0^N))$. Now consider what happens if aggregate demand expands, say from Y_0 to Y_1 ($>Y_0$). Ceteris paribus the nominal wage rate (W_0^N) and the price index for the composite consumption good (P),[12] the level of profit rises for all values of P_j and the entire profit function shifts up, say from $\Pi_j(P_j, P, Y_0, W_0^N)$ to $\Pi_j(P_j, P, Y_1, W_0^N)$.[13] The output expansion leads to an increase in marginal costs (provided $\gamma < 1$) and thus to an increase in the optimal price of firm j (see (13.64)–(13.65)). Hence, the top of the new profit hill (point B) lies north-east of the top of the old profit hill (point A).[14]

But this is not the end of the story. Following the shock to aggregate demand, firm j experiences a boost in the demand for its product and increases its production level

[12] We hold constant the prices charged by all other firms and conclude that this renders the price index, P, constant. In doing so, we ignore the fact that firm j's price also features in the price index P. This is allowed because there are many firms and each individual firm is extremely small and its price thus carries a small weight in the price index.

[13] Formally, (13.62) implies that $\partial \Pi_j(.)/\partial Y = [P_j - MC_j]\partial Y_j/\partial Y$. A necessary condition for firm j to have positive profits (as drawn in Figure 13.3) is that its price must cover at least marginal cost, i.e. $P_j > MC_j$. Furthermore, (13.59) implies that firm j's demand expands if aggregate demand increases, i.e. $\partial Y_j/\partial Y$. Combining these results yields $\partial \Pi_j(.)/\partial Y > 0$. Firms like aggregate demand expansions because it raises their profits.

[14] In contrast, if the marginal product of labour is constant ($\gamma = 1$), point B lies directly above point A. This strong result follows from the pricing rule (13.64) in combination with the fact that the demand elasticity (θ) and thus the gross markup (μ) of firm j are both constant. The optimal price is then proportional to the given nominal wage. As a result, for a given nominal wage there is no need for firm j to change its price and the envelope result (13.67) holds exactly.

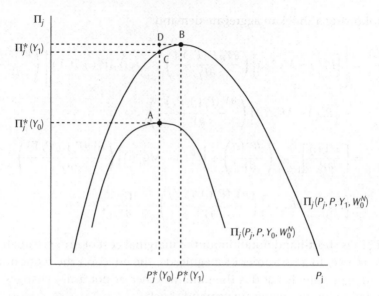

Figure 13.3. Menu costs

accordingly. But this means that it needs to employ more workers. Since all firms are in exactly the same position as firm j they will also want to employ more workers so that aggregate demand for labour will rise. This is where the labour market comes in. Clearly, if the labour supply elasticity is very large ($\sigma \to \infty$), firm j (and all other firms) can obtain the additional units of labour at the initial nominal wage rate (W_0^N). In that case the real wage is rigid (see (T3.5)) and thus, if the price index P does not change neither will the nominal wage rate W^N. So all we need to show now is why the price index would be rigid.

Assuming for the time being that labour supply is infinitely elastic ($\sigma \to \infty$) it is possible to demonstrate the menu-cost insight graphically with the aid of Figure 13.3. For given values of P and W^N, the aggregate demand shock would increase the profits of firm j from $\Pi_j^*(P, Y_0, W_0^N)$ to $\Pi_j^*(P, Y_1, W_0^N)$ if it adjusted its price optimally (which is the move from A to B). If instead firm j keeps its price unchanged, the profit increase would be the vertical distance between points C and A and the envelope theorem suggests that the profit loss due to non-adjustment of the price is second order, i.e. the vertical distance DC in Figure 13.3 is very small. But that suggests that small menu costs can make non-adjustment of the price a profitable option for firm j. Indeed, provided the menu costs (Z) are larger than the vertical distance DC, keeping P_j unchanged is the optimal choice for firm j, i.e. P_j will be set equal to its old optimal level ($P_j^*(P, Y_0, W_0^N)$) if the following condition is satisfied:

$$\Pi_j(P_j^*(P, Y_0, W_0^N), P, Y_1, W_0^N) > \Pi_j^*(P, Y_1, W_0^N) - Z, \tag{13.68}$$

where the left-hand side of (13.68) is the profit level of firm j when it charges the old price and faces the higher aggregate demand, Y_1. The right-hand side of (13.68) is the net profit of firm j if it changes its price in the face of higher demand and incurs the menu cost. Since by assumption all firms are in exactly the same position as firm j, they also do not change their price if (13.68) holds and the maintained assumption that P is constant is thereby confirmed. Hence, for the infinitely elastic labour supply case ($\sigma \to \infty$) a menu-cost equilibrium exists for which an aggregate demand shock has no effect on prices and the nominal (and real) wage rate.

The effects of fiscal and monetary policy in a menu-cost equilibrium can be computed as follows. The model consists of equations (T3.1) and the second expression in (T3.2). Since aggregate profit income equals revenue minus the wage bill ($\Pi \equiv PY - W^N L$) we can write the system as:

$$Y = C + G, \tag{13.69}$$

$$C = \left(\frac{\alpha}{1-\alpha}\right)(M_0/P) = \alpha\left[Y + M_0/P - G\right]. \tag{13.70}$$

Fiscal policy is highly effective in the menu-cost equilibrium:

$$\left(\frac{dY}{dG}\right)_T^{MCE} = 1, \ \left(\frac{dC}{dG}\right)_T^{MCE} = \left(\frac{d(M_0/P)}{dG}\right)_T^{MCE} = 0, \tag{13.71}$$

where the superscript "MCE" stands for menu-cost equilibrium. The increase in government consumption raises aggregate demand and thus each individual firm's demand and profit level. Due to the menu costs all firms keep their price unchanged and because of the horizontal labour supply curve ($\sigma \to \infty$) the nominal wage does not change either. The firms can hire all the additional units of labour they need at the old real wage rate. The representative household receives the additional firm revenue in the form of additional wage payments and profit income. The additional income exactly covers the higher taxes levied by the government so that private consumption is unchanged and the output effect is simply the effect due to public consumption as in the original Haavelmo (1945) story. In view of the production function (13.61) the employment expansion can be written as:

$$(W^N/P)\left(\frac{dL}{dG}\right)_T^{MCE} = \frac{1}{\mu}\left(\frac{dY}{dG}\right)_T^{MCE} = \frac{\theta - 1}{\theta} > 0, \tag{13.72}$$

where we have used symmetry ($L_j = L/N$ for $j = 1, \ldots, N$) plus the fact that firms have set their prices as a markup over marginal cost in the **initial** (pre-shock) equilibrium.

Monetary policy, consisting of a helicopter drop of nominal money balances ($dM_0 > 0$) stimulates output, employment, and consumption, and the existence of menu costs thus destroys monetary neutrality:

$$P \left(\frac{dY}{dM_0} \right)^{MCE} = P \left(\frac{dC}{dM_0} \right)^{MCE} = \mu W^N \left(\frac{dL}{dM_0} \right)^{MCE} = \frac{\alpha}{1 - \alpha} > 0. \tag{13.73}$$

The increase in money balances leads to an increase in consumption spending and further multiplier effects via the expanded income of the representative household, i.e. after n rounds of the multiplier process spending has increased by $P\,dY = P\,dC = [\alpha + \alpha^2 + \cdots + \alpha^n]\,dM_0$ and the demand for money has increased by $dM = (1 - \alpha)[1 + \alpha + \alpha^2 + \cdots + \alpha^n]\,dM_0$. Since the marginal propensity to consume is less than unity, the multiplier process converges to the expressions in (13.73).

In summary, we have succeeded in demonstrating that with a very high labour supply elasticity ($\sigma \to \infty$, so that the labour supply curve is horizontal), small menu costs can lead to nominal price and wage inflexibility, which in turn drastically alters the qualitative properties of the model. Indeed, as was shown in the previous sub-section, the flex-price version of the model possesses extremely classical properties in that money is neutral and fiscal policy only affects the price level. In contrast, in a menu cost equilibrium, both fiscal and monetary policy affect output and employment thus giving the model a much more Keynesian flavour. Below we demonstrate that both the **nominal rigidity** (price stickiness due to menu costs in price adjustment) and the **real rigidity** (constant real wage due to a horizontal labour supply curve) are of crucial importance in this result. Before doing so, however, we must demonstrate part (c) of our menu-cost investigation by demonstrating that there are first-order welfare effects associated with the aggregate demand effects we found above (see page 384 above).

As before, we use the indirect utility function to compute the welfare effects of aggregate demand shocks in a menu-cost equilibrium. By using (13.69)–(13.70) in (13.52) (with $\sigma \to \infty$ imposed) we find a number of alternative expressions for indirect utility:

$$\begin{aligned}
V &= \alpha^\alpha (1 - \alpha)^{1 - \alpha} \left[Y + \frac{M_0}{P} - G \right] - \gamma_L L \\
&= \alpha^\alpha (1 - \alpha)^{1 - \alpha} \left[\frac{M_0 + \Pi}{P} - G \right] + \left[\alpha^\alpha (1 - \alpha)^{1 - \alpha} \left(\frac{W^N}{P} \right) - \gamma_L \right] L \\
&= \alpha^\alpha (1 - \alpha)^{1 - \alpha} \left[\frac{M_0 + \Pi}{P} - G \right].
\end{aligned} \tag{13.74}$$

In going from the first to the second expression we have used the definition for aggregate profit income ($\Pi \equiv PY - W^N L$) and in going from the second to the third expression we have used the labour supply equation (T3.5). Fiscal policy clearly has first-order welfare effects. Using the first line of (13.74) and noting (13.69) we derive:

$$\left(\frac{dV}{dG}\right)_T^{MCE} = \alpha^\alpha (1-\alpha)^{1-\alpha} \left(\frac{dC}{dG}\right)_T^{MCE} - \gamma_L \left(\frac{dL}{dG}\right)_T^{MCE}$$

$$= -\frac{\gamma_L}{\mu}\left(\frac{P}{W^N}\right) = -\frac{\alpha^\alpha(1-\alpha)^{1-\alpha}}{\mu} < 0, \tag{13.75}$$

where the second equality makes use of (13.71) and (13.72). The increase in government consumption raises output one-for-one but does not come for free (as in Keynes' story in section 1.5 above) as the representative household has to supply more hours of work. Since the labour market is competitive the household derives no surplus from supplying labour; the additional wage income exactly compensates the household for having to work harder (Blanchard and Kiyotaki, 1987, p. 654). Hence, only the additional profit income mitigates the welfare loss due to additional government spending somewhat. Indeed, the welfare effect (13.75) can be restated in terms of MCPF as:

$$0 < MCPF_T^{MCE} \equiv -\frac{1}{U_C}\left(\frac{dV}{dG}\right)_T^{MCE} = \frac{1}{\mu} = \frac{\theta-1}{\theta} < 1, \tag{13.76}$$

where we have used the fact that the marginal utility of consumption equals $U_C = \alpha^\alpha(1-\alpha)^{1-\alpha}$. The existence of market power in the goods market mitigates but does not obliterate the social costs associated with a public spending shock.

Monetary policy also has first-order welfare effects in the menu-cost equilibrium. Indeed, using the final expression in (13.74) we derive:

$$\left(\frac{dV}{dM_0}\right)^{MCE} = \alpha^\alpha(1-\alpha)^{1-\alpha}\left[\frac{1}{P} + \left(\frac{d(\Pi/P)}{dM_0}\right)^{MCE}\right]$$

$$= \frac{\alpha^\alpha(1-\alpha)^{1-\alpha}}{P}\left[1 + P\left(\frac{dY}{dM_0}\right)^{MCE} - W^N\left(\frac{dL}{dM_0}\right)^{MCE}\right]$$

$$= \frac{\alpha^\alpha(1-\alpha)^{1-\alpha}}{P}\left[1 + \left(\frac{1}{\theta}\right)\left(\frac{\alpha}{1-\alpha}\right)\right] > 0. \tag{13.77}$$

The term outside the brackets on the right-hand side of (13.77) represents the marginal utility of nominal income. Inside the square brackets on the right-hand side of (13.77) there are two effects which may be labelled, respectively, the *liquidity effect* and the *profit effect*. As is pointed out by Blanchard and Kiyotaki, the liquidity effect exists because even the competitive equilibrium (for which $1/\theta = 0$) is suboptimal if real money enters utility (1987, p. 654 n. 13). As is explained in Chapter 12, the inefficiency results from the fact that people economize on a resource (fiat money) which is not scarce from a societal point of view. For that reason, ceteris paribus consumption, an increase in real money balances constitutes a welfare gain because it lowers the marginal utility of real money balances and brings the economy closer to Friedman's satiation point. This effect operates regardless of the nature of competition in the goods market.

In contrast to the liquidity effect, the profit effect in (13.77) is only operative under monopolistic competition (i.e. if $1/\theta$ is finite). This works via the profit income of households. An increase in the money stock boosts output and profit income and this causes an additional welfare gain to the representative household over and above the liquidity effect. Since both effects work in the same direction, the total welfare effect of an increase in nominal money balances in a menu-cost equilibrium is unambiguously positive and first order.

Some simulations

In the previous subsection it was demonstrated (for the case with a horizontal labour supply curve, i.e. $\sigma \to \infty$), that with small menu costs both monetary and fiscal policy can have first-order effects on welfare. We have thus confirmed the basic menu-cost insight of Akerlof and Yellen (1985a, 1985b). In Tables 13.4 and 13.5 we present some numerical simulations with a more general version of the menu-cost model. In particular, we investigate the robustness of the menu-cost insight with respect to changes in key parameters such as the labour supply elasticity (σ), the markup (μ), and the elasticity of the marginal cost function ($\sigma_Y \equiv (1 - \gamma)/\gamma$).

In order to perform the simulations, numerical values must be chosen for all the parameters that appear in Table 13.3. The following so-called *calibration approach* is adopted. We set up the model such that the parameters of special interest (σ, σ_Y, and μ) can be varied freely. We adopt a number of quantities/shares that are held constant (at economically reasonable values) throughout the simulations. In particular, the number of firms is $N_0 = 1000$ (large), the steady-state revenue share of overhead labour cost is $\omega_F \equiv W^N NF/PY = 0.05$, the output share of government consumption is $\omega_G \equiv G/Y = 0.1$, and the velocity of money $v_M \equiv M_0/(PY)_0 = 6$. We assume that the initial money supply is $M_0 = 1$ and that initial output and employment are normalized at unity, $Y_0 = L_0 = 1$. For a given configuration of (σ, σ_Y, μ) it is possible to compute the initial steady state for the endogenous variables ($Y, C, P, W^N/P, L, \Pi/P$) by using the calibration parameters (α, γ_L, F, k) appropriately, i.e. in such a way that the steady state is consistent with the share and parameter information we have imposed above.

Since this way of calibrating a theoretical model may not be familiar to all readers, we show in detail how we can retrieve the remaining variables and parameters. We denote the initial steady-state value with a subscript "0". It follows from (T3.1) that $C_0 = (1 - \omega_G)Y_0 = 0.9$ and $G_0 = \omega_G Y_0 = 0.1$. By rewriting the money velocity definition we find $P_0 = M_0/(v_M Y_0) = 1/6$. From (T3.2) we derive $\omega_C \equiv C/Y = \alpha v_M/(1 - \alpha)$ which can be solved for $\alpha = \omega_C/(\omega_C + v_M) \approx 0.13$. By defining the pure profit share as $1 - \epsilon_L \equiv [\Pi/(PY)]_0$, it follows from (T3.3) and the definition of ω_F that $\epsilon_L = \gamma/\mu + \omega_F$ (where $\gamma \equiv 1/(1 + \sigma_Y)$). By definition $\epsilon_L \equiv [W^N L/(PY)]_0$ from which we derive an expression for the initial real wage $(W^N/P)_0 = \epsilon_L$. We can make this expression for the real wage consistent with (T3.5) by setting $\gamma_L = (W^N/P)_0 \alpha^\alpha (1 - \alpha)^{1-\alpha}$. In view of the definition of ω_F we find that $F = (Y/N)_0/(W^N/P)_0 = (N_0 \epsilon_L)^{-1}$. The value for

k is retrieved from (T3.4): $k = \gamma \left[\epsilon_L \mu (Y/N)_0^{\sigma_Y} \right]^{-1}$ and Π_0 is obtained from (T3.3). To give an example, for the case with $\mu = 1.25$, $\sigma_Y = 0.1$, and $\sigma = 10^6$, the calibration approach yields the following results for the variables and parameters.

$$
\begin{array}{llll}
Y_0 = 1 & C_0 = 0.9 & G_0 = 0.1 & L_0 = 1 \\
N_0 = 1000 & (W^N/P)_0 = 0.777 & P_0 = 0.167 & \Pi_0 = 0.0371 \\
\alpha = 0.130 & \gamma_L = 0.528 & k = 1.867 & F = 6.433 \times 10^{-5}
\end{array} \qquad (13.78)
$$

In order to numerically investigate the menu cost insight, we follow Blanchard and Kiyotaki (1987, p. 658) by administering a non-trivial monetary shock, taking the form of a 5% increase in the money supply. We study the economy under two pure scenarios. In the *full-adjustment* case, all firms pay the menu cost and adjust the price of their product in the light of the higher level of aggregate demand. In contrast, in the *no-adjustment* case, all firms keep their price unchanged and expand output to meet the aggregate demand expansion.

Assuming that the menu cost takes the form of overhead labour (e.g. workers are employed to change price tags), under full adjustment, the model consists of equations (T3.1)–(T3.2) and (T3.4)–(T3.5) plus the augmented profit function:

$$
\Pi^{FA} = \left(\frac{\mu - \gamma}{\mu} \right) PY - W^N N (F + Z), \qquad (13.79)
$$

where the superscript "*FA*" stands for full adjustment. For a given value of Z, this system can be solved numerically for the endogenous variables Π^{FA}, Y, L, P, C, and W^N.

In contrast, in the no-adjustment case all firms keep their price unchanged ($P = P_0$) and the system consists of equations (T3.1)–(T3.2), (T3.5), and the profit function under no adjustment (superscript "*NA*"):

$$
\Pi^{NA} = P_0 Y - W^N \left[k Y^{1/\gamma} N^{1-1/\gamma} + NF \right]. \qquad (13.80)
$$

This system of equations can be solved numerically for the endogenous variables Π^{NA}, Y, L, C, and W^N.

In the final step, we compare profit levels under the two scenarios and find the lowest value of menu costs, Z_{MIN}, for which non adjustment of prices is an equilibrium, i.e. for which Π^{FA} just falls short of Π^{NA}. In Tables 13.4 and 13.5 we report a number of indicators for different parameter combinations. In Table 13.4 we consider four different values for the markup ($\mu \in \{1.1, 1.25, 1.5, 2\}$) and six different values for the labour supply elasticity ($\sigma \in \{0.2, 0.5, 1, 2.5, 5, 10^6\}$). In each case the entry labelled "menu costs" reports the revenue share of menu costs for which non-adjustment is an equilibrium for all firms, i.e. the entry equals:

$$
\text{menu costs} = 100 \times \left(\frac{N_0 \left(W^N \right)^{NA} Z_{MIN}}{P_0 Y^{NA}} \right), \qquad (13.81)
$$

where $\left(W^N \right)^{NA}$ and Y^{NA} are, respectively, the nominal wage and output when the price is not adjusted. So, for example, if $\mu = 1.1$, $\sigma_Y = 0.1$, and $\sigma = 10^6$, the results

Table 13.4. Menu costs and the markup

$\Delta M = 0.05$ $\sigma_Y = 0.1$	menu costs	welfare gain	ratio	menu costs	welfare gain	ratio
	$\mu = 1.10$			$\mu = 1.25$		
$\sigma = 0.2$	20.44	28.6	1.40	18.10	29.1	1.61
$\sigma = 0.5$	7.85	28.9	3.68	6.96	29.4	4.22
$\sigma = 1$	3.95	29.0	7.35	3.51	29.5	8.40
$\sigma = 2.5$	1.69	29.1	17.18	1.51	29.5	19.49
$\sigma = 5$	0.94	29.1	30.80	0.86	29.6	34.37
$\sigma = 10^6$	0.20	29.1	146.12	0.20	29.6	145.73
	$\mu = 1.50$			$\mu = 2$		
$\sigma = 0.2$	15.23	29.8	1.96	11.53	30.6	2.65
$\sigma = 0.5$	5.87	30.0	5.11	4.55	30.8	6.76
$\sigma = 1$	2.99	30.1	10.06	2.35	30.8	13.12
$\sigma = 2.5$	1.32	30.1	22.80	1.06	30.8	29.12
$\sigma = 5$	0.76	30.1	39.56	0.63	30.9	48.68
$\sigma = 10^6$	0.21	30.1	144.67	0.21	30.9	144.95

in Table 13.4 show that menu costs amounting to no more than 0.20% of revenue will make non-adjustment of prices an equilibrium in the sense that $\Pi^{NA} > \Pi^{FA}$. The entry labelled "welfare gain" measures the gain in welfare (expressed in terms of an output share) which results from the monetary shock when there is no adjustment in prices:

$$\text{welfare gain} = 100 \times \left(\frac{V^{NA} - V_0}{U_C Y^{NA}} \right), \tag{13.82}$$

where $U_C \equiv \alpha^\alpha (1 - \alpha)^{1-\alpha}$ is the marginal utility of income, V_0 is initial welfare, and V^{NA} is welfare following the shock but in the absence of price adjustment. So, if $\mu = 1.1$, $\sigma_Y = 0.1$, and $\sigma = 10^6$, the monetary shock gives rise to a huge 29.1% rise in welfare. Finally, the entry labelled "ratio" is the ratio of the welfare gain and the macroeconomic menu costs. For the particular case considered here, the ratio is 146.12, so that a small menu cost gives rise to very large welfare effects.

In Table 13.4 we hold the elasticity of marginal cost constant (at $\sigma_Y = 0.1$) and consider various combinations of the markup (μ) and the substitution elasticity of labour supply (σ). Just like Blanchard and Kiyotaki (1987, p. 658) we find a number of key features in these simulations. First, the welfare measure does not vary a lot with the different parameter combinations. Second, for a given value of σ, the markup does not affect menu costs and the ratio very much. Third, for a given value of μ, menu costs are strongly dependent on the value of the labour elasticity.

Table 13.5. Menu costs and the elasticity of marginal cost

$\Delta M = 0.05$ $\mu = 1.25$	menu costs	welfare gain	ratio	menu costs	welfare gain	ratio
	$\sigma_Y = 0$			$\sigma_Y = 0.05$		
$\sigma = 0.2$	17.44	29.2	1.67	17.72	29.2	1.65
$\sigma = 0.5$	6.61	29.4	4.45	6.76	29.4	4.35
$\sigma = 1$	3.17	29.5	9.31	3.34	29.5	8.84
$\sigma = 2.5$	1.19	29.5	24.73	1.36	29.5	21.69
$\sigma = 5$	0.52	29.6	56.72	0.70	29.6	42.23
$\sigma = 10^6$	$\to 0$	29.6	$\to \infty$	0.04	29.6	672.74
	$\sigma_Y = 0.1$			$\sigma_Y = 0.2$		
$\sigma = 0.2$	18.10	29.1	1.61	18.54	29.1	1.57
$\sigma = 0.5$	6.96	29.4	4.22	7.34	29.4	4.00
$\sigma = 1$	3.51	29.5	8.40	3.84	29.5	7.67
$\sigma = 2.5$	1.51	29.5	19.49	1.83	29.5	16.16
$\sigma = 5$	0.86	29.6	34.37	1.15	29.5	25.60
$\sigma = 10^6$	0.20	29.6	145.73	0.49	29.6	60.60

Take, for example, the empirically reasonable case for which the net markup is 25%, i.e. $\mu = 1.25$. If labour supply is infinitely elastic ($\sigma \to \infty$), menu costs of 0.2% of revenue suffice to make non-adjustment of prices optimal and the ratio is 145.73. This ratio drops very rapidly for lower, empirically more reasonable, values of σ. For example, if $\sigma = 1$ then only unreasonably high menu costs (amounting to 3.51% of revenue) can stop the firm from finding price adjustment advantageous. Intuitively, if labour supply is not very elastic, the output expansion under non-adjustment drives up wages (and thus production costs) very rapidly and thus makes it more likely that price adjustment is profitable.

In Table 13.5 we hold the markup constant (at $\mu = 1.25$) and consider various combinations of the elasticity of marginal cost (σ_Y) and the labour supply elasticity (σ). Essentially the same picture emerges from this table as from the previous one: the welfare gain is rather insensitive to (σ, σ_Y)-combinations, the value of σ_Y does not affect menu costs and the ratio very much, and the labour supply elasticity exerts a major effect on menu costs and the ratio.

Evaluation

The simulation results graphically illustrate that the standard menu-cost model runs into trouble because non-adjustment of prices after a monetary shock is only an equilibrium if labour supply is highly elastic (Blanchard and Kiyotaki, 1987, p. 663). For an empirically reasonable value of the labour supply elasticity, there are very strong incentives to adjust prices and nominal frictions produce only small non-neutralities.[15] Ball and Romer (1990) argue that the menu-cost argument can be rescued if the economy has both real and nominal rigidities. By real rigidity they mean the phenomenon that "real wages or prices are unresponsive to changes in economic activity" (Ball and Romer, 1990, p. 183). Nominal rigidity can either take the form of small menu costs or departures from full rationality (as in Akerlof and Yellen, 1985a, 1985b). Taken in isolation, real rigidity does not imply price inflexibility. But in combination with nominal rigidity, a high degree of real rigidity translates into substantial effects of monetary shocks. In the model considered in the previous subsection, a high labour supply elasticity leads to substantial real rigidity. Indeed, for $\sigma \to \infty$, the real wage is constant (see equation (T3.5)) and thus completely insensitive to economic activity. Ball and Romer (1990) discuss a number of alternative models leading to real rigidities, such as the efficiency-wage model of the labour market and the imperfect-information customer-market model of the goods market.

Rotemberg (1987, pp. 80–81) has identified a number of problematic aspects of the menu-cost insight. First, the menu-cost equilibrium may not be unique. In the context of our model, his argument runs as follows. Recall that Z_{MIN} represents the minimum amount of menu costs for which it is profitable for an individual firm j not to adjust its price *given that all other firms also keep their prices unchanged*! But if one firm changes its price when $Z = Z_{MIN}$, it generally becomes profitable for *all* other firms to change their prices also, so we have two equilibria: the firms either all adjust their prices or they all keep them unchanged. Let us now define Z_{MIN}^* as the minimum amount of menu costs for which an individual firm j keeps its price unchanged *even if all other firms would change their prices*. Clearly, Z_{MIN}^* exceeds Z_{MIN}. Furthermore, if $Z \geq Z_{MIN}^*$ the menu cost equilibrium is unique. For the intermediate case, however, with $Z \in (Z_{MIN}, Z_{MIN}^*)$ there are three equilibria: one with no firm adjusting, another with all firms adjusting, and an intermediate case in which a fraction ϕ of the firms adjusts ($0 < \phi < 1$). Rotemberg (1987, p. 90) argues that the multiplicity of equilibria is a weakness for any economic model. Essentially, with multiple equilibria it is impossible to predict the economy's reaction to particular policy shocks.

A second problem with the menu-cost insight is that it could equally well be applied to quantities instead of prices. Indeed, if there are costs of adjusting quantities (e.g. because capital has to be installed in advance of the price-setting decision, as in Shapiro, 1989, pp. 350–351) it may well be optimal for the firm to adjust its price and leave output unchanged (Rotemberg, 1987, p. 77).

---

[15] As we show in Chapter 15, the competitive real business cycle (RBC) model runs into the same problem because it can only generate large output movements following real shocks if the (intertemporal) labour supply elasticity is very large.

Finally, as is argued by Rotemberg (1987, pp. 85–91) and Blanchard (1990, p. 822) an important practical disadvantage of the menu-cost approach to price adjustment is that it does not generalize easily to a dynamic setting.[16] For that reason we now turn to two approaches which do not have this disadvantage.

13.3.2 Quadratic price adjustment costs

In an influential article, Rotemberg (1982) has formulated a rather attractive dynamic model of price adjustment in which adjustment costs are assumed to be quadratic (just as in the investment literature surveyed in Chapters 2 and 4 above). Intuitively, his model solves the problem of dynamic price adjustments in two (conceptual) steps. In the first step, a path of "equilibrium" prices is determined consisting of the solution that firm j would choose if there were no costs of adjusting prices. Normalizing the current (planning) period by $t = 0$, this equilibrium path for firm j is denoted by the sequence $\{P_{j,\tau}^*\}_{\tau=0}^{\infty}$. In the second step, Rotemberg takes a quadratic approximation of the firm's profit function around this equilibrium path and incorporates adjustment costs. He shows that the dynamic objective function of the firm can then be written as follows:

$$\Omega_0 = \sum_{\tau=0}^{\infty} \left(\frac{1}{1+\rho}\right)^\tau \left[\left(p_{j,\tau} - p_{j,\tau}^*\right)^2 + c \left(p_{j,\tau} - p_{j,\tau-1}\right)^2\right], \tag{13.83}$$

where $(1 + \rho)^{-1}$ is the firm's discount factor, c is a constant, $p_{j,\tau} \equiv \log P_{j,\tau}$, and $p_{j,\tau}^* \equiv \log P_{j,\tau}^*$. In the presence of price adjustment costs, the firm chooses a sequence of actual prices, $\{P_{j,\tau}\}_{\tau=0}^{\infty}$, in order to *minimize* the costs of deviating from the optimum in the absence of price adjustment costs (Ω_0). Equation (13.83) shows that these "deviation costs" are composed of two terms. The first quadratic term on the right-hand side of (13.83) represents the *intra*temporal cost of setting the price at a "suboptimal" level, i.e. at a level different from $P_{j,\tau}^*$. The second quadratic term on the right-hand side of (13.83) parameterizes the *inter*temporal costs to the firm that are due to price adjustment costs. The higher is c, the more severe are the price adjustment costs.

The first-order condition for the optimal price in period τ is readily obtained by using (13.83) and setting $\partial\Omega_0/\partial p_{j,\tau} = 0$:

$$\frac{\partial\Omega_0}{\partial p_{j,\tau}} = \left(\frac{1}{1+\rho}\right)^\tau \left[2\left(p_{j,\tau} - p_{j,\tau}^*\right) + 2c\left(p_{j,\tau} - p_{j,\tau-1}\right)\right]$$

$$- \left(\frac{1}{1+\rho}\right)^{\tau+1} \left[2c\left(p_{j,\tau+1} - p_{j,\tau}\right)\right] = 0. \tag{13.84}$$

---

[16] See Danziger (1999) for a recent example of a dynamic general equilibrium model with menu costs.

After some straightforward manipulation we find that (13.84) can be simplified to:

$$p_{j,\tau+1} - \left[1 + (1+\rho)\left(\frac{1+c}{c}\right)\right]p_{j,\tau} + (1+\rho)p_{j,\tau-1} = -\left(\frac{1+\rho}{c}\right)p_{j,\tau}^* \qquad (13.85)$$

Equation (13.85) is a second-order difference equation in $p_{j,\tau}$ with constant coefficients and a potentially time-varying forcing term $p_{j,\tau}^*$. In order to solve this equation we need two boundary conditions. The first is an initial condition which results from the fact that when the firm decides on its price $p_{j,\tau}$, the price it charged in the previous period $(p_{j,\tau-1})$ is predetermined. The second boundary condition is a terminal condition saying that the firm expects to charge a price close to $p_{t,\tau}^*$ in the distant future (see Rotemberg (1982, pp. 523–524) for details):

$$\lim_{\tau \to \infty}\left[\left(p_{j,\tau} - p_{j,\tau}^*\right) + c\left(p_{j,\tau} - p_{j,\tau-1}\right)\right] = 0. \qquad (13.86)$$

It is shown by Kennan (1979, p. 1443) and Rotemberg (1987, p. 92) that the solution for the price in the planning period, $p_{j,0}$, can be written as:

$$p_{j,0} = \lambda_1 p_{j,-1} + (1 - \lambda_1)\left[\left(\frac{\lambda_2 - 1}{\lambda_2}\right)\sum_{\tau=0}^{\infty}\left(\frac{1}{\lambda_2}\right)^{\tau} p_{j,\tau}^*\right], \qquad (13.87)$$

where $0 < \lambda_1 < 1$ and $\lambda_2 > 1$.[17] The economic intuition behind the pricing-setting rule (13.87) is as follows. In the presence of price adjustment costs, the firm finds it optimal to adjust its price gradually over time. As a result, the optimal price in any period is the weighted average of the last period's price $p_{j,-1}$ and the long-run "target" price given in square brackets on the right-hand side of (13.87). This target price itself depends on the present and future equilibrium prices ($p_{j,\tau}^*$, for $\tau = 0, 1, \ldots$). In the special case where the equilibrium price is (expected to be) constant indefinitely, we have $p_{j,\tau}^* = p_j^*$ and it follows that the target price is equal to p_j^*. In the general case, however, the firm knows that it chases a moving (rather than a stationary) target because it recognizes future variability in the equilibrium price (say due to anticipated policy shocks).

13.3.3 Staggered price contracts

In a number of papers, Calvo has proposed an alternative approach to modelling sluggish aggregate prices (see e.g. Calvo, 1982, 1983, 1987 and Calvo and Végh, 1994). His basic idea, which derives from the early papers by Phelps (1978) and Taylor (1980), makes use of the notion that price contracts are staggered. Calvo (1987, p. 144) adopts the following price-setting technology. Each period of time "nature" draws a signal to the firm which may be a "green light" or a "red light" with probabilities π and $1 - \pi$, respectively. These probabilities are the same for all

---

[17] Readers of the Mathematical Appendix will recognize that λ_1 and λ_2 are, respectively, the stable and unstable characteristic roots of the difference equation in (13.85).

firms in the economy. A firm which has just received a green light can change its price optimally in that period but must maintain that price until the next green light is received.

In order to solve the pricing problem of a firm which has just received a green light we can follow the same approach as in the previous subsection. In the absence of the pricing friction firm j would always want to set its price equal to its equilibrium price P_j^*. But with the pricing friction the firm aims to minimize the deviation cost, Ω_0, given in equation (13.83) but with $c = 0$ (there are no price adjustment costs). By substituting the assumptions about the pricing technology into the objective function (13.83) we obtain:

$$\Omega_0 = \left(p_{j,0} - p_{j,0}^*\right)^2 + \left(\frac{1}{1+\rho}\right)\left[\pi\left(p_{j,1} - p_{j,1}^*\right)^2 + (1-\pi)\left(p_{j,0} - p_{j,1}^*\right)^2\right]$$

$$+ \left(\frac{1}{1+\rho}\right)^2 [\pi^2\left(p_{j,2} - p_{j,2}^*\right)^2 + \pi(1-\pi)\left(p_{j,1} - p_{j,2}^*\right)^2$$

$$+ (1-\pi)^2\left(p_{j,0} - p_{j,2}^*\right)^2] + \text{higher-order terms.} \qquad (13.88)$$

The interpretation of this expression is as follows. In the current period ($\tau = 0$) the firm has a green light so it can set its price. The first term on the right-hand side of (13.88) gives the cost of deviating from $p_{j,0}^*$ in the current period. In the next period ($\tau = 1$) the firm may or may not get a green light again. If it does (with probability π) it will again be able to set its price in the light of the then relevant equilibrium price $p_{j,1}^*$. If it gets a red light, however, it will have to keep its price unchanged (at $p_{j,0}$) and face the deviation costs associated with this choice made in the previous period. In period $\tau = 2$ there are three different possibilities depending on when the firm last received a green signal.

Since the pattern should be clear by now and we are only interested in the price to be set by the firm in the planning period, we can rewrite (13.88) by gathering all terms involving $p_{j,0}$:

$$\Omega_0 = \left(p_{j,0} - p_{j,0}^*\right)^2 + \left(\frac{1-\pi}{1+\rho}\right)\left(p_{j,0} - p_{j,1}^*\right)^2 + \left(\frac{1-\pi}{1+\rho}\right)^2\left(p_{j,0} - p_{j,2}^*\right)^2 + \cdots$$

$$= \sum_{\tau=0}^{\infty}\left(\frac{1-\pi}{1+\rho}\right)^\tau\left(p_{j,0} - p_{j,\tau}^*\right)^2 + \cdots, \qquad (13.89)$$

where the remaining terms do not involve $p_{j,0}$. The pricing friction thus shows up in the discounting factor employed by the firm. The higher is the probability of a green light in any period, the less severe is the friction, and the lower is the weight attached to future equilibrium prices.

The firm chooses $p_{j,0}$ in order to minimize Ω_0. The first-order condition is given by $\partial \Omega_0 / \partial p_{j,0} = 0$ which can be written as:

$$p_{j,0}\sum_{\tau=0}^{\infty}\left(\frac{1-\pi}{1+\rho}\right)^\tau = \sum_{\tau=0}^{\infty}\left(\frac{1-\pi}{1+\rho}\right)^\tau p_{j,\tau}^*. \qquad (13.90)$$

Since the infinite sum on the left-hand side of (13.90) converges to $(1+\rho)/(\pi+\rho)$ we can rewrite (13.90) as follows:

$$p_0^n = \left(\frac{\pi+\rho}{1+\rho}\right) \sum_{\tau=0}^{\infty} \left(\frac{1-\pi}{1+\rho}\right)^\tau p_\tau^*, \tag{13.91}$$

where p_0^n denotes the common "new" price set in period 0 by all firms facing a green light in that period. Note that we have assumed that all firms are identical so that the firm index no longer features in (13.91). The firms facing a red light in the planning period ($\tau = 0$) keep their prices as set in some past period using a rule like (13.91), i.e.:

$$p_{-s}^n = \left(\frac{\pi+\rho}{1+\rho}\right) \sum_{\tau=0}^{\infty} \left(\frac{1-\pi}{1+\rho}\right)^\tau p_{\tau-s}^*, \tag{13.92}$$

for $s = 1, 2, \cdots \infty$. Since $\pi(1-\pi)^s$ is the fraction of firms which last adjusted prices s periods before the planning period, we can define the aggregate price level in the planning period as follows:

$$
\begin{aligned}
p_0 &= \pi p_0^n + \pi(1-\pi)p_{-1}^n + \pi(1-\pi)^2 p_{-2}^n + \pi(1-\pi)^3 p_{-3}^n + \cdots \\
&= \pi \sum_{s=0}^{\infty} (1-\pi)^s p_{-s}^n \\
&= \pi p_0^n + (1-\pi)p_{-1}.
\end{aligned} \tag{13.93}
$$

The actual aggregate price level in the planning period (p_0) is thus the weighted average of the aggregate price in the previous period (p_{-1}) and the newly set price (p_0^n). By substituting (13.91) in (13.93) we get the following expression for p_0:

$$p_0 = (1-\pi)p_{-1} + \pi \left[\left(\frac{\pi+\rho}{1+\rho}\right) \sum_{\tau=0}^{\infty} \left(\frac{1-\pi}{1+\rho}\right)^\tau p_\tau^* \right]. \tag{13.94}$$

As is pointed out by Rotemberg (1987, p. 93), the pricing rule that results from the Calvo friction (given in (13.94)) is indistinguishable from the aggregate version of the pricing rule under adjustment costs (given in (13.87)). The nice thing about both pricing rules is that they can be readily estimated using time series data for actual economies. Rotemberg (1987, p. 93) for example, cites evidence that 8% of all prices are adjusted every quarter in the US, implying a mean time between price adjustments of about three years.[18]

[18] The expected time of price fixity (ETPF) is:

$$ETPF = \pi \times 1 + \pi(1-\pi) \times 2 + \cdots + \pi(1-\pi)^{n-1}n + \cdots$$

$$= \pi \sum_{s=0}^{\infty} (1-\pi)(1+s) = 1/\pi.$$

See King and Wolman (1996, p. 10).

13.4 Punchlines

We started this chapter by constructing a small general equilibrium model with monopolistic competition in the goods market. On the supply side of the goods market there are many small firms who each produce slightly unique product variety and thus possess a small amount of market power. Each firm sets its price to optimally exploit its market power.

The model provides microeconomic foundations for the multiplier. In the short run the number of firms is fixed and a tax-financed increase in government consumption boosts output, though by less than one-for-one. The tax increase makes households poorer which prompts them to decrease consumption and leisure (and thus to increase labour supply). The increase in output raises profit income which partially mitigates the fall in consumption. In the long run the short-run increase in profits prompts entry of new firms which continues until all firms exactly break even (the Chamberlinian tangency solution). If households like product diversity then the increase in the number of product varieties causes an increase in the real consumer wage. The multiplier is not very Keynesian as the output expansion relies critically on the labour supply response (a new classical feature).

Under monopolistic competition, there exists an intimate link between the multiplier and the welfare effect of public spending which is absent under perfect competition. Under monopolistic competition there is a distortion in the goods market and the economy is "too small" from a societal point of view. By raising government spending output rises and that in itself constitutes a move in the right, welfare-enhancing, direction.

Next we introduce money into the model by assuming that households derive utility from real money balances. (This money-in-the-utility-function approach is discussed in detail in Chapter 12 and constitutes the simplest way to ensure that fiat money is held by economic agents.) Monopolistic competition in and of itself does not invalidate the classical dichotomy. Indeed, a helicopter drop of money balances simply inflates all nominal variables equi-proportionally and leaves all real variables unchanged.

Money ceases to be a mere veil if prices are sticky. Here the assumption of monopolistic competition is essential because it explicitly recognizes that it is the individual firms (and not some anonymous auctioneer) who are responsible for setting prices in the economy. We study three major approaches under which price stickiness emerges as an equilibrium phenomenon. The menu-cost approach postulates the existence of small costs associated with changing prices. Since profit functions are flat at the top, it may be optimal for an individual firm not to increase its price in the wake of an expansionary (monetary or fiscal) shock and instead to expand its output. Provided labour supply is sufficiently elastic (and there is thus a sufficient degree of real rigidity) small menu costs (a source of nominal rigidity) can rationalize the fixity of both wages and prices in general equilibrium. In the menu-cost equilibrium, both fiscal and monetary policy are highly effective and money is not neutral. The Achilles heel of the menu-cost model is that it hinges on a highly elastic labour supply equation, a feature which is not supported by the empirical evidence.

A more pragmatic approach to price stickiness assumes that there are convex costs associated with changing prices. In this approach, the individual firm tries to steer the actual sequence of its price as close as possible to its "ideal" price path which would be attained in the absence of adjustment costs. The presence of adjustment costs ensures that the firm sets its actual price as a weighted average of last period's price and some long-run target price which is explicitly forward looking. At a macroeconomic level, the adjustment cost approach thus provides a microeconomic foundation for the expectations-augmented Phillips curve of Friedman and Phelps.

In the third approach to aggregate price stickiness, the pricing friction is stochastic. Each period of time "nature" draws a signal to the firm which may be a "green light" or a "red light" with given probabilities. These probabilities are the same for all firms in the economy. A firm which has just received a green light can change its price optimally (without adjustment costs) in that period but must maintain that price until the next green light is received. Although this theory differs substantially from the adjustment-cost approach at the microeconomic level, the two approaches give rise to an observationally equivalent macroeconomic pricing equation.

Further Reading

Mankiw and Romer (1991) is a collection of key articles on new Keynesian economics. Also see Gordon (1990) and Benassi, Chirco, and Colombo (1994) for overviews of new Keynesian economics. On monopolistic competition as a foundation for the multiplier, see Ng (1982), Hart (1982), Solow (1986), Blanchard and Kiyotaki (1987), Dixon (1987), Mankiw (1988), and Startz (1989). Recent contributions include Molana and Moutos (1992), Dixon and Lawler (1996), Heijdra and Ligthart (1997), and Heijdra, Ligthart, and van der Ploeg (1998). On the welfare properties of the monopolitically competitive equilibrium, see Mankiw and Whinston (1986). Bénassy (1991a,b, 1993b), Silvestre (1993), and Matsuyama (1995) give excellent surveys of the early literature.

On price adjustment costs, see Mankiw (1985), Poterba, Rotemberg, and Summers (1986), Parkin (1986), Dixon and Hansen (1999), and Danziger (1999). Levy et al. (1997) present empirical evidence on the size of menu costs in supermarket chains. For the envelope theorem, see Dixit (1990). On the new Keynesian Phillips curve, see Ball, Mankiw, and Romer (1988) and Roberts (1995). The Calvo approach to price stickiness is widely used in monetary economics. See, for example, King and Wolman (1996, 1999), Clarida, Galí, and Gertler (1999), Goodfriend and King (1997), Rotemberg and Woodford (1999), and Yun (1996).

Kiyotaki (1988) and Bénassy (1993a) show that under monopolistic competition it may not be optimal for households to have rational expectations. There is a large literature on multiple equilibria and coordination failures. See Diamond (1982, 1984a,b), Howitt (1985), Shleifer (1986), Diamond and Fudenberg (1989, 1991), Cooper and John (1988), Weil (1989a), and Benhabib and Farmer (1994). An excellent survey of some of this literature is presented by Cooper (1999). The classic source on multiple equilibria and animal spirits is Keynes (1937).

14

Theories of Economic Growth

The purpose of this chapter is to discuss the following issues:

1. What are some of the most important stylized facts of economic growth?
2. How well does the Solow–Swan model explain these stylized facts?
3. What are the key implications of adding human capital to the Solow–Swan model?
4. What are the most important features of the growth model based on dynamically optimizing consumers?
5. How do fiscal policy and Ricardian equivalence work in various traditional growth models?
6. Under which conditions can endogenous growth emerge?

14.1 Stylized Facts of Economic Growth

According to Kaldor (1961, pp. 178–179), a satisfactory theory of economic growth should be able to explain the following six "stylized facts" by which we mean results that are broadly observable in most capitalist countries.

(SF1) (*) Output per worker shows continuing growth "with no tendency for a falling rate of growth of productivity".

(SF2) Capital per worker shows continuing growth.

(SF3) The rate of return on capital is steady.

(SF4) (*) The capital-output ratio is steady.

(SF5) (*) Labour and capital receive constant shares of total income.

(SF6) (*) There are wide differences in the rate of productivity growth across countries.

Note that not all these stylized facts are independent: (SF1) and (SF4) are easily seen to imply (SF2). In a similar fashion, (SF4) and (SF5) imply (SF3). Hence, the starred facts are fundamental. Romer (1989, p. 55) argues that there is evidence which leads him to disbelieve (SF5), but the remaining facts can be considered stylized even four decades after Kaldor's original claims.

Romer (1989, p. 55) suggests five more stylized facts that growth theorists should be able to explain:

(SF7) In cross-section, the mean growth rate shows no variation with the level of per capita income.

(SF8) The rate of growth of factor inputs is not large enough to explain the rate of growth of output; that is, growth accounting always finds a residual.

(SF9) Growth in the volume of trade is positively correlated with growth in output.

(SF10) Population growth rates are negatively correlated with the level of income.

(SF11) Both skilled and unskilled workers tend to migrate towards high-income countries.

Although we shall have very little to say about the last three stylized facts, the other facts will be referred to regularly.

14.2 The Solow–Swan Model

The neoclassical growth model was developed independently by Solow (1956) and Swan (1956). The central element of their theory is the notion of an aggregate production function (which has been used throughout the book). It can be written in a very general form as:

$$Y(t) = F[K(t), L(t), t],$$ (14.1)

where t is the time index which appears separately in the production function to indicate that the technology itself may not be constant over time. We retain the assumption of perfectly competitive behaviour of firms which implies that the production function must obey constant returns to scale. We label this first property of technology (P1):[1]

$$F[\lambda K(t), \lambda L(t), t] = \lambda F[K(t), L(t), t], \quad \text{for } \lambda > 0.$$ (P1)

---

[1] See the Intermezzo on production theory in Chapter 4 above.

405

It is assumed that the household sector as a whole (or the representative household) consumes a constant fraction of output and saves the rest. Aggregate saving in the economy is then:

$$S(t) = sY(t), \quad 0 < s < 1, \tag{14.2}$$

where s is the constant propensity to save which is assumed to be exogenously given. In a closed economy, output is exhausted by household consumption $C(t)$ and investment $I(t)$:

$$Y(t) = C(t) + I(t), \tag{14.3}$$

where we have assumed that government consumption is zero for now. Aggregate gross investment is the sum of replacement investment, $\delta K(t)$ (where δ is the constant depreciation rate), and the net addition to the capital stock, $\dot{K}(t)$:

$$I(t) = \delta K(t) + \dot{K}(t). \tag{14.4}$$

We assume that labour supply is exogenous but that the population grows as a whole at a constant exponential rate n_L:

$$\frac{\dot{L}(t)}{L(t)} = n_L \quad \Leftrightarrow \quad L(t) = L(0)e^{n_L t}, \tag{14.5}$$

where we can normalize $L(0) = 1$.

14.2.1 No technological progress

We first look at the case for which technology itself is time-invariant, so that the production function (14.1) has no separate time index:

$$Y(t) = F[K(t), L(t)]. \tag{14.6}$$

In addition to linear homogeneity (property (P1)), the production function features positive but diminishing marginal products to both factors:

$$F_K, F_L > 0, \quad F_{KK}, F_{LL} < 0, \quad F_{KL} > 0. \tag{P2}$$

A more controversial assumption, but one we will make nevertheless, is that $F(.)$ obeys the so-called *Inada conditions* (after Inada (1963)) which ensure that it has nice curvature properties around the origin (with K or L equal to zero) and in the limit (with K or L approaching infinity):[2]

$$\lim_{K \to 0} F_K = \lim_{L \to 0} F_L = +\infty, \quad \lim_{K \to \infty} F_K = \lim_{L \to \infty} F_L = 0. \tag{P3}$$

As we shall demonstrate below, these conditions are far from innocuous and actually preclude a number of interesting non-standard cases.

---

[2] Ironically these are the two points about which we humans know the least. The question "Where do we come from and what are we heading for?" is perhaps better dealt with by theologians than by macroeconomists. The Inada conditions obviate the need for a deep study of theology.

The model consists of equations (14.2)–(14.5) plus the savings-investment identity, $S(t) \equiv I(t)$. Because the labour force grows, it is impossible to attain a steady state in *levels* of output, capital, etc., but this problem is easily remedied by measuring all variables in per capita or *intensive form*, i.e. we define $y(t) \equiv Y(t)/L(t)$, $k(t) \equiv K(t)/L(t)$, etc. The model can then be condensed into a single differential equation in the per capita capital stock:

$$\dot{k}(t) = sf(k(t)) - (\delta + n_L)k(t), \tag{14.7}$$

where $f(k(t))$ is the intensive form of the production function and use has been made of the linear homogeneity property (P1):

$$f(k(t)) \equiv F[K(t)/L(t), 1]. \tag{14.8}$$

We can obtain insight into the properties of the model by working with a phase diagram for $k(t)$—see Figure 14.1. In that figure, the straight line $(\delta + n_L)k(t)$ represents the amount of investment required to replace worn-out capital *and* to endow each existing worker with the same amount of capital. Since the work force grows, the line features the growth rate of the labour force, n_L. Since the savings rate, s, is constant by assumption, the per capita saving curve has the same shape as the intensive-form production function. To draw this curve we need to know what happens for $k(t) = 0$ and $k(t) \to \infty$. We obtain from (14.8):

$$f'(k(t)) \equiv F_K[k(t), 1], \quad f''(k(t)) \equiv L(t)F_{KK}[k(t), 1], \tag{14.9}$$

about which the Inada conditions (P3) say all we need to know: $f(k(t))$ is vertical at the origin, is concave, and flattens out as more and more capital per worker is accumulated. Hence $f(k(t))$ and $sf(k(t))$ are as drawn in Figure 14.1.[3]

It follows in a straightforward fashion from the diagram that the model is stable. From any initial position $k(t)$ will converge to the unique equilibrium at point E_0. In the steady state capital per worker is constant and equal to $k(t) = k^*$. This implies that the capital stock itself must grow at the same rate as the work force, i.e. $\dot{K}(t)/K(t) = \dot{L}(t)/L(t) = n_L$. The intensive-form production function says that steady-state output per worker, y^*, satisfies $y^* = f(k^*)$ and is thus also constant. Hence, output itself also grows at the same rate as the work force, i.e. $\dot{Y}(t)/Y(t) = n_L$, and since the savings rate is constant, the same holds for the levels of saving and investment. In the *balanced growth path* we thus have:

$$\frac{\dot{Y}(t)}{Y(t)} = \frac{\dot{K}(t)}{K(t)} = \frac{\dot{I}(t)}{I(t)} = \frac{\dot{S}(t)}{S(t)} = \frac{\dot{L}(t)}{L(t)} = n_L. \tag{14.10}$$

Since the rate of population growth is exogenous, the long-run growth rate of the economy is exogenously determined and thus cannot be influenced by government

[3] Barro and Sala-i-Martin (1995, p. 52) show that both inputs are *essential* if the properties (P1)–(P3) are satisfied. Hence, $F(0, L) = F(K, 0) = f(0) = 0$.

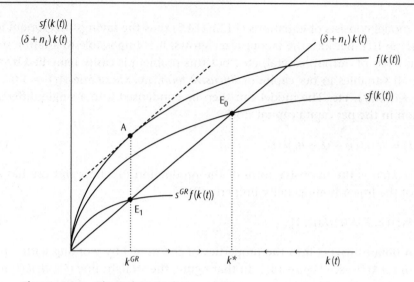

Figure 14.1. The Solow–Swan model

policy or household behaviour. For example, an increase in the savings rate rotates the savings function counter-clockwise and gives rise to a higher steady-state capital-labour ratio but it does not affect the rate of economic growth along the balanced growth path.

Before turning to a detailed examination of the properties of the Solow–Swan model we first expand the model by re-introducing technological change into the production function.

14.2.2 Technological progress

Technical change can be *embodied* or *disembodied* (see Burmeister and Dobell, 1970, ch. 3). Embodied technical change is only relevant to newly acquired and installed equipment or workers and therefore does not affect the productivity of existing production factors. Disembodied technical progress takes place if, independent of changes in the production factors, isoquants of the production function shift inwards as time progresses (Burmeister and Dobell, 1970, p. 66). Reasons for this inward shift may be improvements in techniques or organization which increase the productivity of new and old factors alike. We focus on disembodied technical progress in the first part of this chapter but will return to examples of embodied technical progress later on.

We can represent different cases of factor-augmenting disembodied technical change by writing the production function (14.1) in the following form:

$$Y(t) = F\left[A_K(t)K(t), A_L(t)L(t)\right], \tag{14.11}$$

where $A_K(t)$ and $A_L(t)$ only depend on time, and $A_K(t)K(t)$ and $A_L(t)L(t)$ are "effective capital" and "effective labour" respectively. Technical progress is purely labour augmenting if $\dot{A}_K(t) \equiv 0$ and $\dot{A}_L(t) > 0$, purely capital augmenting if $\dot{A}_L(t) \equiv 0$ and $\dot{A}_K(t) > 0$, and equally capital and labour augmenting if $\dot{A}_K(t) \equiv \dot{A}_L(t) > 0$.

Three different concepts of neutrality in the process of technical advance exist in the literature (Burmeister and Dobell, 1970, p. 75; Barro and Sala-i-Martin, 1995, p. 33). Technological change is (a) *Harrod neutral* if the relative input share $F_K K / F_L L$ is constant over time for a given capital-output ratio, K/Y, (b) *Hicks neutral* if this share is constant over time for a given capital-labour ratio, K/L, and (c) *Solow neutral* if this share is constant over time for a given labour-output ratio, L/Y. In terms of equation (14.11), the three cases correspond to, respectively, $A_K(t) \equiv 1$, $A_K(t) \equiv A_L(t)$, and $A_L(t) \equiv 1$.

Of course, for the Cobb–Douglas production function the three concepts of neutrality are indistinguishable, since:

$$
\begin{aligned}
Y(t) \quad &= [A_K(t)K(t)]^\alpha \, L(t)^{1-\alpha} \quad \Leftrightarrow \\
&= K(t)^\alpha \, [A_L(t)L(t)]^{1-\alpha} \quad \text{for } A_L(t) \equiv A_K(t)^{\alpha/(1-\alpha)} \quad \Leftrightarrow \\
&= A(t)K(t)^\alpha L(t)^{1-\alpha} \quad \text{for } A(t) = A_K(t)^\alpha.
\end{aligned}
\tag{14.12}
$$

For non-Cobb–Douglas cases, however, the different neutrality concepts have different implications for balanced growth. Barro and Sala-i-Martin (1995, pp. 54–55) show, for example, that technical progress must be Harrod neutral (labour augmenting) for the model to have a steady state with a constant growth rate. In a steady state we must have a constant capital-output ratio and it can be shown that for forms of technological progress that are not Harrod neutral, one of the factor shares approaches zero if the capital-output ratio is to be constant. So if we wish to have balanced growth **and** be able to consider a non-unitary substitution elasticity between capital and labour, we must assume Harrod-neutral technical progress. The remainder of the discussion in this section will thus assume that Harrod neutrality holds.

The production function is written as:

$$
Y(t) = F[K(t), N(t)],
\tag{14.13}
$$

where $N(t)$ measures the effective amount of labour ($N(t) \equiv A(t)L(t)$) and we assume that technical progress occurs at a constant exponential rate:

$$
\frac{\dot{A}(t)}{A(t)} = n_A, \quad A(t) = A(0)e^{n_A t}.
\tag{14.14}
$$

Since the labour force itself grows exponentially at a constant rate n_L (see (14.5)), the *effective* labour force grows at a constant exponential rate $n_L + n_A$.

By measuring output and capital per unit of effective labour, i.e. $y(t) \equiv Y(t)/N(t)$ and $k(t) \equiv K(t)/N(t)$, and following the standard solution procedure explained above, the fundamental differential equation for $k(t)$ is obtained:

$$\dot{k}(t) = sf(k(t)) - (\delta + n_L + n_A)k(t). \tag{14.15}$$

In the steady state, $k^* = sy^*/(\delta + n_L + n_A)$, so that output and the capital stock grow at the same rate as the effective labour input. Hence, equation (14.10) is changed to:

$$\frac{\dot{Y}(t)}{Y(t)} = \frac{\dot{K}(t)}{K(t)} = \frac{\dot{I}(t)}{I(t)} = \frac{\dot{S}(t)}{S(t)} = \frac{\dot{N}(t)}{N(t)} = \frac{\dot{L}(t)}{L(t)} + \frac{\dot{A}(t)}{A(t)} = n_L + n_A. \tag{14.16}$$

Hence, exactly the same qualitative conclusions are obtained as in the model without technological advance. Long-term balanced growth merely depends on the exogenous factors n_L and n_A.

14.3 Properties of the Solow–Swan Model

In this section we study the most important properties of the Solow–Swan model. In particular, we look at (a) the golden rule and the issue of over-saving, (b) the transitional dynamics implied by the model as well as the concept of absolute versus conditional convergence, and (c) the speed of dynamic adjustment.

14.3.1 The golden rule of capital accumulation

One of the implications of the model developed thus far is that, even though long-term balanced *growth* is exogenous (and equal to $n \equiv n_L + n_A$), the *levels* of output, capital, and consumption are critically affected by the level of the savings rate. In other words, even though s does not affect long-term growth it does affect the path along which the economy grows. This prompts the issue concerning the relative welfare ranking for these different paths. To the extent that the policy maker can affect s, he/she can also select the path on which the economy finds itself. We first consider steady-state paths.

In the steady state, equation (14.15) implies a unique implicit relationship between the savings rate and the equilibrium capital-labour ratio which can be written as:

$$k^* = k^*(s), \tag{14.17}$$

with $dk^*/ds = y^*/[\delta + n - sf'(k^*)] > 0$. Suppose that the policy maker is interested in steady-state per capita consumption and, to keep things simple, assume that there is no technical progress (i.e. $n_A = 0$ and $n = n_L$). Consumption per capita can then be written as:

$$c(s) = (1 - s)f[k^*(s)] = f[k^*(s)] - (\delta + n)k^*(s), \tag{14.18}$$

which in Figure 14.1 represents the vertical distance between the production function and the required-replacement line in the steady state. In Figure 14.2 we plot $c(s)$ for different savings rates. Any output not needed to replace the existing capital stock per worker in the steady state can be consumed. Per capita consumption is at its maximum if the savings rate satisfies $dc(s)/ds = 0$, or:

$$\frac{dc(s)}{ds} = [f'[k^*(s)] - (\delta + n)]\frac{dk^*(s)}{ds} = 0. \tag{14.19}$$

In terms of Figure 14.1, per capita consumption is at its maximum at point A where the slope of the production function equals the slope of the required-replacement function. In view of (14.19), the *golden rule* savings rate, s^{GR}, satisfies:

$$f'[k^*(s^{GR})] = \delta + n. \tag{14.20}$$

The golden rule savings rate is associated with point E_1 in Figure 14.2. Burmeister and Dobell (1970, pp. 52–53) provide the intuition behind the result in (14.20). The produced asset (the physical capital stock) yields an own-rate of return equal to $f' - \delta$, whereas the non-produced primary good (labour) can be interpreted as yielding an own-rate of return $n_L = n$. Intuitively, the efficient outcome occurs if the rates of return on the two assets are equalized, i.e. if the equality in (14.20) holds.

Note that the expression in (14.20) can be rewritten as:

$$s^{GR} = \frac{(\delta + n)k^*(s^{GR})}{f[k^*(s^{GR})]} = \frac{k^*(s^{GR})f'[k^*(s^{GR})]}{f[k^*(s^{GR})]}. \tag{14.21}$$

Equation (14.21) shows that the golden rule savings rate should be equated to the share of capital income in national income (which itself in general depends on the golden rule savings rate). In the Cobb–Douglas case, with $f(.) = k(t)^\alpha$, α represents the capital income share so that the golden rule savings rate equals $s^{GR} = \alpha$.

We are now in a position to discuss the concept of *dynamic inefficiency*. We call an economy dynamically inefficient if it is possible to make everybody at least as well off (and some strictly better off) by reducing the capital stock. Consider the situation in Figure 14.2, and assume that the actual steady-state savings rate is s_0 so that the economy is at point E_0. Since this savings rate exceeds the golden rule savings rate ($s_0 > s^{GR}$), per capita consumption is lower that under the golden rule. It is not difficult to show that point E_0 is dynamically inefficient in the sense that higher per capita consumption can be attained by reducing the savings rate. Figure 14.2 shows that a reduction in the savings rate from s_0 to s^{GR} would move the steady state from E_0 to E_1 and lead to higher per capita steady-state consumption. With the aid of Figure 14.3 we can figure out what happens to per capita consumption

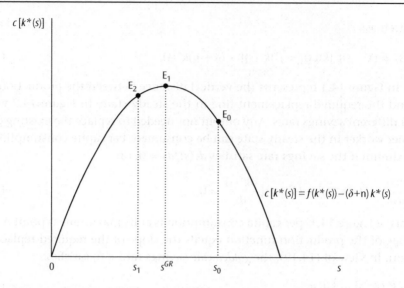

Figure 14.2. Per capita consumption and the savings rate

during the transitional phase. The economy is initially at point E_0 and the initial steady-state capital-labour ratio is k_0^*. A reduction in the savings rate (from s_0 to s^{GR}) rotates the per capita consumption schedule in a counter-clockwise fashion and the economy jumps from E_0 to A at impact. Since the transition towards the golden-rule capital-labour ratio k^{GR} is stable, the economy moves from A to the new steady-state point E_1 as $k(t)$ falls towards k^{GR} during transition. Hence, as a result of the decrease in the savings rate, consumption is higher than it would have been, both during transition and in the new steady state, i.e. the reduction in s is thus Pareto-improving. As a result, we can conclude that savings rates exceeding s^{GR} are dynamically inefficient.

The same conclusion does not hold if the savings rate falls short of s^{GR} as the Pareto-optimality property cannot be demonstrated unambiguously. Consider an economy in which the savings rate is too low, i.e. $s_1 < s^{GR}$. In terms of Figures 14.2 and 14.3, the economy is initially at point E_2. An increase in the savings rate from s_1 to s^{GR} still leads to an increase in steady-state per capita consumption. During transition, however, per capita consumption will have to fall before it can settle at its higher steady-state level prescribed by the golden rule. In terms of Figure 14.3, at impact the economy jumps from E_2 to B as the savings rate is increased. During part of the transition consumption is lower than it would have been in the absence of the shock. Since we have no welfare function to evaluate the uneven path of per capita consumption we cannot determine whether the increase in s is Pareto-improving in this case.

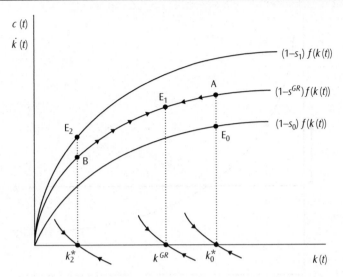

Figure 14.3. Per capita consumption during transition to its golden rule level

14.3.2 Transitional dynamics and convergence

Up to now attention has been focused on steady-state issues. We now return to the model with exogenous technical change, the fundamental equation of which is given in (14.15). By defining the growth rate of $k(t)$ as $\gamma_k(t) \equiv \dot{k}(t)/k(t)$, we derive from (14.15):

$$\gamma_k(t) \equiv sf(k(t))/k(t) - (\delta + n), \tag{14.22}$$

where $n \equiv n_L + n_A$. In Figure 14.4 this growth rate is represented by the vertical difference between the two lines.[4] An immediate implication of (14.22), or Figure 14.4 for that matter, is that countries with little capital (in efficiency units) grow faster than countries with a lot of capital. In other words, poor and rich countries should converge!

Note that the growth rate of output in efficiency units of labour, $\gamma_y(t)$, is uniquely linked to $\gamma_k(t)$:

$$\gamma_y(t) \equiv \frac{\dot{y}(t)}{y(t)} = \frac{f'[k(t)]\dot{k}(t)}{y(t)} \equiv \omega_K(t)\gamma_k(t), \tag{14.23}$$

where $\omega_K(t) \equiv f'(k(t))k(t)/y(t)$ is the capital share in national income (see below). For a Cobb–Douglas production function this share is constant ($\omega_K(t) = \alpha$) but this does not hold if the substitution elasticity between capital and labour is unequal to unity.

---

[4] The Inada conditions ensure that $\lim_{k \to 0} sf(k)/k = \infty$ and $\lim_{k \to \infty} sf(k)/k = 0$.

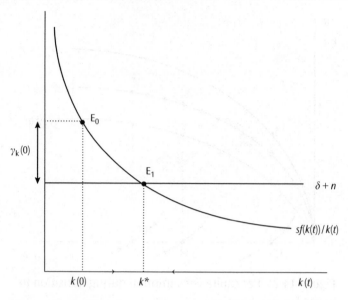

Figure 14.4. Growth convergence

Take, for example, the CES production function:

$$F[K(t), N(t)] \equiv \left[\alpha K(t)^{(\sigma_{KL}-1)/\sigma_{KL}} + (1-\alpha)N(t)^{(\sigma_{KL}-1)/\sigma_{KL}} \right]^{\sigma_{KL}/(\sigma_{KL}-1)} \Leftrightarrow$$

$$f[k(t)] \equiv \left[1 - \alpha + \alpha k(t)^{(\sigma_{KL}-1)/\sigma_{KL}} \right]^{\sigma_{KL}/(\sigma_{KL}-1)}, \tag{14.24}$$

where σ_{KL} (>0) represents the substitution elasticity between capital and labour. The capital share implied by (14.24) is given by $\omega_K(t) \equiv \alpha[f(k(t))/k(t)]^{(\sigma_{KL}-1)/\sigma_{KL}}$, which thus depends on $k(t)$ according to:

$$\frac{d\omega_K(t)}{\omega_K(t)} = \left(\frac{\sigma_{KL}-1}{\sigma_{KL}} \right) [1 - \omega_K(t)] \left(\frac{dk(t)}{k(t)} \right). \tag{14.25}$$

It follows that for $\sigma_{KL} > 1$ (<1), an increase in $k(t)$ results in an increase (decrease) in the share of capital in national income. By using (14.23) and (14.25) we obtain the result linking output growth to the output level in efficiency units of labour:

$$d\gamma_y(t) = -\left(1 - \omega_K(t)\right) \left[\frac{\gamma_k(t)}{\sigma_{KL}} + n + \delta \right] \left(\frac{dy(t)}{y(t)} \right). \tag{14.26}$$

For economies with positive growth in $k(t)$ (for which $\gamma_k(t) > 0$) the term in square brackets on the right-hand side of (14.26) is guaranteed to be positive, so that a higher output level in efficiency units of labour is associated with a lower growth rate in output. The same holds for declining economies (for which $\gamma_k(t) < 0$) operating to the right of their steady-state position, provided they are not too far from this steady state (i.e. $\gamma_k(t)$ must not be too negative).

This suggests that there is a simple empirical test of the Solow–Swan model which is based on the convergence property of output in a cross-section of many different countries. We take a group of closed economies (since the Solow–Swan model refers to the closed economy) and assume that they are similar in the sense that they possess the same structural parameters, s, n, and δ, and the same production function, so that in theory they have the same steady state. The so-called *absolute convergence hypothesis* (ACH) then suggests that poor countries should grow faster than rich countries. Barro and Sala-i-Martin (1995, p. 27) show the results of regressing of $\gamma_y(t)$ on $\log y(t)$ for a sample of 118 countries. The results are dismal: instead of finding a negative effect as predicted by the ACH, they find a slight positive effect, i.e. initially rich countries grow faster than poor countries. Absolute convergence does not seem to hold and (Romer's) stylized fact (SF7) is verified by the data.

This rejection of the ACH does not necessarily mean that the Solow–Swan model is refuted because one of the identifying assumptions underlying the regression results could be false. For example, if a rich country has a higher savings rate than a poor country, it could actually be further from its (higher) steady state than the poor country is from its steady state. The Solow–Swan model then predicts that the rich country will be growing faster than the poor country, as indeed the empirical results of Barro and Sala-i-Martin (1995) suggest. We demonstrate this result in Figure 14.5 where s_P and s_R are the savings rates of the poor and the rich country, respectively, and $(k^*)^P$ and $(k^*)^R$ are the corresponding steady states. If the poor country is initially at $k^P(0)$ and the rich country at $k^R(0)$, the former will grow slower than the latter (the vertical distance CD is larger than AB).

A refined test of the Solow–Swan model makes use of the *conditional convergence hypothesis* (CCH) according to which *similar* countries should converge. Barro and

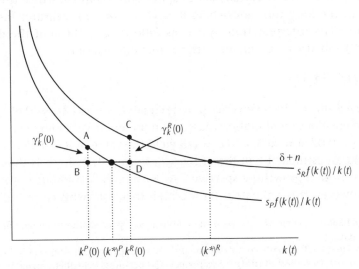

Figure 14.5. Conditional growth convergence

Sala-i-Martin (1995, pp. 27–28) show that convergence does appear to take place for the twenty original OECD countries and *a fortiori* for the different states in the US. This suggests that the CCH is not grossly at odds with the data, which is good news for the Solow–Swan model (and bad news for some of the endogenous growth models discussed below).

14.3.3 The speed of adjustment

The convergence property is not the only testable implication of the Solow–Swan model. Apart from testing *whether* economies converge, another issue concerns *how fast* they converge. In order to study this issue further we follow Burmeister and Dobell (1970, pp. 53–56) and Barro and Sala-i-Martin (1995, pp. 37–39, 53) by focusing on the Cobb–Douglas case for which $f(.) = k(t)^\alpha$, and the fundamental differential equation (14.15) becomes:

$$\dot{k}(t) = sk(t)^\alpha - (\delta + n)k(t). \tag{14.27}$$

An exact solution to this differential equation can be obtained by using a transformation of variables, i.e. by rewriting (14.27) in terms of the capital-output ratio, $x(t) \equiv k(t)/y(t) = k(t)^{1-\alpha}$:

$$\dot{x}(t) = (1 - \alpha)\left[s - (\delta + n)x(t)\right]. \tag{14.28}$$

The solution to (14.28) is obtained by standard methods:

$$x(t) = x(\infty) + [x(0) - x(\infty)]\, e^{-\beta t}, \tag{14.29}$$

where $x(\infty) \equiv s/(\delta + n)$ is the steady-state capital-output ratio to which the economy converges in the long run, and where $\beta \equiv (1 - \alpha)(\delta + n)$ measures the speed of convergence. The interpretation of β is as follows: $\zeta \times 100\%$ of the divergence between $x(t)$ and $x(\infty)$ is eliminated after a time interval of t_ζ:

$$t_\zeta \equiv -(1/\beta)\log(1 - \zeta). \tag{14.30}$$

Hence, the half-life of the divergence ($\zeta = \frac{1}{2}$) equals $t_{1/2} = \log 2/\beta = 0.693/\beta$.[5] Some back-of-the-envelope computations based on representative values of $n_L = 0.01$ (per annum), $n_A = 0.02$, $\delta = 0.05$, and $\alpha = 1/3$ yield the value of $\beta = 0.0533$ (5.33% per annum) and an estimated half-life of $t_{1/2} = 13$ years. Transition is thus relatively fast, at least from a growth perspective.[6] As Barro and Sala-i-Martin (1995, p. 38) indicate, however, this estimate is far too high to accord with empirical evidence.

---

[5] See also Chapter 7 where we compute the convergence speed of the unemployment rate in a discrete-time setting.

[6] Note that Sato (1963) actually complains about the startlingly low transition speed implied by the Solow–Swan model. His object of study is fiscal policy and business cycle phenomena. In this context convergence of 5% per annum is slow. Hence the different conclusion.

They suggest that β is more likely to be in the range of 2% per annum (instead of 5.33%). So here is a real problem confronting the Solow–Swan model. In order for it to generate a realistic convergence rate of 2%, for given values of δ and n, the capital share must be unrealistically high (a value of $\alpha = \frac{3}{4}$ actually yields an estimate of $\beta = 0.02$)! One way to get the Solow–Swan model in line with reality is to assume a broad measure of capital to include human as well as physical capital. This is indeed the approach taken by Mankiw, Romer, and Weil (1992).

14.3.4 Human capital to the rescue

Mankiw, Romer, and Weil (1992, p. 415) start their highly influential analysis by using real world data to estimate the textbook Solow model. They show that, though the model appears to fit the data quite well, some of the parameter estimates are not entirely satisfactory. For example, the estimated capital coefficient is much larger than the actual capital share of about one third. So either their Cobb–Douglas technology assumption is inappropriate or there is a serious mis-measurement of the capital input. They adopt the latter stance and suggest that the convergence conundrum of the Solow–Swan model disappears if the production function is modified to include human capital:

$$Y(t) = K(t)^{\alpha_K} H(t)^{\alpha_H} [A(t)L(t)]^{1-\alpha_K-\alpha_H}, \quad 0 < \alpha_K + \alpha_H < 1, \tag{14.31}$$

where $H(t)$ is the stock of human capital and α_K and α_H are the efficiency parameters of the two types of capital ($0 < \alpha_K, \alpha_H < 1$). In close accordance with the Solow–Swan model, productivity and population growth are both exponential ($\dot{A}(t)/A(t) = n_A$ and $\dot{L}(t)/L(t) = n_L$) and the accumulation equations for the two types of capital can be written in effective labour units as:

$$\dot{k}(t) = s_K y(t) + (\delta + n)k(t), \tag{14.32}$$

$$\dot{h}(t) = s_H y(t) + (\delta + n)h(t), \tag{14.33}$$

where $h(t) \equiv H(t)/[A(t)L(t)]$, $n \equiv n_A + n_L$, and s_K and s_H represent the propensities to accumulate physical and human capital, respectively. The production functions as well as the depreciation rate of the two types of capital are assumed to be equal. Since there are decreasing returns to the two types of capital in combination ($\alpha_K + \alpha_H < 1$) the model possesses a steady state for which $\dot{k}(t) = \dot{h}(t) = 0$, $k(t) = k^*$, and $h(t) = h^*$. By using (14.31)–(14.33) we obtain:

$$k^* = \left(\frac{s_K^{1-\alpha_H} s_H^{\alpha_H}}{\delta + n} \right)^{1/(1-\alpha_K-\alpha_H)}, \quad h^* = \left(\frac{s_K^{\alpha_K} s_H^{1-\alpha_K}}{\delta + n} \right)^{1/(1-\alpha_K-\alpha_H)}. \tag{14.34}$$

By substituting k^* and h^* into the (logarithm of the) production function (14.31) we obtain an estimable expression for per capita output along the balanced growth path:

$$\log \left[Y(t)/L(t) \right] = \log A(0) + n_A t - \left(\frac{\alpha_K + \alpha_H}{1 - \alpha_K - \alpha_H} \right) \log (n + \delta)$$

$$+ \left(\frac{\alpha_K}{1 - \alpha_K - \alpha_H} \right) \log s_K + \left(\frac{\alpha_H}{1 - \alpha_K - \alpha_H} \right) \log s_H. \qquad (14.35)$$

Mankiw et al. (1992, p. 417) suggest approximate guesses for $\alpha_K = \frac{1}{3}$ and α_H between $\frac{1}{3}$ and $\frac{4}{9}$. The latter guess is based on the observation that in the US manufacturing sector the minimum wage is between a third and a half of the average wage. By interpreting the minimum wage as the return to labour without any human capital (so-called "raw" labour), this means that between half and two thirds of the total payment to labour represents the return to human capital. Since an income share of $(1 - \alpha_K)$ is left after payments to owners of physical capital are taken care of, this implies $\frac{1}{2}(1 - \alpha_K) < \alpha_H < \frac{2}{3}(1 - \alpha_K)$ or $\frac{1}{3} < \alpha_H < \frac{4}{9}$.[7]

As a result of the inclusion of human capital, the model is much better equipped to explain large cross-country income differences for relatively small differences between savings rates (s_K and s_H) and population growth rates (n). This is apparent from equation (14.35). An increase in s_K, for example, induces higher income in efficiency units just as in the standard Solow–Swan model (see (14.32)) but also raised the stock of human wealth in efficiency units. By adding human capital to the model, the elasticity of s_K in (14.35) is of the order of unity rather than one half which is predicted by the standard Solow–Swan model. A similar conclusion holds for a change in n. An increase in n reduces income because both physical and human capital are spread out over more souls and the elasticity of $(n + \delta)$ is not $-\frac{1}{2}$, as in the Solow–Swan model, but a staggering -2! See Romer (1996, pp. 134–135) for a further numerical example.

Not surprisingly, the inclusion of a human capital variable works pretty well empirically; the estimated coefficient for α_H is highly significant and lies between 0.28 and 0.37 (Mankiw et al., 1992, p. 420). The convergence property of the augmented Solow–Swan model is also much better. The convergence speed is now defined as $\beta \equiv (1 - \alpha_K - \alpha_H)(n + \delta)$ which can be made in accordance with the observed empirical estimate of $\hat{\beta} = 0.02$ without too much trouble. Hence, by this very simple and intuitively plausible adjustment the Solow–Swan model can be salvaged from the dustbin of history. The speed of convergence it implies can be made to fit the real world.

---

[7] Ingenious as it is, this approach to estimating the income share of human capital is not without dangers, especially in Europe where the minimum wage is policy manipulated rather than market determined.

14.4 Macroeconomic Applications

The Solow–Swan model can also be used to study traditional macroeconomic issues such as the effect of fiscal policy and the issue of debt versus tax financing and Ricardian equivalence. In order to keep things simple, we return to the standard Solow–Swan model in which there is only physical capital.

14.4.1 Fiscal policy in the Solow model

Suppose that the government consumes $G(t)$ units of output so that aggregate demand in the goods market is:

$$Y(t) = C(t) + I(t) + G(t). \tag{14.36}$$

Aggregate saving is proportional to after-tax income, so that (14.2) is modified to:

$$S(t) = s[Y(t) - T(t)], \tag{14.37}$$

where $T(t)$ is the lump-sum tax. Since $S(t) \equiv Y(t) - C(t) - T(t)$ any primary government deficit must be compensated for by an excess of private saving over investment, i.e. $G(t) - T(t) = S(t) - I(t)$. The government budget identity is given by:

$$\dot{B}(t) = r(t)B(t) + G(t) - T(t), \tag{14.38}$$

where $B(t)$ is government debt and $r(t)$ is the real interest rate which, under the competitive conditions assumed in the Solow–Swan model, equals the net marginal productivity of capital:[8]

$$r(t) = f'(k(t)) - \delta. \tag{14.39}$$

By writing all variables in terms of effective labour units, the model can be condensed to the following two equations:

$$\dot{k}(t) = f(k(t)) - (\delta + n)k(t) - c(t) - g(t)$$
$$= sf(k(t)) - (\delta + n)k(t) + (1 - s)\tau(t) - g(t), \tag{14.40}$$
$$\dot{b}(t) = [f'(k(t)) - \delta - n]b(t) + g(t) - \tau(t), \tag{14.41}$$

where $\tau(t) \equiv T(t)/N(t)$, $g(t) \equiv G(t)/N(t)$, and $b(t) \equiv B(t)/N(t)$.

Under *pure tax financing* and in the absence of initial government debt ($\dot{b}(t) = b(t) = 0$), the government budget identity reduces to $g(t) \equiv \tau(t)$. By substituting

---

[8] This result is demonstrated more formally below. See section 5.2.

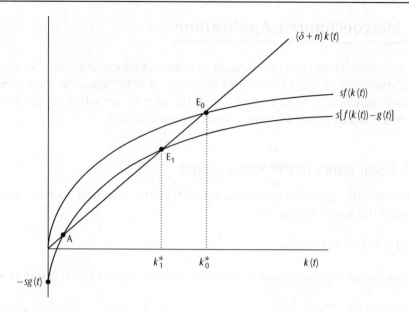

Figure 14.6. Fiscal policy in the Solow–Swan model

this expression into (14.40) we obtain:

$$\dot{k}(t) = sf(k(t)) - (\delta + n)k(t) - sg(t). \tag{14.42}$$

The economy can be analysed with the aid of (14.40) alone—see Figure 14.6. In the absence of government consumption, the unique (and stable) steady-state equilibrium is at point E_0. An increase in government consumption shifts the net investment line down which results in multiple equilibria (or even no equilibria). Of these equilibria, the one at point A is unstable and that at E_1 is stable. Fiscal policy crowds out the physical capital stock. At impact, private consumption and net investment (in efficiency units of labour) both fall ($dc(0) < 0$ and $d\dot{k}(0) < 0$) but output is unchanged ($dy(0) = 0$). Over time, as the capital stock dwindles, output and private consumption per effective labour unit fall:

$$\frac{dy(\infty)}{dg} = \frac{f'\,dk(\infty)}{dg} = \frac{sf'}{sf' - (\delta + n)} < 0, \tag{14.43}$$

$$\frac{dc(\infty)}{dg} = (1-s)\left[1 - \frac{dy(\infty)}{dg}\right] = \frac{(1-s)(\delta+n)}{sf' - (\delta+n)} < 0. \tag{14.44}$$

Next we consider the issue of *bond financing*. If the government increases its consumption without at the same time raising $\tau(t)$ by the same amount, a primary deficit will be opened up which, according to (14.41), will lead to an ever-increasing explosive process for government debt (since $r > n$ by assumption in (14.41)). In order to avoid this economically rather uninteresting result, we postulate a debt

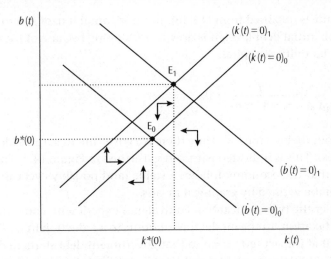

Figure 14.7. Ricardian non-equivalence in the Solow–Swan model

stabilization rule, a variation of which was suggested by Buiter (1988, p. 288):

$$\tau(t) = \tau_0 + \xi b(t), \quad \xi > r - n. \tag{14.45}$$

By substituting (14.45) into (14.41) we obtain a stable debt process:[9]

$$\dot{b}(t) = \left[f'(k(t)) - \delta - n - \xi\right] b(t) + g(t) - \tau_0. \tag{14.46}$$

The dynamic properties of the economy can be illustrated with the aid of a phase diagram in (k, b) space—see Figure 14.7. By combining (14.40) and (14.45) we obtain the following expression:

$$\dot{k}(t) = sf(k(t)) - (\delta + n)k(t) + (1 - s)\left[\tau_0 + \xi b(t)\right] - g(t). \tag{14.47}$$

The slope of the $\dot{k} = 0$ line is obtained from (14.47) in the usual fashion:

$$\left(\frac{db(t)}{dk(t)}\right)_{\dot{k}(t)=0} = \frac{(1 - s)\xi}{\delta + n - sf'} > 0. \tag{14.48}$$

The $\dot{k} = 0$ line is upward sloping and points above (below) this line are associated with positive (negative) net investment, i.e. $\dot{k} > 0$ (< 0). Ceteris paribus the capital stock, an increase in the level of debt raises tax receipts (by (14.45)), reduces consumption, and renders net investment positive. As a result, the new capital stock equilibrium features a higher capital stock. The dynamic forces are indicated by horizontal arrows in Figure 14.7.

---

[9] Equation (14.46) is stable because the coefficient for $b(t)$ on the right-hand side is equal to $(r-n)-\xi$, which is negative.

The $\dot{b} = 0$ line is obtained from (14.46). It is horizontal if debt is zero initially but with a positive initial debt level, it is downward sloping because of the diminishing marginal productivity of capital:

$$\left(\frac{db(t)}{dk(t)}\right)_{\dot{b}(t)=0} = \frac{bf''}{\xi - (r - n)} < 0. \tag{14.49}$$

For points above (below) the $\dot{b} = 0$ line there is a government surplus (deficit) so that debt falls (rises). This is indicated with vertical arrows in Figure 14.7. The Buiter rule thus ensures that the economy follows a stable (and possibly cyclical) adjustment pattern, as can be verified by graphical means.

Now consider the typical Ricardian equivalence experiment, consisting of a postponement of taxation. In the model this amounts to a reduction in τ_0. This creates a primary deficit at impact ($g(t) > \tau_0$) so that government debt starts to rise. In terms of Figure 14.7, both the $\dot{k} = 0$ line and the $\dot{b} = 0$ line shift up, the former by more than the latter. In the long run, government debt, the capital stock, and output (all measured in efficiency units of labour) rise as a result of the tax cut.

$$\frac{dy(\infty)}{d\tau_0} = \frac{f'dk(\infty)}{d\tau_0} = -\frac{(1 - s)(r - n)f'}{|\Delta|} < 0, \tag{14.50}$$

$$\frac{db(\infty)}{d\tau_0} = \frac{sf' - (\delta + n) + (1 - s)bf''}{|\Delta|} < 0, \tag{14.51}$$

where $|\Delta| \equiv \lambda_1\lambda_2 = [\xi - (r - n)][n + \delta - sf'] - (1 - s)b\xi f'' > 0$ is the determinant of the Jacobian matrix of the two-by-two system of differential equations, and λ_1 and λ_2 are the two characteristic roots. As $\text{tr}(\Delta) \equiv \lambda_1 + \lambda_2 = -[\xi - (r - n)] - [n + \delta - sf'] < 0$, both roots are negative, i.e. as we already verified by graphical means, the system is stable. Clearly, Ricardian equivalence does not hold in the Solow–Swan model. A temporary tax cut boosts consumption, depresses investment, and thus has real effects.

14.5 The Ramsey Model

Up to now we have assumed an ad hoc savings function according to which aggregate saving is a constant fraction of income (see (14.2)). Whilst the underlying consumption function works rather well empirically, there are serious theoretical objections that can be raised against it. In Chapter 6, for example, it was shown that a forward-looking "representative" agent would condition consumption not on some measure of disposable income but rather on lifetime wealth, comprising the sum of financial and human wealth. In this section we investigate the implications for growth of the intertemporal consumption theory.

14.5.1 The representative consumer

Assume that the representative consumer is infinitely lived[10] and blessed with perfect foresight. The consumer experiences instantaneous utility (or "felicity") which depends on the consumption flow $c(t)$. The felicity function, $U(c(t))$, exhibits positive but diminishing marginal utility and thus satisfies $U'(c(t)) > 0$ and $U''(c(t)) < 0$. In addition the following Inada-style conditions are imposed:

$$\lim_{c(t)\to 0} U'[c(t)] = +\infty, \quad \lim_{c(t)\to\infty} U'[c(t)] = 0. \tag{14.52}$$

The consumer derives no felicity from the consumption of leisure and is assumed to inelastically supply $L(t)$ units of labour to a competitive labour market. As before, labour supply grows over time at a constant exponential rate (i.e. $\dot{L}(t)/L(t) = n_L$).[11] The consumer's utility functional is defined as the discounted integral of present and future felicity. Normalizing the present by $t = 0$ ("today") we obtain:

$$\Lambda(0) \equiv \int_0^\infty U[c(t)]e^{-\rho t}dt, \quad \rho > 0, \tag{14.53}$$

where $\Lambda(0)$ is lifetime utility and ρ is the pure rate of time preference. At time t, the consumer holds financial assets totalling $A(t)$ and yielding a rate of return of $r(t)$. The budget identity is thus given by:

$$C(t) + \dot{A}(t) \equiv r(t)A(t) + W(t)L(t), \tag{14.54}$$

where $W(t)$ is the real wage and $C(t) \equiv c(t)L(t)$ is aggregate consumption. Equation (14.54) says that the sum of income from financial assets and labour (the right-hand side) is equal to the sum of consumption and saving (the left-hand side). By rewriting (14.54) in per capita form we obtain:

$$\dot{a}(t) \equiv [r(t) - n] a(t) + W(t) - c(t), \tag{14.55}$$

where $a(t) \equiv A(t)/L(t)$. As it stands, (14.55) is still no more than an identity, i.e. without further restrictions it is rather meaningless. Indeed, if the household can borrow all it likes at the going interest rate $r(t)$ it will simply accumulate debt indefinitely and thus be able to finance any arbitrary consumption path. To avoid this economically nonsensical outcome, we need to impose a solvency condition:

$$\lim_{t\to\infty} a(t)\exp\left[-\int_0^t [r(\tau) - n]\,d\tau\right] = 0. \tag{14.56}$$

Intuitively, (14.56) says that the consumer does not plan to "expire" with positive assets and is not allowed by the capital market to die hopelessly indebted.[12]

---

[10] Alternatively, one might assume a representative family dynasty, the members of which are linked across time via operative bequests. See Barro and Sala-i-Martin (1995, p. 60) and Chapter 6 for this interpretation.

[11] Under the extended-family interpretation the family grows exponentially at rate n_L.

[12] Compare the discussion in Barro and Sala-i-Martin (1995, pp. 62–66). Strictly speaking (14.56) in equality form is an *outcome* of household maximizing behaviour rather than an a priori restriction.

By integrating (14.55) over the (infinite) lifetime of the agent and taking into account the solvency condition (14.56), we obtain the household lifetime budget constraint:

$$\int_0^\infty c(t)e^{-[R(t)-nt]}\,dt = a(0) + h(0),\qquad(14.57)$$

where $a(0)$ is the initial level of financial assets, $h(0)$ is human wealth, and $R(t)$ is a discounting factor:

$$R(t) \equiv \int_0^t r(\tau)d\tau,\qquad(14.58)$$

$$h(0) \equiv \int_0^\infty W(t)e^{-[R(t)-nt]}\,dt.\qquad(14.59)$$

Equation (14.59) shows that human wealth is the present value of the real wage, i.e. the market value of the agent's time endowment. From the viewpoint of the consumer, the right-hand side of (14.57) is given and acts as a restriction on the time paths for consumption that are feasible.

The consumer chooses a time path for $c(t)$ in order to attain a maximum lifetime utility level $\Lambda(0)$ (given in (14.53)), subject to the lifetime budget restriction (14.57). The first-order conditions are (14.57) and:

$$U'[c(t)]\,e^{-\rho t} = \lambda e^{-[R(t)-nt]},\quad t \in [0,\infty),\qquad(14.60)$$

where λ is the marginal utility of wealth, i.e. the Lagrange multiplier associated with the lifetime budget restriction (14.57). The left-hand side of (14.60) represents the marginal contribution to lifetime utility (evaluated from the perspective of "today", i.e. $t = 0$) of consumption in period t. The right-hand side of (14.60) is the lifetime marginal utility cost of consuming $c(t)$ rather than saving it. The marginal unit of $c(t)$ costs $\exp(-[R(t) - nt])$ from the perspective of today. This cost is translated into utility terms by multiplying it by the marginal utility of wealth.[13]

Since the marginal utility of wealth is constant (i.e. it does not depend on t), differentiation of (14.60) yields an expression for the optimal time profile of consumption:

$$\frac{d}{dt}U'[c(t)] = -\lambda e^{-[R(t)-nt-\rho t]}\left[\frac{dR(t)}{dt} - n - \rho\right] \Leftrightarrow$$

$$U''[c(t)]\frac{dc(t)}{dt} = -U'[c(t)][r(t) - n - \rho] \Leftrightarrow$$

$$\theta[c(t)]\left(\frac{1}{c(t)}\frac{dc(t)}{dt}\right) = r(t) - n - \rho,\qquad(14.61)$$

where we have used the fact that $dR(t)/dt = r(t)$ (see (14.58)) and where $\theta[.]$ is the elasticity of marginal utility which is positive for all positive consumption levels

By using (14.56) we avoid getting bogged down in technical issues. See also Chapter 6 for an intuitive discussion of the solvency condition in macroeconomics.

[13] See Dixit (1990, ch.10) for intuitive discussions of apparently intractable first-order conditions.

because of the strict concavity of $U[.]$:

$$\theta[c(t)] \equiv -\frac{U''[c(t)]c(t)}{U'[c(t)]}. \tag{14.62}$$

The *intertemporal substitution elasticity*, $\sigma[.]$, is the inverse of $\theta[.]$. By using this relationship, the expression in (14.61) can be rewritten to yield the consumption Euler equation:

$$\frac{1}{c(t)}\frac{dc(t)}{dt} = \sigma[c(t)] \, [r(t) - n - \rho] \,. \tag{14.63}$$

Intuitively, if $\sigma[.]$ is low, a large interest gap $(r(t) - n - \rho)$ is needed to induce the household to adopt an upward-sloping time profile for consumption. In that case the willingness to substitute consumption across time is low, the elasticity of marginal utility is high, and the marginal utility function has a lot of curvature. The opposite holds if $\sigma[.]$ is high. Then, the marginal utility function is almost linear so that a small interest gap can explain a large slope of the consumption profile.

As it stands, (14.63) is of little use to us because $\sigma[.]$ still depends on consumption, rendering (14.63) difficult to work with and the derivation of a closed-form solution for consumption impossible. For this reason an explicit form for $U[.]$ is chosen. There are two useful functional forms, i.e. the *exponential utility* function:

$$U[c(t)] \equiv -\alpha e^{-(1/\alpha)c(t)}, \quad \alpha > 0, \tag{14.64}$$

and the *iso-elastic* utility function:[14]

$$U[c(t)] \equiv \begin{cases} \frac{c(t)^{1-1/\sigma}-1}{1-1/\sigma} & \text{for } \sigma > 0, \quad \sigma \neq 1, \\ \log c(t) & \text{for } \sigma = 1. \end{cases} \tag{14.65}$$

It is not difficult to verify that the substitution elasticities corresponding with these two functional forms are, respectively, $\sigma[.] = \alpha/c(t)$ and $\sigma[.] = \sigma$, so that the respective Euler equations are:

$$\frac{dc(t)}{dt} = \alpha \, [r(t) - n - \rho] \quad \text{(exponential felicity)}, \tag{14.66}$$

$$\frac{1}{c(t)}\frac{dc(t)}{dt} = \sigma \, [r(t) - n - \rho] \quad \text{(iso-elastic felicity)}. \tag{14.67}$$

So both these utility functions lead to very simple expressions for the Euler equation. But what about the closed-form solution for consumption itself?

---

[14] The second line in (14.65) is obtained from the first line by letting $1/\sigma$ approach unity. The trick is to use L'Hôpital's rule for calculating limits of the $0 \div 0$ type:

$$\lim_{(1/\sigma)\to 1} \left[\frac{c^{1-1/\sigma}-1}{1-1/\sigma} \right] = \frac{-\lim_{(1/\sigma)\to 1} c^{1-1/\sigma}\log c}{-1} = \log c.$$

We focus on the iso-elastic case, leaving the exponential case as an exercise for the reader. First we note that (14.67) can be integrated to yield future consumption $c(t)$ in terms of current consumption $c(0)$:

$$c(t) = c(0)e^{\sigma[R(t)-nt-\rho t]}.\tag{14.68}$$

By substituting this expression into the household budget constraint (14.57) we obtain in a few steps:

$$\int_0^\infty c(0)e^{\sigma[R(t)-nt-\rho t]}e^{-[R(t)-nt]}\,dt = a(0) + h(0) \quad \Leftrightarrow$$

$$c(0)\int_0^\infty e^{(\sigma-1)[R(t)-nt]-\sigma\rho t}\,dt = a(0) + h(0) \quad \Leftrightarrow$$

$$c(0) \equiv \Delta(0)^{-1}[a(0) + h(0)],\tag{14.69}$$

where $\Delta(0)^{-1}$ is the propensity to consume out of total wealth:

$$\Delta(0) \equiv \int_0^\infty e^{(\sigma-1)[R(t)-nt]-\sigma\rho t}\,dt.\tag{14.70}$$

According to (14.69), consumption in the planning period is proportional to total wealth. Some special cases merit attention. If $\sigma = 1$ (so that $U[.]$ in (14.65) is logarithmic), $\Delta(0)^{-1} = \rho$ and the household consumes a constant fraction of total wealth in the current period. Income and substitution effects of a change in the interest rate exactly cancel in this case (see also Chapter 6). Another special case is often used in the international context. If a country is small in world financial markets and thus faces a constant world interest rate r^* it follows from (14.58) that $R(t) = r^*t$ and from (14.70) that $\Delta(0)^{-1} = \sigma\rho + (1-\sigma)(r^* - n)$. (Of course restrictions on the parameters must ensure that $\Delta(0)$ remains positive.)

14.5.2 The representative firm

Perfectly competitive firms produce a homogeneous good by using capital and labour. Since there are constant returns to scale to the production factors taken together (see (P1)) there is no need to distinguish individual firms and we can make use of the notion of a representative firm, which makes use of technology as summarized by the production function in (14.6). (We abstract from technical progress to keep things simple.)

The stockmarket value of the firm is given by the discounted value of its cash flows:

$$V(0) = \int_0^\infty \big[F[K(t), L(t)] - W(t)L(t) - (1 - s_I)I(t)\big]e^{-R(t)}\,dt,\tag{14.71}$$

where $R(t)$ is the discounting factor given in (14.58), $I(t)$ is gross investment by the firm (see equation (14.4)), and s_I is an investment subsidy to be used below (in this section we assume $s_I = 0$). The firm maximizes its stockmarket value (14.71) subject to the capital accumulation constraint (14.4). Implicit in the formulation of the firm's choice set is the notion that it can vary its desired capital stock at will, i.e. there are no adjustment costs on investment (see Chapter 4 and below for a discussion of such costs). Indeed, by substituting (14.4) into (14.71) and integrating we find that the objective function for the firm can be written as:[15]

$$V(0) = K(0) + \int_0^\infty \left[F\left[K(t), L(t)\right] - (r(t) + \delta)K(t) - W(t)L(t) \right] e^{-R(t)} dt, \qquad (14.72)$$

where $K(0)$ is the initial capital stock. Equation (14.72) shows that the firm's decision about factor inputs is essentially a static one. Maximization of $V(0)$ by choice of $L(t)$ and $K(t)$ yields the familiar marginal productivity conditions for labour and capital:

$$F_L\left[K(t), L(t)\right] = W(t), \quad F_K\left[K(t), L(t)\right] = r(t) + \delta. \qquad (14.73)$$

By substituting the marginal productivity conditions (14.73) into (14.72) and noting the linear homogeneity property of the production function we find that $V(0) = K(0)$. In the absence of adjustment costs on investment the value of the firm equals the (replacement) value of its capital stock and Tobin's q is unity.

By writing the production function in the intensive form (see (14.8)) we can rewrite the marginal products of capital and labour as follows:[16]

$$F_K\left[K(t), L(t)\right] = f'(k(t)), \quad F_L\left[K(t), L(t)\right] = f(k(t)) - k(t)f'(k(t)). \qquad (14.74)$$

We now have all the ingredients of the model and we summarize them for the sake of convenience in Table 14.1. Equation (T1.1) is the rewritten Euler equation associated with an iso-elastic felicity function (see the expression in (14.67)). (T1.2) combines equations (14.3)–(14.5) and is written in the intensive form. Finally, (T1.3) is obtained by combining the relevant conditions in (14.73) and (14.74).

14.5.3 The phase diagram

The model in Table 14.1 can be analysed to a large extent by means of its associated phase portrait which is given in Figure 14.8. The construction of this diagram warrants some additional comment. The $\dot{k}(t) = 0$ line represents points in $(c(t), k(t))$ space for which the per capita capital stock is in equilibrium . The Inada conditions

---

[15] In deriving (14.72) the key thing to note is:

$$\int_0^\infty \left[\dot{K}(t) - r(t)K(t)\right] e^{-R(t)} dt = \int_0^\infty d\left[K(t)e^{-R(t)}\right] = -K(0),$$

where we have used the fact that $\lim_{K(t) \to \infty} K(t)e^{-R(t)} = 0$ in the final step.

[16] We use $F = F_K K + F_L L$, which follows from Euler's theorem, and $F_K = f'$ to derive the second expression.

Table 14.1. The Ramsey growth model

$$\dot{c}(t) = \sigma \left[r(t) - n - \rho \right] c(t), \tag{T1.1}$$
$$\dot{k}(t) = f(k(t)) - c(t) - (\delta + n)k(t), \tag{T1.2}$$
$$r(t) = f'(k(t)) - \delta. \tag{T1.3}$$

Notes: $c(t)$ is per capita consumption, $k(t)$ is the capital-labour ratio, and $r(t)$ is the interest rate. Capital depreciates at a constant rate δ and the population grows exponentially with rate n.

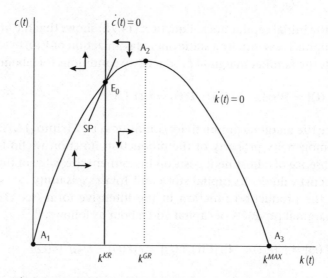

Figure 14.8. Phase diagram of the Ramsey model

ensure that it passes through the origin and is vertical there (see point A_1). Golden rule consumption occurs at point A_2 where the $\dot{k}(t) = 0$ line reaches its maximum:

$$\left(\frac{dc(t)}{dk(t)} \right)_{\dot{k}(t)=0} = 0 : \quad f' \left[k^{GR} \right] = \delta + n. \tag{14.75}$$

The maximum attainable capital-labour ratio, k^{MAX}, occurs at point A_3, where per capita consumption is zero and total output is needed for replacement investment:

$$\frac{f\left(k^{MAX} \right)}{k^{MAX}} = \delta + n. \tag{14.76}$$

Finally, the capital dynamics depends on whether there is more or less capital than the golden rule prescribes:

$$\left(\frac{\partial \dot{k}(t)}{\partial k(t)} \right)_{\dot{k}(t)=0} = f' - (\delta + n) = r - n \gtreqless 0 \quad \text{for } k(t) \lesseqgtr k^{GR}. \tag{14.77}$$

This has been indicated by horizontal arrows in Figure 14.8.

The $\dot{c}(t) = 0$ line represents points for which the per capita consumption profile is flat. In view of (T1.1) this occurs at the point for which the interest rate equals the rate of time preference plus the rate of population growth, $r^{KR} \equiv \rho + n$, where the superscript "KR" refers to "Keynes–Ramsey", who were the first to discover this result. The Keynes–Ramsey interest rate is associated with a unique capital-labour ratio (see (T1.3)). Hence, $r^{KR} = f'(k^{KR}) - \delta$ and k^{KR} thus satisfies:

$$f'(k^{KR}) = \delta + n + \rho. \tag{14.78}$$

The comparison of (14.75) and (14.78) reveals that $f'(k^{KR})$ exceeds $f'(k^{GR})$, i.e. k^{KR} lies to the left of k^{GR}. Finally, we note that the expression determining the Keynes–Ramsey capital–labour ratio (namely (14.78)) is often referred to in the literature as the *modified golden rule*.

14.5.4 Efficiency properties of the Ramsey model

Perhaps the most important property of the Ramsey model is that it precludes the possibility of dynamic inefficiency and oversaving, phenomena which are possible in the Solow–Swan model. Intuitively, this result is perhaps not that surprising because there are no missing markets, distortions, and external effects in the model so there is no reason to suspect violation of the fundamental theorems of welfare economics.

The efficiency property of the Ramsey model can be demonstrated by proving the equivalence of the market outcome (discussed in the previous section) and the solution chosen by a benevolent social planner. Such a social planner would maximize lifetime utility of the representative agent ($\Lambda(0)$ given in (14.53)) subject to the production function (14.6) and the capital accumulation constraint (14.4).[17]

The Hamiltonian associated with the command optimum is given by:

$$\mathcal{H}(t) \equiv U[c(t)]e^{-\rho t} + \mu(t)[f(k(t)) - c(t) - (n + \delta)k(t)], \tag{14.79}$$

where $\mu(t)$ is the co-state variable. The first-order necessary conditions characterizing the social optimum are:

$$\frac{\partial \mathcal{H}(t)}{\partial c(t)} = 0: \quad U'[c^{SO}(t)]e^{-\rho t} = \mu(t), \tag{14.80}$$

$$\dot{\mu}(t) = -\frac{\partial \mathcal{H}(t)}{\partial k(t)} = 0: \quad \dot{\mu}(t) = -[f'[k^{SO}(t)] - (n + \delta)]\mu(t), \tag{14.81}$$

where the superscript "SO" denotes socially optimal values. The socially optimal interest rate can be defined as $r^{SO}(t) \equiv f'[k^{SO}(t)] - \delta$, so that (14.79)–(14.80) can be

---

[17] As well as an initial condition for the capital stock, non-negativity constraints for consumption and capital, and a transversality condition. See Blanchard and Fischer (1989, pp. 38–43) and Intriligator (1971, pp. 405–416).

combined to yield an easily interpretable expression for the optimal time profile of consumption:

$$U'' \left[c^{SO}(t) \right] \frac{dc^{SO}(t)}{dt} = \mu(t) e^{\rho t} \left[\rho + \frac{\dot{\mu}(t)}{\mu(t)} \right]$$

$$= -U' \left[c^{SO}(t) \right] \left[f' \left[k^{SO}(t) \right] - \delta - (\rho + n) \right] \quad \Leftrightarrow$$

$$\frac{1}{c^{SO}(t)} \frac{dc^{SO}(t)}{dt} = \sigma \left[c^{SO}(t) \right] \left[r^{SO}(t) - \rho - n \right], \quad t \in [0, \infty). \tag{14.82}$$

Equation (14.82) has exactly the same form as (14.63) so that the planning solution and market outcome coincide.[18] Hence, by removing the ad hoc saving function from the Solow–Swan model there is no possibility of oversaving any more.

14.5.5 Transitional dynamics and convergence in the Ramsey model

As was demonstrated graphically with the aid of Figure 14.8, the Ramsey model is saddle-point stable. An exact solution for the saddle path can in general not be obtained, however, rendering the study of the convergence properties of the model slightly more complicated than was the case for the Solow–Swan model. By linearizing the model around the initial steady state, E_0, however, the *approximate* transitional dynamics can be studied in a relatively straightforward manner.

After linearizing the model in Table 14.1 we obtain the following system of first-order differential equation:

$$\begin{bmatrix} \dot{c}(t) \\ \dot{k}(t) \end{bmatrix} = \begin{bmatrix} 0 & \sigma c^* f''(k^*) \\ -1 & \rho \end{bmatrix} \begin{bmatrix} c(t) - c^* \\ k(t) - k^* \end{bmatrix}, \tag{14.83}$$

where the superscript "*" denotes initial steady-state values. The Jacobian matrix on the right-hand side of (14.83) is denoted by Δ. Since tr(Δ)$\equiv \lambda_1 + \lambda_2 = \rho > 0$ and $|\Delta| \equiv \lambda_1 \lambda_2 = \sigma c^* f''(k^*) < 0$, where λ_1 and λ_2 are the characteristic roots of Δ, equation (14.83) confirms saddle-point stability, i.e. λ_1 and λ_2 have opposite signs. The absolute value of the stable (negative) characteristic root determines the approximate convergence speed of the economic system. After some manipulation we obtain the following expression:

$$\beta \equiv \left(\frac{\rho}{2} \right) \left[\sqrt{1 - \frac{4 \sigma c^* f''(k^*)}{\rho^2}} - 1 \right]$$

$$= \left(\frac{\rho}{2} \right) \left[\sqrt{1 + \frac{4}{\rho^2} \left(\frac{\sigma}{\sigma_{KL}} \right) \left(\frac{c}{k} \right)^* (r^* + \delta)(1 - \omega_K)} - 1 \right], \tag{14.84}$$

---

[18] We have also used the fact that the initial condition and the capital accumulation constraint are the same for the market and planning solutions. This implies that the *levels* of the interest rate, capital, and consumption also coincide for the two solutions.

Table 14.2. Convergence speed in the Ramsey model

	σ/σ_{KL}			
	0.2	0.5	1	2
$\omega_K = \frac{1}{3}$	4.23	7.38	10.97	16.08
$\omega_K = \frac{1}{2}$	2.41	4.39	6.70	10.00
$\omega_K = \frac{2}{3}$	1.25	2.44	3.88	5.96

where $\sigma_{KL} \equiv (1 - \omega_K)f'/(- kf'')$ is the substitution elasticity between capital and labour in the production function and $\omega_K \equiv kf'/f$ is the capital share in national income (both evaluated in the initial steady state). Recall that the Solow–Swan model predicts a convergence speed which exceeds the empirically relevant estimate of about 2% per annum by quite a margin (see section 3.3). Although it is not immediately apparent from the formula in (14.84) it turns out that the Ramsey model also predicts too high a rate of convergence for realistic values of the parameters. This has been demonstrated by means of some numerical simulations in Table 14.2. We calibrate the steady state of a fictional economy as follows. We set the rate of pure time preference at 3% per annum ($\rho = 0.03$), the rate of population growth at 2% ($n = 0.02$), and the depreciation rate of capital at 5% ($\delta = 0.05$). The steady state implies $r^* = \rho + n$, $(k/y)^* = \omega_K/(r^* + \delta)$, and $(c/y)^* = 1 - (\delta + n)\omega_K/(r^* + \delta)$. By varying the capital share (ω_K) and the ratio of elasticities of the felicity function and the production function (σ/σ_{KL}) we obtain a number of estimates for the convergence speed β. As is clear from the results in Table 14.2, the Ramsey predicts even faster convergence than the Solow model! For example, if both the felicity function and the production function feature a unitary substitution elasticity (so that $\sigma/\sigma_{KL} = 1$) then for the realistic capital share of $\omega_K = \frac{1}{3}$, the convergence speed is a staggering 10.97% per annum. Only if the capital share is unrealistically high *and* the felicity function is relatively inelastic (so that σ/σ_{KL} is low) does the model come anywhere near to matching the empirically observed speed of convergence.

14.5.6 An open-economy Ramsey model

Up to this point we have focused attention on the traditional closed-economy representation of the Ramsey model. In a closed economy, the domestic interest rate clears the domestic rental market for *physical* capital and thus bears a close relationship with the capital-labour ratio; see equation (T1.3). In an open economy, which is small in world financial markets, on the other hand, the interest rate is fully determined abroad and is thus exogenous. It is clear that the marginal productivity condition for capital (equation (T1.3)) can only hold for a small open economy if the physical capital stock is perfectly mobile across countries! Indeed, a small increase in the world interest rate must be accompanied by an immediate and instantaneous outflow of physical capital in order to restore equality between the domestic marginal product of capital and the world interest rate.

Apart from the fact that perfect mobility of physical capital is extremely unrealistic, it also has a very unfortunate implication in that it renders the convergence speed of the economy infinitely large! In technical terms, capital is changed from a slow-moving (predetermined) variable to a jumping variable. The traditional solution to this problem is to assume that physical capital is firm specific and thus cannot move costlessly and instantaneously. *Financial* capital, such as bonds and ownership claims of domestic assets, is of course perfectly mobile in this context so that yields on domestic and foreign assets are equalized. In technical terms imperfect mobility of physical capital is modelled by assuming that the firm must incur installation costs associated with the investment process.

The small open economy assumption also causes a complication on the consumption side of the Ramsey model. Indeed, as was shown above, the representative household chooses its optimal consumption profile according to the Euler equation (T1.1). But if the rate of interest is exogenous (i.e. $r(t) = r^*$, where r^* is the world interest rate) then consumption can only ever attain a steady state ($\dot{c}(t) = 0$) if the world interest rate happens to be equal to the exogenous population growth plus the rate of time preference, i.e. $r^* = \rho + n$ must be satisfied. In any other case, the country either follows an ever-decreasing path of per capita consumption if its citizens are impatient ($\rho + n > r^*$) or the country saves so much that it eventually ceases being small in world financial markets (with very patient citizens, $\rho + n < r^*$). In order to avoid these difficulties we assume that the following "knife-edge" condition holds:

$$\rho + n = r^*. \tag{14.85}$$

An immediate consequence of (14.85) in combination with (T1.1) is that per capita consumption of the representative household is completely smoothed over time, i.e. $\dot{c}(t)/c(t) = 0$ for all time periods.

We now consider the behaviour of the representative (domestic) firm facing adjustment costs for investment. The stockmarket value of the firm is still given by (14.71) but net and gross investment are now related according to a concave installation function:

$$\dot{K}(t) = \left[\Phi\left(\frac{I(t)}{K(t)}\right) - \delta \right] K(t), \tag{14.86}$$

where $\Phi(.)$ represents the presence of installation costs associated with investment. We assume that the installation cost function satisfies the usual properties: $\Phi(0) = 0$, $\Phi'(.) > 0$, and $\Phi''(.) < 0$.[19]

The firm chooses time paths for investment, labour demand, and the capital stock in order to maximize $V(0)$ subject to the capital accumulation identity (14.86), an initial condition for the capital stock, and a transversality condition. The first-order necessary conditions are the constraint (14.86) and:[20]

$$W(t) = F_L\left[K(t), L(t)\right],$$ (14.87)

$$q(t)\Phi'\left(\frac{I(t)}{K(t)}\right) = 1 - s_I,$$ (14.88)

$$\dot{q}(t) = \left[r(t) + \delta - \Phi\left(\frac{I(t)}{K(t)}\right)\right]q(t)$$

$$- F_K\left[K(t), L(t)\right] + (1 - s_I)\left(\frac{I(t)}{K(t)}\right),$$ (14.89)

where $q(t)$ is Tobin's q (its current value, $q(0)$, measures the marginal (and average) value of installed capital, $K(0)$, i.e. $V(0) = q(0)K(0)$).

As was demonstrated in Chapter 11, gross domestic product in an open economy can be written as follows:

$$Y(t) \equiv C(t) + I(t) + X(t),$$ (14.90)

where $X(t)$ is net exports (i.e. the trade balance) and gross investment (inclusive of installation costs) appears in the national income identity. Note furthermore that we abstract from government consumption for convenience. Designating $A_F(t)$ as the stock of net foreign assets in the hands of domestic agents, gross national product is equal to gross domestic product plus interest earnings on net foreign assets, $r^*A_F(t)$. The current account of the balance of payments is equal to net exports plus interest earnings on foreign assets. The dynamic equation for the stock of net foreign assets is thus:

$$\dot{A}_F(t) = r^*A_F(t) + X(t) = r^*A_F(t) + Y(t) - C(t) - I(t),$$ (14.91)

which can be written in per capita form as:

$$\dot{a}_F(t) = \rho a_F(t) + y(t) - c(t) - i(t),$$ (14.92)

where we have used the fact that $\rho = r^* - n$ (see (14.85)). Although the country can freely borrow from (or lend to) the rest of the world, it must obey an intertemporal

---

[19] See Chapters 2 and 4 for an extensive discussion of the theory of investment based on adjustment costs.

[20] See the Intermezzo on Tobin's q-theory of investment in Chapter 4 for a derivation of these first-order conditions.

solvency condition of the form:

$$\lim_{t \to \infty} a_F(t)e^{-\rho t} = 0. \tag{14.93}$$

Equations (14.92) and (14.93) in combination imply that there is a relationship between the initial level of net foreign assets per capita, $a_{F,0}$, and the present value of future trade balances:

$$a_{F,0} = \int_0^\infty [c(t) + i(t) - y(t)] e^{-\rho t} dt. \tag{14.94}$$

To the extent that the country possesses positive net foreign assets ($a_{F,0} > 0$), it can afford to run present and future trade balance deficits. All that nation-wide solvency requires is that the present value of these trade balance deficits (the right-hand side of (14.94)) add up to the initial level of net foreign assets (left-hand side of (14.94)).

We now possess all the ingredients of the open-economy Ramsey model and we restate its key equations for the sake of convenience in Table 14.3.

Equation (T3.1) shows that per capita consumption is completely smoothed over time. As was pointed out above, this result is a direct consequence of the assumption expressed in (14.85). Equation (T3.2) implicitly determines the optimal investment–capital ratio as a function of (subsidy-adjusted) Tobin's q. Equation (T3.3) gives the dynamic evolution of Tobin's q and (T3.4) does the same for the capital stock per worker. Finally, (T3.5) is the current account equation which is obtained by substituting the production function, $f(k(t))$, into (14.92).

Model solution and convergence speed

The model is quite unlike the growth models that were studied up to this point because it contains a zero root and thus displays hysteretic properties in the sense that the steady state depends on the initial conditions.[21] Technically, the model

Table 14.3. The Ramsey model for the open economy

$\frac{\dot{c}(t)}{c(t)} = 0$	(T3.1)
$q(t)\Phi'\left(\frac{i(t)}{k(t)}\right) = 1 - s_I$	(T3.2)
$\dot{q}(t) = \left[\rho + n + \delta - \Phi\left(\frac{i(t)}{k(t)}\right)\right] q(t) - f'(k(t)) + (1 - s_I)\left(\frac{i(t)}{k(t)}\right)$	(T3.3)
$\dot{k}(t) = \left[\Phi\left(\frac{i(t)}{k(t)}\right) - n - \delta\right] k(t)$	(T3.4)
$\dot{a}_F(t) = \rho a_F(t) + f(k(t)) - c(t) - i(t)$	(T3.5)

Notes: $c(t)$ is per capita consumption, $k(t)$ is the capital-labour ratio, $q(t)$ is Tobin's q, $i(t)$ is gross investment per worker, s_I is an investment subsidy, and $A_F(t)$ is net foreign assets per worker. See also Table 14.1.

[21] See Turnovsky (1995, ch. 12), Sen and Turnovsky (1990), and Giavazzi and Wyplosz (1985) for a further discussion. See also Chapter 2 above for an example of a hysteretic model in discrete time.

solution proceeds as follows. First, we note that equations (T3.2)–(T3.4) form an autonomous subsystem determining the dynamics of $i(t)$, $q(t)$, and $k(t)$. Second, once the solutions for investment and capital are known, they can be substituted into the nation-wide solvency condition (14.94) which can then be solved for per capita consumption.

Since the model is non-linear, it can only be solved analytically by first linearizing it around the steady state. We start with the investment system consisting of (T3.2)–(T3.4). To keep the model as simple as possible we postulate an iso-elastic installation function:

$$\Phi\left(\frac{i(t)}{k(t)}\right) \equiv \frac{1}{1 - \sigma_I}\left(\frac{i(t)}{k(t)}\right)^{1-\sigma_I}, \tag{14.95}$$

with $0 < \sigma_I < 1$. The parameter σ_I regulates the curvature of the installation function. The lower is σ_I, the closer $\Phi(.)$ resembles a straight line, and the higher is the international mobility of physical capital—see Bovenberg (1994, p. 122). The investment demand implied by (T3.2) in combination with (14.95) is also iso-elastic:

$$\frac{i(t)}{k(t)} = g(q(t), s_I) \equiv \left[\frac{q(t)}{1 - s_I}\right]^{1/\sigma_I}. \tag{14.96}$$

By inserting (14.96) into (T3.3)–(T3.4) and linearizing, we obtain a simple matrix expression for the investment system:

$$\begin{bmatrix} \dot{k}(t) \\ \dot{q}(t) \end{bmatrix} = \begin{bmatrix} 0 & i^*(1 - s_I)/\left[(q^*)^2\sigma_I\right] \\ -f''(k^*) & \rho \end{bmatrix}\begin{bmatrix} k(t) - k^* \\ q(t) - q^* \end{bmatrix}. \tag{14.97}$$

The Jacobian matrix on the right-hand side of (14.97) is denoted by Δ_I and its typical elements by δ_{ij}. The investment system is saddle-point stable because Δ_I has a positive trace (equal to ρ) and a negative determinant (equal to $(1 - s_I)i^*f''(k^*)/[(q^*)^2\sigma_I]$). This implies that the characteristic roots of Δ_I are real, distinct, and opposite in sign.[22] Denoting the stable and unstable roots by, respectively $-\lambda_1 < 0$ and $\lambda_2 > 0$ it follows from (14.97) that:

$$\lambda_2 - \lambda_1 = \text{tr}(\Delta_I) = \rho \quad \Leftrightarrow \quad \lambda_2 = \rho + \lambda_1 > \rho, \tag{14.98}$$

i.e. the unstable root equals the pure rate of time preference (ρ) plus the transition speed in the economy (represented by λ_1). Note that the adjustment speed of the investment system (λ_1) is finite due to the existence of installation costs of investment and the associated short-run immobility of capital.

If the initial capital stock is denoted by k_0, then the system converges to the steady state provided it is on the saddle path. Deferring the technical details of the

---

[22] Recall that the trace and determinant of the Jacobian matrix equal, respectively, the sum and the product of the characteristic roots.

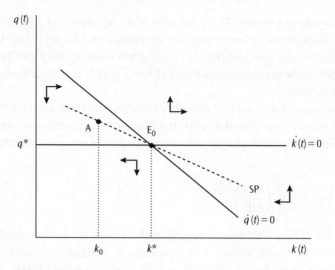

Figure 14.9. Investment in the open economy

derivation to the appendix of this chapter, we find that the solution to (14.97) is:

$$\begin{bmatrix} k(t) - k^* \\ q(t) - q^* \end{bmatrix} = \begin{bmatrix} k_0 - k^* \\ q(0) - q^* \end{bmatrix} e^{-\lambda_1 t}, \tag{14.99}$$

where the initial value of Tobin's q is given by:

$$q(0) = q^* - \left(\frac{\lambda_1}{\delta_{12}} \right) [k_0 - k^*]. \tag{14.100}$$

The solution path is illustrated in Figure 14.9. For the initial capital stock, k_0, Tobin's q is above its equilibrium level and the economy moves gradually towards the steady-state equilibrium E_0.

Now that we know the dynamic paths for the capital stock and Tobin's q (and thus, by (14.96), the implied path for investment) we can work out the restriction implied by national solvency. First, we linearize the production function, $y(t) = f(k(t))$, and the investment function (14.96) around the steady state:

$$\begin{bmatrix} y(t) - y^* \\ i(t) - i^* \end{bmatrix} = \begin{bmatrix} f'(k^*) & 0 \\ g^* & k^* g_q^* \end{bmatrix} \begin{bmatrix} k(t) - k^* \\ q(t) - q^* \end{bmatrix}, \tag{14.101}$$

where $g^* \equiv g(q^*, s_I)$ and $g_q^* \equiv g_q(q^*, s_I)$. By using (14.99)–(14.101) we find the (approximate) path for $i(t) - y(t)$:

$$i(t) - y(t) = i^* - y^* + k^* g_q^* [q(t) - q^*] + [g^* - f'(k^*)][k(t) - k^*]$$

$$= i^* - y^* - \Omega [k_0 - k^*] e^{-\lambda_1 t}, \tag{14.102}$$

where $\Omega \equiv f'(k^*) - g^* + \lambda_1 k^* g_q^* / \delta_{12} > 0$. Equation (T3.1) shows that per capita consumption stays constant during the transition, i.e. $c(t) = c^*$. By using this result as well as equation (14.102) in the nation-wide solvency condition we obtain the following expression:

$$
\begin{aligned}
a_{F,0} &= \frac{c^*}{\rho} + \int_0^\infty \left[i(t) - y(t)\right] e^{-\rho t}\, dt \\
&= \frac{c^* + i^* - y^*}{\rho} - \Omega\left[k_0 - k^*\right] \int_0^\infty e^{-(\rho + \lambda_1)t}\, dt \\
&= \frac{c^* + i^* - y^*}{\rho} - \frac{\Omega\left[k_0 - k^*\right]}{\lambda_2},
\end{aligned}
\tag{14.103}
$$

where we have used the fact that $\lambda_2 = \rho + \lambda_1$ (see (14.98)) in the final step. It follows from the steady-state version of (14.92) that $\rho a_F^* = c^* + i^* - y^*$ (since $\dot{a}_F^* = 0$) so that (14.103) can be rewritten as follows:

$$
a_{F,0} + \left(\frac{\Omega}{\lambda_2}\right) k_0 = a_F^* + \left(\frac{\Omega}{\lambda_2}\right) k^*.
\tag{14.104}
$$

As Sen and Turnovsky (1990, p. 287) point out, the left-hand side of (14.104) represents the initial value of total resources available to the economy and can thus be interpreted as *national wealth*. National wealth consists of initial non-human wealth, $a_{F,0} + k_0$, plus the present value of resources generated by capital accumulation starting from the initial capital stock, k_0.

The striking feature of the open-economy Ramsey model is that its steady state depends on the initial stock of assets, $a_{F,0}$ and k_0. This is the hysteretic property alluded to above. In the steady state we have that $\dot{c}(t) = \dot{q}(t) = \dot{k}(t) = \dot{a}_F(t) = 0$ and the model consists of equation (14.104) as well as:

$$
q^* \Phi'\left(\frac{i^*}{k^*}\right) = 1 - s_I,
\tag{14.105}
$$

$$
f'(k^*) = \rho q^* + (1 - s_I)\left(\frac{i^*}{k^*}\right),
\tag{14.106}
$$

$$
\Phi\left(\frac{i^*}{k^*}\right) = n + \delta,
\tag{14.107}
$$

$$
\rho a_F^* + f(k^*) = c^* + i^*,
\tag{14.108}
$$

which jointly determine the steady-state values q^*, i^*, k^*, c^*, and a_F^*. Given the structure of the model, only consumption and the net stock of foreign assets display hysteresis and are thus a function of the initial conditions.[23]

---

[23] In particular, (14.107) determines i^*/k^* as a function of $n + \delta$, (14.105) then determines q^* and (14.106) determines k^* (and thus i^*). The only variables remaining to be determined by (14.104) and (14.108) are c^* and a_F^*. Sen and Turnovsky (1990) show that if labour supply is endogenous, the hysteretic property extends to investment and the capital stock also.

Effects of an investment subsidy

We are now in the position to use the model to study the effects of an investment subsidy on the macroeconomy. To keep things simple we restrict attention to the case of an unanticipated and permanent increase in the investment subsidy. It is most convenient to determine the long-run effect first. Equation (14.107) shows that i^*/k^* is constant, so that it follows from (14.105) that q^* is proportional to $(1 - s_I)$. Hence, Tobin's q falls in the long run:

$$\frac{dq^*}{ds_I} = -\frac{1}{\Phi'(i^*/k^*)} = -\frac{q^*}{1 - s_I} < 0. \tag{14.109}$$

Equation (14.106) can be used to derive the long-run effect on the stock of capital per worker:

$$\frac{dk^*}{ds_I} = \frac{k^* di^*}{i^* ds_I} = \frac{1}{f''(k^*)}\left[\rho\left(\frac{dq^*}{ds_I}\right) - \frac{i^*}{k^*}\right] = -\frac{f'(k^*)}{(1 - s_I)f''(k^*)} > 0. \tag{14.110}$$

Hence, investment and the capital stock (both measured per worker) rise equi-proportionally in the long run. The national wealth constraint (14.104) shows that the composition of wealth changes also, i.e. the increase in the domestic capital stock leads to a reduction in the long-run stock of net foreign assets:

$$\frac{da_F^*}{ds_I} = -\left(\frac{\Omega}{\lambda_2}\right)\left(\frac{dk^*}{ds_I}\right). \tag{14.111}$$

The net effect on consumption is ambiguous.

The transitional effects of the policy shock can be studied with the aid of Figure 14.10. In that figure, k_0 is the initial capital stock per worker, the economy is at point A and is heading towards the steady state at E_0 (where the steady-state capital stock per worker is k_0^*). The long-run effect on the capital stock is positive (see (14.110)) and saddle-point stability requires that the economy must be on the stable arm of the saddle path. By using the expression for the saddle path (given in (14.100)) we obtain the impact effect for Tobin's q:[24]

$$\begin{aligned}
\frac{dq(0)}{ds_I} &= \frac{dq^*}{ds_I} + \left(\frac{\lambda_1}{\delta_{12}}\right)\left(\frac{dk^*}{ds_I}\right) \\
&= -\frac{q^*}{1 - s_I} - \left(\frac{\lambda_1}{\delta_{12}f''(k^*)}\right)\frac{f'(k^*)}{1 - s_I} \\
&= -\frac{q^*}{1 - s_I} + \left(\frac{1}{\rho + \lambda_1}\right)\frac{f'(k^*)}{1 - s_I} \lessgtr 0.
\end{aligned} \tag{14.112}$$

[24] We have used equations (14.109) and (14.110) in going from the first to the second line. In going from the second to the third line we have used some results for the characteristic roots, i.e. $\lambda_1\lambda_2 = -f''(k^*)\delta_{12}$ and $\lambda_2 = \rho + \lambda_1$.

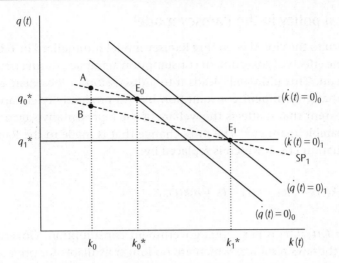

Figure 14.10. An investment subsidy with high mobility of physical capital

The impact effect on Tobin's q is ambiguous because the first term on the right-hand side is negative whilst the second term is positive. The ambiguity arises from the fact that both the $\dot{k}(t) = 0$ line and the $\dot{q}(t) = 0$ lines shift as a result of the increase in the investment subsidy. Recall that the $\dot{k}(t) = 0$ line represents points for which the (i/k) ratio is constant. Since an increase in s_I leads to a higher desired (i/k) ratio (see (14.96)), Tobin's q must fall to restore capital stock equilibrium, i.e. the $\dot{k}(t) = 0$ line shifts down. At the same time, the boost in s_I leads to an upward shift in the $\dot{q}(t) = 0$ line.

In Figure 14.10 the new steady-state equilibrium is at E_1 and the saddle path is drawn under the assumption that the capital stock effect is dominated by the effect on Tobin's q (given in (14.112)), so that $dq(0)/ds_I < 0$. At impact the economy jumps from point A to point B, after which gradual adjustment takes place towards the new steady-state equilibrium E_1.

Why is the impact effect on Tobin's q ambiguous? Equation (14.112) shows that the ambiguity arises because $dq(0)/ds_I$ depends on the adjustment speed in the economy, λ_1. If adjustment costs on investment are relatively low ($\sigma_I \approx 0$), then λ_1 is relatively high, physical capital is highly mobile, and installed and new capital goods are close substitutes. The investment subsidy reduces the price of new capital goods and thus also the value of the installed capital stock in that case (Bovenberg, 1993, p. 13). The opposite holds if adjustment costs are severe ($\sigma_I \approx 1$). As the diagram shows, however, regardless of the sign of $dq(0)/ds_I$, net capital accumulation takes place (as B lies above the new $\dot{k}(t) = 0$ line) and the economy moves from B to E_1 over time.

14.5.7 Fiscal policy in the Ramsey model

We now return to the closed-economy Ramsey model summarized in Table 14.1 and investigate the effects of government consumption at impact, during transition, and in the long run. This ultimately leads into a discussion of Ricardian equivalence. We assume that government consumption has no productivity-enhancing effects and, to the extent that it affects the welfare of the representative agent, does so in a weakly separable manner.[25] The only change that is made to the Ramsey model relates to equation (T1.2) which is replaced by:

$$\dot{k}(t) = f(k(t)) - c(t) - g(t) - (\delta + n)k(t), \qquad (14.113)$$

where $g(t) \equiv G(t)/L(t)$ is per capita government consumption. Government consumption withdraws resources which are no longer available for private consumption or replacement of the capital stock. As a result, for a given level of per capita public consumption, $g(t) = g$, the $\dot{k}(t) = 0$ line can be drawn as in Figure 14.11. Several conclusions can be drawn already. First, the existence of positive government consumption does not reinstate the possibility of dynamic inefficiency in the Ramsey model. The golden-rule capital stock per worker is not affected by g, although of course the golden-rule per capita consumption *level* is affected. Second, the issue of multiple equilibria also does not arise in the Ramsey model with government consumption. In contrast to the situation in the Solow model, provided an equilibrium exists in the Ramsey model it is unique and saddle-point stable.

An *unanticipated* and *permanent* increase in the level of government consumption per worker shifts the $\dot{k}(t) = 0$ line down, say to $(\dot{k}(t) = 0)_1$. Since the shock comes as a complete surprise to the representative household, it reacts to the increased level of taxes (needed to finance the additional government consumption) by cutting back private consumption. The representative household feels poorer as a result of the shock and, as consumption is a normal good, reduces it one-for-one:

$$\frac{dc(t)}{dg} = -1, \quad \frac{dy(t)}{dg} = \frac{dk(t)}{dg} = 0, \qquad (14.114)$$

for all $t \in [0, \infty)$. There is no transitional dynamics because the shock itself has no long-run effect on the capital stock and there are no anticipation effects. In terms of Figure 14.11 the economy jumps from E_0 to E_1.

With a *temporary* increase in g there are non-trivial transition effects. The representative household anticipates the temporarily higher taxes but spreads the negative effect on human wealth out over the entire lifetime consumption path. As a result,

---

[25] See Turnovsky and Fisher (1995) for the more general cases. With weak separability we mean that the marginal utility of private consumption does not depend on the level of government consumption.

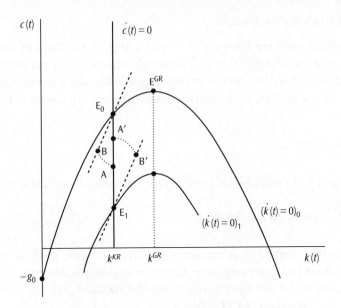

Figure 14.11. Fiscal policy in the Ramsey model

the impact effect on private consumption is still negative but less than one-for-one:

$$-1 < \frac{dc(0)}{dg} < 0. \tag{14.115}$$

In terms of Figure 14.11 the economy jumps from E_0 to point A. Immediately after the shock the household starts to dissave so that the capital stock falls, the interest rate rises, and (by (T1.1)) the consumption path rises over time. The economy moves from A to B which is reached at the time government consumption is cut back to its initial level again. This cut in g (and the associated taxes) releases resources which allow the capital stock to return to its constant steady-state level. As a result of the temporary boost in government consumption, the policy maker has managed to engineer a temporary decline in output per worker.

With an *anticipated* and *permanent* increase in g, the opposite effect occurs during transition. Consumption falls by less than one-for-one (as in (14.115)), but since the government consumption has not risen yet it leads to additional saving and a gradual increase in the capital stock, a reduction in the interest rate, and a downward-sloping consumption profile. At impact the economy jumps from E_0 to A′, after which it gradually moves from A′ to B′ during transition. Point B′ is reached at precisely the time the policy is enacted. As g is increased, net saving turns into net dissaving and the capital stock starts to fall. The economy moves from point B′ to E_1.

441

Ricardian equivalence once again

Ricardian equivalence (see Chapter 6) clearly holds in the Ramsey model as can be demonstrated quite easily. The government budget identity (in per capita form) is given in (14.41). Like the representative household, the government must also remain solvent so that it faces an intertemporal solvency condition of the following form:[26]

$$\lim_{t \to \infty} b(t)e^{-[R(t)-nt]} = 0, \tag{14.116}$$

By combining (14.41) and (14.116), we obtain the government budget restriction:

$$b(0) = \int_0^\infty [\tau(t) - g(t)] e^{-[R(t)-nt]} dt. \tag{14.117}$$

To the extent that there is a pre-existing government debt ($b(0) > 0$), solvency requires that this debt must be equal to the present value of future primary surpluses. In principle, there are infinitely many paths for $\tau(t)$ and $g(t)$ (and hence for the primary deficit), for which (14.117) holds.

The budget identity of the representative agent is given in (14.55). It is modified to take into account that lump-sum taxes are levied on the agent:

$$\dot{a}(t) \equiv [r(t) - n]a(t) + W(t) - \tau(t) - c(t). \tag{14.118}$$

By using (14.118) in combination with the household solvency condition (14.56), the household budget restriction is obtained as in (14.57), but with a tax-modified definition of human wealth:

$$h(0) \equiv \int_0^\infty [W(t) - \tau(t)] e^{-[R(t)-nt]} dt. \tag{14.119}$$

By substituting the government budget restriction (14.117) into (14.119), the expression for human wealth can be rewritten as:

$$h(0) = \int_0^\infty [W(t) - g(t)] e^{-[R(t)-nt]} dt - b(0). \tag{14.120}$$

The path of lump-sum taxes completely vanishes from the expression for human wealth. Since $b(0)$ and the path for $g(t)$ are given, the particular path for lump-sum taxes does not affect the total amount of resources available to the representative agent. As a result, the agent's real consumption plans are not affected either.

---

[26] By substituting (14.39) into (14.41) and integrating the resulting expression we obtain:

$$\lim_{t \to \infty} b(t)e^{-[R(t)-nt]} - b(0) = \int_0^\infty [g(t) - \tau(t)] e^{-[R(t)-nt]} dt,$$

where we have also used (14.58). The first term on the left-hand side is the government solvency condition. By imposing this condition the government budget restriction (14.117) is obtained.

By using (14.120) in (14.57), the household budget restriction can be written as:

$$\int_0^\infty c(t)e^{-[R(t)-nt]}\,dt = [a(0) - b(0)] + \int_0^\infty [W(t) - g(t)]\,e^{-[R(t)-nt]}\,dt. \qquad (14.121)$$

This expression shows clearly why Barro (1974) chose the title he did for his path-breaking article. Under Ricardian equivalence, government debt should not be seen as household wealth, i.e. $b(0)$ must be deducted from total financial wealth in order to reveal the household's true financial asset position, as is in fact done in (14.121).

14.5.8 Overlapping generations of infinitely lived dynasties

In the previous section we saw that the Ramsey model yields classical conclusions *vis-à-vis* fiscal policy and implies the validity of Ricardian equivalence. The question which arises is which aspect of the model can be considered the prime cause for these classical results. In this subsection we show that once we allow for "disconnectedness of generations", debt neutrality no longer holds despite the fact that individual generations live forever.

Up to now we have introduced population growth by assuming growth of the dynastic family. Suppose now, however, that individual agents are infinitely lived (as the dynastic family is in the Ramsey model) but that population growth takes the form of new agents gradually entering the economy. These new agents also have infinite lives but are not linked to any of the agents already alive at the time of their birth. This is the setting of infinitely lived overlapping generations (OLG) suggested by Weil (1989b). Loosely put, growth of the population now occurs at the "extensive" rather than the "intensive" margin.

Since different agents enter life at different moments in historical time, both the birth rate (generational index) and the calendar date must be distinguished. We assume that a representative agent of generational cohort $v \leq t$ chooses a path for consumption in order to maximize lifetime utility,

$$\Lambda(v,t) \equiv \int_t^\infty \log c(v,\tau)e^{\rho(t-\tau)}\,d\tau, \qquad (14.122)$$

subject to the budget identity:

$$\dot{a}(v,\tau) \equiv \frac{da(v,\tau)}{d\tau} = r(\tau)a(v,\tau) + W(\tau) - c(v,\tau), \qquad (14.123)$$

and the intertemporal solvency condition:

$$\lim_{t\to\infty} a(v,\tau)e^{-R(t,\tau)} = 0, \quad R(t,\tau) \equiv \int_t^\tau r(s)\,ds, \qquad (14.124)$$

where $c(v,\tau)$ and $a(v,\tau)$ denote, respectively, consumption and financial assets at time τ of the representative household of vintage v. The felicity function appearing in (14.122) features an intertemporal substitution elasticity of unity. Equation

443

(14.123) shows that the household supplies a single unit of labour inelastically to the competitive labour market and receives a wage, $W(\tau)$, which is age-independent. A new generation is born without any financial assets:

$$a(v, v) = 0. \tag{14.125}$$

In view of the simple structure of preferences, the level and time profile of consumption by a representative household of vintage v are easily computed:

$$c(v, t) = \rho \left[a(v, t) + h(t) \right], \tag{14.126}$$

$$\dot{c}(v, t) = [r(t) - \rho] c(v, t), \tag{14.127}$$

where $h(t)$ is age-independent human wealth:

$$h(t) \equiv \int_t^\infty [W(\tau) - \tau(\tau)] e^{-R(t,\tau)} \, d\tau, \tag{14.128}$$

and $\tau(\tau)$ represents lump-sum taxes per agent. This tax is, by assumption, the same for all agents and thus does not feature a generations index either.

At the beginning of time, the economy starts out with $N(0)$ agents, so that with a constant exponential population growth rate of n, the population size at time t is:

$$N(t) = N(0)e^{nt}. \tag{14.129}$$

The instantaneous arrival rate of new generations is $dN(t)/dt$ so we know that the number of agents of generation $v \leq t$ is given by $N(v, v) \equiv dN(v)/dv$. This suggests that aggregate per capita variables can be measured as follows:

$$x(t) \equiv \frac{1}{N(t)} \left[N(0)x(0, t) + \int_0^t x(v, t) \, dN(v) \right], \tag{14.130}$$

so that aggregate per capita consumption, $c(t)$, can be written as follows:

$$c(t) = \rho \left[a(t) + h(t) \right], \tag{14.131}$$

where we have used (14.126) plus the fact that human wealth is age-independent. The aggregate counterpart to (14.123) is:

$$\dot{a}(t) = [r(t) - n] a(t) + W(t) - c(t), \tag{14.132}$$

and equation (14.128) implies that human wealth (per agent) accumulates according to:

$$\dot{h}(t) = r(t)h(t) - [W(t) - \tau(t)]. \tag{14.133}$$

Human and non-human wealth accumulate at different rates because newborns have no financial wealth, and thus drag down aggregate per capita financial wealth

Table 14.4. The Weil model of overlapping generations

$\dot{c}(t) = [r(t) - \rho]\,c(t) - n\rho k(t)$	(T4.1)
$\dot{k}(t) = f(k(t)) - c(t) - g(t) - (\delta + n)k(t)$	(T4.2)
$r(t) = f'(k(t)) - \delta$	(T4.3)

Notes: See Table 14.1 for definitions of the variables.

accumulation, whilst all generations have the same level of human wealth (see Weil, 1989b, pp. 187–188).

Equations (14.131)–(14.133) can be combined to yield the Euler equation modified for the existence of overlapping generations:

$$\frac{\dot{c}(t)}{c(t)} = [r(t) - \rho] - n\rho \left(\frac{a(t)}{c(t)} \right) \tag{14.134}$$

$$= \frac{\dot{c}(v, t)}{c(v, t)} - n \left[\frac{c(t) - c(t, t)}{c(t)} \right]. \tag{14.135}$$

The first term on the right-hand side of these expressions represents individual consumption growth, whilst the second term indicates how the arrival of new generations affects per capita consumption growth. In the absence of initial government debt ($b(t) = 0$), equilibrium in the financial capital market implies that household non-human wealth is held in the form of productive capital, i.e. $a(t) = k(t)$.[27] The model is completed by the capital accumulation identity (14.113) and the marginal productivity condition (T1.3). For convenience the key equations have been collected in Table 14.4.

The phase diagram for the overlapping-generations (OLG) model has been drawn in Figure 14.12 for the case with zero initial debt and government consumption ($b(t) = g(t) = 0$). The $\dot{k}(t) = 0$ line has already been discussed extensively in section 5.6 above. The $\dot{c}(t) = 0$ line is obtained by combining (T4.3) and (T4.1) and invoking the steady state. The slope of the $\dot{c}(t)$ line can be explained by appealing to equation (14.135) and Figure 14.12. Suppose that the economy is initially at point A in Figure 14.12 and consider point B which lies directly above it. With the same amount of capital per worker, both points feature the same interest rate so that individual consumption growth, $\dot{c}(v, t)/c(v, t)$, coincides at the two points. Equation (14.135) indicates, however, that aggregate consumption growth depends not only on individual growth but also on the *proportional* difference between average consumption and consumption by a newly born generation, i.e. $[c(t) - c(t, t)]/c(t)$. Since newly born generations start without any financial capital, the *absolute difference* between average and new-born consumption depends on the average capital stock (i.e. $c(t) - c(t, t) = \rho k(t)$) and is thus the same at points A and B. Since the *level*

---

[27] There are no adjustment costs of investment so that the stockmarket value of the firm is equal to the capital stock. See (14.72) above.

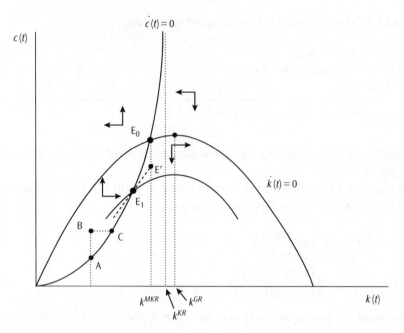

Figure 14.12. Fiscal policy in the overlapping-generations model

of aggregate consumption is larger at B, this point features a smaller proportional difference between average and new-born consumption, thereby raising aggregate consumption growth. In order to restore zero growth of aggregate per capita consumption, the capital stock must rise (to point C, which lies to the right of B). The larger capital stock not only reduces individual consumption growth by decreasing the rate of interest but also raises the drag on aggregate consumption growth due to the arrival of new dynasties because a larger capital stock widens the gap between average wealth and wealth of a newly born.

This argument also explains that for points above (below) the $\dot{c}(t) = 0$ line, consumption rises (falls). This has been indicated with vertical arrows in Figure 14.12. The intersection of the $\dot{c}(t) = 0$ and $\dot{k}(t) = 0$ lines yields a unique, saddle-point stable, equilibrium at point E_0. The capital stock per worker associated with point E_0 is k^{MKR}, where "MKR" stands for **m**odified-**K**eynes–**R**amsey rule. It is clear from the diagram that $k^{MKR} < k^{KR}$ and that the steady-state interest rate exceeds the rate of time preference:

$$\rho < r^{MKR} \equiv f'(k^{MKR}) - \delta < \rho + n. \tag{14.136}$$

The upward-sloping time profile of individual consumption that is implied by (14.136) and (14.127) ensures that new generations, like old generations, accumulate capital. Note that there is nothing preventing the capital-labour ratio from being larger than the golden-rule ratio. Indeed, $k^{MKR} > (<)k^{GR} \Leftrightarrow r^{MKR} < (>)n$.

The "normal case" appears to be, however, that the rate of pure time preference exceeds the rate of population growth ($\rho > n$), so that $r^{MKR} > n$ (see Weil, 1989b, p. 197). This is indeed the case that we will restrict attention to.

It is straightforward to demonstrate that Ricardian equivalence fails in the OLG model. Indeed, the government budget restriction can be written as:

$$b(t) = \int_t^\infty [\tau(\tau) - g(\tau)] e^{-[R(t,\tau)-n(t-\tau)]} d\tau, \tag{14.137}$$

where we now allow there to be a non-zero initial debt. By substituting (14.137) into (14.128) we can derive the following expression for aggregate per capita wealth:

$$
\begin{aligned}
a(t) + h(t) &\equiv k(t) + b(t) + h(t) \\
&= k(t) + b(t) + \int_t^\infty [W(\tau) - g(\tau)] e^{-R(t,\tau)} d\tau \\
&\quad - \left[b(t) + \int_t^\infty [g(\tau) - \tau(\tau)] e^{n(t-\tau)} d\tau \right] \\
&= k(t) + \int_t^\infty [W(\tau) - g(\tau)] e^{-R(t,\tau)} d\tau \\
&\quad + \left[b(t) - \int_t^\infty [\tau(\tau) - g(\tau)] e^{-R(t,\tau)} d\tau \right].
\end{aligned}
\tag{14.138}
$$

By comparing (14.138) to (14.137) it is clear that the term in square brackets on the right-hand side of (14.138) only vanishes if there is no population growth, i.e. if no new unconnected generations enter the economy ($n = 0$). With a positive arrival rate of generations ($n > 0$) Ricardian equivalence fails because total wealth and (by (14.131)) aggregate per capita consumption are both affected by the path of primary deficits and debt.

The intuition behind this result is provided by Weil (1989b, p. 193). A postponement of taxation which is financed by means of government debt makes all existing generations better off not because they don't have to pay taxes in the future, but rather because the future *tax base* will be larger as it includes newly arrived generations to which the present generations are not linked. An important conclusion from the analysis is that it is the economic identity of future taxpayers which determines the validity of Ricardian equivalence. Whether or not agents have finite lives in-and-of itself has no implication for Ricardian equivalence.[28]

The OLG model thus generally refutes the notion of Ricardian equivalence. It does, however, yield classical predictions regarding the effects of government consumption on output, consumption, and capital etc. This can be demonstrated as follows. Assume that lump-sum taxation is used and that there is no initial debt, so that the government budget identity reduces to $g(t) = \tau(t)$. An increase in government consumption shifts the $\dot{k}(t) = 0$ line down by the amount of the shock (dg),

---

[28] See Weil (1989b) and Buiter (1988) on this point. We return to the different versions of the OLG approach in Chapter 16 below.

so that the long-run equilibrium shifts from E_0 to E_1 in Figure 14.12. In contrast to what happens in the Ramsey model, not only consumption but also the capital stock per worker is reduced in the long run:

$$\frac{dc(\infty)}{dg} = \frac{-n\rho + c^*f''(k^*)}{|\Delta|} < -1, \tag{14.139}$$

$$\frac{dk(\infty)}{dg} = \frac{r^* - \rho}{|\Delta|} < 0, \tag{14.140}$$

where c^*, k^*, and r^* are the initial steady-state levels of consumption, capital per worker, and the interest rate, respectively. The denominator appearing in (14.139)–(14.140) is negative by saddle-point stability.[29]

Since the model is saddle-point stable, the economy jumps at impact from E_0 to E', and consumption falls but by less than one-for-one in the impact period:

$$-1 < \frac{dc(0)}{dg} = -\frac{[\lambda_2 - (r^* - \rho)]}{\lambda_2} < 0, \tag{14.141}$$

where $\lambda_2 > 0$ is the unstable root of the Jacobian matrix of the linearized system (footnote 29 shows that $\lambda_2 > r^* - \rho$). Existing generations do not bear the full burden of taxation because they know that future generations will eventually expand the tax base. As a result, present generations cut back consumption by too little and thus save too little to maintain the capital stock per worker at its old level. Over time the capital stock falls, as does the wage. Gradually, new generations are born with a lower level of human wealth due to the decreasing wage. This explains why aggregate per capita consumption falls during transition.

14.6 Endogenous Growth

Up to now we have exclusively worked with a production structure which satisfies the Inada conditions (See (P2) and (P3) for the properties). Although these conditions facilitate the construction of the phase diagrams they are not innocuous (in an economic-theoretic sense) because they imply the existence of diminishing returns to both factors of production. This, in turn, ensures that economic

---

[29] The dynamical system (T4.1)–(T4.3) can be linearized around the initial steady state:

$$\begin{bmatrix} \dot{k}(t) \\ \dot{c}(t) \end{bmatrix} = \begin{bmatrix} r^* - n & -1 \\ c^*f''(k^*) - n\rho & r^* - \rho \end{bmatrix} \begin{bmatrix} k(t) - k^* \\ c(t) - c^* \end{bmatrix},$$

where we have used the fact that $r^* \equiv f'(k^*) - \delta$. The determinant of the Jacobian matrix on the right-hand side is $|\Delta| \equiv (r^* - n)(r^* - \rho) + c^*f''(k^*) - n\rho = r^*[r^* - (\rho + n)] + c^*f''(k^*) < 0$, where the sign follows from the fact that $\rho < r^* < \rho + n$ (see (14.136)). The characteristic roots of Δ are $-\lambda_1 < 0$ and $\lambda_2 > 0$, respectively. Since $\text{tr}(\Delta) = \lambda_2 - \lambda_1 = 2r^* - (\rho + n)$ we find that $\lambda_2 - (r^* - \rho) = \lambda_1 + (r^* - n) > 0$, where the final inequality follows from the assumption of dynamic efficiency ($r^* > n$).

growth eventually settles down to a constant. In terms of Figure 14.4, the steady-state capital–labour ratio is constant and growth equals the sum of exogenously given population growth and technological progress (see equation (14.16)).

As was pointed out above, the Inada conditions have no obvious intrinsic appeal and are certainly difficult to test empirically since they deal with the curvature of the production function for very low and very high levels of capital. For this reason alone, an investigation of the consequences of abandoning (some of) the Inada conditions seems a worthwhile endeavour. As it turns out, this brings us into the realm of so-called "endogenous growth" models.[30]

14.6.1 "Capital-fundamentalist" models

The aspect of traditional growth models which ensures that growth settles down to its exogenously given steady-state rate is the existence of diminishing returns to capital. As $k(t)$ rises, the average product of capital falls:

$$\frac{d\left[f(k(t))/k(t)\right]}{dk(t)} = -\frac{\left[f(k(t)) - k(t)f'(k(t))\right]}{k(t)^2} < 0, \tag{14.142}$$

where the term in square brackets denotes the marginal product of labour, which is positive (see (14.74)). This is not enough to ensure the existence of a constant steady-state capital–labour ratio, however, because this requires equality between $sy(t)/k(t)$ and $(\delta + n)$ in the Solow model. Provided (P2) and (P3) hold, we can derive by l'Hôpital's rule that:

$$\lim_{k(t) \to 0} \frac{f(k(t))}{k(t)} = \lim_{k(t) \to 0} \frac{f'(k(t))}{1} = \infty, \tag{14.143}$$

$$\lim_{k(t) \to \infty} \frac{f(k(t))}{k(t)} = \lim_{k(t) \to \infty} \frac{f'(k(t))}{1} = 0. \tag{14.144}$$

Equation (14.144) shows that $sy(t)/k(t)$ goes to zero (infinity) as the capital–labour ratio becomes very large (small). This ensures the existence of a constant steady-state capital–labour ratio and thus a balanced growth path.

Easy substitution between capital and labour

As was already well known in the 1960s,[31] there are perfectly legitimate production functions which violate the results in (14.143)–(14.144). Consider the CES production function given in (14.24), for which the average product of capital

---

[30] See the symposium on new growth theory in the Winter 1994 issue of the *Journal of Economic Perspectives*. See also Barro and Sala-i-Martin (1995).

[31] See e.g. Burmeister and Dobell (1970, pp. 30–36), and indeed Solow (1956).

equals:

$$\frac{f(k(t))}{k(t)} = \left[(1-\alpha)k(t)^{(1-\sigma_{KL})/\sigma_{KL}} + \alpha\right]^{\sigma_{KL}/(\sigma_{KL}-1)}. \tag{14.145}$$

It is clear from this expression that two separate cases must be distinguished, depending on the ease with which capital and labour can be substituted in production. If substitution is difficult (so that $0 < \sigma_{KL} < 1$) then the average product of capital satisfies:

$$\lim_{k(t)\to 0} \frac{f(k(t))}{k(t)} = \alpha^{\sigma_{KL}/(\sigma_{KL}-1)} > 0, \tag{14.146}$$

$$\lim_{k(t)\to\infty} \frac{f(k(t))}{k(t)} = \lim_{k(t)\to\infty} \frac{f'(k(t))}{1} = 0. \tag{14.147}$$

The average product of capital goes to zero as more and more capital is added but near the origin it attains a finite value, i.e. while (14.144) is still satisfied (14.143) no longer holds. It is therefore not even guaranteed that the average product of capital around the origin is high enough to exceed $((\delta + n)/s)$, so that a situation as illustrated in Figure 14.13 is a distinct possibility. (In that figure, we assume that $0 < \sigma_{KL} < 1$ and $s\alpha^{\sigma_{KL}/(\sigma_{KL}-1)} < \delta + n$.) An economy characterized by Figure 14.13 would never be able to accumulate any capital nor would it be able to produce any output (as both product factors are essential in production). Alternatively, if this economy were to start out with the initial capital–labour ratio k_0 (say because it

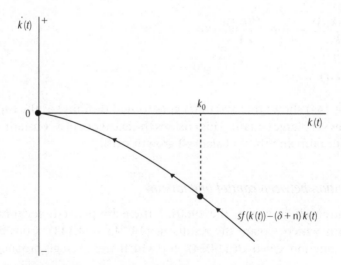

Figure 14.13. Difficult substitution between labour and capital

experienced a higher savings rate in the past), then it would slowly decline towards the origin.

Matters are radically different if capital can be easily substituted for labour, i.e. if σ_{KL} exceeds unity. In that case, the average product of capital satisfies:

$$\lim_{k(t) \to 0} \frac{f(k(t))}{k(t)} = \lim_{k(t) \to 0} \frac{f'(k(t))}{1} = \infty, \tag{14.148}$$

$$\lim_{k(t) \to \infty} \frac{f(k(t))}{k(t)} = \alpha^{\sigma_{KL}/(\sigma_{KL}-1)} > 0. \tag{14.149}$$

The average product of capital starts out very high (as the Inada conditions require) but it approaches a positive limit as more and more capital is added, i.e. (14.144) no longer holds. It follows that the average product of capital may not fall below $((\delta + n)/s)$, so that a steady-state capital–labour ratio may not exist. This is indeed the situation illustrated in Figure 14.14. (In that figure, we assume that $\sigma_{KL} > 1$ and $s\alpha^{\sigma_{KL}/(\sigma_{KL}-1)} > \delta + n$.) Starting from an initial value k_0, the capital–labour ratio grows without bounds. Despite the fact that there are diminishing returns to capital, in the long run the production factors are very much alike and substitute well in production ($\sigma_{KL} > 1$). This means that if capital grows indefinitely the constant growth rate of (effective) labour never becomes a binding constraint. Relatively scarce labour is simply substituted for capital indefinitely. The long-run "endogenous" growth rate of the capital-labour ratio and the output-labour ratio is:

$$\gamma^* = s\alpha^{\sigma_{KL}/(\sigma_{KL}-1)} - (\delta + n) > 0. \tag{14.150}$$

This growth rate is called "endogenous" because it is affected not only by exogenous parameters (α, δ, and n) but also by the savings rate (s), a result which is in stark contrast to the predictions of the standard Solow–Swan model discussed in sections 2–3 above.

It is not difficult to understand that with this kind of labour-substituting endogenous growth, labour becomes less and less important and eventually the income share of capital goes to unity and that of labour goes to zero. This is why this endogenous growth model is an example of the "capital-fundamentalist" class of models (King and Levine, 1994). With $\sigma_{KL} > 1$, labour is not essential in production and in the limit it is possible to produce with (almost) only capital. This prediction is, of course, at odds with the stylized facts (SF3) and (SF5).

The AK model

An even more radical example of a capital-fundamentalist model is the so-called "AK" model proposed by Romer (1986), Barro (1990), Rebelo (1991), and others. In its most rudimentary form, the AK model eliminates (raw) labour from the production function altogether and assumes constant returns to scale on a broad measure

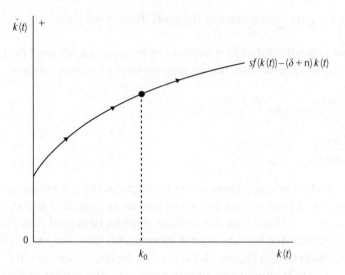

Figure 14.14. Easy substitution between labour and capital

of capital. Hence, equation (14.6) is replaced by:

$$Y(t) = AK(t), \tag{14.151}$$

which of course clearly violates the Inada conditions. The first task at hand is to derive the behavioural equations of firms and households under the technology (14.151).

Following the analysis in section 5.2, we assume that the representative (perfectly competitive) producer chooses its output and investment plans in order to maximize the discounted value of its cash flows, taking the production function (14.151) and the capital accumulation identity (14.4) as given. After some manipulation we find that the rental rate of capital depends on the constant marginal product of capital (A) and both the level and the time change in the investment subsidy.

$$r(t) + \delta = \frac{A}{1 - s_I(t)} - \frac{\dot{s}_I(t)}{1 - s_I(t)}. \tag{14.152}$$

The representative household is assumed to be infinitely lived. As in section 5.1, it maximizes lifetime utility subject to its accumulation identity:

$$\max \Lambda(0) = \int_0^\infty \left[\frac{C(t)^{1-1/\sigma} - 1}{1 - 1/\sigma} \right] e^{-\rho t} \, dt \tag{14.153}$$

$$\text{s.t. } \dot{A}(t) = r(t)A(t) - [1 + t_C(t)] C(t) + Z(t), \tag{14.154}$$

where σ is the constant intertemporal substitution elasticity (see (14.65)), t_C is a consumption tax, $Z(t)$ is a lump-sum transfer from the government (or tax if it is negative), $A(t)$ represents financial assets, and $r(t)$ is the rate of interest. Using the analytical methods discussed in section 5.1, the representative household's Euler equation can be derived:

$$\frac{\dot{C}(t)}{C(t)} = \sigma \left[r(t) - \rho - \frac{\dot{t}_C(t)}{1 + t_C(t)} \right]. \tag{14.155}$$

Since the model deals with a closed economy and there is no government debt, the only financial asset which can be accumulated consists of company shares, i.e. $A(t) = K(t)$. The key equations of the basic AK growth model have been summarized in Table 14.5.

Equations (T5.1) and (T5.3) have been explained above, and (T5.2) is the capital accumulation identity (14.4) combined with the output constraint (14.3) and the production function (14.151). It is now straightforward to demonstrate the existence of perpetual "endogenous" growth in the model. We focus attention on the case for which both the consumption tax and the investment subsidy are (expected by agents to be) constant over time, i.e. $\dot{t}_C(t) = \dot{s}_I(t) = 0$.[32] In that case the interest rate is constant and the growth rate of consumption is fully determined by (T5.1). At the same time, similar arguments to those explained in section 5.1 can be used to show that the propensity to consume out of total wealth is constant also, i.e. it is optimal for the representative household to maintain a constant ratio between consumption and the capital stock.[33] But if $C(t)/K(t)$ is constant, so is $I(t)/K(t)$. Hence, the common growth rate for output, consumption, the capital stock, and investment is given by:

$$\gamma^* = \frac{\dot{C}(t)}{C(t)} = \frac{\dot{Y}(t)}{Y(t)} = \frac{\dot{K}(t)}{K(t)} = \frac{\dot{I}(t)}{I(t)} = \sigma \left[\frac{A}{1 - s_I} - \delta - \rho \right]. \tag{14.156}$$

The striking conclusion is that the *growth rate* of the economy can be permanently affected by the investment subsidy, a result which is impossible in the traditional growth model discussed above. Intuitively, a higher investment subsidy leads to a

Table 14.5. The basic AK growth model

$\dot{C}(t) = \sigma \left[r(t) - \rho - \frac{\dot{t}_C(t)}{1 + t_C(t)} \right] C(t)$	(T5.1)
$\dot{K}(t) = (A - \delta)K(t) - C(t)$	(T5.2)
$r(t) = \frac{A}{1 - s_I(t)} - \frac{\dot{s}_I(t)}{1 - s_I(t)} - \delta$	(T5.3)

Notes: $C(t)$ is consumption, $K(t)$ is the capital stock, $r(t)$ is the interest rate, $t_C(t)$ is the consumption tax, $s_I(t)$ is an investment subsidy, ρ is the pure rate of time preference, and δ is the depreciation rate of capital.

[32] The key point to note in Table 14.5 is that the *level* of the consumption tax does not influence the growth rate as this tax does not distort the intertemporal consumption decision.

[33] Since there is no labour in the model, human wealth is zero and the capital stock equals total wealth.

higher interest rate, a steeper intertemporal consumption profile, and thus a higher rate of capital accumulation in the economy. Furthermore, taste parameters also exert a permanent effect on the growth rate of the economy. Hence, an economy populated by patient households (a low ρ) or households with a high willingness to substitute consumption intertemporally (a high σ), tends to have a high rate of economic growth.

The level of the different variables can be determined by using the initial condition regarding the capital stock. Indeed, by using $\dot{K}(0)/K(0) = \gamma^*$ in (T5.2) and noting that $K(0)$ is predetermined we find:

$$\frac{C(0)}{K(0)} = A - \delta - \gamma^* = \left(\frac{1 - s_I - \sigma}{1 - s_I}\right) A + (\sigma - 1)\delta + \sigma\rho. \tag{14.157}$$

A number of further properties of the basic AK model must be pointed out. First, the model contains no transitional dynamics. The initial levels of the different macroeconomic variables are tied down by the initial capital stock (see (14.151) and (14.157)), and the rate of growth is constant and the same for all these variables. This result does not hold if the consumption tax or the investment subsidy are time-varying, since in that case the real interest rate will vary over time and the agents will react to this. Second, the equilibrium in the basic AK model is Pareto-efficient in that the market outcome and the central planning solution coincide. Intuitively this result holds because there is no source of market failure in the model (Barro and Sala-i-Martin, 1995, p. 144).

In a recent paper, Barro (1990) has proposed a model in which productive government spending has an effect on the economic growth rate. The production function (14.151) is replaced by:

$$Y(t) = AK(t)^\alpha G(t)^{1-\alpha} = AK(t)\left(\frac{G(t)}{K(t)}\right)^{1-\alpha}, \quad 0 < \alpha < 1, \tag{14.158}$$

where $G(t)$ is the flow of public spending. The idea is that productive public spending affects all producers equally, these services are provided free of charge, and there is no congestion effect. Note that (14.158) reinstates diminishing returns to private capital, $K(t)$, because α is less than unity. If somehow the government succeeds in maintaining a constant ratio between its productive spending and the private capital stock, however, the model ends up looking very much like the basic AK model and thus will display endogenous growth.

The government is assumed to finance its spending by means of a tax on output:

$$G(t) = t_Y Y(t), \tag{14.159}$$

where t_Y is the output tax. The representative firm takes the level of $G(t)$ as given and maximizes the present value of after-tax cash flows:

$$V(0) = \int_0^\infty [(1 - t_Y)Y(t) - I(t)] e^{-R(t)} \, dt, \tag{14.160}$$

subject to the capital accumulation identity (14.4), the production function (14.158), an initial condition on the capital stock, and a transversality condition. After some manipulation we find that the rental rate on capital equals the after-tax marginal product of capital:

$$r(t) + \delta = (1 - t_Y) \frac{\partial Y(t)}{\partial K(t)}. \tag{14.161}$$

Since nothing is changed on the household side of the model, the Euler equation is still of the form given in (T5.1) (with $\dot{t}_C(t) = 0$ imposed). The representative firm computes the marginal product of capital for a given level of public spending ($G(t)$):

$$\frac{\partial Y(t)}{\partial K(t)} = \alpha A \left(\frac{G(t)}{K(t)} \right)^{1-\alpha}. \tag{14.162}$$

By using (T5.1) in combination with (14.161)–(14.162) and assuming that the government maintains a constant t_Y and $G(t)/K(t)$-ratio, we find the common growth rate implied by (this version of) the Barro model:

$$\gamma^* = \frac{\dot{C}(t)}{C(t)} = \frac{\dot{Y}(t)}{Y(t)} = \frac{\dot{K}(t)}{K(t)} = \frac{\dot{I}(t)}{I(t)}$$

$$= \sigma \left[\alpha(1 - t_Y)A \left(\frac{G(t)}{K(t)} \right)^{1-\alpha} - \delta - \rho \right]. \tag{14.163}$$

The striking conclusion is that endogenous growth emerges despite the existence of diminishing returns to private capital! Intuitively, by ever increasing its level of productive spending, the government manages to negate the effect of diminishing returns to private capital that would otherwise result from continuing capital accumulation. It is able to do so without ever-increasing (and thus ultimately infeasible) tax rates because the tax base (gross output) grows at the same rate as the capital stock.

By using the production function (14.158) and the government budget constraint (14.159) we can express the $G(t)/K(t)$-ratio in terms of the productivity parameter and the output tax rate, i.e. $G(t)/K(t) = (t_Y A)^{1/\alpha}$. By substituting this result into (14.163), we obtain an expression linking the rate of growth to the tax rate:

$$\gamma^* = \sigma \left[\alpha(1 - t_Y)A^{1/\alpha} t_Y^{(1-\alpha)/\alpha} - \delta - \rho \right], \tag{14.164}$$

which has been plotted in Figure 14.15. There are two offsetting effects of the output tax on the rate of economic growth. First, via the government budget constraint we know that a higher $G(t)/Y(t)$-ratio requires a higher tax rate which is bad for growth. Second, a higher $G(t)/Y(t)$-ratio also raises the marginal product of private capital which is good for growth as it raises the interest rate and makes households save more. For low initial tax rates, the second effect dominates the first effect and the growth rate increases if the output tax is raised, and vice versa for high tax rates.

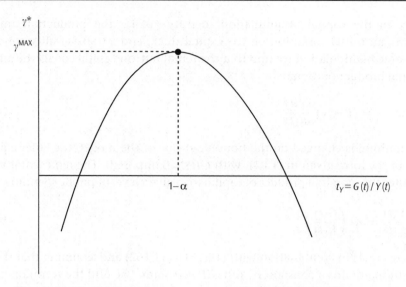

Figure 14.15. Productive government spending and growth

The growth-maximizing tax rate (and share of productive government spending) is obtained by maximizing γ^* with respect to t_Y. After some manipulation we obtain:

$$\frac{d\gamma^*}{dt_Y} = 0 \quad \Leftrightarrow \quad t_Y = \frac{G(t)}{Y(t)} = 1 - \alpha. \tag{14.165}$$

The interpretation of this result is as follows. The social cost of a unit of government spending is unity and the social benefit is $\partial Y(t)/\partial G(t) = (1-\alpha)Y(t)/G(t) = (1-\alpha)/t_Y$. By equating marginal costs and benefits we obtain the expression in (14.165) (see Barro and Sala-i-Martin, 1995, p. 155).

14.6.2 Human capital formation

In a path-breaking early contribution to the literature, Uzawa (1965) argued that (labour-augmenting) technological progress should not be seen as some kind of "manna from heaven" but instead should be regarded as the outcome of the intentional actions by economic agents employing scarce resources in order to advance the state of technological knowledge. Uzawa (1965) formalized his notions by assuming that all technological knowledge is embodied in labour, i.e. in terms of the aggregate production function (14.11) he sets $A_K(t) = 1$ for all t and proposes a theory which endogenizes $A_L(t)$ (and thus n_A in (14.14)). Uzawa postulates the existence of a broadly defined educational sector which uses labour, $L_E(t)$, in order to augment the state of knowledge in the economy according to the following knowledge production function:

$$\frac{\dot{A}_L(t)}{A_L(t)} = \Psi\left(\frac{L_E(t)}{L(t)}\right), \tag{14.166}$$

where $L(t) = L_E(t) + L_P(t)$ is the total labour force, $L_P(t)$ is labour employed in the production of goods, and $\Psi(x)$ satisfies $\Psi'(x) > 0 > \Psi''(x)$ for $0 < x < 1$. It is clear that there are now two stocks that can be accumulated in this economy, namely the stock of physical capital goods ($K(t)$) and the stock of knowledge ($A_L(t)$). Uzawa shows how a benevolent social planner would optimally choose these stocks for the special case of a linear felicity function (i.e. under the assumption that $U[c(t)] = c(t)$ in (14.53)). One of the trade-offs which the planner must make is of course the optimal assignment of labour to the production and educational sectors. By raising the proportion of workers in the educational sector the growth of knowledge will increase but production of goods (and thus the rate of investment) will decrease.

Uzawa's ideas lay dormant for two decades until they were taken up again and extended by Romer (1986), Lucas (1988, 1990b), and Rebelo (1991). The aim of this section is to discuss (a simplified version of) the Lucas model in order to demonstrate that human capital accumulation can serve as the engine of (endogenous) growth.

Lucas (1988) modifies and extends Uzawa's analysis in various directions. First, whereas Uzawa interprets $A_L(t)$ very broadly as consisting of activities like education, health, construction and maintenance of public goods (1965, p. 18), Lucas adopts a more specific interpretation by interpreting $A_L(t)$ as human capital. Second, Lucas cites Rosen (1976) whose findings suggests that the empirical evidence on individual earnings is consistent with a linear knowledge production function. Despite the fact that in reality people tend to accumulate human capital mainly early on in life, this does not necessarily imply that there are diminishing returns to knowledge accumulation (as is assumed in (14.166)) but rather may be due to the fact that agents' lives are finite (Lucas, 1988, p. 19). It simply makes no sense for an octogenarian to go to school as the time during which he can cash in on his additional skills is too short for the investment to be worthwhile. On the basis of the above considerations, Lucas adopts the following specification for the human capital accumulation function:

$$\frac{\dot{H}(t)}{H(t)} = \psi_E\left(\frac{L_E(t)}{L(t)}\right), \tag{14.167}$$

where $\psi_E > 0$ is a constant. The third modification that Lucas makes is to assume a curved (rather than linear) felicity function. The lifetime utility function for the representative infinitely lived household is thus given by:

$$\Lambda(0) = \int_0^\infty \left[\frac{C(t)^{1-1/\sigma} - 1}{1 - 1/\sigma}\right] e^{-\rho t}\, dt, \tag{14.168}$$

where σ is the intertemporal substitution elasticity, ρ is the rate of time preference, and $C(t)$ is consumption. The remainder of the model is fairly standard. To keep things simple we abstract from population growth and normalize the size of the population to unity ($L(t) = 1$). This means that the time constraint can be written as:

$$L_E(t) + L_P(t) = 1. \tag{14.169}$$

Following Lucas we assume that the aggregate production function is Cobb–Douglas:

$$Y(t) = F[K(t), N(t)] = N(t)^{1-\alpha_K} K(t)^{\alpha_K}, \tag{14.170}$$

where $N(t)$ is *effective* labour used in goods production, i.e. skill-weighted man-hours:[34]

$$N(t) \equiv H(t) L_P(t). \tag{14.171}$$

We are now in a position to solve the model and to demonstrate that it contains a mechanism for endogenous growth. The institutional setting is as follows. Perfectly competitive firms hire capital and labour from the household sector. Households receive rental payments on the two production factors and decide on the optimal accumulation of physical and human capital and the optimal time profile for consumption.

Since technology is linearly homogeneous and competition is perfect it is appropriate to postulate the existence of a representative firm. This firm hires units of labour and capital from the household in order to maximize profit, $\Pi(t) \equiv Y(t) - W(t)L_P(t) - R^K(t)K(t)$, subject to the technology (14.170) and the definition of effective labour (14.171). This yields the familiar expressions for the rental rate on capital $R^K(t)$ and the wage rate $W(t)$:

$$R^K(t) = F_K[K(t), N(t)] = \alpha_K \left(\frac{K(t)}{N(t)} \right)^{\alpha_K - 1}, \tag{14.172}$$

$$W(t) = H(t)F_N[K(t), N(t)] = (1 - \alpha_K)H(t) \left(\frac{K(t)}{N(t)} \right)^{\alpha_K}. \tag{14.173}$$

Equation (14.172) is the standard condition equating the marginal product of capital to the rental rate. The key thing to note about (14.173) is that, for a given capital-effective-labour ratio, K/N, the wage rate increases as the skill level increases. This gives the household a clear incentive to accumulate human capital.

The representative household chooses sequences for consumption and the stocks of physical and human capital in order to maximize lifetime utility (14.168) subject

---

[34] In adopting (14.169)–(14.171) we have simplified the Lucas model by assuming that the population is constant and that there is no external effect of human capital. See Lucas (1988, p. 18) for the latter effect.

to the time constraint (14.169), accumulation identities (14.4) and (14.167), and the following budget identity:

$$I(t) + C(t) = H(t)F_N(.)L_P(t) + R^K(t)K(t), \tag{14.174}$$

where $I(t)$ is gross investment in physical capital and we have substituted the expression for the real wage from (14.173).[35] The crucial thing to note is that, from the point of the individual agent described here, the marginal product of effective labour (F_N) is taken as given as it depends on the aggregate ratio between physical capital and effective labour.

The Hamiltonian associated with the representative household's decision problem is given by:

$$\mathcal{H}(t) = \frac{C(t)^{1-1/\sigma} - 1}{1 - 1/\sigma} + \mu_H(t)\psi_E L_E(t)H(t)$$
$$+ \mu_K(t)\big[\big(R^K(t) - \delta\big)K(t) + H(t)F_N(.)(1 - L_E(t)) - C(t)\big], \tag{14.175}$$

where $\mu_K(t)$ and $\mu_H(t)$ are the co-state variables for, respectively, $K(t)$ and $H(t)$. The first-order necessary conditions are:[36]

$$C(t)^{-1/\sigma} = \mu_K(t), \tag{14.176}$$

$$\mu_K(t)F_N(.) = \psi_E\mu_H(t), \tag{14.177}$$

$$\frac{\dot{\mu}_K(t)}{\mu_K(t)} = \rho + \delta - F_K[K(t), N(t)], \tag{14.178}$$

$$\frac{\dot{\mu}_H(t)}{\mu_H(t)} = \rho - \psi_E L_E(t) - \left(\frac{\mu_K(t)}{\mu_H(t)}\right)[1 - L_E(t)]F_N[K(t), N(t)], \tag{14.179}$$

$$0 = \lim_{t\to\infty} e^{-\rho t}\mu_K(t)K(t) = \lim_{t\to\infty} e^{-\rho t}\mu_H(t)H(t), \tag{14.180}$$

where we have used (14.172) to simplify (14.178) and (14.180) are the transversality conditions (explained in detail by e.g. Benhabib and Perli (1994, p. 117)). The intuition behind these expressions is as follows. First, according to (14.176) goods must on the margin be equally valuable in their two uses, namely consumption and capital accumulation. Similarly, (14.177) says that time must be equally valuable in its two uses, namely the accumulation of physical and human capital (Lucas, 1988, p. 21). The intuition behind (14.178)–(14.179) is best understood by rewriting them slightly and appealing to the fundamental principle of valuation according to which the rate of return on different assets (dividends plus capital gains) must be equalized

---

[35] Since, capital and effective labour receive their respective marginal products, it follows that profit is zero ($\Pi(t) = 0$).

[36] The first-order conditions are $\partial\mathcal{H}/\partial x = 0$ for the control variables ($x \in \{C, L_E\}$) and $-\partial\mathcal{H}/\partial x = \dot{\mu}_x - \rho\mu_x$ for the state variables ($x \in \{K, H\}$).

(cf. Miller and Modigliani, 1961, p. 412).

$$\rho = \frac{\dot{\mu}_K(t) + D_K(t)}{\mu_K(t)} = \frac{\dot{\mu}_H(t) + D_H(t)}{\mu_H(t)}, \tag{14.181}$$

where $D_K(t) \equiv F_K[K(t), N(t)] - \delta$ is the "dividend" on physical capital, consisting of the net marginal product of physical capital, and $D_H(t)$ stands for the "dividend" on human capital. The latter can be written in a number of different (but equivalent) ways:

$$D_H(t) \equiv \mu_K(t) F_N(.) = \psi_E \mu_H(t). \tag{14.182}$$

Recall that $\mu_K(t)$ and $\mu_H(t)$ are the imputed shadow prices of the two assets owned by the household. According to the fundamental principle of valuation, the rate of return (consisting for each asset of dividends plus capital gains expressed in terms of the value of the asset) must be equalized across assets. This is essentially what (14.181) says in the context of the household's choice regarding physical and human capital. The expressions in (14.182), which are obtained by substituting (14.177) into (14.179), show that the dividend on human capital can be written in terms of the additional wage payments it causes (first equality) or in terms of the increase in the marginal productivity of educational activities it gives rise to (second term).

We now have all the ingredients of the model and proceed to characterize its balanced growth path (BGP).[37] Along the BGP consumption and physical and human capital are all growing at constant exponential growth rates, the fraction of labour used in education is constant, and the shadow prices decline at constant exponential rates. We define the exponential growth rate of a variable along the BGP as $\gamma_x \equiv \dot{x}/x$ (for $x \in \{K, C, H, Y\}$). First we note that by differentiating (14.176) with respect to time and substituting (14.178) we obtain:

$$\frac{\gamma_C}{\sigma} + \rho + \delta = F_K\left[\frac{K}{N}, 1\right], \tag{14.183}$$

where we have incorporated the fact that $F[.]$ is homogeneous of degree one (so that $F_K[.]$ is homogeneous of degree zero). Equation (14.183) implies that the capital-effective-labour ratio is constant along the BGP, i.e. $\gamma_K = \gamma_N = \gamma_H$, where the final equality follows from (14.171) plus the fact that L_P is constant along the BGP. It follows from (14.177) that $\mu_H/\mu_K = F_N$ is constant also, so that (14.177)–(14.179) together imply that $F_K = \delta + \psi_E$. Using this value for F_K in (14.183) we find that $\gamma_C = \sigma(\psi_E - \rho)$. The macroeconomic resource constraint along the BGP can be written as follows:

$$\gamma_K + \frac{C}{K} = \frac{Y}{K} - \delta. \tag{14.184}$$

Since $Y/K = F[1, N/K]$ is constant along the BGP (as K/N is constant) it follows from (14.184) that C/K is constant also. Hence, consumption, human and physical

---

[37] The issue of transitional dynamics is studied by, among others, Mulligan and Sala-i-Martin (1993), Benhabib and Perli (1994), Xie (1994), and Bond et al. (1996).

capital, and output all grow at the same exponential rate:

$$\gamma_K = \gamma_Y = \gamma_C = \gamma_H = \sigma(\psi_E - \rho). \tag{14.185}$$

It remains to be checked that the (common) growth rate given in (14.185) is actually feasible. According to (14.167) the maximum growth rate of human capital (equalling ψ_E) occurs if the entire labour stock is devoted to educational activities ($L_E = 1$ and $L_P = 0$). Hence, the growth rate in (14.185) is feasible if and only if $\gamma_H < \psi_E$. The feasibility requirement thus places an upper limit on the allowable intertemporal substitution elasticity:

$$\sigma < \frac{\psi_E}{\psi_E - \rho}. \tag{14.186}$$

We have thus demonstrated that endogenous growth can result from the purposeful accumulation of human capital by maximizing agents. No "manna from heaven" assumption is needed to generate this result. The model studied by Lucas (1988) is more complex than the one studied here because he introduces (exogenous) population growth n_L and, more importantly, because he argues that knowledge may have a positive external effect on productivity. Instead of (14.170) he uses the production function $Y(t) = N(t)^{1-\alpha_K} K(t)^{\alpha_K} \bar{H}(t)^{\alpha_S}$, where $\bar{H}(t)$ is the average skill level in society and $\alpha_S > 0$. Intuitively, his formulation attempts to capture the notion that the formation of human capital is, in part, a social activity. Since individual households are infinitesimally small (relative to the economy) they will not recognize the link between their own human capital choice and the resulting level of average economy-wide human capital. As a result, the market economy will not be efficient. Lucas (1990b) uses this extended model to explain why there can be persistent differences in the marginal product of capital across countries even if there are no barriers to international capital flows.

14.6.3 Endogenous technology

In the previous subsection we showed that the purposeful accumulation of human capital ("skills") forms the key ingredient of the Uzawa–Lucas theory of economic growth. In this subsection we briefly review a branch of the (huge) literature in which the purposeful conduct of research and development (R&D) activities forms the key source of growth.[38] In order to demonstrate the key mechanism by which R&D affects economic growth we follow Grossman and Helpman (1991, ch. 3) and Bénassy (1998) by abstracting from physical and human capital altogether. In such a setting all saving by households is directed towards the creation of new technology.

There are three production sectors in the economy. The *final goods sector* produces a homogeneous good using varieties of a differentiated intermediate good

---

[38] Key contributions to this literature are Romer (1987, 1990), Aghion and Howitt (1992), and Grossman and Helpman (1991).

as productive inputs. Production is subject to constant returns to scale (in these inputs) and perfect competition prevails. The *R&D sector* is also perfectly competitive. In this sector units of labour are used to produce blueprints of new varieties of the differentiated input. Finally, the *intermediate goods sector* is populated by a large number of small firms, each producing a single variety of the differentiated input, who engage in Chamberlinian monopolistic competition (see Chapter 13 for a detailed account of this market structure).

The production function in the final goods sector is given by the following (generalized) Dixit–Stiglitz (1977) form:

$$Y(t) \equiv N(t)^{\eta} \left[N(t)^{-1} \int_0^{N(t)} X_j(t)^{1/\mu} dj \right]^{\mu}, \quad \mu > 1, \ \eta \geq 1, \tag{14.187}$$

where $N(t)$ is the number of different varieties that exist at time t, $X_j(t)$ is variety j, and μ and η are parameters.[39] Note that, holding constant the number of varieties, doubling all inputs leads to a doubling of output in (14.187), i.e. constant returns to scale prevail. The specification in (14.187) implies that, provided $\eta > 1$, there are *returns to specialization* of the form emphasized by Ethier (1982). This can be demonstrated as follows. Suppose that the same amount is used of all inputs (as will indeed be the case in the symmetric equilibrium discussed below), i.e. $X_j(t) = \bar{X}(t)$ for $j \in [0, N(t)]$. Then total output in the final goods sector will be $Y(t) = N(t)^{\eta-1}(L_X(t)/k_X)$, where $L_X(t) = k_X N(t)\bar{X}(t)$ represents the total amount of labour used up in the intermediate goods sector (see below). Ceteris paribus $L_X(t)$, output in the final goods sector rises with the number of intermediate inputs provided η exceeds unity. By having a larger number of varieties, producers in the final goods sector can adopt a more "round-about" method of production and thus produce more.

The representative producer in the final goods sector minimizes its costs and sets the price of final goods equal to the marginal (equals average) cost of production:

$$P_Y(t) \equiv N(t)^{-\eta} \left[N(t)^{\mu/(1-\mu)} \int_0^{N(t)} P_j(t)^{1/(1-\mu)} dj \right]^{1-\mu}, \tag{14.188}$$

where $P_j(t)$ is the price of input variety j. The cost-minimizing demand for input j is given by:

$$\frac{X_j(t)}{Y(t)} = N(t)^{(\eta-\mu)/(\mu-1)} \left(\frac{P_j(t)}{P_Y(t)} \right)^{\mu/(1-\mu)}, \quad j \in [0, N(t)], \tag{14.189}$$

where $\mu/(1 - \mu)$ thus represents the (constant) price elasticity of the demand for variety j.

---

[39] Note that (14.187) is similar to (13.2) in Chapter 13 with the summation sign replaced by an integral sign. Strictly speaking $N(t)$ is now the "measure" of products invented before time t. Following convention we will continue to refer to $N(t)$ as the number of firms. See Romer (1987) and Grossman and Helpman (1991, p. 45) for details.

In the intermediate goods sector there are many monopolistically competitive firms which each hold a blueprint telling them how to produce their own, slightly unique, variety $X_j(t)$. The operating profit of firm j is defined as follows:

$$\Pi_j(t) \equiv P_j(t)X_j(t) - W(t)L_j(t), \tag{14.190}$$

where $W(t)$ is the wage rate (common to all firms in the economy as labour is perfectly mobile) and $L_j(t)$ is the amount of labour used by firm j. Firm chooses its output level, $X_j(t)$, given the demand for its output (14.189), the production function $X_j(t) = (1/k_X)L_j(t)$, and taking the actions of all other producers in the intermediate goods sector as given. As is familiar from the detailed discussion in Chapter 13, the optimal choice of the firm is to set price according to a fixed markup over marginal production cost:

$$P_j(t) = \mu W(t)k_X, \tag{14.191}$$

where μ thus represents the constant markup. Since all active firms in the intermediate sector possess the same technology and face the same input price and markup, they all choose the same amount of output and charge the same price. Hence, from here on we can suppress the firm subscript, as $X_j(t) = \bar{X}(t)$, $P_j(t) = \bar{P}(t)$, and $\Pi_j(t) = \bar{\Pi}(t)$ for $j \in [0, N(t)]$, and let the barred variables denote the choices of the representative firm in the intermediate sector. By substituting (14.191) into (14.190) and invoking the symmetry results we obtain the following expression for the profit of a representative firm in the intermediate goods sector:

$$\bar{\Pi}(t) = \left[\bar{P}(t) - W(t)k_X\right]\bar{X}(t) = \left(\frac{\mu - 1}{\mu}\right)\bar{P}(t)\bar{X}(t). \tag{14.192}$$

In the R&D sector competitive firms use labour (researchers) to produce new blueprints. Since $N(t)$ is the stock of existing blueprints, its time rate of change, $\dot{N}(t)$, represents the new blueprints. It is assumed, following Bénassy (1998) that the production function for new blueprints is given by:

$$\dot{N}(t) = (1/k_R)N(t)L_R(t), \tag{14.193}$$

where $L_R(t)$ is the amount of labour employed in the R&D sector and $1/k_R$ is a productivity parameter. By employing more labour in the R&D sector, more new blueprints are produced per unit of time. Furthermore, equation (14.193) incorporates the assumption, due to Romer (1990), that the stock of existing blueprints positively affects the productivity of researchers. As Romer puts it, "[t]he engineer working today is more productive because he or she can take advantage of all the additional knowledge accumulated as design problems were solved during the last 100 years" (1990, pp. S83–84). Since the R&D sector is competitive the price of a new blueprint, $P_N(t)$, is equal to the marginal cost of producing it:

$$P_N(t) = \frac{k_R W(t)}{N(t)}. \tag{14.194}$$

It remains to describe the optimal behaviour of the representative, infinitely lived, household. This household has a utility function as in (14.168) and faces the following budget identity:

$$P_Y(t)C(t) + P_N(t)\dot{N}(t) = W(t)L + N(t)\bar{\Pi}(t), \tag{14.195}$$

where L is the exogenous supply of labour of the household. Total spending on consumption goods plus investment in new blueprints (left-hand side) equals total labour income plus the total profits the household receives from firms in the differentiated sector (right-hand side). By using the price of final output as the numeraire ($P_Y(t) = 1$) we obtain the household budget identity in real terms, $C(t) + P_N(t)\dot{N}(t) = W(t)L + N(t)\bar{\Pi}(t)$.

The current-value Hamiltonian associated with the representative household's decision problem is given by:

$$\mathcal{H}(t) = \frac{C(t)^{1-1/\sigma} - 1}{1 - 1/\sigma} + \mu_N(t) \left[\frac{W(t)L + N(t)\bar{\Pi}(t) - C(t)}{P_N(t)} \right], \tag{14.196}$$

where $\mu_N(t)$ is the co-state variable for $N(t)$. The first-order necessary conditions are:[40]

$$C(t)^{-1/\sigma} = \frac{\mu_N(t)}{P_N(t)}, \tag{14.197}$$

$$\frac{\dot{\mu}_N(t)}{\mu_N(t)} = \rho - \frac{\bar{\Pi}(t)}{P_N(t)}. \tag{14.198}$$

By combining these two expressions we obtain the conventional consumption Euler equation:

$$\frac{\dot{C}(t)}{C(t)} = \sigma \left[r(t) - \rho \right], \tag{14.199}$$

where $r(t)$ is the rate of return on blueprints:

$$r(t) = \frac{\bar{\Pi}(t) + \dot{P}_N(t)}{P_N(t)}. \tag{14.200}$$

The return on blueprints is the dividend plus the capital gain expressed in terms of the purchase price of the blueprint.

---

[40] The first-order conditions are $\partial \mathcal{H}/\partial x = 0$ for the control variables ($x \in \{C, L_E\}$) and $-\partial \mathcal{H}/\partial x = \dot{\mu}_x - \rho \mu_x$ for the state variables ($x \in \{K, H\}$).

The model is closed by two market clearing conditions. The final goods market clears provided output equals consumption:

$$Y(t) = C(t). \tag{14.201}$$

The labour market equilibrium condition requires the total supply of labour to equal the sum of labour demand in the intermediate and R&D sectors, i.e. $L_X(t) + L_R(t) = L$. Since $L_X(t) = k_X N(t)\bar{X}(t)$ and $L_R(t) = k_R \dot{N}(t)/N(t)$ we can rewrite this labour market equilibrium condition as:

$$\frac{\dot{N}(t)}{N(t)} = \frac{L - k_X N(t)\bar{X}(t)}{k_R}, \tag{14.202}$$

where we assume implicitly that the differentiated sector is not too large and thus does not absorb all available labour (i.e. the numerator on the right-hand side is strictly positive).

Growth

We are now in a position to determine the growth rate in the economy. We follow the solution approach of Bénassy (1998). In the first step, we note a number of intermediate results:

$$\frac{\bar{\Pi}(t)}{P_N(t)} = (\mu - 1)\left(\frac{k_X N(t)\bar{X}(t)}{k_R}\right), \tag{14.203}$$

$$\frac{\dot{P}_N(t)}{P_N(t)} = (\eta - 2)\left(\frac{\dot{N}(t)}{N(t)}\right), \tag{14.204}$$

$$C(t) = N(t)^{\eta-1}N(t)\bar{X}(t). \tag{14.205}$$

Equation (14.203) expressed the real dividend rate on blueprints in terms of the monopoly markup (μ) and the total amount of labour absorbed by the final goods sector. It is obtained by using (14.194) and (14.191) in (14.192) and imposing the symmetry results. Equation (14.204) shows that the capital gains rate on blueprints is proportional to the growth rate of varieties, i.e. the rate of innovation. It is obtained by using (14.191) and (14.188) in (14.194), setting $P_Y(t) = 1$ and imposing symmetry. This yields $P_N(t) = [k_R/(\mu k_X)]N(t)^{\eta-2}$ which can be differentiated with respect to time to obtain (14.204). Finally, (14.205) is the goods market clearing condition in the symmetric equilibrium.

In the second step we write the dynamics of the model as follows:

$$\gamma_C(t) = \sigma\left[\left(\frac{\mu - 1}{k_R}\right)L_X(t) + (\eta - 2)\gamma_N(t) - \rho\right], \tag{14.206}$$

$$\gamma_C(t) = (\eta - 1)\gamma_N(t) + \dot{L}_X(t), \tag{14.207}$$

$$\gamma_N(t) = \frac{L - L_X(t)}{k_R}, \tag{14.208}$$

where we use the conventional notation for growth rates, i.e. $\gamma_x \equiv \dot{x}(t)/x(t)$. Equation (14.206) is the consumption Euler equation. It is obtained by combining (14.199)–(14.200) and (14.203)–(14.204) and noting that $L_X(t) = k_X N(t)\bar{X}(t)$. Equation (14.207) is the time derivative of (14.205) and (14.208) is a rewritten version of (14.202).

In the third step we eliminate $\gamma_N(t)$ and $\gamma_C(t)$ from (14.206)–(14.208) to derive a single differential equation for $L_X(t)$:

$$\dot{L}_X(t) = \left[\frac{\sigma\mu + (1-\sigma)(\eta-1)}{k_R}\right] L_X(t) - \left[\frac{\eta - 1 + \sigma(2-\eta)}{k_R}\right] L - \sigma\rho. \qquad (14.209)$$

The crucial thing to note about this expression is that the coefficient for $L_X(t)$ on the right-hand side is positive, i.e. (14.209) is an unstable differential equation.[41] This, of course, means that the only economically sensible solution is such that $L_X(t)$ jumps immediately to its steady-state value:

$$L_X = \frac{[\eta - 1 + \sigma(2-\eta)]L + \sigma\rho k_R}{\sigma\mu + (1-\sigma)(\eta-1)}. \qquad (14.210)$$

Since there is no transitional dynamics in $L_X(t)$ (and thus $\dot{L}_X(t) = 0$ for all t) the same hold for the growth rates of the number of varieties and consumption. Indeed, by using (14.210) in (14.206) and (14.208) we obtain:

$$\gamma_N = \frac{\sigma(\mu-1)(L/k_R) - \sigma\rho}{\sigma\mu + (1-\sigma)(\eta-1)} > 0, \quad \gamma_C = \gamma_Y = (\eta - 1)\gamma_N, \qquad (14.211)$$

where the sign follows from our assumption made in the text below equation (14.202). This expression generalizes the results of Grossman and Helpman (1991, p. 59), Bénassy (1998, p. 66), and de Groot and Nahuis (1998, p. 293) to the case of a non-unitary elasticity of intertemporal substitution. Like these authors, we find that the rate of innovation increases with the monopoly markup ($\partial\gamma_N/\partial\mu > 0$) and the size of the labour force ($\partial\gamma_N/\partial L > 0$) and decreases with the rate of time preference ($\partial\gamma_N/\partial\rho < 0$). The partial equilibrium effect for the intertemporal substitution elasticity is:

$$\frac{\partial\gamma_N}{\partial\sigma} = \frac{(\eta-1)\gamma_N}{\sigma[\sigma\mu + (1-\sigma)(\eta-1)]}. \qquad (14.212)$$

Provided the returns to specialization are operative (so that $\eta > 1$), an increase in the willingness of the representative household to substitute consumption across time raises the rate of innovation ($\partial\gamma_N/\partial\sigma > 0$). As is evident from (14.211), the growth rate in consumption and output also depends critically on whether or not the technology in the final goods sector is characterized by returns from specialization.

[41] Recall that $\mu > 1$ and $\eta \geq 1$. For low values of the intertemporal substitution elasticity, $0 < \sigma < 1$, it follows immediately that the coefficient is positive. If $\sigma > 1$ we write the numerator of the coefficient as $\sigma(\mu-1) + \eta - 1 + \sigma(2-\eta)$. This expression is positive provided a mild sufficient condition on η holds, i.e. $\eta < 2$.

Efficiency

One of the classic questions in economics concerns the welfare properties of the decentralized market equilibrium. In the context of the model we wish to know whether the market rate of innovation is too high or too low. To study this problem we follow the usual procedure by computing the social optimum and comparing it to the decentralized market equilibrium.

As is pointed out by Bénassy (1998, p. 66), computation of the social optimum is quite a lot easier than that of the market solution because we can impose symmetry up front and work in terms of aggregates like consumption, the number of firms, and labour used in the intermediate sector. The social planner is assumed to maximize lifetime utility of the representative agent (14.168), subject to the constraints (14.202) and (14.205). By using $L_X(t) = k_X N(t) \bar{X}(t)$ in the various expressions we find that the Hamiltonian for the social welfare programme is given by:

$$\mathcal{H}(t) = \frac{\left[N(t)^{\eta-1} k_X^{-1} L_X(t)\right]^{1-1/\sigma} - 1}{1 - 1/\sigma} + \mu_N(t) N(t) \left[\frac{L - L_X(t)}{k_R}\right], \tag{14.213}$$

where $\mu_N(t)$ is the co-state variable for $N(t)$. The first-order necessary conditions are:

$$\left(\frac{\mu_N(t)}{k_R}\right) = \frac{N(t)^{\eta-2}}{k_X \left[N(t)^{\eta-1} k_X^{-1} L_X(t)\right]^{1/\sigma}}, \tag{14.214}$$

$$\dot{\mu}_N(t) = \rho \mu_N(t) - \frac{(\eta-1) L_X(t) N(t)^{\eta-2}}{k_X \left[N(t)^{\eta-1} k_X^{-1} L_X(t)\right]^{1/\sigma}} - \mu_N(t) \left[\frac{L - L_X(t)}{k_R}\right]. \tag{14.215}$$

By combining these two expressions we obtain (after a number of tedious but straightforward steps) a differential equation in $L_X(t)$:

$$\frac{\dot{L}_X(t)}{L_X(t)} = \left[\frac{\eta-1}{k_R}\right] L_X(t) - \left[\frac{(\eta-1)(1-\sigma)}{k_R}\right] L - \sigma\rho. \tag{14.216}$$

Provided there are returns to specialization ($\eta > 1$), the coefficient for $L_X(t)$ on the right-hand side of (14.216) is positive so that the differential equation is unstable and the socially optimal solution is to jump immediately to the steady state ($\dot{L}_X(t) = 0$):

$$L_X^{SO} = (1-\sigma)L + \frac{\sigma\rho k_R}{\eta-1}, \tag{14.217}$$

where the superscript "SO" denotes the socially optimal value and we assume implicitly that L_X^{SO} is feasible (positive). The socially optimal rate of innovation associated with (14.217) is:

$$\gamma_N^{SO} = \sigma(L/k_R) - \frac{\sigma\rho}{\eta - 1} > 0, \quad \gamma_C^{SO} = \gamma_Y^{SO} = (\eta - 1)\gamma_N^{SO}. \tag{14.218}$$

The striking conclusion that can be drawn from (14.218) is that the socially optimal rate of innovation does not depend on the markup (μ) at all but rather on the parameter regulating the returns to specialization (η). This result is obvious when you think of it—in the symmetric equilibrium (14.187) collapses to $Y(t) = N(t)^{\eta-1}(L_X(t)/k_X)$ from which we see that the social return to research depends critically on $\eta - 1$ (Bénassy, 1998, p. 67).

We can now compare the socially optimal and market rate of innovation (given, respectively, in (14.211) and (14.218)) and answer our question regarding the welfare properties of the decentralized market equilibrium. To keep things simple we set $\sigma = 1$ (logarithmic felicity) for which case γ_N and γ_N^{SO} are:

$$\gamma_N = \frac{(\mu - 1)(L/k_R) - \rho}{\mu}, \quad \gamma_N^{SO} = \frac{(\eta - 1)(L/k_R) - \rho}{\eta - 1}. \tag{14.219}$$

These expressions can be used to derive the following result:

$$\mu\left[\gamma_N^{SO} - \gamma_N\right] = \frac{L}{k_R} - \rho\left[\frac{\mu - (\eta - 1)}{\eta - 1}\right]. \tag{14.220}$$

No general conclusion can be drawn from (14.220) and both $\gamma_N^{SO} > \gamma_N$ (underinvestment in R&D) and $\gamma_N^{SO} < \gamma_N$ (overinvestment in R&D) are distinct possibilities as is the knife-edge case for which the parameters are such that the market yields the correct amount of investment in R&D ($\gamma_N^{SO} = \gamma_N$).[42] The literature tends to stress the underinvestment case but that result is not robust as it is based on the implicit assumption that the markup equals the returns to specialization parameter. Indeed, for that special case, $\eta = \mu$, and (14.220) reduces to:

$$\mu\left[\gamma_N^{SO} - \gamma_N\right] = \frac{L}{k_R} - \rho\left[\frac{1}{\eta - 1}\right] \equiv \gamma_N^{SO}. \tag{14.221}$$

Hence, if $\eta = \mu$ and $\gamma_N^{SO} > 0$ the "traditional" result obtains and the market yields too little R&D and the innovation growth rate is too low (Bénassy, 1998, p. 68; de Groot and Nahuis, 1998, p. 294).[43]

---

[42] Recall that $\mu > 1$ and $1 < \eta < 2$ so that the term in square brackets on the right-hand side of (14.220) is positive.

[43] The example in this paragraph serves to demonstrate that, even though the standard Dixit-Stiglitz preferences (for which $\eta = \mu$) are convenient to work with, they are restrictive and may impose too much structure. Ethier (1982) stresses the need to distinguish η and μ. Weitzman (1994) provides some micro-foundations for assuming η and μ to be different. Broer and Heijdra (2001) study diversity and markup effects in a traditional growth model with capital accumulation.

Human and physical capital

Romer (1990) extends the R&D model by recognizing physical capital accumulation and by assuming that a given stock of human capital is used in both the final goods sector and in the R&D sector. In his model the production function for final output (14.187) is modified to:

$$Y(t) \equiv H_Y(t)^{\alpha_H} L^{\alpha_L} \left[\int_0^{N(t)} X_j(t)^{1-\alpha_H-\alpha_L} dj \right], \quad 0 < \alpha_H, \alpha_L, \alpha_H + \alpha_L < 1, \quad (14.222)$$

where L and $H_Y(t)$ are, respectively, the amounts of labour and human capital used in the final goods sector. Labour is only used in the final goods sector and its total stock is constant. The total stock of human capital, H, is also constant, but it is used both in the final goods sector ($H_Y(t)$) and in the R&D sector ($H_R(t)$):

$$H = H_Y(t) + H_R(t). \quad (14.223)$$

A further notable difference between (14.187) and (14.222) is that in the latter formulation the technology coefficient, $1-\alpha_H-\alpha_L$, performs no less than three roles: it parameterizes the returns to specialization, the monopoly markup, and the capital efficiency parameter (i.e. $1/\eta = 1/\mu = 1 - \alpha_H - \alpha_L$).

Any output of final goods which is not consumed is added to the stock of (non-depreciating) "general" capital, $K(t)$. Hence, the accumulation identity for general capital is:

$$\dot{K}(t) = Y(t) - C(t), \quad (14.224)$$

where $C(t)$ is aggregate consumption. The representative household maximizes its lifetime utility function (14.168) using both general capital and new technology as assets to smooth consumption over time. Since these assets attract the same net rate of return, $r(t)$, the consumption Euler equation is still as given by (14.199).

General capital (or "cumulative foregone output" as Romer calls it) is rented (from the representative household) by the monopolistically competitive producers in order to produce units of the differentiated input. The production function in the differentiated sector is $K_j(t) = (1/k_X)X_j(t)$. Romer (1990, p. S80) furthermore assumes that the differentiated inputs, $X_j(t)$, are durable and non-depreciating "specialized capital goods". Capital is "putty-putty" in the sense that specialized capital can be converted back into general capital if the need arises (1990, p. S86). Romer defines the following accounting measure for general capital:

$$K(t) \equiv (1/k_X) \int_0^{N(t)} X_j(t) \, dj, \quad (14.225)$$

where the left-hand side of (14.225) denotes the total stock of general capital and the right-hand side is the total amount of general capital used in the differentiated sector.

The R&D sector uses human capital, $H_R(t)$, in order to produce new designs. Hence, equation (14.193) is replaced by:

$$\dot{N}(t) = (1/k_R)N(t)H_R(t). \tag{14.226}$$

Apart from the fact that raw labour ($L_R(t)$) appears in (14.193) and human capital appears in (14.226), the two expressions for the R&D technology are essentially the same. The engine of growth in both cases is furnished by the fact that the number of designs, $N(t)$, appears linearly in both expressions (see also Romer, 1990, p. S84).

On the balanced growth path consumption, final output, general capital, and the number of designs all grow at the same exponential rate, i.e. $\gamma_C = \gamma_Y = \gamma_K = \gamma_N$, where γ_N is given by (Romer, 1990, p. S92):

$$\gamma_N = \frac{H/k_R - \rho\Lambda}{1 + \Lambda/\sigma}, \quad \Lambda \equiv \frac{\alpha_H}{(1 - \alpha_H - \alpha_L)(\alpha_H + \alpha_L)}, \tag{14.227}$$

where it is assumed that this growth rate is positive ($H_R(t) > 0$ in the balanced growth path). Comparing (14.211) and (14.227) reveals a number of differences and similarities. Both models give rise to similar effects on the rate of innovation of preference and technology parameters like s, ρ, and k_R. An important difference between the two models concerns the scale factor. In (14.211) the stock of raw labour (L) determines the growth rate whereas in (14.227) it is the stock of human capital (H) which determines the rate of innovation. This key difference is, of course, directly attributable to the different specifications of the R&D sector (namely (14.193) and (14.226)).

Scale effect

In the previous subsections we have developed two R&D-type growth models which have in common the prediction that the *scale* of an economy is an important determinant of that economy's balanced *growth rate* in the economy. This so-called *scale effect* is in fact a common feature of many important R&D growth models such as Grossman and Helpman (1991) and Aghion and Howitt (1992). In a recent paper, Jones (1995) has argued that the prediction of scale effects is easily falsified empirically. In the US, for example, the amount of labour employed in R&D activities grew from 160,000 in 1950 to about 1,000,000 in 1988 whereas total factor productivity growth stayed the same (or even declined somewhat) during that period (Jones, 1995, p. 762). Similar data can be quoted for other industrialized countries such as France, West Germany, and Japan. On the basis of the empirical evidence, Jones concludes that "the assumption embedded in the R&D equation that the growth rate of the economy is proportional to the level of resources devoted to R&D is obviously false" (1995, p. 762).

Jones suggests that, since the R&D equation is clearly the cause of the empirical refutation, it should be replaced by the following specification:

$$\dot{N}(t) = (1/k_R)L_R(t)N(t)^{\phi_1} \left[\bar{L}_R(t)\right]^{\phi_2-1}, \quad 0 < \phi_1, \; \phi_2 \leq 1, \tag{14.228}$$

where $\bar{L}_R(t)$ captures an external effect due to unintended duplication of work in the R&D sector. In equilibrium $\bar{L}_R(t) = L_R(t)$, and the production of new designs features diminishing returns to labour provided $\phi_2 < 1$. Individual R&D firms, however, take $\bar{L}_R(t)$ as given and operate under the assumption that the R&D production function is linear in $L_R(t)$. Apart from a *duplication externality*, (14.228) also features a more general specification of the *knowledge externality* which operates across time via the stock of invented product varieties. Indeed, whereas $N(t)$ enters linearly in the standard R&D equation (14.193), it features in the augmented R&D equation with an exponent ϕ_1 which may or may not equal unity. An attractive feature of the generalized R&D equation (14.228) is that it contains the standard R&D equation (14.193) as a special case. Indeed, if $\phi_1 = \phi_2 = 1$ the duplication externality is absent and the R&D equation is linear in $N(t)$ and the two expressions coincide.

We now demonstrate the implications for economic growth of adopting the more general specification of the R&D function. As we have seen in the previous sub-section, the accumulation of physical capital does not play an essential role in the determination of the steady-state growth rate. For that reason we use our first R&D model (without physical capital) and derive the steady-state growth rate when (14.228) is used as the R&D function. We augment our simple R&D model, however, by assuming non-zero population growth.

The key ingredients of the model are as follows. The production function for final output is as given in (14.187) except that we follow convention by assuming that the specialization parameter equals the markup ($\eta = \mu$):

$$Y(t) \equiv \left[\int_0^{N(t)} X_j(t)^{1/\mu}\, dj\right]^{\mu}, \quad \mu > 1. \tag{14.229}$$

The simplifications that result from assuming $\eta = \mu$ are easily incorporated in equations (14.188)–(14.189). Equations (14.190)–(14.192) are unchanged, (14.193) is replaced by (14.228), and (14.194) is replaced by:

$$P_N(t) = \frac{k_R W(t)}{N(t)^{\phi_1}} \left[\bar{L}_R(t)\right]^{1-\phi_2}. \tag{14.230}$$

The price of a new design is equal to the *private* marginal cost of producing. As in our first R&D model, labour is used in both the intermediate goods sector and in the R&D sector. In contrast to what was assumed in that model, the stock of labour is now postulated to grow at a constant exponential rate, i.e. $\dot{L}(t)/L(t) = n_L$. The representative household is assumed to care about its per capita consumption,

471

$c(t) \equiv C(t)/L(t)$, and has the following lifetime utility function:

$$\Lambda(0) = \int_0^\infty \left[\frac{c(t)^{1-1/\sigma} - 1}{1 - 1/\sigma} \right] e^{-\rho t} \, dt. \tag{14.231}$$

Finally, since the number of family members of the household grows, the budget identity for the household is changed from (14.195) to:

$$L(t)c(t) + P_N(t)\dot{N}(t) = W(t)L(t) + N(t)\bar{\Pi}(t), \tag{14.232}$$

where we once again assume that final output is the numeraire commodity (so that $P_Y(t) = 1$). The representative household chooses the optimal per capita consumption path in order to maximize (14.231) subject to (14.232) (plus an NPG—no-Ponzi-game—condition). The consumption Euler equation that results from this choice problem is given by:

$$\frac{\dot{c}(t)}{c(t)} = \sigma \left[r(t) - (\rho + n_L) \right], \tag{14.233}$$

where the rate of interest ($r(t)$, representing the yield on blueprints) is given by (14.200). The remaining equations of the model are the final goods market clearing condition (14.201) and the labour market condition:

$$L(t) = L_X(t) + L_R(t) = L_X(t) + \left[k_R N(t)^{1-\phi_1} \left(\frac{\dot{N}(t)}{N(t)} \right) \right]^{1/\phi_2}, \tag{14.234}$$

where the second equality uses (14.228) and incorporates the fact that $\bar{L}_R(t) = L_R(t)$ in equilibrium.

Although we could, in principle, retrace the steps leading from the simplified model to the expression in (14.211), we skip the details of dynamic adjustment here and simply compute the steady-state growth rates implied by the augmented model. We are looking for a balanced growth path in which (a) the proportions of labour going into the intermediate and R&D sectors (L_X/L and L_R/L) are both constant, and (b) the proportional rates of growth in $N(t)$, $c(t)$, and $y(t) \equiv Y(t)/L(t)$ are all constant. The steady-state innovation rate is easily found by rewriting (14.228) in steady-state format and substituting $\bar{L}_R = L_R$:

$$[\gamma_N \equiv] \frac{\dot{N}}{N} = (1/k_R)N^{\phi_1 - 1}L_R^{\phi_2}. \tag{14.235}$$

The left-hand side of (14.235) is constant (as γ_N is constant). By differentiating the left-hand side of (14.235) with respect to time and noting that $\dot{L}_R/L_R = n_L$ we obtain $0 = (\phi_1 - 1)\gamma_N + \phi_2 n_L$ which can be solved for γ_N:

$$\gamma_N = \frac{\phi_2 n_L}{1 - \phi_1}. \tag{14.236}$$

By using the steady-state version of (14.229) (and imposing symmetry) we find $Y = N^\mu \bar{X}$ which can be rewritten as $Y/L = (1/k_X)N^{\mu-1}L_X/L$ (where $L_X = k_X N\bar{X}$).

From this last expression we find:

$$\gamma_y = \gamma_Y - n_L = (\mu - 1)\gamma_N. \tag{14.237}$$

Finally, from the final goods market clearing condition (14.202) we find the growth rate for (per capita) consumption:

$$\gamma_c = \gamma_C - n_L = \gamma_y. \tag{14.238}$$

We reach a rather striking conclusion. By modifying the R&D equation suggested by Jones (namely (14.228)) instead of the standard one (14.193) we have managed to eliminate the scale effect altogether (compare (14.211) and (14.236)). The economy still grows and innovation continues to take place in the modified model but growth is *exogenous*, i.e. it is explained by the rate of population growth just as in the good old Solow model! With a stable population ($n_L = 0$) innovation ceases in the long run because as $N(t)$ rises over time, more and more labour has to be devoted to the R&D sector to sustain a given rate of innovation.

14.7 Punchlines

We started this chapter by presenting some of the most important stylized facts about growth as they were presented four decades ago by Kaldor. These are: (i) output per worker shows continuous growth, (ii) the capital-output ratio is constant, (iii) labour and capital receive constant shares of total income, and (iv) the rate of productivity growth differs across countries. Together these stylized facts also explain that (v) capital per worker grows continuously and that (vi) the rate of return on capital is steady.

Next we presented the neoclassical growth model as it was developed by Solow and Swan in the mid-1950s. The key elements of this model are the neoclassical production function, featuring substitutability between capital and labour, and the "Keynesian" savings function according to which households save a constant fraction of their income. Although the Solow–Swan model is able to explain all of Kaldor's stylized facts, some economists are disturbed by its prediction that long-run growth is determined entirely by exogenous factors, such as the rate of population growth and the rate of labour-augmenting technological progress. For this reason the Solow–Swan model is often referred to as an "exogenous" growth model. The model is inconsistent with Ricardian equivalence. Further important features of the model are that it allows for the possibility of oversaving (dynamic inefficiency) and that it is consistent with the conditional convergence hypothesis according to which similar countries converge. The standard Solow–Swan model predicts too high a convergence speed but this counterfactual prediction of the model is easily fixed by incorporating human capital into the model.

Several extensions and applications of the Solow–Swan model are discussed. In the most important extension, the ad hoc savings function is endogenized by introducing infinitely lived optimizing consumers into the model. This approach, which was pioneered by Ramsey more than seven decades ago, precludes the possibility of oversaving and implies the validity of Ricardian equivalence. (Ricardian equivalence fails, even with infinitely lived agents, if population growth consists of the arrival of disconnected generations.) The growth properties of the Ramsey model are very similar to those of the Solow–Swan model.

The final section of the chapter deals with the recent literature on so-called "endogenous" growth. Three major approaches can be distinguished in this literature. The so-called "capital-fundamentalist" models generate perpetual growth by abandoning one of the key elements of the Solow–Swan model, namely the assumption that the average product of capital goes to zero as the capital stock gets very large. If it is easy to substitute labour for capital then the average product of capital reaches a finite limiting value. It is possible to produce without any labour at all and long-run growth depends, among other things, on the savings rate. Similar results are obtained for the *AK*-model in which labour plays no role at all and production features constant returns to a broad measure of capital.

The second major approach in the endogenous growth literature emphasizes the purposeful accumulation of human capital as the engine of growth. This approach was pioneered by Uzawa in the mid-1960s and further developed by Lucas. The model features infinitely lived households and technology exhibits constant returns to scale in capital and effective labour. The rate of growth in human capital depends on the fraction of time households spend on educational purposes. Even without population growth, consumption, human and physical capital, and output all grow at the same exponential rate.

The third group of studies in the field of endogenous growth is based on the notion that research and development (R&D) activities by firms constitute the engine of growth in the economy. Studies in this vein abandon the assumption of perfect competition and instead analyse monopolistically competitive firms. We present a very simple model (without physical and human capital) in which the R&D sector produces blueprints for new differentiated inputs. In the intermediate goods sector there are many monopolistically competitive firms which each hold a blueprint telling them how to produce their own, slightly unique, input variety. Production of final goods features returns to specialization, i.e. a broader range of differentiated inputs raises productivity because a more roundabout production process can be adopted. The model features a constant rate of innovation which depends positively on the monopoly markup and the scale of the economy. The scale effect is a problematic feature of many R&D based models because it is easily falsified empirically. Elimination of the scale effect is possible but renders the rate of innovation proportional to the rate of population growth, just as in the standard Solow–Swan model.

Further Reading

The first wave of growth theory is well surveyed by Burmeister and Dobell (1970), Hamberg (1971), and Hacche (1979). Key contributions to the Ramsey model are Ramsey (1928), Cass (1965), and Koopmans (1965, 1967). Important early papers on endogenous growth are by Arrow (1962), Uzawa (1965), Sheshinski (1967), Shell (1967), and Conlisk (1969).

Recent textbooks on economic growth include Barro and Sala-i-Martin (1995), Aghion and Howitt (1998), Jones (1998), and Gylfason (1999). Good survey articles are Stern (1991), van de Klundert and Smulders (1992), van der Ploeg and Tang (1992), and Jones and Manuelli (1997). Key references to the R&D literature are Grossman and Helpman (1991) and Aghion and Howitt (1998). The classic source on the idea of creative destruction is Schumpeter (1934).

Lucas (1990a) studies capital taxation in a growth model. Temple (1999) presents a survey of the recent empirical growth literature. On the issue of transitional dynamics, see King and Rebelo (1993), Mulligan and Sala-i-Martin (1993), Xie (1994), Benhabib and Perli (1994), and Bond, Wang, and Yip (1996).

There is a large literature on money and growth. The key references are Tobin (1955, 1965), Sidrauski (1967), Fischer (1979), and Ireland (1994). Key contributions to the literature on public investment include Barro (1981, 1990), Aschauer and Greenwood (1985), Uzawa (1988), Aschauer (1988, 1989), Baxter and King (1993), Glomm and Ravikumar (1994), Turnovsky (1996), Turnovsky and Fisher (1995), and Fisher and Turnovsky (1998). On the scale effect, see Young (1998) and Segerstrom (1998). On R&D and education, see Griliches (2000). Rivera-Batiz and Romer (1991) study the growth effects of economic integration.

Appendix

In this appendix we show how the expressions in (14.99)–(14.100) are derived. In the first step we postulate a trial solution for capital and Tobin's q:

$$\left[\begin{array}{c} k(t) - k^* \\ q(t) - q^* \end{array} \right] = \left[\begin{array}{c} \pi_{k1} \\ \pi_{q1} \end{array} \right] e^{-\lambda_1 t} + \left[\begin{array}{c} \pi_{k2} \\ \pi_{q2} \end{array} \right] e^{\lambda_2 t}, \tag{A14.1}$$

where π_{ki} and π_{qi} ($i = 1, 2$) are coefficients to be determined and where $-\lambda_1 < 0$ and $\lambda_2 > 0$ are, respectively, the stable (negative) and unstable (positive) characteristic root of Δ_I. To eliminate the effects of the unstable root we must set:

$$\left[\begin{array}{c} \pi_{k2} \\ \pi_{q2} \end{array} \right] = \left[\begin{array}{c} 0 \\ 0 \end{array} \right]. \tag{A14.2}$$

By differentiating (A14.1) with respect to time and noting (A14.2) we obtain:

$$\left[\begin{array}{c} \dot{k}(t) \\ \dot{q}(t) \end{array} \right] = -\lambda_1 \left[\begin{array}{c} \pi_{k1} \\ \pi_{q1} \end{array} \right] e^{-\lambda_1 t}, \tag{A14.3}$$

where we have also used the fact that $\dot{k}^* = \dot{q}^* = 0$ (constant steady state). By substituting (A14.1)–(A14.3) into (14.97) we obtain:

$$
\begin{bmatrix} -(\lambda_1 + \delta_{11}) & -\delta_{12} \\ -\delta_{21} & -(\lambda_1 + \delta_{22}) \end{bmatrix} \begin{bmatrix} \pi_{k1} \\ \pi_{q1} \end{bmatrix} = \begin{bmatrix} 0 \\ 0 \end{bmatrix},
\tag{A14.4}
$$

where δ_{ij} represents element (i, j) of the Jacobian matrix Δ_I. Since $-\lambda_1$ is an eigenvalue of Δ_I, the matrix on the left-hand side of (A14.4) is singular so either row of (A14.4) can be used to solve π_{q1} in terms of π_{k1}. Noting that $\delta_{11} = 0$ we obtain from the first row:

$$
\pi_{q1} = -\left(\frac{\lambda_1}{\delta_{12}}\right)\pi_{k1}.
\tag{A14.5}
$$

Next we exploit the fact that the capital stock is predetermined, i.e. its value at time $t = 0$, denoted by k_0, is given. Substituting this initial condition in the first equation of (A14.1) and noting (A14.2) we obtain:

$$
k(0) - k^* = k_0 - k^* = \pi_{k1}.
\tag{A14.6}
$$

The second equation of (A14.1) in combination with (A14.2) and (A14.5)–(A14.6) yields the solution for Tobin's q on the saddle path:

$$
q(0) - q^* = \pi_{q1} = -\left(\frac{\lambda_1}{\delta_{12}}\right)[k_0 - k^*].
\tag{A14.7}
$$

By substituting (A14.2), (A14.6)–(A14.7) into (A14.1) the expressions in (14.99)–(14.100) are obtained.

The solution method used here is valid provided the forcing term of the dynamical system is time invariant. This covers both the transition path of an economy which starts outside the steady state and the adjustment path following an unanticipated and permanent shock to the investment subsidy (both are discussed in section 5.6 above). In the Mathematical Appendix we present a solution method which can handle more general shock patterns.

15

Real Business Cycles

The purpose of this chapter is to achieve the following aims:

1. To introduce an endogenous labour supply decision into the Ramsey model and to study the effects of fiscal policy, both theoretically and quantitatively;

2. To turn the extended Ramsey model into a prototypical real business cycle (RBC) model by assuming that technology is stochastic;

3. To analyse the theoretical properties of the RBC model by means of its impulse-response functions;

4. To study the quantitative performance of the RBC model by showing how well it can be made to fit real world data;

5. To briefly discuss some of the extensions that have been proposed in recent years to improve the model's empirical performance.

15.1 Introduction

In this chapter we study two major themes which were pursued by predominantly new classical economists in the wake of the rational expectations revolution of the early 1970s. The first theme studies the effects of fiscal policy in an optimizing equilibrium framework. Pioneering contributions to this branch of the literature were made by Hall (1971, 1980), Barro (1981), and Aschauer (1988), and more recently by Baxter and King (1993).

The second theme concerns the general equilibrium approach to economic fluctuations. Pioneering contributions to this so-called real business cycle (RBC) approach were made by Kydland and Prescott (1982), Long and Plosser (1983), and Prescott (1986).

15.2 Extending the Ramsey Model

In this section we extend the deterministic Ramsey model (see Chapter 14) by endogenizing the labour supply decision of households. In the model a representative household makes optimal decisions regarding present and future consumption, labour supply, and saving. The representative firm hires the factors of production from the household sector and produces output. The government levies taxes and consumes goods. All agents in the economy operate under perfect foresight. The model can be used to study how the economy reacts to shocks in government spending. Throughout the chapter we abstract from population growth.

15.2.1 Households

The representative agent makes a dynamically optimal decision regarding consumption of goods and leisure both for the present and for the indefinite future. The agent has a time endowment of unity which is allocated over labour and leisure. The agent is infinitely lived and lifetime utility in period t, $\Lambda(t)$, is given by the discounted integral of present and future utility:

$$\Lambda(t) \equiv \int_t^\infty \Phi(\tau) e^{\rho(t-\tau)} \, d\tau, \tag{15.1}$$

where ρ is the pure rate of time preference ($\rho > 0$), and $\Phi(\tau)$ is *instantaneous utility* (or *felicity*) in period τ. Following Campbell (1994, p. 482) and King and Rebelo (1999, p. 954) we assume that the felicity function takes the following form:

$$\Phi(\tau) \equiv \epsilon_C \log C(\tau) + (1 - \epsilon_C) \left[\frac{[1 - L(\tau)]^{1-1/\sigma_L} - 1}{1 - 1/\sigma_L} \right], \quad \sigma_L > 0, \tag{15.2}$$

where $C(\tau)$ is consumption and $1 - L(\tau)$ is leisure. The felicity function is convenient to work with because it nests the two most commonly used specifications in the RBC literature as special cases. The first special case assumes that leisure, like consumption, enters felicity in a logarithmic fashion, i.e. $\sigma_L = 1$ in (15.2). The second special case is based on the assumption that leisure enters felicity linearly, i.e. $\sigma_L \to \infty$ in (15.2). The main emphasis in this chapter will focus on the logarithmic case. (In section 15.5.4 below we present the linear case.)

The agent's dynamic budget identity is:

$$\dot{A}(\tau) \equiv r(\tau)A(\tau) + W(\tau)L(\tau) - T(\tau) - C(\tau), \tag{15.3}$$

where $r(\tau)$ is the real rate of interest, $A(\tau)$ is real financial assets, $W(\tau)$ is the real wage rate, $L(\tau)$ is labour supply, $T(\tau)$ is real lump-sum taxes, and $C(\tau)$ is consumption of a homogeneous good. A dot above a variable designates the derivative with respect to time, i.e. $\dot{A}(\tau) \equiv dA(\tau)/d\tau$. As it stands, equation (15.3) simply says that the income from assets and labour is either consumed, paid to the government in the form of taxes, or saved. Provided the agent has free access to the capital market, the choice problem defined so far is not meaningful: the agent can simply borrow an infinite amount ($A(\tau) \to -\infty$), service the debt with further borrowings ($\dot{A}(\tau) < 0$), and live in a state of utmost bliss (presumably that would mean "all fun and no work", i.e. $C(\tau) \to +\infty$ and $L(\tau) = 0$). Obviously, something is missing in the story up to now to make for interesting macroeconomics. The key to the puzzle is obtained by integrating (15.3):

$$A(t) = \int_t^\infty [C(\tau) - W(\tau)L(\tau) + T(\tau)]\, e^{-R(t,\tau)} d\tau + \left[\lim_{\tau \to \infty} A(\tau) e^{-R(t,\tau)}\right], \tag{15.4}$$

where $R(t, \tau) \equiv \int_t^\tau r(s)\, ds$ is a discounting factor.[1] A heuristic argument can be used to motivate why the term in square brackets on the right-hand side of (15.4) should be zero. It is not in the agent's interest to 'die' with a positive wealth position. Hence, the term in square brackets cannot be positive. Similarly, although the agent may wish to 'die' heavily indebted, the capital market will not allow this. Hence, the term cannot be negative either. The only possibility that remains is that the term vanishes, i.e. the agent remains solvent. This condition is often referred to as the no-Ponzi-game (NPG) condition (Blanchard and Fischer, 1989, p. 49):

$$\lim_{\tau \to \infty} A(\tau) e^{-R(t,\tau)} = 0 \quad \text{(NPG condition).} \tag{15.5}$$

When (15.5) is substituted in (15.4), the household intertemporal budget constraint is obtained. It says that the value of financial assets that the agent possesses in period t (left-hand side of (15.4)) equals the present discounted value of the excess of consumption over after-tax labour income (first term on the right-hand side of (15.4)). Hence, an agent who has negative assets (i.e. debt) in period t must eventually consume less than his after-tax labour income at some time in the future.

The household chooses paths for consumption, labour supply, and assets in order to maximize lifetime utility (15.1) subject to the budget identity (15.3), and the NPG condition (15.5), taking as given the initial level of assets. The current-value Hamiltonian for this problem is:

$$\mathcal{H}(\tau) \equiv \epsilon_C \log C(\tau) + (1 - \epsilon_C) \left[\frac{[1 - L(\tau)]^{1 - 1/\sigma_L} - 1}{1 - 1/\sigma_L} \right]$$

$$+ \mu(\tau)[r(\tau)A(\tau) + W(\tau) - T(\tau) - C(\tau) - W(\tau)[1 - L(\tau)]], \tag{15.6}$$

---

[1] Equation (15.4) is derived as follows. We multiply (15.3) by $e^{-R(t,\tau)}$ and find:

$$\left[\dot{A}(\tau) - r(\tau)A(\tau)\right] e^{-R(t,\tau)} = [W(\tau)L(\tau) - T(\tau) - C(\tau)] e^{-R(t,\tau)}$$

$$\frac{d}{d\tau}\left[A(\tau)e^{-R(t,\tau)}\right] = [W(\tau)L(\tau) - T(\tau) - C(\tau)] e^{-R(t,\tau)}, \tag{a}$$

where we have used the fact that $dR(t,\tau)/d\tau \equiv r(\tau)$. By bringing $d\tau$ to the right-hand side of (a) and integrating over the interval $[t, \infty)$ we obtain (15.4).

where $\mu(\tau)$ is the co-state variable. The interesting first-order necessary conditions are:[2]

$$\frac{\epsilon_C}{C(\tau)} = \mu(\tau), \tag{15.7}$$

$$\frac{1 - \epsilon_C}{[1 - L(\tau)]^{1/\sigma_L}} = \mu(\tau)W(\tau), \tag{15.8}$$

$$\frac{\dot{\mu}(\tau)}{\mu(\tau)} = \rho - r(\tau). \tag{15.9}$$

By using (15.7) in (15.8)–(15.9) we can eliminate $\mu(\tau)$ and $\dot{\mu}(\tau)$ and write the first-order conditions as follows:

$$\frac{C(\tau)}{[1 - L(\tau)]^{1/\sigma_L}} \left(\frac{1 - \epsilon_C}{\epsilon_C} \right) = W(\tau), \tag{15.10}$$

$$\frac{\dot{C}(\tau)}{C(\tau)} = r(\tau) - \rho. \tag{15.11}$$

Equation (15.10) requires the marginal rate of substitution between leisure and consumption to be equated to the wage rate in each period. This is essentially a static decision which is made in each period. According to (15.10) labour supply depends negatively on consumption and positively on the real wage.[3] The dynamic part of the solution is contained in (15.11) which is the consumption Euler equation. If the real interest rate exceeds (falls short of) the pure rate of time preference, the household chooses an upward (downward) sloping consumption profile over time (see Chapter 14 for further details).

15.2.2 Firms

Perfectly competitive firms produce a homogeneous good by using capital and labour. Since there are constant returns to scale to the production factors, there is no need to distinguish individual firms and we can make use of the notion of a "representative firm". In the interest of simplicity, the production function features the following Cobb–Douglas form:

$$Y(\tau) = F(K(\tau), L(\tau)) \equiv Z_0 L(\tau)^{\epsilon_L} K(\tau)^{1 - \epsilon_L}, \tag{15.12}$$

where Z_0 is an index of general productivity, $Y(\tau)$ is aggregate output, and $K(\tau)$ and $L(\tau)$ are, respectively, the amounts of capital and labour used in production.

---

[2] The first-order conditions are $\partial \mathcal{H}/\partial x = 0$ for the control variables ($x \in \{C, 1 - L\}$) and $-\partial \mathcal{H}/\partial x = \dot{\mu} - \rho\mu$ for the state variable ($x = A$).

[3] By differentiating (15.10) we obtain:

$$\frac{dL}{L} = \sigma_L \omega_{LL} \left[\frac{dW}{W} - \frac{dC}{C} \right],$$

where $\omega_{LL} \equiv (1 - L)/L$. Hence, the wage elasticity of labour supply is given by $\sigma_L \omega_{LL}$. For a given ω_{LL}, this elasticity rises with σ_L.

The stockmarket value of the firm is given by the discounted value of its cash flows:

$$V(t) = \int_t^\infty [Y(\tau) - W(\tau)L(\tau) - I(\tau)] e^{-R(t,\tau)} d\tau, \tag{15.13}$$

where $R(t, \tau)$ is the discounting factor (defined below (15.4)) and $I(\tau)$ is gross investment:

$$\dot{K}(\tau) = I(\tau) - \delta K(\tau), \tag{15.14}$$

where δ is the depreciation rate of capital. The firm maximizes its stockmarket value (15.13) subject to the capital accumulation constraint (15.14). Implicit in the formulation of the firm's choice set is the notion that the firm can vary its desired capital stock at will, i.e. there are no adjustment costs on investment. It is not very surprising, therefore, that the firm's decision about how much labour and capital to hire is essentially a static one. Hence, the familiar marginal conditions for labour and capital hold:

$$\frac{\partial Y(\tau)}{\partial L(\tau)} = W(\tau), \quad \frac{\partial Y(\tau)}{\partial K(\tau)} = r(\tau) + \delta. \tag{15.15}$$

In view of the fact that both factors are paid their respective marginal products, and the production function exhibits constant returns to scale, excess profits are zero and the stockmarket value of the firm is equal to the replacement value of its capital stock, i.e. $V(t) = K(t)$.

15.2.3 Equilibrium

Output can be used for private consumption, public consumption, or for investment purposes. Hence, the condition for goods market equilibrium is:

$$Y(\tau) = C(\tau) + I(\tau) + G(\tau). \tag{15.16}$$

Finally, the model is completed by the government budget restriction which simply states that public consumption is paid for by lump-sum taxes levied on the representative household:

$$G(\tau) = T(\tau). \tag{15.17}$$

15.3 The Unit-elastic Model

In the previous section we have constructed a fairly simple dynamic general equilibrium model of the closed economy. In section 15.5 this model will be used to

Table 15.1. The unit-elastic model

$$\dot{K}(t) = I(t) - \delta K(t) \tag{T1.1}$$

$$\frac{\dot{C}(t)}{C(t)} = r(t) - \rho \tag{T1.2}$$

$$G(t) = T(t) \tag{T1.3}$$

$$W(t) = \epsilon_L \left(\frac{Y(t)}{L(t)} \right) \tag{T1.4}$$

$$r(t) + \delta = (1 - \epsilon_L) \left(\frac{Y(t)}{K(t)} \right) \tag{T1.5}$$

$$Y(t) = C(t) + I(t) + G(t) \tag{T1.6}$$

$$W(t)[1 - L(t)] = \left(\frac{1 - \epsilon_C}{\epsilon_C} \right) C(t) \tag{T1.7}$$

$$Y(t) = Z_0 L(t)^{\epsilon_L} K(t)^{1 - \epsilon_L} \tag{T1.8}$$

Definitions: Y real national income, C private consumption, L employment, K capital stock, I gross investment, G public consumption, W real wage rate, r real interest rate, ϵ_C taste parameter for consumption, T lump-sum taxes, ρ pure rate of time preference, δ depreciation rate of capital, ϵ_L efficiency parameter of labour.

simulate the effects of stochastic productivity shocks. In this section, however, we demonstrate some of the theoretical properties of a special case of the model in which the substitution elasticity for labour supply equals unity, i.e. $\sigma_L = 1$. This *unit-elastic* version of the model is often used in the RBC literature (see e.g. Baxter and King, 1993 and King and Rebelo, 1999) because it is relatively easy to analyse and yet does quite a decent job when confronted with the data (see below). For convenience, the complete unit-elastic model has been summarized in Table 15.1.

Equations (T1.1), (T1.2), (T1.3), (T1.6), and (T1.8) restate, respectively, equations (15.14), (15.11), (15.17) (15.16), and (15.12). Equation (T1.7) is obtained by setting $\sigma_L = 1$ in (15.10). Finally, (T1.4)–(T1.5) are obtained by using (15.12) in (15.15).

In the appendix to this chapter we present the full derivation of the phase diagram for the unit-elastic model. The derivation proceeds under the assumption that the output share of government consumption is held constant. The phase diagram is presented graphically in Figure 15.1. The $\dot{K} = 0$ line represents combinations in (C, K) space for which net investment is zero. For each (C, K) combination there exists a unique equilibrium employment level. Indeed, for points near the origin employment is low whilst for points near the horizontal intercept (K_K) employment is close to its upper limit of unity. The golden-rule capital stock is K^{GR} and the associated consumption level is C^{GR} (see point A). For points above (below) the $\dot{K} = 0$ line, consumption is too high (low) and net investment is negative (positive). These dynamic effects have been illustrated with horizontal arrows in Figure 15.1.

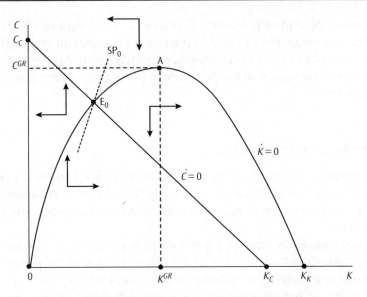

Figure 15.1. Phase diagram of the unit-elastic model

The $\dot{C} = 0$ line represents (C, K) combinations for which consumption is constant over time, i.e. for which the interest rate equals the rate of time preference. Since the interest rate depends on the marginal product of capital, and production features constant returns to scale, consumption equilibrium pins down a unique capital–labour ratio and thus a unique output–capital ratio and real wage rate. It follows (from (T1.7)) that the ratio between consumption and labour supply is constant also. The $\dot{C} = 0$ line is linear and slopes downward. Ceteris paribus the capital stock, an increase (decrease) in consumption decreases (increases) labour supply and equilibrium employment, and decreases (increases) the output–capital ratio and the rate of interest. Hence, consumption falls (rises) at points above (below) the $\dot{C} = 0$ line. This has been indicated with vertical arrows in Figure 15.1.

It follows from Figure 15.1 that the two equilibrium loci intersect only once, at point E_0. The arrow configuration shows that E_0 is saddle-point stable. The saddle path associated with the steady-state equilibrium E_0, denoted by SP_0, is upward sloping.

15.4 Fiscal Policy

In this section we demonstrate some illustrative properties of the deterministic unit-elastic model developed in the previous sections. In doing so we prepare the way for the numerical simulations of the stochastic model in the next section. In the first subsection we study the impact, transitional, and long-run effects of a permanent and unanticipated increase in government consumption. In the second subsection we study how the economy reacts to a temporary fiscal shock. Throughout this section we assume that the government finances its consumption by means of lump-sum taxes.

15.4.1 Permanent fiscal policy

This section studies the effect on the main macroeconomic variables of an increase in public consumption financed by means of lump-sum taxes. We assume that the policy shock is unanticipated and permanent, and that the economy is initially in the steady state.

Although the model in Table 15.1 may look rather complex, it was demonstrated recently by Baxter and King (1993) that the *long-run* effects of the policy shock can be determined in a relatively straightforward fashion. For that reason, we first study the long-run effects, before investigating the somewhat more demanding short-run and transitional effects of fiscal policy.

Long-run multipliers

Computation of the long-run "new classical multiplier" is a back-of-the-envelope exercise due to the fact that the economy is structurally characterized by a number of *great ratios* that are independent of public consumption (see Baxter and King, 1993, p. 319). In our model this can be demonstrated as follows. In the steady state, both the capital stock and consumption are constant, i.e. $\dot{K} = \dot{C} = 0$. Equation (T1.1) and (T1.2) in Table 15.1 then imply, respectively, that the investment–capital ratio and the rate of interest are constant, i.e. $I/K = \delta$ and $r = \rho$. The marginal productivity condition for capital, (T1.5), then pins down the equilibrium capital intensity of production, $y^* \equiv (Y/K)^*$, as a function of structural parameters only ($y^* \equiv (\rho + \delta)/(1 - \epsilon_L)$). But, since the production function, (T1.8), features constant returns to scale, the equilibrium capital intensity also determines a unique capital–labour ratio, (K/L). This, in turn, pins down the real wage and thus (by (T1.7)) the ratio between goods and leisure consumption, $C/(1 - L)$.

The long-run constancy of the various ratios can be exploited to find the long-run effect of an increase in public consumption. By totally differentiating the goods market clearing condition, (T1.6), we obtain:

$$\frac{dY(\infty)}{Y} = \omega_C \left(\frac{dC(\infty)}{C} \right) + \omega_I \left(\frac{dI(\infty)}{I} \right) + \omega_G \left(\frac{dG}{G} \right), \tag{15.18}$$

where $\omega_I \equiv I/Y = \delta K/Y = \delta/y^*$, $\omega_C \equiv C/Y$, and $\omega_C + \omega_I + \omega_G \equiv 1$. Following the shock to public spending, eventually the various ratios will be restored. This implies the following long-run relationships (in loglinearized form):

$$\frac{dY(\infty)}{Y} = \frac{dK(\infty)}{K} = \frac{dI(\infty)}{I} = \frac{dL(\infty)}{L} = -\omega_{LL}\left(\frac{dC(\infty)}{C}\right), \qquad (15.19)$$

where $\omega_{LL} \equiv [1-L]/L$. By substituting the relevant results from (15.18) into (15.19) we find an expression for $dY(\infty)/Y$ which can be rewritten in a multiplier format:

$$\frac{dY(\infty)}{dG} = \frac{1}{1 - \omega_I + \omega_C/\omega_{LL}} > 0. \qquad (15.20)$$

In a similar fashion, the long-run multipliers for consumption, investment, and the capital stock can be derived:

$$-1 < \frac{dC(\infty)}{dG} = -\frac{\omega_C/\omega_{LL}}{1 - \omega_I + \omega_C/\omega_{LL}} < 0, \qquad (15.21)$$

$$\frac{dK(\infty)}{dG} = \frac{1}{\delta}\frac{dI(\infty)}{dG} = \frac{\omega_I/\delta}{1 - \omega_I + \omega_C/\omega_{LL}} > 0. \qquad (15.22)$$

A number of observations can be made about these results. First, the endogeneity of the labour supply decision plays a crucial role for the new classical multiplier. Indeed, if labour supply is exogenous ($\epsilon_C = 1$ so that $L = 1$ and $\omega_{LL} = 0$) equation (15.19) gives the immediate result that output, investment, and the capital stock are unchanged. Equation (15.21) shows that there is one-for-one crowding out of private by public consumption in that case. Second, the elasticity of labour supply (σ_L) also plays a crucial role. Note that the great ratios result also holds for the general model developed in section 2 above. Indeed, by replacing ω_{LL} by $\sigma_L\omega_{LL}$ in (15.20)–(15.22) the long-run effects for the more general model are obtained. Consequently, the more elastic is labour supply (i.e. the higher is σ_L), the larger are the long-run effects on output, capital, and investment, and the smaller is the crowding-out effect on consumption.[4]

Short-run multipliers

The impact and transitional effects of the fiscal shock can be studied graphically with the aid of Figure 15.2. In this figure, CE_0 is the initial consumption equilibrium line,

---

[4] The intertemporal substitution effect in labour supply can be eliminated by using the felicity function suggested by Greenwood et al. (1988):

$$\Phi(\tau) \equiv \log U(\tau), \quad U(\tau) \equiv C(\tau) - \left(\frac{\gamma_L}{1+\theta_L}\right)L(\tau)^{1+\theta_L}.$$

The first-order conditions for this case are:

$$W(\tau) = \gamma_L L(\tau)^{\theta_L}, \quad \frac{\dot{U}(\tau)}{U(\tau)} = r(\tau) - \rho.$$

Employment only depends on the wage rate which is pinned down by the steady-state interest rate ($r = \rho$). It follows that fiscal policy does not affect output and the capital stock either, and that crowding out of consumption is one for one. See Heijdra (1998, pp. 687–688).

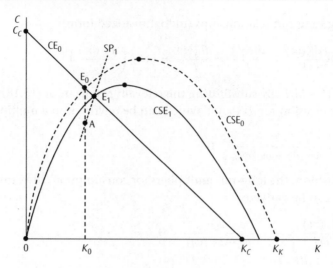

Figure 15.2. Effects of fiscal policy

CSE_0 is the initial capital stock equilibrium line, and E_0 is the initial steady state. As a result of the shock, the CSE line changes to CSE_1. Since lump-sum taxes are used to balance the budget, the position of the CE line is unaffected and the long-run equilibrium shifts from E_0 to E_1 (see (15.20)–(15.22)). At impact, the economy jumps from E_0 to point A on the new saddle path SP_1. Agents cut back consumption of both goods and leisure because they are faced with a higher lifetime tax bill and thus feel poorer. The boost in employment causes an expansion in aggregate output and an increase in the marginal product of capital, and hence the interest rate, despite the fact that the capital stock is fixed in the short run. The increase in the real interest rate not only results in an upward-sloping time profile for consumption but also creates a boom in saving-investment by the representative household, so that both consumption and the capital stock start to rise over time. This is represented in Figure 15.2 by the gradual movement along the saddle path SP_1 from A to the new equilibrium at E_1. The long-run effect on the capital stock is positive (see (15.22)) and consumption falls. Since the representative agent reacts to the fiscal shock by accumulating a larger capital stock and supplying more labour, steady-state output rises and crowding out is less than full (see (15.21)).

Though we can get a good feel for the *qualitative* properties of the model by graphical means such methods are useless to obtain *quantitative* results. For example, it is clear from Figure 15.2 that consumption overshoots its long-run effect at impact and is crowded out ($dC(0)/dG < dC(\infty)/dG < 0$). It is impossible, however, to deduce how large the overshooting and crowding-out effects are. In order to compute the impact and transitional effects on the economy, the standard practice in the RBC literature is to *loglinearize* the model around the steady state so that it can be analysed more easily.[5]

Intermezzo

Loglinearization. Strangely enough, loglinearization of a non-linear *dynamic* model often confuses people. For that reason we show in detail how we loglinearize the model in Table 15.1. Campbell (1994) and Uhlig (1999) provide further examples. We first define the variable $\tilde{x}(t)$:

$$\tilde{x}(t) \equiv \log\left[x(t)/x\right] \quad \Leftrightarrow \quad x(t)/x \equiv e^{\tilde{x}(t)}, \tag{a}$$

where x is the steady-state value for $x(t)$. Provided $x(t)$ is near its steady-state value ($x(t)/x \approx 1$ and $\tilde{x}(t) \approx 0$) we have $e^{\tilde{x}(t)} \approx 1 + \tilde{x}(t)$ so that it follows from (a) that:

$$x(t)/x \approx 1 + \tilde{x}(t). \tag{b}$$

Furthermore, in view of the definition of $\tilde{x}(t)$ (given in (a)) we have:

$$\dot{\tilde{x}}(t) \equiv \frac{\dot{x}(t)}{x(t)} \approx \frac{\dot{x}(t)}{x}. \tag{c}$$

We now apply these intermediate results to the unit-elastic model. In Table 15.1 there are three "basic types" of equations, namely dynamic equations (like (T1.1) and (T1.2)), equations that need no approximation because they are multiplicative and thus loglinear (like (T1.3), (T1.4), and (T1.8)), and linear equations (like (T1.6)).

Consider first a dynamic equation like (T1.1). We obtain in a few steps:

$$\frac{\dot{K}(t)}{K} = \left(\frac{I}{K}\right)\left(\frac{I(t)}{I}\right) - \delta\left(\frac{K(t)}{K}\right)$$

$$\approx \delta\left[1 + \tilde{I}(t)\right] - \delta\left[1 + \tilde{K}(t)\right]$$

$$\dot{\tilde{K}}(t) \approx \delta\left[\tilde{I}(t) - \tilde{K}(t)\right],$$

where we have used (b) (plus the steady-state relation $I = \delta K$) in going from the first to the second line and (c) in going from the second to the third line.

---

[5] In this chapter, we make use of the method of *comparative dynamics*. This method loglinearizes the non-linear model and tackles the issue of dynamics in the much easier linear world. The method is explained in more detail in the Mathematical Appendix. Intuitively, it is appropriate and gives relatively accurate answers, provided the changes in the forcing terms (the exogenous variables) are not "too large" and the model is not "too non-linear". See also Dotsey and Mao (1992).

Next we consider an equation like (T1.8). By taking logarithms on both sides we get:

$$\log Y(t) = \log Z_0 + \epsilon_L \log L(t) + (1 - \epsilon_L) \log K(t). \tag{d}$$

In the steady state we have:

$$\log Y = \log Z_0 + \epsilon_L \log L + (1 - \epsilon_L) \log K. \tag{e}$$

Deducting (e) from (d) and noting the definitions of $\tilde{Y}(t)$, $\tilde{L}(t)$, and $\tilde{K}(t)$ we obtain the desired expression (which no longer contains the constant $\log Z_0$):

$$\tilde{Y}(t) = \epsilon_L \tilde{L}(t) + (1 - \epsilon_L) \tilde{K}(t).$$

Third, we consider a linear equation like (T1.6). We derive in a few steps:

$$\frac{Y(t)}{Y} = \left(\frac{C}{Y}\right)\left(\frac{C(t)}{C}\right) + \left(\frac{I}{Y}\right)\left(\frac{I(t)}{I}\right) + \left(\frac{G}{Y}\right)\left(\frac{G(t)}{G}\right)$$

$$1 + \tilde{Y}(t) \approx \left(\frac{C}{Y}\right)\left[1 + \tilde{C}(t)\right] + \left(\frac{I}{Y}\right)\left[1 + \tilde{I}(t)\right] + \left(\frac{G}{Y}\right)\left[1 + \tilde{G}(t)\right]$$

$$\tilde{Y}(t) \approx \left(\frac{C}{Y}\right)\tilde{C}(t) + \left(\frac{I}{Y}\right)\tilde{I}(t) + \left(\frac{G}{Y}\right)\tilde{G}(t),$$

where we have used (b) in going from the first to the second line and note that in the steady state $Y = C + I + G$.

Finally, consider an equation like (T1.7) which is loglinear in leisure (but not in labour). Indeed, we obtain in a straightforward fashion $\tilde{W}(t) + [\widetilde{1 - L(t)}] = \tilde{C}(t)$. But in the rest of the model we work with $\tilde{L}(t)$. Using (b) we can relate $\tilde{L}(t)$ and $[\widetilde{1 - L(t)}]$:

$$\widetilde{1 - L(t)} \equiv \log\left(\frac{1 - L(t)}{1 - L}\right) \approx \frac{[1 - L(t)] - [1 - L]}{1 - L} = -\left(\frac{L(t) - L}{1 - L}\right)$$

$$\tilde{L}(t) \equiv \log\left(\frac{L(t)}{L}\right) \approx \frac{L(t) - L}{L},$$

from which it follows that $[\widetilde{1 - L(t)}] = -[L/(1 - L)]\tilde{L}(t)$.

The loglinearized version of the unit-elastic model is given in Table 15.2. All variables with a tilde ("~") are defined as proportional rates of change relative to the initial steady state, i.e. $\tilde{x}(t) \equiv \log[x(t)/x]$. Variables with a tilde and a dot are time rates of change of the variable, again expressed in terms of the initial steady-state level of the variable, i.e. $\dot{\tilde{x}}(t) \equiv \dot{x}(t)/x$. This notation is used throughout the remainder of this chapter.

Table 15.2. The loglinearized model

$$\dot{\tilde{K}}(t) = \delta\left[\tilde{I}(t) - \tilde{K}(t)\right] \tag{T2.1}$$

$$\dot{\tilde{C}}(t) = \rho\tilde{r}(t) \tag{T2.2}$$

$$\tilde{G}(t) = \tilde{T}(t) \tag{T2.3}$$

$$\tilde{W}(t) = \tilde{Y}(t) - \tilde{L}(t) \tag{T2.4}$$

$$\rho\tilde{r}(t) = (\rho + \delta)\left[\tilde{Y}(t) - \tilde{K}(t)\right] \tag{T2.5}$$

$$\tilde{Y}(t) = \omega_C\tilde{C}(t) + \omega_I\tilde{I}(t) + \omega_G\tilde{G}(t) \tag{T2.6}$$

$$\tilde{L}(t) = \omega_{LL}\left[\tilde{W}(t) - \tilde{C}(t)\right] \tag{T2.7}$$

$$\tilde{Y}(t) = \epsilon_L\tilde{L}(t) + (1 - \epsilon_L)\tilde{K}(t) \tag{T2.8}$$

Definitions: $\omega_G \equiv G/Y$: output share of public consumption; $\omega_C \equiv C/Y$: output share of private consumption; $\omega_I \equiv I/Y$: output share of investment, $\omega_C + \omega_I + \omega_G = 1$, $\delta/\omega_I = y^* \equiv (\rho + \delta)/(1 - \epsilon_L)$. $\omega_{LL} \equiv (1 - L)/L$: ratio between leisure and labour. $\tilde{x}(t) \equiv \dot{x}(t)/x$, $\tilde{x}(t) \equiv \log[x(t)/x]$.

The state variables are the aggregate capital stock, $\tilde{K}(t)$, which is predetermined, and consumption, $\tilde{C}(t)$, which is a jump variable. The dynamic behaviour of the model can be studied most easily by first condensing it as much as possible. This is done by expressing $\tilde{Y}(t)$, $\tilde{C}(t)$, $\tilde{I}(t)$, $\tilde{W}(t)$, and $\tilde{L}(t)$ in terms of the state variables. Labour demand (T2.4), labour supply (T2.7), and the production function (T2.8) are used to compute the *conditional* equilibrium levels of employment, real wages, and real output:

$$\epsilon_L\tilde{L}(t) = (\phi - 1)\left[(1 - \epsilon_L)\tilde{K}(t) - \tilde{C}(t)\right], \tag{15.23}$$

$$\epsilon_L\tilde{W}(t) = (1 - \epsilon_L)\left[[1 - \phi(1 - \epsilon_L)]\tilde{K}(t) + (\phi - 1)\tilde{C}(t)\right], \tag{15.24}$$

$$\tilde{Y}(t) = \phi(1 - \epsilon_L)\tilde{K}(t) - (\phi - 1)\tilde{C}(t), \tag{15.25}$$

where ϕ is a crucial parameter representing the effects intertemporal substitution in labour supply:

$$1 \leq \phi \equiv \frac{1 + \omega_{LL}}{1 + \omega_{LL}(1 - \epsilon_L)} < \frac{1}{1 - \epsilon_L}. \tag{15.26}$$

The expressions in (15.23)–(15.25) are easy to understand intuitively. First, for a given capital stock, a rise in the level of consumption reduces labour supply (and hence employment), drives up the real wage rate, and reduces output. Second, for a given level of consumption, a rise in the capital stock boosts labour demand and employment and raises the real wage. Output is stimulated both because of the increase in the capital stock and because of the induced effect on employment.

By using the output expression (15.25) in (T2.5) and (T2.6) the conditional equilibrium results for investment and the interest rate are obtained:

$$\omega_I \tilde{I}(t) = \phi(1 - \epsilon_L)\tilde{K}(t) - (\omega_C + \phi - 1)\tilde{C}(t) - \omega_G \tilde{G}, \tag{15.27}$$

$$\left(\frac{\rho}{\rho + \delta}\right)\tilde{r}(t) = -\left[[1 - \phi(1 - \epsilon_L)]\tilde{K}(t) + (\phi - 1)\tilde{C}(t)\right], \tag{15.28}$$

where we have incorporated the assumption (made throughout this section) that the shock in government consumption is constant over time, i.e. $\tilde{G}(t) = \tilde{G}$. The rate of interest depends negatively on both the capital stock and consumption. For a given level of consumption, an increase in the capital stock raises employment, as labour demand is boosted. This raises the marginal product of capital and hence the interest rate. This positive effect on the interest rate is more than offset, however, by the fact that marginal returns to capital decline as more capital is added. For a given capital stock, an increase in consumption lowers labour supply and employment, and hence lowers the marginal product of capital and the interest rate.

Of course, since there are constant returns to scale in production, there exists a unique inverse relationship between factor prices. This *factor price frontier* is obtained by substituting (T2.4) and (T2.5) into (T2.8):

$$\epsilon_L \tilde{W}(t) + \left(\frac{\rho}{\rho + \delta}\right)(1 - \epsilon_L)\tilde{r}(t) = 0. \tag{15.29}$$

By substituting (15.27) into (T2.1) and (15.28) into (T2.2), the dynamical system can be written in a condensed form as:

$$\begin{bmatrix} \dot{\tilde{K}}(t) \\ \dot{\tilde{C}}(t) \end{bmatrix} = \Delta \begin{bmatrix} \tilde{K}(t) \\ \tilde{C}(t) \end{bmatrix} + \begin{bmatrix} \gamma_K(t) \\ \gamma_C(t) \end{bmatrix}, \tag{15.30}$$

where Δ is the Jacobian matrix of the system:

$$\Delta \equiv \begin{bmatrix} y^*(\phi(1 - \epsilon_L) - \omega_I) & -y^*(\omega_C + \phi - 1) \\ -(\rho + \delta)[1 - \phi(1 - \epsilon_L)] & -(\rho + \delta)(\phi - 1) \end{bmatrix}, \tag{15.31}$$

and $\gamma_K(t)$ and $\gamma_C(t)$ are the shock terms:

$$\begin{bmatrix} \gamma_K(t) \\ \gamma_C(t) \end{bmatrix} \equiv \begin{bmatrix} -y^*\omega_G \tilde{G} \\ 0 \end{bmatrix}. \tag{15.32}$$

Saddle-point stability of the loglinearized system can be demonstrated formally by computing the determinant and the trace of the Jacobian matrix, Δ. After some

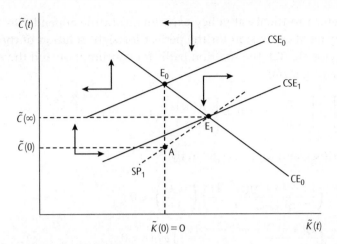

Figure 15.3. Phase diagram of the loglinearized model

manipulation we find:[6]

$$|\Delta| = -(\rho + \delta)y^* \left[\omega_G(\phi - 1) + \phi\omega_C\epsilon_L\right] < 0, \tag{15.33}$$

$$\text{tr}(\Delta) = \rho > 0. \tag{15.34}$$

As $|\Delta|$ is equal to the product of the characteristic roots, it follows from (15.33) that there must be one negative (stable) root and one positive (unstable) root. Throughout this chapter the stable root is designated by $-\lambda_1$ (< 0) and the unstable root by λ_2 (> 0). When written in this way, λ_1 also represents the adjustment speed of the economic system (see Chapter 14 for details). Furthermore, since $\text{tr}(\Delta)$ is the sum of the characteristic roots, it follows from (15.34) that $\lambda_2 = \rho + \lambda_1$.

The loglinearized model has been illustrated in Figure 15.3, where the loglinearized CSE and CE schedules are given by, respectively:

$$\tilde{C}(t) = \left(\frac{\phi(1 - \epsilon_L) - \omega_I}{\omega_C + \phi - 1}\right)\tilde{K}(t) - \left(\frac{\omega_G}{\omega_C + \phi - 1}\right)\tilde{G}, \tag{15.35}$$

and:

$$\tilde{C}(t) = -\left(\frac{1 - \phi(1 - \epsilon_L)}{\phi - 1}\right)\tilde{K}(t). \tag{15.36}$$

(Equations (15.35)–(15.36) are obtained from (15.30)–(15.32) by imposing the steady state $\dot{\tilde{K}}(t) = \dot{\tilde{C}}(t) = 0$.)

---

[6] By noting that $y^* \equiv (\rho + \delta)/(1 - \epsilon_L)$, the trace of Δ can be simplified as follows:

$$\text{tr}(\Delta) = y^* \left[\phi(1 - \epsilon_L) - \omega_I\right] - (1 - \epsilon_L)y^*(\phi - 1) = y^*\omega_A = \rho,$$

where $\omega_A \equiv \rho K/Y = 1 - \epsilon_L - \omega_I = \rho/y^*$ is the net steady-state capital income share.

491

We now return to the fiscal policy experiment. In the appendix to this chapter we derive a general expression for the perfect foresight solution of the model. For the shock vector (15.32), the solution paths for consumption and the capital stock take the following form:

$$\begin{bmatrix} \tilde{K}(t) \\ \tilde{C}(t) \end{bmatrix} = \begin{bmatrix} 0 \\ \tilde{C}(0) \end{bmatrix} e^{-\lambda_1 t} + \begin{bmatrix} \tilde{K}(\infty) \\ \tilde{C}(\infty) \end{bmatrix} (1 - e^{-\lambda_1 t}), \tag{15.37}$$

where $\tilde{C}(0)$, $\tilde{C}(\infty)$, and $\tilde{K}(\infty)$ are given by:

$$\tilde{C}(0) = -\left(\frac{\lambda_2 + (\rho + \delta)(\phi - 1)}{\phi + \omega_C - 1} \right) \left(\frac{\omega_G \tilde{G}}{\lambda_2} \right) < 0, \tag{15.38}$$

$$\tilde{C}(\infty) = -\left(\frac{(\rho + \delta)\left[1 - \phi(1 - \epsilon_L)\right] y^*}{\lambda_1 \lambda_2} \right) \omega_G \tilde{G} < 0, \tag{15.39}$$

$$\tilde{K}(\infty) = \left(\frac{(\rho + \delta)(\phi - 1) y^*}{\lambda_1 \lambda_2} \right) \omega_G \tilde{G} > 0. \tag{15.40}$$

Equations (15.37)–(15.40) represent the so-called *impulse-response functions* for capital and consumption with respect to a permanent and unanticipated shock in government consumption which occurs at time $t = 0$. Equation (15.37) shows that the effect of the shock as of time t can be written as the weighted average of the impact effect and the long-run effect with respective time-varying weights $e^{-\lambda_1 t}$ and $1 - e^{-\lambda_1 t}$. The impulse-response function for the remaining variables of the model (i.e. $\tilde{L}(t)$, $\tilde{W}(t)$, $\tilde{Y}(t)$, $\tilde{I}(t)$, and $\tilde{r}(t)$) are obtained by using (15.37)–(15.40) in (15.23)–(15.25) and (15.27)–(15.28).

Since the capital stock is predetermined in the impact period ($\tilde{K}(0) = 0$), the impact effects for employment, output, the wage, and the interest rate are all proportional to $\tilde{C}(0)$. The decrease in consumption causes labour supply (and employment) to increase.

$$W\left(\frac{dL(0)}{dG} \right) = \frac{\lambda_2 + (\rho + \delta)(\phi - 1)}{\lambda_2(\phi + \omega_C - 1)} > 0. \tag{15.41}$$

As a result of the increase in employment, output also expands:

$$\frac{dY(0)}{dG} = \frac{(\phi - 1)\left[\lambda_2 + (\rho + \delta)(\phi - 1)\right]}{\lambda_2(\phi + \omega_C - 1)} > 0. \tag{15.42}$$

Since output expands and goods consumption falls, investment unambiguously rises:

$$\frac{dI(0)}{dG} = \lambda_1 \left(\frac{dK(\infty)}{dG} \right) = \frac{(\rho + \delta)(\phi - 1)}{\lambda_2} > 0. \tag{15.43}$$

Equation (15.43) shows the *accelerator mechanism* that is operative in the model (see also Baxter and King, 1993, p. 321): the impact effect on investment is proportional to the long-run effect on the capital stock, with the adjustment speed of the economy acting as the factor of proportionality. Because the output–capital ratio expands at impact, the marginal product of capital and thus the real interest rate rises:

$$Y\left(\frac{dr(0)}{dG}\right) = \frac{(\rho + \delta)(\phi - 1)\left[\lambda_2 + (\rho + \delta)(\phi - 1)\right]}{\lambda_2(\phi + \omega_C - 1)} > 0. \tag{15.44}$$

Finally, the expansion of labour supply implies that the real wage rate falls as the demand for labour is downward sloping:

$$L\left(\frac{dW(0)}{dG}\right) = -\frac{(1 - \epsilon_L)(\phi - 1)\left[\lambda_2 + (\rho + \delta)(\phi - 1)\right]}{\lambda_2(\phi + \omega_C - 1)} < 0. \tag{15.45}$$

Of course, what happens to the wage rate can also be determined by combining (15.44) with the factor price frontier (15.29).

Quantitative evidence

Now that the *qualitative* effects of the fiscal shock have been fully characterized analytically, the next question concerns the *quantitative* size of the various effects. In order to cast some light on this issue we must now *calibrate* the model by using information that is more or less plausible for a typical advanced market economy. The calibrated model is then used to compute the various impact, transitional, and long-run effects.

Essentially calibration amounts to choosing the parameters of the theoretical model in such a way that the model replicates certain outcomes about which sufficiently robust information is available. Take, for example, the unit-elastic model given in Tables 15.1 (in levels) and 15.2 (in loglinearized format). The structural parameters appearing in that model are the pure rate of time preference ρ, the rate of depreciation of the capital stock δ, the efficiency parameter of labour ϵ_L, the preference parameter ϵ_C, and the general productivity parameter Z_0.

Some of these parameters are not hard to guess. For example, under the maintained hypothesis that the economy is in (or near) a steady state, it follows from (T1.2) that the real rate of interest must be (nearly) equal to the rate of pure time preference, i.e. $r = \rho$. King and Rebelo (1999, p. 953) suggest that the average real rate of return to capital in the US has been 6.5% per annum over the period 1948–1986. On a quarterly basis this would give us the estimate $r = \rho = (1.065)^{1/4} - 1 = 0.0159$ (1.59% on a quarterly basis). The annual rate of depreciation of the capital stock is set at 10% per annum by King and Rebelo, i.e. $\delta = (1.1)^{1/4} - 1 = 0.0241$. Of course, for buildings this figure is far too high (most buildings last longer than ten years) but for machines (e.g. personal computers) it may be far too low. As an average guess, however, it may not be too widely off the mark. With Cobb-Douglas technology ϵ_L equals the share of labour income in output (see (T1.4)) which King and Rebelo set equal to two-thirds, i.e. $\epsilon_L = 2/3$ (1999, p. 954). But now that we know ρ and ϵ_L, we can infer the implied estimate for the equilibrium output–capital ratio from (T1.5), i.e. $y^* \equiv (Y/K)^* = (\rho + \delta)/(1 - \epsilon_L) = 3(0.0159 + 0.0241) = 0.12$. By imposing the steady state in (T1.1) we obtain the implied investment share of output, i.e. $\omega_I \equiv I/Y = \delta/y^* = 0.0241/0.12 = 0.201$. Baxter and King (1993, p. 320) suggest that the average postwar share of government consumption in output was 20% in the US, i.e. $\omega_G = 0.2$. We now have estimates for almost all parameters of interest. By using (T1.6) we observe that the consumption share in output is $\omega_C \equiv C/Y = 1 - \omega_I - \omega_G = 0.599$. By combining (T1.4) and (T1.6) we derive:

$$\omega_{LL} \equiv \frac{1-L}{L} = \left(\frac{\omega_C}{\epsilon_L}\right)\left(\frac{1-\epsilon_C}{\epsilon_C}\right), \tag{15.46}$$

so choosing ϵ_C implies choosing L (and thus ω_{LL}) and vice versa. King and Rebelo suggest that 20% of total available time has been dedicated to working in the postwar period in the US, i.e. $L = 0.2$ and $\omega_{LL} = 4$, so that it follows from (15.46) and the other estimates that $\epsilon_C = \omega_C/[\omega_C + \epsilon_L\omega_{LL}] = 0.183$. Finally, we observe that Z_0 is a "free parameter" in the sense that it merely fixed the scale of the economy. In the next section we shall set $Z_0 = 1$ but here we normalize Z_0 such that output is unity in the initial steady state, i.e. we set $Z_0 = L^{-\epsilon_L}(y^*)^{1-\epsilon_L} = 1.442$.[7]

In summary, we have now calibrated the model using the following values for the *structural parameters*:

$$\begin{aligned} \rho = 0.0159 \quad & \delta = 0.0241 \quad \epsilon_L = 2/3 \\ \epsilon_C = 0.183 \quad & Z_0 = 1.442 \quad \omega_G = 0.2 \end{aligned} \tag{15.47}$$

The resulting initial steady state is given by:

$$\begin{aligned} Y = 1 \qquad & C = 0.599 \quad I = 0.201 \quad G = T = 0.2 \\ r = 0.0159 \quad & L = 0.2 \qquad K = 8.337 \quad W = 3.333 \end{aligned} \tag{15.48}$$

Using these calibration values in (15.31)–(15.32) and noting (15.26) we obtain the implied estimates for the Jacobian matrix, Δ, and the shock terms, $\gamma_K(t)$ and $\gamma_C(t)$:[8]

$$\Delta \equiv \begin{bmatrix} 0.06156 & -0.20892 \\ -0.01142 & -0.04569 \end{bmatrix}, \tag{15.49}$$

$$\begin{bmatrix} \gamma_K(t) \\ \gamma_C(t) \end{bmatrix} \equiv \begin{bmatrix} -0.02399 \\ 0 \end{bmatrix} \tilde{G}. \tag{15.50}$$

The characteristic roots of Δ are, respectively, $-\lambda_1 = -0.0646$ and $\lambda_2 = 0.0805$. What do these figures mean? Recall that λ_1 represents the adjustment speed in the economy—see (15.37). Using the reasoning explained in Chapter 14, the half-life of the adjustment process in the economy is $t_{1/2} \equiv (1/\lambda_1) \log 2 = 10.7$. Since we

---

[7] Most numerical solution algorithms work best when the endogenous variables are all of the same order of magnitude. For that reason it is wise to normalize output such that this is indeed the case.

[8] We present the actual numerical estimates here not to test the reader's patience but rather to enable replication and to give a 'feel' for the magnitudes and dimensions involved.

Table 15.3. Government consumption multipliers

Variable	Impact effect	Long-run effect
$\dfrac{dY}{dG}$	1.029	1.054
$\dfrac{dC}{dG}$	−0.539	−0.158
$\dfrac{dI}{dG}$	0.568	0.212
$\left(\dfrac{dK}{K}\right) / \left(\dfrac{dG}{G}\right)$	0	0.211
$\left(\dfrac{dL}{L}\right) / \left(\dfrac{dG}{G}\right)$	0.309	0.211
$\left(\dfrac{dr}{r}\right) / \left(\dfrac{dG}{G}\right)$	0.518	0
$\left(\dfrac{dW}{W}\right) / \left(\dfrac{dG}{G}\right)$	−0.103	0

have calibrated on quarterly observations for the interest rate and the depreciation rate on capital, this figure means, for example, that half of the adjustment in the non-jumping variable (the capital stock) is completed almost eleven quarters after the shock occurred.

Using the information from (15.49)–(15.50) in the various analytical expressions (15.37)–(15.45) we obtain the numerical estimates for the impact and long-run effects on the different variables. These results have been summarized in Table 15.3. There is severe crowding out of private by public consumption at impact. For every $1 of extra government consumption private consumption falls by $0.54 at impact. Because the representative agent cuts back on leisure consumption—by supplying more hours to the labour market—household labour income rises. The additional (saving equals) investment at impact is $0.57 out of every $1 of extra government consumption so that the output multiplier exceeds unity at impact. Let us look at some of the other magnitudes involved. At impact a 1% increase in government spending gives rise to a 0.3% increase in employment and a 0.1% fall in the wage rate. The interest rate rises proportionally by 0.5%, i.e. in absolute terms the interest rate rises by 0.0082 percentage points from 1.587% to 1.595% on a quarterly basis.

In the long run the interest rate, the wage rate (see the factor price frontier (15.29)), and the capital–labour ratio all return to their respective initial equilibrium values. For a 1% increase in government consumption the capital stock increases by 0.211%. In the long-run **net** investment ceases as the initial investment–capital ratio is restored. Consumption crowding out remains but is less severe than at impact and the output multiplier is a little higher than at impact.

In summary, the results in this subsection show that large output multipliers due to permanent government consumption are quite possible in the representative-agent model. The mechanism behind the multiplier is, however, quite classical and originates from the dynamic interaction of the supply of labour and capital (Baxter and King, 1993, pp. 323–324). The additional lump-sum taxes make people poorer which leads them to increase labour supply both at impact and in the long run. In the long run the capital–labour ratio is restored so that the capital stock rises also. In the short run the investment accelerator (see (15.43)) explains that the public consumption shock is accompanied by an investment boom.

15.4.2 Temporary fiscal policy

One of the recurrent themes in the study of fiscal policy is the difference between the effects of temporary and permanent policy. Baxter and King, for example, employ numerical methods to study to what extent the impact multiplier for output depends on the duration for which the fiscal policy impulse is in operation (1993, p. 315). In this subsection we show how a temporary (but unanticipated) fiscal spending shock affects the economy. To keep things simple we assume that the government raises its consumption level unexpectedly at some time $t_0 = 0$ and then gradually lets it fall back to the initial level. In terms of (15.32), the shock term for the CE line is unaffected (i.e. $\gamma_C(t) \equiv 0$ because lump-sum taxes continue to be used in this experiment) but the shock term affecting the CSE line is changed to:

$$\gamma_K(t) \equiv -e^{-\xi_K t} y^* \omega_G \tilde{G}, \tag{15.51}$$

where $\xi_K > 0$ is the exponential rate at which government consumption returns to its initial level. At impact the shock is the same as before (since $\gamma_K(0) = -y^* \omega_G \tilde{G}$) but eventually the shock vanishes ($\lim_{t \to \infty} \gamma_K(t) = 0$). Since agents in the economy are assumed to know the path of government consumption they will condition their behaviour accordingly and will change their plans optimally. Note that ξ_K parameterizes the *persistence* of the shock. For example, if $\xi_K \approx 0$ then the shock is highly persistent and $\gamma_K(t)$ falls only very slowly towards zero. In contrast, if ξ_K is large, then $\gamma_K(t)$ drops off rapidly as time goes by and the shock is very transitory. The time path for $\gamma_K(t)$ is illustrated in Figure 15.4 for different values of ξ_K, ranging from $\xi_K = 0$ (permanent shock) to $\xi_K = 0.5$ (very transitory shock).

Using the methods explained in the appendix to this chapter, the perfect foresight solution of the model is obtained:

$$\begin{bmatrix} \tilde{K}(t) \\ \tilde{C}(t) \end{bmatrix} = \begin{bmatrix} 0 \\ \tilde{C}(0) \end{bmatrix} e^{-\lambda_1 t} - \begin{bmatrix} \xi_K - (\rho + \delta)(\phi - 1) \\ (\rho + \delta)[1 - \phi(1 - \epsilon_L)] \end{bmatrix}$$
$$\times \, T(\xi_K, \lambda_1, t) \left(\frac{y^* \omega_G \tilde{G}}{\lambda_2 + \xi_K} \right), \tag{15.52}$$

where the impact effect on consumption, $\tilde{C}(0)$, is:

$$\tilde{C}(0) = - \left(\frac{\lambda_2 + (\rho + \delta)(\phi - 1)}{\omega_C + \phi - 1} \right) \left(\frac{\omega_G \tilde{G}}{\lambda_2 + \xi_K} \right) < 0, \tag{15.53}$$

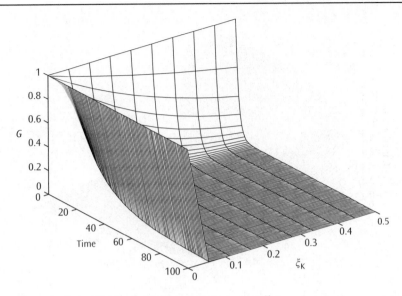

Figure 15.4. The path for government spending

and where $T(\xi_K, \lambda_1, t)$ is a temporary transition term which is defined as follows:

$$T(\xi_K, \lambda_1, t) \equiv \begin{cases} \frac{e^{-\lambda_1 t} - e^{-\xi_K t}}{\xi_K - \lambda_1} & \text{for } \xi_K \neq \lambda_1 \\ \\ te^{-\lambda_1 t} & \text{for } \xi_K = \lambda_1 \end{cases} \tag{15.54}$$

Before developing the economic interpretation of the solutions for consumption and the capital stock, as given in (15.52)–(15.53), it is useful to first look at the shape of the temporary transition term $T(\xi_K, \lambda_1, t)$. In Figure 15.5 we illustrate the shape of this term for a range of values of ξ_K. In this figure, the adjustment speed of the economy is set at the value implied by the calibration, i.e. $\lambda_1 = 0.0646$ (see the text below equation (15.50)).

We observe from Figure 15.5 that, provided ξ_K is strictly positive, the transition term is a non-negative bell-shaped function of time. Furthermore, this term is zero both at the time of the shock ($t = 0$) and in the long run ($t \to \infty$). The lower is the value of ξ_K, the later is the time at which the transition terms reaches its peak and the slower is the decline towards zero as time goes on. In the limiting case, with $\xi_K = 0$, the shock is permanent and the transition term is proportional to an adjustment term of the form $A(\lambda_1, t) \equiv 1 - e^{-\lambda_1 t}$. Hence, for $\xi_K = 0$ the transition function is not bell-shaped—see the back ridge in Figure 15.5.

We are now in a position to study the intuition behind the macroeconomic effects of a temporary public spending shock. The aim is to firmly establish the link between the impulse-response diagrams contained in Figures 15.7–15.10 and the analytical results given in (15.52)–(15.53). This task is facilitated by considering the phase diagram presented in Figure 15.6.

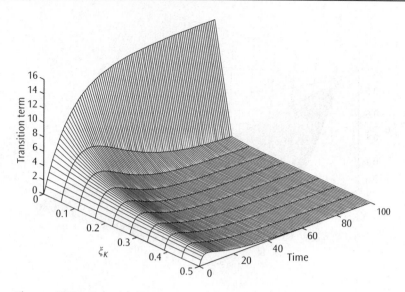

Figure 15.5. Transition term

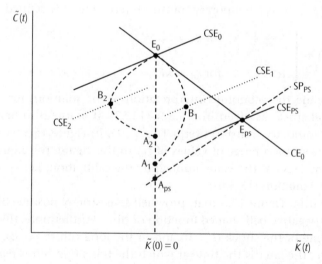

Figure 15.6. Phase diagram for temporary shock

In Figure 15.6, CSE_0 and CE_0 are, respectively, the initial capital stock equilibrium and consumption equilibrium curves, and E_0 is the initial equilibrium. The effect of a permanent shock, which was also studied in Figure 15.4, is to shift the CSE curve to CSE_{ps}. The economy adjusts by jumping from E_0 to A_{ps} at impact and by moving gradually along the saddle path, SP_{ps}, from A_{ps} to E_{ps}.

Next we consider what the adjustment path looks like when the shock is temporary. It follows from the comparison of (15.38) and (15.53) that the impact reduction in consumption is larger for a permanent than for a temporary shock. In Figure 15.6 this means that for a temporary shock the economy jumps somewhere along the vertical dashed line connecting E_0 and A_{ps}. In order to study the qualitative effects of shock persistence, we postulate two values for ξ_K, say ξ_K^1 and ξ_K^2, and we assume that $\xi_K^1 < \xi_K^2$, i.e. the shock is relatively more persistent for ξ_K^1. The consumption jumps associated with the two ξ_K values are illustrated in Figure 15.6 by, respectively, points A_1 and A_2.

Consumption falls regardless of the degree of shock persistence. The additional lump-sum taxes make the representative agent poorer as a result of which he cuts back on goods consumption and leisure. This negative human wealth effect is larger the more persistent is the shock. Next we consider whether the agents react to the shock by accumulating or decumulating assets. The diagram in and of itself does not provide an unambiguous answer because it is not a priori clear which region the economy jumps to. This is where the analytical results can provide further guidance.

It follows from the first expression in (15.52) that the impact effect on net investment is given by:[9]

$$\dot{K}(0) = [(\rho + \delta)(\phi - 1) - \xi_K]\left(\frac{y^* \omega_G \tilde{G}}{\lambda_2 + \xi_K}\right). \tag{15.55}$$

The impact effect on net investment depends on the interplay of two mechanisms working in opposite directions. If labour supply is highly elastic (ϕ high) and the shock is very persistent (ξ_K low), then the term in square brackets on the right-hand side of (15.55) is positive and net investment rises at impact ($\dot{K}(0) > 0$). Intuitively, since consumption falls and output increases strongly (because of the large boost in labour supply), the increase in government consumption does not cause any crowding out of private investment. Hence, for $\xi_K^1 < (\rho + \delta)(\phi - 1)$, the transition path at impact is upward sloping—see the dashed line from point A_1 in Figure 15.6. The phase diagram can now be used to characterize the transition path. Over time, the capital stock equilibrium locus starts to shift back towards CSE_0. During the early part of the transition the equilibrium trajectory runs in a north-easterly direction, say from A_1 to B_1 in Figure 15.6. By the time the equilibrium trajectory catches up with the then relevant capital stock equilibrium locus (CSE_1), net capital accumulation ceases, i.e. the trajectory is vertical at point B_1. After that time, the economy returns to the old equilibrium along the trajectory from B_1 to E_0.

If the labour supply is not very elastic (ϕ close to unity) or the shock is very transient (ξ_K high), then the term in square brackets on the right-hand side of (15.55) is negative and net investment falls at impact ($\dot{K}(0) < 0$). In that case, $\xi_K^2 > (\rho + \delta)(\phi - 1)$, and the economy jumps at impact from E_0 to A_2, after which it

[9] This expression is obtained by differentiating the first expression in (15.52) with respect to time and noting that $dT/dt = 1$ for $t = 0$.

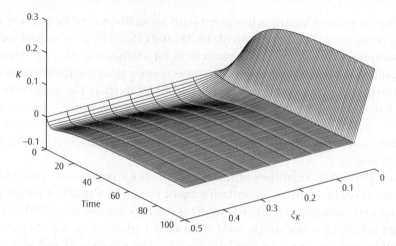

Figure 15.7. Capital stock

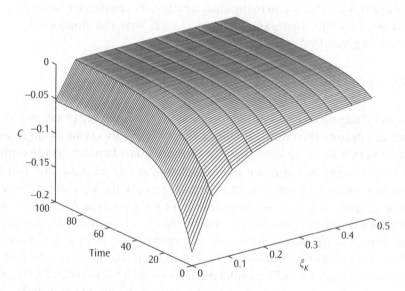

Figure 15.8. Consumption

moves gradually from A_2 via B_2 to the initial equilibrium E_0. The transition paths for the capital stock and consumption have been illustrated in the time domain and for a range of ξ_K values in, respectively, Figures 15.7 and 15.8. As is evident from both the phase diagram (Figure 15.6) and the time domain picture (Figure 15.8) the adjustment of consumption is monotonic.

The adjustment paths for employment, wages, output, and the interest rate are obtained by substituting the solutions for consumption and the capital stock, given in (15.52)–(15.53), into the quasi-reduced form expressions (15.23)–(15.25) and

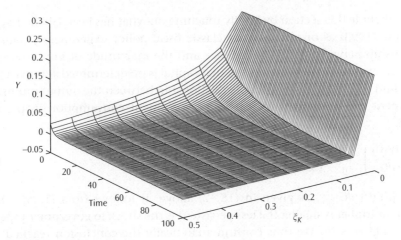

Figure 15.9. Output

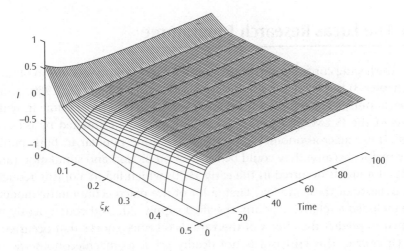

Figure 15.10. Investment

(15.28). In a similar fashion, the adjustment path for gross private investment is obtained by using (T2.6) and noting that $\tilde{G}(t) = e^{-\xi_K t}\tilde{G}$. In Figures 15.9 and 15.10 we illustrate the paths for, respectively, output ($\tilde{Y}(t)$) and gross private investment ($\tilde{I}(t)$). Output jumps up at impact and thereafter monotonically drops back to its initial level. The more transient the shock, the faster is the transition in output.[10] Gross investment jumps up (down) when the shock persistence is high (low) and thereafter returns monotonically to its initial level.

[10] Comparing Figures 15.4 and 15.9 reveals that the output response looks almost identical to the spending shock itself. The model has little *internal propagation* (Cogley and Nason, 1995). We return to this problematic feature of the unit-elastic model (and other RBC models like it) below.

501

We conclude this section by briefly touching on what has been labelled by Baxter and King (1993) as one of the four classic fiscal policy experiments, namely the relationship between policy persistence and the magnitude of impact effects. By using (15.25) and (15.53) and noting that capital is predetermined at impact ($\tilde{K}(0) = 0$), we find that there exists a simple relationship between the output multiplier for permanent and temporary increases in government consumption in the impact period:

$$\left[\frac{dY(0)}{dG}\right]_{\xi_K>0} = \left(\frac{\lambda_2}{\lambda_2 + \xi_K}\right)\left[\frac{dY(0)}{dG}\right]_{\xi_K=0} > 0, \tag{15.56}$$

where $[dY(0)/dG]_{\xi_K=0}$ is given in (15.42) above. It follows from (15.56) that the impact multiplier is smaller the less persistent is the shock to government spending, i.e. the higher is ξ_K. We thus confirm analytically the conclusion reached on the basis of numerical simulations by Baxter and King (1993, p. 326).[11]

15.5 The Lucas Research Programme

One of the lasting contributions of the rational expectations revolution of the 1970s (see Chapter 3) has been a methodological one. Throughout the 1950s and 1960s macroeconomists engaged in a huge model construction programme in which the insights of the IS-LM model and its refinements were estimated by econometric means. These macroeconometric models were quite popular in both public and private sectors because they could be used for prediction and simulation purposes. Two developments occurred in the early 1970s which led to a drastic reduction in the popularity of these models. First, a lot of the macroeconometric models then in use included a relatively poorly specified supply side and consequently were ill equipped to predict the effects of the various oil price shocks that occurred at the time. Of course, this criticism is not deadly *per se* as macroeconometric models can be (and indeed, have been) re-specified to better deal with shocks affecting the supply side of the economy.

A second—potentially much more lethal—criticism was raised by Lucas (1976). The so-called *Lucas critique* was discussed above–see Chapter 3. Loosely put, it states that macroeconometric models that are not based on a consistent set of optimizing foundations are *non-structural* and cannot be used for policy evaluation. The reason is that the estimated parameters of the model's equations are mixtures of structural and policy parameters and are therefore not invariant across different policy regimes (see Chapter 3 for a simple example of this point). To avoid the critique that now carries his name, Lucas (1980, 1987) argued forcefully and eloquently

---

[11] In the classic analyses of Hall (1980) and Barro (1981), exactly the opposite result holds, i.e. temporary spending shocks have larger effects than permanent ones. The reason for this discrepancy is that these papers do not allow for capital accumulation. See Baxter and King (1993, p. 326).

that macroeconomists should build structural models, i.e. models that are based on optimizing behaviour of the various agents in the economy. In doing so he proposed what Christiano, Eichenbaum, and Evans (1999) have recently labelled the *Lucas (research) programme*.

As Lucas (1980, p. 272) argues, well-articulated structural models are of necessity unrealistic and artificial. They should be tested "as useful imitations of reality by subjecting them to shocks for which we are fairly certain how actual economies ... would react. The more dimensions on which the model mimics the answers actual economies give to simple questions, the more we trust its answers to harder questions". He goes on to argue that:

On this general view of the nature of economic theory then, a "theory" is not a collection of assertions about the behavior of the actual economy but rather an explicit set of instructions for building a parallel or analogue system–a mechanical, imitation economy. A "good" model, from this point of view, will not be exactly more "real" than a poor one, but will provide better imitations. (1980, p. 272)

In a seminal paper, Kydland and Prescott (1982) accepted the challenge posed by Lucas and his co-workers by building a full-scale structural model with maximizing agents doing as well as they can in a world in which technology is subject to stochastic shocks. Their model can be seen as the starting point of the real business cycle (RBC) research programme (see also Prescott (1986)). As their testing procedure they ask themselves the following question: can shocks to productivity explain fluctuations in actual economies using a model that is plausibly calibrated, i.e. that uses parameter estimates that are not inconsistent with micro observations (Kydland and Prescott, 1982, p. 1359)? The performance of the model is not gleaned by estimating its equations econometrically and testing its implied restrictions. Indeed, as Kydland and Prescott (1982, p. 1360) suggest, the model would undoubtedly have been rejected statistically both because of measurement problems and because of its abstract nature. Instead, the model is tested by comparing *model-generated* and *actual* statistics characterizing fluctuations in the economy. "Failure of the theory to mimic the behavior of the post-war US economy with respect to these stable statistics ... would be ground for its rejection".

The aim of this section is to illustrate to what extent RBC models have been successful in passing the tests proposed by Kydland and Prescott (1982). Since the Kydland-Prescott model is rather complex, we start our assessment with a much simpler RBC model based on Prescott (1986). It is shown that even this relatively simple model does surprisingly well in mimicking the fluctuations in the US economy. At the end of this section we show some deficiencies of the simple model and survey some of the possible extensions that can potentially fix them.[12]

---

[12] Of necessity, our discussion of the RBC methodology is far from complete. The interested reader is referred to Plosser (1989), Danthine and Donaldson (1993), Stadler (1994), Cooley (1995), and King and Rebelo (1999) for much more extensive surveys of the literature.

15.5.1 The unit-elastic RBC model

The model constructed in section 2 can be viewed as a deterministic version of an RBC model. To turn that model into a conventional RBC model we must reformulate it in discrete time, introduce a stochastic technology shock, and derive the rational expectations solution for the loglinearized version of the model.

In much of the early RBC literature attention was restricted to competitive models without distortions (like tax rates, useless government consumption, etc.) or externalities (like congestion, pollution, etc.). As Prescott (1986, p. 271) argues, the advantage of working with such models is that the competitive equilibrium is Pareto-optimal and unique. The solution algorithm can then exploit this equivalence between the decentralized market outcome and the social planning problem by solving the latter (easy) problem rather than the former (more difficult) problem. Here we do not pursue this approach because we wish to emphasize the link with the theoretical framework used throughout the book. As a result of this, we need to spell out the decentralized economy. (An additional advantage of doing so is that distortions, such as taxes, are easily introduced in and analysed with the model.)

The decentralized economy

The basic setup is as follows. The representative firm is perfectly competitive and produces homogeneous output, Y_τ, by renting capital, K_τ, and labour, L_τ, from the household sector. The production function is linearly homogeneous in capital and labour and features a unit elasticity of substitution:

$$Y_\tau = F(Z_\tau, K_\tau, L_\tau) \equiv Z_\tau L_\tau^{\epsilon_L} K_\tau^{1-\epsilon_L}, \quad 0 < \epsilon_L < 1, \tag{15.57}$$

where Z_τ is the state of general technology at time τ, which is known to the firm at the time of its production decision. The firm thus faces the static problem of maximizing profit, $\Pi_\tau \equiv F(K_\tau, L_\tau) - W_\tau L_\tau - R_\tau^K K_\tau$, where W_τ is the wage rate and R_τ^K is the rental charge on capital services. The first-order conditions are:

$$F_L(Z_\tau, K_\tau, L_\tau) = W_\tau, \quad F_K(Z_\tau, K_\tau, L_\tau) = R_\tau^K, \tag{15.58}$$

and the linear homogeneity of the production function ensures that profits are zero ($\Pi_\tau = 0$).

There is a large number of consumer–investor households. Each individual household is infinitely small and is a price taker on all markets in which it operates. By normalizing the population size to unity we can develop the argument on the basis of a single representative agent. The representative household is infinitely lived and has an objective function based on expected lifetime utility. Denoting the planning period by t, expected lifetime utility, $E_t \Lambda_t$, is given by:

$$E_t \Lambda_t \equiv E_t \sum_{\tau=t}^{\infty} \left(\frac{1}{1+\rho} \right)^{\tau-t} [\epsilon_C \log C_\tau + (1 - \epsilon_C) \log[1 - L_\tau]], \tag{15.59}$$

where E_t is the expectations operator, C_τ and $1 - L_\tau$ are, respectively, consumption and leisure in period τ, and $1/(1 + \rho)$ is the discounting factor due to time preference. Equation (15.59) is the discrete-time analogue to (15.1)–(15.2) modified for the existence of uncertainty (and with $\sigma_L = 1$ imposed). The notation for the expectation operator, E_t, indicates that the household bases its decisions on information available at time t.

The household receives wage and rental payments from the firm, pays lump-sum taxes to the government, and uses its after-tax income for consumption and investment purposes. The budget identity is given in discrete time (for $\tau = t, t + 1, t + 2, \ldots$) by:

$$C_\tau + I_\tau = W_\tau L_\tau + R_\tau^K K_\tau - T_\tau, \tag{15.60}$$

where I_τ is gross investment. The capital stock carried over from one period to the next equals gross investment plus the undepreciated part of the existing capital stock:

$$K_{\tau+1} = I_\tau + (1 - \delta)K_\tau, \tag{15.61}$$

with $0 < \delta < 1$. Equations (15.60) and (15.61) are the discrete-time counterparts to, respectively, (15.3) and (15.14). In the planning period, the household knows W_t and R_t^K but future rental payments on labour and capital are stochastic variables because of the future technology shocks (see (15.58) and below). The household can borrow and lend freely on the capital market and chooses sequences for consumption, labour supply, investment, and capital $\{C_\tau, L_\tau, I_\tau, K_{\tau+1}\}_t^\infty$ in order to maximize expected utility (15.59) subject to (15.60)–(15.61) and taking its initial capital stock, K_t, as given.

We follow Chow (1997) by tackling this problem with the Lagrangian methods used throughout this book. The Lagrangian expression is:

$$\mathcal{L}_t^H \equiv E_t \sum_{\tau=t}^\infty \left(\frac{1}{1+\rho}\right)^{\tau-t} \Big[\epsilon_C \log C_\tau + (1 - \epsilon_C)\log[1 - L_\tau] \tag{15.62}$$

$$- \lambda_\tau \big(K_{\tau+1} - W_\tau + T_\tau - (R_\tau^K + 1 - \delta)K_\tau + C_\tau + W_\tau[1 - L_\tau]\big)\Big],$$

where λ_τ is the Lagrange multiplier for the budget identity in period τ. The first-order conditions for this problem (for $\tau = t, t + 1, t + 2, \ldots$) are:

$$\frac{\partial \mathcal{L}_t^H}{\partial C_\tau} = \left(\frac{1}{1+\rho}\right)^{\tau-t} E_t \left[\frac{\epsilon_C}{C_\tau} - \lambda_\tau\right] = 0, \tag{15.63}$$

$$\frac{\partial \mathcal{L}_t^H}{\partial[1 - L_\tau]} = \left(\frac{1}{1+\rho}\right)^{\tau-t} E_t \left[\frac{1 - \epsilon_C}{1 - L_\tau} - \lambda_\tau W_\tau\right] = 0, \tag{15.64}$$

$$\frac{\partial \mathcal{L}_t^H}{\partial K_{\tau+1}} = \left(\frac{1}{1+\rho}\right)^{\tau-t} E_t \left[-\lambda_\tau + \left(\frac{R_{\tau+1}^K + 1 - \delta}{1 + \rho}\right)\lambda_{\tau+1}\right] = 0. \tag{15.65}$$

For the planning period ($\tau = t$) these first-order conditions can be combined to obtain one static and one dynamic equation:

$$W_t = \left(\frac{1 - \epsilon_C}{1 - L_t}\right) / \left(\frac{\epsilon_C}{C_t}\right), \tag{15.66}$$

$$\left(\frac{\epsilon_C}{C_t}\right) = E_t \left(\frac{1 + r_{t+1}}{1 + \rho}\right) \left(\frac{\epsilon_C}{C_{t+1}}\right), \tag{15.67}$$

$$r_{t+1} \equiv R^K_{t+1} - \delta. \tag{15.68}$$

Equation (15.66), which is obtained by combining (15.63) and (15.64) for period t, is the familiar condition calling for an equalization of the wage rate and the marginal rate of substitution between consumption and leisure. Note that the expectations operator does not feature in this expression. As Mankiw, Rotemberg, and Summers (1985, p. 231) explain, this is the case because (15.66) is a purely static condition as the household knows the wage rate at time t and simply chooses the optimal mix of consumption and leisure appropriately.

Equation (15.67) is obtained by using (15.63) twice (for periods t and $t + 1$) in (15.65) for period t and substituting (15.68). It is the discrete-time consumption Euler equation. Intuitively (15.67) says that along the optimal path the representative household cannot change his/her expected lifetime utility by consuming a little less and investing a little more in period $\tilde{t}$, and consuming the additional resources thus obtained in period $t+1$. The left-hand and right-hand sides of (15.67) represent, respectively, the (marginal) utility cost of giving up present consumption and the expected utility gain of future consumption (Mankiw, Rotemberg, and Summers, 1985, p. 231).

The remainder of the model is quite standard. The government is assumed to finance its consumption with lump-sum taxes, i.e. $G_\tau = T_\tau$. Finally, the goods market clearing condition is given in each period by: $Y_\tau = C_\tau + I_\tau + G_\tau$. The last two expressions are the discrete-time counterparts to, respectively, (15.16) and (15.17).

Loglinearized model

The model consists of the capital accumulation identity (15.61), the consumption Euler equation (15.67), the factor demand equations (15.58), the definition of the real interest rate (15.68), the labour supply equation (15.66), the production function (15.57), plus the goods market clearing condition and the government budget restriction.

We follow Campbell (1994) by looking for analytical solutions to the loglinearized model. The advantage of this approach is that it allows us to study the economic mechanisms behind our simulation results in a straightforward fashion. The loglinearized model is reported in Table 15.4. As before we loglinearize the model around the steady state and use the notation $\tilde{x}_t \equiv \log[x_t/x]$, where x is the steady-state value of x_t.

Table 15.4. The log-linearized stochastic model

$$\tilde{K}_{t+1} - \tilde{K}_t = \delta \left[\tilde{I}_t - \tilde{K}_t \right] \tag{T4.1}$$

$$E_t \tilde{C}_{t+1} - \tilde{C}_t = \left(\frac{\rho}{1+\rho} \right) E_t \tilde{r}_{t+1} \tag{T4.2}$$

$$\tilde{G}_t = \tilde{I}_t \tag{T4.3}$$

$$\tilde{W}_t = \tilde{Y}_t - \tilde{L}_t \tag{T4.4}$$

$$\rho \tilde{r}_t = (\rho + \delta) \left[\tilde{Y}_t - \tilde{K}_t \right] \tag{T4.5}$$

$$\tilde{Y}_t = \omega_C \tilde{C}_t + \omega_I \tilde{I}_t + \omega_G \tilde{G}_t \tag{T4.6}$$

$$\tilde{L}_t = \omega_{LL} \left[\tilde{W}_t - \tilde{C}_t \right] \tag{T4.7}$$

$$\tilde{Y}_t = \tilde{Z}_t + \epsilon_L \tilde{L}_t + (1 - \epsilon_L) \tilde{K}_t \tag{T4.8}$$

Definitions: $\omega_G \equiv G/Y$: output share of public consumption; $\omega_C \equiv C/Y$: output share of private consumption; $\omega_I \equiv I/Y$: output share of investment, $\omega_C + \omega_I + \omega_G = 1$, $\delta/\omega_I = y^* \equiv (\rho + \delta)/(1 - \epsilon_L)$. $\omega_{LL} \equiv (1 - L)/L$: ratio between leisure and labour. $\tilde{x}_t \equiv \log[x_t/x]$.

Comparing the discrete-time model of Table 15.4 to the continuous-time model of Table 15.2 reveals the close connection between the two models. Apart from the technology term appearing in (T4.8) but not in (T2.8), the only significant difference between the two models lies in the consumption Euler equation. In the continuous time model agents are blessed with perfect foresight and thus actual consumption growth ($\dot{C}(t)$) appears in the Euler equation. In contrast, in the discrete-time model the representative household does not know the future interest rate ($\tilde{r}_{t+1}$) because future general technology ($\tilde{Z}_{t+1}$) is stochastic. As a result, the expectations operator features in the Euler equation (T4.2).

The derivation of the loglinearized Euler equation (T4.2) from its level counterpart (15.67) is not straightforward and warrants some further comment. First we note that (15.67)–(15.68) can be combined to:

$$1 = E_t \left(\frac{1 + r_{t+1}}{1 + \rho} \right) \left(\frac{C_t}{C_{t+1}} \right). \tag{15.69}$$

By definition we have that $(1 + r_{t+1})/(1 + \rho) = \exp[\widetilde{1 + r_{t+1}}]$, $C_t/C = e^{\tilde{C}_t}$ and $C_{t+1}/C = e^{\tilde{C}_{t+1}}$ so we can rewrite (15.69) in a number of steps:

$$1 = E_t \exp \left[(\widetilde{1 + r_{t+1}}) + \tilde{C}_t - \tilde{C}_{t+1} \right]$$

$$= E_t \left[1 + (\widetilde{1 + r_{t+1}}) + 1 + \tilde{C}_t - 1 - \tilde{C}_{t+1} \right],$$

$$0 = E_t \left[\left(\frac{\rho}{1+\rho} \right) \tilde{r}_{t+1} + \tilde{C}_t - \tilde{C}_{t+1} \right]. \tag{15.70}$$

In going from the first to the second line, we have used the approximation $e^{\tilde{x}_t} \approx 1 + \tilde{x}_t$, and in going from the second to the third line, we relate $\widehat{1 + r_{t+1}}$ to $\tilde{r}_{t+1}$.[13]

As was the case for the deterministic continuous-time model of section 4.1, the stochastic discrete-time model of Table 15.4 can best be solved by first condensing it. This procedure yields a system of stochastic difference equations in the state variables $\tilde{K}_t$ and $\tilde{C}_t$, of which the former is a predetermined variable and the latter is a jumping variable.

By using labour demand (T4.4), labour supply (T4.7), and the production function (T4.8), we solve for the equilibrium levels of employment $\tilde{L}_t$, wages $\tilde{W}_t$, and output $\tilde{Y}_t$, *conditional* upon the two state variables *and* the existing state of general productivity $\tilde{Z}_t$:

$$\epsilon_L \tilde{L}_t = (\phi - 1)\left[\tilde{Z}_t + (1 - \epsilon_L)\tilde{K}_t - \tilde{C}_t\right], \tag{15.71}$$

$$\epsilon_L \tilde{W}_t = [1 - \phi(1 - \epsilon_L)]\left[\tilde{Z}_t + (1 - \epsilon_L)\tilde{K}_t\right] + (\phi - 1)(1 - \epsilon_L)\tilde{C}_t, \tag{15.72}$$

$$\tilde{Y}_t = \phi\left[\tilde{Z}_t + (1 - \epsilon_L)\tilde{K}_t\right] - (\phi - 1)\tilde{C}_t, \tag{15.73}$$

where ϕ is defined in (15.26) above. Ceteris paribus consumption and capital, a higher than average level of general productivity ($\tilde{Z}_t > 0$) implies that labour demand is higher than average. As a result, employment, wages, and output are also higher than average.

By using (15.73) in (T4.6) and (T4.5), respectively, we obtain the relevant expressions for investment $\tilde{I}_t$ and the interest rate $\tilde{r}_t$:

$$\omega_I \tilde{I}_t = \phi(1 - \epsilon_L)\tilde{K}_t - (\omega_C + \phi - 1)\tilde{C}_t + \phi\tilde{Z}_t - \omega_G\tilde{G}_t, \tag{15.74}$$

$$\left(\frac{\rho}{\rho + \delta}\right)\tilde{r}_t = -[1 - \phi(1 - \epsilon_L)]\tilde{K}_t - (\phi - 1)\tilde{C}_t + \phi\tilde{Z}_t. \tag{15.75}$$

General productivity affects investment and the interest rate positively because, ceteris paribus, output and capital productivity are both higher than average if $\tilde{Z}_t > 0$. By leading (15.75) by one period and taking expectations we obtain the following expression:

$$\left(\frac{\rho}{\rho + \delta}\right)E_t\tilde{r}_{t+1} = -[1 - \phi(1 - \epsilon_L)]\tilde{K}_{t+1} - (\phi - 1)E_t\tilde{C}_{t+1} + \phi E_t\tilde{Z}_{t+1}. \tag{15.76}$$

---

[13] An alternative derivation, mentioned by Campbell (1994, p. 469) and Uhlig (1999, p. 33), is due to Hansen and Singleton (1983, p. 253). (See also Attanasio, 1999, p. 768.) Under the assumption that (C_{t+1}/C_t) and $(1 + r_{t+1})$ are jointly distributed lognormally with a constant variance-covariance matrix, (15.69) can be rewritten as:

$$E_t \log (1 + r_{t+1}) = E_t \log [C_{t+1}/C_t] + \log (1 + \rho) - \frac{\sigma^2}{2},$$

where σ^2 is the (constant) variance of $\log [(C_t/C_{t+1})(1 + r_{t+1})]$. The σ^2 term is subsequently ignored by Campbell (1994) and Uhlig (1999).

Since investment is known in period t, the household knows exactly what next period's capital stock will be. Hence, the *actual* future capital stock ($\tilde{K}_{t+1}$) features in (15.76). Furthermore, the household must form expectations regarding next period's general productivity level ($E_t \tilde{Z}_{t+1}$) and labour supply. The latter effect explains why $E_t \tilde{C}_{t+1}$ enters in (15.76).

Finally, by using (15.74) in (T4.1) and (15.76) in (T4.2) we obtain the following expression for the (condensed) dynamic system of stochastic difference equations:

$$
\begin{bmatrix} \tilde{K}_{t+1} - \tilde{K}_t \\ E_t \tilde{C}_{t+1} - \tilde{C}_t \end{bmatrix} = \Delta \begin{bmatrix} \tilde{K}_t \\ \tilde{C}_t \end{bmatrix} + \begin{bmatrix} \gamma_t^K \\ \gamma_t^C \end{bmatrix},
\tag{15.77}
$$

where $\Delta \equiv \Gamma^{-1} \Delta^*$ is the Jacobian matrix and Δ^* and Γ are defined, respectively, as:

$$
\Delta^* \equiv \begin{bmatrix} \gamma^* \left(\phi(1 - \epsilon_L) - \omega_I \right) & -\gamma^*(\omega_C + \phi - 1) \\ -\zeta \left[1 - \phi(1 - \epsilon_L) \right] & -\zeta(\phi - 1) \end{bmatrix}, \quad \Gamma \equiv \begin{bmatrix} 1 & 0 \\ \gamma_{21} & 1 \end{bmatrix}
\tag{15.78}
$$

with:

$$
\gamma_{21} \equiv \zeta \left[1 - \phi(1 - \epsilon_L) \right], \quad 0 < \zeta \equiv \frac{\rho + \delta}{1 - \delta + \phi(\rho + \delta)} < 1,
\tag{15.79}
$$

and γ_t^K and γ_t^C are the shock terms:

$$
\begin{bmatrix} \gamma_t^K \\ \gamma_t^C \end{bmatrix} \equiv \Gamma^{-1} \begin{bmatrix} \gamma^* \left(\phi \tilde{Z}_t - \omega_G \tilde{G}_t \right) \\ \phi \zeta E_t \tilde{Z}_{t+1} \end{bmatrix}.
\tag{15.80}
$$

A number of things should be noted about the dynamical system defined in (15.77). First we note that the determinants of Δ and Δ^* are identical.[14] It is straightforward to verify that $|\Delta|$ equals:

$$
|\Delta| = |\Delta^*| = -\zeta \gamma^* \left[\omega_G(\phi - 1) + \phi \omega_C \epsilon_L \right] < 0.
\tag{15.81}
$$

Second, since the determinant is the product of the characteristic roots it follows from (15.81) that the system in (15.77) possesses one negative characteristic root, denoted by $-\lambda_1 < 0$, and one positive characteristic root which we denote by $\lambda_2 > 0$. If, in addition, the parameters of the problem are such that $\lambda_1 < 1$ it follows that the system is saddle-point stable.[15]

---

[14] Denoting the typical elements of Δ and Δ^* by, respectively, δ_{ij} and δ_{ij}^* we find:

$$
\Delta \equiv \Gamma^{-1} \Delta^* = \begin{bmatrix} \delta_{11}^* & \delta_{12}^* \\ \delta_{21}^* - \gamma_{21}\delta_{11}^* & \delta_{22}^* - \gamma_{21}\delta_{12}^* \end{bmatrix}.
$$

From matrix algebra we know that the subtraction of a multiple of any row from another row leaves the determinant unchanged, so it follows that $|\Delta| = |\Delta^*|$. See Mathematical Appendix.

[15] Checking saddle-point stability is thus more involved in a discrete-time setting than in a continuous-time context. With continuous time, the only thing that must be checked is the *sign* of the characteristic roots. In contrast, with discrete time, the *magnitude* of the roots matters, i.e. one must

The shock process

Our description of the unit-elastic RBC model is completed once particular specifications are adopted for the exogenous variables, $\tilde{Z}_t$ and $\hat{G}_t$. To keep things simple, we assume that government consumption is constant, so that $\hat{G}_t = 0$ for all t, and that the technology shock takes the following first-order autoregressive form:

$$\log Z_t = \alpha_Z + \rho_Z \log Z_{t-1} + \epsilon_t^Z, \quad 0 < \rho_Z < 1, \tag{15.82}$$

where α_Z is a constant, ρ_Z is the autoregressive parameter, and ϵ_t^Z is a stochastic "innovation" term. The parameter ρ_Z parameterizes the persistence in the productivity term–the closer ρ_Z is to unity, the higher is the degree of persistence. It is assumed that the innovation term, ϵ_t^Z, is identically and independently distributed with mean zero and variance σ_Z^2. In the absence of stochastic shocks, technology would settle in a steady state for which $(1 - \rho_Z) \log Z = \alpha_Z$. Since, by definition, we have that $\tilde{Z}_t \equiv \log [Z_t/Z]$, equation (15.82) can be rewritten as follows:

$$\tilde{Z}_t = \rho_Z \tilde{Z}_{t-1} + \epsilon_t^Z. \tag{15.83}$$

Recall that agents must form an expectation at time t about technology in the next period $(E_t \tilde{Z}_{t+1})$ in order to forecast the interest rate featuring in their Euler equation $(E_t \tilde{r}_{t+1}$, see (15.76)). Since agents are aware of the shock process for technology (given in (15.83)) they will use this information to compute their forecast, i.e. they will base their decisions on the forecast $E_t \tilde{Z}_{t+1} = \rho_Z \tilde{Z}_t$ (since $E_t \epsilon_{t+1}^Z = 0$ this is the best they can do).

The model is now fully specified and consists of (15.77), (15.80), and (15.83). There exist several methods that can be used to solve for the rational expectations solution of the model. Campbell (1994, pp. 470–472), for example, uses the method of undetermined coefficients. Intuitively, this method works as follows. First, we guess a solution for consumption in terms of the state variables $(\tilde{K}_t, \tilde{Z}_t)$ and unknown parameters (π_{ck}, π_{cz}), of the form $\tilde{C}_t = \pi_{ck} \tilde{K}_t + \pi_{cz} \tilde{Z}_t$. Next, we use all the structural information contained in the model plus the assumption of rational expectations in order to relate the unknown coefficients to the structural parameters of the model. Another method is due to Blanchard and Kahn (1980)—see Uhlig (1999, pp. 54–56) for an example.

check whether they are inside or outside the unit circle. Note that (15.77) is conventionally written as:

$$\begin{bmatrix} \tilde{K}_{t+1} \\ E_t \tilde{C}_{t+1} \end{bmatrix} = \bar{\Delta} \begin{bmatrix} \tilde{K}_t \\ \tilde{C}_t \end{bmatrix} + \begin{bmatrix} \gamma_t^K \\ \gamma_t^C \end{bmatrix},$$

where $\bar{\Delta} \equiv I + \Delta$ has characteristic roots $\bar{\lambda}_1 \equiv 1 - \lambda_1$ and $\bar{\lambda}_2 \equiv 1 + \lambda_2$ (see Mathematical Appendix). A stable (unstable) root satisfies $|\bar{\lambda}_i| < 1$ $(|\bar{\lambda}_i| > 1)$. Saddle-point stability thus obtains provided $|1 - \lambda_1| < 1$ and $|1 + \lambda_2| > 1$. See Azariadis (1993, pp. 39 and 62–67) for a very thorough discussion of the discrete-time case. In the text we simply assume that $\lambda_1 < 1$ and we ensure that this assumption is satisfied in the simulations.

15.5.2 Impulse-response functions

In the appendix to this chapter we work out the general rational expectations solution of the model in terms of its state variables, following the approach suggested by Campbell (1994). Here, we focus directly on the impulse-response functions for the different variables. The advantage of doing so is twofold. First, it facilitates the comparison with the analytical discussion in the first half of this chapter. Second, the impulse-response functions nicely visualize the key properties of our prototypical RBC model, especially those related to the degree of persistence of the shock.

We compute the impulse-response functions as follows. We normalize the time of the shock at $t = 0$, and assume that $\epsilon_0^Z > 0$ and $\epsilon_t^Z = 0$ for $t = 1, 2, \ldots$ Assuming that technology was at its steady-state level in the previous period ($\tilde{Z}_{-1} = 0$) we can use (15.83) to solve for the implied path of $\tilde{Z}_t$ that results from the innovation at time $t = 0$:

$$\tilde{Z}_t = \rho_Z^t \epsilon_0^Z. \tag{15.84}$$

By using (15.84) in (15.80) (and recalling that $\tilde{G}_t = 0$ and $E_t \tilde{Z}_{t+1} = \rho_Z \tilde{Z}_t$) we find that the shock term affecting the dynamical system takes the following, time-varying, form:

$$\begin{bmatrix} \gamma_t^K \\ \gamma_t^C \end{bmatrix} \equiv \phi \Gamma^{-1} \begin{bmatrix} \gamma^* \tilde{Z}_t \\ \zeta \rho_Z \tilde{Z}_t \end{bmatrix} = \phi \begin{bmatrix} \gamma^* \\ \zeta [\rho_Z - \gamma^* [1 - \phi(1 - \epsilon_L)]] \end{bmatrix} \epsilon_0^Z \rho_Z^t. \tag{15.85}$$

It follows from (15.85) that the productivity shock affects both the CSE and CE curves. Since $0 < \rho_Z < 1$, the shock eventually dies out as time goes by, i.e. $\gamma_\infty^K = \gamma_\infty^C = 0$. The innovation therefore does not have a long-run effect but the impact and transition results are non-zero. In the appendix to this chapter we derive the impulse-response function for the capital stock and consumption:

$$\begin{bmatrix} \tilde{K}_t \\ \tilde{C}_t \end{bmatrix} = \begin{bmatrix} 0 \\ \tilde{C}_0 \end{bmatrix} (1 - \lambda_1)^t + \begin{bmatrix} \gamma^* [(1 - \rho_Z)(1 - \zeta(\phi - 1)) + \rho_Z \zeta \omega_C] \\ \zeta \rho_Z [1 - \rho_Z + (1 - \omega_I)\gamma^*] \end{bmatrix}$$

$$\times \left(\frac{\phi \epsilon_0^Z}{\lambda_2 + 1 - \rho_Z} \right) T_t(\rho_Z, 1 - \lambda_1), \tag{15.86}$$

where the impact jump in consumption is given by:

$$\tilde{C}_0 = \left(\frac{\lambda_2 + \zeta [(1 - \rho_Z)(\phi - 1) - \rho_Z \omega_C]}{\omega_C + \phi - 1} \right) \left(\frac{\phi \epsilon_0^Z}{\lambda_2 + 1 - \rho_Z} \right), \tag{15.87}$$

and $T_t(\alpha_1, \alpha_2)$ is a non-negative bell-shaped term:

$$T_t(\alpha_1, \alpha_2) \equiv \begin{cases} 0 & \text{for } t = 0 \\ \begin{cases} \dfrac{\alpha_1^t - \alpha_2^t}{\alpha_1 - \alpha_2} & \text{for } \alpha_1 \neq \alpha_2 \\ t\alpha_1^{t-1} & \text{for } \alpha_1 = \alpha_2 \end{cases} & \text{for } t = 1, 2, \ldots \end{cases} \tag{15.88}$$

Although these expressions look rather complex, it turns out that quite a lot can be understood about them by first focusing on some special cases that have received a lot of attention in the literature. In doing so we are able to demonstrate the crucial role of shock persistence in the unit-elastic RBC model.

A purely temporary shock ($\rho_Z = 0$)

We follow King and Rebelo (1999, pp. 964–967) by first considering the effects of a purely transitory productivity shock. In terms of our model this means that the shock displays no serial correlation at all (i.e. $\rho_Z = 0$ in (15.83)) and we study the response of the system to a technology shock of the form $\tilde{Z}_0 = \epsilon_0^Z$ and $\tilde{Z}_t = 0$ for $t = 1, 2, \ldots$ Clearly, such a shock has no long-run effect on the macroeconomy as technology only deviates in the impact period from its steady-state level. The impact effect on consumption, and thus on the other variables, is, however, non-zero. Indeed, by setting $\rho_Z = 0$ in (15.87) we obtain the expression for the consumption jump with a purely transitory shock:

$$\tilde{C}_0 = \frac{\phi \left[\lambda_2 + \zeta(\phi - 1) \right] \epsilon_0^Z}{(1 + \lambda_2) \left[\omega_C + \phi - 1 \right]} > 0. \tag{15.89}$$

Intuitively, consumption rises in the impact period because the technology shock, brief though it may be, makes the agent richer. Since leisure, like consumption, is a normal good, the shock also causes a wealth effect in labour supply. In terms of Figure 15.11 the labour supply curve shifts up and to the left (from the solid to the dashed line). At the same time, however, the shock raises labour productivity and thus labour demand. Hence, even though the capital stock is predetermined in the impact period, the labour demand curve shifts up and to the right. As is clear from the diagram, the impact effect on the wage rate is unambiguously positive, but the impact effect on employment appears to be ambiguous as it depends on the relative magnitudes of the labour supply and demand effects.

By using (15.89) and $\tilde{Z}_0 = \epsilon_0^Z$ in (15.71)–(15.73) we obtain the following analytical expressions for $\tilde{L}_0$, $\tilde{W}_0$, and $\tilde{Y}_0$:

$$\tilde{L}_0 = \left(\frac{\phi - 1}{\epsilon_L} \right) \left[1 - \frac{\phi \left[\lambda_2 + \zeta(\phi - 1) \right]}{(1 + \lambda_2) \left[\omega_C + \phi - 1 \right]} \right] \epsilon_0^Z, \tag{15.90}$$

$$\tilde{W}_0 = \left[\frac{1 - \phi(1 - \epsilon_L)}{\epsilon_L} \right] \epsilon_0^Z + \left[\frac{(\phi - 1)(1 - \epsilon_L)}{\epsilon_L} \right] \tilde{C}_0 > 0, \tag{15.91}$$

$$\tilde{Y}_0 = \left[\frac{(1 + \lambda_2)\omega_C + (\phi - 1) \left[1 - \zeta(\phi - 1) \right]}{(1 + \lambda_2) \left[\omega_C + \phi - 1 \right]} \right] \phi \epsilon_0^Z > 0. \tag{15.92}$$

For realistic calibrations of the model the labour-demand effect dominates the labour-supply effect, so that employment increases in the impact period as illustrated in Figure 15.11. The wage rate increases at impact regardless of the parameter values as the labour-demand and supply effects work in the same direction. Finally, despite the fact that the employment effect is ambiguous in general, the output

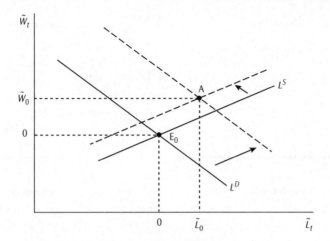

Figure 15.11. A shock to technology and the labour market

effect is unambiguously positive.[16] Since output rises and capital is predetermined at impact, the immediate effect on the interest rate is positive (see e.g. (T4.5)). Finally, the impact effect on investment is obtained by using (15.89) and setting $\tilde{Z}_0 = \epsilon_0^Z$ and $\tilde{G}_t = 0$ in (15.74). After some manipulation we obtain:

$$\tilde{I}_0 = \left[\frac{1 - \zeta(\phi - 1)}{\omega_I (1 + \lambda_2)} \right] \phi \epsilon_0^Z > 0, \tag{15.93}$$

where the sign follows from the fact that $0 < \zeta(\phi - 1) < 1$ (see footnote 16).

By substituting $\rho_Z = 0$ into (15.86) and (15.88) (and noting (15.93)) we find the transition paths for the capital stock and consumption:

$$\begin{bmatrix} \tilde{K}_t \\ \tilde{C}_t \end{bmatrix} = \begin{bmatrix} \left(\frac{\delta}{1 - \lambda_1} \right) \tilde{I}_0 \\ \tilde{C}_0 \end{bmatrix} (1 - \lambda_1)^t, \quad \text{for } t = 1, 2, 3, \dots \tag{15.94}$$

In Figure 15.12 we plot the impulse-response functions for the purely transitory shock, using the calibration values discussed above (see page 493). One period after the shock has occurred, technology is back to its steady-state level (as $\tilde{Z}_t = 0$ for $t = 1, 2, \dots$). It follows from (15.94) that the economy has a slightly higher capital stock in period 1 (since $\tilde{K}_1 = \delta \tilde{I}_0 > 0$) which is gradually run down over time. Consumption also gradually returns to its initial steady-state value. As the simulations confirm, investment and employment fall below their respective steady-state levels during transition ($\tilde{I}_t < 0$ and $\tilde{L}_t < 0$ for $t = 1, 2, \dots$). The real interest rate also falls below its steady-state level in period $t = 1$ after which it gradually returns to

---

[16] The sign of the output effect follows in a straightforward fashion from the fact that ζ, defined in (15.79), satisfies $0 < \zeta(\phi - 1) < 1$.

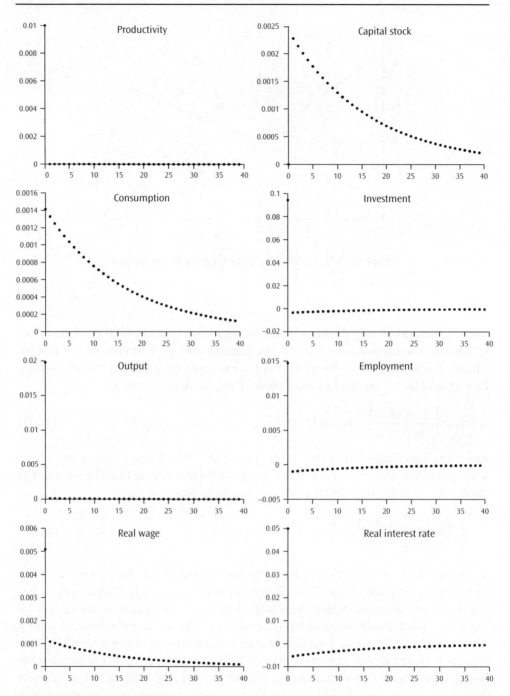

Figure 15.12. Purely transitory productivity shock

this level. Since $\tilde{r}_t < 0$ for $t = 1, 2, \ldots$ it is optimal for the household to choose a downward-sloping consumption profile.[17]

A permanent shock ($\rho_Z = 1$)

The second special case that can be distinguished assumes that the technology shocks are permanent, i.e. the technology process (15.83) features a unit root ($\rho_Z = 1$). The impact effect on consumption is obtained from (15.87):

$$\tilde{C}_0 = \frac{\phi [\lambda_2 - \zeta \omega_C] \epsilon_0^Z}{\lambda_2 [\omega_C + \phi - 1]} > 0. \tag{15.95}$$

Consumption rises at impact because the permanent technology shock makes the representative agent wealthier. By substituting (15.95) into (15.71)–(15.73) we obtain the impact effects for employment, the wage, and output:

$$\tilde{L}_0 = \left(\frac{\phi - 1}{\epsilon_L} \right) \left[1 - \frac{\phi [\lambda_2 - \zeta \omega_C]}{\lambda_2 [\omega_C + \phi - 1]} \right] \epsilon_0^Z, \tag{15.96}$$

$$\tilde{W}_0 = \left[\frac{1 - \phi(1 - \epsilon_L)}{\epsilon_L} \right] \epsilon_0^Z + \left[\frac{(\phi - 1)(1 - \epsilon_L)}{\epsilon_L} \right] \tilde{C}_0 > 0, \tag{15.97}$$

$$\tilde{Y}_0 = \left[\frac{\lambda_2 + \zeta(\phi - 1)}{\lambda_2 [\omega_C + \phi - 1]} \right] \phi \omega_C \epsilon_0^Z > 0. \tag{15.98}$$

As for the purely temporary shock, the employment effect is ambiguous in general but positive for realistic calibrations. The wage rate rises unambiguously as does output. Finally, the impact effect on investment is obtained by using (15.95) and setting $\tilde{Z}_0 = \epsilon_0^Z$ and $\tilde{G}_t = 0$ in (15.74):

$$\tilde{I}_0 = \frac{\zeta \phi \omega_C \epsilon_0^Z}{\omega_I \lambda_2} > 0. \tag{15.99}$$

By setting $\rho_Z = 1$ in (15.86) and (15.88) we obtain analytical expressions for the transition paths of the capital stock and consumption:

$$\begin{bmatrix} \tilde{K}_t \\ \tilde{C}_t \end{bmatrix} = \begin{bmatrix} 0 \\ \tilde{C}_0 \end{bmatrix} (1 - \lambda_1)^t + \begin{bmatrix} \tilde{K}_\infty \\ \tilde{C}_\infty \end{bmatrix} \left[1 - (1 - \lambda_1)^t \right], \tag{15.100}$$

where $\tilde{C}_0$ is given in (15.95) above, and $\tilde{K}_\infty$ and $\tilde{C}_\infty$ are given by:

$$\tilde{K}_\infty = \left(\frac{\omega_C}{1 - \omega_I} \right) \tilde{C}_\infty = \frac{\phi \omega_C \epsilon_0^Z}{\omega_G(\phi - 1) + \phi \omega_C \epsilon_L} > 0. \tag{15.101}$$

As equation (15.100) shows, $\tilde{K}_t$ and $\tilde{C}_t$ (and thus all other variables also) can be written as the weighted average of the relevant impact and long-run effects. The

---

[17] King and Rebelo (1999, pp. 966–967) incorrectly argue that the interest rate falls in the impact period. Since output rises and the capital stock is unchanged at impact, it must be the case that the interest rate rises at impact also.

transition speed of the economy, $(1-\lambda_1)$, determines the time-varying weights. With a permanent productivity shock both consumption and the capital stock increase in the long run—see (15.101). The intuition behind this result follows readily from the steady-state constancy of the great ratios (see also above). Imposing the steady state in equations (T4.1)–(T4.2) (and ignoring the expectations operator) we find $\tilde{I}_\infty = \tilde{K}_\infty$ and $\tilde{r}_\infty = 0$. But this implies, by (T4.5), that $\tilde{Y}_\infty = \tilde{K}_\infty$, and by (T4.4) and (T4.8) that $\tilde{K}_\infty - \tilde{L}_\infty = \tilde{W}_\infty = (1/\epsilon_L)\tilde{Z}_\infty$, where $\tilde{Z}_\infty = \epsilon_0^Z$. With constant government spending ($\tilde{G}_t = 0$), the steady-state versions of (T4.6) and (15.73) can be solved for $\tilde{C}_\infty$ and $\tilde{Y}_\infty$:

$$\tilde{Y}_\infty = \left(\frac{\omega_C}{\omega_C + \omega_G}\right)\tilde{C}_\infty = \frac{\phi\omega_C \tilde{Z}_\infty}{\omega_G(\phi - 1) + \phi\omega_C\epsilon_L} > 0, \tag{15.102}$$

and (T4.7) can be solved for $\tilde{L}_\infty$:

$$\tilde{L}_\infty = \frac{\tilde{Y}_\infty - \tilde{C}_\infty}{1 + \omega_{LL}} = -\left(\frac{\omega_G}{\omega_C + \omega_G}\right)\left(\frac{\tilde{C}_\infty}{1 + \omega_{LL}}\right) \leq 0. \tag{15.103}$$

In the long run a permanent productivity improvement makes the representative agent wealthier which prompts him to increase consumption. The investment–capital ratio and the output–capital ratio are unchanged but the capital–labour ratio rises as does the real wage. In the absence of government consumption ($\omega_G = 0$) the income and substitution effects in labour supply exactly cancel out and employment is unchanged (see (15.103)). With positive government consumption the income effect dominates the substitution effect and labour supply goes down (i.e. the household consumes more leisure).

In Figure 15.13 we present the impulse-response functions for the permanent shock, again using the calibration values discussed above (see page 493). Following their initial jumps, consumption and the wage both gradually increase further during transition. Investment and employment both overshoot their respective long-run levels. Though the impact effect on employment is positive, employment falls in the long run because the calibration is based on a positive share of government consumption (see (15.103)). The real interest jumps up at impact and gradually returns to its initial level. This explains why the time profile of consumption is upward sloping.

A realistic shock

Now that we have discussed the impulse-response functions for purely transitory and permanent technology shock, we can proceed and study the reaction of the economy to *realistic* productivity shocks. The seminal work by Solow (1957) has been used by RBC proponents to estimate the nature of technological change. Solow (1957) tried to determine how much of economic growth can be accounted for by fluctuations in the production factors capital and labour. He found that the

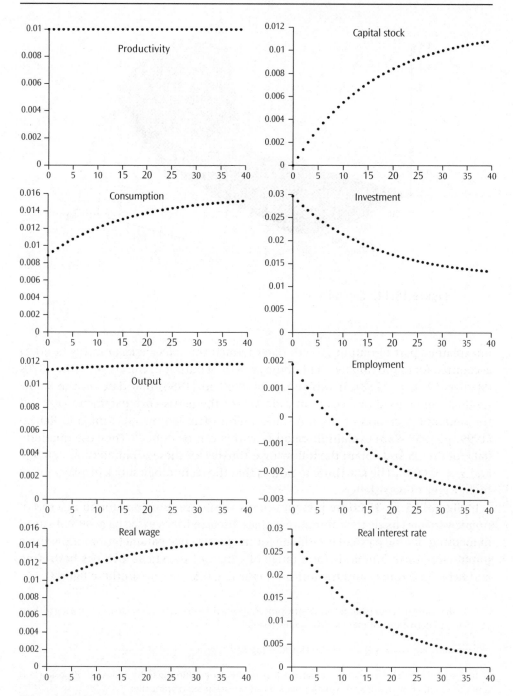

Figure 15.13. Permanent productivity shock

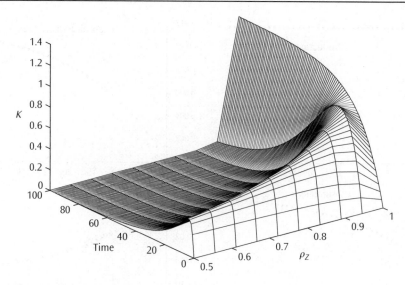

Figure 15.14. Capital stock

unexplained part of output growth (later termed the *Solow residual* in his honour) accounted for approximately half of the growth of output in the US since the 1870s (Stadler, 1994, p. 1753). It was shown by Prescott (1986) that data on the Solow residual can be used to recover an estimate for the persistence parameter (ρ_Z) and the standard deviation of the innovation term (denoted by σ_Z). King and Rebelo (1999, pp. 952–953) explain in detail how this can be done.[18] They use quarterly data for the US and obtain the following estimates for these parameters: $\rho_Z = 0.979$ and $\sigma_Z = 0.0072$. The key thing to note is that the technology shock displays a very high degree of persistence.

In Figures 15.14–15.20 we present impulse-response functions for all macroeconomic variables using the calibration values discussed above (see page 493). Instead of focusing on one particular estimate for the persistence parameter, we show these impulse-response functions for a range of values of ρ_Z which includes both King and Rebelo's estimate and the unit-root case (i.e. $0.5 \leq \rho_Z \leq 1$ in these figures).

---

[18] In the context of our (simple) model the procedure would work as follows. First, we take logarithms of (15.57) to derive the estimate for the Solow residual:

$$\log SR_t \equiv \log Y_t - \epsilon_L \log L_t - (1 - \epsilon_L) \log K_t = \log Z_t.$$

Hence, in our model the Solow residual is equal to the general productivity index Z_t. By using this result in (15.82) one obtains an equation which can be estimated empirically:

$$\log SR_t = \alpha_Z + \rho_Z \log SR_{t-1} + \epsilon_t^Z.$$

The procedure of King and Rebelo (1999) is a little more complicated because they also allow for labour-augmenting technological change.

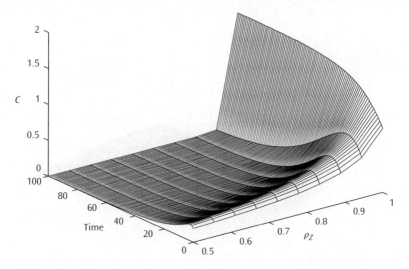

Figure 15.15. Consumption

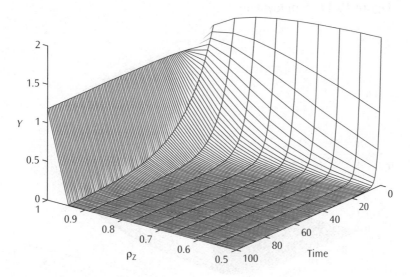

Figure 15.16. Output

As King and Rebelo (1999, p. 969) point out, the shape of each impulse-response function is very sensitive to ρ_Z for the high-persistence case (i.e. if ρ_Z is near unity). Hence, impulse responses associated with, respectively, $\rho_Z = 0.979$ and $\rho_Z = 1$, are very different in shape. In contrast, for relatively transient shocks this non-linearity does not show up in Figures 15.14–15.20, i.e. impulse responses for $\rho_Z = 0.5$ and $\rho_Z = 0.7$ look very much alike. Intuitively, the non-linearity in the high-persistence case is due to the fact that permanent shocks cause non-zero long-run effects whilst transitory shocks (no matter how persistent they are) do not.

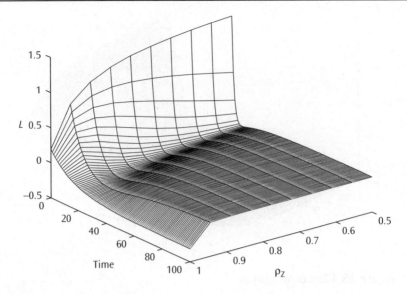

Figure 15.17. Employment

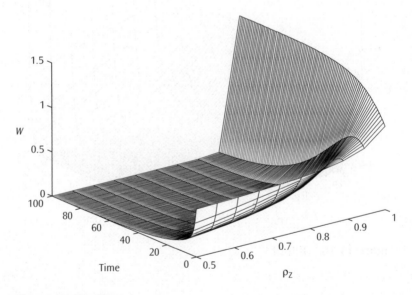

Figure 15.18. Wage

Lack of propagation

Perhaps the most important (and somewhat disappointing) feature of the unit-elastic RBC model is its *lack of internal propagation*, a point first made in a more general setting by Cogley and Nason (1995). For example, as is clear from

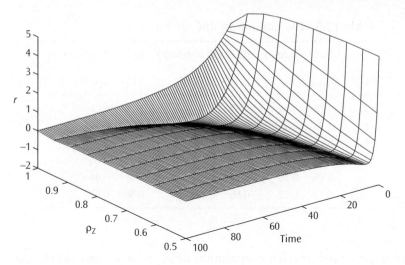

Figure 15.19. Interest rate

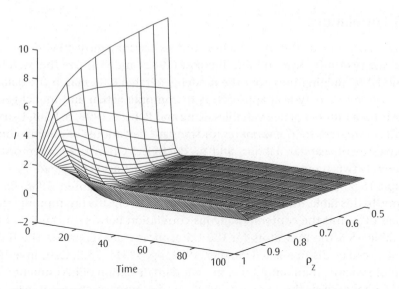

Figure 15.20. Investment

Figure 15.12 the impulse-response function of output looks virtually identical to the exogenous productivity shock itself. Although it is impossible to see in the figure, there is some transitional dynamics in output after period $t = 1$ but it is of a very small magnitude. Exactly the same result is found in Figure 15.13 which deals with permanent shocks. For this reason, research has focused in recent years on

Table 15.5. The unit-elastic RBC model

x_t:	(a) US economy		(b) Model economy I		(c) Model economy II	
	$\sigma(x_t)$	$\rho(x_t, Y_t)$	$\sigma(x_t)$	$\rho(x_t, Y_t)$	$\sigma(x_t)$	$\rho(x_t, Y_t)$
Y_t	1.76		1.35		1.76	
C_t	1.29	0.85	0.42	0.89	0.51	0.87
I_t	8.60	0.92	4.24	0.99	5.71	0.99
K_t	0.63	0.04	0.36	0.06	0.47	0.05
L_t	1.66	0.76	0.70	0.98	1.35	0.98
Y_t/L_t	1.18	0.42	0.68	0.98	0.50	0.87

ways to improve the internal propagation mechanism of the model. Some of this literature will be discussed briefly below.

15.5.3 Correlations

As was pointed out in the introduction to this section, most RBC modellers follow the suggestion by Kydland and Prescott (1982) and evaluate the usefulness of their model by judging how well the model-generated data match the data for an actual economy. The typical approach is to compute actual and model-generated moments for a number of key variables (King and Rebelo, 1999, p. 956). Usually the moments of interest are the *variances* (or standard deviations) of output, consumption, investment, capital, labour, and productivity. Often the contemporaneous *correlations* between output and the other variables are also compared.[19]

In Table 15.5 we show the results that were computed by Hansen (1985) for the US economy. In this table, $\sigma(x_t)$ and $\rho(x_t, Y_t)$ are, respectively, the (asymptotic) standard deviation of x_t and the contemporaneous correlation between x_t and Y_t. In panel (a) of Table 15.5 the indicators for the US economy are reported. The following regularities can be distinguished (Stadler, 1994, pp. 1751–1752). First, investment is much more volatile than output, i.e. the standard deviation of investment is $\sigma(I_t) = 8.60$ which far exceeds the standard deviation of output which equals $\sigma(Y_t) = 1.76$. Second, consumption is somewhat less volatile than output ($\sigma(C_t) = 1.29$). Third, the capital stock is much less volatile than both consumption and output ($\sigma(K_t) = 0.63$). Fourth, employment is approximately as volatile as output ($\sigma(L_t) = 1.66$). Fifth, productivity is less volatile than output ($\sigma(Y_t/L_t) = 1.18$). Sixth, all variables are positively correlated with output, although the correlation is rather weak for the capital stock.

---

[19] In the appendix to this chapter we show how these various indicators can be computed for the theoretical model without having to use statistical simulation methods.

Chapter 15: Real Business Cycles

In panel (b) of Table 15.5 the model-generated standard deviations and correlations are reported. Hansen (1985, pp. 319–320) uses the unit-elastic model to generate these results and employs the following calibration parameters: $\omega_G = 0$, $\epsilon_L = 0.64$, $\rho = 0.01$, $\delta = 0.025$, and $\epsilon_C = 1/3$. These parameters imply: $y^* = (\rho + \delta)/(1 - \epsilon_L) = 0.097$, $\omega_I = \delta/y^* = 0.257$, $\omega_C = 1 - \omega_I = 0.743$, and (by (15.46)) $\omega_{LL} = 2.321$. The persistence parameter and standard deviation of the technology shock (ϵ_t^Z in (15.83)) are set at, respectively, $\rho_Z = 0.95$ and $\sigma_Z = 0.00712$.

A comparison of panels (a) and (b) reveals that the model captures the facts that consumption is less and investment is more volatile than the aggregate output. It also matches the output correlations of consumption, investment, capital, and employment quite well but it overpredicts the correlation between output and productivity. Given the extremely simple structure of the unit-elastic model, the match between actual and model-generated moments is quite impressive. There are, however, also a number of facts that are not well explained by the model. Following Stadler (1994, pp. 1757–1761) we focus on some stylized facts about the labour market which the model is unable to mimic.

Employment variability puzzle

In reality employment and output are almost equally variable (see Table 15.5), and employment is strongly procyclical, whilst wages are only mildly procyclical. If general productivity shocks are the source of the variability, then a positive shock should shift labour demand, and for a given upward-sloping labour supply curve, there should be a reaction in both wages and employment. Microeconomic evidence, however, suggests that the labour supply curve is almost vertical, so that the variability in wages should be high and that in employment should be low. In panel (b) of Table 15.5 we therefore observe that the unit-elastic model underpredicts the variability of employment by a significant factor, i.e. the model predicts $\sigma(L_t) = 0.70$ whereas in reality for the US $\sigma(L_t) = 1.66$.[20]

Procyclical real wage

The unit-elastic model with productivity shocks as the source of fluctuations predicts a high correlation between productivity and output (in panel (b) of Table 15.5 $\rho(Y_t/L_t, Y_t) = 0.87$). In reality, however, this correlation is much weaker. Since technology is represented by a Cobb-Douglas production function in the unit-elastic model, the real wage is proportional to productivity (see (T4.4) above). It thus follows that the unit-elastic model generates wage fluctuations that are much more procyclical than is consistent with reality.

---

[20] Below we discuss Hansen's (1985) approach to bringing the model outcomes closer to reality. See section 15.5.4 as well as Hansen and Wright (1994) and Stadler (1994, pp. 1757–1762).

Productivity puzzle

If productivity shocks are the predominant source of fluctuations, the shifts in labour demand would imply that hours worked and productivity move closely together. If real wage changes are small, all variation in employment is due to labour demand shocks, and the correlation between productivity and both hours worked and output should be high. In reality, however, the first correlation (productivity-hours) is absent or even negative and the second correlation (productivity-output) is much weaker than predicted.

Unemployment

Since there is no unemployment in the unit-elastic model, all variation in employment is explained by fluctuations in the supply of labour by the representative household. In reality, however, about two thirds of the variation in hours is due to movements into (and out of) employment and only one third is explained by variation in the number of hours worked per employed worker (Stadler, 1994, p. 1758).

15.5.4 Extending the model

Stadler (1994), Hansen and Wright (1994), and King and Rebelo (1999) discuss the several model extensions that have been proposed in the RBC literature over the past two decades. Here, we focus attention on just some of the ways in which RBC modellers have responded to the various puzzles discussed above.

Employment variability puzzle

One would observe a realistic correlation between real wages and employment if the labour supply curve is relatively flat. There are several ways to get this. First, there may be strong intertemporal substitution effects in labour supply, but this is rejected by the econometric evidence to date (Card, 1994). Second, the dominant RBC solution to the employment variability puzzle is provided by Hansen (1985) who incorporated the insights of Rogerson (1988) into an RBC model. His argument makes use of the fact that in reality about two thirds of the variation of total hours worked is due to movements into and out of employment, whilst only one third is explained by variation in the number of hours worked. Hansen (1985) assumes that the length of the working week is constant: you either have a job and work for, say, 38 hours per week, or you do not work at all. This non-convexity in the form of *indivisible labour* (IL) ensures that workers wish to work as much as possible when wages are high. Hansen shows that even if individual agents have a zero intertemporal labour supply elasticity, the aggregate economy behaves as if the (average) "representative agent" has an infinite intertemporal labour supply elasticity. Individual households do not choose the number of working hours per period, but rather the probability of working. Who actually works is determined by a lottery. There is a contract between the firm and a household that specifies that the household must work $\bar{L}$ hours with probability π_t in period t. The firm provides complete insurance to the worker and the lottery contract is traded, so that each household gets the same amount from the firm, regardless of whether it works or not in any particular period. Actual per capita employment in period t will be $L_t = \pi_t \bar{L}$, and each household gets paid as if it worked L_t hours in period t.

The IL model is obtained by setting $\sigma_L \to \infty$ in (15.2) so that the felicity function appearing in (15.59) is linear in labour supply:

$$\Phi(\tau) \equiv \epsilon_C \log C_\tau - (1 - \epsilon_C) L_\tau. \tag{15.104}$$

With this modification, the consumption Euler equation continues to be given by (15.67) but leisure drops out of equation (15.66) which becomes:

$$\frac{W_t}{C_t} = \frac{1 - \epsilon_C}{\epsilon_C}. \tag{15.105}$$

In the IL model, consumption is proportional to the wage, i.e. the labour supply equation is horizontal. In terms of the loglinearized model of Table 15.4, equation (T4.7) is replaced by $\tilde{W}_t = \tilde{C}_t$. Hence, in formal terms, the IL model is a special case of the model presented in Table 15.4 with $\omega_{LL} \to \infty$.

In panel (c) of Table 15.5 we show the results that were obtained by Hansen's (1985) calibration of the IL model. With the exception of ϵ_C (and thus ω_{LL}) the calibration parameters are the same as for panel (b). The parameter ϵ_C is chosen such that employed individuals spend 53 percent of their time endowment on work, i.e. $\bar{L} = 0.53$ (Hansen, 1985, p. 320).[21] This yields the value of $\epsilon_C = 0.381$. It is clear from Table 15.5 that the IL model provides a much better match between the model-generated and actual variability of employment than the standard model does.[22] By incorporating the assumption of indivisible labour in the unit-elastic model, the model-generated standard deviation of employment rises from $\sigma(L_t) = 0.70$ (in panel (b)) to $\sigma(L_t) = 1.35$ (in panel (c)). The IL model is thus able to dispose of the employment variability puzzle but not of the procyclical real wage. Indeed, the results in panel (c) of Table 15.5 show that the IL model predicts a very similar correlation between productivity and output as the standard unit-elastic

---

[21] By manipulating (15.105) we find that the value of ϵ_C can be written as follows:

$$\epsilon_C = \left[1 + \frac{\epsilon_L}{\bar{L}\omega_C} \right]^{-1}.$$

Since ω_C and ϵ_L are known, the value of ϵ_C is readily obtained from this expression.

[22] Note that the actual and model-generated standard deviation of output are the same in panels (a) and (c) of Table 15.5. This cannot be counted as a success for the unit-elastic model because it is a feature of the calibration procedure. The standard deviation of the productivity shock (σ_Z) is chosen such that the variation in aggregate output is perfectly matched (Hansen, 1985, p. 320). In a model with divisible labour (given in panel (b)) a larger standard deviation of the innovation term is needed to match the observed standard deviation of output.

model does (i.e. $\rho(Y_t/L_t, Y_t) = 0.87$ in panel (c) and $\rho(Y_t/L_t, Y_t) = 0.98$ in panel (b)). Because it largely solves the employment variability puzzle, Hansen's approach has nevertheless become standard practice in the RBC literature.

Productivity puzzle

RBC theorists have also found creative solutions to the productivity puzzle, which are often based on introducing shift factors in the labour supply equation. Examples that are found in the literature include the existence of nominal wage contracts, taste shocks, government spending shocks, labour hoarding by firms, and the existence of a non-market production sector that is also subject to technology shocks (see Stadler, 1994, pp. 1759–1761). In home production models, for example, households divide their labour over market and non-market activities. If market productivity rises, agents not only intertemporally substitute labour, but also shift labour intratemporally from the non-market to the market sector.

Unemployment

In recent years, a number of authors have introduced voluntary unemployment into the RBC framework by making use of the search-theoretic approach of Diamond, Mortensen, and Pissarides (see Chapter 9).[23] Andolfatto (1996, p. 113) shows that the introduction of labour market search into an RBC model leads to three major improvements. First, the model is able to predict that labour hours fluctuate more than wages. Second, the model predicts a lower correlation between labour hours and productivity. Third, the model predicts a more realistic impulse-response function for output.

Involuntary unemployment can be built into RBC-style models as well. Danthine and Donaldson (1990), for example, use the device of efficiency wages (see Chapter 7) to explain equilibrium unemployment. In such models, the real wage does not clear the labour market but rather is used to induce high effort by the workers. Such models typically predict some kind of real wage rigidity which can help explain the low correlation between wages and employment and magnifies the impact of shocks on output. The latter effect also ensures that productivity shocks do not have to be unrealistically large in order to explain given fluctuations in output.

15.6 Punchlines

This chapter deals with the two major themes which have been developed by new classical economists over the last two decades, namely the equilibrium approach to

[23] See, e.g. Andolfatto (1996), Merz (1995, 1997, 1999), and Cole and Rogerson (1999).

fiscal policy and real business cycle theory. These two themes build on and extend the insights that were obtained as a result of the rational expectations revolution of the 1970s.

In order to discuss the equilibrium approach to fiscal policy, we started this chapter by extending the deterministic Ramsey model that was studied in detail in the previous chapter. To make this model more suitable for fiscal policy analysis the labour supply decision of households is endogenized. We use (a simple version of) the extended Ramsey model to study the effects of a lump-sum tax financed increase in government consumption. Both permanent and temporary policy shocks are considered. Furthermore, the impact, transitional, and long-run effects are characterized both analytically and quantitatively.

With a permanent increase in government consumption, the increase in taxes causes households to cut back goods consumption and to supply more labour because they feel poorer (the wealth effect). Output and investment both rise and the capital stock starts to increase during transition and consumption recovers somewhat. In the long run, consumption is still crowded out (though by less than one for one) and output, capital, employment, and investment all increase equi-proportionally due to the constancy of a number of "great ratios". A plausibly calibrated version of the model shows that the long-run output multiplier may well exceed unity. Though this result is superficially reminiscent of the Keynes–Haavelmoo multiplier, the mechanism behind the output multiplier is distinctly new classical in nature. Whereas the marginal propensity to consume out of income plays the vital role in the former multiplier, it is the wealth effect in labour supply which determines the latter multiplier.

When the increase in government consumption is only temporary there are no long-run effects. Consumption is crowded out and labour supply and thus output rise in the impact period. These effects are stronger the more persistent is the policy shock. If labour supply is highly elastic and the shock is relatively persistent then the household starts to accumulate capital during the early part of the transition. The increase in output and decrease in consumption together more than compensate the increased government consumption and investment is crowded in at impact. If the labour supply effect is weak and the shock is highly transitory then the capital stock falls during the early phases of the transition.

In the second half of the chapter we turn the extended Ramsey model into a prototypical real business cycle model by reformulating it in discrete time, introducing a stochastic process for general productivity, and imposing the assumption of rational expectations. We study the properties of the so-called unit-elastic RBC model by computing the analytical impulse-response functions for the different macroeconomic variables. Just as for the deterministic model, the degree of persistence of the technology shock exerts a critical influence on the shape of the impulse-response functions.

For a purely transitory technology shock, consumption, employment, investment, and output all rise in the impact period. The employment response is explained not so much by the wealth effect (which is rather weak) but rather by the incentive to substitute labour supply across time. The technology shock makes it attractive to work in the current period because the current wage is high relative to future wages. After technology has returned to its initial level, capital and consumption gradually fall back over time.

With a permanent productivity shock, consumption, capital, output, investment, and the real wage all rise in the long run. In the absence of government consumption (and the concomitant lump-sum taxes), employment stays the same because the income and substitution effects of the wage change cancel out. With positive lump-sum taxes the former dominates the latter effect and employment falls. The intuition behind the long-run results is again provided by the constancy of a number of great ratios. Consumption jumps up at impact and thereafter increases further during transition.

Next we study the impulse-response functions for a "realistic" shock persistence parameter. Most RBC modellers use the so-called Solow residual to obtain an estimate for this persistence parameter. The typical finding is that productivity shocks (thus measured) are very persistent, i.e. the persistence parameter is close to (but strictly less than) unity.

An important, somewhat disappointing, feature of the unit-elastic RBC model is its lack of internal propagation. For all cases considered, the impulse-response function for output is virtually identical to the exogenous technology shock itself. The lack of propagation plagues not just the uni-elastic model but many other RBC models as well. For this reason, one of the currently active areas of research in the RBC literature concerns the development of models with stronger and more realistic internal propagation mechanisms.

It is standard practice to evaluate the quantitative performance of a given RBC model in terms of the quality of the match it provides between model-generated and actual data. Typically, the statistics of interest are the standard deviations (and correlations with aggregate output) of some key macroeconomic variables. Despite its simplicity, the unit-elastic model is able to capture quite a few features of the real world data. For example, it correctly predicts that investment is more and consumption is less volatile than aggregate output. It also matches the output correlations of consumption, investment, capital, and employment quite closely. There are also a number of empirical facts that are difficult or impossible to reconcile with the unit-elastic model. For that reason a huge literature has emerged over the last two decades which aims to improve the empirical fit of RBC models.

Perhaps the most important contribution of the RBC approach is a methodological one. Recall that in the traditional macroeconometric approach, weakly founded relationships were typically estimated with the aid of time series data. RBC modellers have largely abandoned the macroeconometric approach and have instead forged a link with micro-founded stochastic computable equilibrium models. Attention has shifted from estimation to simulation. The approach has proved to be quite flexible. RBC models now exist which include alternative market structures (on goods and labour markets), price and wage stickiness, open-economy features, more than just technology shocks, and heterogeneous households. The broad range of applications indicates that the RBC methodology has received widespread acceptance from classical and Keynesian economists alike.

Further Reading

Some of the most important early articles on the RBC approach have been collected in Miller (1994). For survey articles, see King, Plosser, and Rebelo (1987, 1988a, 1988b), McCallum (1989b), Plosser (1989), Eichenbaum (1991), Danthine and Donaldson (1993), Campbell (1994), Stadler (1994), Cooley (1995), and King and Rebelo (1999). Early critics of the approach are Summers (1986) and Mankiw (1989). For a recent discussion on the method of calibration, see Kydland and Prescott (1996), Hansen and Heckman (1996), and Sims (1996). Watson (1993) develops a measures of fit for calibrated models. Cogley and Nason (1995) and Rotemberg and Woodford (1996) document the weak propagation mechanisms of a number of standard RBC models.

There is a huge and growing literature on various labour market aspects. The intertemporal substitution mechanism is studied in detail by Hall (1991, 1997) and Mulligan (1998). On family labour supply, see Cho and Rogerson (1988) and Cho and Cooley (1994). Nominal wage contracts are studied by Cho and Cooley (1995) and Huang and Liu (1999). On search unemployment, see Andolfatto (1996), Merz (1995, 1997, 1999), and Cole and Rogerson (1999). Efficiency wage theories are used by Danthine and Donaldson (1990), Kimball (1994), and Georges (1995).

Early papers on the macroeconomic effects of government purchases, using a deterministic approach, include Foley and Sidrauski (1971), Hall (1971), Miller and Upton (1974), Barro (1981), and Aschauer (1988). Recent stochastic models include Cassou and Lansing (1998) (on public infrastructure), Christiano and Eichenbaum (1992), McGrattan (1994), Braun (1994), Jonsson and Klein (1996), and Canton (2001). Edelberg, Eichenbaum, and Fisher (1998) study the empirical effects of a shock to government purchases.

Temporary shocks and the interaction between the graphic and mathematical approaches are also studied by Judd (1985) and Bovenberg and Heijdra (forthcoming). Key articles on home production are Benhabib, Rogerson, and Wright (1991) and Greenwood and Hercowitz (1991). Models with distorting taxes are presented by Greenwood and Huffman (1991) and McGrattan (1994). Ljungqvist and Uhlig (2000) introduce habit formation in household consumption. Studies focusing on firm investment include Greenwood, Hercowitz, and Huffman (1988) and Gilchrist and Williams (2000). Models including a monopolistically competitive goods market are formulated by Bénassy (1996a), Hornstein (1993), Chatterjee and Cooper (1993),Rotemberg and Woodford (1992, 1996), Devereux, Head, and Lapham (1996a, 1996b), Heijdra (1998), and Galí (1999). On models with money and price stickiness, see Hairault and Portier (1993), King and Watson (1986), Yun (1996), Rotemberg and Woodford (1999), and Chari, Kehoe, and McGrattan (2000). King (1991) develops a method to decompose impulse-response functions into wealth and substitution effects.

Appendix

Phase diagram for the unit-elastic model

In this appendix we derive the phase diagram for the unit-elastic model. We drop the superfluous time index and hold the output share of government consumption, $\omega_G \equiv G/Y$, constant.

Employment as a function of the state variables

By using labour demand (T1.4), labour supply (T1.7), and the production function (T1.8), we obtain an expression relating equilibrium employment to consumption and the capital stock ("LME" designates labour market equilibrium).

$$\text{LME:} \qquad \left(f(L) \equiv\right)(1 - L)L^{\epsilon_L - 1} = \left(\frac{1 - \epsilon_C}{\epsilon_C \epsilon_L Z_0}\right) CK^{-(1 - \epsilon_L)}, \tag{A15.1}$$

with $f'(L) < 0$ and $f''(L) > 0$ in the *economically meaningful* interval $L \in [0, 1]$. Hence, $f(L)$ is as drawn in Figure A15.1.

Capital stock equilibrium

Using (T1.6) in (T1.1) we observe that $\dot{K} = 0$ holds if and only if $\delta K = (1 - \omega_G)Y - C$. By using (T1.4) and (T1.7), and assuming $0 < \epsilon_C < 1$, the capital stock equilibrium (CSE) locus ($\dot{K} = 0$) can be written as:

$$\delta K = \left[1 - \omega_G - \left(\frac{\epsilon_C \epsilon_L}{1 - \epsilon_C}\right)\left(\frac{1 - L}{L}\right)\right]Y. \tag{A15.2}$$

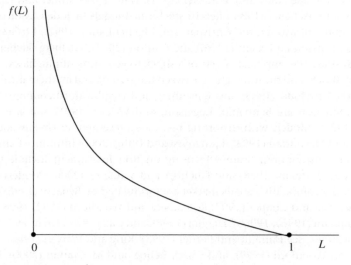

Figure A15.1. Labour market equilibrium

We are clearly only interested in positive values of output and capital so that the term in square brackets on the right-hand side of (A15.2) must be non-negative. This furnishes a lower bound for employment:

$$L \geq L_{MIN} \equiv \frac{\epsilon_C \epsilon_L}{\epsilon_C \epsilon_L + (1 - \omega_G)(1 - \epsilon_C)}, \quad 0 < L_{MIN} < 1. \tag{A15.3}$$

By using L_{MIN} and (T1.8) we can rewrite (A15.2):

$$\text{CSE:} \quad K^{\epsilon_L} = \left(\frac{\epsilon_C \epsilon_L Z_0}{\delta(1 - \epsilon_C)} \right) \left(\frac{L - L_{MIN}}{L_{MIN}} \right) L^{\epsilon_L - 1}. \tag{A15.4}$$

Equation (A15.4) represents an implicit function, $L = g(K)$, over the interval $L \in [L_{MIN}, 1]$ relating K and L. In order to compute the slope of the implicit function we totally differentiate (A15.4):

$$K^{\epsilon_L} \left(\frac{dK}{K} \right) = \left(\frac{\epsilon_C Z_0}{\delta(1 - \epsilon_C)} \right) \left[\frac{\epsilon_L L + (1 - \epsilon_L) L_{MIN}}{L_{MIN}} \right] L^{\epsilon_L - 1} \left(\frac{dL}{L} \right). \tag{A15.5}$$

Since $L \geq L_{MIN} > 0$ the term in square brackets on the right-hand side is strictly positive so that $g'(K) > 0$. It follows from (A15.4) that $K = 0$ for $L = L_{MIN}$, so as L rises from $L = L_{MIN}$ to $L = 1$, K rises from $K = 0$ to $K = K_K \equiv ((1 - \omega_G)Z_0/\delta)^{1/\epsilon_L} > 0$. We now have two zeros for the CSE line, i.e. both $(K, L) = (0, L_{MIN})$ and $(K, L) = (K_K, 1)$ solve equation (A15.2). By using (A15.1) we find the corresponding values for C, i.e. $(C, K, L) = (0, 0, L_{MIN})$ and $(C, K, L) = (0, K_K, 1)$ are both zeros for the CSE line. In Figure 15.1 these points have been drawn in (C, K) space.

The slope of the CSE line is computed as follows. We note that the CSE line can be written as:

$$C = (1 - \omega_G) Z_0 g(K)^{\epsilon_L} K^{1 - \epsilon_L} - \delta K, \tag{A15.6}$$

where $L = g(K)$ is the implicit function defined by (A15.4). By taking the derivative of (A15.6) we obtain in a few steps:

$$\left(\frac{dC}{dK} \right)_{K=0} = (1 - \omega_G) Z_0 \left[1 - \epsilon_L \left(1 - \eta_g(K) \right) \right] \left(\frac{g(K)}{K} \right)^{\epsilon_L} - \delta, \tag{A15.7}$$

where $\eta_g(K)$ is the elasticity of the $g(.)$ function:

$$\eta_g(K) \equiv \left(\frac{K g'(K)}{g(K)} \right) = \frac{\epsilon_L \left(g(K) - L_{MIN} \right)}{\epsilon_L g(K) + (1 - \epsilon_L) L_{MIN}}. \tag{A15.8}$$

It follows from (A15.8) that $\eta_g(0) = 0$ so that the term in square brackets on the right-hand side of (A15.7) goes to $(1 - \epsilon_L)$ as $K \to 0$. But since $\lim_{K \to 0} g(K)/K = +\infty$ it follows that the

CSE line is vertical near the origin (see Figure 15.1):

$$\lim_{K \to 0} \left(\frac{dC}{dK} \right)_{\dot{K}=0} = +\infty. \tag{A15.9}$$

The *golden-rule point* (for which consumption is at its maximum value) is obtained by setting $dC/dK = 0$ in (A15.7):

$$(1 - \omega_G)\left[1 - \epsilon_L(1 - \eta_g(K^{GR}))\right] \left(\frac{Y^{GR}}{K^{GR}} \right) = \delta, \tag{A15.10}$$

where Y^{GR} is given by:

$$Y^{GR} \equiv Z_0 \left[g(K^{GR})\right]^{\epsilon_L} \left[K^{GR}\right]^{1-\epsilon_L}, \tag{A15.11}$$

and $\eta_g(K)$ is given in (A15.8). The golden rule occurs at point A in Figure 15.1. For points to the right of the golden-rule point, the CSE line is downward sloping.[24] The capital stock dynamics follows from (T1.1) in combination with (T1.6), (T1.8), and using the implicit function $L = g(K)$:

$$\dot{K} = (1 - \omega_G)Z_0 g(K)^{\epsilon_L} K^{1-\epsilon_L} - \delta K - C, \tag{A15.12}$$

from which we derive $\partial \dot{K} / \partial C < 0$. See the horizontal arrows in Figure 15.1.

Consumption equilibrium

The consumption equilibrium (CE) line describes combinations of C and K for which $\dot{C} = 0$. By using (T1.2) (in steady-state format), (T1.5), and (T1.8), we can write the CE line as follows:

$$\text{CE:} \quad y \left[\equiv \left(\frac{Y}{K} \right) = Z_0 \left(\frac{K}{L} \right)^{-\epsilon_L} \right] = y^*, \tag{A15.13}$$

where $y^* \equiv (\rho + \delta)/(1 - \epsilon_L)$ is the equilibrium output-capital ratio for which the rate of interest equals the rate of time preference ($r = \rho$). It follows from (A15.13) that consumption equilibrium pins down a unique capital-labour ratio, $(K/L)^* \equiv (Z_0/y^*)^{1/\epsilon_L}$. By substituting this ratio into (A15.1) we obtain the expression for the CE line in the (C, K) plane:

$$C = y^* \left(\frac{\epsilon_C \epsilon_L}{1 - \epsilon_C} \right) \left[\left(\frac{Z_0}{y^*} \right)^{1/\epsilon_L} - K \right]. \tag{A15.14}$$

It follows from (A15.14) that the CE line is linear and passes through the coordinates $(C, K) = (0, K_C)$ and $(C, K) = (C_C, 0)$ in Figure 15.1:

$$K_C \equiv \left(\frac{Z_0}{y^*} \right)^{1/\epsilon_L}, \quad C_C \equiv y^* \left(\frac{\epsilon_C \epsilon_L}{1 - \epsilon_C} \right) K_C. \tag{A15.15}$$

[24] For exogenous labour supply $\eta_g(K) = 0$ for all K and the formula for K^{GR} collapses to the usual expression $(1 - \omega_G)F_K = \delta$ or $(1 - \omega_G)(1 - \epsilon_L)(Y/K)^{GR} = \delta$.

Provided $\omega_G < \epsilon_L$, the CE line crosses the K-axis to the left of the K-intercept of the CSE line.[25]

The consumption dynamics can be deduced by noting that (T1.2) can be rewritten in the following fashion: $\dot{C}/C = (1 - \epsilon_L)[y - y^*]$, where y^* is defined below (A15.13). From (A15.13) we find:

$$\frac{\partial y}{\partial C} = \epsilon_L Z_0 \left(\frac{K}{L}\right)^{-(1+\epsilon_L)} \left(\frac{K}{L^2}\right) \left(\frac{\partial L}{\partial C}\right) < 0, \tag{A15.16}$$

where (A15.1) shows that $\partial L/\partial C < 0$. It follows that $\partial[\dot{C}/C]/\partial C = (1 - \epsilon_L)\partial y/\partial C < 0$. This has been indicated with vertical arrows in Figure 15.1.

Derivation of (15.52)–(15.53)

We wish to solve the dynamical system (15.30) given that $\gamma_C(t) \equiv 0$ (for all t) and $\gamma_K(t)$ is as defined in (15.51). In the Mathematical Appendix we show that the solution can be written in Laplace transforms as:

$$(s + \lambda_1) \left[\begin{array}{c} \mathcal{L}\{\tilde{K}, s\} \\ \mathcal{L}\{\tilde{C}, s\} \end{array} \right] = \left[\begin{array}{c} \mathcal{L}\{\gamma_K, s\} \\ \tilde{C}(0) \end{array} \right]$$
$$+ \left[\begin{array}{c} \lambda_2 - \delta_{22} \\ \delta_{21} \end{array} \right] \left(\frac{\mathcal{L}\{\gamma_K, s\} - \mathcal{L}\{\gamma_K, \lambda_2\}}{s - \lambda_2} \right). \tag{A15.17}$$

The impact jump for consumption, $\tilde{C}(0)$, is:

$$\tilde{C}(0) = -\left(\frac{\lambda_2 - \delta_{22}}{\delta_{12}}\right) \mathcal{L}\{\gamma_K, \lambda_2\} \tag{A15.18}$$

The shock term (15.51) can be written in general terms as:

$$\gamma_K(t) \equiv \eta_K e^{-\xi_K t}, \quad \eta_K \equiv -y^* \omega_G \tilde{G}, \quad \xi_K \geq 0. \tag{A15.19}$$

The shock occurs at time $t = 0$ and is permanent (transitory) if $\xi_K = 0$ ($\xi_K > 0$). In view of (A15.19), the Laplace transform appearing in (A15.17) can be written as:

$$\mathcal{L}\{\gamma_K, s\} = \frac{\eta_K}{s + \xi_K}, \tag{A15.20}$$

$$\frac{\mathcal{L}\{\gamma_K, s\} - \mathcal{L}\{\gamma_K, \lambda_2\}}{s - \lambda_2} = -\frac{\eta_K}{(s + \xi_K)(\lambda_2 + \xi_K)}. \tag{A15.21}$$

---

[25] To show this result, we note that K_C can be related to K_K (defined in the text below (A15.5)):

$$\left(\frac{K_C}{K_K}\right)^{\epsilon_L} = \left(\frac{\delta}{\rho + \delta}\right)\left(\frac{1 - \epsilon_L}{1 - \omega_G}\right).$$

Both terms in round brackets on the right-hand side are between zero because $\rho > 0$ and $\omega_G < \epsilon_L$. Hence, we conclude that $K_C < K_K$.

By using these expressions in (A15.17) we obtain:

$$
\begin{bmatrix} \mathcal{L}\{\tilde{K}, s\} \\ \mathcal{L}\{\tilde{C}, s\} \end{bmatrix} = \begin{bmatrix} 0 \\ \tilde{C}(0) \end{bmatrix} \frac{1}{s + \lambda_1}
$$

$$
+ \left(\frac{\eta_K}{\lambda_2 + \xi_K} \right) \begin{bmatrix} \delta_{22} + \xi_K \\ -\delta_{21} \end{bmatrix} \frac{1}{(s + \xi_K)(s + \lambda_1)}. \tag{A15.22}
$$

The impact effect is obtained by substituting (A15.20) in (A15.18):

$$
\tilde{C}(0) = - \left(\frac{\lambda_2 - \delta_{22}}{\delta_{12}} \right) \left(\frac{\eta_K}{\lambda_2 + \xi_K} \right). \tag{A15.23}
$$

By inverting (A15.22) and noting that $\mathcal{L}\{e^{-at}, s\} = 1/(s + a)$ and $\mathcal{L}\{T(\alpha_1, \alpha_2, t), s\} = [(s + \alpha_1)(s + \alpha_2)]^{-1}$ we obtain the expression for the transition paths of $\tilde{K}(t)$ and $\tilde{C}(t)$:

$$
\begin{bmatrix} \tilde{K}(t) \\ \tilde{C}(t) \end{bmatrix} = \begin{bmatrix} 0 \\ \tilde{C}(0) \end{bmatrix} e^{-\lambda_1 t} + \left(\frac{\eta_K}{\lambda_2 + \xi_K} \right) \begin{bmatrix} \delta_{22} + \xi_K \\ -\delta_{21} \end{bmatrix} T(\xi_K, \lambda_1, t), \tag{A15.24}
$$

where $T(\xi_K, \lambda_1, t)$ is a temporary bell-shaped transition term with properties covered by the following lemma.

Lemma 1 *Let* $T(\alpha_1, \alpha_2, t)$ *be a single transition function of the form:*

$$
T(\alpha_1, \alpha_2, t) \equiv \begin{cases} \dfrac{e^{-\alpha_2 t} - e^{-\alpha_1 t}}{\alpha_1 - \alpha_2} & \text{for } \alpha_1 \neq \alpha_2 \\ t e^{-\alpha_1 t} & \text{for } \alpha_1 = \alpha_2, \end{cases}
$$

with $\alpha_1 > 0$ *and* $\alpha_2 > 0$. *Then* $T(\alpha_1, \alpha_2, t)$ *has the following properties: (i) (positive)* $T(\alpha_1, \alpha_2, t) > 0$ *for* $t \in (0, \infty)$, *(ii)* $T(\alpha_1, \alpha_2, t) = 0$ *for* $t = 0$ *and in the limit as* $t \to \infty$, *(iii) (single-peaked)* $dT(\alpha_1, \alpha_2, t)/dt > 0$ *for* $t \in (0, \hat{t})$, $dT(\alpha_1, \alpha_2, t)/dt < 0$ *for* $t \in (\hat{t}, \infty)$, $dT(\alpha_1, \alpha_2, t)/dt = 0$ *for* $t = \hat{t}$ *and in the limit as* $t \to \infty$, *and* $dT(\alpha_1, \alpha_2, 0)/dt = 1$, *(iv)* $\hat{t} \equiv \ln(\alpha_1/\alpha_2)/(\alpha_1 - \alpha_2)$ *if* $\alpha_1 \neq \alpha_2$ *and* $\hat{t} \equiv 1/\alpha_1$ *if* $\alpha_1 = \alpha_2$; *(v) (point of inflexion)* $d^2T(\alpha_1, \alpha_2, t)/dt^2 = 0$ *for* $t^* = 2\hat{t}$; *(vi) if* $\alpha_i \to \infty$ *then* $T(\alpha_1, \alpha_2, t) = 0$ *for all* $t \geq 0$.

Lemma 2 *If* $\alpha_2 = 0$ *the transition function is proportional to a monotonic adjustment function:* $T(\alpha_1, 0, t) = (1/\alpha_1)A(\alpha_1, t)$, *where* $A(\alpha_1, t) \equiv 1 - e^{-\alpha_1 t}$ *has the following properties:* $0 < A(\alpha_1, t) < 1$ *for* $t \in (0, \infty)$, *(ii)* $A(\alpha_1, 0) = 0$ *and* $\lim_{t \to \infty} A(\alpha_1, t) = 1$, *(iii) (monotonic)* $dA(\alpha_1, t)/dt > 0$ *for* $t \in [0, \infty)$, $\lim_{t \to \infty} dA(\alpha_1, t)/dt = 0$.

It follows from Lemma A15.2 that for permanent shocks ($\xi_K = 0$) (A15.24) can be rewritten as:

$$
\begin{bmatrix} \tilde{K}(t) \\ \tilde{C}(t) \end{bmatrix} = \begin{bmatrix} 0 \\ \tilde{C}(0) \end{bmatrix} [1 - A(\lambda_1, t)] + \begin{bmatrix} \tilde{K}(\infty) \\ \tilde{C}(\infty) \end{bmatrix} A(\lambda_1, t), \tag{A15.25}
$$

where the long-run effects are given by:

$$
\begin{bmatrix} \tilde{K}(\infty) \\ \tilde{C}(\infty) \end{bmatrix} = \frac{\text{adj } \Delta}{\lambda_1 \lambda_2} \begin{bmatrix} \eta_K \\ 0 \end{bmatrix}. \tag{A15.26}
$$

Derivation of (15.86)–(15.87)

We compute the impulse-response function associated with the innovation ϵ_0^Z by solving the following system:

$$
\left[\begin{array}{c} \tilde{K}_{t+1} - \tilde{K}_t \\ \tilde{C}_{t+1} - \tilde{C}_t \end{array} \right] = \Delta \left[\begin{array}{c} \tilde{K}_t \\ \tilde{C}_t \end{array} \right] + \left[\begin{array}{c} \gamma_t^K \\ \gamma_t^C \end{array} \right],
\tag{A15.27}
$$

where the shock vector is given in (15.85). The key thing to note is that (A15.27) is the deterministic counterpart to (15.77). The expectations operator, E_t, can be dropped from (15.77) when we compute the impulse-response function because we have already incorporated the rational expectations assumption by substituting the path for $\tilde{Z}_t$ that results from the innovation ϵ_0^Z into the shock term.

In the Mathematical Appendix we show how a system like (A15.27) can be solved with the aid of the z-transform method. Assuming that Δ possesses real characteristic roots, $-1 < -\lambda_1 < 0$ and $\lambda_2 > 0$, the general solution of (A15.27) is:

$$
[z - (1 - \lambda_1)] \left[\begin{array}{c} \mathcal{Z}\{\tilde{K}_t, z\} \\ \mathcal{Z}\{\tilde{C}_t, z\} \end{array} \right] = \left[\begin{array}{c} \mathcal{Z}\{\gamma_t^K, z\} \\ z\tilde{C}_0 + \mathcal{Z}\{\gamma_t^C, z\} \end{array} \right]
\tag{A15.28}
$$

$$
+ \frac{\text{adj}\Lambda(\lambda_2) \left[\begin{array}{c} \mathcal{Z}\{\gamma_t^K, z\} - \left(z/(1+\lambda_2)\right)\mathcal{Z}\{\gamma_t^K, 1+\lambda_2\} \\ \mathcal{Z}\{\gamma_t^C, z\} - \left(z/(1+\lambda_2)\right)\mathcal{Z}\{\gamma_t^C, 1+\lambda_2\} \end{array} \right]}{z - (1+\lambda_2)},
$$

where $\Lambda(\lambda_2) \equiv \lambda_2 I - \Delta$ and we have used the fact that capital cannot jump at impact (i.e. $\tilde{K}_0 = 0$). The impact jump in consumption ($\tilde{C}_0$) is:

$$
\tilde{C}_0 = -\frac{\mathcal{Z}\{\gamma_t^C, 1+\lambda_2\}}{1+\lambda_2} - \left(\frac{\lambda_2 - \delta_{22}}{\delta_{12}}\right) \left[\frac{\mathcal{Z}\{\gamma_t^K, 1+\lambda_2\}}{1+\lambda_2} \right]
\tag{A15.29}
$$

The shock term (15.85) can be written in general format as:

$$
\left[\begin{array}{c} \gamma_t^K \\ \gamma_t^C \end{array} \right] = \left[\begin{array}{c} \eta_K \\ \eta_C \end{array} \right] \rho_Z^t, \qquad \left[\begin{array}{c} \eta_K \\ \eta_C \end{array} \right] \equiv \phi \left[\begin{array}{c} y^* \\ \zeta[\rho_Z - y^* [1 - \phi(1 - \epsilon_L)]] \end{array} \right] \epsilon_0^Z.
\tag{A15.30}
$$

The z-transform for γ_t^i can then be written as:

$$
\mathcal{Z}\{\gamma_t^i, z\} = \eta_i \left(\frac{z}{z - \rho_Z} \right), \quad i \in \{K, C\}.
\tag{A15.31}
$$

Using (A15.31) in (A15.29) we obtain the following expression for $\tilde{C}_0$:

$$
\tilde{C}_0 = -\frac{\eta_C}{\lambda_2 + (1 - \rho_Z)} - \left(\frac{\lambda_2 - \delta_{22}}{\delta_{12}}\right) \left(\frac{\eta_K}{\lambda_2 + (1 - \rho_Z)}\right).
\tag{A15.32}
$$

By substituting η_C and η_K in (A15.32) we obtain equation (15.87) in the text. We derive from (A15.31) that:

$$
\frac{\mathcal{Z}\{\gamma_t^i, z\} - \left(\frac{z}{1+\lambda_2}\right)\mathcal{Z}\{\gamma_t^i, 1+\lambda_2\}}{z - (1+\lambda_2)} = -\left(\frac{\eta_i}{1+\lambda_2 - \rho_Z}\right)\left(\frac{z}{z - \rho_Z}\right),
\tag{A15.33}
$$

so that (A15.28) can be rewritten as:

$$
\begin{bmatrix} \mathcal{Z}\{\tilde{K}, z\} \\ \mathcal{Z}\{\tilde{C}, z\} \end{bmatrix} = \begin{bmatrix} 0 \\ \tilde{C}_0 \end{bmatrix} \left(\frac{z}{z - (1 - \lambda_1)} \right) + \begin{bmatrix} \delta_{22} + (1 - \rho_Z) & -\delta_{12} \\ -\delta_{21} & \delta_{11} + (1 - \rho_Z) \end{bmatrix}
$$

$$
\times \left(\frac{1}{\lambda_2 + (1 - \rho_Z)} \right) \begin{bmatrix} \eta_K \\ \eta_C \end{bmatrix} \left(\frac{z}{(z - \rho_Z)[z - (1 - \lambda_1)]} \right). \tag{A15.34}
$$

We recognize that $\mathcal{Z}^{-1}\{z/(z-\alpha)\} = \alpha^t$ and $\mathcal{Z}^{-1}\{z/[(z-\alpha_1)(z-\alpha_2)]\} = T_t(\alpha_1, \alpha_2)$, where $T_t(.)$ is a temporary bell-shaped transition term:

$$
T_t(\alpha_1, \alpha_2) \equiv \begin{cases} \dfrac{\alpha_1^t - \alpha_2^t}{\alpha_1 - \alpha_2} & \text{for } \alpha_1 \neq \alpha_2 \\ t\alpha_1^{t-1} & \text{for } \alpha_1 = \alpha_2, \end{cases} \tag{A15.35}
$$

with $\alpha_i \neq 0$ (see Ogata (1995, p. 30)). This term is the discrete-time counterpart to the single transition function whose properties are similar to the ones covered in Lemma A15.1 above. A result we use in the analysis of permanent shocks is that $T_t(1, \alpha_2) = (1 - \alpha_2)^{-1} A_t(\alpha_2)$, where $A_t(\alpha_2) \equiv 1 - \alpha_2^t$ is a discrete-time adjustment term. For purely transitory shocks we have:

$$
T_t(0, \alpha_2) \equiv \begin{cases} 0 & \text{for } t = 0 \\ \alpha_2^{t-1} & \text{for } t = 1, 2, \ldots \end{cases} \tag{A15.36}
$$

(Note that in the text we combine (A15.35) and (A15.36) into (15.88).) By inverting (A15.34) we find the solution in the time domain:

$$
\begin{bmatrix} \tilde{K}_t \\ \tilde{C}_t \end{bmatrix} = \begin{bmatrix} 0 \\ \tilde{C}_0 \end{bmatrix} (1 - \lambda_1)^t + \begin{bmatrix} \delta_{22} + (1 - \rho_Z) & -\delta_{12} \\ -\delta_{21} & \delta_{11} + (1 - \rho_Z) \end{bmatrix}
$$

$$
\times \left(\frac{1}{\lambda_2 + (1 - \rho_Z)} \right) \begin{bmatrix} \eta_K \\ \eta_C \end{bmatrix} T_t(\rho_Z, 1 - \lambda_1). \tag{A15.37}
$$

By simplifying (A15.37) somewhat we find the equation (15.86) in the text.

Method of undetermined coefficients

In this subsection we show how the unit-elastic RBC model of section 15.5.1 can be solved using the method of undetermined coefficients. Following Campbell (1994, p. 470), we conjecture the following trial solution:

$$
\tilde{C}_t = \pi_{ck}\tilde{K}_t + \pi_{cz}\tilde{Z}_t, \tag{A15.38}
$$

where π_{ck} and π_{cz} are coefficients to be determined. By substituting (A15.38) in the system (15.77) we obtain:

$$
\begin{bmatrix} 1 & 0 \\ \gamma_{21} & 1 \end{bmatrix} \begin{bmatrix} \tilde{K}_{t+1} \\ \pi_{ck}\tilde{K}_{t+1} + \rho_Z\pi_{cz}\tilde{Z}_t \end{bmatrix} = \begin{bmatrix} 1 + \delta_{11}^* & \delta_{12}^* \\ 0 & 1 + \delta_{22}^* \end{bmatrix} \begin{bmatrix} \tilde{K}_t \\ \pi_{ck}\tilde{K}_t + \pi_{cz}\tilde{Z}_t \end{bmatrix}
$$

$$
+ \begin{bmatrix} \gamma^* \\ \zeta\rho_Z \end{bmatrix} \phi\tilde{Z}_t, \tag{A15.39}
$$

where δ_{ij}^* are the elements of Δ^* (defined in (15.78)) and we have used the fact that $E_t C_{t+1} = \pi_{ck}\tilde{K}_{t+1} + \pi_{cz}E_t\tilde{Z}_{t+1}$ and $E_t\tilde{Z}_{t+1} = \rho_Z\tilde{Z}_t$. The system in (A15.39) gives two expressions for $\tilde{K}_{t+1}$

in terms of $\tilde{K}_t$ and $\tilde{Z}_t$ which must hold for all $(\tilde{K}_t, \tilde{Z}_t)$ combinations. By eliminating $\tilde{K}_{t+1}$ from (A15.39) we find:

$$
0 = \left[1 + \delta_{11}^* + \delta_{12}^* \pi_{ck} - (1 + \delta_{22}^*) \left(\frac{\pi_{ck}}{\gamma_{21} + \pi_{ck}} \right) \right] \tilde{K}_t \tag{A15.40}
$$
$$
+ \left[\delta_{12}^* \pi_{cz} + \phi \gamma^* - \frac{(1 - \rho_Z + \delta_{22}^*) \pi_{cz} + \phi \zeta \rho_Z}{\gamma_{21} + \pi_{ck}} \right] \tilde{Z}_t.
$$

We use π_{ck} to ensure that the term in square brackets in front of $\tilde{K}_t$ is zero. After some manipulation we find the following quadratic function in π_{ck}:

$$
\delta_{12} \pi_{ck}^2 + (\delta_{11} - \delta_{22}) \pi_{ck} - \delta_{21} = 0, \tag{A15.41}
$$

where δ_{ij} are the elements of Δ ($\delta_{11} = \delta_{11}^*$, $\delta_{12} = \delta_{12}^*$, $\delta_{21} = -\gamma_{21} \delta_{11}^* + \delta_{21}^* = -\gamma_{21}(1 + \delta_{11}^*)$, and $\delta_{22} = -\gamma_{21} \delta_{12}^* + \delta_{22}^*$). Given saddle path stability, we solve (A15.41) for the positive root:[26]

$$
\pi_{ck} = \frac{-(\delta_{11} - \delta_{22}) + \sqrt{(\delta_{11} - \delta_{22})^2 + 4\delta_{12}\delta_{21}}}{2\delta_{12}} > 0. \tag{A15.42}
$$

(Note also that $\delta_{12}\pi_{ck} = \delta_{22} - \lambda_2$.) For this value of π_{ck}, the term in square brackets in front of $\tilde{Z}_t$ in (A15.40) can be put to zero by the appropriate choice of π_{cs}:

$$
\pi_{cz} = \frac{\phi \left[\zeta \rho_Z - (\gamma_{21} + \pi_{ck}) \gamma^* \right]}{\delta_{12} \pi_{ck} - \delta_{22} - (1 - \rho_Z)} > 0. \tag{A15.43}
$$

Once we know the coefficients π_{ck} and π_{cz}, we obtain the solution for $\tilde{K}_{t+1}$ by using either row of (A15.39):

$$
\tilde{K}_{t+1} = \pi_{kk} \tilde{K}_t + \pi_{kz} \tilde{Z}_t, \tag{A15.44}
$$

where $\pi_{kk} \equiv 1 + \delta_{11} + \delta_{12}\pi_{ck}$ and $\pi_{kz} \equiv \delta_{12}\pi_{cz} + \phi \gamma^*$. (Note also that $\pi_{kk} = 1 - \lambda_1$.)

Computing correlations

In order to judge the empirical performance of the unit-elastic RBC model we can compute various correlations that are implied by the theoretical model. We approach the problem from an analytical viewpoint in order to stress the link with the rational expectations literature discussed in Chapter 3. We start by computing the statistical properties of the

---

[26] The sign of π_{ck} follows from saddle-point stability. First, we note that the discriminant in (A15.42) can be written as $(\delta_{11} - \delta_{22})^2 + 4\delta_{12}\delta_{21} = (\delta_{11} + \delta_{22})^2 - 4|\Delta| > 0$, where the sign follows from the fact that $|\Delta| < 0$. Hence, the roots are real and distinct. Next we note that $\delta_{12}\delta_{21} = -\gamma_{21}\delta_{12}^*(1 + \delta_{11}^*) > 0$. Hence, the discriminant is larger than $(\delta_{11} - \delta_{22})$ so that (A15.41) has one positive and one negative root. The positive root must be selected in order to ensure that the steady state is stable, i.e. that π_{kk} in (A15.44) lies between zero and one (see also Campbell, 1994, pp. 471–472).

capital stock. We derive from (A15.44) that:

$$E\left[\tilde{K}_{t+1} - E\tilde{K}_{t+1}\right]^2 = \pi_{kk}^2 E\left[\tilde{K}_t - E\tilde{K}_t\right]^2 + \pi_{kz}^2 E\tilde{Z}_t^2 + 2\pi_{kk}\pi_{kz}E\left[\tilde{K}_t - E\tilde{K}_t\right]\tilde{Z}_t \Longleftrightarrow$$

$$\text{Var}(\tilde{K}_{t+1}) = \pi_{kk}^2 \text{Var}(\tilde{K}_t) + \pi_{kz}^2 \text{Var}(\tilde{Z}_t) + 2\pi_{kk}\pi_{kz}\text{Cov}(\tilde{K}_t, \tilde{Z}_t), \tag{A15.45}$$

where we have used the fact that $E\tilde{Z}_t = 0$. Since $\tilde{Z}_t$ is covariance stationary,[27] the same holds for $\tilde{K}_t$ (and all other endogenous variables). Hence, $\text{Var}(\tilde{K}_{t+1}) = \text{Var}(\tilde{K}_t)$ and equation (A15.45) can be simplified to:

$$(1 - \pi_{kk}^2)\text{Var}(\tilde{K}_{t+1}) = \pi_{kz}^2 \text{Var}(\tilde{Z}_t) + 2\pi_{kk}\pi_{kz}\text{Cov}(\tilde{K}_t, \tilde{Z}_t). \tag{A15.46}$$

It is straightforward to derive from (15.83) that:

$$\text{Var}(\tilde{Z}_t) \equiv E\tilde{Z}_t^2 = E\left[\rho_Z^2 \tilde{Z}_{t-1}^2 + 2\rho_Z Z_{t-1}\epsilon_t^Z + (\epsilon_t^Z)^2\right]$$

$$= \rho_Z^2 \text{Var}(\tilde{Z}_{t-1}) + \sigma_Z^2 \Rightarrow$$

$$\text{Var}(\tilde{Z}_t) = \frac{\sigma_Z^2}{1 - \rho_Z^2}, \tag{A15.47}$$

where σ_Z^2 is the (constant) variance of the innovation term (i.e. $\sigma_Z^2 \equiv E(\epsilon_t^Z)^2$) and we have used covariance stationarity of the shock process (so that $\text{Var}(\tilde{Z}_t) = \text{Var}(\tilde{Z}_{t-1})$). Similarly, we find:

$$\text{Cov}(\tilde{Z}_t, \tilde{Z}_{t-j}) \equiv E\tilde{Z}_t\tilde{Z}_{t-j} = \rho_Z^j \text{Var}(\tilde{Z}_t). \tag{A15.48}$$

Next we use (A15.44) to write $\tilde{K}_t$ in terms of $\tilde{Z}_{t-j}$ terms:

$$\tilde{K}_t = \lim_{T\to\infty} \pi_{kk}^T \tilde{K}_{t-T} + \pi_{kz}\left[\tilde{Z}_{t-1} + \pi_{kk}\tilde{Z}_{t-2} + \pi_{kk}^2 \tilde{Z}_{t-3} + \cdots\right]$$

$$= \pi_{kz} \sum_{j=1}^{\infty} \pi_{kk}^{j-1} \tilde{Z}_{t-j}, \tag{A15.49}$$

where we have used the fact that (A15.44) is a stable difference equation so that $\pi_{kk}^T \tilde{K}_{t-T}$ goes to zero as T becomes large. By using (A15.48) and (A15.49) we find the expression for $\text{Cov}(\tilde{K}_t, \tilde{Z}_t)$:

$$\text{Cov}(\tilde{K}_t, \tilde{Z}_t) \equiv E\left[\tilde{K}_t - E\tilde{K}_t\right]\tilde{Z}_t = \pi_{kz} \sum_{j=1}^{\infty} \pi_{kk}^{j-1} E\tilde{Z}_t\tilde{Z}_{t-j}$$

$$= \pi_{kz} \sum_{j=1}^{\infty} \pi_{kk}^{j-1}\rho_Z^j \text{Var}(\tilde{Z}_t) = \rho_Z\pi_{kz}\text{Var}(\tilde{Z}_t) \sum_{j=1}^{\infty} (\rho_Z\pi_{kk})^{j-1}$$

$$= \left(\frac{\rho_Z\pi_{kz}}{1 - \rho_Z\pi_{kk}}\right)\text{Var}(\tilde{Z}_t). \tag{A15.50}$$

---

[27] A stochastic process, $\{x_t\}$, is covariance stationary if the mean is independent of time and the sequence of autocovariance matrices, $E(x_{t+j} - Ex_{t+j})(x_t - Ex_t)^T$ depends only on j but not on t. See Ljungqvist and Sargent (2000, p. 9) and Patterson (2000, ch. 3).

By substituting (A15.48) and (A15.50) into (A15.46) we obtain the final expression for the variance of the capital stock:

$$\text{Var}(\tilde{K}_{t+1}) = \left(\frac{1 + \rho_Z \pi_{kk}}{1 - \rho_Z \pi_{kk}}\right)\left(\frac{\pi_{kz}^2}{1 - \pi_{kk}^2}\right)\text{Var}(\tilde{Z}_t). \tag{A15.51}$$

It follows from (A15.44) that:

$$\text{Cov}(\tilde{K}_{t+1}, \tilde{K}_t) \equiv E\left[\tilde{K}_{t+1} - E(\tilde{K}_{t+1})\right]\left[\tilde{K}_t - E(\tilde{K}_t)\right]$$

$$= \pi_{kk}\text{Var}(\tilde{K}_{t+1}) + \pi_{kz}\text{Cov}(\tilde{K}_t, \tilde{Z}_t)$$

$$= \left(\frac{\rho_Z + \pi_{kk}}{1 - \rho_Z \pi_{kk}}\right)\left(\frac{\pi_{kz}^2}{1 - \pi_{kk}^2}\right)\text{Var}(\tilde{Z}_t). \tag{A15.52}$$

Now that we have expressions for $\text{Var}(\tilde{K}_t)$, $\text{Var}(\tilde{Z}_t)$, and $\text{Cov}(\tilde{K}_t, \tilde{Z}_t)$, the variances and covariances of all remaining variables are easily obtained. For consumption, for example, we derive from (A15.38):

$$\text{Var}(\tilde{C}_t) = \pi_{ck}^2\text{Var}(\tilde{K}_t) + \pi_{cz}\text{Var}(\tilde{Z}_t) + 2\pi_{ck}\pi_{cz}\text{Cov}(\tilde{K}_t, \tilde{Z}_t), \tag{A15.53}$$

$$\text{Cov}(\tilde{C}_t, \tilde{K}_t) = \pi_{ck}\text{Var}(\tilde{K}_t) + \pi_{cz}\text{Cov}(\tilde{K}_t, \tilde{Z}_t). \tag{A15.54}$$

By using (A15.38) in (15.71)–(15.75) we can write employment, wages, output, investment, and the interest rate in terms $\tilde{K}_t$ and $\tilde{Z}_t$ and derive expressions similar to (A15.53)–(A15.54) for these variables. For output, for example, we find the following expression:

$$\tilde{Y}_t = \pi_{yk}\tilde{K}_t + \pi_{yz}\tilde{Z}_t, \tag{A15.55}$$

where $\pi_{yk} \equiv \phi(1 - \epsilon_L) - (\phi - 1)\pi_{ck}$ and $\pi_{yz} \equiv \phi - (\phi - 1)\pi_{cz}$. Equation (A15.55) is useful to compute the covariances of the different variables with output. For example, it follows from (A15.38) and (A15.55) that $\text{Cov}(\tilde{C}_t, \tilde{Y}_t)$ is:

$$\text{Cov}(\tilde{C}_t, \tilde{Y}_t) = \pi_{ck}\pi_{yk}\text{Var}(\tilde{K}_t) + \left[\pi_{ck}\pi_{yz} + \pi_{cz}\pi_{yk}\right]\text{Cov}(\tilde{K}_t, \tilde{Z}_t)$$

$$+ \pi_{cz}\pi_{yz}\text{Var}(\tilde{Z}_t) \tag{A15.56}$$

Similarly, we derive from (A15.55) that $\text{Cov}(\tilde{K}_t, \tilde{Y}_t)$ is:

$$\text{Cov}(\tilde{K}_t, \tilde{Y}_t) = \pi_{yk}\text{Var}(\tilde{K}_t) + \pi_{yz}\text{Cov}(\tilde{K}_t, \tilde{Z}_t). \tag{A15.57}$$

Similar expressions for the other variables are easily found. Finally, note that in the text we report correlation coefficients. These are defined as follows:

$$\rho(x_t, y_t) = \frac{\text{Cov}(x_t, y_t)}{[\text{Var}(x_t)\text{Var}(y_t)]^{1/2}}. \tag{A15.58}$$

16

Intergenerational Economics, I

The purpose of this chapter is to achieve the following goals:

1. To introduce a popular continuous-time overlapping-generations (OG) model and to show its main theoretical properties;

2. To apply this workhorse model to study fiscal policy issues and the role of debt;

3. To extend the continuous-time OG model to the cases of endogenous labour supply, age-dependent labour productivity, and the small open economy.

16.1 Introduction

In this chapter we study one of the "workhorse" models of modern macroeconomics, namely the Blanchard–Yaari model of overlapping generations. This model has proved to be quite useful because it is very flexible and contains the Ramsey model as a special case. The key element which differentiates the Blanchard–Yaari model from the Ramsey model is that the former distinguishes agents by their date of birth, whereas the latter assumes a single representative agent. By incorporating some smart modelling devices, the Blanchard–Yaari model can be solved and analysed at the aggregate macroeconomic level, despite the fact that individual households are heterogeneous.

16.2 The Blanchard–Yaari Model of Overlapping Generations

16.2.1 Yaari's lessons

One of the great certainties in life—apart from taxes—is death. After that things get fuzzy because nobody knows exactly when the Grim Reaper will make his one and only call. In all consumption models discussed so far in this book, *lifetime uncertainty* has been ignored, however. Indeed, in Chapter 6 we introduced the basic two-period consumption-saving model to illustrate the various reasons for the breakdown of the Ricardian Equivalence Theorem. But in that model each agent knows exactly that he/she will only live for two periods. Similarly, in Chapter 14 we explained the Ramsey model in which an infinitely lived representative consumer makes optimal consumption and savings decisions. Again there is no lifetime uncertainty because the agent lives forever in this model.

In a seminal article, Yaari (1965) confronted the issue of lifetime uncertainty in the context of a dynamic consumption-saving model. In doing so, he provided one of the key building blocks of the Blanchard (1985) overlapping generations model which itself has become one of the workhorse models of dynamic macroeconomics. Yaari (1965, pp. 139–140) clearly identified the two complications that arise in a model with lifetime uncertainty. First, if the agent's time of death, T, is random then so is that agent's lifetime utility function. As a result the agent's decision problem is inherently stochastic and maximizing lifetime utility makes no sense. Rather, the expected utility hypothesis must be used and *expected* lifetime utility should be the objective function. Second, the non-negativity constraint on the agent's wealth at the time of death is similarly stochastic as it also depends on the random time of death. In symbols, if $A(t)$ is real assets at time t, then $A(T)$ is stochastic and the solution procedure should ensure that $A(T) \geq 0$ holds with certainty.

Fortunately, Yaari (1965) also proposed appropriate solutions to these two complications. First, though T is a random variable all we need to do to render the expected utility hypothesis operational is to postulate the probability density function for T. Indeed, demographic data can be used to obtain quite detailed estimates of the distribution function for T. Obviously, no one has a negative expected lifetime and there also seems to be a finite upper limit, $\bar{T}$, beyond which nobody lives. So the density function for T is denoted by $f(T)$ and it satisfies:

$$f(T) \geq 0, \ \forall T \geq 0, \quad \int_0^{\bar{T}} f(T)\, dT = 1. \tag{16.1}$$

The first property is a general requirement for densities and the second one says that the random variable T lies in the interval $[0, \bar{T}]$ with probability 1 (i.e. $\Pr\{0 \leq T \leq \bar{T}\} = 1$).

The consumer's lifetime utility is denoted by $\Lambda(T)$ and is defined as follows:

$$\Lambda(T) \equiv \int_0^T U[C(\tau)]\, e^{-\rho\tau}\, d\tau, \tag{16.2}$$

where $U[C(\tau)]$ is instantaneous utility (or "felicity") at time τ, $C(\tau)$ is private consumption,[1] and ρ is the pure rate of time preference. Using this notation, the

---

[1] Labour supply is taken to be inelastically supplied. Hence, the consumption-leisure decision is not part of the consumer's optimization problem. Later on we will relax this.

expected lifetime utility can be written as:[2]

$$E\Lambda(T) \equiv \int_0^{\bar{T}} f(T)\Lambda[T]\,dT$$

$$= \int_0^{\bar{T}} \left[\int_\tau^{\bar{T}} f(T)dT \right] U[C(\tau)]\,e^{-\rho\tau}\,d\tau$$

$$= \int_0^{\bar{T}} [1 - F(\tau)]\,U[C(\tau)]\,e^{-\rho\tau}\,d\tau, \tag{16.3}$$

where $1 - F(\tau)$ is the probability that the consumer will still be alive at time τ, i.e.

$$1 - F(\tau) \equiv \int_\tau^{\bar{T}} f(T)\,dT. \tag{16.4}$$

The crucial thing to note about (16.3) is that the consumer's objective function is now in a rather standard format. Apart from containing some additional elements ($\bar{T}$ and $F(\tau)$) resulting from lifetime uncertainty, the expression in (16.3) is very similar to the utility function of the representative consumer (namely (14.53) in Chapter 14).

The second complication identified by Yaari (1965) and discussed above can also be easily dealt with. Assume that the household budget identity can be written as follows:

$$\dot{A}(\tau) = r(\tau)A(\tau) + W(\tau) - C(\tau), \tag{16.5}$$

where $\dot{A}(\tau) \equiv dA(\tau)/d\tau$, $r(\tau)$ is the rate of interest, and $W(\tau)$ is non-interest income, all expressed in real terms (units of output). Both $r(\tau)$ and $W(\tau)$ are known to the consumer as lifetime uncertainty is (by assumption) the only stochastic element in the model. The final wealth constraint, $\Pr\{A(T) \geq 0\} = 1$, is then equivalent to:[3]

$$A(\bar{T}) = 0, \quad C(\tau) \leq W(\tau) \text{ whenever } A(\tau) = 0. \tag{16.6}$$

The consumer maximizes expected lifetime utility ($E\Lambda(T)$ in (16.3)) subject to (16.5) and (16.6), the non-negativity constraint on consumption ($C(\tau) \geq 0$), and given the initial wealth level ($A(0)$). The interior solution for this optimization problem is summarized by the following expressions:

$$[1 - F(\tau)]\,U'[C(\tau)] = \lambda(\tau) \tag{16.7}$$

$$\frac{\dot{\lambda}(\tau)}{\lambda(\tau)} = \rho - r(\tau), \tag{16.8}$$

where $\lambda(\tau)$—the co-state variable associated with (16.5)—represents the expected marginal utility of wealth. Intuitively, (16.7) says that in the interior solution the

---

[2] In going from the first to the second line in (16.3) we have changed the order of integration.

[3] Yaari (1965, pp. 142–143) shows this result as follows. We know for sure that the constraint $A(\tau) \geq 0$ must hold with equality for $\tau = \bar{T}$, i.e. $A(\bar{T}) = 0$. For other values of τ it follows that $A(\tau) \geq 0$ is equivalent to $\dot{A}(\tau) = W(\tau) - C(\tau) \geq 0$ if $A(\tau) = 0$, i.e. no dissaving is allowed if no wealth remains.

consumer equates the expected marginal utility of consumption to the expected marginal utility of wealth. Equation (16.8) is the standard expression summarizing the optimal dynamics.

By combining (16.7) and (16.8) we obtain the household's consumption Euler equation in the presence of lifetime uncertainty:

$$\frac{\dot{C}(\tau)}{C(\tau)} = \sigma\,[C(\tau)]\,[r(\tau) - \rho - \beta(\tau)], \tag{16.9}$$

where $\sigma\,[C(\tau)] \equiv -U'\,[C(\tau)]\,/\,[C(\tau)U''\,[C(\tau)]] > 0$ is the intertemporal substitution elasticity (see Chapter 14) and $\beta(\tau) \equiv f(\tau)/\,[1 - F(\tau)] > 0$ is the so-called "hazard rate" or *instantaneous probability of death* at time τ. Compared to the case of an infinitely lived consumer, the hazard rate is the additional term appearing in the Euler equation.[4] This is the *first lesson* from Yaari (1965, p. 143): the uncertainty of survival leads the household to discount the future more heavily, i.e. the subjective discount rate in the presence of lifetime uncertainty is $\rho + \beta(\tau)$ rather than just ρ. This makes intuitive sense. If there is a positive probability that you will not live long enough to enjoy a given planned future consumption path, then you tend to discount the utility stream resulting from it more heavily.

Up to this point we have studied the optimal behaviour of the consumer when no insurance possibilities are available. But in reality various forms of life insurance exist so a relevant question is how this institutional feature would change the consumer's behaviour. Yaari (1965, pp. 140–141) suggests a particular kind of life insurance based on so-called *actuarial notes* issued by the insurance company. An actuarial note can be bought or sold by the consumer and is cancelled upon the consumer's death. The instantaneous rate of interest on such notes is denoted by $r^A(\tau)$ and non-zero trade in such notes only occurs if $r^A(\tau)$ exceeds $r(\tau)$. A consumer who *buys* an actuarial note in fact buys an annuity which stipulates payments to the consumer during life at a rate higher than the rate of interest. Upon the consumer's death the insurance company has no further obligations to the consumer's estate. Reversely, a consumer who *sells* an actuarial note is getting a life-insured loan. During the consumer's life he/she must pay a higher interest rate on the loan than the market rate of interest, but upon death the consumer's estate is held free of any obligations, i.e. the principal does not have to be paid back to the insurance company.

In order to determine the rate of return on actuarial notes, Yaari makes the (simplest possible) assumption of *actuarial fairness*. To derive the expression for $r^A(\tau)$ implied by this assumption, assume that one dollar's worth of actuarial notes is bought at time τ. These notes are either redeemed with interest at time $\tau + d\tau$ (if the consumer survives) or are cancelled (if the consumer dies between τ and $\tau + d\tau$).

---

[4] In the standard Ramsey model no lifetime uncertainty exists. See e.g. Chapters 14 and 15.

Actuarial fairness then implies:

$$[1 + r^A(\tau) \, d\tau] \left(\frac{1 - F(\tau + d\tau)}{1 - F(\tau)} \right) = 1 + r(\tau) \, d\tau, \tag{16.10}$$

where the equality holds as $d\tau \to 0$. The right-hand side of (16.10) shows the yield if the dollar is invested in regular market instruments whereas the left-hand side shows the yield on the actuarial note purchase. The term in round brackets is less than unity and corrects for the fact that the consumer may pass away between τ and $\tau + d\tau$. By solving for $r^A(\tau)$ and taking the limit as $d\tau \to 0$ we obtain the following—rather intuitive—no-arbitrage equation between the two kinds of financial instruments:[5]

$$r^A(\tau) = r(\tau) + \beta(\tau). \tag{16.11}$$

Recall that τ is not only the time index but also stands for the age of the consumer so (16.11) has the sensible implication that $r^A(\tau) \to \infty$ as $\tau \to \bar{T}$. The closer the consumer gets to the maximum possible age $\bar{T}$, the higher will be the instantaneous probability of death and thus the higher will be the required excess yield on actuarial notes.

Let us now return to the consumer's choice problem. As Yaari (1965, p. 145) points out, the consumer will always hold his/her financial assets in the form of actuarial notes, i.e. he/she will fully insure against the loss of life and the budget identity will be:

$$\dot{A}(\tau) = r^A(\tau)A(\tau) + W(\tau) - C(\tau). \tag{16.12}$$

Hence the restriction on the terminal asset position is trivially met as all actuarial notes are automatically cancelled when the consumer dies. The intuition behind this *full-insurance* result is best understood by looking at the two cases. If the consumer has positive net assets at any time then they will be held in the form of actuarial notes because these yield the highest return (which is all the consumer is interested in in the absence of a bequest motive). Conversely, if the consumer had any negative outstanding net assets in other than actuarial notes, he/she would be violating the constraint on terminal assets mentioned above (i.e. the requirement that $\Pr\{A(T) \geq 0\} = 1$).

We are not out of the forest of complications yet as we also need to ensure that the consumer is unable to beat the system by engaging in unlimited borrowing (sales of actuarial notes) and covering the ever increasing interest payments with

---

[5] Equation (16.11) is derived as follows. We note that (16.10) can be rewritten as:

$$r^A(\tau) = \left(\frac{1 - F(\tau)}{1 - F(\tau + d\tau)} \right) r(\tau) + \frac{[F(\tau + d\tau) - F(\tau)] / d\tau}{1 - F(\tau + d\tau)}.$$

By letting $d\tau \to 0$, the first term on the right-hand side goes to $r(\tau)$ and the second approaches $\beta(\tau) \equiv f(\tau) / [1 - F(\tau)]$.

yet further borrowings. This prompts the consumer's solvency condition (see Yaari, 1965, p. 146 for a detailed derivation):

$$A(0) + \int_0^{\bar{T}} e^{-\int_0^\tau r^A(s)ds} [W(\tau) - C(\tau)] d\tau = 0. \tag{16.13}$$

Intuitively, the condition says that the present value of the consumption stream must be equal to the sum of initial financial assets plus the present value of current and future non-interest income (i.e. "human wealth"), using the rate on actuarial notes for discounting.

The consumer maximizes expected lifetime utility ($E\Lambda(T)$ in (16.3)) subject to the solvency condition (16.13) and the non-negativity constraint on consumption ($C(\tau) \geq 0$). The interior solution to this problem is characterized by the following Euler equation:

$$\frac{\dot{C}(\tau)}{C(\tau)} = \sigma\left[C(\tau)\right]\left[r^A(\tau) - \rho - \beta(\tau)\right]$$

$$= \sigma\left[C(\tau)\right]\left[r(\tau) - \rho\right], \tag{16.14}$$

where we have used (16.11) in going from the first to the second line. The striking thing to note about (16.14)—and thus Yaari's *second lesson*—is the fact that the Euler equation with fully insured lifetime uncertainty is identical to the Euler equation when no lifetime uncertainty exists! It should be observed, however, that the consumption levels will differ between the two scenarios as the lifetime consumption possibility frontier will differ between the two cases.

16.2.2 Turning lessons into a workhorse

Yaari's crucial insights lay dormant for twenty years until Blanchard (1985) made them the core elements of his continuous-time overlapping-generations model which subsequently became one of the workhorse models of modern macroeconomics. Blanchard simplified the Yaari setup substantially by assuming that the probability density function for the consumer's time of death is *exponential*, i.e. $f(T)$ in (16.1) is specified as:

$$f(T) = \begin{cases} \beta e^{-\beta T} & \text{for } T \geq 0 \\ 0 & \text{for } T < 0 \end{cases}, \tag{16.15}$$

so that $1 - F(\tau) \equiv \int_\tau^\infty f(T) dT = f(\tau)/\beta$ and $\beta(\tau) \equiv f(\tau)/[1 - F(\tau)] = \beta$. Hence, instead of assuming an age-dependent instantaneous death probability—as Yaari did—Blanchard assumes that the hazard rate is constant and independent of the consumer's age. This approach has several advantages. First and foremost, it leads to optimal consumption rules that are easy to aggregate across households (see below). We are thus able to maintain a high level of aggregation in the model despite the fact that the underlying population of consumers is heterogeneous by age. Second, it follows from (16.15) that the *expected remaining lifetime* of any agent is equal to $1/\beta$. By setting $\beta = 0$, the Blanchard model thus coincides with the representative-agent model studied extensively in Chapters 14 and 15 above.[6]

Individual households

The first task at hand is to derive the expressions for consumption and savings for an individual household at an arbitrary time during its life. Assume that the utility function at time t of a consumer born at time $v < t$ is given by $E\Lambda(v, t)$:

$$E\Lambda(v, t) \equiv \int_t^\infty [1 - F(\tau - t)] \log C(v, \tau) e^{\rho(t-\tau)} d\tau$$

$$= \int_t^\infty \log C(v, \tau) e^{(\rho+\beta)(t-\tau)} d\tau, \tag{16.16}$$

where we have used the property of the exponential distribution in (16.15) to deduce that $1 - F(\tau - t) = e^{\beta(t-\tau)}$. Furthermore, in going from (16.3) to (16.16) we have assumed a logarithmic felicity function (featuring a unit intertemporal substitution elasticity), and we have added indexes for the agent's date of birth (v) and the time to which the decision problem refers (t). Consequently, $C(v, \tau)$ stands for planned consumption at time τ by an agent born at time v. The agent's budget identity is:

$$\dot{A}(v, \tau) = [r(\tau) + \beta] A(v, \tau) + W(\tau) - T(\tau) - C(v, \tau), \tag{16.17}$$

where $r(\tau)$, is the interest rate, $W(\tau)$ is the wage rate, $T(\tau)$ is the lump-sum tax levied by the government, and $A(v, \tau)$ are real financial assets. Equation (16.17) incorporates the Yaari notion of actuarially fair life-insurance contracts and is a straightforward generalization of (16.12) with (16.11) substituted in. Specifically, during life agents receive $\beta A(v, \tau)$ from the life-insurance company but at the time of the agent's death the entire estate $A(v, \tau)$ reverts to that company. To avoid the agent from running a Ponzi game against the life-insurance company, the following *solvency condition* must be obeyed.

$$\lim_{\tau \to \infty} e^{-R^A(t,\tau)} A(v, \tau) = 0, \quad R^A(t, \tau) \equiv \int_t^\tau [r(s) + \beta] ds. \tag{16.18}$$

By combining (16.17) and (16.18) the household's lifetime budget restriction is obtained:

$$A(v, t) + H(t) = \int_t^\infty C(v, \tau) e^{-R^A(t,\tau)} d\tau, \tag{16.19}$$

---

[6] Of course, the modelling simplification does not come without a price tag. The main disadvantage of assuming a constant instantaneous death probability is that it leads to a consumption model that—like the representative-agent model—is at odds with the typical life-cycle consumption pattern observed in empirical studies. We will return to this issue below.

where $H(t)$ is the human wealth of the agents consisting of the present value of lifetime after-tax wage income using the annuity factor, $R^A(t, \tau)$, for discounting:

$$H(t) \equiv \int_t^\infty [W(\tau) - T(\tau)]\, e^{-R^A(t,\tau)}\, d\tau. \tag{16.20}$$

Equation (16.19) is the counterpart to (16.13) above. Intuitively, it says that the present value of the household's consumption plan must be equal to the sum of financial and human wealth.

Intermezzo

Intuition behind the household's solvency condition. The intuition behind the household's solvency condition (16.18) can be explained as follows. We note that (16.17) can be premultiplied by $e^{-R^A(t,\tau)}$ and rearranged to:

$$\left[\dot{A}(v, \tau) - [r(\tau) + \beta] A(v, \tau)\right] e^{-R^A(t,\tau)} = [W(\tau) - T(\tau) - C(v, \tau)] e^{-R^A(t,\tau)}$$

$$\frac{d}{d\tau}\left[A(v, \tau)e^{-R^A(t,\tau)}\right] = [W(\tau) - T(\tau) - C(v, \tau)] e^{-R^A(t,\tau)}, \tag{a}$$

where we have used the fact that $dR^A(t, \tau)/d\tau = r(\tau) + \beta$ (Leibnitz's rule) in going from the first to the second line. By integrating both sides of (a) over the interval $[t, \infty)$ we obtain:

$$\int_t^\infty dA(v, \tau)e^{-R^A(t,\tau)} = \int_t^\infty [W(\tau) - T(\tau) - C(v, \tau)] e^{-R^A(t,\tau)}\, d\tau$$

$$\lim_{\tau \to \infty} e^{-R^A(t,\tau)}A(v, \tau) - A(v, t) = H(t) - \int_t^\infty C(v, \tau)e^{-R^A(t,\tau)}\, d\tau, \tag{b}$$

where we have used (16.20) and have noted that $e^{-R^A(t,t)} = 1$. The insurance companies will ensure that the limit on the left-hand side of (b) (loosely referred to as "terminal assets") will be non-negative. Similarly, it is not in the best interest of the consumer to plan for positive terminal assets as he/she has no bequest motive and does not get satiated from consuming goods (as the marginal felicity of consumption remains strictly positive—see (16.16)). Hence, planned terminal assets will be strictly equal to zero. This yields the solvency condition (16.18). By using it in (b) the expression for the household's lifetime budget restriction (16.19) is obtained. See Chiang (1992, pp. 101–103) for a more formal discussion of the transversality condition in an infinite-horizon optimal control problem.

The consumer maximizes expected lifetime utility (16.17) subject to its lifetime budget restriction (16.19). The first-order conditions are (16.19) and:

$$\left(\frac{1}{C(v,\tau)}\right)e^{(\rho+\beta)(t-\tau)} = \lambda(t)e^{-R^A(t,\tau)}, \quad \tau \in [t,\infty), \tag{16.21}$$

where $\lambda(t)$, the Lagrange multiplier associated with the lifetime budget restriction (16.19), represents the marginal expected lifetime utility of wealth.[7] Intuitively, the optimality condition (16.21) instructs the consumer to plan consumption at each time to be such that the appropriately discounted marginal utility of consumption (left-hand side) and wealth (right-hand side) are equated (see also the discussion following). By using (16.21) for the planning period ($\tau = t$) we see that $C(v,t) = 1/\lambda(t)$. Using this result and (16.19) in (16.21) we can express $C(v,t)$ in terms of total wealth:

$$\int_t^\infty C(v,t)e^{(\rho+\beta)(t-\tau)}\,d\tau = \int_t^\infty C(v,\tau)e^{-R^A(v,\tau)}\,d\tau$$

$$\left(\frac{C(v,t)}{\rho+\beta}\right)\left[-e^{(\rho+\beta)(t-\tau)}\right]_t^\infty = A(v,t)+H(t) \quad\Leftrightarrow$$

$$C(v,t) = (\rho+\beta)\left[A(v,t)+H(t)\right]. \tag{16.22}$$

Optimal consumption in the planning period ($\tau = t$) is proportional to total wealth, and the marginal propensity to consume out of total wealth is constant and equal to the "effective" rate of time preference, $\rho + \beta$.

Aggregate households

Now that we know what the consumption rules for individual households look like, the next task at hand is to describe the demographic structure of the Blanchard model. To keep things simple, Blanchard assumes that at each instant in time a *large* cohort of new agents is born. The size of this cohort of newborns is $P(\tau,\tau) = \beta P(\tau)$, where $P(\tau)$ stands for the aggregate population size at time τ. These newborn agents start their lives without any financial assets as they are unlinked to any existing agents and thus receive no bequests, i.e. $A(\tau,\tau) = 0$. Of course, at each instant in time a fraction of the existing population dies. Since each individual agent faces an instantaneous probability of death equal to β and the number of agents $P(\tau)$ is large, "frequencies and probabilities coincide" and the number of deaths at each instant will be equal to $\beta P(\tau)$. Since births and deaths exactly match, the size of the population is constant and can be normalized to unity ($P(\tau) = 1$).[8]

---

[7] Note that by differentiating (16.21) with respect to τ we obtain the household's Euler equation:

$$\frac{\dot{C}(v,\tau)}{C(v,\tau)} = r(\tau) - \rho.$$

In the OG model we also need to solve for the consumption *level* in the planning period.

[8] Net population change can easily be incorporated in the Blanchard model by allowing the birth and death rates to differ—see Buiter (1988).

Another very useful consequence of the large-cohort assumption is that we can exactly trace the size of any particular cohort over time. For example, a cohort born at time v will be of size $\beta e^{\beta(v-t)}$ at time $t \geq v$, because $\beta\left[1 - e^{\beta(v-t)}\right]$ of the cohort members will have died in the time interval $[v, t]$. Since we know the size of each cohort it is possible to work with aggregate variables. For example, by aggregating the consumption levels of all existing agents in the economy we obtain the following expression for aggregate consumption at time t:

$$C(t) \equiv \beta \int_{-\infty}^{t} e^{\beta(v-t)} C(v, t)\, dv. \tag{16.23}$$

Of course, (16.23) is simply a definition and is not of much use in and of itself. But because the optimal consumption rule (16.22) features a propensity to consume out of total wealth which is independent of the generations index v, equation (16.23) gives rise to a very simple aggregate consumption rule:

$$\begin{aligned}
C(t) &\equiv \beta \int_{-\infty}^{t} e^{\beta(v-t)}(\rho + \beta)\,[A(v, t) + H(t)]\, dv \\
&= (\rho + \beta)\left[\beta \int_{-\infty}^{t} e^{\beta(v-t)} A(v, t)\, dv + \beta \int_{-\infty}^{t} e^{\beta(v-t)} H(t)\, dv\right] \\
&= (\rho + \beta)\,[A(t) + H(t)], \tag{16.24}
\end{aligned}$$

where aggregate financial wealth is defined analogously to aggregate consumption (given in (16.23)). It cannot be overemphasized that the aggregation property follows from the assumption that each agent faces a constant instantaneous death probability (see (16.16)). If instead the hazard rate varies with age—as in the Yaari (1965) model—then the optimal household consumption rule no longer features a generation-independent marginal propensity to consume out of total wealth and exact aggregation is impossible.

What does the aggregate asset accumulation identity look like? By definition we have that $A(t) \equiv \beta \int_{-\infty}^{t} A(v, t) e^{\beta(v-t)}\, dv$ from which we derive (by application of Leibnitz's rule):

$$\dot{A}(t) = \beta A(t, t) - \beta A(t) + \beta \int_{-\infty}^{t} \dot{A}(v, t) e^{\beta(v-t)}\, dv, \tag{16.25}$$

where the first term on the right-hand side represents assets of newborns ($A(t, t) = 0$), the second term is the wealth of agents who die, and the third term is the change in assets of existing agents. By substituting (16.17) into (16.25) and simplifying we obtain the aggregate asset accumulation identity:

$$\begin{aligned}
\dot{A}(t) &= -\beta A(t) + \beta \int_{-\infty}^{t} [[r(t) + \beta]\,A(v, t) + W(t) - T(t) - C(v, t)] e^{\beta(v-t)}\, dv \\
&= -\beta A(t) + [r(t) + \beta]\,A(t) + W(t) - T(t) - C(t) \\
&= r(t) A(t) + W(t) - T(t) - C(t). \tag{16.26}
\end{aligned}$$

Whereas individual wealth attracts the actuarial interest rate, $r(t)+\beta$, for agents that stay alive (see 16.17), equation (16.26) shows that aggregate wealth accumulates at the rate of interest, $r(t)$. The amount $\beta A(t)$ does not represent aggregate wealth accumulation but is a transfer—via the life-insurance companies—from those who die to those who remain alive.

In the formal analysis of the model it is useful to have an expression for the "aggregate Euler equation". It follows from (16.23) that:

$$\dot{C}(t) = \beta C(t,t) - \beta C(t) + \beta \int_{-\infty}^{t} \dot{C}(v,t) e^{\beta(v-t)} \, dv. \tag{16.27}$$

According to (16.22) newborn agents consume a fraction of their human wealth at birth, i.e. $C(t,t) = (\rho+\beta)H(t)$. Equation (16.24) shows that aggregate consumption is proportional to total (human and financial) wealth, i.e. $C(t) = (\rho + \beta)[A(t) + H(t)]$. Finally, it follows from (16.21) that individual households' consumption growth satisfies $\dot{C}(v,\tau)/C(v,\tau) = r(\tau) - \rho$ for $\tau \in [t, \infty)$ (see footnote 7). By using all these results in (16.27) we obtain the aggregate Euler equation modified for the existence of overlapping generations of finitely lived agents:

$$\frac{\dot{C}(t)}{C(t)} = r(t) - \rho - \beta(\rho + \beta)\left(\frac{A(t)}{C(t)}\right) \tag{16.28}$$

$$= \frac{\dot{C}(v,t)}{C(v,t)} - \beta\left(\frac{C(t) - C(t,t)}{C(t)}\right). \tag{16.29}$$

Equation (16.28) has the same form as the Euler equation for individual households except for the correction term due to the distributional effects caused by the turnover of generations. Optimal consumption *growth* is the same for all generations (since they face the same interest rate) but older generations have a higher consumption *level* than younger generations (since the former generations are wealthier). Since existing generations are continually being replaced by newborns who hold no financial wealth, aggregate consumption growth falls short of individual consumption growth. The correction term appearing on the right-hand side of (16.28) thus represents the difference in average consumption and consumption by newborns, i.e. (16.28) can be re-expressed as in (16.29).

Firms

The production sector is characterized by a large number of firms that produce an identical good under perfect competition. Output, $Y(t)$, is produced according to a linearly homogeneous technology with labour, $L(t)$, and physical capital, $K(t)$, as homogeneous factor inputs which are rented from households:

$$Y(t) = F\left(K(t), L(t)\right), \tag{16.30}$$

Table 16.1. The Blanchard–Yaari model

$$\dot{C}(t) = [r(t) - \rho]\, C(t) - \beta(\rho + \beta)\, [K(t) + B(t)] \tag{T1.1}$$

$$\dot{K}(t) = F(K(t), L(t)) - C(t) - G(t) - \delta K(t) \tag{T1.2}$$

$$\dot{B}(t) = r(t)B(t) + G(t) - T(t) \tag{T1.3}$$

$$r(t) + \delta = F_K(K(t), L(t)) \tag{T1.4}$$

$$W(t) = F_L(K(t), L(t)) \tag{T1.5}$$

$$L(t) = 1 \tag{T1.6}$$

Notes: $C(t)$ is consumption, $K(t)$ is the capital stock, $B(t)$ is government debt, $W(t)$ is the wage rate, $T(t)$ is lump-sum taxes, and $r(t)$ is the interest rate. Capital depreciates at a constant rate δ, β is the birth rate (equals death rate), and ρ is the pure rate of time preference.

where $F(.)$ satisfies the usual Inada conditions (see Chapter 14). The stockmarket value of the representative firm is:

$$V(t) = \int_t^\infty [Y(\tau) - W(\tau)L(\tau) - I(\tau)]\, e^{-R(t,\tau)}\, d\tau, \quad R(t, \tau) \equiv \int_t^\tau r(s)\, ds. \tag{16.31}$$

The firm chooses labour and capital in order to maximize (16.31) subject to the production function (16.30) and the capital accumulation constraint:

$$\dot{K}(t) = I(t) - \delta K(t), \tag{16.32}$$

where $I(t)$ denotes gross investment, and δ is the constant rate of depreciation of capital. There are no adjustment costs associated with investment. The first-order conditions imply that the marginal productivity of labour and capital equal the producer costs of these factors—see, respectively, equations (T1.4) and (T1.5) in Table 16.1. Finally, we recall from Chapter 14 that the market value of the firm is equal to the replacement value of its capital stock, i.e. $V(t) = K(t)$.

The government and market equilibrium

The government budget identity is given in (T1.3) in Table 16.1. The government consumes $G(t)$ units of the good and levies lump-sum taxes on households $T(t)$. Government debt is $B(t)$ so that $r(t)B(t)$ is interest payments on outstanding debt. Like the private sector, the government must remain solvent and obey a no-Ponzi-game condition like:

$$\lim_{\tau \to \infty} e^{-R(t,\tau)}B(\tau) = 0. \tag{16.33}$$

By using (T1.3) and (16.33) the government budget restriction is obtained:

$$B(t) = \int_t^\infty [T(\tau) - G(\tau)] e^{-R(t,\tau)} d\tau. \tag{16.34}$$

Intuitively, government solvency means that if there is a pre-existing government debt (positive left-hand side) it must be covered in present-value terms by present and future primary surpluses (right-hand side).

At each instant of time, factor and goods markets clear instantaneously. In this closed economy households can only accumulate domestic assets so that, as a result, financial market equilibrium requires that $A(t) = K(t) + B(t)$. Wage flexibility ensures that the aggregate supply of labour ($L(t) = 1$) by households matches labour demand by firms. Goods market equilibrium is obtained when the supply of goods equals aggregate demand, which consists of private and public consumption plus investment: $Y(t) = C(t) + I(t) + G(t)$. For convenience, the key equations of the model have been gathered in Table 16.1.

The phase diagram

In order to illustrate some of the key properties of the model we now derive the phase diagram in Figure 16.1. We assume for simplicity that lump-sum taxes, government consumption, and public debt are all zero in the initial situation ($T(t) = G(t) = B(t) = 0$). The $\dot{K}(t) = 0$ line represents points for which the capital stock is in equilibrium. The Inada conditions (see Chapter 14) ensure that it passes through the origin and is vertical there (see point A_1 in Figure 16.1). Golden-rule

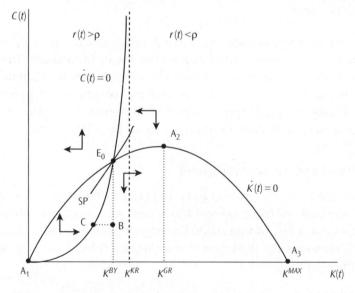

Figure 16.1. Phase diagram of the Blanchard–Yaari model

(GR) consumption occurs at point A_2 where the $\dot{K}(t) = 0$ line reaches its maximum:

$$\left(\frac{dC(t)}{dK(t)}\right)_{\dot{K}(t)=0} = 0: \quad F_K\left(K^{GR}, 1\right) = \delta. \tag{16.35}$$

The maximum attainable capital stock, K^{MAX}, occurs at point A_3, where consumption is zero and total output is used for replacement investment ($F\left(K^{MAX}, 1\right)/K^{MAX} = \delta$). For points above (below) the $\dot{K}(t) = 0$ line consumption is too high (too low) to be consistent with a capital stock equilibrium and consequently net investment is negative (positive). This has been indicated by horizontal arrows in Figure 16.1.

The derivation of the $\dot{C}(t) = 0$ line is a little more complex because its position and slope depend on the interplay between effects due to capital scarcity and those attributable to intergenerational-distribution effects. Recall from Chapter 14 that the "Keynes-Ramsey" (KR) capital stock, K^{KR}, is such that the rate of interest equals the exogenously given rate of time preference, i.e. $r^{KR} = F_K(K^{KR}, 1) - \delta \equiv \rho$. Since K^{GR} is associated with a zero interest rate and there are diminishing returns to capital ($F_{KK} < 0$), K^{KR} lies to the left of the golden-rule point as is indicated in Figure 16.1. Furthermore, for points to the left (right) of the dashed line, capital is relatively scarce (abundant), and the interest rate exceeds (falls short of) the pure rate of time preference.

When agents have finite lives ($\beta > 0$) the $\dot{C} = 0$ line is upward sloping because of the turnover of generations. Its slope can be explained by appealing directly to equations (16.28) (with $A = K$ as we set $B = 0$), (16.29), and Figure 16.1. Suppose that the economy is initially on the $\dot{C} = 0$ curve, say at point E_0. Now consider a lower level of consumption, say at point B. With the same capital stock, both points feature the same rate of interest. Accordingly, individual consumption growth, $\dot{C}(v, t)/C(v, t)$ $[= r - \rho]$, coincides at the two points.

Expression (16.29) indicates, however, that aggregate consumption growth depends not only on individual growth but also the *proportional* difference between average consumption and consumption by a newly born generation, i.e. $[C(t) - C(t, t)]/C(t)$. Since newly born generations start without any financial capital, the absolute difference between average consumption and consumption of a newly born household depends on the average capital stock and is thus the same at the two points. Since the level of aggregate consumption is lower at B (than it is at E_0), this point features a larger proportional difference between average and newly born consumption, thereby decreasing aggregate consumption growth (i.e. $\dot{C}(t) < 0$). In order to restore zero growth of aggregate consumption, the capital stock must fall (to point C). The smaller capital stock not only raises individual consumption growth by increasing the rate of interest but also lowers the drag on aggregate consumption growth due to the turnover of generations because a smaller capital stock narrows the gap between average wealth (i.e. the wealth of the generations that pass away) and wealth of the newly born. In summary, for points above (below) the $\dot{C}(t) = 0$ line, the capital-scarcity effect dominates (is dominated by) the intergenerational-redistributional effect and consumption rises (falls) over time.[9] This is indicated with vertical arrows in Figure 16.1.

In terms of Figure 16.1, steady-state equilibrium is attained at the intersection of the $\dot{K}(t) = 0$ and $\dot{C}(t) = 0$ lines at point E_0. Given the configuration of arrows, it is clear that this equilibrium is saddle-point stable, and that the saddle path, SP, is upward sloping and lies between the two equilibrium loci.

16.3 Applications of the Basic Model

16.3.1 The effects of fiscal policy

As a first application of the Blanchard–Yaari model we now consider the effects of a typical fiscal policy experiment, consisting of an unanticipated and permanent increase in government consumption. We abstract from debt policy by assuming that the government balances its budget by means of lump-sum taxes only, i.e. $\dot{B}(t) = B(t) = 0$ and $G(t) = T(t)$ in equation (T1.3). We also assume that the economy is initially in a steady state and that the time of the shock is normalized to $t = 0$.

In terms of Figure 16.2, the $\dot{K}(t) = 0$ line is shifted downward by the amount of the shock dG. In the short run the capital stock is predetermined and the economy jumps from point E_0 to A on the new saddle path SP_1. Over time the economy gradually moves from A to the new steady-state equilibrium at E_1. As is clear from the figure, there is less than one-for-one crowding out of private by public consumption in the impact period, i.e. $-1 < dC(0)/dG < 0$. In contrast, there is more than one-for-one crowding out in the long run, i.e. $dC(\infty)/dG < -1$.

The reason for these crowding-out results is that the change in the lump-sum tax induces an intergenerational redistribution of resources away from future towards present generations (Bovenberg and Heijdra, forthcoming). At impact, all households cut back on private consumption because the higher lump-sum tax reduces the value of their human capital. Since households discount present and future tax liabilities at the annuity rate ($r(\tau) + \beta$, see (16.20)) rather than at the interest rate, existing households at the time of the shock do not feel the full burden of the additional taxes and therefore do not cut back their consumption by a sufficient amount. As a result, private investment is crowded out at impact ($\dot{K}(t) < 0$ at point A) and the capital stock starts to fall. This in turn puts downward pressure on before-tax wages and upward pressure on the interest rate so that human capital falls over time. So, future generations are poorer than newborn generations at the

---

[9] Since the economy features positive initial assets (as $K > 0$), the $\dot{C} = 0$ line lies to the left of the dashed line representing K^{KR} and approaches this line asymptotically as C gets large (and the intergenerational-redistribution effect gets small). If there is very little capital, the rate of interest is very high and the $\dot{C} = 0$ line is horizontal.

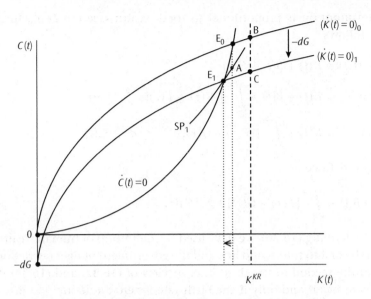

Figure 16.2. Fiscal policy in the Blanchard–Yaari model

time of the shock because they have less capital to work with and thus receive lower wages (since $F_{LK} < 0$).

If the birth rate is zero ($\beta = 0$) there is a single infinitely lived representative consumer and intergenerational redistribution is absent. Crowding out of consumption is one-for-one, there is no effect on the capital stock, and thus no transitional dynamics. In terms of Figure 16.2, the only effect on the economy consists of a downward jump in consumption from point B to point C.

16.3.2 The non-neutrality of government debt

The previous subsection has demonstrated that lump-sum taxes cause intergenerational redistribution of resources in the Blanchard–Yaari model. This suggests that Ricardian equivalence does not hold in this model, i.e. the timing of taxes is not intergenerationally neutral and debt has real effects. Ricardian non-equivalence can be demonstrated by means of some simple "bookkeeping" exercises (see also Chapter 14). The result that must be proved is that, ceteris paribus the time path of government consumption ($G(\tau)$ for $\tau \in [t, \infty)$), aggregate consumption ($C(t)$) depends on pre-existing debt ($B(t)$) and the time path of taxes ($T(\tau)$ for $\tau \in [t, \infty)$) (Buiter, 1988, p. 285).

Total consumption is proportional to total wealth (see (16.24)) which can be written as follows:

$$A(t) + H(t) \equiv K(t) + B(t) + H(t)$$

$$= K(t) + B(t) + \int_t^\infty [W(\tau) - T(\tau)] e^{-R^A(t,\tau)} \, d\tau$$

$$= K(t) + \int_t^\infty [W(\tau) - G(\tau)] e^{-R^A(t,\tau)} \, d\tau + \Omega(t), \tag{16.36}$$

where $\Omega(t)$ is defined as:

$$\Omega(t) \equiv B(t) - \int_t^\infty [T(\tau) - G(\tau)] e^{-R^A(t,\tau)} \, d\tau. \tag{16.37}$$

Note that in deriving (16.36), we have used the definition of human wealth (16.20) to go from the first to the second line and the government budget restriction (16.34) to get from the second to the third line. In view of (16.37) and (16.34) it follows that $\Omega(t)$ vanishes if and only if the birth rate is zero and $R^A(t, \tau) = R(t, \tau)$. If the birth rate is positive, $\Omega(t)$ is non-zero and Ricardian equivalence does not hold.

Recall that in the Blanchard–Yaari model the birth rate of new generations is equal to the instantaneous death probability facing existing generations. As a result it is not a priori clear which aspect of the model is responsible for the failure of Ricardian equivalence. The analysis of Weil (1989b) provides the strong hint that it is the arrival rate of new generations which destroys Ricardian equivalence (see Chapter 14 above). This suggestion was formally demonstrated by Buiter (1988) who integrates and extends the Blanchard–Yaari-Weil models by allowing for differential birth and death rates (β_B and β_D) and Hicks-neutral technical change. In his model the population grows at an exponential rate $n \equiv \beta_B - \beta_D$. Buiter (1988, p. 285) demonstrates that a zero birth rate ($\beta_B = 0$) is indeed necessary and sufficient for Ricardian equivalence to hold.

16.4 Extensions

In this section we demonstrate the flexibility of the Blanchard—Yaari model—and thus document its workhorse status—by showing how easily it can be extended in various directions. These extensions are by no means the only ones possible—some others are mentioned in the Further Reading section of this chapter.

16.4.1 Endogenous labour supply

As we have seen throughout the book, an endogenous labour supply response often plays a vital role in the various macroeconomic theories. In Chapter 15, for example, it was demonstrated that the intertemporal substitutability of household leisure forms one of the key mechanisms behind most models in the real business cycle (RBC) tradition. The aim of this subsection is therefore to extend the basic Blanchard–Yaari model by allowing for an endogenous labour supply decision of the households. We follow Heijdra and Ligthart (2000) by introducing various taxes and assuming simple functional forms for preferences and technology in order to keep the discussion as simple as possible. We analyse the effects of a consumption tax in order to demonstrate some of the key properties of the model.

Extending the model

Assume that the utility function used so far (see (16.16)) is replaced by:

$$E\Lambda(v, t) \equiv \int_t^\infty \log\left[C(v, \tau)^{\epsilon_C}\left[1 - L(v, \tau)\right]^{1-\epsilon_C}\right] e^{(\rho+\beta)(t-\tau)}\, d\tau, \tag{16.38}$$

with $0 < \epsilon_C \leq 1$. Leisure is defined as the consumer's time endowment (which is normalized to unity) minus labour supply, $L(v, \tau)$. Note that (16.16) is obtained as a special case of (16.38) setting $\epsilon_C = 1$. Since labour supply is now endogenous, the agent's budget identity (16.17) is replaced by:

$$\dot{A}(v, \tau) = [r(\tau) + \beta] A(v, \tau) + W(\tau)(1 - t_L) + Z(\tau) - X(v, \tau), \tag{16.39}$$

$$X(v, \tau) \equiv (1 + t_C)C(v, \tau) + W(\tau)(1 - t_L)\left[1 - L(v, \tau)\right], \tag{16.40}$$

where $X(v, \tau)$ represents *full consumption*, i.e. the sum of spending on goods consumption and leisure, t_C is a proportional tax on private consumption, t_L is a proportional tax on labour income, and $Z(\tau)$ are age-independent transfers received from the government. The household's solvency condition is still given by (16.18).

Following Marini and van der Ploeg (1988) we solve the household's optimization problem by using *two-stage budgeting*. We have encountered this technique several times before in this book, albeit in the context of static models—see for example Chapters 11 and 13. The procedure is, however, essentially the same in dynamic models. Intuitively the procedure works as follows. In the first stage we determine how the consumer chooses an optimal mix of consumption and leisure conditional upon a given level of full consumption ($X(v, \tau)$). Then, in the second stage, we determine the optimal time path for full consumption itself. The procedure is valid provided the utility function is *intertemporally separable*.[10]

In *stage 1* the consumer chooses $C(v, \tau)$ and $[1 - L(v, \tau)]$ in order to maximize instantaneous felicity, $\log\left[C(v, \tau)^{\epsilon_C}[1 - L(v, \tau)]^{1-\epsilon_C}\right]$, given the restriction (16.40) and conditional upon the level of $X(v, \tau)$. This optimization problem yields the familiar first-order condition calling for the equalization of the marginal rate of

---

[10] Preferences are intertemporally separable if the marginal utility of consumption and leisure at time τ only depends on time τ dated variables. Intertemporal separability is commonly assumed in the macro literature and indeed holds for (16.38). See also Deaton and Muellbauer (1980, p. 124).

substitution between leisure and consumption and the relative price of leisure and consumption:

$$\frac{(1 - \epsilon_C)/[1 - L(v, \tau)]}{\epsilon_C/C(v, \tau)} = W(\tau)\left(\frac{1 - t_L}{1 + t_C}\right). \tag{16.41}$$

By substituting (16.41) into (16.40), we obtain expressions for consumption and leisure in terms of full consumption:

$$(1 + t_C)C(v, \tau) = \epsilon_C X(v, \tau), \tag{16.42}$$

$$W(\tau)(1 - t_L)[1 - L(v, \tau)] = (1 - \epsilon_C)X(v, \tau). \tag{16.43}$$

Since sub-felicity—the term in square brackets in (16.38)—is Cobb–Douglas and thus features a unit substitution elasticity, spending shares on consumption and leisure are constant. To prepare for the second stage we substitute (16.42)–(16.43) into the lifetime utility functional (16.38) to obtain the following expression:

$$E\Lambda(v, t) \equiv \int_t^\infty [\log X(v, \tau) - \log P_\Omega(\tau)] e^{(\rho+\beta)(t-\tau)} d\tau, \tag{16.44}$$

where $P_\Omega(\tau)$ is a true cost-of-living index relating sub-felicity to full consumption:

$$P_\Omega(\tau) \equiv \left(\frac{1 + t_C}{\epsilon_C}\right)^{\epsilon_C} \left(\frac{W(\tau)(1 - t_L)}{1 - \epsilon_C}\right)^{1-\epsilon_C}. \tag{16.45}$$

In *stage 2*, the consumer chooses the path of full consumption in order to maximize (16.44) subject to the dynamic budget identity (16.39) and the solvency condition (16.18). This problem is essentially the same as the one that was solved in Section 16.2.2 above so it should therefore not surprise the reader that the solution takes the following form:

$$X(v, t) = (\rho + \beta)[A(v, t) + H(t)], \tag{16.46}$$

$$\frac{\dot{X}(v, \tau)}{X(v, \tau)} = r(\tau) - \rho, \quad \text{for } \tau \in [t, \infty), \tag{16.47}$$

$$H(t) \equiv \int_t^\infty [W(\tau)(1 - t_L) + Z(\tau)] e^{-R^A(t, \tau)} d\tau. \tag{16.48}$$

Equation (16.46) says that full consumption is proportional to total wealth (the sum of financial and human wealth) whereas (16.47) shows that optimal full consumption growth depends on the difference between the interest rate and the pure rate of time preference. Finally, (16.48) is the definition of human wealth. It differs from (16.20) because labour income is taxed at a proportional rate and because the household receives transfers.

By aggregating (16.46) and (16.47) across surviving generations and making use of (16.42)–(16.43), expressions for aggregate consumption growth and labour supply are obtained—see equations (T2.1) and (T2.6) in Table 16.2. Compared to the basic

Table 16.2. The extended Blanchard–Yaari model

$$\frac{\dot{C}(t)}{C(t)} = r(t) - \rho - \epsilon_C \beta(\rho + \beta) \left[\frac{K(t)}{(1 + t_C)C(t)} \right], \tag{T2.1}$$

$$\dot{K}(t) = Y(t) - C(t) - \delta K(t) \tag{T2.2}$$

$$Z(t) = t_L W(t)L(t) + t_C C(t) \tag{T2.3}$$

$$r(t) + \delta = (1 - \epsilon_L) \left(\frac{Y(t)}{K(t)} \right) \tag{T2.4}$$

$$W(t) = \epsilon_L \left(\frac{Y(t)}{L(t)} \right) \tag{T2.5}$$

$$W(t) [1 - L(t)] = \left(\frac{1 - \epsilon_C}{\epsilon_C} \right) \left(\frac{1 + t_C}{1 - t_L} \right) C(t), \quad 0 < \epsilon_C \le 1. \tag{T2.6}$$

$$Y(t) = K(t)^{1-\epsilon_L} L(t)^{\epsilon_L}, \quad 0 < \epsilon_L < 1 \tag{T2.7}$$

Notes: $C(t)$ is consumption, $K(t)$ is the capital stock, $L(t)$ is labour supply, $Y(t)$ is aggregate output, $W(t)$ is the wage rate, $Z(t)$ are lump-sum transfers, and $r(t)$ is the interest rate. There are proportional taxes on consumption (t_C) and on wage income (t_L). Capital depreciates at a constant rate δ, β is the birth rate (equals death rate), and ρ is the pure rate of time preference.

Blanchard–Yaari model we have introduced the following simplifications. First, we abstract from government spending and debt ($G(t) = B(t) = \dot{B}(t) = 0$) and assume that all tax revenues are rebated to households in a lump-sum fashion. As a result, the government budget identity is static—see (T2.3) in Table 16.2. Second, we have simplified the production structure of the extended model somewhat by assuming a Cobb-Douglas technology—see (T2.7). Using this specification in (T1.2), (T1.4), and (T1.5) yields the expressions (T2.2), (T2.4), and (T2.5), respectively.

Phase diagram

The phase diagram of the model is drawn in Figure 16.3. The endogeneity of the labour supply decision considerably complicates the derivation of the phase diagram. For that reason we report the details of this derivation in a mathematical appendix to this chapter and focus here on a graphical and intuitive discussion.

The capital stock equilibrium locus (CSE) represents the (C, K) combinations for which net investment is zero ($\dot{K} = 0$). Apart from the fact that the model now includes various tax rates and government consumption is set equal to zero, the CSE line is identical to the one discussed in detail in Chapter 15. The CSE line is

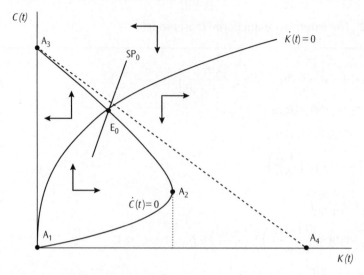

Figure 16.3. Phase diagram for the extended Blanchard–Yaari model

concave and for points above (below) this line consumption is too high (low) and net investment is negative (positive).[11]

The consumption equilibrium (CE) locus represents the (C, K) combinations for which *aggregate* consumption is constant ($\dot{C} = 0$). In the representative-agent model of Chapter 15, aggregate and individual consumption coincide and CE is simply the locus of points for which the interest rate equals the rate of time preference ($r = \rho$) and the output-capital ratio is constant (see Chapter 15 for details). For convenience, the CE line for the representative-agent model is included in the figure as the dashed line connecting points A_3 and A_4 (see Figure 16.3).

In contrast, in the overlapping-generations model, individual and aggregate consumption do not coincide and as a result, the position and slope of the CE curve are affected by two conceptually distinct mechanisms, namely the *factor scarcity effect* (FS, which explains the slope of the CE curve for the representative-agent model) and the *generational turnover effect* (GT). The interplay between these two effects ensures that CE has the shape of a rather prominent nose. Along the lower branch, $A_1 A_2$, consumption is low, equilibrium employment is close to unity ($L \approx 1$), and CE is upward sloping. In contrast, along the upper branch, $A_2 A_3$, consumption is high, equilibrium employment is low ($L \approx 0$), and CE slopes downward. The dynamic

---

[11] We have only drawn the upward-sloping part of the CSE line. Recall from Chapter 15 that CSE reaches a maximum for the "golden-rule" capital stock, K^{GR}, and then becomes downward sloping.

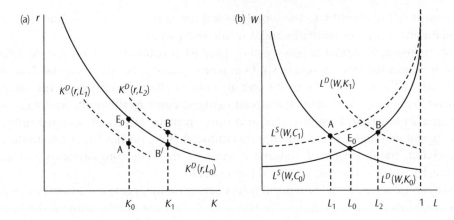

Figure 16.4. Factor markets

forces at work can be studied by writing (T2.1) as follows:

$$\frac{\dot{C}(t)}{C(t)} = r(t) - \rho - \beta \left(\frac{C(t) - C(t,t)}{C(t)} \right)$$

$$= r(C(t), K(t)) - \rho - \left(\frac{\beta \epsilon_C (\rho + \beta)}{1 + t_C} \right) \left(\frac{K(t)}{C(t)} \right), \tag{16.49}$$

where $r(C, K)$ is short-hand notation for the dependence of the real interest rate on consumption and the capital stock. Simple intuitive arguments can be used to motivate the signs of the partial derivatives of the $r(C, K)$ function, which are denoted by r_C and r_K, respectively. Some simple graphs can clarify matters.

Consider Figure 16.4 which depicts the situation in the rental market for capital and the labour market. In panel (a), the supply of capital is predetermined in the short run—say at K_0. The demand for capital is downward sloping—due to diminishing returns to capital—and depends positively on the employment level—because the two factors are cooperative in production. Panel (b) depicts the situation in the labour market. There are diminishing returns to labour—so labour demand slopes downwards—and additional capital boosts labour demand. The labour supply curve follows from the optimal leisure-consumption choice (T2.6). It slopes upwards because (T2.6) isolates the pure substitution effect of labour supply.[12]

Let us now use Figure 16.4 to deduce the signs of r_C and r_K. Ceteris paribus the capital stock, an increase in consumption shifts labour supply to the left so that the wage rises and employment falls. The reduction in employment shifts the demand for capital to the left so that—for a given inelastic supply of capital—the real interest

---

[12] Normally, in static models of labour supply, the income and substitution effects work in opposite directions thus rendering the slope of the labour supply curve ambiguous. Here we do not have this "problem" because the income effect is incorporated in C. Technically speaking, (T2.6) is a so-called *Frisch demand* curve for leisure. See also Judd (1987b).

561

rate must fall to equilibrate the rental market for capital, i.e. $r_C < 0$. The thought experiment compares points E_0 and A in the two panels.

An increase in capital supply—ceteris paribus consumption—has a *direct effect* which pushes the interest rate down (a movement along the initial capital demand schedule, $K^D(r, L_0)$ from E_0 to B′) and an *induced effect* operating via the labour market. The boost in K shifts the labour demand curve to the right, leading to an increase in wages and employment and thus (in panel (a)) to an outward shift in the capital demand curve. Although this induced effect pushes the interest rate up somewhat, the direct effect dominates and $r_K < 0$.[13] The comparison is between points E_0 and B in the two panels of Figure 16.4.

We can now study the dynamical forces acting on aggregate consumption along the two branches of the CE curve in Figure 16.3. First consider a point on the lower branch of this curve (for which $L \approx 1$). Holding capital constant, an increase in aggregate consumption leads to a small decrease in labour supply[14] and thus a small decrease in the interest rate. At the same time, however, the capital-consumption ratio falls so that aggregate consumption growth increases, i.e. $\dot{C}/C > 0$ for points above the lower branch of CE:

$$\underbrace{\frac{\dot{C}}{C}}_{\uparrow} = \underbrace{r(C,K)}_{\downarrow} - \rho - \left(\frac{\beta\epsilon_C(\rho + \beta)}{1 + t_C}\right)\underbrace{\left(\frac{K}{C}\right)}_{\downarrow\downarrow}. \qquad \text{(lower branch of CE)}$$

Now consider a point on the upper branch of the CE curve (for which $L \approx 0$). Ceteris paribus K, a given increase in C has a strong negative effect on labour supply and thus causes a large reduction in the interest rate which offsets the effect operating via the capital-consumption ratio, i.e. $\dot{C}/C < 0$ for points above the upper branch of CE:

$$\underbrace{\frac{\dot{C}}{C}}_{\downarrow} = \underbrace{r(C,K)}_{\downarrow\downarrow} - \rho - \left(\frac{\beta\epsilon_C(\rho + \beta)}{1 + t_C}\right)\underbrace{\left(\frac{K}{C}\right)}_{\downarrow}. \qquad \text{(upper branch of CE)}$$

These dynamic effects have been illustrated with vertical arrows in Figure 16.3.

[13] This follows directly from the *factor price frontier*, which is obtained by substituting (T2.4) and (T2.5) into (T2.7):

$$1 = \left(\frac{r + \delta}{1 - \epsilon_L}\right)^{1 - \epsilon_L}\left(\frac{W}{\epsilon_L}\right)^{\epsilon_L}.$$

The boost in the wage is associated with a higher capital labour ratio and thus relatively more abundant capital. This translates itself into a lower return to capital.

[14] Holding constant the tax rates we can use (T2.6) to derive:

$$\frac{dL}{L} = \left(\frac{1 - L}{L}\right)\left[\frac{dW}{W} - \frac{dC}{C}\right].$$

Hence, for $L \approx 1$ ($L \approx 0$) the labour supply curve in Figure 16.4 is relatively steep (flat) and a given change in consumption shifts the curve by a little (a lot). This explains why the parameter $\omega_{LL} \equiv (1 - L)/L$ plays a vital role in the analysis of the loglinearized model below.

In summary, the CE curve is very similar to the one for the standard Blanchard model with exogenous labour supply (see Figure 16.1) for values of L close to unity (the lower branch in Figure 16.3). At the same time, it is very similar to the CE curve for the representative-agent model with endogenous labour supply for values of L close to zero (compare the upper branch of CE in Figure 16.3 with the dashed line). Put differently, on the lower branch of the CE curve the generational turnover effect dominates whereas on the upper branch the factor scarcity effect dominates.

It follows from the configuration of arrows that the unique equilibrium E_0 in Figure 16.3 is saddle-point stable. Although we have drawn Figure 16.3 such that the equilibrium occurs on the downward-sloping part of the CE curve (for which the factor scarcity effect dominates the generational turnover effect), there is nothing to prevent the opposite occurring, i.e. it is quite possible that the structural parameters are such that E_0 lies on the lower branch of CE.

Raising the consumption tax

We now illustrate how the model can be used for policy analysis. We focus attention on the effects of an unanticipated and permanent increase in the consumption tax, t_C. Using the methods explained in detail in Chapter 15, the model can be loglinearized along an initial steady state (such as E_0). The resulting expressions are collected in Table 16.3.

Table 16.3. The loglinearized extended model

$$\dot{\tilde{C}}(t) = r\tilde{r}(t) + (r - \rho)\left[\tilde{C}(t) + \tilde{t}_C - \tilde{K}(t)\right] \tag{T3.1}$$

$$\dot{\tilde{K}}(t) = (\delta/\omega_I)\left[\tilde{Y}(t) - \omega_C\tilde{C}(t) - \omega_I\tilde{K}(t)\right] \tag{T3.2}$$

$$\tilde{Z}(t) = (1 + t_C)\omega_C\left[\tilde{t}_C + \left(\frac{t_C}{1 + t_C}\right)\tilde{C}(t)\right] + \epsilon_L t_L\tilde{Y}(t) \tag{T3.3}$$

$$r\tilde{r}(t) = (r + \delta)\left[\tilde{Y}(t) - \tilde{K}(t)\right] \tag{T3.4}$$

$$\tilde{W}(t) = \tilde{Y}(t) - \tilde{L}(t) \tag{T3.5}$$

$$\tilde{L}(t) = \omega_{LL}\left[\tilde{W}(t) - \tilde{t}_C - \tilde{C}(t)\right] \tag{T3.6}$$

$$\tilde{Y}(t) = \epsilon_L\tilde{L}(t) + (1 - \epsilon_L)\tilde{K}(t) \tag{T3.7}$$

Definitions: $\omega_C \equiv C/Y$: output share of private consumption; $\omega_I \equiv I/Y$: output share of investment, $\omega_C + \omega_I = 1$, $\delta/\omega_I = y \equiv (r + \delta)/(1 - \epsilon_L)$; $\omega_{LL} \equiv (1 - L)/L$: ratio between leisure and labour; $\tilde{x}(t) \equiv \dot{x}(t)/x$, $\tilde{x}(t) \equiv \log[x(t)/x]$, $\tilde{t}_C \equiv dt_C/(1 + t_C)$, $\tilde{Z}(t) \equiv dZ(t)/Y$.

Solving the loglinearized model is child's play and proceeds along much the same lines as in Chapter 15. First we use (T3.5)–(T3.7) to compute the "quasi-reduced-form" expression for output:

$$\tilde{Y}(t) = \phi(1 - \epsilon_L)\tilde{K}(t) - (\phi - 1)\left[\tilde{C}(t) + \tilde{t}_C\right], \tag{16.50}$$

where ϕ summarizes the intertemporal labour supply effects (see also equation (15.26) above):

$$1 \le \phi \equiv \frac{1 + \omega_{LL}}{1 + \omega_{LL}(1 - \epsilon_L)} < \frac{1}{1 - \epsilon_L}. \tag{16.51}$$

Second, we use (16.50) in (T3.2) and impose $\dot{\tilde{K}}(t) = 0$ to get the loglinearized CSE line:

$$\tilde{C}(t) = \left(\frac{\phi(1 - \epsilon_L) - \omega_I}{\omega_C + \phi - 1}\right)\tilde{K}(t) - \left(\frac{\phi - 1}{\omega_C + \phi - 1}\right)\tilde{t}_C. \tag{16.52}$$

The CSE curve is upward sloping (since $rK/Y = 1 - \epsilon_L - \omega_I > 0$ and $\phi \ge 1$) and an increase in the consumption tax shifts the curve down—see the shift from CSE_0 to CSE_1 in Figures 16.5 and 16.6. For a given capital stock, an increase in t_C reduces labour supply, and thus employment and output. To restore capital stock equilibrium, employment and output must return to their former levels, i.e. consumption must fall.

Finally, we obtain the loglinearized CE line by substituting (16.50) and (T3.4) into (T3.1) and setting $\dot{\tilde{C}}(t) = 0$:

$$\tilde{C}(t) = -\left(\frac{(r + \delta)\left[1 - \phi(1 - \epsilon_L)\right] + r - \rho}{(\phi - 1)(r + \delta) - (r - \rho)}\right)\tilde{K}(t) - \tilde{t}_C. \tag{16.53}$$

As was apparent from our discussion concerning Figure 16.3 above, the slope of the CE line around the initial steady state is ambiguous and depends on the relative strength of the factor scarcity and generational turnover effects. These two effects show up in the denominator of the coefficient for $\tilde{K}(t)$ on the right-hand side as, respectively, $(\phi - 1)(r + \delta)$ (for the FS effect) and $(r - \rho)$ (for the GT effect). There are thus two cases of interest. First, if $(r - \rho)$ exceeds $(\phi - 1)(r + \delta)$ then the GT effect dominates the FS effect, and the CE line is upward sloping as in Figure 16.5. Second, if the reverse holds and $(\phi - 1)(r + \delta)$ is larger than $(r - \rho)$ then the FS effect dominates the GT effect so that the CE curve is downward sloping as in Figure 16.6.

It turns out that the effect of the consumption tax on the long-run capital stock depends critically on the relative strength of the GT and FS effects. Indeed, by solving (16.52) and (16.53) we obtain the following expression for the steady-state

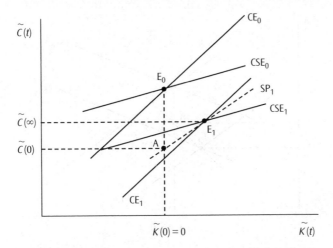

Figure 16.5. Consumption taxation with a dominant GT effect

effect on capital of the consumption tax change:

$$\tilde{K}(\infty) = \left(\frac{(r - \rho) - (\phi - 1)(r + \delta)}{\phi \epsilon_L \left[(r + \delta)\omega_C + r - \rho \right]} \right) \omega_C \tilde{t}_C. \tag{16.54}$$

If the GT effect is stronger (weaker) than the FS effect, an increase in the consumption tax leads to an increase (decrease) in the long-run capital stock. The intuition behind these results can be explained with the aid of Figures 16.5 and 16.6.

In Figure 16.5 the GT effect is dominant $(r - \rho > (\phi - 1)(r + \delta))$, the CSE curve shifts down by less than the CE curve does, and the steady state shifts from E_0 to E_1. At impact the tax shock causes a redistribution from old to young existing generations. The old generations are wealthy and thus have a high consumption level, whereas the young generations consume very little and thus face only a small increase in their tax bill. Since the additional tax revenue is recycled to all generations in an age-independent lump-sum fashion, older generations are hit harder by the tax shock than younger generations are and the proportional difference in consumption between the old and young agents falls. In terms of (16.49), $r(t)$ changes hardly at all (because the FS effect is weak) but the generational turnover term, $[C(t) - C(t, t)]/C(t)$, falls so that aggregate consumption growth increases at impact, i.e. $\tilde{C}(0) < 0$ and $\dot{\tilde{C}}(0) > 0$ at point A. The reduction in aggregate consumption outweighs the fall in production (which is slight because labour supply changes by very little), net investment takes place ($\dot{\tilde{K}}(0) > 0$ at point A) and the economy gradually moves from point A to the new steady state in E_1.

Matters are quite different if the FS effect dominates the GT effect, a situation which is depicted in Figure 16.6. Now the downward shift in CE dominates the downward shift in CSE and the new steady state, E_1, is associated with a lower

565

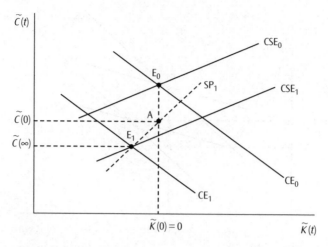

Figure 16.6. Consumption taxation with a dominant FS effect

capital stock. This long-run effect is best understood by noting that with a dominant FS effect, the long-run capital-labour ratio is more or less unchanged. Since the consumption tax reduces labour supply this can only occur if the capital stock falls also.[15] In the impact period the reduction in consumption is dominated by the fall in output and net investment is negative. At the same time, the reduction in labour supply reduces the capital-labour ratio at impact so that the interest rate falls and the aggregate consumption profile becomes downward sloping. In summary, it follows that both $\dot{K}(0) < 0$ and $\dot{C}(0) < 0$ at point A. Over time, the economy gradually moves from point A to the new steady state at E_1.

Discussion

We have demonstrated that the qualitative effects of a consumption tax in the extended Blanchard–Yaari model depend critically on the relative importance of the GT and FS effects. A simple (rough and ready) calibration exercise suggests that the empirically relevant case is likely to be such that the FS effect is dominant. Consider for this purpose the parameters used to calibrate the unit-elastic RBC model discussed in Chapter 15. In that chapter we used $r = 0.0159$ per quarter (6.5% annual rate of interest), $\delta = 0.0241$ (10% per annum), $\epsilon_L = 2/3$ so that $y = (r + \delta)/(1 - \epsilon_L) = 0.12$ and $\omega_I = I/Y = \delta/y = 0.201$. Since we abstract from government consumption, the output share of consumption is $\omega_C = 1 - \omega_I = 0.799$. Just as in Chapter 15, we assume that 20% of available time is used for working, so that $\omega_{LL} \equiv (1 - L)/L = 4$.

---

[15] If the GT effect is absent altogether ($\beta = 0$), the steady-state interest rate equals the rate of time preference ($r = \rho$) and the capital-labour ratio does not change at all. See the discussion surrounding the *great ratios* in Chapter 15 above.

Using the calibration values of ϵ_L and ω_{LL} in the definition of ϕ (given in (16.51) above) we get $\phi = 2.143$ and:

$$(\phi - 1)(r + \delta) = 0.0457 \qquad \text{(Calibrated FS effect)}$$

It remains to find a plausible value for $(r - \rho)$ in the overlapping generations model. This is where we need more detailed information on the variables affecting the household sector. We assume that the initial tax rates are $t_C = 0.1$ and $t_L = 0.3$. By using (T2.5)–(T2.6) we get the implied estimate for ϵ_C:

$$\epsilon_C = \left[1 + \left(\frac{\epsilon_L \omega_{LL}}{\omega_C}\right)\left(\frac{1 - t_L}{1 + t_C}\right)\right]^{-1} = 0.320. \qquad (16.55)$$

From the steady-state version of (T2.1) we can then derive:

$$r - \rho = \beta(\rho + \beta)\left(\frac{\epsilon_C}{1 + t_C}\right)\left(\frac{K/Y}{C/Y}\right) = \beta(\rho + \beta) \times 3.037. \qquad (16.56)$$

This expression still contains two parameters, namely the pure rate of time preference (ρ) and the birth rate (β), neither of which is directly observable.[16] Recall, however, that in the Blanchard setting $1/\beta$ represents the expected remaining lifetime of all agents. As a result, we do not expect β to be very high. Suppose that agents have a planning horizon of 200 quarters, so that the implied birth/death rate is $\beta = 0.005$. Plugging this value into (16.56) and recalling that $r = 0.0159$ we obtain the implied value for the pure rate of time preference, $\rho = 0.0156$, so that:

$$r - \rho = 0.000312. \qquad \text{(Calibrated GT effect)}$$

Hence, for this value of β the FS effect is much stronger than the GT effect. In Table 16.4 we compute the GT effect for a number of alternative values of β. The results indicate that the FS effect continues to dominate even for quite high (and unrealistic) values for the birth rate. For example, even if $\beta = 0.04$ so that households' expected remaining lifetime is only 25 quarters, the FS effect still dominates the GT effect. We conclude that for reasonable parameters the GT effect is quite weak and is dominated by the FS effect.[17]

16.4.2 Age-dependent productivity

In the standard Blanchard–Yaari model labour supply is exogenous and workers of all ages have the same productivity, i.e. a 60-year old worker produces the same amount

[16] Of course the actual birth and mortality rates in an economy can be observed. It is not possible to directly link actual demographic data to the Blanchard–Yaari model, because in reality (1) the birth and mortality rates are typically not equal, (2) the death hazard is not age-independent, and (3) immigration typically explains part of the population increase.

[17] The fact that the OG effect is of negligible order for plausible birth rates suggests that the extended Blanchard–Yaari model has all the properties of an RBC model. Rios-Rull (1994) confirms this result using a much more complicated OG model which is plausibly calibrated for the US economy.

Table 16.4. The birth rate and the GT effect

β	$1/\beta$	ρ	GT effect	FS effect
0.005	200	0.0156	0.000312	0.0457
0.01	100	0.0151	0.000762	0.0457
0.02	50	0.0138	0.002054	0.0457
0.04	25	0.0098	0.006051	0.0457
0.07229	13.83	0	0.015868	0.0457

of output in a unit of time as his 25-year old colleague does. We now consider what happens if worker productivity is age-dependent. To keep things simple, we assume that agents supply one unit of "raw" labour throughout their lives but that the productivity of their labour declines exponentially with age.

With age-dependent productivity, the aggregate production function (16.30) is replaced by:

$$Y(\tau) = F(K(\tau), N(\tau)), \tag{16.57}$$

where $N(\tau)$ is the aggregate labour input in *efficiency units*:

$$N(\tau) \equiv \int_{-\infty}^{\tau} N(v, \tau)dv = \int_{-\infty}^{\tau} E(\tau - v)L(v, \tau)dv. \tag{16.58}$$

In this equation, $E(\tau - v)$ represents the efficiency of a worker of generation v at time τ (whose *age* is thus $\tau - v$) and $L(v, \tau)$ is the total number of raw labour units supplied by generation-v workers at time τ. Since all workers supply one unit of raw labour during life and generations die at a proportional rate β, it follows that:

$$L(v, \tau) = e^{-\beta(\tau-v)}L(v, v) = \beta e^{-\beta(\tau-v)}. \tag{16.59}$$

We assume that efficiency falls exponentially with the age of the worker:

$$E(\tau - v) \equiv \left(\frac{\alpha + \beta}{\beta}\right) e^{-\alpha(\tau-v)}, \tag{16.60}$$

where $\alpha > 0$ is the proportional rate at which worker productivity declines with age (Note that the term in round brackets represents a convenient normalization). According to (16.60), a 20-year old worker is $e^{10\alpha}$ times as productive as a 30-year old worker. By substituting (16.59)–(16.60) into (16.58) and integrating we derive that the aggregate supply of labour in efficiency units equals unity:

$$N(\tau) = 1. \tag{16.61}$$

The objective function of the representative firm is changed from (16.31) to:

$$V(t) = \int_{t}^{\infty} \left[F(K(\tau), N(\tau)) - \int_{-\infty}^{\tau} W(v, \tau)L(v, \tau)dv - I(\tau) \right] e^{-R(t,\tau)}d\tau, \tag{16.62}$$

where $N(\tau)$ is defined in (16.58) and the capital accumulation constraint is given in (16.32). The firm hires raw units of labour from all age groups in the economy $(L(v, \tau))$ but pays an age-dependent wage $(W(v, \tau))$ because it knows that labour productivity depends on age. The first-order conditions for an optimum are:

$$r(\tau) + \delta = F_K(K(\tau), N(\tau)), \tag{16.63}$$

$$W(v, \tau) = E(\tau - v)F_N(K(\tau), N(\tau)). \tag{16.64}$$

The first-order condition for capital is the same as before (compare (T1.4) and (16.63)) but the one for labour is different (compare (T1.5) and (16.64)). Ceteris paribus the aggregate capital-effective-labour ratio $(K(\tau)/N(\tau))$, the wage rate declines with the age of the worker. Hence, even in the steady state households will face a downward-sloping profile of wage income over their lives. Since households want to consume both when they are young and when they are old, they formulate their savings decisions during youth taking into account that they will have little or no labour income later on in life. As Blanchard (1985, p. 235) points out, a declining path of labour income loosely captures the notion of "saving for retirement".

To keep things simple, we assume that the household has a logarithmic felicity function and maximizes lifetime utility (given in (16.16) above) subject to the budget identity (16.17) (with $W(\tau)$ replaced by $W(v, \tau)$) and the solvency condition (16.18). Abstracting from government taxes and transfers, private consumption in the planning period is:

$$C(v, t) = (\rho + \beta)[A(v, t) + H(v, t)], \tag{16.65}$$

where human wealth, $H(v, t)$, is now age-dependent:[18]

$$H(v, t) \equiv \int_t^\infty W(v, \tau)e^{-R^A(t, \tau)} \, d\tau$$

$$= \int_t^\infty \left(\frac{\alpha + \beta}{\beta}\right) e^{\alpha(v - \tau)} W(\tau)e^{-R^A(t, \tau)} \, d\tau$$

$$= e^{\alpha(v - t)} H(t, t), \tag{16.66}$$

where $H(t, t)$ is the human wealth of a newborn at time t:

$$H(t, t) \equiv \left(\frac{\alpha + \beta}{\beta}\right) \int_t^\infty W(\tau) \exp\left\{-\int_t^\tau [r(s) + \alpha + \beta] \, ds\right\} d\tau. \tag{16.67}$$

---

[18] In going from the first to the second line we make use of the fact that $W(v, \tau)$ can be rewritten as:

$$W(v, \tau) = \left(\frac{\alpha + \beta}{\beta}\right) e^{-\alpha(\tau - v)} W(\tau),$$

where $W(\tau) = F_N(., .)$ is the aggregate wage. To get from the second to the third line we have used the definition of $R^A(t, \tau)$ as given in (16.18).

Aggregate human wealth in the economy is given by:

$$H(t) \equiv \beta \int_{-\infty}^{t} e^{\beta(v-t)} H(v,t)\, dv$$

$$= H(t,t) \int_{-\infty}^{t} \beta e^{(\alpha+\beta)(v-t)}\, dv$$

$$= \left(\frac{\beta}{\alpha+\beta} \right) H(t,t)$$

$$= \int_{t}^{\infty} W(\tau) \exp \left\{ -\int_{t}^{\tau} [r(s)+\alpha+\beta]\, ds \right\} d\tau. \tag{16.68}$$

The important lesson to be drawn from (16.68) is that the decline in the labour income of individual generations results in a higher discounting of future aggregate labour income in the definition of aggregate human wealth. Not only do current generations face a risk of dying but they also get a smaller share of aggregate wage income as they get older.

In summary, the aggregate household model developed in this subsection is given by:

$$C(t) = (\rho + \beta) [A(t) + H(t)], \tag{16.69}$$

$$\dot{A}(t) = r(t)A(t) + W(t) - C(t), \tag{16.70}$$

$$\dot{H}(t) = [r(t) + \alpha + \beta] H(t) - W(t). \tag{16.71}$$

By differentiating (16.69) with respect to t and substituting (16.70)–(16.71) we obtain the Euler equation for aggregate consumption:

$$\frac{\dot{C}(t)}{C(t)} = [r(t) + \alpha - \rho] - (\alpha + \beta)(\rho + \beta) \left(\frac{A(t)}{C(t)} \right). \tag{16.72}$$

This expression reduces to the Euler equation for the standard Blanchard–Yaari model (given in equation (16.28)) if productivity is constant throughout life and $\alpha = 0$.

The dynamical system characterizing the economy is:

$$\dot{C}(t) = [F_K(K(t), 1) + \alpha - (\rho + \delta)]C(t) - (\alpha + \beta)(\rho + \beta)K(t) \tag{16.73}$$

$$\dot{K}(t) = F(K(t), 1) - C(t) - \delta K(t), \tag{16.74}$$

where we assume that government debt and consumption are both zero ($B(t) = G(t) = 0$). Equation (16.73) is obtained by substituting $A(t) = K(t)$, (16.61), and (16.63) into the aggregate Euler equation (16.72). Equation (16.74) is simply the standard expression for capital accumulation in the absence of government consumption.

Figure 16.7 shows the phase diagram for the model given in (16.73)–(16.74). We make the usual Inada-style assumptions regarding the production function.

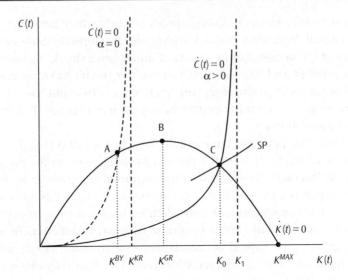

Figure 16.7. Dynamic inefficiency and declining productivity

In Figure 16.7, the $\dot{K}(t) = 0$ line and the dashed $\dot{C}(t) = 0$ line, labelled "$\alpha = 0$", reproduce the equilibrium loci for the standard Blanchard–Yaari model illustrated in Figure 16.1. Point A is the standard Blanchard–Yaari (BY) equilibrium for which the steady-state capital stock is K^{BY}. The golden-rule capital stock (K^{GR}, for which consumption is at its maximum) is defined in (16.35). Since $K^{BY} < K^{GR}$ the standard Blanchard–Yaari model is *dynamically efficient*. Now consider the effects of declining productivity. It is clear from (16.74) that the $\dot{K}(t) = 0$ line is not affected by α. It follows from (16.73), however, that the $\dot{C}(t) = 0$ line rotates in a clockwise fashion around the origin as α is increased. If α is not very large then the relevant $\dot{C}(t) = 0$ line will intersect the $\dot{K}(t) = 0$ line along the line segment AB and the equilibrium will still be dynamically efficient. There is nothing, however, preventing the occurrence of dynamic inefficiency as depicted in Figure 16.7.[19] The equilibrium at point C is saddle-point stable but there is overaccumulation of capital. Intuitively, because labour income is high early on in life, agents save a lot during youth as a result of which the aggregate capital stock can become too large.

16.4.3 The open economy

As a final extension we now consider how the Blanchard–Yaari approach can be used to model the open economy. In the interests of space we restrict attention to the

---

[19] In Figure 16.7, K_1 is such that $r_1 \equiv F_K(K_1, 1) - \delta = \rho - \alpha$ so a necessary condition for dynamic inefficiency to occur is $\alpha > \rho$ (so that $r_1 < 0$). Abel et al. (1989) show how to test empirically for dynamic inefficiency. Their results suggest that the US economy is dynamically efficient.

case of a small open economy in a single-product world which faces perfect mobility of financial capital. We use this model, which was developed by Matsuyama (1987), to investigate the macroeconomic effects of an oil price shock. To keep the model as simple as possible we follow Heijdra and van der Horst (2000) by assuming simple functional forms for technology and preferences. To avoid the counterfactual phenomenon of perfect mobility of *physical* capital it is assumed that investment is subject to adjustment costs.

The representative perfectly competitive firm has a Cobb-Douglas production function, reported in (T5.7), which is linearly homogeneous in the private production factors, capital ($K(t)$), labour ($L(t)$), and imported energy (e.g. oil, $O(t)$), where $Y(t)$ is gross output and the parameters satisfy $0 < \epsilon_L, \epsilon_K, \epsilon_O < 1$ and $\epsilon_L + \epsilon_K + \epsilon_O = 1$. The firm faces convex adjustment costs defined on gross investment. We follow Uzawa (1969) and Hayashi (1982) by postulating an installation function, $\phi(.)$, which links gross to net capital accumulation—see equation (T5.1), where $I(\tau)$ is gross investment and δ is the depreciation rate. The firm maximizes the present value of its cash flow,

$$V(t) = \int_t^\infty [Y(\tau) - W(\tau)L(\tau) - P_O(\tau)O(\tau) - I(\tau)] e^{r(t-\tau)} d\tau, \tag{16.75}$$

subject to the production function (T5.7) and the installation cost function (T5.1), where $P_O(\tau)$ is the relative price of energy which is determined in world markets and taken as given by the agents in the small open economy. The resulting optimality conditions yield expressions for labour demand, (T5.3), energy demand, (T5.4), investment demand, (T5.6), and the shadow value of installed capital (namely Tobin's q), (T5.2). Since the installation cost function, $\phi(.)$, is homogeneous of degree zero in $I(\tau)$ and $K(\tau)$ and the production technology is linear-homogeneous in the factors of production, Tobin's marginal and average q coincide, and the stockmarket value of the firm equals $V(t) = q(t)K(t)$ (see Hayashi, 1982).

The household sector of the model is as in the standard Blanchard–Yaari model. Labour supply is exogenous—see equation (T5.5). Individual households consume according to (16.22) and aggregate household consumption is given by (16.24). Since the country is small in world financial markets and there is perfect mobility of financial capital, the interest rate appearing in, respectively, the individual and aggregate budget equations (namely (16.17) and (16.26)) is taken as given by the domestic agents. In the remainder we assume that the world rate of interest is also constant over time, i.e. $r(t) = r$. For that reason the aggregate consumption Euler equation (16.28) can be written as follows:

$$\frac{\dot{C}(t)}{C(t)} = r - \rho - \beta(\rho + \beta)\left(\frac{A(t)}{C(t)}\right). \tag{16.76}$$

It follows from this expression that for a country populated with relatively patient (impatient) households, the rate of time preference falls short of (exceeds) the world interest rate, and steady-state financial wealth (A) is positive (negative). We follow

Table 16.5. The small open economy model

(a) Investment subsystem

$$\dot{K}(t) = \left[\phi\left(\frac{I(t)}{K(t)}\right) - \delta\right]K(t) \tag{T5.1}$$

$$\dot{q}(t) = \left[r + \delta - \phi\left(\frac{I(t)}{K(t)}\right)\right]q(t) + \frac{I(t)}{K(t)} - F_K(L(t), K(t), O(t)) \tag{T5.2}$$

$$W(t) = F_L(L(t), K(t), O(t)) \tag{T5.3}$$

$$P_O(t) = F_O(L(t), K(t), O(t)) \tag{T5.4}$$

$$L(t) = 1 \tag{T5.5}$$

$$1 = q(t)\phi'\left(\frac{I(t)}{K(t)}\right) \tag{T5.6}$$

$$Y(t) = F(L(t), K(t), O(t)) = L(t)^{\epsilon_L} K(t)^{\epsilon_K} O(t)^{\epsilon_O} \tag{T5.7}$$

(b) Saving subsystem

$$\dot{H}(t) = (r + \beta)H(t) - W(t) \tag{T5.8}$$

$$\dot{A}(t) = (r - \rho - \beta)A(t) - (\rho + \beta)H(t) + W(t) \tag{T5.9}$$

(c) Net foreign assets

$$A_F(t) = A(t) - q(t)K(t) \tag{T5.10}$$

Note: $\epsilon_L + \epsilon_K + \epsilon_O = 1$

Matsuyama (1987, p. 306) by restricting attention to the case of a *creditor country* for which $r > \rho$ and thus $A > 0$.[20]

The government plays no role in the model, i.e. lump-sum taxes, public debt, and government consumption are all zero ($T(t) = B(t) = G(t)$). Household can hold their wealth in the form of shares in domestic firms ($V(t) = q(t)K(t)$) and in net foreign assets ($A_F(t)$) so that equilibrium in the asset markets is given by equation (T5.10). By differentiating this expression with respect to time and using (T5.1)–(T5.7) we obtain:

$$\dot{A}_F(t) = rA_F(t) + [Y(t) - C(t) - I(t) - P_O(t)O(t)]. \tag{16.77}$$

Equation (16.77) is the current account of the balance of payments, showing the evolution of the stock of net foreign assets. The term in square brackets on the

---

[20] See Blanchard (1985, pp. 230–231) for the analysis of both creditor ($r > \rho$) and debtor ($r < \rho$) nations in a world without physical capital. Giovannini (1988) considers both cases in a two-commodity model in which physical capital is perfectly mobile across borders.

Table 16.6. The loglinearized small open economy model

(a) Investment subsystem

$$\dot{\tilde{K}}(t) = \left(\frac{r\omega_I}{\omega_V}\right)\left[\tilde{I}(t) - \tilde{K}(t)\right] \tag{T6.1}$$

$$\dot{\tilde{q}}(t) = r\tilde{q}(t) - \left(\frac{r\epsilon_K}{\omega_V}\right)\left[\tilde{Y}(t) - \tilde{K}(t)\right] \tag{T6.2}$$

$$\tilde{W}(t) = \tilde{Y}(t) \tag{T6.3}$$

$$\tilde{P}_O(t) = \tilde{Y}(t) - \tilde{O}(t) \tag{T6.4}$$

$$\tilde{q}(t) = \sigma_A\left[\tilde{I}(t) - \tilde{K}(t)\right] \tag{T6.5}$$

$$\tilde{Y}(t) = \epsilon_K\tilde{K}(t) + \epsilon_O\tilde{O}(t) \tag{T6.6}$$

(b) Saving subsystem

$$\dot{\tilde{H}}(t) = (r + \beta)\tilde{H}(t) - r\epsilon_L\tilde{W}(t) \tag{T6.7}$$

$$\dot{\tilde{A}}(t) = (r - \rho - \beta)\tilde{A}(t) - (\rho + \beta)\tilde{H}(t) + r\epsilon_L\tilde{W}(t) \tag{T6.8}$$

(c) Net foreign assets

$$\tilde{A}_F(t) = \tilde{A}(t) - \omega_V\left[\tilde{K}(t) + \tilde{q}(t)\right] \tag{T6.9}$$

Definitions: $\omega_C \equiv C/Y$: output share of private consumption; $\omega_I \equiv I/Y$: output share of investment, $\omega_C + \omega_I = 1$; $\omega_V \equiv rqK/Y$: income from shares as a ratio of total output; and $\omega_F \equiv rA_F/Y$: income from net foreign assests as a ratio of total output.

right-hand side of (16.77) is the trade balance consisting of domestic value added $(Y(t) - P_O(t)O(t))$ minus domestic absorption $(C(t) + I(t))$.

Since aggregate consumption is given by $C(t) = (\rho + \beta)[A(t) + H(t)]$ and $T(t) = 0$, the aggregate household budget identity (16.26) can be written as in (T5.9). Finally, the path for human wealth is obtained by differentiating (16.20) with respect to time, noting that $dR^A(t, \tau)/d\tau = r(t) + \beta = r + \beta$, and setting $T(t) = 0$. The resulting expression is given in equation (T5.8).

In order to study the effects of an oil price shock we loglinearize the model around an initial steady state. The resulting expressions are found in Table 16.6, where we use the following notational conventions. (i) $\tilde{x}(t) \equiv \log[x(t)/x]$ and $\dot{\tilde{x}}(t) \equiv \dot{x}(t)/x$ for $x \in \{C, K, q, Y, I, W, P_O\}$, and (ii) $\tilde{x}(t) \equiv r[x(t) - x]/Y$ and $\dot{\tilde{x}}(t) \equiv r\dot{x}(t)/Y$ for $x \in \{A, H, A_F\}$.

The key thing to note about the model is that it can be solved recursively, i.e. the total system can be subdivided into an *investment subsystem*, describing the dynamics of physical capital and Tobin's q, and a *savings subsystem*, describing the dynamics of human and financial wealth (and thus of aggregate household consumption). So even though the full system contains four dynamic variables (K, q, H, and A), the dynamics of (K, q) decouples from that of (H, A).[21] In order to find the relevant expressions for the two subsystems we first summarize the static part of the model as much as possible. By using (T6.6) and (T6.4) we obtain the quasi-reduced form expression for aggregate output, the wage rate, and energy usage:

$$\tilde{Y}(t) = \tilde{W}(t) = \frac{\epsilon_K \tilde{K}(t) - \epsilon_O \tilde{P}_O(t)}{\epsilon_L + \epsilon_K}, \tag{16.78}$$

$$\tilde{O}(t) = \frac{\epsilon_K \tilde{K}(t) - \tilde{P}_O(t)}{\epsilon_L + \epsilon_K}. \tag{16.79}$$

According to these expressions, an increase in the capital stock (or a decrease in the energy price) boosts the demand for both labour and energy (because all factors are cooperative in production) and leads to an increase in output, wages, and energy usage.

By using the output expression from (16.78) in (T6.2) and (T6.5) in (T6.1) we obtain a simple representation for the investment subsystem.

$$\begin{bmatrix} \dot{\tilde{K}}(t) \\ \dot{\tilde{q}}(t) \end{bmatrix} = \begin{bmatrix} 0 & \frac{r\omega_I}{\sigma_A \omega_V} \\ \frac{r\epsilon_L \epsilon_K}{\omega_V (\epsilon_L + \epsilon_K)} & r \end{bmatrix} \begin{bmatrix} \tilde{K}(t) \\ \tilde{q}(t) \end{bmatrix} + \begin{bmatrix} 0 \\ \frac{r\epsilon_K \epsilon_O}{\omega_V (\epsilon_L + \epsilon_K)} \end{bmatrix} \tilde{P}_O(t). \tag{16.80}$$

The Jacobian matrix on the right-hand side of (16.80) has the following characteristic polynomial:

$$p_I(\lambda) = \lambda(\lambda - r) - \frac{r^2 \epsilon_K \epsilon_L \omega_I}{\sigma_A \omega_V^2 (\epsilon_L + \epsilon_K)}, \tag{16.81}$$

which has distinct roots $-\lambda_1^I < 0$ (stable) and $\lambda_2^I = r + \lambda_1^I > r$ (unstable). This shows that the investment subsystem is saddle-point stable with the capital stock and Tobin's q acting as, respectively, the predetermined and jumping variables.

---

[21] Some authors prefer to analyse the savings subsystem by expressing it in terms of (C, A_F) dynamics (see e.g. Matsuyama, 1987 and Bovenberg, 1993, 1994). We prefer the approach adopted here because it stresses the link between, on the one hand, the current account and on the other hand, the behaviour of domestic savers and investors. This makes the interpretation of the results easier.

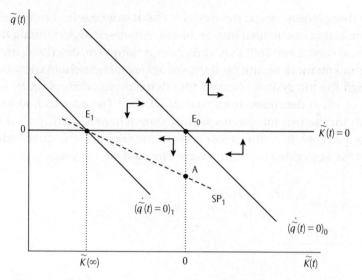

Figure 16.8. The effect of an oil shock on the investment subsystem

Similarly, the savings subsystem (T6.7)–(T6.8) can be written in a compact format as follows:

$$\begin{bmatrix} \dot{\tilde{H}}(t) \\ \dot{\tilde{A}}(t) \end{bmatrix} = \begin{bmatrix} r+\beta & 0 \\ -(\rho+\beta) & r-(\rho+\beta) \end{bmatrix} \begin{bmatrix} \tilde{H}(t) \\ \tilde{A}(t) \end{bmatrix} - \begin{bmatrix} 1 \\ -1 \end{bmatrix} r\epsilon_L \tilde{W}(t). \qquad (16.82)$$

The Jacobian matrix on the right-hand side of (16.82) has the following characteristic polynomial:

$$p_S(\lambda) = [\lambda - (r+\beta)][\lambda + (\rho+\beta - r)], \qquad (16.83)$$

from which it follows that the savings subsystem has one stable root, $-\lambda_1^S = r - (\rho + \beta) < 0$, and one unstable root, $\lambda_2^S = r + \beta > 0$.[22] Financial and human wealth act as, respectively, the predetermined and jumping variables.

Investment dynamics

Let us now consider the macroeconomic effects of an unanticipated and permanent increase in the world price of energy. We normalize the time at which the shock occurs at $t = 0$ and the shock to the system is represented by $\tilde{P}_O(t) = \tilde{P}_O$ for $t \geq 0$. We

---

[22] The determinant of the Jacobian matrix in (16.82) is: $|\Delta^S| = -(r+\beta)[\rho + \beta - r]$. Since $\text{tr}(\Delta^S) = 2r - \rho > 0$ it follows that there is at least one positive root. Saddle-point stability requires there to be one stable and one unstable root, i.e. $|\Delta^S| < 0$ and thus (since $r + \beta > 0$) that $r < \rho + \beta$. See Blanchard (1985, p. 230) and Matsuyama (1987, p. 305).

find the solution as follows. First we solve the response of the investment subsystem to the shock. Next, by substituting the implied solution path for the wage rate ($\tilde{W}(t)$) and the initial condition for financial wealth (i.e. the capital loss term on domestic shares) into the savings subsystem we obtain the solution paths for human and financial wealth. Finally, the path of net foreign assets then follows residually from (T6.9).

In order to explain the intuition behind our results, we use the diagrammatic apparatus of Figure 16.8, which is the graphical representation of the (loglinearized) investment system (16.80). The $\dot{\tilde{K}}(t) = 0$ locus represents ($\tilde{q}, \tilde{K}$)-combinations for which the capital stock is in equilibrium, i.e. for which net investment is zero. It is horizontal because Tobin's q is constant in the steady state.[23] For points above (below) the $\dot{\tilde{K}}(t) = 0$ line, Tobin's q is larger (smaller) than its steady-state value, and net investment is positive (negative). This is illustrated with horizontal arrows in Figure 16.8.

The $\dot{\tilde{q}}(t) = 0$ locus represents ($\tilde{q}, \tilde{K}$)-combinations for which Tobin's q is constant over time. It is downward sloping because a higher capital stock leads to a fall in the marginal product of capital and thus to a lower dividend to the owners of shares. For points to the right (left) of the line the marginal product of capital is too low (high) so that part of the return on shares is explained by capital gains (losses). Hence, $\dot{\tilde{q}}(t) > 0$ (< 0) to the right (left) of the line, as has been shown with vertical arrows in Figure 16.8. The arrow configuration in Figure 16.8 confirms that the initial equilibrium at E_0 is saddle-point stable.

The increase in the price of energy reduces the marginal product of capital because energy usage is adjusted downward—see (16.79). To restore the equilibrium value of Tobin's q, the marginal product of capital must rise, i.e. the capital stock must fall and the $\dot{\tilde{q}}(t) = 0$ line shifts to the left. The steady-state equilibrium shifts from E_0 to E_1, there is no long-run effect on Tobin's q (see above), $\tilde{q}(\infty) = 0$, and the long-run effect on the stock of capital is:

$$\tilde{K}(\infty) = -\left(\frac{\epsilon_O}{\epsilon_L}\right)\tilde{P}_O < 0. \tag{16.84}$$

It follows from (16.78) and (16.79) that output and wages fall equi-proportionally with the capital stock, $\tilde{Y}(\infty) = \tilde{W}(\infty) = \tilde{K}(\infty)$, and that energy usage falls:

$$\tilde{O}(\infty) = -\left(\frac{\epsilon_L + \epsilon_O}{\epsilon_L}\right)\tilde{P}_O < 0. \tag{16.85}$$

At impact, the capital stock is predetermined ($\tilde{K}(0) = 0$) and the economy jumps from point E_0 to point A on the new saddle path SP_1. The impact jump in Tobin's

---

[23] Note that equation (T5.1) defines a unique steady-state value for I/K, such that $\phi(I/K) = \delta$. By substituting this I/K value in (T5.6) we obtain the unique steady-state value for Tobin's q.

q is given by:

$$\tilde{q}(0) = - \left(\frac{\epsilon_K \epsilon_0}{\omega_V \left[\epsilon_L + \epsilon_K\right]} \right) \left(\frac{r}{r + \lambda_1^I} \right) \tilde{P}_0 < 0,$$ (16.86)

where the speed of adjustment, λ_1^I, refers to the stable root of the investment sub-system (16.80) (see above). The increase in the energy price hurts capital owners at impact. The fall in Tobin's q is caused by the fact that the marginal product of capital is below its equilibrium level (dictated by the exogenous world rate of interest) during transition. Though the capital stock is predetermined ($\tilde{K}(0) = 0$), output and wages fall at impact because domestic firms cut back on the use of energy—see (16.78) and (16.79). Gross investment collapses, the capital stock starts to fall, and the economy gradually moves along the saddle path from point A towards E_1. The transition path takes the following form:

$$\begin{bmatrix} \tilde{K}(t) \\ \tilde{q}(t) \end{bmatrix} = e^{-\lambda_1^I t} \begin{bmatrix} 0 \\ \tilde{q}(0) \end{bmatrix} + \left[1 - e^{-\lambda_1^I t} \right] \begin{bmatrix} \tilde{K}(\infty) \\ 0 \end{bmatrix}.$$ (16.87)

The degree of physical capital mobility, as parameterized by σ_A [$\equiv -(I/K)(\phi''/\phi') \geq 0$], is an important determinant of the transition path. Indeed, the lower is σ_A, the more mobile is physical capital, the more approximate is the saddle path to the $\dot{\tilde{K}}(t) = 0$ line, and the higher is the adjustment speed λ_1^I. In the limiting case with $\sigma_A = 0$ (perfect mobility), the saddle path coincides with the $\dot{\tilde{K}}(t) = 0$ line, transition is immediate ($\lambda_1^I = \infty$), capital is a jumping variable, and Tobin's q is identically equal to unity precluding any capital gains or losses.[24]

Wage dynamics

By using the solution path for $\tilde{K}(t)$ (given in (16.87) above) in the quasi-reduced form expression (16.78) we obtain the transition path for the wage rate:

$$\tilde{W}(t) = e^{-\lambda_1^I t} \tilde{W}(0) + \left[1 - e^{-\lambda_1^I t} \right] \tilde{W}(\infty),$$ (16.88)

where the impact response is $\tilde{W}(0) = -\epsilon_0 \tilde{P}_0 / (\epsilon_L + \epsilon_K) < 0$ (see (16.78)) and the long-run effect is $\tilde{W}(\infty) = -\epsilon_0 \tilde{P}_0 / \epsilon_L < 0$ (see the text below (16.84)). At impact, the wage rate falls because the energy price increase prompts a decrease in the demand for labour. In the long run the reduction of the capital stock leads to a further decrease in the demand for labour and thus the wage.

---

[24] See also Bovenberg (1994, p. 122) and Barro and Sala-i-Martin (1995, ch. 3) on this point. See also our discussion of the Sen and Turnovsky (1990) model in Chapter 14 above.

Financial and human wealth

We now turn to the savings subsystem in order to determine the effects of the energy price shock on financial and human wealth. Because the shock term hitting the savings subsystem, $\tilde{W}(t)$, is time-varying, a graphical analysis of the $(\tilde{H}, \tilde{A})$ dynamics, though feasible, is not very insightful. For that reason we simply state the solution and focus in the text on the economic intuition behind the results. All technical derivations are placed in a short appendix to this chapter.

In the long run both human and financial wealth fall as a result of the reduction in wages:

$$\tilde{H}(\infty) = \left(\frac{r\epsilon_L}{r+\beta} \right) \tilde{W}(\infty) < 0, \tag{16.89}$$

$$\tilde{A}(\infty) = \left(\frac{r-\rho}{\rho+\beta-r} \right) \left(\frac{r\epsilon_L}{r+\beta} \right) \tilde{W}(\infty) < 0, \tag{16.90}$$

where $\tilde{W}(\infty) < 0$ (see above). Steady-state human wealth is the perpetuity value of wage income using the annuity rate of interest, $r + \beta$, for discounting. Since wages fall and the interest rate is constant, human wealth unambiguously goes down. The effect on financial wealth is fully explained by the fact that the proportion of financial and human wealth is constant in the steady state of this model (i.e. equations (T5.8)–(T5.9) together imply $A/H = (r - \rho)/(\rho + \beta - r)$).

Since the stocks of net foreign assets and physical capital are both predetermined at impact ($\tilde{A}_F(0) = \tilde{K}(0) = 0$) it follows from (T6.9) that the impact jump in financial wealth is:

$$\tilde{A}(0) = \omega_V \tilde{q}(0) < 0, \tag{16.91}$$

where the sign follows from (16.86). As a result of the energy price shock, owners of shares in domestic firms suffer a capital loss on their share holdings.

Since human wealth is the present value of the transition path of wage income (given in (16.88)) it exhibits a discrete jump at impact as well:

$$\tilde{H}(0) = \left(\frac{r\epsilon_L}{r+\beta} \right) \left[\left(\frac{r+\beta}{r+\beta+\lambda_1^I} \right) \tilde{W}(0) + \left(\frac{\lambda_1^I}{r+\beta+\lambda_1^I} \right) \tilde{W}(\infty) \right] < 0, \tag{16.92}$$

where $\tilde{W}(\infty) < \tilde{W}(0) < 0$ (see above). The jump in human wealth is proportional to a weighted average of the impact and long-run effects on the wage rate with the weights depending on the speed of adjustment in the investment subsystem (λ_1^I) relative to the annuity rate of interest ($r + \beta$). If agents are short lived (β high) and/or the adjustment costs of investment are severe (σ_A high and thus λ_1^I low) then the weight attached to the impact effect on wages is high. Intuitively, transition in the capital stock and wages is slow and short-lived agents mainly care about what happens to the wage rate at impact in the computation of human wealth. The opposite effect occurs, of course, if the birth rate is low (long-lived agents) and capital transition is fast (mild adjustment costs of investment).

The adjustment path for human wealth displays a pattern similar to that of the wage rate (namely (16.88)):

$$\tilde{H}(t) = e^{-\lambda_1^I t}\tilde{H}(0) + \left[1 - e^{-\lambda_1^I t}\right]\tilde{H}(\infty), \tag{16.93}$$

where the key thing to note is that the adjustment speed of human capital is governed by the speed of transition in the investment system (λ_1^I). Since both the impact and long-run effects on human wealth are negative it follows that $\tilde{H}(t) < 0$ for all $t \geq 0$. Furthermore, since wages decline monotonically during transition the same holds for human wealth, i.e. $\dot{\tilde{H}}(t) < 0$ during transition and $\tilde{H}(\infty) < \tilde{H}(0) < 0$.

The transition path for financial wealth may be non-monotonic and can be written as:

$$\tilde{A}(t) = \tilde{A}(0)e^{-\lambda_1^S t} + \left[1 - e^{-\lambda_1^S t}\right]\tilde{A}(\infty)$$
$$+ T(\lambda_1^S, \lambda_1^I, t)\left[\frac{r\epsilon_L(r - \rho + \lambda_1^I)\left[\tilde{W}(0) - \tilde{W}(\infty)\right]}{r + \beta + \lambda_1^I}\right], \tag{16.94}$$

where $\lambda_1^S \equiv \rho + \beta - r$ is the transition speed of the savings subsystem (see the text below (16.83)), and $T(\lambda_1^S, \lambda_1^I, t)$ is a bell-shaped transition term, which is zero at impact and in the long run and positive during transition.[25] The first two terms on the right-hand side of (16.94) show that part of the transition in the stock of financial assets is explained by a weighted average of the impact and long-run effect on financial wealth. The final term on the right-hand side of (16.94) represents the transitory effect of the energy price shock on the aggregate accumulation of financial wealth. As was explained (for a different kind of shock) by Bovenberg (1993), this transitory effect is due to a temporary, additional macroeconomic incentive to accumulate financial assets due to intergenerational distributional effects.

We complete the characterization of the macroeconomic effects of an energy price shock by determining what happens to consumption and net foreign assets. Since $C(t) = (\rho + \beta)[A(t) + H(t)]$ we find that:

$$\left(\frac{r\omega_C}{\rho + \beta}\right)\tilde{C}(t) = \tilde{A}(t) + \tilde{H}(t). \tag{16.95}$$

It follows from (16.91)–(16.92) and (16.95) that the impact jump in consumption is negative ($\tilde{C}(0) < 0$). All existing generations at the time of the shock cut back their consumption level. Old agents, for whom financial wealth is the major wealth component, cut back consumption because they suffer a capital loss on their share possessions. Young agents, for whom human wealth is the major wealth component, cut back consumption because they suffer a capital loss on this wealth type due to the lower path of wages. By using (16.89)–(16.90) in (16.95) we find that

---

[25] See Lemma A15.1 of the appendix to Chapter 15 for the properties of the transition term.

consumption also falls in the long run:

$$\left(\frac{r\omega_C}{\rho+\beta}\right)\tilde{C}(\infty) = \left(\frac{\beta}{\rho+\beta-r}\right)\left(\frac{r\epsilon_L}{r+\beta}\right)\tilde{W}(\infty) < 0. \tag{16.96}$$

Since the path of financial wealth may be non-monotonic (see above) the same holds for consumption.

The long-run effect on the stock of net foreign assets is obtained by substituting (16.84) and (16.90) in (T6.9) and noting that $\tilde{q}(\infty) = 0$:

$$\tilde{A}_F(\infty) = \left[\left(\frac{r-\rho}{\rho+\beta-r}\right)\left(\frac{r\epsilon_L}{r+\beta}\right) - \omega_V\right]\tilde{K}(\infty). \tag{16.97}$$

The long-run effect on net foreign assets may be positive or negative. See Matsuyama (1997, p. 311–312) for a detailed explanation.

16.5 Punchlines

In this chapter we study one of the key models of modern macroeconomics, namely the continuous-time overlapping-generations model of Blanchard and Yaari. This model is important not only because it has proved to be quite flexible and easy to work with, but also because it nests the Ramsey (growth) model as a special case.

We start the chapter by studying the seminal insights of Yaari who studied optimal consumption behaviour in the presence of lifetime uncertainty. When an agent's lifetime (and thus his planning horizon) is uncertain two complications arise. First, the agent's decision problem becomes inherently stochastic and the expected utility hypothesis must be employed. Second, the non-negativity constraint on the agent's wealth position at the time of death is also stochastic and should be ensured to hold with certainty. Yaari showed that the key implication of uncertain lifetimes is that the instantaneous probability of death (the so-called "death hazard rate") enters the consumption Euler equation of the expected-utility maximizing agent. Intuitively, the uncertainty of survival leads the rational agent to discount the future more heavily.

Yaari makes the analysis of terminal wealth more tractable by postulating the existence of a kind of life insurance based on actuarial notes. Such a note can be bought or sold by the consumer and is cancelled upon the consumer's death. A consumer who *buys* an actuarial note in fact buys an annuity which stipulates payments to the consumer during life at a rate higher than the rate of interest. Upon the consumer's death the insurance company has no further obligations to the consumer's estate. Reversely, a consumer who *sells* an actuarial note is getting a life-insured loan. During the consumer's life he/she must pay a higher interest rate on the loan than the market rate of interest but upon death the consumer's estate is held free of any obligations, i.e. the principal does not have to be paid back to the insurance company. Under actuarial fairness the rate of return on actuarial notes equals the rate of interest plus the death hazard. Yaari shows that households have the incentive to fully insure against the loss of life. He thus reaches the striking result that, with actuarially fair life insurance, the death hazard drops out of the consumption Euler equation altogether.

Yaari's insights lay dormant for two decades before Blanchard embedded them in his dynamic general equilibrium model with overlapping generations. In order to allow for an aggregate treatment, Blanchard made two modelling choices. First, he assumed that the death hazard is age-independent. This ensures that the optimal decision rules are "linear in the generations index" and can thus be aggregated. Second, he assumed the arrival of large cohorts of newborn agents at each instant. This ensures that frequencies and probabilities coincide. (To ensure a constant population the birth and death rates are assumed to be equal.)

The Blanchard–Yaari model has a number of important properties. First, the standard Ramsey model (based on the notion of an infinitely lived representative household) is obtained as a special case of the Blanchard–Yaari model by setting the birth rate equal to zero. Second, the steady-state capital stock is smaller in the Blanchard–Yaari model than in the Ramsey model. Due to the turnover of generations, aggregate consumption growth falls short of individual consumption growth. This means that in the steady state the interest rate exceeds the rate of time preference. It also means that the equilibrium is dynamically efficient. Third, fiscal policy, taking the form of a permanent and unanticipated lump-sum tax financed increase in government consumption, causes less (more) than one-for-one crowding out of private consumption in the short (long) run. In the short run, households do not feel the full burden of the additional taxes because they discount present and future tax liabilities at the annuity rather than the market rate of interest. As a result they do not cut back consumption by enough so that private investment is crowded out. In the long run the capital stock and output are smaller, wages are lower, and the interest rate is higher. Intuitively, the shock redistributes resources away from future generations towards present generations. Finally, Ricardian equivalence does not hold in the Blanchard–Yaari model. It is the positive birth rate (and not the agents' finite planning horizon) which causes the rejection of Ricardian equivalence.

In the second half of the chapter we show three extensions to the Blanchard–Yaari model. In the first extension we endogenize the household's labour supply decision. We use the model to study the effects of an increase in the consumption tax. In the Ramsey version of the extended model, the tax increase unambiguously leads to a decrease in the long-run capital stock because the household cuts back labour supply. With finite lives, however, the tax redistributes resources from present to future generations which tends to increase the capital stock in the long run. The net effect of the tax shock thus depends on the relative strength of the generational turnover effect *vis-à-vis* the factor scarcity effect.

In the second extension to the Blanchard–Yaari model we assume that a worker's productivity declines with age. The declining path of labour income mimics the notion of saving for retirement—even though the agent continues to work the same number of hours during life, the decline in productivity makes these hours less valuable over time. If the productivity profile declines steeply then the steady-state equilibrium may be dynamically inefficient. Because labour income is high during youth and agents practise consumption smoothing, they save a lot early on in life and the economy as a whole may oversave.

Finally, in the third extension we study a small open economy version of the Blanchard–Yaari model. We use the model to study the effects on the macroeconomy of an oil price shock. An attractive feature of the open-economy Blanchard–Yaari model is that it can be used to study both creditor nations (populated by patient citizens) and debtor countries (inhabited by impatient households). (Recall from Chapter 14 that in the corresponding Ramsey model, the steady-state equilibrium only exists for a knife-edge case in which the world interest rate equals the rate of time preference of residents.)

Further Reading

The Blanchard–Yaari model has been applied in a large number of areas. Open economy models are presented by inter alia Blanchard (1983, 1984), Frenkel and Razin (1986), Buiter (1987), Matsuyama (1987), Giovannini (1988), and Heijdra and van der Horst (2000). The closely related Weil (1989b) model is used for the analysis of tax policy by Bovenberg (1993, 1994) and Nielsen and Sørenson (1991) and for the study of current account dynamics by Obstfeld and Rogoff (1995b, pp. 1759–1764).

Alogoskoufis and van der Ploeg (1990) and Saint-Paul (1992) introduce endogenous growth into the model. Weil (1991) and Marini and van der Ploeg (1988) study monetary neutrality. Aschauer (1990a) introduces endogenous labour supply in the Blanchard–Yaari model. On public infrastructure, see Heijdra and Meijdam (forthcoming). Marini and Scaramozzino (1995) and Bovenberg and Heijdra (1998, forthcoming) study environmental issues. Nielsen (1994) introduces social security into the model. Gertler (1999) generalizes the model by assuming that workers move into retirement according to a stochastic Poisson process. The International Monetary Fund's MULTIMOD model includes insights from the Blanchard–Yaari framework–see Laxton et al. (1998).

Appendix

Derivation of Figure 16.3

In this appendix we derive the phase diagram for the extended Blanchard–Yaari model with endogenous labour supply and various tax rates. In doing so, we follow the general approach discussed in detail in the appendix to Chapter 15.

Employment as a function of the state variables

By using labour demand (T2.5), labour supply (T2.6), and the production function (T2.7)—and dropping the time index where no confusion is possible—we obtain an expression relating (labour-market-clearing) equilibrium employment to the state variables (C and K) and the exogenous variables:

$$(\Gamma(L) \equiv) \ (1-L)L^{\epsilon_L-1} = \left(\frac{(1-\epsilon_C)(1+t_H)}{\epsilon_C\epsilon_L}\right) CK^{-(1-\epsilon_L)}, \tag{A16.1}$$

where $t_H \equiv (t_C+t_L)/(1-t_L)$ is the tax wedge directly facing households, and $\Gamma(L)$ is a decreasing function in the feasible interval $L \in [0,1]$ with $\Gamma'(L) = -L^{\epsilon_L-2}[(1-\epsilon_L)(1-L)+L] < 0$ and $\Gamma''(L) = (1-\epsilon_L)L^{\epsilon_L-3}[2-\epsilon_L(1-L)] > 0$. In summary, (A16.1) shows that equilibrium employment depends negatively on consumption and the tax wedge (via labour supply) and positively on the capital stock (via labour demand).

Capital stock equilibrium

The capital stock equilibrium (CSE) locus represents points in (C,K)-space for which $\dot{K} = 0$ and thus $\delta K = Y - C$. We note from (T2.5) and (T2.6) that:

$$\frac{1-L}{L} = \left(\frac{(1-\epsilon_C)(1+t_H)}{\epsilon_C\epsilon_L}\right)\left(\frac{C}{Y}\right), \tag{A16.2}$$

so that along the CSE line we have:

$$\delta K = \left[1 - \left(\frac{\epsilon_C\epsilon_L}{(1-\epsilon_C)(1+t_H)}\right)\left(\frac{1-L}{L}\right)\right]Y. \tag{A16.3}$$

We require the term in square brackets on the right-hand side to be non-negative, so that the lower bound for employment is:

$$L \geq L_{MIN} \equiv \frac{\epsilon_C\epsilon_L}{\epsilon_C\epsilon_L + (1-\epsilon_C)(1+t_H)}, \quad 0 < L_{MIN} < 1. \tag{A16.4}$$

By using (A16.4) and (T2.7) in (A16.3) we can write the CSE curve as follows:

$$K^{\epsilon_L} = \left(\frac{\epsilon_C\epsilon_L}{\delta(1-\epsilon_C)(1+t_H)}\right)\left(\frac{L-L_{MIN}}{L_{MIN}}\right)L^{\epsilon_L-1}. \tag{A16.5}$$

Equation (A16.5) represents an implicit function, $L = g(K)$, over the interval $L \in [L_{MIN}, 1]$ relating K and L. In order to compute the slope of the implicit function we totally differentiate (A16.5):

$$K^{\epsilon_L}\left(\frac{dK}{K}\right) = \left(\frac{\epsilon_C}{\delta(1-\epsilon_C)(1+t_H)}\right)\left[\frac{\epsilon_L L + (1-\epsilon_L)L_{MIN}}{L_{MIN}}\right]L^{\epsilon_L-1}\left(\frac{dL}{L}\right). \tag{A16.6}$$

Since $L \geq L_{MIN} > 0$ the term in square brackets on the right-hand side is strictly positive so that $g'(K) > 0$. It follows from (A16.5) that $K = 0$ for $L = L_{MIN}$, so as L rises from $L = L_{MIN}$ to $L = 1$, K rises from $K = 0$ to $K = K_K \equiv \delta^{-1/\epsilon_L} > 0$. We now have two zeros for the CSE line, i.e. both $(K,L) = (0, L_{MIN})$ and $(K,L) = (K_K, 1)$ solve equation (A16.3). By using (A16.1) we find the corresponding values for C, i.e. $(C,K,L) = (0,0,L_{MIN})$ and $(C,K,L) = (0,K_K,1)$ are both zeros for the CSE line—see Figure 16.3.

The slope of the CSE line is computed as follows. We note that this line can be written as:

$$C = g(K)^{\epsilon_L} K^{1-\epsilon_L} - \delta K, \tag{A16.7}$$

where $L = g(K)$ is the implicit function defined by (A16.5). By taking the derivative of (A16.7) we obtain in a few steps:

$$\left(\frac{dC}{dK}\right)_{\dot{K}=0} = \left[1 - \epsilon_L \left(1 - \eta_g(K)\right)\right] \left(\frac{g(K)}{K}\right)^{\epsilon_L} - \delta, \tag{A16.8}$$

where $\eta_g(K)$ is the elasticity of the $g(.)$ function:

$$\eta_g(K) \equiv \left(\frac{Kg'(K)}{g(K)}\right) = \frac{\epsilon_L \left(g(K) - L_{MIN}\right)}{\epsilon_L g(K) + (1 - \epsilon_L)L_{MIN}}, \tag{A16.9}$$

from which it follows that $\eta_g(0) = 0$ so that the term in square brackets on the right-hand side of (A16.8) goes to $(1 - \epsilon_L)$. But since $\lim_{K \to 0} g(K)/K = +\infty$ it follows that the CSE line is vertical near the origin (see Figure 16.3):

$$\lim_{K \to 0} \left(\frac{dC}{dK}\right)_{\dot{K}=0} = +\infty. \tag{A16.10}$$

The capital stock dynamics follows by substituting (T2.7) and $L = g(K)$ into (T2.2):

$$\dot{K} = g(K)^{\epsilon_L} K^{1-\epsilon_L} - \delta K - C. \tag{A16.11}$$

For point above (below) the CSE line, consumption is too high (low) and net investment is negative (positive). These dynamic effects have been illustrated with horizontal arrows in Figure 16.3.

Consumption flow equilibrium

The consumption equilibrium (CE) locus represents points in (C, K)-space for which the aggregate flow of consumption is in equilibrium ($\dot{C} = 0$). By using (T2.1) in steady state, (T2.4), (T2.7) and (A16.2) we can write the CE locus as follows:

$$\beta(\rho + \beta) = \left(\frac{\epsilon_L(1 - \epsilon_L)(1 - t_L)}{1 - \epsilon_C}\right) \left(\frac{1 - L}{L}\right) y \left[y - y^*\right], \tag{A16.12}$$

$$y = \left(\frac{L}{K}\right)^{\epsilon_L}, \tag{A16.13}$$

where $y \equiv Y/K$ is the output–capital ratio and $y^* \equiv (\rho + \delta)/(1 - \epsilon_L)$. Equations (A16.12)–(A16.13) define consumption flow equilibrium in (K, L)-space.

In the *representative-agent model* (with $\beta = 0$) the CE locus represents points for which $y = y^*$. By using this in (A16.13) and (A16.1) we get after a few steps:

$$
\begin{aligned}
C &= \left(\frac{\epsilon_C \epsilon_L}{(1 - \epsilon_C)(1 + t_H)} \right) \left(\frac{K}{L} \right)^{1-\epsilon_L} (1 - L) \\
&= \left(\frac{\epsilon_C \epsilon_L}{(1 - \epsilon_C)(1 + t_H)} \right) (y^*)^{(\epsilon_L - 1)/\epsilon_L} \left[1 - (y^*)^{1/\epsilon_L} K \right] \\
&= \left(\frac{(\rho + \delta)\epsilon_C \epsilon_L}{(1 - \epsilon_C)(1 - \epsilon_L)(1 + t_H)} \right) \left[(y^*)^{-1/\epsilon_L} - K \right].
\end{aligned}
\tag{A16.14}
$$

Hence, the CE curve for the RA model (CE^{RA}) is linear and downward sloping—see the dashed line from A_3 to A_4 in Figure 16.3.

For the *overlapping-generations model* the CE line can only be described *parametrically*, i.e. by varying L in the feasible interval $[0, 1]$. We first write (A16.12) in a more convenient format:

$$
\zeta_0 \left[\equiv \frac{\beta(\rho + \beta)(1 - \epsilon_C)}{\epsilon_L(1 - \epsilon_L)(1 - t_L)} \right] = \left(\frac{1 - L}{L} \right) y [y - y^*],
\tag{A16.15}
$$

where $\zeta_0 > 0$. Solving (A16.15) for the positive (economically sensible) root yields the equilibrium output–capital ratio for the overlapping-generations (OG) model as a function of L:

$$
\frac{y}{y^*} = \frac{1}{2} + \sqrt{\frac{1}{4} + \frac{\zeta_0}{(y^*)^2} \left(\frac{L}{1 - L} \right)} \geq 1.
\tag{A16.16}
$$

Using (A16.16) in (A16.13) yields an expression for the capital-labour ratio:

$$
\left(\frac{K}{L} \right) = y^{-1/\epsilon_L} = (y^*)^{-1/\epsilon_L} \left[\frac{1}{2} + \sqrt{\frac{1}{4} + \frac{\zeta_0}{(y^*)^2} \left(\frac{L}{1 - L} \right)} \right]^{-1/\epsilon_L},
\tag{A16.17}
$$

from which we derive the following limiting results:

$$
\lim_{L \to 0} \left(\frac{K}{L} \right) = (y^*)^{-1/\epsilon_L}, \quad \lim_{L \to 1} \left(\frac{K}{L} \right) = 0.
\tag{A16.18}
$$

The labour market equilibrium condition (A16.1) yields an expression for consumption:

$$
C = \left(\frac{\epsilon_C \epsilon_L}{(1 - \epsilon_C)(1 + t_H)} \right) \left(\frac{K}{L} \right)^{1-\epsilon_L} (1 - L),
\tag{A16.19}
$$

from which we derive the following limiting results:

$$
\begin{aligned}
\lim_{L \to 0} C &= \left(\frac{\epsilon_C \epsilon_L}{(1 - \epsilon_C)(1 + t_H)} \right) \lim_{L \to 0} \left(\frac{K}{L} \right)^{1-\epsilon_L} \\
&= \left(\frac{\epsilon_C \epsilon_L}{(1 - \epsilon_C)(1 + t_H)} \right) (y^*)^{(\epsilon_L - 1)/\epsilon_L},
\end{aligned}
\tag{A16.20}
$$

$$
\lim_{L \to 1} C = 0.
\tag{A16.21}
$$

Hence, the CE line for the OG model has the same vertical intercept as CE^{RA} as $L \to 0$ and goes through the origin as $L \to 1$.

It is straightforward—though somewhat tedious—to prove that CE^{OLG} is horizontal near the origin (where $L \approx 1$) and downward sloping and steeper than CE^{RA} near the vertical intercept (where $L \approx 0$).

Uniqueness

The uniqueness of the equilibrium can be established most easily in the (K, L) plane. First we rewrite (A16.17) as:

$$K^{\epsilon_L} = \frac{h(L)}{y^*}, \quad h(L) \equiv L^{\epsilon_L} \left[\frac{1}{2} + \sqrt{\frac{1}{4} + \frac{\zeta_0}{(y^*)^2} \left(\frac{L}{1-L} \right)} \right]^{-1}. \tag{A16.22}$$

It is not difficult to show that $h(0) = \lim_{L \to 1} h(L) = 0$, $\lim_{L \to 0} h'(L) = +\infty$ and $\lim_{L \to 1} h'(L) = -\infty$. These properties ensure that the CSE curve (equation (A16.5)) and the CE curve (equation (A16.22)) cross only once thus determining unique equilibrium values (K^*, L^*). Equilibrium consumption, C^*, then follows from (A16.1), and equilibrium output, Y^*, follows from the production function (T2.7). All other variables are determined uniquely also.

Savings dynamics in the open economy

In this appendix we solve the savings subsystem (16.82) given that wages evolve according to (16.88). We use the Laplace transform technique that is discussed in detail in the Mathematical Appendix and was also used in the appendix to Chapter 15. By imposing the steady state in (16.82) ($\dot{\tilde{H}}(\infty) = \dot{\tilde{A}}(\infty) = 0$) we find (16.89)–(16.90). To compute the impact and transitional effects we note that the savings system is itself recursive and can be solved in two steps. In the first step we solve for the dynamics of human wealth which is described by the first line of (16.82). In the second step we substitute the solution path for human wealth into the second line of (16.82) and solve the dynamics for financial wealth.

Taking the Laplace transform of the first line of (16.82) and noting that $\mathcal{L}\{\dot{\tilde{H}}, s\} = s\mathcal{L}\{\tilde{H}, s\} - \tilde{H}(0)$ we obtain:

$$\mathcal{L}\{\tilde{H}, s\} = \frac{\tilde{H}(0) - r\epsilon_L \mathcal{L}\{\tilde{W}, s\}}{s - (r + \beta)}, \tag{A16.23}$$

where $\tilde{H}(0)$ is the impact jump in human wealth. The only way to avoid the instability arising from the instable root ($\lambda_2^S = r + \beta$) is to ensure that the numerator on the right-hand side of (A16.23) is zero when $s = r + \beta$. This implies that the impact jump in human capital is:

$$\tilde{H}(0) = r\epsilon_L \mathcal{L}\{\tilde{W}, r + \beta\}. \tag{A16.24}$$

By substituting the Laplace transform of the transition path for wages (16.88) we obtain (16.92), where we have used the fact that $\lambda_2^S = r + \beta$, $\mathcal{L}\{e^{-at}, s\} = 1/(s+a)$, and $\mathcal{L}\{1, s\} = 1/s$. The transition path for human wealth is obtained as follows. First we substitute (A16.24) into (A16.23) and invert the Laplace transform:

$$\tilde{H}(t) = r\epsilon_L \mathcal{L}^{-1}\left\{\frac{\mathcal{L}\{\tilde{W}, r+\beta\} - \mathcal{L}\{\tilde{W}, s\}}{s-(r+\beta)}\right\}. \tag{A16.25}$$

By substituting (the Laplace transform of) (16.88) into (A16.25) we obtain the desired expression in a few steps:

$$\tilde{H}(t) = r\epsilon_L \mathcal{L}^{-1}\left\{\left(\tilde{W}(0) - \tilde{W}(\infty)\right)\left[\frac{\frac{1}{r+\beta+\lambda_1^I} - \frac{1}{s+\lambda_1^I}}{s-(r+\beta)}\right] + \tilde{W}(\infty)\left[\frac{\frac{1}{r+\beta} - \frac{1}{s}}{s-(r+\beta)}\right]\right\}$$

$$= r\epsilon_L \mathcal{L}^{-1}\left\{\frac{\tilde{W}(0) - \tilde{W}(\infty)}{(r+\beta+\lambda_1^I)(s+\lambda_1^I)} + \frac{\tilde{W}(\infty)}{(r+\beta)s}\right\}$$

$$= e^{-\lambda_1^I t}\tilde{H}(0) + \left(1 - e^{-\lambda_1^I t}\right)\tilde{H}(\infty), \tag{A16.26}$$

where we have used (16.92) and (16.89) in going from the second to the third line.

By taking the Laplace transform of the second line of (16.82), noting that $\mathcal{L}\{\dot{\tilde{A}}, s\} = s\mathcal{L}\{\tilde{A}, s\} - \tilde{A}(0)$ and substituting (A16.23)–(A16.24) we obtain:

$$(s + \lambda_1^S)\mathcal{L}\{\tilde{A}, s\} = \tilde{A}(0) + r\epsilon_L \mathcal{L}\{\tilde{W}, s\}$$

$$- (\rho + \beta)r\epsilon_L\left\{\frac{\mathcal{L}\{\tilde{W}, r+\beta\} - \mathcal{L}\{\tilde{W}, s\}}{s-(r+\beta)}\right\}, \tag{A16.27}$$

where we recall that $-\lambda_1^S \equiv r - (\rho + \beta) < 0$ is the stable root of the savings subsystem. By using the path of wages in (A16.27) we obtain (16.94) after some manipulations.

17

Intergenerational Economics, II

The purpose of this chapter is to achieve the following goals:

1. To introduce and study a popular discrete-time overlapping-generations (OG) model and to show its main theoretical properties;

2. To apply the discrete-time model to study things like (funded or unfunded) pensions and the macroeconomic effects of ageing;

3. To extend the model to account for (private versus public) human capital accumulation and public investment;

4. To illustrate the method of intergenerational accounting.

17.1 The Diamond–Samuelson Model

As the previous chapter has demonstrated, the continuous-time Blanchard–Yaari framework is quite flexible and convenient and therefore fully deserves its current workhorse status. It yields useful and intuitive macroeconomic results and does so in a simple fashion. This is not to say that the framework has no shortcomings. Indeed, as Blanchard himself points out, the main drawback of the perpetual youth approach is that, though it captures the finite-horizon aspect of life, it fails to account for life-cycle aspects of consumption (1985, p. 224). Indeed, in the standard Blanchard model, a household's age affects the level and composition of its wealth (first aspect) but not its propensity to consume out of wealth (life-cycle aspect). In the absence of a bequest motive and with truly finite lives, one would expect an old agent to have a much higher propensity to consume out of wealth than a young agent, simply because the old agent has a shorter planning horizon (a higher death hazard) than the young agent has.

A simple model which captures both the finite-horizon and life-cycle aspects of household behaviour was formulated by Diamond (1965) using the earlier insights of Samuelson (1958).[1] The Diamond–Samuelson model is formulated in discrete time and has been *the* workhorse model in various fields of economics for almost four decades. In the remainder of this section we describe (a simplified version of) the Diamond (1965) model in detail.

17.1.1 Households

Individual agents live for two periods. During the first period (their "youth") they work and in their second period (their "old age") they are retired from the labour force. Since they want to consume in both periods, agents save during youth and dissave during old age. We abstract from bequests and assume that the population grows at a constant rate n.

A representative young agent at time t has the following lifetime utility function:

$$\Lambda_t^Y \equiv U(C_t^Y) + \left(\frac{1}{1+\rho} \right) U(C_{t+1}^O), \tag{17.1}$$

where the subscript identifies the time period and the superscript the period of life the agent is in, with "Y" and "O" standing for, respectively, youth and old age. Hence, C_t^Y and C_{t+1}^O denote consumption by an agent born in period t during youth and old age, respectively, and Λ_t^Y is lifetime utility of a young agent from the perspective of his birth. As usual, $\rho > 0$ captures the notion of pure time preference and we assume that the felicity function, $U(.)$, satisfies Inada-style conditions ($U' > 0 > U''$, $\lim_{x \to 0} U'(x) = +\infty$, and $\lim_{x \to \infty} U'(x) = 0$).

During the first period the agent inelastically supplies one unit of labour and receives a wage W_t which is spent on consumption, C_t^Y, and savings, S_t. In the second period, the agent does not work but receives interest income on his savings, $r_{t+1} S_t$. Principal plus interest are spent on consumption during old age, C_{t+1}^O. The household thus faces the following budget identities:

$$C_t^Y + S_t = W_t, \tag{17.2}$$

$$C_{t+1}^O = (1 + r_{t+1}) S_t. \tag{17.3}$$

By substituting (17.3) into (17.2) we obtain the consolidated (or lifetime) budget constraint:

$$W_t = C_t^Y + \frac{C_{t+1}^O}{1 + r_{t+1}}. \tag{17.4}$$

The young agent chooses C_t^Y and C_{t+1}^O to maximize (17.1) subject to (17.4). The first-order conditions for consumption in the two periods can be combined after

---

[1] An even earlier overlapping-generations model was developed by Allais (1947). Unfortunately, due to the non-trivial language barrier, it was not assimilated into the Anglo-Saxon literature.

which we obtain the familiar consumption Euler equation:

$$\frac{U'(C_{t+1}^O)}{U'(C_t^Y)} = \frac{1+\rho}{1+r_{t+1}}. \tag{17.5}$$

Together, (17.4)–(17.5) determine implicit functions relating C_t^Y and C_{t+1}^O (and thus S_t) to the variables that are exogenously given to the agents, i.e. W_t and r_{t+1}. The key expression is the savings equation:

$$S_t = S(W_t, r_{t+1}), \tag{17.6}$$

which has the following partial derivatives:

$$0 < S_W \equiv \frac{\partial S}{\partial W_t} = \frac{\theta\left[C_t^Y\right]/C_t^Y}{\theta\left[C_{t+1}^O\right]/S_t + \theta\left[C_t^Y\right]/C_t^Y} < 1, \tag{17.7}$$

$$S_r \equiv \frac{\partial S}{\partial r_{t+1}} = \frac{1 - \theta\left[C_{t+1}^O\right]}{(1+r_{t+1})\left[\theta\left[C_{t+1}^O\right]/S_t + \theta\left[C_t^Y\right]/C_t^Y\right]} \gtrless 0, \tag{17.8}$$

where $\theta[x] \equiv -U''(x)x/U'(x)$ is the elasticity of marginal utility (which is positive, given the assumption made regarding $U(.)$ above). Recall from Chapter 14 that the inverse of $\theta[x]$ is the intertemporal substitution elasticity, denoted by $\sigma[x] \equiv 1/\theta[x]$. According to (17.7), an increase in the wage rate increases savings. It follows from (17.2) and (17.3) that both consumption goods are normal, i.e. $\partial C_t^Y/\partial W_t = 1 - \partial S/\partial W_t > 0$ and $\partial C_{t+1}^O/\partial W_t = (1+r_{t+1})\partial S_t/\partial W_t > 0$. The response of savings with respect to the interest rate is ambiguous as the income and substitution effects work in opposite directions (see Chapter 6). On the one hand an increase in r_{t+1} reduces the relative price of future goods which prompts the agent to substitute future for present consumption and to increase savings. On the other hand, the increase in r_{t+1} expands the budget available for present and future consumption which prompts the agent to increase both present and future consumption and to decrease savings. Equation (17.8) shows that, on balance, if the intertemporal substitution elasticity exceeds (falls short of) unity then the substitution (income) effect dominates and savings depend positively (negatively) on the interest rate:

$$S_r \gtrless 0 \quad \Leftrightarrow \quad \theta\left[C_{t+1}^O\right] \lessgtr 1 \quad \Leftrightarrow \quad \sigma\left[C_{t+1}^O\right] \equiv \frac{1}{\theta\left[C_{t+1}^O\right]} \gtrless 1. \tag{17.9}$$

17.1.2 Firms

The perfectly competitive firm sector produces output, Y_t, by hiring capital, K_t, from the currently old agents, and labour, L_t, from the currently young agents. The production function is linearly homogeneous:

$$Y_t = F(K_t, L_t), \tag{17.10}$$

and profit maximization ensures that the production factors receive their respective marginal physical products (and that pure profits are zero):

$$W_t = F_L(K_t, L_t), \tag{17.11}$$

$$r_t + \delta = F_K(K_t, L_t), \tag{17.12}$$

where $0 < \delta < 1$ is the depreciation rate of capital.[2] The crucial thing to note about (17.12) is its timing: capital that was accumulated by the currently old, K_t, commands the rental rate $r_t + \delta$. It follows that the rate of interest upon which the currently young agents base their savings decisions (i.e. r_{t+1} in (17.3) and (17.6)) depends on the *future* capital stock and labour force:

$$r_{t+1} + \delta = F_K(K_{t+1}, L_{t+1}). \tag{17.13}$$

Since the labour force grows at a constant rate and we ultimately wish to study an economy which possesses a well-defined steady-state equilibrium, it is useful to rewrite (17.9)–(17.10) and (17.13) in per capita form (see Chapter 14 for details):

$$y_t = f(k_t), \tag{17.14}$$

$$W_t = f(k_t) - k_t f'(k_t), \tag{17.15}$$

$$r_{t+1} + \delta = f'(k_{t+1}), \tag{17.16}$$

where $y_t \equiv Y_t/L_t$, $k_t \equiv K_t/L_t$, and $f(k_t) \equiv F(k_t, 1)$.

17.1.3 Market equilibrium

The resource constraint for the economy as a whole can be written as follows:

$$Y_t + (1 - \delta)K_t = K_{t+1} + C_t, \tag{17.17}$$

where C_t represents aggregate consumption in period t. Equation (17.17) says that output plus the undepreciated part of the capital stock (left-hand side) can be either consumed or carried over to the next period in the form of capital (right-hand side). Alternatively, (17.17) can be written as $Y_t = C_t + I_t$ with $I_t \equiv \Delta K_{t+1} + \delta K_t$ representing gross investment.

---

[2] Most authors follow Diamond (1965, p. 1127) by assuming that capital does not depreciate at all ($\delta = 0$). Since the model divides human life into two periods, each period is quite long (in historical time) and it is thus defensible to assume that capital fully depreciates with the period ($\delta = 1$). Blanchard and Fischer (1989, p. 93) circumvent the choice of δ by assuming that (17.10) is a *net* production function, with depreciation already deducted. In their formulation, δ vanishes from the capital demand equation (17.12).

Aggregate consumption is the sum of consumption by the young and the old agents in period t:

$$C_t \equiv L_{t-1}C_t^O + L_t C_t^Y. \tag{17.18}$$

Since the old, as a group, own the capital stock, their total consumption in period t is the sum of the undepreciated part of the capital stock plus the rental payments received from the firms, i.e. $L_{t-1}C_t^O = (r_t + \delta)K_t + (1 - \delta)K_t$. For each young agent consumption satisfies (17.2) so that total consumption by the young amounts to: $L_t C_t^Y = W_t L_t - S_t L_t$. By substituting these two results into (17.18), we obtain:

$$C_t = (r_t + \delta)K_t + (1 - \delta)K_t + W_t L_t - S_t L_t$$
$$= Y_t + (1 - \delta)K_t - S_t L_t, \tag{17.19}$$

where we have used the fact that $Y_t = (r_t + \delta)K_t + W_t L_t$ in going from the first to the second line. Output is fully exhausted by factor payments and pure profits are zero.

Finally, by combining (17.17) and (17.19) we obtain the expression linking this period's savings decisions by the young to next period's capital stock:

$$S_t L_t = K_{t+1}. \tag{17.20}$$

The population is assumed to grow at a constant rate,

$$L_t = L_0(1 + n)^t, \quad n > -1, \tag{17.21}$$

so that (17.20), in combination with (17.6), can be rewritten in per capita form as:

$$S(W_t, r_{t+1}) = (1 + n)k_{t+1}. \tag{17.22}$$

The capital market is represented by the demand for capital by entrepreneurs (equation (17.16)) and the supply of capital by households (equation (17.22)).

17.1.4 Dynamics and stability

The dynamical behaviour of the economy can be studied by substituting the expressions for W_t and r_{t+1} (given in, respectively, (17.15) and (17.16)) into the capital supply equation (17.22):

$$(1 + n)k_{t+1} = S\left[f(k_t) - k_t f'(k_t), f'(k_{t+1}) - \delta\right]. \tag{17.23}$$

This expression relates the future to the present capital stock per worker and is thus suitable to study the stability of the model. By totally differentiating (17.23) we obtain:

$$\frac{dk_{t+1}}{dk_t} = \frac{-S_W k_t f''(k_t)}{1 + n - S_r f''(k_{t+1})}, \tag{17.24}$$

where S_W and S_r are given, respectively, in (17.7) and (17.8). We recall from Chapter 2 that local stability requires that the deviations from a steady state must be dampened (and not amplified) over time. Mathematically this means that a steady state is locally stable if $|dk_{t+1}/dk_t| < 1$. It is clear from (17.24) that we are not going to obtain clearcut results on the basis of the most general version of our model. Although we know that the numerator of (17.24) is positive (because $S_W > 0$ and $f'' < 0$), the sign of the denominator is indeterminate (because S_r is ambiguous).

Referring the interested reader to Galor and Ryder (1989) for a rigorous analysis of the general case, we take the practical way out by illustrating the existence and stability issues with the *unit-elastic* model. Specifically, we assume that technology is Cobb–Douglas, so that $y_t = k_t^{1-\epsilon_L}$, and that the felicity function is logarithmic, so that $U(x) = \log x$ and $\sigma(x) = 1/\theta(x) = 1$. With these simplifications imposed the savings function collapses to $S_t = W_t/(2 + \rho)$, the wage rate is $W_t = \epsilon_L k_t^{1-\epsilon_L}$, and (17.23) becomes:

$$k_{t+1} = g(k_t) \equiv \left(\frac{\epsilon_L}{(1+n)(2+\rho)} \right) k_t^{1-\epsilon_L}. \tag{17.25}$$

Equation (17.25) has been drawn in Figure 17.1. Since $\lim_{k \to 0} g'(k) = \infty$ and $\lim_{k \to \infty} g'(k) = 0$, the steady state, satisfying $k^* = g(k^*)$, is unique and stable. The diagram illustrates one stable trajectory from k_0. The tangent of $g(.)$ passing through the steady-state equilibrium point E_0 is the dashed line AB. It follows from the diagram (and indeed from (17.25)) that the unit-elastic Diamond–Samuelson model satisfies the stability condition with a positive slope for $g(.)$, i.e. $0 < g'(k^*) < 1$.

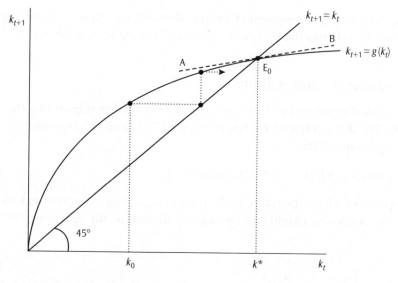

Figure 17.1. The unit-elastic Diamond–Samuelson model

17.1.5 Efficiency

It is clear from the discussion surrounding Figure 17.1 that there is a perfectly reasonable setting in which the Diamond–Samuelson model possesses a stable and
unique steady-state equilibrium. We now assume for convenience that our most
general model also has this property and proceed to study its welfare properties. To
keep things simple, and to prepare for the discussion of social security issues below,
we restrict attention to a steady-state analysis. Indeed, following Diamond (1965)
we compare the market solution to the so-called *optimal golden-age path*.

A golden-age path is such that the capital-labour ratio is constant over time, i.e.
$k_{t+1} = k_t = k$. Such a path is called *optimal* if (i) each individual agent has the
highest possible utility, and (ii) all agents have the same utility level (Diamond,
1965, p. 1128). Formally, the optimal golden-age path maximizes the lifetime utility
of a "representative" individual,

$$\Lambda^Y \equiv U(C^Y) + \left(\frac{1}{1+\rho}\right)U(C^O), \tag{17.26}$$

subject to the economy-wide steady-state resource constraint:

$$f(k) - (n+\delta)k = C^Y + \frac{C^O}{1+n}. \tag{17.27}$$

Note that we have dropped the time subscripts in (17.26)–(17.27) in order to stress
the fact that we are looking at a steady-state situation only.[3] An important thing to
note about this formulation is the following. In (17.26) C^Y and C^O refer, respectively,
to consumption during youth and retirement *of a particular individual*. In contrast, in
(17.27) C^Y and C^O refer to consumption levels of young and old agents, respectively,
at a *particular moment in time*. This does, of course, not mean that we are comparing
apples and oranges—for the purposes of selecting an optimal golden-age path we
can ignore these differences because all individuals are treated symmetrically.

The first-order conditions for the optimal golden-age path consist of the steady-
state resource constraint and:

$$\frac{U'(C^O)}{U'(C^Y)} = \frac{1+\rho}{1+n}, \tag{17.28}$$

$$f'(k) = n + \delta. \tag{17.29}$$

Samuelson (1968a) calls these conditions, respectively, the biological-interest-rate
consumption golden rule and the production golden rule. Comparing (17.28)—
(17.29) with their respective market counterparts (17.5) and (17.16) reveals that

---

[3] The steady-state resource constraint (17.27) is obtained as follows. First, (17.18) is substituted in
(17.17) and the resulting expression is divided by L_t. Then (17.14) is inserted, the steady state is imposed
$(k_{t+1} = k_t = k)$, and all time indexes are dropped.

they coincide if the market rate of interest equals the rate of population growth:

$$r = f'(k) - \delta = n \qquad \text{(golden rule)}$$

As is stressed by Samuelson (1968a, p. 87) the two conditions (17.28)–(17.29) are analytically independent: even if k is held constant at some suboptimal level, so that production is inefficient as $f'(k) \neq n + \delta$, the optimum consumption pattern must still satisfy (17.28). Similarly, if the division of output among generations is suboptimal (e.g. due to a badly designed pension system), condition (17.28) no longer holds but the optimal k still follows from the production golden rule (17.29).

If the steady-state interest rate is less than the rate of population growth ($r < n$) then there is overaccumulation of capital, k is too high, and the economy is dynamically inefficient. A quick inspection of our unit-elastic model reveals that such a situation is quite possible for reasonable parameter values. Indeed, by computing the steady-state capital-labour ratio from (17.25) and using the result in (17.16) we find that the steady-state interest rate for the unit-elastic model is:

$$r = \frac{(1 - \epsilon_L)(2 + \rho)(1 + n)}{\epsilon_L} - \delta. \qquad (17.30)$$

Blanchard and Fischer (1989, p. 147) suggest the following numbers. Each period of life is 30 years and the labour share is $\epsilon_L = 3/4$. Population grows at 1% per annum so $n = 1.01^{30} - 1 = 0.348$. Capital depreciates at 5% per annum so $\delta = 1 - (0.95)^{30} = 0.785$. With relatively impatient agents, the pure discount rate is 3% per annum, so $\rho = (1.03)^{30} - 1 = 1.427$ and (17.30) shows that $r = 0.754$ which exceeds n by quite a margin. With more patient agents, whose pure discount rate is 1% per annum, $\rho = (1.01)^{30} - 1 = 0.348$ and $r = 0.269$ which is less than n.

17.2 Applications of the Basic Model

In this section we show how the standard Diamond–Samuelson model can be used to study the macroeconomic and welfare effects of old-age pensions. A system of social security was introduced in Germany during the 1880s by Otto von Bismarck, purportedly to stop the increasingly radical working class from overthrowing his conservative regime. It did not help poor Otto—he was forced to resign from office in 1890—but the system he helped create stayed. Especially following the Second World War, most developed countries have similarly adopted social security systems. Typically such a system provides benefit payments to the elderly which continue until the recipient dies.

In the first subsection we show how the method of financing old-age pensions critically determines the effects of such pensions on resource allocation and welfare. In the second subsection we study the effects of a demographic shock, such as an ageing population, on the macroeconomy.

17.2.1 Pensions

In order to study the effects of public pensions we must introduce the government into the Diamond–Samuelson model. Assume that, at time t, the government provides lump-sum transfers, Z_t, to old agents and levies lump-sum taxes, T_t, on the young. It follows that the budget identities of a young household at time t are changed from (17.2) and (17.3) to:

$$C_t^Y + S_t = W_t - T_t, \tag{17.31}$$

$$C_{t+1}^O = (1 + r_{t+1})S_t + Z_{t+1}, \tag{17.32}$$

so that the consolidated lifetime budget constraint of such a household is now:

$$W_t - T_t + \frac{Z_{t+1}}{1 + r_{t+1}} = C_t^Y + \frac{C_{t+1}^O}{1 + r_{t+1}}. \tag{17.33}$$

The left-hand side of (17.33) shows that lifetime wealth consists of after-tax wages during youth plus the present value of pension receipts during old age.

Depending on the way in which the government finances its transfer scheme, we can distinguish two prototypical social security schemes. In a *fully funded* system the government invests the contributions of the young and returns them with interest in the next period in the form of transfers to the then old agents. In such a system we have:

$$Z_{t+1} = (1 + r_{t+1})T_t. \tag{17.34}$$

In contrast, in an unfunded or *pay-as-you-go* (PAYG) system, the transfers to the old are covered by the taxes of the young *in the same period*. Since, at time t, there are L_{t-1} old agents (each receiving Z_t in transfers) and L_t young agents (each paying T_t in taxes) a PAYG system satisfies $L_{t-1}Z_t = L_t T_t$ which can be rewritten by noting (17.21) to:

$$Z_t = (1 + n)T_t. \tag{17.35}$$

Fully funded pensions

A striking property of a fully funded social security system is its neutrality. With this we mean that an economy with a fully funded system is identical in all relevant aspects to an economy without such a system. This important neutrality result can be demonstrated as follows.

First, we note that, by substituting (17.34) into (17.33), the fiscal variables, T_t and Z_{t+1}, disappear from the lifetime budget constraint of the household. Consequently, these variables also do not affect the household's optimal life-cycle consumption plan, i.e. C_t^Y and C_{t+1}^O are exactly as in the pension-less economy described in section 17.1.1 above. It follows, by a comparison of (17.2) and (17.31), that with a fully funded pension system saving plus tax payments are set according to:

$$S_t + T_t = S(W_t, r_{t+1}), \tag{17.36}$$

where $S(W_t, r_{t+1})$ is the same function as the one appearing in (17.6).

As a second preliminary step we must derive an expression linking savings of the young to next period's stock of productive capital. The key aspect of a fully funded system is that the government puts the tax receipts from the young to productive use by renting them out in the form of capital goods to firms. Hence, the economy-wide capital stock, K_t, is:

$$K_t = K_t^H + K_t^G, \tag{17.37}$$

where K_t^H and $K_t^G \equiv L_{t-1} T_{t-1}$ denote capital owned by households and the government, respectively. The economy-wide resource constraint is still as given in (17.17) but the expression for total consumption is changed from (17.19) to:[4]

$$C_t = Y_t + (1 - \delta)K_t - L_t(S_t + T_t). \tag{17.38}$$

Finally, by using (17.17), (17.38), and (17.36) we find that the capital market equilibrium condition is identical to (17.22). Since the factor prices, (17.15)–(17.16), are also unaffected by the existence of the social security system, economies with and without such a system are essentially the same. Intuitively, with a fully funded system the household knows that its contributions, T_t, attract the same rate of return as its own private savings, S_t. As a result, the household only worries about its total saving, $S_t + T_t$, and does not care that some of this saving is actually carried out on its behalf by the government.[5]

---

[4] Equation (17.38) is derived as follows. Consumption by the old agents is $L_{t-1} C_t^O = (r_t + \delta)K_t^H + (1 - \delta)K_t^H + L_{t-1} Z_t$. For young agents we have $L_t C_t^Y = L_t [W_t - S_t - T_t]$ so that aggregate consumption is:

$$
\begin{aligned}
C_t &= (r_t + \delta)K_t^H + (1 - \delta)K_t^H + L_{t-1} Z_t + L_t [W_t - S_t - T_t] \\
&= Y_t + (1 - \delta)K_t^H - (r_t + \delta)K_t^G + L_{t-1} Z_t - L_t(S_t + T_t) \\
&= Y_t + (1 - \delta)K_t - L_t(S_t + T_t) + \left[L_{t-1} Z_t - (1 + r_t)K_t^G \right].
\end{aligned}
$$

This final expression collapses to (17.38) because the term in square brackets on the right-hand side vanishes:

$$L_{t-1} Z_t - (1 + r_t)K_t^G = L_{t-1} [Z_t - (1 + r_t)T_{t-1}] = 0.$$

[5] An important proviso for the neutrality result to hold is that the social security system should not be too severe, i.e. it should not force the household to save more than it would in the absence of social security. In terms of the model we must have that $T_t < (1 + n)k_{t+1}$ (see Blanchard and Fischer, 1989, p. 111).

Pay-as-you-go pensions

Under a PAYG system there is a transfer from young to old in each period according to (17.35). Assuming that the contribution rate per person is held constant over time (so that $T_{t+1} = T_t = T$), (17.35) implies that $Z_{t+1} = (1 + n)T$ so that consolidation of (17.31)–(17.32) yields the following lifetime budget constraint of a young household:

$$\hat{W}_t \equiv W_t - \left(\frac{r_{t+1} - n}{1 + r_{t+1}} \right) T_t = C_t^Y + \frac{C_{t+1}^O}{1 + r_{t+1}}. \tag{17.39}$$

This expression is useful because it shows that, ceteris paribus the factor prices, the existence of a PAYG system contracts (expands) the consumption possibility frontier for young agents if the interest rate exceeds (falls short of) the growth rate of the population. Put differently, if $r_{t+1} > n$ ($r_{t+1} < n$) the contribution rate is seen as a lump-sum tax (subsidy) by the young household.

The household maximizes lifetime utility (17.1) subject to its lifetime budget constraint (17.39). Since the rate of return on household saving is r_{t+1}, the consumption Euler equation is still given by (17.5). To keep matters as simple as possible we now restrict attention to the simple unit-elastic model for which utility is logarithmic (and technology is Cobb–Douglas). In that case, the optimal consumption plan satisfies $C_t^Y = (1 + \rho)\hat{W}_t/(2 + \rho)$ and $C_{t+1}^O = (1 + r_{t+1})\hat{W}_t/(2 + \rho)$ and the savings function is:

$$
\begin{aligned}
S_t &= W_t - T - C_t^Y \\
&= W_t - T - \left(\frac{1 + \rho}{2 + \rho} \right) \left[W_t - \left(\frac{r_{t+1} - n}{1 + r_{t+1}} \right) T \right] \\
&= \left(\frac{1}{2 + \rho} \right) W_t - \left[1 - \left(\frac{1 + \rho}{2 + \rho} \right) \left(\frac{r_{t+1} - n}{1 + r_{t+1}} \right) \right] T \equiv S(W_t, r_{t+1}, T). \tag{17.40}
\end{aligned}
$$

It is easy to verify that the partial derivatives of the savings function satisfy $0 < S_W < 1$, $S_r > 0$, $-1 < S_T < 0$ (if $r_{t+1} > n$), and $S_T < -1$ (if $r_{t+1} < n$).

Since the PAYG pension is a pure transfer from co-existing young to old generations it does not itself lead to the formation of capital in the economy. Since only private saving augments the capital stock, equation (17.20) is still relevant.[6] By combining (17.20) with (17.40) we obtain the expression linking the future

---

[6] Consumption by the old agents is $L_{t-1} C_t^O = (r_t + \delta)K_t + (1 - \delta)K_t + L_{t-1}Z_t$. For young agents we have $L_t C_t^Y = L_t [W_t - S_t - T_t]$ so that aggregate consumption is:

$$C_t = (r_t + \delta)K_t + (1 - \delta)K_t + L_{t-1}Z_t + L_t [W_t - S_t - T_t]$$
$$= Y_t + (1 - \delta)K_t + [L_{t-1}Z_t - L_t T_t] - L_t S_t.$$

This final expression collapses to (17.19) because the term in square brackets on the right-hand side vanishes under the PAYG scheme. Combining (17.17) and (17.19) yields (17.20).

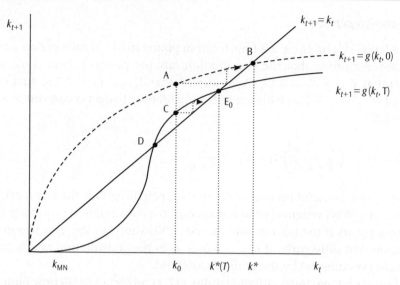

Figure 17.2. PAYG pensions in the unit-elastic model

capital stock to current saving plans:

$$S(W_t, r_{t+1}, T) = (1+n)k_{t+1}. \tag{17.41}$$

With Cobb–Douglas technology ($y_t \equiv k_t^{1-\epsilon_L}$) equations (17.15) and (17.16) reduce to, respectively, $W_t \equiv W(k_t) = \epsilon_L k_t^{1-\epsilon_L}$ and $r_{t+1} \equiv r(k_{t+1}) = (1-\epsilon_L)k_{t+1}^{-\epsilon_L} - \delta$. By using these expressions in (17.41) we obtain the fundamental difference equation (in implicit form) characterizing the economy under a PAYG system, $k_{t+1} = g(k_t, T)$. The partial derivatives of this function are:

$$g_k \equiv \frac{\partial g}{\partial k_t} = \frac{S_W W'(k_t)}{1+n - S_r r'(k_{t+1})} > 0, \tag{17.42}$$

$$g_T \equiv \frac{\partial g}{\partial T} = \frac{S_T}{1+n - S_r r'(k_{t+1})} < 0, \tag{17.43}$$

where S_W and S_r are obtained from (17.40). We illustrate the fundamental difference equation in Figure 17.2.[7]

---

[7] The fundamental difference equation can be written as:

$$(1+n)k_{t+1} = \frac{W(k_t) - T}{2 + \rho} - \left(\frac{1+\rho}{2+\rho}\right)\frac{(1+n)T}{1 + r(k_{t+1})}.$$

The second term on the right-hand side vanishes as $k_{t+1} \to 0$ (since $r(k_{t+1}) \to +\infty$ in that case). Hence, $W(k_{MIN}) = T$. For $k_t < k_{MIN}$ the wage rate is too low ($W(k_t) < T$) and the PAYG scheme is not feasible. By differentiating the fundamental difference equation we obtain:

$$\frac{dk_{t+1}}{dk_t} = \frac{W'(k_t)}{(1+n)[2 + \rho + (1+\rho)T\psi(k_{t+1})]} \geq 0, \quad \psi(k_{t+1}) \equiv \frac{-r'(k_{t+1})}{[1 + r(k_{t+1})]^2}.$$

In Figure 17.2, the dashed line, labelled "$k_{t+1} = g(k_t, 0)$" characterizes the standard unit-elastic Diamond–Samuelson model without social security, i.e. it reproduces Figure 17.1 and point B is the steady state to which the economy converges in the absence of social security. Suppose now that the PAYG system is introduced at time $t = 0$ when the economy has an initial (non-steady-state) capital–labour ratio of k_0. Members of the old generation at time $t = 0$ cannot believe their luck. They have not contributed anything to the PAYG system but nevertheless receive a pension of $Z = (1 + n)T$ (see equation (17.35)). Since the old do not save this *windfall gain* is spent entirely on additional consumption. Consumption by each old household at time $t = 0$ is now:

$$C_0^O = (1 + n)[(1 + r(k_0))k_0 + T], \tag{17.44}$$

and, since k_0 is predetermined, so is the interest rate and $dC_0^O/dT = (1 + n)$.

In contrast, members of the young generation at time $t = 0$ are affected by the introduction of the PAYG system in a number of different ways. On the one hand, they must pay T in the current period in exchange for which they receive a pension $(1 + n)T$ in the next period. Since the wage rate at time $t = 0$, $W(k_0)$, is predetermined, the net effect of these two transactions is to change the value of lifetime resources ($\hat{W}_0$ defined in (17.39)) according to:

$$\frac{\partial \hat{W}_0}{\partial T} = -\left(\frac{r(k_1) - n}{1 + r(k_1)}\right) \lesseqqgtr 0, \tag{17.45}$$

where the sign is ambiguous because $r(k_1)$ may exceed or fall short of the population growth rate n. Furthermore, (17.45) is only a partial effect because the interest rate depends on the capital stock in the next period (k_1), which is itself determined by the savings behaviour of the young in period $t = 0$. It follows from (17.41) and (17.43), however, that the total effect of the introduction of the PAYG system is to reduce saving by the young and thus to reduce next period's capital stock, i.e. $dk_1/dT = g_T < 0$. This adverse effect on the capital stock is represented in Figure 17.2 by the vertical difference between points A and C.

As a result of the policy shock, the economy now follows the convergent path from C to the ultimate steady state E_0. It follows from Figure 17.2 that k_t is less than it would have been without the PAYG pension, both during transition and in the new steady state (i.e. the path from C to E_0 lies below the path from A to B). Hence, since $W'(x) > 0$ and $r'(x) < 0$, the steady-state wage is lower and the interest rate is higher than it would have been. The long-run effect on the capital–labour ratio is

It is straightforward to show that $\psi(k_{t+1}) \to +\infty$ for $k_{t+1} \to 0$, $\psi(k_{t+1}) \to 0$ for $k_{t+1} \to \infty$, $W'(k_t) \to 0$ for $k_t \to \infty$, and $W'(k_{MIN}) > 0$. It follows that $g(k_t, T)$ is horizontal in $k_t = k_{MIN}$, is upward sloping for larger values of k_t, and becomes horizontal as k_t gets very large. Provided T is not too large there exist two intersections with the $k_{t+1} = k_t$ line.

obtained by using (17.41) and imposing the steady state ($k_{t+1} = k_t$):

$$\frac{dk}{dT} = \frac{g_T}{1 - g_k} < 0, \tag{17.46}$$

where $0 < g_k < 1$ follows from the stability condition.

The upshot of the discussion so far is that, unlike a fully funded pension system, a PAYG system is not neutral but leads to crowding out of capital, a lower wage rate, and a higher interest rate in the long run. Is that good or bad for households? To answer that question we now study the welfare effect on a *steady-state generation* of a change in the contribution rate, T. As in our discussion of dynamic efficiency above we thus continue to ignore transitional dynamics for the time being by only looking at the steady state.

To conduct the welfare analysis we need to utilize two helpful tools, i.e. the *indirect utility function* and the *factor price frontier*. The indirect utility function is defined in formal terms by:

$$\bar{\Lambda}^Y(W, r, T) \equiv \max_{\{C^Y, C^O\}} \left\{ \Lambda^Y(C^Y, C^O) \text{ subject to } \hat{W} = C^Y + \frac{C^O}{1+r} \right\}, \tag{17.47}$$

where $\Lambda^Y(C^Y, C^O)$ is the direct utility function (i.e. (17.1)). The lack of subscripts indicates steady-state values and $\hat{W}$ represents lifetime household resources under the PAYG system:

$$\hat{W} = W - \left(\frac{r - n}{1 + r} \right) T. \tag{17.48}$$

For example, for the logarithmic felicity function (employed regularly in this chapter) the indirect utility function takes the following form:

$$\bar{\Lambda}^Y = \omega_0 + \left(\frac{2 + \rho}{1 + \rho} \right) \log \hat{W} + \left(\frac{1}{1 + \rho} \right) \log (1 + r), \tag{17.49}$$

where ω_0 is a constant.[8]

---

[8] The explicit functional form of the indirect utility is obtained by plugging the optimal consumption levels, as chosen by the household, back into the direct utility function (17.1). The reader should verify the properties stated in (17.50)–(17.52).

The indirect utility function (17.47) has a number of properties which will prove to be very useful below:[9]

$$\frac{\partial \bar{\Lambda}^Y}{\partial W} = \frac{\partial \Lambda^Y}{\partial C^Y} > 0, \tag{17.50}$$

$$\frac{\partial \bar{\Lambda}^Y}{\partial r} = \left(\frac{S}{1+r}\right)\frac{\partial \Lambda^Y}{\partial C^Y} > 0, \tag{17.51}$$

$$\frac{\partial \bar{\Lambda}^Y}{\partial T} = -\left(\frac{r-n}{1+r}\right)\frac{\partial \Lambda^Y}{\partial C^Y} \gtreqless 0. \tag{17.52}$$

According to (17.50)–(17.51), steady-state welfare depends positively on both the wage rate and the interest rate. Since we saw above that the wage falls ($dW/dT = W'(k)dk/dT < 0$) but the interest rate rises ($dr/dT = r'(k)dk/dT > 0$) in the long run, the effects of factor prices on welfare work in opposite directions even in the absence of a PAYG system (if $T = 0$).

But both W and r depend on the capital-labour ratio (as in the standard neo-classical model) and are thus not independent of each other. By exploiting this dependency we obtain the factor price frontier, $W_t = \phi(r_t)$, which has a very useful property:

$$W_t = \phi(r_t), \qquad \frac{dW_t}{dr_t} \equiv \phi'(r_t) = -k_t. \tag{17.53}$$

The slope of the factor price frontier is obtained as follows. In general, by differentiating (17.15) and (17.16) (for r_t) we get $dr_t = f''(k_t)dk_t$ and $dW_t = -k_t f''(k_t)dk_t$ so that $dW_t/dr_t = -k_t$. From this it follows that $d^2 W_t/dr_t^2 = -dk_t/dr_t = -1/f''(k_t)$.[10]

---

[9] These properties are derived as follows. We start with the identity $\bar{\Lambda}^Y(W, r, T) \equiv \Lambda^Y\left[C^Y(W, r, T), C^O(W, r, T)\right]$, where $C^i(W, r, T)$ are the optimal consumption levels during the two periods of life. By using this identity, partially differentiating (17.1), and using (17.5) we obtain:

$$\frac{\partial \bar{\Lambda}^Y}{\partial W} = \frac{\partial \Lambda^Y}{\partial C^Y}\left[\frac{\partial C^Y}{\partial W} + \left(\frac{1}{1+r}\right)\frac{\partial C^O}{\partial W}\right].$$

It follows from the constraint in (17.47) that the term in square brackets is equal to unity. Using the same steps we obtain for $\partial \bar{\Lambda}^Y/\partial r$:

$$\frac{\partial \bar{\Lambda}^Y}{\partial r} = \frac{\partial \Lambda^Y}{\partial C^Y}\left[\frac{\partial C^Y}{\partial r} + \left(\frac{1}{1+r}\right)\frac{\partial C^O}{\partial r}\right] = \frac{\partial \Lambda^Y}{\partial C^Y}\left(\frac{C^O - (1+n)T}{(1+r)^2}\right).$$

Using $C^O - (1+n)T = (1+r)S$ we obtain (17.51). Finally, we obtain for $\partial \bar{\Lambda}^Y/\partial T$:

$$\frac{\partial \bar{\Lambda}^Y}{\partial T} = \frac{\partial \Lambda^Y}{\partial C^Y}\left[\frac{\partial C^Y}{\partial T} + \left(\frac{1}{1+r}\right)\frac{\partial C^O}{\partial T}\right] = -\left(\frac{r-n}{1+r}\right)\frac{\partial \Lambda^Y}{\partial C^Y},$$

where the final result follows from the constraint in (17.47).

[10] The factor price frontier for the Cobb–Douglas technology is given by:

$$W = \epsilon_L\left(\frac{1-\epsilon_L}{r+\delta}\right)^{(1-\epsilon_L)/\epsilon_L},$$

where the reader should verify the property stated in (17.53).

We now have all the necessary ingredients to perform our welfare analysis. By differentiating the indirect utility function with respect to T we obtain in a few steps:

$$
\begin{aligned}
\frac{d\Lambda^Y}{dT} &= \frac{\partial \bar{\Lambda}^Y}{\partial W}\frac{dW}{dT} + \frac{\partial \bar{\Lambda}^Y}{\partial r}\frac{dr}{dT} + \frac{\partial \bar{\Lambda}^Y}{\partial T} \\
&= \frac{\partial \Lambda^Y}{\partial C^Y}\left[\frac{dW}{dT} + \left(\frac{S}{1+r}\right)\frac{dr}{dT} - \left(\frac{r-n}{1+r}\right)\right] \\
&= -\left(\frac{r-n}{1+r}\right)\left(\frac{\partial \Lambda^Y}{\partial C^Y}\right)\left[1 + k\left(\frac{dr}{dT}\right)\right] \propto \mathrm{sgn}(n-r),
\end{aligned}
\tag{17.54}
$$

where we have used (17.48) and (17.50)–(17.52) in going from the first to the second line and (17.53) as well as $S = (1+n)k$ in going from the second to the third line. The term in square brackets on the right-hand side of (17.54) shows the two channels by which the PAYG pension affects welfare. The first term is the partial equilibrium effect of T on lifetime resources and the second term captures the general equilibrium effects that operate via factor prices.

The expression in (17.54) is important because it illustrates in a transparent fashion the intimate link that exists between, on the one hand, the steady-state welfare effect of a PAYG pension and, on the other hand, the dynamic (in)efficiency of the initial steady-state equilibrium. If the economy happens to be in the golden-rule equilibrium (so that $r = n$) then it follows from (17.54) that a *marginal* change in the PAYG contribution rate has no effect on steady-state welfare (i.e. $d\Lambda^Y/dT = 0$ in that case). Since the yield on private saving and the PAYG pension are the same in that case, a small change in T does not produce a first-order welfare effect on steady-state generations despite the fact that it causes crowding out of capital (see (17.46)) and thus an increase in the interest rate (since $r'(k) < 0$).

Matters are different if the economy is initially not in the golden-rule equilibrium (so that $r \neq n$) because the capital crowding out does produce a first-order welfare effect in that case. For example, if the economy is initially dynamically inefficient ($r < n$), then an increase in the PAYG contribution rate actually raises steady-state welfare! The intuition behind this result, which was first demonstrated in the pensions context and with a partial equilibrium model by Aaron (1966), is as follows. In a dynamically inefficient economy there is oversaving by the young generations as a result of which the market rate of interest is low. By raising T the young partially substitute private saving for saving via the PAYG pension. The latter has a higher yield than the former because the biological interest rate, n, exceeds the market interest rate, r. The reduction in the capital stock lowers the wage but this adverse effect on welfare is offset by the increase in the interest rate in a dynamically inefficient economy. To put it bluntly, capital crowding out is good in such an economy.

Equivalence PAYG and deficit financing government debt

As was shown by Auerbach and Kotlikoff, a PAYG social security scheme can also be reinterpreted as a particular kind of government debt policy (1987, pp. 149–150).

In order to demonstrate this equivalency result, we now introduce government debt into the model. This model extension also allows us to further clarify the link between the pension insights of Aaron (1966) and the macroeconomic effects of debt as set out by Diamond (1965).

Assume that the government taxes the young generations, provides transfers to the old generations, and issues one-period (indexed) debt which yields the same rate of interest as capital. Ignoring government consumption, the government budget identity is now:

$$B_{t+1} - B_t = r_t B_t + L_{t-1} Z_t - L_t T_t, \tag{17.55}$$

where B_t is the stock of public debt at the beginning of period t. Interest payments on existing debt $(r_t B_t)$ plus transfers to the old are covered by the revenues from the tax on the young and/or additional debt issues $(B_{t+1} - B_t)$.

Because government debt and private capital attract the same rate of return, the household is indifferent about the *composition* of its savings over these two assets. Consequently, the young choose consumption in the two periods and *total* saving in order to maximize lifetime utility (17.1) subject to the budget identities (17.31) and (17.32). The savings function that results takes the following form:

$$S_t = S(\hat{W}_t, r_{t+1}), \tag{17.56}$$

where $\hat{W}_t$ is given by the left-hand side of (17.33) which is reproduced here for convenience:

$$\hat{W}_t = W_t - T_t + \frac{Z_{t+1}}{1 + r_{t+1}}. \tag{17.57}$$

It remains to derive the expression linking private savings plans and aggregate capital formation. There are L_t young agents who each save S_t so that aggregate saving is $S_t L_t$. Saving can be in the form of private capital or public debt. Hence the capital market equilibrium condition is now:[11]

$$L_t S_t = B_{t+1} + K_{t+1}. \tag{17.58}$$

We are now in the position to present an important equivalence result which was proved *inter alia* by Wallace (1981), Sargent (1987a), and Calvo and Obstfeld (1988). Buiter and Kletzer state the equivalence result as follows: "... any equilibrium with government debt and deficits can be replicated by an economy in

---

[11] Consumption by old agents is $L_{t-1} C_t^O = (r_t + \delta) K_t + (1 - \delta) K_t + (1 + r_t) B_t + L_{t-1} Z_t$. For young agents we have $L_t C_t^Y = L_t [W_t - T_t - S_t]$ so that aggregate consumption is:

$$C_t = (r_t + \delta) K_t + (1 - \delta) K_t + (1 + r_t) B_t + L_{t-1} Z_t + L_t [W_t - T_t - S_t]$$
$$= Y_t + (1 - \delta) K_t + [(1 + r_t) B_t + L_{t-1} Z_t - L_t T_t] - L_t S_t$$
$$= Y_t + (1 - \delta) K_t + B_{t+1} - L_t S_t.$$

By combining the final expression with the resource constraint (17.17) we obtain (17.58).

which the government budget is balanced period-by-period (and the stock of debt is zero) by appropriate age-specific lump-sum taxes and transfers" (1992, pp. 27–28). A corollary of the result is that if the policy maker has access to unrestricted age-specific taxes and transfers then public debt is redundant in the sense that it does not permit additional equilibria to be supported (1992, p. 28).

The model developed in this subsection is fully characterized (for $t \geq 0$) by the following equations:

$$C_t^O = (1 + r(k_t))(1 + n)(k_t + b_t) + Z_t \tag{17.59}$$

$$U'(C_t^Y) = \left(\frac{1 + r(k_{t+1})}{1 + \rho}\right) U'(C_{t+1}^O) \tag{17.60}$$

$$W(k_t) - T_t - C_t^Y = (1 + n)[k_{t+1} + b_{t+1}] \tag{17.61}$$

$$(1 + n)b_{t+1} = (1 + r(k_t))b_t + \frac{Z_t}{1 + n} - T_t, \tag{17.62}$$

where $b_t \equiv B_t/L_t$ is per capita government debt and where k_0 and b_0 are both given. Equation (17.59) is consumption of an old household, (17.60) is the consumption Euler equation for a young household (see also (17.5)), (17.61) is (17.31) combined with (17.58), and (17.62) is the government budget identity (17.55) expressed in per capita form. Finally, we have substituted the rental expressions $W_t = W(k_t)$ and $r_t = r(k_t)$ in the various equations (see (17.15) and (17.16) above).

The first thing we note is that the fiscal variables only show up in two places in the dynamical system. In (17.59) there is a resource transfer from the government to each old household (Γ_t^{GO}) consisting of debt service and transfers:

$$\Gamma_t^{GO} \equiv (1 + r(k_t))(1 + n)b_t + Z_t. \qquad \text{(government to old)}$$

Similarly, in (17.61) there is a resource transfer from each young household to the government (Γ_t^{YG}) in the form of purchases of government debt plus taxes:

$$\Gamma_t^{YG} \equiv (1 + n)b_{t+1} + T_t. \qquad \text{(young to government)}$$

Since there are L_{t-1} old and L_t young households, the net resource transfer to the government is $L_t \Gamma_t^{YG} - L_{t-1} \Gamma_t^{GO} = 0$, where the equality follows from the government budget constraint (17.62). Hence, in the absence of government consumption, what the government takes from the young it must give to the old. Once you know Γ_t^{YG} you also know $\Gamma_t^{GO} \equiv (1 + n)\Gamma_t^{YG}$ and the individual components appearing in the government budget identity (such as b_{t+1}, b_t, Z_t, and T_t) are irrelevant for the determination of the paths of consumption and the capital stock (Buiter and Kletzer, 1992, p. 17).

The equivalence result is demonstrated by considering two paths of the economy which, though associated with different paths for bonds, taxes, and transfers, nevertheless give rise to the same paths for the real variables, namely the capital stock and consumption by the young and the old. For the reference path, the sequence $\{\hat{b}_t, \hat{Z}_t, \hat{T}_t\}_{t=0}^{\infty}$ gives rise to a sequence for the real variables denoted by $\{\hat{C}_t^Y, \hat{C}_t^O, \hat{k}_t\}_{t=0}^{\infty}$ given k_0 and b_0. We can then show that for any other debt sequence $\{\check{b}_t\}_{t=1}^{\infty}$ we can always find sequences for taxes and transfers $\{\check{Z}_t, \check{T}_t\}_{t=0}^{\infty}$ such that the resulting sequences for the real variables are the same as in the reference path, i.e. $\{\hat{C}_t^Y\}_{t=0}^{\infty} = \{\check{C}_t^Y\}_{t=0}^{\infty}$, $\{\hat{C}_t^O\}_{t=0}^{\infty} = \{\check{C}_t^O\}_{t=0}^{\infty}$, and $\{\hat{k}_t\}_{t=0}^{\infty} = \{\check{k}_t\}_{t=0}^{\infty}$.

The key ingredient of the proof is to construct the alternative path such that the resource transfers from the young to the government (Γ_t^{YG}) and from the government to the old (Γ_t^{GO}) are the same for the two paths. These requirements give rise to the following expressions:

$$\hat{Z}_t - \check{Z}_t = (1 + n)\left[(1 + r(\check{k}_t))\check{b}_t - (1 + r(\hat{k}_t))\hat{b}_t\right], \tag{17.63}$$

$$\check{b}_{t+1} - \hat{b}_{t+1} = \left(\frac{1}{1+n}\right)\left[\hat{T}_t - \check{T}_t\right]. \tag{17.64}$$

By using (17.63) in (17.59) and (17.64) in (17.61) we find that these equations solve for the same real variables. As a result, the Euler equation (17.60) is the same for both paths. Obviously the government budget identity still holds. Finally, if the reference path satisfies the government solvency condition then so will the alternative path.

As a special case of the equivalence result we can take as the reference path the PAYG system (studied above), which has $\hat{b}_t = 0$, $\hat{T}_t = T$, and $\hat{Z}_t = (1+n)T$ for all t. One (of many) alternative paths is the deficit path in which there are only taxes on the young generations, i.e. $\check{Z}_t = 0$, $\check{b}_t = T/(1+r_t)$, and $\check{T}_t = T - (1+n)\check{b}_{t+1}$ for all t.

From PAYG to a funded system

In the previous subsection we have established the equivalence between traditional deficit financing and a PAYG social security system. As a by-product of the analysis there we showed how public debt affects the equilibrium path of the economy. In this section we continue our analysis of the welfare effects of a PAYG system, first without and then with bond policy.

Up to this point we have only unearthed the welfare effect of a PAYG system on steady-state generations (see (17.54)) and we have ignored the initial conditions facing the economy, i.e. we have not yet taken into account the costs associated with the transition from the initial growth path to the golden-rule path. As both Diamond (1965, pp. 1128–1129) and Samuelson (1975b, p. 543) stress, ignoring transitional welfare effects is not a very good idea.

As we argued above, the introduction of a PAYG system (or the expansion of a pre-existing one) affects different generations differently. The welfare of old generations at the time of the shock unambiguously rises because of the windfall gain the shock confers on them. From the perspective of their last period of life, they gain utility to the tune of $U'(C_1^O)dC_0^O/dT = U'(C_1^O) > 0$ (see (17.44)). The welfare effect on generations born in the new steady state is ambiguous as it depends on whether or not the economy is dynamically efficient (see (17.54)). In a dynamically inefficient economy, $r < n$, all generations, including those born in the new steady state, gain from the pension shock. Intuitively, the PAYG system acts like a "chain letter" system which ensures that each new generation passes resources to the generation immediately preceding it. In such a situation a PAYG system which moves the economy in the direction of the golden-rule growth path is surely "desirable" for society as a whole.

As Abel et al. (1989) suggest, however, actual economies are not likely to be dynamically inefficient. If the economy is dynamically efficient, so that $r > n$, then it follows from, respectively, (17.44) and (17.54) that whilst an increase in T still makes the old initial generation better off, it leaves steady-state generations worse off than they would have been in the absence of the shock. Since some generations gain and other lose out, it is no longer obvious whether a pension-induced move in the direction of the golden-rule growth path is "socially desirable" at all.

There are two ways in which the concept of social desirability, which we have deliberately kept vague up to now, can be made operational. The first approach, which was pioneered by Bergson (1938) and Samuelson (1947), makes use of a so-called *social welfare function*. In this approach, a functional form is typically postulated which relates an indicator for social welfare (SW) to the welfare levels experienced by the different generations. Using our notation, an example of a social welfare function would be:

$$SW_t = w(\Lambda_{t-1}^Y, \Lambda_t^Y, \dots, \Lambda_\infty^Y). \tag{17.65}$$

Once a particular form for the social welfare function is adopted, the social desirability of different policies can be ranked. If policy A is such that it yields a higher indicator of social welfare than policy B, then it follows that policy A is *socially preferred* to policy B (i.e. $SW_t^A > SW_t^B$). Note that, depending on the form of the social welfare function $w(.)$, it may very well be the case that some generations are worse off under policy A than under policy B despite the fact that A is socially preferred to B. What the social welfare function does is establish marginal rates of substitution between lifetime utility levels of different generations (i.e. $(\partial w / \partial \Lambda_{t-1}^Y)/(\partial w / \partial \Lambda_t^Y)$, etc.).[12]

The second approach to putting into operation the concept of social desirability makes use of the concept of *Pareto-efficiency*. Recall that an allocation of resources in the economy is called Pareto-optimal (or Pareto-efficient) if there is no other feasible allocation which (i) makes no individual in the economy worse off and (ii) makes at least one individual strictly better off than he/she was. Similarly, a policy is called *Pareto-improving vis-à-vis* the initial situation if it improves welfare for at least one agent and leaves all other agents equally well off as in the status quo.

Recently, a number of authors have applied the Pareto-criterion to the question of pension reform. Specifically, Breyer (1989) and Verbon (1989) ask themselves

---

[12] An application of the social welfare function approach is given in the next subsection.

the question whether it is possible to abolish a pre-existing PAYG system (in favour of a fully funded system) in a Pareto-improving fashion in a dynamically efficient economy. This is a relevant question because in such an economy, steady-state generations gain if the PAYG system is abolished or reduced (since $r > n$ it follows from equation (17.54) that $d\Lambda^Y/dT < 0$ in that case) but the old generation at the time of the policy shock loses out (see (17.44)). This generation paid into the PAYG system when it was young in the expectation that it would receive back $1 + n$ times its contribution during old age. Taken in isolation, the policy shock is clearly not Pareto-improving.

Of course bond policy constitutes a mechanism by which the welfare gains and losses of the different generations can be redistributed. This is the case because it breaks the link between the contributions of the young ($L_t T_t$) and the pension receipts by the old in the same period ($L_{t-1} Z_t$)—compare (17.35) and (17.55). The key issue is thus whether it is possible to find a bond path such that the reduction in the PAYG contribution is Pareto-improving. As it turns out, no such path can be found. It is thus not possible to compensate the old generation at the time of the shock without making at least one future generation worse off (Breyer, 1989, p. 655).

17.2.2 PAYG pensions and endogenous retirement

In a very influential article, Feldstein (1974) argued that a PAYG system not only affects a household's savings decisions (as is the case in the model studied up to this point) but also its decision to retire from the labour force. We now augment the model in order to demonstrate the implications for allocation and welfare of endogenous retirement. Following the literature, we capture the notion of retirement by assuming that labour supply during the first period of life is endogenous. To keep the model as simple as possible, we continue to assume that households do not work at all during the second period of life. To bring the model closer to reality, we assume furthermore that the contribution to the PAYG system is levied in the form of a proportional tax on labour income and that the pension is *intragenerationally fair*, i.e. an agent who works a lot during youth gets a higher pension during old age than an agent who has been lazy during youth. Within the augmented model it is possible that the PAYG system distorts the labour supply decisions by households.

Households

The lifetime utility function of a young agent i who is born at time t is given in general form by:

$$\Lambda_t^{Y,i} \equiv \Lambda^Y(C_t^{Y,i}, C_{t+1}^{O,i}, 1 - N_t^i), \tag{17.66}$$

where N_t^i is labour supply ($1 - N_t^i$ is leisure) and $\Lambda^Y(.)$ satisfies the usual Inada-style conditions. The agent faces the following budget identities:

$$C_t^{Y,i} + S_t^i = W_t N_t^i - T_t^i, \tag{17.67}$$

$$C_{t+1}^{O,i} = (1 + r_{t+1})S_t^i + Z_{t+1}^i, \tag{17.68}$$

where T_t^i and Z_{t+1}^i are defined as follows:

$$T_t^i = t_L W_t N_t^i, \tag{17.69}$$

$$Z_{t+1}^i = \left(t_L W_{t+1} \sum_{j=1}^{L_{t+1}} N_{t+1}^j \right) \left(\frac{N_t^i}{\sum_{j=1}^{L_t} N_t^j} \right), \tag{17.70}$$

where $0 < t_L < 1$. According (17.69), the individual agent's contribution to the PAYG system is equal to a proportion of his labour income, where the proportional tax, t_L, is assumed to be the same for all individuals and constant over time. Equation (17.70) shows that the pension is intragenerationally fair (as in Breyer and Straub, 1993, p. 81). The first term on the right-hand side of (17.70) is the total tax revenue that is available for pension payments in the next period. Agent i gets a share of this revenue that depends on his *relative* labour supply effort during youth (the second term on the right-hand side).[13]

Household i is fully aware of the features of the pension system (as formalized in (17.69)–(17.70)) so that the consolidated lifetime budget constraint, upon which the household bases its decisions, is given by:

$$W_t N_t^i - t_L \left(1 - \frac{W_{t+1} \sum_{j=1}^{L_{t+1}} N_{t+1}^j}{W_t(1 + r_{t+1}) \sum_{j=1}^{L_t} N_t^j} \right) W_t N_t^i = C_t^{Y,i} + \frac{C_{t+1}^{O,i}}{1 + r_{t+1}}. \tag{17.71}$$

The key thing to note about (17.71) is that in the current setting the household's pension depends not only on future wages but also on the aggregate supply of labour *by future young agents*. To solve its optimization problem, the household must thus form expectations regarding these variables and, as usual, by suppressing the expectations operator we have implicitly assumed in (17.71) that the agent is blessed with perfect foresight.

---

[13] Since we assume that all agents are identical below, all agents of the same generation will supply the same amount of labour ($N_t^i = N_t$) and (17.69)–(17.70) will be simplified to:

$$T_t^i = T_t = t_L W_t N_t, \quad Z_{t+1}^i = Z_{t+1} = (1 + n)t_L W_{t+1} N_{t+1}. \tag{a}$$

Working directly with (a) would obscure the fact that the pension is intragenerationally fair.

Assuming an interior optimum, the first-order conditions for consumption during the two periods and labour supply are:

$$\frac{\partial \Lambda^Y}{\partial C_{t+1}^{O,i}} = \left(\frac{1}{1+r_{t+1}}\right)\left(\frac{\partial \Lambda^Y}{\partial C_t^{Y,i}}\right), \tag{17.72}$$

$$\left[-\frac{\partial \Lambda^Y}{\partial N_t^i}\right] = \frac{\partial \Lambda^Y}{\partial(1-N_t^i)} = (1-t_{L,t}^E)W_t\left(\frac{\partial \Lambda^Y}{\partial C_t^{Y,i}}\right), \tag{17.73}$$

$$t_{L,t}^E \equiv t_L\left[1-\left(\frac{W_{t+1}}{W_t}\right)\left(\frac{\sum_{j=1}^{L_{t+1}} N_{t+1}^j}{\sum_{j=1}^{L_t} N_t^j}\right)\left(\frac{1}{1+r_{t+1}}\right)\right]. \tag{17.74}$$

Equation (17.72) is the familiar consumption Euler equation in general functional form. The optimal labour supply decision is characterized by (17.73)–(17.74). Equation (17.73) is the usual condition calling for an equalization of the after-tax wage rate and the marginal rate of substitution between leisure and consumption during youth. Equation (17.74) shows to what extent the PAYG system has the potential to distort the labour supply decision. It is not the *statutory* tax rate, t_L, which determines whether or not the labour supply decison is distorted but rather the *effective* tax rate, $t_{L,t}^E$. By paying the PAYG premium during youth one obtains the right to a pension. Ceteris paribus labour supply, the effective tax rate may actually be negative, i.e. it may in fact be an employment subsidy (Breyer and Straub, 1993, p. 82).

Since all agents of a particular generation are identical in all aspects we can now drop the index i. In such a symmetric equilibrium we have $N_t^i = N_t$ and with a constant growth rate of the population ($L_{t+1} = (1+n)L_t$) (17.74) simplifies to:

$$t_{L,t}^E \equiv t_L\left[1-\left(\frac{W_{t+1}}{W_t}\right)\left(\frac{N_{t+1}}{N_t}\right)\left(\frac{1+n}{1+r_{t+1}}\right)\right]. \tag{17.75}$$

Holding constant labour supply we find that the pension system acts like an employment subsidy (and $t_{L,t}^E < 0$) if the so-called *Aaron condition* holds, i.e. if the growth of the population and wages exceeds the rate of interest (Aaron, 1966).

In the symmetric equilibrium, equations (17.71)–(17.73) define the optimal values of C_t^Y, C_{t+1}^O, and N_t as a function of the variables that are exogenous to the representative agent (W_t, r_{t+1}, and $t_{L,t}^E$). We write these solutions as $C_t^Y = C^Y(W_t^N, r_{t+1})$, $C_{t+1}^O = C^O(W_t^N, r_{t+1})$, and $N_t = N(W_t^N, r_{t+1})$, where $W_t^N \equiv W_t(1-t_{L,t}^E)$. The (partial-equilibrium) effect of a change in the statutory tax rate, t_L, on the household's labour supply decision can thus be written in elasticity format as:

$$\frac{t_L}{N_t}\frac{\partial N_t}{\partial t_L} = -\epsilon_{WN}^N\left(\frac{t_{L,t}^E}{1-t_{L,t}^E}\right), \qquad \epsilon_{WN}^N \equiv \frac{W^N}{N}\frac{\partial N}{\partial W^N}, \tag{17.76}$$

where ϵ_{WN}^N is the uncompensated elasticity of labour supply. It follows from (17.76) that the effect of the contribution rate on labour supply is ambiguous for two reasons. First, it depends on whether the Aaron-condition is satisfied ($t_{L,t}^E < 0$) or violated ($t_{L,t}^E > 0$). Second, it also depends on the sign of ϵ_{WN}^N. We recall that $\epsilon_{WN}^N > 0$ (<0) if the substitution effect in labour supply dominates (is dominated by) the income effect. If the labour supply is upward sloping and the Aaron condition is satisfied then, for given factor prices, an increase in the statutory tax rate decreases labour supply.

The macroeconomy

We must now complete the description of the model and derive the fundamental difference equation for the economic system. We follow the approach of Ihori (1996, pp. 36–37). With endogenous labour supply, the number of agents (L_t) no longer coincides with the amount of labour used in production ($L_t N_t$). By redefining the capital-labour ratio as $k_t \equiv K_t/(L_t N_t)$, however, the expressions for the wage and the interest rate are still as in (17.15)–(17.16) and the factor price frontier is still as given in (17.53). Current savings leads to the formation of capital in the next period, i.e. $L_t S_t = K_{t+1}$. In terms of the redefined capital-labour ratio we get:

$$S_t = (1 + n)N_{t+1}k_{t+1}. \tag{17.77}$$

To characterize this fundamental difference equation we note that the labour supply and savings equations can be written in general functional form as:

$$N_t = N(W_t(1 - t_{L,t}^E), r_{t+1}) \tag{17.78}$$

$$S[.] \equiv \frac{C^O(W_t(1 - t_{L,t}^E), r_{t+1}) - (1 + n)t_L W_{t+1}N_{t+1}}{1 + r_{t+1}}. \tag{17.79}$$

By using these expressions in (17.77) we obtain the following expression:

$$S\left[W_t(1 - t_{L,t}^E), r_{t+1}, t_L W_{t+1}N_{t+1}\right] = (1 + n)N(W_{t+1}(1 - t_{L,t+1}^E), r_{t+2})k_{t+1}. \tag{17.80}$$

Clearly, since $W_t = W(k_t)$ and $r_t = r(k_t)$, this expression contains the terms k_t, k_{t+1}, and k_{t+2} so one is tempted to conclude that it is a second-order difference equation in the capital stock. As Breyer and Straub (1993, p. 82) point out, however, the presence of future pensions introduces an infinite regress into the model, i.e. since $t_{L,t}^E$ depends on N_{t+1} (see (17.75)), it follows that $t_{L,t+1}^E$ depends on N_{t+2} which itself depends on k_{t+2}, k_{t+3}, and $t_{L,t+2}^E$. As a result, (17.80) depends on the entire sequence of present and future capital stocks, $\{k_{t+\tau}\}_{\tau=0}^{\infty}$ so that, even though we assume perfect foresight, the model has a continuum of equilibria.[14] Since we assume that the population growth rate is constant, however, we can skip over the indeterminacy issue by first studying the steady state.

---

[14] Indeterminacy and multiple equilibria are quite common phenomena in overlapping-generations models of the Diamond–Samuelson type. Azariadis (1993) gives a general discussion and Reichlin (1986) deals specifically with the case of endogenous labour supply.

The steady state

We study two pertinent aspects of the steady state. First, we show how the endogeneity of labour supply affects the welfare effect of the PAYG pension. Second, we show that in the unit-elastic model the pension crowds out capital in the long run. As before, the long-run welfare analysis makes use of the indirect utility function which is defined as follows:

$$
\bar{\Lambda}^Y(W, r, t_L) \equiv \max_{\{C^Y, C^O, N\}} \Lambda^Y(C^Y, C^O, 1 - N)
$$

$$
\text{subject to: } WN\left[1 - t_L\left(\frac{r-n}{1+r}\right)\right] = C^Y + \frac{C^O}{1+r}. \tag{17.81}
$$

Retracing our earlier derivation we can derive the following properties of the indirect utility function:

$$
\frac{\partial \bar{\Lambda}^Y}{\partial W} = N\left(\frac{\partial \Lambda^Y}{\partial C^Y}\right)\left[1 - t_L\left(\frac{r-n}{1+r}\right)\right], \tag{17.82}
$$

$$
\frac{\partial \bar{\Lambda}^Y}{\partial r} = \left(\frac{S}{1+r}\right)\left(\frac{\partial \Lambda^Y}{\partial C^Y}\right), \tag{17.83}
$$

$$
\frac{\partial \bar{\Lambda}^Y}{\partial t_L} = -WN\left(\frac{r-n}{1+r}\right)\left(\frac{\partial \Lambda^Y}{\partial C^Y}\right). \tag{17.84}
$$

The effect of a marginal change in the statutory tax rate on steady-state welfare is now easily computed:

$$
\begin{aligned}
\frac{d\Lambda^Y}{dt_L} &= \frac{\partial \bar{\Lambda}^Y}{\partial W}\frac{dW}{dt_L} + \frac{\partial \bar{\Lambda}^Y}{\partial r}\frac{dr}{dt_L} + \frac{\partial \bar{\Lambda}^Y}{\partial t_L} \\
&= \frac{\partial \Lambda^Y}{\partial C^Y}\left[N\left(1 - t_L\left(\frac{r-n}{1+r}\right)\right)\frac{dW}{dt_L} + \left(\frac{S}{1+r}\right)\frac{dr}{dt_L} - \left(\frac{r-n}{1+r}\right)WN\right] \\
&= -N\left(\frac{r-n}{1+r}\right)\left(\frac{\partial \Lambda^Y}{\partial C^Y}\right)\left[W + (1 - t_L)k\left(\frac{dr}{dt_L}\right)\right], \tag{17.85}
\end{aligned}
$$

where we have used (17.82)–(17.84) in going from the first to the second line and (17.53) and (17.77) in going from the second to the third line. There are two noteworthy conclusions that can be drawn on the basis of (17.85). First, if the economy is initially in the golden-rule equilibrium ($r = n$), then a marginal change in t_L does not produce a first-order welfare effect on steady-state generations. Intuitively, the labour supply decision is not distorted because the effective tax on labour is zero in that case ($t_L^E = t_L(r - n)/(1 + r) = 0$). Second, if the economy is not in the golden-rule equilibrium ($r \neq n$), then the sign of the welfare effect is determined by the sign of the term in square brackets on the right-hand side of (17.85). Just as for the case with lump-sum contributions (see (17.54)), the PAYG pension affects welfare through lifetime resources (first term in brackets) and via the capital-labour ratio (second term). It turns out, however, that with endogenous labour supply the sign of dr/dt_L (and thus the sign of $d\Lambda^Y/dt_L$) is ambiguous (Ihori, 1996, p. 237).

Matters are simplified quite a lot if Cobb–Douglas preferences are assumed, i.e. if (17.66) is specialized to:

$$\Lambda_t^Y \equiv \log C_t^Y + \lambda_C \log[1 - N_t] + \left(\frac{1}{1+\rho}\right) \log C_t^O, \tag{17.86}$$

where ρ is the rate of time preference and λ_C (≥ 0) regulates the strength of the labour supply effect. The following solutions for the decision variables are then obtained by maximizing (17.86) subject to (17.71):

$$C_t^Y = \left(\frac{1+\rho}{2+\rho+\lambda_C(1+\rho)}\right) W_t^N, \tag{17.87}$$

$$C_{t+1}^O = \left(\frac{1+r_{t+1}}{2+\rho+\lambda_C(1+\rho)}\right) W_t^N, \tag{17.88}$$

$$N_t = \frac{2+\rho}{2+\rho+\lambda_C(1+\rho)}, \tag{17.89}$$

where $W_t^N \equiv W_t(1 - t_{L,t}^E)$ is the effective after-tax wage. In the unit-elastic model, consumption during youth and old age are both normal goods and labour supply is constant because income and substitution effects cancel out. Since the current workers know that future workers will also supply a fixed amount of labour ($N_{t+1} = N_t = N$), the expression for the after-tax wage simplifies to:

$$W_t^N \equiv W_t(1 - t_{L,t}^E) \equiv W_t\left[1 - t_L\left(1 - \left(\frac{W_{t+1}}{W_t}\right)\left(\frac{1+n}{1+r_{t+1}}\right)\right)\right]. \tag{17.90}$$

Note furthermore that in (17.87) the presence of pension payments during old age ensures that consumption during youth depends negatively on the interest rate—via the effective tax rate—despite the fact that logarithmic preferences are used. According to (17.88) old-age consumption depends positively on the interest rate and negatively (positively) on the tax rate if the Aaron condition is violated (holds) $t_{L,t}^E > 0$ ($t_{L,t}^E < 0$). Finally, in (17.89) the standard model is recovered by setting $\lambda_C = 0$, in which case labour supply is exogenous and equal to unity.

We can now determine the extent to which capital is crowded out by the PAYG system. In view of (17.88) and (17.90), the fundamental difference equation for the model (17.80) can be written as follows:

$$(1+n)k_{t+1} = \frac{W_t(1-t_L)}{2+\rho} - \left(\frac{1+\rho}{2+\rho}\right)\left(\frac{t_L(1+n)W_{t+1}}{1+r_{t+1}}\right). \tag{17.91}$$

Since $W_t = W(k_t)$ and $r_t = r(k_t)$, equation (17.91) constitutes a first-order difference equation in the capital-labour ratio. Hence, in the unit-elastic model the indeterminacy of the transition path (that was mentioned above) disappears because the uncompensated labour supply elasticity is zero.

The stability condition and the long-run effect of the PAYG system on the capital-labour ratio are derived in the usual manner by finding the partial derivatives of the implicit function, $k_{t+1} = g(k_t, t_L)$, around the steady state. After some manipulation we obtain:

$$g_k \equiv \frac{\partial k_{t+1}}{\partial k_t} = \frac{(1 - t_L)W'}{(1 + n)(2 + \rho)\left[1 + t_L\left(\frac{1+\rho}{2+\rho}\right)\frac{(1+r)W'-Wr'}{(1+r)^2}\right]} > 0, \qquad (17.92)$$

$$g_t \equiv \frac{\partial k_{t+1}}{\partial t_L} = -\frac{W[1 + r + (1 + \rho)(1 + n)]}{(1 + r)(1 + n)(2 + \rho)\left[1 + t_L\left(\frac{1+\rho}{2+\rho}\right)\frac{(1+r)W'-Wr'}{(1+r)^2}\right]} < 0. \qquad (17.93)$$

Since g_k is positive (as $W' > 0 > r'$), stability requires it to be less than unity ($0 < g_k < 1$). As a result, the long-run effect on the capital-labour ratio is unambiguously negative in the unit-elastic model:

$$\frac{dk}{dt_L} = \frac{g_t}{1 - g_k} < 0. \qquad (17.94)$$

Welfare effects

We are now in a position to compare and contrast the key results of this subsection to those that hold when labour supply is exogenous and the pension contribution is levied in a lump-sum fashion (see subsection 17.2.1). At first view, the assumption of a distorting pension contribution does not seem to change the principal conclusions very much—at least in the unit-elastic model. In both cases, the PAYG contribution leads to long-run crowding out of the capital-labour ratio (compare (17.46) and (17.94)) and a reduction (increase) in steady-state welfare for a dynamically efficient (inefficient) economy (compare (17.54) and (17.85)). Intuitively, this similarity is only moderately surprising in view of the fact that in the unit-elastic model (optimally chosen) labour supply is constant (see (17.89)).

There is a very important difference between the two cases, however, because the pension contribution, t_L, causes a distortion of the labour supply decision of households which is absent if the contribution is levied in a lump-sum fashion. The resulting loss to the economy of using a distorting rather than a non-distorting tax is often referred to as the *deadweight loss* (or burden) of the distorting tax (Diamond and McFadden, 1974, p. 5). Following Diamond and McFadden we define the deadweight loss (DWL) associated with t_L as the difference between, on the one hand, the income one must give a young household to restore it to its pre-tax indifference curve and, on the other hand, the tax revenue collected from it (1974, p. 5).

In Figure 17.3 we illustrate the DWL of the pension contribution for a steady-state generation in the unit-elastic model. We hold factor prices (W and r) constant and assume that the economy is dynamically efficient ($r > n$). We follow the approach of Belan and Pestieau (1999) by solving the model in two stages. In the first stage we define lifetime income as:

$$X \equiv WN\left[1 - t_L\left(\frac{r - n}{1 + r}\right)\right] \equiv WN(1 - t_L^E), \qquad (17.95)$$

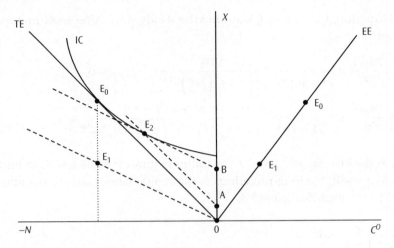

Figure 17.3. Deadweight loss of taxation

and let the household choose current and future consumption in order to maximize:

$$\log C^Y + \left(\frac{1}{1+\rho}\right) \log C^O, \tag{17.96}$$

subject to the constraint $C^Y + C^O/(1+r) = X$. This yields the following expressions:

$$C^Y = \left(\frac{1+\rho}{2+\rho}\right) X, \qquad C^O = \left(\frac{1+r}{2+\rho}\right) X. \tag{17.97}$$

In the right-hand panel of Figure 17.3 the line EE relates old-age consumption to life-time income. In that panel the value of consumption during youth can be deduced from the fact that it is proportional to lifetime income.

By substituting the expressions (17.97) into, respectively, the utility function (17.86) and the budget constraint (given in (17.81)) we obtain:

$$\Lambda^Y \equiv \left(\frac{2+\rho}{1+\rho}\right) \log X + \lambda_C \log[1 - N_t] + \log\left[\left(\frac{1+\rho}{2+\rho}\right)\left(\frac{1+r}{2+\rho}\right)^{1/(1+\rho)}\right], \tag{17.98}$$

$$X = WN(1 - t_L^E). \tag{17.99}$$

In the second stage, the household chooses its labour supply and lifetime income in order to maximize (17.98) subject to (17.99). The solution to this second-stage problem is, of course, that N takes the value indicated in (17.89) and X follows from the constraint. The second-stage optimization problem is shown in the left-hand panel of Figure 17.3. In that panel, TE represents the budget line (17.99) in the absence of taxation ($t_L^E = 0$). It is upward sloping because we measure *minus N* on the horizontal axis. The indifference curve which is tangent to the pre-tax budget line is given by IC and the initial equilibrium is at E_0. In the right-hand panel E_0 on the EE line gives the corresponding optimal value for old-age consumption.

Now consider what happens if a positive effective tax is levied ($t_L^E > 0$). Nothing happens in the right-hand panel but in the left-hand panel the budget line rotates in a counter-clockwise fashion. The new budget line is given by the dashed line from the origin. We know that in the unit-elastic model income and substitution effects in labour supply cancel out so that labour supply does not change (see (17.89)). Hence, the new equilibrium is at E_1 in the two panels. By shifting the new budget line in a parallel fashion and finding a tangency along the pre-tax indifference curve we find that the pure substitution effect of the tax change is given by the shift from E_0 to E_2 (the income effect is thus the shift from E_2 to E_1). Hence, the vertical distance OB represents the income one would have to give the household to restore it to its pre-tax indifference curve. We call this hypothetical transfer Z_0. What is the tax revenue which is collected from the agent? To answer that question we draw a line, that is parallel to the pre-tax budget line, through the compensated point E_2. This line has an intercept with the vertical axis at point A. We now have two expressions for lines that both pass through the compensated point E_2, namely $X + W(1 - t_L^E)(-N) = Z_0$ and $X + W(-N) = Z_0 - T$, where T is the vertical distance AB in Figure 17.3. By deducting the two lines we find that $T = t_L^E W N$ so that AB represents the tax revenue collected from the agent. Since the required transfer is OB the DWL of the tax is given by the distance OA.

Reform

As a number of authors have recently pointed out, the distorting nature of the pension system has important implications for the possibility of designing Pareto-improving reform (see e.g. Homburg, 1990, Breyer and Straub, 1993, and the references to more recent literature in Belan and Pestieau, 1999). Recall from the discussion at the end of section 17.2.1 that a Pareto-improving transition from PAYG to a fully funded system is not possible in the standard model because the resources cannot be found to compensate the old generations at the time of the reform without making some future generation worse off. Matters are different if the PAYG system represents a distorting system. In that case, as Breyer and Straub (1993) point out, provided lump-sum (non-distorting) contributions can be used during the transition phase, a gradual move from a PAYG to a fully funded system can be achieved in a Pareto-improving manner. Intuitively, by moving from a distortionary to a non-distortionary scheme, additional resources are freed up which can be used to compensate the various generations (Belan and Pestieau, 1999).[15]

---

[15] The distortive nature of the PAYG scheme does not have to result from endogenous labour supply. Demmel and Keuschnigg (1999), for example, assume that union wage-setting causes unemployment which is exacerbated by the pension contribution. Efficiency gains then materialize because pension reform reduces unemployment. In a similar vein, Belan et al. (1998) use a Romer-style (1986,

Table 17.1. Age composition of
the population

	1950	1990	2025
World			
0–19	44.1	41.7	32.8
20–65	50.8	52.1	57.5
65+	5.1	6.2	9.7
OECD			
0–19	35.0	27.2	24.8
20–64	56.7	59.9	56.6
65+	8.3	12.8	18.6
US			
0–19	33.9	28.9	26.8
20–65	57.9	58.9	56.0
65+	8.1	12.2	17.2

17.2.3 The macroeconomic effects of ageing

Up to this point we have assumed that the rate of population growth is constant and equal to n (see equation (17.21) above). This simplifying assumption of course means that the age composition of the population is constant also. A useful measure to characterize the economic impact of demography is the so-called (old-age) *dependency ratio*, which is defined as the number of retired people divided by the working-age population. In our highly stylized two-period overlapping-generations model the number of old and young people at time t are, respectively, L_{t-1} and $L_t = (1 + n)L_{t-1}$ so that the dependency ratio is $1/(1 + n)$.

Of course, as all members of the baby-boom generation will surely know, the assumption of a constant population composition, though convenient, is not a particularly realistic one. Table 17.1, which is taken from Weil (1997, p. 970), shows that significant demographic changes have taken place between 1950 and 1990 and are expected to take place between 1990 and 2025.

The figures in Table 17.1 graphically illustrate that throughout the world, and particularly in the group of OECD countries and in the US, the proportion of young people (0–20 years of age) is on the decline whilst the fraction of old people (65 and over) steadily increases. Both of these phenomena are tell-tale signs of an ageing population.

1989) endogenous growth model and show that reform may be Pareto-improving because it helps to internalize a positive externality in production. See also Corneo and Marquardt (2000).

In this subsection we show how the macroeconomic effects of demographic composition changes can be analysed with the aid of a simple overlapping-generations model. We only stress some of the key results, especially those relating to the interaction between demography and the public pension system. The interested reader is referred to Weil (1997) for an excellent survey of the literature on the economics of ageing.

In the absence of immigration from abroad, population ageing can result from two distinct sources, namely a decrease in *fertility* and a decrease in *mortality*. In the two-period overlapping-generations model used so far the length of life is exogenously fixed but we can nevertheless capture the notion of ageing by reducing the rate of population growth, n. In order to study the effects on allocation and welfare of such a demographic shock we first reformulate the model of subsection 17.2.1 in terms of a variable growth rate of the population, n_t. Hence, instead of (17.21) we use:

$$L_t = (1 + n_t)L_{t-1}. \tag{17.100}$$

Assuming a constant contribution rate per person ($T_t = T$), the pension at time t equals $Z_t = (1 + n_t)T$. Redoing the derivations presented in subsection 17.2.1 yields the following fundamental difference equation of the model:

$$S(W_t, r_{t+1}, n_{t+1}, T) = (1 + n_{t+1})k_{t+1}, \tag{17.101}$$

where the savings function is the same as in (17.40) but with n_{t+1} replacing n. Ceteris paribus, saving by the young depends negatively on the (expected) rate of population growth, n_{t+1}, because the pension they receive when old depends on it (as $Z_{t+1} = (1 + n_{t+1})T$). An anticipated reduction in fertility reduces the expected pension and lifetime income, and causes the agent to cut back on both present and future consumption and to increase saving. Hence, $S_n \equiv \partial S/\partial n_{t+1} < 0$. The right-hand side of (17.101) shows that a decrease in the population growth rate makes it possible to support a higher capital-labour ratio for a given amount of per capita saving.

Following the solution method discussed in subsection 17.2.1, we can derive that (17.101) defines an implicit function, $k_{t+1} = g(k_t, n_{t+1})$, with partial derivatives $0 < g_k < 1$ (see equation (17.42)) and $g_n < 0$:

$$g_n \equiv \frac{\partial g}{\partial n_{t+1}} = \frac{S_n - k_{t+1}}{1 + n_{t+1} - S_r r'(k_{t+1})} < 0. \tag{17.102}$$

It follows that a permanent reduction in the population growth rate, say from n_0 to n_1, gives rise to an increase in the long-run capital stock, i.e. $dk/dn = g_n/(1 - g_k) < 0$. The transition path of the economy to the steady state is illustrated in Figure 17.4. In that figure, the dashed line labelled "$k_{t+1} = g(k_t, n_0)$" reproduces the initial transition path with social security in Figure 17.2. The reduction in fertility boosts saving at impact so that, if the economy starts out with a capital stock k_0, the new transition path is the dotted line from B to the new equilibrium at E_1. During transition

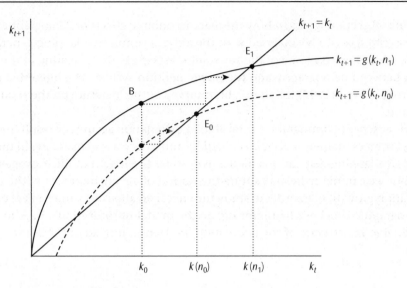

Figure 17.4. The effects of ageing

the wage rate gradually rises and the interest rate falls. The intuition behind the long-run increase in the capital-labour ratio is straightforward. As a result of the demographic shock there are fewer young households, who own no assets, and more old households, who own a lot of assets which they need to provide income for their retirement years (Auerbach and Kotlikoff, 1987, p. 163).

The effect of a permanent reduction in fertility on steady-state welfare can be computed by differentiating the indirect utility function (17.47) with respect to n, using (17.50)–(17.51) and (17.54), and noting that $\partial \bar{\Lambda}^Y / \partial n = T \left(\partial \Lambda^Y / \partial C^Y \right) / (1 + r)$:

$$
\begin{aligned}
\frac{d\Lambda^Y}{dn} &= \frac{\partial \bar{\Lambda}^Y}{\partial W} \frac{dW}{dn} + \frac{\partial \bar{\Lambda}^Y}{\partial r} \frac{dr}{dn} + \frac{\partial \bar{\Lambda}^Y}{\partial n} \\
&= \frac{\partial \Lambda^Y}{\partial C^Y} \left[\frac{dW}{dn} + \left(\frac{S}{1+r} \right) \frac{dr}{dn} + \frac{T}{1+r} \right] \\
&= \left(\frac{\partial \Lambda^Y}{\partial C^Y} \right) \left[-k \left(\frac{r-n}{1+r} \right) \left(\frac{dr}{dn} \right) + \frac{T}{1+r} \right] \lessgtr 0.
\end{aligned}
\tag{17.103}
$$

In a dynamically efficient economy (for which $r > n$ holds) there are two effects which operate in opposite directions. The first term in square brackets on the right-hand side of (17.103) represents the effect of fertility on the long-run interest rate. Since $dr/dn = r' dk/dn > 0$, a fall in fertility raises long-run welfare on that account. The second term in square brackets on the right-hand side of (17.103) is the PAYG-yield effect. If fertility falls so does the rate of return on the PAYG contribution. Since the yield effect works in the opposite direction to the interest rate effect, the overall effect of a fertility change is ambiguous. If the PAYG contribution is very small ($T \approx 0$) and the economy is not close to the golden-rule point ($r \gg n$), then a drop in fertility raises long-run welfare.

Although our results are based on a highly stylized (and perhaps oversimplified) model, they nevertheless seem to bear some relationship to reality. Indeed, Auerbach and Kotlikoff (1987, ch. 11) simulate a highly detailed computable general equilibrium model for the US economy and find qualitatively very similar results: wages rise, the interest rate falls, and long-run welfare increases strongly (see their Table 11.3). In their model, households live for 75 years, labour supply is endogenous, productivity is age-dependent, households' retirement behaviour is endogenous, taxes are distorting, and demography is extremely detailed.

17.3 Extensions

17.3.1 Human capital accumulation

Human capital and growth

Following the early contributions by Arrow (1962) and Uzawa (1965), a number of authors have drawn attention to the importance of human capital accumulation for the theory of economic growth. The key papers that prompted the renewed interest in human capital in the 1980s are Romer (1996) and Lucas (1988). In this subsection we show how the Diamond–Samuelson overlapping-generations model can be extended by including the purposeful accumulation of human capital by households. We show how this overlapping-generations version of the celebrated Lucas (1988) model can give rise to endogenous growth in the economy (see also Chapter 14 above).

As in the standard model, we continue to assume that households live for two periods, but we deviate from the standard model by assuming that the household works full-time during the second period of life and divides its time between working and training during youth. Following Lucas (1988) human capital is equated to the worker's level of skill at producing goods. We denote the human capital of worker i at time t by H_t^i and assume that producers can observe each worker's skill level and will thus pay a skill-dependent wage (just as in the continuous-time model discussed in Chapter 14 above).

The lifetime utility function of a young agent who is born at time t is given in general terms by:

$$\Lambda_t^{Y,i} \equiv \Lambda^Y(C_t^{Y,i}, C_{t+1}^{O,i}). \tag{17.104}$$

This expression incorporates the notion that the household does not value leisure and attaches no utility value to training *per se*. The household is thus only interested in improving its skills because it will improve its income later on in life. The budget identities facing the agent are:

$$C_t^{Y,i} + S_t^i = W_t H_t^i N_t^i, \tag{17.105}$$

$$C_{t+1}^{O,i} = (1 + r_{t+1})S_t^i + W_{t+1}H_{t+1}^i, \tag{17.106}$$

where W_t denotes the going wage rate for an efficiency unit of labour at time t, and N_t^i is the amount of time spent working (rather than training) during youth. Since the agent has one unit of time available in each period we have by assumption that $N_{t+1}^i = 1$ (there is no third period of life so no point in training during the second period). The amount of training during youth is denoted by E_t^i and equals:

$$E_t^i = 1 - N_t^i \geq 0. \tag{17.107}$$

To complete the description of the young household's decision problem we must specify how training augments the agent's skills. As a first example of a *training technology* we consider the following specification:

$$H_{t+1}^i = G(E_t^i)H_t^i, \tag{17.108}$$

where $G' > 0 \geq G''$ and $G(0) = 1$. This specification captures the notion that there are positive but non-increasing returns to training in the production of human capital and that zero training means that the agent keeps his initial skill level.

The household chooses $C_t^{Y,i}$, $C_{t+1}^{O,i}$, S_t^i, N_t^i, and E_t^i in order to maximize lifetime utility $\Lambda_t^{Y,i}$ (given in (17.104)) subject to the constraints (17.105)–(17.107), and given the training technology (17.108), the expected path of wages W_t, and its own initial skill level H_t^i. The optimization problem can be solved in two steps. In the first step the household chooses its training level, E_t^i, in order to maximize its lifetime income, I_t^i, i.e. the present value of wage income:

$$I_t^i(E_t^i) \equiv H_t^i \left[W_t(1 - E_t^i) + \frac{W_{t+1}G(E_t^i)}{1 + r_{t+1}} \right]. \tag{17.109}$$

The first-order condition for this optimal human capital investment problem, taking explicit account of the inequality constraint (17.107), is:

$$\frac{dI_t^i}{dE_t^i} = H_t^i \left[-W_t + \frac{W_{t+1}G'(E_t^i)}{1 + r_{t+1}} \right] \leq 0, \quad E_t^i \geq 0, \quad E_t^i \left(\frac{dI_t^i}{dE_t^i} \right) = 0. \tag{17.110}$$

This expression shows that it may very well be in the best interest of the agent not to pursue any training at all during youth. Indeed, this no-training solution will hold if the first inequality in (17.110) is strict. Since there are non-increasing returns to training (so that $G'(0) \geq G'(E_t^i)$ for $E_t^i \geq 0$) we derive the following implication from (17.110):

$$G'(0) < \frac{W_t(1 + r_{t+1})}{W_{t+1}} \quad \Rightarrow \quad E_t^i = 0. \tag{17.111}$$

If the training technology is not very productive ($G'(0)$ low) then the corner solution will be selected.

An internal solution with a strictly positive level of training is such that $dI_t^i/dE_t^i = 0$. After some rewriting we obtain the investment equation in arbitrage format:

$$E_t^i > 0 \Rightarrow \quad 1 + r_{t+1} = \left(\frac{W_{t+1}}{W_t}\right) G'(E_t^i). \tag{17.112}$$

This expression shows that in the interior optimum the agent accumulates physical and human capital such that their respective yields are equalized. By investing in physical capital during youth the agent receives a yield of $1 + r_{t+1}$ during old age (left-hand side of (17.112)). By working a little less and training a little more during youth, the agent upgrades his human capital and gains $W_{t+1}G'(E_t^i)$ during old age. Expressed in terms of the initial investment (foregone wages in the first period) we get the yield on human capital (right-hand side of (17.112)).

In the second step of the optimization problem the household chooses consumption for the two periods and its level of savings in order to maximize lifetime utility (17.104) subject to its lifetime budget constraint:

$$C_t^{Y,i} + \frac{C_{t+1}^{O,i}}{1 + r_{t+1}} = I_t^i, \tag{17.113}$$

where I_t^i is now maximized lifetime income. The savings function which results from this stage of the optimization problem can be written in general form as:

$$S_t^i = S(r_{t+1}, (1 - E_t^i)W_t H_t^i, W_{t+1}H_{t+1}^i). \tag{17.114}$$

In order to complete the description of the decision problem of household i we must specify its initial level of human capital at birth, i.e. H_t^i in the training technology (17.108). Following Azariadis and Drazen (1990, p. 510) we assume that each household born in period t "inherits" (is born with) the average stock of currently available knowledge at that time, i.e. $H_t^i = H_t$ on the right-hand side of (17.108). With this final assumption it follows that all individuals in the model face the same interest rate and learning technology so that they will choose the same consumption, saving, and investment plans. We can thus drop the individual index i from here on and study the symmetric equilibrium.

We assume that there is no population growth and normalize the size of the young and old populations to unity ($L_{t-1} = L_t = 1$). Total labour supply in efficiency units is defined as the sum of efficiency units supplied by the young and the old, i.e. $N_t = (1 - E_t)H_t + H_t$. For convenience we summarize the key expressions of the (simplified) Azariadis–Drazen model below.

$$N_{t+1}k_{t+1} = S(r_{t+1}, (1 - E_t)W_tH_t, W_{t+1}H_{t+1}) \tag{17.115}$$

$$r_{t+1} + \delta = f'(k_{t+1}) \tag{17.116}$$

$$W_t = f(k_t) - k_tf'(k_t) \tag{17.117}$$

$$N_t = (2 - E_t)H_t \tag{17.118}$$

$$1 + r_{t+1} = \left(\frac{W_{t+1}}{W_t}\right)G'(E_t) \tag{17.119}$$

$$H_{t+1} = G(E_t)H_t, \tag{17.120}$$

Equation (17.115) relates saving by the representative young household to next period's stock of physical capital. Note that the capital-labour ratio is defined in terms of efficiency units of labour, i.e. $k_t \equiv K_t/N_t$. With this definition, the expressions for the wage rate and the interest rate are, respectively (17.116) and (17.117). Equation (17.118) is labour supply in efficiency units, (17.119) is the investment equation for human capital (assuming an internal solution), and (17.120) is the accumulation for aggregate human capital in the symmetric equilibrium.

It is not difficult to show that the model allows for endogenous growth in the steady state. In the steady-state growth path the capital-labour ratio, the wage rate, the interest rate, and the proportion of time spent training during youth, are all constant over time (i.e. $k_t = k$, $W_t = W$, $r_t = r$, and $E_t = E$). The remaining variables grow at a common growth rate $\gamma \equiv G(E) - 1$. Referring the reader for a general proof to Azariadis (1993, p. 231), we demonstrate the existence of a unique steady-state growth path for the unit-elastic model for which technology is Cobb–Douglas ($y_t = k_t^{1-\epsilon_L}$) and the utility function (17.104) is log-linear ($\Lambda_t^Y = \log C_t^Y + (1/(1+\rho))\log C_{t+1}^O$). For the unit-elastic case the savings function can be written as:

$$S_t = \left[\left(\frac{1}{2+\rho}\right)(1 - E_t)W_t - \left(\frac{1+\rho}{2+\rho}\right)\frac{W_{t+1}G(E_t)}{1+r_{t+1}}\right]H_t. \tag{17.121}$$

By using (17.121), (17.118), and (17.120) in (17.115) and imposing the steady state we get an implicit relationship between E and k for which savings equals investment:

$$(2 + \rho)\left(\frac{k}{W(k)}\right) = \left(\frac{1}{2 - E}\right)\left[\frac{1 - E}{G(E)} - \frac{1+\rho}{1+r(k)}\right]. \tag{17.122}$$

Similarly, by using (17.116) and (17.118) in the steady-state we get a second expression, again relating E and k, for which the rates of return on human and physical capital are equalized:

$$[1 + r(k) =] \quad G'(E) = f'(k) + 1 - \delta. \tag{17.123}$$

The joint determination of E and k in the steady-state growth path is illustrated in the upper panel of Figure 17.5. The portfolio-balance (PB) line is upward sloping because both the production technology and the training technology exhibit

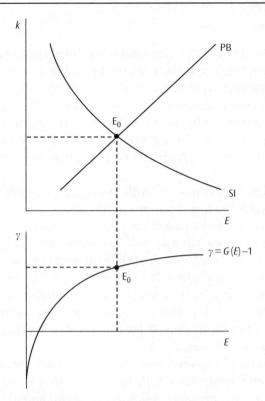

Figure 17.5. Endogenous growth due to human capital formation

diminishing returns ($f''(k) < 0$ and $G''(E) < 0$). The savings-investment (SI) line is downward sloping with Cobb–Douglas technology. The right-hand side of (17.122) is downward sloping in both k and E. With Cobb–Douglas technology we have that $k/W(k) = (1/\epsilon_L)k^{\epsilon_L}$ which ensures that the left-hand side of (17.122) is increasing in k. Together these result imply that SI slopes down. In the upper panel the steady state is at E_0. In the bottom panel we relate the equilibrium growth rate to the level of training.

The *engine of growth* in the Azariadis–Drazen model is clearly the training technology (17.120) which ensures that a given steady-state *level* of training allows for a steady-state *rate of growth* in the stock of human capital. Knowledge and technical skills are *disembodied*, i.e. they do not die with the individual agents but rather they are passed on in an automatic fashion to the newborns. The newborns can then add to the stock of knowledge by engaging in training. It should be clear that endogenous growth would disappear from the model if skills were *embodied* in the agents themselves. In that case young agents would have to start all over again and "re-invent the wheel" the moment they are born.

Human capital and education

Whilst it is undoubtedly true that informal social interactions can give rise to the transmission of knowledge and skills (as in the Azariadis–Drazen (1990) model) most developed countries have had formal educational systems for a number of centuries. A striking aspect of these systems is that they are compulsory, i.e. children up to a certain age are forced by law to undergo a certain period of basic training. This prompts the question why the adoption of compulsory education has been so widespread, even in countries which otherwise strongly value their citizens' right to choose.

Eckstein and Zilcha (1994) have recently provided an ingenious answer to this question which stresses the role of parents in the transmission of human capital to their offspring. They use an extended version of the Azariadis–Drazen model and show that compulsory education may well be welfare-enhancing to the children if the parents do not value the education of their offspring to a sufficient extent. The key insight of Eckstein and Zilcha (1994) is thus that there may exist a significant *intra-family* external effect which causes parents to underinvest in their children's human capital. Note that such an effect is not present in the Azariadis–Drazen model because in that model the agent *himself* bears the cost of training during youth and reaps the benefits during old age.

We now develop a simplified version of the Eckstein–Zilcha model to demonstrate their important underinvestment result. We assume that all agents are identical. The representative parent consumes goods during youth and old age (C_t^Y and C_{t+1}^O, respectively), enjoys leisure during youth (Z_t), is retired during old age, and has $1+n$ children during the first period of life. Fertility is exogenous so that the number of children is exogenously given ($n \geq 0$). The lifetime utility function of the young agent at time t is given in general form as:

$$\Lambda_t^Y \equiv \Lambda^Y(C_t^Y, C_{t+1}^O, Z_t, O_{t+1}), \tag{17.124}$$

where $O_{t+1} \equiv (1+n)H_{t+1}$ represents the total human capital of the agent's offspring. Since the agent has $1+n$ kids, each child gets H_{t+1} in human capital (knowledge) from its parent. There is no formal schooling system so the parent cannot purchase education services for its offspring in the market. Instead, the parent must spend (part of its) leisure time during youth to educate its children and the training function is given by:

$$H_{t+1} = G(E_t)H_t^\beta, \tag{17.125}$$

where E_t is the educational effort per child, $G(.)$ is the training curve (satisfying $0 < G(0) \leq 1$, $G(1) > 1$, $G' > 0 \geq G''$) and $0 < \beta \leq 1$. Equation (17.125) is similar in format to (17.120) but its interpretation is different. In (17.120) H_{t+1} and E_t are chosen by and affect the same agent. In contrast, in (17.125) the parent chooses H_{t+1} and E_t and the consequences of this choice are felt by both the parent and his/her offspring.

The agent has two units of time available during youth, one of which is supplied inelastically to the labour market (Eckstein and Zilcha, 1994, p. 343), and the other of which is spent on leisure and educational activities:

$$Z_t + (1+n)E_t = 1. \tag{17.126}$$

The household's consolidated budget constraint is of a standard form:

$$C_t^Y + \frac{C_{t+1}^O}{1+r_{t+1}} = W_t H_t, \tag{17.127}$$

where the left-hand side represents the present value of consumption and the right-hand side is labour income. Competitive firms hire capital, K_t, and efficiency units of labour, $N_t \equiv L_t H_t$, from the households, and the aggregate production function is $Y_t = F(K_t, N_t)$. The wage and interest rate then satisfy, respectively, $W_t = F_N(K_t, N_t)$ and $r_t + \delta = F_K(K_t, N_t)$.

The representative parent chooses C_t^Y, C_{t+1}^O, Z_t, E_t, and H_{t+1} in order to maximize lifetime utility (17.124) subject to the training technology (17.125), the time constraint (17.126), and the consolidated budget constraint (17.127). By substituting the constraints into the objective function and optimizing with respect to the remaining choice variables (C_t^Y, C_{t+1}^O, and E_t) we obtain the following first-order conditions:

$$\frac{\partial \Lambda^Y / \partial C_t^Y}{\partial \Lambda^Y / \partial C_{t+1}^O} = 1 + r_{t+1} \tag{17.128}$$

$$\frac{\partial \Lambda^Y}{\partial O_t} G'(E_t) H_t^\beta - \frac{\partial \Lambda^Y}{\partial Z_t} < 0 \quad \rightarrow \quad E_t = 0 \tag{17.129}$$

$$\frac{\partial \Lambda^Y}{\partial O_t} G'(E_t) H_t^\beta - \frac{\partial \Lambda^Y}{\partial Z_t} = 0 \quad \leftarrow \quad E_t > 0 \tag{17.130}$$

Equation (17.128) is the standard consumption Euler equation, which we encountered time and again, and (17.129)–(17.130) characterizes the optimal educational activities of the parent. The left-hand side appearing in (17.129)–(17.130) represents the net marginal benefit of child education. If the (marginal) costs outweigh the benefits this term is negative and the parent chooses not to engage in educational activities at all (see (17.129)). Conversely, a strictly positive (interior) choice of E_t implies that the net marginal benefit of child education is zero. In the remainder we assume that conditions are such that $E_t > 0$ is chosen by the representative parent.

A notable feature of the parent's optimal child education rule (17.130) is that it only contains the costs and benefits as they accrue to the parent. But if a child receives a higher level of human capital from its parents, then it will have a higher labour income and will thus be richer and enjoy a higher level of welfare. By assumption, however, the parent only cares about the level of education it passes on to its children and therefore disregards any welfare effects that operate directly on its offspring. This is the first hint of the under-investment problem. Loosely put, by disregarding some of the positive welfare effects its own educational activities have on its children, the parent does not provide "enough" education.

As was explained above, in our discussion regarding pension reform, there are several ways in which we can tackle the efficiency issue of under-investment in a more formal manner. One way would be to look for Pareto-improving policy interventions. For example, in the present context one could investigate whether a system of financial transfers to parents could be devised which (a) would induce parents to raise their child-educational activities and (b) would make no present or future generation worse off and at least one strictly better off. If such a transfer system can be found we can conclude that the status quo is inefficient and there is underinvestment.

An alternative approach, one which we pursue here, makes use of a social welfare function. Following Eckstein and Zilcha (1994, pp. 344–345) we postulate a specific form for the social welfare function (17.65) which is linear in the lifetime utilities of present and future agents:

$$SW_0 \equiv \sum_{t=0}^{\infty} \lambda_t \Lambda_t^Y = \sum_{t=0}^{\infty} \lambda_t \Lambda^Y(C_t^Y, C_{t+1}^O, Z_t, O_{t+1}), \tag{17.131}$$

where SW_0 is social welfare in the planning period ($t = 0$) and $\{\lambda_t\}_{t=0}^{\infty}$ is a positive monotonically decreasing sequence of weights attached to the different generations which satisfies $\sum_{t=0}^{\infty} \lambda_t < \infty$. In the social optimum, the social planner chooses sequences for consumption ($\{C_t^Y\}_{t=0}^{\infty}$ and $\{C_{t+1}^O\}_{t=0}^{\infty}$), the stocks of human and physical capital ($\{K_{t+1}\}_{t=0}^{\infty}$ and $\{H_{t+1}\}_{t=0}^{\infty}$), and the educational effort ($\{E_t\}_{t=0}^{\infty}$) in order to maximize (17.131) subject to the training technology (17.125), the time constraint (17.126), and the following resource constraint:

$$C_t^Y + \frac{C_t^O}{1+n} + (1+n)k_{t+1} = F(k_t, H_t) + (1-\delta)k_t, \tag{17.132}$$

where $k_t \equiv K_t/L_t$ is capital per worker.

The Lagrangian associated with the social optimization problem is given by:

$$\mathcal{L}_0 \equiv \sum_{t=0}^{\infty} \lambda_t \Lambda^Y(C_t^Y, C_{t+1}^O, Z_t, (1+n)H_{t+1})$$

$$- \sum_{t=0}^{\infty} \mu_t^R \left[C_t^Y + \frac{C_t^O}{1+n} + (1+n)k_{t+1} - F(k_t, H_t) - (1-\delta)k_t \right]$$

$$- \sum_{t=0}^{\infty} \mu_t^T [Z_t + (1+n)E_t - 1] - \sum_{t=0}^{\infty} \mu_t^H \left[H_{t+1} - G(E_t)H_t^\beta \right], \tag{17.133}$$

where μ_t^R, μ_t^T, and μ_t^H are the Lagrange multipliers associated with, respectively, the resource constraint, the time constraint, and the training technology.

After some manipulation we find the following first-order conditions for the social optimum for $t = 0, \ldots, \infty$:

$$\frac{\partial \mathcal{L}_0}{\partial C_t^Y} = \lambda_t \frac{\partial \Lambda^Y}{\partial C_t^Y} - \mu_t^R = 0, \tag{17.134}$$

$$\frac{\partial \mathcal{L}_0}{\partial C_{t+1}^O} = \lambda_t \frac{\partial \Lambda^Y}{\partial C_{t+1}^O} - \frac{\mu_{t+1}^R}{1+n} = 0, \tag{17.135}$$

$$\frac{\partial \mathcal{L}_0}{\partial Z_t} = \lambda_t \frac{\partial \Lambda^Y}{\partial Z_t} - \mu_t^T = 0, \tag{17.136}$$

$$\frac{\partial \mathcal{L}_0}{\partial E_t} = -(1+n)\mu_t^T + \mu_t^H G'(E_t)H_t^\beta = 0, \tag{17.137}$$

$$\frac{\partial \mathcal{L}_0}{\partial H_{t+1}} = (1+n)\lambda_t \frac{\partial \Lambda^Y}{\partial O_t} - \mu_t^H + \beta \mu_{t+1}^H G(E_{t+1})H_{t+1}^{\beta-1}$$

$$+ \mu_{t+1}^R F_N(k_{t+1}, H_{t+1}) = 0, \tag{17.138}$$

$$\frac{\partial \mathcal{L}_0}{\partial k_{t+1}} = -(1+n)\mu_t^R + \mu_{t+1}^R [F_K(k_{t+1}, H_{t+1}) + (1-\delta)] = 0. \tag{17.139}$$

By combining (17.134)–(17.135) and (17.139) we obtain the socially optimal consumption Euler equation:

$$(1+n)\frac{\mu_t^R}{\mu_{t+1}^R} = \frac{\partial \Lambda^Y(\hat{x}_t)/\partial C_t^Y}{\partial \Lambda^Y(\hat{x}_t)/\partial C_{t+1}^O} = F_K(\hat{k}_{t+1}, \hat{H}_{t+1}) + (1-\delta)\left[\equiv 1 + \hat{r}_{t+1}\right], \tag{17.140}$$

where $x_t \equiv [C_t^Y, C_{t+1}^O, Z_t, O_{t+1}]$, hats ("^") denote socially optimal values, and $\hat{r}_{t+1}$ thus represents the socially optimal interest rate. Similarly, by using (17.134) for period $t+1$ and (17.135) we obtain an expression determining the socially optimal division of consumption between old and young agents living at the same time:

$$\frac{\lambda_{t+1}}{\lambda_t} = (1+n)\frac{\partial \Lambda^Y(\hat{x}_t)/\partial C_{t+1}^O}{\partial \Lambda^Y(\hat{x}_{t+1})/\partial C_{t+1}^Y}. \tag{17.141}$$

This expression shows that, by adopting a particular sequence of generational weights $\{\lambda_t\}_{t=0}^\infty$, the social planner in fact chooses the generational consumption profile between the young and the old (see Calvo and Obstfeld, 1988, p. 417).

Intermezzo

Dynamic Consistency. There are some subtle issues that must be confronted when using a social welfare function like (17.131). If we are to attach any importance to the social planning exercise we must assume that either one of the following two situations holds:

Commitment the policy maker only performs the social planning exercise once and can credibly commit never to re-optimize. Economic policy is a one-shot event and no further restrictions on the generational weights are needed.

Consistency the policy maker can re-optimize at any time but the generational weights are such that the socially optimal plan is dynamically consistent, i.e. the mere evolution of time itself does not make the planner change his mind.

This intermezzo shows how dynamic consistency can be guaranteed in the absence of credible commitment. We study dynamic consistency in the context of the standard Diamond–Samuelson model. The social welfare function in the planning period 0 is given in general terms by:

$$SW_0 \equiv \lambda_{0,-1} \Lambda^Y(C_{-1}^Y, C_0^O) + \sum_{\tau=0}^{\infty} \lambda_{0,\tau} \Lambda^Y(C_\tau^Y, C_{\tau+1}^O), \tag{a}$$

where $\lambda_{0,\tau}$ is the weight that the planner in time 0 attaches to the lifetime utility of the generation born in period τ (for $\tau = -1, 0, 1, 2, \ldots$). The social planner chooses sequences for consumption during youth and old age ($\{C_\tau^Y\}_{\tau=0}^{\infty}$ and $\{C_\tau^O\}_{\tau=0}^{\infty}$) and the capital stock ($\{k_{\tau+1}\}_{\tau=0}^{\infty}$) in order to maximize social welfare (a) subject to the resource constraint:

$$C_\tau^Y + \frac{C_\tau^O}{1+n} + (1+n)k_{\tau+1} = f(k_{\tau+1}) + (1-\delta)k_\tau, \tag{b}$$

and taking the initial capital stock, k_0, as given. Obviously, since past things cannot be undone, consumption during youth of the initially old generation (C_{-1}^Y) is also taken as given. After some straightforward computations we find the following first-order conditions characterizing the social optimum:

$$\frac{\partial \Lambda^Y(\hat{x}_\tau)/\partial C_\tau^Y}{\partial \Lambda^Y(\hat{x}_\tau)/\partial C_{\tau+1}^O} = f'(\hat{k}_{\tau+1}) + 1 - \delta, \tag{c}$$

$$\frac{\partial \Lambda^Y(\hat{x}_\tau)/\partial C_\tau^Y}{\partial \Lambda^Y(\hat{x}_{\tau-1})/\partial C_\tau^O} = \frac{(1+n)\lambda_{0,\tau-1}}{\lambda_{0,\tau}}, \quad \tau = 0, 1, 2, \ldots \tag{d}$$

where $x_\tau \equiv [C_\tau^Y, C_{\tau+1}^O]$ and hats denote socially optimal values.

Now consider a planner who performs the social planning exercise at some later planning period $t > 0$. The social welfare function in planning period t is:

$$SW_t \equiv \lambda_{t,t-1} \Lambda^Y(C_{t-1}^Y, C_t^O) + \sum_{\tau=t}^{\infty} \lambda_{t,\tau} \Lambda^Y(C_\tau^Y, C_{\tau+1}^O), \tag{e}$$

where $\lambda_{t,\tau}$ is the weight that the planner in time t attaches to the lifetime utility of the generation born in period τ (for $\tau = t - 1, t, t + 1, t + 2, \ldots$). The social planner chooses sequences for consumption during youth and old age ($\{C_\tau^Y\}_{\tau=t}^\infty$ and $\{C_\tau^O\}_{\tau=t}^\infty$) and the capital stock ($\{k_{\tau+1}\}_{\tau=t}^\infty$) in order to maximize social welfare (e) subject to the resource constraint (b). The (interesting) first-order conditions consist of (c) and:

$$\frac{\partial \Lambda^Y(\hat{x}_\tau)/\partial C_\tau^Y}{\partial \Lambda^Y(\hat{x}_{\tau-1})/\partial C_\tau^O} = \frac{(1+n)\lambda_{t,\tau-1}}{\lambda_{t,\tau}}, \quad \tau = t, t+1, t+2, \ldots \tag{f}$$

The crucial thing to note is that conditions (d) and (f) overlap for the time interval $\tau = t, t+1, t+2, \ldots$. The sequences $\{C_\tau^Y\}_{\tau=0}^{t-1}$, $\{C_\tau^O\}_{\tau=0}^{t-1}$, and $\{k_{\tau+1}\}_{\tau=0}^{t-1}$ are chosen by the planner at time 0 but taken as given ("water under the bridge") by the planner at time t. But the sequences $\{C_\tau^Y\}_{\tau=t}^\infty$, $\{C_\tau^O\}_{\tau=t}^\infty$, and $\{k_{\tau+1}\}_{\tau=t}^\infty$ are chosen by both planners. Unless the planner at time 0 can commit to his plan (and thus can stop any future planner from re-optimizing the then relevant social welfare function), the sequences chosen by the planners at time 0 and at time t will not necessarily be the same. If they are not the same we call the social plan dynamically inconsistent (see Chapter 10).

Following the insights of Strotz (1956), Burness (1976) has derived conditions on the admissible pattern of generational weights, $\lambda_{t,\tau}$, that ensure that the optimal social plan is dynamically consistent. Comparing (d) and (f) reveals that dynamic consistency requires the following condition to hold for any planning period t:

$$\frac{\lambda_{t,\tau-1}}{\lambda_{t,\tau}} = \frac{\lambda_{0,\tau-1}}{\lambda_{0,\tau}}, \quad \tau = t, t+1, t+2, \ldots \tag{g}$$

Condition (g) means that $\lambda_{t,\tau}$ must be multiplicatively separable in time (τ) and the planning date (t), i.e. it must be possible to write $\lambda_{t,\tau} = g(t)\lambda_\tau$, where g is some function of t. A simple example of such a multiplicatively separable function is:

$$\lambda_{t,\tau} = \left(\frac{1}{1+\lambda}\right)^{\tau-t}, \tag{h}$$

where $\lambda > 0$ is the planner's constant discount rate. By using (h) we normalize the weight attached to the young in the planning period to unity ($\lambda_{t,t} = 1$). It follows necessarily, that in order to preserve dynamic consistency, there must be reverse discounting applied to the old generation in the planning period. Indeed, the dynamic consistency requirement (g) combined with (h) implies $\lambda_{t,\tau-1}/\lambda_{t,\tau} = 1+\lambda$ so that $\lambda_{t,t-1} = (1+\lambda)\lambda_{t,t} = 1+\lambda$. Calvo and Obstfeld (1988) apply this notion of reverse discounting in the context of the Blanchard–Yaari model of overlapping generations.

Finally, by using (17.135)–(17.137), and (17.141) in (17.138) we can derive the following expression:

$$
\frac{\partial \Lambda^Y(\hat{x}_t)}{\partial Z_t} = G'(\hat{E}_t)\hat{H}_t^\beta \left[\left(\frac{\partial \Lambda^Y(\hat{x}_t)}{\partial O_t} \right) \right.
$$

$$
+ \left(\frac{\partial \Lambda^Y(\hat{x}_t)}{\partial C_{t+1}^O} \right) F_N(\hat{k}_{t+1}, \hat{H}_{t+1}) \tag{17.142}
$$

$$
\left. + \frac{\beta(1+n)\hat{H}_{t+2}}{G'(\hat{E}_{t+1})\hat{H}_{t+1}^{1+\beta}} \left(\frac{\partial \Lambda^Y(\hat{x}_t)}{\partial C_{t+1}^O} \right) \left(\frac{\partial \Lambda^Y(\hat{x}_{t+1})/\partial Z_{t+1}}{\partial \Lambda^Y(\hat{x}_{t+1})/\partial C_{t+1}^Y} \right) \right].
$$

In the social optimum the marginal social cost of educational activities (left-hand side of (17.142)) should be equated to the marginal social benefits of these activities (right-hand side of (17.142)). The marginal social costs are just the value of leisure time of the parent, but the marginal social benefits consist of three terms. All three terms on the right-hand side of (17.142) contain the expression $G'(\hat{E}_t)\hat{H}_t^\beta$, which represents the marginal product of time spent on educational activities in the production of human capital (see (17.125)). The first line on the right-hand side of (17.142) is the "own" effect of educational activities on the parent's utility. This term also features in the first-order condition for the privately optimal (internal) child-education decision, namely (17.130). The second and third lines show the additional effects that the social planner takes into account in determining the optimal level of child education. The second line represents the effect of the parent's decision on the children's earnings: by endowing each child with more human capital they will have a higher skill level and thus command a higher wage. The third line represents the impact of the parent's investment on the children's incentives to provide education for their own children (i.e. the parent's grandchildren).

Eckstein and Zilcha are able to prove that (a) the competitive allocation is suboptimal, and (b) that under certain reasonable assumptions regarding the lifetime utility function there is underinvestment of human capital. Intuitively, this result obtains because the parents ignore some of the benefits of educating their children (1994, pp. 345–346). To internalize the externality in the human capital investment process, the policy maker would need to construct a rule such that the parent's decision regarding educational activities would take account of the effect on the children's wages and education efforts. As Eckstein and Zilcha argue, it is not likely that such a complex rule can actually be instituted in the real world. For that reason, the institution of compulsory education, which is practicable, may well achieve a welfare improvement over the competitive allocation because it imposes a minimal level of educational activities on parents (1994, pp. 341, 346).

17.3.2 Public investment

At least since the seminal work by Arrow and Kurz (1970), macroeconomists have known that the stock of public infrastructure is an important factor determining the productive capacity of an economy. Somewhat surprisingly, however, the public capital stock has played only a relatively minor role in the literature up until recently. This unfortunate state of affairs changed dramatically a decade ago when the pathbreaking and provocative empirical research of Aschauer (1989, 1990b) triggered a veritable boom in the econometric literature on public investment (see Gramlich, 1994 for an excellent survey of this literature). Aschauer (1989) showed that public capital exerts a strong positive effect on the productivity of private capital and argued that the slowdown in productivity growth in the US since the early 1970s is due to a shortage of investment in public infrastructure. Indeed, his estimates suggest implicit rates of return on government capital of 100% or more, values which are seen as highly implausible by many commentators (see e.g. Gramlich, 1994, p. 1186). Although Aschauer's results were controversial and many subsequent studies have questioned their robustness, it is nevertheless fair to conclude that economists generally support the notion that public capital is indeed productive.

In this subsection we show how productive public capital can be introduced into the Diamond–Samuelson model. We show how the dynamic behaviour of the economy is affected if the government adopts a constant infrastructural investment policy. Finally, we study how the socially optimal capital stock can be determined. To keep things simple we assume that labour supply is exogenous, and that the government has access to lump-sum taxes. We base our discussion in part on Azariadis (1993, pp. 336–340).

Prototypical examples of government capital are things likes roads, bridges, airports, hospitals, etc., which all have the stock dimension. Just as with the private capital stock, the public capital stock is gradually built up by means of infrastructural investment and gradually wears down because depreciation takes place. Denoting the stock of government capital by G_t we have:

$$G_{t+1} - G_t = I_t^G - \delta_G G_t, \tag{17.143}$$

where I_t^G is infrastructural investment and $0 < \delta_G < 1$ is the depreciation rate of public capital. Assuming that the population grows at a constant rate as in (17.21), per capita public capital evolves according to:

$$(1+n)g_{t+1} = i_t^G + (1 - \delta_G)g_t, \tag{17.144}$$

where $g_t \equiv G_t/L_t$ and $i_t^G \equiv I_t^G/L_t$.

We assume that public capital enters the production function of the private sector, i.e. instead of (17.10) we have:

$$Y_t = F(K_t, L_t, g_t), \tag{17.145}$$

where we assume that $F()$ is linearly homogeneous in the *private* production factors, K_t and L_t. This means that we can express per capita output ($y_t \equiv Y_t/L_t$) as follows:

$$y_t = f(k_t, g_t), \tag{17.146}$$

633

where $k_t \equiv K_t/L_t$ and $f(k_t, g_t) \equiv F(K_t/L_t, 1, g_t)$. We make the following set of assumptions regarding technology:

$$f_k \equiv \frac{\partial f}{\partial k_t} > 0, \quad f_g \equiv \frac{\partial f}{\partial g_t} > 0, \tag{P1}$$

$$f_{kk} \equiv \frac{\partial^2 f}{\partial k_t^2} < 0, \quad f_{gg} \equiv \frac{\partial^2 f}{\partial g_t^2} < 0, \tag{P2}$$

$$f(0, g_t) = f(k_t, 0) = 0, \tag{P3}$$

$$f_{kg} \equiv \frac{\partial^2 f}{\partial k_t \partial g_t} > 0, \tag{P4}$$

$$f_g - k f_{kg} > 0. \tag{P5}$$

Private and public capital both feature positive (property (P1)) but diminishing marginal productivity (property (P2)). Both types of capital are essential in production, i.e. output is zero if either input is zero (property (P3)). Finally, properties (P4)–(P5) ensure that public capital is complementary with both private capital and labour. This last implication can be seen by noting that perfectly competitive firms hire capital and labour according to the usual rental expressions $r_t + \delta = F_K(K_t, L_t, g_t)$ and $W_t = F_L(K_t, L_t, g_t)$. These can be expressed in per capita form as:

$$r_t = r(k_t, g_t) \equiv f_k(k_t, g_t) - \delta, \tag{17.147}$$

$$W_t = W(k_t, g_t) \equiv f(k_t, g_t) - k_t f_k(k_t, g_t), \tag{17.148}$$

where $0 < \delta < 1$ is the depreciation rate of the private capital stock. We can deduce from Properties (P4)–(P5) that $r_k \equiv \partial r/\partial k_t < 0$ and $W_k \equiv \partial W/\partial k_t > 0$ (as in the standard model) and $r_g \equiv \partial r/\partial g_t > 0$ and $W_g \equiv \partial W/\partial g_t > 0$ (public capital positively affects both the interest rate and the wage rate). To illustrate the key properties of the model we shall employ a simple Cobb–Douglas production function below of the form $Y_t = K_t^{1-\epsilon_L} L_t^{\epsilon_L} g_t^{\eta}$, with $0 < \eta < \epsilon_L$. This function satisfies properties (P1)–(P5) and implies $W(k_t, g_t) = \epsilon_L k_t^{1-\epsilon_L} g_t^{\eta}$ and $r(k_t, g_t) = (1 - \epsilon_L) k_t^{-\epsilon_L} g_t^{\eta} - \delta$.

To keep things simple, we assume that the representative young agent has the following lifetime utility function:

$$\Lambda_t^Y = \log C_t^Y + \left(\frac{1}{1+\rho}\right) \log C_{t+1}^O. \tag{17.149}$$

The budget identities facing the household are:

$$C_t^Y + S_t = W_t - T_t^Y, \tag{17.150}$$

$$C_{t+1}^O = (1 + r_{t+1}) S_t - T_{t+1}^O, \tag{17.151}$$

where T_t^Y and T_{t+1}^O are lump-sum taxes paid by the agent during youth and old age respectively. The consolidated budget constraint is:

$$\hat{W}_t \equiv W_t - T_t^Y - \frac{T_{t+1}^O}{1 + r_{t+1}} = C_t^Y + \frac{C_{t+1}^O}{1 + r_{t+1}}, \tag{17.152}$$

where $\hat{W}_t$ is after-tax non-interest lifetime income. The optimal household choices are $C_t^Y = c\hat{W}_t$ and $C_{t+1}^O/(1+r_{t+1}) = (1-c)\hat{W}_t$, where $c \equiv (1+\rho)/(2+\rho)$. The savings function can then be written as follows:

$$S_t \equiv S(W_t, r_{t+1}, T_t^Y, T_{t+1}^O) = (1-c)\left(W_t - T_t^Y\right) + c\left(\frac{T_{t+1}^O}{1+r_{t+1}}\right). \qquad (17.153)$$

It follows that, ceteris paribus, lump-sum taxes during youth reduce private saving whilst taxes during old age increase saving. As before, private saving by the young is next period's stock of private capital, i.e. $L_t S_t = K_{t+1}$. In per capita form we have:

$$S_t = (1+n)k_{t+1}. \qquad (17.154)$$

The government budget constraint is very simple and states that government infrastructural investment (I_t^G) is financed by tax receipts from the young and the old, i.e. $I_t^G = L_t T_t^Y + L_{t-1} T_t^O$ which can be written in per capita form as:

$$i_t^G = T_t^Y + \frac{T_t^O}{1+n}. \qquad (17.155)$$

We now have a complete description of the economy. The key expressions are the accumulation identity for the public capital stock (17.144), the government budget constraint (17.155), and the accumulation expression for private capital. The latter can be written in the following format by using (17.147), (17.148), and (17.153) in (17.154):

$$(1+n)k_{t+1} = (1-c)\left[W(k_t, g_t) - T_t^Y\right] + \frac{cT_{t+1}^O}{1+r(k_{t+1}, g_{t+1})}. \qquad (17.156)$$

Once a path for public investment and a particular financing method are chosen, (17.144) and (17.156) describe the dynamical evolution of the public and private capital stocks. We derive the phase diagram for the case of Cobb–Douglas technology and a constant public investment policy (so that $i_t^G = i^G$ for all t) financed by taxes on only the young generations (so that $T_t^Y = i^G$ and $T_t^O = 0$ for all t). The consequences of alternative assumptions regarding financing are left as an exercise for the reader.

The phase diagram has been drawn in Figure 17.6. The GE line is the graphical representation of (17.144) for the constant public investment policy $i_t^G = i^G$, i.e. along the line we have $g_{t+1} = g_t$. The GE line is horizontal and defines a unique steady-state equilibrium value for the stock of public capital equal to $g = i^G/(n+\delta_G)$. The dynamics for public capital are derived from the rewritten version of (17.144):

$$g_{t+1} - g_t = \frac{i^G - (n+\delta_G)g_t}{1+n} = -\left(\frac{n+\delta_G}{1+n}\right)[g_t - g], \qquad (17.157)$$

from which we conclude that for points above (below) the GE line, $g_t > g$ $(< g)$ and the public capital stock falls (rises) over time, $g_{t+1} < g_t$ $(> g_t)$. This (stable) dynamic pattern has been illustrated with vertical arrows in Figure 17.6.

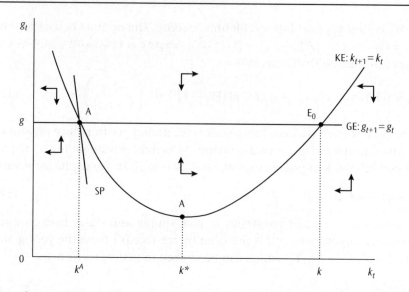

Figure 17.6. Public and private capital

The KE line in Figure 17.6 is the graphical representation of (17.156), with the constant investment policy and the financing assumption both substituted in and imposing the steady state, $k_{t+1} = k_t$. For the Cobb–Douglas technology, the KE line has the following form:

$$g_t = \left(\frac{1+n}{\epsilon_L(1-c)}\right)^{1/\eta} \left[k_t^{\epsilon_L} + i^G \left(\frac{1-c}{1+n}\right) k_t^{\epsilon_L - 1}\right]^{1/\eta}, \tag{17.158}$$

from which we derive that $\lim_{k_t \to 0} g_t = \lim_{k_t \to \infty} g_t = \infty$ and that g_t reaches its minimum value along the KE curve for $k_t = k^*$, where k^* is defined as:

$$k^* \equiv i^G \left(\frac{1-c}{1+n}\right) \left(\frac{1-\epsilon_L}{\epsilon_L}\right). \tag{17.159}$$

Hence, the KE line is as drawn in Figure 17.6. There are two steady-state equilibria (at A and E_0, respectively). The dynamics of the private capital stock are obtained by rewriting (17.156) as:

$$k_{t+1} - k_t = \left(\frac{1-c}{1+n}\right)\left(\epsilon_L k_t^{1-\epsilon_L} g_t^\eta - i^G\right) - k_t, \tag{17.160}$$

and noting that $\partial[k_{t+1} - k_t]/\partial g_t > 0$. Hence, since the wage rate increases with public capital and future consumption is a normal good, private saving increases with g_t. Hence, the capital stock is increasing (decreasing) over time for points above (below) the KE line. These dynamic forces have been illustrated with horizontal arrows in Figure 17.6.

It follows from the configuration of arrows (and from a formal local stability analysis of the linearized model) that the low-private-capital equilibrium at A is a saddle point whereas the high-private-capital equilibrium at E_0 is a stable node. For the latter equilibrium it holds that, regardless of the initial stocks of private and public capital, provided the economy is close enough to E_0 it will automatically return to E_0.

What about the steady-state equilibrium at A? Is it stable or unstable? In the typical encounters that we have had throughout this book with two-dimensional saddle-point equilibria, we called such equilibria stable because there always was one predetermined and one non-predetermined variable. By letting the non-predetermined variable jump onto the saddle path, stability was ensured. For example, in Chapter 4 we studied Tobin's q theory of private investment and showed that K and q are, respectively, the predetermined and jumping variables. In the present application, however, both K and G are predetermined variables so neither can jump. Only if the initial stocks of private and public capital by pure coincidence happen to lie on the saddle path (SP in Figure 17.6), will the equilibrium at A eventually be reached given the constant investment policy employed by the government. Appealing to the Samuelsonian correspondence principle we focus attention in the remainder of this subsection on the truly stable equilibrium at E_0.

Now consider what happens if the government increases its public investment. It follows from, respectively (17.157) and (17.158), that both the GE and KE lines shift up. Clearly, the higher public investment level will lead to a higher long-run stock of public capital, i.e. $dg/di^G = 1/(n + \delta_G) > 0$. The long-run effect on the private capital stock is ambiguous and depends on the relative scarcity of public capital. By imposing the steady state in (17.160) and differentiating we obtain:

$$\left[1 - \left(\frac{1-c}{1+n} \right) W_k \right] \left(\frac{dk}{di^G} \right) = \left(\frac{1-c}{1+n} \right) \left[W_g \left(\frac{dg}{di^G} \right) - 1 \right], \tag{17.161}$$

where the term in square brackets on the left-hand side is positive because the model is outright stable around the initial steady-state equilibrium E_0.[16] The first term in square brackets on the right-hand side represents the positive effect on the pre-tax wage of the young households whilst the second term is the negative tax effect. Since $W_g = \eta W/g$, $W = \epsilon_L y$, and $g = i^G/(n + \delta_G)$, it follows from (17.161) that the steady-state private capital stock rises (falls) as a result of the shock if $i^G/y < \eta \epsilon_L$ ($> \eta \epsilon_L$), i.e. if public capital is initially relatively scarce (abundant).

---

[16] Recall that for a constant level of public capital, the model is stable provided the following stability condition is satisfied around the initial steady state, E_0:

$$0 < \frac{\partial k_{t+1}}{\partial k_t} \equiv \left(\frac{1-c}{1+n} \right) W_k < 1.$$

Modified golden rules

Now that we have established the macroeconomic effects of public capital, we can confront the equally important question regarding the socially optimal amount of public infrastructure. Just as in the previous subsection on education, we study this issue by computing the public investment plan that a social planner would choose. Following Calvo and Obstfeld (1988, p. 414) and Diamond (1973, p. 219) we assume that the social welfare function takes the following Benthamite form:[17]

$$SW_0 \equiv \left(\frac{1+n}{1+\rho_G}\right)^{-1} \Lambda^Y(C^Y_{-1}, C^O_0) + \sum_{t=0}^{\infty} \left(\frac{1+n}{1+\rho_G}\right)^t \Lambda^Y(C^Y_t, C^O_{t+1}), \qquad (17.162)$$

where we assume that $\rho_G > n$. Equation (17.162) is a special case of (17.131) with the generational weight set equal to $\lambda_t \equiv [(1+n)/(1+\rho_G)]^t$. This means that the social planner discounts the lifetime utility of generations at a constant rate ρ_G which may or may not be equal to the rate employed by the agents to discount their own periodic utility (namely ρ). The social planner chooses sequences for consumption for young and old ($\{C^Y_t\}_{t=0}^{\infty}$ and $\{C^O_t\}_{t=0}^{\infty}$), the per capita stocks of public and private capital ($\{g_{t+1}\}_{t=0}^{\infty}$ and $\{k_{t+1}\}_{t=0}^{\infty}$), in order to maximize (17.162) subject to the following resource constraint:

$$C^Y_t + \frac{C^O_t}{1+n} + (1+n)[k_{t+1} + g_{t+1}] = f(k_t, g_t) + (1-\delta)k_t + (1-\delta_G)g_t, \qquad (17.163)$$

and taking as given k_0 and g_0. The Lagrangean associated with the social optimization problem is given by:

$$\begin{aligned}
\mathcal{L}_0 &\equiv \left(\frac{1+n}{1+\rho_G}\right)^{-1} \Lambda^Y(C^Y_{-1}, C^O_0) + \sum_{t=0}^{\infty} \left(\frac{1+n}{1+\rho_G}\right)^t \Lambda^Y(C^Y_t, C^O_{t+1}) \\
&\quad - \sum_{t=0}^{\infty} \mu^R_t \Big[C^Y_t + \frac{C^O_t}{1+n} + (1+n)[k_{t+1} + g_{t+1}] - f(k_t, g_t) \\
&\quad - (1-\delta)k_t - (1-\delta_G)g_t\Big],
\end{aligned} \qquad (17.164)$$

where μ^R_t is the Lagrange multiplier associated with the resource constraint.

---

[17] This name for the social welfare function derives from the classical economist Jeremy Bentham (1748–1832) who argued that "it is the greatest happiness of the greatest number that is the measure of right and wrong" (quoted by Harrison, 1987, p. 226). This explains why the rate of population growth enters (17.162).

After some manipulation we find the following first-order conditions for the social optimum for $t = 0, \ldots, \infty$:

$$\frac{\partial \mathcal{L}_0}{\partial C_t^Y} = \left(\frac{1+n}{1+\rho_G}\right)^t \frac{\partial \Lambda^Y(x_t)}{\partial C_t^Y} - \mu_t^R = 0, \tag{17.165}$$

$$\frac{\partial \mathcal{L}_0}{\partial C_t^O} = \left(\frac{1+n}{1+\rho_G}\right)^{t-1} \frac{\partial \Lambda^Y(x_{t-1})}{\partial C_t^O} - \frac{\mu_t^R}{1+n} = 0, \tag{17.166}$$

$$\frac{\partial \mathcal{L}_0}{\partial g_{t+1}} = -(1+n)\mu_t^R + \mu_{t+1}^R \left[f_g(k_{t+1}, g_{t+1}) + 1 - \delta_G\right] = 0, \tag{17.167}$$

$$\frac{\partial \mathcal{L}_0}{\partial k_{t+1}} = -(1+n)\mu_t^R + \mu_{t+1}^R \left[f_k(k_{t+1}, g_{t+1}) + 1 - \delta\right] = 0, \tag{17.168}$$

where $x_t \equiv [C_t^Y, C_{t+1}^O]$. By combining (17.165)–(17.168) to eliminate the Lagrange multipliers we find some intuitive expressions characterizing the social optimum:

$$\frac{\partial \Lambda^Y(\hat{x}_t)/\partial C_t^Y}{\partial \Lambda^Y(\hat{x}_t)/\partial C_{t+1}^O} = f_k(\hat{k}_{t+1}, \hat{g}_{t+1}) + 1 - \delta = f_g(\hat{k}_{t+1}, \hat{g}_{t+1}) + 1 - \delta_G, \tag{17.169}$$

$$\frac{\partial \Lambda^Y(\hat{x}_t)/\partial C_t^Y}{\partial \Lambda^Y(\hat{x}_{t-1})/\partial C_t^O} = 1 + \rho_G, \tag{17.170}$$

where hatted variables once again denote socially optimal values. The first equality in (17.169) is the socially optimal consumption Euler equation calling for an equalization of, on the one hand, the marginal rate of substitution between present and future consumption and, on the other hand, the socially optimal gross interest factor, $1 + \hat{r}_{t+1}$, where $\hat{r}_{t+1} \equiv f_k(\hat{k}_{t+1}, \hat{g}_{t+1}) - \delta$. The second equality in (17.169) says that the socially optimal stock of public capital per worker should be such that the yields on private and public capital are equalized, i.e. $\hat{g}_{t+1}$ should be set in such a way that $\hat{r}_{t+1}^G = \hat{r}_{t+1}$, where $\hat{r}_{t+1}^G \equiv f_g(\hat{k}_{t+1}, \hat{g}_{t+1}) - \delta_G$. Finally, equation (17.170) determines the socially optimal *intratemporal* division of consumption. Its intuitive meaning, and especially the interplay between the agent's and the planner's discount rate, can best be understood by considering the case of intertemporally separable preferences (which has been used throughout this chapter). By using $\Lambda_t^Y(x_t) \equiv U(C_t^Y) + (1 + \rho)^{-1}U(C_{t+1}^O)$ we can rewrite (17.170) in terms of the agent's felicity function ($U(.)$) and the pure rate of time preference (ρ):

$$\frac{U'(\hat{C}_t^Y)}{U'(\hat{C}_t^O)} = \frac{1 + \rho_G}{1 + \rho}. \tag{17.171}$$

It follows from (17.171) that if the planner's discount rate exceeds (falls short of) the agent's rate of time preference, $\rho_G > \rho \ (< \rho)$, then the social planner ensures that $U'(\hat{C}_t^Y)$ exceeds (falls short of) $U'(\hat{C}_t^O)$, and thus (since $U'' < 0$) that $\hat{C}_t^Y$ falls short of (exceeds) $\hat{C}_t^O$. If $\rho_G = \rho$, the planner chooses the egalitarian solution ($\hat{C}_t^O = \hat{C}_t^Y$).

Intermezzo

Calvo–Obstfeld two-step procedure. Calvo and Obstfeld (1988) have shown that with intertemporally separable preferences, the social planning problem can be solved in two stages. In the first stage, the planner solves a static problem and in the second stage a dynamic problem is solved. Their procedure works as follows. Aggregate consumption at time τ, expressed per worker, is defined as:

$$C_\tau \equiv C_\tau^Y + \left(\frac{1}{1+n}\right) C_\tau^O \tag{a}$$

With intertemporally separable preferences (and ignoring a constant like $U(C_{-1}^Y)$) the social welfare function in period t can be rewritten as:

$$SW_t \equiv \left(\frac{1+\rho_G}{(1+n)(1+\rho)}\right) U\left(C_t^O\right)$$

$$+ \sum_{\tau=t}^{\infty} \left(\frac{1+n}{1+\rho_G}\right)^{\tau-t} \left[U\left(C_\tau^Y\right) + \left(\frac{1}{1+\rho}\right) U\left(C_{\tau+1}^O\right)\right]$$

$$= \sum_{\tau=t}^{\infty} \left(\frac{1+n}{1+\rho_G}\right)^{\tau-t} \left[U\left(C_\tau^Y\right) + \left(\frac{1+\rho_G}{(1+n)(1+\rho)}\right) U\left(C_\tau^O\right)\right], \tag{b}$$

where the term in square brackets in (b) now contains the weighted felicity levels of old and young agents living in the same time period. The special treatment of period-t felicity of the old is to preserve dynamic consistency (see the Intermezzo above). We can now demonstrate the two-step procedure.

In the first step, the social planner solves the static problem of dividing a given level of aggregate consumption, C_τ, over the generations that are alive at that time:

$$\bar{U}(C_\tau) \equiv \max_{\{C_\tau^Y, C_\tau^O\}} \left[U\left(C_\tau^Y\right) + \left(\frac{1+\rho_G}{(1+n)(1+\rho)}\right) U\left(C_\tau^O\right)\right], \quad \text{s.t. (a),} \tag{c}$$

where $\bar{U}(C_\tau)$ is the (indirect) social felicity function. The first-order condition associated with this optimization problem is:

$$\frac{U'(C_\tau^Y)}{U'(C_\tau^O)} = \frac{1+\rho_G}{1+\rho}, \tag{d}$$

which is the same as (17.171). Furthermore, by differentiating (c) and using (a) and (d) we find the familiar envelope property:

$$\bar{U}'(C_\tau) \equiv \frac{d\bar{U}(C_\tau)}{dC_\tau} = U'(C_\tau^Y). \tag{e}$$

For the special case of logarithmic preferences, for example, individual felicity is $U(x) \equiv \log x$ and the social felicity function would take the following form:

$$
\bar{U}(C_\tau) = \log \left[\frac{(1+n)(1+\rho)C_\tau}{(1+n)(1+\rho) + 1 + \rho_G} \right]
$$

$$
+ \left(\frac{1 + \rho_G}{(1+n)(1+\rho)} \right) \log \left[\frac{(1+n)(1+\rho_G)C_\tau}{(1+n)(1+\rho) + 1 + \rho_G} \right]
$$

$$
\equiv \omega_0 + \left(\frac{(1+n)(1+\rho) + 1 + \rho_G}{(1+n)(1+\rho)} \right) \log C_\tau. \tag{f}
$$

In the second step the social planner chooses sequences of aggregate consumption and the two types of capital in order to maximize social welfare:

$$
SW_t = \sum_{\tau=t}^{\infty} \left(\frac{1+n}{1+\rho_G} \right)^{\tau-t} \bar{U}(C_\tau), \tag{g}
$$

subject to the initial conditions (k_t and g_t given) and the resource constraint:

$$
C_\tau + (1+n)\left[k_{\tau+1} + g_{\tau+1}\right] = f(k_\tau, g_\tau) + (1-\delta)k_\tau + (1-\delta_G)g_\tau, \tag{h}
$$

where we have used (a) in (17.163) to get (h). Letting μ_τ^R denote the Lagrange multiplier for the resource constraint in period τ we obtain the following first-order conditions:

$$
\frac{(1+n)\mu_\tau^R}{\mu_{\tau+1}^R} = f_k(k_{t+1}, g_{t+1}) + 1 - \delta = f_g(k_{t+1}, g_{t+1}) + 1 - \delta_G, \tag{i}
$$

$$
\mu_\tau^R = \left(\frac{1+n}{1+\rho_G} \right)^{\tau-t} \bar{U}'(C_\tau). \tag{j}
$$

By using (j) for period $t + 1$ and noting (d) and (e) we find that (i) coincides with (17.169).

We now return to the general first-order conditions (17.169)–(17.170) and study the steady state. In the steady state we have $C_t^Y = C^Y$, $C_t^O = C^O$, $k_t = k$, $g_t = g$, and $\hat{x}_t = \hat{x}$ for all t so that (17.169)–(17.170) simplify to:

$$
\frac{\partial \Lambda^Y(\hat{x})/\partial C^Y}{\partial \Lambda^Y(\hat{x})/\partial C^O} = 1 + \rho_G, \tag{17.172}
$$

$$
[\hat{r} \equiv] f_k(k, g) - \delta = \rho_G = f_g(k, g) - \delta_G [\equiv \hat{r}_G]. \tag{17.173}
$$

Equation (17.172) calls for an optimal division of consumption over the young and the old. The first equality in (17.173) is the *modified golden rule* (MGR) equating the steady-state yield on the private capital stock (the steady-state rate of interest) to the rate of time preference of the social planner. There is an important difference between this version of the MGR and the one encountered in Chapter 14 in the context of the Ramsey representative-agent model. In the OLG setting, the planner's rate of time preference features in the MGR whereas in the Ramsey model the representative agent's own rate of time preference is relevant (compare (17.173) with (14.78)).

The second equality in (17.173) is a modified golden rule for public capital that was initially derived by Pestieau (1974). It calls for an equalization of the public rate of return and the planner's rate of time preference. The two equalities in (17.173) together determine the optimal per worker stocks of public and private capital. For example, for Cobb–Douglas technology we have $y_t = k_t^{1-\epsilon_L} g_t^\eta$ (with $\eta < \epsilon_L$) so that $k/y = (1 - \epsilon_L)/(\rho_G + \delta)$, $g/y = \eta/(\rho_G + \delta_G)$. It follows from these results that output per worker is:

$$y = \left[\left(\frac{k}{y} \right)^{1-\epsilon_L} \left(\frac{g}{y} \right)^\eta \right]^{1/(\epsilon_L - \eta)} = \left[\left(\frac{1 - \epsilon_L}{\rho_G + \delta} \right)^{1-\epsilon_L} \left(\frac{\eta}{\rho_G + \delta_G} \right)^\eta \right]^{1/(\epsilon_L - \eta)} \tag{17.174}$$

Now that we have characterized the necessary conditions for the steady-state social optimum, a relevant question concerns the *decentralization* of this optimum. Can the policy maker devise a set of policy tools in such a way that the private sector choices concerning consumption and private capital accumulation coincide exactly with their respective values in the social optimum? The answer is affirmative provided the policy maker has access to the right kind of policy instruments. In the present context, for example, the first-best social optimum can be mimicked in the market place if (i) the level of public investment (and thus the public capital stock) is chosen to be consistent with (17.173), and (ii) there are age-specific lump-sum taxes available (see Pestieau, 1974 and Ihori, 1996, p. 114). The latter instrument is needed to ensure that the market replicates the socially optimal mix of consumption by the young and the old (cf. (17.172)).

17.3.3 Intergenerational accounting

One of the most hotly debated concepts in macroeconomic policy circles has been the correct definition and measurements of the government budget deficit. Throughout the book we have encountered several examples pointing at a fundamental ambiguity in the concept of the deficit. For example, in Chapter 6 we saw that government investment which yields the market rate of return represents no net liability of the government. Yet, depending on the way in which these expenditures are treated by the government's accountants, they either do or do not feature in the government budget deficit (in the standard accounting approach they are typically treated as government consumption and thus feature in the deficit).

Haveman (1994, p. 95) gives an impressive list of further items for which proposals have been made to change the way in which these items are treated in the government's accounting system. They include things like federal credit and loan programmes, future commitments of programmes like medicare and social security, changes in the value of government assets, government retirement liabilities, etc. It is fair to say that there is no consensus as to how to measure the deficit.

Auerbach, Gokhale, and Kotlikoff (1991, p. 57) give the most radical statement of the problem to date by arguing that "... every dollar the government takes in or pays out is labeled in a manner that is economically arbitrary". They suggest doing away with the concept of the government deficit altogether and to focus instead on what they label the *generational accounts*. The background to their proposal is the notion that "[t]he conceptual issue associated with the word 'deficit' is the intergenerational distribution of welfare". Auerbach et al. (1991, p. 57) and that the intertemporal budget constraint of the government should be the focus of attention. In words, this constraint says that "the government's current net wealth plus the present value of the government's net receipts from all current and future generations (the generational accounts) must be sufficient to pay for the present value of the government's current and future consumption" (1991, p. 58).

Auerbach et al. (1991, 1994) claim a number of advantages that a system of generational accounts has over the traditional government budget deficit: (i) generational accounts are invariant to changes in accounting labels, (ii) they bring out the zero-sum feature of the intertemporal government budget constraint (what some generation gets will have to be paid for by some other generation), and (iii) they can be used to study the fiscal and intergenerational consequences of alternative policies.

In this subsection we follow Buiter (1997) by illustrating the system of generational accounts in a simple version of the Diamond–Samuelson model. Assuming that the population is constant (so that $L_{t-1} = L_t = 1$), the government (flow) budget identity is given by:

$$B_{t+1} = (1 + r_t)B_t + G_t^O + G_t^Y - T_t^O - T_t^Y, \tag{17.175}$$

where T_t^O and T_t^Y are the taxes paid by the old and young respectively, and G_t^O and G_t^Y are pure public consumption goods that the government provides free of charge to, respectively, the old and the young. Following Buiter (1997, p. 607) we assume that these public goods are non-rival and non-excludable. Iterating (17.175) forwards in time yields the following expression:

$$B_t = \prod_{s=0}^{T}\left(\frac{1}{1+r_{t+s}}\right)B_{t+T+1} + \sum_{\tau=0}^{T}\prod_{s=0}^{\tau}\left(\frac{1}{1+r_{t+s}}\right)[T_{t+\tau}^O + T_{t+\tau}^Y - (G_{t+\tau}^O + G_{t+\tau}^Y)]$$

$$\equiv R_{t-1,T}B_{t+T+1} + \sum_{\tau=0}^{T} R_{t-1,\tau}[T_{t+\tau}^O + T_{t+\tau}^Y - (G_{t+\tau}^O + G_{t+\tau}^Y)], \tag{17.176}$$

where $R_{t-1,\tau}$ is a discounting factor:

$$R_{t-1,\tau} = \prod_{s=0}^{\tau}\left(\frac{1}{1+r_{t+s}}\right). \tag{17.177}$$

By letting $T \to \infty$ in (17.176) we find that the government NPG condition is:

$$\lim_{T \to \infty} R_{t-1,T} B_{t+T+1} = 0, \tag{17.178}$$

so that the government budget constraint is:

$$B_t = \sum_{\tau=0}^{\infty} R_{t-1,\tau} \left[T^O_{t+\tau} + T^Y_{t+\tau} - \left(G^O_{t+\tau} + G^Y_{t+\tau} \right) \right]. \tag{17.179}$$

If there is government debt outstanding at time t ($B_t > 0$ on the left-hand side of (17.179)), then the solvent government must ultimately run primary surpluses. Note that (17.178) does not require the government to pay off its debt eventually. All that solvency requires is that government debt must not grow faster in the long run than the rate of interest.

The household sector is standard. Households consume during youth and old age (C^Y_t and C^O_{t+1}, respectively), practise consumption smoothing by saving (S_t) which can be in the form of physical capital or government bonds. The relevant expressions characterizing the household sector are:

$$C^Y_t + S_t = W_t - T^Y_t, \tag{17.180}$$

$$C^Y_{t+1} = (1 + r_{t+1}) S_t - T^O_{t+1}, \tag{17.181}$$

$$S_t = B_{t+1} + K_{t+1}. \tag{17.182}$$

Equations (17.180)–(17.182) are the same as (17.150)–(17.151) and (17.182) is the same as (17.58) but with the size of the (young) population set equal to unity ($L_t = 1$). The consolidated budget constraint facing households is obtained in the usual manner by combining (17.180) and (17.181):

$$C^Y_t + \frac{C^O_{t+1}}{1 + r_{t+1}} = W_t - T_{t,t}, \tag{17.183}$$

where $T_{t,t}$ is the present value of (lump-sum) taxes that a generation born in period t (second subscript) must pay over the course of its life seen from the perspective of period t (first subscript):

$$T_{t,t} \equiv T^Y_t + \frac{T^O_{t+1}}{1 + r_{t+1}}. \tag{17.184}$$

We can now develop the generational accounts for existing and future generations by decomposing the government budget constraint (17.179). Because it is very easy indeed to get tangled up in the different subscripts identifying time and generations we show some of the details of the derivation.[18] First we note that by using (17.177)

[18] A more direct derivation makes use of the fact that the discount factor in (17.169) satisfies the following property:

$$R_{t-1,\tau+1} = \left(\frac{1}{1 + r_{t+\tau+1}} \right) R_{t-1,\tau}.$$

Using this property in (17.179) yields (17.186) in a single step.

equation (17.179) can be written as follows:

$$
B_t = \left(\frac{1}{1+r_t} \right) [T_t^O + T_t^Y] + \left(\frac{1}{1+r_t} \right) \left(\frac{1}{1+r_{t+1}} \right) [T_{t+1}^O + T_{t+1}^Y]
$$

$$
+ \left(\frac{1}{1+r_t} \right) \left(\frac{1}{1+r_{t+1}} \right) \left(\frac{1}{1+r_{t+2}} \right) [T_{t+2}^O + T_{t+2}^Y]
$$

$$
+ \left(\frac{1}{1+r_t} \right) \left(\frac{1}{1+r_{t+1}} \right) \left(\frac{1}{1+r_{t+2}} \right) \left(\frac{1}{1+r_{t+3}} \right) [T_{t+3}^O + T_{t+3}^Y] + \cdots
$$

$$
- \sum_{\tau=0}^{\infty} R_{t-1,\tau} [G_{t+\tau}^O + G_{t+\tau}^Y]. \tag{17.185}
$$

Next we look for terms pertaining to the same generation and group these together:

$$
B_t = \left(\frac{1}{1+r_t} \right) T_t^O + \left(\frac{1}{1+r_t} \right) \left[T_t^Y + \frac{T_{t+1}^O}{1+r_{t+1}} \right]
$$

$$
+ \left(\frac{1}{1+r_t} \right) \left(\frac{1}{1+r_{t+1}} \right) \left[T_{t+1}^Y + \frac{T_{t+2}^O}{1+r_{t+2}} \right]
$$

$$
+ \left(\frac{1}{1+r_t} \right) \left(\frac{1}{1+r_{t+1}} \right) \left(\frac{1}{1+r_{t+2}} \right) \left[T_{t+2}^Y + \frac{T_{t+3}^O}{1+r_{t+3}} \right] + \cdots
$$

$$
- \sum_{\tau=0}^{\infty} R_{t-1,\tau} [G_{t+\tau}^O + G_{t+\tau}^Y]. \tag{17.186}
$$

In the first line of (17.186) we find the remaining taxes to be paid by the old at time t and the lifetime taxes, $T_{t,t}$, of the young at time t. Both these terms are, however, expressed in present-value terms, i.e. they are discounted back to the end of period $t-1$. The same holds for all the other terms pertaining to future generations (namely the second and third lines in (17.186)). The reason for this discounting is that B_t is debt at the beginning of period t (which was accumulated at the end of period $t-1$), over which interest must be paid at the beginning of period t.

Equation (17.186) gives the generational accounts for the different generations. The first line contains the accounts for the two existing generations at time t, whilst lines two and three contain the generational accounts for future generations. Kotlikoff and co-authors often write the generational accounts in a more compact format as:

$$
B_t + \sum_{\tau=0}^{\infty} R_{t-1,\tau} [G_{t+\tau}^O + G_{t+\tau}^Y] = \sum_{k=t-1}^{\infty} T_{t-1,k}, \tag{17.187}
$$

where the $T_{t-1,k}$ terms are defined as follows:

$$T_{t-1,t-1} \equiv \left(\frac{1}{1+r_t}\right) T_t^O, \qquad \text{(existing old)}$$

$$T_{t-1,t} \equiv \left(\frac{1}{1+r_t}\right) T_{t,t} = \left(\frac{1}{1+r_t}\right)\left[T_t^Y + \frac{T_{t+1}^O}{1+r_{t+1}}\right], \qquad \text{(existing young)}$$

$$T_{t-1,k} \equiv R_{t-1,k-1} T_{k,k} = R_{t-1,k-t}\left[T_k^Y + \frac{T_{k+1}^O}{1+r_{k+1}}\right], \qquad \text{(future generations)}$$

where $k = t+1, t+2, \ldots$. Equation (17.187) says that the sum of outstanding government debt plus the present value of government consumption (left-hand side) must equal the sum of the generational accounts of existing and future generations (right-hand side).

Having completed our description of the generational accounting system in the context of the Diamond–Samuelson model we can now turn to an actual empirical implementation of the method. Auerbach et al. (1991, pp. 65–75) explain in detail how the method of generational accounting can be applied to actual economies. Table 17.2 contains the 1991 generational accounts for US males. (This table is an abbreviated version of Table 1 of Auerbach et al., 1994, p. 80.) Of course, for the method to have any practical use, an actual implementation must contain much more detail than is contained in our stylized model. Table 17.2 therefore distinguishes ten (rather than just two) existing generations and gives the accounts for males only because females are different in labour force participation, family structure, and mortality. (Auerbach et al., 1994, give figures for nineteen five-year cohorts

Table 17.2. Male generational accounts

Generation's age in 1991	Net payments	Tax payments	Transfer receipts
	×$1000	×$1000	×$1000
0	78.9	99.3	20.4
10	125.0	155.3	30.3
20	187.1	229.6	42.5
30	205.5	258.5	53.0
40	180.1	250.0	69.9
50	97.2	193.8	96.6
60	−23.0	112.1	135.1
70	−80.7	56.3	137.0
80	−61.1	30.2	91.3
90	−3.5	8.8	12.3
Future	166.5		

and also present generational accounts for females.) Furthermore, Auerbach et al. allow for transfers, distorting taxes etc. that were abstracted from in the stylized model.

In Table 17.2 the first column gives the age of the particular generation of US males in 1991, e.g. the row marked '0' pertains to agents born in 1991 whereas the row marked '40' gives the data for agents who were 40 years of age in 1991 (who were thus born in 1951). The second column gives the net generational accounts for the different generations whilst the third and fourth columns distinguishes, respectively, the underlying tax payments and transfer receipts. A positive entry in the second column means that the particular generation will pay more in present value to the government than it will receive. For example, for a 40–year old male in 1991, the present value of taxes to be paid during his remaining lifetime amount to $250,000 whilst the present value of transfers is $69,900. In contrast, a 70-year old in 1991 has a negative generational account of $80,700 because the present value of transfers (on disability, health, and welfare transfers) far exceeds the present value of taxes.

The final row labelled 'Future' in Table 17.2 gives the generational account for the typical future generation. For future generations, the generational account measures the present value of net payments over their entire lives. Since the same holds for newborns in 1991, the figures for newborns and future generations can be meaningfully compared. As Auerbach et al. (1994, p. 82) point out, there is a striking generational imbalance in US fiscal policy in the sense that future newborns have a generational account of $166,500, which is a whopping $87,600 more than newborns in 1991 have to pay.

Discussion

Buiter (1997) agrees with the proponents of the generational accounting method that the traditional measure of the government deficit is a meaningless indicator for the effects of fiscal policy not only on aggregate demand and private saving but also on the intergenerational distribution of resources. He is nevertheless quite critical of the method of generational accounting. Buiter's objections centre on the following three issues. First, the usefulness of generational accounts "lives or dies with the validity of the life-cycle model" (1997, p. 606), of which the Diamond model is a simple representation. The validity of the life-cycle model depends critically on the following assumptions (which must all hold): (i) households have finite lives, (ii) generations are not linked via operative bequests, and (iii) markets are complete (no borrowing constraints). If condition (ii) is violated and Ricardian equivalence is valid (see Chapter 6), then the generational accounts are completely uninformative about the effect of the government budget on both the intergenerational distribution of resources and on saving (see Buiter, 1997, p. 612 and Bohn, 1992). A similar conclusion follows if condition (iii) is violated and households face binding liquidity constraints because in that case the timing of tax payments over the life cycle matters (in addition to the present value of these taxes).

Second, even if the strict life-cycle model is valid, generational accounts should be interpreted quite carefully. Indeed, existing applications of the generational accounting method say nothing about the intergenerational distribution of benefits from government spending on public goods. Take, for example, the case of a government abatement programme aimed at cleaning up the natural environment. If the environment improves only slowly over time, future generations may be the principal beneficiaries of the policy measure even though the current generations have paid for it. In generational accounts, the tax payments associated with the programme feature prominently but the benefits to future generations are not included.

Third, the method of generational accounting does not take into account the general equilibrium repercussions of alternative budgetary policies. In particular, the method ignores (i) the endogeneity of the various tax (and subsidy) bases and (ii) the endogeneity of pre-tax factor prices and incomes. Buiter gives several examples for which the general equilibrium effects turn out to be quite important (1997, pp. 616–622).[19]

In principle all the issues raised above can be studied with the aid of a computable dynamic general equilibrium model although the construction of such a model is clearly not a trivial task. On the one hand, such models can readily deal with the general equilibrium repercussions of alternative budgetary policies (see Auerbach and Kotlikoff, 1987) and can be extended to include all kinds of market imperfections and alternative intergenerational linkages. On the other hand, there are huge practical difficulties in quantifying the (intergenerational) welfare effects of public spending. In this context, the method of generational accounting is valuable because its data can provide some of the inputs needed for a realistic simulation model.

17.4 Punchlines

In this chapter we study the discrete-time overlapping-generations model that was developed by Diamond and Samuelson. Just as in the Blanchard–Yaari model (studied in the previous chapter), the demographic structure of the population plays a central role in the Diamond–Samuelson model. One of the attractive features of the model is its ability to capture the life-cycle aspects of economic behaviour in an analytically tractable fashion. Because of its flexibility and simplicity, the model has played a central role during the last four decades in such diverse fields as

---

[19] Fehr and Kotlikoff (1995), on the other hand, present a number of general equilibrium examples where the generational accounting method appears to work quite well.

macroeconomics, monetary theory, public finance, international economics, and environmental economics.

We start this chapter by formulating a simplified version of the Diamond–Samuelson model featuring time-separable preferences. In this model households live for two periods, called "youth" and "old age" respectively. They consume during both periods of life but they work only during youth, when they inelastically supply one unit of labour. Young households save part of their labour income in order to finance their consumption during old age (life-cycle saving). In the basic model there is no public debt and household saving takes the form of capital formation. This means that saving by the young in one period equals the capital stock available for production in the next period. Perfectly competitive firms use capital and labour to produce the homogeneous good. The model has a well-defined steady state provided the relevant stability condition is satisfied. There is a distinct possibility of oversaving occurring. Indeed, if the households are relatively patient, and thus have a low rate of time preference, they may well save too much for retirement and thus accumulate too much capital and render the steady state dynamically inefficient.

We next apply the basic model to study the macroeconomic and welfare effects of old-age pensions. Two prototypical pension systems are distinguished, namely the *fully funded* system and the *pay-as-you-go* (PAYG) system. In a fully funded system the government taxes the young, invests the tax receipts in the capital market, and returns principal plus interest to the old in the form of a pension in the next period. The fully funded system is neutral and does not affect consumption, capital, factor prices, or welfare. Intuitively, the household knows that its pension contributions during youth attract the same rate of return as its own private savings. The household therefore does not care that some of its saving is actually carried out on its behalf by the government.

Matters are different under a PAYG system. In such a system the taxes levied on the young are used to finance the pension payments to the old living in the same period. The yield that the household earns on its pension contributions is not the market rate of interest (as in the fully funded system) but rather the rate of population growth. The PAYG system is not neutral. Indeed, the introduction of such a system (or the expansion of an existing one) crowds out capital, lowers the wage rate, and increases the interest rate. Steady-state welfare decreases (increases) if the economy is dynamically efficient (inefficient), i.e. if the interest rate exceeds (falls short of) the rate of population growth. Intuitively, in a dynamically efficient (inefficient) economy, crowding out of capital reduces (increases) the welfare of the generations born in the new steady-state generations.

Two further aspects of the PAYG system are discussed. First, a PAYG system can be reinterpreted as a particular kind of debt policy. Second, in a dynamically efficient economy it is impossible to abolish a pre-existing PAYG system (in favour of a fully funded system) in a Pareto-improving fashion. Intuitively, it is not possible in the standard model to compensate the old generation at the time of the policy initiative without making at least one other (present or future) generation worse off. (Pareto-improving reform may be possible, however, if the reform reduces a pre-existing distortion in the economy. We consider the particular example where labour supply is endogenous and the pension contribution is distorting.)

The basic model can also be used to study the macroeconomic effects of population ageing. A useful measure to characterize the economic impact of demography is the dependency ratio, which is defined as the number of retired people divided by the working-age population. A reduction in the growth rate of the population leads to an increase in the dependency ratio. Under a PAYG system an anticipated reduction in fertility reduces expected pensions and lifetime income, and causes households to increase saving. As a result, the long-run capital-labour ratio rises.

In the second half of the chapter we consider a number of extensions and further applications of the Diamond–Samuelson model. In the first extension we introduce human capital into the model and study the implications for economic growth. Young agents are born with the average stock of currently available knowledge and can spend time during youth engaged in training. Provided the training technology is sufficiently productive, the young choose to accumulate human capital. In the aggregate this mechanism provides the engine of growth for the economy.

In the second extension we augment the human capital model by assuming that the parent must choose the level of training of its offspring. If the parent derives utility from the human capital of its offspring then it is quite possible that the parent will not devote the socially optimal amount of time on training its children. Intuitively, the underinvestment result follows from the fact that the parent fails to take into account all welfare effects (on its children and grandchildren) of its training efforts. In such a situation it may well be socially optimal to have a system of mandatory public education.

In the third extension we show how public infrastructure can be introduced into the overlapping generations model. We show how public investment affects the macroeconomy and derive simple modified-golden-rule expressions calling for an equalization of the rate of return on public and private capital and the social planner's rate of time preference. In the final extension we illustrate and evaluate the pros and cons of the method of generational accounting in the context of a simple Diamond–Samuelson model.

Further reading

Classic papers on pensions are Samuelson (1975a, b) and Feldstein (1974, 1976, 1985, 1987). In recent years a large literature has been developed on the issue of pension system reform. See Diamond (1997, 1999), Feldstein (1997, 1998), and Sinn (2000). For a recent survey on the economic effects of ageing, see Bosworth and Burtless (1998).

The Diamond–Samuelson model has been generalized in a number of directions. Barro (1974) studies intergenerational linkages. Jones and Manuelli (1992) consider the growth effects of finite lives. Tirole (1985) and O'Connell and Zeldes (1988) consider the possibility of asset bubbles. Grandmont (1985) presents a model exhibiting endogenous business cycles. Michel and de la Croix (2000) study the model properties under both myopic foresight and perfect foresight. Bierwag, Grove, and Khang (1969) show that a full set of age-specific taxes renders debt policy redundant. Abel (1986) and Zilcha (1990, 1991) introduce uncertainty into the model. On intergenerational risk sharing, see Gordon and Varian (1988). Barro and Becker (1989) present a model of endogenous fertility. For applications of endogenous fertility models, see Wildasin (1990), Zhang (1995), Robinson and Srinivasan (1997), and Nerlove and Raut (1997). Galor (1992) and Nourry (2001) study a two-sector version of the Diamond–Samuelson model.

The Diamond–Samuelson model has been applied in a large number of fields. For public finance applications, see Auerbach (1979a), Kotlikoff and Summers (1979), and Ihori (1996). On the economics of education, see Loury (1981), Glomm and Ravikumar (1992), Zhang (1996), Buiter and Kletzer (1993), and Kaganovich and Zilcha (1999). Environmental policy applications include Howarth (1991, 1998), Howarth and Norgaard (1990, 1992), John and Pecchenino (1994), John et al. (1995), and Mourmouras (1993).

There is a large literature on generational accounting. Some key references are Auerbach, Gokhale, and Kotlikoff (1991, 1994), Kotlikoff (1993a, b), and Fehr and Kotlikoff (1995). For critical papers on the topic, see Bohn (1992), Haveman (1994), and Buiter (1997). International applications of the method are collected in Auerbach, Kotlikoff, and Leibfritz (1999).

Epilogue

Changes

The field of macroeconomics has certainly changed a lot over the past twenty five years. When we took our first courses in macroeconomics in the mid-1970s, the leading textbooks were Branson (1972) at the intermediate level and Turnovsky (1977) at the graduate end of the spectrum. Both of these books contain extensive treatments of the IS-LM model and all its variations and extensions. In contrast, at the beginning of the new millennium, though the IS-LM model is still treated in most intermediate texts, it has vanished almost completely from the advanced texts.[1]

A comparison between the past and the present thus reveals that the once dominant IS–LM model, with its emphasis on the demand side of the economy, has fallen on hard times in recent years. There is no doubt that the rational expectations revolution of the 1970s has a lot to do with the reduced role of the IS-LM model. In part as a result of this revolution, macroeconomists started to develop dynamic models which are based on explicit microeconomic foundations and give more attention to the supply side of the economy. Modern graduate textbooks therefore contain extensive discussions of dynamically optimizing representative agents (households, firms, the government) endowed with perfect foresight (or rational expectations).[2]

To outsiders it may appear that macroeconomics is a field in disarray, with proponents of two competing approaches battling it out to achieve the position once held by the IS-LM model. According to this view, current macroeconomics is somewhat like a boxing match. In the blue corner of the boxing ring, we find the "new classicals" who stress flexible prices and wages and emphasize market clearing. In the red corner we find the "new Keynesians" who like to work with models incorporating sticky prices and wages and are willing to assume various degrees of market imperfection.

---

[1] Most intermediate texts still make use of the IS-LM model. See e.g. Mankiw (2000a) and Blanchard (2000a). Most graduate texts barely mention the IS-LM model. See Romer (2001), Turnovsky (1997, 2000), and Ljungqvist and Sargent (2000).

[2] Intermediate texts incorporating the optimization approach are Barro (1997) and Auerbach and Kotlikoff (1998).

Even though this picture of macroeconomics as a boxing match may bear some similarity with the reality of the late 1970s through to the early 1990s, we agree with Goodfriend and King (1997) who argue that the subject has been moving towards a new synthesis over the last decade or so. Goodfriend and King (1997, p. 255) identify the key aspects of, what they call, the New Neoclassical Synthesis (NNS):

- The NNS takes from the new classicals the notion that macroeconomic models should be explicitly dynamic, and should incorporate rational expectations and intertemporal optimization.
- The NNS takes from the new Keynesians the assumptions of imperfect competition and costly price adjustment.
- The NNS takes from the RBC approach the insistence on quantitative models of economic fluctuations.

Just like the old neoclassical synthesis (see Chapter 1), the NNS thus contains elements from new classicals and new Keynesians alike. Instead of as a boxing match, it appears as if the current intellectual debate in macroeconomics is more aptly characterized as a tango. In one sense this is true. For example, there is not much debate about the usefulness of the rational expectations hypothesis any more. Similarly, economists of all signatures routinely construct models based on dynamically optimizing behaviour of the economic agents. In another sense the metaphor of macroeconomics as a tango is somewhat flawed.

In his comment on Goodfriend and King (1997), Blanchard (1997) agrees that macroeconomists need to use three ingredients to study economic fluctuations, namely intertemporal optimization, nominal rigidities, and imperfect competition. He argues that putting together these ingredients and understanding their interaction constitutes the core business of all macroeconomists.[3] He goes on to argue that what distinguishes us macroeconomists is the relative weight one places on the different ingredients and the short-cuts one is willing to make.

Blanchard suggests that a useful way to think about these ingredients (and their interaction) is by means of a triangle, like in Figure E.1. In the top corner one could place the approach of Prescott (1986) with its emphasis on dynamically optimizing behaviour. In the bottom left corner one could place the approaches of Fischer (1977) and Taylor (1980) which emphasize nominal wage or price stickiness. Finally, in the bottom right corner one could think of Blanchard and Kiyotaki (1987) and Akerlof and Yellen (1985a) who focus on imperfections in the goods and labour markets.

Blanchard argues that most economists are located somewhere in the triangle, but he finds it an overstatement to infer from this phenomenon that a synthesis has

[3] Blanchard (1997, p. 290) argues that this is exactly what the "old" neoclassical synthesis was all about: "In rather schizophrenic fashion, intertemporal optimization was at the core of the formalization of consumption and investment, imperfect competition the underlying rationale for markup pricing, and nominal rigidities used as a general justification for the Phillips curve. Since then, we have tried to improve on the shortcomings. But the goal is the same".

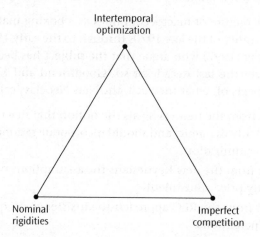

Figure E.1. Aspects of macro models

been achieved. The triangle is not a small one and diverse views can be accommodated within its boundaries. In particular, economists with classical leanings would probably locate themselves in the top half of the triangle whereas their Keynes-inspired colleagues would be more comfortably located in the bottom half of the triangle. To the extent that there is a synthesis, it mainly refers to methods and not to particular applications of these methods.

Threads

Blanchard's triangle is quite useful for showing how the topics in this book fit together. To prepare students for the explicitly dynamic framework adopted in the later chapters of the book we start in Chapter 2 by studying the intrinsic dynamics that exist in IS-LM type models. The choice of the IS-LM model as a vehicle of exposition is a natural one in view of the fact that this model is still used widely in the intermediate textbooks (see above). Chapter 2 also presents a first view of the dynamic optimization approach in the form of Tobin's q theory of investment which is based on the notion of adjustment costs of investment. This investment theory is extended in Chapter 4 and applied in Chapters 14, 16, and 17.

Chapter 3 follows logically from Chapter 2 and shows some of the key implications of the rational expectations hypothesis (REH) within the context of (loglinear) IS-LM models. This chapter and the next also alert students to the crucial difference that exists between backward-looking and forward-looking stability. Both types of stability are encountered in the later chapters of the book within the context of dynamically optimizing models.

In Chapter 5 the student has a first encounter with nominal rigidities and with micro-based macroeconomics. The IS-LM model is no longer used and the behavioural equations of households and firms are based on maximizing behaviour. Some of the insights from the quantity rationing literature are further developed in Chapter 13, where we show how the assumption of imperfect competition in the goods market can, in combination with price adjustment costs, provide a rationale for price stickiness.

In Chapter 6 we present the student with a first view of intertemporal consumption theory. This chapter allows us to familiarize the student with important notions such as the Ricardian Equivalence Theorem and the neoclassical theory of tax smoothing within a relatively simple model. In addition, the student has a first encounter with the notion of intertemporal substitution of consumption. The intertemporal household model is further extended in the later chapters of the book.

In Chapters 7–9 we present the various theories concerning the aggregate labour market. We first show how the competitive model can be used to interpret various features of the labour market. Next we show how imperfect competition (in the form of trade unions) and other kinds of imperfections (such as informational frictions) impinge on this market.

Chapter 10 introduces the notion of dynamic inconsistency, especially as it applies to economic policy. This chapter is a logical sequel to Chapter 3, and shows yet another implication of the REH, namely that economic policy may not be credible to the economic agents affected by it. Note that the credibility problem did not arise in the pre-REH literature because there agents were typically assumed to form expectations adaptively, i.e. not taking into account the structure of the economic environment. In this chapter we also show how an intertemporal reputation mechanism can potentially resolve the problem of dynamic inconsistency.

In Chapter 11 we tie up some loose ends held over from the first ten chapters. First we extend the analysis from Chapter 1 by showing how the standard IS–LM can be opened up for trade in goods and financial assets. Next we study the transmission of monetary and fiscal policy in a two-country world experiencing various kinds of labour market rigidities (i.e. real or nominal wage rigidity). Finally, we show the main implications for prices, output, and exchange rate fluctuations of introducing rational expectations (or, rather, perfect foresight) in the open economy IS-LM model.

In Chapter 12 we discuss a number of micro-founded models of money based on intertemporal optimization by households. This chapter also allows us to introduce the student to a simple model of money demand based on uncertainty. Finally, we study the optimal quantity of money (and Friedman's famous "full liquidity rule") within the context of a simple dynamic model. Together with Chapter 6, this chapter forms the stepping stone for the multi-period dynamic analyses which are found in Chapter 14–17.

In Chapter 13 we discuss some of the recent literature on new Keynesian economics. As was pointed out above, new Keynesians can be placed somewhere in the bottom half of the Blanchard triangle so it is not surprising that the chapter features an extensive discussion of imperfect competition and price stickiness. We show how the assumption of monopolistic competition in the goods market can provide the micro-foundations for the multiplier. We also demonstrate with the aid of an explicitly forward-looking theory of firm behaviour how price adjustment costs can provide the microeconomic foundations behind short-term price stickiness.

In Chapter 14 we present a brief overview of the main theories of economic growth that have been developed over the last forty-five years. We start with the classic analysis of Solow and Swan which is based on a Keynesian savings function. Next we replace the ad hoc savings function by explicitly modelling the consumption-savings decisions of an infinitely lived representative household. (This chapter thus completes our discussion of the forward-looking theory of consumption commenced in Chapter 6.) The growth properties of the model are not much affected by this switch to a micro-based savings theory. Once the theory with forward-looking consumers has been developed, it is relatively straightforward to show how endogenous human capital accumulation or the accumulation of patents (and new product varieties) can give rise to so-called endogenous growth.

In Chapter 15 we give a brief overview of the recent RBC literature. Especially the early proponents to this approach are firmly located in the top half of the Blanchard triangle. More recently RBC practitioners have started to explore the interior parts of the triangle. We start this chapter by extending the dynamic consumption theory (of the previous chapter) to include a joint decision regarding the consumption of goods and leisure. In the extended model the household substitutes leisure across time, i.e. there is an intertemporal substitution effect in the supply of labour. We demonstrate the macroeconomic implications of this intertemporal labour supply effect both for deterministic shocks in government consumption (fiscal policy) and for stochastic technology shocks.

In Chapters 16–17 we study the macroeconomic and welfare-theoretic implications of abandoning the representative-agent framework on the household side. In both chapters we assume that individual households have finite lives and that they are not linked with each other via operative bequests. The resulting overlapping-generations structure implies another kind of imperfection, namely the incompleteness of markets. At any point in time, only the currently living generations are active in the market place but their economic behaviour affects the conditions facing future generations. This property of overlapping-generations models implies that virtually all policy measures affect both efficiency and the intergenerational distribution of resources.

Views

To the astute observer it is clear from our choice of topics where we ourselves are located within the Blanchard triangle—somewhere in the middle. We conclude this book with some final observations on what in our view constitutes macroeconomics and what we expect to be major themes in the years to come.

We find it a bad idea to scrap models merely because their micro-foundations are unavailable or incomplete. Although we acknowledge that a micro-based model is aesthetically pleasing, a weakly founded model may better capture pertinent aspects of the world we happen to live in than a model with the wrong micro-foundations. There is, for example, ample evidence suggesting that nominal prices and/or wages are rigid (see e.g. Blinder, 1994 and Bewley, 1999), that current income is a strong determinant of consumption (Mankiw, 2000b), and that agents do "suffer" from money illusion (Shafir et al., 1997). Furthermore, as is demonstrated by Galí (1992), the ad hoc IS-LM-AS model does quite a decent job at matching postwar US data. It seems to us that a good macro model should pay attention to this kind of evidence.

Another reason for tolerating weakly founded models is that it may well be possible eventually to come up with credible microeconomic foundations for such models. In this context one can think of the remarkable comeback (like Phoenix from its ashes) of the IS-LM model initiated by McCallum and Nelson (1999). We suspect that large advances will be made in the coming years on the link between the microeconometric evidence and their macroeconomic implications (cf. the plea in this direction by Browning et al., 1999). With the ongoing technological advance in computing hardware and software, it will be feasible to strengthen the empirical content of computable equilibrium models by paying more attention to agent heterogeneity, market imperfections, and nominal rigidities.

In our view, good macroeconomics is not designed from the armchair and blindly following some simple methodological prescriptions will not lead to good policy advice. Macroeconomics is not only a science but also an art form. This book focuses merely on one of the necessary skills that any good macroeconomist should possess, namely a firm grasp of the technical tools of the trade. The other skills that are needed are a good understanding of the empirical evidence, of actual institutions, and of history. Some of the best macro theoreticians have also made their mark in applied macroeconomics and in policy circles. Names that spring to mind in this context are John Maynard Keynes (him again), Robert Mundell, Stanley Fischer, Rudiger Dornbusch, Larry Summers, Michael Bruno, and Joe Stiglitz. A good macroeconomist should not be blind to the real world and periodicals such as *The Economist*, the *Brookings Papers on Economic Activity*, and *Economic Policy* should feature prominently in the macro curriculum. By reading the works of the great macroeconomic artists, the tools discussed in this book should come to life.

Mathematical Appendix

A.1 Introduction

In this mathematical appendix we give a brief overview of the main techniques that are used in this book. In order to preserve space, for most cases we simply state the results and refer the interested reader to various sources—of differing levels of sophistication—where the mathematical background for these results is explained in more detail. The transform methods used in sections A.6.1 and A.7.2 are explained in more detail because they are somewhat unfamiliar to most economists. Klein (1998) and Pemberton and Rau (2001) are both good single sources for the mathematical techniques employed in this book, both in terms of coverage and the level of sophistication. Sydsæter et al. (2000) is a very convenient reference book describing most of the tricks used by economists.

A.2 Matrix Algebra

A.2.1 General

A *matrix* is a rectangular array of numbers a_{ij} where $i = 1, 2, \ldots, m$ is the row index and $j = 1, 2, \ldots, n$ is the column index. A matrix of dimension m by n thus has m rows and n columns:

$$A_{m \times n} \equiv \begin{bmatrix} a_{11} & a_{12} & \cdots & \cdots & a_{1n} \\ a_{21} & a_{22} & \cdots & \cdots & a_{2n} \\ \vdots & \vdots & \vdots & \vdots & \vdots \\ a_{m1} & a_{m2} & \cdots & \cdots & a_{mn} \end{bmatrix}. \tag{A.1}$$

If $m = n = 1$ then A is a *scalar*, if $m = 1$ and $n > 1$ it is *row vector*, and if $n = 1$ and $m > 1$ it is a *column vector*. If $m = n$ then the matrix A is *square* and we call the diagonal containing the elements $a_{11}, a_{22}, \ldots, a_{nn}$ the *principal diagonal*. There are a number of special matrices. The *zero matrix* contains only elements equal to zero

($a_{ij} = 0$ for $i = 1, 2, \ldots, m$ and $j = 1, 2, \ldots, n$). The *identity matrix*, I_n is a square n by n matrix with ones on the principal diagonal and zeros elsewhere.

A.2.2 Addition, subtraction, multiplication

Two matrices A and B can be added if and only if they have the same dimension. If A has elements $[a_{ij}]$ and B has elements $[b_{ij}]$ then the matrix $C \equiv A + B$ is obtained by adding corresponding elements:

$$A + B = C, \quad \text{with } c_{ij} = a_{ij} + b_{ij}, \tag{A.2}$$

for $i = 1, 2, \ldots, m$ and $j = 1, 2, \ldots, n$. Subtracting matrices works the same way:

$$A - B = D, \quad \text{with } d_{ij} = a_{ij} - b_{ij}, \tag{A.3}$$

for $i = 1, 2, \ldots, m$ and $j = 1, 2, \ldots, n$.

Matrices can be multiplied by a scalar, k, by multiplying all elements of the matrix by that scalar, i.e. $B \equiv kA$ then $b_{ij} \equiv ka_{ij}$ for $i = 1, 2, \ldots, m$ and $j = 1, 2, \ldots, n$. Some rules and properties follow immediately (k and l are both scalars):

$$
\begin{aligned}
kA &= Ak \\
k(A + B) &= kA + kB \\
(k + l)A &= kA + lA \\
(kl)A &= k(lA) \\
(-1)A &= -A \\
A + (-1)B &= A - B.
\end{aligned}
\tag{A.4}
$$

Two matrices can be multiplied if they are *conformable* for that operation. The matrix product AB is defined if the column dimension of the matrix on the left (matrix A) is the same as the row dimension of the matrix on the right (the B matrix). If A is m by r and B is r by n then by this rule AB is defined as follows:

$$AB = C, \quad c_{ij} = \sum_{k=1}^{r} a_{ik} b_{kj}, \tag{A.5}$$

for $i = 1, 2, \ldots, m$ and $j = 1, 2, \ldots, n$. Unless $m = n$ the product BA is not defined. Even if BA is defined it is not equal to AB in general. So premultiplying B by A (yielding AB) does not give the same matrix in general as premultiplying A by B (an operation yielding BA). Some properties of matrix multiplication are the following (A, B, and C are conformable matrices, 0 is the zero matrix, and k is a scalar):

$$
\begin{aligned}
A(B + C) &= AB + AC \\
(A + B)C &= AC + AB \\
A(BC) &= (AB)C \\
k(AB) &= A(kB) \\
A0 &= 0A = 0 \\
AI &= IA = A
\end{aligned}
\tag{A.6}
$$

A.2.3 Transposition

The *transpose* of matrix A is denoted by A^T (or sometimes by A'). It is obtained by interchanging the rows and columns of matrix A. Hence, if A is m by n and $B \equiv A^T$ then B is n by m and $b_{ij} \equiv a_{ji}$. Some properties of transposes are:

$$
\begin{aligned}
(A^T)^T &= A \\
(kA)^T &= kA^T \\
(A + B)^T &= A^T + B^T \\
(AB)^T &= B^T A^T
\end{aligned}
\tag{A.7}
$$

A.2.4 Square matrices

In this subsection we gather the key results pertaining to square matrices (for which the row and column dimensions are the same). The *trace* of the n by n matrix A, denoted by $\text{tr}(A)$, is the sum of the elements on its principal diagonal:

$$
\text{tr}(A) \equiv \sum_{i=1}^{n} a_{ii}.
\tag{A.8}
$$

The following properties can be derived:

$$
\begin{aligned}
\text{tr}(I_n) &= n \\
\text{tr}(0) &= 0 \\
\text{tr}(A^T) &= \text{tr}(A) \\
\text{tr}(AA^T) &= \text{tr}(A^T A) = \sum_{i=1}^{n} \sum_{j=1}^{n} a_{ij}^2 \\
\text{tr}(kA) &= k\text{tr}(A) \\
\text{tr}(AB) &= \text{tr}(BA)
\end{aligned}
\tag{A.9}
$$

The *determinant* of a square matrix A, denoted by $|A|$ (sometimes by $\det(A)$) is a unique scalar associated with that matrix. For a two-by-two matrix the determinant is:

$$
A \equiv \begin{bmatrix} a_{11} & a_{12} \\ a_{21} & a_{22} \end{bmatrix}, \quad |A| \equiv a_{11}a_{22} - a_{12}a_{21}.
\tag{A.10}
$$

For a three-by-three matrix the determinant can be computed as follows:

$$
|A| \equiv \begin{vmatrix} a_{11} & a_{12} & a_{13} \\ a_{21} & a_{22} & a_{23} \\ a_{31} & a_{32} & a_{33} \end{vmatrix} = a_{11} \begin{vmatrix} a_{22} & a_{23} \\ a_{32} & a_{33} \end{vmatrix} - a_{12} \begin{vmatrix} a_{21} & a_{23} \\ a_{31} & a_{33} \end{vmatrix} + a_{13} \begin{vmatrix} a_{21} & a_{22} \\ a_{31} & a_{32} \end{vmatrix}
$$

$$
= a_{11} \left[a_{22}a_{33} - a_{23}a_{32} \right] - a_{12} \left[a_{21}a_{33} - a_{23}a_{31} \right] + a_{13} \left[a_{21}a_{32} - a_{22}a_{31} \right]
$$

$$
= a_{11}a_{22}a_{33} - a_{11}a_{23}a_{32} - a_{12}a_{21}a_{33} + a_{12}a_{23}a_{31} + a_{13}a_{21}a_{32} - a_{13}a_{22}a_{31}.
\tag{A.11}
$$

We have computed $|A|$ by going along the first row and seeking two-by-two determinants associated with each element on that first row. For element a_{11} we find the associated two-by-two determinant by deleting the row and column in which a_{11} is located. The resulting two-by-two determinant is called the *minor* of element a_{11}. In a similar fashion, the minor of element a_{12} is found by deleting row 1 and column 2 from the original determinant, and the minor of a_{13} is obtained by deleting row 1 and column 3 from the original determinant. Denoting the minor of element a_{ij} by $|M_{ij}|$ we can define the *cofactor* of that element by $|C_{ij}| = (-1)^{i+j} |M_{ij}|$. A cofactor is a minor with a sign in front of it. The sign is determined as follows: if the sum of the row and column indices $(i + j)$ is even, then the sign is positive and the cofactor is equal to the minor. Conversely, if $i + j$ is uneven, then the cofactor is minus the minor. Using these definitions we can now see that the determinant of the three-by-three matrix in (A.11) can be written as: $|A| \equiv a_{11} |C_{11}| + a_{12} |C_{12}| + a_{13} |C_{13}| = \sum_{j=1}^{3} a_{1j} |C_{1j}|$. Of course, we could have computed $|A|$ by going along row 2 ($|A| = \sum_{j=1}^{3} a_{2j} |C_{2j}|$) or row 3 ($|A| = \sum_{j=1}^{3} a_{3j} |C_{3j}|$) or by going along any of the columns of the original determinant ($|A| = \sum_{i=1}^{3} a_{ij} |C_{ij}|$ for $j = 1, 2, 3$). It is not difficult to verify that in each case we would have found the same value for $|A|$.

The procedure we have just followed to compute $|A|$ is called a *Laplace expansion*. The Laplace expansion of an n by n matrix is given by:

$$|A| = \sum_{i=1}^{n} a_{ij} |C_{ij}|, \quad \text{for } j = 1, \dots, n \quad \text{(column expansion)}, \tag{A.12}$$

$$= \sum_{j=1}^{n} a_{ij} |C_{ij}|, \quad \text{for } i = 1, \dots, n \quad \text{(row expansion)}, \tag{A.13}$$

The determinant has a number of useful properties (k is scalar):

$$
\begin{aligned}
&|I| = 1 \\
&|0| = 0 \\
&|A| = |A^T| \\
&|A| = (-1)^n |-A| = k^{-n} |kA| \\
&|AB| = |BA|
\end{aligned}
\tag{A.14}
$$

- If any row (column) is a non-trivial linear combination of all the other rows (columns) of A then $|A| = 0$.
- If B results from A by interchanging two rows (or columns) then $|B| = -|A|$.
- If B results from A by multiplying one row (or one column) by k then $|B| = k|A|$.
- The addition (subtraction) of a multiple of any row to (from) another row leaves $|A|$ unchanged.
- The addition (subtraction) of a multiple of any column to (from) another column leaves $|A|$ unchanged.

The *adjoint matrix* of matrix A is denoted by adj A. It is defined as the transposed matrix of cofactors:

$$\text{adj}\,A \equiv \begin{bmatrix} |C_{11}| & |C_{12}| & \cdots & \cdots & |C_{1n}| \\ |C_{21}| & |C_{22}| & \cdots & \cdots & |C_{2n}| \\ \vdots & \vdots & \vdots & \vdots & \vdots \\ |C_{n1}| & |C_{n2}| & \cdots & \cdots & |C_{nn}| \end{bmatrix}^{T} \tag{A.15}$$

If $|A| \neq 0$ then the matrix A is *non-singular* and possesses a unique *inverse*, denoted by A^{-1}:

$$A^{-1} = \frac{1}{|A|}\text{adj}\,A. \tag{A.16}$$

If the matrix A has an inverse it follows that $A^{-1}A = AA^{-1} = I$.

Intermezzo

Matrix inversion. For example, let A be:

$$A \equiv \begin{bmatrix} 1 & 2 \\ 3 & 4 \end{bmatrix},$$

then we find by applying the rules that $|A| = 4 - 6 = -2$ (non-singular matrix) so that the inverse matrix exists and is equal to:

$$A^{-1} = \frac{1}{-2}\begin{bmatrix} 4 & -2 \\ -3 & 1 \end{bmatrix} = \begin{bmatrix} -2 & 1 \\ \frac{3}{2} & -\frac{1}{2} \end{bmatrix}.$$

To check that we have not made any mistakes we compute AA^{-1} and $A^{-1}A$ (both should equal the identity matrix).

$$AA^{-1} = \begin{bmatrix} 1 & 2 \\ 3 & 4 \end{bmatrix}\begin{bmatrix} -2 & 1 \\ \frac{3}{2} & -\frac{1}{2} \end{bmatrix}$$

$$= \begin{bmatrix} -2 + 2\left(\frac{3}{2}\right) & 1 + 2\left(-\frac{1}{2}\right) \\ -6 + 4\left(\frac{3}{2}\right) & 3 + 2\left(-\frac{1}{2}\right) \end{bmatrix} = \begin{bmatrix} 1 & 0 \\ 0 & 1 \end{bmatrix}$$

$$A^{-1}A = \begin{bmatrix} -2 & 1 \\ \frac{3}{2} & -\frac{1}{2} \end{bmatrix}\begin{bmatrix} 1 & 2 \\ 3 & 4 \end{bmatrix}$$

$$= \begin{bmatrix} -2 + 3 & -4 + 4 \\ 1\left(\frac{3}{2}\right) - 3\left(\frac{1}{2}\right) & 2\left(\frac{3}{2}\right) + 4\left(-\frac{1}{2}\right) \end{bmatrix} = \begin{bmatrix} 1 & 0 \\ 0 & 1 \end{bmatrix}$$

Assuming that the indicated inverses exist (and the matrices A and B are thus non-singular), we find the following properties:

$$I^{-1} = I$$
$$(A^{-1})^{-1} = A$$
$$(A^T)^{-1} = (A^{-1})^T \tag{A.17}$$
$$(AB)^{-1} = B^{-1}A^{-1}$$
$$|A^{-1}| = |A|^{-1}$$

A.2.5 Cramer's Rule

Suppose we have a linear system of n equations in n unknowns:

$$
\begin{aligned}
a_{11}x_1 + a_{12}x_2 + \cdots + a_{1n}x_n &= b_1 \\
a_{21}x_1 + a_{22}x_2 + \cdots + a_{2n}x_n &= b_2 \\
\vdots\ &=\ \vdots \\
a_{n1}x_1 + a_{n2}x_2 + \cdots + a_{nn}x_n &= b_n
\end{aligned}
\tag{A.18}
$$

where a_{ij} are the coefficients, b_i are the exogenous variables, and x_i are the endogenous variables. We can write this system in the form of a single matrix equation as:

$$Ax = b, \tag{A.19}$$

where A is an n by n matrix, and x and b are n by 1 (column) vectors:

$$
A \equiv \begin{bmatrix}
a_{11} & a_{12} & \cdots & \cdots & a_{1n} \\
a_{21} & a_{22} & \cdots & \cdots & a_{2n} \\
\vdots & \vdots & \vdots & \vdots & \vdots \\
a_{n1} & a_{n2} & \cdots & \cdots & a_{nn}
\end{bmatrix}, \quad
x \equiv \begin{bmatrix}
x_1 \\ x_2 \\ \vdots \\ x_n
\end{bmatrix}, \quad
b \equiv \begin{bmatrix}
b_1 \\ b_2 \\ \vdots \\ b_n
\end{bmatrix}.
\tag{A.20}
$$

Provided the coefficient matrix A is non-singular (so that $|A| \neq 0$) the solution of the matrix equation is:

$$x = A^{-1}b. \tag{A.21}$$

Instead of inverting the entire matrix A we can find the solutions for individual variables by means of *Cramer's Rule* (which only involves determinants):

$$x_j = \frac{|A_j|}{|A|}, \quad \text{for } j = 1, 2, \ldots, n \tag{A.22}$$

where $|A_j|$ is the determinant of the matrix A_j which is obtained by replacing column j of A by the vector of exogenous variables, for example A_1 is:

$$A_1 \equiv \begin{bmatrix} b_1 & a_{12} & a_{13} & \cdots & a_{1n} \\ b_2 & a_{22} & a_{23} & \cdots & a_{2n} \\ \vdots & \vdots & \vdots & \vdots & \vdots \\ b_n & a_{n2} & a_{n3} & \cdots & a_{nn} \end{bmatrix}. \tag{A.23}$$

If the vector b consists entirely of zeros we call the system *homogeneous*. If $|A| \neq 0$ then the unique solution to the matrix equation is the trivial one: $x = A^{-1}b = 0$. The only way to get a non-trivial solution to a homogeneous system is if the coefficient matrix is singular, i.e. if $|A| = 0$. In that case Cramer's Rule cannot be used. An infinite number of solutions nevertheless exist (including the trivial one) in that case. Take, for example, the following homogeneous system:

$$\begin{bmatrix} 1 & 2 \\ 2 & 4 \end{bmatrix} \begin{bmatrix} x_1 \\ x_2 \end{bmatrix} = \begin{bmatrix} 0 \\ 0 \end{bmatrix}. \tag{A.24}$$

Clearly, $|A| = 4 - 4 = 0$ so the system is singular (row 2 is two times row 1). Nevertheless, both the trivial solution ($x_1 = x_2 = 0$) and an infinite number of non-trivial solutions (any combination for which $x_1 + 2x_2 = 0$) exist. Intuitively, we have infinitely many solutions because we have a single equation but two unknowns.

A.2.6 Characteristic roots and vectors

A characteristic vector of an n by n matrix A is a non-zero vector x which, when premultiplied by A yields a multiple of the same vector:

$$Ax = \lambda x, \tag{A.25}$$

where λ is called the *characteristic root* (or *eigenvalue*) of A. By rewriting equation (A.25) we find:

$$(\lambda I - A)x = 0, \tag{A.26}$$

which constitutes a homogeneous system of equations which has non-trivial solutions provided the determinant of its coefficient matrix, $\lambda I - A$, is zero:

$$|\lambda I - A| = 0 \tag{A.27}$$

This expression is called the *characteristic equation* of A. For a 2 by 2 matrix the characteristic equation can be written as:

$$|A - \lambda I| = \begin{bmatrix} \lambda - a_{11} & a_{12} \\ a_{21} & \lambda - a_{22} \end{bmatrix} = (\lambda - a_{11})(\lambda - a_{22}) - a_{12}a_{21}$$

$$= \lambda^2 - (a_{11} + a_{22})\lambda + a_{11}a_{22} - a_{12}a_{21}$$

$$= \lambda^2 - \text{tr}(A)\lambda + |A| = 0, \tag{A.28}$$

where tr(A) and |A| are, respectively, the trace and the determinant of matrix A. Hence, for such a matrix the characteristic equation is quadratic in λ and thus possesses two roots:

$$\lambda_{1,2} = \frac{\text{tr}(A) \pm \sqrt{[\text{tr}(A)]^2 - 4|A|}}{2}. \tag{A.29}$$

These roots are distinct if the discriminant, $[\text{tr}(A)]^2 - 4|A|$, is non-zero. They are real (rather than complex) if the discriminant is positive (this is certainly the case if $|A| < 0$). For an n by n matrix the characteristic equation is an n-th order polynomial with n roots, $\lambda_1, \lambda_2, \ldots, \lambda_n$ which may not all be distinct or real. Some properties of characteristic roots are:

$$\begin{aligned} \sum_{i=1}^{n} \lambda_i &= \text{tr}(A) \\ \prod_{i=1}^{n} \lambda_i &= |A| \end{aligned} \tag{A.30}$$

Associated with each characteristic root is a *characteristic vector* (or *eigenvector*), which is unique up to a constant. The characteristic vector $x^{(i)}$ associated with λ_i solves (A.26). If a matrix has distinct characteristic roots then it can be *diagonalized* as follows:

$$P^{-1}AP = \Lambda \quad \Leftrightarrow \quad A = P\Lambda P^{-1}, \tag{A.31}$$

where P is the matrix with the characteristic vectors, $x^{(i)}$, as columns and Λ is the diagonal matrix with characteristic roots, λ_i, on the principal diagonal. Diagonalization is useful in the context of difference and differential equations—see Chapter 2 and below.

Intermezzo

Eigenvalues, eigenvectors, and matrix diagonalization. Suppose that A is defined as:

$$A = \begin{bmatrix} 6 & 10 \\ -2 & -3 \end{bmatrix}.$$

The characteristic equation is $\lambda^2 - 3\lambda + 2 = (\lambda - 1)(\lambda - 2) = 0$ so that the characteristic roots are $\lambda_1 = 1$ and $\lambda_2 = 2$. The characteristic vector associated with λ_1 is obtained by noting from (A.26) that:

$$(\lambda_1 I - A)x = 0$$

$$\left(\begin{bmatrix} 1 & 0 \\ 0 & 1 \end{bmatrix} - \begin{bmatrix} 6 & 10 \\ -2 & -3 \end{bmatrix} \right) \begin{bmatrix} x_1 \\ x_2 \end{bmatrix} = \begin{bmatrix} 0 \\ 0 \end{bmatrix}$$

$$\begin{bmatrix} -5 & -10 \\ 2 & 4 \end{bmatrix} \begin{bmatrix} x_1 \\ x_2 \end{bmatrix} = \begin{bmatrix} 0 \\ 0 \end{bmatrix}.$$

Any solution for which $2x_1 + 4x_2 = 0$ will do. Hence, by setting $x_1 = c$ (a non-zero constant) we find that $x_2 = -c/2$ so that the characteristic vector associated with λ_1 is:

$$x^{(1)} \equiv \begin{bmatrix} c \\ -c/2 \end{bmatrix}.$$

Similarly, for $\lambda_2 = 2$ we find:

$$(\lambda_2 I - A)x = 0$$

$$\left(\begin{bmatrix} 2 & 0 \\ 0 & 2 \end{bmatrix} - \begin{bmatrix} 6 & 10 \\ -2 & -3 \end{bmatrix} \right) \begin{bmatrix} x_1 \\ x_2 \end{bmatrix} = \begin{bmatrix} 0 \\ 0 \end{bmatrix}$$

$$\begin{bmatrix} -4 & -10 \\ 2 & 5 \end{bmatrix} \begin{bmatrix} x_1 \\ x_2 \end{bmatrix} = \begin{bmatrix} 0 \\ 0 \end{bmatrix}.$$

Any combination for which $2x_1 + 5x_2 = 0$ will do. Hence, the characteristic vector associated with λ_2 is:

$$x^{(2)} \equiv \begin{bmatrix} c \\ -2c/5 \end{bmatrix}.$$

In the example matrix we have:

$$P \equiv \begin{bmatrix} c & c \\ -c/2 & -2c/5 \end{bmatrix} \quad \text{and} \quad \Lambda \equiv \begin{bmatrix} 1 & 0 \\ 0 & 2 \end{bmatrix},$$

from which we verify the result:

$$P\Lambda P^{-1} = \frac{10}{c^2} \begin{bmatrix} c & c \\ -c/2 & -2c/5 \end{bmatrix} \begin{bmatrix} 1 & 0 \\ 0 & 2 \end{bmatrix} \begin{bmatrix} -2c/5 & -c \\ c/2 & c \end{bmatrix}$$

$$= 10 \begin{bmatrix} 1 & 1 \\ -1/2 & -2/5 \end{bmatrix} \begin{bmatrix} 1 & 0 \\ 0 & 2 \end{bmatrix} \begin{bmatrix} -2/5 & -1 \\ 1/2 & 1 \end{bmatrix}$$

$$= 10 \begin{bmatrix} 1 & 2 \\ -1/2 & -4/5 \end{bmatrix} \begin{bmatrix} -2/5 & -1 \\ 1/2 & 1 \end{bmatrix} = 10 \begin{bmatrix} 3/5 & 1 \\ -1/5 & -3/10 \end{bmatrix} = A$$

It works!

A.2.7 Literature

Basic: Klein (1998, chs. 4–5), Chiang (1984, chs. 4–5), Sydsæter and Hammond (1995, chs. 12–14). Intermediate: Intriligator (1971, appendix B), Kreyszig (1999, chs. 6–7), and Strang (1988). Advanced: Ayres (1974), Lancaster and Tismenetsky (1985), and Ortega (1987).

A.3 Implicit Function Theorem

A.3.1 Single equation

Suppose we have the following equation relating the endogenous variable of interest, y, to one or more exogenous variables, x_i:

$$F(y, x_1, x_2, \ldots, x_m) = 0. \tag{A.32}$$

Assume that (a) F has continuous partial derivatives (denoted by $F_y \equiv \partial F / \partial y$, $F_j \equiv \partial F / \partial x_j$ for $j = 1, 2, \ldots, m$) and (b) $F_y \neq 0$ around a point $[y^0, x^0]$ which satisfies (A.32). Then according to the *implicit function theorem*, there exists an m-dimensional neighbourhood of $[x_j^0]$ in which y is an implicitly defined function of the exogenous variables:

$$y = f(x_1, x_2, \ldots, x_m). \tag{A.33}$$

The implicit function is continuous and has continuous partial derivatives, denoted by $f_j \equiv \partial f / \partial x_j$, which can be computed as follows:

$$\frac{\partial y}{\partial x_j} = f_j = -\frac{F_j}{F_y}, \quad \text{for } j = 1, 2, \ldots, m. \tag{A.34}$$

As an example, consider $F(y, x) = y^2 + x^2 - 9$. We find that $F_y = 2y$ and $F_x = 2x$, so that $\partial y / \partial x = -F_x / F_y = -x/y$ provided $y \neq 0$.

A.3.2 System of equations

Next we consider the system of n equations in n endogenous variables $(y_1, y_2, \ldots, y_n)$:

$$
\begin{aligned}
F^1(y_1, y_2, \ldots, y_n; x_1, x_2, \ldots, x_m) &= 0 \\
F^2(y_1, y_2, \ldots, y_n; x_1, x_2, \ldots, x_m) &= 0 \\
\vdots &= \vdots \\
F^n(y_1, y_2, \ldots, y_n; x_1, x_2, \ldots, x_m) &= 0
\end{aligned}
\tag{A.35}
$$

We assume that (a) the functions F^i all have continuous partial derivatives with respect to all y_i and x_j and (b) at a point $[y_i^0; x_j^0]$ the following determinant (of the

Jacobian matrix) is non-zero:

$$|J| \equiv \begin{vmatrix} \partial F^1/\partial y_1 & \partial F^1/\partial y_2 & \cdots & \cdots & \partial F^1/\partial y_n \\ \partial F^2/\partial y_1 & \partial F^2/\partial y_2 & \cdots & \cdots & \partial F^2/\partial y_n \\ \vdots & \vdots & \vdots & \vdots & \vdots \\ \partial F^n/\partial y_1 & \partial F^n/\partial y_2 & \cdots & \cdots & \partial F^n/\partial y_n \end{vmatrix} \neq 0. \tag{A.36}$$

Then, according to the *generalized implicit function theorem* there exists an *m*-dimensional neighbourhood of $[x_j^0]$ in which the variables y_i are implicitly defined functions of the exogenous variables:

$$\begin{aligned} y_1 &= f^1(x_1, x_2, \ldots, x_m) \\ y_2 &= f^2(x_1, x_2, \ldots, x_m) \\ \vdots &= \qquad \vdots \\ y_n &= f^n(x_1, x_2, \ldots, x_m) \end{aligned} \tag{A.37}$$

These implicit functions are continuous and have continuous partial derivatives, denoted by $f_j^i \equiv \partial f^i / \partial x_j$, which can be computed as follows:

$$\frac{\partial y_i}{\partial x_j} = f_j^i = \frac{|J_j^i|}{|J|}, \quad \text{for } i = 1, 2, \ldots, n, \tag{A.38}$$

where J_j^i is the matrix obtained by replacing column i of matrix J by the following vector of partial derivatives:

$$\begin{bmatrix} -\partial F^1/\partial x_j \\ -\partial F^2/\partial x_j \\ \vdots \\ -\partial F^n/\partial x_j \end{bmatrix} \tag{A.39}$$

Intermezzo

Generalized implicit function theorem. As a example, consider the IS-LM model:

$$Y = C(Y - T(Y)) + I(r) + G_0$$
$$M_0 = L(r, Y),$$

where Y is output, C is consumption, I is investment, r is the interest rate, T is taxes. The endogenous variables are r and Y and the exogenous variables are government consumption G_0 and the money supply M_0. By differentiating with respect to G_0 we get:

$$\begin{bmatrix} 1 - C_{Y-T}(1-T_Y) & -I_r \\ L_Y & L_r \end{bmatrix} \begin{bmatrix} \partial Y/\partial G_0 \\ \partial r/\partial G_0 \end{bmatrix} = \begin{bmatrix} 1 \\ 0 \end{bmatrix}.$$

The Jacobian determinant is:

$$|J| \equiv L_r \left[1 - C_{Y-T}(1-T_Y) \right] + I_r L_Y < 0,$$

where the sign follows from the fact that both money demand and investment depend negatively on the interest rate ($L_r < 0$ and $I_r < 0$), the marginal propensity to consume and the marginal tax rate are between zero and unity (so that $0 < C_{Y-T}(1 - T_Y) < 1$), and money demand depends positively on output ($L_Y > 0$). By Cramer's Rule we get the partial derivatives:

$$\frac{\partial Y}{\partial G_0} = \frac{1}{|J|} \begin{vmatrix} 1 & -I_r \\ 0 & L_r \end{vmatrix} = \frac{L_r}{L_r\left[1 - C_{Y-T}(1-T_Y)\right] + I_r L_Y} > 0$$

$$\frac{\partial r}{\partial G_0} = \frac{1}{|J|} \begin{vmatrix} 1 - C_{Y-T}(1-T_Y) & 1 \\ L_Y & 0 \end{vmatrix} = \frac{-L_Y}{L_r\left[1 - C_{Y-T}(1-T_Y)\right] + I_r L_Y} > 0.$$

These expressions, of course, accord with intuition (see Chapter 1).

A.3.3 Literature

Basic: Klein (1998, pp. 239–245), Chiang (1984, ch. 8), and Sydsæter and Hammond (1995, pp. 591–593). Advanced: De la Fuente (2000, ch. 5).

A.4 Static Optimization

A.4.1 Unconstrained optimization

Suppose we wish to find an optimum (minimum or maximum) of the following function:

$$y = f(x), \tag{A.40}$$

where we assume that this function is continuous and possesses continuous derivatives. The necessary condition for a (relative) extremum of the function at point

$x = x_0$ is

$$f'(x_0) = 0. \tag{A.41}$$

To test whether $f(x)$ attains a relative maximum or a relative minimum at $x = x_0$ we compute the second derivative. The second-order sufficient condition is:

$$\text{if } f''(x_0) \begin{Bmatrix} < \\ > \end{Bmatrix} 0, \quad f(x_0) \text{ is a relative } \begin{Bmatrix} \text{maximum} \\ \text{minimum} \end{Bmatrix}. \tag{A.42}$$

Now suppose that the function depends on n arguments (choice variables):

$$y = f(x_1, x_2, \ldots, x_n), \tag{A.43}$$

where $f(.)$ is continuous and possesses continuous derivatives. The first-order necessary conditions for a relative extremum are:

$$f_i = 0, \quad i = 1, 2, \ldots, n, \tag{A.44}$$

where $f_i \equiv \partial f / \partial x_i$ are the partial derivatives of $f(.)$ with respect to x_i. To study the second-order sufficient conditions we define the *Hessian matrix* of second-order derivatives, H:

$$H_{n \times n} \equiv \begin{bmatrix} f_{11} & f_{12} & \cdots & \cdots & f_{1n} \\ f_{21} & f_{22} & \cdots & \cdots & f_{2n} \\ \vdots & \vdots & \vdots & \vdots & \vdots \\ f_{n1} & f_{n2} & \cdots & \cdots & f_{nn} \end{bmatrix}, \tag{A.45}$$

where $f_{ii} \equiv \partial^2 f / \partial x_i^2$ and $f_{ij} \equiv \partial^2 f / \partial x_i \partial x_j$ are second-order partial derivatives. By Young's theorem we know that $f_{ij} = f_{ji}$ so the Hessian matrix is symmetric. We define the following set of principal minors of H:

$$|H_1| \equiv f_{11}, \quad |H_2| \equiv \begin{vmatrix} f_{11} & f_{12} \\ f_{21} & f_{22} \end{vmatrix}, \quad \ldots, \quad |H_n| \equiv \begin{vmatrix} f_{11} & f_{12} & \cdots & \cdots & f_{1n} \\ f_{21} & f_{22} & \cdots & \cdots & f_{2n} \\ \vdots & \vdots & \vdots & \vdots & \vdots \\ f_{n1} & f_{n2} & \cdots & \cdots & f_{nn} \end{vmatrix}. \tag{A.46}$$

Then, provided the first-order conditions hold at a point $[x_1^0, x_2^0, .., x_n^0]$, the second-order sufficient condition for $f(x_i^0)$ to be a relative maximum is:

$$|H_1| < 0, \quad |H_2| > 0, \quad \ldots, \quad (-1)^n |H_n| > 0, \tag{A.47}$$

whilst for a relative minimum the condition is:

$$|H_1|, \quad |H_2|, \quad \ldots, \quad |H_n| > 0 \tag{A.48}$$

See Chiang (1984, pp. 337–353) for the relation between concavity–convexity of $f(.)$ and the second-order conditions.

A.4.2 Equality constraints

We focus on the case with multiple choice variables and a single equality constraint. As in the unconstrained case, the objective function is given by (A.43). The constraint is given by:

$$g(x_1, x_2, \ldots, x_n) = c, \tag{A.49}$$

where c is a constant. We assume that $g(.)$ is continuous and possesses continuous derivatives. The *Lagrangian* is defined as follows:

$$\mathcal{L} \equiv f(x_1, x_2, \ldots, x_n) + \lambda [c - g(x_1, x_2, \ldots, x_n)], \tag{A.50}$$

where λ is the Lagrange multiplier. The first-order necessary conditions for an extremum are:

$$\begin{aligned} \mathcal{L}_i &= 0, \quad i = 1, 2, \ldots, n, \\ \mathcal{L}_\lambda &= 0, \end{aligned} \tag{A.51}$$

where $\mathcal{L}_i \equiv \partial \mathcal{L}/\partial x_i$ and $\mathcal{L}_\lambda \equiv \partial \mathcal{L}/\partial \lambda$ are the partial derivatives of the Lagrangean with respect to x_i and λ, respectively. To study the second-order conditions we formulate a so-called *bordered Hessian matrix*, denoted by $\bar{H}$:

$$\bar{H}_{(n+1)\times(n+1)} \equiv \begin{bmatrix} 0 & g_1 & g_2 & \cdots & \cdots & g_n \\ g_1 & f_{11} & f_{12} & \cdots & \cdots & f_{1n} \\ g_2 & f_{21} & f_{22} & \cdots & \cdots & f_{2n} \\ \vdots & \vdots & \vdots & \vdots & \vdots & \vdots \\ g_n & f_{n1} & f_{n2} & \cdots & \cdots & f_{nn} \end{bmatrix}. \tag{A.52}$$

The bordered Hessian consists of the ordinary Hessian but with the borders made up of the derivatives of the constraint function (g_i). We define the following set of principal minors of $\bar{H}$:

$$|\bar{H}_2| \equiv \begin{vmatrix} 0 & g_1 & g_2 \\ g_1 & f_{11} & f_{12} \\ g_2 & f_{21} & f_{22} \end{vmatrix}, \quad \ldots, \quad |H_n| \equiv \begin{vmatrix} 0 & g_1 & g_2 & \cdots & \cdots & g_n \\ g_1 & f_{11} & f_{12} & \cdots & \cdots & f_{1n} \\ g_2 & f_{21} & f_{22} & \cdots & \cdots & f_{2n} \\ \vdots & \vdots & \vdots & \vdots & \vdots & \vdots \\ g_n & f_{n1} & f_{n2} & \cdots & \cdots & f_{nn} \end{vmatrix}. \tag{A.53}$$

Then provided the first-order conditions hold at a point $[x_1^0, x_2^0, \ldots, x_n^0]$ the second-order sufficient conditions for $f(x_i^0)$ to be a relative constrained maximum are:

$$(-1)^k |\bar{H}_k| > 0, \quad k = 2, \ldots, n, \tag{A.54}$$

whilst for the conditions for a relative constrained minimum are:

$$|\bar{H}_k| < 0, \quad k = 2, \ldots, n. \tag{A.55}$$

If there are multiple constraints then additional Lagrange multipliers are added to the Lagrangian (one per constraint) and the first-order condition for each Lagrange multiplier, λ_j, takes the form $\mathcal{L}_{\lambda_j} \equiv \partial \mathcal{L}/\partial \lambda_j = 0$. See Chiang (1984, pp. 385–386) for the appropriately defined bordered Hessian for the multi-constraint case.

Interpretation of the Lagrange multiplier

We now return to the single constraint case in order to demonstrate the interpretation of the Lagrange multiplier in the optimum. Using the superscript "0" to denote optimized values, we can write the optimized value of the Lagrangian as:

$$\mathcal{L}^0 \equiv f(x_1^0, x_2^0, \ldots, x_n^0) + \lambda^0 \left[c - g(x_1^0, x_2^0, \ldots, x_n^0) \right]. \tag{A.56}$$

Next, we ask the question what happens if the constraint is changed marginally. Obviously, both λ^0 and x_i^0 are expected to change if c does. Differentiating (A.56) we get:

$$\frac{d\mathcal{L}^0}{dc} = \sum_{i=1}^{n} \mathcal{L}_i \left(\frac{dx_i^0}{dc} \right) + \mathcal{L}_\lambda \left(\frac{d\lambda^0}{dc} \right) + \lambda^0 \left(\frac{dc}{dc} \right) = \lambda^0, \tag{A.57}$$

where we have used the necessary conditions for an optimum ($\mathcal{L}_\lambda = \mathcal{L}_i = 0$ for $i = 1, 2, \ldots, n$) to get from the first to the second equality. Recall that the constraint holds with equality ($c = g(.)$) so that λ^0 measures the effect of a small change in c on the optimized value of the objective function $f(.)$. For example, if the objective function is utility and c is income, then λ^0 is the marginal utility of income.

A.4.3 Inequality constraints

We now briefly study some key results from non-linear programming. We first look at the simplest case with non-negativity constraints on the choice variables. Then we take up the more challenging case of general inequalities. We focus on first-order conditions and ignore some of the subtleties involved (like constraint qualifications and second-order conditions).

Non-negativity constraints

Suppose that the issue is to maximize a function $y = f(x)$ subject only to the non-negativity constraint $x \geq 0$. There are three situations which can arise. These have been illustrated in Figure A.1 which is taken from Chiang (1984, p. 723).

Panel (a) shows the case we have studied in detail above. The function attains a maximum for a strictly positive value of x. We call this an *interior solution* because the solution lies entirely within the feasible region (and not on a boundary). The constraint $x \geq 0$ is *non-binding* and the first-order condition is as before:

$$f'(x_0) = 0. \qquad \text{(interior solution)}$$

Panels (b) and (c) deal with two types of *boundary solutions*. In panel (b) the function happens to attain a maximum for $x = x_0 = 0$, i.e. exactly on the boundary of the

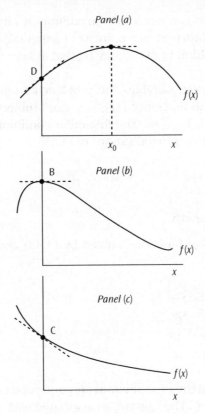

Figure A.1. Non-negativity constraints

feasible region. In panel (b) we thus have:

$$f'(x_0) = 0 \quad \text{and} \quad x_0 = 0. \qquad \text{(boundary solution)}$$

Finally, in panel (c) we also have a boundary solution but one for which the function $f(x)$ continues to rise for negative (infeasible) values of x. Hence, at that point we have:

$$f'(x_0) < 0 \quad \text{and} \quad x_0 = 0. \qquad \text{(boundary solution)}$$

These three conditions, covering the interior solution and both types of boundary solutions, can be combined in a single statement:

$$f'(x_0) \le 0, \quad x_0 \ge 0, \quad x_0 f'(x_0) = 0. \qquad \text{(A.58)}$$

There are two key things to note about this statement. First, as is evident from Figure A.1, we can safely exclude the case of $f'(x_0) > 0$ from consideration. If $f'(x_0) > 0$

even for $x_0 = 0$ then this can never be a maximum as raising x by a little would also raise the objective function (see point D in panel (a)). The second key result concerns the third condition in (A.58), saying that at least one of x_0 or $f'(x_0)$ must be zero.

When there are n choice variables the problem becomes one of choosing x_i $(i = 1, 2, \ldots, n)$ in order to maximize $f(x_1, x_2, \ldots, x_n)$ subject to the non-negativity constraints $x_i \geq 0$ $(i = 1, 2, \ldots, n)$. The first-order conditions associated with this problem are straightforward generalizations of (A.58):

$$f_i \leq 0, \quad x_i \geq 0, \quad x_i f'(x_i) = 0, \quad i = 1, 2, \ldots, n. \tag{A.59}$$

General inequality constraints

Suppose that the objective function is given by (A.43) and the set of non-linear constraints is given by:

$$
\begin{aligned}
g^1(x_1, x_2, \ldots, x_n) &\leq c_1, \\
g^2(x_1, x_2, \ldots, x_n) &\leq c_2, \\
&\vdots \quad \leq \quad \vdots \\
g^m(x_1, x_2, \ldots, x_n) &\leq c_m,
\end{aligned}
\tag{A.60}
$$

where c_j are constants and the $g^j(.)$ functions are continuous and possess continuous derivatives $(j = 1, 2, \ldots, m)$. The Lagrangian associated with the problem is:

$$\mathcal{L} \equiv f(x_1, x_2, \ldots, x_n) + \sum_{j=1}^{m} \lambda_j \left[c_j - g^j(x_1, x_2, \ldots, x_n) \right], \tag{A.61}$$

where λ_j is the Lagrange multiplier associated with the inequality constraint $c_j \geq g^j(.)$. The first-order conditions for a constrained maximum are:

$$
\begin{aligned}
\mathcal{L}_i \leq 0 \quad x_i \geq 0 \quad x_i \mathcal{L}_i = 0 \quad i = 1, 2, \ldots, n, \\
\mathcal{L}_{\lambda_j} \geq 0 \quad \lambda_j \geq 0 \quad \lambda_j \mathcal{L}_{\lambda_j} = 0 \quad j = 1, 2, \ldots, m,
\end{aligned}
\tag{A.62}
$$

where $\mathcal{L}_i \equiv \partial \mathcal{L}/\partial x_i$ and $\mathcal{L}_{\lambda_j} \equiv \partial \mathcal{L}/\partial \lambda_j$.

For a minimization problem, the Lagrangian is the same as before but the first-order conditions are:

$$
\begin{aligned}
\mathcal{L}_i \geq 0 \quad x_i \geq 0 \quad x_i \mathcal{L}_i = 0 \quad i = 1, 2, \ldots, n, \\
\mathcal{L}_{\lambda_j} \leq 0 \quad \lambda_j \geq 0 \quad \lambda_j \mathcal{L}_{\lambda_j} = 0 \quad j = 1, 2, \ldots, m.
\end{aligned}
\tag{A.63}
$$

We refer the reader to Chiang (1984, pp. 731–755) for a detailed discussion of second-order conditions and the restrictions that the constraint functions must satisfy (the so-called constraint qualification proviso).

A.4.4 Literature

Basic: Klein (1998, chs 9–11), Chiang (1984, chs 9–12, 21), and Sydsæter and Hammond (1995, chs 17–18). Intermediate: Dixit (1990, chs 2–8) and Intriligator (1971, chs 2–4). Advanced: de la Fuente (2000, chs 7–8).

A.5 Single Differential Equations

In this section we show how to solve the most commonly encountered differential equations. We follow standard procedure in the economics literature by using the Newtonian 'dot' notation to indicate derivatives with respect to time, i.e. $\dot{y}(t) \equiv dy(t)/dt$ and $\ddot{y}(t) \equiv d^2y(t)/dt^2$ etc.

A.5.1 First-order (constant coefficients)

Homogeneous

Suppose we have the following differential equation in $y(t)$:

$$\dot{y}(t) + ay(t) = 0, \tag{A.64}$$

where a is a constant. This is called a *homogeneous* differential equation because the constant on the right-hand side is zero. To solve this equation, we must find a path for $y(t)$, such that the exponential rate of growth in $y(t)$ is constant, i.e. $\dot{y}(t)/y(t) = -a$. Since growth must be exponential it is logical to try a solution of the exponential type:

$$y(t) = Ae^{\alpha t}, \tag{A.65}$$

where $A \neq 0$ and α are constants to be determined. Clearly the trial solution must solve (A.64). This implies that:

$$\alpha Ae^{\alpha t} + aAe^{\alpha t} = 0$$
$$(\alpha + a) Ae^{\alpha t} = 0 \quad \Rightarrow \quad \alpha = -a, \tag{A.66}$$

where the result follows from the fact that $Ae^{\alpha t} \neq 0$. Suppose we are also given an initial value for $y(t)$, say $y(0) = y_0$ (a constant). Then it follows from our trial solution, $y(t) = Ae^{-at}$ that $y(0) = A = y_0$ (since $e^{-at} = 1$ for $t = 0$) so that the full solution of the homogeneous differential equation is:

$$y(t) = y_0 e^{-at}. \tag{A.67}$$

Mathematical Appendix

Non-homogeneous

Now suppose that the differential equation is non-homogeneous:

$$\dot{y}(t) + ay(t) = b, \tag{A.68}$$

where $b \neq 0$. We look for the solution in two steps. First we find the *complementary function*, $y_C(t)$, which is the path for $y(t)$ which solves the homogeneous part of the differential equation. Next, we find the so-called *particular solution*, $y_P(t)$, to the general equation. By adding the complementary function and the particular solution we obtain the general solution. In case we want to impose the initial condition this can be done after the general solution is found.

Since the complementary function solves the homogeneous part of the differential equation it makes sense to try $y_C(t) = Ae^{-at}$. The particular integral is found by trial and error starting with the simplest possible case. Try $y_P(t) = k$ (a constant) and substitute it in the differential equation:

$$\dot{y}_P(t) + ay_P(t) = b$$

$$0 + ak = b \quad \Rightarrow \quad k = \frac{b}{a} \quad \text{(for } a \neq 0). \tag{A.69}$$

Hence, provided $a \neq 0$, our simplest trial solution works and the general solution is given by:

$$y(t) \left[= y_C(t) + y_P(t)\right] = Ae^{-at} + \frac{b}{a} \quad \text{(for } a \neq 0). \tag{A.70}$$

If we have the initial condition $y(0) = y_0$ (as before) then we find that $A = y_0 - b/a$.

What if $a = 0$? In that case the complementary function is $y_C(t) = Ae^{-0t} = A$, a constant, so it makes no sense to assume that the particular solution is also a constant. Instead we guess that $y_P(t) = kt$ (a time trend). Substituting it in the differential equation (A.64) (with $a = 0$ imposed) we obtain:

$$\dot{y}_P(t) + ay_P(t) = b \quad \Rightarrow \quad k = b \quad \text{(for } a = 0). \tag{A.71}$$

Hence, the trial works and the general solution is:

$$y(t) = A + bt, \quad \text{(for } a = 0). \tag{A.72}$$

(Imposing the initial condition $y(0) = y_0$ we obtain that $A = y_0$.) The thing to note about the general solution is that we could have obtained it by straightforward integration. Indeed, by rewriting (A.68) and setting $a = 0$ we get $dy(t) = bdt$ which can be integrated:

$$\int dy(t) = \int bdt \quad \Rightarrow \quad y(t) = A + bt, \tag{A.73}$$

where A is the constant of integration. Of course, equations (A.72) and (A.73) are the same but in the derivation of the latter no inspired guessing is needed.

A.5.2 First-order (variable coefficients)

Assume that the differential equation has the following form:

$$\dot{y}(t) + a(t)y(t) = b(t), \tag{A.74}$$

where a and b are now both functions of time. Though the expression does not have constant coefficients it is nevertheless linear in the unknown function $y(t)$ and its time derivative $\dot{y}(t)$. This linearity property makes the solution relatively straight-forward. We first solve the homogeneous equation for which $b(t) \equiv 0$. Assuming that $a(t)$ is continuous we can rewrite equation (A.74) as:

$$\frac{dy(t)/dt}{y(t)} = -a(t), \tag{A.75}$$

from which we conclude that:

$$\log |y(t)| = A - \int a(t)\, dt, \tag{A.76}$$

where we have used the fact that $\int dy(t)/y(t) = \log |y(t)|$ and where A is the constant of integration. Assuming that $y(t) > 0$, as is often the case in economic applications, we find that the general solution for $y(t)$ is:

$$y(t) = Ae^{-\int a(t)\, dt}. \tag{A.77}$$

The non-homogeneous equation (A.74) can also be solved readily because it possesses an *integrating factor*, $e^{F(t)}$, where $F(t)$ is given by:

$$F(t) \equiv \int a(t)\, dt. \tag{A.78}$$

First we note the following result:

$$\frac{d}{dt}\left[e^{F(t)}y(t)\right] = e^{F(t)}\dot{y}(t) + y(t)e^{F(t)}\dot{F}(t) = e^{F(t)}\left[\dot{y}(t) + a(t)y(t)\right], \tag{A.79}$$

where we have used the fact that $\dot{F}(t) = a(t)$. Next, by multiplying both sides of (A.74) by the integrating factor $e^{F(t)}$ and using (A.79) we obtain:

$$\frac{d}{dt}\left[e^{F(t)}y(t)\right] = b(t)e^{F(t)}. \tag{A.80}$$

Finally, by integrating both sides of (A.80) we obtain:

$$e^{F(t)}y(t) = A + \int b(t)e^{F(t)}\, dt \quad \Rightarrow$$

$$y(t) = e^{-F(t)}\left[A + \int b(t)e^{F(t)}\, dt\right], \tag{A.81}$$

where A is again the constant of integration.

A.5.3 Leibnitz's rule

In the text we occasionally make use of *Leibnitz's rule* for differentiation under the integral sign (Spiegel, 1974, p. 163). Suppose that the function $f(x)$ is defined as follows:

$$f(x) \equiv \int_{u_1(x)}^{u_2(x)} g(t, x)\, dt, \quad a \leq x \leq b. \tag{A.82}$$

Then, if (i) $g(t, x)$ and $\partial g / \partial x$ are continuous in both t and x (in some region including $u_1 \leq t \leq u_2$ and $a \leq x \leq b$) and (ii) $u_1(x)$ and $u_2(x)$ are continuous and have continuous derivatives (for $a \leq x \leq b$), then df/dx is given by:

$$\frac{df(x)}{dx} = \int_{u_1(x)}^{u_2(x)} \frac{\partial g(t, x)}{\partial x} dt + g(u_2, x)\frac{du_2}{dx} - g(u_1, x)\frac{du_1}{dx}. \tag{A.83}$$

Often u_1 and/or u_2 are constants so that one or both of the last two terms on the right-hand side of (A.83) vanish. See also Sydsæter and Hammond (1995, pp. 547–549) for examples of Leibnitz's rule.

A.5.4 Literature

Basic: Klein (1998, ch. 14), Chiang (1984, chs. 13–15), Sydsæter and Hammond (1995, ch. 21). Intermediate: Apostol (1967, ch. 8), Kreyszig (1999, chs. 1–5), Boyce and DiPrima (1992), and de la Fuente (2000, chs. 9–11).

A.6 Systems of Differential Equations

The main purpose of this section is to demonstrate how useful Laplace transform techniques can be to (macro) economists. Whilst the technique is not much more difficult than the method of comparative statics—that most students are familiar with—it enables one to study thoroughly (the properties of) low-dimensional[1] dynamic models in an analytical fashion.

A.6.1 The Laplace transform

The Laplace transform is a tool used extensively in engineering contexts and a very good source is the engineering mathematics textbook by Kreyszig (1999). The

---

[1] By "low dimensional" we mean that the characteristic polynomial of the Jacobian matrix of the system must be of order four or less. For such polynomials closed-form solutions for the roots are available. For higher-order polynomials Abel's Theorem proves that finite algebraic formulae do not exist for the roots. See the amusing historical overview of this issue in Turnbull (1988, pp. 114–115).

Laplace transform is extremely useful for solving (systems of) differential equations. Intuitively, the method works in three steps: (i) the difficult problem is transformed into a simple problem, (ii) we use (matrix) algebra to solve the simple problem, and (iii) we transform back the solution obtained in step (ii) to obtain the ultimate solution of our hard problem. Instead of having to work with difficult operations in calculus (in step (i)) we work with algebraic operations on transforms. This is why the Laplace transform technique is called *operational calculus*.

The major advantage of the Laplace transform technique lies in the ease with which time-varying shocks can be studied. In economic terms this makes it very easy to identify the propagation mechanism that is contained in the economic model. As we demonstrate in Chapter 15 this is important, for example, in models in the real business cycle (RBC) tradition.

Suppose that $f(t)$ is a function defined for $t \geq 0$. Then we can define the Laplace transform of that function as follows:[2]

$$\mathcal{L}\{f, s\} \equiv \int_0^\infty e^{-st} f(t)\, dt. \tag{A.84}$$

In economic terms $\mathcal{L}\{f, s\}$ is the discounted present value of the function $f(t)$, from present to the indefinite future, using s as the discount rate. Clearly, provided the integral on the right-hand side of (A.84) exists, $\mathcal{L}\{f, s\}$ is well-defined and can be seen as a function of s.

Here are some simple examples. Suppose that $f(t) = 1$ for $t \geq 0$. What is $\mathcal{L}\{f, s\}$? We use the definition in (A.84) to get:

$$\mathcal{L}\{f, s\} = \mathcal{L}\{1, s\} = \int_0^\infty 1 \times e^{-st}\, dt = \left. -\frac{1}{s} e^{-st} \right|_0^\infty = \frac{1}{s},$$

for $s > 0$. We have found our first Laplace transform, i.e. $\mathcal{L}\{1, s\} = 1/s$. Despite the ease with which it was derived, the transform of unity, $\mathcal{L}\{1, s\}$, is an extremely useful one to remember. Let us now try to find a more challenging one. Suppose that $f(t) = e^{at}$ for $t \geq 0$. What is $\mathcal{L}\{f, s\}$? We once again use the definition in (A.84) and get:

$$\mathcal{L}\{f, s\} = \mathcal{L}\{e^{at}, s\} = \int_0^\infty e^{at} e^{-st}\, dt = \int_0^\infty e^{-(s-a)t}\, dt$$

$$= \left. -\frac{1}{s-a} e^{-(s-a)t} \right|_0^\infty = \frac{1}{s-a},$$

provided $s > a$ (otherwise the integral does not exist and the Laplace transform is not defined).

---

[2] Some authors prefer to use the notation $F(s)$ for the Laplace transform of $f(t)$. Yet others use notation similar to ours but suppress the s argument and write $\mathcal{L}\{f\}$ for the Laplace transform of $f(t)$. We adopt our elaborate notation since we shall need to evaluate the transforms for particular values of s below.

Table A.1. Commonly used Laplace transforms

$f(t)$	$\mathcal{L}\{f,s\}$	valid for:
1	$\dfrac{1}{s}$	$s > 0$
t	$\dfrac{1}{s^2}$	$s > 0$
$\dfrac{t^{n-1}}{(n-1)!}$	$\dfrac{1}{s^n}$	$n = 1, 2, \ldots; s > 0$
e^{at}	$\dfrac{1}{s-a}$	$s > a$
$t e^{at}$	$\dfrac{1}{(s-a)^2}$	$s > a$
$\dfrac{t^{n-1} e^{at}}{(n-1)!}$	$\dfrac{1}{(s-a)^n}$	$n = 1, 2, \ldots; s > a$
$\dfrac{e^{at} - e^{bt}}{a-b}$	$\dfrac{1}{(s-a)(s-b)}$	$s > a, s > b, a \neq b$
$\dfrac{a e^{at} - b e^{bt}}{a-b}$	$\dfrac{1}{(s-a)(s-b)}$	$s > a, s > b, a \neq b$
$\mathcal{U}(t-a) \equiv \begin{cases} 0 & \text{for } 0 \leq t < a \\ 1 & \text{for } t > a \end{cases}$	$\dfrac{e^{-as}}{s}$	

So now we have found our second Laplace transform and in fact we already possess the two transforms used most often in economic contexts. Of course there are very many functions for which the technical work has been done already by others and the Laplace transforms are known. In Table A.1 we show a list of commonly used transforms. Such a table is certainly quite valuable but even more useful are the *general properties* of Laplace transforms which allow us to work with them in an algebraic fashion. Let us look at some of the main properties.

Property 1 *Linearity. The Laplace transform is a linear operator. Hence, if the Laplace transforms of $f(t)$ and $g(t)$ both exist, then we have for any constants a and b that:*

$$\mathcal{L}\{af + bg, s\} = a\mathcal{L}\{f, s\} + b\mathcal{L}\{g, s\}. \tag{P1}$$

The proof is too obvious to worry about.

The usefulness of (P1) is easily demonstrated: it allows us to deduce more complex transforms from simple transforms. Suppose that we are given a Laplace transform and want to figure out the function in the time domain which is associated with it. Assume that $\mathcal{L}\{f, s\} = 1/((s-a)(s-b))$, $a \neq b$. What is $f(t)$? We use the method of partial fractions to split up the Laplace transform:

$$\frac{1}{(s-a)(s-b)} = \frac{1}{a-b}\left[\frac{1}{s-a} - \frac{1}{s-b}\right]. \tag{A.85}$$

Now we apply (P1) to equation (A.85)–which is in a format we know—and derive:

$$\mathcal{L}\{f,s\} = \frac{1}{a-b}\left[\frac{1}{s-a} - \frac{1}{s-b}\right] = \frac{1}{a-b}\left[\mathcal{L}\{e^{at},s\} - \mathcal{L}\{e^{bt},s\}\right], \tag{A.86}$$

where we have used Table A.1 to get to the final expression. But (A.86) can now be inverted to get our answer:

$$f(t) = \frac{e^{at} - e^{bt}}{a-b}. \tag{A.87}$$

This entry is also found in Table A.1.

But we have now performed an operation (inverting a Laplace transform) for which we have not yet established the formal validity. Clearly, going from (A.87) to (A.86) is valid but is it also allowed to go from (A.86) to (A.87), i.e. is the Laplace transform unique? The answer is "no" in general but "yes" for all cases of interest. Kreyszig (1999, p. 256) states the following sufficient condition for existence.

Property 2 *Existence. Let $f(t)$ be a function that is piecewise continuous on every finite interval in the range $t \geq 0$ and satisfies:*

$$|f(t)| \leq Me^{\gamma t},$$

for all $t \geq 0$ and for some constants γ and M. Then the Laplace transform exists for all $s > \gamma$.

With "piecewise continuous" we mean that, on a finite interval $a \leq t \leq b$, $f(t)$ is defined on that interval and is such that the interval can be subdivided into finitely many sub-intervals in each of which $f(t)$ is continuous and has finite limits (Kreyszig, 1999, p. 255). Figure A.2 gives an example of a piecewise continuous function. The requirement mentioned in the property statement is that $f(t)$ is of exponential order γ as $t \to \infty$. Functions of exponential order cannot grow in absolute value more rapidly than $Me^{\gamma t}$ as t gets large. But since M and γ can be as large as desired the requirement is not much of a restriction (Spiegel, 1965, p. 2).

Armed with these results we derive the next properties. The first one says that discounting very heavily will wipe out the integral (and thus the Laplace transform) of any function of exponential order. The second one settles the uniqueness issue.

Property 3 *If $\mathcal{L}\{f,s\}$ is the Laplace transform of $f(t)$, then:*

$$\lim_{s \to \infty} \mathcal{L}\{f,s\} = 0 \tag{P3}$$

Property 4 *Unique inversion [Lerch's theorem]. If we restrict ourselves to functions $f(t)$ which are piecewise continuous in every finite interval $0 \leq t \leq N$ and of exponential order for $t > N$, then the inverse Laplace transform of $\mathcal{L}\{f,s\}$, denoted by $\mathcal{L}^{-1}\{\mathcal{L}\{f,s\}\} = f(t)$, is unique.*

Let us now push on and study some more properties that will prove useful later on.

Mathematical Appendix

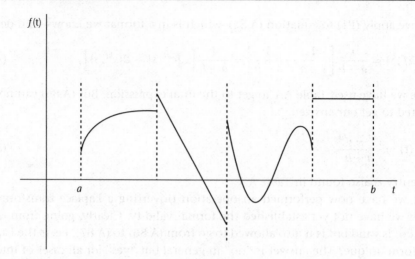

Figure A.2. Piecewise continuous function

Property 5 *Transform of a derivative. If $f(t)$ is continuous for $0 \le t \le N$ and of exponential order γ for $t > N$ and $f'(t)$ is piecewise continuous for $0 \le t \le N$ then:*

$$\mathcal{L}\{\dot{f}, s\} = s\mathcal{L}\{f, s\} - f(0), \tag{P5}$$

for $s > \gamma$.

PROOF: Note that we state and prove the property for the simple case with $f(t)$ continuous for $t \ge 0$. Then we have by definition:[3]

$$\mathcal{L}\{\dot{f}, s\} = \int_0^\infty e^{-st}\dot{f}(t)dt$$

$$= e^{-st}f(t)\big|_0^\infty + s\int_0^\infty e^{-st}f(t)dt$$

$$= \lim_{t \to \infty} e^{-st}f(t) - f(0) + s\mathcal{L}\{f, s\}.$$

But for $s > \gamma$ the discounting by s dominates the exponential order of $f(t)$ so that $\lim_{t \to \infty} e^{-st}f(t) = 0$ and the result follows.

Of course, we can use (P5) repeatedly. For second- and third-order time derivatives of $f(t)$ we obtain:

$$\mathcal{L}\{\ddot{f}, s\} = s\mathcal{L}\{\dot{f}, s\} - \dot{f}(0) = s\,[s\mathcal{L}\{f, s\} - f(0)] - \dot{f}(0)$$

$$\mathcal{L}\{\dddot{f}, s\} = s^3\mathcal{L}\{f, s\} - s^2 f(0) - s\dot{f}(0) - \ddot{f}(0). \tag{P6}$$

We can now illustrate the usefulness of the properties deduced so far and introduce the three-step procedure mentioned above (on page 679) by means of the following prototypical example.

---

[3] We use integration by parts, i.e. $\int u\,dv = uv - \int v\,du$, and set $u = e^{-st}$ and $v = f(t)$.

A.6.2 Simple applications

Suppose we have the following differential equation:

$$\ddot{y}(t) + 4\dot{y}(t) + 3y(t) = 0, \tag{A.88}$$

which must be solved subject to the initial conditions:

$$y(0) = 3, \quad \dot{y}(0) = 1. \tag{A.89}$$

Here goes the three-step procedure:

Step 1: Set up the subsidiary equation. By taking the Laplace transform of (A.88) and noting (P6) we get:

$$\mathcal{L}\{\ddot{y}, s\} + 4\mathcal{L}\{\dot{y}, s\} + 3\mathcal{L}\{y, s\} = 0 \Leftrightarrow$$

$$\left[s^2 \mathcal{L}\{y, s\} - sy(0) - \dot{y}(0)\right] + 4\left[s\mathcal{L}\{y, s\} - y(0)\right] + 3\mathcal{L}\{y, s\} = 0 \Leftrightarrow$$

$$\left[s^2 + 4s + 3\right]\mathcal{L}\{y, s\} = (s + 4)y(0) + \dot{y}(0). \tag{A.90}$$

By substituting (A.89) in (A.90) we obtain the *subsidiary equation* of the differential equation including its initial conditions.

$$\left[s^2 + 4s + 3\right]\mathcal{L}\{y, s\} = 3s + 13. \tag{A.91}$$

Step 2: Solve the subsidiary equation. We now do the easy stuff of algebraically manipulating the expression (A.91) in s-space. We notice that the quadratic on the left-hand side of (A.91) can be written as $s^2 + 4s + 3 = (s + 1)(s + 3)$ so we can solve for $\mathcal{L}\{y, s\}$ quite easily:[4]

$$\mathcal{L}\{y, s\} = \frac{3s + 13}{(s + 1)(s + 3)} = \frac{3(s + 1) + 10}{(s + 1)(s + 3)}$$

$$= \frac{3}{s + 3} + \frac{10}{(s + 1)(s + 3)}$$

$$= \frac{3}{s + 3} + \frac{10}{3 - 1}\left[\frac{1}{s + 1} - \frac{1}{s + 3}\right]$$

$$= \frac{5}{s + 1} - \frac{2}{s + 3}. \tag{A.92}$$

Step 3: Invert the transform to get the solution of the given problem. We have now written the (Laplace transform of the) solution in terms of known transforms. Inversion of (A.92) is thus straightforward and results in:

$$y(t) = \mathcal{L}^{-1}\{\mathcal{L}\{y, s\}\} = 5\mathcal{L}^{-1}\left\{\frac{1}{s + 1}\right\} - 2\mathcal{L}^{-1}\left\{\frac{1}{s + 3}\right\} = 5e^{-t} - 2e^{-3t}. \tag{A.93}$$

Of course we could have obtained this solution quite easily using the standard techniques so for this simple example the Laplace transform technique is not that

---

[4] We show the trivial steps leading to the final result in order to demonstrate that the algebra involved in s-space is indeed trivial. In general, the work involved in step 2 of the procedure is always easier than tackling the problem directly in t-space.

useful. It has some value added but not a lot. The thing to note, however, is that the method is essentially unchanged for much more complex problems. We now study two such cases.

Assume that the differential equation (A.88) is replaced by:

$$\ddot{y}(t) + 4\dot{y}(t) + 3y(t) = g(t), \tag{A.94}$$

where $g(t)$ is some (piecewise continuous) *forcing function* which is time-dependent and has a unique Laplace transform $\mathcal{L}\{g, s\}$. The initial conditions continue to be as given in (A.89). Using the same procedure as before we derive the solution of the subsidiary equation in terms of the Laplace transforms:

$$\underbrace{\mathcal{L}\{y, s\}}_{\text{output}} = \underbrace{\frac{3s + 13}{(s + 1)(s + 3)}}_{\text{initial conditions}} + \underbrace{\frac{\mathcal{L}\{g, s\}}{(s + 1)(s + 3)}}_{\text{input}}. \tag{A.95}$$

The first term on the right-hand side is the same as before (see (A.92)) and results from the initial conditions of the problem. The second term on the right-hand side represents the influence of the time-varying forcing term. Two further things must be noted about equation (A.95). First, the expression is perfectly general. A whole class of shock terms can be used in (A.95) to solve for $y(t)$ after inversion. Second, it should be noted that all of the model's dynamic properties are contained in the quadratic function appearing in the denominator. In fact, $H(s) \equiv \frac{1}{(s+1)(s+3)}$ is often referred to as the *transfer function* in the engineering literature since it transfers the shock (the "input") to the variable of interest (the "output")—see for example Boyce and DiPrima (1992, p. 312). The inverse of $H(s)$, denoted by $h(t) \equiv \mathcal{L}^{-1}\{H(s)\}$, is called the *impulse response function* of the system.

A.6.3 Systems of differential equations

The transform method is equally valuable for systems of differential equations. Suppose that the dynamic model is given in matrix form by:

$$\begin{bmatrix} \dot{K}(t) \\ \dot{Q}(t) \end{bmatrix} = \Delta \begin{bmatrix} K(t) \\ Q(t) \end{bmatrix} + \begin{bmatrix} g_K(t) \\ g_Q(t) \end{bmatrix}, \tag{A.96}$$

where Δ is the two-by-two Jacobian matrix with typical element δ_{ij}, and $g_i(t)$ are (potentially time-varying) shock terms. Note that a system like (A.96) occurs quite regularly in analytical low-dimensional macro models.

By taking the Laplace transform of (A.96), and noting property (P5) we get:

$$\begin{bmatrix} s\mathcal{L}\{K, s\} - K(0) \\ s\mathcal{L}\{Q, s\} - Q(0) \end{bmatrix} = \Delta \begin{bmatrix} \mathcal{L}\{K, s\} \\ \mathcal{L}\{Q, s\} \end{bmatrix} + \begin{bmatrix} \mathcal{L}\{g_K, s\} \\ \mathcal{L}\{g_Q, s\} \end{bmatrix} \Leftrightarrow$$

$$\Lambda(s) \begin{bmatrix} \mathcal{L}\{K, s\} \\ \mathcal{L}\{Q, s\} \end{bmatrix} = \begin{bmatrix} K(0) + \mathcal{L}\{g_K, s\} \\ Q(0) + \mathcal{L}\{g_Q, s\} \end{bmatrix}, \tag{A.97}$$

where $\Lambda(s) \equiv sI - \Delta$ is a two-by-two matrix depending on s and the elements of Δ. We know from matrix algebra that the inverse of this matrix, $\Lambda(s)^{-1}$, can be written as:

$$\Lambda(s)^{-1} = \frac{1}{|\Lambda(s)|} \text{adj}\Lambda(s), \tag{A.98}$$

where $\text{adj}\Lambda(s)$ is the adjoint matrix (see above in section A.2.4) of $\Lambda(s)$ and $|\Lambda(s)|$ is the determinant of $\Lambda(s)$. For the simple two-by-two model $\text{adj}\Lambda(s)$ and $|\Lambda(s)|$ are:

$$\text{adj}\Lambda(s) \equiv \begin{bmatrix} s - \delta_{22} & \delta_{12} \\ \delta_{21} & s - \delta_{11} \end{bmatrix}, \tag{A.99}$$

and:

$$\begin{aligned} |\Lambda(s)| &= (s - \delta_{11})(s - \delta_{22}) - \delta_{12}\delta_{21} \\ &= s^2 - (\delta_{11} + \delta_{22})s + \delta_{11}\delta_{22} - \delta_{12}\delta_{21} \\ &= s^2 - s\,\text{tr}(\Delta) + |\Delta|, \end{aligned} \tag{A.100}$$

where $\text{tr}(\Delta)$ and $|\Delta|$ are, respectively, the trace and the determinant of the matrix Δ. The quadratic equation in (A.100) can be factored as follows:

$$|\Lambda(s)| = (s - \lambda_1)(s - \lambda_2), \tag{A.101}$$

where λ_1 and λ_2 are the characteristic roots of the matrix Δ:

$$\lambda_{1,2} = \frac{\text{tr}(\Delta) \pm \sqrt{[\text{tr}(\Delta)]^2 - 4|\Delta|}}{2}. \tag{A.102}$$

Before going on we note—by comparing (A.100) and (A.101)—that for the two-by-two case we have:

$$\text{tr}(\Delta) = \lambda_1 + \lambda_2, \quad |\Delta| = \lambda_1\lambda_2, \tag{A.103}$$

i.e. the sum of the characteristic roots equals the trace of the Jacobian matrix Δ and the product of these roots equals the determinant of this matrix. This property is often very useful for deducing the signs of these roots. It is not difficult to see why this is so by looking at (A.102). We note that the roots are real (imaginary) if $[\text{tr}(\Delta)]^2 > (<) 4|\Delta|$ and that they are distinct provided $[\text{tr}(\Delta)]^2 \neq 4|\Delta|$. Also, if $\text{tr}(\Delta) > 0$ there must be at least one positive root. Finally, if $|\Delta| < 0$ there is exactly one positive (unstable) and one negative (stable) real characteristic root.[5]

Let us now consider the two cases encountered most often in the economics literature for which the roots are real and distinct, i.e. $[\text{tr}(\Delta)]^2 > 4|\Delta|$.

---

[5] These characteristic roots are going to show up in exponential functions, $e^{\lambda_i t}$, in the solution of the (system of) differential equation(s). If the root is positive (negative) $e^{\lambda_i t} \to \infty$ ($\to 0$) as $t \to \infty$ so positive (negative) roots are unstable (stable). The knife-edge case of a zero root is also stable as $e^{0t} = 1$ for all t. See section A.6.4 below.

Both roots negative $(\lambda_1, \lambda_2 < 0)$

We can use (A.97), (A.98), and (A.101) to derive the following expression in Laplace transforms:

$$\begin{bmatrix} \mathcal{L}\{K, s\} \\ \mathcal{L}\{Q, s\} \end{bmatrix} = \frac{\text{adj } \Lambda(s) \begin{bmatrix} K(0) + \mathcal{L}\{g_K, s\} \\ Q(0) + \mathcal{L}\{g_Q, s\} \end{bmatrix}}{(s - \lambda_1)(s - \lambda_2)}, \tag{A.104}$$

which is in the same format as (A.95), with $H(s) \equiv \text{adj } \Lambda(s)/[(s - \lambda_1)(s - \lambda_2)]$ acting as the transfer function. To solve the model for particular shocks it is useful to re-express the transfer function. We note that for the two-by-two case $\text{adj}\Lambda(s)$ has the following properties:

$$\text{adj } \Lambda(s) = \text{adj } \Lambda(\lambda_i) + (s - \lambda_i)I, \quad (i = 1, 2), \tag{A.105}$$

$$I = \frac{\text{adj } \Lambda(\lambda_1) - \text{adj } \Lambda(\lambda_2)}{\lambda_1 - \lambda_2},$$

where the second result follows from the first. We can now perform a partial fractions expansion of the transfer matrix:

$$\begin{aligned}
\frac{\text{adj } \Lambda(s)}{(s - \lambda_1)(s - \lambda_2)} &= \frac{\text{adj } \Lambda(s)}{\lambda_1 - \lambda_2} \left[\frac{1}{s - \lambda_1} - \frac{1}{s - \lambda_2} \right] \\
&= \frac{1}{\lambda_1 - \lambda_2} \left[\frac{\text{adj } \Lambda(s)}{s - \lambda_1} - \frac{\text{adj } \Lambda(s)}{s - \lambda_2} \right] \\
&= \frac{1}{\lambda_1 - \lambda_2} \left[I + \frac{\text{adj } \Lambda(\lambda_1)}{s - \lambda_1} - I - \frac{\text{adj } \Lambda(\lambda_2)}{s - \lambda_2} \right] \\
&= \frac{1}{\lambda_1 - \lambda_2} \left[\frac{\text{adj } \Lambda(\lambda_1)}{s - \lambda_1} - \frac{\text{adj } \Lambda(\lambda_2)}{s - \lambda_2} \right]. \tag{A.106}
\end{aligned}$$

By using (A.106) in (A.104) we obtain the following general expression in terms of the Laplace transforms:

$$\begin{bmatrix} \mathcal{L}\{K, s\} \\ \mathcal{L}\{Q, s\} \end{bmatrix} = \frac{1}{\lambda_1 - \lambda_2} \left[\frac{\text{adj } \Lambda(\lambda_1)}{s - \lambda_1} - \frac{\text{adj } \Lambda(\lambda_2)}{s - \lambda_2} \right] \begin{bmatrix} K(0) + \mathcal{L}\{g_K, s\} \\ Q(0) + \mathcal{L}\{g_Q, s\} \end{bmatrix}. \tag{A.107}$$

Suppose that the shocks are step functions and satisfy $g_i(t) = g_i$ for $i = K, Q$ and $t \geq 0$. The Laplace transform for such step functions is $\mathcal{L}\{g_i, s\} = g_i/s$ which can be substituted in (A.107). After some manipulation we obtain the following result:

$$\begin{bmatrix} \mathcal{L}\{K, s\} \\ \mathcal{L}\{Q, s\} \end{bmatrix} = \left[\frac{B}{s - \lambda_1} + \frac{I - B}{s - \lambda_2} \right] \begin{bmatrix} K(0) \\ Q(0) \end{bmatrix} \tag{A.108}$$

$$- \left[\frac{B}{\lambda_1} \left(\frac{-\lambda_1}{s(s - \lambda_1)} \right) + \frac{I - B}{\lambda_2} \left(\frac{-\lambda_2}{s(s - \lambda_2)} \right) \right] \begin{bmatrix} g_K \\ g_Q \end{bmatrix},$$

where $B \equiv \text{adj}\Lambda(\lambda_1)/(\lambda_1 - \lambda_2)$ and $I - B \equiv -\text{adj}\Lambda(\lambda_2)/(\lambda_1 - \lambda_2)$ are weighting matrices.[6] The expression is now in terms of known Laplace transforms so that inversion is child's play:

$$
\begin{bmatrix} K(t) \\ Q(t) \end{bmatrix} = \left[Be^{\lambda_1 t} + (I - B)e^{\lambda_2 t} \right] \begin{bmatrix} K(0) \\ Q(0) \end{bmatrix} \tag{A.109}
$$

$$
- \left[\frac{B}{\lambda_1} \left(1 - e^{\lambda_1 t} \right) + \frac{I - B}{\lambda_2} \left(1 - e^{\lambda_2 t} \right) \right] \begin{bmatrix} g_K \\ g_Q \end{bmatrix}.
$$

Equation (A.109) constitutes the full solution of the problem. It yields impact, transition, and long-run results of the shock. To check that we have done things correctly we verify that we can recover from (A.109) the initial conditions by setting $t = 0$ and the long-run steady state by letting $t \to \infty$. The first result is obvious: for $t = 0$ we have that $e^{\lambda_i t} = 1$ so that $K(t) = K(0)$ and $Q(t) = Q(0)$. Similarly, for $t \to \infty$, $e^{\lambda_i t} \to 0$ (since both roots are stable) and we get from (A.109):

$$
\begin{bmatrix} K(\infty) \\ Q(\infty) \end{bmatrix} = - \left[\frac{B}{\lambda_1} + \frac{I - B}{\lambda_2} \right] \begin{bmatrix} g_K \\ g_Q \end{bmatrix} = \frac{-\text{adj}\Lambda(0)}{-\lambda_1 \lambda_2} \begin{bmatrix} g_K \\ g_Q \end{bmatrix}
$$

$$
= \frac{\text{adj}\Delta}{-|\Delta|} \begin{bmatrix} g_K \\ g_Q \end{bmatrix} = -\Delta^{-1} \begin{bmatrix} g_K \\ g_Q \end{bmatrix}, \tag{A.110}
$$

which is the same solution we would have obtained by substituting the permanent shock in (A.96) and imposing the steady state. So at least the initial and ultimate effects check out!

We could have checked our results also by working directly with the solution in terms of Laplace transforms (i.e. (A.107) in general and (A.108) for the particular shocks). We need the following two properties to do so.

Property 6 *If the indicated limits exist then the initial-value theorem says:*

$$
\lim_{t \to 0} f(t) = \lim_{s \to \infty} s\mathcal{L}\{f, s\} \tag{P7}
$$

and the final-value theorem says:

$$
\lim_{t \to \infty} f(t) = \lim_{s \to 0} s\mathcal{L}\{f, s\} \tag{P8}
$$

PROOF: See Spiegel (1965, p. 20).

---

[6] These weighting matrices also satisfy:

$$
\frac{B}{\lambda_1} + \frac{I - B}{\lambda_2} = \frac{\text{adj}\Lambda(0)}{-\lambda_1 \lambda_2} = \frac{\text{adj}\Delta}{\lambda_1 \lambda_2} = \Delta^{-1}.
$$

These results are used below. Note that we have used the fact that $\text{adj}\Lambda(0) = \text{adj}(-\Delta) = (-1)^{n-1}\text{adj}\Delta$, where n is the order of Δ ($n = 2$ here). See Lancaster and Tismenetsky (1985, p. 43).

Applying Property (P7) directly to (A.108) we obtain:

$$
\lim_{s \to \infty} \begin{bmatrix} s\mathcal{L}\{K, s\} \\ s\mathcal{L}\{Q, s\} \end{bmatrix} = \left[B \underbrace{\lim_{s \to \infty} \left(\frac{s}{s - \lambda_1} \right)}_{=1} + (I - B) \underbrace{\lim_{s \to \infty} \left(\frac{s}{s - \lambda_2} \right)}_{=1} \right] \begin{bmatrix} K(0) \\ Q(0) \end{bmatrix}
$$

$$
- \left[\frac{B}{\lambda_1} \underbrace{\lim_{s \to \infty} \left(\frac{-\lambda_1 s}{s(s - \lambda_1)} \right)}_{=0} + \frac{I - B}{\lambda_2} \underbrace{\lim_{s \to \infty} \left(\frac{-\lambda_2 s}{s(s - \lambda_2)} \right)}_{=0} \right] \begin{bmatrix} g_K \\ g_Q \end{bmatrix}
$$

$$
= [B + I - B] \begin{bmatrix} K(0) \\ Q(0) \end{bmatrix} = \begin{bmatrix} K(0) \\ Q(0) \end{bmatrix}.
$$

Similarly, applying Property (P8) to (A.108) we get:

$$
\lim_{s \to 0} \begin{bmatrix} s\mathcal{L}\{K, s\} \\ s\mathcal{L}\{Q, s\} \end{bmatrix} = \left[B \underbrace{\lim_{s \to 0} \left(\frac{s}{s - \lambda_1} \right)}_{=0} + (I - B) \underbrace{\lim_{s \to 0} \left(\frac{s}{s - \lambda_2} \right)}_{=0} \right] \begin{bmatrix} K(0) \\ Q(0) \end{bmatrix}
$$

$$
- \left[\frac{B}{\lambda_1} \underbrace{\lim_{s \to 0} \left(\frac{-\lambda_1 s}{s(s - \lambda_1)} \right)}_{=1} + \frac{I - B}{\lambda_2} \underbrace{\lim_{s \to 0} \left(\frac{-\lambda_2 s}{s(s - \lambda_2)} \right)}_{=1} \right] \begin{bmatrix} g_K \\ g_Q \end{bmatrix}
$$

$$
= - \left[\frac{B}{\lambda_1} + \frac{I - B}{\lambda_2} \right] \begin{bmatrix} g_K \\ g_Q \end{bmatrix} = \begin{bmatrix} K(\infty) \\ Q(\infty) \end{bmatrix}.
$$

Roots alternate in sign $(\lambda_1 < 0 < \lambda_2)$

A situation which occurs quite regularly in dynamic macro models is one in which the Jacobian matrix Δ in (A.96) has one negative (stable) root and one positive (unstable) root. The way to check for such saddle-point stability is either by means of (A.102) or (A.103). From (A.102) we observe that if $|\Delta| < 0$ then we have distinct and real roots for sure since $\sqrt{(\mathrm{tr}\Delta)^2 - 4|\Delta|} > 0$. Also, since $|\Delta| < \lambda_1 \lambda_2 < 0$ it must be the case that $\lambda_1 < 0 < \lambda_2$. Of course we also see this directly from (A.103).

The beauty of the Laplace transform technique is now that (A.104) is still appropriate and just needs to be solved differently. Let us motivate the alternative solution method heuristically by writing (A.104) as follows:

$$
(s - \lambda_1) \begin{bmatrix} \mathcal{L}\{K, s\} \\ \mathcal{L}\{Q, s\} \end{bmatrix} = \frac{\mathrm{adj}\, \Lambda(s) \begin{bmatrix} K(0) + \mathcal{L}\{g_K, s\} \\ Q(0) + \mathcal{L}\{g_Q, s\} \end{bmatrix}}{s - \lambda_2}. \tag{A.111}
$$

In a two-by-two saddle-point stable system there is one predetermined and one non-predetermined (or "jumping") variable so we need to supply only one initial condition (and not two as before). Let us assume that K is the predetermined variable (the value of which is determined in the past, e.g. a stock of human or physical capital, assets, etc.) so that $K(0)$ is given. But then Q is the non-predetermined variable (e.g. a (shadow) price) so we must somehow figure out its initial condition.[7] It is clear from (A.111) how we should do this.

Note that the instability originates from the unstable root λ_2. For $s = \lambda_2$ we have that the denominator on the right-hand side of (A.111) is zero. The only way we can still obtain bounded (and thus economically sensible) solutions for $\mathcal{L}\{K, s\}$ and $\mathcal{L}\{Q, s\}$ is if the numerator on the right-hand side of (A.111) is also zero for $s = \lambda_2$, i.e. if:

$$\text{adj}\Lambda(\lambda_2) \begin{bmatrix} K(0) + \mathcal{L}\{g_K, \lambda_2\} \\ Q(0) + \mathcal{L}\{g_Q, \lambda_2\} \end{bmatrix} = \begin{bmatrix} 0 \\ 0 \end{bmatrix}. \tag{A.112}$$

All except one of the variables appearing in (A.112) are determined so $Q(0)$ must be such that (A.112) holds. At first view it appears as if (A.112) represents two equations in one unknown but that is not the case. A theorem from matrix algebra says that, since $\Lambda(\lambda_2)$ is of rank 1 so is $\text{adj}\Lambda(\lambda_2)$.[8] So, in fact, we can use either row of (A.112) to compute $Q(0)$:

$$\begin{bmatrix} 0 \\ 0 \end{bmatrix} = \begin{bmatrix} \lambda_2 - \delta_{22} & \delta_{12} \\ \delta_{21} & \lambda_2 - \delta_{11} \end{bmatrix} \begin{bmatrix} K(0) + \mathcal{L}\{g_K, \lambda_2\} \\ Q(0) + \mathcal{L}\{g_Q, \lambda_2\} \end{bmatrix} \Rightarrow$$

$$Q(0) = -\mathcal{L}\{g_Q, \lambda_2\} - \left(\frac{\lambda_2 - \delta_{22}}{\delta_{12}}\right)[K(0) + \mathcal{L}\{g_K, \lambda_2\}] \tag{A.113}$$

$$= -\mathcal{L}\{g_Q, \lambda_2\} - \left(\frac{\delta_{21}}{\lambda_2 - \delta_{11}}\right)[K(0) + \mathcal{L}\{g_K, \lambda_2\}]. \tag{A.114}$$

We next use (A.105), (A.111), and (A.112) to get:

$$(s - \lambda_1) \begin{bmatrix} \mathcal{L}\{K, s\} \\ \mathcal{L}\{Q, s\} \end{bmatrix} = \frac{\text{adj}\Lambda(\lambda_2) \begin{bmatrix} K(0) + \mathcal{L}\{g_K, s\} \\ Q(0) + \mathcal{L}\{g_Q, s\} \end{bmatrix}}{s - \lambda_2} + \begin{bmatrix} K(0) + \mathcal{L}\{g_K, s\} \\ Q(0) + \mathcal{L}\{g_Q, s\} \end{bmatrix}$$

$$= \begin{bmatrix} K(0) + \mathcal{L}\{g_K, s\} \\ Q(0) + \mathcal{L}\{g_Q, s\} \end{bmatrix} + \text{adj}\Lambda(\lambda_2) \begin{bmatrix} \dfrac{\mathcal{L}\{g_K, s\} - \mathcal{L}\{g_K, \lambda_2\}}{s - \lambda_2} \\ \dfrac{\mathcal{L}\{g_Q, s\} - \mathcal{L}\{g_Q, \lambda_2\}}{s - \lambda_2} \end{bmatrix}, \tag{A.115}$$

---

[7] Of course, economic theory suggests which variables are predetermined and which ones are not.

[8] In general, if the n-square matrix Δ has distinct eigenvalues its eigenvectors are linearly independent and the rank of $\Lambda(\lambda_i) \equiv \lambda_i I - \Delta$ is $n-1$ (Ayres, 1974, p. 150). Furthermore, for any n-square matrix A of rank $n-1$ we have that $\text{adj}A$ is of rank 1 (Ayres, 1974, p. 50).

where we have used (A.112) in the last step. Note that in (A.115) all effects of the unstable root have been incorporated and only the stable dynamics remains (represented by the term involving $s - \lambda_1$).

Suppose again that the shocks satisfy $g_i(t) = g_i$ for $i = K, Q$ and $t \geq 0$ so that $\mathcal{L}\{g_i, s\} = g_i/s$ and:

$$\frac{\mathcal{L}\{g_i, s\} - \mathcal{L}\{g_i, \lambda_2\}}{s - \lambda_2} = \frac{g_i/s - g_i/\lambda_2}{s - \lambda_2} = -\frac{g_i}{s\lambda_2}.$$

By using these results in (A.115) we obtain the full solution of the saddle-point stable model:

$$(s - \lambda_1) \begin{bmatrix} \mathcal{L}\{K, s\} \\ \mathcal{L}\{Q, s\} \end{bmatrix} = \begin{bmatrix} K(0) \\ Q(0) \end{bmatrix} - \frac{1}{\lambda_2} [\operatorname{adj} \Lambda(\lambda_2) - \lambda_2 I] \begin{bmatrix} g_K \\ g_Q \end{bmatrix} \frac{1}{s} \Leftrightarrow$$

$$\begin{bmatrix} \mathcal{L}\{K, s\} \\ \mathcal{L}\{Q, s\} \end{bmatrix} = \begin{bmatrix} K(0) \\ Q(0) \end{bmatrix} \left(\frac{1}{s - \lambda_1} \right) - \frac{\operatorname{adj} \Lambda(0)}{-\lambda_1 \lambda_2} \begin{bmatrix} g_K \\ g_Q \end{bmatrix} \left(\frac{-\lambda_1}{s(s - \lambda_1)} \right)$$

$$= \begin{bmatrix} K(0) \\ Q(0) \end{bmatrix} \left(\frac{1}{s - \lambda_1} \right) + \begin{bmatrix} K(\infty) \\ Q(\infty) \end{bmatrix} \left(\frac{-\lambda_1}{s(s - \lambda_1)} \right), \qquad \text{(A.116)}$$

where we have used (A.105) and the result in footnote 6, and where $Q(0)$ is obtained by substituting the shock terms in either (A.113) or (A.114). By inverting (A.116) we obtain the solution in the time dimension.

$$\begin{bmatrix} K(t) \\ Q(t) \end{bmatrix} = \begin{bmatrix} K(0) \\ Q(0) \end{bmatrix} e^{\lambda_1 t} + \begin{bmatrix} K(\infty) \\ Q(\infty) \end{bmatrix} (1 - e^{\lambda_1 t}). \qquad \text{(A.117)}$$

The key point to note is that the stable root determines the speed of transition between the respective impact and long-run results.

A.6.4 Hysteretic models

We now consider a special class of models that have the *hysteresis* property. With hysteresis we mean a system whose steady state is not given, but can wander about and depends on the past path of the economy. Mathematically, this property implies that the Jacobian matrix of a continuous-time system has, apart from some "regular" (non-zero) eigenvalues, a zero eigenvalue.[9] Hysteretic systems are important in macroeconomics because they allow us to depart from the rigid framework of equilibrium, ahistorical, economics. Put differently: history matters in such systems.

---

[9] Note that in a discrete-time setting a model displays hysteresis if it contains a unit root. Amable et al. (1994) argue that it is inappropriate to equate zero-root (or unit-root) dynamics with "true" hysteresis. Strong hysteresis is a much more general concept in their view and they suggest that zero-root dynamics at best captures some aspects of this concept.

In the remainder of this section we show that the Laplace transform methods studied above can easily be applied in low-dimensional hysteretic models also. We restrict attention to the two cases encountered most frequently in the economics literature, namely two-dimensional models with both roots non-positive and non-negative, respectively.

Non-positive roots ($\lambda_1 < 0 = \lambda_2$)

Suppose that the matrix Δ in (A.96) satisfies $|\Delta| = \lambda_1\lambda_2 = 0$ and $\text{tr}(\Delta) = \lambda_1 + \lambda_2 < 0$ so that the system has a zero root and is hysteretic, i.e. $\lambda_1 = \text{tr}(\Delta) < 0$ and $\lambda_2 = 0$. Clearly, since $|\Delta| = 0$, the inverse matrix Δ^{-1} does not exist and we cannot compute the long-run results of a shock by imposing the steady state in (A.96) and inverting Δ. However, the derivations leading from (A.104) to (A.107) are all still valid even for $\lambda_2 = 0$, i.e. the general solution in Laplace transforms is:

$$\begin{bmatrix} \mathcal{L}\{K, s\} \\ \mathcal{L}\{Q, s\} \end{bmatrix} = \begin{bmatrix} \dfrac{B}{s - \lambda_1} + \dfrac{I - B}{s} \end{bmatrix} \begin{bmatrix} K(0) + \mathcal{L}\{g_K, s\} \\ Q(0) + \mathcal{L}\{g_Q, s\} \end{bmatrix}, \tag{A.118}$$

where $B \equiv \text{adj}\,\Lambda(\lambda_1)/\lambda_1$ and $I - B \equiv -\text{adj}\,\Lambda(0)/\lambda_1$ are weighting matrices. Now assume that there is a *temporary* shock, i.e. $g_i(t) = g_i e^{-\xi_i t}$ for $i = K, Q$, $\xi_i > 0$, and $t \geq 0$. In a non-hysteretic model such a temporary shock has no effect in the long run as the system will eventually just return to its initial steady state which is uniquely determined by the long-run values of the shock terms.

In stark contrast, in a hysteretic model, a temporary shock does have permanent effects. In order to demonstrate this result we first substitute $\mathcal{L}\{g_i, s\} = g_i/(s + \xi_i)$ into (A.118):

$$\begin{bmatrix} \mathcal{L}\{K, s\} \\ \mathcal{L}\{Q, s\} \end{bmatrix} = \begin{bmatrix} \dfrac{B}{s - \lambda_1} + \dfrac{I - B}{s} \end{bmatrix} \begin{bmatrix} K(0) + g_K/(s + \xi_K) \\ Q(0) + g_Q/(s + \xi_Q) \end{bmatrix}. \tag{A.119}$$

Equation (A.119) constitutes the full solution for $K(t)$ and $Q(t)$ once the (history-determined) initial conditions are plugged in. Using the final-value theorem (P8) we derive from (A.119):

$$\lim_{s \to 0} \begin{bmatrix} s\mathcal{L}\{K, s\} \\ s\mathcal{L}\{Q, s\} \end{bmatrix} = \begin{bmatrix} B \underbrace{\lim_{s \to 0} \left(\dfrac{s}{s - \lambda_1} \right)}_{=0} + (I - B) \underbrace{\lim_{s \to 0} \left(\dfrac{s}{s} \right)}_{=1} \end{bmatrix}$$

$$\times \begin{bmatrix} K(0) + \lim_{s \to 0} \left(g_K/(s + \xi_K) \right) \\ Q(0) + \lim_{s \to 0} \left(g_Q/(s + \xi_Q) \right) \end{bmatrix}$$

$$= \frac{\text{adj}\,\Delta}{\lambda_1} \begin{bmatrix} K(0) + g_K/\xi_K \\ Q(0) + g_Q/\xi_Q \end{bmatrix} = \begin{bmatrix} K(\infty) \\ Q(\infty) \end{bmatrix}, \tag{A.120}$$

where we have used the fact that $\text{adj}\,\Lambda(0) = -\text{adj}\,\Delta$ in going from the first to the second line. Equation (A.120) shows that the hysteretic system does not return to its initial state following the temporary shock. It is not unstable, however, because it does settle down in a new "steady state" (for which $\dot{K}(\infty) = \dot{Q}(\infty) = 0$) but the position of this new steady state depends on the entire path of the shock terms, i.e. in our example on ξ_K and ξ_Q. The ultimate steady state is thus "path dependent" which explains why another term for hysteresis is *path dependency*.

Intermezzo

Pegging the nominal interest rate. Giavazzi and Wyplosz (1985, p. 355) give a simple example of a hysteretic system. Consider the following simple macroeconomic model:

$$m(t) - p(t) = ay(t) - bi_0 \tag{LM}$$

$$i_0 = r(t) + \dot{p}(t) \tag{Fisher}$$

$$y(t) = y_0^D(t) - \eta r(t) \tag{IS}$$

$$\dot{y}(t) = \theta \left[\bar{y}_0 - y(t) \right], \tag{AS}$$

where m, y, $\bar{y}$, and p are, respectively, the money supply, actual output, full employment output, and the price level (all in logarithms), r and i are the real and nominal interest rate, respectively, and y_0^D represents the exogenous elements of aggregate demand. The monetary authority uses monetary policy to peg the nominal interest rate (at $i(t) = i_0$) so the LM curve residually determines the money supply. By combining the Fisher relation with the IS curve we obtain $\dot{p}(t) = (1/\eta)[y(t) - y_0^D(t)] + i_0$. By differentiating this expression and the AS curve—keeping the other exogenous variables constant—we obtain the system in the required format:

$$
\begin{bmatrix} d\dot{p}(t) \\ d\dot{y}(t) \end{bmatrix} = \begin{bmatrix} 0 & 1/\eta \\ 0 & -\theta \end{bmatrix} \begin{bmatrix} dp(t) \\ dy(t) \end{bmatrix} + \begin{bmatrix} -(1/\eta)dy_0^D(t) \\ 0 \end{bmatrix},
$$

where the Jacobian matrix has characteristic roots $\lambda_1 = -\theta$ and $\lambda_2 = 0$ and it is assumed that both p and y are predetermined variables (so that $dp(0) = dy(0) = 0$). Now consider the effects of a temporary boost in aggregate demand, i.e. $dy_0^D(t) = e^{-\xi_D t}$ for $\xi_D > 0$ and $t \geq 0$. Using the methods developed in this subsection we derive:

$$
\begin{bmatrix} \mathcal{L}\{dp, s\} \\ \mathcal{L}\{dy, s\} \end{bmatrix} = \begin{bmatrix} -1/(\eta \xi_D) \\ 0 \end{bmatrix} \left(\frac{1}{s} - \frac{1}{s + \xi_D} \right).
$$

Despite the fact that the shock is purely transitory it has a permanent effect on the price level.

Non-negative roots ($\lambda_1 = 0 < \lambda_2$)

We now assume that Δ in (A.96) satisfies $|\Delta| = \lambda_1\lambda_2 = 0$ and $\text{tr}(\Delta) = \lambda_1 + \lambda_2 > 0$ so that $\lambda_1 = 0$ and $\lambda_2 = \text{tr}(\Delta) > 0$. For this hysteretic case the analysis in subsection A.6.3 is relevant. The general solution in Laplace transforms is obtained by setting $\lambda_1 = 0$ in (A.115):

$$
s\left[\begin{array}{c} \mathcal{L}\{K, s\} \\ \mathcal{L}\{Q, s\} \end{array}\right] = \left[\begin{array}{c} K(0) + \mathcal{L}\{g_K, s\} \\ Q(0) + \mathcal{L}\{g_Q, s\} \end{array}\right] + \text{adj}\,\Lambda(\lambda_2)\left[\begin{array}{c} \dfrac{\mathcal{L}\{g_K, s\} - \mathcal{L}\{g_K, \lambda_2\}}{s - \lambda_2} \\[2mm] \dfrac{\mathcal{L}\{g_Q, s\} - \mathcal{L}\{g_Q, \lambda_2\}}{s - \lambda_2} \end{array}\right].
$$

(A.121)

Let us once again assume that the shock is temporary and has a Laplace transform $\mathcal{L}\{g_i, s\} = g_i/(s + \xi_i)$ for $i = K, Q$ so that:

$$
\frac{\mathcal{L}\{g_i, s\} - \mathcal{L}\{g_i, \lambda_2\}}{s - \lambda_2} = \frac{-g_i}{(\lambda_2 + \xi_i)(s + \xi_i)}.
$$

(A.122)

Equation (A.121) can then be rewritten as:

$$
s\left[\begin{array}{c} \mathcal{L}\{K, s\} \\ \mathcal{L}\{Q, s\} \end{array}\right] = \left[\begin{array}{c} K(0) + g_K/(s + \xi_K) \\ Q(0) + g_Q/(s + \xi_Q) \end{array}\right] - \text{adj}\,\Lambda(\lambda_2)\left[\begin{array}{c} \dfrac{g_K}{(\lambda_2 + \xi_K)(s + \xi_K)} \\[2mm] \dfrac{g_Q}{(\lambda_2 + \xi_Q)(s + \xi_Q)} \end{array}\right],
$$

(A.123)

where $Q(0)$ follows from either (A.113) or (A.114). By using the final-value theorem (P8) in (A.123) we derive the hysteretic result:[10]

$$
\lim_{s \to 0} s\left[\begin{array}{c} \mathcal{L}\{K, s\} \\ \mathcal{L}\{Q, s\} \end{array}\right] = \left[\begin{array}{c} K(0) + g_K/\xi_K \\ Q(0) + g_Q/\xi_Q \end{array}\right] - \text{adj}\,\Lambda(\lambda_2)\left[\begin{array}{c} \dfrac{g_K}{\xi_K(\lambda_2 + \xi_K)} \\[2mm] \dfrac{g_Q}{\xi_Q(\lambda_2 + \xi_Q)} \end{array}\right]
$$

$$
= \frac{\text{adj}\,\Delta}{\lambda_2}\left[\begin{array}{c} K(0) + g_K/\xi_K \\ Q(0) + g_Q/\xi_Q \end{array}\right] = \left[\begin{array}{c} K(\infty) \\ Q(\infty) \end{array}\right].
$$

(A.124)

As in the outright stable case (see (A.120)) parameters of the shock path determine the ultimate long-run result.

Intermezzo

Current account dynamics. Consider the simple representative-agent model of a small open economy suggested by Blanchard (1985, p. 230). There is no

---

[10] In going from the first to the second line we use (A.112), note that (A.105) implies $\lambda_2 I = \text{adj}\,\Lambda(\lambda_2) - \text{adj}\,\Lambda(0)$, and recall that $\text{adj}\,\Lambda(0) = -\text{adj}\,\Delta$.

capital and labour supply is exogenously fixed (at unity) so that output, Y, and the wage rate, $W = Y$, are exogenous. The model is:

$$\dot{C}(t) = [r(t) - \alpha]\, C(t)$$

$$\dot{F}(t) = r(t)F(t) + W(t) - C(t),$$

where F is net foreign assets, and C and r are, respectively, consumption and the exogenous interest rate. As is well known, a steady state only exists in this model if the steady-state interest rate equals the rate of time preference, i.e. if $r(t) = \alpha$. After loglinearizing the model around an initial steady state we obtain:

$$\begin{bmatrix} \dot{\tilde{F}}(t) \\ \dot{\tilde{C}}(t) \end{bmatrix} = \begin{bmatrix} \alpha & -\alpha(1 + \omega_F) \\ 0 & 0 \end{bmatrix} \begin{bmatrix} \tilde{F}(t) \\ \tilde{C}(t) \end{bmatrix} + \begin{bmatrix} \omega_F \\ 1 \end{bmatrix} \alpha \tilde{r}(t),$$

where $\omega_F \equiv \alpha F/Y = C/Y - 1$ is the initial share of foreign asset income in national output, $\dot{\tilde{F}}(t) \equiv \alpha\, d\dot{F}/Y$, and $\tilde{F}(t) \equiv \alpha\, dF/Y$. The Jacobian matrix on the right-hand side has characteristic roots $\lambda_1 = 0$ and $\lambda_2 = \alpha$ and it is assumed that F is the predetermined variable and C is the jumping variable. Now consider a temporary change in the world interest rate, $\tilde{r}(t) = e^{-\xi_R t}$ for $\xi_R > 0$ and $t \geq 0$. By using (A.113) and making the obvious substitutions we obtain the jump in consumption:

$$\tilde{C}(0) = -\frac{\alpha}{(\alpha + \xi_R)(1 + \omega_F)} < 0.$$

In a similar fashion, the long-run results can be obtained by using (A.124):

$$\begin{bmatrix} \tilde{F}(\infty) \\ \tilde{C}(\infty) \end{bmatrix} = \begin{bmatrix} 0 & 1 + \omega_F \\ 0 & 1 \end{bmatrix} \begin{bmatrix} \alpha \omega_F/\xi_R \\ \tilde{C}(0) + \alpha/\xi_R \end{bmatrix}$$

$$= \begin{bmatrix} 1 + \omega_F \\ 1 \end{bmatrix} \left(\frac{\alpha\,[\alpha + \omega_F(\alpha + \xi_R)]}{\xi_R(\alpha + \xi_R)(1 + \omega_F)} \right).$$

In the impact period the household cuts back consumption to boost its savings. In the long run both consumption and net foreign assets are higher than in the initial steady state (provided $\omega_F > -\alpha/(\alpha + \xi_R)$ in the initial steady state).

A.6.5 Literature

The most accessible intermediate sources to the Laplace transform method are to be found in the engineering literature. Kreyszig (1999, ch. 5) and Boyce and DiPrima (1992, ch. 6) are particularly illuminating. An advanced and encyclopedic source on Laplace transforms is Spiegel (1965). Judd (1982, 1985, 1987a, 1987b) was the first to apply the method to saddle-point stable perfect foresight models, and to note the close link with welfare evaluations along the transition path.

A.7 Difference Equations

Although continuous-time models are quite convenient to work with, economists often work with models formulated in discrete time. Most RBC models fall under this category as does the class of overlapping-generations models in the Samuelson (1958)–Diamond (1965) tradition. In this section we briefly introduce the z-transform method. This method plays the same role in discrete-time models that the Laplace transform method performs in continuous-time models. In order to avoid unnecessary duplication, only the basic elements of the z-transform are introduced. The student should be able to "translate" the insights obtained above to the discrete-time setting after reading this section. Extremely lucid expositions of the z-transform method are Ogata (1995) and Elaydi (1996). Meijdam and Verhoeven (1998) apply the techniques in an economic setting.

A.7.1 Basic methods

The basic first-order linear difference equation takes the following form:

$$y_{t+1} + ay_t = b, \tag{A.125}$$

where a and b are constant parameters. If $b = 0$ ($\neq 0$) the equation is homogeneous (non-homogeneous). Equation (A.125) can be seen as the discrete-time counterpart to (A.64). Just as for the continuous case we can solve the difference equation in two steps. In step 1 we solve the complementary function, y_t^C, which solves the homogeneous part of (A.125). In step 2 we then look for the particular solution, y_t^P. The general solution is then given by $y_t = y_t^C + y_t^P$.

To solve the homogeneous part of the difference equation we are looking for a function for which $y_{t+1}/y_t = -a$ which suggests that a good trial solution is $y_t^C = A\alpha^t$. Substituting this trial in (A.125) and setting $b = 0$ we obtain $A\alpha^t[\alpha + a] = 0$ or $\alpha = -a$. Hence, the complementary function is:

$$y_t^C = A(-a)^t. \tag{A.126}$$

To find the particular solution we first try the simplest possible guess, $y_t^P = k$ (a constant). Substituting this trial solution into (A.125) we find $(1 + a)k = b$ which can be solved for k provided $a \neq -1$: $k = b/(1 + a)$. The general solution of the difference equation is thus:

$$y_t = A(-a)^t + \frac{b}{1+a} \quad \text{(for } a \neq -1\text{).} \tag{A.127}$$

This expression is the discrete time counterpart to (A.70).

Whereas a zero coefficient necessitates a different trial for the particular solution in the continuous time case, the same holds for the discrete-time case when the coefficient is minus unity. If $a = -1$ we use the trial solution $y_t^P = kt$, after which we find that $k = b$ so that the general solution is:

$$y_t = A + bt \quad \text{(for } a = -1\text{)}. \tag{A.128}$$

Initial conditions can be imposed just as for the continuous-time case. Suppose that y_0 is some given constant. Then we obtain from (A.127) that $A = y_0 - b/(1+a)$ and from (A.128) that $A = y_0$.

Just as in the continuous-time case, there exists a very convenient transformation method for solving difference equations. We now briefly explain how this z-transform method works.

A.7.2 The z-transform

Suppose we have a discrete-time function, f_t, which satisfies $f_t = 0$ for $t = -1, -2, \dots$. The (one-sided) z-transform of the function is then defined as follows:[11]

$$\mathcal{Z}\{f_t, z\} \equiv \sum_{t=0}^{\infty} f_t z^{-t}. \tag{A.129}$$

Provided the sum on the right-hand side converges, $\mathcal{Z}\{f_t, z\}$ exists and can be seen as a function of z. The region of convergence is determined as follows. Suppose that f_t satisfies:

$$\lim_{t \to \infty} \left| \frac{f_{t+1}}{f_t} \right| = R. \tag{A.130}$$

Then the infinite sum in (A.129) converges provided:

$$\lim_{t \to \infty} \left| \frac{f_{t+1} z^{-(t+1)}}{f_t z^{-t}} \right| < 1, \tag{A.131}$$

and diverges if the inequality is reversed. Together, (A.130) and (A.131) imply that (A.129) converges—and $\mathcal{Z}\{f_t, z\}$ exists—in the region $|z| > R$ ("heavy discounting"). In the region $|z| < R$, on the other hand, discounting is "light" and $\mathcal{Z}\{f_t, z\}$ does not exist. R is referred to as the *radius of convergence* of $\mathcal{Z}\{f_t, z\}$.

---

[11] By comparing (A.84) and (A.129) we cannot help but notice the close relation that exists between the Laplace transform and the z-transform. Indeed, assuming that $f(t)$ in (A.84) is continuous we obtain by discretizing $\mathcal{L}\{f, s\} = \sum_{t=0}^{\infty} e^{-st} f_t$. By setting $z = e^s$ we obtain (A.129). See also Elaydi (1996, p. 254).

Table A.2. Commonly used z-transforms

f_t	$\mathcal{Z}\{f,z\}$	valid for:
1 for $t = 0$ 0 for $t = 1, 2, \ldots$	1	
1	$\dfrac{z}{z - 1}$	$|z| > 1$
t	$\dfrac{z}{(z - 1)^2}$	$|z| > 1$
a^t	$\dfrac{z}{z - a}$	$|z| > |a|$
a^{t-1}	$\dfrac{1}{z - a}$	$|z| > |a|$
ta^{t-1}	$\dfrac{z}{(z - a)^2}$	$|z| > |a|$
$\dfrac{a^t - b^t}{a - b}$	$\dfrac{z}{(z - a)(z - b)}$	$|z| > |a|,\ |z| > |b|,\ a \neq b$

Here are some examples. Suppose that $f_t = 1$ for $t = 0, 1, 2, \ldots$ (and $f_t = 0$ otherwise). Then $\mathcal{Z}\{f_t, z\}$ is:

$$\mathcal{Z}\{f_t, z\} \equiv \mathcal{Z}\{1, z\} = \sum_{t=0}^{\infty} 1 \times z^{-t} = 1 + (1/z) + (1/z)^2 + \ldots$$

$$= \frac{1}{1 - 1/z} = \frac{z}{z - 1},$$

provided $|z| > 1$. Now a slightly harder one: Suppose that $f_t = a^t$ for $t = 0, 1, 2, \ldots$ (and $f_t = 0$ otherwise). Then $\mathcal{Z}\{f_t, z\}$ is:

$$\mathcal{Z}\{f_t, z\} \equiv \mathcal{Z}\{a^t, z\} = \sum_{t=0}^{\infty} a^t z^{-t} = 1 + (a/z) + (a/z)^2 + \ldots$$

$$= \frac{1}{1 - a/z} = \frac{z}{z - a},$$

provided $|z| > |a|$.

In Table A.2 we have gathered some often-used z-transforms. The student should verify that both the form of each transform and its associated radius of convergence are correct.

The z-transform has a number of properties which allow us to perform algebraic calculations with them. The most important of these are the following. Notice that in each case we assume that f_t possesses a z-transform and that $f_t = 0$ for $t = -1, -2, \ldots$

Property 7 *Multiplication by a constant. If $\mathcal{Z}\{f, s\}$ is the z-transform of f_t then $\mathcal{Z}\{af, z\} = a\mathcal{Z}\{f, z\}$.*

Property 8 *If f_t and g_t both have a z-transform then we have for any constants a and b that:*

$$\mathcal{Z}\{af + bg, z\} = a\mathcal{Z}\{f, z\} + b\mathcal{Z}\{g, z\} \tag{P9}$$

Property 9 *Left-shifting.*

$$\mathcal{Z}\{f_{t+1}, z\} = z\mathcal{Z}\{f_t, z\} - zf_0 \tag{P10}$$

$$\mathcal{Z}\{f_{t+2}, z\} = z\mathcal{Z}\{f_{t+1}, z\} - zf_1 = z^2\mathcal{Z}\{f_t, z\} - z^2 f_0 - zf_1 \tag{P11}$$

$$\ldots$$

$$\mathcal{Z}\{f_{t+k}, z\} = z^k \mathcal{Z}\{f_t, z\} - \sum_{r=0}^{k-1} z^{k-r} f_r \tag{P12}$$

Property 10 *Initial-value and final-value theorems:*

$$\lim_{|z|\to\infty} \mathcal{Z}\{f_t, z\} = f_0 \tag{P13}$$

$$\lim_{z\to 1} (z - 1)\mathcal{Z}\{f_t, z\} = \lim_{t\to\infty} f_t \tag{P14}$$

A.7.3 Simple application

Suppose we wish to solve the following difference equation:

$$x_{t+2} + 3x_{t+1} + 2x_t = 0, \quad x_0 = 0, \quad x_1 = 1. \tag{A.132}$$

By using properties (P10) and (P11) we obtain the subsidiary equation in a few steps:

$$0 = \left[z^2 \mathcal{Z}\{x_t, z\} - z^2 x_0 - zx_1\right] + 3\left[z\mathcal{Z}\{x_t, z\} - zx_0\right] + 2\mathcal{Z}\{x_t, z\} \quad \Leftrightarrow$$

$$\left(z^2 + 3z + 2\right)\mathcal{Z}\{x_t, z\} = z^2 x_0 + zx_1 + 3zx_0 = z \quad \Leftrightarrow$$

$$\mathcal{Z}\{x_t, z\} = \frac{z}{(z+1)(z+2)} = \frac{z}{z+1} - \frac{z}{z+2}. \tag{A.133}$$

Inverting (A.133) yields the solution in the time domain:

$$x_t = (-1)^t - (-2)^t, \tag{A.134}$$

for $t = 0, 1, 2, \ldots$

   This example is—of course—rather unexciting apart from the fact that it gives us a hint as to the stability properties of difference equations. Asymptotic stability of (a system of) difference equations is obtained if the roots lie inside the unit circle, i.e. terms like $\frac{z}{z+a}$ are (un) stable if $|a| < 1$ ($|a| > 1$).

A.7.4 The saddle-path model

We now consider the following system of difference equations (by analogy with (A.96)):

$$
\begin{bmatrix} K_{t+1} - K_t \\ Q_{t+1} - Q_t \end{bmatrix} = \Delta \begin{bmatrix} K_t \\ Q_t \end{bmatrix} + \begin{bmatrix} g_{K,t} \\ g_{Q,t} \end{bmatrix},
\tag{A.135}
$$

where $g_{K,t}$ and $g_{Q,t}$ are shock terms (possessing a z-transform) and Δ has typical element δ_{ij}. Taking the z-transform of (A.135) yields:

$$
\Lambda(z-1) \begin{bmatrix} \mathcal{Z}\{K_t, z\} \\ \mathcal{Z}\{Q_t, z\} \end{bmatrix} = \begin{bmatrix} zK_0 + \mathcal{Z}\{g_{K,t}, z\} \\ zQ_0 + \mathcal{Z}\{g_{Q,t}, z\} \end{bmatrix},
\tag{A.136}
$$

where $\Lambda(z-1) \equiv (z-1)I - \Delta$. We assume that the characteristic roots of Δ are both real and that $-1 < \lambda_1 < 0$ and $\lambda_2 > 0$.[12] As before, K_t is deemed to be predetermined (so that K_0 is given) whilst Q_t is a non-predetermined variable (so that Q_0 can jump). Since $\Lambda(z-1)^{-1} = \mathrm{adj}\,\Lambda(z-1)/[(z-(1-\lambda_1))(z-(1+\lambda_2))]$ we can rewrite (A.136) as:

$$
[z - (1-\lambda_1)] \begin{bmatrix} \mathcal{Z}\{K_t, z\} \\ \mathcal{Z}\{Q_t, z\} \end{bmatrix} = \frac{\mathrm{adj}\,\Lambda(z-1) \begin{bmatrix} zK_0 + \mathcal{Z}\{g_{K,t}, z\} \\ zQ_0 + \mathcal{Z}\{g_{Q,t}, z\} \end{bmatrix}}{z - (1+\lambda_2)}.
\tag{A.137}
$$

To ensure saddle-point stability the denominator and numerator on the right-hand side of (A.137) must both go to zero as z goes to $1 + \lambda_2$. This furnishes the expression for Q_0:

$$
\mathrm{adj}\,\Lambda(\lambda_2) \begin{bmatrix} (1+\lambda_2)K_0 + \mathcal{Z}\{g_{K,t}, 1+\lambda_2\} \\ (1+\lambda_2)Q_0 + \mathcal{Z}\{g_{K,t}, 1+\lambda_2\} \end{bmatrix} = \begin{bmatrix} 0 \\ 0 \end{bmatrix}.
\tag{A.138}
$$

By rewriting (A.138) we finally obtain:

$$
Q_0 = -\frac{\mathcal{Z}\{g_{Q,t}, 1+\lambda_2\}}{1+\lambda_2} - \left(\frac{\lambda_2 - \delta_{22}}{\delta_{12}}\right)\left[K_0 + \frac{\mathcal{Z}\{g_{K,t}, 1+\lambda_2\}}{1+\lambda_2}\right]
\tag{A.139}
$$

$$
= -\frac{\mathcal{Z}\{g_{Q,t}, 1+\lambda_2\}}{1+\lambda_2} - \left(\frac{\delta_{21}}{\lambda_2 - \delta_{11}}\right)\left[K_0 + \frac{\mathcal{Z}\{g_{K,t}, 1+\lambda_2\}}{1+\lambda_2}\right].
\tag{A.140}
$$

---

[12] We write the system in a form which emphasizes the close analogy with (A.96). Of course, we can also re-express (A.135) as:

$$
\begin{bmatrix} K_{t+1} \\ Q_{t+1} \end{bmatrix} = \Delta^* \begin{bmatrix} K_t \\ Q_t \end{bmatrix} + \begin{bmatrix} g_{K,t} \\ g_{Q,t} \end{bmatrix},
$$

where $\Delta^* \equiv I + \Delta$. The characteristic roots of Δ^* and Δ are related according to $\lambda_i^* = 1 + \lambda_i$. Azariadis (1993, p. 65) gives the conditions for saddle-point stability.

Similarly, the general expression for the solution can be written as:

$$[z - (1 + \lambda_1)] \begin{bmatrix} \mathcal{Z}\{K_t, z\} \\ \mathcal{Z}\{Q_t, z\} \end{bmatrix} = \begin{bmatrix} zK_0 + \mathcal{Z}\{g_{K,t}, z\} \\ zQ_0 + \mathcal{Z}\{g_{Q,t}, z\} \end{bmatrix}$$

$$+ \frac{\text{adj } \Lambda(\lambda_2) \begin{bmatrix} \mathcal{Z}\{g_{K,t}, z\} - \left(\frac{z}{1+\lambda_2}\right) \mathcal{Z}\{g_{K,t}, 1 + \lambda_2\} \\ \mathcal{Z}\{g_{Q,t}, z\} - \left(\frac{z}{1+\lambda_2}\right) \mathcal{Z}\{g_{Q,t}, 1 + \lambda_2\} \end{bmatrix}}{z - (1 + \lambda_2)},$$

(A.141)

where the analogy with (A.115) should be obvious. In the appendix to Chapter 15 equations (A.139)–(A.141) are used to solve the impulse-response functions for the unit-elastic RBC model with technology shocks.

A.7.5 Literature

Basic: Klein (1998, ch. 13), Chiang (1984, chs. 16–17), Sydsæter and Hammond (1995, ch. 20). Intermediate: de la Fuente (2000, chs. 9–11). Advanced: Azariadis (1993), Elaydi (1996), and Ogata (1995).

A.8 Dynamic Optimization

In this section we present the key results from optimal control theory as they are used in this book. We focus on infinite-horizon maximization problems in continuous time and gloss over second-order conditions. Discrete-time problems are solved in the text by making use of the Lagrangian methods discussed above in this appendix. Intriligator (1971, pp. 346–348) shows the link between the method of Lagrange multipliers and optimal control theory.

A.8.1 Unconstrained

The proto-typical optimal control problem encountered in economics takes the following form. The objective function is defined as:

$$y(0) = \int_0^\infty F[x(t), u(t), t] e^{-\rho t} dt,$$

(A.142)

where $x(t)$ is the state variable, $u(t)$ is the control variable, $e^{-\rho t}$ is the discount factor, and t is time. The state and control variable are related according to the following *state equation:*

$$\dot{x}(t) = f\,[x(t), u(t), t]\,. \tag{A.143}$$

The state equation thus describes the equation of motion for the state variable. The initial condition for the state variable is given by:

$$x(0) = x_0, \tag{A.144}$$

where x_0 is a given constant (e.g. the accumulated stock of some resource). The objective is to find a time path for the control variable, $u(t)$ for $t \in [0, \infty]$, such that the objective function (A.142) is maximized given the state equation (A.143) and the initial condition (A.144).

To solve this problem one formulates a so-called *Hamiltonian* which takes the following form:

$$\mathcal{H} \equiv F\,[x(t), u(t), t]\,e^{-\rho t} + \lambda(t) f\,[x(t), u(t), t]\,, \tag{A.145}$$

where $\lambda(t)$ is the co-state variable which plays the role similar to the Lagrange multiplier encountered in static optimization problems. The Maximum Principle furnishes the following conditions (for $t \in [0, \infty]$):

$$\frac{\partial \mathcal{H}}{\partial u(t)} = 0, \tag{A.146}$$

$$\dot{x}(t) = \frac{\partial \mathcal{H}}{\partial \lambda(t)}, \tag{A.147}$$

$$\dot{\lambda}(t) = -\frac{\partial \mathcal{H}}{\partial x(t)}. \tag{A.148}$$

The first condition says that the control variable should be chosen such that the Hamiltonian is maximized, the second condition gives the equation of motion for the state variable, whilst the third equation gives the equation of motion for the co-state variable.

An equivalent way of solving the same problem is to work with the *current-value Hamiltonian*, which is defined as follows:

$$\mathcal{H}_C\,[\equiv \mathcal{H}e^{\rho t}] = F\,[x(t), u(t), t] + \mu(t) f\,[x(t), u(t), t]\,, \tag{A.149}$$

where $\mu(t) \equiv \lambda(t) e^{\rho t}$ is the redefined co-state variable. The first-order conditions expressed in terms of the current-value Hamiltonian are:

$$\frac{\partial \mathcal{H}_C}{\partial u(t)} = 0, \tag{A.150}$$

$$\dot{x}(t) = \frac{\partial \mathcal{H}_C}{\partial \mu(t)}, \tag{A.151}$$

$$\dot{\mu}(t) - \rho\mu(t) = -\frac{\partial \mathcal{H}_C}{\partial x(t)}. \tag{A.152}$$

If there are n state variables and m controls then the same methods carry over except, of course, that $x(t) \equiv [x_1(t), \ldots, x_n(t)]$ and $u(t) \equiv [u_1(t), \ldots, u_m(t)]$ must be interpreted as vectors and the set of conditions is suitable expanded:

$$\frac{\partial \mathcal{H}_C}{\partial u_j(t)} = 0, \tag{A.153}$$

$$\dot{x}_i(t) = \frac{\partial \mathcal{H}_C}{\partial \mu_i(t)}, \tag{A.154}$$

$$\dot{\mu}_i(t) - \rho \mu_i(t) = -\frac{\partial \mathcal{H}_C}{\partial x(t)}, \tag{A.155}$$

where $\lambda_i(t)$ is the co-state variable corresponding to the state variable $x_i(t)$, $j = 1, \ldots, m$, and $i = 1, \ldots, n$.

A.8.2 (In)equality constraints

Suppose the problem is as in (A.142)–(A.144) but that there is an additional constraint in the form of:

$$g\,[x(t), u(t), t] \le c, \tag{A.156}$$

where c is some constant. Suppose furthermore that there is a non-negativity constraint on the control variable, i.e. $u(t) \ge 0$ is required. The way to deal with these inequalities is to form the following current-value Lagrangian:

$$\mathcal{L}_C = F\,[x(t), u(t), t] + \mu(t)f\,[x(t), u(t), t] + \theta(t)[c - g\,[x(t), u(t), t]], \tag{A.157}$$

where $\theta(t)$ is the Lagrange multiplier associated with the inequality constraint (A.156). The first-order conditions are now:

$$\frac{\partial \mathcal{L}_C}{\partial u(t)} \le 0, \quad u(t) \ge 0, \quad u(t)\frac{\partial \mathcal{L}_C}{\partial u(t)} = 0, \tag{A.158}$$

$$\frac{\partial \mathcal{L}_C}{\partial \theta(t)} \ge 0, \quad \theta(t) \ge 0, \quad \theta(t)\frac{\partial \mathcal{L}_C}{\partial \theta(t)} = 0, \tag{A.159}$$

$$\dot{x}(t) = \frac{\partial \mathcal{L}_C}{\partial \mu(t)}, \tag{A.160}$$

$$\dot{\mu}(t) - \rho \mu(t) = -\frac{\partial \mathcal{L}_C}{\partial x(t)}. \tag{A.161}$$

Equation (A.158) gives the Kuhn-Tucker conditions taking care of the non-negativity constraint on the control variable. The second equation gives the Kuhn-Tucker conditions for the inequality constraint (A.156). Finally, (A.160) and (A.161) give the laws of motion of, respectively, the state variable and the co-state variable.

A.8.3 Second-order conditions

The second-order sufficient conditions are given by Chiang (1992, p. 290).

A.8.4 Literature

Basic: Klein (1998, ch. 15) and Chiang (1992). Intermediate: Dixit (1990, chs 10–11), Intriligator (1971, chs 11–14), Léonard and Long (1992), and de la Fuente (2000, chs 12–13). Advanced: Kamien and Schwartz (1991), Seierstad and Sydsæter (1987), and Chow (1997).

Bibliography

Aaron, H. J. (1966). The social insurance paradox. *Canadian Journal of Economics and Political Science*, 32:371–374.

Abel, A. B. (1981). A dynamic model of investment and capacity utilization. *Quarterly Journal of Economics*, 96:379–403.

—— (1982). Dynamic effects of permanent and temporary tax policies in a q model of investment. *Journal of Monetary Economics*, 9:353–373.

—— (1986). Capital accumulation and uncertain lifetimes with adverse selection. *Econometrica*, 54:1079–1097.

—— (1990). Consumption and investment. In Friedman, B. M. and Hahn, F. H., editors, *Handbook of Monetary Economics*. North-Holland, Amsterdam.

—— and Bernanke, B. S. (2001). *Macroeconomics*. Addison Wesley, Boston, MA, fourth edition.

——, Dixit, A. K., Eberly, J. C., and Pindyck, R. S. (1996). Options, the value of capital, and investment. *Quarterly Journal of Economics*, 111:753–777.

—— and Eberly, J. C. (1994). A unified model of investment under uncertainty. *American Economic Review*, 84:1369–1384.

——, Mankiw, N. G., Summers, L. H., and Zeckhauser, R. (1989). Assessing dynamic efficiency: Theory and evidence. *Review of Economic Studies*, 56:1–19.

Agénor, P.-R., Bhandari, J. S., and Flood, R. P. (1992). Speculative attacks and models of balance of payments crises. *IMF Staff Papers*, 39:357–394.

Aghion, P. and Howitt, P. (1992). A model of growth through creative destruction. *Econometrica*, 60:323–351.

—— and Howitt, P. (1998). *Endogenous Growth Theory*. MIT Press, Cambridge, MA.

Akerlof, G. and Yellen, J. (1985a). Can small deviations from rationality make significant differences to economic equilibria? *American Economic Review*, 75:708–721.

—— and Yellen, J. (1985b). A near-rational model of the business cycle with wage and price inertia. *Quarterly Journal of Economics, Supplement*, 100:823–838.

—— and Yellen, J. L., editors (1986). *Efficiency Wage Models of the Labor Market*. Cambridge University Press, Cambridge.

Alesina, A. and Grilli, V. (1992). The European central bank: Reshaping monetary politics in Europe. In Canzoneri, M., Grilli, V., and Masson, P., editors, *Establishing a Central Bank. Issues in Europe and Lessons from the US*. Cambridge University Press, Cambridge.

Allais, M. (1947). *Économie et Intérêt*. Imprimerie Nationale, Paris. Second edition with a new introduction, 1998, Paris: Clement Juglar.

Allen, R. G. D. (1967). *Macro-Economic Theory: A Mathematical Treatment*. Macmillan, London and Basingstoke.

Alogoskoufis, G. and van der Ploeg, F. (1990). Endogenous growth and overlapping generations. Discussion Paper 9072, CentER, Tilburg University.

Amable, B., Henry, J., Lordon, F., and Topol, R. (1994). Strong hysteresis versus unit-root dynamics. *Economics Letters*, 44:43–47.

Anderson, S. P. and Devereux, M. (1988). Trade unions and the choice of capital stock. *Scandinavian Journal of Economics*, 90:27–44.

Andolfatto, D. (1996). Business cycle and labor market search. *American Economic Review*, 86:112–132.

Aoki, M. (1986). Dynamic adjustment behaviour to anticipated supply shocks in a two-country model. *Economic Journal*, 96:80–100.

Apostol, T. M. (1967). *Calculus*, volume I. John Wiley, New York, second edition.

Argy, V. and Salop, J. (1979). Price and output effects of monetary and fiscal policy under flexible exchange rates. *IMF Staff Papers*, 26:224–256.

Armington, P. S. (1969). A theory of demand for products distinguished by place of production. *IMF Staff Papers*, 16:159–178.

Arrow, K. J. (1959). Towards a theory of price adjustment. In Abramovitz, M. et al., editors, *The Allocation of Economic Resources*. Stanford University Press, Stanford, CA.

—— (1962). The economic implications of learning by doing. *Review of Economic Studies*, 29:155–173.

—— (1965). *Aspects of the Theory of Risk-Bearing*. Yrjö Jahnssonin Säätio, Helsinki.

—— and Kurz, M. (1970). *Public Investment, the Rate of Return, and Optimal Fiscal Policy*. Johns Hopkins Press, Baltimore, MD.

Aschauer, D. (1988). The equilibrium approach to fiscal policy. *Journal of Money, Credit, and Banking*, 20:41–62.

Aschauer, D. A. (1989). Is public expenditure productive? *Journal of Monetary Economics*, 23:177–200.

—— (1990a). Finite horizons, intertemporal substitution, and fiscal policy. *Public Finance Quarterly*, 18:77–91.

—— (1990b). Why is infrastructure important? In Munnell, A. H., editor, *Is There a Shortfall in Public Investment?*, pages 21–68. Federal Reserve Bank of Boston, Boston.

—— and Greenwood, J. (1985). Macroeconomic effects of fiscal policy. *Carnegie-Rochester Conference Series on Public Policy*, 23:91–138.

Atkinson, A. B. and Stern, N. H. (1974). Pigou, taxation, and public goods. *Review of Economic Studies*, 41:119–128.

—— and Stiglitz, J. E. (1980). *Lectures on Public Economics*. McGraw-Hill, New York.

Attanasio, O. P. (1999). Consumption. In Taylor, J. B. and Woodford, M., editors, *Handbook of Macroeconomics*, volume 1B. North-Holland, Amsterdam.

Attfield, C. L. F., Demery, D., and Duck, N. W. (1985). *Rational Expectations in Macroeconomics*. Basil Blackwell, Oxford.

Auerbach, A. J. (1979a). The optimal taxation of heterogeneous capital. *Quarterly Journal of Economics*, 94:589–612.

—— (1979b). Wealth maximization and the cost of capital. *Quarterly Journal of Economics*, 94:433–446.

Bibliography

Auerbach, A. J., Gokhale, J., and Kotlikoff, L. J. (1991). Generational accounts: A meaningful alternative to deficit accounting. In Bradford, D., editor, *Tax Policy and the Economy*, volume 5, pages 55–110.

——, Gokhale, J., and Kotlikoff, L. J. (1994). Generational accounting: A meaningful way to evaluate fiscal policy. *Journal of Economic Perspectives*, 8:73–94.

——and Kotlikoff, L. J. (1987). *Dynamic Fiscal Policy*. Cambridge University Press, Cambridge.

——and Kotlikoff, L. J. (1998). *Macroeconomics: An Integrated Approach*. MIT Press, Cambridge, MA, second edition.

——, Kotlikoff, L. J., and Leibfritz, W., editors (1999). *Generational Accounting around the World*. University of Chicago Press, Chicago.

Axelrod, R. (1984). *The Evolution of Cooperation*. New York.

Ayres, F. (1974). *Theory and Problems of Matrices*. McGraw-Hill, New York.

Azariadis, C. (1975). Implicit contracts and underemployment equilibria. *Journal of Political Economy*, 83:1183–1202.

——(1981). Implicit contracts and related topics: A survey. In Hornstein, Z., Grice, J., and Webb, A., editors, *The Economics of the Labour Market*. Her Majesty's Stationary Office, London.

——(1993). *Intertemporal Macroeconomics*. Basil Blackwell, Oxford.

——and Drazen, A. (1990). Threshold externalities in economic development. *Quarterly Journal of Economics*, 105:501–526.

——and Stiglitz, J. E. (1983). Implicit contracts and fixed price equilibria. *Quarterly Economic Journal, Supplement*, 98:1–22.

Backus, D. and Driffill, J. (1985). Inflation and reputation. *American Economic Review*, 75:530–538.

Bailey, M. J. (1956). The welfare costs of inflationary finance. *Journal of Political Economy*, 64:93–110.

Ball, L., Mankiw, N. G., and Romer, D. (1988). The new Keynesian economics and the output-inflation trade-off. *Brookings Papers on Economic Activity*, pages 1–65.

——and Romer, D. (1990). Real rigidities and the non-neutrality of money. *Review of Economic Studies*, 57:183–203.

Barro, R. J. (1974). Are government bonds net wealth? *Journal of Political Economy*, 82:1095–1117.

——(1976). Rational expectations and the role of monetary policy. *Journal of Monetary Economics*, 2:1–32.

——(1977). Long-term contracting, sticky prices, and monetary policy. *Journal of Monetary Economics*, 3:305–316.

——(1979a). On the determination of the public debt. *Journal of Political Economy*, 87:940–971.

——(1979b). Second thoughts on Keynesian economics. *American Economic Review, Papers and Proceedings*, 69:54–59.

——(1981). Output effects of government purchases. *Journal of Political Economy*, 89:1086–1121.

——(1989). The Ricardian approach to budget deficits. *Journal of Economic Perspectives*, 3:37–54.

——(1990). Government spending in a simple model of endogenous growth. *Journal of Political Economy*, 98:S103–S125.

——(1997). *Macroeconomics*. MIT Press, Cambridge, MA, fifth edition.

——and Becker, G. S. (1989). Fertility choice in a model of economic growth. *Econometrica*, 57:481–501.

——and Gordon, D. B. (1983a). A positive theory of monetary policy in a natural rate model. *Journal of Political Economy*, 91:589–610.

——and Gordon, D. B. (1983b). Rules, discretion, and reputation in a model of monetary policy. *Journal of Monetary Economics*, 12:101–120.

——and Grossman, H. I. (1971). A general disequilibrium model of income and employment. *American Economic Review*, 61:82–93.

——and Grossman, H. I. (1976). *Money, Employment, and Inflation*. Cambridge University Press, Cambridge.

——and Sala-i-Martin, X. (1995). *Economic Growth*. McGraw-Hill, New York.

Barsky, R. B., Mankiw, N. G., and Zeldes, S. P. (1986). Ricardian consumers with Keynesian propensities. *American Economic Review*, 76:676–691.

Batina, R. G. and Ihori, T. (2000). *Consumption Tax Policy and the Taxation of Capital Income*. Oxford University Press, Oxford.

Baumol, W. (1952). The transactions demand for cash: An inventory theoretic approach. *Quarterly Journal of Economics*, 67:545–556.

Baumol, W. J. (1959). *Economic Dynamics: An Introduction*. Macmillan, New York, second edition.

Baxter, M. and King, R. G. (1993). Fiscal policy in general equilibrium. *American Economic Review*, 83:315–334.

Bean, C. R. (1994). European unemployment: A survey. *Journal of Economic Literature*, 32:573–619.

Belan, P., Michel, P., and Pestieau, P. (1998). Pareto improving social security reform. *Geneva Papers on Risk and Insurance Theory*, 23:119–125.

Belan, P. and Pestieau, P. (1999). Privatizing social security: A critical assessment. *Geneva Papers on Risk and Insurance Theory*, 24:114–130.

Benassi, C., Chirco, A., and Colombo, C. (1994). *The New Keynesian Economics*. Basil Blackwell, Oxford.

Bénassy, J.-P. (1982). *The Economics of Market Disequilibrium*. Academic Press, New York.

——(1991a). Monopolistic competition. In Hildenbrand, W. and Sonnenschein, H., editors, *Handbook of Mathematical Economics*, volume IV. North-Holland, Amsterdam.

——(1991b). Optimal government policy in a macroeconomic model with imperfect competition and rational expectations. In Barnett, W. et al., editors, *Equilibrium Theory and Applications*. Cambridge University Press, Cambridge.

——(1993a). Imperfect competition and the suboptimality of rational expectations. *European Economic Review*, 37:1315–1330.

——(1993b). Non-clearing markets: Microeconomic concepts and macroeconomic applications. *Journal of Economic Literature*, 31:732–761.

——(1996a). Monopolistic competition, increasing returns to specialisation and output persistence. *Economics Letters*, 52:187–191.

——(1996b). Taste for variety and optimum production patterns in monopolistic competition. *Economics Letters*, 52:41–47.

Bibliography

Bénassy, J.-P. (1998). Is there always too little research in endogenous growth with expanding product variety? *European Economic Review*, 42:61–69.

Benhabib, J. and Farmer, R. E. A. (1994). Indeterminacy and increasing returns. *Journal of Economic Theory*, 63:19–41.

—— and Perli, R. (1994). Uniqueness and indeterminacy: Transitional dynamics in a model of endogenous growth. *Journal of Economic Theory*, 63:113–142.

——, Rogerson, R., and Wright, R. (1991). Homework in macroeconomics: Household production and aggregate fluctuations. *Journal of Political Economy*, 99:1166–1187.

Bergson, A. (1938). A reformulation of certain aspects of welfare economics. *Quarterly Journal of Economics*, 42:310–334.

Bernheim, B. D. (1987). Ricardian equivalence: An evaluation of theory and evidence. *Macroeconomics Annual*, 2:263–304.

Bewley, T. (1980). The optimum quantity of money. In Kareken, J. H. and Wallace, N., editors, *Models of Monetary Economies*. Federal Reserve Bank of Minneapolis, Minneapolis.

Bewley, T. F. (1999). *Why Wages Don't Fall During a Recession*. Harvard University Press, Cambridge, MA.

Bierwag, G. O., Grove, M. A., and Khang, C. (1969). National debt in a neoclassical growth model: Comment. *American Economic Review*, 59:205–210.

Binmore, K. and Dasgupta, P., editors (1987). *The Economics of Bargaining*. Basil Blackwell, Oxford.

Blackburn, K. and Sola, M. (1993). Speculative currency attacks and models of balance of payments crises. *Journal of Economic Surveys*, 7:119–144.

Blanchard, O. J. (1981). Output, the stock market, and interest rates. *American Economic Review*, 71:132–143.

—— (1983). Debt and the current account in Brazil. In Aspe Armella, P., Dornbusch, R., and Obstfeld, M., editors, *Financial Policies and the World Capital Market: The Problem of Latin American Countries*. University of Chicago Press, Chicago.

—— (1984). Current and anticipated deficits, interest rates and economic activity. *European Economic Review*, 25:7–27.

—— (1985). Debts, deficits, and finite horizons. *Journal of Political Economy*, 93:223–247.

—— (1990). Why does money affect output? A survey. In Friedman, B. M. and Hahn, F. H., editors, *Handbook of Monetary Economics*, volume II. North-Holland, Amsterdam.

—— (1991). Wage bargaining and unemployment persistence. *Journal of Money, Credit, and Banking*, 23:277–292.

—— (1997). Comment. *Macroeconomics Annual*, 12:289–293.

—— (2000a). *Macroeconomics*. Prentice-Hall, Upper Saddle River, NJ, second edition.

—— (2000b). What do we know about macroeconomics that Fisher and Wicksell did not? *Quarterly Journal of Economics*, 115:1375–1409.

—— and Diamond, P. (1989). The Beveridge curve. *Brookings Papers on Economic Activity*, 1:1–76.

—— and Diamond, P. (1994). Ranking, unemployment duration, and wages. *Review of Economic Studies*, 61:417–434.

—— and Fischer, S. (1989). *Lectures on Macroeconomics*. MIT Press, Cambridge, MA.

—— and Kahn, C. M. (1980). The solution of linear difference models under rational expectations. *Econometrica*, 48:1305–1311.

—— and Kiyotaki, N. (1987). Monopolistic competition and the effects of aggregate demand. *American Economic Review*, 77:647–666.

—— and Summers, L. H. (1986). Hysteresis and the European unemployment problem. *Macroeconomics Annual*, 1:15–89.

—— and Summers, L. H. (1987a). Fiscal increasing returns, hysteresis, real wages and unemployment. *European Economic Review*, 31:543–566.

—— and Summers, L. H. (1987b). Hysteresis in unemployment. *European Economic Review*, 31:288–295.

Blinder, A. S. (1994). On sticky prices: Academic theories meet the real world. In Mankiw, N. G., editor, *Monetary Policy*, pages 117–154. University of Chicago Press, Chicago.

—— and Solow, R. M. (1973). Does fiscal policy matter? *Journal of Public Economics*, 2:319–337.

—— and Solow, R. M. (1976). Does fiscal policy still matter? A reply. *Journal of Monetary Economics*, 6:501–510.

Bohn, H. (1992). Budget deficits and government accounting. *Carnegie-Rochester Conference Series on Public Policy*, 37:1–84.

Bond, E. W., Wang, P., and Yip, C. K. (1996). A general two-sector model of endogenous growth with human and physical capital: Balanced growth and transitional dynamics. *Journal of Economic Theory*, 68:149–173.

Booth, A. L. (1995). *The Economics of the Trade Union*. Cambridge University Press, Cambridge.

Bosworth, B. and Burtless, G., editors (1998). *Aging Societies: The Global Dimension*. Brookings Institution Press, Washington.

Bovenberg, A. L. (1993). Investment-promoting policies in open economies: The importance of intergenerational and international distributional effects. *Journal of Public Economics*, 51:3–54.

—— (1994). Capital taxation in the world economy. In van der Ploeg, F., editor, *Handbook of International Macroeconomics*. Basil Blackwell, Oxford.

—— and Heijdra, B. J. (1998). Environmental tax policy and intergenerational distribution. *Journal of Public Economics*, 67:1–24.

—— and Heijdra, B. J. (forthcoming). Environmental abatement and intergenerational distribution. *Environmental and Resource Economics*.

Boyce, W. E. and DiPrima, R. C. (1992). *Elementary Differential Equations and Boundary Value Problems*. Wiley, New York, fourth edition.

Branson, W. H. (1972). *Macroeconomic Theory and Policy*. Harper and Row, New York.

—— and Rotemberg, J. J. (1980). International adjustment with wage rigidity. *European Economic Review*, 13:309–332.

Braun, R. A. (1994). Tax disturbances and real economic activity in the postwar United States. *Journal of Monetary Economics*, 33:441–462.

Breyer, F. (1989). On the intergenerational Pareto efficiency of pay-as-you-go financed pension systems. *Journal of Institutional and Theoretical Economics*, 145:643–658.

—— and Straub, M. (1993). Welfare effects of unfunded pension systems when labor supply is endogenous. *Journal of Public Economics*, 50:77–91.

Brock, W. A. (1975). A simple perfect foresight monetary model. *Journal of Monetary Economics*, 1:133–150.

Bibliography

Broer, D. P. and Heijdra, B. J. (2001). The investment tax credit under monopolistic competition. *Oxford Economic Papers*, 53:318–351.

Browning, M., Hansen, L. P., and Heckman, J. J. (1999). Micro data and general equilibrium models. In Taylor, J. B. and Woodford, M., editors, *Handbook of Macroeconomics*, volume 1A. North-Holland, Amsterdam.

Buiter, W. H. (1980). The macroeconomics of Dr. Pangloss. *Economic Journal*, 90:34–50.

——(1981). Time preference and international lending and borrowing in an overlapping generations model. *Journal of Political Economy*, 89:769–797.

——(1985). A guide to public sector debt and deficits. *Economic Policy*, 1:13–79.

——(1987). Fiscal policy in open, interdependent economies. In Razin, A. and Sadka, E., editors, *Economic Policy in Theory and Practice*. Macmillan, London.

——(1988). Death, productivity growth and debt neutrality. *Economic Journal*, 98:279–293.

——(1990). *Principles of Budgetary and Financial Policy*. Harvester Wheatsheaf, New York.

——(1997). Generational accounts, aggregate saving and intergenerational distribution. *Economica*, 64:605–626.

——, Corsetti, G., and Roubini, N. (1993). Maastricht's fiscal rules. *Economic Policy*, 16:57–100.

——and Kletzer, K. M. (1992). Government solvency, Ponzi finance and the redundancy and usefulness of public debt. Working Paper 4076, NBER, Cambridge, MA.

——and Kletzer, K. M. (1993). Permanent international productivity growth differentials in an integrated global economy. *Scandinavian Journal of Economics*, 95:467–493.

——and Miller, M. (1981). Monetary policy and international competitiveness: The problems of adjustment. *Oxford Economic Papers, Supplement*, 33:143–175.

——and Miller, M. (1982). Real exchange rate overshooting and the output cost of bringing down inflation. *European Economic Review*, 33:143–175.

Bulow, J. and Summers, L. H. (1986). A theory of dual labor markets with applications to industrial policy, discrimination, and Keynesian unemployment. *Journal of Labor Economics*, 4:376–414.

Burda, M. and Wyplosz, C. (1997). *Macroeconomics: A European Text*. Oxford University Press, Oxford, second edition.

Burmeister, E. and Dobell, A. R. (1970). *Mathematical Theories of Economic Growth*. Macmillan, London.

Burness, H. S. (1976). A note on consistent naive intertemporal decision making and an application to the case of uncertain lifetime. *Review of Economic Studies*, 43:547–549.

Caballero, R. J. (1999). Aggregate investment. In Taylor, J. B. and Woodford, M., editors, *Handbook of Macroeconomics*, volume 1B. North-Holland, Amsterdam.

——and Leahy, J. V. (1996). Fixed costs: The demise of marginal q. Working Paper 5508, NBER, Cambridge, MA.

Calmfors, L. and Driffill, J. (1988). Centralisation of wage bargaining. *Economic Policy*, 6:14–61.

Calvo, G. A. (1982). Staggered contracts and exchange rate policy. In Frenkel, J., editor, *Exchange Rates and International Economics*. University of Chicago Press, Chicago.

——(1983). Staggered prices in a utility-maximizing framework. *Journal of Monetary Economics*, 12:383–398.

——(1987). Real exchange rate dynamics with nominal parities, structural change and overshooting. *Journal of International Economics*, 22:141–155.

—— and Obstfeld, M. (1988). Optimal time-consistent fiscal policy with finite lifetimes. *Econometrica*, 56:411–432.

—— and Rodriguez, C. A. (1977). A model of exchange rate determination under currency substitution and rational expectations. *Journal of Political Economy*, 85:617–625.

—— and Végh, C. A. (1994). Stabilization dynamics and backward-looking contracts. *Journal of Development Economics*, 43:59–84.

Campbell, J. Y. (1994). Inspecting the mechanism: An analytical approach to the stochastic growth model. *Journal of Monetary Economics*, 33:463–506.

Canton, E. (2001). Fiscal policy in a stochastic model of endogenous growth. *Economic Modelling*, 18:19–47.

Canzoneri, M. and Henderson, D. W. (1991). *Monetary Policy in Interdependent Economies*. MIT Press, Cambridge, MA.

Card, D. (1994). Intertemporal labour supply: An assessment. In Sims, C., editor, *Advances in econometrics: Sixth world congress*, volume II. Cambridge University Press, Cambridge.

Cass, D. (1965). Optimum growth in an aggregative model of capital accumulation. *Review of Economic Studies*, 32:233–240.

—— and Yaari, M. E. (1966). A re-examination of the pure consumption loans model. *Journal of Political Economy*, 74:353–367.

Cassou, S. P. and Lansing, K. J. (1998). Optimal fiscal policy, public capital, and the productivity slowdown. *Journal of Economic Dynamics and Control*, 22:911–935.

Chadha, B. (1989). Is increased price flexibility stabilizing? *Journal of Money, Credit, and Banking*, 21:481–497.

Chamley, C. (1985). On a simple rule for the optimal inflation rate in second best taxation. *Journal of Public Economics*, 26:35–50.

Chari, V. V., Christiano, L. J., and Kehoe, P. J. (1996). Optimality of the Friedman rule in economies with distorting taxes. *Journal of Monetary Economics*, 37:203–223.

——, Kehoe, P. J., and McGrattan, E. (2000). Sticky price models of the business cycle: Can the contract multiplier solve the persistence problem. *Econometrica*, 68:1151–1179.

Chatterjee, S. and Cooper, R. W. (1993). Entry, exit, product variety and the business cycle. Working Paper 4562, NBER, Cambridge, MA.

Chiang, A. C. (1984). *Fundamental Methods of Mathematical Economics*. McGraw-Hill, New York, third edition.

—— (1992). *Elements of Dynamic Optimization*. McGraw-Hill, New York.

Cho, J. O. and Cooley, T. F. (1994). Employment and hours over the business cycle. *Journal of Economic Dynamics and Control*, 18:411–432.

—— and Cooley, T. F. (1995). The business cycle with nominal contracts. *Economic Theory*, 6:13–33.

—— and Rogerson, R. (1988). Family labor supply and aggregate fluctuations. *Journal of Monetary Economics*, 21:233–245.

Chow, G. C. (1997). *Dynamic Economics: Optimization by the Lagrange Method*. Oxford University Press, New York and Oxford.

Christiano, L. J. and Eichenbaum, M. (1992). Current real-business-cycle theories and aggregate labour-market fluctuations. *American Economic Review*, 82:430–450.

——, Eichenbaum, M., and Evans, C. L. (1999). Monetary policy shocks: What have we learned and to what end? In Taylor, J. B. and Woodford, M., editors, *Handbook of Macroeconomics*, volume 1B. North-Holland, Amsterdam.

Bibliography

Chung, J. W. (1994). *Utility and Production Functions*. Basil Blackwell, Oxford.

Clarida, R., Galí, J., and Gertler, M. (1999). The science of monetary policy: A new Keynesian perspective. *Journal of Economic Literature*, 37:1661–1707.

Clower, R. (1965). The Keynesian counter-revolution: A theoretical appraisal. In Hahn, F. H. and Brechling, F., editors, *The Theory of Interest Rates*. Macmillan, London.

Clower, R. W. (1967). A reconsideration of the microfoundations of monetary theory. *Western Economic Journal*, 6:1–8.

Cogley, T. and Nason, J. M. (1995). Output dynamics in real-business-cycle models. *American Economic Review*, 85:492–511.

Cole, H. L. and Rogerson, R. (1999). Can the Mortensen-Pissarides matching model match the business-cycle facts? *International Economic Review*, 40:933–959.

Conlisk, J. (1969). A neoclassical growth model with endogenously positioned technological change frontier. *Economic Journal*, 79:348–362.

Cooley, T. F. (1995). *Frontiers of Business Cycle Research*. Princeton University Press, Princeton, NJ.

Cooper, R. N. (1968). *The Economics of Interdependence*. McGraw-Hill, New York.

Cooper, R. W. (1999). *Coordination Games: Complementarities and Macroeconomics*. Cambridge University Press, Cambridge.

—— and John, A. (1988). Coordinating coordination failures in Keynesian models. *Quarterly Journal of Economics*, 103:441–464.

Corneo, G. and Marquardt, M. (2000). Public pensions, unemployment insurance, and growth. *Journal of Public Economics*, 75:293–311.

Correia, I. and Teles, P. (1996). Is the Friedman rule optimal when money is an intermediate good? *Journal of Monetary Economics*, 38:223–244.

Cross, R., editor (1988). *Unemployment, Hysteresis and the Natural Rate Hypothesis*. Basil Blackwell, Oxford.

Cuddington, J. T., Johansson, P.-O., and Löfgren, K.-G. (1984). *Disequilibrium Macroeconomics in Open Economies*. Basil Blackwell, Oxford.

Cukierman, A. (1992). *Central Bank Strategy, Credibility, and Independence: Theory and Evidence*. MIT Press, Cambridge, MA.

—— and Meltzer, A. H. (1986). A theory of ambiguity, credibility, and inflation under discretion and asymmetric information. *Econometrica*, 54:1099–1128.

Danthine, J. P. and Donaldson, J. B. (1990). Efficiency wages and the business cycle puzzle. *European Economic Review*, 34:1275–1301.

—— and Donaldson, J. B. (1993). Methodological and empirical issues in real business cycle theory. *European Economic Review*, 37:1–35.

Danziger, L. (1999). A dynamic economy with costly price adjustment. *American Economic Review*, 89:878–901.

Davies, G. (1994). *A History of Money: From Ancient Times to the Present Day*. University of Wales Press, Cardiff.

Davis, S. J., Haltiwanger, J. C., and Schuh, S. (1996). *Job Creation and Destruction*. MIT Press, Cambridge, MA.

Deaton, A. (1992). *Understanding Consumption*. Oxford University Press, Oxford.

—— and Muellbauer, J. (1980). *Economics and Consumer Behavior*. Cambridge University Press, Cambridge.

DeCanio, S. J. (1979). Rational expectations and learning from experience. *Quarterly Journal of Economics*, 93:47–57.

Demmel, R. and Keuschnigg, C. (1999). Funded pensions and unemployment. Economic Series Discussion Paper 9911, University of Saarland, Saarbruecken.

Devereux, M. B., Head, A. C., and Lapham, B. J. (1996a). Aggregate fluctuations with increasing returns to specialisation and scale. *Journal of Economic Dynamics and Control*, 20:627–656.

—— (1996b). Monopolistic competition, increasing returns, and the effects of government spending. *Journal of Money, Credit, and Banking*, 28:233–253.

—— and Lockwood, B. (1991). Trade unions, non-binding wage agreements, and capital accumulation. *European Economic Review*, 35:1411–1426.

Diamond, P. A. (1965). National debt in a neoclassical growth model. *American Economic Review*, 55:1126–1150.

—— (1973). Taxation and public production in a growth setting. In Mirrlees, J. A. and Stern, N. H., editors, *Models of Economic Growth*. Macmillan, London.

—— (1982). Aggregate demand management in search equilibrium. *Journal of Political Economy*, 90:881–894.

—— (1984a). Money in search equilibrium. *Econometrica*, 52:1–20.

—— (1984b). *A Search-Equilibrium Approach to the Micro Foundations of Macroeconomics*. MIT Press, Cambridge, MA.

—— (1997). Macroeconomic aspects of social security reform. *Brookings Papers on Economic Activity*, 2:1–87.

——, editor (1999). *Issues in Privatizing Social Security*. MIT Press, Cambridge, MA.

—— and Fudenberg, D. (1989). Rational expectations business cycles in search equilibrium. *Journal of Political Economics*, 97:606–619.

—— and Fudenberg, D. (1991). Rational expectations business cycles in search equilibrium: A correction. *Journal of Political Economics*, 99:218–219.

—— and McFadden, D. L. (1974). Some uses of the expenditure function in public finance. *Journal of Public Economics*, 3:3–21.

Dixit, A. K. (1978). The balance of trade in a model of temporary equilibrium with rationing. *Review of Economic Studies*, 45:393–404.

—— (1990). *Optimization in Economic Theory*. Oxford University Press, Oxford, second edition.

—— (1996). *The Making of Economic Policy: A Transaction-Cost Perspective*. MIT Press, Cambridge, MA.

—— and Pindyck, R. S. (1994). *Investment under Uncertainty*. Princeton University Press, Princeton, NJ.

—— and Stiglitz, J. E. (1977). Monopolistic competition and optimum product diversity. *American Economic Review*, 67:297–308.

Dixon, H. D. (1987). A simple model of imperfect competition with Walrasian features. *Oxford Economic Papers*, 39:134–160.

—— and Hansen, C. T. (1999). A mixed industrial structure magnifies the importance of menu costs. *European Economic Review*, 43:1475–1499.

—— and Lawler, P. (1996). Imperfect competition and the fiscal multiplier. *Scandinavian Journal of Economics*, 98:219–231.

713

Bibliography

Dixon, H. D. and Rankin, N., editors (1995). *The New Macroeconomics, Imperfect Markets and Policy Effectiveness*. Cambridge University Press, Cambridge.

Dorfman, R. (1969). An economic interpretation of optimal control theory. *American Economic Review*, 59:817–831.

Dornbusch, R. (1976). Expectations and exchange rate dynamics. *Journal of Political Economy*, 84:1161–1176.

—— (1980). *Open Economy Macroeconomics*. Basic Books, New York.

—— (1983). Flexible exchange rates and interdependence. *IMF Staff Papers*, 30:3–30.

Dotsey, M. and Mao, C. S. (1992). How well do linear approximation methods work? The production tax case. *Journal of Monetary Economics*, 29:25–58.

Drazen, A. (1980). Recent developments in macroeconomic disequilibrium theory. *Econometrica*, 48:283–306.

—— (2000). *Political Economy in Macroeconomics*. Princeton University Press, Princeton, NJ.

—— and Helpman, E. (1990). Inflationary consequences of anticipated macroeconomic policies. *Review of Economic Studies*, 57:147–164.

Drèze, J. and Modigliani, F. (1972). Consumption decisions under uncertainty. *Journal of Economic Theory*, 5:308–335.

Dunlop, J. (1944). *Wage Determination under Trade Unions*. Macmillan, New York.

Eckstein, Z. and Zilcha, I. (1994). The effects of compulsory schooling on growth, income distribution and welfare. *Journal of Public Economics*, 54:339–359.

Edelberg, W., Eichenbaum, M., and Fisher, J. D. M. (1998). Understanding the effects of a shock to government purchases. Working Paper 6737, NBER, Cambridge, MA.

Eichenbaum, M. (1991). Real business-cycle theory: Wisdom or whimsey? *Journal of Economic Dynamics and Control*, 15:607–626.

Einzig, P. (1949). *Primitive Money in Its Ethnological, Historical and Economic Aspects*. Eyre and Spottiswood, London.

Eisner, R. and Strotz, R. H. (1963). Determinants of business investment. In Commission on Money and Credit, editor, *Impacts of Monetary Policy*. Prentice-Hall, Englewood Cliffs, NJ.

Elaydi, S. N. (1996). *An Introduction to Difference Equations*. Springer, New York.

Ethier, W. J. (1982). National and international returns to scale in the modern theory of international trade. *American Economic Review*, 72:389–405.

Farber, H. S. (1986). The analysis of union behavior. In Ashenfelter, O. and Layard, R., editors, *Handbook of Labor Economics*. North-Holland, Amsterdam.

Farmer, R. E. A. (1993). *The Macroeconomics of Self-Fulfilling Expectations*. MIT Press, Cambridge, MA.

Favero, C. and Hendry, D. F. (1992). Testing the Lucas critique: A review. *Econometric Reviews*, 11:265–306.

Feenstra, R. C. (1986). Functional equivalence between liquidity costs and the utility of money. *Journal of Monetary Economics*, 17:271–291.

Fehr, H. and Kotlikoff, L. (1995). Generational accounting in general equilibrium. Working Paper 5090, NBER, Cambridge, MA.

Feldstein, M. S. (1974). Social security, induced retirement, and aggregate capital accumulation. *Journal of Political Economy*, 82:905–926.

—— (1976). Social security and saving: The extended life cycle theory. *American Economic Review, Papers and Proceedings*, 66:77–86.

714

—— (1985). The optimal level of social security benefits. *Quarterly Journal of Economics*, 100:303–320.

—— (1986). Supply side economics: Old truths and new claims. *American Economic Review, Papers and Proceedings*, 76:26–30.

—— (1987). Should social security benefits be means tested? *Journal of Political Economy*, 95:468–484.

—— (1988). The effects of fiscal policies when incomes are uncertain: A contradiction to Ricardian equivalence. *American Economic Review*, 78:14–23.

—— (1994). Tax policy and international capital flows. *Weltwirtschaftliches Archiv*, 130:675–697.

—— (1997). Transition to a fully funded pension system: Five economic issues. Working Paper 6149, NBER, Cambridge, MA.

——, editor (1998). *Privatizing Social Security*. University of Chicago Press, Chicago.

—— and Horioka, C. (1980). Domestic saving and international capital flows. *Economic Journal*, 90:314–329.

Ferguson, C. E. (1969). *The Neoclassical Theory of Production and Distribution*. Cambridge University Press, Cambridge.

Fischer, S. (1974). Money in the production function. *Economic Inquiry*, 12:518–533.

—— (1977). Long-term contracts, rational expectations, and the optimal money supply rule. *Journal of Political Economy*, 85:191–205.

—— (1979). Capital accumulation on the transition path in a monetary optimizing model. *Econometrica*, 47:1433–1439.

—— (1980a). Dynamic inconsistency, cooperation, and the benevolent dissembling government. *Journal of Economic Dynamics and Control*, 2:93–107.

——, editor (1980b). *Rational Expectations and Economic Policy*. University of Chicago Press, Chicago.

Fisher, I. (1913). *The Purchasing Power of Money*. Macmillan, New York. Reprinted by Augustus M. Kelley, Fairfield, NJ, 1985.

—— (1930). *The Theory of Interest*. Macmillan, New York. Reprinted by Augustus M. Kelley, Fairfield, NJ, 1986.

Fisher, W. H. and Turnovsky, S. J. (1998). Public investment, congestion, and private capital accumulation. *Economic Journal*, 108:399–413.

Fleming, J. M. (1962). Domestic financial policies under fixed and flexible exchange rates. *IMF Staff Papers*, 9:369–379.

Foley, D. K. and Sidrauski, M. (1971). *Monetary and Fiscal Policy in a Growing Economy*. Macmillan, London.

Frenkel, J. A. and Razin, A. (1986). Fiscal policies in the world economy. *Journal of Political Economy*, 34:564–594.

—— and Razin, A. (1987). The Mundell-Fleming model: A quarter century later. *IMF Staff Papers*, 34:567–620.

—— and Rodriguez, C. (1982). Exchange rate dynamics and the overshooting hypothesis. *IMF Staff Papers*, 29:1–30.

Friedman, B. M. (1979). Optimal expectations and the extreme information assumption of 'rational expectations' macromodels. *Journal of Monetary Economics*, 5:23–41.

Friedman, M. (1968). The role of monetary policy. *American Economic Review*, 58:1–17.

—— (1969). *The Optimal Quantity of Money and Other Essays*. Aldine, Chicago.

Bibliography

Frydman, R. and Phelps, E. S., editors (1983). *Individual Forecasting and Aggregate Outcomes.* Cambridge University Press, Cambridge.

Fuente, A. de la (2000). *Mathematical Methods and Models for Economists.* Cambridge University Press, Cambridge.

Gahvari, F. (1988). Lump-sum taxation and the superneutrality and optimum quantity of money in life cycle growth models. *Journal of Public Economics,* 36:339–367.

Galí, J. (1992). How well does the IS-LM model fit postwar U.S. data? *Quarterly Journal of Economics,* 107:709–739.

——(1999). Technology, employment, and the business cycle: Do technology shocks explain aggregate fluctuations? *American Economic Review,* 89:249–271.

Galor, O. (1992). A two-sector overlapping-generations model: A global characterization of the dynamical system. *Econometrica,* 60:1351–1386.

——and Ryder, H. E. (1989). Existence, uniqueness, and stability of equilibrium in an overlapping-generations model with productive capital. *Journal of Economic Theory,* 49:360–375.

Gärtner, M. (1993). *Macroeconomics under Flexible Exchange Rates.* Harvester Wheatsheaf, New York.

Georges, C. (1995). Adjustment costs and indeterminacy in perfect foresight models. *Journal of Economic Dynamics and Control,* 19:39–50.

Gertler, M. (1999). Government debt and social security in a life-cycle model. *Carnegie-Rochester Series on Public Policy,* 50:61–117.

Giavazzi, F. and Wyplosz, C. (1985). The zero root problem: A note on the dynamic determination of the stationary equilibrium in linear models. *Review of Economic Studies,* 52:353–357.

Gilchrist, S. and Williams, J. C. (2000). Putty-clay and investment: A business cycle analysis. *Journal of Political Economy,* 108:928–960.

Giovannini, A. (1988). The real exchange rate, the capital stock, and fiscal policy. *European Economic Review,* 32:1747–1767.

Glomm, G. and Ravikumar, B. (1992). Public versus private investment in human capital: Endogenous growth and income inequality. *Journal of Political Economy,* 100:818–834.

——and Ravikumar, B. (1994). Public investment in infrastructure in a simple growth model. *Journal of Economic Dynamics and Control,* 18:1173–1187.

Goodfriend, M. and King, R. G. (1997). The new neoclassical synthesis and the role of monetary policy. *Macroeconomics Annual,* 12:231–283.

Gordon, R. H. and Varian, H. R. (1988). Intergenerational risk sharing. *Journal of Public Economics,* 37:185–202.

Gordon, R. J., editor (1974). *Milton Friedman's Monetary Framework: A Debate with His Critics.* University of Chicago Press, Chicago.

——(1990). What is New-Keynesian economics? *Journal of Economic Literature,* 28:1115–1171.

Gottfries, N. and Horn, H. (1987). Wage formation and the persistence of unemployment. *Economic Journal,* 97:877–884.

Gould, J. P. (1968). Adjustment costs in the theory of investment of the firm. *Review of Economic Studies,* 35:47–55.

Gramlich, E. M. (1994). Infrastructure investment: A review essay. *Journal of Economic Literature,* 32:1176–1196.

Grandmont, J.-M. (1985). On endogenous competitive business cycles. *Econometrica*, 53:995–1045.

Gray, J. A. (1976). Wage indexation: A macroeconomic approach. *Journal of Monetary Economics*, 2:221–235.

——(1978). On indexation and contract length. *Journal of Political Economy*, 86:1–18.

Greenwood, J. and Hercowitz, Z. (1991). The allocation of capital and time over the business cycle. *Journal of Political Economy*, 99:1188–1214.

——and Huffman, G. W. (1988). Investment, capacity utilization, and the real business cycle. *American Economic Review*, 78:402–417.

——and Huffman, G. W. (1991). Tax analysis in a real business cycle model: On measuring Harberger triangles and Okun gaps. *Journal of Monetary Economics*, 27:167–190.

Griliches, Z. (2000). *R & D, Education, and Productivity: A Retrospective*. Harvard University Press, Cambridge, MA.

Groot, H. L. F. de and Nahuis, R. (1998). Taste for diversity and the optimality of economic growth. *Economics Letters*, 58:291–295.

Grossman, G. M. and Helpman, E. (1989). Product development and international trade. *Journal of Political Economy*, 97:1261–1283.

——and Helpman, E. (1990). Comparative advantage and long-run growth. *American Economic Review*, 80:796–815.

——and Helpman, E. (1991). *Innovation and Growth in the Global Economy*. MIT Press, Cambridge, MA.

Grossman, S. J. and Stiglitz, J. E. (1980). On the impossibility of informationally efficient markets. *American Economic Review*, 70:393–408.

Grout, P. A. (1984). Investment and wages in the absence of binding contracts. *Econometrica*, 52:449–460.

Gylfason, T. (1999). *Principles of Economic Growth*. Oxford University Press, Oxford.

Haavelmoo, T. (1945). Multiplier effects of a balanced budget. *Econometrica*, 13:311–318.

Hacche, G. (1979). *The Theory of Economic Growth: An Introduction*. Macmillan, London.

Hairault, J.-O. and Portier, F. (1993). Money, New-Keynesian macroeconomics and the business cycle. *European Economic Review*, 37:1533–1568.

Hall, R. E. (1971). The dynamic effects of fiscal policy in an economy with foresight. *Review of Economic Studies*, 38:229–244.

——(1980). Labor supply and aggregate fluctuations. *Carnegie-Rochester Series on Public Policy*, 12:7–33.

——(1991). Substitution over time in consumption and work. In McKenzie, L. W. and Zamagni, S., editors, *Value and Capital Fifty Years Later*. Macmillan, London.

——(1997). Macroeconomic fluctuations and the allocation of time. *Journal of Labor Economics*, 15:S223–S250.

Hamberg, D. (1971). *Models of Economic Growth*. Harper and Row, New York.

Hamermesh, D. S. (1993). *Labor Demand*. Princeton University Press, Princeton, NJ.

——and Pfann, G. A. (1996). Adjustment costs in factor demand. *Journal of Economic Literature*, 34:1264–1292.

Hansen, G. D. (1985). Indivisible labour and the business cycle. *Journal of Monetary Economics*, 16:309–327.

Hansen, G. D. and Wright, R. (1994). The labor market in real business cycle theory. In Miller, P. J., editor, *The Rational Expectations Revolution: Readings from the Front Line*. MIT Press, Cambridge, MA.

Hansen, L. P. and Heckman, J. J. (1996). The empirical foundations of calibration. *Journal of Economic Perspectives*, 10:87–104.

—— and Singleton, K. J. (1983). Stochastic consumption, risk aversion, and the temporal behavior of asset returns. *Journal of Political Economics*, 91:249–265.

Harrison, R. (1987). Jeremy Bentham. In Eatwell, J., Milgate, M., and Newman, P., editors, *The New Palgrave: A Dictionary of Economics*. Macmillan, London.

Hart, O. D. (1982). A model of imperfect competition with Keynesian features. *Quarterly Journal of Economics*, 97:109–138.

Haveman, R. (1994). Should generational accounts replace public budgets and deficits? *Journal of Economic Perspectives*, 8:95–111.

Hayashi, F. (1982). Tobin's marginal q and average q: A neoclassical interpretation. *Econometrica*, 50:213–224.

Heijdra, B. J. (1998). Fiscal policy multipliers: The role of market imperfection and scale economies. *International Economic Review*, 39:659–696.

—— and Ligthart, J. E. (1997). Keynesian multipliers, direct crowding out, and the optimal provision of public goods. *Journal of Macroeconomics*, 19:803–826.

—— and Ligthart, J. E. (2000). The dynamic macroeconomic effects of tax policy in an overlapping generations model. *Oxford Economic Papers*, 52:677–701.

——, Ligthart, J. E., and van der Ploeg, F. (1998). Fiscal policy, distortionary taxation, and direct crowding out under monopolistic competition. *Oxford Economic Papers*, 50:79–88.

—— and Meijdam, A. C. (forthcoming). Public investment and intergenerational distribution. *Journal of Economic Dynamics and Control*.

—— and van der Horst, A. (2000). Taxing energy to improve the environment: Efficiency and distributional effects. *De Economist*, 148:45–69.

—— and van der Ploeg, F. (1996). Keynesian multipliers and the cost of public funds under monopolistic competition. *Economic Journal*, 106:1284–1296.

Hicks, J. R. (1937). Mr Keynes and the Classics: A suggested interpretation. *Econometrica*, 5:147–159.

Hirshleifer, J. and Riley, J. G. (1992). *The Analytics of Uncertainty and Information*. Cambridge University Press, Cambridge.

Hoel, M. (1990). Efficiency wages and income taxes. *Journal of Economics*, 51:89–99.

Homburg, S. (1990). The efficiency of unfunded pension systems. *Journal of Institutional and Theoretical Economics*, 146:640–647.

Homer (1946). *The Odyssey*. Penguin, Harmondsworth. Edition used: E.V. Rieu, Ed.

Hoover, K. D., editor (1992). *The New Classical Macroeconomics*. Edward Elgar, Aldershot.

Hornstein, A. (1993). Monopolistic competition, increasing returns to scale, and the importance of productivity shocks. *Journal of Monetary Economics*, 31:299–316.

Hosios, A. J. (1990). On the efficiency of matching and related models of search and unemployment. *Review of Economic Studies*, 57:279–298.

Howarth, R. B. (1991). Intergenerational competitive equilibria under technological uncertainty and an exhaustible resource constraint. *Journal of Environmental Economics and Management*, 21:225–243.

—— (1998). An overlapping generations model of climate-economy interactions. *Scandinavian Journal of Economics*, 100:575–591.

—— and Norgaard, R. B. (1990). Intergenerational resource rights, efficiency, and social optimality. *Land Economics*, 66:1–11.

—— and Norgaard, R. B. (1992). Environmental valuation under sustainable development. *American Economic Review, Papers and Proceedings*, 82:473–477.

Howitt, P. (1985). Transaction costs in the theory of unemployment. *American Economic Review*, 75:88–100.

Huang, K. X. D. and Liu, Z. (1999). Staggered contracts and business cycle persistence. Discussion Paper 127, Federal Reserve Bank of Minneapolis, Minneapolis, MN.

Ihori, T. (1996). *Public Finance in an Overlapping Generations Economy*. Macmillan Press, London.

Inada, K.-I. (1963). On a two-sector model of economic growth: Comments and a generalisation. *Review of Economic Studies*, 30:119–127.

Intriligator, M. D. (1971). *Mathematical Optimization and Economic Theory*. Prentice Hall, Englewood Cliffs, NJ.

Ireland, P. N. (1994). Money and growth: An alternative approach. *American Economic Review*, 84:47–65.

Jevons, W. S. (1875). *Money and the Mechanism of Exchange*. King, London. Reprinted by Augustus M. Kelley, Fairfield, NJ.

John, A., Pecchenino, R., Schimmelpfennig, D., and Schreft, S. (1995). Short-lived agents and the long-lived environment. *Journal of Public Economics*, 58:127–141.

—— and Pecchenino, R. A. (1994). An overlapping generations model of growth and the environment. *Economic Journal*, 104:1393–1410.

Jones, C. I. (1995). R & D-based models of economic growth. *Journal of Political Economy*, 103:759–784.

—— (1998). *Introduction to Economic Growth*. W.W. Norton, New York and London.

Jones, L. E. and Manuelli, R. E. (1992). Finite lifetimes and growth. *Journal of Economic Theory*, 58:171–197.

—— (1997). The sources of growth. *Journal of Economic Dynamics and Control*, 21:75–114.

—— and Rossi, P. E. (1997). On the optimal taxation of capital income. *Journal of Economic Theory*, 73:93–117.

Jones, R. A. (1976). The origin and development of media of exchange. *Journal of Political Economy*, 84:757–775.

Jonsson, G. and Klein, P. (1996). Stochastic fiscal policy and the Swedish business cycle. *Journal of Monetary Economics*, 38:245–268.

Judd, K. L. (1982). An alternative to steady-state comparisons in perfect foresight models. *Economics Letters*, 10:55–59.

—— (1985). Short-run analysis of fiscal policy in a simple perfect foresight model. *Journal of Political Economy*, 93:298–319.

—— (1987a). Debt and distortionary taxation in a simple perfect foresight model. *Journal of Monetary Economics*, 20:51–72.

—— (1987b). The welfare cost of factor taxation in a perfect-foresight model. *Journal of Political Economy*, 95:675–709.

—— (1998). *Numerical Methods in Economics*. MIT Press, Cambridge, MA.

Bibliography

Kaganovich, M. and Zilcha, I. (1999). Education, social security, and growth. *Journal of Public Economics*, 71:289–309.

Kahn, R. F. (1931). The relation of home investment to unemployment. *Economic Journal*, 41:173–198.

Kaldor, N. (1961). Capital accumulation and economic growth. In Lutz, F. A. and Hague, D. C., editors, *The Theory of Capital*, pages 177–222. St Martin's Press, New York.

Kamien, M. I. and Schwartz, N. L. (1991). *Dynamic Optimization: The Calculus of Variations and Optimal Control in Economics and Management*. North-Holland, Amsterdam, second edition.

Katz, L. F. (1986). Efficiency wage theories: A partial evaluation. *NBER Macroeconomics Annual*, 1:235–290.

Kennan, J. (1979). The estimation of partial adjustment models with rational expectations. *Econometrica*, 47:1441–1455.

Keynes, J. M. (1930). *A Treatise on Money*. Macmillan, London.

——(1936). *The General Theory of Employment, Interest, and Money*. Macmillan, London.

——(1937). The general theory of employment. *Quarterly Journal of Economics*, 51:209–223.

Killingsworth, M. R. and Heckman, J. J. (1986). Female labor supply: A survey. In Ashenfelter, O. and Layard, R., editors, *Handbook of Labor Economics*. North-Holland, Amsterdam.

Kimball, M. S. (1994). Labor-market dynamics when unemployment is a worker discipline device. *American Economic Review*, 84:1045–1059.

King, R. G. (1991). *Value and Capital* in the equilibrium business cycle programme. In McKenzie, L. W. and Zamagni, S., editors, *Value and Capital Fifty Years Later*. Macmillan, London.

——and Levine, R. (1994). Capital fundamentalism, economic development and economic growth. *Carnegie-Rochester Series on Public Policy*, 40:259–292.

——, Plosser, C. I., and Rebelo, S. (1987). Production, growth and business cycles: Technical appendix. Working paper, University of Rochester, Rochester, NY.

——, Plosser, C. I., and Rebelo, S. (1988a). Production, growth and business cycles I: The basic neoclassical model. *Journal of Monetary Economics*, 21:195–232.

——, Plosser, C. I., and Rebelo, S. (1988b). Production, growth and business cycles II: New directions. *Journal of Monetary Economics*, 21:309–341.

——and Rebelo, S. (1993). Transitional dynamics and economic growth in the neoclassical model. *American Economic Review*, 83:908–931.

——and Rebelo, S. (1999). Resuscitating real business cycles. In Taylor, J. B. and Woodford, M., editors, *Handbook of Macroeconomics*, volume 1B. North-Holland, Amsterdam.

——and Watson, M. W. (1986). Money, prices, interest rates and the business cycle. *Review of Economics and Statistics*, 78:35–53.

——and Wolman, A. L. (1996). Inflation targeting in a St. Louis model of the 21st century. Working Paper 5507, NBER, Cambridge, MA.

——and Wolman, A. L. (1999). What should the monetary authority do when prices are sticky? In Taylor, J. B., editor, *Monetary Policy Rules*. University of Chicago Press, Chicago.

Kiyotaki, N. (1988). Multiple expectational equilibria under monopolistic competition. *Quarterly Journal of Economics*, 103:695–713.

——and Wright, R. (1993). A search-theoretic approach to monetary economics. *American Economic Review*, 83:63–77.

Klamer, A. (1984). *The New Classical Macroeconomics*. Wheatsheaf, Brighton.

Klein, M. W. (1998). *Mathematical Methods for Economics*. Addison Wesley, Reading, MA.

Klundert, Th. van de and Smulders, S. (1992). Reconstructing growth theory: A survey. *De Economist*, 140:177–203.

Koopmans, T. C. (1965). On the concept of optimal economic growth. In *The Econometric Approach to Development Planning*. Rand-McNally, Chicago.

—— (1967). Intertemporal distribution and 'optimal' aggregate economic growth. In *Ten Economic Studies in the Tradition of Irving Fisher*. Wiley, New York.

Koskela, E. and Vilmunen, J. (1996). Tax progression is good for employment in popular models of trade union behaviour. *Labour Economics*, 3:65–80.

Kotlikoff, L. J. (1993a). From deficit delusion to the fiscal balance rule: Looking for an economically meaningful way to assess fiscal policy. In Felderer, B., editor, *Public Pension Economics*. Springer Verlag, New York.

—— (1993b). *Generational Accounting*. Free Press, New York.

—— and Summers, L. H. (1979). Tax incidence in a life cycle model with variable labor supply. *Quarterly Journal of Economics*, 94:705–718.

—— and Summers, L. H. (1987). Tax incidence. In Auerbach, A. J. and Feldstein, M., editors, *Handbook of Public Economics*, volume I. North-Holland, Amsterdam.

Kouri, P. J. K. (1976). The exchange rate and the balance of payments in the short run and in the long run: A monetary approach. *Scandinavian Journal of Economics*, 78:280–304.

Kreyszig, E. (1999). *Advanced Engineering Mathematics*. John Wiley, New York, eighth edition.

Krugman, P. (1994). *Peddling Prosperity: Economic Sense and Nonsense in the Age of Diminished Expectations*. W.W. Norton, New York and London.

Kydland, F. E. and Prescott, E. C. (1977). Rules rather than discretion: The inconsistency of optimal plans. *Journal of Political Economy*, 85:473–491.

—— (1982). Time to build and aggregate fluctuations. *Econometrica*, 50:1345–1370.

—— (1996). The computational experiment: An econometric tool. *Journal of Economic Perspectives*, 10:69–85.

Laidler, D. (1991). *The Golden Age of the Quantity Theory*. Philip Alland, New York.

Lancaster, P. and Tismenetsky, M. (1985). *The Theory of Matrices*. Academic Press, San Diego, CA, second edition.

Laxton, D., Isard, P., Faruqee, H., Prasad, E., and Turtelboom, B. (1998). *MULTIMOD Mark III: The Core Dynamic and Steady-State Models*. International Monetary Fund, Washington.

Layard, R., Nickell, S., and Jackman, R. (1991). *Unemployment: Macroeconomic Performance and the Labour Market*. Oxford University Press, Oxford.

Leijonhufvud, A. (1968). *On Keynesian Economics and the Economics of Keynes*. Oxford University Press, New York.

Léonard, D. and Long, N. V. (1992). *Optimal Control Theory and Static Optimization in Economics*. Cambridge University Press, Cambridge.

Leontief, W. (1946). The pure theory of the guaranteed annual wage contract. *Journal of Political Economy*, 54:76–79.

Levy, D., Bergen, M., Dutta, S., and Venable, R. (1997). The magnitude of menu costs: Direct evidence from large U.S. supermarket chains. *Quarterly Journal of Economics*, 112:791–825.

Lindbeck, A. and Snower, D. J. (1988). *The Insider-Outsider Theory of Employment and Unemployment*. MIT Press, Cambridge, MA.

Liviatan, N. (1984). Tight money and inflation. *Journal of Monetary Economics*, 13:5–15.

Bibliography

Ljungqvist, L. and Sargent, T. J. (2000). *Recursive Macroeconomic Theory*. MIT Press, Cambridge, MA.

——and Uhlig, H. (2000). Tax policy and aggregate demand management under catching up with the Joneses. *American Economic Review*, 90:356–366.

Long, J. B. and Plosser, C. I. (1983). Real business cycles. *Journal of Political Economy*, 91:39–69.

Loury, G. C. (1981). Intergenerational transfers and the distribution of earnings. *Econometrica*, 49:843–867.

Lucas, R. E. (1967). Adjustment costs and the theory of supply. *Journal of Political Economy*, 75:321–334.

——(1972). Expectations and the neutrality of money. *Journal of Economic Theory*, 4:103–124. Reprinted in: R. E. Lucas (1981).

——(1973). Some international evidence on the output-inflation tradeoffs. *American Economic Review*, 63:326–334. Reprinted in: R. E. Lucas (1981).

——(1976). Econometric policy analysis: A critique. *Carnegie-Rochester Conference on Public Policy*, 1:19–46. Reprinted in: R. E. Lucas (1981).

——(1980). Methods and problems in business cycle theory. *Journal of Money, Credit, and Banking*, 12:696–715. Reprinted in: R. E. Lucas (1981).

——(1981). *Studies in Business-Cycle Theory*. MIT Press, Cambridge, MA.

——(1987). *Models of Business Cycles*. Basil Blackwell, Oxford.

——(1988). On the mechanics of economic development. *Journal of Monetary Economics*, 22:3–42.

——(1990a). Supply-side economics: An analytical review. *Oxford Economic Papers*, 42:293–316.

——(1990b). Why doesn't capital flow from rich to poor countries? *American Economic Review, Paper and Proceedings*, 80:92–96.

——and Sargent, T. J., editors (1981). *Rational Expectations and Econometric Practice*. George Allen and Unwin, London.

——and Stokey, N. L. (1983). Optimal fiscal and monetary policy in an economy without capital. *Journal of Monetary Economics*, 12:55–93.

Maddock, R. and Carter, M. (1982). A child's guide to rational expectations. *Journal of Economic Literature*, 20:39–51.

Malinvaud, E. (1977). *The Theory of Unemployment Reconsidered*. Basil Blackwell, Oxford.

Mankiw, N. G. (1985). Small menu costs and large business cycles: A macroeconomic model of monopoly. *Quarterly Journal of Economics*, 100:529–539.

——(1987). The optimal collection of seigniorage: Theory and evidence. *Journal of Monetary Economics*, 20:327–341.

——(1988). Imperfect competition and the Keynesian cross. *Economics Letters*, 26:7–13.

——(1989). Real business cycles: A new Keynesian perspective. *Journal of Economic Perspectives*, 3:79–90.

——(2000a). *Macroeconomics*. Worth Publishers, New York, fourth edition.

——(2000b). The savers-spenders theory of fiscal policy. *American Economic Review, Papers and Proceedings*, 90:120–125.

——and Romer, D., editors (1991). *New Keynesian Economics*. MIT Press, Cambridge, MA.

——, Romer, D., and Weil, D. N. (1992). A contribution to the empirics of economic growth. *Quarterly Journal of Economics*, 107:407–437.

——, Rotemberg, J. J., and Summers, L. H. (1985). Intertemporal substitution in macroeconomics. *Quarterly Journal of Economics*, 100:225–251.

——and Whinston, M. D. (1986). Free entry and social inefficiency. *Rand Journal of Economics*, 17:48–58.

Manning, A. (1987). An integration of trade union models in a sequential bargaining framework. *Economic Journal*, 97:121–139.

Marini, G. and Scaramozzino, P. (1995). Overlapping generations and environmental control. *Journal of Environmental Economics and Management*, 29:64–77.

——and van der Ploeg, F. (1988). Monetary and fiscal policy in an optimising model with capital accumulation and finite lives. *Economic Journal*, 98:772–786.

Marschak, J. (1953). Economic measurement for policy and prediction. In Hood, W. C. and Koopmans, T. C., editors, *Studies in Econometric Method*. Wiley, New York.

Matsuyama, K. (1987). Current account dynamics in a finite horizon model. *Journal of International Economics*, 23:299–313.

——(1995). Complementarities and cumulative processes in models of monopolistic competition. *Journal of Economic Literature*, 33:701–729.

McCallum, B. T. (1980). Rational expectations and macroeconomic stabilization policy: An overview. *Journal of Money, Credit, and Banking*, 12:716–746.

——(1983a). The liquidity trap and the Pigou effect: A dynamic analysis with rational expectations. *Economica*, 50:395–405.

——(1983b). The role of overlapping-generations models in monetary economics. *Carnegie-Rochester Conference Series on Public Policy*, 18:9–44.

——(1989a). *Monetary Economics: Theory and Policy*. Macmillan, New York.

——(1989b). Real business cycle models. In Barro, R. J., editor, *Modern Business Cycle Theory*. Basil Blackwell, Oxford.

——and Goodfriend, M. S. (1987). Demand for money: Theoretical studies. In Eatwell, J., Milgate, M., and Newman, P., editors, *The New Palgrave: A Dictionary of Economics*. Macmillan, London.

——and Nelson, E. (1999). An optimizing IS-LM specification for monetary policy and business cycle analysis. *Journal of Money, Credit, and Banking*, 31:296–316.

McDonald, I. M. and Solow, R. M. (1981). Wage bargaining and employment. *American Economic Review*, 71:896–908.

McGrattan, E. R. (1994). The macroeconomic effects of distortionary taxation. *Journal of Monetary Economics*, 33:573–601.

McKibbin, W. and Sachs, J. (1991). *Global Linkages: Macroeconomic Interdependence and Cooperation in the World Economy*. The Brookings Institution, Washington, DC.

McKibbin, W. J. (1988). The economics of international policy coordination. *Economic Record*, 64:241–265.

Meijdam, A. C. and Verhoeven, M. J. (1998). Comparative dynamics in perfect-foresight models. *Computational Economics*, 12:115–124.

Menger, C. (1892). On the origin of money. *Economic Journal*, 2:239–255.

Merton, R. C. (1971). Optimum consumption and portfolio rules in a continuous-time model. *Journal of Economic Theory*, 3:373–413. Reprinted in: R.C. Merton, Continuous-Time Finance. Oxford: Basil Blackwell, 1990.

Merz, M. (1995). Search in the labor market and the real business cycle. *Journal of Monetary Economics*, 36:269–300.

Merz, M. (1997). A market structure for an environment with heterogeneous job-matches, indivisible labour and persistent unemployment. *Journal of Economic Dynamics and Control*, 21:853–872.

—— (1999). Heterogeneous job-matches and the cyclical behavior of labor turnover. *Journal of Monetary Economics*, 43:91–124.

Michel, P. and de la Croix, D. (2000). Myopic and perfect foresight in the OLG model. *Economics Letters*, 67:53–60.

Miller, M. H. (1977). Debt and taxes. *Journal of Finance*, 32:261–275.

—— and Modigliani, F. (1961). Dividend policy, growth, and the valuation of shares. *Journal of Business*, 34:411–433.

—— and Orr, D. (1966). A model of the demand for money by firms. *Quarterly Journal of Economics*, 79:413–435.

—— and Upton, C. W. (1974). *Macroeconomics: A Neoclassical Introduction*. University of Chicago Press, Chicago.

Miller, P. J., editor (1994). *The Rational Expectations Revolution: Readings from the Front Line*. MIT Press, Cambridge, MA.

Mitchell, B. R. (1998a). *International Historical Statistics: Europe, 1750–1993*. Macmillan, London.

—— (1998b). *International Historical Statistics: The Americas, 1750–1993*. Macmillan, London.

Modigliani, F. (1944). Liquidity preference and the theory of interest and money. *Econometrica*, 12:45–88.

—— and Miller, M. H. (1958). The cost of capital, corporation finance and the theory of investment. *American Economic Review*, 48:261–297.

Molana, H. and Moutos, T. (1992). A note on taxation, imperfect competition, and the balanced-budget multiplier. *Oxford Economic Papers*, 44:68–74.

Mortensen, D. T. (1978). Specific capital and labor turnover. *Bell Journal of Economics*, 9:572–586.

—— (1982a). The matching process as a noncooperative bargaining game. In McCall, J. J., editor, *The Economics of Information and Uncertainty*. University of Chicago Press, Chicago.

—— (1982b). Property rights and efficiency in mating, racing, and related games. *American Economic Review*, 72:968–979.

—— (1986). Job search and labor market analysis. In Ashenfelter, O. and Layard, R., editors, *Handbook of Labor Economics*. North-Holland, Amsterdam.

—— (1989). The persistence and indeterminacy of unemployment in search equilibrium. *Scandinavian Journal of Economics*, 91:347–370.

—— and Pissarides, C. A. (1994). Job creation and job destruction in the theory of unemployment. *Review of Economic Studies*, 61:397–415.

—— and Pissarides, C. A. (1999a). Job reallocation, employment fluctuations and unemployment. In Taylor, J. B. and Woodford, M., editors, *Handbook of Macroeconomics*, volume 1B. North-Holland, Amsterdam.

—— and Pissarides, C. A. (1999b). New developments in models of search in the labor market. In Ashenfelter, O. and Card, D., editors, *Handbook of Labor Economics*, volume 3B. North-Holland, Amsterdam.

Mourmouras, A. (1993). Conservationist government policies and intergenerational equity in an overlapping generations model with renewable resources. *Journal of Public Economics*, 51:249–268.

Muellbauer, J. and Portes, R. (1978). Macroeconomic models with quantity rationing. *Economic Journal*, 88:788–821.

Mueller, D. C. (1989). *Public Choice II*. Cambridge University Press, Cambridge.

Mulligan, C. B. (1998). Microfoundations and macro implications of indivisible labor. Discussion Paper 126, Federal Reserve Bank of Minneapolis, Minneapolis, MN.

—— and Sala-i-Martin, X. (1993). Transitional dynamics in two-sector models of endogenous growth. *Quarterly Journal of Economics*, 108:739–773.

Mundell, R. A. (1968). *International Economics*. Macmillan, New York.

Mussa, M. (1979). Macroeconomic interdependence and the exchange rate regime. In Dornbusch, R. and Frenkel, J. A., editors, *International Economic Policy: Theory and Evidence*. Johns Hopkins University Press, Baltimore, MD.

Muth, J. F. (1961). Rational expectations and the theory of price movements. *Econometrica*, 29:315–335.

Neary, J. P. (1980). Nontraded goods and the balance of trade in a neo-Keynesian temporary equilibrium. *Quarterly Journal of Economics*, 95:403–429.

—— (1990). Neo-Keynesian macroeconomics in an open economy. In van der Ploeg, F., editor, *Advanced Lectures in Quantitative Economics*. Academic Press, San Diego, CA.

—— and Stiglitz, J. E. (1983). Toward a reconstruction of Keynesian economics: Expectations and constrained equilibria. *Quarterly Journal of Economics*, 98:199–228.

Nerlove, M. and Raut, L. K. (1997). Growth models with endogenous population: A general framework. In Rosenzweig, M. R. and Stark, O., editors, *Handbook of Population and Family Economics*. North-Holland, Amsterdam.

Ng, Y.-K. (1982). Macroeconomics with non-perfect competition. *Economic Journal*, 90:598–610.

Nickell, S. J. (1986). Dynamic models of labour demand. In Ashenfelter, O. and Layard, R., editors, *Handbook of Labor Economics*. North-Holland, Amsterdam.

Niehans, J. (1977). Exchange rate dynamics with stock/flow interaction. *Journal of Political Economy*, 85:1245–1257.

—— (1978). *The Theory of Money*. Johns Hopkins University Press, Baltimore, MD.

Nielsen, S. B. (1994). Social security and foreign indebtedness in a small open economy. *Open Economies Review*, 5:47–63.

—— and Sørensen, P. B. (1991). Capital income taxation in a growing open economy. *European Economic Review*, 34:179–197.

Nourry, C. (2001). Stability of equilibria in the overlapping generations model with endogenous labour supply. *Journal of Economic Dynamics and Control*, 25:1647–1663.

Obstfeld, M. (1982). Aggregate spending and the terms of trade: Is there a Laursen-Metzler effect? *Quarterly Journal of Economics*, 97:251–270.

—— and Rogoff, K. (1984). Exchange rate dynamics with sluggish prices under alternative price-adjustment rules. *International Economic Review*, 25:159–174.

—— and Rogoff, K. (1995a). Exchange rate dynamics redux. *Journal of Political Economy*, 103:624–660.

Bibliography

Obstfeld, M. and Rogoff, K. (1995b). The intertemporal approach to the current account. In Grossman, G. M. and Rogoff, K., editors, *Handbook of International Economics*, volume 3. North-Holland, Amsterdam.

——and Rogoff, K. (1996). *Foundations of International Macroeconomics*. MIT Press, Cambridge, MA.

O'Connell, S. A. and Zeldes, S. P. (1988). Rational Ponzi games. *International Economic Review*, 29:431–450.

OECD (1994). *Employment Outlook*. OECD, Paris. Organisation for Economic Co-operation and Development.

——(2001). *Economic Outlook, 69, June*. OECD, Paris. Organisation for Economic Co-operation and Development.

Ogata, K. (1995). *Discrete-Time Control Systems*. Prentice Hall, Upper Saddle River, NJ, second edition.

Ortega, J. M. (1987). *Matrix Theory: A Second Course*. Plenum Press, New York.

Oswald, A. J. (1982). The microeconomic theory of the trade union. *Economic Journal*, 97:269–283.

——(1985). The economic theory of trade unions: An introductory survey. *Scandinavian Journal of Economics*, 87:160–193.

Parkin, M. (1986). The output-inflation trade-off when prices are costly to change. *Journal of Political Economy*, 94:200–224.

Patinkin, D. (1965). *Money, Interest, and Prices*. Harper and Row, New York, second edition.

Patterson, K. (2000). *An Introduction to Applied Econometrics: A Time Series Approach*. Macmillan, London.

Pemberton, M. and Rau, N. (2001). *Mathematics for Economists: An Introductory Textbook*. Manchester University Press, Manchester.

Pencavel, J. (1986). Labor supply of men: A survey. In Ashenfelter, O. and Layard, R., editors, *Handbook of Labor Economics*. North-Holland, Amsterdam.

——(1991). *Labor Markets under Trade Unionism: Employment, Wages, and Hours*. Blackwell, Oxford.

Persson, T. and Svensson, L. E. O. (1983). Is optimism good in a Keynesian economy? *Economica*, 50:291–300.

——and Tabellini, G. (1989). *Macroeconomic Policy, Credibility and Politics*. Harwood, London.

——and Tabellini, G., editors (1994a). *Monetary and Fiscal Policy, I: Credibility*. MIT Press, Cambridge, MA.

——and Tabellini, G. (1994b). Representative democracy and capital taxation. *Journal of Public Economics*, 55:53–70.

——and Tabellini, G. (2000). *Political Economics: Explaining Economic Policy*. MIT Press, Cambridge, MA.

Pesaran, M. H. (1987). *The Limits to Rational Expectations*. Basil Blackwell, Oxford.

Pestieau, P. M. (1974). Optimal taxation and discount rate for public investment in a growth setting. *Journal of Public Economics*, 3:217–235.

Petrongolo, B. and Pissarides, C. A. (2001). Looking into the black box: A survey of the matching function. *Journal of Economic Literature*, 39:390–431.

Phelps, E. S. (1967). Phillips curves, expectations of inflation and optimal unemployment over time. *Economica*, 34:254–281.

—— (1972). *Inflation Policy and Unemployment Theory*. Macmillan, London.

—— (1973). Inflation in theory of public finance. *Scandinavian Journal of Economics*, 75:67–82.

—— (1978). Disinflation without recession: Adaptive guideposts and monetary policy. *Weltwirtschaftliches Archiv*, 100:783–809.

—— et al. (1970). *Microeconomic Foundations of Employment and Inflation Theory*. Macmillan, London.

—— and Taylor, J. B. (1977). Stabilizing powers of monetary policy under rational expectations. *Journal of Political Economy*, 85:163–317.

Pissarides, C. A. (1990). *Equilibrium Unemployment Theory*. Basil Blackwell, Oxford.

—— (1992). Loss of skill during unemployment and the persistence of employment shocks. *Quarterly Journal of Economics*, 107:1371–1391.

—— (1994). Search unemployment with on-the-job search. *Review of Economic Studies*, 61:457–475.

—— (2000). *Equilibrium Unemployment Theory*. MIT Press, Cambridge, MA, second edition.

Ploeg, F. van der (1987a). Rationing in open economy and dynamic macroeconomics: A survey. *De Economist*, 135:488–519.

—— (1987b). Trade unions, investment, and employment: A non-cooperative approach. *European Economic Review*, 31:1465–1492.

—— (1995). Political economy of monetary and budgetary policy. *International Economic Review*, 36:427–439.

—— and Tang, P. J. G. (1992). The macroeconomics of growth: An international perspective. *Oxford Review of Economic Policy*, 8:15–28.

Plosser, C. I. (1989). Understanding real business cycles. *Journal of Economic Perspectives*, 3:51–77.

Poole, W. (1970). Optimal choice of monetary policy instruments in a simple stochastic macro model. *Quarterly Journal of Economics*, 84:197–216.

Poterba, J. M., Rotemberg, J., and Summers, L. H. (1986). A tax-based test for nominal rigidities. *American Economic Review*, 76:659–675.

Pratt, J. W. (1964). Risk aversion in the small and in the large. *Econometrica*, 32:122–136.

Prescott, E. C. (1986). Theory ahead of business cycle measurement. *Federal Reserve Bank of Minneapolis Quarterly Review*, 10:9–22. Reprinted in: Miller (1994).

Ramsey, F. P. (1927). A contribution to the theory of taxation. *Economic Journal*, 37:47–61.

—— (1928). A mathematical theory of savings. *Economic Journal*, 38:543–559.

Rebelo, S. (1991). Long-run policy analysis and long-run growth. *Journal of Political Economy*, 99:500–521.

Reichlin, R. (1986). Equilibrium cycles in an overlapping generations economy with production. *Journal of Economic Theory*, 40:89–102.

Ricardo, D. (1817). *On the Principles of Political Economy and Taxation*. John Murray, London. Edition used: P. Sraffa, editor, *The Works and Correspondence of David Ricardo*, volume I. Cambridge: Cambridge University Press, 1951.

Rios-Rull, J. V. (1994). On the quantitative importance of market completeness. *Journal of Monetary Economics*, 34:463–496.

Rivera-Batiz, L. A. and Romer, P. M. (1991). Economic integration and endogenous growth. *Quarterly Journal of Economics*, 106:531–555.

Bibliography

Roberts, J. M. (1995). New Keynesian economics and the Phillips curve. *Journal of Money, Credit, and Banking*, 27:975–984.

Robinson, J. A. and Srinivasan, T. N. (1997). Long-term consequences of population growth: Technological change, natural resources, and the environment. In Rosenzweig, M. R. and Stark, O., editors, *Handbook of Population and Family Economics*. North-Holland, Amsterdam.

Rogerson, R. (1988). Indivisible labor, lotteries and equilibrium. *Journal of Monetary Economics*, 21:3–16.

Rogoff, K. (1985). The optimal degree of commitment to an intermediate monetary target. *Quarterly Journal Economics*, 100:1169–1190.

Romer, D. (1986). A simple general equilibrium version of the Baumol-Tobin model. *Quarterly Journal of Economics*, 101:663–686.

—— (1987). The monetary transmission mechanism in a general equilibrium version of the Baumol-Tobin model. *Journal of Monetary Economics*, 20:105–122.

—— (1996). *Advanced Macroeconomics*. McGraw-Hill, New York.

—— (2001). *Advanced Macroeconomics*. McGraw-Hill, New York, second edition.

Romer, P. M. (1986). Increasing returns and long-run growth. *Journal of Political Economy*, 94:1002–1037.

—— (1987). Growth based on increasing returns due to specialization. *American Economic Review, Papers and Proceedings*, 77:56–62.

—— (1989). Capital accumulation in the theory of long-run growth. In Barro, R. J., editor, *Modern Business Cycle Theory*, pages 51–127. Basil Blackwell, Oxford.

—— (1990). Endogenous technological change. *Journal of Political Economy*, 98:S71–S101.

Rosen, S. (1976). A theory of life earnings. *Journal of Political Economy*, 84:545–567.

—— (1985). Implicit contracts: A survey. *Journal of Economic Literature*, 23:1144–1175.

Ross, S. M. (1993). *Introduction to Probability Models*. Academic Press, San Diego, CA, fifth edition.

Rotemberg, J. J. (1982). Monopolistic price adjustment and aggregate output. *Review of Economic Studies*, 49:517–531.

—— (1987). The New Keynesian microfoundations. *NBER Macroeconomics Annual*, 2:69–104.

—— and Woodford, M. (1992). Oligopolistic pricing and the effects of aggregate demand on economic activity. *Journal of Political Economy*, 100:1153–1207.

—— and Woodford, M. (1996). Real-business-cycle models and forecastable movements in output, hours, and consumption. *American Economic Review*, 86:71–89.

—— and Woodford, M. (1999). Interest-rate rules in an estimated sticky price model. In Taylor, J. B., editor, *Monetary Policy Rules*. University of Chicago Press, Chicago.

Sachs, J. D. (1981). The current account and macroeconomic adjustment in the 1970s. *Brookings Papers on Economic Activity*, 1:201–268.

Saint-Paul, G. (1992). Fiscal policy in an endogenous growth model. *Quarterly Journal of Economics*, 107:1243–1259.

—— (2000). The "new political economy": Recent books by Drazen and Persson and Tabellini. *Journal of Economic Literature*, 38:915–925.

Samuelson, P. A. (1947). *Foundations of Economic Analysis*. Harvard University Press, Cambridge, MA.

——(1958). An exact consumption-loan model of interest with or without the social contrivance of money. *Journal of Political Economics*, 66:467–482.

——(1965). Proof that properly anticipated prices fluctuate randomly. *Industrial Management Review*, 6:41–49.

——(1968a). The two-part golden rule deduced as the asymptotic turnpike of catenary motions. *Western Economic Journal*, 6:85–89.

——(1968b). What classical and neoclassical monetary theory really was. *Canadian Journal of Economics*, 1:1–15.

——(1969a). Lifetime portfolio selection by dynamic stochastic programming. *Review of Economics and Statistics*, 51:239–246.

——(1969b). Nonoptimality of money holding under laissez faire. *Canadian Journal of Economics*, 2:303–308.

——(1975a). The optimum growth rate for population. *International Economic Review*, 16:531–538.

——(1975b). Optimum social security in a life-cycle growth model. *International Economic Review*, 16:539–544.

Sandmo, A. (1969). Capital risk, consumption, and portfolio choice. *Econometrica*, 37:586–599.

——(1970). The effect of uncertainty on saving decisions. *Review of Economic Studies*, 37:353–360.

Sargent, T. and Wallace, N. (1982). The real-bills doctrine versus the quantity theory: A reconsideration. *Journal of Political Economics*, 90:1212–1236.

Sargent, T. J. (1973). Rational expectations, the real rate of interest, and the natural rate of unemployment. *Brookings Papers on Economic Activity*, 2:169–183.

——(1987a). *Dynamic Macroeconomic Theory*. Harvard University Press, Cambridge, MA.

——(1987b). *Macroeconomic Theory*. Academic Press, Boston, second edition.

——(1993). *Rational Expectations and Inflation*. Harper Collins College Publishers, New York, second edition.

——and Wallace, N. (1975). Rational expectations, the optimal monetary instrument, and the optimal money supply rule. *Journal of Political Economy*, 83:241–254.

——and Wallace, N. (1976). Rational expectations and the theory of economic policy. *Journal of Monetary Economics*, 2:169–183.

——and Wallace, N. (1993). Some unpleasant monetarist arithmetic. In Sargent, T., editor, *Rational Expectations and Inflation*. Harper Collins, New York, second edition.

Sato, R. (1963). Fiscal policy in a neoclassical growth model: An analysis of time required for equilibrating adjustment. *Review of Economic Studies*, 30:16–23.

Saving, T. R. (1971). Transactions costs and the demand for money. *American Economic Review*, 61:407–420.

Scarth, W. M. (1988). *Macroeconomics: An Introduction to Advanced Methods*. Harcourt Brace Jovanovich, Toronto.

Schumpeter, J. A. (1934). *The Theory of Economic Development*. Harvard University Press, Cambridge, MA. Reprinted by Transaction Publishers, New Brunswick, NJ, 1983.

Seater, J. J. (1993). Ricardian equivalence. *Journal of Economic Literature*, 31:142–190.

Segerstrom, P. S. (1998). Endogenous growth without scale effects. *American Economic Review*, 88:1290–1310.

Bibliography

Seierstad, A. and Sydsæter, K. (1987). *Optimal Control Theory with Economic Applications*. North-Holland, Amsterdam.

Sen, P. and Turnovsky, S. J. (1990). Investment tax credit in an open economy. *Journal of Public Economics*, 42:277–299.

Shafir, E., Diamond, P., and Tversky, A. (1997). Money illusion. *Quarterly Journal of Economics, Supplement*, 112:341–374.

Shapiro, C. (1989). Theories of oligopoly behavior. In Schmalensee, R. and Willig, R. D., editors, *Handbook of Industrial Organization*, volume II. North-Holland, Amsterdam.

——and Stiglitz, J. E. (1984). Equilibrium unemployment as a worker discipline device. *American Economic Review*, 74:433–444.

Shell, K. (1967). A model of inventive activity and capital accumulation. In Shell, K., editor, *Essays on the Theory of Optimal Economic Growth*. MIT Press, Cambridge, MA.

Sheshinski, E. (1967). Optimal accumulation with learning by doing. In Shell, K., editor, *Essays on the Theory of Optimal Economic Growth*. MIT Press, Cambridge, MA.

Shleifer, A. (1986). Implementation cycles. *Journal of Political Economy*, 94:1163–1190.

Sidrauski, M. (1967). Rational choice and patterns of growth in a monetary economy. *American Economic Review*, 57:534–544.

Silberberg, E. (1987). Envelope theorem. In Eatwell, J., Milgate, M., and Newman, P., editors, *The New Palgrave: A Dictionary of Economics*. Macmillan, London.

Silvestre, J. (1993). The market-power foundations of macroeconomic policy. *Journal of Economic Literature*, 31:105–141.

Sims, C. A. (1996). Macroeconomics and methodology. *Journal of Economic Perspectives*, 10:105–120.

Sinn, H.-W. (1987). *Capital Income Taxation and Resource Allocation*. North-Holland, Amsterdam.

Sinn, H.-W. (2000). Why a funded pension system is useful and why it is not useful. *International Tax and Public Finance*, 7:389–410.

Snowdon, B., Vane, H., and Wynarczyk, P. (1994). *A Modern Guide to Macroeconomics*. Edward Elgar, Aldershot.

Solow, R. M. (1956). A contribution to the theory of economic growth. *Quarterly Journal of Economics*, 70:65–94.

——(1957). Technical change and the aggregate production function. *Review of Economics and Statistics*, 39:312–320.

——(1986). Monopolistic competition and the multiplier. In Heller, W. P., Starr, R. M., and Starrett, D. A., editors, *Equilibrium Analysis: Essays in Honour of Kenneth J. Arrow, Vol. II*. Cambridge University Press, Cambridge.

——(1998). *Monopolistic Competition and Macroeconomic Theory*. Cambridge University Press, Cambridge.

Spence, M. (1976). Product selection, fixed costs, and monopolistic competition. *Review of Economic Studies*, 43:217–235.

Spiegel, M. R. (1965). *Laplace Tranforms*. McGraw-Hill, New York.

——(1974). *Advanced Calculus*. McGraw-Hill, New York.

Stadler, G. W. (1994). Real business cycles. *Journal of Economic Literature*, 32:1750–1783.

Startz, R. (1989). Monopolistic competition as a foundation for Keynesian macroeconomic models. *Quarterly Journal of Economics*, 104:737–752.

Stern, N. H. (1991). The determinants of growth. *Economic Journal*, 101:122–133.

Stiglitz, J. E. (1986). Theories of wage rigidity. In Butkiewicz, J. L., Koford, K. J., and Miller, J. B., editors, *Keynes' Economic Legacy: Contemporary Economic Theories*. Praeger, New York.

Strang, G. (1988). *Linear Algebra and Its Applications*. Harcourt Brace Jovanovich, San Diego, CA, third edition.

Strotz, R. H. (1956). Myopia and inconsistency in dynamic utility maximization. *Review of Economic Studies*, 23:165–180.

Summers, L. H. (1981). Taxation and corporate investment: A q-theory approach. *Brookings Papers on Economic Activity*, 1:67–140.

—— (1986). Some skeptical observations on real business cycle theory. *Federal Reserve Bank of Minneapolis Quarterly Review*, 10:23–27. Reprinted in: Miller (1994).

—— (1988). Relative wages, efficiency wages and unemployment. *American Economic Review, Papers and Proceedings*, 78:383–388.

Svensson, L. E. O. and Razin, A. (1983). The terms of trade and the current account: The Harberger-Laursen-Metzler effect. *Journal of Political Economy*, 91:97–125.

Swan, T. W. (1956). Economic growth and capital accumulation. *Economic Record*, 32:334–361.

Sydsæter, K. and Hammond, P. J. (1995). *Mathematics for Economic Analysis*. Prentice-Hall, Englewood Cliffs, NJ.

——, Strøm, A., and Berck, P. (2000). *Economists' Mathematical Manual*. Springer, Berlin, third edition.

Taylor, J. B. (1979). Staggered wage setting in a macro model. *American Economic Review*, 69:108–113.

—— (1980). Aggregate dynamics and staggered contracts. *Journal of Political Economy*, 88:1–17.

—— and Woodford, M., editors (1999). *Handbook of Macroeconomics*. North-Holland, Amsterdam.

Temple, J. (1999). The new growth evidence. *Journal of Economic Literature*, 37:112–156.

Tirole, J. (1985). Asset bubbles and overlapping generations. *Econometrica*, 53:1071–1100.

Tobin, J. (1955). A dynamic aggregative model. *Journal of Political Economy*, 63:103–115.

—— (1956). The interest elasticity of the transactions demand for cash. *Review of Economics and Statistics*, 38:241–247.

—— (1958). Liquidity preference as behavior towards risk. *Review of Economic Studies*, 25:65–86.

—— (1965). Money and economic growth. *Econometrica*, 33:671–684.

—— (1969). A general equilibrium approach to monetary theory. *Journal of Money, Credit, and Banking*, 1:15–29.

—— and Buiter, W. H. (1976). The long-run effects of fiscal and monetary policy on aggregate demand. In Stein, J., editor, *Monetarism*. North-Holland, Amsterdam.

Treadway, A. B. (1969). On rational entrepreneurial behaviour and the demand for investment. *Review of Economic Studies*, 36:227–239.

Trejos, A. and Wright, R. (1995). Search, bargaining, and prices. *Journal of Political Economy*, 103:118–141.

Turnbull, H. W. (1988). The great mathematicians. In Newman, J. R., editor, *The World of Mathematics*. Tempus Books, Redmond, WA.

Turnovsky, S. J. (1977). *Macroeconomic Analysis and Stabilization Policies*. Cambridge University Press, Cambridge.

Bibliography

Turnovsky, S. J. (1995). *Methods of Macroeconomic Dynamics*. MIT Press, Cambridge, MA.

—— (1996). Optimal tax, debt, and expenditure policies in a growing economy. *Journal of Public Economics*, 60:21–44.

—— (1997). *International Macroeconomic Dynamics*. MIT Press, Cambridge, MA.

—— (2000). *Methods of Macroeconomic Dynamics*. MIT Press, Cambridge, MA, second edition.

—— and Brock, W. A. (1980). Time consistency and optimal government policies in perfect foresight equilibrium. *Journal of Public Economics*, 13:183–212.

—— and Fisher, W. H. (1995). The composition of government expenditure and its consequences for macroeconomic performance. *Journal of Economic Dynamics and Control*, 19:747–786.

Uhlig, H. (1999). A toolkit for analysing nonlinear dynamic stochastic models easily. In Marimon, R. and Scott, A., editors, *Computational Methods for the Study of Dynamic Economies*, pages 30–61. Oxford University Press, Oxford.

Uzawa, H. (1965). Optimum technical change in an aggregative model of economic growth. *International Economic Review*, 6:18–31.

—— (1969). Time preference and the Penrose effect in a two-class model of economic growth. *Journal of Political Economy*, 77:628–652.

—— (1988). On the economics of social overhead capital. In Uzawa, H., editor, *Preference, production, and capital*. Cambridge University Press, Cambridge.

Varian, H. R. (1992). *Microeconomic Analysis*. W. W. Norton, New York, third edition.

Verbon, H. A. A. (1989). Conversion policies for public pension plans in a small open economy. In Gustafsson, B. A. and Klevmarken, N. A., editors, *The Political Economy of Social Security*. North-Holland, Amsterdam.

Viner, J. (1931). Cost curves and supply curves. *Zeitschrift für Nationalökonomie*, 3:23–46. Reprinted with supplementary note in: G.J. Stigler and K.E. Boulding, editors, *Readings in Price Theory*. London: Allen and Unwin, 1953.

Von Neumann, J. and Morgenstern, O. (1944). *Theory of Games and Economic Behavior*. Princeton University Press, Princeton, NJ.

Wallace, N. (1980). The overlapping generations model of fiat money. In Kareken, J. H. and Wallace, N., editors, *Models of Monetary Economies*. Federal Reserve Bank of Minneapolis, Minneapolis.

—— (1981). A Modigliani-Miller theorem for open-market operations. *American Economic Review*, 71:267–274.

Walsh, C. E. (1998). *Monetary Theory and Policy*. MIT Press, Cambridge, MA.

Watson, M. W. (1993). Measures of fit for calibrated models. *Journal of Political Economy*, 101:1011–1041.

Weil, D. N. (1997). The economics of population aging. In Rosenzweig, M. and Stark, O., editors, *Handbook of Population and Family Economics*. North-Holland, Amsterdam.

Weil, P. (1989a). Increasing returns and animal spirits. *American Economic Review*, 79:889–894.

—— (1989b). Overlapping families of infinitely-lived agents. *Journal of Public Economics*, 38:183–198.

—— (1991). Is money net wealth? *International Economic Review*, 37:37–53.

Weiss, A. (1991). *Efficiency Wages: Models of Unemployment, Layoffs, and Wage Dispersion*. Oxford University Press, Oxford.

Weitzman, M. L. (1982). Increasing returns and the foundation of unemployment theory. 92:787–804.

——(1984). *The Share Economy: Conquering Stagflation*. Harvard University Press, Cambridge, MA.

——(1994). Monopolistic competition with endogenous specialization. *Review of Economic Studies*, 61:57–80.

Wicksell, K. (1935). *Lectures on Political Economy*, volume II. George Routledge and Sons, London. Reprinted by Augustus M. Kelley, Fairfield, NJ, 1978.

Wildasin, D. E. (1990). Non-neutrality of debt with endogenous fertility. *Oxford Economic Papers*, 42:414–428.

Woodford, M. (1990). The optimum quantity of money. In Friedman, B. M. and Hahn, F. H., editors, *Handbook of Monetary Economics*, volume II. North-Holland, Amsterdam.

——(forthcoming). Revolution and evolution in twentieth-century macroeconomics. In Gifford, P., editor, *Frontiers of the Mind in the Twenty-First Century*. Harvard University Press, Cambridge, MA.

Xie, D. (1994). Divergence in economic performance: Transitional dynamics with multiple equilibria. *Journal of Economic Theory*, 63:97–112.

Yaari, M. E. (1965). Uncertain lifetime, life insurance, and the theory of the consumer. *Review of Economic Studies*, 32:137–150.

Young, A. (1998). Growth without scale effects. *Journal of Political Economy*, 106:41–63.

Yun, T. (1996). Nominal price rigidity, money supply endogeneity, and business cycles. *Journal of Monetary Economics*, 37:345–370.

Zhang, J. (1995). Social security and endogenous growth. *Journal of Public Economics*, 58:185–213.

——(1996). Optimal public investments in education and endogenous growth. *Scandinavian Journal of Economics*, 98:387–404.

Zilcha, I. (1990). Dynamic efficiency in overlapping generations models with stochastic production. *Journal of Economic Theory*, 52:364–379.

——(1991). Characterizing efficiency in stochastic overlapping generations models. *Journal of Economic Theory*, 55:1–16.

Index

Index

Index

Index

Index

Index